A HISTORY OF GREECE

A HISTORY OF
GREECE

TO THE DEATH OF ALEXANDER THE GREAT

J. B. BURY, D.Litt., LL.D., F.B.A.

*Late Regius Professor of Modern History and
Fellow of King's College in the University of Cambridge*

and

RUSSELL MEIGGS, F.B.A.

Formerly Fellow of Balliol College, Oxford

FOURTH EDITION
(with revisions)

First Edition July 1900
Reprinted October 1900, 1902, 1904, 1906, 1908, 1909, 1911, 1912
Second Edition July 1913
Reprinted 1914, 1916, 1917, 1920, 1922, 1924, 1927, 1929, 1931, 1938, 1941, 1945
Third Edition 1951
Reprinted 1951, 1952, 1955, 1956, 1959, 1963, 1966, 1967, 1970, 1972
Fourth Edition 1975
Reprinted 1976, 1977
Reprinted with revisions and corrections 1978, 1979

Published by
THE MACMILLAN PRESS LTD
London and Basingstoke
Associated companies in Delhi Dublin
Hong Kong Johannesburg Lagos Melbourne
New York Singapore and Tokyo

ISBN 0 333 15492 4 (hard cover)
0 333 15493 2 (paper cover)

Printed in Hong Kong

Preface to the Fourth Edition

The first edition of this History of Greece was published in 1900, on the eve of Sir Arthur Evans' dramatic excavations at Cnossus in Crete. In the second edition, published in 1913, Bury rewrote the first chapter in the light of the new evidence. Outside Chapter I a few minor changes only were made.

In the 1951 edition radical changes again had to be made in the first chapter. The increasing scale of excavation on the Greek mainland had considerably advanced our understanding of the Mycenaeans and modifications were needed in the section on Crete. The accumulation of new evidence from archaeology and the changing assessment of early evidence also required revision at many points in other chapters. The nature and extent, however, of the changes were restricted by the economic requirement of using the existing plates.

By 1970 these plates were showing their age and the resetting has provided the opportunity for a more comprehensive revision. The need for a new edition had become urgent, for in the twenty years since the publication of the third edition dramatic discoveries had been made by excavation, and an expanding number of learned journals had encouraged and sustained lively controversy on topics old and new. Once again our understanding of the Bronze Age has gained most from new evidence, and particularly from the excavation of the palace in Messenia from which it is generally believed that Homer's Nestor ruled his wide Kingdom. This discovery revived interest in the relation of the traditions recorded by Homer to history, and also threw interesting light on the last phase of Mycenaean history; but the most important of the objects unearthed were a large number of clay tablets, baked by the fire which destroyed the palace. These tablets were at once seen to resemble tablets from Cnossus and both were written in the same script, which Evans had called Linear B as distinct from the earlier Linear A script. It was a Pylos tablet which enabled Michael Ventris, an English architect, who had worked on the decipherment since his schooldays, to convince the great majority of classical scholars that the Linear B tablets were written in an early form of Greek.

This discovery involved a rethinking of many issues. The use of Greek by the palace administration at Minoan Cnossus showed unexpectedly that Greeks had gained control of Cnossus before the palace was destroyed. This at once raised the problem of the destruction of the other Cretan palaces, and controversy became more lively when the excavation of a settlement near Akrotiri on the island of Santorini seemed to strengthen a thesis that Marinatos had tentatively outlined in 1939. Many would now agree with him that a violent volcanic eruption on Santorini was responsible for the widespread destruction of palaces and settlements on Crete. The archaeological evidence, however, raises difficulties and the alternative explanation that it was the Greeks who were the destroyers still has strong support.

On the mainland the new evidence has been less sensational, but excavations at Lerna in the Argolid and at Lefkandi on Euboea have undermined the widely accepted view that there was a major invasion of Greece from the north at the end of the early Helladic period. The pattern of change is now seen to be much less simple. The Mycenaeans have also come more into their own as new evidence accumulates. It is natural that Evans, who had discovered the richness of Minoan culture, should have exaggerated the dependence of the Mycenaeans on Crete. We now have a better appreciation of the native roots and development of Mycenaean culture. There is in fact a danger that the reaction will go too far and underrate the power of Crete before the fifteenth century B.C.

Such unexpected developments could not be accommodated by patchwork revision; the first chapter has therefore been completely rewritten. There has also been considerable rewriting in the history of the archaic period; for in 1950 the restrictions imposed by the use of the original plates made it impossible to do justice to the new light thrown on the period by the redating of the introduction of coinage and of the Greek alphabet, and the excavation of Al-Mina. Elsewhere the main structure remains essentially Bury's. His text has been changed when new evidence makes it necessary, or when continuing debate has turned decisively against him, but I have tried not to impose my own views in issues that are still controversial and have used the notes to show alternatives. One other principle needs to be stated. In the seventy years since Bury wrote his history language usage has changed considerably. Some words and phrases that were common currency in 1900 now have a period flavour which many regard as a distraction. In such cases the text has been adapted to modern usage.

Though the number of students who learn Greek has been sadly reduced in recent years, the number of people interested in Ancient History has steadily increased, and among the new readers are many who wish to get nearer to the sources and to current controversy. It is mainly for such readers that the notes have been expanded, and bibliographies added. A glossary has also been included of words that are essentially Greek words transliterated. All the maps have been reconsidered and new ones added including a pull-out map of the Greek world at the end of the book; I have good reason to be grateful to Messrs Lovell Johns for their patience, cheerfulness and skill. A considerable number of new photographs have also been introduced and notes have been added on those whose significance may not be apparent. Due acknowledgement is made in the list of photographs, but I must record my special gratitude to Alison Frantz. I have had generous help from friends too numerous to catalogue, especially in my struggle with the Bronze Age. In this field of many problems the opportunity of discussing their excavations with Professor Caskey and Mr. Popham was invaluable and I remain very grateful for their patience and encouragement. I have also learnt much from the doctoral thesis of Oliver Dickinson on the Mycenaeans, and subsequent discussion with him. He was one of a lively and distinguished group of Oxford graduates working on the Bronze Age who provided a most congenial background. I was also very fortunate to be able to enjoy the hospitality and stimulus of the British School at Athens at a critical period in the revision. Rosamund Broadley, who is the only person known to me, other than my wife, who can read more than half of my writing, has struggled through a difficult manuscript with an efficiency and tolerance that I hardly deserve, but keenly appreciate.

Throughout this complex revision Rex Allen of Macmillan has been my constant guide and comforter. His advice and practical help have been invaluable and I have thoroughly enjoyed our working partnership.

Garsington
November 1973

RUSSELL MEIGGS

Extracts from the Preface to First Edition

In determining the form and character of this book, I have been prompted by two convictions. One is that while, in writing a history based on the original authorities and from one's own personal point of view, it is natural and certainly easier to allow it to range into several volumes, its compression into a single volume often produces a more useful book. In the case of a new history of Greece, it seemed worth while to undertake the more laborious task. The other opinion which I venture to hold is this. So far as history is concerned, those books which are capable of enlisting the interest of mature readers seem to me to be best also for informing younger students. Therefore, while my aim is to help education, this book has in view a wider circle than those merely who are going through a course of school or university discipline.

It was a necessary consequence of the limitations of space which I imposed upon myself, that literature and art, philosophy and religion, should be touched upon only when they directly illustrate, or come into some specially intimate connection with, the political history. It will be found that I have sometimes interpreted this rule liberally; but it is a rule which could be the more readily adopted as so many excellent works dealing with art, literature, and philosophy are now easily accessible. The interspersion, in a short political history, of a few unconnected chapters dealing, as they must deal, inadequately with art and literature seems useless and inartistic.

The existence of valuable handbooks, within the reach of all, on constitutional antiquities has enabled me, in tracing the development of the Athenian state or touching on the institutions of other cities, to omit minor details. The reader must also seek elsewhere for the sagas of Hellas, for a geographical description of the country, for the topography of Athens. On the topography of Athens, and on the geography of Greece, he will find excellent works to his hand.

There are two cautions which I must convey to the reader, and it will be most convenient to state them here. The first concerns the prehistoric age, which is the subject of the first chapter of this work. The evidence gathered by the researches of archaeologists on the coasts and islands of the Aegean during the last twenty years, as to the civilisation of prehistoric Greece, brought historians face to face with a set of new problems, for which no solutions that can be regarded as certain have yet been discovered. The ablest investigators differ widely in their views. Fresh evidence may at any hour upset tentative conclusions and force us to seek new interpretations of the data. The excavations which are now to be undertaken in Crete, at last restored to its own Greek world, may lead to unexpected results that may transform the whole question. Thus prehistoric Greece cannot be treated satisfactorily except by the method of discussion, and in a work like this, since discussion lies outside its scope, a writer can only describe the main features of the culture which excavation has revealed, and state with implied reserve the chief general conclusions, which he considers probable, as to the correlation of the archaeological evidence with the literary traditions of the Greeks. He must leave much vague and indefinite. The difficulty of the problems is increased by the circumstance that the literary evidence concerning the doings and goings of the early Greek folks is largely embedded in myth and harder to extract from its bed than buried walls or tombs from their coverings of earth. The importance of the pre-Greek inhabitants of Greece, the mixed ethnical character of the historical Greeks, the comparatively early date of the 'Ionian' migration, the continuity of Aegean civilisation, the relation of the so-called 'Mycenaean' culture to the culture described by Homer—these are the main points which I have been content to emphasise.

The second caution applies to all histories of Greece that have been written since the days of Ephorus. The early portion of Greek history, which corresponds to the seventh and sixth centuries B.C., is inevitably distorted and placed in a false perspective through the strange limitations of our knowledge. For at that time (as well as in the centuries immediately preceding, which are almost quite withdrawn from our vision) the cities of the western coast of Asia Minor formed the most important and enlightened part of the Hellenic world, and of those cities in the days of their greatness we have only some disconnected glimpses. Our knowledge of them hardly begins till Persia advances to the Aegean and they sink to a lower place in Greece. Thus the pages in which the Greeks of Asia should have the supreme place are monopolised by the development of elder Greece; and the false impression is produced that the history of Hellas in the seventh and sixth centuries consisted merely or mainly of the histories of Sparta and Athens and their immediate neighbours. Darkness also envelops the growth of the young Greek communities of Italy and Sicily during the same period. The wrong, unfortunately, cannot be righted by a recognition of it. Athens and Sparta and their fellows abide in possession. *Les absents ont toujours tort.*

In the Notes and References at the end of the volume I have indicated obligations to modern research on special points. Here I must acknowledge my more general obligations to the histories of Grote, Freeman (*History of Sicily*), Busolt, Beloch, E. Meyer (*Geschichte des Altertums*), and Droysen. Though other histories of high reputation, both English and foreign, have been respectfully consulted, it is to those mentioned that I am chiefly indebted. But I owe perhaps a deeper debt to the writings of one who, though he has never written a formal history of Greece, has made countless invaluable contributions to its study—Professor U. von Wilamowitz-Möllendorff. With some of his conclusions I do not agree, but I would express here deep sympathy with his methods and admiration for the stimulating virtue of his writings.

J. B. BURY

Contents

INTRODUCTION

GREECE AND THE AEGEAN

CHAPTER 1

THE BEGINNINGS OF GREECE AND THE HEROIC AGE

CHAPTER 2

CHAPTER 3

CHAPTER 4

CHAPTER 5

CONTENTS

CHAPTER 6

THE ADVANCE OF PERSIA TO THE AEGEAN 141

CHAPTER 7

THE PERILS OF GREECE. THE PERSIAN AND PUNIC INVASIONS 167

CHAPTER 8

THE FOUNDATION OF THE ATHENIAN EMPIRE 200

CHAPTER 9

THE ATHENIAN EMPIRE UNDER THE GUIDANCE OF PERICLES 215

CHAPTER 10

THE WAR OF ATHENS WITH THE PELOPONNESIANS
(431-421 B.C.) 245

CHAPTER 11

THE DECLINE AND DOWNFALL OF THE ATHENIAN EMPIRE 288

CONTENTS

CHAPTER 12

THE SPARTAN SUPREMACY AND THE PERSIAN WAR 323

CHAPTER 13

THE REVIVAL OF ATHENS AND HER SECOND LEAGUE 346

CHAPTER 14

THE HEGEMONY OF THEBES 366

CHAPTER 15

CHAPTER 16

CHAPTER 17

CHAPTER 18

THE CONQUEST OF THE FAR EAST 473

List of Illustrations

LIST OF ILLUSTRATIONS

List of Maps

xix

Introduction

Greece and the Aegean

The rivers and valleys, the mountains, bays and islands of Greece will become familiar as our story unfolds itself, and we need not enter here into any minute description. But it is useful at the very outset to grasp some general features which went to make the history of the Greeks what it was, and what otherwise it could not have been. The character of their history is so intimately connected with the character of their dwelling-places that we cannot conceive it apart from their land and seas.

The Illyrian (or Balkan) peninsula

Of Spain, Italy, and Illyricum, the three massive promontories of which southern Europe consists, Illyricum in the east would have closely resembled Spain in the west if it had stopped short at the north of Thessaly, and if its offshoot Greece had been sunk beneath the waters. It would then have been no more than a huge block of solid land, at one corner almost touching the shores of Asia, as Spain almost touches the shores of Africa. But Greece, its southern continuation, has totally different natural features, which distinguish it alike from Spain the solid square and Italy the solid wedge, and make the eastern basin of the Mediterranean strikingly unlike the western.

Character of Greece:

Greece gives the impression of a group of nesses and islands, yet in truth it might have been as solid and unbroken a block of continent, on its own smaller scale, as the massive promontory from which it juts. Greece may be described as a mountainous headland broken

the Gulf of Corinth;

across the middle into two parts by a huge rift, and with its whole eastern side split into fragments. We can trace the ribs of the framework, which a convulsion of nature bent and shivered—for the service, as it turned out, of the human race.

the mountain ribs;

The mountains which form Thessaly's eastern barrier: Olympus, Ossa, and Pelion; the mountains of the long island of Euboea; and the string of islands which seem to hang to Euboea as a sort of tail, should have formed a perpetual mountainous chain—the rocky eastern coast of a solid promontory. Again, the ridges of Pindus which divide Thessaly from Epirus find their prolongation in the heights of Tymphrestus and Corax, and then, in an oblique south-eastward line, deflected from its natural direction, the chain is continued in Parnassus, Helicon, and Cithaeron, in the hills of Attica, and in the islands which would be part of Attica, if Attica had not dipped beneath the waters. In the same way the mountains of the Peloponnese are a continuation of the mountains of Epirus. Thus

imaginary reconstruction

restoring the framework in our imagination and raising the dry land from the sea, we reconstruct, as the Greece that might have been, a lozenge of land, ribbed with chains of hills stretching south-eastward far out into the Aegean. If nature had given the Greeks a land like this, their history would have been entirely changed; and by imagining it we are helped to understand how much they owed to the accidents of nature. In a land of capes and deep bays and islands it was determined that waterways should be the ways of their expansion. They were driven as it were into the arms of the sea.

Important geographical features. I. The Great Inlet (Gulf of Corinth)

The most striking feature of continental Greece is the deep gulf which has cleft it asunder into two parts. The southern half ought to have been an island—as its Greek name, 'the island of Pelops', suggests—but it

1

holds on to the continent by a narrow bridge of land at the eastern extremity of the great cleft. Now this physical feature had the utmost significance for the history of Greece; and its significance may be viewed in three ways, if we consider the existence of the dividing gulf, the existence of the isthmus, and the fact that the isthmus was at the eastern and not at the western end.

1. The double effect of the gulf itself is clear at once. It let the sea in upon a number of folks who would otherwise have been inland mountaineers, and increased enormously the length of the seaboard of Greece. Further, the gulf constituted southern Greece a world by itself, so that it could be regarded as a separate land from northern Greece—an island practically, with its own insular interests.

2. But if the island of Pelops had been in very truth an island, if there had been no isthmus, there would have been from the earliest ages direct and constant intercourse between the coasts which are washed by the Aegean and those which are washed by the Ionian Sea. The eastern and western lands of Greece would have been brought nearer to one another, when the ships of trader or warrior, instead of tediously circumnavigating the Peloponnese, could have sailed from the eastern to the western sea through the middle of Greece. The disappearance of the isthmus would have revolutionised the roads of traffic and changed the centres of commerce; and the wars of Greek history would have been fought out on other lines. How important the isthmus was may perhaps be best illustrated by a modern instance on a far mightier scale. Remove the bridge which joins the southern to the northern continent of America, and contemplate the changes which ensue in the routes of trade and in the conditions of naval warfare in the great oceans of the globe.

3. Again, if the bridge which attached the Peloponnese to the mainland had been at the western end of the gulf, the lands along either shore of the inlet would have been accessible easily, and sooner, to the commerce of the Aegean and the orient; the civilisation of north-western Greece might have been more rapid and intense; and the history of Boeotia and Attica, unhooked from the Peloponnese, would have run a different course.

II. The Aegean

The character of the Aegean basin was another determining condition of the history of the Greeks. Strewn with countless islands, it seems meant to promote the intercourse of folk with folk. The Cyclades, which, as we have seen, belong properly to the framework of the Greek continent, pass imperceptibly into the isles which the Asiatic coast throws out, and there is formed a sort of island bridge, inviting ships to pass from Greece to Asia. The western coast of Asia Minor belongs, in truth, more naturally to Europe than to its own continent; it soon became part of the Greek world, and the Aegean might be considered then as the true centre of Greece.

The west side of Greece, too, was well *The west* furnished with good harbours, and though not as rich in bays and islands as the east, was a favourable scene for the development of trade and civilisation. It was no long voyage from Corcyra to the heel of Italy, and the inhabitants of western Greece had a whole world open to their enterprise. But that world was barbarous in early times and had no civilising gifts to offer, whereas the peoples of the eastern seaboard looked towards Asia and were drawn into contact with the immemorial civilisations of the Orient. The backward condition of western as contrasted with eastern Greece in early ages did not depend on the conformation of the coast, but on the fact that it faced away from Asia, and in later days we find the Ionian Sea a busy scene of commerce and lined with prosperous communities which are fully abreast of Greek civilisation.

The northern coast of Africa, confronting *III.* and challenging the three peninsulas of the *Position of* Mediterranean, has played a remarkable part *Greece in* in the history of southern Europe. From the *regard to* earliest times it has been historically associated *Africa.* with Europe, and the story of geology illus- *Land-* trates the fitness of this connection. Western *bridges in* Europe and northern Africa were once in days *the Medi-* long past united together by bridges of con- *terranean* tinuous land; and this ancient continent, which *in the* we might call Europo-Libya, was perhaps *pliocene* inhabited by peoples of a homogeneous race, *period:* who were severed from one another when the *(1) at* ocean was let in and the Mediterranean as- *Gibraltar;* sumed its present shape. Sicily, a remnant of *(2) Italy—* the old land-bridge, has always been for Italy *Sicily—* a step to, or a step from, Africa; while Spain *Tunis* needs no island to bridge her strait.

Greece is a land of mountains and small *IV. Greece* valleys; it has few plains of even moderate size *suitable for* and no considerable rivers. It is therefore well *small* adapted to be a country of separate com- *states* munities, each protected against its neighbours by hilly barriers; and the history of the Greeks, a story of small independent states, could not have been wrought out in a land of dissimilar formation. The political history of all countries is in some measure under the influence of geography, but in Greece geography made itself pre-eminently felt, and fought along with other forces against the accomplishment of national unity. The islands formed states in themselves—but though seas, like mountains, may sever, they may also, unlike mountains, unite: it was less difficult, here, to form a sea empire than a land one. In the same way, the hills prevented the development of a brisk land traffic, while, as we have seen, the broken character of the coast and the multitude of islands facilitated intercourse by water.

Climate and productivity

There is no barrier to break the winds which sweep over the Euxine from the Asiatic continent towards the Greek shores and render Thrace a chilly land. Hence the Greek climate has a certain severity and bracing quality, which promoted the vigour and energy of the people. Again, Greece is by no means a rich and fruitful country. It has few well-watered plains of large size; the cultivated valleys do not yield the due crop to be expected from the area; whilst the soil, though good for barley, is not rich enough for wheat to grow freely. Thus the tillers of the earth had hard work. And the nature of the land had consequences which tended to promote maritime enterprise. On one hand, richer lands beyond the seas attracted the adventurous, especially when the growth of the population began to press on the means of support. On the other hand, it ultimately became necessary to supplement home-grown corn by wheat imported from abroad. But if Demeter denied her highest favours, the vine and the olive grew abundantly in most parts of the country, and their cultivation was one of the chief features of ancient Greece.

CHAPTER 1

The beginnings of Greece and the Heroic age

The Origins of the Greeks

As late as the 1870s Greek mythology, and in particular the great epics of Homer, were the only witnesses of the history of Greece before the coming of the Dorians. When Schliemann, the German banker who taught himself Greek and was emotionally carried away by the Iliad and Odyssey, set out to find the world of Homer he opened a new epoch. At Hissarlik he found a rich settlement with gold in many of the houses, and at Mycenae a series of shaft graves with a fabulous wealth of gold and silver, ceremonial daggers and swords, jewelry and pottery of high quality. Schliemann thought that he had found Priam's Troy and the bodies of Agamemnon and his peers, but it was not long before it was realised that the Trojan gold and the Mycenaean graves were hundreds of years earlier than the traditional dates of Homer's Trojan War. The shaft graves were a positive embarrassment to archaeologists, for there was nothing in the Greek archaeological record to suggest such wealth so early; a special explanation seemed to be needed. Sir Arthur Evans, then Keeper of the Ashmolean Museum in Oxford, thought that the answer might be found in Crete. He was impressed by the mixed contents of the shaft graves, and particularly the non-classical elements, and he was led to Crete by the writing on seals which were being sold by dealers in Athens and were said to come from Crete. There was also a strong Greek tradition as early as Thucydides and Herodotus of a great King Minos of Cnossus who ruled the Aegean. Evans succeeded in acquiring the site of Cnossus, and in a series of campaigns beginning in 1900 he opened a completely new chapter of history. Evans was convinced that it was to Crete that the Greeks of the mainland owed their culture, and he even suggested that at the peak of her power Cnossus controlled part of Greece. With the extension of excavation to other Cretan palaces, Evans's view won wide assent; but as more and more sites on the Greek mainland were excavated it became increasingly clear that the mainland civilisation, which for convenience is called Mycenaean from its most important centre, though strongly influenced by Crete, had a character of its own, and was also carrying Mycenaean wares to the east and west.

For the history of the Aegean during the second millennium we have two sources— archaeology, and oral tradition in later myth and legend. Both have their limitations. Those of legend are clear enough: stories grow and are distorted as they are handed down; circumstantial detail often derives only from the storyteller's imagination; generations can easily be telescoped, the chronology is rarely reliable. But legend can be useful as a control and can raise useful questions. It was Homer who led Schliemann to Mycenae, and the importance of Mycenaean Thebes in later tradition is a reasonable ground for archaeologists and historians to look forward to the complete excavation of the Theban Acropolis. Archaeology deals directly with the raw material of

Archaeology and tradition

4

history, but, though the objects which it unearths are facts, the more delicate and vulnerable part of the archaeologist's work is the interpretation of the facts. Excavation can reveal the widespread destruction of a site, but the strong and continuing difference of opinions suggests that it is not always easy to distinguish between earthquakes and human violence. Conclusions often have to depend on samples, and the samples may be unrepresentative or insufficient; new excavations in the last ten years have radically changed our picture of the Neolithic period in Greece. There is a temptation to be too schematic in classifying objects and styles, and on these depends in large part our chronology. In attempting to understand the convulsions that end the Mycenaean period dates are of particular importance, and they depend primarily on the evidence of pottery. It is very doubtful whether we can yet place the series of destructions in a secure sequence. We might hope at least to be able to trace changes of population from the material record, but the dark ages still remain very dark. However, the archaeological findings must be the basis of any historical reconstruction, and though there are still major problems to be resolved the historical outline of the prehistoric period has become considerably firmer in the last twenty years.

Neolithic Age

A generation ago it was thought that human occupation in Greece did not begin until developed Neolithic times, but in 1961 the skull of a Neanderthal man was found in Chalcidice and there is already enough material to study the development of Palaeolithic tools. The beginnings of Neolithic settlement have been pushed back to the seventh millennium, and the earliest sites known, at Nea Nikomedia in Macedonia and the Franchthi Cave in the Argolid, show a remarkably early development. At Nea Nikomedia the earliest pottery has been dated between *c.* 6500 and 6000.[1] The houses, of irregular shape, seem to have been built on a framework of timber posts with walls of mud and roofs probably of brushwood covered with clay. Central hearths of mud were built up inside, and outside pits were dug for storage and for rubbish. The settlers grew barley and wheat and kept sheep and goats, supplementing their food supplies by hunting and fishing. In the Franchthi Cave in the Argolid, which has a width at the mouth of 30 m. and a length of 150 m., occupation can be followed from the Pleistocene through the Mesolithic to the Neolithic period.[2] The Mesolithic tenants were hunters, and more than three-quarters of the bones they have left

behind are from red deer. With the transition to the Neolithic period, dated by radiocarbon–14 to the first half of the sixth millennium, the bones of sheep and goats predominate but oxen and pigs also had been domesticated by the middle of the Neolithic period; the economy was based on these domestic animals and on agriculture. After a short period without pottery they made their own pots, at first without decoration, later with linear patterns painted or incised, becoming increasingly sophisticated. But the most impressive evidence of the excavations is the presence of obsidian in the earliest Neolithic levels, increasing considerably through the middle and late periods. Flint, and strong flint particularly, is very rare in Greece and the best available material for knives, razors, sickles and other small tools which need a sharp edge was the hard volcanic glass-like obsidian. According to our present knowledge there is no obsidian in Greece, and the island of Melos in the southern Cyclades had a virtual monopoly.[3] With the primitive tools available for boat or raft building in the sixth millennium a journey to Melos must have been a hazardous adventure requiring considerable enterprise.

Less is known about the Neolithic period in Crete and in the Aegean islands, but what has been found in the large settlement under the Palace at Cnossus and elsewhere suggests that a broadly similar way of life was spread over the mainland, the Cyclades and Crete. Most settlements were small villages living on a combination of stock-raising, mainly sheep and goats, a rudimentary agriculture, and hunting. There was a surprisingly wide-scale trade in obsidian. Stone and bone were the standard materials for other tools. There was ample room for the small population, and these agricultural communities had probably more to fear from animals than from men.

Bronze Age

With the coming of the Bronze Age our evidence becomes fuller, and social and economic changes proceed more quickly. The main incentive was the increasing use of metals and the development of metallurgy, though the transition was not abrupt. Before the end of the Neolithic period there was a limited use of copper and a little silver has been found. From the beginning of the Bronze Age copper was much more widely used, but it was the discovery that an admixture of tin (or, less satisfactory, arsenic) with copper produced in bronze a much harder metal which revolutionised both fighting and farming.[4]

Throughout the Bronze Age which lasts from *c.* 2800 B.C. to *c.* 1050 B.C. when iron begins to replace bronze no events in Greece, Crete or the Aegean can be firmly dated by contemporary sources. Unlike the civilisations of Egypt and Mesopotamia the peoples of these areas were illiterate through the third millennium and when they developed a script they did not record historical events in permanent form. All that survives in writing are the ephemeral records of palace bureaucracies on clay tablets accidentally preserved by destructive fires which baked them. We therefore have to rely for our chronology almost entirely on the dating of material objects. Of these pottery is by far the most widespread and the most resistant. It is used at all levels of society for cooking, eating, drinking and storing, and in all grades of quality. Even when pots are broken the pieces survive and fire does not destroy them. As in modern times different generations tend to have different tastes: there are changes in the style of decoration and changes in ·popular shapes. These can be classified and, with the help of stratified deposits which show which pots are contemporaries, arranged in sequence.

Chron-ology   In order to establish a framework for converting his Cretan excavations into history Evans divided his Bronze Age pottery into three main periods which he called Early, Middle, and Late Minoan, taking the name from the Cretan Minos of tradition. These three periods were then further divided into three phases each, and some of these phases have in turn been subdivided. And so we read of LM III B, referring to the second half of the third phase of late Minoan pottery, and the difference between LM III A and B is crucial in determining the sequence of important events. The same principle has been applied to the other two areas which mainly concern 'us—the mainland of Greece and the islands of the Aegean. The mainland Bronze Age is divided into Early, Middle, and Late Helladic, the last phase of which is often called Mycenaean since Mycenae was the dominant state in Greece at the time, and the islands into Early, Middle, and late Cycladic. The framework that Evans devised has stood up to continuous testing remarkably well, and at a time when some of his most cherished views have crumbled under the weight of new evidence it is well to remember the remarkable achievement of his basic classification.

These labels would not in themselves provide dates because the rhythm of change is not constant and some styles will have been retained much longer than others, but some dates can be given by reference to Egyptian objects which are themselves dated precisely or, more often, approximately by the recorded dates of kings. For example, in several tomb wall-paintings from the early part of the eighteenth dynasty Cretan envoys are included among the peoples who bring gifts or tribute to the Egyptian king. The dress they wear and the vessels they carry suggest that the Cretan period LM I B corresponds roughly with the reign of Thotmes III. Similarly, a great deal of Mycenaean pottery was found at Tel-el-Amarna, and that artificial city established by the heretic Akhenaten was occupied for a short period only, from 1372–1354 B.C. (or possibly 1358 to 1340) so providing approximate dates for Late Helladic III A. Unfortunately some of the Egyptian dates have become less secure than they seemed to be and there is considerable support for lowering the dates in the fourteenth to twelfth centuries, which for our purpose is the most important period.[5] The difference at issue, however, is only fourteen years, and does not affect the sequence of events.

One cannot expect changes of style in all these areas to coincide precisely, but the Cretan pattern provides a fairly satisfactory framework for the mainland also. The same dates can be accepted for both, provided that it is clearly understood that all dates are approximate only and subject to revision as the pottery is more closely analysed and new evidence found. Since the narrative will often be concerned with the evidence of pottery a simplified table at this stage may be convenient:

Approximate dates for Bronze Age Pottery Styles

Early Minoan		Early Helladic
I	2800–2500	I
II	2500–2200	II
III	2200–2000	III

Middle Minoan		Middle Helladic
I	2000–1900	I
II	1900–1700	II
III	1700–1550	III

Late Minoan		Late Helladic
IA	1550–1500	IA
IB	1500–1450	IB
II	1450–1400	II
IIIA	1400–1300	IIIA
IIIB	1300–1200	IIIB
IIIC	1200–1050	IIIC

There is no firm evidence that there was a major change of population at the beginning of the Bronze Age. There are no signs of widespread destruction, nor of the introduction of new customs. There is indeed little observable change from Neolithic to Early Helladic I, though there is a gradual extension of the use of metals. By contrast the second period of the Early Helladic is a period of impressive growth. There is a significant increase in population, and there is more trade between the mainland, Crete, and the islands, and more within each area. The development of metallurgy together with the growth of trade increases specialisation and creates more complex societies. It is in this period that we first see the emergence of dominant buildings and fortifications suggesting a stronger authority and increased resources, accompanied by a growing danger from neighbours or pirates. For these new features the main evidence comes from coastal or island sites. There are good examples of both fortifications and a large building at Chaliandri on the island of Syros and at Lerna in the Argolid. The so-called House of the Tiles at Lerna seems to anticipate on a much smaller scale the later palaces and the tiles from which it is named reflect an important step forward in roof construction.[6] They have been found also at Tiryns and Asine, both near to Lerna, and under the palace at Tiryns there are the remains of a very large circular building.

New arrivals in Greece

By the end of the first phase of Middle Helladic there had been great cultural changes over wide areas of the mainland. What has often been regarded as the first significant feature of the new culture is a new style of pottery which Schliemann called Minyan because he first found it at Orchomenus, the legendary home of King Minyas. It is different in shape, colour and texture from the Early Helladic pottery which preceded it; the dominant shapes are the long-stemmed goblet and the two-handled cup, both reflecting the shapes of metal vessels; the commonest colour is grey; and the texture has not unfairly been described as soapy. Precisely similar pottery was also found of roughly the same period in Troy. Another new type of pottery is usually called matt-painted because the designs, normally geometric, are applied directly to the clay. Other features that were attributed to this phase were the potter's wheel which increased the range and speed of pottery production, the domesticated horse, and the megaron. It was widely believed that these changes were due to a large scale invasion of people from the north, some of whom moved at the same time into Asia Minor. This invasion, it was thought, first

Minyan ware

brought the Greek people and the Greek language into Greece at the end of the second period of the Early Helladic Age (*c.* 2200 B.C.).

Any such reconstruction now seems invalid, and the evidence which has done most to undermine it comes from Caskey's excavations at Lerna. There, before the beginning of the last phase of the Early Helladic, the impressive House of Tiles and the settlement that surrounded it were violently destroyed and further destructions, thought to be of approximately the same date, have been found at Asine, Zygouries, and Tiryns in the Argolid, at Cirrha across the Corinthian Gulf, and at Hagios Cosmas on the southern coast of Attica: in the next generation no major destructions have yet been found. The destruction of Lerna led to occupation by new people with different customs and different houses.[7] When the settlement was restored the area occupied by the House of Tiles, which had been burnt to the ground, was not built over; the ruins were heaped together and covered with a memorial mound until successive rebuilding had reached the top of the mound, when the site was again built over.[4] There is little likelihood that these newcomers came from the north. The importance of Minyan ware in the argument is also becoming questionable. A crude form of Minyan hand-made is found in post-destruction Lerna, and is also made by people, apparently from Anatolia, who occupied Lefkandi between Chalcis and Eretria in Euboea at about this time.[8] The Minyan ware of Troy on the other hand is at a more developed stage. Nor can much importance be attached to the megaron at this period, because definitions have been much too flexible. We should also even retain an open mind on the date of the arrival of the Greeks. All that can be said securely is that there are numerous place names that survived in Greece but are not Greek. The clearest examples have the suffixes *nth* and *ss,* as Corinth and Tiryns, and the rivers Kephissus and Ilissus; these suffixes are also found in Crete as in Cnossus and Tylissus, and in the south-west of Asia Minor, where *nth* becomes *nd,* as in Alinda, and Halicarnassus.[9] At some time before the Greeks came, this non-Greek people must have been widely spread on both sides of the Aegean and in Crete.

New settlers at Lerna

and Lefkandi

Pre-Greek names

The Middle Helladic Age, from *c.* 2000 to 1550 B.C., shows at first an unspectacular development. In contrast with Crete and even with some of the Cyclades mainland Greece could almost be regarded as a backward area, but from *c.* 1600 progress was quickened, largely under the influence of Crete. For some two hundred years Crete exercised a powerful influence on the mainland and to Crete we must first turn.

Crete

Natural resources

Through the third millennium there was no question of Crete exercising influence outside her own island; but early in the second millennium, in the Middle Minoan period, she made spectacular advances. She enjoyed useful resources for development: her mountains were thickly wooded with cypress, cedar, pine and fir which could provide ample material for the building of ships and perhaps for export to Egypt, which was chronically short of good timber. The combination of mountain and valley encouraged stock-breeding, and her coastal plains—particularly the Mesara on the south side of the central mountain backbone—could provide good crops. Technologically, the time was well suited for a major advance. Bronze was ceasing to become a precious metal and was coming into general use: among the tools that it produced were the impressive long saws up to nearly four feet in length, which were made primarily to cut the larger timbers

1.1   Vase with palm trees

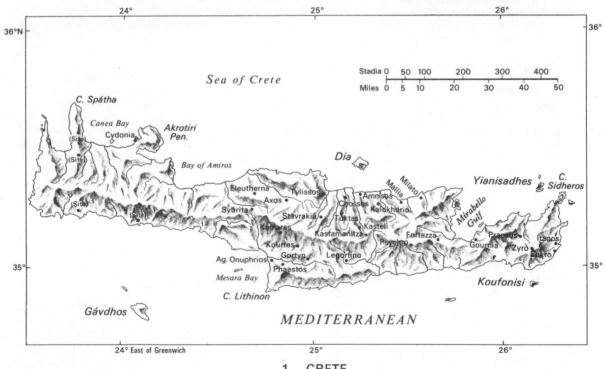

1.   CRETE

but could also saw through the softer stones.[10] This also was the time when the potter's wheel came into use, quickened the speed of production, and extended the range of shapes. But however favourable the circumstances may have been, the pottery of this period, known as Kamares ware because it was first found in the Kamares cave on the south side of Mount Ida near the summit, is an astonishing revelation. Technically the pots are very well fired. The designs are bold, semi-abstract, but recognisably related to nature; the colours are emphatic—black, white, orange and red; and there is no conflict between decoration and shape.

The first palaces

But the most striking development of this period in Crete is the building of palaces, which were to set the pattern of organisation for Crete and Greece for nearly a thousand years. The palaces imply a concentration of political and religious authority, and an increase in wealth, and they pave the way for further expansion by strong direction. Soon after *c.* 2000 they were built at Cnossus some five miles from the coast, in the middle of the north side of the island; at Mallia thirty miles to the east; at Phaestus opposite Cnossus on the south side of the mountains, commanding the Mesara plain; and, later, at Zakro on the coast at the east end of the island. These first palaces mark a sharp break with the pattern of the Neolithic village and they follow eastern models such as can be seen at Ugarit (the modern Ras Shamra) on the Syrian coast and Mari on the upper Euphrates. It was not until the Greeks developed the city state that a sharp political and institutional contrast developed between east and west.

It was probably the introduction of palace organisation that provided the main incentive for the development of writing and in this field also the models were in the east and particularly in Egypt. The first Cretan script was pictorial and, borrowing Egyptian terms, is called hieroglyphic, though there was nothing religious about it. The pictures were at first recognisable representations of natural objects, but they gradually became increasingly schematic. Before the end of the second Middle Minoan period a syllabic script had been developed at Phaestus which Evans called Linear A, to be distinguished from a later development which he called Linear B. These first palaces were all destroyed or severely damaged in the course of the second Middle Minoan period and as no substantial traces of fire were found it is generally assumed that one or more earthquakes were responsible. Crete has always been liable to earthquakes and the construction of the palaces could not withstand severe shocks.

By the third Middle Minoan period the palaces had been rebuilt on a grander scale, though apparently without any radical change of plan, and the period of the second palaces, roughly from 1650 to 1450, marks the height of Cretan prosperity. Though no two palaces are precisely alike in plan, they all have certain basic features in common. The most important of these, and the most emphatic in the plan, is the impressively large central court, which at Cnossus, Phaestus and Mallia is some 170 feet long and 80 feet wide (at Zakro it is smaller). It is almost certainly designed for public ceremonies and spectacles. Round the court separate blocks provide for the various functions of the palace. There are the big state rooms and, separate from them, the royal family's residential quarters. Storage capacity is required not only to meet the needs of the palace itself but also to carry the stocks of oil, wool or other commodities needed to exchange in trade for what cannot be locally produced. There are also working quarters for the skilled craftsmen required to maintain the buildings and provide some of the amenities of palace life.

Palace of Cnossus

Of the second palaces that of Cnossus was considerably the largest, covering three acres with its main building and five acres if separate but associated buildings are included. The state rooms are on the west side of the court and the more important and grander are on an upper floor approached by a monumental staircase: among the ground floor rooms is a complex devoted to ritual cult. To the west of the state rooms are the main stores of the palace occupying no less than nineteen rooms, in which the dominant feature is the series of large *pithoi,* storage jars of varying heights up to five feet tall. Most of these were for the storage of oil, which has always been one of the main products of Crete; but some will have contained wine, and others might have been used for wool, also important in the economy, or grain. In the floor of the corridor flanking these store-rooms were a series of cists, originally lined with lead, which were used for the storage of small and more valuable objects. The living quarters of the royal family are on the opposite side of the court, taking advantage of the terraced slope down to the river Keiretos which provided two floors below ground level. The rooms of the ground floor of this wing include a bathroom and a toilet; the main rooms here also are on an upper floor approached by a second monumental staircase.

1.2   Store-jars in the palace of Cnossus

By later Greek standards the plan is not tidy but the organisation of the space is practical.

Cretan building

The building techniques used at Cnossus are typical of Cretan palaces. Most of the walls have their foundations and lowest courses in stone, but the main structure is built with large unbaked bricks, interlaced with vertical and horizontal timbers and tie-beams holding together the two sides. The roof is flat with a thick layer of clay over brushwood resting on the rafters. Considerable care is taken to brighten internal rooms by light-wells, and columns of wood, many of them fluted, are used as weight-bearers to help support upper floors as well as to add dignified variety to the architecture.

Most of the principal chambers and corridors were decorated with fresco paintings, representing solemn processions, gay groups of men and women, scenes of town-life, less often of war. The fashions of the time are vividly portrayed in a series of miniature frescoes, showing women, idling in courts or on balconies, with their hair elaborately dressed, wearing costumes which look as if they had been modelled on quite modern fashions—puffed sleeves, flounced skirts, bodices tightly drawn

in round the waist and leaving the bosom exposed. One of the most striking pictures which have survived is that of a tall handsome cup-bearer, strongly resembling the Cretans (Keftiu) who are represented in a painting of Egyptian Thebes bringing offerings to King Thothmes III in the fifteenth century. Near the northern entrance to their palace the later lords of Cnossus constructed a theatre, capable of holding about 400 spectators. This was not a new thing; a theatre of an earlier period has been discovered in the palace of Phaestus. The orchestral area in these early theatres was not circular as in those of later times, but rectangular; and the performances were probably religious dances.

The rebuilding of the palace of Phaestus fell perhaps in the sixteenth century. Like that of Cnossus it was unfortified, and it was built on a very similar plan, and in the same fashion of architecture. Here, too, there was a large court in the centre, surrounded by pillared reception halls and store-rooms, and a smaller court in the west of the building. The palace of Phaestus was distinguished by an imposing entrance, with a flight of twelve steps forty-five feet broad; and though it was smaller in extent

Palace of Phaestus

1.3   Staircase in the palace of Cnosses

than the rival palace of Cnossus, and its walls were not adorned with such rich and various paintings, its external appearance seems to have been more imposing, for it was built upon the top of a hill and dominated the wide plain of the Mesara. About two miles off, at a place now called Hagia Triada, a palace-like building has been found which seems to have served as a pleasure-residence for the princes of the neighbouring palace.

In the period of the second palaces prosperity was by no means confined to the palaces; there was also a widespread improvement in the general standard of living. The little town of Gournia, built on rising ground overlooking Mirabello Bay, near but not on the sea, was a small and unimportant settlement probably dependent on agriculture; but its streets were paved, and the houses were built on the same principles as many parts of the palaces, walls of unbaked bricks resting on a few courses of rough stones. House plans were ingeniously adapted to the slope of the ground and the 'squire's house' at the top of the hill is a miniature palace with well-coursed blocks of

Gournia town

cut stone. A carpenter's stock of tools implies developed craftsmanship and the pottery fragments that were found in the ruins included some fine pieces. On the north-east coast the port of Palaikastro, probably more concerned with trade, had larger and more elaborate houses and finer pottery. That these two settlements were not especially favoured is shown by the even more impressive house remains at Tylissus and Mallia. From the low walls of all these houses little can be clearly grasped except the plan of the ground floor, but a fair idea of facades can be seen from the houses on mosaic plaques of porcelain discovered in the palace of Cnossus. These houses have several storeys, they are well-windowed, and there are un-windowed openings on upper storeys which may have served as balconies.

The prosperity of Crete during this period was based in part on the development of her own resources, primarily wool and oil, in part on the expansion of trade. Thucydides and Herodotus preserve the tradition of the thalassocracy of Minos king of Cnossus and the archaeological evidence has given substance

Crete and the Aegean

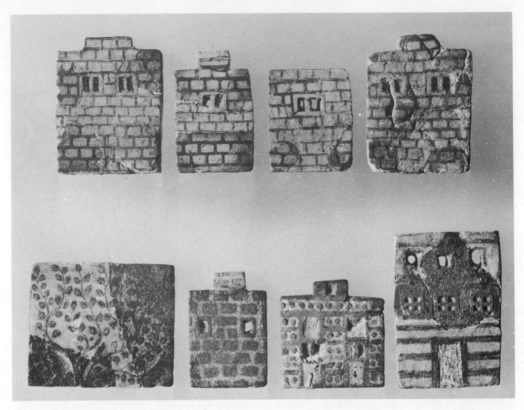

1.4 Faience plaques, Cnossus (see note, page 551)

and colour to the tradition.[11] Minoan pottery has been found in Egypt and Syria and Cretan influence is apparent on the development of the earliest Cypriot script.[12] On the way to the east there was a Cretan settlement at Trianda on the island of Rhodes, near to the site of the later Dorian Ialysus, and sufficient Minoan pottery has been found on Samos and at Miletus to suggest a settlement or at least strong trading connections.[13] There is far less evidence of Cretan interest in the west but Minoan pottery has been found in Sicily and Herodotus preserves a tradition of a disastrous expedition to Sicily to avenge the killing of Minos.[14] Nearer home the influence of Crete radiated strongly over the Aegean, though it is not easy to distinguish between Minoan influence, Minoan control and Minoan settlement. In the fifth century Minos king of Cnossus was firmly rooted in tradition. To Herodotus, writing at a time when Athenian power was based on a navy which controlled the Aegean, Minos was the first ruler to exercise thalassocracy and Thucydides, who could not resist any opportunity to correct his predecessor, accepts the same tradition.[11] There is little doubt that he saw in Minos the precursor of Athens, clearing the sea of pirates and so increasing the flow of trade. He adds that Minos also colonised most of the islands.

There is no doubt that at the least Crete exercised a strong influence on the Cyclades and that they were one of her most important markets. The islanders were the main customers for the stone vases which were a Cretan speciality; comparatively few have been found on the mainland or in the Near East. Minoan pottery was more widely distributed but a considerable quantity of Cretan pots have been found in the islands. Imports from Crete, however, even in large quantities, do not necessarily imply a colony nor subject status. In later history we are so accustomed to the poverty and helplessness of most of the Cyclades that we are apt to overlook the high quality of their culture in the prehistoric period. In the Early Bronze Age they were indeed ahead of the mainland in the use of metals and in the attractiveness of their pottery.

There is only one island colony which is not seriously questioned. In the Early Helladic period a small settlement was established at

Colony on Cythera

1.5   Hagia Eirene, Ceos

Kastri on a small headland on the south coast of the island of Cythera which lies off the southern shore of the Peloponnese. These settlers were undoubtedly from Crete. All their pottery whether for the kitchen, the table or display, were Minoan in form and style though little of it was actually imported from Crete. In Cretan style they set up a purple dye industry and were probably useful to Cretan merchants as a depot through which Cretan goods could be carried to the Peloponnese, where there is a significant import of Cretan pottery in the Middle Helladic period. It is also significant that the settlement of Kastri was abandoned at approximately the same time as Cretan power in Cnossus collapsed.[15]

Melos Strong claims have also been made for Cretan colonies on Melos, Thera, and Ceos, but none of these is certain. The excavations at Phylakopi on Melos revealed a prosperous community with its own individual character, influenced but not submerged by Cretan influences.[16] The island had sufficient resources in her agriculture to remain prosperous even when obsidian, in which she had held a virtual monopoly, was devalued by the increasing use of bronze and later of iron. The influence of Crete is no less clearly shown on *Thera* Thera (the modern Santorini), not far from

Melos. Here the most revealing excavations are those that were begun in 1967 at Akrotiri on the eastern side of the island. The Bronze Age settlements of Thera were overwhelmed by a volcanic eruption of catastrophic violence and now lie buried under a mountain of ash, in some places up to a hundred feet in depth. But at Akrotiri excavation, though costly and extremely difficult, has been practicable and the results already achieved are a striking tribute to the ingenuity and skill of the excavator, Sp. Marinatos, and his team. The area uncovered is still small, and most of their treasures were taken away by the inhabitants when they decided to evacuate before it was too late, but enough evidence remains to encourage speculation on the nature of the settlement. The buildings are certainly very similar to Cretan workmanship and the frescoes in style and subject are reminiscent of Crete. Minoan pottery has also been found in the houses, but there are also pots of excellent quality from the islands and the swallows that figure so delightfully on two of the frescoes and also on one of the pots recall Melos rather than Cnossus.[17]

Hagia Eirene is the name given to a small *Ceos* settlement on Ceos (the modern Kea) occupying a promontory in the harbour of Vourkari at the inner end of the bay of Hagios Nikolaos.

It was established in the Early Bronze Age, reached its peak in the sixteenth and fifteenth centuries, but was largely destroyed by earthquake at the end of the second phase of Middle Helladic and never fully recovered. Situated near Attica and Euboea and having an excellent harbour it was well situated to trade with central Greece and the islands, and became a flourishing trading station. In the Early Helladic period there is no trace of Cretan influence and the pottery suggests close relations with the mainland and the islands. From the first two phases of the Middle Helladic a few fragments of Kamares ware from Crete have been found, but imports from Crete remain inconsiderable until the sixteenth century. It is probably no coincidence that Hagia Eirene's most prosperous period coincides with the great days of the Cretan second palaces. Cretan influence can then be seen in the increasing import of Minoan pottery and the setting up of a workshop for the production of stone vessels on the Cretan model. But pottery imports from Crete are balanced by continuing imports from the mainland and the islands. Caskey's fruitful excavations have revealed nothing that cannot be explained by the independent development of a lively and hard-working native community taking full advantage of a site admirably suited for trade. It is true that there was a tradition known to Bacchylides and Pindar that King Minos slept with a Cean princess and that their son became King of the island, but without some clearer confirmation from archaeology it would be dangerous to infer more than a close relationship between Crete and Ceos.[18]

Athens   Athens also is linked with Crete in the famous story of Theseus and the minotaur. According to this story Athens was at the time subject to Crete and was required to pay an annual tribute of seven boys and seven girls to be sacrificed to the man-bull in the labyrinth attached to the palace at Cnossus. The Athenian hero Theseus with the collusion of the king's daughter Ariadne slew the minotaur and by using a thread to mark his way through the labyrinth escaped with Ariadne whom he somewhat ungallantly deserted when they reached the island of Naxos. This account of the liberation of Athens from the Cretan yoke is a good story, but very doubtful history. According to the main tradition Theseus was a contemporary of Heracles two generations before the Trojan War, but by that time the power of Cretan Cnossus had been broken for nearly a hundred years. Ariadne is the name of a Cretan goddess and the cruelty implied in King Minos is barely consistent

1.6   Cretan bull and acrobat

with the wise lawgiver of tradition. A minotaur is represented on Cretan seals and rings, but there are very few examples and he seems to be merely one of many animal-headed demons introduced from Egypt. The minotaur and his victims are probably echoes of the bull-leaping displays by young men and women which figure so prominently in frescoes and figurines, but these seem to be athletes specially trained for this dangerous game rather than the human tribute from subject states. The legend of the labyrinth may derive from the Carian word for the double-axe, *labrys,* for the palace, where the double-axe was the dominant symbol on the walls, could well be called the house of the double-axe, and its intricate plan might suggest a maze. It is very doubtful whether Athens at any time was paying annual tribute to Cnossus.[19] It is possible that the decipherment of the language of the earlier series of tablets, most of which were found in the Cretan palaces, and the extension of excavation may throw clearer light on the means by which Cnossus exercised her influence, but in the present state of the evidence it is sound policy to avoid such words as imperialist and empire, and to be sceptical about the proliferation of colonies. But whatever the nature of the relationship the islands prospered in the heyday of the Cretan palaces, and Cretan culture played an important part in civilising the Greeks.

Cretan civilisation in its prime is extremely *Cretan* attractive. The best pottery of the Middle *culture* Minoan period has rarely been equalled, beginning with the semi-abstract style of the Kamares ware and then moving through a naturalistic phase, in which most designs are taken from marine life or nature. The octopus and the dolphin become favourite subjects for delightfully varied designs: palms, lilies, iris and poppy are ingeniously adapted to the shape of the vase. Even the most sophisticated pieces give the impression of spontaneity. There is the same sensitivity in their frescoes.

Though it would be rash to argue from the attractiveness of their pottery, painting and jewelry, that the Bronze Age Cretans were a humane and peace-loving people, it is reasonable to argue from the lack of emphasis on arms and armour in their tombs and in palace decoration that they did not regard fighting as the nobleman's primary occupation. If Cretan fleets dominated the seas there may have been no need for elaborate protection against invaders from outside, but the defencelessness of the palaces implies that they did not expect dangerous raids from rival princes in the island. Their frescoes, pottery and gems suggest a delight in the world of nature, and there seems to be more gaiety than fear in their religion.

1.7   Vase with octopus, Cnossus

1.8   Harvesters in Song

Religian

There is no evidence yet of public temples in Crete at this date: the sacred places were in caves and on the peaks of certain mountains. Here the people brought offerings, and there was some form of public cult. There were also rustic shrines where some form of tree cult was maintained, with ritual dances to stimulate the epiphany of goddess or god. In palaces and some private houses there were domestic sanctuaries, but the palace seems also to have been the focal point of the people's religion.

Religion centred on the forces of nature, and nature demons in the form of animals recur on paintings and on gems. The most popular divinity seems to have been a nature goddess, mistress of animals, who is sometimes guarded by lions, and sometimes associated with doves. The very beautiful snake-entwined figurines found in the palace at Cnossus are probably the goddess who protects the palace, or her priestess. Minoan religion seems to have been dominated by goddesses; the few representatives of gods suggest that they had a very secondary role, though in later times the Greeks

1.9 Snake-goddess

1.10 Ivory figurine of a boy god, southern Crete

gave a Cretan origin to Zeus, son of Rhea and nurtured in the Idaean cave. Two symbols were particularly associated with Cretan cults: the horns of consecration emphasised the religious nature of a place, and the double-axe was both a religious symbol and a cult object. It is represented in painting on the palace walls at Cnossus and is widely used by potters as a decorative element in their designs; double-axes are a favourite form of dedication, and miniatures are manufactured for this purpose—some even in gold. There is very little evidence of a darker side of religion, and it is significant that the Cretans seem to attach little importance to their burials; they do not need a rich store of possessions to accompany them to another world.[20]

Destruction of palaces

The great days of the Cretan palaces lasted until approximately the middle of the fifteenth century when, at the height of Cretan power, the palaces of Phaestus, Mallia and Zakro became masses of rubble and ash. The destruction also spread to country villas and can be traced at the small towns of Gournia and Palaikastro. Cnossus alone of the excavated palaces survived. What was the cause of such a dramatic disaster? Twenty years ago there was a natural answer: it was then thought that the destruction of Cnossus was contemporary with that of the other palaces, and it was reasonable to infer that the Mycenaeans, who seemed to have profited most from the eclipse of Crete, had invaded the island and destroyed the main centres of power. Such a simple answer is no longer possible. More concentrated study of the pottery has shown beyond doubt that Cnossus survived the holocaust and was not destroyed until after 1400. A much more serious shock was the discovery that at the time of its destruction the palace of Cnossus was controlled by Greeks. Features that had already been noted might have led to this conclusion—a new emphasis on weapons in burials, the adoption of the Mycenaean chamber tomb, and what seemed to be mainland influence on pottery—but the decisive evidence was in writing.

Greeks control Cnossus

In the ruins of the palace Evans had found over three thousand clay tablets, baked by the fire which accompanied the destruction. The writing on these tablets was different from that on tablets which had been found in the other palaces, and it was considered by Evans to be a later development from the first. Linear A and linear B seemed appropriate names. Literacy had always been one of Evans's

Decipherment of Linear B tablets

1.11   Painted sarcophagus, Hagia Triada (see note, page 551)

dominant interests, but the decipherment of the tablets eluded him. In 1939, however, a new palace was found by Blegen on the Greek mainland, at Epano Englianos in Messenia, and one of his first discoveries was a mass of tablets, clearly from an archive room, which used the same signs and figures as the linear B tablets from Cnossus. This new material enabled a young British architect, Michael Ventris, who had been working from his schooldays on the decipherment, to demonstrate that the linear B tablets spoke a pre-Homeric form of Greek.[21] Unfortunately the tablets are all concerned with detailed administration. They throw interesting though rather fitful and controversial light on economic and social conditions but they do not tell us when and how the Greeks won Cnossus and what their relations were with the natives.

Volcanic eruption on Thera

The question of Cnossus cannot be separated from that of the other palaces. To the question why they were destroyed, various answers have been given, and the most exciting introduces the great volcanic eruption on Thera (Santorini). This island has always been known to owe its present form to volcanic action; there is now evidence which suggests that there was an eruption of tremendous force at some point near 1500 B.C. The violence of the eruption is not in dispute. All the settlements on the island were buried beneath mountains of pumice and ash and when the crater had blown itself out the sea rushed in and, breaking through the ring of land that surrounded the volcano, made of Thera three separate islands.

The repercussions of the eruption could have affected settlements over a very wide area as was shown by the eruption in 1882 of Krakatoa in the channel between Java and Sumatra. The volume of matter ejected at Santorini was very considerably larger and the force of the explosion must have blown an enormous cloud of pumice and ash miles into the air and this could have drifted a very considerable distance with the wind. Borings in the sea bed show deep deposits on both sides of the eastern end of Crete: it is virtually certain that a thick layer of ash fell over east Crete and this could have made the land unusable for some time. The inrush of sea into the vacuum left by the eruption would create an immense wave up to a hundred feet in height which could travel hundreds of miles and be very destructive. The great obstacle to associating either of these dangers with the destruction of the Cretan palaces comes from the dating of pottery.[22]

We have seen how the settlement of Akrotiri on the east side of Thera was evacuated before it was too late and the immediate cause was an earthquake. Traces of small-scale reoccupation have been found but no evidence of substantial rebuilding.[23] In the deep sealing of pumice and ash there are normally three layers: at the bottom mainly pumice *c*. 12–15 feet deep; above, a thinner layer (*c*. four feet) with narrow bands of pink or white ash and grey-white pumice; on top, a huge deposit of white ash. There is evidence of an interval after the first in traces of erosion in the pumice, but the fact that no soil had accumulated suggests that the interval was short. The pottery that was being used in Akrotiri at the time of the evacuation clearly belongs to Late Minoan 1A, indicating a date *c*. 1500; the pottery from the destruction levels in the palaces belongs no less clearly to Late Minoan 1B some fifty years later.

There is a natural temptation to try and bridge the gap and D. L. Page has advanced an interpretation which is at first sight attractive.[24] His hypothesis is that the earthquake which led to the evacuation of Akrotiri was a preliminary warning of the disaster that was threatened, but that the actual eruption came some twenty or more years later and was accompanied by a major earthquake which was the cause of the destructions, while the deep cover of ash explains why, with minor exceptions, the destroyed buildings were not reoccupied. This is an ingenious tour de force, but there are strong technical and logical objections. Expert opinion, arguing from known parallels, considers that the total process of eruption would be compressed within a very short period, and that the evidence of erosion in the layer of pumice at Akrotiri is not inconsistent with this assumption. Page's interpretation does not satisfactorily explain the evidence of fire at almost all the destroyed sites, for though fire is not incompatible with earthquake we should expect it to be the exception rather than the rule. We should not expect the palace of Cnossus to survive, as it did, when buildings at Tylissus only seven miles away were destroyed. But the most serious objection is the long interval between the preliminary warning at Akrotiri and the great eruption. The original excavators of Phaestus and Mallia were satisfied that human violence was responsible for the destruction; they were probably right.

There is, however, good reason to believe that the repercussions of the eruption on Crete were serious. The immense wave generated by the inrush of the sea into the crater could have done considerable damage to settlements on the north coast and to shipping in their harbours and the fall of ash may have, temporarily at least, paralysed agricultural production in the east of the island. Considerable damage was done by earthquake to the palace at Cnossus at about this time, and Hood has suggested that a massive deposit of the LMIA period from two votive pits on a hill above Zakro may have been designed to appease the gods after the cataclysm.[25]

De-
struction
of palaces
by Greeks?

If human violence was responsible for the destructions the destroyers must have been either Cretans, or Greeks, or other foreigners. We can dismiss the view that the destructions reflect a social revolution, the underprivileged turning on their masters. This would not explain the destruction of Gournia, a small town of mainly modest houses, nor does wealth seem to have been concentrated too narrowly in Cretan society. The large number of seals that have been found on most sites shows that many of the middle class had property which they wanted to identify as their own or to sell, and in the towns there is no marked segregation of large houses from small. In the period between *c.*1230 and *c.*1170 there is evidence from Egypt and Ugarit that loosely associated bands of different peoples were operating by sea and land and leaving a trail of destruction on their way to Egypt. There could have been such plundering raids on Crete in the fifteenth century but the expansion of trade with the east in the fourteenth century is barely consistent with large organised piratical fleets as early as this. Perhaps the least unlikely solution is that Greeks from the mainland, and probably from the Argolid, got control of Cnossus without serious fighting and systematically destroyed political rivals.

Destruc-
tion of
palace of
Cnossus

This, however, leaves another very awkward question. Some fifty or more years after the destruction of the other palaces Cnossus itself was largely destroyed. Evans thought that an earthquake was responsible, but had that been so the palace would have been rebuilt. Perhaps the Mycenaeans of the mainland thought that Cnossus was interfering with their interests. A very different historical sequence would have to be accepted if we could follow Palmer's interpretation of the evidence from Cnossus. He would date the major destruction of Cnossus to *c.*1200 B.C., at the time when the great Mycenaean centres on the mainland were being destroyed; at the earlier date, he thinks, only minor damage was done. The Mycenaean Greeks, on this view, would have controlled Cnossus for more than 200 years, and the Cnossus tablets would be contemporary with the tablets from Pylos. This, he thinks, would explain why there are only insignificant differences in the language from the two centres. To make his case Palmer analysed Evans's notebooks, compared them with the later publication, and showed that there were mistakes and inconsistencies.[26] But however attractive the historical implications of this dating may seem, the decisive evidence is the pottery. Here the historian is out of his depth, but the last detailed analysis, by Popham, should persuade waverers that in his interpretation of the evidence Evans was basically right.[27] There was a major destruction before 1350, though rather later than Evans's 1400, and only an impoverished partial occupation afterwards.

But for some seventy years after the destruction of the eastern palaces Cnossus remained a powerful and prosperous centre ruled by Greeks whose control probably extended at least over the areas previously ruled from Phaestus, Mallia and Zakro. The west remains comparatively unexplored and much work has to be done before we get a comprehensive picture of developments in Crete at this critical period. It will be particularly interesting to know whether Cydonia shared the fate of the eastern palaces. No systematic exploration has been possible because the Minoan city is buried under Khania, the modern capital of the island, but Cydonia was an important harbour town in the archaic and classical periods and casual finds show that its importance goes back to the Minoan period.

When the palace of Cnossus was destroyed it was still enjoying prosperity. Fine objects were still being made by resident craftsmen and it has been calculated that there was storage capacity for more than 25,000 gallons of oil, mainly in the great *pithoi* in the western wing. It was perhaps with this oil that the palace was able to import in exchange the metals and precious stones needed for the work of the craftsmen and the amenities of palace life. All this was as it had been before the Greeks came. It was probably with the help of Cretans that the script of the linear B tablets was devised for the Greek language, and the form of the records of routine administration was also probably derived from the Cretans. It was the Greek experience in Cnossus that led to the building of large palaces on the mainland and the development of palace-based economics on the Cretan model. But the palace of Cnossus was destroyed before Mycenae and Thebes reached their prime, and it was probably the Greeks of the mainland who destroyed it in order to remove a rival.

Mycenaean Civilisation
(1600–1100 B.C.)

The highly developed civilisation of Crete began to exercise a dominant influence on the Greek mainland from about 1600 B.C., and the first clear evidence comes from the shaft graves of Mycenae. Mycenae was well placed to be a centre of power in an insecure age. Some twelve miles inland, at the north-east corner of the Argive plain, it had good corn land to support it, a strong defensive and strategic position, and an adequate water-supply. Built on a hill rising some 900 feet above sea-level, it overlooked the Argive plain and commanded easy routes to the Isthmus. There are only faint traces of settlement on the site in Neolithic times, but the population had grown considerably by the Middle Helladic period. There is, however, no reason to believe that Mycenae was then more powerful or prosperous than several of the other settlements round the Argive plain. Certainly nothing had been found to prepare archaeologists for the dazzling wealth of the shaft graves: it was Homer and not the archaeological evidence that led Schliemann to Mycenae.

Shaft graves Circle A The graves that Schliemann discovered were of a distinctive type that had not been found before and it was to have a very short history. Shafts up to three and a half metres deep were sunk in the soft rock and supports were added in the form of inset ledges or attached walls to carry roof timbers roughly a metre above the floor. The body, elaborately dressed, was laid on the floor of the shaft and beside the body were placed food, wine and prized possessions to accompany the dead. The grave was then roofed and the timbers were covered with brushwood which was then sealed with a thick coat of clay. Earth was thrown back to fill the shaft and a small mound was raised on which a stone was erected, sometimes plain, more often with linear designs or crude figured scenes of fighting or the hunt. Some of the graves were reused for later burials in which case the whole process was repeated. There were six graves containing altogether nineteen burials; two of the graves had single burials and one had as many as five. The special distinction of the dead was marked by a circular wall enclosing their graves and this circle was preserved and respected for more than 200 years.

The most astonishing feature of the shaft graves is their wealth of precious materials, particularly gold, and their abundance of weapons.[28] Of the six graves three are pre-eminently rich (III, IV, V). These are probably the graves of kings with their queens and immediate family, covering a period of roughly one hundred years (c. 1600–1500 B.C.); the other three may have been for more distant relatives. The richest of all was grave IV in which three men and two women were buried: with them were two magnificent golden crowns, eight golden diadems, five golden cups, including one with a repoussé dolphin design, and another with birds perched on its two handles, faintly reminiscent of Nestor's cup in Homer, and two gold rings. There were also vessels of silver, alabaster, faience and electrum as well as the more common bronze and copper. No less impressive is the glut of weapons in graves

1.12   Inlaid dagger blade, Mycenae

IV and V, including more than 50 swords for five burials together with smaller numbers of daggers, hacking-knives and spears, and arrowheads of bronze, obsidian, and bone.

Among the swords are several that were primarily decorative, to be hung in the hall rather than carried to battle, and on some of the dagger blades there are delicately designed scenes with silver and gold inlays on a background of dark niello. The most ambitious vividly depicts a lion hunt. On the right are three lions: the first on the right is in full flight, the second follows but turns his head round, the third boldly attacks the hunters. The leading hunter has fallen to the ground, the second stands fast holding his shield to protect him, the third and the fifth advance with their long spears poised to strike, while between them is an archer with a bow, unprotected by shield because he will keep at a safe distance. On another blade there is a contrasting scene of a duck hunt in the marshes. But most of the weapons were meant to kill. Fighting is also the theme on a large amphora with figures of silver on a background of niello; two groups, each of four warriors, fight with their spears, over a man who has fallen in battle.[29] A silver rhyton of which only tantalising fragments survive has a more complex scene of women

1.13 Silver rhyton with siege scene, Mycenae (see note, page 551)

behind battlements, archers in action, and perhaps a boat manned with armed men. It is called the Siege Rhyton and may illustrate a typical raid on an eastern town.

Grave III, in which three women and one child (or perhaps two) were buried, presents a very different picture. Here there were no weapons, but a massive display of gold and jewelry, and attachments to dresses—in particular wafer-thin gold disks with designs ranging from various spiral forms to conventionalised octopus, butterfly and other creatures. The three poorer graves had very much less gold and silver but correspondingly more pottery.

Some of the objects found in the graves were locally made, but most of the finer treasures are the work of Cretan craftsmen, including perhaps some who may have been working on the mainland. Alabaster and faience vases are a Cretan speciality and the gold repoussé work and scenes inlaid on daggers are Cretan in spirit and beyond the skills of contemporary mainland craftsmen. There is no clear evidence of direct contact with the Near East or Egypt. Most of the gold may have come from Egypt, the ivory from Syria, the lapis-lazuli from Afghanistan, but the vessels made from these were probably made in Crete and came to the mainland through Crete. The amber beads, however, did not pass through Crete; they came from the Baltic region of the far north.

The contrast of the shaft grave treasures with the earlier archaeological material from Mycenae was so striking that it was commonly believed that this was a dynasty of newcomers who owed their position to their superior weapons, including chariots, and their fighting strength. Evans believed that they were Cretan conquerors, others suggested that they were mercenaries who had enriched themselves by helping the Egyptians to drive the Hyksos out of Egypt (the dates could fit). But the shaft graves are radically different from Cretan burials, and their barbaric display of wealth and emphasis on fighting are incompatible with the civilised ways of the Cretans. Mercenaries rewarded by Egypt should have had considerably more Egyptian souvenirs than are found. With the further extension of excavation revealing growing wealth in other centres it became easier to believe that these were Mycenaeans who established Mycenaean supremacy over the Argive plain and perhaps raided further afield.

This solution was easier to accept when a second circle of shaft graves was discovered at Mycenae. This series (known as Circle B to

Circle B

1.14 Gold disks from shaft graves, Mycenae (see note, page 551)

1.15 Grave in Circle B, Mycenae

which were earlier. The construction of these shaft graves and the general character of the grave contents closely resemble those of Circle A, but their display of precious metals and weapons was less spectacular. These were probably the graves of leading nobles, the king's companions rather than kings themselves. It is significant that while Circle A was respected and renovated as a public memorial when during the thirteenth century it was included within an extension of the citadel walls, Circle B was neglected and partly buried under a large mound of earth from a later tomb.

From *c.* 1600 to 1400 Cretan influence was dominant on the mainland. In pottery Cretan subjects and shapes are taken over by the mainland potter. At first the subjects, mainly drawn from plant and marine life—iris, lily, palm, octopus, dolphin—are treated naturalistically and a single theme covers the whole vessel; later the subjects are more stylised and the surface is divided into panels. In metal Cretan styles and subjects are similarly followed. But the shaft grave, which has not yet been found

Cretan influence on mainland

distinguish it from Schliemann's graves, now Circle A) had begun earlier, but overlapped with Circle A (from *c.* 1650 to *c.* 1550 B.C.). There were fourteen shaft graves in the circle and a number of modest cist graves, most of outside the Argolid, owes nothing to Crete. It is probably a development from the common cist, which is a shallow grave covered by a stone slab and sometimes lined with stone inside. It may have been the richness of their funeral furnishings that encouraged these generations of Mycenaean chiefs to adopt a form of grave which would damp the spirits of tomb robbers. No shaft grave has been found at Mycenae later than Circle A; a new type of tomb had by then become the recognised tomb for princes. This was the tholos tomb, which *Tholos* is first found in Messenia and subsequently *tombs* spreads throughout the Peloponnese and central Greece. Unlike the cist and shaft grave and the later chamber tomb it was round in form with a beehive roof formed by successive rings of stones gradually narrowing and covered at the top by a large roof-stone. It was approached by a long passage, *dromos,* and the whole was covered by a mound of earth. Some think that the ancestor of this tomb is the circular enclosure for multiple burials in the Mesara plain of southern Crete, but there are significant differences and if the model was Cretan, the mainland adapter has made his own considerable contribution.[30]

While Minoan civilisation was at its height Mycenae and the other mainland centres could not compare with Cnossus, Phaestus, and the other Cretan palace-cities, but when Cnossus had been occupied by Greeks and most at least of the other Cretan palaces destroyed, the mainland Greeks were well prepared to develop independently, though it was probably not until Greek Cnossus was crushed that they could expand without serious competition. Their increasing prosperity is reflected in their buildings, nor was this prosperity confined to Mycenae. A common culture spreads through the Peloponnese and Central Greece, developed from the same basic organisation. In pottery styles there are minor local variations but the same shapes and decorative patterns are produced in all the main centres. What were to become city states in Classical Greece are now palace states which carry on the bureaucratic system of administration developed in Minoan Crete, taken over by Greeks at Cnossus, and from Cnossus spreading to the mainland. The palaces of the mainland are a development of the fourteenth century and, unlike the Cretan palaces, they are built on defensible hills, and their citadels are fortified by strong walls. The fortified citadel is reserved for the palace and a limited number of nobles on whom the king particularly relies for counsel in peace and fighting in war. The agricultural workers and the craftsmen who are not working for the palace normally live outside the walls.

In building techniques the Mycenaeans *Building* follow Cretan practice, with only minor varia- *materials* tions. Most walls are built with their bottom *and plans* courses in stone and the rest of the wall in crude brick, strengthened by a framework of vertical and horizontal timbers. The roof is flat, sealed by a thick coat of clay over a layer of brushwood. But there are significant differences in plan. In Minoan palaces the dominant feature is the large court, probably designed for public spectacles; the Mycenaean court is considerably smaller, as it serves primarily as a forecourt to the megaron or great hall. This hall is the heart of the palace, emphasised by porch and vestibule. It has an open hearth and a throne. It is here that the king receives distinguished visitors and takes counsel with his advisers, and this is where royal banquets would be held, and public sacrifices made. The disposition and function of public rooms in Cretan palaces is more obscure, and there is a strong case for believing that at Cnossus and Phaestus the most important public rooms were over the ground floor. There was also a different attitude to lighting. The light wells designed to give as much light as possible to the more important rooms in Crete are not found in Mycenaean palaces which must have been considerably darker. In both, however, the economic aspect of the palace is abundantly clear from the ample storage capacity provided on the ground floor; this, as in Crete, implies trading to procure the essential goods and luxuries that were not available at home. The large storage jars for oil and wine are the most conspicuous reminders of this side of palace organisation. The Mycenaean palace also, like the Cretan, had to provide working accommodation for skilled craftsmen who were probably concerned not only with meeting the needs of the palace itself but also with providing a surplus for trade.

The linear B tablets that were found at *Palace* Cnossus and Pylos throw a little more explicit *administra-* light on the palace system of administration, *tion* but decipherment is still so incomplete that the most interesting questions cannot yet be answered with any certainty.[31] A wider measure of agreement among philologists is needed before historians can feel confidence, and inferences about the system of land tenure or the nature of Mycenaean religion need to be particularly guarded. The tablets from the two centres are more than a hundred years apart, for the palace at Cnossus was destroyed before

1350 and the Pylos palace was destroyed after 1250, but in content and style they are very similar and the few tablets that have been added from Mycenae and Thebes add nothing fundamentally new. The documents include lists of personal names, inventories, allocation of materials, lists of offerings to be made to various gods, and of land holdings with quantities of seed required. It seems clear that the religious calendar is controlled by the palace, though each cult has its priest or priestess. The palace also is responsible for organising the production of weapons and holding a reserve stock. At Cnossus there were more than 120 chariots with wheels, 41 without wheels, and 237 not assembled when the palace was destroyed: at Pylos there is provision for the supply of bronze arrow-heads. The basic words that govern the system of land tenure are still controversial, but it seems that land can be held 'from the demos' which should mean from the local community and could imply something like the open field system. In contrast there may be other land to which definite services are attached. The king, *wanax*, has his own *temenos*, his own special reservation, but both at Cnossus and at Pylos he is concerned with the produce and flocks of very considerable areas.[32]

Social structure

The tablets also throw a little light on the social structure of the Mycenaean state. Beneath the king the most important official is the *lawagetas*, leader of the people, who also has his own *temenos*, apparently a third of the size of the king's; he is generally thought to be the commander of the army under the king (but see p. 52). The king also has *hepetai* who probably correspond to the *hetairoi* of later Greece and the *comites* of the Roman Empire, the men closest to the king in peace and war. The tablets also refer to *pasireu*, the precursor of the later Greek *basileus*, king, but in Mycenaean times the king is *wanax* and the *basileus* is probably a provincial officer with local responsibilities, a usage which survives in Hesiod's 'gift-devouring *basileis*', who were local lords dispensing justice—at a price. Among the workers there is a surprising degree of specialisation, including chariot builders, wheelwrights, and woodcutters. Among them are some potters, fullers and armourers who are described as being *wa-ner-ka-te-ro* which presumably means belonging to the king, producing exclusively for the palace.

The number of palaces and tholos tombs testifies to the wide spread of prosperity in Greece during the Late Helladic period. Between *c*. 1400 and *c*. 1250 the Peloponnese and central Greece were probably more prosperous than they were to be again for more than five hundred years, and this period is with good reason called the Mycenaean Age. In Greek tradition Mycenae was 'rich in gold', and archaeology has confirmed the aptness of the epithet. No other centre can compete with the number of its great tholos tombs of which nine have been discovered and more may yet be found. The princes of the shaft graves presumably lived on the citadel but their residence cannot be identified in the scanty remains that survive beneath the rebuilding of the fourteenth and thirteenth centuries. It was not until the fourteenth century that the first true palace was built and it was probably at the same time that strong walls, following the contours, were built round the citadel. These walls, averaging some six metres in thickness, were constructed with huge irregular blocks of limestone packed with small stones and clay.

Mycenae

Towards the middle of the next century important changes were made in the line of the walls. A long stretch on the west side was pulled down and replaced on a different line by blocks of conglomerate hammer-dressed and laid in regular courses. The new line extended the defended area by incorporating the royal circle of shaft graves. At this point the ground level was raised, the gravestones carefully re-erected, and the area enclosed in a circle of stone uprights to mark its religious character. The most striking feature of the new wall was the western gate ensconced in a corner of the wall, which at this point ran in south-eastward and then turned outward due west, thus enclosing and commanding the approach to the gate. The lintel of the doorway is formed by a huge square block of stone, and the weight of the wall resting on it is lightened by the device of leaving a triangular space. This opening is filled by a sculptured relief in hard limestone representing two lionesses standing opposite each other on either side of a pillar, on whose pedestal their forepaws rest. They are, as it were, watchers who ward the castle, and from them the gate is known as the Lion Gate. The composition admirably fits the space and, with strict economy, combines realism of treatment with a strong architectural sense. The unknown artist, working with crude tools of bronze, has created a masterpiece. To protect the gate a strong bastion was built on the west to threaten the shieldless side of an attacking enemy.

From the west gate a monumental ramp led to the King's palace at the top of the citadel,

The palace

1.16 Lion Gate, Mycenae

which was thoroughly reconstructed and enlarged; by bold terracing and levelling the architect adapted the difficult site to his ambitious plan, so that the most important apartments could be laid out in the most suitable and commanding position. The detailed plan of the palace cannot be recovered but the main sequence of Throne Room, Great Court, and Megaron, preceded by columned porch and vestibule, can be traced. These public quarters were gaily decorated. Fragments of frescoes show women, elaborately dressed, in procession; others are decorated with spirals, lotus and rosettes. The floors of

1.17 Mycenae from the air

vestibule and megaron were covered with painted stucco with coloured linear designs, bordered with blocks of gypsum. To the north of the megaron were the domestic quarters; evidence has been found of store-rooms and a shrine, and recent excavation has shown that large buildings which were separately named as the House of the Columns and the House of the Artisans were in fact an eastern wing of the palace used primarily for storage.[33]

The Treasury of Atreus

Mycenae's most famous monument, the great tholos tomb which still carries the name used by Pausanias in the second century, the Treasury of Atreus, should be dated between the original building of the walls and their reconstruction. What marks it out from its predecessors, apart from its great size, is the fine workmanship of its walling, the monumental character of the entrance, and the magnificent proportions and decoration of the chamber. The entrance passage or *dromos* which runs into the side of the hill, floored with cement, is 6 m. wide and 36 m. long. The walls of the passage, over 10 m. high at the inner end, are built of well-coursed blocks of con-

glomerate, and at the west end are irregularly bonded with the face of the tomb. The doorway into the tholos is 5·4 m. high and 2·7 m. wide, narrowing at the top. It is framed by two tall engaged half-columns of green stone from Laconia, carved in relief with a zigzag pattern of spirals, beading and flutes, and crowned with capitals of similar pattern. In a relieving triangle over the door, reminiscent of the Lion Gate, was set a large block of red stone, also from Laconia, chosen for its decorative effect and probably linked, by a design which cannot be precisely recovered, with two smaller half-columns continuing the line of the lower pair that frame the door. The doorway is 5·4 m. deep and the inner lintel is formed by a massive block of conglomerate, calculated to weigh about a hundred tons. This huge block, brought into place no doubt by rollers along the hillside rather than raised from below, overlaps considerably the jambs on either side, and is clearly intended to sustain at each end the downward thrust of the upper vault—one sign among many of the considerable skill of the architect. The tholos, which is 14·5 m. across and 13·2 m.

1.18   Entrance to the Treasury of Atreus

south-west which were built in the thirteenth century. Three have been named from their contents: the House of the Oil Merchant, the House of Shields, and the House of the Sphinxes; the fourth, in which more pottery was found but which is without any distinctive feature has the more colourless name of the West House. In the House of the Oil Merchant the excavators found some thirty stirrup jars, most of which still had stoppers in their spouts with the original seals still over them; they had once been full of oil. In another room there were eleven large *pithoi* for the storage of oil, set on small bases in alcoves along the two main walls, with a moveable heating apparatus under one of them which could be used to prevent the oil from congealing. Only the basement of the house remains, but traces can be seen of a stairway cut partially in the rock that led to the main entrance. The House of the Sphinx takes its name from a finely carved ivory plaque showing two sphinxes facing each other heraldically, as the lions of the Lion Gate, with their forepaws resting on the capital of a fluted column. This was one of several ivory plaques and inlays, including many models of columns. Ivories were also the most significant feature of the third house which took its name from the large number of figure-of-eight shields in ivory.

The interest of these houses is considerably increased by the discovery of clay tablets similar in form and style to those that were found in the palaces at Cnossus and Pylos. Like the palaces these houses had been destroyed by violence and the fire which completed the destruction baked the records. The texts, so far as they can be deciphered are not very revealing. There is a list of names, and there are references to oil and to various herbs and spices used in giving more character to some of the oil, and also to wool. These are not simply household records as the quantity of oil shows, but the function of these houses is in dispute. Mylonas who has directed most of the recent work at Mycenae, considers that this was a subsidiary branch of the palace administration, but there are serious objections to this view. Would any such branch of palace organisation have been built in the thirteenth century outside the protection of the walls and the citadel, and would such handsome establishments have been built for storage, distribution and accounts? Unfortunately nothing remains of the upper floors but fragments of frescoes which had fallen down into the basement when the buildings collapsed suggest well furnished rooms. Wace, who excavated

high, is built of large blocks of conglomerate, hammer-dressed and laid in regular courses, narrowing gradually to the summit, where the chamber is crowned with a large roof-stone. The stones of the walls are roughly triangular in shape, with only the inner surface prepared: in the heart of the wall the spaces are filled with small stones and clay, and to make the structure water-tight the upper part of the dome, which stood above the level of the hill, was covered with clay. The walls of the vaulted chamber were decorated with a pattern of bronze rosettes, and a door, similar to that of the main portal, admits to a side-chamber hewn in the rock, its walls decorated with sculptured alabaster plates.

Houses outside the walls   Of the buildings outside the walls other than tombs the most interesting are a group of four substantial houses below the citadel to the these houses, is more probably right in regard-ing them as the homes of rich merchants. If this is right we can believe that not all trade was controlled from the palace, and that the linear B script was neither a secret system nor a palace monopoly.[34] Similar questions arise about another building, nearer to the walls, on the north slope of the ridge of the Lion Tomb.

period as the building of the new palace and city wall date the remains of a network of prepared roads radiating from Mycenae, marked by the bridges that carried them over streams and culverts, and by low embankments on hillsides. Northwards three roads ran to the isthmus fortresses, the two western joining at Cleonae, the eastern going by Tenea; from

Control of the Argive plain

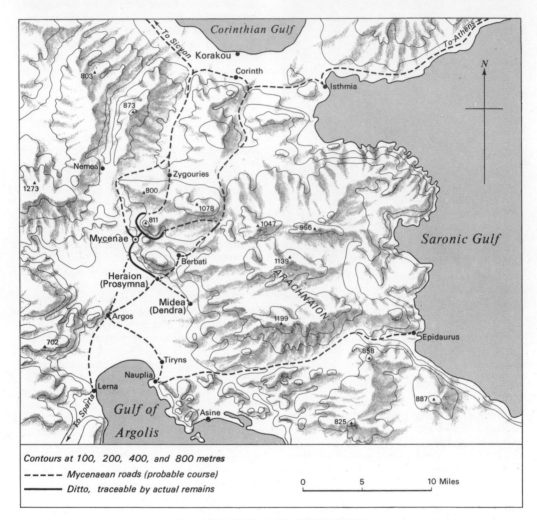

Contours at 100, 200, 400, and 800 metres

- - - - Mycenaean roads (probable course)

———— Ditto, traceable by actual remains

0   5   10 Miles

2. ARGOLIS AND CORINTHIA

This building also dates from the thirteenth century and its main feature was the large number of stirrup jars and *pithoi* in the ruins. The House of the Wine Merchant, as it is called, is a more appropriate name than 'The Imperial Wine-cellar'.

The immediate sphere of Mycenae's in-fluence can be clearly traced. From the same

the other side of the Corinthian gulf roads ran to the fortresses of Boeotia. Southwards, traces have been found of a road going to the site of the later temple of Hera, and the other settlements on the borders of the Argive plain were doubtless linked up by similar roads. For Mycenae's special domain was the Argive plain, guarded at crucial points by fortresses under vassal princes. The Larissa above Argos guarded the entry from the west; Tiryns held guard over the open coastline of the gulf. Nauplia, at the south-west corner, was a useful settlement at Asine. Reflections of Mycenae's wealth have been found at most of these sites, and tombs from Dendra have yielded particularly rich treasures.

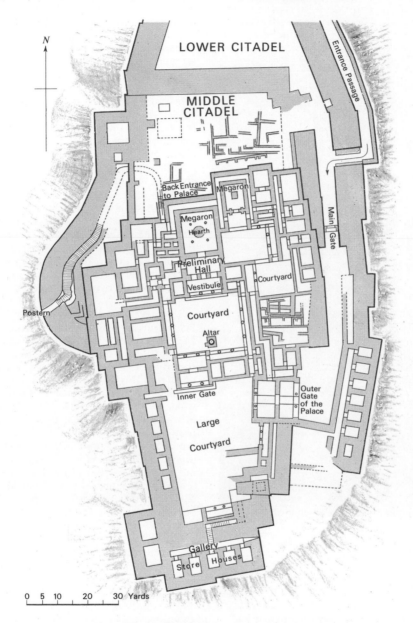

3. THE UPPER CITADEL, PALACE OF TIRYNS

port, and on the east side of the plain there was a settlement at Prosymna, the site of the later Heraeum, while princes ruled at Dendra (Midea), which guarded the route to another

But of them all, Tiryns has the longest history and the most revealing monuments. Tiryns stands on a long low rock about a mile and a half from the sea and was probably

Tiryns

29

1.19   Gallery in the palace of Tiryns

altar. From this inner courtyard a vestibule and fore-hall lead into the main megaron with its central hearth, surrounded by four wooden pillars to support a flat roof. Beside the large megaron, and approached separately, with a separate courtyard, is a much smaller megaron. The view that this represents the women's megaron we may discard, for in Mycenaean art there is no evidence of the segregation of the sexes typical of classical Greece. We should think rather perhaps of the large megaron as the public reception room, and the smaller as the private quarters of the royal family. While the megaron is the central feature marking a sharp difference from the palaces of Crete, there are a number of rooms, including a bathroom, built beside the megaron, which are more reminiscent of the arrangement of the palace of Cnossus; and as at Cnossus, there are signs of stairs, showing that some parts of the palace had one or more upper storeys. More reminiscent of Crete are the frescoes on the walls and the patterned decoration of the floors, inspired from Crete if not the work of Cretans. The hill was monopolised by the palace; the people lived in the plain below.

Messenia

The development of western and northern Peloponnese is considerably more obscure. Messenia, which attracted little attention in the early days of excavation, has now been shown to be one of the most progressive areas of Greece in the Early and Middle Helladic periods. It was here that the tholos tomb, whatever its origins, seems to have been first introduced and more than twenty have already been discovered in Messenia. When unrobbed tombs have been found their contents have been impressive, with gold and silver vessels, though not in the profusion of the Mycenaean shaft graves, and amber beads from the Baltic. More than a hundred Bronze Age settlements have been located and the wide distribution of tholos tombs suggests that the area was divided into small principalities. But one of these, on the hill of Ano Englianos, was to become the administrative centre of a large kingdom. This site is nine miles inland and commands a good view of the coast. By the end of the fourteenth century it had become a significant settlement. The top of the hill was fortified by a protective wall and the growth of population had led to an extension below the hill. Two tholos tombs in the near neighbourhood are a sign of the importance of the settlement, but there were other more impressive sites in Messenia until it was transformed by a new dynasty.

occupied before Mycenae. The ruins of the great palace still enable us to trace the main ground plan in its final phase. The south, and higher, end of the hill was surrounded with a strong wall of fortification, and within the walls was built the great palace. The main entrance, on the east side, was approached by a long passage between the inner wall of the fortress and the wall of the palace. A portico leads into a large courtyard, from which an inner gate gives entrance to an inner courtyard with an

Palace of Pylos

At the end of the first phase of the Late Helladic IIIA (*c.* 1300 B.C.) the buildings on the hilltop were destroyed and a substantial palace was built, which with subsequent extensions came to occupy more than half the hilltop while the other half was kept free of buildings. This palace was totally destroyed at the end of LH IIIB (*c.* 1200) and as the site was never reoccupied, Blegen's excavations have provided a more vivid impression of Mycenaean palace life than we can find in the ruins of Tiryns or Mycenae.[35] There were three main parts to the palace but the east and west

as at Tiryns. On the walls were attractive frescoes and the pavement was covered with stucco and divided into squares with coloured linear designs, except in the second square in front of the throne, which was decorated with a naturalistic octopus.

This Megaron was essentially the state room. The king's more private living rooms were on the south-east corner of the block. Here the largest room also had a permanent central hearth, and later an outside court was added to it. It is called the Queen's Megaron, but whether the king would have agreed to such a

1.20 Megaron in the palace of Pylos (from the north, entrance at top)

quarters were very loosely linked with the central block and considerably less important. The plan of the central block is very similar, on a smaller scale, to the palace at Tiryns. The main entrance leads into a courtyard from which one passes through a porch with two columns into a vestibule which leads into the Megaron. This room, which is the public heart of the palace, measures 12·90 × 11·00 m. and has a large central hearth with four columns round it to support a balcony. Against the centre of the right wall as you enter traces can still be seen where the royal throne was placed,

title is perhaps doubtful; he might have preferred 'Private Megaron'. Among the smaller rooms on the ground floor is an elegant bathroom with a built-in terracotta bathtub and two large water-containers permanently installed. Stone stairs led to an upper floor over this part of the building which was probably occupied mainly by bedrooms. Most of the rest of the ground floor was used for storage. In the north-west corner five rooms contained the main stock of pottery in everyday use—cups, bowls, and dippers, among which by far the commonest were *kylikes,* cups not

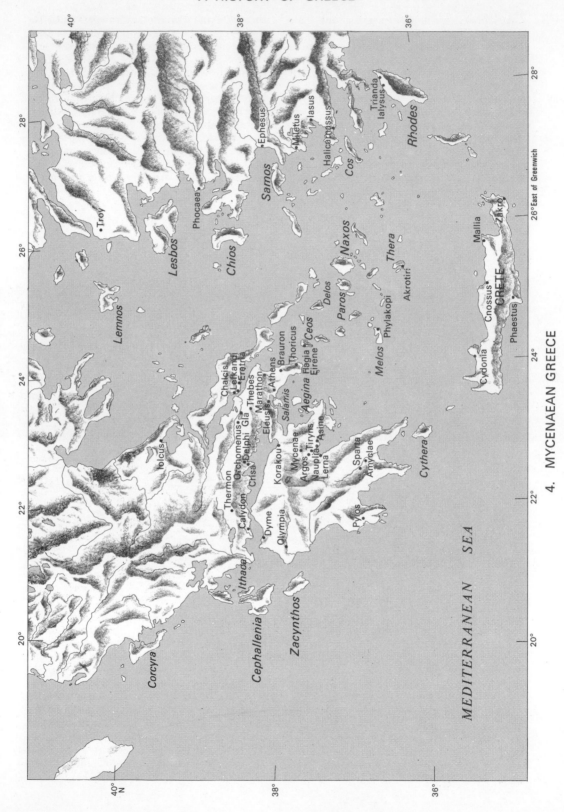

4. MYCENAEAN GREECE

unlike champagne glasses in shape, with conspicuously long stems. Of these 2853 were actually counted in one room and the total number found in the building was more than 3000. In another room there were more than 1000 bowls. The numbers, particularly of *kylikes,* is at first unexpected but the palace had to provide for public ceremonies which required ample reserves.

No less conspicuous were the large number of *pithoi* for the storage of oil. In two large rooms behind the Megaron there were 33 of these large storage jars and further supplies were kept in two other rooms, one of which was reserved for specially treated oil. The main wine cellar was in a separate building northeast of the main block. Here 35 *pithoi* were found and several clay sealings wrapped around strings which had been used to tie on the lids

Nestor's kingdom. Homer preserves a tradition that Neleus, quarrelling with his brother in Thessalian Iolcus, left his home and established himself in Pylos. His son Nestor was an old man, wise in counsel but past active fighting when he accompanied Agamemnon to Troy: the dates could fit. The tablets show that the control of the palace of Ano Englianos extended over a very large area; there is no trace of such a centre elsewhere in the west of the Peloponnese.

Laconia presents a strong contrast with *Laconia* Messenia. There are fewer sites that show clear traces of occupation during the Mycenaean period. There is some evidence of a cult centre at Amyclae where a famous temple of Apollo was later built, but the settlement was small. Near the site of classical Sparta there was a larger settlement but no palace has yet

(a)   *(b)*

1.21   Gold cup from Vapheio (a) The decoy cow, (b) The bull captured (see note, page 551)

or stoppers of the containers in which the wine was brought for storage. The main office of the palace seems to have been a small room on the left side of the main entrance, for this is where the majority of the tablets were found.

There is no clear evidence where the slaves who prepared the food, cleaned the rooms and attended on the royal family slept. They may have had crowded quarters on the upper floor of the west wing or in light shanties outside the main building. The two other blocks in the palace complex are considerably less well preserved, but the south-west block was residential and well equipped, with its own storage capacity, and handsome decoration. The rooms to the north-east included a large workshop in which tablets dealing with repairs to chariots were found.

It was not long before Blegen was convinced that this was the capital of Pylian

been found. There is, however, one striking exception to a colourless picture at Vapheio on the lower slopes of Mount Taygetus south of Sparta. Here a tholos tomb was excavated as long ago as 1888, and from it came one of the richest archaeological harvests from a single tomb, though it had already been robbed. The robbers must have found plenty of treasures on the floor of the tomb, because there still remained several small objects of considerable value, but they had failed to discover the main burial which was in a stone-lined cist beneath the centre of the floor, preserving its treasures intact. It is here that the two famous golden cups were found which have, deservedly, been illustrated in more books than any other objects of the Mycenaean period: they show two different methods of catching wild bulls. By any standard these are remarkable works of art, naturalistic, but beautifully designed to fit their space, almost certainly the work of Cretan craftsmen. Their reputation, however, has obscured the rest of the contents of this grave. These included vessels in silver, bronze and clay, amethyst and amber beads, rings of gold, bronze and iron (for iron was still a rare and precious metal), a sword, several knives and daggers including one inlaid with swimming figures, and, most interesting of all, a large collection of gems of Cretan and mainland workmanship. The somewhat odd mixture of objects may be explained, as has been suggested by E. Vermeule, by two burials, a man followed later by a woman.[36] This rich tomb implies an important settlement in the neighbourhood, but none has yet been found. The Vapheio tomb is probably less than a century later than the shaft graves of Mycenae. It is possible that both Messenia and Laconia were in decline during the great days of Mycenae in the fourteenth and thirteenth centuries.

Elis and Achaea

In Elis and Achaea there has been much less investigation, but an increasing amount of pottery of the period has been found, and there is enough evidence to show that Olympia, which was to become one of the great Panhellenic centres, was already inhabited though there is no firm evidence of continuity of cult. Across the Corinthian Gulf Mycenaean influence extends to Thermon in Aetolia and up the west coast, but their importance in the Mycenaean period is very secondary. Delphi which was to become the most influential religious centre in Greece was already occupied, but of only local influence.

Athens

North of the Isthmus, Athens would seem to have had strong advantages. Her ample Acropolis rises sharply from the plain and the steep cliffs offer little comfort to the attacker. Traces of a Mycenaean palace have been found towards the centre of the north side, and strong polygonal walls were built round the circuit in the thirteenth century; these seem to have been strongly influenced by the walls of the Argolid, which they closely resemble. The Athenians later boasted that they were autochthonous and had never been overrun by enemies: Thucydides acidly comments that this was because the soil of Attica was of poor quality, but the natural strength of the Acropolis was surely not irrelevant.[37] Rich tombs of the fourteenth and thirteenth centuries have been found near the foot of the south side of the Acropolis and they include imports from Crete, Egypt and the Near East, but though Athens later did what she could to build up her Bronze Age history, it is clear that Mycenae and Thebes outmatched her in power and wealth. In the earliest traditions Thebes was a much more important centre. The story of Oedipus and of the War between Argos and Thebes gave rise to three epics and a long succession of tragedies, and the richness of Thebes was proverbial. According to the epic tradition the Argives had attacked Thebes and been defeated, but a generation later seven Argive heroes, descendants of men who had fought in the unsuccessful war, succeeded in capturing the city. This was a generation before the Trojan War.

Thebes

Archaeology cannot yet make a full commentary on the tradition because the Cadmeia (the Theban acropolis) is buried under modern buildings in the busy centre of the town, but there have been limited opportunities for restricted investigations during rebuilding operations. Such opportunities occurred in 1906 and 1921 when Keramopoullos thought he had found part of the remains of a palace which had been destroyed and not rebuilt. His finds included a large number of stirrup jars, agate and other materials for the working of gems and fragments of large-scale frescoes of fine quality. Discoveries in 1964 were even more sensational. In what was thought to be a second palace were found linear B tablets, beads of onyx, gold and other precious materials and, biggest and most interesting surprise, 36 oriental cylinder seals of lapis-lazuli, with dates ranging from the third millennium to the middle of the fourteenth century, mainly from Babylon in the Kassite period, but also including examples from Sumeria, Mitanni and Anatolia. These naturally invited new speculation about Cadmus the Phoenician who, according to Herodotus, brought writing to Greece and was generally regarded as the founder of Thebes. These seals, however, are a collector's hoard and do not necessarily mean anything more than that some Theban prince was attracted by oriental seals, especially when they were made of lapis-lazuli; but it is at least a nice coincidence, and could be more.[38]

Keramopoullos thought that his palace had been destroyed early in the fourteenth century. Platon, who supervised the 1964 exploration, was provisionally inclined to infer that there were two destructions, the first early in the thirteenth century, the second towards the end of the century. This could be an interesting confirmation of tradition, but before the evidence is published in detail and widely discussed it would be wise to suspend judgement. Meanwhile it has been reported that the largest chamber tomb yet known in Greece, with frescoes fit for a king's burial place, has been found at Thebes.[39]

Orchomenus also, according to tradition, was once very wealthy, though in the classical period it played a very secondary role to Thebes, but the nineteenth-century excavations of Schliemann and his German successors were inconclusive. There can still, however, be seen at Orchomenus one of the finest tholos tombs in Greece, strikingly similar to the Treasury of Atreus at Mycenae. Built probably in the thirteenth century, it had a second chamber covered by a stone ceiling with an elegant design in low relief combining meandering spirals with fan-shaped leaves bordered by rosettes. Fragments of frescoes were found which might have come from a palace, but the palace itself has almost certainly been the victim of erosion. Orchomenus should also probably be associated with the drainage of the Copaic lake and the mysterious fortress of Gla. To the east of Orchomenus lies a large area that, unless properly drained, becomes lake in winter and marsh in summer. In modern times it has been systematically drained and is now the most fertile land in Boeotia, producing crops that would make any Attic farmer very jealous. It is one of the greatest achievements of Mycenaean engineers that they were able to design a drainage system of ditches and dykes which restored this land to agriculture: in their dykes have been found Mycenaean sherds which date the work to the fourteenth or thirteenth century, and it was probably at the same period that a large outcrop of rock near the south-east corner of the 'lake' was converted into a fortress. A strong wall was built round the edge of the plateau with four well-fortified gates. The whole circuit survives to a length of nearly 2 miles; the citadel of Mycenae would go seven times into the area enclosed. This enormous enclosure is no ordinary settlement, nor is there any sign of large-scale occupation. At the north-west corner is an L-shaped building which has been called a palace, but there is no megaron and none of the normal signs of palace architecture. The only other building complex whose foundations have been found has been called the Agora, but no satisfactory explanation of its form or purpose has been found. This fortress probably had two functions—to provide a refuge for men and flocks from the neighbouring hills in time of trouble, and to guard the drainage system of the 'lake' near its vulnerable points where the water was carried into *katavothra* (emissaries).[40] Further north, on the southern edge of Thessaly, Iolcus

had its tholos tomb and palace, but the results of current investigations have not yet been published.

The Mycenaean states were not self-sufficient. From their corn crops, stock-raising, fishing and hunting they may have been able to feed themselves, but the raw materials for weapons and tools had to come from without. There was little copper and no tin in Greece, and without them there could be no bronze.[41] The silver of the Laurion peninsula in Attica, which was to play such an important part in the Athenian economy in the classical period, was being worked already, but only on a very limited scale. For precious metals the Mycenaeans had to go further afield. Trade was a necessity; they proved to be very successful traders. In the period of the shaft graves their most significant foreign contacts were with the Lipari islands, where sufficient pottery has been found to suggest regular trading.[42] Further north, off the west coast of Italy, a few Mycenaean sherds have been found on the island of Ischia, anticipating the first Greek colony of the archaic period in the west. In both periods the metals of the mainland were the main attraction. In Sicily a substantial number of vases have been found at Thapsus on the east coast, and a thin scatter in the south-east corner of the island; it is possible that the Mycenaeans were interested in Sicilian corn. But by far the largest quantity of Mycenaean pottery in the west comes from Scoglio del Tonno, just outside Taranto, where there may have been a Mycenaean settlement.[43]

In the east there are a few scattered finds of Mycenaean early pottery, but it was not until Cretan power collapsed that Mycenaean ships could sail with full confidence into the eastern Mediterranean. From *c.* 1400 Mycenaean pottery increasingly replaces Minoan in Egypt, Syria, Palestine and Cyprus. Egypt could supply gold from Nubia, her own wide range of exotic stones for jewelry and ornaments, and other luxuries; on the more practical plane her papyrus was invaluable for the making of sails and rope, and her flint for arrowheads. From Syria came attractive textiles and the ivory which Mycenaean craftsmen, taking their lessons from the eastern schools, worked with such delicacy and skill. Cyprus was the great centre of copper production, and for that reason was of continuing concern to the Mycenaeans. The copper was exported in the form of oxhide ingots, and a lively illustration of the trade on a small scale can be seen in a merchantman sunk off Cape Gelidonya on the south coast of Asia Minor, probably on a voyage

1.22   Ivory group, Mycenae (see note, page 551)

commercial centre and, like sixth-century Tyre, vividly described by Ezekiel, she traded with Egypt and Mesopotamia.[45] From Ugarit and other Syrian ports, and from Askalon, Greek merchandise found its way to the hinterland of Syria and Palestine, where the finds of Mycenaean sherds are steadily increasing. In Egypt at Tel-el-Amarna in the second quarter of the fourteenth century there is so much Mycenaean pottery that a small trading community may possibly have settled there and similar evidence comes from Gurob. But after the end of Tel-el-Amarna's short period of flourishing as the Pharaoh's new capital, Mycenaean trade with Egypt declined sharply.

in Asia Minor

The Mycenaean penetration of the eastern Mediterranean is coherent and well attested. We know very much less of relations with the western coast of Asia Minor. Miletus alone has been examined in depth and it is clear that Minoan influence and possibly settlement was there succeeded by a Mycenaean settlement for which there is the firm evidence of a cemetery of chamber tombs. On Samos it is likely that Mycenaeans followed and supplanted Minoans. Traces of Mycenaean settlers have been found in the area of the Heraeum; the Cretan evidence comes from the site of the later town, some 5 miles distant.[46] South of Miletus the Italians excavating at Iasus have found the same succession of Minoan and Mycenaean, and at Halicarnassus there is a cemetery of Mycenaean tombs; Miletus may have been a Mycenaean principality with dependencies to the south. North of Miletus there is little to record. A tholos tomb was found at Colophon and a Mycenaean tomb at Ephesus, but at neither site has there been any large-scale excavation to the prehistoric level. It would be very unwise to argue from archaeological silence until there is much more archaeology to argue from.

Relations with the Hittites

In Miletus and in Syria the Mycenaeans were on the fringes of the Hittite empire. The Hittites had established themselves as the dominant people in Asia Minor about 2000 B.C., with their capital at Boghazkoi. At roughly the time of the fall of Cnossus they were reaching the height of their power and even penetrating southwards to compete with Egypt for the control of the rich lands of Syria. The struggle which ensued between the two powers weakened both, and the Hittite empire in Asia Minor collapsed about 1200 B.C., though the immediate cause is still uncertain. Their capital was looted and destroyed, but a substantial part of the imperial archives inscribed on clay tablets has been preserved and deciphered.

to the Aegean. The boat was only about 10 m. long and the cargo barely more than a ton in weight, but it was composed entirely of metal. Copper ingots took up most of the room, but the ship also carried bronze tools, bronze scrap for re-smelting and a little tin. The wreck cannot be closely dated, but 1220–1100 B.C. would be safe limits.[44]

Mycenaean settlements in the East,

The considerable trade with the east led to, and was further encouraged by, settlements on the route. On Rhodes, Mycenaeans settled in some strength near Minoan Trianda. There was not room for both, and Trianda was evacuated, possibly without violence. A substantial cemetery of Mycenaean tombs is witness to a sister settlement in neighbouring Cos, and there is some evidence of Mycenaeans on Carpathos and along the coast of Pamphylia; but the great Cilician plain, a more attractive area for settlement, was for long closed by the Hittite fortresses of Mersin at the western edge and Tarsus in the centre. At Ugarit (Ras-Shamra) in Syria, sufficient Mycenaean pottery has been found to confirm regular trading connections: we can imagine Mycenaean traders advising their homeland about the requirements of the local market and exchanging the products of the Aegean for the luxuries of the east. For Ugarit was a brisk

These documents refer frequently to the King of Ahhiyava and his relations with the Hittite King. The contexts in which the Kingdom of Ahhiyava appears imply that this Kingdom is on the coast or over the seas, and nearly all scholars are now agreed that we have here the first documentary evidence for the Achaeans, the name most commonly applied to the Greeks by Homer. One of the main problems raised by these documents is the identification of place-names. Very few can be securely identified, and the location of incidents in which the Achaeans are involved should be postponed until further evidence makes the picture clearer. But though at best we can make only attractive guesses about detailed incidents, the general style of the correspondence is important. The powerful King of the Hittites, a world power of the first rank, addresses the Achaean King as 'brother' and with some respect. On one tablet the King of Ahhiyava was even recognised as a great King on a level with the Kings of Egypt, of Mitanni, and Assyria (though the entry for some reason was later erased). At some point on the periphery of the Hittite empire, probably in south-west Asia Minor, the brother of the King of Ahhiyava is in control, but he has to recognise his rule as a gift of the Hittite King. Negotiations are delicate, the Achaeans encroach upon the territory of the Lycians, the threat of counteraction follows. All is patched up again. We hear of enemies of the Hittite King banished to Ahhiyava, but also of protests against the reception of disloyal servants of the Hittite King. The presents of the King of Ahhiyava are welcome at the great king's court. The god of the King of Ahhiyava is summoned for help when the Hittite King is ill. Relations are outwardly friendly but often strained. We feel that the Achaeans are making the most of their opportunities without risking an open breach.[47]

These records, fragmentary and tantalising as they are, show clearly that the King of Ahhiyava wielded considerable power and could be held responsible for his vassals. The identification of this Kingdom of Ahhiyava has for long been controversial. The case for Rhodes has been most fully argued by D. L. Page and is still supported by E. Vermeule and other scholars,[48] but it is extremely doubtful whether the Mycenaean community in Rhodes, especially at the time of the earliest references, was sufficiently strong to be taken so seriously by the King who ruled virtually the whole of Asia Minor. An identification with Greece would not imply that Greece was firmly united politically. There is, however, nothing in the archaeological evidence to conflict with the relationships suggested by Homer's *Iliad*. Agamemnon is leader of the Greek forces, but the kings of the other states are not his servants and he has to be careful how he handles them. Thucydides, reviewing Homer's story of the Trojan War, says that Agamemnon led the Greek forces against Troy because he was the most powerful of the kings, ruling more widely than any other. It is a fair inference from the archaeological evidence that Mycenae was the most powerful of the cities and that there was a remarkable homogeneity of fashions in palace architecture, fortifications, armour, pottery and burial customs throughout the Peloponnese and central Greece. There is an elaborate road system linking the various settlements that ring the Argive plain; we should not expect Tiryns, Asine, Dendra, Argos, Prosymna and Lerna to be fully independent of the more powerful Mycenae. It is very much less certain whether, for instance, the kings of Pylos and Thebes would have accepted instructions from Mycenae; but they might have been willing to be persuaded. Correspondence between the King of the Hittites and the King of Mycenae would be no more strange than the much later alliance in the sixth century of Sparta with the Kings of Lydia, Babylon and Egypt. (p. 144)

It used to be thought that these documents were to be dated in the fourteenth and thirteenth centuries, but this chronology is no longer secure. New evidence has made it probable that one of the most important in the series, the so-called Maduwatta letter, was written in the late fifteenth century, and this may carry with it the redating of others. The earlier dating would make the identification with Rhodes even more difficult because it is unlikely that Mycenaeans replaced Cretans on Rhodes before the palaces were destroyed c. 1450, and the settlers would have needed more than two generations to establish the prestige and power implied by the Hittite documents. On the other hand the Mycenaeans of the mainland were already strong enough and sufficiently interested in the east to be a cause of concern to the Hittites. One of the main results of the destruction of the Cretan palaces was the intensification of Mycenaean activity in the east. Cretans were supplanted in Miletus and Rhodes, and Mycenaean trade with Cyprus and the eastern Mediterranean expanded vigorously.[49] The main evidence for Mycenaean enterprise in the west and east comes from Mycenaean pottery, which was clearly very popular with the upper classes.

Pottery alone, however, will not account for all the gold, silver, ivory and other luxuries that were imported. In the fifth century, Herodotus tells us, large quantities of Greek wine were marketed in Egypt, and wine was probably already a staple product in the Mycenaean period. Similarly oil, which later was one of the most important Greek exports, was probably also widely traded. Much of this trade was conducted directly by the palaces, to judge by the large number of huge storage vessels that are found in them all, containing far more than was needed by the palace staff alone. But though the king was the largest trader there is no indication that all trade was centralised in the palace. There was probably ample room for private initiative, which may be illustrated, as we have seen, by the House of the Oil Merchant and the House of the Wine Merchant at Mycenae.

In the period between the shaft graves and the destruction of the Cretan palaces the influence of Crete on the mainland was paramount; from *c.* 1400 the mainland becomes increasingly independent. Mycenaean pots of the sixteenth and fifteenth centuries closely followed Cretan models. Mycenae now reverts to the linear designs that preceded the strong Minoan influence and also develops a new

pictorial style, the main feature of which is a *Pictorial* frieze of figures running round the top of the *vases* vase. Charioteers are the most common subject; bulls, goats and deer are almost equally attractive. These vases were particularly popular in the east, and most of the surviving examples have been found in Cyprus and Syria. They have indeed often been regarded as evidence of substantial Greek settlement in Cyprus during the fourteenth century, but the analysis of the clay seems to show that they were made in Greece, and more recently a pottery of the Mycenaean period has been found at Berbati in the Argolid which was making vases of this pictorial style.[50]

Religion may have followed a somewhat *Religion* similar pattern, but it is not easy to tell from material objects what people thought and felt. From dedications and gems it is difficult to draw any sharp distinction between Minoan and Mycenaean. Similar cult scenes in the open air of ritual dance, adoration, and epiphany, are found in both places, and even though many of the gems found in Greece were made in Crete some of them at least must have belonged to Mycenaeans. In votive dedications goddesses seem to dominate in Mycenae, as in Crete. There are, however, differences. The horns of consecration do not play such an important part in Mycenae, and the double axe which is so pervasive in Crete is often little more than a decorative element in Greece. In Cretan palaces it is usually easy to identify special rooms devoted to cult; in Mycenaean palaces there are altars in courts but rooms specifically devoted to cult are elusive. It is generally assumed that the Mycenaeans had no temples and no cult statues.

In this generation new evidence has reminded us sharply how little we know. In Hagia Eirene Caskey found a large building in which several near life-size naturalistic female statues in terracotta were found, with no clear indication whether they were goddesses or priestesses. This temple, as it can legitimately be called, was built in the Early Helladic period and some form of cult survived here into the classical period.[51] There is no near parallel on the mainland but in 1963 British excavators, intending a mere tidying-up operation in one of the houses near the Lion Gate at Mycenae unexpectedly came across a room filled with small clay figures (50 to 60 cm.), male and female, wheel-made like pots with nose, ear, and arms added separately. With them were two coiled snakes complete and fragments of at least four others. These dedications had been hidden in this room, presumably

1.23 Pictorial style vase from Cyprus

Evidence of the tablets

when the citadel was being attacked, but originally they probably stood in an adjoining large room which has a high oblong dais built against one of the walls, and at a lower level a stone platform approached by two square steps.[52]

But the most important new evidence comes from the tablets found at Cnossus and Pylos. In the general archaeological picture Mycenaean cults seemed very similar to the Cretan cults and far removed from the Olympian gods of Homer and the mainstream of later Greek religion. Goddesses of nature and fertility such as were also widespread in Anatolia and the Near East seemed to be much more important than a Zeus or an Apollo. The palace tablets may help to bridge the gap. Zeus and Hera are recorded at both Cnossus and Pylos, and Poseidon at Pylos is probably to be identified with Enesidaone the earthshaker at Cnossus. Enegalios, god of battles, is probably to be

Pigadhia on the island of Carpathos, where there was a Mycenaean settlement, was Poseidion Polis. The evidence of the tablets suggests two strands, Greek side by side with pre-Greek, but it is difficult to sense more than a very blurred outline.

Changes in weapons

It is easier to see Mycenaean man as a fighter than as a worshipper, for the weapons in his tombs and in figured scenes on vases tell a clearer story. At the time of the shaft graves the two main offensive weapons were the rapier or thrusting sword, sometimes up to three feet in length, and the spear. The use of the sword is well illustrated in scenes of duels on seals and rings; such duels between champions were probably an important element in battle and the special pride in the sword is emphasised by their astonishing number in the shaft graves. There are considerably fewer spearheads, but in general fighting they should have been more dependable than the slender

1.24 Mycenaean gems

identified with Ares and Paiawon may be Apollo the healer. At Pylos there are also references to Artemis and Hermes, and, in a very uncertain context, Dionysus though he may not be a god. We cannot be certain that these gods had the same attributes as in the historical period, but they show that the male element was stronger than the archaeological evidence suggested. In particular it is interesting to see the importance of Poseidon at Pylos, for in the *Odyssey* when Telemachus comes to the court of Nestor a feast is being celebrated in honour of Poseidon.[53] The early importance of Poseidon is also illustrated in the tradition of the contest between Athena and Poseidon for the possession of the Athenian Acropolis and Poseidon was the patron god of the league of Ionian cities which traced their descent from Pylian Neleus through Athens, and it may be significant that the name given by Ptolemy to

blade of the rapier and it is significant that in the vase scene already referred to which shows *(p. 21)* two groups of warriors fighting over a fallen man they fight with spears. The most striking feature of the spears in this picture is their great length, more than 8 feet if the drawing is even roughly to scale. A similar length is implied in the hunting scene inlaid on a dagger from one of the shaft graves, and this will account for some remarkable spear heads up to 2 feet in length; but there were also smaller spear heads in the graves, suggesting that there was considerable variation in the length of the shaft. There may have been some javelins for throwing, but the main weapon was a thrusting spear.

The large number of arrowheads in the shaft graves suggests that they were used in war as well as in the hunt, and an archer is included in the battle scene on the vase as well as in the enormous shield, of which there were two standard types, both made of oxhide on a wooden frame: the figure-of-eight, which covered the whole body, was convex with drawn-in waist; the tower shield, which was like the vertical section of a cylinder, had straight sides and rectangular base, curved at the top to protect the face, guarding the sides, but not coming below the knees. In one of the shaft graves there was a fragment of linen fourteen layers thick, presumably from a cuirass; there may also have been some protection for the legs in cloth or leather. The standard helmet was the so-called boar's tusk

1.25 Gravestone from shaft grave, Mycenae (see note, page 552)

lion hunt. The stones over some of the shaft graves show that chariots also had already been adopted at Mycenae. There is no firm evidence of the domesticated horse in Greece before the shaft graves but horse bones are common in the ruins of Troy VI (from c. 1900) and Greece will have grown used to them during the Middle Helladic period. The battle chariot, light and fast, had been developed in the Near East but there may be a Cretan stage in the transmission of the idea. As we have seen there was a large reserve of chariots when Greek Cnossus was destroyed and there are tablets from Pylos recording chariot repairs. In both Cnossus and Pylos the palace was responsible for maintaining chariot strength. They took nobles to battle and the driver's companion could use his thrusting spear from the chariot or dismount, as was the practice of British charioteers when Julius Caesar invaded Britain.[54] Defensive armour was still rudimentary, without any trace of metal. The main defence was an

1.26 Bronze armour from warrior tomb, Dendra

40

helmet; on a foundation of leather or cloth slight plates cut from the tusks of wild boars were sewn in close-fitting rows.

For the period between the shaft graves and the second half of the twelfth century the evidence, and particularly dated evidence, is very meagre, but a chamber tomb found in 1960 at Dendra, in the Argolid, showed an astonishing advance in defensive armour. Buried with the dead man were a bronze-plated cuirass of elaborate but effective design, and a pair of bronze greaves. The date is near 1400, and no other instances of either are known for some 200 years; in fact the next bronze cuirass to have been found comes from Argos towards the end of the eighth century.[55] The pioneering models may have seemed too heavy and too expensive. From roughly the same date a metal helmet, which requires no less skill in the bronze worker, was found at Cnossus, but this too did not set a general fashion. So far as we know there were no major changes in the offensive weapons before the thirteenth century; there were technical improvements in the sword, and the average size was reduced, but it remained a thrusting sword. After c. 1250 there is a radical change with the introduction, probably from the north, of a cut-and-thrust sword, which may have been accompanied by wider changes. At about this time the size of the spear is considerably reduced. The great body shields are now out of date, replaced by a much smaller shield, usually round, but with minor variations in shape; they are made of oxhide and sometimes have a central bronze boss, convex and occasionally with a spike. No metal helmets have been found on the mainland from this period, and the illustrations suggest that oxhide was probably the normal basis. A few bronze greaves have been found and bronze shoulder plates, but no bronze cuirasses. The new equipment is most comprehensively illustrated in the Warrior Vase from Mycenae, dated in the first half of the twelfth century. A woman on the left is bidding farewell to a line of soldiers going to battle. The shield is round, but with a segment cut from the bottom. The helmet is of leather, with a peak projection at the front and back which gives a little added protection against the cutting sword. The horn, possibly one of a pair of boars' tusks, seems, like the plumes, to be primarily decorative; the white spots on helmet and kilt may be metal disks. The cuirass is presumably of leather, but with the kilt it has a pronounced border, which looks like an echo of the boars' tusk helmet. What resemble football stockings

are leather leggings. The only weapon shown is the spear, not fundamentally different from its predecessors of the shaft graves, but shorter. It would be dangerous to argue from such pictures as this that the sword was not used in battle by such men as these; the painter may not have wished to overcrowd his picture. But

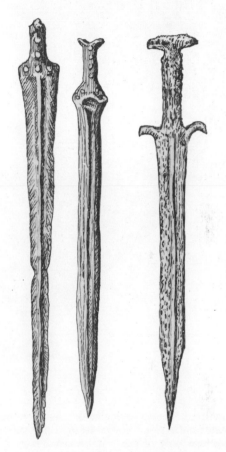

1.27 Mycenaean swords

the men on the Warrior Vase marching in line suggest a very different style of fighting from the single combats illustrated on earlier gems. Allowance must be made for the difference between a small gem and a large pot, but it is to be expected that as wealth became more widely distributed with the growth of Mycenaean trade less emphasis in battle should be placed on the individual. Similar factors were to lead much later to the hoplite phalanx.

The emphasis on weapons in tombs suggests that the Mycenaean Age was one of much fighting, and this is supported by Greek

1.28 Vase with warriors

tradition, which remembers feuds within states and between states. Of fighting overseas we hear only of the war against Troy. The magnificence of Homer's *Iliad* ensured that no rival expedition survived in the tradition and left to archaeologists and historians a series of very embarrassing questions.

The Trojan War

In the poetic tradition Agamemnon, lord of Mycenae, calls on the Achaean princes throughout Greece, who own allegiance to him, to avenge the rape of Helen stolen from his brother Menelaus by Trojan Paris. The combined fleet sails from Aulis on the Euboean strait and lands on the Asiatic shore. The Achaeans build a strong base camp on the Trojan plain,

and for ten years with fluctuating fortunes, helped and hindered by gods and goddesses, they lay siege to Troy. Disaster threatens the Achaeans when Achilles quarrels with Agamemnon and leaves the fight; his return is decisive. The city is finally taken by a cunning ruse and sacked.

Troy had been an important fortress since *The early* the beginning of the Bronze Age, and for much *history of* of the time had been technologically ahead of *Troy* the mainland of Greece. The site has strong natural advantages. Built on a low hill some four miles from the Aegean, and a little less from the Hellespont, it commands a broad and fertile plain, and by it pass two much used routes—the road which follows the western coast and turns east to reach the shortest crossing of the Hellespont, and the sea passage from the Aegean to the Bosphorus and Euxine.

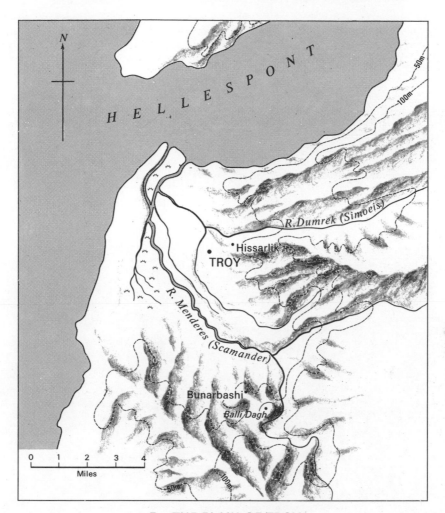

5. THE PLAIN OF TROY

When Schliemann unearthed the many layers of cities he found a formidable wealth of gold in the next to the bottom, Troy II, and this he assumed to be Homer's Troy. It was indeed an impressive fortress, apart from its accumulation of gold; it had strong fortification walls, and houses of the megaron type. Its masons and potters developed considerable skill, and imports show a fairly wide range of contacts. But Troy II was roughly contemporary with the second phase of the Early Helladic period in Greece. The next three cities show no break in culture and are not particularly distinguished, but soon after 2000 there was a movement of new people into Troy who revived its fortunes. The new settlement of Troy VI was the largest of the settlements on

the hill of Hissarlik, and has the hallmarks of a royal fortress. Within the citadel, which was little more than 200 m. long and 150 m. wide, the ground was terraced, and the palace, as at Mycenae, was probably in the centre at the top. Around it were a number of large houses which made no attempt to economise in space; in them presumably lived the king's main officials and advisers. On the outskirts by the walls the houses were more crowded, but the bulk of the agricultural population must, as at Mycenae, have lived outside the walls. Troy VI in its final phase towards the close of the fourteenth century could stand comparison with Mycenae and Tiryns. In the early years of the millennium it had adopted the same grey Minyan ware as the Greeks; in the fourteenth century it imported and copied the latest Mycenaean styles. This Troy was destroyed at some time near 1300, and the absence of any traces of fire, and the pattern of violence reflected in the way the stones fell, point to an earthquake. There is no evidence of a change in the composition or culture of the population in the succeeding settlement. The walls were restored, new houses were built partly with the old material, and Mycenaean pottery was still imported, though not on so large a scale. But there are two significant features which are not paralleled in earlier Troys. The houses are

doubtedly VIIA and so far as the archaeological record goes the Greeks got no immediate gain from their war. They did not occupy the site and they did not destroy Troy for ever. If their main purpose was to extend their economic interests into the Propontis and beyond there is no trace of their success.[56]

But the significance of the Trojan expedition cannot be assessed unless we see its relation to events elsewhere, and before returning to Troy and the date of its destruction we must try to reconstruct events in Greece and in the eastern Mediterranean.

1.29 Troy, sixth city

very crowded, as if it was important to bring as many people as possible within the protection of the walls, and throughout the citadel there are large storage vessels sunk in the ground within the houses. Trouble was clearly expected, though not necessarily from Greece.

Homer's Troy

This settlement also, now known as VIIA, was destroyed, but not by an earthquake. There must have been a devastating fire, and skeletons were found in two of the houses. The next settlement, VIIB, shows no abrupt change at first, but later new people came, bringing with them a new type of knobbed pottery which to people familiar with Mycenaean standards must have seemed very uncouth. If Troy was destroyed by the Greeks it was un-

Troubles in Greece and the Near East

In 1289 the Hittites and the Egyptians fought a great battle at Kadesh in north Syria, and fifteen years later closed hostilities in a comprehensive peace; the mercantile cities of the coast could at last hope for a period of stability and the expansion of their commerce. In Greece all still seemed set fair for the Mycenaeans, who since the collapse of Crete had steadily increased in power and prosperity. Before the end of the century both areas were the scenes of violence, confusion and the movement of peoples, and it was some hundred and fifty years before the new patterns of population were firmly established.

Pressures on Egypt and the Hittites

This period of destructions and invasions is still very difficult to reconstruct in detail, but the sequence of events is clearer in the East. There we have the contemporary records in Egypt of King Merneptah and Rameses III, and the archives of the Hittite capital Boghazkoi and of the trading town of Ugarit on the Syrian coast add their own commentary. The earliest evidence comes from the temple of Amon at Karnak, where Merneptah has briefly described and illustrated his defeat *c.* 1225 (or *c.* 1211) of an attack on the western Delta by Libyans in alliance with 'northerners coming from all lands'.[57] Unfortunately the names of the northerners cannot be securely identified, for they are written in hieroglyphics without vowels. The same people, k-w-sh might be transcribed Ekwesh or Akaiwasha. The first recorded attack on Egypt from the north is made by k-w-sh, t-r-sh, sh-k-l-sh, sh-r-d, l-k. Of these the last are almost certainly Lycians from the south coast of Asia Minor; the sh-r-d, Shardana or Sherden, have by some been identified with Sardinians and the first two with Tyrsenians or Etruscans, and Sicels. These are exciting possibilities but no more; unless further evidence is found the origin of the invaders should be looked for along or not far behind the coast of Asia Minor, Syria or Palestine. Philologically the Ekwesh or Akaiwasha could be Achaeans, and in view of the relations between Hittites and Achaeans, Achaean participation in a plundering attack on Egypt would not be out of character; but the Ekwesh of the Egyptian relief were circumcised and later Greeks were not. A sculptor's error cannot be ruled out but an Achaean participation in the attack on Egypt is not certain.

Ugarit and Cyprus threatened

During the following years fitful light is thrown on the continuing unrest, and a particularly interesting view of the situation is seen from Ugarit. The wealth of Ugarit was based on good land and successful trading, but her position between the major powers of Egypt and the Hittite Kingdom made her policy decisions delicate, and her trade was no longer secure when there were restless bands looking for plunder. In this period her interests coincide with those of Cyprus, and some of the correspondence between the two survives; there was probably a marriage connection, for Ammurapi, who was to be the last king of Ugarit, addresses the king of Cyprus as father. The king of Cyprus writes: 'You have written to me: enemy ships have been seen at sea. Even if it is true remain firm. Where are your troops and chariots? . . . Surround your towns with ramparts, bring in your troops and chariots and await the enemy steadfastly.' This advice was of little comfort: 'Ships of the enemy have come. By fire he has burnt my towns and done much evil in my country. My father does not know that my troops and chariots are all in Hittite country and all my ships in Lycian country. They have not rejoined me yet and the country is left to itself. Let my father know it: yes, seven enemy ships have come and have plundered my land. If there are any more enemy ships now in sight let me somehow know.' Ugarit was a semi-dependent vassal state, expected to follow the policy of the Hittites and to provide military forces when needed. Her fleet has gone into action against the Lycians, who were famous pirates even in classical times; at the battle of Kadesh they fought with the Hittites, but now in spite of the peace they are one of the people threatening Egypt. The troops of Ugarit are in Hittite lands, probably to support Hittite forces against trouble in north Syria. Cyprus was a natural prize for pirate fleets; in another letter we learn that 'twenty enemy ships were left in the mountainous regions (north coast). They have not stayed there. They left hurriedly, we don't know where they have gone.' It was not long before the raiders had sacked Enkomi, the largest and richest town in Cyprus, Sinda and perhaps other settlements. Ugarit may have changed allegiance as Hittite power declined and the northerners became stronger and more united.[58]

The final chapter can be read in the mortuary temple of Rameses III at Medinet Habu. Some forty years after the first major attack on Egypt the northerners again fought their way down by sea and land, leaving a trail of destruction behind them. 'The foreign countries made a conspiracy in their islands. Removed and scattered in the fray were the bands at one time. No land could stand before their arms from Hatti (the Hittites), Quadi, Carchemish, Arzawa, and Alashia (Cyprus), but they were cut off at [one time]. A camp was set up in one place at Amurru (south of Ugarit). They desolated its people, and its land was like that which has never come into being. They were coming, while the flame was prepared before them, forward toward Egypt. They laid their hand upon the land to the (very) circuit of the earth, their hearts confident and trusting: "Our plans will succeed".' The Egyptian king proudly recorded his triumph: 'The peoples of the north were disturbed . . . They were cut off from their countries; advancing, their courage broke . . . Some on

Egypt defeats invaders

land, others on sea. Those that came by land were defeated and massacred. Those who penetrated the mouths of the Nile were caught in the net like birds.'[59]

The peoples from the north had come down with their families and possessions in covered wagons; this was not a plundering raid, but a determination to settle in Egypt, where the Nile guaranteed good harvests. There is evidence that during the period of emergency demands for corn from Egypt and Ugarit for Cilicia and elsewhere and famine or near-famine conditions may have been a part cause of the widespread restlessness. The Egyptian king probably exaggerated his triumph, for the Philistines who were with his enemies were able to settle on a fertile stretch of coast not far from Egypt's eastern border. But so far as we know there were no further massed attacks on Egypt. Her most dangerous rival in the north, the Hittite Kingdom, had already been mortally crippled. At some time near 1200 the capital at Boghazkoi was destroyed and the central control of the empire disintegrated. Asia Minor entered on a confused period of small-scale powers until the Phrygians coming in from the north-west consolidated an empire in the north and centre.

Tension in Greece   The violence and insecurity in the Near East were not irrelevant to the fortunes of the Mycenaeans, for a significant part of their prosperity depended on their trade with the eastern Mediterranean, and if communications with Cyprus were cut it would not be easy to find a sufficient substitute for Cyprian copper. But there were more serious dangers nearer home, where the clouds began to gather towards the end of the thirteenth century. When in the middle of the century Mycenae rebuilt her fortifications and enlarged the circuit of her walls she was not necessarily anxious for the future; the monumental Lion Gate certainly does not suggest anxiety, but when later she built a passage through her wall in the north-east corner with steps down to an extra source of water outside the walls the natural explanation is that an attack might be imminent and that the new water supply was an insurance against a long siege.[60] Nor can it be a coincidence that similar action was taken at roughly the same time at Tiryns and at Athens. At Tiryns underground passages were dug through the walls to a reservoir in the rock outside. At Athens a more difficult engineering feat was achieved: seven flights of steep steps were built to a source of water 100 feet below the level of the Acropolis.[61] A further sign of danger may be the building of

1.30   Entry through wall to outside cistern, Mycenae

a polygonal wall across the Isthmus of Corinth; it has been traced for nearly two miles from the Saronic Gulf, but it is not yet certain whether it was completed.[62]

At or near the end of the century the clouds *Destruc-* burst, and a wave of destruction spread *tions in* through Mycenaean Greece—in the Argolid at *Greece* Tiryns, Mycenae, Zygouries, Dendra; across the Gulf of Corinth at Cirrha; at Pylos in Messenia. North of the Isthmus Athens, as tradition maintained, escaped, but at Thebes there now seems to be evidence of destruction in the same general context. Gla, with which the fate of Orchomenus was bound up, was abandoned at about this time, and one of the gates showed evidence of burning; for Orchomenus itself we must await further excavation; Iolcus at the north frontier of the Mycenaean world was also a victim. For the dating of these destructions we rely on the evidence of pottery and particularly in the classification of shapes and styles towards the end of IIIB and the beginning of IIIC. The evidence of some sites is very tenuous and more detailed work still needs to be done on fixing pottery sequences, but though modifications of details may be needed there is no doubt that within a generation or little more the main Mycenaean centres with the exception of Athens were violently broken.

Owing to the abundance of its pottery the evidence from Pylos is the least controversial. Pylos was destroyed in the transition stage between IIIB and IIIC; for most of the rest a date towards the end of IIIB is given, but with varying degrees of conviction. The latest studies of the evidence at Mycenae, however, are a timely warning against an over-simplification of the general pattern. It has now been established that there were three stages in the eclipse of Mycenae. In the first there was fairly widespread destruction outside the walls, including the House of the Oil Merchant and its three neighbours; in the second there was considerable destruction within the citadel, and this was followed by a final destruction in the middle of IIIC. The first attack is substantially earlier than the destruction of Pylos, but the second attack on Mycenae could be contemporary.[63]

The Isthmus wall

There is one further problem which may be associated with the destructions that needs further examination. For the reconstruction of events in this critical phase the Isthmus wall is of primary importance. The sherds recovered from the interstices in the wall were classified by Broneer as transitional between IIIB and IIIC, which suggests a date later than the late IIIB attributed to most of the destructions. To make historical sense the wall should be a sign of alarm when danger threatened from the north and not when the main work of destruction had been accomplished. The prior question, however, which has to be asked is whether the lengths of wall that have been examined are in fact part of a defensive wall, to bar the passage of the Isthmus. The difficulties raised could be dismissed if we accept the recent suggestion that the remains are part of a retaining wall supporting a road leading to the centre of the Isthmus. This would mean rejecting one stretch of wall which would not fit the road theory;[64] the arguments, however, originally advanced for regarding it as part of the wall still seem sound. Tentatively I conclude that it is part of a defensive wall.

One other major event has to be fitted into

the narrative of dissolution, the Dorian invasion which changed the map of Greece. We have to trace the relation between the Trojan War, the destructions, and the coming of the Dorians with no contemporary records to guide us and with archaeological evidence which seems to make the problem more rather than less difficult. The main literary tradition presents a reasonably coherent general outline. The sack of Troy was the beginning of troubles; the princes returned to unsettled conditions and palace intrigues. Ten years before the Greeks sailed for Troy the Dorians had tried to break into the Peloponnese, where as Heraclids they had a right to settle, but their champion was slain at the Isthmus and the oracle said that they must wait 100 years before returning. Those years were completed two generations after the fall of Troy, and instead of coming over the Isthmus they crossed the Corinthian Gulf from Naupactus to Rhion. Dates for the fall of Troy differed considerably from the 1334 of Douris to the 1138 of Ephorus, but the figure which carried most authority was 1183, the date calculated or accepted by Eratosthenes.

This date cannot be easily reconciled with the archaeological evidence, though there is an embarrassing difference in the interpretation of the evidence. Since in the ruins of Troy VIIA no objects which could be precisely dated were found, pottery remains the only guide, and in a site as disturbed as Troy intrusive sherds can easily find their way into strata to which they do not belong. The majority of sherds which were associated with this level were in the styles of Late Helladic (or Mycenaean) IIIB, which is generally held to run from c. 1300 to c. 1200. Blegen in his basic publication suggested 1240 as the date for the destruction, and later was inclined to move the date back a little, but one of his reviewers after a detailed analysis of the pottery suggests that it should fall near the end of IIIB.[65] It would then be close to the destruction of the palace at Pylos, where the evidence, massive in quantity since the palace was not reoccupied, was clear in its implications. The pottery in use when Pylos fell was IIIB, near the point of transition to IIIC.

On the evidence available it seems possible to put the fall of Troy a generation earlier than the main destructions in Greece and it could even have weakened rather than strengthened their position, but it can no longer be assumed that an Achaean war against Troy is an undisputed episode of Greek history. The modern tendency has been to see more and

47

more of the post-Mycenaean world in Homer and less and less that is genuinely Mycenaean. The question is already being asked whether there ever was a Greek expedition against Troy.[66] Few have been bold enough to take an open stand in support of such a heresy but scepticism can no longer be summarily dismissed. Archaeology has shown that Troy VIIA was violently destroyed either towards the end of the thirteenth or the beginning of the twelfth century, but archaeology throws no light on who destroyed her.

It must be admitted that to stand on the site of Troy with an imagination nourished on Homer is very disillusioning. The plain below the fortress is as impressive as one could expect but the fortress itself is miserably restricted. Where would we place Priam's palace with its multitude of rooms for his family of 50 sons with their 50 princesses? How big a population could in fact be compressed within the walls? Nor did excavation reveal signs of great wealth. Would such an objective have attracted a levy from all the Mycenaean principalities? If we had to rely entirely on the archaeological evidence the destruction of Troy VIIA would seem to be a very minor event and we should assume that the destroyers were either some local power or new people pressing down from the north.

Certainly we must reject the scale of operations that Homer describes, but we expect such exaggeration in epic and we even find it in the fifth century in Herodotus' prose epic of the Persian wars; but national epics are almost always based on actual events, however much they embellish or distort them. If it is difficult to see why the Trojan War happened it is more difficult to see why it should have been invented. It was remembered while more important operations of the fifteenth and fourteenth centuries were forgotten because it was the last signal success of the Mycenaeans. In a time of growing insecurity it was a raid to secure material wealth. Nor does archaeology disprove the relevance of a Spartan princess.

It remains to consider who destroyed the Mycenaean centres. The solution that comes most naturally to mind is to attribute both the anxious attention to new water supplies and the Isthmus wall to the fear of a Dorian invasion, which proved more than justified when the Dorians broke in and destroyed the main centres of Mycenaean power. Any such solution, however, is difficult to reconcile with the archaeological evidence. The Dorians have indeed proved extremely elusive, for they have not been successfully identified with any of the

changes that might seem to indicate a change of population. The iron which was once thought to come with them from the north now seems to be introduced from the east; cremation which also was commonly associated with them is first found in an Athenian cemetery; the replacement of the chamber tomb by the cist grave is more probably a sign of impoverishment rather than of newcomers—they had been common in Greece much earlier and had never died out. We should also expect to see a growth of population in the lands that became Dorian; whereas the evidence suggests that in Laconia and Messenia there was a sharp decline in population. Archaeologically the destroyers cannot be identified. The most comprehensive review of the evidence concludes that they destroyed and withdrew.[67]

On this hypothesis one is naturally reminded of the so-called sea raiders of the eastern Mediterranean who moved down on Egypt by sea and land, destroying as they went. Raiders would be concerned primarily with plunder including prisoners to sell into slavery, and would not necessarily wish to settle. But if they came by sea, there should be evidence of destruction in the islands, whereas the islands seem to be unaffected. And would sea raiders have sailed right round the Peloponnese to destroy Cirrha? If they came by land from the far north there should be evidence of their passage through Macedonia and Thessaly. If they came from the periphery of the Mycenaean world why did they not settle? Other solutions have therefore been offered. Rhys Carpenter made the basic cause a change in climate, by which in a recurring rhythm a wet period was followed by a period of intensified heat accompanied by severe droughts, leading to famine which in turn led to social revolution.[68] This theory, in the extreme form that it is presented, has not been accepted by the experts in climate, and it is difficult to envisage a peasants' revolt succeeding against so many strong fortifications, but a series of bad harvests throughout a wide area may be one of the factors responsible for so much restlessness. Others have suggested that the destructions were the result of inter-city struggles within the Mycenaean sphere, but the destructions are too widespread to have such a single explanation. Moreover none of these three solutions is compatible with a defensive wall across the Isthmus.

It is probably premature to hope for a definitive interpretation of the evidence until there has been a rigorous re-examination of the pottery at all the destroyed sites. It is by no means certain that all reports mean quite the same thing by their terms, and one may suspect that 'the end of IIIB' in particular may sometimes have been loosely used. There is danger in making inferences from fragments that are too small, and from pots that are too few. It has also to be established whether the classification and sequence of pottery from Mycenae applies without modification at other centres. The changes that have been made in establishing the sequence of design and shape at Mycenae suggests that there may be scope for similar work elsewhere.[69] Such detailed work might possibly provide a secure relative chronology of the destructions and this might show that they are spread over a longer period than is generally assumed. If it were found that Pylos was destroyed before Tiryns and Mycenae, or even before Thebes, many current accounts would need to be rewritten.

Invasion from the north

Our reconstruction can therefore only be tentative. The Isthmus wall is good evidence that the Peloponnese was threatened from the north. Formally it could have been designed by the Argolid against Thebes or a coalition based on Thebes but it seems to be directed against a greater danger than this from further north, and since archaeology reveals no clearly intrusive elements the invaders are probably from the periphery of the Mycenaean world in Epirus or Thessaly or both. If no further evidence of destruction can be found contemporary with the first phase at Mycenae when the House of the Oil Merchant and its neighbours were burnt, this Mycenae destruction may be the result of internal conflict rather than enemies from outside. Tradition recorded dynastic troubles at Mycenae when Agamemnon returned from the Trojan War. Since it remains difficult to imagine the destroyers vanishing into thin air when their work of destruction was done, we should think of some of them remaining in the Argolid and being concerned in the final destruction of Mycenae in the middle of IIIC (c. 1150). But there should be some basis in the story that the Heraclids were returning to the Peloponnese after a hundred years. This may refer to the gap between the destruction after which some of the invaders returned home with their loot and the mass movement of newcomers into the Peloponnese. Whatever the sequence of events may have been the basic fact seems certain that Mycenaean power and with it the palace economy was broken near the end of the thirteenth century.

The destruction of the Mycenaean centres in Greece marks the end of a century of dissolution. If we review the scene when the Hittites made peace with Egypt in the early thirteenth century, we see Egypt secure within her own borders and her political frontiers extended into Syria; the Hittites, ruling from Boghazkoi, dominant in Asia Minor and North Syria; Troy commanding the Hellespont, with her power probably reaching along the western fringe of Asia Minor and the north coast of the Aegean; Greece a land of strong principalities recognising the primacy of Mycenae. In all these centres there was wealth and power: little more than a hundred years later they were all broken. Egypt, already weakened by her long struggle with the Hittites, had been further crippled by a series of land and sea raids from west and north, and for many centuries was to be a powerless spectator of events. Boghazkoi lay in ruins, and Asia Minor remained unsettled until the Phrygians consolidated an empire in the north and centre, followed by the Lydians in the west. But, though the power of the Hittites was eclipsed in Asia Minor, the principalities that they had established in Syria in the days of their greatness carried on the Hittite traditions and provided one of the fertilising elements for Greek craftsmen when Greek traders once again sailed into the eastern Mediterrranean. The breaking of the Hittite and Egyptian empires also gave opportunity to the Phoenician cities of the coast to play a greater part in Mediterranean seafaring. Troy never recovered its power: the settlements that followed the Greek sack were poor and powerless. When the Aegean world settled down again the hill of Hissarlik was no longer a strategic site; Sestus and Abydus on the two shores commanded the Hellespont. Greece entered on a dark age, though when the invaders had been assimilated she was to enter a new spring on the way to a more glorious summer; but the centres of power were to be transferred from Mycenae to Sparta and Athens.

The Homeric Poems

The heroic age of Greece may be said to have come to an end with the final destruction of Mycenae, but memories of Mycenaean greatness and the age of heroes were kept alive in song.

The deeds of Achaean princes were celebrated by minstrels in Mycenaean palaces, as in the *Odyssey* by Phemius and the blind Demodocus at the courts of Ithaca and Scheria.

The stories were handed down and added to by nameless bards in the bleak period that followed, until the greatest of them all conceived an epic on a grand scale which eclipsed his predecessors. Homer, who sang of the Achaean war against Troy and the wrath of Achilles, lived long after the Trojan War: he himself tells us that he is composing in an age of lesser men. Herodotus thought that he lived

1.31   Ivory plaque from Delos

in the ninth century, but the material background of the *Iliad* points more strongly to the eighth century. Homer, however, had a long tradition behind him: the epic style and language had already been fashioned, the outlines of the story were fixed. Stock epithets, recurrent lines, whole passages he could take and adapt, while the artistic structure of the work could be wholly his own.

And so Homer gives us vivid reflections of a period as remote from his own day as the Elizabethans from ourselves. He describes a helmet which had gone out of fashion before Mycenae fell—'a helmet made of leather, and with many a thong was it stiffly wrought within, while without the white teeth of a boar of flashing tusks were arranged thick set on either side, well and cunningly, and in the midst was fixed a cap of felt'. Just such a helmet is depicted on an ivory plaque of the period, and fragments of boars' tusks from such helmets have been found in many burials, from the shaft grave period to the early thirteenth century.[70] A gold cup with doves poised at the two handles is faintly reminiscent of Nestor's famous cup in the *Iliad*, 'a rightly good cup, embossed with strands of gold, and four handles there were to it, and round each

Confusion of periods

1.32   Gold cup with doves, Mycenae

two golden doves were feeding, and to the cup were two feet below'.[71] But only Nestor could lift his cup when it was full; the shaft grave cup was less than six inches high. The differences in fact are more striking than the resemblances, but the addition of the birds is an unusual feature, derived from Minoan Crete, which would have been unfamiliar in the eighth century.

There is more specific history in the catalogue of Greek ships, where many cities are included which were of no importance in archaic and classical Greece, but there are apparent anachronisms here too.[72] Argos, which archaeologically seems to be comparatively unimportant in the Mycenaean period, controls Tiryns and the Argive plain while Mycenae's rule is confined to the area to the north extending to the Corinthian Gulf. It is perhaps possible that there was such a change in the balance of power in the course of the twelfth century, but it is hard to believe that the King of Mycenae could be powerful enough in the thirteenth century to be accepted as leader of the Greeks if he did not control his own seafront on the Aegean.[73] The omission of Thebes and inclusion of Lower Thebes is unexpected and convincing: it accords with the tradition that the Cadmeia of Thebes was destroyed by the Epigoni before the Trojan War, a tradition which is strengthened by traces of destruction that have been found in the palace. On the other hand the Boeotians figure both in the catalogue and in the narrative of the fighting at Troy, but according to Thucydides it was not until the sixtieth year after the Trojan War that the Boeotians came into Boeotia.[74] And Crete is regarded as an Achaean island, sending 80 ships, the largest contingent after Agamemnon's 100, led by Idomeneus with his henchman Meriones who both play a conspicuous part in the fighting—but the archaeological evidence suggests that Crete was basically carrying on Minoan traditions until the island was transformed by the arrival of the Dorians not earlier than the end of the twelfth century.[75]

In Homer's weapons and fighting it is vain to look for a consistent pattern; all periods from the sixteenth to the eighth centuries have left their traces. The two great body shields of the shaft-grave period, the figure-of-eight and *The Iliad* the tower shield, are both used by Homer's heroes, but both were out of date by the time of his Trojan War. Though iron was introduced in the eleventh century, and by the eighth century had long been the standard material for weapons and certain tools, the swords of Homer's heroes are still of bronze. Chariots are still retained as a traditional element in heroes' battles, though they probably did not survive in battle into the eighth century. The spear, which in the Mycenaean period was used for thrusting, is primarily a throwing spear in Homer, as it was in the Geometric period. There is much more of the Mycenaean world that has been

forgotten. No mention is made in the *Iliad* of the great tholos tombs, the most striking achievement of the Mycenaean architect; and the burial customs of the poem bear little resemblance to Mycenaean remains. In the Mycenaean period bodies were buried and not burnt; in the *Iliad* cremation is implied throughout as the normal rule. It seems also that Homer regarded his Achaean heroes as illiterate. The only possible reference to writing in the *Iliad* is in the story of Bellerophon who carries from Argos to Lycia 'deadly symbols in a folded tablet', and the strangeness of the expression suggests something most unusual;[76] but from the linear B tablets we know that writing was used at least for the business affairs of the palace. In Mycenaean days iron was still a precious metal, used primarily for jewelry: in Homer it is common in simile and metaphor and is used for axes, pruning-hooks and knives. There is no evidence that the Mycenaeans built temples or made large cult statues: in the *Iliad* they are both implied.

The *Iliad* was followed by the *Odyssey*, *The* which complements it. The *Iliad* is concerned *Odyssey* with fighting and war conditions; in the *Odyssey* we have a wider canvas and more varied social conditions. As with the *Iliad* there is a long history behind it though, like the *Iliad*, it has been fashioned into its final form by a single great poet. Both epics were attributed to the same author by most ancient authorities, but a small minority disagreed; the modern tendency is to be more sceptical. They are at least close together in time and reflect the same composite world. Though echoes of the culture of Mycenae remain, the material world is predominantly the world of the eighth century. The epics are not only witnesses to the glories of the past; they reflect also the reawakening of the present. But before that reawakening could come, the Greek world was to endure a long period of disturbance and poverty.

Political and Social Organisation of the Early Greeks

It is not always easy to unravel the chronological layers in the material world of Homer; it is no less difficult to determine to what extent the political and social system implied by the epics corresponds with Mycenaean conditions. In both epic and history the palace is the main focus of power, as it no longer was in Homer's day, and the great megaron

51

with its porch and vestibule is the dominant feature in Homer's palaces as it is in the excavated palaces of Mycenae, Tiryns and Pylos. Homer's kings are as well supplied as were the Shaft Grave dynasty with treasures of silver and gold, but some of the glory has departed. The frescoes that were such a prominent feature of the excavated palaces have been forgotten and there is nothing in the *Iliad* or *Odyssey* to suggest the great elaboration of the palaces whose plans we know. But though life in Homer's royal homes may seem more homely than royal, there is no shortage of staff. Penelope has her personal attendants, there are special servants responsible for preparing and serving the food, a vague number of slaves to do what house-work is needed and 50 to spin and weave; but there is no hint of the detailed work that the scribes are doing on the tablets from Cnossus and Pylos, making inventories, allocating rations, distributing raw material to craftsmen. It could be argued that such matters are not the stuff of epic poetry, but one might at least expect a passing reference—if not to the scribes, then to the dues in kind paid to the palace, and the great storage jars for oil, wine, and grain. When the palaces were destroyed the palace organisation collapsed, and the art of writing was forgotten; memories of the detailed functioning of the system would soon fade.

The King　　The Homeric king is more Mycenaean than his setting and it is interesting that the Mycenaean title has survived. Both at Cnossus and Pylos the king was *wanax* and the word was still used by Homer, though by his day it was obsolete in its original sense and reserved for gods. The king was now *basileus,* an earlier form of which is also found in the tablets, but referring to local princes as it still does in Hesiod's 'gift-devouring *basileis*'. Beneath the king at Pylos is a *lawagetas,* a word which should mean 'leader of the people'; it is usually understood to mean 'commander of the army', but it is unlikely that the army would have been commanded by anyone but the king. He was more probably a civilian official.

But though Mycenaean organisation was more complex than Homer suggests, it is doubtful whether there are major anachronisms in his portrait of the Mycenaean king. In Homer the king was at once the chief priest, the chief judge, and the supreme warlord of his people. He exercised a general control over religious ceremonies, except in cases where there were special priesthoods; he pronounced judgment and dealt out justice to those who came to his judgment-seat to have their wrongs righted, and he led forth the host to war. He belonged to a family which claimed descent from the gods themselves. His relation to his people was conceived as that of a protecting deity; 'he was revered as a god in the land'. The kingship passed from father to son, but it is probable that personal fitness was recognised as a condition of the kingly office, and the people might refuse to accept a degenerate son who was unequal to the tasks that his father had fulfilled. The sceptred king had various privileges—the seat of honour at feasts, a large and choice share of booty taken in war and of food offered at sacrifices. A special close of land was marked out and set apart for him as a royal domain, distinct from that which his family owned.

The nobles　In Homer Nestor is treated with considerable respect on account of his age and long experience, and throughout the *Iliad* and *Odyssey* it is assumed that the king will consult his senior nobles. This emphasis on consultation has often been thought to reflect the decline of monarchy in the Dark Ages when the gap between the monarch and his nobles had been considerably narrowed and they were soon to take over his power as the aristocratic councils of the early archaic period. This is possible, perhaps probable, but it must remain a hypothesis until we know more about the relation of the Mycenaean king to his nobles than the present state of our evidence discloses. The graves of the second circle of shaft graves (circle B) were not royal graves, but they were almost royal in wealth.

The Assembly　There is also a foreshadowing in Homer of the larger meeting which was to develop into the Assembly of the whole people and to become the corner-stone of democracy. When in the *Odyssey* Alcinous calls the Phaeacians to the place of meeting to hear Odysseus, Pallas Athena seems to urge all Phaeacians to attend, and not only the king's advisers and men of rank. More striking is the meeting by the ships early in the *Iliad*. Nerves are tense and morale is low; there are even serious thoughts of abandoning Troy and sailing for home. Thersites makes a protest that by modern standards is not unreasonable. The war was well enough for Agamemnon who got the lion's share of all the booty and lived in considerable comfort; the common soldier had more than his share of the misery of war and none of the rewards. Let Agamemnon stay and the rest go home. Homer makes it quite clear that men like Thersites should be seen and not heard. He gets a rough handling from Odysseus and in case there should be any sympathy for him Homer describes him in some detail as physically contemptible.[77] This surely is the eighth century breaking in when the divine right of kings and princes was being increasingly questioned, but not by Homer.

The king was surrounded by a body of Companions, or retainers, who were attached to him by personal ties of service, and seem often to have lived in his palace. The Companions are the same institution as the thanes of England. And if kingship had held its ground in Greece, the Companions might possibly, as in England, have developed into a new order of nobility, founded not on birth, but on the king's own choice for his service.

Though the monarchy in this primitive form, as we find it reflected in Homer, generally passed away, it survived in a few outlying regions which lagged behind the rest of the Hellenic world in political development. Thus the Macedonian Greeks in the lower valley of the Axius retained a constitution of the old Homeric type till the latest times— the royal power continually growing. At the close of the tale of Greek conquest and expansion, which began on the Cayster and ended on the Hyphasis, we shall come back by a strange revolution to the Homeric state. When all the divers forms of the rule of the few and the rule of the many, which grew out of the primitive monarchy, have had their day, we shall see the Macedonian warrior, who is to complete the work that was begun by the Achaean conquerors of Troy, attended by his Companions like Agamemnon or Achilles, and ruling his people like an Achaean king of men.

The Dark Ages

The material remains of the period that follows the destruction of the great Mycenaean centres bear eloquent witness to the completeness of the collapse. The architect no longer designs on a monumental scale, for there are no wealthy princes to command his services. Writing, which seems to have been almost confined to palace administration, lapses because there are no rich palaces to be administered. No new fortifications are built, in spite of the violence of the times, because the resources are no longer available to organise and maintain the labour force that such works required. The craftsman, restricted to a narrower world, lacks the precious materials and the skilled refinements of his predecessors, though the potters are an exception to this gloomy picture: during the twelfth century some of their pottery was more interesting and more enterprising than in the period before the destructions. But the burials of the period are those of an impoverished society: in the Peloponnese and central Greece the tholos tomb and the chamber tomb are abandoned in favour of the simpler cist tomb, a shallow grave dug in the ground and lined and roofed with stone slabs. Cremation increasingly replaces burial, encouraged perhaps by a general sense of insecurity.

There will have to be much more excavation and much more detailed study of what has already been excavated, especially the pottery, before the two centuries that follow the final storming of Mycenae become anything but dark. Certain patterns, however, seem to be emerging.[78] Through the twelfth century the evidence suggests a serious decline in population in most areas. There was probably some movement overseas—to Cyprus certainly, probably to Tarsus in Cilicia, and perhaps to the Dodecanese. In the Argolid there was a temporary revival at Mycenae and Tiryns before the final destruction of Mycenae (c. 1150); Argos and Asine seem to have been comparatively unaffected. Achaea seems to have escaped the holocaust, to have received refugees and to have become more Mycenaean than Mycenae. In the west, in Messenia, Laconia, Arcadia, Elis there is a marked decline in population. North of the Isthmus, Thebes and Orchomenus both seem to have been crippled before the Dark Ages start, but Athens remained comparatively unaffected.

While the Argolid and Thebes were strong, Athens seems to have been only a secondary power and the modest place she takes in the Homeric Catalogue of Ships is probably a fair reflection of her standing, but from c. 1150 to c. 1000 she was the least distressed of the major states of Greece. While communications inside Greece were broken or at least weakened she retained contact with the islands and with Cyprus. The cemetery of Perati on the east coast of Attica during this period illustrates her wide range of contacts and comparative prosperity; it is significant that Lefkandi in Euboea also seems to have flourished at the same time, and Hagia Eirene on the island of Ceos is still a busy trading station.[79] Before the middle of the eleventh century the Mycenaean settlement at Miletus which had been destroyed in the twelfth century was occupied again, and the foundation was later attributed to Athens: it is a striking sign of her growing confidence. It was in Athens also

Consequences of the destructions

in the Peloponnese

Athens

again to become much more than a village. In the north of the Peloponnese there may have been serious trouble. At some point the main fortress in the area, Teichos Dymaion, was destroyed and Achaea seems to lose its Mycenaean character. A tradition first recorded by Herodotus says that the people of Achaea, Ionians, were driven out of their country and came to Athens, and from Athens to Ionia. This

1.33 Excavation at Lefkandi (see note, page 552)

1.34 Attic protogeometric vase

that the first new distinctive pottery style was developed, the Protogeometric. This is an austere style of strong shapes and simplified decoration, areas of white and black colour relieved by circles or semi-circles drawn for the first time with compass and multiple brush. The style, originating in Athens, was widely copied in other states, and Athenian pots were traded through the islands and in central Greece and some areas of the Peloponnese.[80] Athens also kept in touch with Cyprus, whose copper remained important in spite of the increasing use of iron, and some Cypriots, descended from Mycenaean emigrants, may have come to settle in Athens.

Achaea   In the Peloponnese, Argos was becoming the main growth point; Mycenae had been temporarily abandoned and Tiryns was never

is an oversimplified schematisation, but it may be basically right. Achaea was Mycenaean in culture as well as name during the twelfth century; the dialect of the district in the archaic period was similar to that of Elis, the so-called north-western dialect, which was the language of newcomers to the Peloponnese.

The reason for the evacuation of Achaea might have been an invasion of the Peloponnese from the north side of the Corinthian Gulf, and this may have been part of what was later called the Dorian invasion which revolutionised the distribution of populations in the Peloponnese. For the Dorian invasion is closely linked in tradition with the colonisation of the eastern seaboard of the Aegean, and though we need much more evidence from more sites it seems that this eastward movement covers the period from *c.* 1050 to *c.* 950.[81]

The Dorian Invasion

Greek tradition kept alive the memory of the Dorian invasion, but legend, invention, and propaganda distorted the details. Already by the fifth century the coming of the Dorians was being interpreted as a reinstatement of the Heraclids rather than an invasion of new-comers. Eurystheus, according to this version, exiled from Mycenae the sons of Heracles and their followers. After various wanderings they found refuge and help in Attica. With the Athenians they fought and defeated the followers of Eurystheus and killed the king. But Atreus, who succeeded to the kingship of Mycenae, led the forces of the Peloponnese to the Isthmus. Hyllus, son of Heracles, challenged the chosen of the enemy to single combat: if he won, the Heraclids should inherit the Kingdom of Mycenae; if he were defeated, they should not return to the Peloponnese for a hundred years. Hyllus was slain by Echemus, an Arcadian king; the Heraclids withdrew, but returned to their heritage after a hundred years had passed. They were led by three Heraclid brothers, Temenus, Aristodemus, and Cresphontes, who divided their conquests into the three kingdoms of Argos, Sparta, and Messenia. This concoction we may dismiss as patriotic fiction; but Herodotus, who reflects this tradition, gives also a version of the Dorian movement which may be closer to history. 'In the time of King Deucalion the Dorians lived in Phthiotis; in the time of Dorus son of Hellen they occupied the land under Ossa and Olympus, which was called Histiaeotis. From Histiaeotis they were expelled by Cadmeians and dwelt in Pindus, being called Macedonians. Thence again they moved to Dryopis (historic Doris) and from Dryopis they came to the Peloponnese and were called Dorians.'[82] That Doris had been their temporary home was believed as early as the seventh century, for Tyrtaeus wrote of Sparta: 'Zeus has granted this city to the Heraclids with whom, leaving wind-swept Erineus (in Doris), we came to the broad island of Pelops.' But the movement was more widespread and less homogeneous than this tradition suggests. The invaders probably came from the north and north-west, but the precise details of their movements cannot yet be disentangled, and matter less than the final results on the map of Greece.

Distribution of Greek dialects

More reliable for the shape of the invasion than legends, which are often inconsistent, is the distribution of dialects which we know from later inscriptions. Two groups of dialects, closely related, the north-western and the Dorian, represent the invaders; the Arcadian, Aeolic, and Ionic dialects derive from the Greeks of the pre-Dorian period. The north-western dialect is spread along the northern shores of the Corinthian gulf through Locris, Doris, Phocis, Aetolia into Acarnania and the islands at the mouth of the gulf. Across the water it is the language of the narrow coastal strip of Achaea and of Elis. These peoples played little part in the history of classical Greece. In Aetolia Homer spoke of 'Pleuron by the sea and rocky Calydon', and the myth of Meleager and the hunting of the Calydonian boar became a part of the heritage of the national legend of Greece. But Mycenaean culture has left little mark on this land of hills and valleys. Aetolia kept pace with mainland Greece in the period of settlement following the invasions, but in the age of colonisation and rapid progress it fell behind. It remained a land of villages, dangerous to the invader, but without influence on the main current of events. Locris suffered eclipse and was split by the establishment of the Phocians, dividing the Locrians into three separate communities, the Ozolian Locrians on the Corinthian gulf, to the west of Phocis; the other two divisions on the Euboean sea, to the north-east. Doris played a rather more important part in the development of Greece, for its territory lay near Delphi, the 'rocky threshold of Apollo' which was to become the most important religious centre in the Greek world. Tradition said that this small territory was the last halting-place of the Dorians before they invaded the Peloponnese, and it was recognised as the mother-country of Dorians everywhere. The tradition may be true, though classical Doris is not strictly Dorian in language, cult, or customs. It was at any rate convenient, for a claim to the championship of Delphic Apollo was not to be despised.

Of those who spoke the north-western dialect the richest prize fell to the invaders of Elis. They settled first in the Peneus Valley, 'Hollow Elis', a land of rich pasture, famous for its horses and good arable. Later they extended their dominion south to the Alpheus Valley, penetrating the religious centre of Olympia, which they transformed by the establishment of the great Olympic festival early in the eighth century. But the Eleans, though good fighters when it was necessary to defend themselves, had no far-reaching ambitions. In their fertile territory they remained primarily a conservative agricultural community independent of trade and colonisation. They did not feel the economic stresses that led to friction and progress elsewhere. The

Aetolia

Locris

Doris

Elis

55

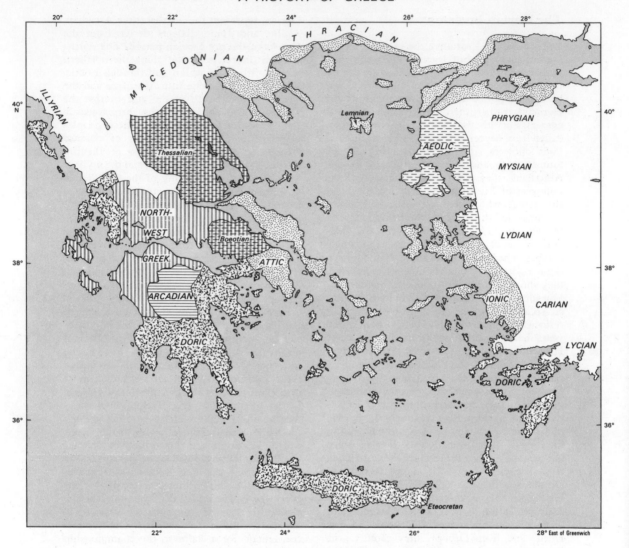

6. LANGUAGE MAP OF THE AEGEAN IN CLASSICAL TIMES

Dorians proper, whose distinguishing marks are the three Dorian tribes, Hylleis, Dymanes, Pamphyloi, and the cult of Apollo Pythaeus, occupied the main seats of power in the Peloponnese, in the Argolid, Laconia, Messenia, Corinth, and Megara. They also occupied the southern islands, Cythera, Melos, Thera, Crete and Rhodes, Cos, and the south-west corner of Asia Minor.

Though remnants of the early population could be identified later in scattered pockets, only one large area in the Peloponnese remained free from invasion. The peoples of mountainous Arcadia, the least inviting of lands to an invader, retained the pre-conquest speech and in historical times spoke the same language as the Greeks of Cyprus, recalling a time when their language was spread throughout the southern coastlands of the Peloponnese. *Arcadia*

North of the Peloponnese Attica and Euboea retained the Ionic dialect, confirming the Athenian tradition that their land though attacked was not occupied, and became a refuge for dispersed peoples and a pierhead for further emigration. Further north, the mixed dialects of Thessaly and Boeotia confirm the tradition of *Attica and Euboea*

Thessaly and Boeotia

two further invasions arising from the main disturbances. In both these countries the mixed dialect shows that an Aeolic population was invaded by peoples speaking a north-western dialect. In Boeotia the two races seem to have amalgamated; in Thessaly the conquered peoples were reduced to serfdom and were known as the *penestae* (labourers), working for overlords who ruled in the strong centres of Pharsalus, Pagasae, Larissa, and Pherae.

Argos

The pressure of the great invasions had come from the north and north-west. Arcadia was left as an island of independence. Elsewhere in the Peloponnese the invaders became the dominant force in history. The first centre of Dorian power was in the Argolid, the immediate sphere of Mycenae's rule, and from the Argolid Phlius on the upper Asopus and Sicyon on the Corinthian gulf were occupied. Argos replaced Mycenae as the centre of power. Temenos in tradition was the leader of these invaders and, recalling her priority in conquest, Argos throughout her history aspired to the hegemony of the Peloponnese. She had her days of greatness, but often she had to struggle hard even for the control of her own plain. In the Argolid the earlier population was submerged but not enslaved, and they probably provided the bulk of the agricultural labour—in time inter-marrying and even being admitted into the citizen body.

Laconia

It was different in Laconia. Here invasion came later, but the conquest was more rigorous. The native population were enslaved and worked the land for their Dorian masters. Further west a thin stream of Dorians may have penetrated Messenia, but their number was too small to dominate the land and Messenia was later to be conquered by the Dorians of Laconia.

The Isthmian states

Corinth and Sicyon were also occupied by the Dorians, and so, perhaps last of the mainland cities, was Megara. From Corinth the Doric dialect was later taken to Corcyra and her other colonies along the north-western seaboard. In Sicyon, Corinth, and Megara, though the Dorians predominated, the native population was not submerged, and when later tyrants arose they were to obtain strong support from the pre-Dorians. The island of Aegina in the Saronic Gulf, which was to play a leading role in Greek trade and for long challenge Athens, also became a Dorian land. It was occupied from Epidaurus after the mainland conquerors had settled down. When Pindar, speaking of Aegina, says 'the Dorian host of Hyllus and Aegimius came here and made our city', he is making full use of poetic licence.

Such may have been the general pattern of the sweeping changes that transformed Greece. To attempt a chronological framework is more hazardous. Literary traditions varied substantially about the direction and composition of the invaders, but felt far less doubt about their date. Even Thucydides, most critical of historians, could say without hesitation that the Boeotians came into their later home in the sixtieth year after the Trojan War, and that in the eightieth year the Dorians occupied the Peloponnese.

Archaeo-logical evidence

Archaeology is here an embarrassment, undermining faith but not yet confident enough to construct a historical record of events. We should expect to find evidence of destruction at the great Mycenaean settlements accompanied by a change in material products and in customs, marking the path of the invaders. And there was indeed a time when the introduction of the geometric style of pottery, of iron, and cremation were thought to be the archaeological clues. But the progress of excavation has shown that the problem is much more complex. A wave of destruction of the Mycenaean palaces at Mycenae, Pylos, and other centres has certainly left its traces, and can be dated at the end of the thirteenth or the beginning of the twelfth centuries. But it is not accompanied by a change in culture. In pottery there is no sharp break between Mycenaean and geometric; the one decays and the other gradually evolves, through sub-Mycenaean and Proto-geometric; it develops in Greece and is not brought from without, for throughout this transitional phase the leading centre of production is Attica, which always boasted of its continuity with the past. Similarly it is in Attica that the first cremations on the mainland are found, and the practice seems to be introduced from the east, finding a receptive background in the insecurity that accompanied the collapse of Mycenae. Nor is iron introduced from the north; it too is first found in Attica, is probably of eastern origin, and only gradually comes into general use. It is likely enough that the invaders had not reached any high standard of material culture but took over and adapted what they found.

For large-scale Dorian elements archaeology provides no evidence in the century following the destruction of the Mycenaean fortresses. In Sparta, where excavation should have yielded firm results, Dorian settlement seems to date only from the tenth century. No signs of Dorian occupation in Corinth have yet been found from the eleventh century. Argos needs more extensive excavation.

Expansion of the Greeks to the Eastern Aegean

Tradition of Ionian origins

Greek tradition associated with the Dorian invasion a great emigration of the dispossessed across the Aegean, which planted the Greek language and Greek customs in Asia. But, like the Dorian invasion, this movement has been simplified and distorted and we cannot yet recover the pattern. Already in Herodotus' day the story of the foundation of the Ionian cities had been schematised. It was said that they derived from the twelve centres of historic Achaea, which stretched along the south shore of the Corinthian gulf. Dispossessed by the invaders, they had fled to Attica and thence sailed east to establish their twelve cities on the western coast of Asia Minor. But Herodotus himself knew that the story was more complex than that. He knew that the settlers were not of common origin, that they included Abantes from Euboea, Minyans from Orchomenos, Dryopes, and many other stocks.[83] And local traditions in these Ionian cities retained memories of their diverse origins: an early poet of Colophon, Mimnermus, who lived at the end of the seventh century, reminded his fellow citizens: 'when we left the city of Neleian Pylos and came in our ships to Asia of our longing and when in lovely Colophon with the might of arms we settled'. Such traditions suggest an uncoordinated stream of refugees fleeing before invaders, and if we could fix the date of this emigration we

Chronology

might in turn illuminate the Dorian invasion itself. But the vital centres in Asia Minor have been only fitfully excavated, and not until their lower levels have been systematically explored can we hope to retrace the main outlines of the movement. But such evidence as we have from Asia Minor is consistent with the late date suggested for the Dorian invasion. The great eastward emigration succeeded because, after the breaking of the Hittite empire at the end of the thirteenth century, there was no longer any strong power to deny the Greeks a foothold.

Evidence of Thucydides

It may even be that the occupation of the coastal lands was a process spreading over some two centuries. For Thucydides seems to imply a date in the eighth century for the Ionian colonisation from Athens. 'A considerable time elapsed before Hellas became finally settled; after a while, however, she recovered tranquillity and began to send out colonies. The Athenians colonised Ionia and most of the islands; the Peloponnesians the greater part of Italy and Sicily, and various places in Hellas.' Perhaps a disordered emigration in the eleventh and tenth centuries from scattered points was followed by a more ordered movement in the early eighth century from Athens. But whenever it ended, the origin of the movement was immediately connected with the Dorian invasion.

Physical character of coast of Asia Minor

The western coast of Asia Minor was well suited to Greek settlement and encouraged the individual development of separate city states, as did the mountain barriers of Greece that separate plain from plain. A series of river valleys are divided by mountain chains which run out into promontories so as to form deep bays; and the promontories are continued in islands. The valleys of the Hermus and the Caicus are bounded on the north by a chain of hills which run out into Lesbos; the valley of the Hermus is parted from that of the Cayster by mountains which are prolonged in Chios; and the valley of the Cayster is separated from the valley of the Maeander by a chain which terminates in Samos. South of the Maeander valley there are bays and islands, but the mountains of the mainland are broken by no rivers. The climate is temperate, the rainfall sufficient, and the river valleys provided natural routes into the interior which were to prove a powerful incentive to trade when secure conditions were established inland and wealthy and powerful kingdoms developed.

The Aeolians

To the north settled the Aeolians. Tradition connected their settlement with Thessaly and Boeotia and their dialect confirms this origin. They settled on the island of Lesbos and the opposite coastland of the Troad, which for much of its history remained in the Lesbian sphere. Further south they occupied strong places which they could defend—Pitane, Myrina, Cyme, Aegae, old Smyrna. They pressed up the rivers, and on the Hermus they founded Magnesia under Mount Sipylus. All this, needless to say, was not done at once. It must have been the work of many years and of successive expeditions from the mother-country.

The Ionians

The Aeolians were to play a less prominent part in history than the emigrants who occupied the coast to the south. These were the Ionians, many of whom could claim kinship with the people of Attica. Simplified tradition, encouraged later by Athenian pretensions, recorded that the Ionian cities were established formally from Athens and took their fire from the Athenian hearth. It is indeed probable that the main body of settlers came through Attica when, before the Dorians, the Ionian-speaking peoples fled from the Peloponnese. But others

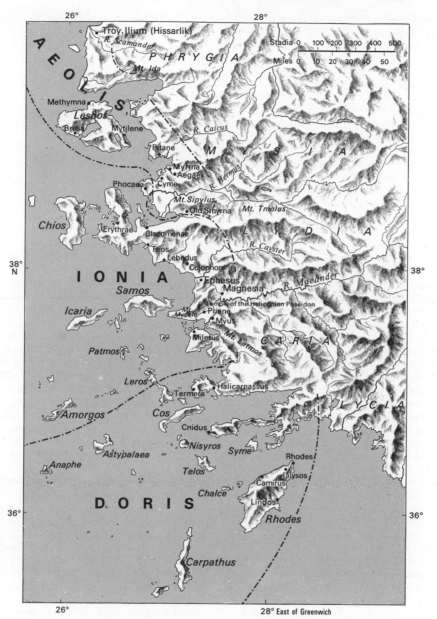

7. GREEK COLONIES IN THE EASTERN AEGEAN

doubtless sailed direct from the Peloponnese—from the Saronic Gulf, the Argolid, and other coastal districts into which the Dorians came. The two-pronged peninsula between the Hermus and Cayster rivers, with the off-lying isle of Chios, the valleys of the Cayster and Maeander with Samos and the peninsula south of Mount Latmos, were studded with com-munities which came to form a group distinct from the Aeolians to the north.

But it would probably be a mistake to regard these two groups as well defined from the first. To begin with, it is possible that they over-lapped chronologically. The latest of the Aeolian settlements may have been founded subsequently to the earliest of the Ionian. In

Distinction of the two groups and their over-lappings

the second place, the original homes of the settlers overlapped. Though the Aeolian colonists mainly came from the lands north of Mount Oeta—apart from those who came from Aetolia—they included some settlers from the coasts of Boeotia and Euboea.[84] Thus Cyme in Aeolis derived its name from Euboean Cyme. And, on the other hand, though the Ionian colonies were chiefly derived from the coasts of Attica and Argolis—apart from some contingents from Crete and other places in the south—there were also some settlers from the north. Thirdly, the two groups ran into each other geographically. Phocaea, for example, which is geographically in Aeolis, standing on the promontory north of the Hermus river, was included in Ionia. And some of the places in north Ionia—Teos, for instance —had received Achaean settlements first, and were then re-settled by Ionians. In Chios, which was afterwards fully in Ionia, a language of Aeolic complexion was once spoken.

*Ionian colonisation*Of the foundation of the famous colonies of Ionia, of the order in which they were founded, and of the relations of the settlers with the Lydian natives, we know as little as of the settlements of the Achaeans. Clazomenae and Teos arose on the north and south sides of the neck of the peninsula which runs out to meet Chios; and Chios, on the east coast of her island, faces Erythrae on the mainland— Erythrae, 'the crimson', so called perhaps from its purple fisheries, the resort of Tyrian traders. Lebedus and Colophon lie on the coast as it retires eastward from Teos to reach the mouth of the Cayster; and there was founded Ephesus, the city of Artemis. By the streams of the Cayster was a plain called 'the Asian meadow', which destiny in some odd way selected to bestow a name upon one of the continents of the earth. South of Ephesus and on the northern slope of Mount Mycale was the religious gathering-place of the Ionians, the temple of the Heliconian Poseidon, which, when once the Ionians became conscious of themselves as a sort of nation and learned to glory in their common name, served to foster a sense of unity among all their cities from Phocaea in the north to Miletus in the south. Samos faces Mount Mycale, and the worship of Hera, which was the religious feature of Samos, is thought to point to men of Argos as participators in its original foundation. South of Mycale the cities of Myus and Priene were planted on the Maeander. Then the coast retires to skirt Mount Latmos and breaks forward again to form the promontory, at the northern point of which was Miletus with its

once splendid harbour. There was one great inland city, Magnesia on the Maeander, which must not be confused with the inland Aeloian city, Magnesia on the Hermus. Though counted in Ionia, it was not of Ionian origin, for it was founded by the Magnētes of Thessaly. And settlers from Euboea and Boeotia took part in the colonisation of Ionia, as well as the Ionians of Argolis and Attica. The old inhabitants—Leleges, Maeonians, Carians— probably offered no prolonged resistance to the invaders, and in some places, as the Carians for example at Miletus, they mixed with the Greek strangers.

The colonists carried with them into the new Greece beyond the seas traditions of the old civilisation which in the mother country was being overwhelmed by the Dorian invaders; and those traditions helped to produce the luxurious Ionian civilisation which meets us some centuries later when we come into the clearer light of recorded history. And they carried with them their minstrelsy, their lays of Troy, celebrating the deeds of Achilles and Agamemnon and Odysseus. The heroic lays of Greece entered upon a new period in Ionia, where a poet of supreme genius arose, and the first and greatest epic poem of the world was created. Homer's date was disputed in *Homer* antiquity and has been disputed ever since, but there is a growing consensus of opinion in favour of the eighth century, for reasons that we have already seen. He probably lived in Chios, for such was the tradition as early as the sixth century, and the Homeridae of Chios derived their origin from him and may at first have been his direct descendants. He seems to have visited the scene of the fighting he describes with a keen eye for significant detail, and he was personally familiar with the geography of the north Aegean. He gives us a local touch when he describes the sun as rising over the sea. The historical importance of Homer is his witness to the early flowering of Ionia after the great emigration. The conscious art of his epic, his keen imagination, and his sense of form show a striking maturity which could not be paralleled on the mainland in his day. In the *Iliad* he took as his main argument the wrath of Achilles leading up to the death of Hector, and wrought into his epic many other episodes derived from the old lays on the theme of Troy. Tradition made Homer the author of both the great epics, the *Odyssey* as well as the *Iliad*. Whether this is so or not, no great length of time need separate the composition of the two poems.

The material background of the *Iliad* shows

a broadening horizon, when contact was again being established with the eastern Mediterranean, and the effect of such contact on Homer's imagination is well illustrated by his description of the shield of Achilles. The shield, wrought in bronze, tin, silver, and gold, is round and has a ringed space in the centre, encompassed by three concentric girdles. In the middle are the earth, the sea, and the heaven, with 'the unwearied sun and the moon at her full, and all the stars wherewith heaven is crowned'. The subject of the first circle is Peace and War. Here are scenes in a city at peace—banquets, brides borne through the streets by torchlight to their new homes, the elders dealing out justice; there is another city besieged, and scenes of battle. The second circle shows scenes from country life at various seasons of the year: ploughing in spring, the ploughman drinking a draught of wine as he reaches the end of the dark furrow; a king watching reapers reaping in his meadows, and the preparations for a harvest festival; a bright vintage scene, 'young men and maids bearing the sweet fruit in wicker baskets', and dancing, while a boy plays a lyre and sings the song of Linus; herdsmen with their dogs pursuing two lions which had carried off an ox from the banks of a sounding river; a pasture and shepherds' huts in a mountain glen. The whole was girdled by the third, outmost circle, through which 'the great might of the river Oceanus' flowed—rounding off, as it were, the life of mortals by its girdling stream. Individual scenes from this shield can be paralleled from the work of Cretan and Mycenaean craftsmen, but neither in Crete nor on the Greek mainland have such decorated shields nor such elaborate compositions been found from the Mycenaean period. It seems that Homer was inspired by the orientalising bronze shields of his own day such as have been found in Crete, but he has gone far beyond his models and infused the composition with a sense of balance and form which is essentially Greek.

The Iliad a national epic

Homer preserved the memory of the Trojan War as a great national enterprise. The *Iliad* was regarded as something of far greater significance than an Ionian poem; it was accepted as a national epic, and was, from the first, a powerful influence in promoting among the Greeks community of feeling and tendencies towards national unity. It was followed, perhaps at no long interval, by the *Odyssey*, which tells of the wanderings of Odysseus after the fall of Troy, and which tradition also attributed to Homer. The

The Epic Cycle, c. 750-600 B.C.

Odyssey reflects the age of bold sea journeys which prepared the way for colonisation, and is a fitting complement to the story of battling armies. The pre-eminence of Homer led to the dominance of the Trojan story in epic tradition, and he was followed by a long line of lesser poets who dealt with events that preceded or followed those described in the *Iliad*. Along with the *Iliad* and *Odyssey* they formed a chronological series which came to be known as the Epic Cycle.

The Ionic settlements did not complete the Greek colonisation of Asia Minor. The Dorian conquest of the eastern Peloponnese was followed by a Dorian expansion beyond the seas and a colonisation of the Asiatic coast, to the south of Ionia. The Carians had spread over this region down to the border of Lycia and had pressed the older inhabitants into the promontory which faces the island of Calymna. Here the Leleges participated in the latest stages of the Aegean civilisation, as we know by the pottery and other things which have been discovered at Termera in chamber-tombs. These round tombs, not hewn out of the earth like the vaulted sepulchres of Mycenae, but built above ground, are found in many parts of the peninsula and remain as the most striking memorial of the Leleges.

New Doris in Asia Minor

The Leleges confined to the Myndian promontory

Chamber-tombs at Termera (Assarlik); 'late Mycenaean.'

The bold promontories below Miletus, the islands of Cos and Rhodes, were occupied by colonists from Argolis, Laconia, Corinth, and Crete. Cnidus was the most important settlement, making with Cos and the three cities of Rhodes (Lindus, Ialysus, Camirus) a Dorian pentapolis. These settlements were independent, but they kept alive their communion of interest and sentiment by the common worship of the Triopian Apollo. Theirs was no small part of the Dorian achievement. Rhodes was to be a pioneer in the reopening of the seaways to east and west, planting settlements as far afield as in France and Spain; Cnidus could boast a wealthy treasury at Delphi and an important part in the opening up of the Adriatic; Cos was to be famous for her school of medicine. Halicarnassus, on the coast opposite Cos, at least was partly Dorian, but she early lost her place in the common Dorian festival; for, as the names of her citizens show, the population had a strong Carian admixture and the language of her documents is Ionian; but Halicarnassus could claim Herodotus among her citizens, and many colourful characters before and after him.[85]

The Carians were a vigorous people. They impressed themselves upon their land, and soon men began to forget that it had not been

Caria

61

always Caria. They took to the sea and formed a maritime power of some strength, so that in later ages a tradition was abroad that there was once upon a time a Carian sea-supremacy, though no one could mention anything that it had achieved. The Carians also claimed to have made contributions to the art of war by introducing shield-handles, and the crested helmet, and the emblazoning of shields—claims which we cannot test.[86]

The Greek fringe of western Asia Minor was complete. It was impossible for Doris to creep round the corner and join hands with Pamphylia; for the Lycians presented an insuperable barrier. The Lycians were not a folk of Aryan speech, as a widely-spread error supposed them to have been; their language is related to the Carian. Their proper name was Trm̃mili; but the name Lycian seems to have been given them by others as well as by the Greeks, who recognised in the chief Tremilian deity their own Apollo Lykios. But, though Lycia was not colonised, the Aegean was now entirely within the Greek sphere, excepting only its northern margin, where Greek enterprise in the future was to find a difficult field. It is important to observe that the process by which Asiatic Greece was created differs in character from the Dorian invasion of the Peloponnese. The settlements of Ionia and Doris are examples of colonisation. Bands of settlers went forth from their homes to find new habitations for themselves, but they left a home-country behind them. The Dorian movements, on the other hand, partake of the character of a folk-wandering. The essential fact is that a whole people dispersed to seek new fields and pastures. For the paltry remnant which remained in the sequestered nook beyond Parnassus could not be called the parent people except by courtesy; the people, as a whole, had gone elsewhere.

Lycia

In this period of the breakdown of a civilisation and violent dislocation of peoples another more distant outpost of Greek civilisation was established. We have already glanced at the early relations of Cyprus with the Aegean world—slight but significant when Minoan Crete was dominant, more intensive in the final period of Mycenaean power. In the fourteenth and thirteenth centuries there is indeed more Mycenaean pottery in Cyprus than in any other comparable area outside Greece, and one type of vessel is particularly popular, the so-called amphoroid crater with figured frieze running round the top. Of these vessels very few have been found in Greece, though they are common in Cyprus and are indeed found

Cyprus

(pp. 37, 45)

8. CYPRUS

elsewhere in the Near East. The pattern of distribution is so peculiar that many scholars have inferred a Mycenaean settlement in Cyprus as early as the fourteenth century; an alternative is to believe that there were Mycenaean traders in Cyprus who informed the potters at home what would be most attractive to eastern markets. This latter is probably the right solution if, as it seems, the clay of the vessels is Greek and not Cypriot.[87]

An influx of Greeks, however, into Cyprus *c.* 1200 is non-controversial and it is probably to be associated with the destructions at Pylos and in the Argolid; there is also a further wave some three or four generations later, which may have been a result of the Dorian invasion. As a result of these infusions the Greeks became the dominant element in the island and were able to impose their own language, which was akin to the Arcadian, showing that the language of this inland people once reached to the coast of the Peloponnese. In Cyprus it was written in a clumsy syllabary even when the rest of the Greek world had adopted the alphabet borrowed from the Phoenicians. A similar conservatism was the long survival into the fifth century and beyond of a kingship tracing direct descent from Mycenaean days, and the royal tombs of the archaic period outside Salamis reflect burial practices of Bronze Age Greece.[88]

In the early Dark Ages Cyprus clung to her connection with Greece, and Cyprian pottery even had an influence on mainland styles, but in the tenth and ninth centuries these links no longer held. In the ninth century the Phoenicians established themselves in Cition, and

1.35 Pictorial style vase from Cyprus

the Phoenician element in the island became stronger in the eighth and seventh centuries. More important were the facts of geography. Cyprus was too far from the Aegean to maintain a close relationship; her natural markets were in Egypt and the Near East, and her policy was bound to be dominated by the great eastern empires—Assyria, Egypt, Persia in turn. The culture of Cyprus reflects the mixture of races, but some of the Greeks kept alive their national consciousness and were proud to renew their association when Greek traders again began to sail regularly into the eastern Mediterranean. In the fifth century Athens even made an attempt to win Cyprus for Greece, but she had not the resources to extend her thalassocracy beyond the Dodecanese. In the fourth century Evagoras of Salamis, with the limited resources of the island, bravely attempted to defy the great Persian empire and to make Cyprus more Greek than Greece, but his gesture was doomed.

Fall of Greek Monarchies and Rise of the Republics

There is already sufficient evidence to trace in broad outline the developments in the Greek world from the destruction of the great Mycenaean centres to the settlement of the western coast of Asia Minor, and further excavation should resolve the major remaining obscurities. The history of the tenth and ninth centuries will remain much darker much longer. It was a period of great poverty dependent almost entirely on agriculture and the number of inhabited sites had shrunk considerably since Mycenaean days. There are no great monuments to attract the archaeologist, or rather the funds for archaeology, and the detailed work needed to retrace the pattern of development will be laborious and unexciting. Though some contact with the outside world must have been maintained to secure essential metals, however limited the supply may have been, Greece was left to grow new roots in comparative isolation. In architecture and sculpture the period has left no memorable achievement. The resources were not available for building on the grand scale, and wood was the standard material for statues and temples. The *xoanon* reflects the poverty of the times, a crude figure roughly shaped with the minimum of detail from the tree trunk. But the potters whose raw material was cheap and accessible were not eclipsed. In the geometric style they showed a remarkable skill in intricate but controlled design which lies at the heart of later Greek architecture, sculpture and painting.

More important than the material products are the social and political changes that transformed Greece during these centuries. With the destruction of the Mycenaean centres the palace system collapsed and kings lacked the material resources to monopolise power. It must be admitted that our understanding of Mycenaean societies is very incomplete. Excavation has not unnaturally been directed mainly to citadels with their palaces, and cemeteries: we know very little about the common people, the size of their settlements or the nature of their housing. How far did the families who worked the land benefit from the increase of prosperity which the palaces suggest? We can form a fair impression of the elaboration of the palace bureaucracy from the Linear B tablets, and there are uncertain glimpses of various forms of land tenure, but not until there has been an archaeological search for the poorer classes shall we be able to have a rounded picture of Mycenaean society. The buildings and the tablets, however, are sufficient to confirm the dominance of the king in wealth and power.

Changing power of kings and nobles

The kings no doubt needed the advice and military assistance of their leading nobles, but, though feuds could be expected between rival families for the succession, the whole nature of palace organisation required a king. When there were no longer the resources to maintain a palace organisation of the Mycenaean type the gap between the king and his nobles must have been considerably reduced. The inevitable result was the gradual weakening of the king's position and the transfer of his power to the nobility. The nobles saw that it was wiser to share the rule rather than fight one another for the faded prestige of a devalued kingship, and by the end of the ninth century most of the Greek states were ruled by aristocracies whose position was based on birth and land. They ruled through elected magistrates responsible to a Council of their peers: where the kingship survived kings retained some of their privileges, especially in religion, but considerably less of their power. Our sources are concerned with these aristocracies mainly when they were coming under increasing pressure from below, and we are apt to underestimate their achievement. It was they who directed the flow of colonisation which widened the Greek horizon and stimulated trade: they brought their states through a very lean period into the prospects of increasing growth.

It was during this period also that the conception of the city state took shape. The period that followed the great movements of peoples seems in many respects like a return to the Greek world before the dynasty of the shaft graves. There seem to have been no large concentrations of population and most people lived in villages; by the end of the ninth century towns were growing up and controlling the villages in their territory. In some areas this change was long delayed. It was not until 471/0 that the Eleans were 'synoecised' in the town of Elis and Mantinea in Arcadia was formed at roughly the same time from a union of villages. Meanwhile Sparta had been formed from five villages before the end of the ninth century. At Athens the pattern was different for there had been no sharp break in her development. It is significant, however, that during this period the inhabited area was extending below the Acropolis where there had earlier been burials.

Kinship organisation

In the Athenian state during this period kinship was the basis of political organisation. The family was composed of households, families combined in clans (*gene*), clans in phratries, and phratries in tribes, of which there were four, and these four Ionic tribes are found also (with others) in the Ionian colonies in Asia Minor. It was not until near the end of the sixth century that the reforms of Cleisthenes changed the basis of representation from blood to place of family origin. That blood-relationships were the basis of political organisation in the archaic period at Athens is

beyond doubt but it remains doubtful whether the system was inherited from the Mycenaean period. The need for it seems considerably less when the king's power was supreme. It implies a general political awareness which seems anachronistic when power and wealth was concentrated in the citadel. But it is odd that neither Homer nor the Linear B tablets throw any light on the social or political organisation of blood-relations.

One other important question needs to be raised. By the time of Hesiod, probably towards the end of the eighth century, invaders and invaded could accept a common name. The Mycenaeans who sailed against Troy were called by Homer Achaeans or, more rarely, Danaans or Argives. By Hesiod's time Dorians, Ionians, Aeolians, and Arcadians were all Hellenes, though why and when a name taken from a small tribe south of Thessaly was adopted for them all remains a mystery. Perhaps the eighth century provides the most suitable context, when the Greeks were breaking out of their isolation: in their increasing contacts with foreigners they will have realised more keenly a common identity.

Phoenician Intercourse with Greece

During the Mycenaean Age the Greeks had been a great seafaring people. They had traded and settled in the eastern Mediterranean and had brought back the luxuries of Syria and Egypt to the palaces of their kings and nobles. The great sea-raids, combined with the collapse of Mycenaean power, had severed these sea lanes, and it was not for some four centuries that they were once again opened up by the Greeks. It was the Phoenicians who first, perhaps in the ninth century, re-established contact between the eastern Mediterranean and the Aegean world. They were the traders of the cities of Sidon and Tyre on the Syrian coast, men of that Semitic stock to which Jew, Arab, and Assyrian alike belonged.

In fifth century Athens it was generally believed that the Phoenicians had been the main traders in the Aegean and in the western Mediterranean from the Bronze Age until the beginning of Greek colonisation in the eighth century. Herodotus prefaces his history of the Persian Wars with a mythical account of the origin of the feud between east and west. In the story of rape and counter-rape it was the Phoenicians who began the feud by seizing Io.

Phoenicians in Greek tradition

They had come to Argos and had set out their cargo for display on the shore and took Io away with them when she came down to look at their wares.[89] Herodotus also tells us that when his curiosity about Heracles took him to Tyre he found that in addition to the main temple of Heracles which was built 2300 years before his visit, there was also a temple of the Thasian Heracles and this, he finds, was built by the Phoenicians who, in their search for Europa, founded Thasos, 'and that was five generations earlier than Heracles son of Amphitryon in Greece'.[90] In a later passage he says that Thasos was the name of the Phoenician founder of the colony and he claims to have seen the mines opened up by the Phoenicians on the east coast of the island facing Samothrace, 'a great mountain turned upside down in the search (for metal)'.[91] In the same vein Herodotus found that the temple of Aphrodite Ourania at Ascalon was the mother-temple of the temples of the goddess on Cyprus and Cythera.[92] He even believes that Cadmus of Tyre brought Phoenicians to 'what is now Boeotia'. Among other things these Phoenicians introduced writing to Greece which was previously illiterate. At first the letters were those used by all Phoenicians, but in the course of time they modified their forms. And Herodotus is proud to add that he had personally seen Cadmeian writing in the temple of Ismenian Apollo at Thebes on three tripods.[93]

Thucydides seems to accept similar traditions. He believes that before Minos controlled the seas the islanders were among the worst pirates, and that most of them were Carians or Phoenicians.[94] In his brief summary of the history of Greek colonisation in Sicily he says that the Phoenicians had trading stations all round the coast but withdrew from the east of the island when the Greeks came.[95] Later sources give very early dates for the foundation of Phoenician colonies in the western Mediterranean: Carthage was said to have been founded in 1123, Cadiz in 1100, and Utica in 1101.

Phoenicians in Homer

With this general impression of the importance of the Phoenicians in the Bronze Age the references to Phoenicians in Homer seem to conform. In both the *Iliad* and the *Odyssey* they are skilled craftsmen and traders. The theme of the *Iliad* does not provide many appropriate contexts, but when Hecuba wishes to find the fairest robe in the palace to present to Athena in her temple she goes to the finely wrought robes that Paris brought home from the land of Sidon, and Achilles selects for one

of the prizes at the funeral games in honour of Patroclus a silver mixing bowl of surpassing beauty, for 'it was well fashioned by skilled Sidonian craftsmen'.[96] Phoenician traders had displayed it for sale, but gave it to Thoas who sold it to one of Priam's sons.

In the *Odyssey* as we should expect, we hear more of the Phoenicians. Menelaus presents to Telemachus a silver mixing bowl with rim of gold which had been given to him by the king of the Sidonians when he stayed with him on his return from Troy.[97] But the Phoenicians are also 'ship-renowned', famous sailors and traders. Eumaeus, Odysseus' faithful swineherd, tells how he was born son of the king of the island of Syrie. The king had living with him a Phoenician woman bought from pirates, who had seized her from Sidon rich in bronze. One day Phoenician traders, 'always greedy for gain', brought a large cargo of trinkets to the island and settled down to sell them. Before leaving they bribed the Phoenician woman with an attractive necklace and a promise to take her back to her home in Sidon if she would bring the king's son down to the boat. And so Eumaeus was carried away; the Phoenician woman came to a bad end in a storm and Eumaeus was sold in Ithaca to Odysseus' father Laertes.[98]

The Phoenicians also find a natural place when Odysseus has to invent plausible accounts of his adventures without revealing his identity. In one version he was enjoying a successful career of plunder when he was required to follow Idomeneus with the Cretan contingent to the Trojan War. When he returned after the war he became restless and led a raid on Egypt. While he was reconnoitring, his men plundered too thoroughly and were caught and killed. He himself was lucky to escape, and for seven years stayed in Egypt, 'collecting much wealth'. Then he was deceived by a Phoenician, 'greedy and wily', who persuaded him to come to his home in Phoenicia. There he stayed for a year after which they set off with a cargo to Libya, where in fact the Phoenician intended to sell him. But when they came to the open sea south of Crete a bad storm sank the vessel, all the others were drowned, but Zeus sent him a mast which enabled him to reach the land of the Thesprotians.[99] In a second version Odysseus is again a Cretan but this time he leaves Crete because he has killed Idomeneus' son. It is again a Phoenician boat that carries him, but these are honest Phoenicians. He asks them to take him to Pylos or Elis but they are carried off course and so bring him to Ithaca. This was no fault of theirs; they even left with him all his belongings.[100]

The Linear B tablets add a little. They show that *phoiniki* was a colour word, used for instance for certain parts of the chariot, and one tablet suggests that Phoenicia and Cyprus are already the Greek names given to lands which in the Near East were called Canaan and Alasia.[101] The Phoenicians probably got their Greek name from the crimson dye for which they were famous. The tablets also show that before the end of the Bronze Age several Semitic words had been incorporated in the Greek language, notably *chrusos* (the word for gold), *chiton* (a sleeveless tunic), and *sesame* and other spices. There would seem to be a coherent body of literary evidence that there were close relations in the Bronze Age between the Mycenaean Greeks and the Phoenicians or other Semites. Unfortunately this evidence is less coherent and less cogent than it appears to be.[102]

Herodotus' story of the Phoenician Cadmus does not bear close examination. The Herodotean date would be in the sixteenth century. If any form of writing was introduced then it would be the Linear B of the tablets which is attested at the latest from the middle of the fourteenth century, but this script is certainly not derived from the Phoenicians. To make sense of his story the letters that Herodotus saw on the Theban tripods cannot have been radically different from the letter forms of his own day. The tripods were probably dedicated in the late eighth or early seventh centuries. Herodotus has in fact conflated the knowledge that the Greeks derived their alphabet from the Phoenicians with what may be an invented story that, as the Danaids came from Egypt to the Argolid, so Cadmus came to Boeotia from Phoenicia. Homer's evidence also raises difficulties. The archaeological evidence suggests strongly that in the Bronze Age the eastern port which was most important to the Mycenaeans was Ugarit on the Syrian coast. Only when Ugarit had been destroyed in the early twelfth century by the peoples moving down against Egypt, and not rebuilt, did Tyre and Sidon become the most important trading centres on this coast. More serious is the increasing doubt whether any of the Near-Eastern peoples came into the Aegean or the western Mediterranean during the Bronze Age.

Carrying trade in the Mycenaean period

There was, as we have seen, a wide distribution of Mycenaean painted pottery in the Near East, and so much was found at Ugarit that a Mycenaean settlement has been widely assumed. The Mycenaeans needed above all the metals that the east could supply, particularly tin, copper and gold, and their ivory probably came from Syria, but Mycenaean palaces and graves have yielded very few eastern objects. Canaanite storage jars, which may have contained eastern wine, have been found at Thebes and Athens, but not enough to suggest a regular trade. And the thin scatter of cylinder seals, Egyptian scarabs and the like could have been brought back by Mycenaean traders. Most archaeologists who are familiar with Bronze Age material feel convinced that the carrying trade was in the hands of the Mycenaeans themselves. Nor has any firm archaeological evidence been found in Spain, Gaul or Africa to support the early dates given for the Phoenician colonies in the west. In Spain there is a steadily increasing amount of Phoenician material from the seventh century but nothing has yet been found in Spain or Gaul which can be firmly dated before the eighth century, and few archaeologists would date the foundation of Carthage earlier than the middle of the eighth century. In Sicily, though wide-scale soundings have been made, no Phoenician material had been found on the east coast of the island and the earliest pottery found at Motya, the first of the Phoenician colonies in the west of Sicily, is later than the earliest pottery from Syracuse.[103]

In the nineteenth century the value of Homer as a historical source for the Mycenaean Age was not seriously questioned. The progress of archaeology with the refinement of its techniques, and the partial decipherment of the Linear B tablets, have induced a growing scepticism. The modern fashion is to see less and less of the Mycenaean Age and more and more of Homer's own contemporary scene. It is current orthodoxy that the Phoenicians in Homer are eighth century Phoenicians and that they reflect the opening up of the sea lanes to the east, which followed the establishment of a Greek settlement at the mouth of the Orontes in Al Mina. The Phoenicians in this view did not sail into the western Mediterranean significantly before the Greeks, perhaps even a little later.

Current reaction against early chronology

Perhaps the reaction is going too far. If Phoenician expansion came so late it would be difficult to understand the Greek conviction that it came so much earlier. That the Phoenicians were prosperous and enterprising in the tenth century is clear from Solomon's negotiations with King Hiram of Tyre. The Phoenician king not only received good payment for the cedars and other timbers provided for the building of temple and palace in Jerusalem, but he also helped Solomon to build a fleet on the Gulf of Aquaba to by-pass Egypt in the carriage of Nubian gold and Arabian luxuries which could be profitably marketed from Tyre.[104] Recent excavations have shown that the establishment of Phoenician Cition in Cyprus, which gave easy access to the rich copper deposits near Tamassus, should be dated not later than the late ninth century and the splendidly decorative bronze shields from the Idaean cave in Cyprus, which are either made by or at least inspired by Phoenician craftsmen have been dated before the end of the eighth century.[105] On the mainland of Greece there is no evidence yet of a stream of goods so early, but a Phoenician bowl from a grave in the Ceramicus at Athens is firmly dated in the middle of the ninth century, and a very similar bowl was found at Olympia. One must also ask how the Greek states got their metals in the early archaic period. More work needs to be done before we know the sources from which they got their iron, and it is possible that all or most of it came from Greece, but for bronze or copper and tin most states must have had to look outside. The most likely source was the east and though Athenian graves suggest that bronze was scarce it is fair to assume that there was some traffic between east and west, and to guess that the ships were Phoenician.

The earliest Phoenician inscription in the west was found at Nora in Sardinia and, though no permanent settlement in the island before the seventh century has been found, informed opinion prefers a date for the Nora inscription before 800. It would be the metals and primarily the copper that attracted the Phoenicians so early. Nor is the late date for the foundation of Carthage universally accepted. Cintas, the French archaeologist with the widest experience of Phoenician material, accepts the date given by the main tradition, 814.[106] Homer's Phoenicians fit well into the tenth and ninth centuries. But the pattern changed in the eighth century when Greeks were settled at Al Mina and in exchange for metals, textiles, and eastern craftsmanship, could distribute their painted pottery and oil as the Mycenaeans had done before them. It was from this point that they became familiar with the arts of Babylon, Syria, Phoenicia and Egypt. The influence of Egypt and Mesopotamia can be seen in statues and reliefs, and the potter's repertoire was enriched with a wide range of animals real and imaginary, and decorative motifs from eastern textiles and reliefs. The strictly disciplined linear designs of the geometric style gradually gave way before the more animated and varied designs of figured scenes. And it was the Phoenicians who provided the ivory and the models which Greek craftsmen translated into their own artistic language.

A much more important debt that the Greeks owed to the Phoenicians was their alphabet. Both the form and the names of the letters of the two alphabets correspond closely and whereas the Phoenician names derive from the forms of the letters—aleph (ox-head), beth (house), gimel (throw-stick)—the corresponding Greek words—alpha, beta, gamma—have no meaning. The debt was publicly acknowledged when the Greeks called letters *phoinikeia*, Phoenician things. As with oriental designs the Greeks adapted the model for their own use. The Phoenician alphabet is an alphabet of consonants; for their indispensable vowels the Greeks used consonantal symbols for which they had no corresponding sound and this added two double consonants, *xi* and *psi*. In different regions various letters had slightly different forms, and the two double letters were differently used, but the basic principles were the same throughout the Greek world. The Greeks in their turn passed the transformed alphabet in the east to Phrygia and in the west to the Etruscans. The date of the adoption by the Greeks of the alphabet is still disputed. It cannot be before they had renewed their links with the Near East and the evidence now available seems to point to a date near the middle of the eighth century.[107] The new alphabet, so much more simple and flexible than the cumbersome Mycenaean syllabary, was to play a fundamental part in the literary and political development of the Greeks.

Phoenician origin of Greek alphabet

CHAPTER 2

The Expansion of Greece

The End of the Dark Ages

The dark ages remain dark for some three hundred years after the destruction of Mycenae, but by the eighth century there is a feeling of spring in the air, or at least in the archaeology. The world of the tenth and ninth centuries seems to be a world of limited horizons, with little evidence of sailings beyond the Aegean or the Corinthian Gulf. In the eighth century

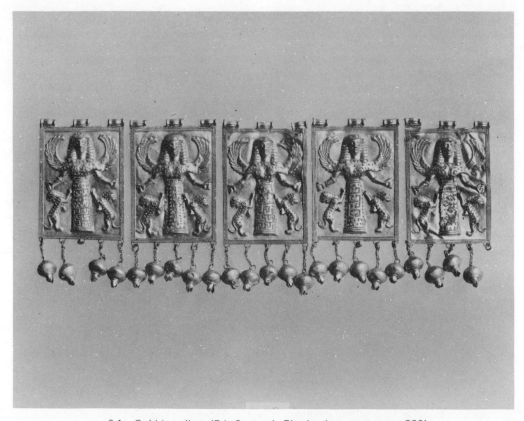

2.1   Gold jewellery (7th Century), Rhodes (see note, page 552)

2.2 Boeotian amphora (c. 700) (see note, page 552)

this isolation is broken down; Greek ships sail again into the eastern Mediterranean and establish a trading station at Al Mina at the mouth of the Orontes, as the Mycenaeans had done long ago at Ras Shamra. The result is seen in the so-called orientalising phase of Greek pottery which breaks away from the somewhat sterile linear designs of the geometric style and introduces eastern animals, mythical and real, and eastern textile patterns into the vase-painters' repertoire. The pioneers in establishing Al Mina were probably the traders of Chalcis and Eretria in Euboea; the potters who made best use of the new opportunities were the Corinthians, whose exports were increasingly widely distributed in east and west. Balancing Al Mina in the east was the bold settlement in the west by Chalcidians and Eretrians on the island of Ischia (Pithecusae), just north of the Bay of Naples. Al Mina was concerned with the luxuries of the east; Pithecusae was intended to tap the mineral resources of the Etruscans on the mainland to the north.

This widening of horizons acted as a valuable solvent in Greece. The sharp increase in trade

2.3 Relief pithos from Myconos (7th century) (see note, page 552)

Reasons

increased the gulf between rich and poor, for the capital needed for trading came from the rich, who grew richer on the profits. At the same time the reopening of the sea-lanes must have had something of the same effect on men's minds as the exploits of Elizabethan sea-captains on the Elizabethan Age. They provided a background against which men would be more prepared to start a new life overseas.

Causes and Character of Greek Colonisation

Land hunger

Thucydides says that the main cause of colonisation was land-hunger, and as a broad generalisation this seems to be right. It is not, however, true of the earliest. Al Mina in the east and Pithecusae in the west, both established before 750, were not designed for peasants or poor labourers seeking land but for merchants seeking profit. Had farming land been the objective, much nearer sites would have been chosen. Conversely in Herodotus' account of the foundation of Cyrene in Africa, the only detailed account we have of the establishment of a colony, the effective cause is a very prolonged drought on the island of Thera. An early fourth-century inscription from Cyrene throws further light on the original settlement. Among the provisions laid down for the colonists by the mother-city was a ban on returning to Thera within five years, except in case of dire necessity. This chilly detail at once explains a passage in Herodotus which records that the original colonists tried to return home, but were driven away.[1] The same grim realism is seen in Plutarch's story of how the Eretrians, when driven out of Corcyra by the Corinthians, tried to return to Eretria but were not allowed to land, which is why they were called the 'slung-out'.[2] This is sufficient to show that, in some cases at least, citizens had to be sent overseas because there was not enough food at home. Similarly the Achaean cities who played a dominant part in the colonisation of south Italy were not well known for their trading, before or afterwards; their land, however, between mountains and Corinthian Gulf was severely restricted.

Trade

There seemed once good ground for believing that at several sites in the west, notably Syracuse, Greek pottery had been imported by the natives before the colonists arrived, and from this it was reasonable to infer that trade was an important, if not decisive, factor in the sending out of the colonists. This can no longer be assumed. Some doubts remain, but the current balance of archaeological opinion is that there are no certain examples of pre-colonial imports of Greek pottery on the sites of any of the Sicilian colonies.[3] There is little doubt, however, that traders played a significant part in the general movement. It was they who knew where land might be available, and traders would be interested in a colony which could also be a market for exchanging goods from the mother-city for raw materials obtained from natives. And though it may be true that political power rested in most cities with the landed nobility and not with merchants, the nobles of Corinth and other coastal cities were not blind to the wealth that could come from busy harbours.

Political conditions

We have seen that at this time the aristocratic form of government generally prevailed. Sometimes a king was formally at the head, but he was really no more than the first of peers; a body of nobles were the true masters. Sometimes there was an aristocracy within an aristocracy; or a large clan, like the Bacchiads at Corinth, held the power. In all cases the distinction between the members of the ruling class and the mass of free citizens was widened and deepened. It was the tendency of the rulers to govern in their own interest, and they cared little to disguise their contempt for the mass of the people. At Mytilene things went so far that the Penthilids, who had secured the chief power, went about in the streets, armed with clubs, and knocked down citizens whom they disliked. Under these conditions there were strong inducements for men to leave their native city where they were of little account and had to endure the slights, if nothing worse, of their rulers, and to join in the foundation of a new *polis* where they might themselves rule. The same inducement drew nobles who did not belong to the inner oligarchical circle. In fact, political discontent was an immediate cause of Greek colonisation and conversely it may be said that colonisation was a palladium of aristocracy. If this outlet had not existed, or if it had not suited the Hellenic temper, the aristocracies might not have lasted so long, and they wisely discerned that it was in their own interest to encourage colonisation.

Colonisation a security to aristocratic states

But while we recognise the operation of general causes we must not ignore special causes. We must, for instance, take into account the fact that Miletus and the south Ionian cities were unable to expand in Caria,

Special causes

as the north Ionian cities expanded in Lydia, because the Carians were too strong for them; and Lycia presented the same kind of barrier to Rhodes. Otherwise, perhaps neither Rhodes nor Miletus would have sent settlers to distant lands.

Relation of the colony to the mother-city

Wherever the Greek went, he retained his customs and language, and made a Greek 'polis'. It was as if a bit of Greece were set down on the remote shores of the Euxine or in the far west on the wild coasts of Gaul or Iberia. The colony was a public enterprise, and the bond of kinship with the 'mother-city' was carefully fostered. Though political discontent might have been the cause which drove the founders forth, yet that solemn departure for a distant land, where a new city-state, protected by the same gods, was to spring up, always sealed a reconciliation. The emigrants took fire from the public hearth of their city to light the fire on that of their new home. Intercourse between colonies and the mother-country was specially kept up at the great religious festivals of the year, and various marks of filial respect were shown by the daughter to the mother. When, as frequently happened, the colony determined herself in turn to throw off a new shoot, it was the recognised custom that she should seek the *oecist* or leader of the colonists from the mother-city. Thus the Megarian colony, Byzantium, when it founded its own colony, Mesembria, must have sought an oecist from Megara. The political importance of colonisation was sanctified by religion, and it was a necessary formality, whenever a settlement was to be made, to ask the approbation of the Delphic god. The most ancient oracular god of Greece was Zeus of Dodona. The Selli, his priests and 'interpreters', are mentioned in the

Oracles

Iliad; and in the *Odyssey* Dodona appears as a place to which a king of the west might go to ask the will of Zeus 'from the lofty oak', where the god was supposed to dwell. But the oak-shrine in the highlands of Epirus was too remote to become the chief oracle of Greece, and the central position of Delphi enabled the astute priests of the Pythian Apollo to exalt the authority of their god as a true prophet to the supreme place in the Greek world. There were other oracular deities who foretold the future: there was, not far off, Trophonius at Boeotian Lebadea; there was Amphiaraus in the land of the Graii, not yet Boeotian. But none of these ever became even a rival of the Delphian Apollo, who by the seventh century at least had won the position of adviser to Greece.

It is worthy of notice that colonisation tended to promote a feeling of unity among the Greek peoples, and it did so in two ways. By the wide diffusion of their race on the fringe of barbarous lands, it brought home to them more fully the contrast between Greek and barbarian, and, by consequence, the community of the Greeks. The Greek dwellers in Asia Minor, neighbours of not-Greek peoples, were naturally impressed with their own unity in a way which was strange to dwellers in Boeotia or Attica, who were surrounded on all sides by Greeks and were therefore alive chiefly to local differences. With the diffusion of their sons over various parts of the world, the European Greeks acquired a stronger sense of unity. In the second place, colonisation led to the association of Greeks of different cities. An oecist who decided to organise a party of colonists could not always find in his own city a sufficient number of men willing to take part in the enterprise. He therefore enlisted comrades from other cities, and thus many colonies were joint undertakings and contained a mixture of citizens of various nationality. This feature was not indeed confined to the later epoch of colonisation: it is one of the few facts about the earlier settlements on the Asiatic coast of which we can be certain.

Consciousness of Greek unity promoted by colonisation, through (1) intercourse with non-Greeks;

(2) joint enterprises

Colonies on the Coasts of the Euxine, Propontis and North Aegean

The voyage of the Argonauts in quest of the golden fleece commemorates in a delightful legend the memorable day on which Greek sailors for the first time burst into the waters of the Euxine Sea. Accustomed to the island straits and short distances of the Aegean, they fancied that when they had passed the Bosphorus they were embarking on a boundless ocean, and they called it the 'Main', *Pontos*. Even when they had circumnavigated its shores it might still seem boundless, for they did not know where the great rivers, the Ister, the Tanais, the Danapris, might lead. The little preliminary sea into which the Hellespont widens, to contract again into the narrow passage of the Bosphorus, was appropriately named the 'vestibule of the Pontus' —*Propontis*. Full of creeks and recesses, it is happily described by Euripides as the 'bayed water-key of the boundless Sea'. The Pontus was a treacherous field for the ships of even experienced mariners, and it was supposed to have received for this reason its name 'Euxine', or Hospitable, in accordance with a habit of

Legend of the Argo

The Pontos (Black Sea)

Propontis

*Signifi-
cance of
the
Odyssey*

the Greeks to seek to propitiate adverse powers by pleasant names.[4] It was when the compass of the Euxine was still unknown, and men were beginning shyly to explore its coasts, that the tale of the wanderings of Odysseus took form. He was imagined to have sailed from Troy into the Pontus, and, after having been driven about in its waters, to have at last reached Ithaca by an overland journey through Thrace and Epirus. In the *Odyssey* as we have it now, compounded of many different legends and poems, this is disguised; the island of Circe has been removed to the far west, and the

direction. But the original wanderings of Odysseus were connected not with the west, but with the exploration of the Euxine.

A mist of obscurity hangs about the beginnings of the first Greek cities which arose on the Pontic shores. Here Miletus was the pioneer. Merchants carrying the stuffs which were manufactured from the wool of Milesian sheep may have established trading-stations along the southern coast. Flax from Colchis, steel and silver and slaves were among the chief products which their wool bought. But the work of colonisation beyond

*Megarian
colonies:*

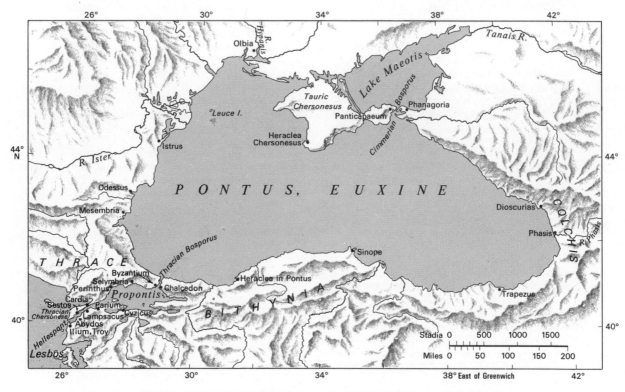

9. EXPANSION OF GREECE IN THE PROPONTIS AND PONTUS

*(Straits of
Azov)*

scene of the Descent to the Underworld translated to the Atlantic Ocean. But Circe, the daughter of the Sun, and sister of King Aeetes who possessed the golden fleece, belongs to the seas of Colchis; and the world of shades beyond the Cimmerians is to be sought near the Cimmerian Bosphorus. The mention of Sicily in some of the later parts of the poem, and the part played by Ithaca, which, with the other islands of the Ionian Sea, lay on the road to the western Mediterranean, reflect the beginning of the expansion of Greece in that

the gate of the Bosphorus can hardly have fully begun until the gate itself was secured by the enterprise of Megara, which sent out men, in the first part of the seventh century, to found the towns of Chalcedon and Byzantium. Byzantium could command the trade of the Black Sea, but the great commercial and political importance of her situation was not fully appreciated until a thousand years had passed, when she became the rival and successor of Rome and took, in honour of her second founder, the name Constantinople.

*Byzantium
[660 B.C.]*

This is the first appearance of the little state of Megara in Greek history and none of her contemporaries took a step that was destined to lead to greater things than the settlement on the Bosphorus. The story was that Chalcedon was founded first, before the Megarians perceived the striking advantages of the opposite shore; and the Delphic oracle, which they consulted as a matter of course, rebuked them as 'blind men'. To the west of Byzantium they also founded Selymbria, on the north coast of the Propontis; eastward they established 'Heraclea in Pontus', on the coast of Bithynia.

Chalcedon

Selymbria
Heraclea

The enterprise of the Megarians stimulated Miletus, and she determined to anticipate others in seizing the best sites on the Pontic shore.[5] At the most northerly point of the southern coast a narrow-necked cape forms two natural harbours, an attractive site for settlers, and here the Milesians planted the city Sinope. Farther east, half-way to that extreme eastern point of the sea where the Phasis flows out at the foot of Mount Caucasus, arose another Milesian colony, Trapezus. At the Bosphorus the Milesians had been anticipated by Megara, but they partly made up for this by planting Abydos on the Hellespont opposite Sestos, and they also seized a jutting promontory on the south coast of the Propontis, where a narrow neck, as at Sinope, forms two harbours. The town was named Cyzicus, and the peninsula was afterwards transformed into an island; the tunny-fish on the coins of the city shows what was one of the chief articles of her trade. Lampsacus, at the northern end of the Hellespont, was colonised by another Ionian city, Phocaea, about the same time, and the winged sea-horse on Lampsacene coins speaks of naval enterprise which led afterwards to wealth and prosperity. The foundation of Parion was due to a joint undertaking of Miletus and Erythrae; and Clazomenae joined Miletus in planting Cardia at the neck of the Thracian Chersonese, in the important position of an advance fort against Thrace. On the southern side of the Hellespont the lands of the Scamander invited the Greeks of Lesbos, and a number of small Aeolian settlements arose.

Milesian colonies:

Sinope

Trebizond

Abydos

Cyzicus

Phocaean colony: Lampsacus

Milesian and Erythraean colony: Parion Cardia

Greek settlements also sprang up in the more remote parts of the Euxine. Dioscurias and Phasis were founded in the far east, in the fabled land of Colchis. On the Tauric Chersonesus or 'peninsula' (now the Crimea), Panticapaeum was founded opposite Phanagoria at the entrance to the Maeotic lake, and Tanais at the mouth of the like-named river. Heraclea, or Chersonesus, on the western side of the peninsula, was destined to preserve the

Other settlements on the Pontus: Dioscurias, Phasis, Panticapaeum, Tanais, Heraclea, Olbia, Odessus, Mesembria

municipal forms of an old Greek city for more than a thousand years. Olbia at the mouth of the Dnieper, Odessus, Istrus, Mesembria were only some of the Greek settlements which complete the circuit of the Black Sea.

This sea and the Propontis were the special domain of the sea-god Achilles, whose fame grew greater by his association as a hero with the legend of Troy. He was worshipped along the coasts as 'lord of the Pontus'; and in Leuce, the 'shining island' near the Danube's mouth, the lonely island where no man dwelt, he had a temple, and the birds of the sea were said to be its warders.

Worship of Achilles in the Pontus

If Miletus and Megara took the most prominent part in extending the borders of the Greek world eastward of the Hellespont, the north-western corner of the Aegean was the special domain of Euboea. The barren islands of Sciathus and Peparethus were the bridge from Euboea to the coast of Macedonia, which, between the rivers Axius and Strymon, runs out into a huge three-pronged promontory. Here Chalcis planted so many towns that the whole promontory was named Chalcidice. Some of the chief cities, however, were founded by other states, notably Corinthian Potidaea on the most westerly of the three prongs, which was called Pallene. Sithonia was the central prong, and Acte, ending in Mount Athos, the eastern. Some of the colonies on Pallene were founded by Eretria, and those north of Acte by Andros, which was at one time dependent on Eretria. Hence we may regard this group of cities as Euboean rather than Chalcidian. On the west side of the Thermaic Bay, two Euboean colonies were planted, Pydna and Methone, on Macedonian soil.

Chalcidian colonisation

Chalcidice

Corinthian colony: Potidaea

Pydna and Methone

Colonies in the Western Mediterranean

The earliest mention of Sicilian and Italian regions in literature is to be found in some later passages of the *Odyssey*, which should perhaps be referred to the eighth century. There we meet with the Sicels, and with the island of Sicania; while Temesa, where Greek traders could buy Tuscan copper, has the distinction of being the first Italian place mentioned by name in a literary record. By the end of the seventh century Greek states stood thick on the east coast of Sicily and round the sweep of the Tarentine Gulf. These colonies naturally fall into three groups:

(1) The Euboean, which were both in Sicily and in Italy.

(2) The Achaean, which were altogether on Italian soil.

(3) The Dorian, which were, with few exceptions, in Sicily.

Odysseus in the west

The oldest stories of the adventures of Odysseus were laid, as we have seen, in the half-explored regions of the Black Sea. Nothing shows more impressively the life of this poetry, and the power it had won over the hearts of the Greeks, than the fact that when the navigation of the Italian and Sicilian seas began, these adventures were transferred from the east to the west; and in the further growth of this cycle of poems a new mythical geography was adopted. At a time when the Greeks knew so little of Italy that the southern promontories could be designated as 'sacred islands', the straits of Messana were identified with Scylla and Charybdis, Lipara became the island of Aeolus, the home of the Cyclopes was found in the fiery mount of Etna. Then Scheria, the isle of the Phaeacians, was fancied to be Corcyra; an entrance to the underworld was placed at Cumae; and the rocks of the Sirens were sought near Sorrento. And not only did the first glimpses of western geography affect the transmutation of the *Odyssey* into its final shape, but the *Odyssey* reacted on the geography of the west. The fact that the promontory of Circei in Latin territory bears the name of the sorceress of Colchis is evidence of the spell of Homeric song. Odysseus was not the only hero who was borne westward with Greek ships in the eighth century. Cretan Minos and Daedalus, for example, had links with Sicily. Above all, the earliest navigation of the western seas was ascribed to Heracles, who reached the limits of the land of the setting sun, and stood on the ledge of the world looking out upon the stream of Oceanus. From him the opposite cliffs which form the gate of the Mediterranean were called the Pillars of Heracles.

The earliest Greek settlement in the western seas was on the island of Pithecusae (Ischia) just north of the Bay of Naples. An island offered greater security to pioneers than a mainland site, and the settlement was on a promontory whose neck could be easily defended. The settlers are said to have come from Chalcis and Eretria, and the pottery from the earliest graves confirms that they were the earliest Greek colonists in the west, established before the middle of the eighth century. It was not long before most of the settlers moved to Cyme on the opposite mainland, whose acropolis is conspicuous from the island, and the name suggests that, in addition to Chalcis and Eretria, Cyme, a town on the east coast of Euboea which later sank into obscurity, played an important part in the new venture; the colonists also included some Graeans who lived on the opposite mainland in the neighbourhood of Tanagra. There was a native settlement on the site which had imported Greek pottery before the colonists came; they continued to live there, but were moved away from the acropolis. The new site was happily chosen. It was a strong post, and, though there was no harbour, ships could be hauled up on a stretch of sand below.[6] But when trade developed and larger merchantmen were built an open strand was no longer adequate. The Cymaeans then occupied the harbour which was just inside the promontory, and established there the town of Dicaearchia, which afterwards became Puteoli; farther east they founded Naples, 'the new city'.

Dicaearchia Neapolis

The people in whose midst this outpost of Greek civilisation was planted were the Opicans, one of the chief branches of the Italic race. The colonists were eminently successful in their intercourse with the natives; and the solitary position of Cyme in these regions made her influence both wide and noiseless, for no Greek settlement could be made northward on account of the great Etruscan power, and there was no rival southward until the later establishment of Posidonia. Her external history is uneventful—there are no striking wars or struggles to record—but the work she did holds an important and definite place in the history of European civilisation. To the Euboeans of Cyme we may say that we owe the alphabet which we use today, for it was from them that the Latins learned to write. The Etruscans also got their alphabet independently from the same masters, and, having modified it in certain ways to suit themselves, passed it on to the Oscans and Umbrians. Again, the Cymaeans introduced the neighbouring Italian peoples to a knowledge of the Greek gods and Greek religion. Heracles, Apollo, Castor, and Polydeuces became such familiar names in Italy that they came to be regarded as original Italian deities. The oracles of the Cymaean Sibyl, prophetess of Apollo, were believed to contain the destinies of Rome.

Importance of Cyme in European history

Italian alphabet

Introduction of Greek gods

To Cyme, too, western Europe probably owes the name by which we call Hellas and the Hellenes. The Greeks, when they first came into contact with Latins, had no common name; Hellenes, the name which afterwards united them, was as yet merely associated with

Origin of the name Greece—

a particular tribe. It was only natural that strangers should extend the name of the first Greeks with whom they came in contact to others whom they fell in with later, and so to all Greeks. But the curious circumstance is that the settlers of Cyme were known not by the name of Chalcis or Eretria or Cyme itself, but by that of Graia. *Graii* was the term which the Latins and their fellows applied to the colonists, and the name *Graeci* is a derivative of a usual type from Graii. It was doubtless

from the Boeotian Graeans

to civilise western Europe and rule it for centuries.

The next settlement of the Euboean Greeks was on Sicilian, not Italian, ground. The island of Sicily is geographically a continuation of Italy, just as the Peloponnese is a continuation of the great eastern peninsula. But its historical importance depends much more on another geographical fact—it is the centre of the Mediterranean: it parts the eastern from the western waters. It has been thus marked out by

Sicily; its position in history

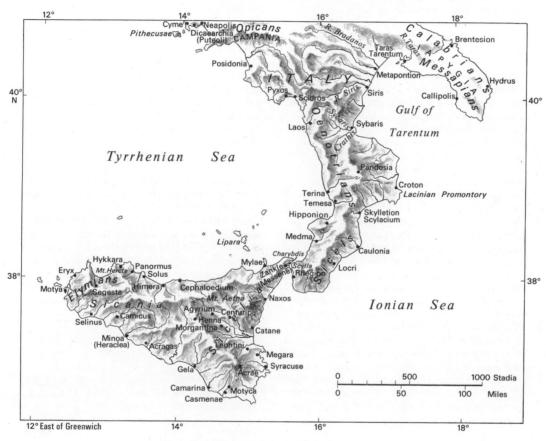

10. SICILY AND MAGNA GRAECIA

some trivial accident which ruled that we today call Hellas 'Greece', instead of knowing it by some name derived from Cyme, Eretria, or Chalcis. The west has got its 'Greece' from an obscure district in Boeotia; Greece itself got its 'Hellas' from a small territory in Thessaly. This was accidental. But it was no accident that western Europe calls Greece by a name connected with that city in which Greeks first came into touch with the people who were destined

nature as a meeting-place of nations; and the struggle between European and Asiatic peoples, which has been called the 'Eternal Question', has been partly fought out on Sicilian soil. There has been in historical times no native Sicilian power. The greatness of the island was due to colonisation—not migration—from other lands. Lying as a connecting link between Europe and Africa, it attracted settlers from both sides, while its close proximity to Italy

Sicans

Sicels

Were Sicans and Sicels kinsfolk?

always rendered it an object of acquisition to those who successively ruled in that peninsula.

The earliest inhabitants of the island were the Sicans. They believed themselves to be autochthonous, and we have no record at what time they entered the island or whence they came or to what race they belonged. The nature of things makes it probable that they entered from Italy. From them the island was called Sicania. The next comers were the Sicels, of whom we can speak with more certainty. As we find Sicels in the toe of Italy, we know that tradition correctly described them as settlers from the Italian peninsula, and there is some slight evidence to show that they spoke the same language as that group of Italic peoples to which the Latins belonged. The likeness of the names Sicel and Sican has naturally led to the view that these two folks were akin in race and language. But likeness of names is deceptive; and it is a remarkable fact that the Greeks, who were only too prone to build up theories on resemblances of words, always carefully distinguished the Sican from the Sicel as ethnically different. Still a connection is possible, if we suppose that the Sicels were Sicans who, remaining behind in Italy, had in the course of centuries become Italicised by intercourse with the Latin and kindred peoples, and then, emigrating in their turn to the island, met without recognition the brethren from whom they had parted in the remote past. But all this is uncertain. The Sicels, however, wrested from the Sicans the eastern half of the island, which was thus cut up into two countries—Sicania in the west, Sicelia in the east. In the *Odyssey* we read of Sicania; perhaps the Greeks of Cyme knew it by this name. At a very early time Sicania was invaded by a mysterious people named *Elymians*, variously said to have come from Italy and from the north of Asia Minor. The probability is that they were of Iberian race. They occupied a small territory in the north-west of the island.

Elymians

These were the three peoples who inhabited this miniature continent, soon about to become the battlefield of Greek and Phoenician. The Sicels were the most numerous and most important. The only Sican town of any significance in historical times was Hykkara, on the north-west promontory. Minôa, originally Sican on the south coast, became Greek. Camicus, at some distance inland in the same region, was in early days an important stronghold. The Elymian settlements at Segesta and Eryx became of far greater importance than the Sican. The eastern half of the isle, the

Sican places

Elymian towns

original Sicelia, was thickly set with Sicel fortresses from Cephaloedium (the modern Cefalù), at the centre of the northern coast, to Motyca, an inland town in the south-eastern corner. Among the most famous were Agyrium, Centuripa, Morgantina, and above all Henna.

Sicel towns

Thucydides says that before the arrival of the Greeks the Phoenicians had occupied headlands and islands all round the coast to trade with the Sicels, but that when the Greeks came they abandoned most of them and concentrated in Motya, Solus and Panormus near the Elymians; for they trusted the Elymians, and these towns were the nearest in Sicily to Carthage. In spite of Thucydides' explicit statement no trace of the Phoenicians has been found in east Sicily before the Greek colonisation, and the earliest evidence from the earliest of the Phoenician colonies, Motya, is rather later than the first Greek colonies.[7] The argument from silence, however, is perhaps not decisive. Temporary trading stations with temporary buildings would not have left much for the archaeologist, and the Phoenicians have in fact proved extremely elusive elsewhere. They are said to have traded in the far west of the Mediterranean during the Bronze Age, especially at Cadiz, but no Phoenician objects earlier than the eighth century have yet been found in Spain; a Phoenician inscription from Nora in Sardinia, however, usually dated to the ninth century, is a warning of the danger of arguing from archaeological silence. The lack of serious opposition to the Greeks in Sicily shows at any rate that the Phoenicians were not yet strong rivals; it was only when Carthage had grown up that the Greeks had to fear Phoenician hostility. At the time of their colonisation Carthage was probably less than two generations old.

Sicilian history, like Italian, really opens with the coming of the Greeks.[8] They came under the guidance of Chalcis and the auspices of Apollo. It was naturally on the east coast, which faces Greece, that the first Greek settlement was made, and it is to be noticed that of the coasts of Sicily the east is that which most resembles in character the coast-line of Greece. The site which was chosen by the Chalcidians, and the Ionians of Naxos who accompanied them, was not a striking one. A little tongue of land, north of Mount Etna, very different from the height of Cyme, was selected for the foundation of Naxos. Here, as in the case of Cyme, the Chalcidians who led the enterprise surrendered the honour of naming the new city to their less prominent fellow-founders. The first of all the Greek towns of Sicily, Naxos

Greeks

Naxos [traditional date 735 B.C.]

Its destruction

was not destined to live for much more than three hundred years. It was to be destroyed not by the fire of the dangerous mountain which dominated it, but by a human enemy. A sort of consecration was always attached to Naxos as the first homestead of the Hellenes in the island which was to become a brilliant part of Hellas.

The altar of Apollo Archegetes

To Apollo Archĕgĕtes an altar was erected on the spot where the Greeks first landed—driven, as the legend told, by contrary winds, through Apollo's dispensation, to the Sicilian shores. It was the habit of ambassadors from old Greece as soon as they arrived in Sicily to offer sacrifice on this altar. In the fertile plain south of Etna the Chalcidians soon afterwards founded Catane, close to the sea and protected by a low range of hills behind, but under the power of Etna which was to unmake the place again and again; and inland Leontini at the south end of her plain between two hills, with an eastern and a western acropolis. These sites, Leontini certainly if not Catane, were wrested from the Sicels. The Chalcidians also won possession of the north-east corner, and thus obtained command of the straits between the island and the mainland. Here Cymaeans and Chalcidians planted Zancle on a low rim of land, which resembles a reaping-hook and gave the place its name. The haven is formed by the curving blade, and when Zancle came later to mint money she engraved on her coins a sickle representing her harbour and a dolphin floating within it. Some two hundred years later, under the influence of Anaxilas of Rhegion, new immigrants were brought in, including Messenians, and ultimately the old local name was ousted in favour of Messana. From Zancle the Euboeans established the fortress of Mylae on the other side of the north-eastern promontory; and in the middle of the seventh century they founded Himera, the only Greek city on the northern coast, destined to live for scarce two centuries and a half, and then to be swept away by the Phoenician. It was important for Zancle that the land opposite her, the extreme point of the Italian peninsula, should be in friendly hands, and therefore the men of Zancle incited their mother-city to found Rhegion; and in this foundation Messenians took part.

Catane [728 B.C.]

Leontini [728 B.C.]

Zancle [c. 715 B.C.?] (ζάγκλον, δάγκλον)

= Messênê

Mylae Himera [648 B.C.]

Rhegion

Dorian colonies.

While this group of Chalcidian colonies was being formed in north-eastern Sicily, Dorian Greeks began to obtain a footing in south-eastern Sicily, which history decided should become the Dorian quarter. The earliest of the Dorian cities was also the greatest. Syracuse, destined to be the head of Greek Sicily, was

Syracuse [trad. date, 734 B.C.]

founded by Corinthian emigrants under the leadership of Archias before the end of the eighth century. Somewhere about the same time Corinth also colonised Corcyra; the Ionian islands were half-way stations to the west. Which colony was the elder, we do not know; tradition did not attempt to decide, for it placed both in the same year. Force was needed for both enterprises. Eretrians had to be driven from Corcyra, Sicels from Syracuse.[9]

Corcyra [trad. date, 734 B.C.]

The great Haven of Syracuse, with its island and its hill, formed the most striking site on the east coast, and could not fail to invite the earliest colonists. The island of Ortygia was first occupied, and the colony was soon to spread extensively on the mainland opposite. There is an alternative tradition in Ephorus that Syracuse was not founded until a generation later than Naxos, but the earlier date has the earlier and more reliable testimony of Thucydides. By holding Syracuse, Corinth effectually prevented any Chalcidian expansion south of Leontini.

The island, Ortygia

At an early date Megarians also sailed into the west to find a new home. After various unsuccessful attempts to establish themselves, they finally built their city on the coast north of Syracuse, beside the hills of Hybla, and perhaps Sicel natives joined in founding the western Megara. It was the most northerly Dorian town on the east coast. But, like her mother, the Hyblaean Megara was destined to found a colony more famous than herself. In the middle of the seventh century the Megarians sent to their metropolis to invite co-operation in planting a settlement in the south-western part of the island. This settlement, which was to be the farthest outpost of Greek Sicily, was Selinus, the town named after wild celery as its own coins boasted, situated on a low hill on the coast. Megara had been occupied with the goodwill of the Sicel; Selinus was probably held at the expense of the Sican. In the meantime the south-eastern corner was being studded with Dorian cities, though they did not rise by any means so rapidly as the Chalcidian in the north. The Sicels seem to have offered a stouter resistance here. At the beginning of the seventh century Gela—the name is Sicel—was planted by Rhodian colonists with Cretans in their train. This city was set on a long narrow hill which stretched between the sea and an inland plain. At a later time Acrae and Casmenae were founded by Syracuse. They were overshadowed by the greatness of the mother-city, and never attained as much independence as more distant

Megara (Hyblaean) [trad. date, 728 B.C.]

Selinus [628 B.C.]

Rhodian Gela [trad. date, 688 B.C.]

Syracusan Acrae and Casmenae and Camarina [595 B.C.]

77

Camarina, which was planted from the same metropolis about half a century later.

The latest Dorian colony of Sicily was only less conspicuous than the first. The Geloans sought an oecist from their Rhodian metropolis and founded, half-way between their own city and Selinus, the lofty town of Acragas, which soon took the second place in Greek Sicily and became the rival of Syracuse. The acropolis, standing back from the coast, covered an area which today satisfies a town of 25,000, but occupation soon extended down the hill. The walls enclose an area of 900 acres and they date from within a generation of the foundation. The small harbour was some distance from the town: 'flock-feeding Acragas' never became a maritime power. But the surrounding country of hill and valley was well suited to olive, vine and grazing, and an easy track led to the rich corn land of the interior.

Geloan Acragas (Roman Agrigentum) [580 B.C.]

In planting their colonies and founding their domination in Sicily, the Greeks had mainly to reckon with the Sicels. In their few foundations in the farther west they had to deal with the Sicans. These older inhabitants were forced to retire from the coasts, but they lived on in their fortresses on the inland hills. The island was too large and its character too continental to invite the newcomers to attempt to conquer the whole of it. With the Phoenicians the Greeks had no trouble. They installed themselves in the western corner of the island and there they maintained three places which assumed the character of cities. These were Panormus, Solus, and Motya—the Haven, the Rock, and the Island. Panormus or 'All-haven' in a fertile plain is protected on the north by Mount Hercte, now the Pilgrim Mount, and on the east by Solus. Motya is on an island in a small bay on the west coast. The Elymian country lay between Motya and Panormus. The chief town of the Elymians, Segesta (which in Greek mouths became Egesta), was essentially a city, while Eryx farther west, high above the sea but not actually on it, was their outpost of defence. On Eryx they worshipped some goddess of nature, soon to be identified with the Greek Aphrodite. The Elymians were on good terms with the Phoenicians, and western Sicily became a Phoenician corner. While the inland country was left to Sicel and Sican, the coasts were to be the scene of struggles between Phoenician and Greek. In the seventh century this struggle was still a long way off, Sicily was still large enough to hold both. The first great trial of strength was to coincide with the Persian invasion of Greece.

The Sicans

Three Phoenician cities: Panormus,

Solus, Motya

The Elymians and their towns

The name by which we know the central of the three great peninsulas of the Mediterranean did not extend as far north as the Po in the time of Julius Caesar, and originally it covered a very small area indeed. In the fifth century Thucydides applies the name Italy to the modern Calabria—the western of the two extremities into which the peninsula divides. This extremity was inhabited, when the Greeks first visited it, by Sicels and Oenotrians. But the heel was occupied by peoples of that Illyrian race which had played, as we dimly see, a decisive part in the earliest history of the Greeks. The Illyrian was now astride the Adriatic; he had reached Italy before the Greek. The Calabrians, who gave their name to the heel, were of Illyrian stock; and along with these were the Messapians, some of whose brethren on the other side of the water seem to have thrown in their fortunes with the Greeks and penetrated into Locris and Boeotia and perhaps into the Peloponnese. It was on the seaboard of the Sicels and Oenotrians that the Achaeans of the Peloponnese, probably towards the close of the eighth century, found a field for colonisation. It has been already remarked that the Ionian islands are a sort of stepping-stone to the west, and just as we find Corinthians settling in Corcyra, so we find Achaeans settling in Zacynthus. The first colonies which they planted in Italy were perhaps Sybaris and Croton, famous for their wealth and their rivalry. Sybaris on the river Crathis, in an unhealthy but most fruitful plain, soon extended her dominion across the narrow peninsula and, founding the settlements of Laos and Scidros on the western coast, commanded two seas. Thus having in her hands an overland route to the western Mediterranean, she could forward to her ports on the Tyrrhenian sea the valuable merchandise of the Milesians, whom Chalcidian jealousy excluded from the straits between Italy and Sicily. Thus both agriculture and traffic formed the basis of the remarkable wealth of Sybaris, and the result was an elaboration of luxury which caused the Sybarite name to pass into a proverb. Posidonia, famous for its temples and its roses, was another colony on the western sea, founded from Sybaris.[10] It is said to have been formed by Troezenians, who were driven out from that city by the Achaeans.

A good way to the south of Sybaris you come to Croton, before the coast, in its southern trend, has yet reached the Lacinian promontory, on which a stately temple of Hera formed a central place of worship for the Greek

Achaean colonies Original meaning of the name Italy

Messapioi or Metapioi

Sybaris [trad. date, 721 B.C.]

Posidonia

Croton [trad. date, 703 B.C.]

settlers in Italy. Unlike the other Achaean colonies, Croton had a good harbour, the only good harbour on the west side of the gulf, but her prosperity, like that of her fellows, rested not on maritime traffic but on the cultivation of land and the rearing of cattle. The Delphic god seems to have taken a more than wonted interest in the foundation of this city, if we may judge from the Delphic tripod which appears on its earliest coins. Like Sybaris, Croton widened its territory and planted colonies of its own. On the Tyrrhenian sea Terina and Temesa were to Croton what Laos and Scidros were to Sybaris.

Caulonia Locrian colonies Epizephyrian Locri

Caulonia, perhaps also a Crotoniate settlement, was the most southerly Achaean colony and was the neighbour of the western Locri. This town was founded in the territory of the Sicels, it is not certain by which of the three Locrian states; perhaps it was a joint enterprise of all three. It was agricultural, like its Achaean neighbours, and like them it pushed over to the western sea and founded Medma and Hipponion on the other coast.

Medma Hipponion

The Achaeans and Locrians might quarrel among themselves, but they had more in common with each other than either had with the Dorians, and we may conveniently include Locri in the Achaean group. Thus the southern coast of Italy would have been almost a homogeneous circle if a Dorian colony had not been established in a small sheltered bay at the extreme north point of the gulf, to which it gave the name it still bears, Taras or Tarentum. Taras was remarkable as the only foreign settlement ever made by the greatest of all the Dorian peoples. The site had long been in contact with the Greek world. There are traces of settlement from the Aegean in the Mycenaean period, and contact was maintained after the Dorian invasion. But the Spartan colony was founded at the end of the First Messenian War. The story is that in the war with the Messenians, when the Spartans were for many years absent from home, the women bore sons to Helots, and that this progeny, called Partheniae or 'Maidens' Children', conspired against the state, and being driven out of the country were directed by the oracle to settle at Taras. But even if there was some non-Dorian blood in the colonists, the official Spartan origin of the colony was not questioned in antiquity, and archaeological evidence shows that the relations between Sparta and Taras were close. Laconian geometric pottery has been found on the site and imports continued in the sixth century. The cults of the colony are almost

Dorian colonies Taras [trad. date, 707 B.C.]

exclusively Spartan, and the dialect is predominantly Dorian. Phalanthus, who was reported to be the leader of the colonists, and who appears on the coinage riding a dolphin, has by some been regarded as a local sea-god but he may well be a historical figure.

Phalanthus— Poseidon

The prosperity of the Tarentines depended partly on the cultivation of a fruitful territory, but mainly on their manufacturing industry. Their fabrics and dyed wools became renowned, and their pottery was widely distributed. Taras in fact must be regarded as an industrial rather than as an agricultural state. Her position brought her into contact with inhabitants of the Calabrian peninsula, and she had an enemy in the Messapian town of Brentesion. She founded the colonies of Callipolis and Hydrus on the eastern coast, where she had no Greek rivals. But on the other side, her possible advance was foreseen and hindered by the prudence of the Sybarites. They feared that the Dorian city might creep round the coast and occupy the fertile lands which are watered by the Bradanus and the Siris. So they induced the Achaeans of old Greece to found a colony at Metapontion on the Bradanus, a place which had derived its name from Messapian settlers; and this, the most northerly of the Achaean cities, flourished as an agricultural community and cut off the westward expansion of Taras. But in the meantime another rival seized the very place from which the Achaeans had desired to exclude the Dorians. In the middle of the seventh century Colophonians, fleeing before Lydian pressure, planted a colony at Siris, and this Ionian state threatened to interrupt the Achaean line of cities and cut off Metapontion from her sisters. 'No land so fair as the land by the waters of Siris', wrote Archilochus, but the colony was short-lived. There are reasons for thinking, though the evidence is not clear, that a hundred years later the place was destroyed by its Achaean neighbours and became an Achaean town. Siris, like Sybaris, Croton, and Locri, had her helpmate, though not a daughter, on the Tyrrhenian sea. By the persuasion of common interest she formed a close connection with Pyxus: the two cities issued common coins, and perhaps organised a rival overland route.

Brundisium

Achaean Metapontion, Metapontum (= 'place of the Metapians,' or Messapians)

Siris

Pyxus (Policastro)

Thus the western coast of the Tarentine gulf was beset with a line of Achaean cities, flanked at one extremity by Western Locri, on the other by Dorian Taras. The common feature which distinguished them from the cities settled by the men of Chalcis and Corinth was that their wealth depended on the mainland, not on the sea. Their rich men were landowners, not merchants; it was not traffic but rich soil that had originally lured them to the far west. The unwarlike Sicels and Oenotrians seem to have laid no obstacles in the way of their settlements and to have submitted to their rule. The Iapygians and Messapians of Calabria were of different temper, and it is significant that it was men from warlike Sparta who succeeded in establishing Taras. But there were destined to be bitter and costly struggles with the natives.

ἡ μεγάλη Ἑλλάς (Magna Graecia)

These cities, with their dependencies beyond the hills, on the shores of the Tyrrhenian sea, came to be regarded as a group, and the country came to be called Great Hellas. We might rather have looked to find it called Great Achaia, by contrast to the old Achaean lands in Greece; but here, as in other cases, it is the name of a lesser folk which prevails. If the Hellenes, the old Greek inhabitants of the plain of the Spercheus, had been conquered by the Achaeans, the conquest was forgotten, and the two peoples had gone out together to found new cities in the west; and here the Hellenic name rose to celebrity and honour. It was no small thing in itself that the belt of Greek settlements on the Tarentine gulf should come to be called Great Hellas. But it was a small thing compared with the extension of the name Hellenes to designate all peoples of Greek race.

Con-jectured origin of the name Hellenes = Greeks

There was nothing to lead the Greeks of their own accord to fix on Hellenes as a common name; if they had sought such a name deliberately, their natural choice would have been Achaeans, which Homer had already used in a wide sense. The name must have been given to them from without. Just as the barbarian peoples in central Italy had taken hold of the name of the Graii, so the barbarians in the southern peninsulas took hold of the name of the Hellenes, and used it to denote all settlers and strangers of the same race. Such a common name, applied by barbarian lips to them all alike, brought home to Greek traders the significance of their common race; and they adopted the name themselves. So the name Hellenes, obscure when it had gone forth to the west, travelled back to the east in a new sense, and won its way into universal use. The fictitious ancestor Hellên became the forefather of the whole Greek race; and the fictitious ancestors of the Dorians, Ionians, and Aeolians were all derived from him. The original Hellenes lost their separate identity as completely as the original Aeolians and Ionians had lost theirs; but their name was destined to live for ever in the speech of men, while those of their greater fellows had passed into a memory.

Growth of Trade and Maritime Enterprise

The age of the aristocratic republics saw the face of the Greek world completely transformed. The colonial expansion of Greece eastward and westward was itself part of this transformation, but it also helped signally to bring about other changes. For, while the colonies were politically independent of their mother-states, they reacted in many ways on the mother-country.

Family system of property in land

The family system of dividing property between sons favoured colonial enterprise. But the colonists, who had suffered under that system, were not likely to introduce it in their new settlements, and thus the institution of personal landownership was probably first established and regulated in the colonies. Their example reacted on the mother-country, where other natural causes were also gradually undermining the family system. In the first place, as the power of the state grew greater the power of the family grew less; and when the head of the state, whether king or republican government, was felt as a formidable authority, the prestige of the head of the family, overshadowed by the power of the state, became imperceptibly weaker. In the second place, it was common to assign a portion of an estate to one member of the family, to manage and enjoy the undivided use of it; and although it did not become his and he had no power of disposing of it, yet the natural tendency would have been to allow it on his death to pass to his son on the same conditions. It is clear that such a practice tended to the ultimate establishment of personal proprietorship of the soil. Again, side by side with the undivided family estate, personal properties were actually acquired. At this period there was much wild unallotted land, 'which wild beasts haunt', especially on the hill-slopes, and when a man of energy reclaimed a portion of this land for tillage, the new fields became his own, for they had belonged to no man. We can thus see generally how inevitable it was that the old system should disappear and the large family estates break up into private domains; but the change was not accomplished by legislation, and the gradual process by which it was brought about cannot be recovered in detail. It was only when private landownership had become an established fact, that the law came in and recognised it by regulating sales of land and allowing men to bequeath it freely.

The life of farmers in Boeotia, eighth century, described in Hesiod's Works and Days

The Boeotian poet Hesiod has given us a picture of rural life in Greece at this period. He was a husbandman himself near Ascra, where his father, who had come as a stranger from Cyme in Aeolis, had put under cultivation a strip of waste land on the slopes of Helicon. The farm was divided between his two sons, Perses and Hesiod, but in unequal shares; and Hesiod accuses Perses of winning the larger part by bribing the lords of the district. But Perses managed his farm badly and it did not prosper. Hesiod wrote his poem the *Works* to teach such unthrifty farmers as his brother true principles of agriculture and economy. His view of life is profoundly gloomy, and suggests a condition of grave social distress in Boeotia. This must have been mainly due to the oppression of the nobles, 'gift-devouring' princes as he calls them. The poet looks back to the past with regret. The golden age, the silver, and the bronze have all gone by, and the age of the heroes who fought at Troy; and mankind is now in the iron age, and 'will never cease by day or night from weariness and woe'. 'Would that I did not live in this generation, would that I had died before, or were born hereafter!' The poem gives minute directions for the routine of the husbandman's work, the times of sowing and reaping and the other labours of the field, the design of farm implements; and all this is accompanied by maxims of proverbial wisdom.

Historical significance of Hesiod's poem

Apart from the value of his poem as a social picture, Hesiod has a great significance as the first spokesman of the common folk. In the history of Europe, his is the first voice raised from among the toiling classes and claiming the interest of mankind in their lot. It is a voice indeed of acquiescence, counselling fellow-toilers to make the best of an evil case; the stage of revolt has not yet been reached. But the grievances are aired, and the lords who wield the power are exhorted to deal just judgements, that the land may prosper. The new poet is, in form and style, under the influence of the Homeric poems, but he is acutely conscious that he is striking new notes and has new messages for men. He comes forward, unlike Homer, in his own person; he contrasts himself with Homer when he claims that the Muses can teach truth as well as beautiful fiction. In another poem, the *Theogony*, we are told that the daughters of Zeus taught Hesiod as he fed sheep on the hillsides of Helicon; they gave him for staff a branch of bay. The staff was now the minstrel's

The Theogony

emblem; for the epic poems were no longer sung to the lyre, but were recited by the 'rhapsode' standing with a staff in his hand. Then the Muses breathed into the shepherd of Ascra the wizard power of declaring the future and the past, and set him the task of singing the race of the blessed gods. In the *Theogony* he performs this task. He sings how the world was made, the gods and the earth, the rivers and the ocean, the stars and the heaven; how in infinite space which was at the beginning there arose Earth and Tartarus and Love the cosmic principle; and it is notable how he introduces amongst the eldest-born powers of the world such abstractions as love itself, memory, sleep. These speculations on the origin of the universe, and the attempt to work up the popular myths into a system, mark a new stage in the intellectual development of Greece. There were other works composed by various bards who merged their identities under Hesiod's name; and, as we have seen, these Hesiodic poems had a decisive influence in moulding the ideas of the Greeks as to the early history of their race.

Hesiod's cosmic system

Hesiodic school

Boeotia was always an unenterprising country of husbandmen, and Hesiod had no sympathy with trade or foreign venture, though his father had come from Aeolis. But the growth of trade was the most important fact of the time, and here too the colonies reacted on the mother-country. By enlarging the borders of the Greek world they invited and facilitated the extension of Greek trade and promoted the growth of industries. Hitherto the Greeks had been mainly an agricultural and pastoral people; many of them were now becoming industrial. They had to supply their western colonies with oil and wool, with metal and pottery, and they began to enter into serious competition with the Phoenician trader and to drive eastern goods from the market.

Roads in Greece

Greek trade moved chiefly along waterways, and this is illustrated by the neglect of road-making in Greece. There were no paved roads, even in later times, except the Sacred Ways to frequented sanctuaries like that from Athens to Eleusis and Delphi, or that from the sea-coast to Olympia. Yet the Greeks were still timorous navigators, and it was thought hazardous to sail even in the most familiar waters, except in the summer. Hesiod expresses in vivid verses the general fear of the sea: 'For fifty days after the solstice, till the end of the harvest, is the tide for sailing; then you will not wreck your ship, nor will the sea wash down your crew, unless Poseidon or Zeus wills their destruction. In that season winds are

Danger of navigation

steady and Ocean kind; with mind at rest, launch your ship and stow your freight; but make all speed to return home, and await not the new wine and the rain of the vintage-tide, when the winter approaches, and the terrible South-wind stirs the waves, in fellowship with the heavy autumnal rain of Zeus, and makes the sea cruel.' About this time, however, an important advance was made in seacraft by the invention of the anchor.

Development of ship-building

Seafaring states found it needful to build warships for protection against pirates. The usual type of the early Greek warship was the penteconter or 'fifty-oar', a long, narrow galley with 25 benches, on each of which two oarsmen sat. The penteconter hardly came into use in Greece before the eighth century. The Homeric Greeks had only smaller vessels of 20 oars, but we can see in the Homeric poems the penteconter coming within their ken as a strange and wonderful thing. The ocean deity, Briareos, called by the name of the Aegean, appears in the *Iliad;* and he is probably no other than the new racer of the seas, sped by a hundred hands. In the *Odyssey* the Phaeacians, who are the kings of seacraft, have ships of 50 oars. But before the end of the eighth century a new idea revolutionised shipbuilding in Phoenicia. Vessels were built with two rows of benches, one above the other, so that the number of oarsmen and the speed were increased without adding to the length of the ship. The 'bireme', however, never became common in Greece, for the Phoenicians had soon improved it into the 'trireme', by the superposition of another bank of oars. The trireme, propelled by 170 rowers, was ultimately to come into universal use as the regular Greek warship, though for a long time after its first introduction, probably in the sixth century, the old penteconters were still generally used;[11] but the unknown shipwright who invented the bireme deserves the credit of the new idea. Whatever naval battles were fought in the seventh century were fought mainly, we may be sure, with penteconters. But penteconters and triremes alike were affected by the new invention of the bronze ram on the prow, a weapon of attack which determined the future character of Greek naval warfare.

The penteconter

Aegaeeus

The bireme

The trireme comes into more general use in Greece not long before 500 B.C.

The beak (embolos)

Tradition of an ancient naval battle between Corinth and Corcyra (664 B.C.)

The Greeks believed that the first regular sea-fight between two Greek powers was fought before the middle of the seventh century between Corinth and her daughter-city Corcyra.[12] If the tradition is true, we may be sure that the event was an incident in a struggle for the trade with Italy and Sicily and along the Adriatic coasts. The chief competitors, however, with Corinth in the west were the Euboean cities, Chalcis and Eretria. In the traffic in eastern seas the island city of Aegina, though she had no colonies of her own, took an active part, and became one of the richest mercantile states of Greece. Athens too had ships, but her industries were still on a comparatively small scale, and it was not till a much later period that her trade was sufficient to involve her in serious rivalry with her neighbours. In the east particularly, the Greeks of Ionia were strong competitors.

Influence of Lydia on Greece

The Greeks of the Asiatic coast were largely dependent, for good or evil, on the adjacent inland countries. The inland trade added to their prosperity, but at any moment if a strong barbarian power arose their independence might be gravely menaced. At the beginning of the seventh century active intercourse was maintained between the Greeks and the kingdoms of Phrygia and Lydia. The Phrygian king Midas dedicated a throne to the god of Delphi; both the Phrygians and the Lydians adopted the Greek alphabet, while the Greeks adopted their modes of music and admitted Phrygian legends into Greek mythology.

Dedication of Midas (c. 700?)

A considerable Phrygian element had won its way into Lydia, and had gained the upper hand. In the Homeric poems we nowhere read of Lydians but only of Maeonians, and there can be no doubt that this name represents the Phrygian settlers or conquerors. A Maeonian dynasty ruled in Lydia at the beginning of the seventh century, and the king bears a Maeonian name, Candaules, 'hound-choker'. The Aryan conquerors—conquerors, that is, who spoke an Aryan tongue—had occupied the throne for centuries; and Greek tradition afterwards derived the origin of the family of Candaules from Heracles himself. But they had become degenerate, and Gyges, a native Lydian, of the clan of the Mermnadae, succeeded in slaying Candaules and seizing the crown. This revolution ushered in a new period for the Lydian kingdom, now no longer called Maeonian. The dominion of the Maeonian sovereign had probably extended southward to the valley of the Maeander. Gyges extended his power northward to the shores of the Propontis, where he founded Dascylion, and conquered the Troad. But he also planned to make the Aegean his western boundary and bring the Greek cities under his lordship. He pressed

The Maeonian dynasty (so-called Heraclidae) of Lydia

Usurpation of Gyges 687-652 B.C.

His conquests

down the valley of the Hermus against Smyrna; down the valley of the Cayster against Colophon; down the valley of the Maeander against Miletus and Magnesia. Of these enterprises only the faintest hints have come down to us. It may be that Colophon was actually captured, and perhaps Magnesia; but the other cities beat back the enemy. The poet Mimnermus sings how a warrior, perhaps his own grandfather, wrought havoc in the ranks of the Lydian horsemen in the plain of the Hermus.

But the plans of Gyges against his Greek neighbours were suddenly interrupted by a blow which descended, as it were from the other side of the world, upon Greeks and Lydians alike. The regions round about Lake Maeotis, on the northern coast of the Black Sea, were inhabited by the Cimmerians, who appear in the marvellous wanderings of Odysseus. They were now driven forth from their abodes, to which, however, their name clung and still clings, by a Scythian folk, the Scolotae, who came from the east. Homeless, the Cimmerians wandered to the opposite side of the Euxine; but whether they travelled by the eastern or the western route, by the Caucasus or by the Danube, is not known for certain. On one hand, they seem to have appeared first in eastern Asia Minor; on the other, they seem to have associated with themselves some Thracian peoples—the Trerians, Edonians, and Thynians. The truth may be that they came round by the eastern coast; and that afterwards, when they made their incursions into western Asia Minor, they invited allies from Thrace to help them. They made Sinope their base and ventured to attack the great Assyrian empire; King Assarhaddon himself tells how 'I smote the Cimmerian Teuspa with all his army'. But they overthrew the realm of Phrygia under its last king Midas, and towards the middle of the seventh century they attacked Lydia. To meet this danger, Gyges sought help from Assyria. The warlike Assarhaddon had been succeeded at Nineveh by Assurbanipal, a peaceful and literary prince, whose refined luxury is caricatured in the Greek conception of Sardanapalus. The lord-of Lydia acknowledged the overlordship of the lord of Assyria. He gained a victory over the Cimmerians and sent their chiefs in chains to Nineveh. But he was not content for long to be the vassal of another sovereign. He threw off his allegiance to Assyria and sent Ionian and Carian mercenary soldiers to Egypt, to help that country also to free itself from Assyrian dominion. At this moment, perhaps, Gyges was at the height of his power. His wealth was famous, and he too, like Phrygian Midas, sent gifts—among them six golden mixing-bowls—to the Delphian god. The poet Archilochus, who witnessed his career, makes one of his characters declare that he 'cares not for the wealth of golden Gyges'.

But the Cimmerians soon renewed their attack, and fortune changed. Gyges was slain in battle; his capital Sardis was taken, except the citadel; and it was some satisfaction to Assurbanipal to record that Lydia was in the hands of the Cimmerians.[13] It was not long before they swooped down upon the Greek cities. Callinus, a poet of Ephesus, heard the trample of their horses and roused his fellow-citizens to battle; Ephesus defied their attack, but the temple of Artemis outside the walls was burned down. They and their allies from Thrace destroyed Magnesia on the Maeander. The barbarians made a deep impression. But the danger passed away. Ardys succeeded Gyges on the Lydian throne, and he finally not only drove out the Cimmerians from the land, but perhaps succeeded in extending his power into Cappadocia, as far as the Halys. The expulsion of the Cimmerians was of profound importance to the Greeks no less than to the Lydians. For the Greek cities depended largely on the Lydian kingdom for their prosperity. Sardis provided a market and an incentive for Greek craftsmanship, and the Lydian kings protected and encouraged the trade that came along the great caravan routes across Asia Minor. Had the Cimmerians established themselves permanently, western Asia Minor would have relapsed into a new dark age. Happily the invasion was a passing whirlwind only, doing much temporary damage but little permanent harm. Herodotus, comparing it with the later subjection by Croesus, could describe it as a plundering raid.

In the meantime Lydia had made an invention which revolutionised commerce. It is to Lydia that Europe owes the invention of coinage. The Babylonians, Phoenicians, and Egyptians made use of weighed gold and silver as a medium of exchange, a certain ratio being fixed between the two metals. A piece of weighed metal becomes a coin when it is stamped by the State and is thereby warranted to have its professed weight and purity. This step was first taken in Lydia, where the earliest money was coined somewhere about the middle of the seventh century, probably by Gyges.[14] These Lydian coins were made of the native white gold, or *electron*—a mixture of gold and silver in which the proportion of gold

Power and wealth of Gyges

Death of Gyges

Cimmerian attack on Ionia

Ardys, king of Lydia

Lydian coinage

Electron staters

Cimmerian invasions

(Crimea)

Cim-merians defeated by Assyrians, 679 B.C.

was greater. A bar of the white gold of Sardis was regarded as ten times the value of a silver bar, and three-fourths of the value of a gold bar, of the same weight. Miletus and Samos soon adopted the new invention, which then spread to other Asiatic towns. Then Aegina and the two great cities of Euboea instituted monetary systems, and by degrees all the states of Greece gave up the primitive custom of estimating value in heads of cattle, and most of them had their own mints. As gold was very rare in Greece, not being found except in the islands of Siphnos and Thasos, the Greeks coined in silver. This invention, coming at the very moment when the Greeks were entering upon a period of great commercial activity, was of immense importance, not only in facilitating trade, but in rendering possible the accumulation of capital. Yet it took many generations to supersede completely the old methods of economy by the new system.

The Aeginetan and Euboit silver standards

The Greeks had derived their systems of weight from Babylonia and Phoenicia. But, when Aegina and the Euboean cities fixed the standard of their silver coinage, they did not adopt the silver standard of either of those countries. The heavier statêr (as the standard silver coin was named) of Aegina weighed 194 grains, and this system was adopted throughout the Peloponnese and in northern Greece. The lighter statêr of Euboea weighed 130 grains, which was the Babylonian standard of gold. This system, at first confined to Euboea, Samos, and a few other places, was adopted by Corinth in a modified form, and afterwards by Athens. From Corinth it spread to Corcyra and her other colonies in the north-west, and, in a modified form, to the cities of south Italy. These cities, having no easy access to supplies of silver, often melted down Corinthian coins for reminting, and in some surviving specimens traces of the Corinthian Pegasus can still be seen.[15]

Secular character of Greek coinage

It was highly characteristic of the Greeks that their coinage was from the first secular in character; it was the work of merchants and magistrates, not of priests. And so the types of Greek coins are rarely religious. Some states chose their civic badge such as the bee of Ephesus, the lion's scalp of Samos; others made good propaganda by illustrating their exports—the tunny fish of Cyzicus, the silphium of Cyrene, the grapes of Maronea; others recalled local legends, the Pegasus of Corinth, the labyrinth of Cretan Cnossus. In sixth-century Athens, when aristocrats were struggling for power, the coin types often represent the heraldic devices of the competing families of nobles. Coin types offered an attractive field for the artist and nowhere was the opportunity more richly exploited than in the western colonies.

The Opening of Egypt

Thus the merchants of Miletus and her fellows grew rich. They were the intermediaries between Lydia and the Mediterranean; while the Lydians carried *their* wares to the interior parts of Asia Minor and the far east. Their argosies sailed to the far west, as well as to the coasts of the Euxine. But a new field for winning wealth was opened to them, much about the same time as the invention of coinage revealed a new prospect to the world of commerce. The jealously guarded gates of Egypt were unbarred to Greek trade.

Assyrian conquest of Egypt, c. 672. Egypt recovers independence, c. 655

The greatest exploit of the Assyrian monarch Assarhaddon was the conquest of Egypt. The land had been split up into an endless number of small kingdoms, and the kings continued to govern as vassals of Assyria. But the foreign domination did not last for much more than a quarter of a century. One of the kings, Psammetichus of Sais, in Lower Egypt, probably of Libyan stock, revolted against Assurbanipal, who, in the last year of his reign, was occupied in subduing an insurrection of the Elamites of Susiana. We have seen how mail-clad soldiers of Ionia and Caria were sent by the lord of Lydia to assist Psammetichus.

Psammetich I

With the help of these 'bronze men who came up from the sea', he reduced the other kings and brought the whole of Egypt under his sway. This Libyan dynasty kept Sais as their capital, and their power was supported by foreign mercenaries, Greeks and Carians, Syrians and Phoenicians. A fortress was built at Daphnae—for so Greek speech graciously altered into Greek shape the Egyptian name Defenneh—and entrusted to Greek mercenaries. Relics of this foreign garrison have been dug up among the ruins of Daphnae. Psammetichus and his successors completely departed from the narrow Egyptian policy of the Pharoahs and were the forerunners in some respects of the Greek dynasty of the Ptolemies, who three centuries later were to rule the land. They opened Egypt to the trade of the world and allowed Greeks to settle permanently in the country. Necho, the son of Psammetichus, connected the Red Sea with the Nile by a canal, and began a work which was completed only a century ago—the cutting of a channel through the isthmus which parts the Red Sea from the

Fort of Defenneh, c. 570 B.C.

Mediterranean. His war-fleets sailed both in the Cypriot and in the Arabian seas; and a party of Phoenician explorers sent out by him accomplished the circumnavigation of Africa —a feat which two thousand years later was regarded as a wild dream.

Foundation of Naucratis

The Milesians founded a factory on the western or Canobic channel of the Nile, not

2.4 East Greek vase, c. 600

very far from Sais; and around it a Greek city grew up, which received the name of Naucratis, 'sea-queen'. This colony became the haven of all Greek traders; for though at first they seem to have moved freely, restrictions were afterwards placed upon them and they were not permitted to enter Egypt except by the Canobic mouth.[16] At Naucratis, the Milesians, the Samians, and the Aeginetans had each their own separate quarter and their own sanctuaries; all the other Greek settlers had one

common enclosure called the Hellenion, girt by a thick brick wall and capable of holding 50,000 men. Here were their market-place and their temples. All the colonists of Naucratis were Greeks of the Asiatic coast, whether Ionians, Dorians, or Aeolians, excepting alone the Aeginetans.

c. 620 B.C.

Egypt, as we see, offered a field not only for traders but for adventurous soldiers, and thus helped to relieve the pressure of over-population in Ionia. At Abu Simbel in Upper Egypt we have a relic of the Greek mercenaries, who accompanied King Psammetichus II, Necho's successor, in an expedition against Ethiopia. Some of them scratched their names on the colossal statues of the temple;[17] and the very triviality of this relic, at such a distance of time, perhaps makes it the more interesting.

Greek soldiers at Abu Simbel [Psammetich II, 594-89 B.C.]

They write their names

Cyrene

Not long after Egypt was thrown open to Greek trade, there arose to the west of Egypt a new Greek city. On the island of Thera in the southern Cyclades there was a prolonged drought which prompted a mission to Delphi to ask for advice. Apollo bade them settle in Libya. Having no overseas experience the Theraeans enlisted the help of a Cretan who knew the African coast and, led by him, they made their first settlement on the little island of Platea off the coast, their second on the opposite coast of the mainland; and when this too proved a failure, they founded their permanent settlement about eight miles from the sea near an abundant spring of water, on two white hills, which commanded the encompassing plain. The city was named Cyrene, and it was the only Greek colony on the coast of Africa which attained to eminence and wealth. The man who led the island folk to their new home became their king; his name seems to have been Aristoteles, but he took the strange name of Battus, which is said to mean 'king' in the Libyan language, while its resemblance to the Greek word for 'stammer' gave rise to the legend that Battus I stammered in his speech. His son was Arcesilas; and in the line of the Cyrenean kings Battus and Arcesilas succeeded each other in alternation. Under Battus II the new city was reinforced by a large incoming of new settlers whom he invited, chiefly from the Peloponnese and Crete; and this influx changed the character of the place, since the original 'Minyan' element was outnumbered. The lands which the Greeks took from the Libyan inhabitants were made

Foundation of Cyrene, c. 630 B.C.

Arcesilas

fruitful by the winter rains; Pindar describes them as plains over which dark clouds hover. The chief source of the wealth of the Cyrenaean kings was the royal monopoly in the export of silphium, a plant which acquired a high repute for medicinal virtues and was richly prized throughout the Greek world. In the early days of the Greek colony it grew

packed. [19] It was in the reign of this king that Barca was founded, farther west. He quarrelled with his brothers, and they left Cyrene and founded a town for themselves.

Cyrene held her head high in the Greek world, though she was somewhat apart from it. A Cyrenaean poet arose, and continued the *Odyssey* and described the last adventures of

2.5   Arcesilas cup (see note, page 552)

The Arcesilas cup

luxuriantly in the district; but it was already dying out in the Roman period and is now extinct. There was also excellent pasturage, and the men of Cyrene became famous for rearing horses and for skill as riders and charioteers. Cyrene's sheep too were famous.[18] On a fine Laconian cup we can see Arcesilas II himself watching the wool being weighed and

Odysseus. His poem was accepted by Greece as winding up the Epic Cycle which was associated with the name of Homer. His work was distinguished by local pride and local colouring. He gave Odysseus a son Arcesilaus, and connected the royal line of Cyrene with the great wanderer. And he introduced a flavour of those Libyan influences which

The Telegony of Eugammon, c. 600 B.C.

modified Cyrenaean civilisation, just as the remote cities of the Euxine received influences from Scythia.

Gaul and Spain

When the Therans were completing their preparations to send out a colony the party left on the island of Platea ran out of supplies; they were saved, according to Herodotus, by Colaeus, a Samian merchant who was driven off course on a voyage to Egypt. Having re-stocked the island party Colaeus continued his voyage, but was driven by the wind beyond the pillars of Hercules and reached Tartessus. There he found a virgin market and brought back a cargo from which he could afford to make a magnificent dedication in the temple of Hera on Samos: a bronze mixing bowl in the Argolic style with griffin heads around the rim, supported by three ten-foot bronze kneeling figures. Tartessus, near Cadiz, was the main outlet for the rich silver mines of south-west Spain; though Colaeus may have discovered the market it was the Phocaeans who system-atically exploited it.

Herodotus tells us that the Phocaeans were the first to open up the Adriatic and Etruscan seas, and they used penteconters rather than merchantmen, presumably because they might have to fight for their trade.[20] They established a colony at Massalia (Marseilles) *c.* 600, which was to have a long and distinguished history and retain much of its Greek character well into the Roman period. It had a good harbour and commanded the trade route into the interior up the river Rhone; and it was by this route that a great bronze crater, probably made in Sparta towards the end of the sixth century, came to a native chief in the centre of France.[21] From Massalia the Phocaeans extended their lines of communication through Emporiae (Ampurias) on the Costa Brava to Tartessus (near Cadiz) and their relations with the king of Tartessus were so friendly that he asked them to settle in his country; the Greeks had a deserved reputation throughout the Mediter-ranean as fighters, and a strong Greek garrison could have been a comforting insurance for a king whose great wealth invited attack. When the Phocaeans declined he paid for them to build a new wall round their city. The Phocaeans may also have had colonies in Sardinia at Cagliari and Olbia, but when the Carthaginians gained control of the island these early Greek colonies were forgotten. Alalia, a Phocaean colony in Corsica, was remembered because a great sea-battle was fought there between Phocaeans and a com-bined fleet of Etruscans and Carthaginians. The Phocaeans are said to have more than held their own, but their losses were serious and they had to evacuate Corsica.

Popular Discontent in Greece

The advance of the Greeks in trade and industry produced many important con-sequences for their political and social devel-opment. *Increase of trade and industry* The manufactures required labour, and a sufficient number of free labourers was not to be had. Slaves were therefore indis-pensable, and they were imported in large *Slavery* numbers from Asia Minor and Thrace and the coasts of the Euxine. The slave-trade became a profitable enterprise, and the men of Chios made it their chief pursuit. The existence of household slaves, generally war-captives, such as we meet in Homer, was an innocent in-stitution which would never have had serious results; but the new organised slave-system which began in the seventh century was destined to prove one of the most fatal causes of disease and decay to the states of Greece.

At first the privileged classes of the aristo-cratic republics benefited by the increase of commerce; for the nobles were themselves the chief speculators. But the wealth which they acquired by trade undermined their political position. For in the first place their influence *Decrease of importance of agriculture* depended largely on their domains of land, and when industries arose to compete with agriculture, the importance of land necessarily declined. In the second place, wealth intro-duced a new political standard; and aristo-cracies resting on birth tended to transform *Wealth becomes a power in politics* themselves into aristocracies resting on wealth. The proverb 'money makes the man' now came into vogue. As nobility by birth cannot be acquired, whereas wealth can, such a change is always a step in the direction of democracy.

On the other hand, the poorer freemen at first suffered, and their distress and discontent *The voice of the people begins to be heard* drove them into striving for radical changes. The second half of the seventh century is marked in many parts of Greece by struggles between the classes; and the wiser and better of the nobles began themselves to see the necessity of extending political privileges to their fellow-citizens. The centralisation in towns, owing to the growth of industries and the declining importance of agriculture, created a new town population and doubtless helped on the democratic movement.

In this agitated period lived a poet of great genius, Archilochus of Paros. It has been truly said that Archilochus is the first Greek 'of flesh and blood' whom we can grasp through the mists of antiquity. Son of a noble by a slave mother he left Paros to seek a better livelihood in its recently established colony of Thasos. But he had no love of the sea and sang of the 'bitter gifts of Poseidon' and the mariner's prayers for 'sweet home'. In Thasos he was involved in party struggles which rent the island. It has been thought that he witnessed at Thasos an eclipse of the sun at noontide which he describes, the eclipse of April 648 B.C., but it is very doubtful whether he is really referring to this eclipse. All the evils of all Hellas are here, he exclaims; and 'Thasos is not a fair place nor desirable, like the land round the stream of Siris.' He announces that he is 'the servant of the lord of battle and skilled in the delicious gift of the Muses'. But when he fought in a war which the Thasians waged with the Thracians of the opposite coast, he ran for his life and dropped his shield; 'never mind', he said, 'I will get me another as good'. Poor, with a stain on his birth, tossed about the world, soured by adversity, Archilochus in his poetry gave full expression to his feelings, and used it to utter his passionate hatred against his enemies, such as the Parian Lycambes, for instance, who refused him his daughter Neobule. Had fortune favoured him, he would have been a noble of the nobles; ill-luck drove him to join the movement against aristocracy. His poems present a complete contrast to the epic style and even to Hesiod. He addressed himself to the people, used colloquial language, and perfected iambic and trochaic measures for literary purposes. His influence may be judged from the fact that his poems were recited by the rhapsodes along with Homer and Hesiod.

The ills of Greece, which were reflected in the poems of Archilochus, were to lead to the development of equality and freedom. But success in the struggle would in most cases depend on military efficiency; and a revolution in the art of warfare, which was brought about at the same period, was therefore of immense importance. This takes us to the history of Sparta.

CHAPTER 3

The Growth of Sparta. Fall of the Aristocracies

Sparta and her Constitution

In the *Iliad* and *Odyssey* Sparta is one of the most important centres of Mycenaean Greece, ruled by Menelaus, brother of Agamemnon who led the Greek forces against Troy and husband of Helen who was the cause of all the troubles. In the *Odyssey*, when Telemachus is determined to find out what he can about the fate of his father Odysseus, it is to the palace of Menelaus that he goes and Menelaus entertains him royally. Thucydides seems to have had no doubt that the Dorians occupied the Peloponnese eighty years after the fall of Troy, which would be roughly a generation later than the destruction of the main Mycenaean centres, and fifth century Spartans accepted a king list which begins with the Dorian invasion. According to Thucydides and Herodotus Sparta was very unsettled for a long time, but Thucydides thought that she reached stability near 800 B.C. The story is too tidy to fit the archaeological evidence.

Mycenaean Laconia has been much less explored than Messenia or the Argolid, but surface surveys suggest that she had considerably fewer settlements and very few important settlements. From the site of classical Sparta nothing has been found to suggest that it was an important Mycenaean site, but some two miles to the north on rising ground overlooking the river Eurotas there was found the remains of a post-Mycenaean shrine of Menelaus and Helen and the accompanying settlement is thought to have been destroyed at roughly the same time as Pylos, *c.* 1200 B.C. From surface surveys it has been inferred that during the two following centuries there was a marked decline in the population of Laconia and that some at least of the destroyed Mycenaean sites were not reoccupied.[1] The Dorians seem to have taken possession near 1000 B.C. and at first lived in small villages. What was probably Mycenaean Sparta seems to have been abandoned and Dorian Sparta on the Eurotas was formed by the amalgamation of four villages. Pausanias records that under king Teleclus, probably in the eighth century, Sparta conquered the pre-Dorian Amyclae after a heroic resistance; Amyclae was incorporated in Sparta, but not admitted to the important Spartan cult of Artemis Orthia. Sparta, however, respected the cult of pre-Dorian, and possibly pre-Greek, Hyacinthus at Amyclae and identified him with Apollo. This tradition about Amyclae can probably be controlled when the settlement as distinct from the site of the cult is excavated, and archaeology may also throw more light on the chronology and nature of the Dorian penetration of Laconia and the reduction of the whole of Laconia under Spartan control. By the time that Spartan domination was complete the pre-Dorian population were *helots*, serfs working their masters' land, and other Dorian settlements were graded as *perioeci*, 'dwellers round about', dependent on Sparta for external relations and giving military service when required, but preserving their own organisation for internal affairs.

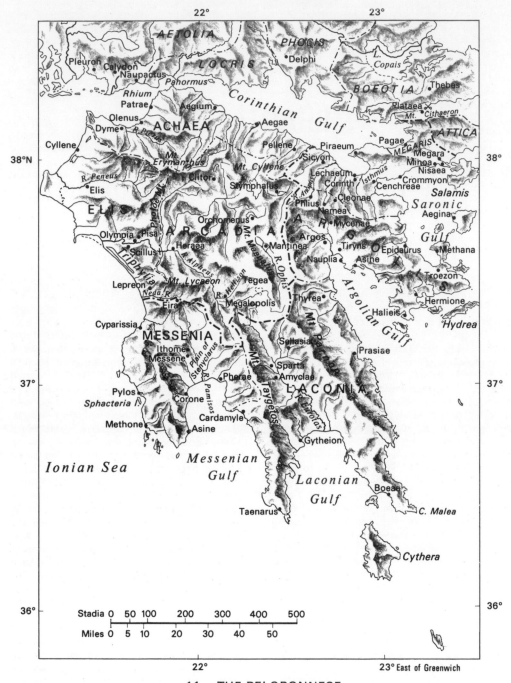

11. THE PELOPONNESE

Spartan belief in the antiquity of the constitution

In the classical period the Spartans differed sharply from all other Greek states in their constitution and in their way of life, and they liked to think and make others think that their constitution had existed from very ancient times in just the same shape and feature which it displayed in the days of recorded history. We are, however, forced to suspect that this was not the case. There can be little doubt that the Spartan state developed up to the end of

90

the seventh century on the same general lines as other Greek states, though with some remarkable peculiarities. There can be little doubt that, like most other states, it passed through the stages of royalty and aristocracy; and that the final form of the constitution was the result of a struggle between the nobles and the people. The remarkable thing was that throughout these changes hereditary kingship survived.

The machine of the Spartan constitution, as we know it when it was fully developed, had four parts: the Kings, the Council, the Assembly, and the Ephors. The first three are institutions, which were common to the whole Greek race; the Ephors were peculiar to Sparta and states derived from Sparta.

I. The kings

We saw that towards the end of the Homeric period the powers of the king were limited, and that this limited monarchy then died out, sometimes leaving a trace behind it, perhaps in the name of a magistracy—like the king-archon at Athens. In a few places it survived, and Sparta was one of them. But if it survived here, its powers were limited in a twofold way. It was limited not only by the other institutions of the state, but by its own dual character. For there were two kings at Sparta, and had been since the memory of men. It seems possible that the origin of this double kingship lay in the coalition of two distinct communities, each of which had its own king. One tribe dwelt about Sparta, and its kings belonged to the clan of the Agidae. The other tribe, we may guess, was settled somewhere in southern Laconia, and its royal clan was that of the Eurypontidae. These two tribes must have united to form a large city-state at Sparta; and the terms of the union may have been that neither tribe should give up its king, but two kings, with coequal authority, should rule over the joint community. The kingship passed from father to son in the two royal houses of the Agids and Eurypontids; and if the Agid kings possessed a slight superiority in public estimation over their colleagues, this may have been due to the fact that the Eurypontids were the strangers who migrated to Sparta. According to a pedigree which was made out for them in later days, when the myth of the Return of the Heraclidae had become current, both dynasties traced themselves back to Heracles.

Origin of the dual kingship

(At Amyclae?)

It seems probable that it was partly because there were two kings, the one a check upon the other, that kingship was not abolished in Sparta, or reduced to a mere magistracy. But the powers of the kings were largely

Limitation of the royal powers

curtailed; and we may suppose that the limitations were introduced by degrees during that epoch in which, throughout Greece generally, monarchies were giving way to aristocratic republics. Of the religious, military, and judicial functions, which belonged to them and to all other Greek kings, they lost some and retained others.

They were privileged to hold certain priesthoods; they offered solemn sacrifices for the city every month to Apollo; they prepared the necessary sacrifices before warlike expeditions and battles; they were priests, though not the sole priests, of the community.

Religious functions

They were the supreme commanders of the army. They had originally the right of making war upon whatever country they chose, and penalties were laid on any Spartan who presumed to hinder them. In the field they had unlimited right of life and death, and they had a bodyguard of a hundred men. It is clear that these large powers were always limited by the double nature of the kingship. But at a later period it was defined by law that only one of the kings, to be chosen on each occasion by the people, should lead the army in time of war, and moreover they were made responsible to the community for their conduct in their campaigns.[2]

Military functions

c. 500 B.C.

But while they enjoyed this supreme position as high priests and leaders of the host, they could hardly be considered judges any longer. The right of dealing out dooms like the Homeric Agamemnon had passed away from them; only in three special cases had they still judicial or legal powers. They presided at the adoption of children; they decided who was to marry an heiress whose father had died without betrothing her; and they judged in all matters concerning public roads.

Judicial functions

There were royal domains in the territory of the *perioeci* from which the kings derived their revenue. But they also had perquisites at public sacrifices; on such occasions they were (like Homeric kings) given the first seat at the banquet, were served first, and received a double portion of everything, and the hides of the slaughtered beasts. The pious sentiment with which royalty, as a hallowed institution, was regarded, is illustrated by the honours which were paid to the kings when they died. 'Horsemen,' says Herodotus, 'carry round the tidings of the event through all Laconia, and in the city women go about beating a cauldron. And at this sign, two free persons of each house, a man and a woman, must put on mourning garb, and if any fail to do this great pains are imposed.' The funeral was attended

Funeral honours

by a fixed number of the perioeci, and it was part of the stated ceremony that the dead king should be praised by the mourners as better than all who had gone before him. Public business was not resumed for ten days after the burial. The king was succeeded by his eldest son, but a son born before his father's accession to the kingship had to give way to the eldest of those who were born after the accession. If there were no children, the succession fell to the nearest male kinsman, who was likewise the regent in the case of a minority.

II. Gerusia, or Council of Elders (or Gerontia)

The *gerontes* or elders, whom we find in Homer advising the king and also acting as judges, have developed at Sparta into a body of fixed number, forming a definite part of the constitution, called the *gerusia*. This Council consisted of 30 members, including the two kings, who belonged to it by virtue of their kingship. The other 28 had to be over sixty years of age, so that the council was a body of elders in the strict sense of the word. They held their office for life and were chosen by acclamation in the general assembly of citizens, whose choice was supposed to fall on him whose moral merits were greatest; membership of the Council was described as a 'prize for virtue'. The Council prepared matters which were to come before the Assembly; it exercised, as an advising body, a great influence on political affairs; and it formed a court of justice for criminal cases.

But though the Councillors were elected *by* the people, they were not elected *from* the people. Nobility of birth retained at Sparta its political significance; and only men of the noble families could be chosen members of the Council. And thus the Council formed an oligarchical element in the Lacedaemonian constitution.

III. Assembly of the People

Every Spartan who had passed his thirtieth year was a member of the Assembly of Citizens, which met every month between the bridge of Babyka and the stream of Knakion. In old days, no doubt, it was summoned by the kings, but in historical times we find that this right has passed to the ephors. The assembly did not debate, but having heard the proposals of kings or ephors, signified its will by acclamation. If it seemed doubtful to which opinion the majority of voices inclined, recourse was had to a division. The people elected the members of the Gerusia, the ephors and other magistrates; determined questions of war and peace and foreign politics; and decided disputed successions to the kingly office. Thus, theoretically, the Spartan constitution was a democracy. No Spartan was excluded from the Assembly of

the people; and the will of the people expressed at their Assembly was supreme. 'To the people,' runs an old statute, 'shall belong the decision and the power.' But the same statute granted to the executive authorities—'the elders and leaders'—a power which restricted this apparent supremacy of the people. It allowed them 'to be dissenters, if the people make a crooked decree'. It seems that the will of the people, declared by their acclamations, did not receive the force of law unless it were then formally proclaimed before the Assembly was formally dissolved.[3] If the elders and magistrates did not approve of the decision of the majority of the Assembly, they could annul the proceedings by refusing to proclaim it—'seceding' and dissolving the meeting, without waiting for the regular dissolution by king or ephor.

Ephorate

The five ephors were the most characteristic part of the political constitution of Sparta. The origin of the office is veiled in obscurity; it was supposed to have been instituted in the first half of the eighth century. But we must distinguish between the first institution of the office and the beginning of its political importance. It is probable that in the course of the eighth century the kings, finding it impossible to attend to all their duties, were constrained to give up the civil jurisdiction, and that the ephors or 'overseers' were appointed for this purpose.[4] The number of the ephors would seem to be connected with the number of the five demes or villages whose union formed the city; and perhaps each one of the ephors was assigned originally to one of the villages. But it cannot have been till the seventh century that the ephors won their great political power. They must have won that power in a conflict between the nobility who governed in conjunction with the kings and the people who had no share in the government. In that struggle the kings represented the cause of the nobility, while the ephors were the representatives of the people. A compromise, as the result of such a conflict, is implied in the oaths which were every month exchanged between the kings and the ephors. The king swore that he would observe the laws of the state in discharging his royal functions; the ephor that he would maintain the royal power undiminished, so long as the king was true to his oath. In this ceremony we have the record of an acute conflict between the government and people. The democratic character of the ephorate appears from the fact that any Spartan might be elected. The mode of election, which is described by Aristotle as 'very childish', was practically equivalent to an election by lot. When the five ephors did not agree among themselves, the minority gave way.

The ephors entered upon their office at the beginning of the Laconian year, which fell on the first new moon after the autumnal equinox. As chosen guardians of the rights of the people, they were called upon to watch jealously the conduct of the kings. With this object, two ephors always accompanied the king on warlike expeditions. They had the power of indicting the king and summoning him to appear before them. The judicial functions which the kings lost passed partly to the ephors, partly to the Council. The ephors were the supreme civil court, and the Council, as we have seen, formed the supreme criminal court. But in the case of the Perioeci the ephors were criminal judges also. They were moreover responsible for the strict maintenance of the order and discipline of the Spartan state, and, when they entered upon office, they issued a proclamation to the citizens to 'shave their upper lips and obey the laws'.

Character of Spartan constitution

This unique constitution cannot be placed under any general head, cannot be called kingdom, oligarchy or democracy, without misleading. None of these names is applicable to it, but it participated in all three. A stranger who saw the kings going forth with power at the head of the host, or honoured above all at the public feasts in the city, would have described Sparta as a kingdom. If one of the kings themselves had been asked to define the constitution, it is probable that he would have regretfully called it a democracy. Yet the close Council, taken from a privileged class, exercising an important influence on public affairs, and deferring to an Assembly which could not debate, might be alleged to prove that Sparta was an oligarchy. The secret of this complex character of the Spartan constitution lies in the fact that, while Sparta developed on the same general path as other states and had to face the same political crises, she overcame each crisis with less violence and showed a more conservative spirit. When she ought to have passed from royalty to aristocracy, she diminished the power of the kings, but she preserved hereditary kingship as a part of the aristocratic government. When she ought to have advanced to democracy, she gave indeed enormous power to the representatives of the people, but she still preserved both her hereditary kings and the Council of her nobles.

Spartan Conquest of Messenia

Messenia

In the growth of Sparta the first and most decisive step was the conquest of Messenia. The southern portion of the Peloponnese is divided into two parts by Mount Taygetus. Of these, the eastern part is again severed by Mount Parnon into two regions: the vale of the river Eurotas, and the rugged strip of coast between Parnon and the sea. The western country is less mountainous, more fruitful, and blessed by a milder climate. Nor is it divided in the same way by a mountain chain: the hills rise irregularly, and the river Pamisus waters the central plain of Stenyclarus where the Greek invaders are said to have fixed their abode. The natural fortress of the country was the lofty rock of Ithome which rises to the west of the river. It is probable that under its protection a town grew up at an early period, whose name Messene was afterwards transferred to the whole country.

Early conquest of Messenia

The fruitful soil of Messenia, 'good to plant and good to plough', as a Spartan poet sang, could not but excite the covetousness of her martial neighbours. The First Messenian War may be dated to the last quarter of the eighth century.[5] Legends grew up freely as to its causes and its course. All that we know with certainty is that the Spartan king, under whose auspices it was waged, was named Theopompus; that it was decided by the capture of the great fortress of Ithome; and that the eastern part of the land became Laconian. A poet writing at the beginning of the seventh century would have naturally spoken of Messene or Pherae as being 'in Lacedaemon'. When the Second War broke out towards the middle of the seventh century, it was history or legend that the previous war had lasted twenty years. Legends grew up around it in which the chief figure was a Messenian hero named Aristodemus. The tale was that he offered his daughter as a sacrifice to save his country, in obedience to the demand of an oracle. Her lover made a despairing effort to save her life by spreading a report that the maiden was about to become a mother, and the calumny so incensed Aristodemus that he slew her with his own hand. Afterwards, terrified by evil dreams and portents, and persuaded that his country was doomed, he killed himself upon his daughter's tomb. All this is later romance; but the conquest of Messenia is historical, and of fundamental importance in Sparta's development.

Legend of Aristodemus

As the object of the Spartans was to increase the number of the lots of land for their citizens,

Condition of the Messenians

many of the conquered Messenians were reduced to the condition of Helots. Servitude was hard, though their plight might have been harder, for they paid to their lords only one-half of the produce of the lands which they tilled. The Spartan poet Tyrtaeus describes how the Messenians endured the insolence of their masters:

> As asses worn by loads intolerable,
> So them did stress of cruel force compel,
> Of all the fruits the well-tilled land affords,
> The moiety to bear to their proud lords.

Their rebellion: 'Second War' (c. mid-seventh century)

For two generations they submitted patiently, but at length, when victorious Sparta felt secure, a rebellion was organised in the northern district of Andania.[6] The rebels were supported by their neighbours in Arcadia and Pisatis, and they are said to have found an able and ardent leader in Aristomenes, sprung from an old Messenian family. The revolt was at first successful. The Spartans fared ill, and their young men experienced the disgrace of defeat. The hopes of the serfs rose, and Sparta despaired of recovering the land. But a leader and a poet arose amongst them. The lame

Tyrtaeus

Tyrtaeus is recorded to have inspired his countrymen with such martial vigour that the tide of fortune turned, and Sparta began to retrieve her losses and recover her reputation. Some scraps of the poems of Tyrtaeus have been preserved, and they supply the only trust-worthy material we have for the history of the Messenian wars; and he won such fame by the practical successes of his art that at a later time the Athenians sought to claim him as one of their sons and gave out that Sparta, by the counsel of an oracle, had sent for him. The warriors advanced to battle singing his 'marches' to the sound of flutes, while his elegies, composed in the conventional epic dialect, are said to have been recited in the tents after the evening meal. But we learn from himself that his strategy was as effective as his poetry, and the Messenians were presently defeated in the Battle of the Great Foss. They then retired to the northern stronghold of Eira on the river Nedon, which plays the same part in the second war that Ithome played in the first, while Aristomenes takes the place of Aristodemus. As to Eira, indeed, we possess no record on the contemporary authority of Tyrtaeus, whose extant fragments notice none of the adventures, nor even the name, of the hero Aristomenes. Yet Eira may well have been the place where the last stand was made, for the Spartans had razed the fortifications of Ithome, which is not mentioned in connection with the second war. At Eira the defenders were near their Arcadian supporters and within reach of Pylos, which seems not to have been yet Lacedaemonian. But Eira fell; legend says that it was beleaguered for eleven years. Aristomenes was the soul of the defence, and his wonderful escapes became the argument of a stirring tale. On one occasion he was thrown, with 50 fellow-countrymen captured by the Spartans, into a deep pit. His comrades perished, and Aristomenes awaited certain death. But by following the track of a fox he found a passage in the rocky wall of his prison and appeared on the following day at Eira. When the Spartans surprised that fortress, he made his escape wounded to Arcadia. He died in Rhodes, but two hundred and fifty years later, on the field of Leuctra, he reappeared against the Spartans to avenge his defeat.

Capture of Eira

Tales of Aristomenes

Those Messenians who were left in the land were mostly reduced again to the condition of Helots, but the maritime communities and even a few in the interior remained free, as perioeci, in the possession of their estates. Many escaped to Arcadia, while some of the inhabitants of the coast towns may have taken ship and sailed to other places.

At this time Sparta, like most other Greek states, suffered from domestic discontent. There was a pressing land question, with which Tyrtaeus dealt in a poem named *Eunomia*, or *Law and Order*. This question was partly solved by the conquest of the whole land of Messenia, which may have given opportunity for a new distribution of land and perhaps the incorporation of new citizens who had helped in the war but were not of pure Spartan descent, and so did not enjoy full privileges.[7]

Pressure of population on the land

The Messenian war, as recorded by Tyrtaeus, shows us that the power of the privileged classes had already been undermined by a great change in the method of warfare. The fighting is done, and the victory won, by regiments of mailed foot-lancers, who march and fight together in close ranks. The secret had been discovered that the well-drilled phalanx of hoplites, as they were called, was superior to the aristocratic method of fighting on horse, or the hurling of spears at long range, such as is seen on geometric vases of the ninth and eighth centuries. The change in tactics was bound up with a change in armour. The two throwing spears were replaced by a single thrusting spear, metal corselet and metal greaves were added, and the shield was no longer strapped to the body but held securely on the left arm, valuable in the clash of the two battle lines, useless in retreat. The progress of metalsmiths

Revolution in warfare

Hoplites

Political significance of this change

3.1   Hoplites on a Corinthian vase (c. 650) (see note, page 552)

3.2   Bronze breastplate and helmet, Argos (c. 720)

in their trade, which accompanied the general industrial advance of Greece, rendered possible this transformation in the art of war. Every well-to-do citizen could now provide himself with an outfit of armour and go forth to battle in panoply. The transformation was distinctly levelling and democratic; for it placed the noble and the ordinary citizen on an equality in the field.[8] We shall not be wrong in connecting this military development with those aspirations of the people for a popular constitution which resulted in the investment of the ephorate with its great political powers.

The new tactics were firmly established by the middle of the seventh century. They spread rapidly through Greece, and their natural tendency everywhere was to promote the progress towards democracy. It is significant that in Thessaly, where the system of hoplites was not introduced and cavalry was always the kernel of the army, democratic ideas never made way, and the peasants remained a depressed class.

Internal Development of Sparta and her Institutions

In the seventh century one could not have foretold what Sparta was destined to be. Her nobles lived luxuriously, like the nobles of other lands; the individual was free, as in other cities, to order his life as he willed. She showed some promise of other than military interests. Lyric poetry was transported from its home in Lesbos to find for a while a second home on

Character of Sparta in early times

95

the banks of the Eurotas. Songs to be sung at banquets, at weddings, at harvest feasts and at festivals of the gods, by single singers or choirs of men or maidens, were older than memory could reach; but with the development of music and the improvement of musical instruments the composition of these songs became an art, and lyric poetry was created. The lyre of seven strings was an ancient invention, but it was attributed to Terpander of Lesbos, who was at all events an historical person, and both a poet and a musician. He visited Sparta and is said to have instituted the musical contest at the Carnea, the great festival of Lacedaemon. His music was certainly welcomed there, and Sparta soon had a poet who, though not her own, was at least her adopted son. Alcman from Lydian Sardis made Sparta his home, and we have some fragments of songs which he composed for choirs of Laconian maidens. Sparta had her epic poet too in Cinaethon. But this promise of a school of music and poetry was not to be fulfilled.

Terpander (c. 700 B.C.) [Feast of Carnean Apollo]

Material culture

Excavation has added colour and detail to the picture of early Sparta drawn from literary sources. Imports of ivory and amber, scarabs and gold and silver jewelry show that Sparta had wide contacts in the seventh century; and Laconian craftsmen in ivory, bone and, later, pottery could compare with the best in Greece. In the sixth century the stream of imports gradually dries up, but Laconian pottery, which is found as far afield as Sardis and Etruria, reaches its peak in the second quarter of the sixth century and rapid deterioration only sets in after *c.* 550.⁹ While other states developed industrial and artistic production, Sparta gradually lost the material refinements of living. But though there is no sudden break in the development to suggest that the decline in culture was the result of formal enactment, the ultimate cause was the retention by Sparta of an obsolete currency of iron bars. The new silver coinage spread rapidly through mainland Greece during the sixth century. The conservatism of Sparta was deliberate choice.

Army reform

That Sparta was taking careful stock of her position after the crushing of the Messenian revolt is suggested by the reorganisation in her army. In the early archaic period the Spartan army had fought in Dorian tribal divisions. At the battle of Plataea in 479 Herodotus speaks of a Pitanate division and Pitane was one of the villages that together made Sparta.¹⁰ The changes in organisation from a tribal to a local basis was probably associated with the Messenian revolt.

Transformation of Sparta (seventh-sixth centuries)

When Sparta emerges into the full light of history we find her under an iron discipline, which invades every part of a man's life and controls all his actions from his cradle to his deathbed. Everything is subordinated to the art of war, and the sole aim of the state is to create invincible warriors. The martial element was doubtless, from the very beginning, stronger in Sparta than in other states; and as a city ruling over a large discontented population of subjects and serfs, she must always be prepared to fight; but we shall probably never know how, and under what influences, the singular Spartan discipline which we have now to examine was introduced. Nor can we, in describing the Spartan society, distinguish always between older and later institutions.

The whole Spartan people formed a military caste; the life of a Spartan citizen was devoted to the service of the state. In order to carry out this ideal it was necessary that every citizen should be freed from the care of providing for himself and his family. The nobles owned family domains of their own; but the Spartan community also came into possession of common land, which was divided into a number of lots. Each Spartan obtained a lot, which passed from father to son, but could not be either sold or divided; thus a citizen could never be reduced to poverty. The original inhabitants, whom the Lacedaemonians dispossessed and reduced to the state of serfs, cultivated the land for their lords. Every year the owner of a lot was entitled to receive seventy medimni of corn for himself, twelve for his wife, and a stated portion of wine and fruit. All that the land produced beyond this, the Helot was allowed to retain for his own use. Thus the Spartan need take no thought for his support; he could give all his time to the affairs of public life. Though the Helots were not driven by taskmasters and had the right of acquiring private property, their condition seems to have been hard; at all events, they were always bitterly dissatisfied and ready to rebel, whenever an occasion presented itself. The system of Helotry was a source of danger from the earliest times, but especially after the conquest of Messenia; and the state of constant military preparation in which the Spartans lived may have been partly due to the consciousness of this peril perpetually at their doors. The *Krypteia* or secret police was instituted—it is uncertain at what date—to deal with this danger. Young Spartans were sent into the country and empowered to kill every Helot whom they had reason to regard with suspicion. Closely connected with this system was the remarkable custom that the ephors, in whose

Land: private and public

Lots

The Helots

(105 bushels?)

Krypteia

hands lay the general control over the Helots, should every year on entering office proclaim war against them. By this device, the youths could slay dangerous Helots without any scruple or fear of the guilt of manslaughter. But notwithstanding these precautions serious revolts broke out again and again. A Spartan had no power to grant freedom to the Helot who worked on his lot, nor yet to sell him to another. Only the state could emancipate. As the Helots were called upon to serve as light-armed troops in time of war, they had then an opportunity of exhibiting bravery and loyalty in the service of the city, and those who conspicuously distinguished themselves might be rewarded by the city with the meed of freedom. Thus arose a class of freedmen called *Neo-damōdes* *neodamōdes*, or new demesmen. There was also *and* another class of persons, neither serfs nor *Mothōnes* citizens, called *mothōnes*, who probably sprang *(or Mothakes)* from illegitimate unions of citizens with Helot women.

Education Thus relieved from the necessity of gaining *(ἀγωγή)* a livelihood, the Spartans devoted themselves to the good of the state, and the aim of the state was the cultivation of the art of war. Sparta was a large military school. Education, marriage, the details of daily life were all strictly regulated with a view to the maintenance of a perfectly efficient army. When a child was born it was submitted to the inspection of the heads of the tribe and, if they judged it to be unhealthy or weak, it was exposed to die on the wild slopes of Mount *(Paido-* Taygetus. At the age of seven years, the boy *nómos)* was consigned to the care of a state-officer, and the course of his education was entirely determined by the purpose of inuring him to bear hardships, training him to endure an exacting discipline, and instilling into his heart a sentiment of devotion to the state. From the age of eighteen to twenty the young men were marshalled in a huge school formed on the *Iranes* model of an army. The captains and prefects who instructed and controlled them were young men who had passed their twentieth year, but had not yet reached the thirtieth, which admitted them to the rights of citizenship. Warm friendships often sprang up between the young men and the boys whom they were training.

At the age of twenty the Spartan entered upon military service and was permitted to marry. But he could not yet enjoy home life; he had to live in 'barracks' with his companions, and could only pay stolen and fugitive visits to his wife. In his thirtieth year, having completed his training, he became a 'man', and

obtained the full rights of citizenship. The *Homoioi* or peers, as the Spartan citizens were called, dined together in tents in the Hyacinthian Street. These public messes were in old days called *andreia*, or 'men's meals', and in later times *phiditia*. Each member of a common *Phiditia* tent made a fixed monthly contribution, derived from the produce of his lot, consisting of barley, cheese, wine and figs, and the members of the same mess-tent shared the same tent in the field in time of war. These public messes are a survival, adapted to military purposes, of the old custom of public banquets, at which all the burghers gathered together at a table spread for the gods of the city. Of the organisation of the Spartan hoplites *Army* in early times we have no definite knowledge. Three hundred 'horsemen', chosen from the Spartan youths, formed the king's bodyguard; but though, as their name shows, they were originally mounted, in later times they fought on foot. The light infantry was supplied by the Perioeci and Helots.

Spartan discipline extended itself to the *Spartan* women too, with the purpose of producing *women* mothers who should be both physically strong and saturated with the Spartan spirit. The girls, in common with the boys, went through a gymnastic training, and it was not considered immodest for them to practise their exercises almost nude. They enjoyed a freedom which was in marked contrast with the seclusion of women in other Greek states. They had a high repute for chastity; but if the government directed them to breed children for the state, they had no scruples in obeying the command even though it might involve a violation of the sanctity of the marriage-tie. They were, proverbially, ready to sacrifice their maternal instincts to the welfare of their country. Such was the spirit of the place.

Thus Sparta was a camp in which the highest object of every man's life was to be ready at any moment to fight with the utmost efficiency for his city. The aim of every law, the end of the whole social order, was to fashion good soldiers. Private luxury was strictly forbidden; Spartan simplicity became proverbial. The individual man, entirely lost in the state, had no life of his own; he had no problems of human existence to solve for himself. Sparta was not a place for thinkers or theorists; the whole duty of man and the highest ideal of life were contained for a Spartan in the laws of his city. Warfare being the object of all the Spartan *Motive of* laws and institutions, one might expect to find *Spartan* the city in a perpetual state of war. One might *discipline* look to see her sons always ready to strive with their neighbours without any ulterior object, war being for them an end in itself. But it was not so; they did not wage war more lightly than other men; we cannot rank them with barbarians who care only for fighting and hunting. We may attribute the original motive of their institutions, in some measure at least, to the situation of a small dominant class in the midst of ill-contented subjects and hostile serfs. They must always be prepared to meet a rebellion of Perioeci or a revolt of Helots, and a surprise would have been fatal. Forming a permanent camp in a country which was far from friendly, they were compelled to be always on their guard. But there was something more in the vitality and conservation of the Spartan constitution than precaution against the danger of a possible insurrection. It appealed to the Greek sense of beauty. There was a certain completeness and simplicity about the constitution itself, a completeness and simplicity about the manner of life enforced by the laws, a completeness and simplicity too about the type of character developed by them, which Greeks of other cities never failed to contemplate with genuine, if distant, admiration. Shut away in 'hollow many-clefted Lacedaemon', out of the world and not sharing in the progress of other Greek cities, Sparta seemed to remain at a standstill; and a stranger from Athens or Miletus in the fifth century visiting the straggling villages which formed her unwalled unpretentious city must have had a feeling of being transported into an age long past, when men were braver, better and simpler, unspoiled by wealth, undisturbed by ideas. To a philosopher like Plato, speculating in political science, the Spartan state seemed the nearest approach to the ideal. The ordinary Greek looked upon it as a structure of severe and simple beauty, a Dorian city stately as a Dorian temple, far nobler than his own abode but not so comfortable to live in. If this was the effect produced upon strangers, we can imagine what a perpetual joy to a Spartan peer was the contemplation of the Spartan constitution; how he felt a sense of superiority in being a citizen of that city, and a pride in living up to its ideal and fulfilling the obligations of his nobility. In his mouth 'not beautiful' meant 'contrary to the Spartan laws', which were believed to have been inspired by Apollo. This deep admiration for their constitution as an ideally beautiful creation, the conviction that it was incapable of improvement—being, in truth, wonderfully effective in realising its aims—is bound up with the conservative spirit of the Spartans,

Greek admiration of Sparta

shown so conspicuously in their use of their old iron bars down to the time of Alexander the Great.

It was inevitable that, as time went on, there should be many fallings away, and that some of the harder laws should, by tacit agreement, be ignored. The other Greeks were always happy to point to the weak spots in the Spartan armour. From an early period it seems to have been a permitted thing for a citizen to acquire land in addition to his original lot. As such lands were not, like the original lot, inalienable, but could be sold or divided, inequalities in wealth necessarily arose, and the 'communism' which we observed in the life of the citizens was only superficial. But it was specially provided by law that no Spartan should possess wealth in the form of gold or silver. This law was at first eluded by the device of depositing money in foreign temples, and it ultimately became a dead letter; Spartans even gained throughout Greece an evil reputation for avarice. By the fourth century they had greatly degenerated, and those who wrote studies of the Lacedaemonian constitution contrasted Sparta as it should be and used to be with Sparta as it was.

Degeneration of Sparta

There is no doubt that the Spartan system of discipline grew up by degrees; yet the argument from design might be plausibly used to prove that it was the original creation of a single lawgiver. We may observe how well articulated and how closely interdependent were its various parts. The whole discipline of the society necessitated the existence of Helots; and on the other hand the existence of Helots necessitated such a discipline. The ephorate was the keystone of the structure; and in the dual kingship one might see a cunning intention to secure the powers of the ephors by perpetual jealousy between the kings. In the whole fabric one might trace an artistic unity which might be thought to argue the work of a single mind. And until lately this was generally believed to be the case; many still maintain the belief. A certain Lycurgus was said to have framed the Spartan institutions and enacted the Spartan laws about the beginning of the ninth century.

Unity of the constitution

Traditional date of Lycurgus 885 B.C.

But the grounds for believing that a Spartan lawgiver named Lycurgus ever existed have been questioned. The earliest statements as to the origin of the constitution date from the fifth century, and their discrepancy shows that they were mere guesses and that the true origins were buried completely in the obscurity of the past. Pindar attributed the Lacedaemonian institutions to Aegimius, the mythical

Statements of Pindar, Hellanicus, Thucydides

*and
Herodotus*

ancestor of the Dorian tribes; the historian Hellanicus regarded them as the creation of the two first kings of Sparta, Procles and Eurysthenes. The more critical Thucydides, less ready to record conjectures, contents himself with saying that the Lacedaemonian constitution had existed for rather more than four hundred years at the end of the Peloponnesian war. Herodotus states that the Spartans declared Lycurgus to have been the guardian of one of their early kings and to have introduced from Crete their laws and institutions. But the divergent accounts of this historian's contemporaries, who ignore Lycurgus altogether, suggest that it was only one of many guesses and not a generally accepted tradition. It may be added that if the old Spartan poet Tyrtaeus had mentioned Lycurgus as a lawgiver, his words would certainly have been quoted by later writers, and therefore it is argued that he knew nothing of such a tradition.

*Silence of
Tyrtaeus*

*Lycurgus
deified*

Hence the theory has arisen that Lycurgus (*Lyco-vorgos*) was not a man; he was only a god. He was an Arcadian deity or 'hero'—perhaps some form of the Arcadian Zeus Lycaeus, god of the wolf-mountain; and his name meant 'wolf-repeller'. He was worshipped at Lacedaemon, where he had a shrine, and it is conjectured that his cult was adopted by the Spartans from the older inhabitants whom they displaced. He may have also been connected with Olympia, for his name was inscribed on a very ancient quoit—the so-called quoit of Iphitus—which was preserved there and perhaps dated from the seventh century. The belief that this deity was a Spartan lawgiver, promoted by the Delphic oracle, gradually gained ground and in the fourth century generally prevailed.[11] Aristotle believed it, and made use of the old quoit to fix the date of the Lycurgean legislation to the first half of the eighth century. But while everybody regarded Lycurgus as unquestionably an historical personage, candid investigation confessed that nothing certain was known concerning him, and the views about his chronology were many and various.

*Quoit of
Iphitus*

The Cretan Constitutions

Ancient Greek students of constitutional history were struck by some obvious and remarkable resemblances between the Spartan and the Cretan states, and it was believed by many that the Spartan constitution was derived from Crete, though there are notable differences as well as notable likenesses. It will be convenient to glance here at the political condition of this island, to which we shall seldom have to recur, since owing to its geographical situation and the lack of political union it was isolated and withdrawn from the main course of Greek history.

*Genuine
Cretans*

In a passage in the *Odyssey* the inhabitants of Crete are divided into five classes: Achaeans, Eteo-Cretans, Cydonians, Dorians and Pelasgians.[12] Of these the Eteo-Cretans may represent the original people who dwelt in the island before the Greeks came, like the Eteo-Carpathians of Carpathos. They survived chiefly in the eastern part of the island, and they continued to speak their own tongue in historical times, writing it, however, not in their ancient linear script but in Greek characters. A specimen of it—but we have no key to the meaning—has been preserved in some inscriptions found at Praesus, their most important city. The people of Cydonia were perhaps also a remnant of the old population. The Achaeans and Pelasgians point to Thessaly, and there are some links which seem to connect Cretan towns with Perrhaebia. It is probable that early settlers from Thessaly found their way to Crete.

But the most important settlers belonged to the Dorian branch of the Greek race, easily recognised by the three tribes, Hylleis, Pamphyli and Dymanes, which always accompanied its migrations. These three tribes can be traced in many Cretan cities; new settlers came from Argolis and Laconia and mingled with the older inhabitants, refounding many cities. Thus Gortyn in the south of the island, in the valley of the river Lethaeus, was resettled; and her neighbour Phaestos, distinguished by a mention in Homer, was invaded by newcomers from Argolis. 'Well-built Lyttus', in its central site, also of Homeric fame, and Polyrrhenion, 'rich in sheep', in the north-western corner, a haunt of the divine huntress Dictynna, were both colonised from Laconia. Cnossus 'the great city' of Minos, Cnossus 'the broad', was repeopled by Dorians, and though it never attained to its former splendour, it remained the leading city in Crete. In the Cretan cities there were of course many local divergences, but the general resemblances are so close, wherever we can trace the facts, that for our purpose we may safely follow the example of the ancients in assuming a general type of Cretan polity.

*(Od. iii.
293.)*

*(Od. xix.
178; Il.
xviii. 591.)*

The population of a Cretan state consisted of two classes, warriors and serfs. In a few cases, where one city had subjugated another,

99

The serfs

the people of the subject city held somewhat the same position as the Laconian Perioeci and formed a third class, but these cases were exceptional. In general, one of the main differences between a Cretan state and Sparta was that the Cretan state had no perioeci. There were two kinds of serfs, *mnoitai* and *aphamiotai*. The *mnoites* belonged to the state, while the *aphamiotes,* also called *clarotes* or 'lot-man', were attached to the lots of the citizens, and belonged to the owners of the lots. These bondsmen cultivated the land themselves and could possess private property, like the Spartan Helots, but though we do not know exactly what their obligations were, they seem to have been in some ways in a better condition than the bondsmen of Laconia. If the *pastas* or lord of a Cretan serf died childless, the serf had an interest in his property. He could contract a legal marriage, and his family was recognised by law. The two privileges from which he was always jealously excluded were the carrying of arms and the practice of athletic exercises in the gymnasia. Unlike the Helots, the Cretan serfs found their condition tolerable, and we never hear that they revolted. The geographical conditions of the Cretans enabled them to excuse their slaves from military service.

Of the monarchical period in Crete we know nothing. In the sixth century we find that monarchy has been abolished by the aristocracies, and that the executive governments are in the hands of boards of ten annual magistrates, entitled *kosmoi*. The *kosmoi* were chosen from certain important clans (*startoi*), and the military as well as the other functions of the king had passed into their hands. They were assisted by the advice of

(Gerusia)

the Council of elders, which was elected from those who had filled the office of *kosmos*. The resolves of the *kosmoi* and Council were laid before the *agorai* or general assemblies of citizens, who merely voted and had no right to propose or discuss.

Comparison of Crete and Sparta

There is a superficial resemblance between this constitution, which prevailed in most Cretan cities, and that of Sparta. The Cretan *agora* answers to the Spartan Assembly, the Cretan to the Spartan *gerusia*, and the *kosmoi* to the ephors. The most obvious difference is that in Crete there was no royalty. But there is another important difference: the democratic feature of the Spartan constitution is absent in Crete. While the ephors were chosen from all the citizens, in a Cretan state only certain noble families were eligible to the office of *kosmos*; and, as the *gerusia* was chosen from

the *kosmoi*, it is clear that the whole power of the state resided in a privileged class consisting of those families or clans. Thus the Cretan state was a close aristocracy.

The true likeness between Sparta and Crete lies in the circumstance that the laws and institutions of both countries aimed at creating a class of warriors. Boys were taught to read and write, and to recite certain songs ordained by law; but the chief part of their training was physical, with a view to making them good soldiers. At the age of seventeen they were admitted into 'herds', *agelai*, answering to the Spartan *buai,* which were organised by sons of noble houses and supported at the expense of the state. The members of these associations went through a training in the public gymnasia or *dromoi*, and hence were called *dromeis*. Great days were held, on which sham fights took place between these 'herds' to the sound of lyres and flutes. The *dromeus* was of age in the eyes of the law, and he was bound to marry, but his wife continued to live in the house of her father or kinsmen, until he passed out of the state of a *dromeus* and became a 'man'. The citizens were divided into *hetairiai,* and each *hetairia* had its own *andreion*, corresponding to the Spartan *phiditia* but the boys were also permitted to join them. These meals were not defrayed altogether, as at Sparta, by the contributions of the members, but were at least partly paid for by the state; and the state also made provision for the sustenance of the women. The public income, which defrayed these and other such burdens and maintained the worship of the gods, must have been derived from public land cultivated by the *mnoites,* and distinct from the land which was apportioned in lots among the citizens.

Cretan education

We see then that in the discipline and education of the citizens, in the common meals of the men, in general political objects, there is a close and significant likeness between Sparta and Crete. But otherwise there are great differences. (1) In Crete there were, as a rule, no Perioeci; (2) the Cretan serfs lived under more favourable conditions than the Helots, and were not a constant source of danger; (3) kingship did not survive in Crete, and consequently (4) the functions which in Sparta were divided between kings and ephors were in Crete united in the hands of the *kosmoi;* (5) the Cretan state was an aristocracy, while Sparta, so far as the city itself was concerned, was a limited democracy—a difference which clearly reveals itself in (6) the modes of electing *kosmoi* and ephors; (7) there is a more advanced form of communism in Crete, in so far as state stores contribute largely to the maintenance of the citizens. If one city had become dominant in Crete and reduced the others to subjection, the resemblance between Laconia and Crete would have been much greater. A class of Cretan perioeci would have forthwith been formed.

The Supremacy and Decline of Argos. The Olympian Games

The rebellion of Messenia had been especially formidable to Sparta, because the rebels had been supported by two foreign powers, Arcadia and Pisa. Part of Arcadia seems to have been united at this time under the lordship of the king of the Arcadian Orchomenus. The king of Pisa on the Alpheus had recently risen to new power and honour with the help of Argos; and Argos itself had been playing a prominent part in the peninsula under the leadership of *Pheidon of* her king Pheidon. The reign of this king was *Argos* the last epoch of Argos as an active power of *(middle of* the first rank. We know little about him, but *seventh* his name became so famous that in later times *century)* the royal house of distant Macedonia, when it reached the height of its success in Alexander the Great, was anxious to connect its line of descent with Pheidon. Under his auspices a system of measures was introduced into Argos and the Peloponnesus. These measures were *Phei-* called after his name *Pheidonian*, and were *donian* likewise adopted at Athens; they seem to have *measures* been closely linked with the Aeginetan system of weights. But the only clear action of Pheidon *Pheidon at* is his expedition to the west. He led an Argive *Olympia* army across Arcadia to the banks of the Alpheus and presided there over the celebration of the Olympian festival, which is now for the first time heard of in the history of Greece.[13]

The Altis The *altis* or sacred grove of Olympia lay *at Olympia* under the wooded mount of Cronus, where the river Cladeus flows into the Alpheus, in the angle between the two streams. It was dedicated to the worship of Zeus; but the spot was probably sacred to Pelops before Zeus claimed it for himself, and Pelops, degraded to the rank of a hero, kept his own sacred precinct *Belongs to* within the larger enclosure. The sanctuary was *the Pisans* in the territory of Pisa, and it is possible that the care of the worship and the conduct of the festivals belonged originally to the Pisan community. But the men of Elis, the northern neighbours of Pisa, set their hearts on having the control of the Olympian sanctuary, which,

though it is not once mentioned, as are Delphi and Dodona in the poems of Homer, must by the seventh century have won a high prestige in the Peloponnese and drawn many visitors. As Elis was stronger than Pisa, the Eleans *Usurped* finally succeeded in usurping the conduct of *by Eleans,* the festival.[14] Games were the chief feature of *572 B.C.* the festival, which was held every fourth year, at the time of the second full moon after midsummer's day. The games at first included foot-races, boxing and wrestling; chariot-races were added later. Such contests were an ancient institution in Greece. We do not know how far back they go, or in what circumstances they were first introduced, but the funeral games of Patroclus, described in the *Iliad*, suggest that they were a feature of Ionian life in the eighth century. We can see but dimly into the political relations of Pheidon's age, but we can discern at least that Sparta lent her countenance to Elis in this usurpation, and that Argos, jealous of the growing power of Sparta, espoused the cause of Pisa. This was the purpose of king Pheidon's expedition to Olympia. He took the management of the *Pheidon* games out of the hands of Elis and restored it *restores* to Pisa. And for many years Pisa maintained *Olympia* her rights. She maintained them so long as *to Pisa* Sparta, absorbed in the Messenian strife, had no help to spare for Elis; and during that time she did what she could to help the enemies of Sparta. But when the revolt was suppressed, it was inevitable that Elis should again, with Spartan help, win the control of the games, for Argos, declining under the successors of Pheidon, could give no aid to Pisa.

When king Pheidon held his state at *The temple* Olympia, the most impressive shrine in the *of Hera* altis was the temple of Hera and Zeus; and this *and Zeus* is the most ancient temple of which the founda- *(Heraeum)* tions are still preserved on the soil of Hellas. It was built of sun-baked bricks, upon lower courses of stone, and the Doric columns were of wood. Pausanias dated the foundation in *c.* 1096, but the archaeological evidence indi- cates that the first temple was built near the end of the eighth century and replaced *c.* 600 by a stone temple with the same plan.[15] The original dedication was to Hera and Zeus, but in the middle of the fifth century a grander temple, eclipsing the Heraeum, was built for Zeus. The mythical institution of the games was ascribed to Pelops or to Heracles, and when the Eleans usurped the presidency the story gradually took shape that the celebration *The* had been revived by the Spartan Lycurgus and *traditional* the Elean Iphitus in the year 776 B.C.; and *first* this year was reckoned as the first Olympiad.[16] *Olympiad,* *776 B.C.*

3.3 Temple of Hera, Olympia

From that year until the visit of Pheidon, the Eleans professed to have presided over the feast, and their account of the matter won its way into general belief.

The games become Pan-hellenic

It is possible that king Pheidon reorganised the games and inaugurated a new stage in the history of the festival. At all events, by the beginning of the sixth century the festival was no longer an event of merely Peloponnesian interest. It had become famous wherever the Greek tongue was spoken, and when the festival came round in each cycle of four years the banks of the Alpheus were thronged with athletes and horses and spectators from all quarters of the Greek world. During the celebration of the festival a sacred truce was observed, and the men of Elis claimed that in those days their territory was inviolable. The prize for victory in the games was a wreath of wild olive, but rich rewards always awaited the victor when he returned home in triumph and laid the Olympian crown in the chief temple of his city.

Geo-graphical position of Olympia facing westward

It may seem strange that the greatest and most glorious of all Panhellenic festivals should have been celebrated near the western shores of the Peloponnese. One might have looked to find it nearer the Aegean. But situated where it was, the scene of the great games was all the nearer to the Greeks beyond the western sea; and none of the peoples of the mother-country vied more eagerly or more often in the contests of Olympia than the colonists who had found new homes far away on Sicilian and Italian soil. This nearness of Olympia to the western colonies comes into one's thoughts when, standing in the sacred altis, one sees the terrace on the northern side of the precinct and the scanty remains of the row of 12 treasure-houses which once stood there. For of those 12 treasuries five at least were dedicated by Sicilian and Italian cities. Thus the Olympian festival helped the colonies of the west to keep in touch with the mother-country; it furnished a centre where Greeks of all parts met and exchanged their ideas and experiences; it was one of the institutions which expressed and quickened the consciousness of fellowship among the scattered folks of the Greek race; and it became a model, as we shall see, for other festivals of the same kind which concurred in promoting a feeling of national unity.

The treasuries

Festival promotes national feeling in Greece

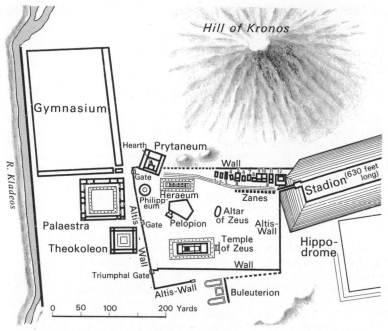

Hill of Kronos

Gymnasium

R. Kladeos

Hearth · Prytaneum

Wall

Gate

Heraeum

Philippeum

Palaestra

Gate · Pelopion

Altis-Wall

Theokoleon

Zanes

Altar of Zeus

Temple of Zeus

Altis-Wall

Stadion (630 feet long)

Hippo-drome

Triumphal Gate

Altis-Wall

Wall

Buleuterion

0   50   100   200 Yards

12.   OLYMPIA

a Treasure Houses

1 *Sicyon (5th Cent.)*	**8** *Cyrene (early 6th Cent.)*
4 *Syracuse (end of 6th Cent.)*	**9** *Selinus (late 6th Cent.)*
5 *Epidamnos*	**10** *Metapontion*
6 *Byzantium*	**11** *Megara (late 6th Cent.)*
7 *Sybaris (6th Cent.)*	**12** *Gela (6th Cent.)*

3.4   Model of Olympia

Democratic Movements: Lawgivers and Tyrants

Demand for written laws

There can be no assurance that equal justice will be meted out to all, so long as the laws by which the judge is supposed to act are not accessible to all. A written code of laws is a condition of just judgement, however just the laws themselves may be. It was therefore natural that one of the first demands the people in Greek cities pressed upon their aristocratic governments, and one of the first concessions those governments were forced to make was a written law. It must be borne in mind that in those days acts which injured only the individual, and did not touch the gods or the state, were left to the injured person to deal with as best he could. The state did not interfere. Even in the case of blood-shedding, it devolved upon the kinsfolk of the slain man to exact punishment from the slayer. Then, as social order developed along with centralisation, the state took justice partly into its own hands, and the injured man, before he could punish the wrongdoer, was obliged to charge him before a judge, who decided the punishment. But it must be noted that no crime could come before a judge unless the injured person came forward as accuser. The case of blood-shedding was exceptional, owing to the religious ideas connected with it. It was felt that the shedder of blood was not only impure himself, but had also defiled the gods of the community; so that, as a consequence of this theory, manslaughter of every form came under the class of crimes against the religion of the state.

Early lawgivers (seventh century)

The work of writing down the laws, and fixing customs in legal shape, was probably in most cases combined with the work of re-forming, and thus the great codifiers of the seventh century were also lawgivers. Among them the most famous were the misty figures of Zaleucus who made laws for the western Locrians, and Charondas the legislator of Catane; the clearer figure of the Athenian Draco, of whom more will be said later, and, most famous of all, Solon the Wise. But other cities had their lawgivers too, men of knowledge and experience; the names of some are preserved but they are mere names. It is probable that the laws of Sparta herself, which she afterwards attributed to a god, were first shaped and written down at this period. The cities of Crete too were affected by the prevalent spirit of law-shaping, and some fragments are preserved of the early laws of Gortyn, which were the beginning of an epoch of legislative activity culminating in the Gortynian Code which has come down to us on tablets of stone.

Political struggles: democratic movements

In many cases the legislation was accompanied by political concessions to the people, and it was part of the lawgiver's task to modify the constitution. But for the most part this was only the beginning of a long political conflict, the people striving for freedom and equality, the privileged classes struggling to retain their exclusive rights. The social distress, touched on in a previous chapter, was the sharp spur which drove the people on in this effort towards popular government. The struggle was in some cases to end in the establishment of a demo-cracy; in many cases, the oligarchy succeeded in maintaining itself and keeping the people down; in most cases, perhaps, the result was a perpetual oscillation between oligarchy and democracy—an endless series of revolutions, too often sullied by violence. But though democracy was not everywhere victorious—though even the states in which it was most firmly established were exposed to the danger of oligarchical conspiracies—yet everywhere the people aspired to it; and we may say that the chief feature of the domestic history of most Greek cities, from the end of the seventh century forward, is an endeavour, here success-ful, there frustrated, to establish or maintain popular government. In this sense then we have now reached a period in which the Greek world is striving and tending to pass from the aristocratic to the democratic commonwealth. The movement passed by some states, like Thessaly, while remote kingdoms like Mace-donia and Molossia were not affected.

Rise of new un-constitu-tional mon-archies in some states

As usually, or at least frequently, happens in such circumstances, the popular movement received help from within the camp of the adversary. It was help indeed for which there was no reason to be grateful to those who gave it, for it was not given for love of the people. In many cities feuds existed between some of the power-holding families, and when one family was in the ascendant its rivals were tempted to make use of the popular discontent in order to subvert it. Thus discontented nobles came forward to be the leaders of the discontented masses. But when the govern-ment was overthrown, the revolution generally resulted in a temporary return to monarchy. The noble leader seized the supreme power and maintained it by armed might. The mass of the people were not yet ripe for taking the power into their own hands, and they were generally glad to entrust it to the man who had helped them to overthrow the hated govern-ment of the nobles. This new kind of monarchy was very different from the old, for the position of the monarch did not rest on hereditary right but on physical force.

The tyrannis

Such illegitimate monarchs were called tyrants, to distinguish them from the hereditary kings, and this form of monarchy was called a *tyrannis*. The name 'tyrant' was perhaps derived from Lydia, and first used by Greeks in designating the Lydian monarchs; Archilochus, in whose fragments we first meet 'tyrannis', applied it to the sovereignty of Gyges. The word was in itself morally neutral and did not imply that the monarch was bad or cruel; there was nothing self-contradictory in a good tyrant, and many tyrants were beneficent. But the isolation of these rulers who, being without the support of legitimacy, depended on armed force, so often urged them to be suspicious and cruel that the *tyrannis* came into bad odour; arbitrary acts of oppression were associated with the name, and 'tyrant' inclined to the evil sense in which modern languages have adopted it. For the Greek dislike of the *tyrannis* there was however a deeper cause than the fact that many tyrants were oppressors. It placed in the hands of an unconstitutional ruler arbitrary control, whether he exercised it or not, over the lives and fortunes of the citizens. It was thus repugnant to the Greek love of freedom, and it seemed to arrest their constitutional growth. As a matter of fact, this temporary arrest during the period when the first tyrannies prevailed may have been useful; for the *tyrannis*, though its direct political effect was retarding, forwarded the progress of the people in other directions. And even from a constitutional point of view it may have had its uses at this period. In some cases it secured an interval of repose and growth, during which the people won experience and knowledge to fit them for self-government.

No such thing in Greek history as an age of tyrannies

The period which saw the fall of the aristocracies is often called the age of the tyrants. The expression is unhappy, because it might easily mislead. The *tyrannis* did indeed first come into existence at this period; there was a large crop of tyrants at much about the same time in different parts of Greece; they all performed the same function of overthrowing aristocracies, and in many cases they paved the way for democracies. But on the other hand, the *tyrannis* was not a form of government which appeared only at this transitional crisis, and then passed away. There is no age in the subsequent history of Greece which might not see, and did not actually see, the rise of tyrants here and there. Tyranny was always with the

Greeks. It, as well as oligarchy, was a danger by which their democracies were threatened at all periods.

Tyrants in Asiatic Greece

Ionia may have been the original home of the *tyrannis*, influenced by the seductive example of the rich court of the Lydian 'tyrants' at Sardis. But of the Ionian tyrannies we know little. We hear of factions and feuds in the cities, of aristocratic houses overthrown and despotisms established in various states. A tyrant of Ephesus marries the daughter of the Lydian monarch Alyattes. The most famous of these tyrants was Thrasybulus of Miletus, under whose rule that city held a more brilliant position than ever. Abroad, he took part in planting some of the colonies on the Black Sea, and successfully resisted the menaces of Lydia. At home, he developed the craft of tyranny to a fine art.

Thrasybulus, c. 610 B.C.

Mytilene

In Lesbian Mytilene we see the *tyrannis*, and also a method by which it might be avoided. Mytilene had won great commercial prosperity; its ruling nobles, the Penthilids, were wealthy and luxurious and oppressed the people. Tyrants rose and fell in rapid succession; the echoes of hatred and jubilation still ring to us from relics of the lyric poems of Alcaeus. 'Let us drink and reel, for Myrsilus is dead'. The poet was a noble and a fighter; but in a war with the Athenians on the coast of the Hellespont he threw away his shield, like Archilochus, and it hung as a trophy at Sigeum. He plotted with Pittacus against the tyrant, but Pittacus was not a noble and his friendship with Alcaeus was not enduring. Pittacus, however, who distinguished himself for bravery in the same war with Athens, was to be the saviour of the state. He gained the trust of the people and was elected ruler for a period of ten years in order to heal the sores of the city. Such a governor, possessing supreme power but for a limited time, was called an *aesymnētes*. Pittacus gained the reputation of a wise lawgiver and a firm, moderate ruler. He banished the nobles who opposed him, among others the two most famous of all Lesbians, the poets Alcaeus and Sappho. At the end of ten years he laid down his office, to be enrolled after his death in the number of the Seven Wise Men. The ship of state had reached the haven, to apply a metaphor of Alcaeus, and the exiles could safely be allowed to return.

Myrsilus, tyrant

Alcaeus (c. 600-570 B.C.)

Pittacus

Holds office of aesymnētes [first years of sixth century?]

This was the brilliant period of the history of Lesbos, and a few surviving fragments of its two great poets, who struck new notes and devised new cadences of lyric song, give a glimpse of the free and luxurious life of the Aeolian island. The radiant genius of Sappho was inspired by her passionate attachments to young Lesbian maidens; the songs of Alcaeus, mirroring the commotions of party warfare, rang with the clatter of arms and the clinking of drinking-cups.

The Tyrannies of Central Greece

The three Isthmian tyrannies

About the middle of the seventh century, three tyrannies arose in central Greece in the neighbourhood of the Isthmus: at Corinth, at Sicyon and at Megara. In each case the development was different and is in each case instructive. In Sicyon the tyranny is brilliant and beneficent, in Corinth brilliant and oppressive, in Megara short-lived and followed by long internal conflict.

I. Corinth

In the eighth and early seventh centuries Corinth had been the wealthiest city on the Greek mainland. Her situation commanding the land route north and south and the narrow stretch of isthmus, which linked the Aegean with the Corinthian Gulf and offered the safest route to the west, encouraged the development of trade. Already before the end of the eighth century Corinthian pottery, Corinthian perfumes and other products were being widely distributed in Italy and Sicily. Corinth's potters were the first mainlanders to exploit the opportunities offered by renewed contact with the east and to enrich their repertoire with a wide range of oriental motifs.[17] Her early power is witnessed by the foundation of Corcyra and Syracuse, and even more by the change in the nature of imports to the west which follows the first wave of colonisation. In the early stages of this trade, pottery from many widely scattered production centres in the Aegean and on the mainland was being carried to the west. By the beginning of the seventh century Corinth seems to have won a virtual monopoly which lasted until the rise of Athenian export towards the middle of the sixth century. But her colonies were becoming increasingly independent, and towards the middle of the seventh century she could do no more than hold her own in a sea battle with Corcyra. The weakening in the leadership of Corinth invited challenge from within.

Cypselus: legend of his birth and name

The ruling clan of the Bacchiads was overthrown by Cypselus, who had put himself at the head of the people. A characteristic legend was formed at an early time about the birth of Cypselus, suggested by the connection of his name with κυψέλη, a jar. His mother was a Bacchiad lady named Labda, who, being lame and consequently compelled to marry out of

her own class, married a certain Eetion, a man of the people. Having no children and consulting the Delphic oracle on the matter, Eetion received this reply:

> High honour is thy due, Eetion,
> Yet no man doth thee honour, as were right.
> Labda thy wife will bear a huge millstone,
> Destined to fall on them who rule alone,
> And free thy Corinth from their rightless might.

The prophecy came to the ears of the Bacchiads and was confirmed to them by another oracle. So, as soon as Labda's child was born, they sent ten men to slay it. When the men came to the court of Eetion's dwelling they found that he was not at home, and they asked Labda for the infant. Suspecting nothing, she gave it to one of them to take in his arms, but, as he was about to dash it to the ground, the child smiled at him, and he had not the heart to slay it. He passed it on to the second, but he too was moved with pity; and so it was passed round from hand to hand, and none of the ten could find it in his heart to destroy it. Then giving the infant back to the mother, and going out into the courtyard, they reviled each other for their weakness, and resolved to go in again and do the deed together. But Labda listening at the door overheard what they said and hid the child in a jar, where none of them thought of looking. Thus the boy was saved, but the men falsely reported to the Bacchiads that they had performed their errand.

The Bacchiads were banished and their property confiscated; dangerous persons were executed, and Cypselus took the reins of government into his own hands. But after his preliminary purge Cypselus seems to have ruled with moderation and he was sufficiently popular to be able to dispense with a bodyguard. He gave new direction to policy by attempting to build up a new kind of colonial empire. Syracuse and Corcyra had been established, like other early Greek colonies, as independent states and, as we have seen, Corcyra was independent enough towards the end of Bacchiad rule to challenge her mother city in a naval battle. Cypselus now built up a network of colonies along the north-west coast directly controlled by Corinth and ruled in her interests by members of the tyrant's family. The Acarnanian peninsula of Leucas was settled and, for greater security, was made an island under Cypselus' successor by the cutting of a canal through the narrow isthmus. Further north Anactorion was founded on the south side of the Ambraciot Gulf and inland, on the north side, Ambracia. There may be evidence that Corcyra actively resisted this colonisation at first in the epitaph of a Corcyraean who died 'fighting beside the ships by the waters of the (river) Arachthus';[18] but before Cypselus died an understanding had been reached and the two states shared in the colonisation of Epidamnus on the Adriatic coast north of Corcyra.

The trade that developed with the natives through these new colonies increased the popularity that Cypselus had won by breaking the exclusive rule of the Bacchiads. He had also increased the prestige of Corinth as well as of his own house by his lavish generosity to the great Panhellenic sanctuaries at Delphi and Olympia. Since in the Greek aristocratic states, as later in early Rome, the control of religion rested primarily with a nobility of birth, it was natural that tyrants should seek a higher sanction for their rule from religious centres that were recognised throughout the Greek world. Delphi, realising that the days of the aristocracies were numbered, had given oracles favourable to Cypselus: he repaid Apollo handsomely by building a Corinthian treasury at Delphi. In the fifth century the inscription said that it was the Corinthians who made the dedication; Herodotus knew that it was the personal gift of Cypselus, whose name was erased when the Cypselid tyranny had outlived its usefulness and was overthrown.[19] At Olympia Cypselus dedicated a colossal gilded statue of Zeus and more than seven hundred years later a large chest of cedarwood decorated with mythological scenes in relief was still one of the most admired treasures in the temple of Hera. It was called the chest of Cypselus and was said to have been the hiding-place in which Labda hid her baby.[20] It would have been a very poor hiding-place indeed, and the style of the reliefs suggests that it is more probably a dedication of Periander, selected for its magnificent craftsmanship.

Cypselus ruled for some thirty years and was succeeded by his eldest son. Periander continued his father's policies and extended them, and under his direction Corinth was relatively more prosperous and powerful than she was ever to become again. But tyranny by its very nature was almost bound to be less popular in the second than in the first generation: Periander had to face increasing opposition at home and towards the end of his life had to rely on repression. His total achievement, however, was very considerable. Cypselus had concentrated his expansion in the west; Periander

added Apollonia on the Adriatic coast between Corcyra and Epidamnus. He also broke new ground by sending one of his sons to establish a colony at Potidaea on the westernmost promontory of Chalcidice. More important was his deliberate promotion of Corinthian influence in the east of which there are several scattered hints in the sources.

Periander's main ally in the east was Thrasybulus, tyrant of Miletus. This was a reversal of relationships under the Bacchiads, for towards the end of the eighth century a Corinthian shipwright had built ships for Samos and the incident was of sufficient importance to be included by Thucydides in his very brief summary of the growth of sea power; and in the great war for the Lelantine plain in Euboea Miletus and Samos were on opposite sides. This war was singled out by Thucydides in his account of early Greek history because of its large scale and widespread alliances. Herodotus tells us that Miletus supported Eretria and Samos Chalcis, and Thucydides implies that other states were also involved: it was probably at this time that Samos raided Aegina, a natural enemy of Corinth. How soon Corinth changed her allegiance we do not know, but for trade expansion in the east Miletus was the more attractive partner. While both Samos and Miletus were strongly represented in Egypt the influence of Miletus in the Euxine was paramount and, after her war with Alyattes, she was on good terms with the rich Lydian court at Sardis. It is not coincidence that Corinthian pottery is more widely distributed in the east in the early sixth century, and it may have been with Corinthian assistance that Miletus developed such close ties with Sybaris in south Italy that she went into public mourning when Sybaris was destroyed by Croton.[21]

Herodotus also recalls the diplomatic assistance given by Periander to Miletus when she was hard pressed by the Lydians. In the course of one of their annual invasions the Lydians accidentally burnt down a temple of Athena. Alyattes sought the advice of Delphi and was told to rebuild the temple. Periander got to know this and passed the information to Thrasybulus. As a result, when Alyattes sent envoys to negotiate a truce while he rebuilt the temple, the Milesians had devised a scenario which convinced the Lydians that Miletus had unlimited food and could hold out indefinitely. The close ties between the two tyrants is even better illustrated by the well-known story of the ears of corn. According to Herodotus, Periander, early in his tyranny, sent to

Thrasybulus for political advice. Thrasybulus made no comment but took the Corinthian messenger through a field of wheat and as they passed through he cut off the tallest ears, telling the messenger to report what he had seen to his master. The story is repeated by Aristotle with the roles reversed, a more appropriate version in view of Periander's reputation for strong action and cunning. Periander's reputation in the Aegean world is confirmed by the acceptance of his arbitration when he supported the Athenian occupation of Sigeum at the entrance to the Hellespont which Mytilene had challenged in war.

Periander's interest in Egypt is reflected in the name of his nephew and successor, Psammetichus, a pretty compliment to the Egyptian king, and it may have been the canal works of Necho which suggested to Periander the cutting which made Leucas an island. He also had designs of cutting a canal through the Isthmus to link the Corinthian Gulf with the Aegean, but the rock was too hard and his resources too limited to achieve what even the Romans found too formidable. Periander did, however, devise an alternative which partially fulfilled the function of a canal. A stone-paved way was built across the isthmus with two parallel grooves to fit a carriage on which light boats could be transported from one sea to the other. This *Diolkos* (drag-way), as it was called, could not take larger merchantmen but their cargoes could be carried across and reloaded on another ship.[22]

The Cypselid period and particularly the rule of Periander saw important developments in the arts and crafts at Corinth. A new form of poetry, the dithyramb, which derived from the crude songs at vintage feasts in honour of Dionysus, were brought to Corinth by Arion from Methymna in the island of Lesbos. The dithyramb was destined to encourage some fine poems, and anything that contributed to the cult of Dionysus was politically valuable, for Dionysus belonged to the whole people.

In architecture, Corinthian skill had made an important contribution to the development of the temple. In the course of the seventh century men began to translate into stone the old shrine of brick and wood; and stone temples arose in all parts of the Greek world— the lighter 'Ionic' form in Ionia, the heavier 'Doric' in the elder Greece. By the re-discovery of roof-tiles, Corinthian workmen rendered it practicable to give a considerable inclination to the roof; and thus in each gable of the temple a large triangular space was left, inviting the sculptor to fill it with a story in marble. The pediment, as we name it, was called by the Greeks the 'eagle'; and thus it was said that Corinth had discovered the eagle. Corinthian pottery, which had developed remarkably under the Bacchiads, won even wider markets under the tyrants; but quantity seems to have undermined quality. The controlled vigour and imagination of the Proto-Corinthian and early Corinthian styles is gradually replaced by fluent mediocrity; and not long after the fall of the tyranny the finer quality of Attic black-figure vases was beginning to eclipse the Corinthian potter. By the end of the sixth century Attic pots had virtually conquered the western market, once almost a Corinthian preserve, though the continued friendship of Corinth with Athens suggests that the Athenians may have used Corinthian ships to carry their goods to the west until the fifth century. The seven great limestone columns, which for long were the only sign to mark the site of ancient Corinth, were thought to be a relic of Periander's rule, but systematic exploration of the foundations has shown that this temple of Apollo was built a generation after the fall of the tyranny.

Judged by modern standards, the government of Periander was strict, though in

Invention of roof-tiles

ἀετός *Pottery*

Periander

3.5 The Diolkos (see note, page 553)

3.6   Columns of the temple of Apollo, Corinth

Laws restricting individual liberty

accordance with the practice in other cities and with the Greek views of the time. There were laws forbidding men to acquire large numbers of slaves or to live beyond their income; suppressing excessive luxury and idleness; hindering country people from fixing their abode in the city.

Tyranny at Epidaurus

In his home-life Periander was unlucky. He married Melissa, the daughter of Procles, who had made himself tyrant of Epidaurus. It was believed that he put her to death, and this led to an irreconcilable quarrel with his son Lycophron. The story is that Procles invited his two grandchildren, Lycophron and an elder brother, to his court. When they were departing he said to them, 'Do you know, boys, who killed your mother?' The elder was dull and did not understand; but the words sank into the heart of Lycophron, and henceforward he showed dislike and suspicion towards his father. Periander, pressing him, discovered what Procles had said; and the affair ended, for the time, in a war with Epidaurus in which Procles was captured, and the banishment of Lycophron to Corcyra. As years went on and Periander was growing old, seeing that his elder son was dull of wit, he desired to hand over the government to Lycophron. But the

Tale of Lyco-phron, son of Periander

Periander reduces Epidaurus

Lycophron at Corcyra

son was implacable and did not deign even to answer his father's messenger. Then Periander sent his daughter to intercede, but Lycophron replied that he would never come to Corinth while his father was there. Periander then decided to go himself to Corcyra and leave Corinth to his son, but the Corcyraeans were so terrified at the idea of having the tyrant among them that they slew Lycophron in order to foil the plan. For this act Periander took savage vengeance.[23]

The great tyrant died and was succeeded by his nephew Psammetichus, who having ruled for a few years was slain. With him the tyranny of the Cypselids came to an end, and a moderate oligarchy was firmly established. At the same time the Cypselid colonial system partly broke down, for Corcyra became independent and hostile, while the Ambraciots set up a democracy. But over her other colonies Corinth retained her influence, and was on friendly terms with all of them.

c. 586 B.C.

End of the tyranny

Of the Orthagorid tyranny at Sicyon, which was roughly contemporary with the Cypselids at Corinth, we know much less, but it was remembered for its long duration (a hundred years, it was said) and Aristotle emphasised the moderation of the dynasty. Orthagoras and

2. Sicyon

his two successors are mere names to us but Cleisthenes was one of the great figures of his day and could stand comparison with Periander. The character of Sicyon was very different from that of Corinth. While Corinth was primarily a trading city with restricted farm land and had played a leading part in colonisation, Sicyon had sent out no colonies. Her land was rich and expansive; she was well known for her fruit and vegetables, and her peasants were probably better off than those of Corinth or Megara. But she had a larger element of pre-Dorian stock in her population and friction between Dorian and non-Dorian seems to have been a major issue in the early years of Cleisthenes' tyranny. Sicyon had originally been occupied by Dorians from Argos and was regarded by Argos as part of the heritage of Temenus. It was probably an Argive attempt to control Sicyon that led to war and to a strong anti-Dorian reaction in Sicyon.

The most conspicuous expression of this reaction was the expulsion from Sicyon of the hero Adrastus who had led the seven Argive heroes against Thebes before the Trojan War and had claimed to inherit the throne of Sicyon from his grandfather. To emphasise his point Cleisthenes brought to Sicyon the hero Melanippus of Thebes, who had been the main enemy of Adrastus. At the same time, according to Herodotus, as part of his anti-Dorian policy he changed the names of the Sicyonian tribes. His own tribe Aigialeis became Archelaoi, rulers of the people, and the three Dorian tribes—Hylleis, Pamphyloi, Dymanes—were renamed Swineites, Assites, and Pigites. Herodotus adds the circumstantial detail that these new names were retained until sixty years after the death of Cleisthenes when the Dorian names were restored.[24] This is the kind of story in which we can safely part company with Herodotus. The names would have been too insulting to too many people: all that we can confidently infer is that there was a fourth non-Dorian tribe in Sicyon and that Cleisthenes supported their interests. If Cleisthenes' enemies called his tribe Goat-men (Aigi-aleis) a natural response would have been to go to the farmyard for nicknames for the Dorian tribes.

Cleisthenes was more widely remembered for his championship of the Delphic oracle in the Sacred War that broke out near the beginning of the sixth century.

The temple of Delphi, or Pytho, lay in the territory of the Phocian town of Crisa.[25] A Delphic Hymn tells how Apollo came 'to Crisa,

a hill facing to westward, under snowy Parnassus; a beetling cliff overhangs it, beneath is a hollow, rugged glen. Here,' he said, 'I will make me a fair temple, to be an oracle for men.' The poet's picture is perfect. The sanctuary of 'rocky Pytho' was terraced on a steep slope, hard under the bare sheer cliffs of Parnassus, looking down upon the deep glen of the Pleistus; an austere and majestic scene, supremely fitted for the utterance of the oracles of God. The city of Crisa lay on a vine-tressed hill to the west of the temple, and commanded its own plain which stretched southward to the sea. The men of Crisa claimed control over the Delphians and the oracle, and levied dues on the visitors who came to consult the deity. The Delphians desired to free themselves from the control of the Crisaeans, and they naturally looked for help to the great league of the north, in which the Thessalians, the ancient foes of the Phocians, were now the dominant member. The folks who belonged to this religious union were the 'dwellers around' the shrine of Demeter at Anthela, close to the pass of Thermopylae; and hence they were called the *Amphictiones* of Anthela or Pylae. The league was probably old: it was formed, at all events, before the Thessalians had incorporated Achaean Phthiotis in Thessaly, for the people of Phthiotis were an independent member of the league, which included the Locrians, Phocians, Boeotians and Athenians, as well as the Dorians, Malians, Dolopians, Enianes, Thessalians, Perrhaebians and Magnetes. The members of the league were bound not to destroy, or cut off running water from, any city which belonged to it.

The Amphictions espoused warmly the cause of Apollo and his Delphian servants, and declared a holy war against the men of Crisa who had violated the sacred territory.[26] Cleisthenes led a force from Sicyon across the gulf to join the crusade. Delphi had given him no comfort earlier: under new management he might expect a friendlier attitude. The Athenians also contributed a force under Alcmaeon whose family, as we shall see, had been put under a curse a generation earlier and would also welcome a change in the control of Delphi. It was not enough to conquer Crisa and force her to make terms or promises. As she was situated in such a strong position, commanding the road from the sea to the sanctuary, it was plain that the utter destruction of the city was the only conclusion of the war which could lead to the assured independence of the oracle. The Amphictions

Site of Delphi

Site of Crisa

The Amphictionic league

The Sacred War. c. 590 B.C.

3.7 Delphi

and Sicyonians took the city after a fierce struggle, razed it to the ground, and slew the inhabitants. The Crisaean plain was dedicated to the god; solemn and heavy curses were pronounced against whosoever should till it. The great gulf which sunders northern Greece from the Peloponnese, and whose old name 'Crisaean' testified to the greatness of the Phocian city, received, after this, its familiar name 'Corinthian' from the city of the Isthmus.

One of the consequences of this war was the establishment of a close connection between Delphi and the Amphictiony of Anthela. The Delphic shrine became a second place of meeting, and the league was often called the Delphic Amphictiony. The temple was taken under the protection of the league; the administration of the property of the god was placed in the hands of the Hieromnemones or sacred councillors, who met twice a year in spring and autumn, both at Anthela and at

Consequences for the amphictiony

Delphi. Two Hieromnemones were sent as its representatives by each member of the league. The oracle and the priestly nobles of Delphi thus won a position of independence; their great career of prosperity and power began. The Pythian games were now reorganised on a more splendid scale, and the ordering of them was one of the duties of the Amphictions. The festival became, like the Olympian, a four-yearly celebration, being held in the third year of each Olympiad; gymnastic contests were introduced, whereas before there had been only a musical competition, and a wreath of bay took the place of money-prizes. Cleisthenes won the laurel in the first chariot-race in the new hippodrome which was built in the plain below the ruins of Crisa. Hard by was the stadion or racecourse in which the athletes ran and wrestled; and it was not till after many years had passed that the new stadion was built high up above Delphi itself, close under the cliffs. Cleisthenes was remembered as having taken a prominent part both in the Sacred War and in the institution of the games; and he commemorated the occasion of his victory by founding Pythian games at Sicyon, which afterwards, by a stroke of the irony of history, became associated with the hated hero Adrastus. The Sicyonian treasury whose foundations can be seen at Delphi was built at the end of the sixth century, but it replaced an earlier building which was probably the gift of Cleisthenes. Fragments of the metopes of this earlier building have been recovered, showing that in the days of her great tyrant Sicyon's craftsmen were among the best of the day, with a rhythmic style which distinguished them from other mainland schools.

Pythian games [first Pythiad, 582 B.C.]

Some six years after his victory in the newly established Pythian Games Cleisthenes won with his four-horse chariot at Olympia and this spectacular victory was commemorated in the grand manner by the arrangements made for the wooing and wedding of his daughter Agariste. This was a story much embellished to take on epic stature and Herodotus' account bears as little relation to what actually happened as Homer's portrait of Troy does to the very restricted fortress that excavation has revealed.[27] As he tells the story suitors were invited from all corners of the Greek world to come to the tyrant's court within sixty days to compete for the hand of his daughter: in a year from the sixtieth day the marriage would be announced. During the year Cleisthenes entertained the suitors royally and tested their characters, their pride, their learning, their athletic prowess and their manners, especially at the dinner table. Of all the suitors he most favoured the two from Athens, Megacles and Hippocleides, and of the two he leaned towards Hippocleides whose family was connected with the Cypselids of Corinth. But the long-drawn-out contest had a strange ending. On the day of decision after dinner, when the suitors were doing their best to talk persuasively and make pleasing music, Hippocleides took control and ordered the flute-player to give them a tune, whereupon he danced to the mild discomfiture of Cleisthenes. Hippocleides, now really enjoying himself, demanded a table, danced some Spartan and Attic measures and finally standing on his head 'made his feet hands'. This was altogether too much for Cleisthenes: 'Son of Teisander, you have danced away your marriage.' 'Hippocleides cares not.' And so Agariste was given to Megacles son of Alcmaeon.

This genial story has historical as well as literary interest. In the age of the tyrants and for some time after it was normal practice for leading men to seek marriage alliances in other states, and it is worth noting that all three tyrannies which we are considering had links with Athens. The grandfather of Hippocleides, the unsuccessful rival of Megacles, was Cypselus, taking his name from a family marriage into the Cypselids of Corinth and the daughter of Theagenes, tyrant of Megara, was married to Cylon, a noble who made an unsuccessful bid for tyranny at Athens. Agariste deserved well of her adopted state. From her marriage with Megacles came another Cleisthenes who established democracy on firm foundations when the last of the Pisistratid tyrants was driven from Athens. And the second son of the marriage, Hippocrates, had a daughter named Agariste after her grandmother and she in turn was to be the mother of Pericles who guided Athenian policies in her greatest period. Cleisthenes of Sicyon did not long outlast his daughter's marriage and soon after his death the Sicyonian tyranny was brought to an end under pressure from Sparta.

The Megarian tyranny lasted less long and for that reason may have had a less decisive influence on Megara's development, but it performed the most essential function of tyranny in breaking the power of an exclusive nobility. Megara had been settled last of the chief Dorian cities and had grown up under the shadow of Corinth. She had followed Corinth to Sicily but her colony in east Sicily soon had to be evacuated and moved to Selinus,

3. Megara

dangerously near the Phoenician sphere in the west of the island. It was probably bad relations with Corinth that ended her western ambitions, for we hear of a border war between the two states towards the end of the eighth century and in the seventh century Megara directed her colonists to the approaches to the Euxine, where she founded Chalcedon and Byzantium.

Megara needed to colonise because her territory, squeezed in between Attica and Corinth, could not provide for a growing population and the best land was controlled by the Dorian nobility. It was as champion of the oppressed peasants that Theagenes was able to seize power, and the gesture that led to his tyranny was a massive slaughter of the cattle of the rich (did this also involve a free banquet for the poor?). His most permanent memorial was an aqueduct which brought a good supply of water to the city, but he also undermined the privilege of birth. The nobles, however, fought back; Theagenes was banished and had no successor. The tyranny had been too short to carry through the social revolution and there followed a long period of unsettlement in which the nobles attempted to stand firm against the social and political changes which Theagenes had set in motion. The bitter conflict is reflected in the poems of Theognis who had no sympathy for social change. He wrote in the early sixth century after the end of the tyranny, pouring out his heart to Cyrnus, a young noble:

> Unchanged the walls, but, ah, how changed
> the folk!
> The base, who knew erstwhile nor law nor
> right,
> But dwelled like deer, with goatskin for a cloak,
> Are now ennobled; and, O sorry plight!
> The nobles are made base in all men's sight.

It was not long before the importance of Megara as a power in Greece dwindled. The war with Athens which resulted in the loss of the island of Salamis was to be decisive for her own decline and for the rise of her rival.[28]

By the middle of the century the tyrannies of Corinth, Sicyon and Megara were past history. These three cities had different characters, but there was a common pattern in their tyrannies. They attacked the privileges of birth and were responsible for the political and economic advancement of the under-privileged. They released new energies in their cities and increased their resources by encouraging trade. By generous benefactions to Delphi and Olympia the tyrants of Corinth

and Sicyon (and perhaps Theagenes of Megara) buttressed their position with divine approval, and, expecting no sympathy from the old-established cults whose priests were supplied by the noble houses, they fostered the cult of Dionysus which recognised no class distinctions. When the tyrants took power they were needed, but when they had broken the power of the nobility their unconstitutional position was resented and they had to tighten the reins of government. Opposition grew and the end was usually abrupt.

The Panhellenic Games and Panhellenism

There is one other movement that is associated, if only indirectly, with tyranny. We have seen that at the end of the Sacred War a Pythian festival was instituted to be held every four years. A little later a more elaborate form was given to a local ceremony at Nemea in the territory of Cleonae and a festival to Nemean Zeus, also to be held every two years, was instituted. It was supervised by Cleonae until the middle of the fifth century when Argos, which had been the directing force from the outset, took control herself. Corinth's response was to institute an Isthmian festival, also at intervals of two years, in honour of Poseidon. And so the Olympic festival, held every four years, was joined by three new two-yearly festivals open to all Greeks. The prizes were modest—at Olympia a crown of wild olive, at Nemea and the Isthmus wild celery, and at Delphi bay leaves, but victors at these games were the pride of their cities.

These four Panhellenic festivals helped to maintain a feeling of fellowship among all the Greeks, and we may suspect that the promotion of this feeling was the deliberate policy of the rulers who raised these games to Panhellenic dignity. But it must not be overlooked that the festivals were themselves only a manifestation of a tendency towards unity which had begun in the eighth century. We have already seen how this tendency was promoted by colonisation and confirmed by the introduction of a common name for the Greek race. About the middle of the seventh century, we meet the name 'Panhellenes' in a poem of Archilochus, and the phrase 'Panhellenes and Achaeans' occurs in a passage, which may be still earlier, in the Homeric Catalogue of the Ships. The Panhellenic idea, the conception of a common Hellenic race with common interests, was encouraged by

Growth of Hellenic unity: displayed by

(1) a common name;

(?) the conception of the Trojan War as Panhellenic;

the poetical records of the heroic age. The Trojan War was remembered as a common enterprise, in which northern and southern Greece had joined; and the ancient poets had called the whole host 'Achaeans' or 'Argives' indifferently. The Homeric poems were a bond among all men of Greek speech, and the memory of Troy was an ingredient in a sentiment which, though we cannot call it national, was distinctly a sentiment of com-

(3) the Pan-hellenic position of Delphi (the 'common hearth' of Greece);

munity. The feeling of community was also displayed in the recognition of the Pythian Apollo as the chief and supreme oracle of Greece. The growth of the prestige of the Delphic god might almost have been used as a touchstone for measuring the growth of the feeling of community. As a meeting-place for pilgrims and envoys from all quarters of the Greek world, Delphi served to keep distant cities in touch with one another, and to spread news—purposes which were effected in a less degree by the Panhellenic festivals. The ten-

(4) the Pan-hellenic games; (5) partial minor unions, religious leagues

dencies to unity were also shown by the leagues, chiefly of a religious kind, which were formed among neighbouring states. The maritime league of Calauria is an instance; the northern Amphictiony of Anthela is another; and we shall presently have a glimpse of the Ionic federation of Delos. In the second half of the sixth century we find the cities of south Italy bound together in some form of loose confederacy, which was indicated in the character of their coinage. We shall soon see Sparta uniting a large part of the Peloponnese in a confederacy under her presidency.

These tendencies to unity never resulted in a political union of all Hellas. The Greek race never became a Greek nation; for the Pan-hellenic idea was weaker than the love of local independence. But an ideal unity was realised —in those beliefs and institutions which we have just been considering. They fostered in the hearts of the Greeks a lively feeling of fellowship and a deep pride in Hellas, even though there was no political tie. And it is to be noted that the Delphic oracle made no efforts to promote political unity, though it unintentionally promoted unity of another kind. Greek states did not ask Apollo to originate or direct their policy; they only sought his authority for what they had already determined or at least considered.

Nature of Delphic influence

CHAPTER 4

The Union of Attica and the Foundation of the Athenian Democracy

The Union of Attica

When recorded history begins, the story of Athens is the story of Attica; the inhabitants of Attica are Athenians. But Attica was once occupied by a number of independent states. Some of these little kingdoms are vaguely remembered in legends which tell of the giant Pallas who ruled at Pallene under the north-eastern slopes of Hymettus, of the dreaded Cephalus lord of the southern region of Thoricus, or of Porphyrion of mighty stature whose domain was at Athmonon under Mount Pentelicus. The hill of Munychia was, in the distant past, an island, and was crowned by a stronghold; the name *Piraeus* has been supposed to preserve the memory of days when the lords of Munychia looked across to the mainland and spoke of the 'opposite shore'. At a later stage we find neighbouring villages uniting themselves together by political or religious bonds. Thus in the north, beyond Pentelicus, Marathon and Oenoe and two other towns formed a *tetrapolis*. Again Piraeus, adjacent Phaleron, and two other places joined in the common worship of the god Heracles, and were called the Four-Villages. Of all the lordships between Mount Cithaeron and Cape Sunion the two most important were those of Eleusis and Athens, severed from one another by the hill-chain of Aegaleos.

Tetra-kômoi

It was upon Athens, the stronghold in the midst of the Cephisian plain, 5 miles from the sea, that destiny devolved the task of working out the unity of Attica. This Cephisian plain, on the south side open to the Saronic gulf, is enclosed by hills, on the west by Aegaleos, on the north-west by Parnes, on the east by Hymettus, while the gap in the north-east, between Parnes and Hymettus, is filled by the gable-shaped mass of Pentelicus. The river Cephisus flows westwards, not far from Athens, and was fed by two smaller streams, the Eridanus and Ilissus, to the north and south of the Acropolis. What was later the Acropolis of a large city was originally the city itself, and the site was occupied at least from the Neolithic period. In the Bronze Age, as we have seen, it was one of the strong centres of the Mycenaean world, with a royal palace and walls which could compare with those of Mycenae and Tiryns. The early history, however, of Athens is beyond recovery, though by the fourth century a complete list of kings could be accepted—beginning with Cecrops in the sixteenth century—and later Plutarch could write a biography of King Theseus. But the history of the Athenian kings is even less substantial than Livy's account of the Roman Romulus and his successors, especially as we have no surviving Livy for Greece, but only fragments from fifth-century Hellanicus and the later chroniclers of Athens. It was the proud boast of the Athenians in the classical period that they were autochthonous and of pure race, but this means no more than that in the period of the destruction of Mycenaean centres Athens remained comparatively stable and was not later occupied by Dorians. That even in Athens the race was mixed is suggested

The Acropolis

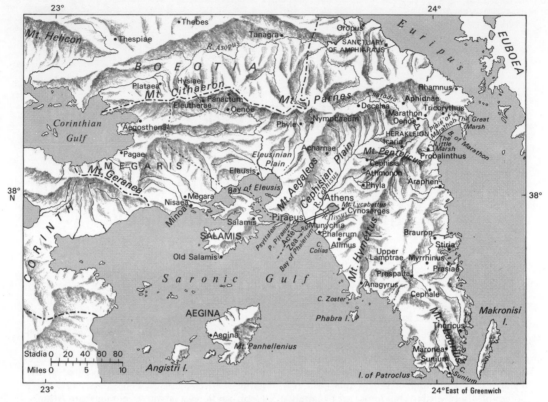

13. ATTICA

Legendary contest of Poseidon and Athena

by the famous contest between Poseidon and Athena for the possession of the Acropolis when Athena had given the sacred olive tree as a token and Poseidon a salt-spring. Athena took possession, but Poseidon-Erechtheus in the shape of a snake was permitted still to live on the hill of Athena.

Synoecism of Attica

More important for its bearing on the future was the union of Attica in a single state. This was not inevitable. To the north Boeotia developed into a land of independent cities; Thebes was the most powerful, but Orchomenus, Tanagra, Thespiae and others were not submerged. But when recorded history begins, the several independent communities of Attica had surrendered their independence to Athens and with her formed a single state. This transference of power was commemorated at Athens by the annual festival of the *Synoikia*, and Thucydides, appreciating its significance, digresses: 'Under Cecrops and the first kings, down to the time of Theseus, Attica was a land of independent communities each with its own town hall and its own magistrates, and they only came to the king at Athens to consult

when they felt insecure; at all other times they managed their own affairs and some of them even went to war with Athens, as the Eleusinians under Eumolpus against Erechtheus. But when Theseus became king, being powerful as well as wise, he put an end to their separate council houses and independent magistracies and concentrated them all in a single council house and a single town hall. They continued to live on their own land but he made them use Athens as their centre; and as a result of this union it was a great city that Theseus handed down to his successors. Formerly the present Acropolis was the city, together with the land to the south of the Acropolis'.[1]

Incorporation of Eleusis

It is certain enough that Athens did become a single state from a number of separate states, but it was not necessarily by a single act; some historians have thought that Eleusis retained her independence into the seventh century, but Eleusis, as an important religious centre, could be a special case.[2] The tradition accepted in the fifth century attributed the reform to Theseus, whom they dated in the thirteenth century, but the earliest traditions about Theseus seem to localise him in the Marathon area and it is very doubtful whether he was ever king at Athens. The approximate date, however, is at least possible. In the insecurity of the second half of the thirteenth century the smaller communities might have felt the need of linking themselves more closely to Athens. Such an atmosphere would form a better context than the impoverishment of the dark ages, and any later date can be rejected, with the possible exception of Eleusis. If there remained independent states in Attica during the archaic period Thucydides would not have accepted a date before the Trojan War for the union.

Aristocratic Government

The early history of the Athenian constitution resembles that of most other Greek states in the general fact that a royalty, subjected to various restrictions, passes into an aristocracy. But the details of the transition are peculiar, and the beginning of the republic seems to have been exceptionally early. The traditional names of the Attic kings who came after the hero Theseus are certainly in some cases, and it may be in most cases, fictitious, the most famous of them being the Neleid Codrus, who was said to have sacrificed himself to save his country on the occasion of an attack by invaders from the Peloponnese. The Athenians said that they had abolished royalty on the death of Codrus, because he was too good to have a successor—a curious reversal of the usual causes of such a revolution. But this story is a late invention. The first limitation of the royal power effected by the aristocracy was the institution of a *polemarch* or military commander. The supreme command of the army, which had belonged to the king, was transferred to him and he was elected from and by the nobles. The next step seems to have been *Fall of the kings* the overthrow of the royal house by the powerful family of the Medontids. The Medontids did not themselves assume the *Rule of the regents for life (Traditional date of Medon, 1088 B.C.)* royal title, nor did they abolish it. They instituted the office of *archon* or regent, and this office usurped the most important functions of the king. Acastus, the Medontid, was the first regent. We know that he was an historical person, for the archons of later days always swore that they would be true to their oath, even as Acastus. He held the post for life, and his successors after him; and thus the Medontids resembled kings, though they did

not bear the kingly name. But they fell short of royalty in another way too, for each regent was elected by the community: the community was only bound to elect a member of the Medontid family. The next step in weakening the power of this kingly magistrate was the *Ten-yearly regents (traditional date 753-2 B.C.)* change of the regency from a life office to an office of ten years. This reform is said to have been effected about the middle of the eighth century. It is uncertain at what time the Medontids were deprived of their prerogative and the regency was thrown open to all the nobles. With the next step we reach firmer ground. The regency became a yearly office, *Annual regents, 683-2 B.C.* and from this time onward an official list of the archons seems to have been preserved.

But meanwhile there were still kings at *Maintenance of the title Basileus* Athens. The Medontids had robbed the kings of their royal power, but they had not done away with the kings; there was to be a king at Athens till the latest days of the Athenian democracy. It seems probable that, as some historical analogies might suggest, the Medontids allowed the shadow of royalty to remain in the possession of the old royal house, so that for some time there would have been life-kings existing by the side of the life-regents; it is not likely that from the very first the kingship was degraded to be a yearly office, filled by election. This, however, was what it ultimately became. The title remained when the power had long since vanished.

The whole course of the constitutional development is uncertain; for it rests upon traditions, of which it is extremely hard to judge the value. But whatever the details of the growth may have been, two important facts are to be grasped. One is that the fall of royalty, which does not imply the abolition of the royal name, happened in Athens at an earlier period than in Greece generally. The other is that the Medontids were not kings, but archons—the chiefs of an aristocracy. The organisation of the Athenian state was based on the four Ionian tribes, which are found also in east Greek states of Ionian origin, and go back far beyond the Dorian invasion. The curious names of these tribes—Geleontes, Argadeis, Aigicoreis, and Hopletes—seem to have been derived from the worship of special deities; for instance, Geleontes from Zeus Geleon. But the original meanings of the names had entirely passed away, and the tribes were affiliated to Apollo Patroös, the paternal Apollo, from whom all Athenians claimed descent.

We can see the clan organisation at Athens better than elsewhere. The families of each clan derived themselves from a common ancestor, and were therefore called *homo-galaktes*, 'milk-fellows', descended from common *mothers,* and most of the clan names are patronymics. The worship of this ancestor was the chief end of the society. All the clans alike worshipped Zeus Herkeios and Apollo Patrōos; many of them had a special connection with other public cults. Each had a regular administration and officers, at the head of whom was an 'archon'. To these clans only members of the noble families belonged; but the other classes, the peasants and the craftsmen, formed similar organisations founded on the worship not of a common ancestor, for they could point to none, but some deity whom they chose. The members of these were called *orgeōnes*. This innovation heralds the advance of the lower classes to political importance.

The orgeōnes or thiasōtai

The *phratriae*, brotherhoods, composed of families whose lands adjoined, united their members in the cult of Zeus Phratrios and Athena Phratria. In early times only clansmen belonged to the brotherhoods, but here again a change takes place in the seventh century, and *orgeōnes* are admitted. The organisation is now used for the purposes of census. Every child whose parents were citizens must be admitted into a brotherhood; and if this rite is neglected he is regarded as illegitimate. It should be observed that illegitimacy at Athens did not deprive a man of political rights, but he could not lay claim by right of birth to his father's inheritance.

Later mis-apprehen-sion

At a much later time the constitutional historians of Athens made out that the clans were artificial subdivisions of the brotherhoods. They said that each tribe was divided into three brotherhoods, each brotherhood into 30 clans, and it was even added that each clan comprised 30 men. This artificial scheme may be true, so far as the relation of the tribe to the brotherhood is concerned; but it is not true in regard to the clan, and is refuted by the circumstance that the tribes consisted of others than clansmen.

Aristocracy in the Seventh Century

The aristocracy

By the middle of the seventh century, the executive at Athens was in the hands of three annually elected officers, the archon, the king and the polemarch. The archon was the supreme judge in all civil suits. When he entered office he published a declaration that he would, throughout the term of his archonship, preserve the property of every citizen

The magistrates: Archon;

intact. At a later time this sphere of judicial power was limited, and he judged mainly cases in which injured parents, orphans, heiresses were involved. He held the chief place among the magistrates, having his official residence in the Prytaneum, where was the public hearth, and his name appeared at the head of official lists, whence he was called *epōnymus*; but the archonship was a later institution than that of polemarch, as is shown by the fact that no old religious ceremonies were performed by the archon, such as devolved upon the polemarch as well as upon the king. The conduct of festivals instituted at later times was, however, entrusted to him. Such was the Thargelia, the late-May feast of the first-fruits, the chief Athenian feast of Apollo, introduced from Delos probably in the seventh century; such was the great Dionysia, which, as we shall see, was founded in the sixth. The polemarch had judicial duties, besides being commander-in-chief of the army. He held a court in the Epilykeion on the banks of the Ilissus, and judged there all cases in which non-citizens were involved. Thus what the archon was for citizens, the polemarch was for the class of foreign settlers who were called 'metics'. The king had his residence in the royal Stoa in the Agora. His functions were confined to the management of the state-religion, and the conduct of certain judicial cases connected with religion. He was president of the Council, and thus had considerable power and responsibility in the conduct of the judicial functions of that body.

Polemarch;

Basileus

The Council was the political organisation through which the nobles carried out, at Athens as elsewhere, the gradual abolition of monarchy. This Council of Elders—a part as we saw of the Aryan inheritance of the Greeks—came afterwards to be called at Athens the Council of the Aeropagus, to distinguish it from other councils of later growth. This name was derived from one of the Council's most important functions. According to early custom, which we find reflected in Homer, murder and manslaughter were not regarded as crimes against the state, but concerned exclusively the family of the slain man, which might either slay the slayer or accept compensation. But gradually, as the worship of the souls of the dead and the deities of the underworld developed, the belief gained ground that he who shed blood was impure and needed cleansing. Accordingly when a murderer satisfied the kinsfolk of the murdered by paying a fine, he had also to submit to a process of purification, and satisfy the Ch-

The Council, called of the Areopagus

thonian gods and the Erinyes or Furies, who were, in the original conception, the souls of the dead clamouring for vengeance. This notion of manslaughter as a religious offence necessarily led to the interference of the state. For when the member of a community was impure, the stain drew down the anger of the gods upon the whole community, if the unclean were not driven out. Hence it came about that the state undertook the conduct of criminal justice. The Council itself formed the court, and the proceedings were closely associated with the worship of the *Semnai*. These Chthonian goddesses had a sanctuary, which served as a refuge for him whose hand was stained with bloodshed, on the north-east side of the Areopagus, outside the city wall. It is possible that the association of this hill with the god Ares is merely due to a popular etymology, for he had no shrine here; but the correct explanation of the name *Areiospagos* is not known. On this rugged spot, apart from but within sight of the dwellings of men, the Council held its sittings for cases of murder, violence with murderous intent, poisoning, and incendiarism. The accuser stood on the stone of Insolence, the accused on the stone of Recklessness, each a huge unhewn block. This function of the Council, which continued to belong to it after it had lost its other powers, procured it the name of the Areopagus.

During the period of the aristocracy this Council was the governing body of Athens. We may be certain that the magistrates were always members; but otherwise we do not know how it was composed, and therefore can form no clear idea how the constitution worked. The Council doubtless exercised some control over the election of the chief magistrates; but we need have small doubt that the king, the archon, and the polemarch were formally elected by the Ecclesia, consisting of the whole body of citizens entitled to vote.

The outline history of Athens under her aristocracy in the eighth and seventh centuries remains dim. In the Dark Ages she was probably the least impoverished of the cities of Greece, for her Acropolis had stood secure and her country had not been overrun. She was able to play a major part in the settlement of Greeks on the east side of the Aegean and she established a new style of pottery which spread through Greece.[3] This Protogeometric pottery was severe but satisfying: it may become a little boring but it certainly does not suggest decadence. The primacy of Athens is illustrated by the wide distribution of her pots on the mainland and through the Aegean. But with the Geometric style (from *c.* 900) the influence of Athens, strong at first, gradually declines and Argos, Corinth, Boeotia tend to go their own different ways.

Reason for Athenian stability

4.1   Attic Late Geometric bowl: (?) Paris abducts Helen (see note, page 553)

In the great surge to colonise at the end of the eighth century and the beginning of the seventh, Athens played no part. Her own citizens had joined in the colonisation of Ionia and probably in strengthening the populations of some of the islands, and she had more farming land than most of the Greek cities; she did not yet feel the pressure of over-population. Her burials during the late ninth and eighth centuries suggest that she was still faring well. It was at this period customary to set up large jars over the grave, through which libations could be poured to the dead. The jars are of excellent quality and richly decorated with geometric patterning and inset figured panels.[4] Scenes of fighting on land and sea are commonly represented, and these presumably commemorate either the manner of death or the main distinction of the dead man. From those that depict ships or action on ships we can infer that Athens was already keenly interested in the sea routes and, a little less securely, that there were men of substance who were directly interested in the development of Athenian trade.

It was probably because Athens had no serious economic problems that the frictions which gave rise to tyranny in Sicyon, Corinth and Megara did not affect her until later. But from the middle of the seventh century she also feels the strain, though it was only after other attempted solutions had failed that Pisistratus made himself tyrant, in 560. The first sign of discontent may be reflected in the appointment of the *thesmothetae,* a college of six judges whose duty was to guard and administer the *thesmoi* or traditional ordinances. They were elected annually and were later associated with the three chief officers of state, the archon, *basileus,* and polemarch in a board of nine archons. Their appointment may have been designed to meet a growing discontent with arbitrary judgements.

Cylon's attempt at tyranny, ? 632 B.C.

A further warning came when an Athenian noble, Cylon, seized the Acropolis. He had married the daughter of Theagenes, tyrant of Megara, and with Megarian help tried to make himself master of the city. Consulting the Delphic oracle, he was advised to seize the Acropolis at the time of the greatest festival of Zeus. Cylon, an Olympic victor himself, had no doubt that the festival of Olympia was meant; but when his plot failed, it was explained that the oracle referred to the Athenian festival of the Diasia in March, which was celebrated outside the city. Cylon enlisted in his enterprise a number of noble youths, and a band of Megarian soldiers were sent by Theagenes. He succeeded in seizing the Acropolis, but the sight of foreign soldiers effectually quenched any lurking sympathy that Athenians might have felt for an effort to overthrow the government. The people rallied to the call. Cylon was blockaded in the citadel, and, after a long siege, when food and water began to fail, he escaped with his brother from the fortress. The rest were soon constrained to capitulate. They had sought refuge in the temple of Athena Polias and left it when they were promised that their lives would be spared. But Megacles, of the Alcmaeonid family, was archon this year; and at his instigation the pledge was disregarded, and the conspirators were put to death. Some feud among the clans may have been at work here.[5]

The curse on the Alcmaeonids

The city was saved from a tyrant, but it had incurred a grave pollution. Such a violation of a solemn pledge to the suppliants who had trusted in the protection of the gods was an insult to the gods themselves, and the city was under a curse till the pollution should be removed. This view was urged by the secret friends of Cylon and those who hated the Alcmaeonids. And so while Cylon, his brother, and their descendants were condemned to disfranchisement and perpetual banishment, the Alcmaeonids and those who had acted with them were also tried on the charge of sacrilege, a curse was laid on them and they were condemned to perpetual exile, with confiscation of their property. And the bodies of those of the clan who had died between the deed of sacrilege and the passing of this sentence were exhumed and cast beyond the boundary of Attica. The banishment of the Alcmaeonids had consequences in the distant future, and we shall see how it came into the practical politics of Athens two hundred years later. The tale is also told that the city required a further purification, and that a priest named Epimenides came from Crete and cleansed it. But it has been thought doubtful whether Epimenides is more than a mythical name like Orpheus, since another story brings him to Athens again, for similar purposes of atonement, more than a century afterwards; and then both tales are conciliated by ascribing to the seer a miraculous sleep of a hundred years.

Such accounts as we have of Cylon's attempted coup suggest that his was primarily a personal bid for power without much popular support, but it seems likely that he thought that there was sufficient unrest in Athens to maintain his position if he was successful. That all was not well is suggested more clearly by the appointment of Draco to draw up a code of laws; the natural implication is that the people were dissatisfied with the arbitrary administration of justice, and insisted that offences and penalties should be defined in writing. It was the same movement as that which a little more than a hundred years later led to the publication of the Twelve Tables of Roman law. Draco was appointed an extraordinary legislator (*thesmothetes*), and empowered to codify and rectify the existing law. We know only the provisions of that part of his criminal law which dealt with the shedding of blood; for these provisions were not altered by subsequent legislation. In later times it was thought that Draco revealed to the Athenians how harsh their laws were, and his name became proverbial for a severe lawgiver. An Athenian orator won credit for his epigram that Draco's laws were written not in ink but in blood. This idea arose from the fact that certain small offences, such as stealing cabbage, were punished by death.

The laws of Draco

A broader view, however, of Draco's code will modify this view. He drew careful distinctions between murder and various kinds of accidental or justifiable manslaughter. In his laws we meet a body of 51 judges, called the *ephetae*. They were chosen from the Eupatrids, but it is not clear whether they formed a part of the Council of the Areopagus or were a wholly distinct body. Those cases of bloodshed which did not come before the court of the Areopagus were tried by the *ephetae,* in a case where the shedder of blood was known. According to the nature of the deed the *ephetae* held their court in different places: in the temple of the Delphinian Apollo, in the Palladion at Phaleron, or at Phreatto, a tongue of land on the Munychian peninsula. This last court was used for those who were tried for manslaughter committed abroad, and, as they might not set foot on the soil of their country, they had to answer the charge standing in a boat drawn up near the shore. When the shedder of blood was not known, the case came before the King Archon in the Prytaneum. It is unfortunate that we are not informed of Draco's other legislation.[6] We know that the laws relating to debtors were stringent; the creditor could claim the person of the insolvent debtor. In general, he was bound to provide for the interests of the rich power-holding class, but it was at all events an enormous gain for the poor that those interests should be defined in writing.

Draco's legislation was not the end of discontent. A generation later the situation was again critical, and a more comprehensive attempt had to be made to solve Athens' problem.

The Legislation of Solon and the Foundation of Democracy

With the appointment of Solon as archon and arbitrator to heal the troubles of the state we at last have access to a contemporary source of first-class value. Solon was the son of Execestides, a noble connected with the house of the Medontids. He left his own record of the political scene, and since prose had not yet become the natural medium for expounding philosophy, politics or economics, there should be no surprise that he addressed his public in verse. Sufficient extracts from his poems were later quoted to give tantalising glimpses of the troubles of Attica and the steps he took to put them right.[7] He also reveals himself: he is the first Athenian whom we feel that we can know. He is a fervent patriot and feels passionately about political morality; he has the indignation of a Hebrew prophet but a better sense of practical politics. In a time of growing tension he was a convinced moderate. He rebukes the rich for their selfishness and indifference to the true interests of the state; he attacks the poor for the extravagance of their demands. They are clamouring for a redistribution of land; he sets himself firmly against such revolutionary steps. But Solon realised that the poorer classes had legitimate grievances and he did not hesitate to take strong measures.

In the background we can see some of the factors that led to the crisis which Solon was called on to cure. The introduction of coinage has less importance than has usually been attributed to it; with the later dating of the first Aeginetan issues it is virtually certain that when Solon drew up his laws Athens had no coinage of her own.[8] There is no question therefore of the small farmer being puzzled by the new-fangled lumps of metal; they were still operating in a barter economy. Goods sold to Aegina, however, would be paid for in Aeginetan turtles and it was more convenient for rich men who wanted luxuries from abroad to purchase them with silver coins rather than with goods. The opening of the eastern trade route had made a widening range of luxuries available, and the rich needed more wealth to maintain the rising standard of living that the new conditions encouraged.

One of their easiest means of increasing wealth was by increasing pressure on those they could control, and the most important

Pressure on hektemoroi

class of dependents were the men on the land who were called *hektemoroi,* sixth-parters. Since Solon's reforms abolished this status, Athenian historians of the fourth century and later had little to go on except the name and general statements in Solon's poems. Sixth-parters can mean either those who keep a sixth part of their crops or those who give up a sixth part, and since the first implies intolerably hard conditions which cannot be paralleled in ancient or modern times we can accept the second. These were men who farmed land and gave a sixth part of their crops every year to a more substantial land-owner. In one of his poems Solon claims that he set the dark earth free by uprooting *horoi* which had been widely planted over the land. The root meaning of *horos* is a witness or marker; its commonest use is as a boundary stone, but in Herodotus, for instance, it is used of the stones set up on the tomb of the Lydian King Alyattes recording how much of the work had been done by the various categories of workers. In the present case they recorded that from the land so marked one sixth of the crops was annually due; when the *horoi* were uprooted the land became the free property of those who worked it. The relationship had been a feudal one. The *hektemoros* had presumably accepted or had virtually forced on him a status whereby he got perhaps his seed corn and the use of ox and plough in return for a regular share of his crops.[9]

? Corn imports needed

Another problem may have been affecting the city more than the countryside. By the fifth century Athens was heavily dependent on imported corn; we have no firm evidence when that dependence started but there may be hints that the position was already becoming precarious. Towards the end of the seventh century Athens planted a small settlement at Sigeum near the entrance to the Hellespont; it may have been intended to stake a claim on the corn route from the north coast of the Euxine which was later to be the main source of Athens' supplies.[10] One of Solon's measures points the same way. He banned the export of all products of the soil except olives and oil. This was not primarily designed to encourage landowners to plant olives, for no encouragement was needed. Olives and oil had already become Athens' most important export. Solon's objective was to stop the sale of corn to Aegina or Megara, both potential enemies. These near neighbours both needed more corn than they could grow themselves and Attic landowners, especially on the Eleusis plain, would find it more attractive to sell their corn for Aeginetan silver rather than to send it by pack-mule or donkey over Mount Aegaleos to Athens. The city population was growing; the food problem was perhaps becoming serious.

4.2   Olive harvest: whipping the trees

Athens' relations with her neighbours was also cause for concern. Megara's open support of Cylon when he made his bid for tyranny will have either created or increased friction, and there was a more important bone of contention. The island of Salamis is equally accessible from Megara and Athens and in the late seventh century it was controlled by Megara. In one of his most famous poems Solon urged the Athenians to end the shame of abandoning Salamis and to return and fight for the island: 'I am come myself as a herald from lovely Salamis with measured verse on my lips and not our common speech.' He blames the people who were prepared 'to let Salamis slip out of our hands'. 'Come, let us go to Salamis and fight for the lovely island, and wipe away our shame.' The implication is that Athens had made an attempt to gain Salamis but had lost hope. The date of this poem is uncertain, because in some accounts Pisistratus also is associated with the capture of Salamis and it has been thought that Solon and Pisistratus were working together shortly before Pisistratus seized the tyranny. But the poem is not that of an old man; it is probably earlier than Solon's appointment to draw up new laws, and the capture of Salamis may be one of the main grounds for his appointment. Not only Megara: Aegina, later to be called by Pericles 'the eyesore of the Piraeus', was hostile and powerful. The feud went back at least to the early seventh century.[11]

Cancellation of debts

Solon was given a special commission in 594 to take such measures as he thought fit. Instead of making the usual declaration of the chief magistrate that he would protect the property of all men undiminished, he made proclamation that all debts were cancelled and all those who had been enslaved for debt were to be free. This measure, called the *Seisactheia*, the shaking off of burdens, covered two groups of people. The normal security for debt had hitherto been the person, and when the debt was not paid the debtor became the bond slave of the creditor. In pre-coinage days a man who could not maintain himself would have little alternative to becoming a bond slave to be fed and maintained in return for his labour. But he could also be sold, and Solon proudly proclaims that he brought back many who had been sold abroad, some of whom had even forgotten their native tongue. The second group were the *hektemoroi* whose condition has been considered. In a sense they too were debtors; they now became free men farming their own land.

Encouragement of trade

Solon also seems to have realised that, since all the best sites for colonies had now been taken, Athens would have to produce more goods for export if she was to procure more corn for a larger population. This is probably why he offered Athenian citizenship to men from other cities who left their homes to settle permanently in Athens with a view to carrying on a trade. He is also credited with a measure absolving sons from the support of their fathers in old age if they had not been taught a trade. In the fourth century tradition Solon was responsible for a more important economic reform. He was thought to have changed Athenian coinage from the Aeginetan standard to the lighter Euboic standard with 100 drachmae to the talent instead of 70, but it is very doubtful indeed whether Athens had her own coinage before 580. But by the fourth century it needed a very sharp critic to distinguish what Solon himself had initiated and what measures had been attributed to him simply because they seemed archaic. There is little doubt that he covered a very wide field, including sumptuary legislation and the definition of crimes and penalties; for the laws of Draco were repealed with the exception of those relating to manslaughter.

Qualifications for office

Solon realised that, if his reforms were to be maintained, changes had to be made in the machinery of government. He had no illusions about the selfishness of the old nobility and hoped to change its spirit by modifications in the structure. The first of these was to replace birth by wealth as the criterion for office. To this end he divided the citizen body into four classes based on the annual produce of the land. Those who harvested 500 *medimni* of corn or more were the 500-bushel men, *pentacosiomedimni*; those whose income was between 300 and 500 *medimni* were knights, *hippeis*; those between 200 and 300 were teamsters, *zeugitae*; those who had less were *thetes*. The last three titles were in current use marking social distinctions; they were now given an economic definition and a further class was added. It is important to note that income was calculated only in terms of produce from the land. It was not until much later that a money equivalent was added, for the capital for trade came ultimately from the land, and the most reliable investment for the profits of trade was still land.

The archonship

The chief offices of state, those of the archon, the polemarch and the king archon had hitherto probably been confined to the Eupatrids, a limited number of noble families, as the higher offices in the Roman republic were long confined to patricians; Solon now opened all offices to all citizens according to their wealth. The chief offices were confined either to the first class or to the first and second class, but the *zeugitae*, who were not made eligible for the archonship until 457–6, were already admitted to lesser offices. The immediate significance of the change in the qualification for office depends on the number of wealthy men who were not Eupatrids, and this we have no means of discovering. But even if the new men were now few, the number would grow and an important principle had been established. One tradition says that Solon changed the form of election to the archonship by combining a preliminary election of 40 candidates, ten from each tribe, with a final selection by lot. The outstanding importance of the chief archonship in the following period makes it much more probable that the archons were directly elected by the popular Assembly.[12]

The Assembly

This Assembly now 'at the latest included the *thetes,* who may have been excluded hitherto. A people's court was also established by Solon, the *Heliaea,* which represented the Assembly as a judicial body in the same way that the *comitia centuriata* at Rome could also try cases. This court was intended as a protection against the abuse of their power by magistrates and an appeal could be made to it, presumably in certain classes of cases.[13] Later writers saw in the *Heliaea* the ancestor of the people's courts of the fully developed Athenian democracy, when all the judicial decisions had passed from the magistrate to the jurors.

A second Council

Another measure, no less important, is controversial. The Aristotelian treatise on the Athenian constitution says, without elaboration, that Solon introduced a new council of four hundred, one hundred from each tribe, and Plutarch speaks of Solon anchoring the state on two councils. In view of the vital importance later of the popular Council, Solon's place in the development of democracy at Athens depends in no small degree on whether he was the original creator of the body. The main arguments against attributing it to Solon are that Aristotle says nothing of it in his *Politics* and that we hear nothing of it at the time of Pisistratus' seizure of power or at any other time before Cleisthenes. Such arguments from silence are dangerous because our record of the sixth century is so very thin. The argument from the narrative of Pisistratus' coup also carries little weight; the atmosphere of the occasion did not encourage nicely constitutional procedures. The main reason for accepting the measure is that in the oligarchic revolution of 411 the oligarchs appealed to tradition in adopting four hundred as the number for their new council.[14] Had the council been first introduced by Cleisthenes, it would have been difficult to impose the tradition. That a democratic council would not be an anachronism is shown by steps taken elsewhere. The Spartan *rhetra* had provided for the preparation of business for the Assembly by the Gerousia. An inscription found at Chios mentions a people's Council and may be dated somewhere near the middle of the sixth century. One of the duties of this Council is to prepare cases that are to be sent up for appeal; the Solonian Council may

similarly have prepared appeal cases for the *Heliaea.*[15] Its main business, however, will have been to prepare business for the regular meetings of the Assembly, presided over by the archon, though the meetings were probably considerably less frequent than in the fifth century.

Solon's laws were inscribed on wooden tables called *axones,* which were numbered, and the laws were quoted by the number of the *axon.* Every citizen was required to take an oath that he would obey these laws, which were to remain in force for ten years.

Solon's moderation

Solon had done his work boldly, but he had done it constitutionally. He had not made himself a tyrant, as he might easily have done, and as many expected him to do. On the contrary, one purpose of his reform was to forestall the necessity, and prevent the possibility, of a tyranny. He had not even become an *aesymnetes*—a legislator (like Pittacus), who for a number of years supersedes the constitution in order to reform it, and rules for that time with the absolute power of a tyrant. He had simply held the office of archon, invested, indeed, with extraordinary powers. To a superficial observer caution seemed the note of his reforms, and men were surprised, and not a few disgusted, by his cautiousness.

His caution

His caution consisted in reserving the highest offices for men of property, and the truth probably is that in his time no others would have been fitted to perform the duties. But Solon has stated his own principle that the privileges of each class should be proportional to the public burdens which it can bear. This was the conservative feature of his legislation; and, seizing on it, democrats could make out a plausible case for regarding his constitution as simply a timocracy. When he laid down his office he was assailed by complaints, and he wrote elegies in which he explains his middle course and professes that he performed the things which he undertook without favour or fear. 'I threw my stout shield,' he says, 'over both parties.' He refused to entertain the idea of any modifications in his measures, and thinking that the reforms would work better in the absence of the reformer, he left Athens soon after his archonship and travelled partly for mercantile ends, but perhaps chiefly from curiosity, to see strange places and strange men.

Character of Solon

Though the remnants of his poems are fragmentary, though the recorded events of his life are meagre, and though the details of his legislation are dimly known and variously interpreted, the personality of Solon leaves a distinct impression on our minds. We know enough to see in him an embodiment of the ideal of intellectual and moral excellence of the early Greeks, and the greatest of their wise men. For him the first of the virtues was moderation, and his motto was 'Avoid excess'. He was in no vulgar sense a man of the world, for he was many-sided—poet and legislator, traveller and trader, noble and friend of the people. He had the insight to discern some of the yet undeveloped tendencies of the age, and could sympathise with other than the power-holding classes. He had meditated too deeply on the circumstances of humanity to find power a temptation; he never forgot that he was a traveller between life and death. It was a promising and characteristic act for a Greek state to commit the task of its reformation to such a man, and empower him to translate into definite legislative measures the views which he expressed in his poems.

The sequel　Solon's social reforms inaugurated a permanent improvement. But his political measures, which he intended as a compromise, displeased many. Party strife broke out again bitterly soon after his archonship—only to end, after thirty years, in the tyranny which it had been his dearest object to prevent. Of this strife we know little. It took the form of a struggle for the archonship, and two years are noted in which, in consequence of this struggle, no archons were elected—hence called years of

Years of anarchia, 589-8 (?) and 584-3 (?) B.C. Damasias, 583-581 B.C.

anarchy. Then a certain archon, Damasias, attempted to convert his office into a permanent tyranny and actually held it for over two years. This attempt frightened the political parties into making a compromise of some sort. It was agreed that ten archons should be chosen, five Eupatrids, three Georgi, and two Demiurgi, all of course possessing the requisite minimum of wealth. It is unknown whether

581-580 B.C.

this arrangement was repeated after the year of its first trial, but it certainly did not lead to a permanent reconciliation.

Two parties:

The two great parties were those who were in the main satisfied with the new constitution of Solon and those who disliked its democratic side and desired to return to the aristocratic government which he had subverted. The latter consisted chiefly of Eupatrids, and were known as the men of the

the Plain (πεδιακοί);

Plain, for the plain round Athens was the stronghold of the old nobility. They were led by Lycurgus and numbered among them the clan of the Philaidae—distinguished as the clan of Hippoclides, the wooer of Agariste, and destined to become more distinguished still as that of more than one Cimon and Miltiades.

4.3　Attic Kouros (c. 600)

the Coast
(πάραλοι)

The opposite party of the Coast included not only the population of the coast, but the bulk of the middle classes. They were led by Megacles, son of Alcmaeon, the same Megacles who married Agariste. For one of Solon's measures was an act of amnesty which was couched in such terms that, while it did not benefit the descendants of Cylon, it permitted the return of the Alcmaeonidae. Their position severed them from the rest of the Eupatrids and associated them with the party which represented Solon's views.

CHAPTER 5

Growth of Athens in the sixth century

The Conquest of Salamis and Nisaea

Though Solon by his legislation had saved Athens from revolution and laid firm foundations for political development, he had in fact, by attempting to satisfy both sides, failed to satisfy either completely and the generation that followed his legislation was one of growing unrest in the political field and continuing trouble with Megara. Of the struggle with Megara we have occasional glimpses. It was to be expected that Megara would attempt to recover Salamis, but Athens seems to have strengthened her position, for we hear of a war a generation later in which Nisaea, the Megarian port on the Saronic Gulf, was captured by the Athenians.[1] The fate of Salamis was finally referred to Sparta, and a commission of five Spartan arbitrators awarded the island to the Athenians. In setting forth her case Athens is said to have based her claim on her place next to Salamis in Homer's catalogue of the Greek forces at Troy in his *Iliad,* an interesting testimony to the authority of Homer.[2]

At this same time or earlier Megara recovered Nisaea, but the more important Salamis remained the secure possession of Athens. Her territory was rounded off; she had complete command of the land-locked Eleusinian bay; it was she who now threatened Megara. The Spartan arbitration was probably made towards the end of the sixth century and it was followed by the granting of land lots on the island to Athenian citizens. Salamis was not incorporated in Attica, but the Athenian lot-

Conflict with Megara

Spartan arbitration over Salamis c. 509

Athenian settlers sent to Salamis

holders had a special status. Their lots were to be rent-free, but they could not be sold or leased to anyone except their relatives. They were to pay the same dues as Athenians in Attica and were to be available for military service when required. A large part of the stone recording the decree of the people which gives these terms has survived. It is the earliest decree of the Athenian democracy that we can read in the original.[3]

Athens under Pisistratus

In the capture of Nisaea the Athenians had been led by Pisistratus, son of Hippocrates, whose home was at Brauron beyond Hymettus. His military success encouraged him to pursue political ambitions. By professing democratic doctrines and practising popular arts, he ingratiated himself with those extreme democrats who, being bitterly opposed to the nobles and not satisfied by the Solonian compromise, were outside both the Plain and the Coast. Pisistratus thus organised a new party which was called the Hill, as it largely consisted of the poor hillsmen of the highlands of Attica; but it also included the poorer classes in the city and many discontented men, who preferred radical measures to the barrenness of oligarchic faction. With this party at his back, Pisistratus aimed at no less a thing than grasping the supreme power for himself. One day he appeared in the Agora, wounded, he said, by a foul attack of his political enemies— his enemies because he was a friend of the people; and he showed his wounds. In the Assembly, packed by his followers, a body-

The Hillsmen (Diakrioi)

Pisistratus seizes the tyranny, 561-0 B.C. Archonship of Comeas (κορυνη- φοροι.)

guard of 50 clubsmen was voted to him on the proposal of Aristion. Having secured his bodyguard—the first step in the tyrant's progress—Pisistratus seized the Acropolis and made himself master of the state.

It was the fate of Solon to live long enough to see the establishment of the tyranny which he dreaded. We do not know what part he had taken in the troubled world of politics since his return to Athens. The story was invented that he called upon the citizens to arm themselves against the tyrant, but called in vain; and that then, laying his arms outside the threshold of his house, he cried, 'I have aided, so far as I could, my country and the constitution, and I appeal to others to do likewise.' Nor has the story that he refused to live under a tyranny and sought refuge with his Cyprian friend the king of Soli any good foundation. We know only that in his later years he enjoyed the pleasures of wine and love, and that he survived but a short time the seizure of the tyranny by Pisistratus.

Death of Solon (c. 560-59 B.C.)

The discord of parties had smoothed the way for the schemes of Pisistratus; but his success led in turn to the union of the two other parties, the Plain and the Coast, against him, and at the end of about five years they succeeded in driving him out. But new disunion followed, and Megacles the leader of the Coast seems to have quarrelled not only with the Plain but with his own party. At all events, he sought a reconciliation with Pisistratus and undertook to help him back to the tyranny on condition that the tyrant wedded his daughter. There is a legend that the partisans of Pisistratus found in Paeania, an Attic village, a woman of loftier than common stature, whom they arrayed in the guise of the goddess Athena. Her name was Phye. Then heralds, on a certain day, entered Athens, crying that Pallas herself was leading back Pisistratus. Presently a chariot arrived bearing the tyrant and Phye; and the trick deceived all the common folk.

First exile of Pisistratus (556-5 B.C.)

Legend of Phye

First restoration and second tyranny (550-49 B.C.?)

But the coalition of Pisistratus with Megacles was not more permanent than that of Megacles with Lycurgus. By a former wife Pisistratus had two sons—Hippias and Hipparchus; and as he desired to create a dynasty, he feared that if he had offspring by a second wife the interests of his older sons might be injured and family dissensions ensue.[4] So, though he went through the form of marriage with the daughter of Megacles, as he had promised, he did not treat her as his wife. Megacles was enraged when the tyrant's neglect reached his ears; he made common cause with the enemies

of Pisistratus and succeeded in driving him out for the second time, perhaps in the same year in which he had been restored.[5]

The second exile lasted for about ten years, and Pisistratus spent it in forming new connections in Macedonia. On the Thermaic gulf he organised the inhabitants of the neighbourhood of Rhaecelus into some sort of a city-state. He exploited the mines of Mount Pangaeus near the Strymon and formed a force of mercenary soldiers, thus providing himself with money and men to recover his position at Athens. He was supported by Lygdamis, a rich Naxian, and by the friendship of other Greek states, including Thessaly, which he had cultivated in the days of his power. The aristocracy of Eretrian horsemen were well disposed to him, and their city was an admirable base for an attack upon Athens. When he landed at Marathon, his adherents flocked to his standard. The citizens who were loyal to the constitutional government marched forth, and were defeated in battle at Pallene. Resistance was at an end, and once more Pisistratus had the power in his hands. This time he kept it.

Second exile (550-49 B.C.?)

Second restoration and third tyranny (540-39-528-7 B.C.)

The rule of Pisistratus may be described as a constitutional tyranny. He did not stop the wheels of the democracy, but he guided the machine entirely at his own will. The constitution of Solon seems to have been preserved in its essential features, though in some details the lapse of time may have brought modifications. Thus it is possible that even before the first success of Pisistratus the assessment according to measures of corn and oil had been converted into an assessment in money. And as money became more plentiful the earlier standards for the division of classes ceased to have the old significance. But it was not to the interest of the tyrant to raise the census for political office. Various measures of policy were adopted by him to protect his position, while he preserved the old forms of government. He managed to influence the appointment of the archons, so as to secure personal adherents, and one of his own family generally held office. The tyrant kept up a standing force of paid soldiers—among them, perhaps, Scythian archers, whom we see portrayed on Attic vases of the time. And he kept in his power, as hostages, the children of some noble families which he suspected. Most indeed of his more prominent opponents, including the Alcmaeonids, had left Attica, and the large estates which they abandoned were at his disposal.

(1) Influence on the magistracies

(2) Mercenaries

(3) Hostages

These estates gave him the means of solving

Land dis-
tribution

The
land-tax

a problem which Solon had left unsolved, and of satisfying the expectations of a large number of his supporters. He divided the vacant lands into lots and gave them to those who had most need.[6] They became peasant proprietors, and they had to pay only the land-tax, amounting to one-tenth of the produce. Land was also given to many needy people who idled in the city, and loans of money to start them. The tax of a tenth, imposed on all estates, formed an important source of the tyrant's revenue, and it is generally supposed that he introduced it. But this is not probable. We may take it that this land-tax was an older institution which continued under Pisistratus until either he or his sons were able, through an increase of revenue from other sources, to reduce it to one-twentieth.[7] It has been plausibly suggested that this increase of revenue came from the silver mines of Laurion, which now perhaps began to be more effectively worked. His possessions on the Strymon were another mainstay of the finance of Pisistratus. He exerted himself to improve agriculture, and under his influence the olive, which had long ago found a home in Attica, was planted more widely.

Under Pisistratus Athens rested from the distractions of party strife, and the old parties gradually disappeared. The development of industry and trade and the tyrant's land policy gave the people a tranquil period of economic and political development. And as the free forms of the constitution were preserved, the masses, in the Assembly and in the Law-courts, received a training in the routine at least of public affairs, which rendered them fit for the democracy which was to ensue when the tyranny was overthrown.

Foreign
policy

Abroad it was the consistent policy of Pisistratus to preserve peaceful relations with other states. Aegina indeed was openly the rival of Athens, and humbled Megara could hardly be other than sullen. But Athens was on friendly terms with both the rival powers of the Peloponnese, Sparta and Argos; and Thebes, and Thessaly, and the Eretrian knights had helped the tyrant in the days of his adversity. His influence extended to the banks of the Strymon and the coast of Macedonia, as we have already seen; and he had a sub-servient friend in Lygdamis of Naxos, whom he had installed as tyrant over the Naxian people. Corinth, later to be the most bitter enemy of Athens, was still friendly.

Athens
in the
Propontis:
the war for
Sigeum

It was doubtless with the object of injuring the Megarian trade in Pontic corn, and gaining some counterpoise to Megarian power in the region of the Propontis, that Athens made her first venture in distant seas. It was about forty years before Pisistratus became tyrant that Athens seized the Lesbian fortress of Sigeum on the shore of the Troad at the entrance to the Hellespont. The friendship of Miletus, mother of many Pontic colonies, favoured this enterprise—which however involved Athens in a conflict with Mytilene, whose power and settlements extended along the shores of the straits. Mytilene, failing to recover the fortress, built another, the Achilleon, close by, which cut off the Athenians from the sea. It has been already told how the statesman Pittacus was engaged in this war and slew an Athenian commander in single combat, and how the poet Alcaeus threw away his shield. It would seem that while Athens was absorbed in her party conflicts at home, Sigeum slipped from her hands, and that the recapture of it was one of the achievements of Pisistratus. The tyrant showed the importance he attached to it by installing one of his sons as governor. The statesmen who first sent Athenian soldiers to the shores of the Hellespont had in truth opened up a new path for Athenian policy, and Pisistratus pursued that path. It was not long before a much greater acquisition than Sigeum was made in the same region; but this acquisition, though made with the good-will, and even under the auspices, of Pisistratus, was made by one who was his political rival and opponent. Miltiades, son of Cypselus, belonged to the noble family of the Philaids, and was one of the leaders of the Plain. It was after the usurpation of Pisistratus that, as he sat one day in the porch of his country-house at Laciadae on the road from Athens to Eleusis, he saw a company of men in Thracian dress, and armed with spears, passing along the road. He called out to them, invited them into his house and offered them hospitality. They were Dolonci, natives of the Thracian Chersonese, and they had come to Greece in search of a helper, who should have the strength and skill to defend them against their northern neighbours, who were pressing them hard in war. They had gone to Delphi, and the oracle had bidden them invite the man who first offered them entertainment after they left the shrine. Miltiades, thus designated by the god, obeyed the call of the Thracians, not reluctant to leave his country fallen under a tyrant's rule.

Acquisi-
tion of the
Thracian
Cher-
sonese
(559-6?)
Miltiades

The circumstances of the foundation of Athenian power in the Chersonese were thus wrought by the story-shaping instinct of the Greeks into a picturesque tale. The simple fact seems to have been that the Dolonci applied directly to Athens, inviting the settlement of an Athenian colony in their midst. Pisistratus was well pleased to promote Athenian influence on the Hellespontine shores; and the selection of Miltiades was not unwelcome to him, since it removed a dangerous subject. We may feel no doubt that it was as a representative of the Athenian state that Miltiades went forth, blessed by the Delphic oracle, to the land of his Thracian guests. But the oecist who went forth, as it was said, to escape tyranny, became absolute ruler in his new country. He ruled as a Thracian prince over the Dolonci; he ruled as a tyrant over his Athenian fellow-settlers. He protected the peninsula against invasions from the north by a wall which he built across the neck from Cardia to Pactye. We hear of his war with Lampsacus and his friendship with the king of Lydia.

It is not too much to say that Pisistratus took the first steps on the path which led Athens to empire. That path had indeed been pointed out to him by nameless predecessors; but it was his sword that conquered Megara, and under his auspices that Athens won a footing on both shores of the Hellespont. We cannot estimate too highly the statesmanship which sought a field for Athenian enterprise in the regions of the Propontis. The Ionian cities had forestalled Athens in venturing into the vast spaces of the eastern sea and winning the products of its shores. But though she entered the contest late, she was destined to outstrip both her friend Miletus, and Megara her enemy. Many years indeed were still to run before her ships dominated the Euxine; but it was much that she now set her posts as a watcher on either side of the narrow gate

> Where the sea-ridge of Helle hangs heavier, and
> east upon west waters break.

Pisistratus strongly asserted the claim of Athens to be the mother and leader of the Ionian branch of the Greek race. The temple of Apollo in Delos, the island of his mythical birth, had long been a religious centre of the Ionians on both sides of the Aegean. There, as an ancient hymn sang, 'the long-robed Ionians gather with their children and their wives', to honour Apollo with dance and song and games: 'a stranger who came upon the Ionians in their throng, seeing the men and the fair-girdled women and the swift ships and all their wealth would say that they were beings free for ever from death and eld'.

Pisistratus 'purified' the sacred spot by digging up all the tombs that were within sight of the sanctuary and removing the bones of the dead to another part of the island.

Thus Athens took the famous Ionian festival under her special care. It was said, and has been believed by many both in ancient and in modern times, that Pisistratus or his enlightened son Hipparchus did a yet more important thing for the great Ionic epics, the *Iliad* and the *Odyssey*. The story is that a commission of literary men was appointed to collect and write down and revise the two poems of Homer, and it has thus been supposed that it was due to the initiative of the tyrants and the labours of the learned men whom they employed that the poems were for the first time written down. If this were so, it would be difficult to explain how the Athenians a generation before, in their dispute with Lesbos over the possession of Sigeum, could appeal to Homer as to the part they had played in the Trojan War, in the absence of a generally recognised text of the *Iliad*. As to the special verse in the Catalogue which they quoted to establish their claim to Salamis against Megara, it was alleged by Megarians in later times that it was spurious, having been fabricated and inserted by the Pisistratean commission in the interests of Athens. This accusation had a certain plausibility, because Onomacritus, who was the most prominent member of the commission, was not above suspicion in the matter of forgery. He was a teacher of the Orphic religion and assisted Hippias, the tyrant's eldest son, in editing a collection of the oracles of soothsayers. But he was detected in introducing into the collection an oracle which he had invented and was banished from Athens. The whole story, however, of the Homeric commission of Pisistratus, implying that our texts of the two poems only go as far back as the sixth century, is without good foundations and is highly improbable.[8]

Pisistratus was indeed interested in Homer in another way. He made Homeric recitations a feature of the great Panathenaic festival, and he made a rule that the rhapsodes who competed should follow strictly the order of the poems in choosing the pieces they recited. The Great Panathenaea had been remodelled shortly before he seized the tyranny, and, on the pattern of the national gatherings at Olympia and Delphi, was held every fourth year. It was celebrated with athletic and musical contests, but the centre and motive of the feast was the great procession which went up to the house of Athena on her hill, to offer her a robe woven by the hands of Athenian maidens. The 'rich fane' of Athena, wherein she accorded Erechtheus a place, had the distinction of passing into the Homeric poems. It was situated on the Acropolis, north of the later Parthenon and close to the site of the old royal palace. Of the original temple but few blocks remain, for early in the tyranny of Pisistratus, or shortly before, it was rebuilt and surrounded by a Doric colonnade. Many of the lowest stones of the walls, still lying in their places, show us the site and shape of this temple, and some of its sculptures have survived. The triangular gables displayed what Attic sculptors of the day could achieve. Hitherto the favourite material of these sculptors had been the soft marly limestone of the Piraeus, and by a curious stroke of luck some striking specimens of such work—Zeus encountering the three-headed Typhon, Heracles destroying the Hydra—have been partly preserved, the early efforts of an art which a hundred and fifty years would bring to perfection. But now—in the second half of the sixth century—Greek sculptors have begun to work in a nobler and harder material; and on one of the pediments of the renovated temple of Athena Polias the battle of the Gods and Giants was wrought in Parian marble. Athena herself in the centre of the composition, slaying Enceladus with her spear, may still be seen and admired.

Peristasis and pediments added probably in Pisistratean age. Pedimental sculptures (?c. 600 B.C.)

Use of marble in sculpture

But the tyrant planned a greater work than the new sanctuary on the hill. Down below, south-eastward from the citadel, on the banks of the Ilissus, he began the building of a great Doric temple for the Olympian Zeus. He began but never finished it, nor did his sons after him. So immense was the scale of his plan that Athens, even when she reached the height of her dominion and fulfilled many of the aspirations of Pisistratus, never ventured to undertake the burden of completing it. A full completion was indeed to come, though in a shape far different from the original plan; but not until Athens and Greece had been gathered under the wings of a power which had all Europe at its feet. The richly ornamented capitals of the few lofty pillars which still stand belong to the work of the Roman emperor Hadrian, but we must remember that the generations of Athenians, with whom this history has to do, saw only plain Doric columns there, the monument of the wealth and ambition of the tyrant who had done more for their city, with his wide-ranging plans, than they cared to think.

Gigantomachy in the Pisistratean pediment

Completed by the Emperor Hadrian

Pisistratus was indeed scrupulous and zealous in all matters concerned with religion, and his sons more than himself. But no act of his was more fruitful in results than what he did for the worship of Dionysus. In the marshes on the south side of the Areopagus the bacchic god had an ancient sanctuary, of which the foundations have been uncovered; but Pisistratus built him a new house at the foot of the Acropolis, and its ruins have not yet wholly disappeared. In connection with this temple Pisistratus instituted a new festival, called the Great Dionysia of the City, and it completely overshadowed the older feast of the Winepress (Lenaea), which still continued to be held in the first days of spring at the temple of the Marshes. The chief feature of the Dionysiac feasts was the choir of satyrs, the god's attendants, who danced around the altar clothed in goat-skins, and sang their 'goat song'. But it became usual for the leader of the dancers, who was also the composer of the song, to separate himself from his fellows and hold speech with them, assuming the character of some person connected with the events which the song celebrated and wearing an appropriate dress. Such performances, which at the rural feasts had been arranged by private enterprise, were made an official part of the Great Dionysia, and thus taken under state protection in the form of a 'tragic' contest, two or more choruses competing for a prize. It was the work of a generation to develop these simple representations into a true drama, by differentiating the satyric element. Legends not connected with Dionysus were chosen for representation, and the dancers appeared not in the bacchic goat-dress but in the costume suitable for their part in the story. This performance was divided into three acts; the dancers changed their costumes for each act, and only at the end did they come forward in their true goat-guise and perform a piece which preserved the original satyric character of 'tragedy'. Then their preponderant importance was by degrees diminished, and a second actor was introduced; and by a development of this kind, hidden from us in its details, the goat song of the days of Pisistratus grew into the tragedy of Aeschylus.

The Lenaeum; the temple of Dionysus in Limnae

Differentiation of tragedy from satyric drama (Trilogy)

(Satyric drama)

The popularity of the worship of Dionysus at Athens in the days of Pisistratus might be observed in the workshops of the potters. No subject was more favoured than Dionysiac scenes by the artists—Exekias and his fellows —who painted the black-figured vases of this period. There is another thing which the student of history may learn among the graceful vessels of the potters of Athens. On the vases of the Pisistratean age the deeds of Heracles are a favourite theme, while Theseus is little regarded. But before the golden age

Dionysiac subjects on vases

Heracles on black-figured amphorae, etc. (c. 570-510 B.C.)

Theseus on red-figured cylixes, etc (c. 510-470 B.C.)

of vase-painting sets in, about the time of the fall of the Pisistratids, Theseus has begun to seize the popular imagination as the great Attic hero, and this is reflected in paintings on the cups of Euphronius and the other brilliant masters of the red-figured style. If we remember that Theseus was specially associated with the hill country of north Attica, which was the stronghold of the Pisistratean party, we may be tempted to infer that the glorification of Theseus was partly due to the policy of Pisistratus.

of the period has been excavated at the southeast corner of the Agora and Dörpfeld found the traces of an aqueduct which brought water from the upper stream of the Ilissus to a cistern in the rocky valley between the Areopagus and the Pnyx.[9] This concern for the public water supply which the aristocracies with their private wells had neglected is a policy typical of tyrants. It is no coincidence that Eupalinus' aqueduct at Megara was built for the tyrant Theagenes, and the Samian aqueduct for Polycrates.

5.1 Athenian fountain scene (c. 520) (see note, page 553)

Water supply

Besides caring for the due honours of the gods, Pisistratus was anxious to improve the living conditions of the people. In the hot summers of eastern Greece few things are more important than a good water supply and Pisistratus seems to have been very active in this field. The spring of Kallirhoe by the Ilissus to the south of the Acropolis, which was previously an open spring was converted into a large fountain house, *Enneakrounos,* with nine heads of water. Another fountain house

Growth of Sparta, and the Peloponnesian League

While a tyrant was moulding the destinies of Athens, the growth of the Spartan power had changed the political aspect of the Peloponnese. About the middle of the sixth century Sparta won successes against her northern neighbours Tegea and Argos; and in consequence of these successes she became the predominant power in the peninsula.

Tegeate
war, c.
560-50 (?)

Legend of
the con-
quest of
Tegea and
the bones
of Orestes

Eastern Arcadia is marked by a large plain, high above the sea-level; the villages in the north of this plain were to coalesce later into the town of Mantinea, those in the south had been united in Tegea. Sparta had gradually pressed up to the borders of the Tegean territory, and a long war was the result. This war is associated with an interesting legend based on the tradition that the Laconian hero Orestes was buried in Tegea. When the Spartans asked the Delphic oracle whether they might hope to achieve the conquest of Arcadia, they received a promise that the god would give them Tegea. Then, on account of this answer, they went forth against Tegea with fetters, but were defeated; and bound in the fetters which they had brought to bind the Tegeates were compelled to till the Tegean plain. Herodotus professed that in his day the very fetters hung in the temple of Athena Alea, the protectress of Tegea. War went on, and the Spartans, invariably defeated, at last consulted the oracle again. The god bade them bring back the bones of Orestes, but they could find no trace of the hero's burying-place, and they asked the god once more. This time they received an oracle couched in obscure enigmatic words:

> Among Arcadian hills a level space
>   Holds Tegea, where blow two blasts perforce
> And woe is laid on woe and face to face
>   Striker and counter-striker; there the corse
> Thou seekest lies, even Agamemnon's son;
> Convey him home and victory is won.

This did not help them much. But during a truce with the Tegeates, a certain Lichas, a Spartan man, was in Tegea and entering a smith's shop saw the process of beating out iron. The smith in conversation told him that wishing to dig a well in his courtyard he had found a coffin 7 cubits long and within it a corpse of the same length, which he replaced. Lichas guessed at once that he had won the solution of the oracular enigma and returning to Sparta communicated his discovery. The courtyard was hired from the reluctant smith, the coffin was found, and the bones brought home to Laconia. Then Tegea was conquered, and here we return from fable to fact. The territory of the Arcadian city was not treated like Messenia; it was not incorporated in the territory of Lacedaemon. It became a dependent state, contributing a military contingent to the army of its conqueror, and it bound itself to harbour no Messenians within its borders.[10] The recovery of the bones of Orestes is to be interpreted as Spartan propaganda. The tyrants of Sicyon had pursued a strong anti-Dorian policy and they may have been followed, to a lesser extent, by the Cypselids at Corinth. Sparta, in extending her influence through the Peloponnese, did not wish to raise issues of race. Later the Spartan King Cleomenes could say at Athens: 'I am no Dorian, but Achaean.'

At this period the counsels of Sparta seem to have been guided by Chilon, whose name became proverbial for wisdom. It was much about the same time, perhaps shortly after the victory over Tegea, that Sparta at length succeeded in rounding off the frontier of Laconia on the north-eastern side by wresting the disputed territory of Thyreatis from Argos. The armies of the two states met in the marchland, but the Spartan kings and the Argive chiefs agreed to decide the dispute by a combat between 300 chosen champions on either side. The story is that all the 600 were slain except three, one Spartan and two Argives; and that while the Argives hurried home to announce their victory, the Spartan— Othryades was his name—remained on the field and erected a trophy. In any case, the trial was futile, for both parties claimed the victory and a battle was fought in which the Argives were utterly defeated. Thyreatis was the last territorial acquisition of Sparta. She changed her policy and, instead of aiming at gaining new territory, she endeavoured to make the whole Peloponnese a sphere of Lacedaemonian influence. This change of policy was exhibited in her dealing with Tegea.

Sparta
conquers
Thyreatis,
c. 550 B.C.

The defeat of Argos placed Sparta at the head of the peninsula. All the Peloponnesian states, except Argos and Achaea, were enrolled in a loose confederacy, engaging themselves to supply military contingents in the common interest, Lacedaemon being the leader. The meetings of the confederacy were held at Sparta, and each member sent representatives. Corinth readily joined; for Corinth was naturally ranged against Argos, while her commercial rival, the island state of Aegina, was a friend of Argos. Periander had already inflicted a blow upon the Argives by seizing Epidaurus and thus cutting off their nearest communication with Aegina. The other Isthmian state, Megara, in which the rule of the nobles had been restored, was also enrolled. Everywhere Sparta exerted her influence to maintain oligarchy, everywhere she discountenanced democracy; so that her supremacy had important consequences for the constitutional development of the Peloponnesian states.

The Pelo-
ponnesian
confed-
eracy and
Sparta's
supremacy

In northern Greece the power of the Thessalians was declining, and thus Sparta became the strongest state in Greece in the second half of the sixth century. She was on friendly terms with Athens throughout the reign of Pisistratus, but the tyrant was careful to maintain good relations with Argos also. With Argos herself indeed Athens had no cause for collision, but the rivalry which existed between Athens and Aegina naturally ranged Athens and Argos in opposite camps. Earlier, probably near the middle of the seventh century, Athens had landed forces in Aegina and had been heavily defeated with Argive help. The policy of Pisistratus avoided a conflict with his island neighbour and courted the friendship of Argos.

Athenian attack on Aegina (first half of 7th cent.?)

Fall of the Pisistratids and Intervention of Sparta

Death of Pisistratus (528-7 B.C.) His sons and their court

When Pisistratus died, his eldest son Hippias took his place. Hipparchus helped him in the government, while Thessalus took little or no share in politics. The new rule opened with a gesture of political reconciliation, for a fragment of an Athenian archon list shows that the Alcmaeonid Cleisthenes, whose family went into exile after the battle of Pallene, was archon in 525/4, and was followed in office by the Philaid Miltiades, whose family had also been hostile to the tyranny.[11] The reconciliation, however, did not last long. Cleisthenes was soon in exile again, and Miltiades in the Chersonese. The general policy of Pisistratus, both in home and foreign affairs, was continued. But the court of Athens seems to have acquired a more distinctive literary flavour. Hippias, who was a learned student of oracles, and Hipparchus were abreast of the most modern culture. The eminent poets of the day came to their court. Simonides of Ceos, famous for his choral odes; Anacreon of Teos, boon companion, singer of wine and love; Lasus of Hermione, who made his mark by novelties in the treatment of the dithyramb, and amused his leisure hours by composing 'hissless hymns', in which the sound *s* did not occur— all these were invited or welcomed by Hipparchus. One of the most prominent figures in this society was Onomacritus, a religious teacher, already mentioned in connection with the alleged edition of Homer.

ὕμνος ἄσιγμος

Conspiracy of Harmodius and Aristogiton

The first serious blow aimed at the power of the tyrants was due to a personal grudge, not to any widespread dissatisfaction, but nevertheless it produced a series of effects which resulted in the fall of the tyranny. It would seem—but conflicting accounts of the affair were in circulation—that Hipparchus gave offence to a comely young man named Harmodius and his lover Aristogiton. It is said that Hipparchus was in love with Harmodius, and, when his wooing was rejected, avenged himself by putting a slight on the youth's sister, refusing to allow her to 'bear a basket' in the Panathenaic procession. Harmodius and Aristogiton then formed the plan of slaying the tyrants and chose the day of that procession, because they could then, without raising suspicion, appear publicly with arms. Very few were initiated in the plot, as it was expected that when the first blow was struck, the citizens would declare themselves for freedom. But, as the hour approached, it was observed that one of the conspirators was engaged in speech with Hippias in the outer Ceramicus. His fellows leapt hastily to the conclusion that their plot was betrayed, and, giving up the idea of attacking Hippias, rushed to the market-place and slew Hipparchus near the Leokorion. Harmodius was cut down and Aristogiton was afterwards captured, tortured, and put to death.

(514 B.C.)

Murder of Hipparchus

At the time no sympathy was manifested, little perhaps felt, for the conspirators. But their act led to a complete change in the government of Hippias. Not knowing what ramifications the plot might have, he became a hard and suspicious despot. It was probably in a purge following the assassination that the Alcmaeonids were expelled or felt forced to leave the city. Hippias fortified Munychia, to have a post on the shore, from which he might at any hour flee overseas, and he began to turn his eyes towards Persia, where a new power had begun to cast its shadow over the Hellenic world. Then many Athenians came to hate him and longed to shake off the reins of tyranny; and they began to cherish the memory of Harmodius and Aristogiton as tyrant-slayers.

Harsh rule of Hippias

The overthrow of the tyranny was chiefly brought about by the Alcmaeonids, who desired to return to Athens and could not win their desire so long as the Pisistratids were in power. They first tried, with other nobles, to win their way back with the sword, but they were defeated at Leipsydrion near Acharnae and realised that they needed stronger support. This they found in the Delphic priesthood with whom the family had long-standing associations, recently strengthened. The old sanctuary of Apollo had been burned down by accident, and it was resolved to build a new

Temple of Delphi built by Alcmaeonids

548-7 B.C.

temple at the enormous cost of 300 talents. A Panhellenic subscription was organised, and by this means about a quarter of the needed money was raised;[12] the rest was defrayed from the resources of Delphi. The Alcmaeonids undertook the contract for the work, and the story went that a frontage of Parian marble was added at their own expense, poros-stone having been specified in the agreement. The temple was not unworthy of the greatest shrine of Hellas. An Athenian poet has sung of the 'glancing light of the two fair faces' of the pillared house of Loxias, and has vividly described sculptured metopes with heroes destroying monsters and a pediment with the gods quelling the giants. It must have been about the time when the new temple was approaching its completion, or soon after, that to the holy buildings of Delphi was added one of the richest of all.

Siphnian Treasury

The islanders of Siphnos spent some of the wealth which they dug out of their gold and silver mines, in making themselves a treasury at the mid-centre of the earth, and its remains show us the richness of its decoration. Perhaps this building marks the height of Siphnian prosperity. Before a hundred years had passed, their supply of precious metal was exhausted; their miners had got below the sea-level, and the water filtering in cut them off from the sources of their wealth.

Large sums of money passed through the hands of the Alcmaeonids during the building of the temple, and their enemies said that this enabled them to hire mercenaries for their design on Attica. Their first attempt was a failure. They and other exiles seized Leipsydrion, a strong position on a spur of Mount Parnes looking down on Paeania and Acharnae; but they were too few to take the field by themselves, and the people had no desire to drive out the tyrant for the sake of setting up an oligarchy of nobles. They were soon forced to abandon their fortress and leave Attica. Convinced that they could only accomplish their schemes by foreign help, they used their influence with the Delphic oracle to put pressure on Sparta. Accordingly, whenever the Spartans sent to consult the god, the response was always: 'First free Athens.'

It has already been said that the Pisistradids cultivated the friendship of Sparta, and after his brother's murder Hippias was more anxious than ever not to break with her. But the diplomacy of the Alcmaeonids, of whose clan Cleisthenes, son of Megacles, was at this time head, supported as it was by the influence of Delphi, finally prevailed, and the Spartans consented to force freedom upon Athens. Perhaps they thought the dealings of Hippias with Persia suspicious; he had married his daughter Archedice to a son of the tyrant of Lampsacus, who was known to have influence at the Persian court.

The Spartans invade Attica

A first expedition of the Spartans under Anchimolius was utterly routed with the help of a body of Thessalian cavalry; but a second led by king Cleomenes defeated the Thessalians, and Hippias was blockaded in the Acropolis.

Fall of the Pisistratids, 510 B.C. (archonship of Harpactides)

When his children, whom he was sending secretly into safety abroad, fell into the hands of his enemies he capitulated and undertook to leave Attica within five days on condition that they were given back. He and all his house departed to Sigeum, and a pillar was set up on the Acropolis, recording the sentence which condemned the Pisistratids to perpetual disfranchisement (*atimia*).

Thus the tyrants had fallen, and with the aid of Sparta Athens was free. It was not surprising that when she came to value her liberty she loved to turn away from the circumstances in which it was actually won and linger over the romantic attempt of Harmodius and Aristogiton, which might be considered at least the prelude to the fall of Hippias. A drinking-song, breathing the spirit of liberty, celebrated the two friends who slew the tyrant; Harmodius and Aristogiton became household words. A skilful sculptor Antenor wrought a commemorative group of the two tyrant-slayers, and it was set up, not very many years later, in the Agora.[13]

Athens in the Peloponnesian league

The Athenian republic had to pay, indeed, something for its deliverance. It was obliged to enter into the Peloponnesian league, of which Sparta was the head; and thus Sparta acquired a certain right of interference in the affairs of Athens. This new obligation was destined to lead soon to another struggle.[14]

King Cleomenes and the Second Spartan Intervention

The birth of Cleomenes, and how he became king

It is necessary here to digress for a moment to tell of the strange manner of the birth of king Cleomenes, who liberated Athens. His father king Anaxandridas was wedded to his niece, but she had no children. The Ephors, anxious that the royal family of the Agids should not die out, urged him to put her away and, when he resisted, they insisted that he should take a second wife into his house. This he did, and Cleomenes was born. But soon afterwards his first wife, hitherto child-less, bore a son, who was named Dorieus. When the old king died, it was ruled that Cleomenes as the eldest should succeed, and *Dorieus* Dorieus, who had looked forward to the king-ship, was forced to leave Sparta. He went forth to seek his fortune in lands beyond the sea; having attempted to plant a settlement in Libya, he led an expedition of adventure to the west, took part in a war of Croton with Sybaris, and then sailed for Sicily, with the *(c. 510* design of founding a new city in the south-*B.C.)* west country. Yet he did not bring his purpose to pass, for he fell in a battle against the Carthaginians and their Elymian allies. After the birth of Dorieus his mother bore Anaxandridas two other sons, Leonidas and Cleombrotus, both of whom we shall meet hereafter.

Situation After the expulsion of the tyrant, the *at Athens,* Athenians had to deal with the political *510-8 B.C.* problems, whose solution, fifty years before, had been postponed by the tyranny. The main problem was to modify the constitution of Solon in such a way as to render it practicable. The old evils which had hindered the realisa-tion of Solon's democracy reared their heads again as soon as Hippias had been driven out and the Spartans had departed. The strife of factions, led by noble and influential families, broke out, and the Coast and Plain seem to have risen again in the parties of the Alcmaeo-nid Cleisthenes and his rival Isagoras. As *Isagoras* Cleisthenes had been the most active promoter *archon,* of the revolution, Isagoras was naturally sup-*508-7 B.C.* ported by the secret adherents of the tyrant's house. The struggle at first turned in favour of Isagoras, who was elected to the chief magistracy in 508, but it was only for a moment. Cleisthenes won the upper hand by appealing to the common people and to those who had been deprived of their citizenship in a revision of the register shortly after the expulsion of Hippias.[15] Thus the victory of Cleisthenes—and the victory of Cleisthenes was the victory of reform—was won by the threat of physical force; and in the year of his rival's archonship he introduced new demo-cratic measures of law. Isagoras was so far out-numbered that he had no recourse but appeal to Sparta. At his instance the Lacedaemonians, who looked with disfavour on democracy, demanded that the Alcmaeonids, as a clan under a curse, should be expelled from Attica; and Cleisthenes, without attempting resist-ance, left the country. But this was not enough. King Cleomenes entered Attica for the second time; he expelled 700 families pointed out by Isagoras, and attempted to dissolve the new constitution and to set up an oligarchy. But the whole people rose in arms; Cleomenes, *Spartans* who had only a small band of soldiers with him, *besieged* was blockaded with Isagoras in the Acropolis, *in the* and was forced to capitulate on the third day *Acropolis* 'in spite of his Spartan spirit'. Cleisthenes could now return with all the other exiles and complete his work. The event was a check for Lacedaemon. It was the first time, but not the last, that Athenian oligarchs sought Spartan intervention and Spartan troops held the hill of Athena.

Reforms of Cleisthenes

Solon created the institutions, and constructed the machinery, of the Athenian democracy. We have seen why this machinery would not work. The fatal obstacle to its success was the political strength of the clans; and Solon, by retaining the old Ionic tribes, had also retained the clan organisation as a base of his constitution. In order therefore to make *Need of a* democracy a reality, it was indispensable to *new or-* deprive the clans of political significance and *ganisation* substitute a new organisation. Another grave evil during the past century had been the growth of local parties; Attica had been split up into political sections. The memorable achievement of Cleisthenes was the invention of a totally new organisation, a truly brilliant and, as the event proved, practical scheme, which replaced the Ionian tribes, based on blood, by territorial tribes as the basis of *Abolition* political organization and so undermined the *of old* political influence of phratries and clans. *tribes* Henceforward the whole body of citizens was to play a decisive and permanent part in the conduct of public affairs.

Taking the map of Attica as he found it, consisting of between one and two hundred demes or small districts, Cleisthenes distin-guished three regions: the region of the city, *Three* the region of the coast, and the inland. In each *regions* of these regions he divided the demes into ten groups called *trittyes,* so that there were thirty *Thirty* such trittyes in all, and each trittys was named *trittyes* after the chief deme which was included in it. Out of the thirty trittyes he then formed ten groups of three, in such a way that no group *Ten tribes* contained two trittyes from the same region. Each of these groups constituted a tribe, and the citizens of all the demes contained in its three trittyes were fellow-tribesmen. Thus Kydathenaion, a trittys of the city region, was combined with Paeania, a trittys of the inland,

Distribution of demes among the tribes

and Myrrhinus, a trittys of the coast, to form the tribe of Pandionis. The ten new tribes thus obtained were called after eponymous heroes chosen by the Delphic priestess. The heroes had their priests and sanctuaries, and their statues stood in front of the Council House in the Agora.[16]

Demarchs (ληξιαρ-χικôυ γραμμα-τειου)

Both the tribes and the demes were corporations with officers, assemblies, and corporate property. The demarch or president of the deme kept the burgess list of the place, in which was solemnly entered the name of each citizen when he reached the age of eighteen. The organisation of the army depended on the tribes, each of which contributed a regiment of hoplites and a squadron of horse. The trittys had no independent constitution of this kind, no corporate existence, and consequently

Import-ance of the trittys

it appears little in official documents. But it was the scarcely visible pivot on which the Cleisthenic system revolved, the link between the demes and the tribes. By its means a number of groups of people in various parts of Attica, without community of local interest, were brought together at Athens and had to

Effect of the new system;

contrast with the old

act in common. The old parties of Plain, Hill, and Coast were thus done away with; there was no longer a means of local political action. Thus an organisation created for a purely political purpose was substituted for an organisation which was originally social and had been adapted to political needs. The ten new tribes, based on artificial geography, took the place of the four old tribes, based on birth. The incorporate trittys, which had no independent existence, but merely represented the relation between the tribe and the deme, took the place of the independent and active phratry. And the deme, a local unit, replaced the social unit of the clan. This scheme of Cleisthenes, with the artificial trittys and the artificially formed tribe, might seem almost too artificial to last. The secret of its permanence lay in the fact that the demes, the units on which it was built up, were natural divisions, which he did not attempt to reduce to a round number.

It must have taken some time to bring this reform into full working order. The first list of demesmen on the new system decided the deme of all their descendants. A man might change his home and reside in another deme, but he still remained a member of the deme to which he originally belonged. All Attica was included in this system except Eleutherae and Oropus on the frontier, which were treated as subject districts and belonged to no tribe.

The political purpose and significance of this reorganisation, which entitles its author to be called the second founder of the democracy, lay in its connection with a reformed Council. As the existing Council of Four Hundred had been based on the four Ionic tribes, Cleisthenes devised a Council of Five Hundred based on his ten new tribes. Each tribe contributed 50 members, of which each deme returned a fixed number, according to its size. They were probably appointed annually by lot from a number of candidates chosen by each deme; but the preliminary election was afterwards abolished, and forty years later they were appointed entirely by lot. All those on whom the lot fell were proved, as to the integrity of their private and public life, by the outgoing Council, which had the right of rejecting the unfit. From 504/3 they took an oath when they entered upon office that they would 'advise what is best for the city'; and they were responsible for their acts when they laid it down.

The new tribal organiza-tion reflected in a new Council of Five Hundred

This Council, in which every part of Attica was represented, was the supreme administrative authority in the state. 'In conjunction with the various magistrates it managed most of the public affairs.' An effective control was exerted on the archons and other magistrates, who were obliged to present reports to the Council and receive the Council's orders. All the finances of the state were practically in its hands, and ten new finance officers called *apodektai* (one from each tribe) later acted under its direction. It seems, moreover, from the very first to have been invested with judicial powers in matters concerning the public finance, and with the right of fining officials. Further, the Council acted as a ministry of public works and even as a ministry of war. It may also be regarded as the ministry of foreign affairs, for it conducted negotiations with foreign states and received their envoys. It had no powers of declaring war or concluding a treaty; these powers resided solely in the sovereign Assembly. But the Council was not only an administrative body; it was a deliberative assembly and had the initiative in all lawmaking. No proposal could come before the Ecclesia unless it had already been considered in the Council. The Council, after discussion, put the business before the Assembly either in the form of a recommendation, *probouleuma*, or without any definite guidance. In either case it was open to any citizen to give his views, supporting, opposing or proposing an amendment. The decision was taken by a show of hands. Again, the Council had some general as well as some special judicial functions. It formed a court before

(1) Adminis-trative functions

(2) De-liberative functions

(3) Judicial functions (εἰσαγ-γελίαι)

which impeachments could be brought, as well as before the Assembly, and in these cases it could either pass sentence itself or hand them over to another court.

It is obvious that the administrative duties could not conveniently be conducted by a body of 500 constantly sitting. Accordingly the year of 360 days was divided into ten parts, and the councillors of each tribe took it in turn to act as a committee for carrying on public business during a tenth of the year. In this capacity, as members of the acting committee of 50, the councillors were called *Prytaneis* or presidents, the tribe to which they belonged was said to be the *presiding*, and the divisions of this artificial year were called *prytanies*. The chairman of the committee was obliged, along with one trittys, to live permanently during his prytany in the Tholos, a round building, where the presidents met and dined at the public expense. The Tholos or Skias was on the south side of the Agora, close to the Council-hall. The old prytaneion still remained in use as the office of the archon and the hearth of the city.[17]

The Prytaneis and the civil year

Epistates

Cleisthenes seems to have retained the Solonian restrictions on eligibility for the higher offices of state. It is just possible that he may have set the knights, in this respect, on a level with the Pentacosiomedimni, but the two lower classes were still excluded from the archonship; the third class remained ineligible for another half-century. But this conservatism of Cleisthenes might be easily misjudged. We must remember that since the days of Solon time itself had been doing the work of a democratic reformer. The money value of 500 medimni was a much lower rating at the end than it had been at the beginning of the sixth century. Trade had increased and people had grown richer.

[Till 458-7 B.C.]

The new tribes of Cleisthenes led to a change in the military organisation. Each of the ten tribes was required to supply a regiment of hoplites and a squadron of horsemen; and the hoplites were commanded by ten generals whom the people elected from each tribe. The office of general was destined hereafter to become the most important in the state, but at first he was merely the commander of the tribal regiment.

Military reforms

Ten generals

The Athenian Council instituted by Cleisthenes shows that Greek statesmen understood the principle of representative government. That Council is an excellent example of representation with a careful distribution of seats according to the size of the electorates, and it was practically the governing body of the state. But though Greek statesmen understood

The Council a popular representative body

the principle, they always hesitated to entrust to a representative assembly sovereign powers of legislation. The reason mainly lay in the fact that, owing to the small size of the city-state, an Assembly which every citizen who chose could attend was a practicable institution; and the fundamental principle, that supreme legislative power is exercised by the people itself, could be literally applied. But while we remember that the Council could not legislate, although its co-operation was indispensable to the making of laws, we may say that its function will be misunderstood if it be either conceived as a sort of Second Chamber or compared to a body like the Roman Senate. It was a popular representative assembly, and from it were taken (though on a totally different principle) committees which performed in part the administrative functions of our 'Government'. It had a decisive influence on legislation; and here the influence of the Council on the Ecclesia must rather be compared to the influence of the Government on our House of Commons. But the ratification given by the Assembly to the proposals sent down by the Council was often as purely formal as the ratification by the Crown of bills passed in Parliament. The Areopagus still retained important powers but, as most of its members had been the nominees of the tyrants, its prestige was temporarily weakened.

First Victories of the Democracy

The Athenian republic had now become a democracy in a fuller sense, and the new government was hardly established before it was called upon to prove its capacity. King Cleomenes, who was the greatest man in Greece at the time, could not rest without attempting to avenge the humiliation which he had recently endured at the hands of the Athenian people. The man who had pulled down one tyrant now proposed to set up another. Isagoras, who had hitherto aimed at establishing an oligarchy, now came forward, it would seem, as an aspirant to the tyranny. Cleomenes arranged with the Boeotians and the Chalcidians a joint attack upon Attica. While the Lacedaemonians and their allies invaded from the south, the Boeotians were to come down from Mount Cithaeron, and the men of Chalcis were to cross the Euripus; the land was to be assailed on three sides at the same moment.

The Peloponnesian army under the two

506 B.C.:
the Pelo-
ponnesians
invade
Attica,

kings, Cleomenes and Demaratus, passed the isthmus and occupied Eleusis; and the Athenians marched to the Eleusinian plain. But the peril on this side passed away without a blow. The Corinthians, on second thoughts, disapproved of the expedition as unjust, and returned to Corinth. At this time Aegina was the most formidable commercial rival of Corinth, and it therefore suited Corinthian interests to encourage the rising power of Aegina's enemy. This action of the Corinthians disconcerted the whole army, and the situation was aggravated by the discord between the Spartan leaders, Cleomenes and Demaratus.

and retire

In the end the army broke up, and there was nothing left for Cleomenes but to return home. His attempt to impose a tyranny had been as unsuccessful as his previous attempt to impose an oligarchy upon Athens. For the second time the Athenian democracy had been saved from Spartan coercion. A hundred years hence, indeed, that coercion was to befall her;

(404 B.C.)

Cleomenes is the forerunner of Lysander, who will amply avenge him.

Plataea
supported
by Athens
against
Thebes

The Theban leaders of Boeotia had readily concurred in the Spartan plan, for they had a recent cause of offence against Athens. The town of Plataea, on the Boeotian slope of Mount Cithaeron, was determined to retain her independence and hold aloof from the Boeotian league, which was under the supremacy of Thebes. The Plataeans applied in the first instance to Sparta; but as Sparta was

510-9 B.C.

unwilling to interfere, they sought and obtained the help of Athens. This was the beginning of a long friendship between Athens and Plataea, based on mutual interest.[18] Plataea depended on the support of Athens to maintain her independence in Boeotia, while it suited Athens to have a small friendly power on the other side of Cithaeron—a sort of watch-tower against Thebes. The Athenians went to the protection of Plataea, but the threatened conflict was averted by the intervention of Corinth. The Corinthian arbitration ruled that

Hysiae
becomes
Athenian

Boeotian cities which did not wish to join the league must not be coerced. But as they were departing the Athenians were treacherously attacked by the Thebans, and, winning a victory, they fixed the river Asopus as the southern boundary of the territory of Thebes. The Athenians acquired, by this expedition, a post in Boeotia itself—the town of Hysiae, on the northern slope of Cithaeron.

Athenians
defeat the
Boeotians
(506 B.C.)

On the approach of the Peloponnesian army, the Boeotians had seized Hysiae, and crossing the pass of Cithaeron above it had taken Oenoe on the upper Attic slopes. When Cleomenes and the Peloponnesians retreated, the Athenian army marched northward to check the knights of Chalcis who were ravaging the northern demes of Attica. The Boeotian forces then withdrew into their own land and moved northwards too, in order to join the Chalcidians. But the Athenians, who must have been generalled by an able polemarch, succeeded in encountering their two enemies separately. They intercepted the Boeotians near the straits and won a complete victory. Then they crossed the straits, for the Chalcidians had retired to their island, and fought another battle, no less decisive, with the horsemen of Chalcis. The defeat of the Chalcidians

and the
Chal-
cidians

was so crushing that they were forced to cede to Athens a large part of that rich Lelantine plain whose possession they had disputed so hotly with Eretria. But this was not all. A multitude of Chalcidians and Boeotians had been made prisoners; they were kept fettered in bitter bondage until their countrymen ransomed them at two minas a man. We cannot withhold our sympathy from the Athenian people if they dealt out hard measure to those whom the Spartan king had so unjustly stirred up against them. The 'gloomy iron chains' in which 'they quenched the insolence' of their foes were proudly preserved on the Acropolis, and with a tithe of the ransom they dedicated to Athena a bronze chariot.

Cleruchy
at Chalcis

The democracy had not only brilliantly defended itself but had won a new territory. The richest part of the Chalcidian plain was divided into lots among 4000 Athenian citizens, who transported their homes to the fertile region beyond the straits—probably under the same conditions as the cleruchs of Salamis. These outsettlers retained all their rights as citizens; they remained members of their demes and tribes. The Salaminians were so near Athens that it was easier for them than for most of the inhabitants of Attica to attend a meeting of the Ecclesia; and the plain of Chalcis was not farther than Sunium from Athens.

Acquisi-
tion of
Oropus

And not only beyond the sea was new territory acquired, but on the borders of Attica itself. This at least is the only occasion to which we can well assign the annexation of the march district of Oropus, the land of the people who gave to the Hellenic race its European name. It had come under the control of Eretria, had adopted the Eretrian dialect which it was to retain throughout all future vicissitudes, and was the last part of Boeotia to be annexed by the Boeotian power of Thebes. This fertile little plain was destined to be a constant subject of discord between Boeotia and Athens, as it had before been a source of strife between Eretria and Boeotia. But it was now to remain subject to Athens for nearly a hundred years—subject to Athens, not Athenian; the men of Oropus, like the men of Eleutherae, never became Athenian citizens.

CHAPTER 6

The Advance of Persia to the Aegean

The Rise of Persia and the Fall of the Lydian Kingdom

While the Greeks were sailing their own seas and working out in their city-states the institutions of law and freedom, untroubled by any catastrophe beyond the shores of the Mediterranean, great despotic kingdoms were waxing and waning in the east. In the seventh century, the mighty empire of Assyria was verging to its end; the power destined to overthrow it had arisen. But the story of Assyria lies outside the story of Greece, since the Greeks, except in one outlying corner, came into no immediate contact with the lords of Nineveh. The Greek communities of Cyprus, as well as the Phoenician, were involved in the fortunes of the Syrian coast-land. When in the last quarter of the eighth century Sargon, under whose sceptre Assyria reached the summit of her power, had conquered the lands of the sea-coast—the Phoenicians and the Philistines—seven kings who lived 'at a distance of seven days in the middle of the western sea' trembled before him and offered their submission. They were the kings of Yatnan, as the Assyrians called Cyprus, and their act of fealty is recorded for us by Sargon himself on a pillar which he set up 'in a valley of the land of Yatnan'. Among the monarchs who submitted there were doubtless Greeks as well as Phoenicians, and a generation later we have the names of ten Cypriot kings who were subject to Assarhaddon and to Assurbanipal—Assarhaddon the great conqueror who voluntarily abdicated his throne, and Assurbanipal the peaceful sover-

eign whom the Greeks remembered as Sardanapalus. Among the names of the vassals whom inscriptions of these two kings enumerate are those of Eteandros of Paphos and Pylagoras of Cition. But if the story of Assyria touches only a remote fringe of the Hellenic world, it is otherwise with the story of those who destroyed the Assyrian empire. The Medes and Persians, folks of Aryan speech like the Greeks, were marked out by destiny to be the adversaries of the Greeks throughout the two chief centuries of Greek history.

The land of Media lies east of Assyria. Its ancient history is shrouded in mist; but there are some reasons for guessing that in the second millennium it was part of a great Aryan kingdom which stretched far north-eastwards over the plains of Bactria, peopled by the Iranian branch, as it is called, of the Aryan stock. The Iranians worshipped the same gods of heaven and light as the other folks of their kindred; but their sun-worship developed into a very different shape from the religion of Zeus. They regarded the element of fire with deeper reverence than other sun-worshippers; they dreaded to pollute it by the touch of a dead body or the overflow of boiling water; their land was full of temples with altars of perpetual fire. But the religion of the fire-worshippers had been moulded into an almost philosophical form by their prophet Zoroaster, who, though his name is encompassed with legend and it is uncertain when he lived, was assuredly a real man and not a creation of myth. He diffused among the Iranians the doctrine that the world is the perpetual scene of a deadly strife between the powers of light and darkness, between

The Medes

Sargon, king of Assyria, 722-705 B.C.

The stele of Sargon (set up at Cition), 709 B.C. Cypriot vassals of Assarhaddon (681-668 B.C.) and Assurbanipal (c. 668-626 B.C.)

Ormuzd the Great Lord and Ahriman the principle of evil.

It was towards the end of the eighth century that the Medes rebelled against the yoke of Assyria. They were led by Deioces, and after a struggle Media gained her independence, the deliverer being elected king by the free vote of his people. He had not only freed but had united his countrymen, and he set the seal on the union of Media by building the great city of Ecbatana. His treasury and palace were in the centre of a fortress, and he is said to have lived in this stronghold, withdrawn from the sight of his people, who could approach him only by written petition.

Deioces (Da-yaukku) founds kingdom of Media, c. 700 B.C.

The first successors of Deioces had enough to do in resisting the efforts of Assyria to recover her power over Media. But presently a king arose who was strong enough to extend his sway beyond the borders of his own land. Phraortes conquered the hilly land of Persia in the south, and thus a large Aryan realm was formed stretching from the Caspian to the Persian Gulf, east of Assyria and Babylonia. The next step was to conquer Assyria itself; and Cyaxares, the successor of Phraortes, prepared for the enterprise by a new organisation of the Median army. It was no hopeless task, for the Assyrian empire had been breaking up. Egypt had thrown off the yoke of the kings of Nineveh, and Nabopolassar had just arisen to do for Babylonia what Deioces had done for Media. Nabopolassar and Cyaxares joined hands, and the united forces of Media and Babylonia defeated the Assyrian army. Nineveh was destroyed in 612 and the remnants of the Assyrian army surrendered at Harran in 606.[1] The conquerors divided the empire. The south-western portion up to the borders of Egypt went to Babylonia; Assyria itself and the lands stretching westward into Asia Minor were annexed to Media.

Phraortes (c. 650-25 B.C.) conquers Persia

New kingdom of Babylonia. Nabo-polassar, 625-605 Fall of Nineveh, 612 B.C.

The restored kingdom of Babylonia, under Nebucadnezar, the successor of its founder, rose into wonderful fame and brilliance. He drove the Egyptians out of Syria, smiting them in the great battle of Carchemish; he stormed Jerusalem and carried the Jews into captivity; he made Tyre on its rock tremble though he failed to take it; he invaded and overran Egypt. But more famous than his conquests abroad were his mighty works in his own land. He made Babylon the greatest city in the world; and the stray Greeks who visited it came back with amazing stories of the palaces and temples, and the 'hanging gardens', a terraced park which was constructed by Nebucadnezar, though report ascribed it to the mythical queen

Babylonia under Nebucad-nezar, 604-562 B.C.

Semiramis. But the gigantic walls which surrounded the city were his mightiest monument; Greek travellers said that the circuit was more than 50 miles. Nebucadnezar went down to his grave, full of honours, after a long reign. He knew well on what side danger was to be feared for his kingdom. One of his works of fortification was a wall from the Tigris to the Euphrates, north of Babylon, to defend Babylonia against Media, her northern neighbour.

The exploits of the great Babylonian king affected Greece little, though Greek mercenaries, including the brother of the poet Alcaeus, served under him.[2] The Greeks of Cyprus must have caught the echoes of the clash of arms at Carchemish; they must have been stirred by the tidings of the storming of Jerusalem and excited by the siege of Tyre. But the changes which had befallen the east were brought nearer to the Greeks by the advance of Media. Cyaxares drew under his power the eastern parts of Asia Minor as far as the banks of the Halys, and this river became the boundary between Media and Lydia. The conquest of Lydia was the next aim in the expansion of the Median power, and a pretext was found for declaring war. In the sixth year of the war a battle was fought, but in the midst of the combat the day was turned suddenly to night; and the darkening of the sun made such a deep impression on the minds of the combatants that they laid down their arms and a peace was concluded. But the solar obscuration of this May day has another association which has a deeper interest for Europe than the warfare of Lydian and Mede. It was the first eclipse which European science foretold. Thales of Miletus, the father of Greek, and thereby of European, philosophy and science, had studied astronomy in Egypt; and he was able to warn the Ionians that before such a year had passed—his lore could not tell the day or the hour—the sun would be darkened. Thales was not only the first man of science; he was also the first philosopher: science and philosophy were not yet separated. If he looks over the ages to Copernicus, Newton, and Laplace, he looks likewise to Descartes, Berkeley, and Kant. He sought for a common substance, a single principle which should explain the variety of nature and reduce the world to unity and system; it is a small matter that he found this principle in water; it is his eternal merit to have sought it.

War of Lydia and Media: battle; eclipse of sun, May 28, 585 B.C.,

predicted by Thales

Beginnings of Greek science and philosophy

The Lydian king Alyattes married his daughter to Astyages, who succeeded to the throne of Media, and the kingdom of Lydia was

Reign of Ardys in Lydia;

saved for a generation, to enjoy the most brilliant period of its history. When Lydia recovered from the Cimmerian invasion, king Ardys renewed the efforts of Gyges to reduce the Greek cities of the coast. His chief success seems to have been the capture of Priene. His successors, Sadyattes and Alyattes, carried on a weary war against Miletus. They harried the Milesian territory every year, destroying the corn crops, and defeated the Milesians in two battles; but the strong walls of the coast-city defied them, as they had no fleet. At length

of Alyattes

Alyattes made peace with Miletus; possibly it was the outbreak of the war with Media that forced him to this step. At all events, he seems to have behaved liberally to his enemy. He built two temples to Athena in the place of one which had been burned down when he was devastating the Milesian land. This act of reparation was quite in accordance with the reverence for the gods of Greece which the Lydian monarchs invariably displayed. The story is that, when Alyattes fell ill and consulted Apollo at Delphi, the oracle enjoined upon him to restore the temple. Ionian Miletus was saved, but Smyrna was not only captured but destroyed, and in this volume its name will occur no more. Alyattes also conquered Bithynia. He might think that Lydia would now take rank with one of the great monarchies of the south or the east, and he built himself an enormous sepulchre, an earth-mound on stone foundations, which in size at least might match the monuments of Egyptian or Babylonian kings.

Reign of Croesus, 560-546 B.C.

It was reserved for Croesus, the son of Alyattes, to carry out fully the design of subjugating the cities of eastern Greece. He attacked and subdued the cities, Ionian and Aeolian, one after another, all except Miletus, whose treaty with his father he respected, while Miletus on her part saved her freedom by withholding all help from her sister cities. The Dorian states of Caria were also forced to submit, and the empire of Croesus extended from the Halys to the Aegean. We saw before that Lydia exercised a distinct influence on the Greeks of Asia, but perhaps their influence upon her was even greater. The Greek language spread in Lydia, and we may suspect that it was heard in Sardis as much as the native idiom; the Greek gods were revered; the Greek oracles were appealed to. The kings were benefactors of Hellenic sanctuaries. In the new temple of Artemis, which arose at Ephesus during his reign, Croesus was the donor of the sculptured reliefs which encircled the Ionic columns, and fragments of the three words,

which recorded the gift 'Dedicated by King Croesus', can still be read on their bases.[3] Hence the Greeks never regarded the Lydians as utter barbarians; and they always cherished a curious indulgence and sympathy for Croesus, though he had enslaved and ruled as despot the cities of Asiatic Hellas. The court of Sardis was in truth more oriental than Hellenic, not only in wealth and luxury, but also in its customs—for instance polygamy and the infliction of cruel punishments. Croesus carded alive a man who had opposed his succession to the throne. The Ionians had marvelled at the treasures of golden Gyges, but the untold wealth of Croesus became proverbial. It was furnished largely by the tributes of the Greek cities, as well as by the white gold of the Pactolus and the products of the mines of Pergamon. Croesus was the first to introduce, instead of the white gold money, a coinage of two metals, pure gold and silver, bearing to each other the fixed proportion of 3 to 40.

Croesus and Delphi

There is no more striking proof of the political importance of the oracle of Delphi at this period than the golden offerings dedicated by Croesus, offerings richer than even the priestly avarice of the Delphians could have dared to hope for. Wealthy though the lord of Lydia was, genuine as was his faith in the inspiration of the oracle, he might hardly have sent such gifts if he had not wished to secure the political support of Apollo and believed that Apollo's support was worth securing. His object was to naturalise himself as a member of the Greek world; to appear, not as an outsider, but as an adopted son of Hellas, ruling over the Greeks whom he had subdued and those whom he still hoped to subdue. Nothing would be more helpful than the good word of the Delphic oracle to create such a reputation. Moreover, if one of the Asiatic cities contemplated rebellion, a discouraging reply from the oracle, which would assuredly be consulted, might stand the despot in good stead.

Having extended his rule to the coast, Croesus conceived the idea of making Lydia a sea-power and conquering the islands. It was a perfectly feasible plan; and it was not till unforeseen events had frustrated it that the islanders could have found much comfort in the epigram that a Lydian king sailing against them with a fleet would be like themselves advancing against Lydia with a host of cavalry. The tale afterwards shaped itself that one of the wise men of Greece—it mattered little whether he was alive at the time or not—used this witticism to dissuade Croesus from the enterprise. But Croesus was diverted from his western designs by something graver than an epigram. Events of great moment were happening in the east. His brother-in-law Astyages was hurled from the throne of Media by a hero, who was to become one of the world's greatest conquerors. The usurper was Cyrus the Great, of the Persian family of the Achaemenids. The revolution signified indeed little more than a change of dynasty; the Persians and Medes were peoples of the same race and the same faith; the realm remained Iranian as before. But the Persians seem to have been the noblest part of the Iranian race; their bravery, temperance, and love of truth extorted the admiration of the Greeks.

The fall of Astyages was an opportunity for the ambitious Lydian to turn his arms to the east. The restoration of his brother-in-law was indeed a sufficient plea; and he might have good cause to fear that, if he were not the first to strike, the Persian usurper would soon advance to the conquest of western Asia. But Croesus certainly cherished hopes of extending the Lydian power into the interior parts of Asia, if not of succeeding himself to the Median throne. In undertaking such an enterprise he had to fear his Greek subjects, who might take advantage of his absence to throw off his yoke, and might even intrigue with the Persian. That the Greeks of Ionia had been long accustomed to regard Media as a resort against Lydia and to intrigue with the Median kings is shown by the word *medism*. For if such intriguing had first come into fashion after the rise of Persia and the fall of Lydia, the name chosen to designate it would naturally have been *persism*. Desirous of probing the hidden event of the future, Croesus consulted some of the oracles of Greece. There can be no question that the Delphic god gave him an answer which was meant to encourage him in his enterprise. Croesus was the wealthiest and most powerful king known to Delphi; Persia was only a name. It is said that the answer was that if he crossed the Halys he would destroy a mighty empire—an answer which need not have been that which was actually given, but may have been circulated afterwards to justify the oracle when the expedition failed. Croesus was also advised to seek the aid of the most powerful state of Greece. An alliance with Sparta was concluded, but no help was sent. Egypt and Babylon, who could not afford to see the balance of power destroyed, joined the alliance but events moved too swiftly for them.

Croesus, at the head of an army which included a force of Ionian Greeks, crossed the fateful Halys and invaded Cappadocia. He took the ancient city of Pteria and in its neighbourhood fought an indecisive battle with the Medes and Persians whom Cyrus had led against him. But the forces of Cyrus seem to have been far superior in numbers, and Croesus retired before him into Lydia. Under the walls of the capital the invader won a decisive victory, and after a short siege Sardis was stormed and plundered. The life of Croesus was spared. Cyrus had given strict injunctions that he was on no account to be slain in the struggle of the capture; and the story went that a soldier, not recognising him, was about to cut him down, when the king's son, who had been dumb from birth, suddenly burst out into speech: 'O man, slay not Croesus'.

This was not the only tale which adorned the fall of the Lydian king. The capture of Sardis was a complete shock. So great had been the wealth and might of Croesus, so dizzy the height of his power, that none thought his overthrow possible; and the sheer and sudden fall into nothingness made perhaps a deeper and more abiding impression on the imagination of Hellas than any other historical event. It was the most illustrious example that the Greeks had ever witnessed of their favourite doctrine that the gods visit with jealousy men who enjoy too great prosperity. And the personality of Croesus himself crept into their sympathies—the admirer of Hellenic art and wisdom, the worshipper of Hellenic gods, the generous giver out of his abundant wealth. Never more than for the memory of Croesus did Greece put forth the power of that genius, which she possessed in such full measure, of weaving round an event of history tales which have a deep and touching import as lessons for the life of men.

Cyrus built a great pyre—so the story is told by Herodotus—and placed thereon Croesus bound in chains, with 14 Lydian boys. And as Croesus was standing on the pile, in this extreme pass, there came into his mind a word which Solon had said to him, that no man could be called happy so long as he was alive. For the Athenian statesman had visited the court of Sardis in his travels—the art of the tale-weaver had no precise regard for the facts of time—and when he had seen the royal treasures and the greatness of the kingdom Croesus asked him whom he deemed the happiest of men. Solon named some obscure Greeks who were dead; and when the king,

6.1   Croesus on his pyre

Then Croesus cried to Apollo for help, and the god sent clouds into the clear sky, and a tempestuous shower of rain extinguished the fire.

Such is the tale as we read it in the history of Herodotus, but we can almost see the story in the making. For, before the episode of Solon was woven in, the fate of Croesus had been wrought into a legend related in a poem of Bacchylides. When the day of doom surprised the king, 'he would not abide to endure the bitterness of bondage, but he raised a pyre before the palace court, and mounted it with his wife and his weeping daughters. He bade the slave kindle the timber; the maidens screamed, and stretched their arms to their mother. But as the might of the fire was springing through the wood, Zeus set a sable cloud above it and quenched the yellow flame. Then Apollo bore the old man with his daughters to the land of the Hyperboreans, to be his abiding place, for his piety's sake, because his gifts to Pytho were greater than all men's gifts'. The moral of the tale clearly was, Bring gifts to Delphi; and we can hardly doubt that it originated under Delphic influence. But in the city of Solon it was transformed by a touch of genius into one of the great stories of the world.

The story of the fate of Croesus, as told by Bacchylides

As for Croesus it is probable that his life was spared, and it is possible that he spent his remaining days in Media, unconscious that a mythical association with the famous Athenian lawgiver would be his best assured claim on the memory of future ages.

Fate of Croesus

The Persian Conquest of Asiatic Greece

The kingdom of Lydia had performed a certain function in the development of Greece. Besides the invention of coinage, which was its one great contribution to the civilisation of mankind; besides the influence which its luxury and 'tyranny' exercised on Ionia; the mere existence of the Lydian realm, in its intermediate position between Greece and the east, was of considerable importance as a bulwark against the great oriental empires. It kept Greece from coming into direct contact with the empire of Assyria; it kept Greece for sixty years from coming into direct contact with the empire of Media.

When the barrier is swept away, a new period is opened in Greek history. The Greeks now stand face to face with the power of a monarch whose dominion stretches far away

unable to hide his wonder and vexation, exclaimed, 'Is our royal fortune so poor, O Athenian, that you set private men before me?', the wise Greek had discoursed on the uncertainty of life and the jealousy of the gods. Then Croesus, remembering this, groaned aloud and called thrice on the name of Solon. But Cyrus heard him call and bade the interpreters ask him on whom he was calling. For a while Croesus would not speak, then he said: 'One whom I would that all tyrants might meet and converse with.' Pressed further he named Solon the Athenian, and repeated the wise man's words. The pyre was already alight, but when Cyrus heard the answer of his prisoner he reflected that he too was a man, and he commanded that the fire should be quenched and the victims set free. The flames were already blazing so strong and high that the men could not quench them.

beyond the Euphrates, beyond the Tigris, into lands which are totally unknown to them. The Asiatic Greeks are now to exchange subjection to a lord of Sardis for subjection to a potentate who holds his court in a city so distant that the length of the journey is told by months. This distance of the centre from the extremities of the empire was of the utmost significance. The king was obliged to leave his conquests in Asia Minor to the government of his satraps; and the Greeks were unable to exercise any influence upon him, as they might have done if he had ruled from Sardis or some nearer capital. This was all the more unfortunate, on account of another difference which distinguished the Persian from the Lydian kingdom. While the Lydians were outside the Aryan family, the Persians and Medes spoke a language of the same stock as that of the Greeks. It may be thought that if the Persians had come under Greek influence, Iranian history would have taken a different course. For the Persians were a people marked out to fall under the influence of others and not to hew an independent path for themselves. In their own highlands, like the Spartans in the Laconian vale, they might live unspotted from the world, a valiant, simple, and truthful race; but when they once went forth to conquer and to rule, it was their inevitable doom to be led captive by their captives and to adopt the manner and ideals of more intellectual and original peoples. If Cyrus had transported the centre of his empire to the west, the Greeks might have been the teachers of their Persian speech-fellows; but such an idea would have occurred to no Mede or Persian. Consequently the new Iranian kingdom fell under the relaxing influences of the corrupt Semitic civilisations of Babylonia and Assyria; and it had soon become a despotism so typically oriental that it is hard to remember that the ruling peoples spoke a tongue akin to the Greek. Hence the struggle of two hundred years, upon which we are now entering, between Greece and Persia, though strictly and literally it was a struggle between Aryan peoples—peoples, that is, of Aryan speech—assumes the larger character of strife between Europe and Asia, between east and west, between Aryan and non-Aryan; and takes its place as the first encounter in that still unclosed debate which has arrayed Europe successively against Babylonian, Phoenician, Saracen, and Turk.

Disunion of Ionia

At the beginning of the campaign against Lydia, Cyrus had invited the Ionians who were in the army of Croesus to change sides. They had refused to 'medize', not perhaps from loyalty to the rule of the Lydian, under which they chafed, but because they did not anticipate his utter overthrow and therefore feared his vengeance. This refusal annoyed Cyrus; and when, after the fall of Sardis, the Greek cities made overtures to the conqueror, he declined to offer terms. Only with Miletus, which had not been subject to Lydia and had stood aloof from the contest, did he conclude an agreement like that in which Croesus had recognised her independence. The others prepared to defend themselves. Cyrus himself had greater projects which recalled him to the far east; and he committed the lesser task of reducing the Asiatic Greeks to the lieutenants whom he left in Lydia. The want of unity among the Ionians was disastrous. They might meet in their Panionic assembly, but they seem to have been without the ability or the organisation to carry out any plan of common action. The most powerful of all the states, Miletus, had gone her own way and stood quite apart, but Thales, the Milesian astronomer and philosopher, whom we have met before, is said to have offered his advice. He saw the weakness of Ionia in its disunion, and the futility of the loose league of the Panionion; and he made the remarkable proposal that Ionia should form itself into a united nation, with one Hall of Council as well as one place of Assembly, each city surrendering her sovereignty and becoming merely a town or deme of the state; and he suggested Teos as the fitting place for the capital. The idea, whether it was put forward by Thales or not, was assuredly suggested by the political development of Attica, the mother country of the Ionians. It was an idea which the proposer can hardly have hoped to persuade the Ionians to adopt, but it had its value as a comment on the disunion of the Greeks in the one part of Greece where, above all others, there was needed a closer unity and a solid serried front, to resist the aggression of the great barbarian powers. Another proposal, which was made in one of the ineffectual meetings of the Panionion, receives the approval of the historian Herodotus. Bias, a statesman of Priene, advised all the Ionians to sail forth together to the west, to the great island of Sardinia, and there found an Ionian state and live happy and free. This proposal illustrates the terror and despair of Ionia at the prospect of Persian rule.

Disunited, the Asiatic Greeks were an easy prey. Harpagus, the general of Cyrus, reduced them one after another; tribute was imposed upon them and the burden of serving in the Persian armies when such service was re-

Persian conquest of Greeks of Asia

quired; but no restrictions were placed upon the freedom of their commerce. To the inhabitants of two cities, exile seemed more endurable than this new slavery and they acted in the spirit of Bias. The people of Phocaea, or the greater part of them, embarked in their pentekonters and sailed to the island of Corsica, where their own settlement of Alalia received them.[4] The Teians did likewise, but found a nearer refuge on the coast of Thrace, where they founded Abdera.

Asiatic Greeks appeal to Sparta

One common effort indeed the Aeolians and Ionians made for their defence. They made a common appeal to the most powerful state in the mother country. They sent an embassy to Lacedaemon, but the Spartans, whose horizon was bounded by the Peloponnese, did as little for them as they had done for Croesus. Sparta had the curiosity, however, to send a ship to Ionia, to spy out the condition of the country and the power of Cyrus. The story is that one of her envoys went up to Sardis and standing before the Persian king forbade him to do harm to any Greek community, 'since the Lacedaemonians will not permit it'. The anecdote was doubtless invented by those who liked a jest at the expense of Sparta; but, if Cyrus might well ask 'who are the Lacedaemonians?', his successors learned the answer to their cost.

Fall of Babylon, 538 B.C.

Having conquered Lydia, Cyrus was now free to deal with the two remaining great powers of the Middle East, Babylon and Egypt, which had both allied with Croesus, but had not realised the urgency of the crisis. Babylon's great days had ended with the death of Nebucadnezar. His son who succeeded him was weak and was removed by his sister's husband who in turn was the victim of a rebellion. The king then elected, Nabonidus, was a conservative scholar who was poorly equipped to give the leadership that Babylon desperately needed. His main preoccupation was the cult of the Moon god at Harran and he spent little time in Babylon itself. His policies led to the increasing estrangement of the priestly hierarchy of Babylon and when in 539 the Persian army was ready Babylon was divided and demoralised. The Persians had no difficulty in winning their first battle, at Opis, and it proved to be their last. The gates of the city of Babylon were opened and the Persians entered unopposed. Cyrus wisely attributed his success to the invitation of Marduk, the supreme god of Babylon, and the priests of the established religion at first welcomed him. Cyrus took to himself the title of 'king of Babel, Sumer, and Accad, and of the four

quarters of the world', thus formally entering into the Babylonian inheritance. The dominion of Cyrus the Great extended in the east over Armenia and Hyrcania, Parthia and Bactria, and into the midst of Afghanistan; from the coasts of the Aegean to the banks of the Jaxartes. But his conquests lie outside our history. His last enterprise was the subjugation of the Massagetae, a Scythian folk near the Aral lake, and one story says that he was slain in battle against them, and that the savage queen placed his head in a basin of blood. All we know with certainty is that his body was buried in Persia, and two hundred years hence we shall visit his tomb at Pasargadae, in the company of a conqueror who was mightier even than he.

Death of Cyrus

The Persian Conquest of Egypt. Polycrates of Samos

The subjugation of Lydia and the Greek seaboard carried the borders of the Iranian empire, under its new dynasty, farther westward than the Assyrian conquest had ever reached. Two lords of Sardis had indeed acknowledged the overlordship of the kings of Nineveh; but that relation had been of brief duration and slight significance, and Lydia can hardly be said to have ever formed a part of the Assyrian dominion. In subduing the Greeks of the coast, at all events, Cyrus broke entirely new ground; they had never paid submission in any shape to Assyria. But while he passed far beyond the utmost limits of Assyria in some directions, he left unconquered the great kingdom of the south, which had once been part of the Assyrian empire. But his son Cambyses repaired the omission; it was inevitable that the new lords of Assyria should seek to bring Egypt under their subjection. We saw how Egypt, like Media itself and Babylonia, threw off the Assyrian yoke and entered upon a new period of national prosperity under enlightened rulers. King Amasis, who climbed the throne by a revolution, maintained his power by a bodyguard of Ionian and Carian mercenaries, like a Greek tyrant. An Egyptian writing tells us how he loved the strong 'wine of Kelebi of Egypt'. Like the Pharaohs of old, he built great temples to the Egyptian gods, but in his patronage of Greece he may be compared to Croesus. He sent gifts to the Greek sanctuaries; he subscribed generously to the rebuilding of the temple at Delphi; he married a Greek princess of Cyrene; and under him Naucratis rose to the

Persian conquest of Egypt by Cambyses

Amasis (Aahmes), 569 B.C.;

a phil-Hellene

147

Naucratis rank of a city, the only one where Greeks were allowed to trade. He had extended his control over the island of Cyprus when the power of Babylonia was declining, but the Cypriots threw off his yoke when Cyrus entered into the Babylonian heritage, and made their submission to the Persian. Amasis was alarmed at the rise of the new power in the east, and he lived to witness with dismay the preparations of Cambyses; but he died a few months before the invasion, and the blow fell upon his son, Psammetichus. A fierce battle near Pelusium delivered Egypt into the hands of the Persians. The conqueror led his army up the Nile, and perhaps he extended the southern frontier of the Egyptian kingdom on the side of Nubia. The Egyptians said that he planned the conquest of all Ethiopia and was compelled to return through want of provisions, so that his enterprise came to nothing. But the Egyptians hated Cambyses, who openly scoffed at their religion, and it is possible that they may have represented as an inglorious failure what was really a successful effort to secure the southern frontier. The conquest of Egypt, which became a Persian satrapy, led to the submission of Greek Cyrene, even as the conquest of Lydia had led to the subjection of the Greeks of the neighbouring coasts.

Death of Amasis, 525 B.C.

(Psammetichus III.) Battle of Pelusium, 525 B.C. Ethiopian expedition of Cambyses

Voluntary submission of Cyrene

Polycrates tyrant of Samos

Amasis and his son might have hoped, when the Persian danger threatened, that they could depend on the support of a powerful Greek friend, the tyrant of Samos. In that island, not long after the Persian conquest of Ionia, a certain Polycrates and his two brothers had established a joint tyranny over the state, with the help of Lygdamis of Naxos. But Polycrates removed his brothers by death and banishment and became sole tyrant. He organised a fleet of a hundred pentekonters and made Samos a strong power; as the Ionian mainland had fallen under Persian dominion, he had perhaps the strongest Greek sea-power in the Aegean and with it he controlled the important religious centre of Delos. His luxurious court was brightened by the presence of the Bacchic poet Anacreon. He continued the building of the great temple of Hera, but the most famous of his works was the aqueduct which supplied the city with water from a spring beyond a hill, by means of a tunnel some 300 m. long. Boring began at both ends and the accuracy of the calculations was a triumph for the engineering skill of Eupalinus of Megara. In all that he put his hand to, Polycrates prospered; he defied the power of Persia; he extended his influence over some of the Ionian cities under Persian rule. It was natural that he and Amasis of Egypt should form a close alliance, based on the common interest of antagonism to Persia. But when the critical hour came, when Cambyses moved upon Egypt, the Samian tyrant altered his policy. He felt that his navy was unequal to coping with the joint armaments of Phoenicia and Cyprus, and instead of coming to the aid of his ally's son he sent forty ships to

526 B.C.

6.2 Hera and Zeus (?) in wood, Samos (see note, page 553)

increase the fleet of the invader. These ships, however, never reached Egypt. The tyrant had manned them with those Samians whom he most suspected of hating himself and his tyranny; but his trick recoiled. At the island of Carpathus the crew resolved to sail back to Samos and overthrow the despot. Defeated in a battle they sought the aid of Sparta, and their appeal was strongly backed by the Corinthians, whose trade probably suffered from the pirate ships of Polycrates. The Spartans sent an expedition to besiege Samos; it was their first expedition to the east, and it was a failure. Repulsed in an engagement outside the walls and despairing of taking the city, they returned home.

Spartan attack on Samos

We cannot charge Polycrates with perfidy in espousing the cause of Persia against Egypt, since we are ignorant of his relations, not only with Psammetichus, but with Amasis in the last years of that monarch's reign. We might indeed gather from Herodotus' story of the ring of Polycrates that the alliance had ceased to exist, and that it was Amasis who had broken it off. Amasis, hearing of his friend's marvellous prosperity, never varied by a reverse, wrote him a letter, expressing misgivings at a good fortune so great and enduring that it could not fail to draw down the envy of heaven, and counselling Polycrates to cast away whatever possession it would give him the most pain to lose: 'Cast it away utterly, out of the world'. Polycrates, taking the words to heart, manned a pentekonter, and having rowed out to sea, cast into the waves the most precious thing he had, an emerald ring engraved by the gem-cutter Theodorus. A few days later a fisherman came to his house and presented him with a huge fish; the ring was found inside it. Polycrates wrote to Amasis an account of what had happened, and Amasis, when he read the letter, discerned that it was impossible for any man to deliver another from that which was destined to befall him. Convinced therefore that Polycrates would come to no good end, and not wishing to have to grieve for a friend's misfortune, Amasis broke off the tie of guest-friendship which bound them. The forecast of the Egyptian was fulfilled. Soon after his repulse of the Lacedaemonian attack, Polycrates fell into a trap laid for him by the Persian satrap of Sardis and was seized and crucified.

Story of the ring of Polycrates

Death of Polycrates, c. 523 B.C.

Ionia under Darius

King Cambyses was recalled from Egypt by a rebellion. He had put to death on suspicions of

Death of Cambyses, 522 B.C.

disloyalty his brother Smerdis, to whom he had entrusted the regency of some of the eastern provinces; and a usurper had arisen, pretending to be the dead Smerdis, to whom he bore a remarkable likeness. Cambyses went in haste to crush the false Smerdis. But as he passed through Syria he 'found death by his own hand', as is related in a great writing on the rock of Behistun.[5] The next heir to the Persian throne was a certain Hystaspes, who was satrap of Parthia and had a son named Darius. But Hystaspes made no attempt to secure his right, and the false Smerdis established himself so firmly that, as Darius wrote afterwards in that famous inscription of the rock, 'No Persian nor Mede dared to oppose him'. But Darius had different thoughts from his father and conspiring with six nobles he killed the usurper and became king himself. In the first years of his reign his force and ability were proved in the task of quelling rebellions which broke out in almost all parts of the wide realm which Cyrus had put together. Elam, Babylonia, Media, Armenia revolted; a new false Smerdis arose; Babylon had to be twice besieged. Having established his power firmly and crushed all resistance, Darius recorded for future ages the hard-won successes of his first years, in an inscription on the lofty rock of Behistun on the upper course of the river Choaspes. The writing is in the Persian, the Susic, and the Babylonian languages.

Accession of Darius (Dûrajavahuš), 521 B.C.

(Babylon taken, (1) Feb. 520 B.C., (2) 519 B.C.) Inscription of Bagistan

By wedding Atossa, the daughter of Cyrus and widow of her brother Cambyses, Darius linked himself closely to the family of his predecessors. He proceeded to reorganise the administration of his dominion. He extended the system of satrapies or governments, and the whole realm was divided into twenty such satrapies. West of the Halys, the old kingdom of Lydia consisted of three provinces, but subject to two satraps: the Ionian and the Lydian under one governor who resided at Sardis; the Phrygian which included the Greek cities of the Propontis under a governor whose seat was at Dascylion. These satraps did not interfere in the local affairs of the Greek cities, which were ruled by despots; and the despots might do much as they pleased, so long as they paid tribute duly and furnished military contingents when required. The despots liked the Persian rule, which secured their power, and this explains the noteworthy fact that the Greeks of Asia Minor made no attempt to shake off the Persian yoke during the troubles which ushered in the reign of Darius. It is possible that their condition under the rule of Cambyses was better than under Darius, for

Atossa

Western satrapies: 1. (a) Ionian, (b) Lydian, 2. Phrygian

Tyrants under Persian rule

6.3   Persian tribute, Persepolis (see note, page 553)

The Royal Road

Darius is said to have instituted a fixed yearly tribute instead of irregular contributions. Trade was furthered by this king's monetary reforms and by his improvement of the road-system in Persia. He adopted the bimetallic coinage which Croesus had introduced in Lydia; the chief piece of Persian gold money was always known in Greece by the name *daric*.

The Royal Road, by which the messengers between Susa and Sardis came and went, was divided into stages marked off by regular stations. Its length was over 1500 miles, and the way was counted a three months' journey for a man on foot. A Greek who had to visit Susa would land at Ephesus and in three days reach Sardis. The road ran through the heart of Phrygia, by the tomb of Midas the golden king, past Pessinus and Ancyra and across the Halys to Pteria the ancient Cappadocian city which Croesus took, then across the Halys again, southward to Mazaka and Comana, to cross the Taurus and reach the Euphrates at Samosata. Beyond the Euphrates, it skirted the mountains which bound Mesopotamia on the north, passing Nisibis and reaching the Tigris at

Nineveh, the ruined capital of Assyria. Beyond Arbela, it went south-eastward to the river Choaspes and Susa. A good and safe road, carefully maintained, brought central Asia nearer to the Aegean, and helped to open the east to western curiosity. The construction of the Royal Road must have had an incalculable effect in widening Greek ideas of geography. Its influence is shown by the importance which it assumed on the first Greek maps. Conceived as a straight line running east and west, it plays on one of the maps which were used by Herodotus practically the same part which is played in the modern Atlas by the Equator. The longitudes were determined by the conception that the Nile and the Danube, the two greatest rivers known within the range of the Greek world, were in the same meridian— the Danube being supposed to flow from north to south. This meridian line passed through Sinope. It was a principle of the early Greek geographers who arose about the end of the sixth century in Ionia that the features of the earth were symmetrically arranged. The attempt to apply mathematical principles to a

Early maps

small portion of the earth, very imperfectly observed, necessarily produced maps which to our fuller knowledge appear grotesque. But it would be hard to overestimate the intellectual activity of the Ionian investigators who made the new departure—Anaximander and Hecataeus, both citizens of Miletus. Anaximander constructed the first map, and Hecataeus wrote a geography which served as a 'text to Anaximander's map'. Hecataeus was himself a traveller—he composed the earliest guide-book to the wonders of Egypt, and he could supplement his own observations by second-hand material gathered, in the great centre of trade where his home was, from travellers and strangers. This development of geography in Ionia was certainly forwarded by the Royal Road, and so far the Persian conquest of eastern Greece was an advantage to European civilisation.

Anaximander

Europe owes so much to the Ionian intellects which at this period were breaking new paths of progress that we may linger a moment longer over the movement of intellectual discovery before resuming the march of events. It was a movement of the most interesting kind, in which the instinct for speculation and the thirst for positive knowledge were closely united. For Anaximander, the first cartographer, map-making is only part of his wider work as a physical philosopher. Dissatisfied with the theory of Thales, who found the first principal of the universe in water, he sought it in a more general conception which he designated, negatively, as the 'Unlimited'—unlimited, that is, by qualities, and so capable of differentiation into all the kinds of definite matter which our senses perceive. Hecataeus is the founder of Greek history. He partly breaks with the old traditions, and criticises the Hesiodic school of theology. The heroes who appeared in legend as sons of the gods he regards as the bastard sons of women who, to shield their shame, ascribed the fatherhood to Zeus or Apollo. 'The stories of the Greeks,' he says, 'are, in my opinion, manifold and absurd.' Thus reason was asserting itself against authority in the religious sphere, and Hecataeus was one of the pioneers. But more effective than he in pressing the claims of reason was another Ionian, his contemporary, Xenophanes of Colophon; and we shall have to consider the importance of his work in another connection.

Hecataeus the logographer

Xenophanes (p. 198)

The remoteness of Susa from the Greek seas, and the homesickness of Greeks whom any chance transported to the far east, find an illustration in the curious story of the physician Democedes of Croton. This man's

The story of Democedes

skill had earned high salaries, as public physician at Aegina and Athens, and higher still in the service of Polycrates of Samos. He was carried off as a prisoner to Susa, in consequence of a series of troubles which followed the death of that tyrant; and he was taken from his dungeon to try his craft for Darius, who had sprained a foot in the chase. His success gained him the king's favour, and there was nothing which he might not ask except the one thing which he desired, permission to return to Greece. One day he was summoned by Queen Atossa, who was suffering from a tumour on the breast, and he made her swear that if he cured her she would do what he asked. Acting by his directions, she stirred up the king to cherish the project of conquering the Greeks, and suggested that he should send spies under the conduct of Democedes to travel through Greece and bring back a report. These counsels of the daughter of Cyrus carried weight with Darius, according to the story; and the plan of Democedes succeeded. He promised to return to Susa, and Darius gave him rich presents for his kinsfolk; the Persians who accompanied him were privately charged to see that he did not escape. When they came to Taras—for the story assumes that Italiot Greece was included in the programme of the journey—the lord of that city arrested the Persians as spies, and kept them in prison until Democedes had time to escape to his native town. When the Persians were released they followed him to Croton, but the Crotoniats refused to give him up; a Persian invasion of Italy was a contingency which they might reasonably risk. Such is the strange story, blended of fact and fiction, which men told of the first Greek physician who practised at the court of Susa. He was not the last; we shall meet hereafter a more famous doctor, who did not yearn back to Greece and wrote the history of his adopted country.

(Ctesias p. 328)

The European Expedition of Darius. Conquest of Thrace

Cyrus had conquered the eastern coasts of the Mediterranean; Cambyses had completed and secured that conquest on the south side by the subjection of Egypt; it remained for Darius to complete and secure his empire on the north side by the reduction of Thrace. The possession of the adjacent part of the European continent was of like importance to the lord of Asia Minor, as the possession of the adjacent part of the African continent to the lord of

Syria. Having spent eight years in setting his house in order, Darius prepared for his European expedition. It seems probable that his original design was first to subdue the Thracian peoples as far as the Danube, so as to make that river the northern boundary of his empire, and secondly to extend his power westward over Macedonia. The Thracian race was warlike and the country is mountainous, so that the Persian enterprise was serious and demanded large forces and careful precautions. *c. 512 B.C.* The skill of a Samian architect named Mandrocles was employed to throw a bridge of boats across the Bosphorus, north of Byzantium; and when the Persian host had passed over Darius ordered two pillars to be set up on the European side, inscribed with the names of the various peoples composing his army, in Greek and cuneiform characters. These pillars were seen by the historian Herodotus. And in the temple of Hera at Samos there was to be seen another monument of the crossing into Europe. Mandrocles spent a part of the reward which Darius gave him in setting up there a painting in which the bridge and the crossing over, with Darius seated in a prominent place, were portrayed. He inscribed on it four verses to this effect: 'Having bridged the fishy Bosphorus, Mandrocles dedicated to Hera a memorial of his raft-bridge. A crown he set upon his own head, and glory upon the men of Samos; for the work he wrought pleased king Darius.' A large fleet was also furnished by the Greek subjects of Persia, to sail along the Thracian coast of the Black Sea as far as the mouths of the Danube, and to support and co-operate with the army. The contingents of the various Greek cities were commanded by their despots, prominent among whom were Histiaeus of Miletus, Hippoclus of Lampsacus, and Miltiades of the Thracian Chersonese.

No details of the warfare in Thrace are preserved. We are told that many tribes submitted, and the Getae signalised their love of freedom by refusing to surrender it without a struggle. It seems probable, however, that the Thracians made some preparations to meet the invader. North of the Danube, in the lands which are now called Wallachia and Moldavia (between the Danube, the Carpathians, and the Pruth), lived tribes which were allied in many respects to the tribes south of the river. The Greeks included these tribes under the general name of Scythian, which they applied to the whole series of peoples who dwelt between the Carpathians and the Caucasus. While the most easterly of them approximated in language to the Persian, the most westerly approximated to the Thracian. Nothing was more natural than that the people south of the Danube, threatened by an Asiatic invasion, should have taken steps to gain help from their neighbours on the north, to oppose the Persian advance. Such help would have been readily given, and Darius doubtless became aware before he reached the Danube that the hostility of the Scythian beyond the Danube—whose frozen waters invited them to cross in winter—might be a frequent trouble to Persian rule in Thrace. The Greek fleet sailed up the mouth of the river and a bridge of boats was thrown across. Darius and his army marched over into Scythia. But both the king's purpose and what he did, in this remote corner of the world, are hidden in a cloud of legend. That he may have wished to make a hostile demonstration and strike terror into the restless neighbours of Thrace is probable; but it is not the whole explanation. We may rather suppose that the chief object of the diversion beyond the Danube was to lay hands upon the gold mines of Dacia, which was then the land of the Agathyrsi, and to secure a route of communication between that land and the mouth of the Danube.[6] For three facts seem to emerge from the mist. The first is that the Agathyrsi were active in opposing the march of the Persians; the second, that he erected forts on a river named the Oaros—a name otherwise unknown, but evidently a tributary of the Danube; the third, that his communications with the fleet which awaited his return were for some time cut off, and the Greek commanders were tempted to sail away and leave him in the lurch. He afterwards showed his gratitude to them for the loyalty with which they supported him in this expedition. The fact is that it would have been entirely contrary to their own interests to inflict a blow on the power which maintained despotism in the Greek cities of Asia Minor. But their loyalty at this juncture was all the more precious to the Persian king when he found on returning through Thrace that Byzantium, Perinthus, and Chalcedon had revolted. These revolts forced him to avoid the Bosphorus. He marched to the Thracian Chersonese and crossed the Hellespont, but left behind him an army under Megabazus, which was ultimately to complete the conquest of Thrace, and immediately to reduce the Greek cities along the northern coast of the Propontis and the Aegean. Megabazus established Persian dominion actually as far as the Strymon, and nominally even farther west; for the Paeonians,

Why Darius crossed the Danube

Persian sway in Europe

between the Strymon and the Axius, were conquered, and Macedonia acknowledged allegiance to the Great King.

The Persian dominion over the eastern part of the Balkan peninsula lasted for about fifteen years, and it was increased by the acquisition of the islands of Lemnos and Imbros. The excursion of Darius beyond the Danube, so far as it was intended to make an impression on the Scythians, seems to have been ineffective. Shortly afterwards we find the Scythians raiding Thrace and driving Miltiades from the Chersonese.

The European expedition of Darius had thus been a distinct success, which might fearlessly be set beside the Egyptian expedition of Cambyses. But it has come down to us in a very different and totally fabulous shape. It is represented as not primarily an expedition against Thrace, but as an attempt to execute the mad project of incorporating the Scythians of the steppes of southern Russia in the Persian empire. In this story, which is told with all the art of Herodotus, Thrace appears merely as the way to Scythia, and the actual conquest of Thrace sinks into insignificance beside the ignominious failure of the Persian army to achieve the ultimate end of their wild enterprise, the conquest of Scythia. Darius, whose purpose is said to have been to take vengeance on the Scythians for their invasion of Media a hundred years before, dispatches the Greek fleet to the Danube simply for the purpose of throwing a bridge of boats across the river. His first idea was to break down the bridge when he had passed over and send the ships home, but by the advice of a prudent Greek he changed his plan. He took a cord, in which he tied sixty knots, and said to the Greek captains: 'Untie one of these knots every day, and remain here and guard the bridge till they are all untied. If I have not returned at the end of that time, sail home.' The Greek historian Herodotus then conducts Darius with his vast host through the steppes of Scythia 'as it were through fairyland', without any regard to the rivers which had to be crossed, the leagues which had to be traversed, the want of supplies. He carries him to regions beyond the Don, and transfers the river Oaros, on which Darius built his forts, from the neighbourhood of the Danube to the neighbourhood of the Maeotic sea, placing this imaginary march of the Persians in the midst of a poetical picture of the Scythian folks and the Scythian land. In returning to the Danube the Persians found themselves in sore straits, chased and harassed by the barbarians, and

meanwhile the sixty days had passed. The Ionians waited at the river beyond the ordained time, and presently a band of Scythians arrived urging them to destroy the bridge, so that they might ensure the destruction of Darius and gain their own freedom. Miltiades, the tyrant of the Chersonese, strongly advocated the proposal of the Scythians, but the counter-arguments of Histiaeus of Miletus prevailed, for he pointed out that the power of the despots in the cities depended on the Persian domination.[7] They pretended however to fall in with the Scythian proposal, and destroyed a part of the bridge on the northern side, so that the Scythians went their ways, satisfied that the retreat of Darius would be cut off. A little later, Darius arrived in the dark hours of the night, and was filled with terror when he could discover no bridge. An Egyptian with a loud voice shouted the name 'Histiaeus!' across the water, and Histiaeus, who was himself keeping guard, heard the cry, brought up his boats, and renewed the missing portion of the bridge. Thus Darius, after an ignominious retreat, was saved by the good offices of Histiaeus; whereas, if the advice of Miltiades had been adopted, the subsequent Persian invasion of Greece might never have taken place.

Thus Greek imagination, inspired by Greek prejudice, has changed a reasonable and successful enterprise into an insane and disastrous expedition.

The Ionian Revolt against Persia

The Persian conquest of Thrace and Macedonia was a step, though there is no reason for supposing it an intentional step, towards a Persian attempt to conquer Greece. The attempt on Greece was not made till more than twenty years later; and for the first twelve years after the return of Darius from Thrace, nothing occurred which seemed likely to bring on a great struggle between Asiatic autocracy and European freedom. Hippias, the banished tyrant of Athens, repaired to Sardis and tried to induce the satrap Artaphernes to aid him in recovering his power. Artaphernes went so far as to threaten the Athenians; envoys from Sardis said at Athens: 'Take back Hippias, if you look for safety.' But he did nothing to enforce his menace.

It was in consequence of events in which Hippias had no part that the expedition of the Persians against Athens was at last undertaken. The condition of politics in the island of Naxos

c. 496 B.C.

Legend of
Scythian
expedition

led indirectly to an insurrection of the subject Greeks against the Persian power; and the part which Athens and Eretria had played in connection with this revolt was the proximate cause of the Persian expeditions against Greece.

Histiaeus, 512 B.C.;

In return for services rendered during the Thracian expedition Histiaeus of Miletus was rewarded by Darius with the grant of Myrcinus, a town with fertile land on the lower Strymon—near the place where the famous Amphipolis was to be built at a later date—where he desired to found a colony. He seems to have accompanied Megabazus in his western march, and he set to work to fortify the place at once. Myrcinus was in the neighbourhood of silver-mines, and there was abundance of wood suitable for shipbuilding. The Persian general thought it would be impolitic to allow a Greek colony to be planted in such a position, and communicated his views to the king who was still at Sardis; and Darius, sending for Histiaeus on the plea that he was a friend whose company was indispensable, carried him off to Susa with the full purpose of never allowing him to return to the Aegean. Thus the schemes of Histiaeus were cut short, and he spent twelve years in regrets at the court of Susa before he had an opportunity of resuming his connection with the politics of the Aegean.

at Susa, 511 B.C.

Aristagoras of Miletus;

Miletus was governed by his son-in-law Aristagoras, a man whose ability fell short of his ambition, but famous in history as the originator of the revolt of the Ionian Greeks. To this man came a number of Naxian oligarchs who had been expelled from their city by a democratic rising, begging for help to put down the people and gain control of the populous and wealthy island. Aristagoras discerned in the request a means for his own aggrandisement; but without Persian assistance the enterprise did not seem feasible. He therefore went up to Sardis and unfolded to Artaphernes a project of reducing all the Cyclades and then perhaps Euboea itself, a project of which the occupation of Naxos was to be the first step. Artaphernes readily entered into the plan, the consent of Darius was obtained, and 200 ships under the command of Megabates were placed at the disposal of the Milesian. There is little doubt that the enterprise would have been entirely successful but for a quarrel between Aristagoras and Megabates. The Persian admiral spitefully warned the Naxians of the approaching danger; the islanders made such effectual preparations that they stood a siege of four months, and as there

his Naxian enterprise;

its failure

was then no likelihood of reducing the city the fleet returned to Ionia. This failure was fatal to the prospects of Aristagoras. He resolved to retrieve his fortunes by inciting a revolt of the Asiatic Greeks against the Persian power.[8]

499 B.C.
Was Histiaeus concerned in the Ionian revolt?

The story was that his father-in-law Histiaeus, weary of his long exile beyond the Tigris, instigated Aristagoras to this step, by a secret message branded on the head of a faithful slave. This message is said to have reached Aristagoras just at the moment when he was meditating a rebellion, and to have decided him. The motive of Histiaeus in desiring the revolt is supposed to have been the conviction that Darius would send him down to Ionia to restore order. But the story sounds improbable. Histiaeus, detained at Susa because he was already deemed dangerous to Persian interests in the Aegean, would rather have had reason to fear that a revolt promoted by his son-in-law would prove fatal to his credit with Darius. It was a surprising thing that Darius was afterwards induced to send down such a near relative of Aristagoras, and we may suspect that the story that Histiaeus instigated the rebellion was suggested by his subsequent conduct—possibly even invented by himself.

There were the seeds of revolt in Ionia and it would be superficial to suppose that the rebellion was due to the ambition of Greek despots. Its indispensable condition was the widespread hatred of a despotic constitution which smouldered in the cities; and the despotic constitutions were part of the Persian system. An ambitious despot was indeed the means of calling this feeling into action; but in order to do so he had first to cease to be a despot. The issue by the rebel cities of coinages on a common standard shows a wide measure of unity and determination in the revolt.[9]

The initial step in promoting the rebellion was to set up democracies in the Greek states and drive out the tyrants. Aristagoras himself resigned his position in Miletus, and in most cases the change seems to have been accomplished without the shedding of blood. Mytilene was an exception; there the tyrant had earned such deep hatred that he was stoned to death.

The next step was to obtain help from free Greece against the Persian power. Aristagoras undertook the mission. He went first to Sparta, but the Spartans refused to send help to free Ionia from Persian oppression, even as they had before refused to aid her against Persian invasion. In later days a delightful story was told of his visit. He went to king Cleomenes and showed him a map of the earth, engraved

Aristagoras at Sparta;

on bronze, displaying the countries of the known world, the seas, and the rivers. Cleomenes had never seen a map before, and the plausible Ionian tried to convince him that Sparta ought to aspire to the conquest of the Persian empire. Cleomenes was impressed, but deferred his reply till the third day, and then asked Aristagoras the distance from Ionia to Susa. 'Three months,' said Aristagoras, off his guard, and he would have described the road, but the king cut him short with the command, 'Begone from Sparta, Milesian stranger, before the sun sets.' Aristagoras made yet another attempt. Entering the house of Cleomenes as a suppliant, he sought to bribe him. Beginning with ten talents, he gradually raised his offers till he reached fifty. Then Gorgo, the king's daughter, a child of eight or nine years, cried out, 'Father, the stranger will corrupt you'; and moved by her words Cleomenes left the room.

at Athens and Eretria. 498 B.C.

The Milesian stranger fared better at Athens and Eretria. Both these cities sent help; Athens twenty ships—ships, says Herodotus, with the solemnity due to the historical significance of the moment, 'which were the beginning of troubles between Greeks and barbarians'—Eretria five.

Advice of Hecataeus

The prospects of success seemed unfavourable to those who were acquainted with the vast resources of the Persian empire. When Aristagoras consulted with the leading men of Miletus, the geographer Hecataeus had tried to dissuade him. Seeing that Aristagoras and the others had made up their minds and disparaged his arguments, Hecataeus gave a second-best counsel; 'If you do revolt, seize the treasure of the temple of Apollo at Didyma, and become masters of the sea; for if you do not, the enemy will.' But the advice was not taken.

The Greeks at Sardis

With his Athenian and Eretrian allies, Aristagoras marched up to Sardis and occupied the city, but they did not take the citadel. While they were there, a fire broke out and the town was burned to the ground. The Greeks left the smoking ruins and marched back to the coast, but near Ephesus they were met by a Persian force and defeated. The Athenians straightaway returned home, and

Part played by Athenians in the revolt

with this battle the part played by Athens in the Ionian revolt comes to an end. The election of Hipparchus, a Pisistratid, to the archonship in 496 suggests a strong reaction against the anti-Persian policy. But the brief episode was to bring serious consequences upon Athens in the future. The burning of Sardis was important, not so much for the course of the revolt itself as for what the revolt was to lead to. It irrevocably compromised two states of European Greece in the eyes of Persia. The story is that Darius, being told that Athenians had helped to burn Sardis, asked, 'The Athenians —who are they?' He then called for a bow and shooting an arrow into the air, called on heaven to allow him to punish the Athenians. Moreover he bade one of his slaves to say to him three times at dinner, 'Sire, remember the Athenians.' The story has no historical value, but it has artistic significance in the narrative of Herodotus.

Anecdote of Darius and the Athenians

The revolt extended southwards to Caria and to Cyprus, northwards to the Propontis. In Cyprus all the cities except Amathus threw off the Persian yoke. The Greek fleet sailed east and controlled the seas, but the Cypriots were defeated on land and the island came again under Persian control. The Hellespontine towns were also subdued. In Caria the insurgents, after suffering two serious defeats, succeeded in destroying a Persian army.

The revolt in the south

But Aristagoras was a man of slight spirit. Seeing that Persia was regaining control, he despaired of his cause and fled to Myrcinus in Thrace. It is said that he called a meeting of his adherents, to decide what they should do and whither they should flee. In that assembly it was proposed to sail to the distant shores of Sardinia; and here again Hecataeus is related to have offered advice, which Aristagoras and his friends rejected—the establishment of a fortress in the neighbouring island of Leros, from which, if fortune favoured, they might easily return to Miletus. Aristagoras soon met his fate at the siege of a Thracian town, but his death did not affect the course of the rebellion, in which he had played a sorry part. He had hardly left the stage when his father-in-law appeared; but the role of Histiaeus is even less important than that of Aristagoras. This adventurer persuaded, or professed that he had persuaded, Darius to send him down to the coast, by promising to suppress the insurrection before he changed his tunic, and to annex Sardinia to the dominion of the Great King. This promise of Histiaeus, though it may not be true to fact, is thoroughly chcrateristic of the Greek adventurers of that time, deceiving themselves and others with speculations on the remote island of Sardinia. When he came down to Sardis, Histiaeus found that he was deeply suspected by the satrap Artaphernes, and feeling himself unsafe he fled to Chios. There he embraced the cause of the rebels, asserting

Flight of Aristagoras

Reappearance of Histiaeus;

155

that *he* had instigated the revolt, and perhaps spreading the famous story of the message written on the slave's head. Having obtained some ships from Lesbos he adopted the congenial business of piracy, occupying Byzantium and seizing the ships that attempted to pass the straits, as long as the revolt lasted. In the end he was taken prisoner and crucified by Artaphernes.

his fate, 493 B.C.

The main and decisive event of the war was the siege of Miletus, on which the Persians at length concentrated all their efforts. The town was blockaded by the Persian fleet, said to number 600 ships, which had reduced Cyprus. The Greek fleet was stationed off the island of Lade. It is said to have numbered 353 ships, but they were ill disciplined, and morale had been undermined by pro-Persian propaganda spread by the tyrants who had been expelled. In the battle which ensued, the Lesbians and Samians deserted; the men of Chios fought splendidly but they were too few. Miletus was then taken by storm; the women and children became slaves and the men who survived were settled by Darius near the mouth of the Tigris. The temple of Apollo at Didyma, one of the chief oracular sanctuaries of the Greek world, was surrendered by the Branchidae, its hereditary priests, and was burnt down.

494 B.C. Battle of Lade and capture of Miletus

Temple of the Branchidae

We may suspect that the burning of Apollo's shrine was not approved of by Darius himself. The respect which the king of kings felt for the oracular god is attested in a letter of admonition which he addressed to a satrap of Phrygia. The text of a Greek version of this letter is partly preserved on a stone, and records the remarkable testimony of the king that Apollo always 'told the truth to the Persians'.[10]

Letter of Darius to Gadates

The capture of Miletus was followed by the reduction of Caria, where the rebels had for a time prospered, and by the conquest of the islands. Presently the Phoenician navy appeared in the waters of the Hellespont, and the attempt of eastern Greece to regain her independence was completely crushed.

End of revolt

For over a hundred years the eastern Greeks had been under increasing pressure, first from Lydia and then from Persia. But from the suffering of Ionia the rest of the Greek world profited. Faced by growing insecurity in the east, individuals and groups left their homes for more congenial surroundings. Already under the Lydian dominance Colophonians had founded Siris in south Italy: we have seen how, when Persia attacked, Phocaeans and Teans sailed to make new homes in Corsica and in Thrace. A stream of emigration

Influence of east Greeks

followed through discontent with Persian rule or local tyranny, and in the crisis of the collapse of the great revolt, Samians, Milesians, Phocaeans and no doubt others sailed to the west. Among the emigrants of this long period were craftsmen and philosophers. Pythagoras abandoned Polycrates' tyranny in Samos and settled in Croton to spread his teaching in the south Italian cities and influence their politics. Xenophanes of Colophon came to Elea, to be the founder of a famous line of philosophers. The influence of east Greek craftsmen is no less marked. It is seen clearly at Acragas in Sicily from the late sixth century and was responsible for the brilliant coinage of Gelon at Leontini and Syracuse. Another Pythagoras came also from Samos to Rhegion to become one of the most famous sculptors of the age.

6.4 Rider in Scythian costume, c. 510 (see note, page 553)

The crushing of the Ionian revolt had a profound effect in Athens. Though the Athenians had withdrawn from the movement in Ionia at an early stage, the tidings of the fall of Miletus produced at Athens a deep feeling of disappointment and sympathy, which found expression in the punishment of Phrynichus, a tragic poet, who made the catastrophe of Miletus the theme of a drama. The Athenians fined him for having recalled to their minds *their own* misfortunes. But in the meantime

Capture of Miletus, Phrynichus fined

Miltiades

Lemnos and Imbros become Athenian

there had been won for them, from the Persian, what was destined to become afterwards a lasting possession. Miltiades, the tyrant of the Chersonese, sympathised with the rebels and during the revolt seized for Athens the isles of Lemnos and Imbros.

Second and Third European Expeditions of Darius. Battle of Marathon

Having suppressed the rebellion, Persia had three things to do. Greek Asia had to be reorganised; Persian Europe had to be consolidated; and those free Greek states which had made war on Persia and occupied Sardis had to be punished.

Reorganisation of Ionia

Artaphernes caused the territories of the Ionian cities to be measured and surveyed, and regulated the tributes accordingly. It was also ordained that the cities should submit their quarrels to arbitration and not make war upon one another. But there was more to be done. The revolt had taught Persia that the system of tyrannies did not answer, and it was now resolved to make an experiment of the opposite policy. The despots were abolished and democratic governments were set up. The world may well have been surprised to see the greatest despotism of all favouring the institution of democracy; it was a concession to the spirit of the Greeks, which reflects credit on the wisdom of Darius.

Thrace and Macedonia conquered by Mardonius, 492 B.C.

The king's son-in-law, Mardonius, was sent to reassert Persian supremacy in Thrace and Macedonia; and through Macedonia he proposed to advance into Greece in order to punish the two cities which had helped the Ionian rebels. A fleet sailed along the coast and subdued the island of Thasos on its way. Thrace was reduced, and Macedonia, then under king Alexander, submitted—a submission which was to be avenged in distant days to come by a descendant and a namesake. But the Greek expedition could not be carried out because disaster had befallen the fleet, which was partly wrecked in a storm off the perilous promontory of Athos. Mardonius returned; he had lost many ships, but he had fulfilled the more important parts of his task.

Darius prepares an expedition against European Greece

But Darius was sternly resolved that Athens and Eretria should not escape unpunished. Their connection with the burning of Sardis had deeply incensed him; it seemed an insult which the Great King's pride could not let pass unnoticed. Moreover Hippias, the banished tyrant, was at the court of Susa, urging an expedition against the city which had cast him

out. It was decided that the new expedition should not be sent by way of Thrace and Macedonia, but should move straight across the Aegean sea. The cities of the Persian seaboard were commanded to equip warships and transports for cavalry, and heralds were sent to the chief cities of free Greece that were not at war with Persia, requiring the tokens of submission, earth and water. In most cases the tokens were given; and among others by Aegina, the enemy of Athens. The command of the army was entrusted to Datis and Artaphernes, a nephew of Darius; and they were accompanied by the aged tyrant Hippias, who hoped to rule once more over his native country. The armament—600 galleys strong, according to Herodotus—setting sail from Samos, made first for Naxos, the island where Aristagoras had failed. The inhabitants abandoned the city and fled up into the hills; and the Persians burned the town. The sacred island of Delos was scrupulously spared; but soon after the Persians had departed it was shaken by an earthquake, and the unwonted event was noted as a sign of coming troubles.

Persians subdue Cyclades and Carystus,

Having sailed from isle to isle, subduing the Cyclades, the fleet went up the channel between Euboea and Attica, and, reducing Carystus by the way, reached the territory of Eretria. It is strange to find that Athens and Eretria had made no common preparations to meet a common danger. Eretria was severed from Attica only by a narrow water, and yet there was no joint action. Athens indeed directed the colonists whom she had settled in the territory of her dependency Chalcis to assist their Eretrian neighbours, but she sent no other help. We hear of sharp engagements outside the walls of the Euboean city, but

burn Eretria,

within seven days it was delivered over to the invaders by the treachery of some leading citizens. The flames which consumed the temples of Eretria were a small set-off against the flames of Sardis. The inhabitants were enslaved. Of all the Greek towns which were involved in the strife between Europe and Asia, none was more ill-fated than Eretria.

land in Attica

The Persian generals had accomplished the lesser half of their task; it now remained to deal with the other city which had defied their king. Crossing over the strait they landed their army in the bay of Marathon. For the second time an exiled tyrant of Athens came down from Eretria to recover his power. The father had come, fifty years before, with but a few mercenaries; the son came now with the forces of Asia. Yet so far as winning support at Athens was concerned, the foreign troops were

Miltiades

the weakest argument of Hippias. The house of the Pisistratids had many bitter enemies, but none was more bitter than one who had also known what it was to rule as a tyrant, Miltiades, son of Cimon who had been forced to return from the Chersonese after the Ionian revolt. His enemies accused him of the crime of oppressive rule in the Chersonese, but he was acquitted by his fellow-citizens, to whom he had brought the gift of Lemnos and Imbros. His hatred of the Pisistratids was natural; they had put to death his father Cimon, celebrated as a victor in the Olympian chariot-race. It is not surprising that Miltiades, who was active as a party man, who was known to be a hot foe of the tyrants, who had probably more first-hand knowledge of the Persians than any other man at Athens, was chosen as the strategos of his tribe. He was the soul of the resistance which his country now offered to the invader.

Energy of free Athens

Athens had changed much since Hippias had been cast out, though less than a generation had passed. Athenian character had been developed under free democratic institutions. It has been said that if the Athenians had not been radically different from their former selves Hippias would easily have recovered Athens. In other words, if the Persian invasion had happened twenty years sooner, the same stand would not have been made against it as Athens now made; the liberty of Greece would have succumbed. But it was no mere accident that the blow had not been aimed twenty years sooner. The Persian invasion was brought about by the same political causes which enabled Athens to withstand it. The Ionian Greeks would not have risen in revolt but for the growth of a strong sentiment against tyrannies—the same cause which overthrew the Pisistratids and created Marathonian Athens. On the other hand, if the Ionian revolt had broken out before the expulsion of Hippias, Athens would have taken no part in it, and the Persian invasion of Greece might not have followed.

As the story is told by Herodotus, one would almost think that the enemy had already landed on Attic soil before the Athenians thought how they were to defend their city and their land. A fast runner was dispatched in hot haste to Lacedaemon to bear the news of the fall of Eretria and the jeopardy of Athens. The Lacedaemonians said that they would help Athens, but religious scruples forbade them to come at once; they must wait till the full moon had passed. But when the full moon had passed, it was too late. The Plataeans alone,

Philippides sent to Sparta

faithful to their new alliance, sent help and fought with the Athenians.

The whole army of the Athenians may have numbered about 9000. The commander-in-chief was Callimachus, the polemarch of the year; and the grave duty of organising the defence rested upon him and the ten generals of the tribal regiments, who formed a Council of War. Fortunately for Athens, Callimachus seems to have been willing to listen to the counsels of Miltiades; and the joint authority of the polemarch and the most influential general outweighed the scruples of their less adventurous colleagues. The enemy had landed near Marathon and clearly intended to advance on unwalled Athens by land and sea. The question was whether the Athenian army should await their approach and give them battle within sight and reach of the Acropolis, or should more boldly go forth to find them. This was a question which the Athenian people itself had to decide. The hour when the Assembly met to deliberate on this question was the most fateful moment in the whole episode. Miltiades proposed that the army should march to Marathon and meet the Persians there. To have proposed and carried this decree is probably the greatest title of Miltiades to his immortal fame.

Calli-machus

Decision to march to Marathon

The plain of Marathon, stretching along a sickle-shaped line of coast, is framed on all other sides by the hills which drop down from Pentelicus and Parnes. In the north-eastern part the soil, now drained, was very marshy, and the plain is cut into two halves by the

Field of Marathon

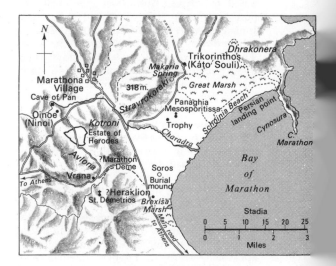

14. MARATHON

path of a torrent coming down from the hills through the northern valley, in which the village of Marathon is situated. Two roads lead from Athens to Marathon. The main road, turning eastward, passes between the mountains of Hymettus and Pentelicus; and, traversing the deme of Pallene, skirting Mount Pentelicus, and then turning due north when it reaches the coast, it enters the plain of Marathon from the south. The other road, which is somewhat shorter but more difficult, continues northward, past the deme of Cephisia, and, running into the hills north of Pentelicus, finds two issues in the Marathonian plain. It divides into two paths which encircle the hill of Kotroni: the northern path goes on to Marathon and descends into the plain from the north along the banks of the torrent; the other, descending the valley of Avlona, issues in the plain at its south-western corner, close to the village which is now called Vraná.

Callimachus probably took the coastal road. Though a little longer it was an easier route and he needed to move quickly; it was also the route which the Persians would naturally take if they decided to move on Athens. When the Athenians reached the plain of Marathon they based their camp on a sanctuary of Heracles at the south end of the plain, commanding the main western outlet from the plain by the coast; there they were joined by the Plataeans, numbering not more than 1000. Meanwhile the Persians had beached their ships at the north-east end of the bay under the shelter of the promontory of Cynosura; their camp was probably north of the great marsh at Kato-Soulo, near a good water supply. The Persians may not have been anxious to force an early battle, for their experience at Eretria will have encouraged them to believe that there would be divisions among the Athenians at Athens, and possibly in the field. The Athenians also had good reason to wait; they had sent for help to Sparta and without the Spartans their numbers were dangerously small. Whatever the reason, it is clear that there was a delay for several days before the battle was joined, and that it was the Athenians who broke the deadlock. In Herodotus' account it was Miltiades who persuaded his fellow generals and Callimachus to give battle, but he then waited until it was his day for the command. This artificial construction we can abandon; it is virtually certain that on the day of battle and before it Callimachus was formally in command, however much he owed to the advice of Miltiades. The probable reason for the Athenian decision to fight is bad news on

the political front from Athens. To realists who looked ahead the chances of the survival of Athens as an independent city must have seemed very slender; it would be surprising if there were no appeasers who preferred to medize before rather than after defeat. As we shall see, there are signs that such a fifth column existed. It was probably the fear of betrayal of the city from within that persuaded Miltiades and Callimachus to risk a decisive battle.

The Athenian line of battle was drawn up at the south end of the plain at right angles to the coast, with the Plataeans on the left wing. Callimachus had the commander's position on the right wing and Aristides and Themistocles, both of whom were to play major parts in Athens' future, are said to have commanded their tribal contingents in the centre. Callimachus probably had some 10,000 men; for the Persian numbers we have no good evidence, but they were at least twice as strong. To avoid envelopment by the much larger Persian line, special dispositions were made; the Athenian centre was thinned and the strength concentrated on the wings. The Persians had crossed the plain and drawn up their forces opposite the Greeks, with their cavalry on the right wing. They relied primarily on their archers to demoralise and break up their enemy's line, after which their cavalry were expected to get to work. These tactics were well known to the Athenian command, and they had worked out the best way to meet them; as soon as they came within range of the arrows they charged 'at a run'. In the centre, as had been anticipated, where they were heavily outnumbered and the Persians had their strongest troops, the Athenians were driven back, but on the wings they quickly broke Persian resistance. They did not, however, follow up their victory but turned back to support their own centre. While the Persian centre was cut to pieces by the combined force of the Athenians, the Persian wings fled across the plain towards their ships. In the last stages of the battle all Persian survivors made for the ships and in the general panic many of them were bogged down in the Great Marsh. The fighting was fiercest by the ships, but the Persians had had time to get most of the men from their wings on board while the main fighting was still at the south end of the plain; only seven ships were captured.

According to Herodotus the Athenians lost only 192 men. The number seems very small, but the names were recorded on the battlefield; it is a figure that should have been widely known. There was no such control for the Persian figure, but Herodotus' 6400 is so surprisingly small in comparison with his normally inflated Persian figures that it may be near the truth; it would imply a total force of some 20,000 fighting men, assuming that the survivors of the Persian centre roughly balanced the light casualties of their two wings. Their losses will have been serious though not crippling. But this was the first major defeat in a pitched battle that the Persians had suffered.[11]

Herodotus tells us that when the Persian ships were standing out at sea a shield signal was seen, and that the Alcmaeonidae were accused of giving this signal to tell the Persians that the city of Athens was ripe for surrender. As a result the Persian fleet set sail, hoping to reach Athens before the Athenian army returned. They rounded Sunion but when they came to Phaleron they found that the Athenians were already back, in good order, at another sanctuary of Heracles in Cynosarges, south of the city, ready to fight again. The Persians sailed back across the Aegean. There is no doubt that they did sail round to Athens after the battle, and Herodotus, though indignantly repudiating the charge against the Alcmaeonidae, admits that there most certainly was a shield signal. This should be accepted; it is doubtful whether, after what was a definite defeat on the plain of Marathon, the Persians would have proceeded to Athens unless they thought it would be betrayed to them. Whether the Alcmaeonidae were traitors at this time is a more open question, which can best be considered in the political context after Marathon.

The mound of Marathon

The Spartans arrived too late for the battle. They visited the field, desiring to gaze upon the Persian corpses, and departed home praising the exploit of the Athenians. The scene of the battle is still marked by the mound at the south end of the plain which the Athenians raised over their own dead; Callimachus was buried there, and Cynegirus (a brother of the poet Aeschylus), who was said to have seized a Persian galley and held it until his arm was severed by an axe; later a victory trophy was set up near the Great Marsh where the Persians had been cut down in their flight, and games in honour of Heracles were instituted to commemorate the encampment before the battle in his sanctuary.[12] Legend grew up quickly round the battle, and there was no historian to record at the time what had actually happened; so that, when a generation had passed, the facts were partly forgotten,

The Marathonian myth

and partly transfigured. Three motives were at work in this transfiguration: the love of the marvellous, the vanity of the Athenians, and the desire of his family to exalt the services of Miltiades. Gods and heroes fought for Athens, ghostly warriors moved among the ranks. The panic terror of the Persians at the Greek charge was ascribed to Pan, and the worship of this god was revived in a cave consecrated to him under the north-west slope of the Acropolis. Out of this grew a story which added a charming incident to the chain of Marathonian memories. The fast runner Philippides, speeding through Arcadia on his way to seek Spartan help, had been accosted by Pan himself, who had asked why the Athenians neglected his worship, and promised them favours in the future. But the supernatural can be easily allowed for. It was more serious that the extraordinarily brilliant strategy and tactics, to which the success was chiefly due, should have faded out of the story, and that Marathon should have been regarded as entirely a soldiers' battle. It was soberly asserted and believed that those wonderful warriors had taken their enemy aback by advancing against them for a whole mile at a run. Miltiades, who was doubtless the heart and soul of the campaign, was raised by the Marathonian myth to be the commander-in-chief on the day of battle; and it was explained that the chief command each day devolved upon the generals in rotation. This was an arrangement which came into force a few years later, when the polemarch lost his importance; but it supplied the legend with a ready means of setting aside Callimachus in favour of Miltiades. We need not follow the myth further. The battle of Marathon was caught up into a cloud of glory, which obscured the truth of the events; and historical criticism has been able to rescue only the barest outline. Callimachus in particular received less than his due, overshadowed by the fame of Miltiades; but chance has preserved his name on an Ionic column once mounted by a figure of Victory. Perhaps it was vowed by the polemarch before battle, and set up after his death.[13]

Worship of Pan

Due thanksgiving was made for the victory at the great religious centre of Delphi. On the expulsion of the tyrants the Athenians, mindful of Apollo's help, had built a little Doric treasury of Pentelic marble. It seems to have been a gem of architecture, worthy of the severe grace of the sculptured reliefs which ran round the inside of the building and have been safely preserved under its ruins. The

The Athenian treasury of Delphi

sculptures represent the deeds of Theseus and of Heracles, and the battle of the gods and giants. After Marathon a long base was built in front of the treasury to carry trophies of the battle.[14]

Memorial at Athens

The victory was also commemorated at Athens. In the life of Aeschylus we are told that in a public competition for an elegy on the Marathon dead Simonides was the victor; Aeschylus, soured by defeat, went to Sicily. The mood of thanksgiving was also expressed on the Acropolis. Under the Periclean temple of Athena, the so-called Parthenon, have been found remains of an earlier temple which was never completed. Some of the drums from its columns can still be seen built into the north wall of the Acropolis; and its ground-plan has been recovered from surviving blocks. Excavation has shown, from pottery fragments at the level of the foundations, that this temple was begun in the eighties, but it was fired by the Persians, during Xerxes' invasion ten years after Marathon, when they sacked the city.[15] No attempt was made to renew the work until peace had been made with Persia in the middle of the century, and the new architect abandoned the old design. To the same period also probably belongs a monumental entrance to the Acropolis, the old Propylon, which was to be superseded by the magnificent Propylaea designed by Mnesicles during the ascendancy of Pericles.

New temple on the Acropolis

Picture of the battle in the Poikilē Stoa

The descendants of the Marathonian warriors derived perhaps their most vivid idea of the combat from a picture of it which was painted about a quarter of a century later—one of the famous battle-pictures in the Stoa Poikilē at the north end of the Agora. In one scene the Athenians and Plataeans advanced against the trousered barbarians; in a second the Persians in their flight pushed each other into the marsh; and in the last, the Phoenician ships were portrayed and the Greeks slaying the Persians who were striving to reach the ships. Callimachus, Miltiades, Datis and Artaphernes, Cynegirus seizing the prow of a ship, could all be recognised; and Theseus, who was believed to have given phantom aid to the warriors, seemed to rise out of the earth. High above the raging strife, the artist—Micon probably—showed the gods and goddesses as they surveyed, from the tranquillity of Olympus, the prowess of their Greeks smiting the profane destroyers of the holy places of Eretria.[16]

What the victory of Marathon meant

The significance of the victory of Marathon, as a triumph for Athens, for Greece, for Europe, cannot be gainsaid; but we must take care not to misapprehend its meaning for Greece and for Athens herself. That significance is unmistakable even if we minimise the immediate peril which was averted. The Asiatic invader had perhaps not yet come to annex; he had come only to chastise; it was enough for him if the rest of the Greeks looked on with respectful awe, while he meted out their doom to the two offending cities. His work in Euboea had been purely a work of demolition; he had not sought to annex territory or add a satrapy to the Persian dominion. The Cyclad islands and Carystus had indeed been compelled to submit to the formal authority of the Great King; but it is not proved that Darius thought of reducing the western coasts of the Aegean to the subject condition of Ionia. Thus the danger which menaced Athens may not have been subjection to an Asiatic despot. Nor was she threatened by the doom of destruction and slavery which befell Eretria. The Persian army had come to restore Hippias; and assuredly Darius did not propose to restore his friend to a city of smouldering temples. The Athenians would be condemned to bow beneath the yoke of their own tyrant; they would not become, like their Eretrian fellows, the bondmen of a barbarian master. To be delivered over to an aged despot, thirsting for power and vengeance, embittered by twenty years of weary exile—this was to have been the punishment of the Athenians, and this was the fate which they escaped by their valour on the field of Marathon. If they had lost that battle and the rule of the Pisistratids had been restored, the work of twenty years earlier would have had to be done again; but that it would have been done again there can be hardly a doubt. The defeat of the Athenians would have arrested, it would not have closed, their development. It might even be argued that it would have saved Greece the terrible trial of the later Persian invasion—if that invasion was undertaken solely to wipe out the ignominy of the repulse at Marathon. Probably, if Datis had been victorious, the subsequent attempt of Persia to conquer Greece would have assumed a different shape. But the attempt would assuredly have been made. The history of the world does not depend on proximate causes. The clash of Greece and Persia, the effort of Persia to expand at the cost of Greece, were inevitable. From the higher point of view it was not a question of vengeance; where Darius stopped, the successors of Darius would undoubtedly go on. The success of Marathon inspired Greece to withstand the

161

later and greater invasion; but the chief consequence was the effect which it wrought upon the spirit of Athens herself. The enormous prestige which she won by the single-handed victory over the host of the Great King gave her new self-confidence and ambition; history seemed to have set a splendid seal on her democracy; she felt that she could trust her constitution and that she might lift her head as high as any state in Hellas. The Athenians always looked back to Marathon as marking an epoch. It was as if on that day the gods had said to them, Go on and prosper.

Expedition to Paros

The great battle immortalised Miltiades; but his latter end was not good. His services at Marathon could not fail to gain for him increased influence and respect at Athens. His fellow-citizens granted him, on his own proposal, a commission to attack the island of Paros. For the Parians had furnished a trireme to the armament of Datis, and had thereby made war upon Athens. Miltiades besieged the city of Paros for twenty-six days, but without success, and then returned home wounded.

Condemnation of Miltiades

The failure was imputed to criminal conduct of the general; his enemies, jealous of his exploits in the Marathonian campaign, accused him of deceiving the people; and he was fined 50 talents, a heavy fine. It is not known what his alleged wrongdoing was, but afterwards, when the legend of Miltiades grew and the part which he played in the campaign of Marathon was unduly magnified, it was foolishly said that he persuaded the Athenians to entrust the fleet to him, promising to take them to a land of gold, and that he deceived them by assailing Paros to gratify a private revenge. At Paros itself, in the temple of Demeter, the tale was told that, when the siege seemed hopeless, he corrupted a priestess of the goddess, named Timo, and that, coming to meet her in a sanctuary to which only women were admitted, he was seized with panic and in his flight, leaping the fence of the precinct, hurt his leg. Certain it is that he returned wounded to Athens, however he came by the chance;

His death

appeared on a couch at his trial; and died soon after his condemnation.

Struggle of Athens and Aegina

Hostility of Aegina and Athens, 506 B.C.

At this time Aegina was the strongest naval power in the Aegean. Hostile feeling had long been the rule between her and Athens, and soon after the fall of the Pisistratids the island had been involved in the quarrel between Athens and Thebes. Legend said that the nymphs Aegina and Theba were sisters; but it was more than sisterly sympathy which drove Aegina to declare a state of standing war—a war without herald, as the Greeks called it—against her continental neighbour. Her ships ravaged Phaleron and the Attic coast. It was to be expected that Aegina would side with the Persian when he sailed against her foe, and would cordially desire the humiliation of Athens. The Athenians had some reason to fear that she would give the invader not only her goodwill but her active help. Accordingly, the Athenians sought the intervention of Sparta, complaining that Aegina was medizing and betraying Greece out of enmity to Athens. The complaint was listened to at Sparta, and king Cleomenes, proceeding to Aegina, seized ten hostages and deposited them with the Athenians. By this means the hands of Aegina were tied; she was hindered from lending help to the Persians or hampering the men of Athens in their preparations to meet the invaders.

(πόλεμος ἀκήρυκτος) 498 B.C.

Appeal of Athens to Sparta;

coercion of Aegina (before 490 B.C.)

This appeal of Athens to Sparta to interfere and exercise coercion in the common interests of Hellas, and the implied recognition of Sparta as the leading power, has been supposed to mark a climax in that feeling of deference towards her which had been growing up both within and without Greece. The episode has been described as 'the first direct and positive historical manifestation of Hellas as an aggregate body with Sparta as its chief'. This description is an exaggeration, for we must not lose sight of the fact—which is too often forgotten, and which Athens took pains to forget—that Athens was, like Aegina, a member of the Peloponnesian league, and the appeal to the head of the league was therefore a matter of course.[17]

Defeat of Argos

The prestige of Sparta had indeed been confirmed and increased by a decisive victory which she had won a few years before over her old rival Argos. The battle was fought at Sêpeia, near the hill of Tiryns. According to the story, the Argive generals acted with extraordinary folly and were easily outmanoeuvred by Cleomenes. They listened for the commands which the herald proclaimed to the army of their enemies, and then issued those same commands to their own men. Learning this, Cleomenes gave secret orders that, when the herald gave the word for dinner, the soldiers should pay no heed but stand prepared for battle. The Argives dined in accordance with the command of the Spartan herald, and were immediately fallen upon and destroyed by their enemies. The disaster lamed the power of Argos for more than twenty years.

494 B.C.

Feud of the Spartan kings

The episode of the hostages of Aegina brought to a final issue the great scandal of Sparta, the bitter feud of her two kings, Cleomenes and Demaratus. King Demaratus entered into a private compact with the Aeginetans to thwart the intervention of king Cleomenes. Accordingly Cleomenes incited Leotychidas, the next heir of the Eurypontid line to which Demaratus belonged, to challenge the legitimacy of his rival's birth. A trial was held; a curious story touching the birth of Demaratus was manufactured and attested; and an oracle came from Delphi, declaring that Demaratus was not the son of his reputed father. Leotychidas consequently became king; Demaratus fled to the court of Darius—refuge of fallen potentates—where as the friend of medizing Aegina he found a good reception. Then Cleomenes and his new colleague went to Aegina and seized the hostages.

Fate of Cleomenes

But the means which Cleomenes used to ruin Demaratus recoiled upon himself. It was discovered that he had tampered with the Pythian priestess at Delphi to bring about the dethronement of his enemy, and fearing the public indignation at this disclosure he fled first to Thessaly and then returned as far as Arcadia, where he conspired against his country. The Spartan government deemed it politic to invite him to return, and he accepted their offer of pardon. But his adventures had unhinged his mind; he became a violent mad-man, striking with his stick every one who approached, and his kinsfolk placed him in chains under the guard of a Helot. One day, having forced his keeper by means of threats to give him a dagger, he wounded himself horribly and died.

[? c. 489 B.C.]

Such was the curiously inglorious end of king Cleomenes, who, if he had not been a Spartan, might have been one of the greater figures in Greek history. But his ambition was cabined and his abilities hampered by the Spartan system; whenever, if left to himself, he might have pursued an effective policy, he was checked by the other king or the Ephorate. On important occasions during his life, Sparta was called upon to take action in foreign affairs; and on each occasion we find that the policy of Cleomenes falls short of the mark owing to the opposition of his royal colleague. Even as it is, he dominates Spartan history for more than twenty years.

War of Athens and Aegina

After his death, the Aeginetans sent envoys to Sparta, demanding the restoration of the hostages whom he and the other king Leotychidas had delivered over to Athens. Leotychidas had been the accomplice of Cleomenes in deposing Demaratus and was consequently at this time under the shadow of public displeasure. The Spartans were ready, it is said, to hand him over to the Aeginetans as a prisoner, but the envoys preferred to ask that he should go with them to Athens and compass the restoration of the hostages. The Athenians flatly refused the demand. Aegina resorted to reprisals, and a war broke out. It began with the conspiracy of an Aeginetan citizen, named *487 B.C.* Nicodromus, who undertook with the help of Athens to overthrow the oligarchical government of his city. His plan failed because the Athenians came a day too late. The delay was due to the necessity of increasing their squadron of 50 ships by a loan of 20 more from Corinth. These ships gained a victory and landed troops on the island to besiege the town. But the Aeginetans on their side obtained some troops from Argos, and overcame the Athenians. This defeat caused disorder in the fleet, which was then attacked and routed by the islanders. But the double repulse was not decisive, and warfare was protracted between the two cities by desultory plundering raids on their respective coasts. The necessity of protecting Attica from Aeginetan depredations, the ambition perhaps of ultimately reducing Aegina to subjection or insignificance, sensibly accelerated the conversion of Athens into a naval power.

Growth of the Athenian Democracy

The Athenian constitution underwent several important modifications in the course of the twenty years which followed its reform by Cleisthenes, and there is reason for thinking that some of the changes which tradition ascribed to Cleisthenes were really not introduced by him. Under his scheme, the power of the archons remained very great; they were usually men deliberately elected for their ability; and if the Council of Cleisthenes was a check upon them, they also were a check upon it. The natural development of things was to strengthen the Council and weaken the magistrates. And at length, some years after Marathon, this step was taken by means of a change in the mode of appointment. Hence- *487-6 B.C.* forward they were appointed by lot from a larger number (possibly 100) previously elected, in the same way in which the members of the Council of Five Hundred were chosen. The result of any system of lot in the appointment to

Change in method of appointing archons

offices is to secure average honesty and exclude more than average ability. Henceforward the chances against any prominent statesmen holding the office of chief archon are very small. It is obvious that the political importance of the chief magistracy now disappears. It is also obvious that a polemarch appointed by lot could no longer hold the post of commander-in-chief. That post must pass to those who were deliberately picked out as competent to hold it. The powers of the polemarch were therefore vested, not in a new officer, but in the body of the ten generals who were hitherto elected each by his own tribe. Either now or not many years later a reform was introduced by which the whole people elected the Generals, one from each tribe. Later still, probably when Pericles dominated the political scene, and his continuous re-election seemed likely to deprive all other men of ability in his tribe of hope of the Generalship, it was made possible for one of the tribes to have two representatives on the Board of Ten. There is no reason, however, to suppose that it ever became the practice at the election of the Generals to assign to one of the ten a position of supreme authority over all his colleagues during their whole term of office. That would have been a reinstitution of the polemarch in another form. The danger of a divided command was avoided by a simpler expedient. Whenever the people voted a military or naval expedition, they decreed which of the Generals should conduct it, and assigned a position of leadership or presidency to one of those whom they chose. But this superior command was limited to the conduct of the particular expedition; and the General to whom it was assigned exercised it only over those of his colleagues who were specially associated with him. Special powers of a wider kind were only voted in an extreme emergency, as for Alcibiades in the crisis of the Ionian war.

We have no record of the attitude of Cleisthenes to the venerable council of the Areopagus, nor do we hear anything about that body for a generation after the fall of the Pisistratids. But a new institution was originated during this period which weakened the position of the Areopagus by depriving it of its most important political function—that of guarding the constitution and protecting the state against the danger of a tyranny. The institution of ostracism is traditionally ascribed to Cleisthenes, but it was not made use of till two years after the battle of Marathon. The ordinance of the *Ostrakismos* was that in the sixth prytany of each civil year the question should be laid before the Assembly of the

people whether they willed that an ostracism should be held or not. If they voted in the affirmative, then an extraordinary Assembly was summoned in the market-place in the eighth prytany. The citizens were grouped in tribes, and each citizen placed in an urn a piece of potsherd *(ostrakon)* inscribed with the name of the person whom he desired to be 'ostracised'. The voting was not valid unless 6000 votes at least were given, and whoever had most ostraka against him was condemned to leave Attica within ten days and not set foot in it again for ten years. He was allowed, however, to retain his property and remained an Athenian citizen.

By this institution the duty of guarding against the dangerous ambitions of influential citizens was transferred from the paternal council of the Areopagus to the sovereign people itself. If this clumsy and, it must be owned, oppressive institution was established by Cleisthenes, it would follow that for about fifteen years the Assembly declined every year to make use of it, though it is stated that the chief object of Cleisthenes was to banish a relation of the Pisistratids, Hipparchus the son of Charmus. And in fact this Hipparchus was ultimately banished, by the first ostracism that was ever practised. This was in 487, two years after the battle of Marathon, and for the next six years ostracism became a major instrument of politics.[18] The Alcmaeonid Megacles, nephew of Cleisthenes, was the second victim in 486, and there was a third in 485. These three, according to the Aristotelian *Constitution of Athens*, were ostracised because they were friends of the tyrants. The more immediate reason was probably the suspicion of treason at the time of Marathon, when Hippias was hoping to recover the tyranny. Hipparchus would naturally be among the first to be suspected, whether guilty or not; the verdict against Megacles is significant in view of Herodotus' statement that the Alcmaeonids were accused of sending a shield signal to the Persians after the battle. A very large number of sherds were also cast during the eighties against another Alcmaeonid, Callixenus son of Aristonymus, and on one sherd he is described as 'the traitor', and votes, though considerably fewer, were cast against Hippocrates son of Alcmaeonides. The name of the victim in 485 is unknown but, judging by the very large number of sherds with his name that have survived, it was probably Callias, son of Cratias, who came from Alopeke, the deme of the Alcmaeonids. After the first three ostracisms the pattern changes; medism and

Polemarch superseded by the Ten Generals

Ostracism

Ostracism 487-82 B.C.

Ostracism of Hipparchus, 487 B.C.; of Megacles, 486 B.C.;

of Xan-
thippus,
484 B.C.;

of
Aristides,
482 B.C.

tyranny are no longer the issues. The ostracism of Xanthippus in 484 may have been influenced by his marriage to the Alcmaeonid Agariste; but in 482 the main issue was the bold naval policy of Themistocles. An excellent anecdote is told of the ostracism of Aristides 'the Just', as he was called. On the day of the voting an illiterate citizen chanced to be close to Aristides who was unknown to him by sight, and requested him to write down the name 'Aristides' on the ostrakon. 'Why,' said Aristides, doing as he was asked, 'do you wish to ostracise him?' 'Because,' said the fellow, 'I am tired of hearing him called "the Just".'

Athens to be a Sea-power

The work
of Themis-
tocles

But the greatest statesman of this critical period in the history of Athens, greater than either of his two rivals Xanthippus and Aristides, greater than the hero of Marathon himself, was Themistocles, the son of Neocles. It may be said that he contributed more than any other single man to the making of Athens into a great state. The pre-eminent importance of his statesmanship was due in the first place to his insight in discerning the potentialities of his city and in grasping her situation before any one else had grasped it; and then to his energy in initiating, and his adroitness and perseverance in following, a policy which raised his city, and could alone have raised her, to the position which she attained before his death. In the sixth century the Athenians were a considerable naval power, as Greek naval powers then went; but the fleet was regarded as subsidiary to the army. The idea of Themistocles was to sacrifice the army to the navy and make Athens a sea-state—the strongest sea-state in Greece. The carrying out of this policy in the face of scepticism and opposition was the great achievement of Themistocles. He began the work when he

493-2 B.C.

was archon, and thus already a man of some prominence, two or three years before the battle of Marathon, by carrying a measure through the Assembly for the fortification of the peninsula of Piraeus. Hitherto the wide exposed strand of Phaleron was the harbour where the Athenians kept their triremes, hauled up on the beach, unprotected against the surprise of an enemy, but within sight of the Acropolis. It was probably the hostility of Aegina that persuaded the people to accept Themistocles' policy, but there is little doubt

6.5   Themistocles (see note, page 553)

that he himself already had primarily the danger from Persia in mind. After the quelling of the Ionian revolt, Persian warships were cruising about the Aegean, and the possibility of an attack on Phaleron seems to have opened the eyes of the Athenians to the need of reforming their naval establishment. The hostility of Aegina was a nearer and more pressing motive. The Athenians had not to seek far for a suitable port. It seems strange that they had not before made use of 'the Piraeus', the large harbour on the west side of the peninsula of Munychia, which could be supplemented by the two smaller harbours on the east side, Munychia and Zea. But the Piraeus was somewhat farther from the city, and was not within sight of the Acropolis like Phaleron. So long, therefore, as there was no fortified harbour, Phaleron was safer. The plan of Themistocles was to fortify the whole circuit of the peninsula by a wall, and prepare docks

Harbours
of Piraeus

Increase
of fleet

(Cama-
reza)
483-2 B.C.
482 B.C.

in the three harbours for the reception of the warships. The work was begun, but it was interrupted by the Persian invasion, and by the party struggles after Marathon. Then the war with Aegina broke out, and this, combined with the fear of another Persian invasion, helped Themistocles to carry to completion another part of his great scheme—the increase of the fleet. A rich bed of silver had been recently discovered at Maronea, in the old mining district of Laurion, and had suddenly brought into the public treasury a large sum, perhaps a hundred talents. It was proposed to distribute this among the citizens, but Themistocles persuaded the Assembly to apply it to the purpose of building new ships. Special contributions for the same object must have been made soon afterwards; more ships were built; and two years later we find Athens with nearly 200 triremes at her command—a navy which could be compared with those of Syracuse and Corcyra. The completion of the Piraeus wall was not attempted at this period, but was accomplished, as we shall see, after the final repulse of the Persians from the shores of Greece.

CHAPTER 7

The Perils of Greece. The Persian and Punic invasions

The Second Persian War

We have now reached the threshold of the second and the greater Persian invasion—the second and the greater triumph of Hellas. The significance of this passage in their history was not lost upon the Greeks. Their defence of Europe against the barbarians of Asia, the discomfiture of a mighty oriental despot by a league of their free states, the defeat of a vast army and a large fleet by their far smaller forces —these surprises made an enduring impression upon the Greek mind and were shaped by Greek imagination into a wonderful dramatic story at a time when the critical instinct had not yet developed. No tale is more delightful than this tale as Herodotus tells it, when we take it simply as a tale; and none illustrates better the story-shaping genius of the Greeks. The historical criticism of it is another matter: we have to seek to extract what actually happened out of the bewildering succession of daring exaggerations, naïve anecdotes, fictitious motives, oracles, not to speak of miracles; in most of which the reflected light of later events is visibly altering the truth, while much is coloured by the prejudices and leanings of the Athenians, from whom Herodotus seems to have derived a great part of his record.

The Preparations and March of Xerxes

(490-80 B.C.)

The chief event in Persia during the ten years which elapsed between the first and second invasions of Greece was the death of King Darius. After the unexpected repulse of his forces at Marathon, he had determined to repeat the experiment and begun to make some preparations. Four years passed and then a revolt broke out in the province of Egypt which demanded immediate attention. But its suppression was delayed in consequence of the king's death and was only accomplished under Xerxes, son of Atossa, who succeeded to the throne. The question then arose whether the design of an expedition against Greece, to avenge those who fell at Marathon and redeem the fame of Persian arms, should be carried out. It is related that Xerxes was himself undecided but was over-persuaded by the impetuous counsels of his cousin Mardonius. On the other hand, his uncle Artabanus appears in the pages of Herodotus as the prudent and experienced adviser who weighs all the obstacles and foresees failure. Xerxes, swayed hither and thither between these opposing counsels, is finally persuaded to yield to the wishes of Mardonius by the peremptory command of a dream, which overcomes even the scruples of Artabanus. In this manner Herodotus pretends to take us behind the curtain of the council chamber at Susa, representing—in the light of later events—the advice of Mardonius as youthful and foolish, although that advice merely amounted to the execution of the design which, according to Herodotus himself, the old and experienced Darius had initiated and prepared. Never-

(486-5 B.C.) Death of Darius, 485 B.C. Subjugation of Egypt, 484-3 B.C.

theless the contrast of Mardonius and Arta-banus, and the dreams divinely sent with evil purpose, are, though not historical, a most effective dramatic introduction to the episode of the invasion. Further pressure was brought to bear on the king by Greeks who visited his court—envoys from the Aleuad princes of Thessaly and members of the Pisistratid family who brought with them the seer Onomacritus to impress Xerxes by favourable oracles.

Canal of Athos, 483 B.C.

It was clear that the expedition must consist of a joint attack by sea and land. Preparations were begun by the difficult enterprise of digging a canal (about a mile and a half long) across the isthmus of Mount Athos. It will be remembered that, on the occasion of the expedition of Mardonius to Thrace and Macedonia, a large part of the fleet had been wrecked in rounding that dangerous headland. But was it necessary for the fleet to venture on this occasion within the proximity of Cape Athos? Might it not sail straight across the Aegean to Greece? On these grounds Herodotus suggested that the cutting of Athos was undertaken for display rather than from necessity. This is an unsound criticism. It was a fundamental principle of Persian strategy in these expeditions that the army and navy should co-operate and never lose touch. The Thracian expedition of Darius, the Macedonian expedition of Mardonius, the Greek expedition of Xerxes illustrate this principle. The canal of Athos was intended to ensure that the ships should safely accompany the land forces along the coasts of Thrace. Once through Athos, the fleet was sheltered from the dangerous north-east winds, and it was not necessary to cut through the flat-shored promontories of Sithonia and Pallene. There is no doubt that the work was completed and used, although later writers threw doubts on the 'velification' of Athos. When it was finished, the workmen proceeded to lay a bridge over the Strymon for the passage of the army, and preparations were made all along the line of route for the feeding of a vast host.

481 B.C.

Story of Pythius

Xerxes came down from Susa to Sardis in the autumn. He met the oriental contingents of his army at Critalla in Cappadocia. At Celaenae it is recorded that Pythius, the richest man in the empire, entertained at his own cost the king and the whole army. His wealth amounted to four million gold darics, all but seven thousand, and Xerxes bestowed upon him seven thousand to make up the full sum. Xerxes spent the winter at Sardis. Pythius was so pleased with the king's graciousness that

when the army was about to start for the Hellespont in the following spring he ventured to request that the eldest of his five sons who were serving in the army might be permitted to remain behind. Great was the king's wrath at what he regarded as the insolent demand of a 'slave'. The body of the eldest son was cut in two; one half was placed at each side of the gate of Sardis, through which the army was about to march forth. The anecdote illustrates the severity with which personal military service was enforced.

Crossing of the Helles-pont, April, 480 B.C.

It is impossible to suppose that the whole army wintered in Sardis with the king; it is probable that the place of mustering was at the Hellespont across which two bridges had been constructed, in the neighbourhood of Sestos and Abydos, by Phoenician and Egyptian engineers. But the strength of these bridges was not sufficient, and a tempest destroyed them. The wrath of Xerxes at this catastrophe was violent. He not only beheaded the engineers, but commanded that 300 lashes should be inflicted on the waters of the Hellespont. Those who carried out this strange order addressed the sea as they scourged it in these words: 'O bitter water, our lord lays this punishment upon you, for having done him wrong, who never did wrong to you. King Xerxes will cross you, whether you will or not. Just is it that no man sacrifices to you, for you are a treacherous and briny river.' These words are censured by Herodotus as 'un-Greek and impious'. The reconstruction of the bridges was entrusted to new engineers. Two lines of ships were moored across the strait by anchors at prow and stern. The line nearer to the Propontis consisted of 360, the other of 314, triremes and pentekonters mixed. Over each of these lines of ships six huge cables—two of flax, four of papyrus—were stretched; and in three places gaps were left between the ships and under the cables for small trading craft to pass between the Euxine and the Aegean. Planks were laid across the cables and kept in their places by a second layer of cables above. On this foundation a road was made with brushwood, wood and earth, and at each side palisades were set, high enough to prevent the animals which passed over from seeing the water. On a marble throne erected on the shore Xerxes is said to have witnessed the passage of his army, which began at the first moment of sunrise. The troops crossed under the lash, and the crossing was accomplished in two days. But when the size of the Persian host was magnified, in later years, to the impossible figure of five millions, the story was that the crossing of the Hellespont required seven days and seven nights—the favourite number of fiction—without a moment's pause.

The army was joined by the fleet at Doriscus in Thrace. Fleet and army were henceforward to act together. In the plain of Doriscus Xerxes reviewed and numbered his forces. 'What nation of Asia,' asks Herodotus, 'did not Xerxes lead against Hellas?' He enumerates forty-six peoples, with a picturesque description of their array. The Persians themselves, who were under the command of Otanes, wore coats of mail and trousers; they had wicker shields, large bows, and short spears. The Medes, Cissians, and Hyrcanians were attired in the same way. Then there were Assyrians with bronze helmets, linen cuirasses, clubs, lances, and short swords; Bactrians with cane bows; trousered Sacae with pointed hats and carrying axes; Indians clad in cotton, Caspians in goatskin; Sarangians wearing dyed garments and high boots; Ethiopians clad in lion skins or leopard skins and armed with arrows whose stone points transport us to a primitive age; Sagartians with dagger and lasso; Thracians with foxskin caps; Colchians with cowskin shields. The fleet was furnished by the Phoenicians, Egyptians, Cypriots, Cilicians, Pamphylians, Lycians, Carians, and subject Greeks. It is said to have consisted of 1207 warships, with 3000 smaller vessels. A curious story was told of the numbering of the army. Ten thousand men were packed together in a close space; a line was drawn round them, and a wall built. All the infantry passed successively into this enclosure. It was filled 170 times, so that the whole number of fighting men was 1,700,000. The number of the cavalry was 80,000 and there were some additional troops not included. Adding to these the crews of the ships—counting 200 to each larger and 80 to each smaller vessel—the total was obtained of 2,317,000 men. This enormous number was further increased by fresh contingents which joined during the march through Thrace and Macedonia. Besides the fighting men were a vast number of servants, sutlers and camp-followers, whom Herodotus considered to be quite as numerous as the soldiers. The whole host would consequently have reached to upwards of 5,000,000, not including eunuchs and concubines.

It is needless to say that these numbers are wholly fabulous. The facts which Herodotus states as to the number of the fighting men are false, and the principle of his conjecture that the total number of the host was double that of the fighting men is also fallacious. The picked body of 10,000 troops, called the Immortals, had the privilege of travelling comfortably with their wives and baggage; but this was an exceptional privilege, and it cannot be supposed that the mass of the troops were accompanied by servants. There is reason for supposing that the land forces may have amounted to perhaps 180,000.[1] A larger force than that would have been unmanageable in a small mountainous country, and the difficulties of provisioning even this were formidable. The number of the fleet must also be considerably reduced—perhaps to 800 triremes.

From Doriscus, Xerxes proceeded to Therma with his fabulous host, in three divisions, drinking rivers dry in their march. At the crossing of the Strymon, near the place called the Nine Roads, he sacrificed nine native youths and virgins. At Therma he was rejoined by his fleet.

Most of the incidents which Herodotus recounts concerning this march of Xerxes are pleasing stories, designed to illustrate the historian's general view as to the great struggle of Greek and barbarian. The cruelty of Xerxes to Pythius, his barbarity and impiety in scourging the Hellespont, serve to characterise the barbarian and the despot. The enormity of the host which rolled over the straits to deluge Europe enhances the danger and the glory of Hellas. And to signify by a solemn portent the destined discomfiture of the Persian host, it is stated that as Xerxes was setting forth from Sardis the sun was darkened. No eclipse was visible at Sardis in the spring of 480. In 481, however, a partial eclipse was visible at Sparta. The tradition which Herodotus follows has moved it forward to heighten the dramatic effect.

The Preparations of Greece

In the meantime Greece was aware of the preparations of the Great King for her enslavement and was making her counter-preparations. The digging at Athos had warned her, and the coming down of the king to Sardis showed that the danger was imminent. Xerxes is said to have dispatched from Sardis heralds to all the Greek states, except Athens and Sparta, to demand earth and water. These two cities now joined hands to resist the invasion. They were naturally marked out as the leaders of Greece in Greece's greatest crisis—Sparta by virtue of that generally acknowledged headship which we have already seen, Athens by the prestige which she had won in resisting the

Autumn
481 B.C.

Mede at Marathon. They jointly convened an Hellenic congress at the Isthmus to consult on the measures to be taken for common resistance to the threatened invasion. We have already observed certain indications of the growth of a Panhellenic feeling, but this is the first instance of anything that can be called a deliberate Panhellenic policy. It is, as Grote observed, an 'attempt to combine all the scattered cities of the Greek world to withstand the power of Persia. It is a new fact in Greek history, opening scenes and ideas unlike to anything which has gone before—enlarging prodigiously the functions and duties connected with that headship of Greece which had hitherto been in the hands of Sparta, but which is about to become too comprehensive for her to manage.' A large number of cities sent delegates to the congress, which was called the *Synedrion of Probuloi* or Congress of Representatives. It met at the Isthmus—a meeting-place marked out by its central position—under the presidency of Sparta. There the states which were represented, thirty-one in number, bound themselves together in a formal confederation by taking a solemn oath that they would 'tithe those who uncompelled submitted' to the barbarian, for the benefit of the Delphic god. This was a way of vowing that they would utterly destroy such traitors. A great many states, the Thessalians, most of the Boeotian cities, besides the smaller peoples of northern Greece—Locrians, Malians, Achaeans, Dolopians, and others—took no part in this congress. Their inaction by no means meant that they had made up their minds to 'medize'. They were only waiting to see how things would turn out, and, considering their geographical position, their policy might be justified by the natural instinct of self-preservation. These northern states would be first invaded by the Persian, and it was hopeless for them to think of withstanding him alone. Unless they could absolutely rely on Sparta and her confederates to support them in defending the northern frontier of Thessaly, nothing would be left for them but to submit. And with this prospect, it would have been imprudent for them to compromise themselves by openly joining the confederacy. Events proved that if they had seriously relied on that confederacy throwing all its strength into the defence of northern Greece, they would have been cruelly deceived. And, as we shall see, they were ready to resist so long as there were hopes of support from the stronger states. In some cases there were parties or classes who were favourable to the Persian cause, for

The congress at the Isthmus

Policy of the northern states

example, the oligarchs of Thebes and the Aleuadae of Thessaly.

One of the great hindrances to joint action was the existence of domestic disputes. There were feuds of old standing between Thessaly and Phocis, Argos and Lacedaemon, Athens and Aegina. The Congress attempted to reconcile such feuds, and Athens and Aegina laid aside their enmity to fight together for Greek freedom. Another important question concerned the command of the confederate forces. The claim of Sparta to the leadership of the army was at once admitted. The question as to the fleet was not so clear. Sparta was not a naval power, and Athens, which would furnish more ships than any other state, had a fair claim. But the other cities were jealous of Athens; they declared that they would submit only to a Spartan leader. The Athenian representatives, when they saw the feeling of the allies, at once yielded the point.

Question of leadership

The Congress made some other provisions. While spies were sent to observe the preparations of Xerxes in Asia Minor, envoys went forth to various Greek states to enlist new confederates—to win over Argos, which had sent no delegates to the Isthmus, and to obtain promises of assistance from Crete, Corcyra, and Syracuse. None of these embassies led to anything. Gelon, the great tyrant of Syracuse, was himself absorbed by the prospect of an attack of the Carthaginians, and could have sent no aid to the mother-country even if he had wished.

Appeal to Syracuse

When the military preparations for the defence of Greece were made and the generals appointed, the Congress of Representatives probably met again in spring, and then consigned the conduct of affairs to the military congresses of the commanders, who used to meet together and decide on each movement under the presidency of the Spartan leaders. King Leonidas was leader of the confederate army, and Eurybiadas, a Spartan who did not belong to either of the royal families, was commander of the confederate fleet.

(480 B.C.)

The Greeks had plenty of time for their preparations—for strengthening their defences and building new ships. Athens probably threw herself with more energy into the work than any other city. One wise measure shows that she had risen to a full apprehension of the truth that a solemn hour in her history had arrived. She recalled those distinguished citizens whom the vote of ostracism had driven into banishment during the last ten years. Aristides and Xanthippus returned home; their feuds with Themistocles were buried in the presence of

Athens recalls ostracised statesmen, spring, 480 B.C.

the great danger; and the city seems to have soon shown its confidence in their patriotism by choosing them as Generals. These leaders will each play his part in the coming struggle.

Battles of Thermopylae and Artemisium

Northern passes left open

About the time when Xerxes reached the Hellespont, the Thessalians sent a message to the confederacy, suggesting that the pass of Tempe should be defended against the invading army. Accordingly 10,000 hoplites were sent. But when they arrived at the spot they found that there were other passes from Macedonia into Thessaly, by which the Persians would be more likely to come. There were the passes of Volustana and Petra which descended into the valley of the river Titaresius, and it was by one of these that Xerxes actually marched. Ten thousand hoplites were not enough to defend the three passes and certain strong elements in Thessaly had no intention of opposing the Persians.[2] It seemed useless and dangerous to occupy this advanced post. Hence the defence of Tempe was abandoned, and the troops left

Thessaly. This desertion necessarily drove all the northern Greeks—between Tempe and Thermopylae—to submit to Xerxes.

Thermopylae, natural features

The next feasible point of defence was Thermopylae, a narrow pass between the sea and mountain, separating Trachis from Locris. It was the gate to all eastern Greece south of Mount Oeta. At the eastern and western ends the pass was in those days extremely narrow, and in the centre the Phocians had constructed a wall as a barrier against Thessalian incursions. Near the western end was Anthela, the meeting-place of the Amphictionic council, while on the Locrian side one emerged from the defile near the village of Alpenoi. The retreat of the sea, and consequent enlargement of the Malian plain, have so altered the appearance of this memorable pass that it is hard to recognise its ancient description; the hot sulphur springs from which it derived its name and the sheer mountain are the two permanent features. It was possible for an active band of men, if they were debarred from proceeding by Thermopylae, to take a rough and steep way over the mountains and so reach the Locrian road at a point east of Alpenoi. It was therefore necessary for a general who undertook the defence of

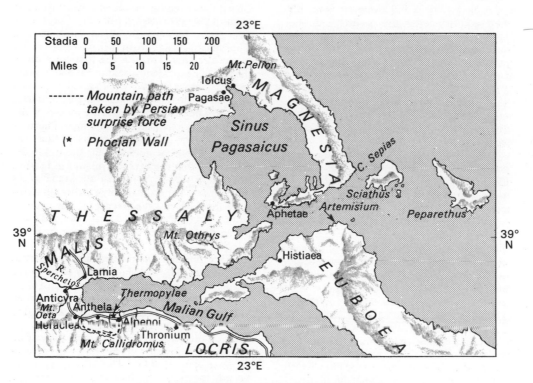

15. ARTEMISIUM AND THERMOPYLAE

Thermopylae to secure this path, lest a detachment should be sent round to surprise him in the rear.

Greek troops at Thermo-pylae

The Greeks determined to defend Thermopylae, and Leonidas marched thither at the head of his army. He had about 7000 men, including 4000 from the Peloponnese, 1000 Phocians, 400 Thebans, 700 Thespians, and the Locrians in full force. It is possible that there may have been some other Boeotians who are not mentioned. Of the Peloponnesians more than half were Arcadians. Mycenae, free at this moment from Argive control, sent 80 men. There were Corinthians and Phliasians; 1000 Laconians, and 300 Spartans. So far as the Peloponnesians were concerned, this was only a small portion of their forces, and we may suspect that but for Athens they would have abandoned northern Greece entirely and concentrated themselves at once on the defence of the Isthmus. But they were dependent on Athens because her fleet was so strong, and they were therefore obliged to consider her interests. To surrender Thermopylae and retire to the Isthmus meant the surrender of Attica. But the hearts of the Spartans were really set on the ultimate defence of the Isthmus and not on the protection of the northern states; their policy was narrow and Peloponnesian. They attempted to cover this selfish and short-sighted policy by the plea that they were hindered from marching forth in full force by the celebration of the Carnean festival, and that the Peloponnesians were delayed by the Olympic games; they alleged that the soldiers of Leonidas were only an advance guard, the rest would soon follow. Yet the feasts did not interfere with the movement of the confederate fleet.

Policy of Sparta

Position of Greek fleet

As the land arm and the sea arm of the Persian force always operated together, it was necessary that while the Greek hoplites held the pass under Mount Oeta, the Greek triremes should oppose the Persian fleet in the straits between Euboea and the mainland. The Persians would naturally attempt to sail between Euboea and Magnesia into the Malian gulf, and thence, accompanying the advance of the army, along the western shore of the long island, to the Euripus. The object of the Greeks was to prevent this and support the garrison of Thermopylae by controlling the Malian gulf.

The Athenian dispositions at this stage have been brought into question by the discovery at Troezen of an inscription which purports to reproduce a decree moved by Themistocles. This decree seems to conflict with the narrative of Herodotus on two important points.

It provides for the deliberate evacuation of Attica before battle is joined at Thermopylae, whereas in Herodotus it is a hasty improvisation after Thermopylae has been lost; and whereas in the account of Herodotus the whole Athenian fleet is stationed at Artemisium, with the exception of fifty-three ships which join the fleet later, the decree prescribes a division of the Athenian ships, one hundred to proceed to Artemisium, the other hundred to remain 'off Salamis and the rest of Attica to guard the land'. These dispositions are intelligible, because there was a danger that part of the Persian fleet might sail down outside Euboea to attack Attica while the main fleet faced the Greeks at Artemisium. The early evacuation of Attica would imply that the Athenians had little confidence that the Persians could be held at Thermopylae. However, other clauses of the decree are considerably less convincing and strongly suggest that the decree was 'composed' later than the fifth century. On balance it seems more likely that Herodotus' account is to be preferred.[3]

According to Herodotus the Greek fleet, which numbered 271 triremes and nine pentekonters—the Athenians contributing 127 manned by their own crews and twenty lent to the Chalcidians—chose its station near Artemisium on the north coast of Euboea.[4] Three ships were sent forward to reconnoitre in the Thermaic gulf, and two of them were destroyed by the Persians. This was the first collision in the war. The incident is said to have so depressed the Greeks that the whole squadron sailed back to the Euripus; but this is highly unlikely, for it was bound to remain at the mouth of the Malian gulf so long as Leonidas held Thermopylae. It was however necessary that the Euripus should be guarded, for there was the possibility that the Persians might send round a detachment by the south of Euboea and so cut off their retreat. As fifty-three Athenian ships were absent during the first conflicts at Artemisium, it may be supposed that they were deputed to the service of keeping watch at the Euripus.

In the month of July the Persian army arrived at Thermopylae, and the Persian navy at the Magnesian coast between Casthanaea and Cape Sepias. Their ships were so many that they could not all be moored at the shore and had to range themselves in eight lines parallel to the coast. While they were in this unsafe position a great storm rose and destroyed a considerable number of their ships. Thus the gods intervened, to lessen the inequality between the Persian and the Greek forces. Encouraged by this disaster, the Greek fleet returned to its station at Artemisium. In this account of Herodotus, the main fact is that the Persians suffered serious loss by a storm off the Magnesian coast. But the loss is exaggerated in proportion to the exaggeration of the original size of the fleet, and the movements of the Greeks are probably misrepresented. The story goes on that cowed by the numerical superiority of the Persians, even after their losses, the Greek commanders wished to retreat again and were restrained from doing so by Themistocles. The Euboeans were naturally anxious that the fleet should remain where it was, as a protection to themselves, and to secure this they gave Themistocles thirty talents. Of this sum Themistocles distributed eight in bribes to his colleagues and kept the rest. The facts of the case throw doubt on this story, which was perhaps suggested by what happened some weeks later at Salamis. For Eurybiadas and the Peloponnesians were bound to stay at Artemisium so long as the land army was at Thermopylae.

After the storm the Persians took up their station at Aphetae. They determined to cut off the Greek retreat, and secretly sent a squadron of 200 vessels to sail round Euboea. The news of this movement was brought to the Greek camp by Scyllias of Scione, the most remarkable diver of his time, who, it was said, plunged into the sea at Aphetae and did not emerge till he reached Artemisium at a distance of 10 miles. Herodotus, indeed, hesitates to accept this tale, and records his private belief that Scyllias arrived at Artemisium in a boat. The Greeks decided that when midnight had passed they would sail to meet the ships which were sailing to the Euripus, but in the afternoon they attacked the enemy, just to see how they fought, and they succeeded in capturing 30 Persian ships. The night was very stormy; the gods had again intervened to aid Greece. The 200 ships, having rounded the southern cape of Euboea, were wrecked off the dangerous coast known as the Hollows. Immediately afterwards the 53 Attic ships which had not yet appeared at Artemisium arrived there, and at the same time came the news of the disaster.[4] The Greeks consequently gave up the intention of retreating. There was some further fighting, and loss on both sides—with no decisive advantage, according to the Greek account, but we may suspect that the Persians had the best of it.

Meanwhile Leonidas had taken up his post at Thermopylae, and the Phocians, who knew the ground, had undertaken the defence of the by-road over the mountains. The old Phocian wall in the centre of the pass was repaired. It was a serious matter for even such a large army as that which was now encamped in the Malian plain to carry the narrow way of Thermopylae against 6000 determined men. For four days Xerxes waited, expecting that they would retreat, awed by the vision of his mighty host. On the fifth he attacked, and in the engagements which took place at the west end of the pass the Hellenic spearmen affirmed their distinct superiority to the Asiatic archers. On the following day the result was the same; the Immortals themselves made no impression on the defenders. Herodotus says that Xerxes 'sprang thrice from his throne in agony for his army'. It was then decided to send round the Immortals—hardly the whole 10,000—under their commander Hydarnes, by the mountain road to take the Greeks in the rear. A Malian Greek named Epialtes guided the band and so won the name of having betrayed Greece. At dawn they reached the highest point of the path, where the Phocians were posted. The Phocians fled to the heights, and the Persians went on, paying no attention to them. Meanwhile deserters informed Leonidas of the Persian stratagem. He hastily called a council of war. The exact plan of action which was decided on is unknown. We only know that the Spartans, Thebans, and Thespians remained in the pass, while the rest of the Greeks retired southward. It was afterwards represented that they had deserted the defence of the position and returned home. But in that case, it was foolish, if splendid, of Leonidas to hold the pass between foes on both sides. The rational courses were either for the whole garrison to abandon the pass, or else, just as the Persians aimed at enclosing the Greeks, so to enclose the band of Hydarnes. We may suspect that this second plan was actually adopted.[5] While part of the force, including Leonidas and the Spartans, remained in the pass, the rest (we may suppose) placed themselves at some distance east of the point where the mountain path descended to the road, so as to take Hydarnes in the rear. Of the 1400 who stood in the pass, some had to guard the eastern entrance against Hydarnes, others the western against the main army. Leonidas and his 300 undertook the western side. But they were no longer content with merely repelling assaults; they now rushed out upon the enemy. Their charge was effective, but Leonidas himself was slain, and a Homeric battle raged over his body. Two brothers of Xerxes fell. Many Persians were driven into the sea. But at length the defenders

Persian losses

Battle of Thermopylae

173

were forced back behind the wall. They drew together on a hillock where they made a last stand, to be surrounded and slain by overwhelming numbers. For the Immortals, having in the meantime routed the Greeks in their rear, had now forced their way into the pass.

The valiant defence of Thermopylae made a deep impression upon Greece, and increased the fame of the Spartans for bravery. It was represented as a forlorn defence—Leonidas and his band devoting themselves to certain death and clinging to their posts from that sense of military duty which was inculcated by the Spartan system from early youth. The brave Thespians would not desert the Spartans, while the Thebans are represented as detained by Leonidas against their will, because they were suspected of secret medism. The malicious tale adds that, having taken only a perfunctory part in the defence, the Thebans advanced to the enemy and asked for quarter, declaring that they were friends of the Great King and had come to Thermopylae against their will. Their lives were spared, but all, including the commander, were forced to suffer the shame of being branded as bad slaves. It is certain that this contrast between the Thespians and Thebans was invented in the light of the subsequent medism of Thebes. Nor is it clear that the defence of Thermopylae, although eminently heroic, was, until the very end, desperate. If, as we suspected, an effort was made to meet the Immortals, then, if that effort had been more effectual, it might have been possible to hold the pass; and in that case a naval battle must have decided whether the Persians or the Greeks would be forced to retreat.

Behaviour of Thebans

A column was afterwards erected at Sparta with the names of Leonidas and his 300. Among them was to be read the name of Diēnekes, reputed as the author of a famous *mot,* which displayed the lightheartedness of a Spartan soldier in the hour of peril. When it was observed to him that the Persian host was so enormous that their arrows hid the sun, he replied, 'so much the better, we shall fight in the shade'.

Retreat of Greek fleet

The news of Thermopylae speedily reached the fleet at Artemisium. The Greeks forthwith weighed anchor and sailed through the Euripus to the shores of Attica.

Battle of Salamis

480 B.C. (August)

Having thus succeeded in breaking through the inner gate of Hellas and slain the king of the leading state, Xerxes continued his way and passed from Locris into Phocis and thence into Boeotia, meeting with no resistance. The Thebans and most of the other Boeotians now, unable to do otherwise, submitted to the Persians. The loss of Thermopylae forced them to this course, as the abandonment of Tempe had forced the Thessalians.

Delphic legend

In later days a story was told at Delphi that a Persian band detached itself from the main host in Phocis, in order to proceed to Pytho and plunder the shrine of the god. 'I think,' says Herodotus, 'that Xerxes knew its treasures better than his own.' The Delphians fled up into the heights of Parnassus, leaving only 60 men and the prophet Acērātus in the temple. They did not remove the treasures, for the god said that he would protect his own. As soon as the barbarians approached, marvels began to happen. The prophet saw the sacred arms, which no man might touch, lying in front of the temple, carried out by some mysterious means. And when the Persians came to the shrine of Athena Pronaea, which stood not far from the Castalian fountain, lightning flashed; two crags rent from Parnassus fell with a loud crash, crushing many of them; and a war-whoop was heard from Athena's temple. The barbarians fled in terror and told how two hoplites of superhuman size pursued them. These were Phylacus and Autonous, the native heroes of Delphi. Such was the legend told at Delphi of the Persian invasion.[6]

The Athenians leave Attica

When the Athenians returned from Artemisium they found that the main body of the Peloponnesian army was gathered at the Isthmus and engaged in building a wall from sea to sea, instead of advancing to the defence of Boeotia as had been previously arranged. Thus Boeotia and Attica were unprotected. Themistocles and his Athenian colleagues decided to evacuate Athens. They made a proclamation that all the citizens should embark in the triremes, and that all who could should convey their families and belongings to places of safety. This was done. The women and children were transported to Troezen, Aegina, and Salamis. The council of the Areopagus helped at this crisis by distributing from the treasury of Athena eight drachmae to each citizen who embarked.[7] At the same time the great natural strength of the Acropolis, encouraged the hope that it might be held against the Persians, and a small garrison was left to defend it. This bold and wise policy of embarkation was dictated by the circumstances, but it was supposed to have been based on an oracle, which foretold the utter destruction of

Attica with the sole exception of a 'wooden wall'. The wooden wall was interpreted to mean the ships. And to suit this view it was represented that the garrison left on the Acropolis was merely a handful of poor citizens who remained behind and barricaded themselves there, because they adopted the more literal interpretation of a wooden barricade. This explanation of the oracle was perhaps suggested by subsequent events.

While the Athenians were thus showing that they were not bound to their soil, the allied fleet had stationed itself in the bay of Salamis, and it was reinforced by new contingents, so that it reached the total strength of 378 triremes and seven pentekonters. The army at the Isthmus was now placed under the command of Cleombrotus, brother of Leonidas and guardian of his son Pleistarchus, who was still a child.

c. Sept. 17

Xerxes arrived at Athens about the same time that his fleet sailed into the roadstead of Phaleron. He found the town empty, but for the small band which had entrenched itself on the Acropolis. Persians troops occupied the lower height of the Areopagus, which is severed from the Acropolis by a broad saddle, and succeeded in setting the wooden barricade on fire by means of burning arrows. The garrison rolled stones down on them, and such is the natural strength of the Acropolis that the siege lasted two weeks. Then the Persians managed to ascend on the precipitous north side by the secret path which emerged close to the shrine of Aglaurus. The Greeks were slain, the temples plundered and burnt.

Persians capture the Acropolis

After the fall of the Acropolis the Greek generals held a council of war, and it was carried by the votes of the majority that they should retreat to the Isthmus and await there the attack of the Persian fleet. The advantage of this seemed to be that they would there be in close touch with the land forces and have the Peloponnese as a retreat in case of defeat; whereas at Salamis they would be entirely cut off. This decision meant the abandonment of Aegina, Salamis, and Megara, and it was strenuously opposed by the Aeginetans, Athenians, and Megarians. Themistocles determined to thwart it. He went privately to Eurybiadas and convinced him that it would be much more advantageous to fight in the narrow waters of the Salaminian channel than in the open bay of the Isthmus, where the superior speed and number of the hostile ships would tell. A new council was summoned at which, it is said, hot words passed between the Athenian and the Corinthian general. When

Will the Greek fleet fight at Salamis or the Isthmus?

Themistocles opened the debate without waiting for the formal introduction of Eurybiadas, the Corinthian Adeimantus said, 'O Themistocles, those who stand up too soon in the games are whipped.' 'Yes,' was the reply, 'but those who start late are not crowned.' It is recorded that Themistocles, in order to carry his point, had to threaten that the Athenians, who were half the fleet, would cease to co-operate with their allies and seek new homes at Siris in South Italy if the retreat to the Isthmus were decided on.[8] Themistocles won his way; and when it was resolved to fight in Salaminian waters, the heroes of the island, Ajax and Telamon, were invoked, and a ship was sent to Aegina to fetch the other Aeacid heroes.

Of all the tales of signs and marvels which befell in these memorable days none perhaps was more attractive to the Athenians than the experience of two Greek exiles as they walked in the Thriasian plain. One was an Athenian named Dicaeus, and his companion was none other than Demaratus, the Spartan king, who had sought refuge at the Persian court. As they went, they saw a great dust afar off near Eleusis, such a dust as they thought might be raised by a host of 30,000 men; and then they heard a voice suddenly from the midst of the dust, and it sounded like the cry of the mystic Iacchus which is cried at the Eleusinian festival. Demaratus asked his companion what it might be. 'It is a token,' said Dicaeus, 'of some great disaster to the King's host. For since the plain is desolate of men, it is clear that the thing which utters the cry is divine—and it is a thing coming from Eleusis to help the Athenians. If it turn to the Peloponnese, the peril menaces the army of the land, but if it moves toward the ships, then are the King's ships endangered.' 'Peace,' said Demaratus, 'for if these words of yours come to the King's ears, you will lose your head.' Then the dust, wherein the voice was, turned to a cloud, and rising aloft moved towards the Greek fleet at Salamis; and so they knew that the fleet of Xerxes was doomed.

What Demaratus and Dicaeus saw in the Thriasian plain

Meanwhile the Persians too had deliberated, and determined to fight. According to a Halicarnassian story told by Herodotus, the Carian queen Artemisia alone gave sound advice—not to risk a sea fight but either to wait for the Greek fleet to disperse from want of provisions, or to advance by land into the Peloponnese.

The southern entrance to the narrow sound between Salamis and Attica is blocked by the islet of Psyttalea and the long promontory which runs out from Salamis towards the mainland. The Greek fleet was anchored close to the town of Salamis, north of this promontory. It would be best for the Greeks if they could lure the Persian fleet to enter the Salaminian bay so that its flank would be exposed as it sailed through the narrow waters. It would be best for the Persians if they could force the Greeks out into the open sea. Xerxes foresaw the possibility that his enemies might attempt to escape at night, and to prevent this he moved his armament so as to enclose the entrances of the two straits on either side of Psyttalea, and landed troops on that island, to rescue Persians and kill Greeks who should happen to swim to its shores in the expected battle. These movements, carried out in the afternoon, alarmed the Greeks; the Peloponnesian commanders brought pressure to bear on Eurybiadas; another council was called, and Themistocles saw that the hard-won result of his previous exertions would now be overthrown. He therefore determined on a bold stroke. Leaving the council, he dispatched a slave named Sicinnus to the Persian camp bearing a message from himself, as a wellwisher to Xerxes, that the Greeks intended to sail away in the night. If they were prevented from doing so, a Persian victory was certain, owing to the disunion which existed in the Hellenic camp. If the Persians attacked the Greeks where they were, the Athenians would turn against their allies. This message was believed, and Xerxes took his measures at nightfall to hinder the Greek fleet from escaping by the western straits between Salamis and the Megarid. He sent his 200 Egyptian ships to round the southern promontory of Salamis and place themselves so that they could bar the straits. And he decided to attack in the morning—a fatal decision, which only the prospect of the treachery of some of his foes could have induced him to take.

Artifice of Themistocles to bring on a battle

The Greek generals meanwhile were engaged in hot discussion. Suddenly Themistocles was called out from the council. It was his rival Aristides who had sailed across from Aegina and brought the news that the fleet was surrounded by the enemy. Themistocles made Aristides inform the generals of what had happened, and the tidings were presently confirmed by a Tenian ship which deserted from the Persians. There is no reason to question the sensational incident that Aristides brought the news; but we need not suppose that this was his first return from ostracism. It seems probable that he had been sent with the ship which fetched the Aeacids from Aegina and that he was one of the ten strategoi.

Themistocles had managed that a naval battle should be fought at Salamis, and under the conditions most favourable to the Greeks. The position and tactics of the two armaments have been the subject of much debate.[9] According to the poet Aeschylus, who was an eyewitness of the battle, the Persian ships were drawn up in three lines outside the entrance into the sound. The extreme left wing was composed of the Ionian Greeks, while the right, towards the Piraeus, was the Phoenician squadron on which Xerxes chiefly relied. The Greek fleet took up its position inside the channel with the Athenians on the left wing opposite the Phoenicians, and the Spartans on the right wing opposite the Ionians. On the mainland shore, under Mount Aegaleos, a high throne was erected, from which Xerxes could survey the battle and watch the conduct of his men.

Position of fleets on day before battle

At break of day the Persians began to advance into the straits. The three lines converted their formation into three columns, and the Phoenicians led the way through the opening between Psyttalea and the mainland. The Ionians on the left would naturally move through the smaller channel between Psyttalea and Salamis. When the Phoenicians came into view, the Athenian squadron immediately advanced, assailed them in the flank, and cut them off from the rest of the fleet, driving them towards the Attic shore. The other Persian divisions crowded through the straits, and a furious mêlée ensued, which lasted till nightfall. There was no room for the exercise of tactical skill in the crowded, narrow waters, where the fairway (between Cynosura and Attica) is little more than a mile in breadth. The valour of the Aeginetans was conspicuous. They seem to have completed the discomfiture of the Phoenicians and to have dispersed the Ionians.

The battle. c. Sept. 20

The Persians, under the eyes of their king, fought with great bravery, but they were badly generalled and the place of the combat was unfavourable to them. By sunset the great armament of Xerxes was partly destroyed, partly put out of action. Aristides, who with a force of Athenian hoplites was watching events on the shore of Salamis, crossed over to Psyttalea and killed the barbarians who had been posted there by Xerxes.

Causes of Persian defeat

Among the anecdotes told about this battle the most famous is that which was current at Halicarnassus, of the signal bravery and no less signal good fortune of the Carian queen Artemisia. She saved herself by the stratagem of attacking and sinking another Carian vessel.

Anecdote of Artemisia

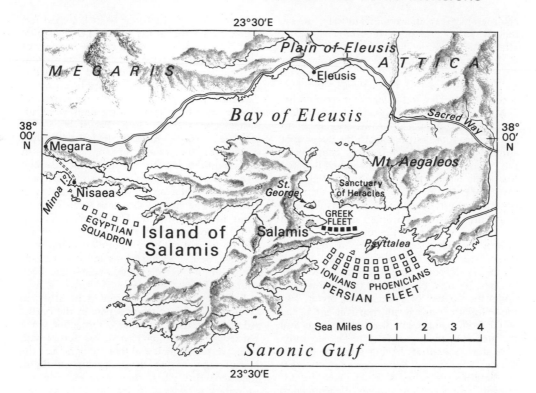

16. BATTLE OF SALAMIS 480 B.C.

Those who stood round Xerxes observed the incident, but supposed the destroyed trireme to be Greek. 'Sire,' they said, 'you see how Artemisia has sunk an enemy's ship?'. And Xerxes exclaimed, 'My men have become women, my women men.'

Consequences of Salamis

Movements of the Persians after the defeat

The Greek victory of Salamis was a heavy, perhaps a decisive, blow to the naval arm of the Persian power, but the prospects of the ultimate success of the invasion were still favourable. The land army had met with no reverse and was overwhelmingly superior in numbers. The only difficulty was to keep it supplied with provisions, and in this respect the loss of the command of the sea was a serious misfortune. The Greeks represented Xerxes as smitten with wild terror, fleeing back overland to the Hellespont and hardly drawing breath till he reached Susa. This dramatic glorification of the victory misrepresents the situation. Xerxes personally was in no jeopardy. The real danger

lay not in Attica but in Ionia. The Persians had good reason to fear the effect which the news of the crushing defeat of their navy might have upon the Greeks of Asia and, if Xerxes dreaded anything, he dreaded the revolt which actually came to pass in the following year. It was all-important for him to secure his line of retreat, while he had no intention of relinquishing his enterprise of conquering Greece. These considerations explain what happened. The Persian fleet was immediately dispatched to the Hellespont to guard the bridge and the line of retreat. The land forces were placed under the command of Mardonius, who, as the season was now advanced, determined to postpone further operations till the spring and to winter in Thessaly. A force of 60,000 men was detached to accompany Xerxes to the Hellespont.

When he arrived the bridge was no longer there. Either it had been destroyed by storm or perhaps its ships had been used as transports. The fleet took him across to Abydos and he proceeded to Sardis, which he made his headquarters. The convoy of 60,000 soldiers returned to the main army in Thessaly, and on their way they laid siege to two towns, which afterwards became famous, Olynthus and Potidaea. Olynthus, then a Bottiaean town, was taken and handed over to the Chalcidians who had remained faithful to Persia. Potidaea successfully withstood a siege of three months.

Meanwhile the Greeks had failed to follow up their victory. Cleombrotus was about to advance from the Isthmus with the purpose of aiming a blow at the retreating columns of the Persian forces before they reached Boeotia. But as he was sacrificing, before setting out, two hours after noon on the 2nd of October, the sun was totally eclipsed, and this ill-omen made him desist from his plan and march back to the Peloponnese. Themistocles tried to induce the naval commanders to follow up their advantage by sailing after the Persian fleet to the Hellespont, and breaking down the bridges. It might be expected that, if this were done, the Greeks of Ionia would revolt. But the Peloponnesians would not consent to sail so far from home while the Isthmus was still threatened by the presence of the Persian army. The story goes that, having failed to get his advice adopted, Themistocles, with that characteristic adroitness which won the admiration of his contemporaries, determined to utilise his failure. The faithful Sicinnus was sent to Xerxes to assure the monarch of the goodwill of Themistocles, who had dissuaded the Greeks from pursuing the Persian fleet. Themistocles might expect that Xerxes, having been deceived before, would now disbelieve his announcement and therefore hasten back with all speed to reach the Hellespont, if possible, before the Greeks. But on a later day of his life, when he was an exile, he claimed Persian gratitude for this service. It was even represented that, with extraordinary long-sightedness or treachery, he had in his view the contingency of being driven to seek Persian help or protection against his countrymen. But the tale need not be seriously criticised; it has all the appearance of an invention suggested by subsequent adventures of the subtle Athenian.

The island of Andros and the Euboean city Carystus had furnished contingents to the Persian fleet. Just as the Athenians, after the battle of Marathon, had sailed against Paros and demanded a war contribution, so now the Greeks acted against Andros and Carystus. They failed at Andros, just as Miltiades had failed at Paros; they devastated the territory of Carystus.

Great was the rejoicing in Greece over the brilliant victory which was so little hoped for. The generals met at the Isthmus to distribute the booty and adjudge rewards. The Aeginetans received the choice lot of the spoil on account of their pre-eminent bravery and dedicated it in the temple of Delphi, on Apollo's express demand, three golden stars set on a mast of bronze. For bravery the Athenians were adjudged the second place. Prizes were also proposed for individuals who had distinguished themselves for valour or for wisdom. In adjudging the prizes for wisdom, each captain wrote down two names in order of merit and placed his tablet on the altar of Poseidon at Isthmus. The story is that each wrote his own name first and that of Themistocles second, and that consequently there was no prize, for a second could not be given, unless a first were also awarded. This ingenious anecdote reflects the reputation for cleverness which had been won by Themistocles.

Later prejudices are reflected in the Athenian version of the Corinthians' part in the battle. Adeimantus, the Corinthian commander, when battle was about to be joined, was seized with panic, raised his sails and took to flight, and the Corinthians, seeing their flagship in flight, followed. But when they were passing the sanctuary of Athena Sciras on Salamis they were miraculously warned that the Greeks were winning the battle, whereupon they turned back and found that the action was finished. Herodotus adds: 'that is the Athenian story, but the Corinthians themselves do not accept it; they think that they were in the fore-front of the battle, and the rest of Greece bears witness to them.' The Corinthians who fell in the battle were buried on the island and the first lines of their epitaph can be read on the stone which was set up over their grave: 'Salamis the isle of Ajax holds us now, who once dwelled in Corinth city of fair water.'[10] They had probably been detached from the main fleet to guard against the Persian squadron that was blocking the western entrance to the Straits. When this squadron did not sail in the Corinthians will have joined the battle.

But the triumph of Hellas had nobler memorials than the unassuming verses of such epitaphs. The barbarian invasion affected art and literature, and inspired the creation of some of the great works of the world. Men seemed to rise at once to the sense of the high historical importance of their experience. The great poets of the day wrought it into their song; the great plastic artists alluded to it in their sculptures. Phrynichus had now a theme which he could treat without any dread of another

*The Phoe-
nissae of
Phrynichus*

*The
Persians of
Aeschylus,
acted
472 B.C.
Herodotus*

*Sculptures
in the
Aeginetan
temple of
Aphaea*

fine. Aeschylus, who had himself fought against the Mede, made the tragedy of Xerxes the argument of a drama, which still remains as the one great historical play dealing with a contemporary event that exists in literature. But the Persian war produced, though not so soon, another and a greater work than the *Persians;* it inspired the 'father of history' with the theme of his book—the contest of Europe with Asia. The idea was afloat in the air that the Trojan war was an earlier act in the same drama—that the warriors of Salamis and Plataea were fighting in the same cause as the heroes who had striven with Hector on the plain of Troy. Men might see, if they cared, this suggestion in the scenes from the two Trojan wars which were wrought by the master sculptors of Aegina to deck the pediments of the temple of Aphaea, whose Doric columns still stand to remind us that Aegina once upon a time was one of the great states of Greece. And in other temples, friezes and pediments spoke in the conventional language of sculptured legend—by the symbols of Lapiths and Centaurs, Gods and Titans—of the struggle of Greek and barbarian.

Preparations for another Campaign

*Prospects
of Greece*

The words of the poet Aeschylus, that the defeat of the Persian sea-host was the defeat of the land-host too, were perfectly true for the hour. But only for the hour. The army, compelled after Salamis to retreat to the north, spent the winter in the plains of Thessaly and was ready for action, though unsupported by a fleet, in the following spring. The liberty of Greece was in greater jeopardy than ever, and the chances were that the success of Salamis would be utterly undone. For in the first place the Greeks, especially the Lacedaemonians and Athenians, found it hard to act together. This had been shown clearly the year before, eminently on the eve of the Salaminian battle. The Peloponnesian interests of the Lacedaemonians rendered them unwilling to meet the enemy in northern Greece; while the northern Greeks, unless they were supported from the Peloponnese, could not attempt a serious resistance and were therefore driven to come to terms with the barbarians. And in the second place, if these difficulties were overcome and a Panhellenic force were opposed to the Persians, the chances were adverse to the Greeks; not from the disparity of numbers, but from the deficiency of the Greeks in cavalry.

In spring Mardonius was joined by Arta- *479 B.C.* bazus and the troops who had conducted Xerxes to the Hellespont. The total number of the forces now at the disposal of Mardonius is unknown; it may have been about 120,000. Meanwhile the Persian fleet, weakened by the absence of the Phoenician ships, was collected at Samos, with the purpose of guarding Ionia. The Greek land forces were not yet assembled, but at the beginning of spring their fleet, now limited to 110 ships, took up its station at Aegina under the command of the Spartan king Leotychidas. Xanthippus, who had returned from ostracism in 480, commanded the Athenian contingent; but Athens' main effort was made on land because the issue would be decided on land. The Greek fleet in 479 had a very subordinate role assigned to it; since the reserves available to the Persians were unknown a Greek fleet had to be ready for action, but it was not intended to assume the offensive. So when Chian envoys appealed first at Sparta and then at Aegina for help to be sent to Ionia, Leotychidas gave them little comfort. He did, however, take the Greek fleet to Delos in the centre of the Cyclades. Herodotus says that he dared go no further, because the Greeks knew nothing of the waters beyond and Samos seemed as distant as the Pillars of Heracles. This of course is fanciful. The Athenians at least were familiar with the eastern Aegean. Leotychidas waited at Delos because his role was intended to be defensive. He could not risk involving his small fleet in battle when he knew so little of the strength of the enemy fleet and the political situation in Ionia. From Delos he could look both ways and follow developments on the mainland and in Ionia.

Mardonius, well aware of the fatal division *Mardonius tempts Athens* of interests between the Athenians and Peloponnesians, made a politic attempt to detach Athens from the Greek league. He sent an honourable ambassador, King Alexander of Macedon himself, with the most generous offers. He undertook to repair all the injuries suffered by Athens from the Persian occupation, to help her to gain new territory, and asked only for her alliance as an equal and independent power. In a desolated land, amid the ruins of their city and its temples, knowing well that their allies, indifferent to the fate of Attica, were busy in completing the walls of Isthmus, the Athenians might be sorely tempted to lend an ear to these seductive overtures. Had they done so, the fate of the Peloponnese would have been sealed—as the Lacedaemonians knew. Accordingly envoys were sent from Sparta to counteract the

The answer of Athens

negotiations of Alexander, and to offer Athens material help in the privations which she was suffering. Tempting as the proposals of Mardonius sounded, and good reason as they had to depend little on the co-operation of their allies, the Athenians were constrained by that instinct of freedom which made them a great people to decline the Persian offer. 'Tell Mardonius,' they said to Alexander, 'that the Athenians say: so long as the sun moves in his present course, we will never come to terms with Xerxes.' This answer utters the spirit of Europe in the 'eternal question' between the East and West—the spirit of the Senate when Hannibal was at the gates of Rome, the spirit of Roman and Goth when they met the riders of Attila on the Catalaunian Plain.

Difficulty of moving Sparta to action

Thus the embassy of Alexander ought to have strengthened rather than weakened the Greek league. It ought to have made the Lacedaemonians more actively conscious of the importance of Athenian co-operation and consequently readier to co-operate with Athens. It enabled Athens to exert stronger pressure on the Peloponnesians, with a view to the defence of northern Greece; and the Spartan envoys promised that an army should march into Boeotia. But still stronger pressure was needed to overcome the selfish policy of the Peloponnesians. Soon after the embassy of Alexander they had completed the walling of the Isthmus, and, feeling secure, they took no thought of fulfilling their promise. The Spartans alleged in excuse the festival of the Hyacinthia, just as the year before they had pleaded the Carnea. And in the meantime Mardonius had set his army in motion and advanced into Boeotia, with the purpose of reoccupying Attica. Once more the Athenians had been cruelly deceived by their allies; once more they had to leave their land and remove their families and property to the refuge of Salamis. Mardonius reached Athens without burning or harrying; he still hoped to detach the Athenians from the Greek cause—herein lay his best chance of success. If they would now accept his former offers he would retreat from their land, leaving it unravaged. But even at this extremity, under the bitter disappointment of the ill-faith of their allies, the Athenians rejected the insidious propositions which were laid by an envoy before the Council of the Five Hundred at Salamis. Immediately the three northern states which had not yielded to the Mede—Athens, Megara, and Plataea—sent ambassadors to Sparta, to insist upon an army marching at once to oppose Mardonius in Attica—a tardy redemption of their promises—

with the threat that otherwise there would be nothing for it but to come to terms with the foe. Even now the narrow Peloponnesian policy of the Ephors almost betrayed Greece. For ten days, it is said, they postponed answering the ambassadors and would have ultimately refused to do anything, but for the intervention of a man of Tegea, named Chileos, who impressively pointed out that the alliance of the Athenian naval power with the Persians would render the Isthmian fortifications on which the Ephors relied absolutely useless. One would have fancied that this was obvious even to an Ephor, without a prophet from Tegea to teach him. However it happened, the Lacedaemonian government suddenly changed its policy and dispatched a force of 5000 Spartans, each attended by some Helots, to northern Greece. Never after, never perhaps before, did so large a body of Spartan citizens take the field at once. They were followed by 5000 perioeci, each attended by one Helot. It was clear that Sparta had risen at last to an adequate sense of the jeopardy of the Peloponnese. The command was entrusted to Pausanias, who was acting as regent for his child-cousin Pleistarchus, son of the hero of Thermopylae. At the Isthmus the Lacedaemonian army was joined by the troops of the Peloponnesian allies and by contingents from Euboea, Aegina, and western Greece; in the Megarid they were reinforced by the Megarians and at Eleusis by Aristides in command of 8000 Athenians and 600 Plataeans. It was entirely an army of foot soldiers, and the total number, including light armed troops, may have approached 100,000. The task of leading this host devolved upon Pausanias.

Sparta acts

The strong fortress of Thebes, abundantly supplied with provisions, was the base of Mardonius; and once the Greek army was in the field, he could not run the risk of having his communications with his base broken off and finding himself shut up in Attica, a land exhausted by the devastation of the preceding autumn. Accordingly he withdrew into Boeotia, having completed the ruin of Athens and having sent a detachment to make a demonstration in the Megarid. He did not take the direct route to Thebes, but marching northward to Decelea and by the north side of Mount Parnes he reached Tanagra and the plain of the Asopus. Marching up this stream, westward, he came to the spot where it is crossed by the road from Athens to Thebes, at the point where that road descends from the heights of Cithaeron. The river Asopus was the boundary

Movements of Mardonius

between the Theban and Plataean territories, and the destruction of Plataea was probably an object of the Persians. But the main purpose of Mardonius in posting himself on the Asopus was that he might fight with Thebes behind him. The Persians had every cause to be sanguine. Not only had they superior, though not overwhelmingly superior forces, but they had a general who was far abler than any commander on the side of the Greeks. Mardonius was not anxious to bring on a battle. He fully realised that his true strategy was to do as little as possible; he knew that the longer the army of the Greeks remained in the field, the more would its cohesion be relaxed through the jealousies and dissensions of the various contingents. We need not take too seriously the story which the Greeks afterwards liked to believe, that at this moment there was a certain dispiritedness and foreboding of disaster in the Persian camp. An anecdote told by one of the guests at a Theban banquet was thought to illustrate this gloomy mood. Attaginus, a Theban noble, made a feast in honour of Mardonius. A hundred guests were present, arranged on double couches, a Persian and a Boeotian on each. Thersander of Orchomenus was among the guests, and in after-days he told the historian Herodotus that his Persian couchfellow spoke these words to him: 'Since we have now shared the same table and wine, I wish to leave you a memorial of my opinion; that being forewarned you may look to your own welfare. You see these Persians feasting— and the host which we left encamped by the river? In a little while you will see few of all these remaining.' The Persian shed tears as he spoke, and Thersander rejoined: 'This you must tell to Mardonius'; but the Persian said: 'Stranger, man cannot avert what God has ordained. No one would believe me. Many of us Persians know it and follow the army under constraint. No human affliction is worse than this: to know and to be helpless.'

Strategic policy of Mardonius

Mardonius had taken up his position and constructed a fortification on the north bank of the river Asopus, before the Greek army had crossed Cithaeron. His plan was to act on the defensive. He would wait for the Greeks to attack him, so that the issue might be tried in a plain, when he would be able to reap the full advantage of his superiority in cavalry. It would, on the contrary, be to the interest of the Greeks, when they descended from Cithaeron, if they could by any means entice the enemy to give battle on the rough and high ground south of the river where cavalry would be of little use.

Battle of Plataea

August 479 B.C.

The field on which the fate of Greece was decided is bounded on the north by the river Asopus, on the south by Mount Cithaeron. The town of Plataea stood in the south-west of this space, on the most westerly of six ridges which connect the lower heights of the mountain with the plain. Three roads descended here into Boeotia: on the extreme east, the road from Athens to Thebes; in the centre, that from Athens to Plataea; on the west, that from Megara to Plataea. The Greek army took the most easterly way, which after a gradual ascent on the Attic side reaches the fortress of Eleutherae and the pass of the Oak's Heads, and then descends steeply into the Boeotian land. They found when they reached the other side that the road passed through the Persian camp, and they were forced to take up a position at the foot of the pass. Their right wing, consisting of the Spartans and Tegeates, rested on the high bastion of the mountain which rises above the town of Erythrae; their centre on lower ground close to the town; and the left wing, where the Athenians and Megarians were posted, was advanced right down to the foot of the descent. Thus the position of the Greeks was astride the road to Thebes. The only assailable point was the left wing, and against it Mardonius sent cavalry under the command of Masistius. Hard pressed by the darts and arrows of the enemy, and with no cavalry to aid them, the Megarians needed help. Three hundred Athenians (for the Athenians were also on the left wing) went down to the scene of battle, and the fortune of the day was at last changed when the general Masistius, a conspicuous figure in the fight, fell from his wounded charger. He was slain with difficulty by a spear which pierced his eye, for his armour was impenetrable; and the Persian horsemen, after a furious and fruitless charge to recover the body of their leader, abandoned the attack. The camp of the Persians was filled with loud wailing and lamentation—echoing, says Herodotus, all over Boeotia—for the death of Masistius.

The roads of Cithaeron

First position of the Greeks

But this success was far from dealing any solid advantage to the Greeks or serious injury to their foes. The Persians were well content to remain where they were; their great host still lay north of the Asopus. The Greeks, in order to obtain a better water supply and knowing that there was no chance that the Persians would attack them in their present position, decided to occupy lower ground in the territory of Plataea. In order to do this they

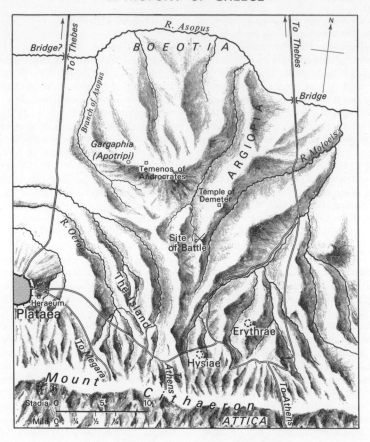

17. BATTLE OF PLATAEA 479 B.C.

moved north-westward along the spurs of Cithaeron, past the towns of Erythrae and Hysiae. To understand the operations which ensued, it is to be observed that the region between Cithaeron and the Asopus falls into two parts separated by a depression in the ground. The southern part is marked by the six ridges already mentioned and the streams which divide them; while the northern tract is also hilly, being marked by three ridges between which rivulets flow into the Asopus. Westward the depression opens out into flat land, the only flat land here, which stretches northward from Plataea to the river and is traversed by the road to Thebes.

Second position of the Greeks The Greek army ultimately arranged itself in order of battle between the Theban road and the Moloeis, a tributary stream of the Asopus. Their position was marked by the spring of Gargaphia, which afforded an abundant supply of fresh water, and the temple of the hero Androcrates. We are told that a dispute arose between the Tegeates and the Athenians for the occupation of the west wing, and that the Lacedaemonians decided in favour of the Athenians, who (as we have seen) were under the command of Aristides. The Tegeates were stationed next the Lacedaemonians on the right. Pausanias had now lost control of the eastern passes across Mount Cithaeron. The Persian general, as soon as the Greeks had left their first position, promptly occupied the roads and cut off a provision train which was on its way to supply the Greek army. The Greek general hoped every day that the enemy would attack; but Mardonius, apart from cavalry skirmishing, remained persistently on the defensive.

It would seem that the Greeks remained for some ten days inactive in this weak position, under continuous attack by the Persian cavalry, which crossed the river, and finally succeeded in choking up the waters of the Gargaphia spring. The only course open to the Greeks was to fall back upon the mountain, and either take up a position on the ridges between Hysiae and Plataea or seek to regain their former position at the foot of the main pass. For they could not venture to cross the Asopus and face the Persian cavalry. Pausanias held a council of war, and it was determined that the army should fall back to a position between Hysiae and Plataea and that one division should move up the mountain slope to recover command of the pass from Plataea to Athens. The whole movement was to be carried out at night. Perhaps Pausanias had received information that the Persian commander was growing impatient and was contemplating an attack. In any case his plan of retreat proved fortunate and, though it was not executed with precision, the Persians, even as at Salamis, were induced to give battle in conditions unfavourable to themselves. We might understand why Mardonius decided to abandon the defensive strategy to which hitherto he had adhered, if we knew something of the intrigues and divisions in the Persian camp. There seems to have been disastrous rivalry between himself and his second in command, Artabazus, who in the ensuing battle did simply nothing and was probably anxious that Mardonius should not win the glory of victory.

A little to the south-east of Plataea, a spur of Cithaeron was enclosed by the two branches of a stream which met again at the foot of the ridge and went by the name of the Island. It was arranged that the Athenians should now occupy the centre next the Lacedaemonians, and they were instructed to retreat to this ridge. The scheme was carried out, as it was planned, by the left wing, who took up their post in front of the temple of Hera, which was just outside the walls of Plataea. But the Athenians, for some unexplained reason, failed to obey orders and remained where they were in a dangerous and isolated position. The Lacedaemonians too seem to have wasted the precious hours of the short night. Their delay is ascribed to the obstinacy of the commander of one of the Spartan divisions, who had not been present at the council of war and refused to obey the order to retreat. His name was Amompharētus; he was a man of blameless valour, and Pausanias could not persuade himself to leave him behind. But the morning was approaching, and at length Pausanias began his march, convinced that his stubborn captain would follow when he found himself deserted. And so it fell out. When they had moved about ten stades, the Spartans saw that Amompharetus was coming, and waited for

him. But the day had dawned; the Persians had perceived that the Greek position was deserted, and Mardonius decided that now was the moment to attack, when the forces of the enemy were divided. His cavalry came up and prevented the Lacedaemonians from proceeding. It was on the slopes under Hysiae, near the modern village of Kriekouki, that Pausanias was compelled to turn and withstand the Persian horsemen, who were speedily supported by the main body advancing under Mardonius himself. The Persians threw up a light barricade of their wicker shields, from behind which they discharged innumerable arrows. Under this fire the Greeks hesitated; for the sacrificial victims were unfavourable. At length Pausanias, looking towards the temple of Hera, invoked the goddess; and after his prayer the prophets obtained good omens from the sacrifices. The Lacedaemonians no longer held back. Along with the Tegeates who were with them they carried the barricade and pressed the Persians backward towards the temple of Demeter which stood on a high slope above them. In this direction the battle raged hotly; but the discipline of the best spearmen of Greece proved itself brilliantly; and when Mardonius fell the battle was decided.

The Lacedaemonians and Tegeates had borne the brunt of the day. At the first attack, Pausanias had dispatched a hasty messenger to the Athenians. As they marched to the scene they were attacked by the Greeks of the right wing of the enemy's army, who effectually hindered them from marching farther. Meanwhile the tidings had reached the rest of the Greek army at Plataea, that a battle was being fought and that Pausanias was winning it. They hastened to the scene, but the action was practically decided before their arrival; some of them were cut off, on the way, by Theban cavalry. The defeated host fled back across the Asopus to their fortified camp; the Greeks pursued, and stormed it. The tent of Mardonius was plundered by the men of Tegea, who dedicated in the temple of Athena Alea in their city the brass manger of his horses; while his throne with silver feet and his scimitar were kept by the Athenians on the Acropolis, along with the breastplate of Masistius, as memorials of the fateful day. The body of Mardonius was respected by Pausanias, but it was mysteriously stolen, and none ever knew the hand that buried it. The slain Greek warriors, among whom was the brave Amompharetus, were buried before the gates of Plataea, and the honour of celebrating their memory by annual sacrifice was assigned to the Plataeans, who

Festival of Eleutheria

also agreed to commemorate the day of the deliverance of Hellas by a 'Festival of Freedom' every four years.[11] Pausanias called the host together, and in the name of the Spartans and all the confederacy guaranteed to Plataea political independence and the inviolability of her town and territory. The hour of triumph for Plataea was an hour of humiliation for Thebes. Ten days after the battle the army advanced against the chief Boeotian city and demanded the surrender of the leaders of the medizing party. On a refusal, Pausanias laid siege to the place, but presently the leaders were given up, by their own wish, for they calculated on escaping punishment by the influence of bribery. But Pausanias caused them to be executed, without trial, at Corinth. A Theban poet who sympathised with the national effort of Hellas might well feel 'distressed in soul'.

(Pindar)

The battle had been won simply and solely by the discipline and prowess of the Spartan hoplites. The plans of the exceptionally able commander, who was matched indeed with a commander abler than himself, were frustrated once and again through the want of unity and cohesion in his army, through the want apparently of tactical skill; and most of all perhaps through the half-heartedness of the Athenians. Never do the Athenians appear in such an ill light, as in the campaign of Cithaeron; and in no case have they exhibited so strikingly their faculty of refashioning history, in no case so successfully imposed their misrepresentations on the faith of posterity. They had no share in the victory; but they told the whole story afterwards so as to exalt themselves and to disparage the Spartans. They represented the night movements planned by Pausanias as a retreat before an expected attack of the enemy, and they invented an elaborate tale to explain how the attack came to be expected. Mardonius, they said, growing impatient of the delay, called a council of war, and it was decided to abandon defensive tactics and provoke a battle. Then Alexander of Macedon showed at this critical moment that his real sympathies were with Hellas and not with his barbarian allies. He rode down to the outposts of the Athenians, and, shouting, we must suppose, across the river, revealed the decision of the Persian council of war. Thus made aware of the Persian resolve to risk a battle, the Spartans proposed to the Athenians to change wings, in order that the victors of Marathon might fight with the Persians, whose ways of warfare they had already experienced, while the Spartans themselves could deal better with the Boeotians and other Greeks, with

The legend of the battle; Athenian misrepresentations

whose methods of fighting they were familiar. The proposal was agreed to, and as day dawned the change was being effected. But the enemy perceived it and immediately began to make a corresponding change in their own array. Seeing their plan frustrated, the Greeks desisted from completing it; and both the adversaries resumed their original positions. Mardonius then sent a message to the Lacedaemonians, complaining that he had been deeply disappointed in them, for though they had the repute of never fleeing or deserting their post, they had now attempted to place the Athenians in the place of danger. He challenged them to stand forth as champions for the whole Greek host and fight against an equal number of Persians. To this proposal the Spartans made no reply. Then Mardonius began his cavalry operations which led to the retreat of the Greeks from their second position. The three incidents of this malicious tale, the night-visit of Alexander, the fruitless attempt of the Spartans to shirk the responsibility of their post on the right wing, the challenge of Mardonius, are all improbable in themselves; but nevertheless this story was circulated and believed, and has received a sort of consecration in the pages of Herodotus.

Battle of Mycale and Capture of Sestos

Significance of battle of Plataea

The battle of Plataea shares with Salamis the dignity of being decisive battles in the world's history. Pindar links them together as the great triumphs of Sparta and Athens respectively, battles 'wherein the Medes of the bent bows were sore afflicted'. Notwithstanding the immense disadvantage of want of cavalry, the Lacedaemonians at Plataea had turned a retreat into a victory. The remarkable feature of the battle was that it was decided by a small part of each army. Sparta and Tegea were the actual victors; and on the Persian side, Artabazus, at the head of 40,000 men, had not entered into the action at all. On the death of Mardonius, that general immediately faced about and began without delay the long march back to the Hellespont. Never again was Persia to make a serious attempt against the liberty of European Greece; 'a god', said a poet of the day—and the poet was a Theban—'turned away the stone of Tantalus imminent above our heads'. For the following century and a half, the dealings between Greece and Persia will only affect the western fringe of Asia, and then the balance of power will have so completely shifted that Persia will succumb to a Greek conqueror, and Alexander of Macedon will achieve against the Asiatic monarchy what Xerxes failed to achieve against the free states of Europe.

The achievement of the Hellenic army under Mount Cithaeron, which rescued Greek Europe from the invader, was followed in a few days by an achievement of the Hellenic fleet which delivered the Asiatic Greeks from their master. Leotychidas at Delos had been persuaded to take the offensive by Samian patriots who assured him that the Ionians were anxious to revolt and that the Persian forces were very vulnerable. Their army was encamped on Cape Mycale with Ionian contingents that could not be trusted; their fleet was at Samos. When the Greek fleet sailed for Samos the Persians decided not to offer battle at sea and dismissed their Phoenician ships, while the small remainder joined the army on Cape Mycale. The Greeks landed, and then attacked, carried and burned the enemy's camp. Their victory was decided by the desertion of the Ionians, who won their freedom on this memorable day. Mycale followed so hard upon Plataea, that the belief easily arose that the two victories were won on the same afternoon. There is more to be said for the tradition that as the Athenians and their comrades assailed the entrenchments on the shore of Mycale the tidings of Plataea reached them and heartened them in their work.

From Mycale the Greeks sailed back to their base on Samos and there debated the future of the east Greeks who had revolted. The Spartans, anxious as always to avoid commitments outside the Peloponnese, suggested that they should be brought back to their mother-country and settled on the lands of the Medizers. The Ionians, however, were very reluctant to leave their homes and good lands, and the Athenians who had played a major part in their colonisation supported them. For the present, however, only the islanders were admitted to the Greek alliance and the fleet sailed to the Hellespont to break down the Persian bridges; but stormy weather had already done this work for them and it remained only to collect the cables, which they dedicated in their temples. At this point Leotychidas with the Peloponnesians sailed home, but the Athenians were determined to recover the Chersonese, which controlled one of the most vital stretches on the corn route from the Euxine. Persian resistance was concentrated in Sestos and the garrison held out through most

of the winter until their supplies were exhausted. With the capture of Sestos, Herodotus closes his history of the Persian Wars. The independence of the Hellespontine regions was a natural consequence of the victory of Mycale, but its historical significance lies in the fact that it was accomplished under the auspices of Athens. The fall of Sestos is the beginning of that Athenian empire to which Pisistratus and the elder Miltiades had pointed the way.

One memorial of the victory of Europe over Asia has survived till today. The votive offering set up at Delphi was a golden tripod standing on a column formed by three intertwining bronze serpents. There had originally been an epigram on the tripod: 'Leader of the Greeks when he destroyed the host of the Medes Pausanias set up this memorial to Phoebus Apollo'. This inscription, Thucydides tells us, which attributed the whole credit to Pausanias, was immediately disowned by the Spartans and erased. Instead the names of the states that had fought for Greece were inscribed and they can still be read on the coils of the serpents. But to see them one now goes to Stamboul to which city the monument was taken when the emperor Constantine refounded Byzantium as Constantinople, his new eastern capital.[12]

The Athenians set up their own memorial at Athens. In the late nineteenth century a fragment from a large marble base was found and the few words that survived suggested an association with the Persian War. Some fifty years later a second fragment was found in the American excavation of the Agora and the nature of the monument became clearer. On the face of the base were two epigrams, each consisting of two elegiac couplets inscribed in two lines, and the lower of the two epigrams was only added at a second stage. Both epigrams were generally thought to commemorate Marathon and the most attractive explanation of this unusual procedure was based on the tradition that Simonides and Aeschylus had competed for the honour of publicly commemorating the great victory of Marathon, and the poem of Simonides had been selected. The upper epigram, it was suggested, was Simonides' poem; it was later decided to add the version of Aeschylus. This popular theory collapsed when Meritt published a fragment from a fourth century copy of the first epigram, which made it virtually certain that this epigram commemorated either Salamis, or, more probably, Salamis and Plataea (and perhaps Mycale): 'These men on foot and in swift-

Battle of Mycale (middle of August, 479 B.C.)

Capture of Sestos, 478 B.C.

7.1 Athenian epigram

moving ships ensured that no part of Greece should see the day of slavery'. The explanation of the later addition of the Marathon epigram could be political. The text is considerably more difficult to restore, but it proclaims that the men of Marathon 'stood their ground outside the city' and it seems to add that by so doing they saved the city from burning. This was in striking contrast to the evacuation of Athens in 480 and the destruction of the city which followed. In this interpretation the contrast could be deliberate, to revive the glory of Cimon's father, Miltiades, at the expense of Themistocles who had guided Athens in 480 but soon found himself politically isolated after the war and then ostracised.[13] There was a more pervasive memorial of the great deliverance from Persia on Athenian coins. The head of their goddess was henceforward to wear a laurel wreath.

Gelon Tyrant of Syracuse

While the eastern Greeks were securing their future development against the Persian enemy and were affirming their possession of the Aegean waters, the western Greeks had been called upon to defend themselves against that Asiatic power which had established itself in the western Mediterranean and was a constant threat to their existence. The Greeks had indeed, on their side, proved a formidable check and hindrance to the expansion of the dominion and trade of Carthage. The endeavours of this vigorous Phoenician state to secure the queenship of the western seas, from Africa to Gaul, from the coast of Spain to the shores of Italy, depended largely for their success on her close connection and identity of interests with her sister-towns in Sicily; and secondly, on her alliance with the strong pirate power of Etruria. The friendly Phoenician ports of western Sicily—Motya, Panormus, and Solus—were an indispensable aid for the African city, both for the maintenance of her communications with Tuscany and for the prosecution of designs upon Sardinia and Corsica. In Corsican waters as well as in Sicily, the Phoenician clashed with the Greek. It was in the first quarter of the sixth century that Dorian adventurers from Cnidus and Rhodes sought to gain a foothold in the barbarian corner of Sicily, at the very gates of the Phoenicians. The name of their leader was Pentathlus. He attempted to plant a

Struggle of Greek and Phoenician in western Mediterranean in sixth century

The enterprise of Pentathlus, c. 580 B.C.

commemorating victories over Persia

settlement on Cape Lilybaeum, near Motya—a direct menace to the communications between Motya and Carthage. The Phoenicians gathered in arms, and they were supported by their Elymian neighbours; the Greeks were defeated and Pentathlus was slain. It was not the destiny of Lilybaeum to be the place of a Hellenic city; but long afterwards it was to become illustrious as the site of a Punic stronghold which would take the place of Motya, when Motya herself had been destroyed by a Greek avenger of Pentathlus. After their defeat the men of Pentathlus, casting about for *Founda-* another place to settle, withdrew to the volcanic *tion of* archipelago off the north coast of Sicily and *Lipara* founded Lipara in the largest of the islands. *Collectiv-* This little state was organised on communistic *ism* principles. The soil was public property: a certain number of the citizens were set apart to till it for the common use; the rest were employed in keeping watch and ward on the coasts against the descents of Tuscan rovers. This system was indeed subsequently modified: the land was portioned out in lots, but was redistributed every twenty years.

Cartha- The attempt of Pentathlus, the occupation *ginian* of the Liparaean group, the recent settlement *expedition* of Acragas, pressed upon Carthage the need of *to Sicily* stemming the Greek advance. Accordingly *under* we find her sending an army to Sicily. The *Malchus,* commander of this expedition, precursor of *c. 560-50* many a greater, was Malchus; and it is possible *B.C.* that he was opposed by Phalaris, who established a tyranny at Acragas. There was a long

war, of which we know nothing except that the invader was successful and Greek territory was lost to the Phoenician. Soon afterwards Carthaginian armies were closing Sardinia, rich in metals and corn, to the Greeks and establishing themselves securely in the island. In the northern seas Carthage was also confronted by the Greeks. The Phocaeans of *The* Massalia planted colonies and won influence on *Phoca-* the coast of Spain. Moreover the new Phocaean *eans: of* settlement at Alalia in Corsica was a challenge *Massalia;* to Carthage in what she regarded as her own *of Alalia* domain. But Greek Alalia was short-lived. Carthage and her powerful Etruscan allies *Battle of* nearly annihilated the Phocaean fleet; and the *Alalia,* crews which escaped were only able to rescue *c. 535 B.C.* their families and goods. Alalia was deserted; Corsica fell under the power of the Etruscans, and the coasts of Sardinia were gradually appropriated by Carthage.[14] Thus the chance of establishing a chain of Greek settlements between Massalia and Sicily was frustrated.

It now remained for Carthage to establish and extend Phoenician power in Sicily. We have seen how Dorieus, son of a Spartan king, *(See* made an attempt to do somewhat the same *above,* thing which the Cnidian adventurer had *p. 136)* essayed—to gain a footing in Sicily within the Phoenician circle. He too failed; but such incidents brought home to Carthage the need of dealing another and a mightier blow at the rival power in Sicily. She was occupied with the conquest of Sardinia and with a Libyan war, and the struggle was postponed; but the hour came at last, and the Carthaginians put forth all their power to annihilate colonial Greece at the very time when the Great King had poured forth the resources of Asia against the mother-country. It was, in the first instance, an accident that the two struggles happened at the same moment. The causes which led to the one were independent of those which led to the other. But the exact moment chosen by Carthage for her attack upon Sicily was probably determined by the attack of Xerxes upon Greece; and although the two struggles ran each its independent course, there is no reason to question the statement that the courts of Susa and Carthage exchanged messages, through the mediation of the Phoenicians, and were conscious of acting in concert against the same enemy.

Sicily menaced by Carthage

Tyrants in Sicily

In the second decade of the fifth century Greek Sicily was dominated by four tyrants. Anaxilas of Rhegion had made himself master of Zancle, which from this time forward is known as Messana, and he thus controlled both sides of the straits, which he secured against the passage of Etruscan pirates.[15] Terillus, his father-in-law, was tyrant of Himera. Over against this family group in the north stood another family group in the south: Gelon of Syracuse and his father-in-law Theron of Acragas.

Gelon had been the general of Hippocrates, a tyrant of Gela, who had extended his sway, whether as lord or over-lord, over Naxos, Zancle, and other Greek cities, and had aimed at winning Syracuse. Hippocrates had defeated the Syracusans on the banks of the Helorus and would have seized their city, if it had not been for the intervention of Corinth and Corcyra. But Syracuse was forced to cede her dependency, Camarina, to the victor. Hippocrates died in besieging Hybla; and the men of Gela had no mind to allow his sons to continue their father's tyranny. But Gelon, son of Deinomenes, a general who had often led the cavalry of Gela to victory, espoused the cause of his master's heirs, and as soon as he had gained possession of the city brushed them aside and took the tyranny for himself. The new lord of Gela achieved what his predecessors had vainly striven to accomplish. The *Gamori* or nobles of Syracuse had been driven out by the commons, and they appealed to Gelon to restore them. The Syracusan people, unable to resist the forces which Gelon brought against them, made terms with him, and he established his power in Syracuse over oligarchs and democrats alike. It seems probable that Gelon was either at once or at a later

Hippocrates, tyrant of Gela Battle of the Helorus, 492 B.C.

Gelon, tyrant of Gela, 491 B.C.;

wins Syracuse:

stage of his rule appointed formally 'General with full powers'; we find his brother Hieron, who succeeded to his position, addressed by the poet Bacchylides as 'General' of the Syracusan horsemen.

his position there

The tyrant of Gela now abandoned his own city and took up his abode in Syracuse, making it the centre of a dominion which embraced the eastern part of the island. Gela had for a short space enjoyed the rank of the first of Sicilian cities; she now surrendered it to Syracuse, which was marked out by its natural site for strength and domination. Gelon may be called the second founder of Syracuse. Soon after the occupation of Ortygia, settlement had extended to the mainland where there was ample room for expansion between the coast and the heights of Epipolae. This district, Achradina, had been linked in the sixth century with the island by a mole. Gelon encompassed the mainland settlement, much enlarged, with a wall. Ortygia remained the 'acropolis'. The chief gate of Syracuse was now in the new wall of Gelon, close to the Harbour; and near it a new agora was laid out, for the old agora in the Island no longer sufficed. Nearby docks were built, for Syracuse was to become a naval power. Until now, in spite of the natural advantages of her position, she had been less wealthy and powerful than Acragas and Gela; her supremacy had been local only. Henceforward she was to become and remain by far the greatest Greek city in the west.

He enlarges Syracuse; his walls and docks;

Gelon, belonging to a proud and noble family, sympathised and most willingly consorted with men of his own class and looked with little favour on the people, whom he described in a famous phrase as 'a thankless neighbour'. He held court at Syracuse like a king, surrounded by men of noble birth. He tolerated the Syracusan commons—he was not unpopular with them—but he showed elsewhere what his genuine feelings were. One of his first needs was to find inhabitants to fill the spaces of his enlarged town. For this purpose he transported men on a large scale from other places of his dominions. His own town Gela was sacrificed to the new capital: half its citizens were removed to Syracuse. Harder was the fate of luckless Camarina, which was now for the second time blotted out from the number of Greek cities. Two generations had hardly passed since she had been swept away by the Syracusan republic; and now the Syracusan tyrant carried off all the inhabitants and made them burgesses of the ruling state. Megara, the next-door neighbour of Syracuse on the north, and Euboea higher

his court and class-prejudice;

his treatment of other cities;

up the coast, also contributed to swell the population of Gelon's capital. Megara became an outpost of Syracuse, while Euboea was so entirely blotted out that its very site is uncertain. But in both these cases the policy of Gelon strikingly displayed the prejudice of his class. He admitted the nobles of Megara and Euboea to Syracusan citizenship; he sold the mass of the commons in the slave market. In abolishing cities and transplanting populations Gelon set an example which we shall see followed by later tyrants. He also invited new settlers from elder Greece, and he gave the citizenship to 10,000 mercenary soldiers.

his family Gelon was supported in his princely power by his three brothers, Hieron, Polyzālus, and Thrasybulus. He entered into close friendship with Theron, his fellow-tyrant, who made Acragas in wealth a power second only to Syracuse itself. Theron, like Gelon, was a noble, belonging to the family of the Emmenids, and his rule was said to have been mild and just. Gelon married Damareta, the daughter of Theron; and Theron married a daughter of Polyzālus. The brilliant lords of Syracuse and Acragas, thus joined by close bonds, were presently associated in the glorious work of delivering Greek Sicily from the terrible danger which was about to come against her from overseas.

The Carthaginian Invasion of Sicily, and the Battle of Himera

A quarrel between Theron of Acragas and Terillus tyrant of Himera led up to the catastrophe which might easily have proved fatal to the freedom of all the Sicilian Greeks. The ruler of Acragas crossed the island and drove Terillus out of Himera. The exiled *Terillus* tyrant had a friend in Anaxilas of Rhegion; *invites* but Rhegion was no match for the combined *interven-* power of Acragas and Syracuse, and so Terillus *tion of* sought the help of Carthage, the common *Carthage* enemy of all.

Carthage was only waiting for the opportunity. She had been making preparations for a descent on Sicily, and the appeal of Terillus merely determined the moment and the point of her attack. Terillus urging the Phoenician against Himera plays the same part as Hippias urging the Persian against Athens, but in neither case is a tyrant's fall the cause of the invasion. The motive of the Carthaginian expedition against Sicily at this particular epoch is to be found in a far higher range of politics than the local affairs of Himera or the interests

of a petty despot. There can hardly be a doubt *Carthage* that the Great King and the Carthaginian *and Persia* republic were acting in concert and that it was deliberately planned to attack eastern and western Greece independently but at the same moment.[16] While the galleys of the elder Phoenicia, under their Persian master, sailed to crush the elder Hellas, the galleys of the younger Phoenician city would cross over on her own account against the younger Hellas. In the Phoenicians of Tyre and Sidon, Xerxes had willing intermediaries to arrange with Carthage the plan of enslaving or annihilating Hellas. The western island mattered little to Xerxes; but what mattered greatly to him was that the lord of Syracuse should be hindered from sending powerful reinforcements of men and ships to the mother-country. We have already seen how the mother-country sought the help of Gelon, and how the danger of Sicily forced him to refuse.

When the preparations were complete, *The Punic* Hamilcar, the shophet of Carthage, sailed with *armament* a large armament and landed at Panormus; for the call of Terillus determined that the recovery of Himera should be the first objective. It is said that the army consisted of 300,000 men, conveyed by more than 200 galleys and 3000 transports; but we can lay no stress on these figures. From Panormus this great host moved along the coast to Himera, accompanied by the warships, and proceeded to besiege the city, which Theron was himself guarding with a large force. Hamilcar made two camps in front of the town. The sea camp lay on the low ground between the hill of Himera and the beach; the land camp stretched along the low hills on the western side of the town. A sally of the besieged resulted in loss, and Theron sent a message to Syracuse to hasten the coming of his son-in-law. With 50,000 foot-soldiers and 5000 horsemen Gelon marched to the rescue without delay. He approached the town on the east side and formed a strong camp on the right bank of the river.

The decisive battle was brought about in a *Battle of* strange way, if we can trust the story. Hamilcar *Himera,* determined to enlist the gods of his foes on his *480 B.C.* own side. He appointed a day for a great sacrifice to Poseidon near the shore of the sea. For this purpose he needed to have Greeks present who understood how the sacrifice should be performed. Accordingly Hamilcar wrote to Selinus, which had become a dependency of Carthage, bidding that city send horsemen to the Punic camp by a fixed day. The letter fell into the hands of Gelon, and he conceived a daring stratagem. On the morning

189

of the appointed day a band of Syracusan horsemen stood at the gate of the sea camp, professing to be the expected contingent from Selinus. The Carthaginians could not distinguish strangers of Syracuse from strangers of Selinus, and they were admitted without suspicion. They cut down Hamilcar by the altar of Poseidon, and they set fire to the ships. All this was visible from the high parts of the town above them, and men posted there signalled to Gelon the success of the plan. The Greek commander immediately led his troops round the south side of the city against the land camp of the enemy. There the battle was fought, a long and desperate struggle, in which the scale was finally turned in favour of the Greeks by a body of men which Theron sent round to take the barbarians in the rear. The victory was complete; the great expedition was utterly destroyed; the chief himself was slain.

Legend of Hamilcar's death

But of the death of Hamilcar the Carthaginians had another and a far grander tale to tell. This tale does not explain how the battle was brought about. It simply gives us a splendid picture. The battle rages 'from the morning till the late evening', and during that long day Hamilcar stands at the altar of Baal, in his camp by the sea. A great fire devours the burnt-offerings to the god; victim after victim, whole bodies of beasts and perhaps of men, are flung into the flames, and the omens are favourable to Carthage. But as he is pouring out a drink-offering, he looks forth, and behold his army is put to flight. The moment for a supreme sacrifice has come; he leaps into the fire and the flames consume him. The offering of his life did not retrieve the day; but hereafter Himera was destined to pay a heavy penalty for the death of Hamilcar.

The common significance of the battles of Salamis and Himera, or the repulse of Asia from Europe, was appreciated at the time and naïvely expressed in the fanciful tradition that the two battles were fought on the same day. But Himera, unlike Salamis, was immediately followed by a treaty of peace. Carthage paid the lord of Syracuse 2000 talents as a war indemnity, but this was a small treasury compared with the booty taken in the camp. Out of a portion of that spoil a beautiful issue of large silver coins was minted and called 'Damareteion', after Gelon's wife; and some pieces of this memorial of the great deliverance of Sicily are preserved.

The Damareteion decadrachms

7.2 Damareteion: *obv.* Chariot crowned by victory; below, running lion, *rev.* Head of Arethusa-Artemis surrounded by dolphins (see note, page 553)

Syracuse and Acragas under Hieron and Theron

Theron and Acragas had played an honourable part in the deliverance of Sicily, though it was a part which was second to that of Gelon and Syracuse. Theron survived the victory by eight years, and during that time he was engaged in doing for Acragas what had been already done for Syracuse by his fellow-tyrant. The area enclosed by the early walls of Acragas needed no enlargement. Theron's task lay in rebuilding the city and particularly its temples on a more magnificent scale. He laid the foundations of the greatness of Acragas in the fifth century but it was not till long after his death that the temples he planned were completed. In all this work, and in the watercourses which he also constructed, Theron had slave-labour in abundance—the barbarians who had been captured after the battle of Himera. Theron placed rescued Himera under the government of his son Thrasydaeus, who however, unlike Theron himself, proved an oppressor and was hated by the citizens.

Meanwhile Gelon died and left the fruits of his enterprise and statesmanship to be enjoyed by his brother Hieron. While Hieron was to have the sovereign power, Gelon desired that Polyzalus, whom he ordered to marry his widow Damareta, should have the supreme command of the Syracusan army. The idea of this dual system was unwise, and it necessarily led to fraternal discord. Polyzalus was popular at Syracuse, and his double connection with Theron secured him the support of that tyrant. To Hieron he seemed a dangerous rival, and in the end he was compelled to seek refuge at Acragas. This led to an open breach between Hieron and Theron, but it did not come to actual war, and it is said that the lyric poet Simonides, who was a favourite at both courts, acted as peacemaker.

Hieron may be said to have completed the work of Himera by the defeat which he inflicted upon the Etruscans at Cyme. The Etruscans were the other rival power which, besides the Carthaginians, threatened the 'Greater Greece' of the west. The possession of Cyme was an important Etruscan objective for it threatened the communications of Etruria with her growing dominion in Campania. Soon after the naval victory at Alalia the Etruscans made a formidable land attack on Cyme, but Aristodemus, who had emerged from faction as a tyrant, saved the city. This check was followed by the driving of the Etruscan kings from Rome and the eclipse of Etruscan power in

7.3 Helmet dedicated by Hieron

Latium, confirmed by the victory of the Latin allies, strongly supported by Cyme, over the Etruscans at Aricia. The cutting of the land route emphasised the need for securing the sea passage along the Italian coast, and some years later an Etruscan fleet sailed against Cyme. Hieron, realising the issues at stake, brought up a Syracusan fleet. The Etruscans were decisively defeated and no longer menaced the development of western Greece. From the booty Hieron sent a bronze helmet to Olympia; and Pindar of Thebes immortalised the victory.[17]

It is perhaps from the hymns of Pindar that we get the most lively impression of the wealth and culture of the courts of Sicily in the fifth century. Pindar, like other illustrious poets of the day, Simonides and Bacchylides, and Aeschylus, visited Sicily, to bask in the smiles, and receive the gifts, of the tyrant. The lord of Syracuse—or king, as he aspired to be styled—sent his race-horses and chariots to contend in the great games at Olympia and Delphi, and he employed the most gifted lyric poets to celebrate these victories in lordly odes.[18] Pindar and Bacchylides were sometimes set to celebrate the same victory in rival strains. These poets give us an impression of the luxury and magnificence of the royal courts and the generosity of the royal victors. Syracuse, on whose adornment her tyrants could spend the Punic spoils, and Acragas, 'fairest of the cities of men', seemed wonderful to the visitors from elder Greece. Yet amid all their own magnificence and amid their absorbing political activity, the princes of this younger western world coveted above all things that their names should be glorious in the mother-country. They still looked to the holy place of Delphi as the central sanctuary of the world, and they enriched it with costly dedications. The golden tripods, which Gelon and his brothers dedicated from Punic treasure, became, like the other golden things of Delphi, the loot of robbers; but we are reminded of that fraternal union by a precious bronze charioteer, which was dug up in the ruins of the Delphic sanctuary. It was dedicated by Polyzalus, perhaps in honour of a Pythian victory.[19]

Ideals of Pindar

It was easy to be blinded by the outward show of these princely tyrants, which the genius of Pindar has invested with a certain dignity. But Pindar, himself born of a noble family, cherished the ideas and prejudices of a bygone generation. He belonged to a class, he wrote chiefly for a class, whose day was past: nobles whose main aim in life was to win victories at the public games. These men were out of sympathy with the new ideas and the political tendencies of their own age; they were belated survivals of an earlier society. Pindar sympathised with them. He liked aristocracies best; he accepted monarchy even in the form of tyranny; but democracy he regarded as the rule of a mob's passions. The despots of Sicily and Cyrene supported the national games of Greece, and that was in truth their great merit in the eyes of the poet. The chariot-race, the athletic contests, seen in the midst of a gay crowd, then the choral dance and song in honour of the victory, and the carouse, in the hall perhaps of some noble Aeginetan burgher, these were 'the delightful things in Hellas' which to Pindar were the breath of life. He was religious to the heart's core; and all these things were invested with the atmosphere of religion. But allowing for this, we feel that he takes the games too seriously and that, when Aeschylus was wrestling with the deep problems of life and death, the day was past for regarding an Olympian victory as the grandest thing in the world. We must not be beguiled by Pindar's majestic art into ascribing to the tyrants any high moral purpose. It was enough that they should aspire to an Olympian crown, and incur the necessary outlay, and seek immortality from the poet's craft; the poet could hardly dare to demand a higher purpose.

Fair as the outside of a Syracusan state might seem to a favoured visitor who was entertained in the tyrant's palace, underneath there was no lack of oppression and suspicion.

The system of spies which Hieron organised to watch the lives of private citizens tells its own tale. One of his most despotic acts was his dealing with the city of Catane. He deported all the inhabitants to Leontini, peopled the place with new citizens, and gave it the name of Aetna. His motive was partly vanity, partly selfish prudence. He aspired to be remembered and worshipped as the founder of a city; and he also intended Aetna to be a stronghold of refuge to himself or his dynasty, in case a day of jeopardy should come. His son Deinomenes was installed as 'King of Aetna'. But the Dorian city of Aetna, so cruelly founded, though it was celebrated in lofty phrases by Pindar and had the still higher honour of supplying the motive of a play of Aeschylus, had but a short duration; it was soon to become Catane again.

Foundation of Aetna

At Acragas, the mild rule of Theron seems to have secured the love and trust of his fellow-citizens; but at Himera he showed what a tyrant might do, by slaughtering without any mercy those who had showed their discontent at the rule of his son. Neither the Syracusan nor the Acragantine dynasty endured long. After Theron's death, Thrasydaeus misruled Acragas, as he had already misruled Himera. But for some unknown reason he had the folly to go to war with Hieron, who discomfited him in a hard-fought battle. This defeat led to his fall. Himera became independent, and Acragas adopted a free constitution. The deliverance of Syracuse came about five years later. When Hieron died, his brother Thrasybulus took the reins of government, and, being a less able and dexterous ruler than Hieron, he soon excited a revolution by his executions and confiscations. The citizens rose in a mass, and obtaining help from other Sicilian cities besieged the tyrant and his mercenaries in Syracuse. He was ultimately forced to surrender and retired into private life in a foreign land. Thus the tyranny at Syracuse came to an end, and the feast of *Eleutheria* was founded to preserve the memory of the dawn of freedom.

Death of Theron, 472-1 B.C. Thrasydaeus: his war with Hieron and his fate 471-0 B.C. Death of Hieron, 467 B.C.

The rule of the despots seems to have wiped out the old feud between the nobles and the commons, but a new strife arose instead. The old citizens, nobles and commons alike, distrusted the new citizens, whom Gelon had gathered together from all quarters. A civil war broke out; for some time the old citizens were excluded from both the Island and Achradina, but in the end all the strangers were driven out, and the democracy of Syracuse was securely established. One good thing the tyrants had done: they had obliterated the class

Republics in Sicily

distinctions which had existed before them, and thus the cities could now start afresh on the basis of political equality for all. The next half-century was a period of increasing prosperity for the republics of Sicily, especially for the greatest among them, Syracuse and Acragas, and for Selinus, freed from the Phoenician yoke. At Acragas the free people carried to completion the works which their beneficent tyrant had begun. The stately row of temples along the southern wall belongs to this period. 'It was a grand conception to line the southern wall, the wall most open to the attacks of mortal enemies, with this wonderful series of holy places of the divine protectors of the city. It was a conception due, we may believe, in the first instance, to Theron, but which the democracy fully entered into and carried out.' But her sacred buildings brought less glory to Acragas than the name of the most illustrious of her sons. The poet and philosopher Empedocles was reared in what he describes as the 'great town above the yellow river of Acragas'. He was not only a profound philosopher, an inspired poet and a skilful physician, but he had lent his hand to the reform of the constitution of his city. Unhappily his personality is lost in the dense covert of legends which quickly grew up around him. The true Empedocles who, banished from his home, died quietly in the Peloponnese, becomes the seer and magician who hurled himself into the bowl of Aetna that he might become a god. A god indeed he proclaims himself to be, going about from city to city, crowned with Delphic wreaths, and worshipped by men and women.

Empedocles

For a time indeed the Siceliots were threatened with a remarkable danger, the revival of the native power of the Sicels. This revival was entirely due to the genius of one man and the danger disappeared on his death. Ducetius organised a federation of the Sicel towns and aspired to bring the Greek cities under Sicel rule. He displayed his talent in the foundation of new cities, which survived the failure of his schemes. His first settlement was on the hill-top of Menaenum, overlooking the sacred lake and temple of the Palici. As his power and ambitions grew, he descended from the hill and founded Palica, close to the national sanctuary, to be the political capital of the nation. He captured Aetna, gained a victory over the Acragantines and Syracusans, but subsequently defeated by Syracuse; and on this defeat his followers deserted him, and the fabric which he had reared collapsed. He boldly took refuge himself at the altar in the

Ducetius and the Sicels, 460-440 B.C. His cities: (1) Menaenum (Mineo), (2) Palica, (3) Kalê Aktê

His failure, 450 B.C.

Syracusan market-place; his case was debated in the Assembly; and by an act of clemency, which we might hardly expect, he was spared and sent to Corinth. Five years later we find him again in Sicily, engaged in the congenial work of founding a third city, Kalê Aktê or Fairshore, on the northern coast, with the approbation of Syracuse. It is uncertain whether he dreamed of repeating his attempt at a national revival or had become convinced that the fortune of the Sicel lay in Hellenisation. His foundations were more abiding than those of Hieron; one of them, Mineo, survives today. The career of Ducetius exhibited the decision of destiny that the Greek was to predominate in the island of the Sicels.

Religious Movements in the Sixth Century

In the latter part of the sixth century, the expansion of the Persian power had suspended a stone of Tantalus over Hellas, and it seemed likely that Greek civilisation might be submerged in an oriental monarchy. We have seen how Greek generals, Greek spearmen, and Greek seamen averted this calamity. We have now to see how another danger was averted, a danger which, though it is not like the Persian invasion written large on the face of history, threatened Greece with a no less terrible disaster. This danger lay in the dissemination of a new religion, which, if it had gained the upper hand, as at one time it seemed likely to do, would have pressed with as dead and stifling a weight upon Greece as any oriental superstition. Spiritually the Greeks might have been annexed to the peoples of the orient.

The age of Solon witnessed not only a social and political movement among the masses in various parts of Greece, but also an intellectual and spiritual stirring. There was an intellectual dissatisfaction with the theogony of Hesiod as an explanation of the origin of the world; and the natural philosophy of Thales and his successors came into being in Ionia. But there was also a moral dissatisfaction with the tales of religious mythology, as they were handed down by the epic bards; and this feeling took the form of interpreting and modifying them, so as to make them conform to ethical ideals. The poet Stesichorus was a pioneer in this direction, and it was he who first imported into the legend of the house of Atreus—the murder of Agamemnon by his wife, and the murder of Clytaemnestra by her son—the terrible moral significance which Aeschylus

Beginning of rationalism

Religious movement

and the Attic tragedians afterwards made so familiar. Further than this, men began to feel a craving for an existence after death, and intense curiosity about the world of shades, and a desire for personal contact with the supernatural. Both the scientific and the religious movements have the same object—to solve the mystery of existence; but the religious craving demanded a short road and immediate satisfaction. The craving led to the propagation of a new religion, which began to spread about the middle of the sixth century. We do not know where it originally took shape, but Attica became its most active centre, and it was propagated to western Hellas beyond the sea.

Elements in the Orphic religion

Based partly on the wild Thracian worship of Dionysus, this religion was called Orphic from Orpheus, poet and priest, who was supposed to have been born in Thrace and founded the bacchic rites; and it exercised a deep influence over not only the people at large but even the thinkers of Greece. The Orphic teachers elaborated a theology of their own; a special doctrine of the future world; peculiar rites and peculiar rules of conduct. But they took up into their system, so far as possible, the old popular beliefs. The Orphic religion might almost be described as based on three institutions: the worship of Dionysus, the mysteries connected with the gods of the underworld, and the itinerant prophets; but Dionysus, the underworld, and the art of the seer and purifier, all acquired new significance in the light of the Orphic theology.

Dionysiac worship

It was perhaps as early as the eighth century that the worship of Dionysus was introduced into northern Greece, and various legends record the opposition which was at first offered to the reception of the stranger. His orgies spread, especially in Boeotia and Attica. The worshippers gathered at night on the mountains, by torchlight, with deer-skins on their shoulders and long ivy-wreathed wands in their hands, and danced wildly to the noise of cymbals and flutes. Men and women tore and devoured the limbs of the sacred victims. They desired to fall, and they often fell, especially the women, into a sort of frenzied ecstasy, in which their souls were thought to be in mystic communion with Dionysus. It was probably the influence of the Dionysiac worship that induced the Delphic god to give his oracles through the mouth of a woman cast into a state of divine frenzy.

Itinerant seers

Men could also deal with the supernatural world through the mediation of seers. Wise men and women, called *bakids* and *sibyls*, attached to no temple or sanctuary, travelled about and made their livelihood by prophesying, purifying, and healing. They practised these three arts through their intimacy with the invisible world of spirits; to which the causes of disease and uncleanness were ascribed. Epimenides was one of the most famous and powerful of these wizards; we saw how he was called upon to purify Athens.

(p. 120)
Mysteries

Mysteries, connected with the cult of the deities of the underworld, supplied another means of approaching the supernatural. The Homeric bards of Ionia may have lived in a society where life yielded so many pleasures that men could look forward with equanimity and resignation to that colourless existence in the grey kingdom of Persephone, which is described in the epics. But the conditions of life were very different in the mother-country in the eighth century. The strife for existence was hard and the Boeotian poet must have echoed the groans of many a wretched peasant when he cried

The earth is full of ills, of ills the sea.

It was a time when men were ready to entertain new views of a future world, suggesting hopes that a tolerable existence, unattainable here, might await them there. These new hopes which began to take shape in the course of the seventh century were naturally connected with the religion of the deities of the underworld. In Homer we find Persephone as queen in the realm of the ghosts, but we meet there no hint of a connection between her worship and that of Demeter, the goddess of the fruits of the earth. But as the earth which yields the sustenance of men's life also receives men into her bosom when they die, Demeter and Persephone came to be associated in many local cults throughout Greece, and there grew up the legend of the rape of Persephone, which was specially developed at Eleusis and was the subject of the Eleusinian Hymn to Demeter, composed in the seventh century. At Eleusis this *chthonian* cult acquired a peculiar character by the introduction of a new doctrine touching the state of souls in the life beyond the grave.

The Eleusinian religion

In the days of Eleusinian independence, the kings themselves were the priests of the two goddesses. When Eleusis became part of the Athenian state, the Eleusinian worship was made part of the Athenian state-religion; a temple of the two goddesses was built under the Acropolis and called the Eleusinion; and the Eleusinian Mysteries became one of the chief festivals of the Attic year, conducted by the king. The Mysteries, which were probably

7.4   Demeter, Triptolemus, Persephone (Eleusis, c. 440)

of a very simple nature in the seventh century, were subsequently transformed under Athenian influence. Two points in this transformation are especially to be noted: the old Eleusinian king Triptolemus is made more prominent and is revered as the founder of agriculture, sent abroad by Demeter herself to sow seed and instruct folk in the art. But far more important is the association of the cult of Iacchus with the Eleusinian worship. Iacchus was a god of the underworld, who had a shrine in Athens. In the Mysteries he was borne to Eleusis and solemnly received there every year. He was originally distinct from the mystic Dionysus, with whom he was afterwards identified.

(1) Tripto-lemus

(2) Iacchus

The rites at Eleusis

The Mysteries seem to have consisted of a representation in dumb show of the story of Persephone and Demeter. Mystic spells were uttered at certain moments in the spectacle, and certain sacred gear was exhibited. There was no explanation of any system of doctrine; the initiated were seers, not hearers. When the scheme of the Mysteries was fully developed the order of the festival, which took place in September, was as follows. On the first day, the cry was heard in the streets of Athens—

Seaward, O mystae, mystae, to the sea!

And the initiated went down to the shore and cleansed themselves in the sea water. The next two days were occupied with offerings and ceremonies at Athens, and on the fourth the image of Iacchus was taken forth from his shrine and carried in solemn procession along the Sacred Way, over Mount Aegaleos to Eleusis. The Mystae, as they went, sang the song of Iacchus, and reached the temple of the goddesses, under the Eleusinian acropolis, late at night, by the light of torches. The great day was when they assembled in the Hall of Initiation, and sat around on the tiers of stone-seats. The Hierophant, who always belonged to the Eleusinian royal family of the Eumolpids, displayed the secret things of the worship. Beside him the Torch-holder, the Herald, and the Priest of the Altar, conducted the mystic ceremonies. The Mysteries are mysterious still, so far as most of the details are concerned. Yet we may perhaps say that no definite dogma was taught, no systematic interpretation was laid on the legends; but the 'acts' were calculated to arouse men's hopes, mysterious enough to impress their imaginations, and vague enough to suggest to different minds different significances. The rites gave to many an assurance of future well-being and even to harder reasoners a certain sense of possibilities

(By the pass of Daphne)

(Tele-sterion)

(τα δρώμενα)

in the unknown. And it was believed that the Mystae had an advantage over the uninitiated not only here but hereafter—an interest as it were with the powers of the other world. So it is said in the old Eleusinian Hymn:

Bliss hath he won whoso these things hath seen,
  Among all men upon the earth that go;
But they to whom those sights have never been
  Unveiled have other dole of weal and woe,
Even dead, shut fast within the mouldy gloom
  below.

The Eleusinian Mysteries became Panhellenic. All Greeks, not impure through any pollution, were welcome to the rites of initiation, women were not excluded by their sex, nor slaves by their condition. It is probable that the development of the Mysteries owed a good deal to the Pisistratids; and the ground plan of the Hall of Ceremonies, which was erected in their time, can be traced at Eleusis.

Spread of the Orphic Religion

The Orphic teachers promulgated a new theory of the creation of the world—a theory which may have derived some suggestions from Babylonia. They taught that Time was the original principle; that then Ether and Chaos came into being; that out of these two elements Time formed a silver egg, from which sprang the first-born of the gods, Phanes god of light; the development of the world is the self-revelation of Phanes. It was necessary to bring this cosmogony into connection with Greek theology. Accordingly, Zeus swallows Phanes and thereby becomes the original force from which the world has to be developed anew. The Thracian god, Dionysus Zagreus, is the son of Zeus and Persephone—and thus closely connected with the underworld. Zeus gives him the kingdom of the universe, while he is still a boy; but he is pursued by the Titans, and when, after many escapes, he takes the shape of a bull, he is rent in pieces by them, but Athena saves his heart. Zeus swallows it and afterwards brings forth the new Dionysus. The Titans, still wet with the blood of their victim, he strikes with lightning, and the race of men springs from their ashes—so the nature of men is compact of Titanic and Dionysiac elements, good and bad. The motive of the myth is to awaken in the human soul a consciousness of its divine origin and help it on its way back to the divine state. To escape from the prison or tomb of the body, to become free from the

Orphic cosmogony

Myth of Dionysus Zagreus

Origin of the human race

Titanic elements, penalties and purifications are necessary, and the soul has to pass through a cycle of incarnations. In the intervals between these incarnations, which recur at fixed times, the soul exists in the kingdom of Hades. To attain a final deliverance, a man must live ascetically according to rules which the Orphics prescribed, and be initiated in the orgies of Dionysus. Thus they prescribed abstinence from animal food and imposed necessary ceremonies of purification. They taught the doctrine of judgment after death, and rewards and punishments in Hades, according to men's deeds in the body.

Thus the Orphics reintroduced, as it were, into Greece the Thracian Dionysus, who seemed almost another god when brought face to face with the Dionysus who had been hellenized and sobered since his admission into the society of the Greek gods of Olympus. They adopted and developed the ideas of the Eleusinian Mysteries; and in a poem on the Descent of Orpheus into Hades they described the geography of the underworld. They also aspired to take the place of the old prophets and purifiers; and they sought out and collected the oracles which those prophets had disseminated. Their doctrines were published in poems which were intended to supersede the Theogony of Hesiod; and the surviving fragments of these works show more poetical power than the compositions of the later successors of Homer.

The Orphics in Attica. Onomacritus

The Orphic religion found a welcome at Athens and was encouraged by Pisistratus and his sons. Onomacritus, one of the most eminent Orphic teachers, reputed the author of a poem on the 'Rites of Initiation', won great credit and influence at the court of the tyrants. We saw how he was supposed to have taken part in preparing an edition of Homer, in which it was suspected that he and his collaborators made interpolations; and how another interpolation led to his banishment, when he was detected in making an addition of his own to a collection of ancient oracles, which were ascribed to the mythical poet Musaeus.

Pytha- goras: goes to Croton, c. 530 B.C.; his scientific work;

The Orphic doctrines were taken up by a man of genius, Pythagoras of Samos, who went to Italy and settled at Croton, where he was well received. His philosophy had two sides, the philosophic and the religious. He made important discoveries in mathematics and the theory of music, he recognised the spherical form of the earth, and his astronomical researches led to a considerable step, taken by his followers, in the direction of the Copernican system—the distinction of real and apparent motions. The Pythagoreans knew that the motion of the sun round the earth was only apparent, but they did not discover the revolution of the earth on its axis. They conceived a fire in the centre of the universe, round which the earth turns in twenty-four hours; the five known planets also revolving round it; and the moon and the sun, in a month and a year respectively. We never see the fire, because we live on the side of the earth which is always turned away from it. The whole world is warmed and lit from that fire—the 'hearth of the universe'. Pythagoras sought to explain the world, spiritual and material, by numbers; and, though he could plausibly defend the idea in general, its absurdity was evident when carried out in detail. His great achievement was the creation of mathematical science.

he founds a brother- hood; its Orphic character;

At Croton he founded a religious sect or brotherhood, organised according to strict rules. The most important doctrine was the transmigration of souls, and the ascetic mode of life corresponded to that of the Orphic sects. In fact, the Pythagoreans were practically an Orphic community. Their brotherhood, which did not exclude women, obtained adherents not only in Croton but in the neighbouring cities and won a decisive political influence in Italiot Greece. But this influence was exerted solely in the interests of oligarchy; it would seem indeed that the nobles became members of the religious organisation, in order to use it as an instrument of political power. It was during the ascendency of the Pythagoreans that a war broke out between Croton and its neighbour Sybaris, which was then subject to a tyranny. The men of Croton harboured the exiles whom Telys, the despot of Sybaris, drove out, and refused his demand for their surrender. Telys led forth a large host; a battle was fought; and the Sybarites were routed. Then the victors captured Sybaris and utterly blotted it out. New cities were to arise near the place; one was for a few months to resume its name; but the old Sybaris, which had become proverbial throughout Greece for its wealth and luxury, disappeared so completely that its exact site has only recently been found. The destruction of the rival city was the chief exploit of the Pythagorean oligarchy of Croton; but a strong opposition arose in Croton against the government and against the Pythagorean order. Pythagoras himself found it prudent to escape from the struggle by leaving Croton, and he ended his life at Metapontion. The democratic party was led by Cylon, but the Cylonians did not get the upper hand till more than half a century had

its political influence

War of Sybaris and Croton

Destruc- tion of Sybaris, 511-10

Pythagoras leaves Croton, c. 510-9(?)

Suppression of the Pythagoreans, c. 450

passed; and the Pythagorean order flourished in Croton and the neighbouring cities. At length a sudden blow dissolved their power. One day 40 brethren were assembled at Croton in the house of Milon. Their opponents set the building on fire, and only two escaped. It was a signal for a general persecution throughout Italy; everywhere the members of the society were put to death or banished.

At the time of the fall of the Pythagoreans, the Orphic religion was no longer a danger to Greece. It was otherwise in the lifetime of Pythagoras himself. Then it seemed as if the Orphic doctrines had been revealed as the salvation which men's minds craved for; and, if those doctrines had taken firm hold of Greece, all the priesthoods of the national temples would have admitted the new religion, become its ministers, and thereby exercised an enormous sacerdotal power. Nor would the Orphic teachers have failed, if there had not been a powerful antidote to counteract their mysticism. Even as it was, they exercised a permanent influence, stimulating the imaginations of poets, like Aeschylus and Pindar, and diffusing a vivid picture of the world of Hades, which has affected all subsequent literature.

Ionian Reason

The antidote to the Orphic religion was the philosophy of Ionia. In Asiatic Greece, that religion never took root; and most fortunately the philosophical movement—the separation of science from theology, of 'cosmogony' from 'theogony'—had begun before the Orphic movement was disseminated. Europe is deeply indebted to Ionia for having founded philosophy; but that debt is enhanced by the fact that she thereby rescued Greece from the tyranny of a religion interpreted by priests. We have met Thales and Anaximander already. Pythagoras, although he and his followers made important advances in science, threw his weight into the scale of mysticism; affected by both the religious and the philosophical movements, he sought to combine them; and in such unions the mystic element always wins the preponderance. But there were others who pursued, undistracted, the paths of reason, and among these the most eminent and influential were Xenophanes and Heraclitus.

Xenophanes (after 545 B.C.)

No man was more active in the cause of reason than Xenophanes of Colophon, who, after the Persian subjugation of Ionia, migrated to Elea, where he died in extreme old age. But he spent his long life in wandering about the world, and none saw and heard more of many lands and many men than he did. The feeble resistance of Ionia to the invader had disgusted him with the Greeks, and produced a reaction in his mind against their religion and their ideals. His experience of many lands helped him to cast away national prejudices, and he spent his strength in warring against received opinions. In the first place he attacked the orthodox religion and showed up the irrational side of gods made in the image of men. If oxen or horses or lions, he said, had hands to make images of their gods, they would fashion them in the shape of oxen, horses, and lions. In the next place, he protested against the accepted teachers of the Greeks, the poets Homer and Hesiod, whom Greece regarded as inspired. All they have taught men, he said, is theft, adultery, and mutual deceit. Again, he ridiculed the conventional ideals of Greek life, the ideal, for instance, of the athlete. He deprecated the folly which showed great honours to a victor in a race or a contest. 'Our wisdom is better than the strength of human animals and horses.' He carried about and spread his revolutionary ideas from city to city in the guise of a musician, attended by a slave with a cithern. But he was not merely destructive; he had something to put in the place of the beliefs which he overthrew. He constructed a philosophy of which the first principle was god—not like mortals in either form or mind—which he identified with the whole cosmos, and which was thus material, existing in space, and not excluding the existence of particular subordinate gods animating nature. He was also distinguished as a geologist; he drew conclusions from fossils as to the past history of the earth. As a fearless thinker, seeking to break through national prejudices, he is one of the most attractive of the pioneers of Greek thought.

But what especially concerns us here is that Xenophanes rejected Orpheus as utterly as he rejected Hesiod. He would have nothing to do with mysticism and divine revelation; he regarded the Orphic priests as impostors, and he inveighed strongly against Pythagoras. We can hardly over-value his services in thus actively fighting the battle of reason and diffusing ideas which counteracted not only the comparatively harmless superstitions of the vulgar but also the more serious and subtle danger of the Orphic religion. Long before he died, Greek philosophy had become a living power which no religion would stifle, a growing force which would hinder sacerdotalism from ever turning back the stream of progress.

Heraclitus

The rationalism of Xenophanes affected Heraclitus of Ephesus, a man of very different temper. Heraclitus heartily despised the vulgar—he was an aristocrat in politics—and he wrote in a hard style, for the few. In old age he retreated to the woods to end his life, having deposited the book of his philosophy in the temple of Artemis. A man of greater genius than any of the Ionian philosophers who preceded him, he thought out the 'doctrine of the flux', which exercised an immense influence on his successors. This principle was the constant change in all things; existence is change; 'we are and we are not'. But the process of change observes a certain law; nature has her measures; and thus, while he had developed the doctrine of relativity—'good and bad', he said, 'are the same'—he had a basis for ethics. His influence was both subversive and conservative, according as one took hold of the doctrine of the flux or the fixed law of the world.

Parmenides

The pantheistic principle of Xenophanes was taken up at Elea by Parmenides, who gave it a new metaphysical meaning. He assumed an eternal unchanging Being, and treated it with the scientific method which he learned from the Pythagoreans. One of the most important services of Parmenides and his followers was their argument that sense is deceptive and leads us into self-contradiction. Here, they said, was the capital error of Heraclitus, who founded his system on the senses.

The religious danger averted

With Parmenides and Heraclitus, philosophy in the strict sense, metaphysics as we call it, was fully founded. We have not to pursue the development here; but we have to realise that the establishment of the study of philosophy was one of the most momentous facts in the history of the Greeks. It meant the triumph of reason over mystery; it led to the discrediting of the Orphic movement; it ensured the free political and social progress of Hellas. A danger averted without noise or bloodshed, not at a single crisis but in the course of many years, is a danger which soon ceases to be realised; and it is perhaps hard to imagine that in the days of Pisistratus the religion which was then moving Greece, and especially Attica, bade fair to gain a dominant influence and secure a fatal power for the priests. The Delphic priesthood had, doubtless, an instinct that the propagation of the Orphic doctrines might ultimately redound to its own advantage. Although the new religion had arisen when the aristocracies were passing away and had addressed itself to the masses, it is certain that, if it had gained the upper hand, it would have lent itself to the support of aristocracy and tyranny. The tyrants of Athens might have made an Orphic priesthood an useful instrument of terror; and the brotherhood of Pythagoras was an unmistakable lesson to Greece what the predominance of a religious order was likely to mean.

We may say, with propriety, that a great peril was averted from Greece by the healthful influence of the immortal thinkers of Ionia. But this, after all, is only a superficial way of putting the fact. If we look deeper, we see that the victory of philosophy over the doctrines of priests was simply the expression of the Greek spirit, which inevitably sought its highest satisfaction in the full expansion of its own powers in the free light of reason.

Legend of the Seven Sages

The sixth century, the most critical period in the mental development of the Greeks, came to be known afterwards as the age of the Seven Sages. The national instinct for shaping legends chose out a number of men who had made some impression by their justice and prudence, and, regardless of dates, invented an ideal community among them, as if they had formed a sort of college; and brought them into connection with great people, like Lydian kings. Periander, the tyrant of Corinth, was curiously added to the list, which included Solon and Thales. To them were attributed wise maxims like 'Know thyself', 'Avoid excess', 'It is hard to be virtuous'. The spirit which the legend ascribes to these sages and which the lives of Solon and Pittacus displayed, reflects the wisdom which sought to solve, or rather to evade, the everlasting problem of the discrepancy between man's ideal of justice and the actual ordering of the world, by enjoining a life of moderation. But it is not without significance that, when the Orphic agitation had abated, Greece should have enshrined the wordly wisdom of men who stood wholly aloof from mystic excitements and sought for no revelation, in the fiction of the Seven Sages.

CHAPTER 8

The Foundation of the Athenian Empire

The Position of Sparta and Career of Pausanias

The Persian war, in its effects on Greece, illustrates the operation of a general law which governs human societies. Pressure from without, whether on a nation or a race, tends to promote unity and cohesion within. In the case of a nation, the danger of foreign attack increases the sense of unity among individual citizens and strengthens the central power. In the case of a race, it tends to weld the individual communities into a nation or a federation. In the latter case, the chance of realising a complete or permanent unity depends partly on the strength and the duration of the external pressure, partly upon the degree of strength in the instinct for independence which has hitherto hindered the political atoms from cohesion. The Persian danger produced a marked tendency towards unity, but the pressure was acute only for a few years, and lasted in any form only for a few decades. On the coast of Asia, where the danger was permanent, a union was made.

Now on these principles a philosopher might have predicted that an Hellenic union, whether whole or partial, whether of short or of long duration, would follow the repulse of the Persians; he might have predicted that such a great joint effort would react upon the domestic development of the victorious peoples. But no one could have foreseen what shape the union would take or how the reaction would be directed. The course of Greek affairs entered upon a new and unexpected way. For *The position of Sparta;* the last forty years, Sparta had been the predominant power in continental Greece.

She had become the head of a Peloponnesian League and had intervened with effect in Greek affairs beyond the limits of the Peloponnese. Her headship in the common resistance to Persia was recognised without murmur or dispute by the allies of northern Greece; in fact, her peninsular league may be said to have widened into the Panhellenic confederacy of the Isthmus. Her admirals had been commanders-in-chief at Salamis and at Mycale; and, if it were said that those naval victories could not be ascribed to Lacedaemonian skill or enterprise, Sparta could point to Thermopylae, where her king had been gloriously defeated, to Plataea where her general and her spearsmen had won what was after all the decisive contest of the war. A political prophet would therefore have been tempted to predict that Sparta, universally acknowledged before the war to be the leading state of Greece, would after the war be able to convert leadership into dominion. A great national enterprise, conducted under her auspices to a splendid conclusion, must immensely increase the moral strength of her position, and might justly stimulate her ambition; moral power, by dexterous management, can soon be converted into material strength; in short, after the battle of Plataea, the Greek world seemed to lie at Sparta's feet. If such calculations were made, they were doomed to disappointment. Lacedaemon had not the means, and the Lacedaemonian government had not the brains or the spirit to create the means, of carrying out an effective imperial policy.

For a state which aspired to a truly imperial *not a sea-* position in Greece must inevitably be a sea- *power;* power. This was determined by the geo-

200

graphical and commercial conditions of the Greek world. So long as the Asiatic Greeks belonged to the Persian dominion, so long as the eastern waters of the Aegean were regarded as a Persian sea, Sparta might indeed hold a dominant position in a Hellas thus restricted. But when the world of free Hellenic states once more extended over the Aegean to the skirts of Asia and to Thrace, Sparta unless she became a sea-power could not extend her influence over this larger sea-bound Greece. She might retain her continental position, but her prestige must ultimately be eclipsed and her power menaced by any city which won imperial authority over the islands and coasts of the Aegean. This was what happened.

her limitations

The Spartans were a people unable to adapt themselves to new conditions. Their city, their constitution, their spirit were survivals from medieval Greece. The government was conservative by tradition; reforms were unwelcome; a man of exceptional ability was regarded with suspicion. They continued to drill their hoplites in the fifth century as they had done in the sixth; the formation of a navy would have seemed to them as unpractical an idea as an expedition against the capital of Persia. And if we follow their conduct of the recent war, we see that their policy was petty and provincial. They had generally acted at the last moment; they had never shown initiative; their view was so limited by the smaller interests of the Peloponnese that again and again they almost betrayed the national cause. Failing to share in the progress of Greece, utterly wanting in the imperial instinct and the quality of imagination which accompanies it, the city of Lacedaemon was not marked out to achieve a political union of the Hellenic states. She was, however, able to prevent a rival from achieving it—though not before that rival had completely thrown her into the shade.

History of these critical years ill-known

Unfortunately the events of the years succeeding the battle of Plataea are but very slightly known. Herodotus, who, about half a century later, completed the story, compact of fiction and history, of the Persian war, ends his work at the capture of Sestos. In the meantime the events of that full and momentous half-century had not been recorded, except by bits and scraps; the dates became confused, the details were forgotten; and when Thucydides, some years after Herodotus, came to investigate the history of this period, the result of his research was a meagre narrative, in a very uncertain chronological setting. The growth of the Athenian empire is the central fact of the period; but before tracing it, we must pause—it will

not be for long—over the misfortunes of Sparta.

Pausanias, the son of Cleombrotus, had shown, it must be allowed, remarkable military ability in conducting the campaign of Plataea. But his talents as a politician were not equal to his talents as a general. Leaping into fame by his victory, he was led into attempting to play a part for which he was too slight a man. Sparta sent him out, in command of a squadron of ships supplied by her allies, to continue the work of emancipating the eastern Greeks. He sailed first to Cyprus and was successful in delivering the greater part of the island from Persian rule. He then proceeded to Byzantium and expelled the Persian garrison. But here his conduct became ambiguous; he began to play a game of his own. He connived at the escape of some kinsmen of Xerxes who were in the city; and he committed various acts of insolence and oppression to the Greeks. He behaved more as a tyrant than as a general; and he completely ruined all chances that his country had of remaining at the head of the confederacy which the Persian invasion had called into being. The eastern Greeks placed themselves under the protection and headship of Athens. This step was inevitable; the maritime power of Athens marked her out to be leader in the prosecution of the war beyond the sea. But the conduct of Pausanias at Byzantium may well have been the occasion of the formal transference of the leadership of the confederacy from Sparta to Athens. At Sparta itself the reports of the doings of the general aroused alarm and anxiety. He was recalled to answer the charges. It was said that he wore Persian dress and was attended by an Asiatic bodyguard in his journey through Thrace. For he had indeed been intriguing with the Persian court. The victor of Plataea offered to enslave his own city and the rest of Hellas to Xerxes and to seal the compact by marrying his daughter. His overtures were welcomed by the Great King; and Pausanias, being a small man and elated by vanity, was unable to refrain from betraying, in little things, his treacherous designs. The Persian intrigue, however, could not at this time be proved against him; he was punished only for some acts of injury which he had done to particular persons. He was not sent out again; but he subsequently hired a trireme for himself and returned to the scene of his former intrigues. He resumed possession of Byzantium and thus controlled the inner gate of the Euxine; and he succeeded almost immediately in capturing Sestos, which gave him control of the outer gate also. This was too much for the Athenians, who were extending

Career of Pausanias

478 B.C.

His medism;

recall and acquittal

Proceeds to Byzantium on his own account, 477 B.C. Takes Sestos;

their political and commercial interests in those regions, and they sent out a squadron under Cimon, the son of Miltiades, who recovered Sestos and drove Pausanias out of Byzantium. The Spartan government, hearing that he was intriguing in the Troad, sent a herald commanding him to return home. He obeyed the summons, believing that he could secure an acquittal by bribes; but it seems that he was already devising a daring and dangerous plan against the constitution of his own city. The Ephors threw him into prison; but it was difficult to procure evidence of his guilt. He was released and challenged inquiry. Everybody knew that he had not only negotiated with Persia but that he had prepared the way for a revolt of the Helots by promising them emancipation. He dreamed of converting the Spartan state into a true monarchy. But there were not clear enough proofs to act upon, until a confidential servant turned informer. Pausanias had entrusted him with a letter to Artabazus, but the man, who had noticed that none of the messengers who had been previously dispatched on the same errand ever returned, broke the seal and read in the letter the order for his death. He showed the letter to the Ephors, and they, wishing to have proof against Pausanias from his own mouth, contrived a stratagem. A hut with a partition was erected at the sanctuary of Taenarus. They concealed themselves in one room and the man remained in the other as a suppliant. Pausanias came to discover why he was there; the man told him of the letter and reproached him. In the conversation, Pausanias admitted the whole truth.[1] But he received a hint of his danger and fled to the temple of Athena of the Brazen House. He took refuge in a small covered building adjoining the shrine. The Ephors had the doors built up and starved him to death. As he was dying they brought him out, and by the command of the Delphic god he was buried at the entrance to the sacred enclosure. But the starvation within the precincts was an offence against the goddess and brought a curse upon the Spartans. To expiate this they dedicated two bronze statues of Pausanias to Athena of the Brazen House.

Though the adventures of Pausanias are of no great consequence, his career is typical of the Spartan abroad; and it throws some light on years of which we know very little. The Spartan government had sent out another general to replace Pausanias in the Hellespont, but the allies would have no more dealings with Spartan generals; the Ionians had appealed to Aristides who commanded the Athenian

driven out by Cimon, ?476 B.C.

recalled to Sparta

The curse of Athena of the Brazen House. (c. 471 B.C.?)

Sending of Dorcis

contingent in the fleet which Pausanias had brought to Byzantium, and through him transferred their allegiance to the Athenians: the Spartans made no further attempt to recover their leadership. On the other hand, they made some attempts at extending their power on the mainland and forming a continental federation. They cast their eyes upon Thessaly and perhaps hoped that if they brought the far north under their control, they could extend their influence southward to the Crisaean gulf and form a Lacedaemonian empire on the basis of the Amphictionic league of northern Greece. They sent out an army under King Leotychidas, who landed in the Pagasaean bay and showed that he could have easily subjugated the Thessalian states. But like many a Spartan general, he could not resist silver and gold; and the Aleuad princes saved their power by bribing the invader. His guilt was evident, and when he returned home he was condemned to death. He saved himself by fleeing to Tegea, where Athena's sanctuary was ever the refuge of a Spartan king in the day of danger. It is possible that Sparta gained some influence in Thessaly by this enterprise, in which she employed a Greek fleet, but she made no conquest. Nor did her attempt to reorganise the Amphictionic federation prosper better. She proposed to expel from this league all those states which had joined the Mede—this was aimed at Thebes and Thessaly; and even the states which had not joined the federation against the Mede—this was aimed at Argos. But through the influence of Themistocles, who represented Athens, the proposal was thrown out. The activity of Themistocles in defeating the designs of Sparta at this period is reflected in the story that he tried to induce the Athenians to set fire to the fleet in Thessalian waters.

Lacedaemonian expedition against Thessaly, 476 B.C.

Lacedaemonian attempt to annex the Amphictionic league (476 B.C.?); thwarted by Themistocles

Sparta was unable to prosecute any further plans of empire beyond her own peninsula; she was soon compelled to fight for her position within the Peloponnese itself. Argos had now recovered somewhat from the annihilating blow which had been dealt her by king Cleomenes, and was entering upon a new constitutional development which was ultimately to shape itself into a democracy. Most of the small towns such as Hysiae and Orneae, which had taken advantage of the prostration of their mistress to throw off her yoke, were brought back to their allegiance. It might have been harder to cast out the slave lords of Tiryns from their Cyclopean fortress, but a prophet from Phigalia came and stirred them up against Argos; they took the offensive, endured a defeat, and Tiryns was recovered.[2] Thus

Argos recovers Tiryns (468-7 B.C. ?)

re-arising, Argos was able to support the Arcadian cities in a combination against the power of Sparta. She entered into alliance with Tegea, but outside the walls of that city the joint forces of the two allies were defeated by the hoplites of Lacedaemon. Yet the city was not taken, and the epitaph of the fallen warriors told how 'their bravery hindered the smoke of blazing Tegea from mounting to the sky'. Soon after this we find all the Arcadian cities leagued against Sparta—all except the Mantineans, who were never ready to join hands with their Tegeate neighbours. This time Argos sent no help. The Arcadian league sustained a crushing defeat at Dipaea, and Tegea was forced to submit.[3] Thus, through the energy of the young king Archidamus, Sparta maintained her position, but there were grave causes of anxiety for the future. She had to behold the synoecism of the villages of Elis into a city with a democratic constitution; that was a danger in the west. Regenerate Argos was a danger in the east. And even in Arcadia, Sparta was constrained reluctantly to recognise the new synoecism of the Mantinean villages, as a mark of gratitude to the community for holding aloof from the Arcadian league.

Thus it was not given to Sparta to strike out a new path; the Persian war left her much where she was before. She had, if anything, diminished rather than increased her prestige, and she had shown the world that she was destined to remain in the old Peloponnesian groove. In the meantime another city had been advancing with rapid strides along a new path, compassing large enterprises, and laying the foundations for a large empire.

The Confederacy of Delos

The lukewarmness of Sparta, exhibited in her failure to follow up the battle of Mycale, had induced the Ionian and other Asiatic Greeks to place themselves under the leader-ship of Athens. Thus was formed the voluntary confederacy on which an Athenian empire was to rise. The object was not only to protect the rescued cities from reconquest by the bar-barian, but also to devastate the country of the Great King, in order to obtain by plunder a set-off against the expenses and losses of the war. The treasury of the league was estab-lished in the sacred island of Delos, the ancient centre of Ionian worship, and it has hence been called the Confederacy of Delos. The recapture of Sestos was its first achievement.

The league included the Ionian and Aeolian cities of Asia; the islands adjacent to the coast from Lesbos to Rhodes; a large number of towns on the Propontis, and some in Thrace; most of the Greek cities of Chalcidice; most of the Cyclades; and Euboea except its southern city Carystus. An oath of loyalty was taken by Aristides on behalf of the Athenians and by representatives of each ally in turn that they would have the same friends and enemies, and they solemnly sank lumps of metal in the sea to signify that the alliance was to be permanent. The purpose of the league was to defend Greeks against Persia and to take vengeance for the sufferings of Greece in the great invasion. For this purpose a strong fleet supported by sound finance was essential and it was left to Athens to decide which states should contribute ships and which money. By the middle of the century only three states were contributing ships, but by then Thasos, and perhaps others, had been required to surrender their fleets after unsuccessful revolts, and a larger number had grown weary of campaigns and preferred to commute to annual tribute. The original league fleet probably included most of the states which had sizeable fleets. For the money-payers an assessment was needed and Aristides, who was popular with the allies and had a great reputation for integrity, was commissioned to decide, after reviewing their resources, how much each state should pay. The first assessment, according to Thucydides, was 460 talents. This is con-siderably more than the later records would lead us to expect, and it is widely believed that Aristides first assessed all states in terms of money and then converted money to ships for the ship contribution; 460 talents on this interpretation would be the grand total reached by Aristides for all the allies, including those who did not at first contribute money.[4] This may be the right solution, but it is not the natural meaning of Thucydides' text. He clearly implies that his figure refers only to the money-payers. Either he has made a mistake (and it would be an easy mistake to make) or the assessments were originally higher than they were by the mid-century.

In the early years the policy of the league was based on meetings of representatives at Delos in which all states large and small had an equal vote. The large number of votes (more than 150) enabled Athens to control the proceedings of the Council; she could influence the smaller states and the number of their votes would overcome the weight of any opposition which the larger states could offer.

And though formally Athens could be outvoted she held all the keys to power.[5] As leader of the league she provided the commanders for all league operations, and the treasurers who received the tribute every year, though called *hellenotamiae,* treasurers of the Greeks, were from the first Athenian officials chosen by Athenians. Thus from the first Athens had in her hands the means of gradually, and without any violent revolution, transforming the naval league into a naval empire. But the allies knew that without Athenian help they would once again become the mere fringe of the Persian empire; they were in no mood to consider carefully ways in which they could protect themselves from an abuse of power by Athens.

While the name of Aristides is connected most closely with the foundation of the Confederacy, there is no doubt that it was due to his rival Themistocles that Athens took the tide of fortune at the flood. Themistocles had made his city a sea-power; and this feat proved him the greatest of all her statesmen. He was a man of genius. The most reserved of all historians, Thucydides, turns aside to praise his unusual natural gifts: his power of divining what was likely to happen, and his capacity for dealing with difficult situations. We should have expected that the guidance of the policy of Athens, and the organisation of the new Confederacy, would have been entirely entrusted to Themistocles. Half a century later, when the democratic development of Athens had advanced farther, this would probably have been the case. But at this time a man without powerful connections could not long maintain his influence over the people. Themistocles had no party behind him, and the exceptional ability of the man is shown by nothing so much as by the fact that in spite of this disadvantage he played such a great part. His rivals, Aristides and Xanthippus, inherited prestige and position; and Xanthippus had married into the Alcmaeonids, the family of Megacles and Cleisthenes. They are the leaders at Plataea and Mycale; the name of Themistocles does not appear in the second year of the Persian war. The circumstance that Themistocles was not a party leader, that there was no protracted period during which Athens submitted to his influence, might easily lead us to underrate his importance. Though he was not formally or officially the founder of the Confederacy, yet, when Athens undertook the leadership and entered upon the new paths which then opened out before her, she was under the spell of a spirit of which he had

Position of Themistocles; he has no party to support him

been the clearest and earliest interpreter. But his influence had not yet passed away; and, while the fleet was building an empire in the east, there was work for him to do amid the ruins of Athens.

The Fortification of Athens and the Piraeus

Themistocles, as we saw, made Athens a sea-power. Under his guidance she threw her chief energy into the development of a navy; but if she had followed that guidance more fully she would have now cut herself more boldly adrift from the ties which attached her to the continent. It often occurred to the Athenians to regret that Athens was not an island; 'if we were islanders', they thought, 'we could defy the world'. There would always be the Boeotian and the Megarian frontiers. But, if a series of strong fortresses had been regularly maintained on these frontiers and if Athenian politicians had resolutely avoided a continental policy, it might have been possible to spend practically all their strength on their ships. In any case, when Athens decided to enter upon a new career, her true policy would have been to come down to the Piraeus. She should have left her old city round the Acropolis and migrated to the shore of the sea which was henceforward to shape her history. The position of the Acropolis was a fatality for Athens; it was too far from the sea and at the same time too near. If it had been as far from the coast as Acharnae, the citizens would almost certainly at this period have transferred their hearths and temples to the hill of Munychia and the shores of the Piraeus. But it was near enough to admit of tolerably quick communication with the harbour; and this geographical circumstance at once saved the old town and weakened the new city. Expediency will induce a monarch, but nothing except necessity will persuade a free people, to take the momentous resolution of leaving the spot where the homes and temples of the community have stood for centuries—the place associated with their dearest memories, their hopes and their fears.

Had Themistocles been a tyrant, we may venture to suppose that he would have left Athens unfortified, built his palace on Munychia, and made Piraeus the centre of government—the city; so that in a few years the old town would have sunk into decay. But since Athens was to remain as before, notwithstanding the new development, and since this

The Acropolis too far from the coast

new development made the Piraeus of greater strategic importance, it became necessary to fortify and defend two towns within five miles' distance of each other.

The walls of Athens

After Plataea, the Athenians brought back their families and goods to their desolate habitation. Little of the old town wall was still standing, and they proceeded to build a new wall. The work was done in haste; the material of older buildings, and even gravestones, were used. The traces of haste can be detected in some of the remains of this wall of Themistocles, near the Dipylon Gate in the north-west of the city. The Peloponnesians looked with jealousy at the rise of the Athenian walls. The activity of Athens in the Persian war, and her strong navy, made them suspect her ambitions. But they could not prevent her from strengthening her town. The Lacedaemonians sent an embassy to deprecate fortifications, and to invite the Athenians instead of fortifying their own town to join Sparta in demolishing all fortifications in Greece. But they were not in a position to do more than remonstrate. As the name of Themistocles was associated with the wall, it was inevitable that an anecdote should be circulated, to illustrate the resources and wiles of the Attic Odysseus.

The trick of Themis- tocles

At his suggestion, the Spartan envoys were sent back with the answer that the Athenians would send an embassy. When they were gone, he started himself, as one of the ambassadors, but his colleagues were to remain behind till the wall had reached the lowest defensible height. In the meantime, the whole population, men, women, and children, were to press on with the work. Having arrived at Sparta, he delayed presenting himself before the assembly, and when he was asked why, he said that his colleagues had been detained and that he expected them every day. Meanwhile persons arriving from Athens assured the Spartans that the wall was being built. Themistocles asked them not to be deceived by such rumours, but to send men of their own to discover whether it was true. At the same time he sent a message to Athens, with instructions that the envoys from Sparta should be detained till he and his colleagues had returned. The wall had now reached a sufficient height; and, the other ambassadors having arrived, Themistocles appeared before the assembly and declared that Athens had walls and could defend her people. 'In future,' he said, 'if the Lacedaemonians or their allies have any communication to make, they must deal with us as with men who are capable of deciding their own and Greece's interests.' The Lacedaemonians had

to put as good a face on the matter as they could. The story has significance in representing Athens as now formally declaring herself the peer of Sparta.

The fortification of Piraeus was likewise taken in hand. A thick wall was built all round the Munychian peninsula, keeping close to the sea, and was continued along the north side of the harbour of Cantharus—or the Harbour, as it was simply called—and out to the promontory of Eetionea. The entrances to this chief Harbour and to the two small havens of Munychia and Zea on the east side of the peninsula were fortified by moles.

In the course of the next twenty years the Athenians came to see the disadvantage of the two towns, which ought to have been one. It was borne in upon their statesmen that, in the case of an enemy invading Attica with a powerful army, the communications between Athens and the Piraeus might be completely severed and the folk of the city be cut off from their ships. In order to meet this danger—which would have been most simply met by deserting Athens—a new device was conceived. It was resolved to transform the two towns into a double town, protected by a continuous line of fortification. Two diverging walls were built, to connect Athens with the sea. The northern joined the Piraeus wall, near the Harbour, the southern ran down to the roadstead of Phaleron. By these Long Walls, costly to build and costly to defend, Athens sought to rectify a mistake and adapt her topography to her role of mistress of the sea.

The Long Walls, 458 B.C.

But though this device of Athens to conciliate her past history with her future seems clumsy enough, it answered its purpose fairly well. Her naval power was based upon the only sure foundation, a growing naval commerce. This, in its turn, depended upon the increase of Attic industries, which may be estimated by the enormous number of resident aliens or metics, who settled in Athens or Piraeus for the purpose of manufacture and trade. These metics, who seem to have ultimately approached the number of 10,000 were liable to the same ordinary burdens as the citizens, and when a property-tax was imposed in time of war they were taxed at a higher rate. We may well believe that Themistocles was concerned to encourage the growth of a class of inhabitants who were directly or indirectly so profitable to the community. But in our scanty and vague records of this momentous period it is impossible to define the activity of Themistocles.

The μέτοικοι

He may have wished to introduce a system by which a certain number of triremes should be added to the fleet every year, but this idea was not adopted; new ships were built from time to time, according as they were needed. But a new system of furnishing them was *Introduction of the trierarchy* introduced. The state supplied only the hull and some of the rigging; the duty and expense of fitting the galley, launching it complete, and training the oarsmen, were laid upon the most wealthy citizens, each in his turn. This public burden was called the trierarchy, and the trierarch, who sailed with his ship, was responsible for the good repair of the trireme at the end of the period of his office. One *Crew: 170 oarsmen, 20 hypêretai* hundred and seventy oarsmen, composed of the poorest class of citizens with metics and, in emergency, slaves, propelled each galley;[6] there was a crew of 20 men, to manage the vessel, *ten epibatai* including the *keleustes* who set the time to the oarsmen; and there were, besides, ten marines.

As their navy was from henceforth to be the chief arm of their military power, the Athenians *Change in the stratêgia* were obliged to make a necessary change in the constitution of their highest military command. Two courses were open to them. They might leave the board of generals as it was, each general being the captain of the hoplites of his own tribe, and institute a new board of admirals. If this arrangement had been made, it would have been necessary to assign to the admirals a higher authority, for the purpose of conducting joint operations by land and sea, so that the position of generals would have been reduced to that of subordinate officers. The other course was to make the generals supreme commanders by land and sea alike— and such had been their virtual position during the Persian invasion. This second plan was adopted, and as a logical consequence the generals were no longer elected by each tribe, but by the whole people, though normally each tribe was represented on the Board of Ten. The old duties of the generals as commanders of the tribal regiments were undertaken for the infantry by new officers called taxiarchs and for the cavalry by the phylarchs.

The fortification of the city and her harbour was the chief, but it was not the only, work that the masons of Athens were set to do. When Mardonius withdrew from Athens before the battle of Plataea he had completed the destruction begun when the city was first captured by the Persians in the previous year. The Athenians returned to find most of their public and private buildings levelled to the ground. After the fortifications had been made *Rebuilding of the city* secure the most pressing problem was to build living quarters for the citizens and to restore such buildings as were essential to the carrying

on of public business. It was on the buildings round the Agora and in the rest of the city below the Acropolis that rebuilding was first concentrated. The temples of the Acropolis *Temples* had also been destroyed, but the main debt to the gods was to be repaid by a later generation. The old temple of Athena Polias, which housed the sacred image of the goddess, was probably brought back into immediate use by temporary improvisation, but no attempt was made to restore the building in its previous form nor to replace the sculptures which had been shattered in the collapse of the temple. Together with fragments of dedications, sculptures from other buildings, and miscellaneous material from the ruins, they were cleared from the site and used as filling to raise the level of the Acropolis, and to preserve thereby for posterity a vivid picture of one of the finest phases of Athenian art. The great new temple of Athena, which had been begun after Marathon, and had been destroyed before it was completed, was not continued. Not until peace had been made with Persia did Athena receive her new home, when the Parthenon arose on the foundations which were intended for a building of wholly different proportions.

Ostracism and Death of Themistocles

For some years Themistocles divided the conduct of public affairs with Aristides and Xanthippus. He superintended the building of the walls, and we have already seen how he effectually opposed the designs of Sparta. But the man of genius had his weaknesses. Like most Greek statesmen, he was accessible to bribes, and perhaps he would hardly have cared to tell how he had become a rich man. It was more serious that his vanity betrayed him into committing public indiscretions. He built near his own house a shrine to 'Artemis wisest in Council', on the ground that the counsels *(Artemis* which he had offered his country had been *Aristobule)* wiser than all others.[7] In themselves such things were of little importance, but they conduced to unpopularity and gave opponents a handle for attack. The time and the immediate causes of the banishment of Themistocles are uncertain. Perhaps he tried to carry through measures which were too revolutionary for Aristides, though Aristides was a decided democrat. More probably his continuous opposition to Sparta was attacked by the philo-Laconian Cimon whose victories gave him great influence in the Assembly.

8.1 Ostraka cast against Themistocles

Flight of Themis-tocles, 471-0 B.C.

Accession of Arta-xerxes, 464 B.C.

an ostracism before 480, but his enemies are not likely to have been more scrupulous now. The exiled statesman took up his abode in Argos and carried his anti-Spartan propaganda through the Peloponnese. The presence there of such a crafty and active enemy was not agreeable to Sparta, and he was not left long in peace. When the Persian intrigues of Pausanias were disclosed, the Lacedaemonians discovered that Themistocles was implicated in the scandal. But though Themistocles held communications with Pausanias, communications of a compromising kind, it is not in the least likely that he was really guilty of any design to betray Greece to Persia; it is rather to be presumed that those communications were concerned with the schemes of Pausanias against the Spartan constitution. He was accused of high treason against his country; men were sent to arrest him and bring him to trial; and he fled to Corcyra. The Corcyraeans refused to keep him and he crossed over to Epirus, pursued by Lacedaemonian and Athenian officers. He was forced to stop at the house of Admetus king of the Molossians, though his previous relations with this king had not been friendly. In these western lands, we seem to be translated into a far older time and to visit the homestead of a Homeric king. Admetus was not at home, but Themistocles supplicated the queen and she directed him to take her child and seat himself by the hearth. When the king returned, Themistocles implored his protection; and Admetus hospitably refused to give him up to the pursuers. The Athenians, disappointed of their prey, condemned him as a traitor to outlawry, confiscating his property and dooming his descendants to loss of citizenship. Admetus sent the fugitive overland to Pydna in Macedonia. A vessel carried him to the shores of Ionia. For some years he lay hidden in towns on the Asiatic coast, but when Xerxes died and Artaxerxes came to the throne, he went up to Susa and intrigued at the Persian court.[9] Thus circumstances drove him to follow the example of Pausanias; and, by a curious irony, the two men who might be regarded as the saviours of Greece, the hero of Salamis and the hero of Plataea, were perverted into framing plans for undoing their own work and enslaving the country which they had delivered. It may well have been, however, that Themistocles, who was an able and far-sighted man, merely intended to ensure his own advantage at the expense of the Great King, and had no serious thought of carrying out any designs against Greece. He was, as we might expect, more

Ostracism of Themis-tocles, c. 472 B.C.

Appeal was made to ostracism and the verdict went against Themistocles. Many sherds bearing his name have been found, and one deposit found in a well-filling is of particular interest. It contains 190 sherds with Themistocles' name, written by a few hands only. These were perhaps sherds prepared by his enemies for distribution, and it is interesting to note that most of them were from vases of good quality.[8] The deposit probably dates from

207

successful than the Spartan schemer. He won high honour in Persia and was given the government of the district of Magnesia, where Magnesia itself furnished[8] his table with bread, Lampsacus with wine, and Myus with meat.[10]

Death of Themis-tocles

Themistocles died in Magnesia, and the Magnesians gave him outside their walls the resting-place which was denied to him in his own country. Nor were they content with this; they sought to associate his fame more intimately with their own city. They paid him the honour of a hero, and erected in their market-place a statue of the saviour of Greece, standing naked in the act of pouring a libation over an altar, below which lay a slain bull. It was not long before this scene was wilfully or ignorantly misunderstood and gave rise to a false story. Half a century after the death of Themistocles it was popularly supposed that he had poisoned himself with bull's blood; and the absurd motive of despair at his inability to fulfil his promises to the Persian king was assigned for his self-slaughter. There can be little doubt that this tale, first circulated perhaps by malicious tongues at Athens, was suggested by the bull and the libation-dish in the monument of the Magnesian market-place.

His statue

Rumoured suicide

The Confederacy of Delos becomes an Athenian Empire

Cimon general of confederate fleet. Capture of Eion, 476-5 B.C.

The conduct of the war which the Confederacy of Delos was waging against Persia had been entrusted to Cimon, the son of Miltiades. We have seen already how he drove Pausanias out of Sestos and Byzantium. His next exploit was to capture Eion, a town near the mouth of the Strymon, and the most important stronghold of the Persians west of the Hellespont. The place was defended to the uttermost by Boges, its gallant commander, who refused all overtures, and when the food ran out he lit a great funeral pyre. He slew his wife and his children, his concubines and his slaves, and hurled them into the fire. He took all his gold and silver to the top of the wall and flung it into the waters of the Strymon. Then he leaped himself into the flames. Thus the Athenians captured and occupied a strong coast-fortress, which gave access to a hinterland rich in timber and silver.[11]

Conquest of Scyros, 474-3 B.C.

Doriscus which commanded the crossing of the Hebrus was still in Persian hands, the attempts of the Athenians to take it were successfully resisted, and we do not know what happened to it. Perhaps it fell into the hands of the Thracians. The next enterprise of Cimon

was the reduction of the rocky island of Scyros, a stronghold of Dolopian pirates. While Athens was winning posts on the fringe of the Aegean, it was no less necessary for her to secure intermediate stations, and the importance of Scyros was its position on the sea-road from Athens to western Thrace. The rude inhabitants were enslaved, and their place was taken by Attic settlers; the island was in fact annexed to Attica. But Cimon won less glory by the conquest than by the discovery of the bones of Theseus. There was a Delphic oracle which bade the Athenians take up the bones of Theseus and keep them in an honourable resting-place, and perhaps there was a legend that the hero was buried in Scyros. In any case, whether by chance or after a search, there was found in the island a grave containing a warrior's corpse of heroic size. It was the corpse of Theseus. Cimon brought it back to Athens, and perhaps none of his exploits earned him greater popularity.

Bones of Theseus

A few years later Cimon achieved what was the most brilliant success of his life. Hitherto he had been busy in the northern waters of the Aegean; it was high time that the fleet should sail southward and strike a blow against the Persian power in the seas of Rhodes and Cyprus. It was not only high time, it was imperative; for Xerxes had equipped a great armament—his last resistance to the triumph of Greek arms. Cimon delivered both the Greek and the native coast towns of Caria from Persian rule, and constrained the Lycian communities to enrol themselves in the Confederacy of Delos. Then at the river Eurymedon in Pamphylia he found the Persian army and the Persian fleet, overcame them in a double battle by land and sea, destroying 200 Phoenician ships, and then eliminated a reinforcing squadron sailing from Cyprus.[12] This victory sealed the acquisition of southern Asia Minor, from Caria to Pamphylia, for the Athenian federation. The booty which was won in this battle was used to build a new south wall to the Acropolis, and a bronze palm tree carrying a gilt statue of Athena was dedicated at Delphi. Themistocles, who laid his hopes on the Piraeus, would have been content that the Acropolis should have remained unwalled; but the conservative policy of Cimon decided otherwise. The south wall was now rebuilt out of the spoils of the Eurymedon.

Carian and Lycian expedition of Cimon, 468 B.C.?

Battle of the Eurymedon

It could not be said that the Confederacy of Delos had failed to do its work. The victory on the Pamphylian river freed Greece from all danger on the side of the Persian empire; and Cimon soon followed up his success by reducing

Cimon captures places on the Hellespont, 466 B.C. (late summer)

208

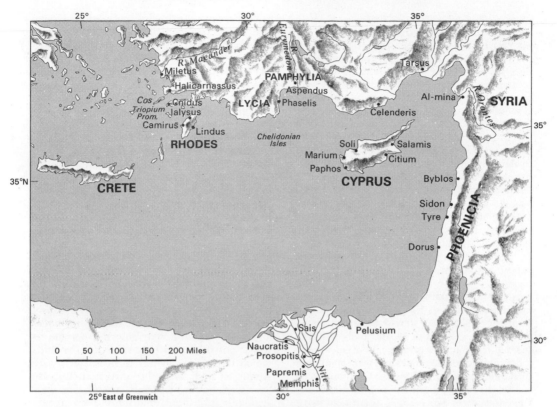

18. THE EASTERN MEDITERRANEAN

8.2   The Cimonian south wall of the Acropolis (see note, page 554)

some places on the Thracian Chersonese which were still held by the barbarians. But in the interval between the conquest of Scyros and the battle of the Eurymedon the confederate fleet had been set to do other work. It had been set to make war upon Greek states which were unwilling to belong to the league. The first case was one of pure and simple coercion of a foreign city. Carystus, unlike the other cities of her island, had held aloof from the Confederacy; and this anomaly seemed intolerable to Athens, especially as the place was so near the shores of Attica. Carystus was subjugated and made, in spite of herself, a member of the league. The second case was that of a confederate state which wished to be confederate no longer. Naxos seceded from the league, and the fleet of the allies reduced her by blockade. In the case of Carystus, the Confederacy could defend its act only by the plea of political necessity; in the case of Naxos, it could reasonably maintain its right of forcing the individual members to fulfil their obligations until the association should be dissolved by the common consent of all. But both acts alike seemed to be acts of tyrannical outrage on the independence of free states and were an offence to public opinion in Greece. The oppression was all the worse, inasmuch as both Naxos and Carystus were deprived of their autonomy. They became in fact subjects of Athens. They are typical examples of the fashion in which the Athenian empire was built up. Athens was already forging the fetters with which she would bind her allies.

Reduction of Carystus, 472-1 B.C.?

Revolt and reduction of Naxos, 469 B.C.?

The victory of the Eurymedon left Athens free to pursue this inevitable policy of transforming the Confederacy into an empire. The most powerful confederate state on the Thracian coast was the island city of Thasos. Possessing a considerable fleet, it was doubtless one of those cities which contributed ships. Athens was making new endeavours to plant a settlement on the Strymon and to lay hands on the traffic in those regions. Her interests collided with those of the Thasians, whose prosperity largely depended upon their trade in Thrace. A dispute arose about a gold mine and the islanders revolted. They hoped for support both from Macedonia and from Thrace, since both those countries were interested in excluding Athens from the coast trade of the northern sea-board. They hoped too for help from Sparta, but the Lacedaemonians were hindered from sending help by a revolt of the Helots. The fleet of the Thasians was defeated by Cimon, and after a long blockade they capitulated. Their walls were

Revolt of Thasos, 465 B.C.

Surrender, 463 B.C.

pulled down, their ships were handed over to Athens, they gave up all claim to the mine and the mainland and agreed to pay whatever tribute was demanded. Meanwhile, however, Athenian and allied settlers had occupied the strategic point of Ennea Hodoi on the Strymon, but while penetrating up country to consolidate their position they were surrounded and annihilated by the native Thracians at Drabescus.

The typical instances of these three island cities, Carystus, Naxos, and Thasos, exhibit the methods which Athenian policy followed in numerous cases which are not recorded. There were now three classes of members in the Confederacy of Delos; there were (1) the non-tributary allies which contributed ships; (2) the tributary allies which were independent; and (3) the tributary allies which were subject. As the Asiatic cities were declining in vigour, and disliked military service and absence from home, they mostly preferred to discharge their obligations by paying tribute. It was obviously in the interest of Athens that as many members as possible should contribute money, and as few as possible contribute ships, for the ships which the tribute money furnished out were simply an addition to her own fleet, because they were under her direct control. She consequently aimed at diminishing the members of the first class, and soon it consisted of only the three large and wealthy islands, Lesbos, Chios, and Samos. Again, it was to the interest of Athens to transfer the members of the second class into the third, and win control over the internal affairs of the cities. New members which were coerced to join were never allowed to preserve absolute autonomy, and all revolting cities were reduced to the condition of subjection. But the degrees of subjection were not the same. The position of each city was determined by a special agreement with Athens, and the terms of these treaties varied. As a rule, Athens prescribed to her subjects the general form of their constitutions, and it need hardly be said that these constitutions were always democratic. The regulations imposed on Erythrae near the middle of the century have been partially preserved in a French traveller's copy of a stone now lost. Emphasis is laid on the appointment, with the aid of Athenian officers, of the Boule, the nerve centre of democratic government; precautions are taken against Medism; an Athenian garrison is to remain; Erythrae is to bring offerings to the Athenian festival of the Great Panathenaea.[13] But there was no general hard and fast system. Each city had its own individual

Three classes of confederates

Erythrae, 453-2 B.C.?

210

arrangements, its own measure of restricted autonomy. The closer dependence of these tributary states on Athens was in many cases marked by the presence of an Athenian garrison and Athenian civil officers. But there was one burden which was common to all, the obligation of furnishing soldiers to the league in time of war. It was a duty which could be demanded only under certain defined conditions, but it was an innovation which altered the original character of the league as a merely maritime confederacy.[14] It seems probable that Athens tried to extend the duty of military service to her autonomous allies, and that this policy caused revolts—a result which was not unwelcome to Athens, as it gave her opportunities to deprive them of autonomy. Ultimately, all the allies seem to have been liable to military service except the three states which furnished ships, Chios, Lesbos, and Samos.

As the process of turning the Alliance into an Empire advanced, Athens found herself able to discontinue the meetings of the Confederate assembly in the island of Delos. She could now act entirely as she deemed good without going through the form of consulting a body whose decisions must necessarily be hers, as the great majority of the members were her own subjects. A further advance in imperialism was made when the treasury was moved from Delos to Athens. The real as well as the declared reason may have been the danger to the Aegean following an Athenian disaster in Egypt. But, however honest the motive, the transfer was to make more easy the use of league funds by Athens for her own purposes. The tribute money thus passed from the protection of the Ionian Apollo to the custody of the goddess of the Acropolis; and, in return for her safe keeping, one mina for every talent of the yearly tribute was paid into her own treasury.

Treasury transferred to Athens, 454 B.C.

(See p. 221)

One-sixtieth as first-fruits to Athena

The Athenian empire in the middle of the century included most of the islands of the Aegean, with the important exceptions of Crete, Melos, and Thera, and most of the cities on and near the coast from Chalcidice in the north-west to Phaselis in the south-east. A careful record was made each year of the *aparche* paid to Athena, the account was audited by the Logistae for the Hellenotamiae, and the annual lists were inscribed on a large stone pillar prominently displayed on the Acropolis. Sufficient fragments of the first two pillars have been found for them to be reconstructed, so that, though gaps remain, we can tell with some accuracy how many states

The tribute

('Quota lists)

brought tribute each year and in many cases how much they paid. From 443-2 B.C. we find the cities arranged in five geographical districts—Thracian, Hellespontine, Ionian, Carian and Islands; but the Carian was soon merged in the Ionian.

At the end of every fourth year, in the years of the Great Panathenaea, the assessment was revised by the Athenians, but the allies had an opportunity to plead in the Athenian courts for a lower assessment. No drastic change was made in the general level until the great Peloponnesian war; and at the assessment of 446, possibly as a measure of conciliation in a dangerous period, a large number of cities had their assessment lowered. In years when Athens was strong some 170 states brought tribute, but some of the lists before 446 are considerably shorter and a number of cities in Caria which were paying in the late fifties are not found again. There is therefore often a considerable gap between the amount of tribute actually received and the total assessment.

One of the most important restrictions on the independence of the cities was the jurisdiction which the Athenians asserted in criminal cases. It was natural that all disputes between Athens and any of her subjects should be decided at Athens; and it was not unreasonable that if the citizen of any allied community committed an act of treason against the empire he should be tried in the imperial city. But with the growth of imperialism Athens claimed further rights of jurisdiction. In her settlement with Chalcis after the revolt of 446, she enacted that all cases in which the penalty was death, banishment, or the loss of civic rights should be subject to appeal to Athens.[15] In this, as in other matters, there were various arrangements with the various cities, and some doubtless had more freedom than others; but from the middle of the century there was a general tendency towards closer control. Lawsuits arising out of breach of contract between citizens of Athens and citizens of the allied states were normally regulated by separate international agreements and decided in the law-courts of the defendant's city. In this matter, and it was important, Athens could take the credit of not using her power for the furtherance of her own interests; and it may sometimes have happened that an Athenian was treated with somewhat less than fairness, when a subject folk had the chance of indulging their bitterness against one of their masters. But this generosity was forgotten in the resentment caused by the use

Jurisdiction of Athens

Chalcis, 446-5 B.C.

of Athenian courts for political cases. This proved an effective instrument of democratic control but it sharpened the opposition of allied oligarchs, who were the main sufferers. The democrats had less to fear, and throughout the period of Athenian rule most of them remained strikingly loyal to Athens.

The Athenian Empire was dissolved half a century after the translation of the treasury from Delos to Athens. The first principles of the political thought and political life of Greece were opposed to such an union. The sovereign city-state was the basis of the civilised Hellenic world, and no city-state was ready, if it could help it, to surrender any part of its sovereignty. In the face of a common danger, cities might be ready to combine together in a league, each parting with some of her sovereign powers to a common federal council but preserving the right of secession; and this was the idea of the Confederacy of Delos in its initial form. But even such a voluntary and partial surrender of sovereignty was regarded as a misfortune, so that when the motives which induced a city to join a federation became less strong and pressing, every member was anxious to gain its complete independence and resume the sovereign rights which it had laid down. Such being the free tendencies which swayed the peoples of Greece, it required a mighty arm and constant vigilance in a ruling state to keep her federation or empire together. An empire, however disguised, was always considered an injustice—a defiance of the political morality of Hellas. A Greek felt it a degradation of his dignity, or an infraction of his freedom, not to be the citizen of a free and sovereign city. And he felt this at many points if he belonged to one of the subject allies of Athens, since their self-government was limited in regard to domestic, as well as foreign affairs. However liberal the general supervision of the mistress might be, the alliance with that mistress was a loss of the best of all good things, liberty, which means the right of governing oneself. If Athens had adopted the policy which was so successfully adopted by Rome, the policy of enlarging herself by admitting the citizens of smaller states to her own citizenship, she might have built up a more enduring fabric of empire. But such a plan was incompatible with the political notions of the Greeks.

Policy and Ostracism of Cimon

As the Persian War had brought out more vividly the contrast between Greek and barbarian, and impressed the Greeks with the ideal unity of their race, so the Confederacy of Delos emphasised a division existing within the Greek race itself, the contrast of Dorian and Ionian. That division was largely artificial. It was the result of mistaken notions about the early history of Greece, and only within very restricted limits did it represent any natural line of cleavage in the Hellenic race. But it had come to be accepted as an axiom and was an important element in the situation. We must probably seek for the origin of the opposition between Dorian and Ionian, as a political doctrine, in the unity of the Peloponnese. The actual geographical unity produced a political unity when, in the sixth century, the Spartan power became dominant; and this was reinforced by the conception of its ethnical unity, as mainly a Dorian country. The identity and exclusiveness of Peloponnesian interests had been apparent at the time of the Persian invasion; and the Peloponnese not only stood aloof from, but had the air of protesting against, the growth of the Athenian Confederacy. And this confederacy had taken upon itself from the very first an Ionian colour. Athens, believing that she was an Ionian city and the mother of the Ionians of Asia, was gathering her children about her. The shrine of the Delian Apollo, the great centre of Ionian worship, was chosen as the centre of the new Ionian union. The treasures of the league were in the Ionian Apollo's keeping, and in his island the allies met to take counsel together. Thus the Dorian federation of the Peloponnese under the headship of Sparta stood over against the Ionian federation of the Aegean under the headship of Athens.

For some years the antagonism lay dormant. Sparta was still an ally of Athens against the Mede, and the danger from Persia had not passed away. But the preservation of peace was also due, in some measure, to the policy of the men who guided the fortunes of Athens— Aristides and Cimon. The son of Miltiades had been at first regarded as a youth of little promise. His grandfather was nicknamed 'Simpleton', and he was supposed to have inherited a wit poorer than that of the ordinary Athenian. Fond of the wine-cup and leading a disorderly life, he was not a man of liberal education; and a writer of memoirs, who knew him, described him as Peloponnesian rather than Athenian—uncultivated but honest and downright. He lived with his step-sister Elpinice, and they both affected Lacedaemonian manners. Aristides seems to have discerned his military ability and to have introduced him to public life. His simplicity, geniality, and lavish hospitality rendered him popular; his military successes confirmed his influence. The two guiding principles of Cimon's policy were the prosecution of the war against Persia and the maintenance of good relations with the Lacedaemonians. He upheld the doctrine of dual leadership: Athens should be mistress of the seas, but she should recognise Sparta as the mistress on the continent. Cimon's sympathy with Sparta and his connections there became an important political fact and undoubtedly helped to postpone a rupture between Sparta and Athens.

In this policy Aristides, the leader of the democracy, and Cimon, who was by no means in sympathy with the development of the democratic constitution, had pulled together. After the ostracism of Themistocles they had the whole power in their hands, Cimon being continually re-elected as Strategos, and Aristides having the moral control of the sovereign Assembly. On the death of Aristides, Cimon remained the most powerful statesman in Athens, but his want of sympathy with democracy rendered it impossible that he should retain his power in a state which was advancing on the lines along which Athens was moving now.[16] Younger statesmen arose and formed a party of opposition against Cimon and the oligarchs who rallied around him. The two chief politicians of this democratic party were Ephialtes, a man of unquestioned probity whom the oligarchs disliked and feared, and Pericles, the son of Xanthippus, who now began to play a prominent part in the Assembly. After the conquest of Thasos they charged Cimon with having received bribes from Alexander, the king of Macedon, and with having failed to act against Macedonia as it was his duty to act. The accusation appears not to have been pressed hard, and Cimon was acquitted. But it was the first movement of an opposition which was speedily to bring about his fall.

Meanwhile Sparta herself had dealt a blow to his policy. When the victory of the Eurymedon dispelled the fears of Persia which had hovered over Greece till then, Sparta felt herself free to unseal her dormant jealousy of Athens at the first suitable opportunity, and she saw her opportunity in the war with Thasos.[17] But unforeseen events at home hindered her, as we saw, from actual intervention against Athens. The Spartan citizens lived over a perpetual volcano—the servitude of their Perioeci and Helots. The fire which Pausanias thought of kindling burst forth not long after his death. An earthquake had laid

Earthquake at Sparta, 464 B.C. Revolt of the Helots

in ruins the villages which composed the town of Sparta, and a large number of the inhabitants were buried in the convulsion. The moment was chosen by the Messenian serfs to shake off the yoke of their detested masters. They annihilated in battle a company of 300 Spartans, but they could not continue to hold their own in the field and sought refuge in the stronghold of Ithome. On that steep hill, full of the memories of earlier struggles, they held out for a few years. The Spartans were driven to ask the aid of allies; Plataea, Aegina, and Mantinea sent troops to besiege Ithome. They even appealed to Athens herself.

The democratic politicians lifted up their voices against the sending of any aid; and the event proved them to be perfectly right. But the Athenian folk listened to the counsels of Cimon, who drove home his doctrine of the dual leadership by two persuasive metaphors: 'We must not leave Hellas lame; we must not allow Athens to lose her yoke-fellow.' Cimon took 4000 hoplites to Messenia, but though the Athenians had a reputation for skill in besieging fortresses their endeavours to take Ithome failed. Then Sparta rounded and smote Athens in the face. She told the Athenians, alone of all the allies who were encamped around the hill, that she required their help no more. We are told that the Lacedaemonians were afraid 'of the adventurous and revolutionary spirit' of the Athenians. But it is strange indeed that they should have dealt thus with a force which was both procured and commanded by a friend so staunch as Cimon.

Expedition of Cimon to Messenia, 462 B.C.

This incident exploded the Laconian policy of Cimon: it exposed the futility of making sacrifices to court Sparta's friendship, and it revealed the depth of Spartan jealousy. The opposition of Ephialtes and his party to the Messenian expedition received its justification. And meanwhile Ephialtes and Pericles had taken advantage of the absence of the conservative statesman to effect a number of radical reforms which were necessary to complete the democratic constitution. These reforms were extremely popular and immensely increased the influence of the statesmen who carried them. When then Cimon returned with his policy discredited, they denounced him as a 'Philo-Laconian' and felt that they could safely attempt to ostracise him. An ostracism was held, and Cimon was banished. Soon afterwards a mysterious crime was committed. Cimon's chief antagonist Ephialtes was murdered, and no one ever ascertained with certainty who the murderers

Ostracism of Cimon, 461 B.C. Murder of Ephialtes

were. He had many bitter foes among the Areopagites, whom he had attacked singly and collectively; and there were perhaps some among them who would not have hesitated to take such vengeance on their assailant.

Capture of Ithome, 459 B.C.?

The Athenians presently had an opportunity of retaliating on Sparta for her arrogance. The blockade of Ithome was continued and the rebels at last capitulated. They were allowed to leave the Peloponnese unharmed, on the condition that they should never return. The Athenians who had helped to besiege them now found them a shelter. They settled the Messenians in a new home at Naupactus, on the Corinthian Gulf, a place where they had recently established a naval station.[18] In the Altis of Olympia we may still see a memorial of this 'Third Messenian War'—the round base of a statue of Zeus which the Lacedaemonians dedicated as a thank-offering for their victory; and we may read the inscribed verses in which they besought the lord Zeus of Olympus to accept the fair image graciously.

Mes-senians settled at Nau-pactus

While the Lacedaemonians were wholly intent upon the long siege of the Messenian fort, the Argives, free from the fear of attack on that side, had seized the occasion to lay siege to Mycenae. In the days of Argive greatness this stronghold can hardly have been other than an Argive fortress, and it was probably after the great victory of Cleomenes that with Spartan help the Mycenaeans won, for a brief space, their ancient independence. During that brief space they had the glory of bearing a hand in the deliverance of Greece. On the summit of their primeval citadel, they had built a temple where the old palace had stood and girdled the city below with a wall. They now defended the fortress for some time, but their supplies were cut off and they were forced to submit. The Argives let them depart whither they would, and some found a refuge in Macedonia; but the old town was destroyed —all except the walls, which were stronger than the forces of destruction. Argos was once more mistress of her plain.

Argos reduces and destroys Mycenae (c. 462-0 B.C.).

(494 B.C.)

CHAPTER 9

The Athenian Empire under the guidance of Pericles

The Completion of the Athenian Democracy

To the Greeks of Cimon's day it might have seemed that the Athenian constitution as it had been fixed by Cleisthenes, and further reformed after the battle of Marathon, was as democratic as it well could be. But the sovereignty of the people was more explicitly emphasised by Ephialtes, whose career was suddenly cut short, and of Pericles, son of *Pericles* Xanthippus, who was to be the most prominent figure in Greece for thirty years.

The mother of Pericles belonged to the family, and bore the name, of the daughter of the Sicyonian tyrant, the Agariste whose wooing had been so famous. She was the niece of Cleisthenes the lawgiver, and sister of *See above,* Megacles who had been ostracised as a friend *p. 164* of the Pisistratids. The young statesman had a military training, but he came under the *His* influence of two distinguished teachers, to *teachers* whom he owed much. One was a countryman of his own, Damon of Oa, one of the most intellectual Athenians of his day and renowned as a master of the theory of music. The other was an outlander and a philosopher, Anaxagoras of Clazomenae, whose mechanical theory of the material universe, once for all set in motion by an act of unchangeable mind, freed Pericles from the superstitions of the multitude whom *His* it was his task to guide. To these masters *reserve* the statesman partly owed his intellectual aloofness; but he did not owe them either his political ideas or the gift of lucid and persuasive speech which was essential to his success. He was indeed a striking contrast to Cimon, the relaxed and genial boon companion. He seldom walked abroad; he was strict in the economy of his household; he avoided convivial parties, and jealously maintained the dignity of his reserve. His portrait was chiselled by Cresilas. *Portrait* It is something to have the round pedestal on which the original image was set, but we also possess a copy of the portrait. It shows us, not the lofty 'Olympian' statesman, but the passionless contemplative face of the friend of Anaxagoras.

The most conservative institution in Athens *The Areo-* was the Council of Areopagus, for it was filled *pagus* up from the archons who were taken from the *loses* two richest classes in the state. This institution *political* was incompatible with the development of *power* democracy, and it was inevitable that it should be ended or mended. Ephialtes had prepared the way for an attack by accusing individual Areopagites of corruption and fraudulent practices; and then, taking advantage of Cimon's absence in Messenia, he introduced a series of laws which deprived the ancient council of all its powers that had any political significance. Its right to punish the public ministers and officers if they violated the laws, and its duties of supervising the administration and seeing that the laws were obeyed, were taken away and transferred to the people. The censorial powers which enabled it to inquire into the lives of private citizens were abolished. Nothing was left to the venerable body but its

9.1 Pericles: copy of the portrait by Cresilas

new democracy that the expenditure on public works should now be publicly recorded for all to see.

We have a notable monument of the excitement which this radical change caused at Athens, in a drama of Aeschylus which was performed a few years later. The *Eumenides* describes the trial of Orestes on the hill of Ares for the murder of his mother and the institution of the court of the Areopagus. The significance of the drama has been often misunderstood. It is no protest after the event; it is no cry to undo what had been done. On the contrary, Aeschylus, so far as his poetical motive permits him to suggest a criticism of recent events, approves of the reform. The Areopagus, he suggests, was instituted as a court, not as a council; its true purpose is to pass a judgement on homicides, like Orestes. The *Eumenides* was calculated to tranquillise those who, awed by the dark and solemn associations which hovered over the hill of Ares, regarded the attack upon it as an impiety.[1]

The Eumenides of Aeschylus, 458 B.C.

The dismantling of the Areopagus was an indirect blow to the dignity of the archons, who, by virtue of their office, became Areopagites. About the same time another step was taken on the path of democracy by making the archonship a paid office. Once this was done, there was no longer any reason for confining the post to the two richer classes. The third class, the Zeugitae, were presently made eligible, perhaps in recognition of the part played by the hoplites in the stubborn battle of Tanagra which had confirmed the confidence of the new democracy.

Archonship becomes a paid office. Admission of Zeugitae to archonship, 458-7 B.C.

The two engines of the democratic development were lot and pay. Lot had been long ago introduced, but it had not been introduced in its purest form. The archons and other lesser officers, and the members of the council, were taken by lot from a select number of candidates, but these candidates were chosen by deliberate election. This mixed system was now abolished; the preliminary election was done away with; and the Council of Five Hundred, as well as the archons, were appointed by lot from all the eligible citizens. By this means every citizen had an equal chance of holding political office and taking a part in the conduct of public affairs.

Lot

It is clear that this system could not work unless the offices were paid, for the poor citizens would have been unable to give up their time to the service of the state. Accordingly pay was introduced not only for the archonship but for the members of the

Payment of offices

jurisdiction in homicidal cases, the care of the sacred olive-trees of Athena, and a voice in the supervision of the property of the Eleusinian deities. The functions which it lost passed to the Council of Five Hundred, the Assembly, and the popular law-courts. All impeachments for crimes which threatened the public interest were henceforward brought before the Council or the Assembly, and henceforward the people tried in their own courts officials who had failed to give a satisfactory account of their administration. In the people's courts the verdict no longer rested with the magistrate but with a majority of the jurors. It was typical also of the

Council. The payment of state offices was the leading feature of the democratic reforms of Pericles.

Pay of the judges, c. 462-1 B.C.

It was a feature which naturally won him popularity with the masses, especially when it was adopted in the case of the popular courts of justice. At the time of the attack on the Areopagus, Pericles carried a measure that the judges should receive a remuneration of two obols, or possibly one, a day.[2] Though the measure had the immediate political object of gaining popular support for the attack on the Areopagus, it was a measure which was ultimately inevitable. The amount of judicial business was growing so enormously that it would have been impossible to find a sufficient number of judges ready to attend day after day in the courts without any compensation. But the easily-earned pay attracted the poor and idle, who found it pleasant to sit in court listening to curious cases, their sense of self-importance tickled by the flattering respect of the pleaders.[3] Every citizen who wished could place his name on a list from which a list of 6000 judges was selected by lot, so many from each tribe; and the courts were empanelled from this list.

Law of citizenship, 451-0 B.C.

It was now to the interest of every Athenian that there should be as few citizens as possible to participate in the new privileges and profits of citizenship. Accordingly, about ten years later the rolls of the citizens were stringently revised, and a decree was introduced by Pericles and passed by the Assembly that in the future the name of no child should be admitted whose father and mother were not Athenian citizens legitimately wedded. It was a law which would have excluded Themistocles, Cimon, and Cleisthenes the lawgiver, whose mothers were foreigners.

The working of the law-courts

It was a matter of course that in cases of a political character the judges of the heliaea should be swayed by their own political opinions and by the eloquence of the pleaders working upon their emotions. It was inevitable that the legal aspect of such cases should be often lost to sight, and the facts often misjudged. It was an essential part of the democratic intention that the sovereign people should make its anger felt; and if its anger were sometimes, like a king's anger, unfair, that could not be helped. But it was far more serious that in private cases the ends of justice were liable to be defeated, not through intention but through ignorance. We can have no better evidence as to the working of the popular courts than the speeches by which the pleaders hoped to influence the decisions of the judges.

Litigants at Athens had to plead their own cases; there was no such institution as court-advocates. But a man might learn off a speech which had been composed for him by another, and recite it in court. Hence there arose a class of professional speech-writers, and many of their speeches have been preserved. From these models of judicial eloquence we learn how pleaders expected to gain decisions in their favour. They make a large use of arguments which are perfectly irrelevant to the case; a plaintiff, for example, will try to demonstrate at great length that he has rendered services to the state and that his opponent has performed none. There was thus no question of simply administering the law. The judges heard each party interpreting the law in its own sense; but they had themselves no knowledge of the law, and therefore, however impartial they sought to be, their decision was unduly influenced by the dexterity of an eloquent pleader, and affected by considerations which had nothing to do with the matter at issue. And there was no appeal from their judgement.

Liturgies, or public burdens

A feature of the Athenian democracy, not to be lost sight of, is that public burdens were laid upon the rich citizens which did not fall upon the poor. These were no regular taxes on income or capital, but burdens which were highly characteristic of ancient society and which might fall to a man's lot only once or twice in his life. We have already seen how trierarchs were taken from the richer classes to equip and man triremes, in which they were themselves obliged to sail, and for which they were entirely responsible. It was a duty which entailed not only an outlay of money but a considerable sacrifice of time and trouble. There were other burdens also. For example, when the city sent solemn deputations on some religious errand, whether to the yearly feast of Apollo at Delos, or to one of the great Panhellenic festivals, or to the oracle of Delphi, a wealthy citizen was chosen to eke out at his cost the money supplied for the purpose by the public treasury, and to conduct the deputation and equip it with magnificence worthy of the occasion. But none of the liturgies, as these public burdens were called, was more important or more characteristic of Athenian life than that of providing the choruses for the festivals of Dionysus. Every year each tribe named one of its wealthy tribesmen to be a *chorêgos*, and his duties were to furnish and array a chorus and provide a skilled trainer to teach it the dances and songs of the drama which it was to perform. Rivalry

The trierarchy

The architheoria

The chorêgia

spurred the *chorêgoi* to ungrudging outlay. He whose chorus was victorious in the tragic or the comic competition was crowned and received a bronze tripod which he used to set up, inscribed with his own name and that of his tribe, upon a pillar, or sometimes upon a miniature round temple. On the east side of the Acropolis, leading to the theatre, a long street of these choregic monuments recorded the public spirit of the citizens, and this Street of Tripods showed, perhaps more impressively than any other evidence, how much significance the state attached to the theatre and to the worship of Dionysus. Never was piety more fully approved as wisdom. The state's endowment of religion turned out to be an endowment of brilliant genius; and the rich men who were called upon to spend their time and money in furnishing the dancers did service to the great masters of tragedy and comedy, and thereby served the whole world.

War of Athens with the Peloponnesians

Alliance of Athens and Argos

The banishment of Cimon was the signal for a complete change in the foreign policy of Athens. She abandoned the alliance with the Lacedaemonians and formed a new alliance with their enemies, Argos and Thessaly. The new friendship of the Athenian and Argive peoples is reflected in the trilogy which Aeschylus composed about this time on the murder of Agamemnon and the vengeance of *(458 B.C.)* Orestes.[4] The dramatist plays pointedly upon the alliance, and perhaps it is a not undesigned compliment to the new ally that he makes Agamemnon lord of Argos and not of newly-destroyed Mycenae. So far, indeed, as the main interests of Athens were concerned, she was not brought into direct collision with Sparta. But these interests forced her into deadly rivalry with two of Sparta's allies. The naval empire of Athens and the growth of her sea-power were rapidly extending her trade and opening new visions of commercial ambition in all quarters of the Greek world. She was competing with, and it seemed likely that she would outstrip, the two great trading cities, Corinth and Aegina. With Aegina there had already been a struggle, and now that Athens had grown in power and wealth another struggle was inevitable. The competition of Athenian merchants with Corinth in the west was active, and it was about this time that an

Athenian general took Naupactus from the Ozolian Locrians and secured a naval station *Capture of Naupactus* which gave Athens a considerable control over the mouth of the Corinthian Gulf. This was a blow which struck home; Athens had now the means of intercepting and harassing the Corinthian merchantmen which sailed forth with cargoes for the west. War was a question of months, and the occasion soon came.

The Megarians, on account of a frontier *Athens* dispute with Corinth, deserted the Pelopon- *wins* nesian league and placed themselves under *Megara,* Athenian protection. Nothing could be more *459 B.C.* welcome to Athens than the adhesion of Megara. Holding Megara, she had a strong frontier against the Peloponnese, commanding the isthmus from Pagae on the Corinthian, to Nisaea on the Saronic Gulf. Without any delays she set about the building of a double line of wall from the hill of Megara down to the haven of Nisaea, which faces Salamis, and she garrisoned these 'Long Walls' with her own troops. Thus the only easy entrance to Attica, by the coast road, was under her control, and between Megara and Pagae on the Corinthian Gulf the mountain range of Geranea was a *Long* formidable barrier which could be easily *Walls of* defended. Attica now had a strong bulwark *Megara* against invasion by land.

The occupation of Megara was a new offence to Corinth; and it was an offence to the mistress of the Peloponnesian league. War soon broke out, but at first Sparta took no active part. On the events of the war we are ill-instructed. We find an Athenian squadron making a descent *Battle of* on Halieis, and receiving a setback from some *Halieis,* Corinthian and Epidaurian troops. Then the *459-8 B.C.* little island of Cecryphalea, which lies between Aegina and the Argive shore, becomes *Battle of* the scene of a naval combat with a Pelopon- *Cecry-* nesian fleet, and the Athenians prevail. At this *phalea* point the Aeginetans enter the struggle, seeing that if Corinth sustained a severe defeat their own fate was sealed: Athens would become absolute mistress in the Saronic sea. A great naval battle was fought near Aegina; the allies *Battle of* of both Aegina and Athens were engaged; and *Aegina,* the Athenians, having taken 70 ships, landed *458 B.C.* on the island and blockaded the town. Thereupon the Peloponnesians sent a force of hoplites to help the Aeginetans, while the Corinthians, advancing over the heights of Geranea, descended into the Megarid, expecting that the Athenians would find it impossible to protect Megara and blockade Aegina at the same time. But they reckoned without a true knowledge of the Athenian spirit. The citizens

Battle in the Megarid, 458 B.C.

who were below and above the regular military age were formed into an extraordinary army and marched to the Megarid under the strategos Myronides. A battle was fought; both sides claimed the victory, but when the Corinthians withdrew the Athenians raised a trophy. Urged by the taunts of their fellow-citizens, the Corinthian soldiers returned in twelve days and began to set up a counter-trophy, but as they were at work the Athenians rushed forth from Megara and inflicted a severe defeat.

This warfare, round the shores and in the waters of the Saronic Gulf, is the prelude to more warfare in other parts of Greece, but it is a prelude which has a unity of its own. Athens is opposed indeed to the Peloponnesian alliance; but the war is, so far, mainly conducted by a concert of three states, whose interests lie in the neighbourhood of the Saronic Gulf—Corinth, Epidaurus, and Aegina. These states have indeed the Peloponnesian league behind them and are helped by 'Peloponnesian ships' and 'Peloponnesian hoplites'; but at the same time, the war has not yet assumed a fully Peloponnesian character.

The year of these successes was a year of intense excitement and strain for Athens; it might fairly be described as an *annus mirabilis* in her history. The victories of Cecryphalea and Aegina were won with only a portion of her fleet. For, in the very hour when she was about to be brought face to face with the armed opposition of rival Greek powers against the growth of her empire and the expansion of her trade, she had embarked in an enterprise beyond the limits of the Greek world. It was an expedition to Egypt, one of the most daring ventures she ever undertook.

Egyptian expedition

A fleet of 200 Athenian and Confederate galleys was operating against Persia in Cyprian seas, when it was invited to cross over to Egypt. The call came from Inaros, a Libyan potentate, who had stirred up the lands of the lower Nile to revolt against their Persian masters. The murder of Xerxes had been followed by troubles at the Persian court, and it was some time before Artaxerxes was safely seated on his throne; the rebellion of Egypt was one of the consequences of this situation. The invitation of Inaros was most alluring. It meant that, if Athens delivered Egypt from Persian rule, she would secure the chief control of the foreign trade with the Nile valley and be able to establish a naval station on the coast; by one stroke she would far outstrip all the rival merchant cities of Hellas. The nameless generals of the Aegean fleet accepted the call of the Libyan prince. As in the days of remote antiquity, the 'peoples of the north' were now to help the Libyans in an attempt to overthrow the lords of Egypt. Of those remote episodes the Greeks knew nothing, but they might remember how Carian and Ionian adventurers had once placed an Egyptian king upon the throne. In another way, an attack on Egypt was a step in a new path. Hitherto the Confederate ships had sailed in waters which were wholly or partly Greek, and had confined their purpose to the deliverance of Greek cities or cities which, like the Carian and Lycian, were in close touch with Greek civilisation. The shores of Cyprus, where Greek and Phoenician were side by side, invited above other shores a squadron of Greek deliverers. But when the squadron crossed over to Egypt, it entered a new sphere and undertook a new kind of work. The Egyptian expedition was an attempt to carry the struggle with Persia into another stage—a stage in which Greece was the aggressor and the invader. This attempt was not destined to prosper; more than a century was still to elapse before the invasion of Xerxes would be avenged. But it is well to remember that the Athenians, in moving on Egypt, anticipated Alexander the Great, and that success was not impossible if Cimon had been their general.

The Athenians sailed up the Nile to find Inaros triumphant, having gained a great victory in the Delta over a Persian army which had been sent to quell him. Sailing up, they won possession of the city of Memphis, except the citadel, the 'White Castle', in which the Persian garrison held out. After this achievement, we lose sight of the war in Egypt for more than two years, and beyond the protracted blockade of the White Castle we have no record how the Athenian forces were employed. But it was a fatal coincidence that the power of Athens should have been divided at this moment. With her full forces she might have inflicted a crushing blow on the Peloponnesians; with her full forces she might have prospered in Egypt. It was a triumph for the political party which had driven Cimon into banishment that, when half the Athenian fleet was on the banks of the Nile, the hostilities of Corinth and Aegina and their friends should have been so bravely repelled. Nothing impresses one more with the energy of Athens at this crisis than the stone which records the names of the citizens belonging to one of the tribes, who fell in this memorable year:

Capture of Memphis, 459 B.C. (autumn)

Erechtheid inscription, 459-8 B.C.

Of the Erechtheid tribe,
These are they who died in the war, in Cyprus, in Egypt, in
Phoenicia, at Halieis, in Aegina, at Megara, in the same year;

and the 177 names follow.[5]

Fall of Aegina, 457-6 B.C. Enrolled in the Confederacy of Delos

The siege of Aegina was continued, and within two years after the battle the Aeginetans capitulated, and agreed to surrender their fleet and pay tribute to Athens. Few successes can have been more welcome or profitable to the Athenians than this. The island which offended their eyes and attracted their desires when they looked forth from their hill across the waters of their gulf was at length powerless in their hands. They had lamed one of their most formidable commercial rivals; they had overthrown one of the most influential cities of Dorian Greece. In the Confederacy, Aegina took her rank with Thasos as the richest of the subject states. For these two island cities the burden of yearly tribute was thirty talents, the largest sum paid at that time by any of the cities whose tribute we know, though much higher tributes were to be imposed later.[6]

Lacedae-monian expedition to northern Greece, 457 B.C.

In the meantime events in another part of Greece had led the Lacedaemonians themselves to take part in the war, and had transported the main interest of the struggle from the Saronic Gulf to Boeotia. The errand of the Lacedaemonians was an errand of piety, to succour their mother people, the Dorians of the north, one of whose three little towns had been taken by the Phocians. To force the aggressors to restore the place was an easy task for a force which consisted of 1500 Lacedaemonian hoplites and 10,000 troops of the allies. The real work of the expedition lay in Boeotia. It was clearly the policy of Sparta to raise up here a powerful state to hold Athens in check; and this could only be effected by strengthening Thebes and making her mistress of the Boeotian federation. Accordingly Sparta now set up the power of Thebes again, revising the league, and forcing the Boeotian cities to join it.[7] When the army had done its work in Boeotia, its return to the Peloponnese was beset by difficulties. To march through the Megarid was dangerous, for the Athenians held the passes and had redoubled their precautions. And it was not safe to cross the Corinthian Gulf—the way by which they probably had come—for Athenian vessels were now on the watch to intercept them. In this embarrassment they seem to have resolved to march straight upon Athens, where the people were now engaged on the building of Long Walls from the city to the harbour.

Restora-tion of the hegemony of Thebes in Boeotia

This course was probably suggested by an Athenian party of oligarchs, who were always awaiting an opportunity to overthrow the democracy. The Peloponnesian army advanced to Tanagra, near the Attic frontier; but before they crossed the borders the Athenians went forth to meet them, 14,000 strong, including 1000 Argives, Thessalian cavalry and troops from the cities of the league. The story was later told that the banished statesman, Cimon, now came to the Athenian camp, pitched on Boeotian soil, and sought leave to fight for his country—against Sparta. The request was hastily referred to the Council of Five Hundred at Athens; it was not granted, and all that Cimon could do was to exhort his partisans to fight valiantly. This act of Cimon prepared the way for his recall; in the battle which followed, his friends fought so stubbornly that none of them survived. The story is doubtless fiction but its main point rings true. Cimon and his followers were first and foremost patriots; they were not the extremists who were prepared to betray the city to the Spartans in order to overthrow the new democracy and restore their own political position. There was great slaughter on both sides, but the Thessalian horsemen deserted during the combat, and the Lacedaemonians gained the victory. Yet the battle saved Athens, and the victory only enabled the victors to return by the Isthmus and cut down the fruit trees of the Megarid. If Cimon's large following among the hoplites had been lukewarm at Tanagra the issue would have been very different.

Battle of Tanagra, 457 B.C. (summer)

The Lacedaemonians celebrated their victory by a golden shield, which they set above the gable of the new temple of Zeus in the altis of Olympia as a gift from the spoils of Tanagra.[8] But the victory did not even secure Boeotia. Two months after the battle, the Athenians made an expedition into Boeotia under the command of Myronides. A decisive battle was fought at Oenophyta, and the Athenians became masters of the whole land except Thebes. This victory seems to have prompted the restoration of a monument that commemorated an earlier victory, in 506, over the Boeotians and Chalcidians. On that occasion a bronze chariot had been dedicated to Athena from the tithe of the prisoners' ransom. This monument had been sent to Susa when the Athenian Acropolis was sacked by the Persians in 480, and a copy was now set up with the order of the two couplets changed to begin with the very topical boast that the sons of the Athenians had quenched the insolence of the Boeotians.[9] The Boeotian

Conquest of Boeotia.

Battle of Oeno-phyta, 457 B.C. (autumn)

cities were not enrolled in the maritime Confederacy of Delos, but their dependence on Athens was expressed in the obligation of furnishing contingents to her armies. At the same time the Phocians entered into the alliance of Athens, and the Opuntian Locrians were constrained to acknowledge her supremacy. Such were the consequences of Oenophyta and Tanagra. Athens could now quietly complete the building of her Long Walls.

These brilliant successes were crowned, as we have seen, by the capture of Aegina; and probably about the same time the acquisition of Troezen gave the Athenians an important post on the Argolic shore. But in the far south *Failure of the Egyptian expedition* their arms were not so prosperous. Since the capture of Memphis no success seems to have been gained, and the White Castle still held out. After an ineffectual attempt to induce Sparta to cause a diversion by invading Attica, king Artaxerxes sent a large army to Egypt *456 B.C.* under Megabyzus, who was supported by a Phoenician fleet. Having won a battle, he drove the Greeks out of Memphis and shut them up in Prosopitis, an island formed by a canal which joined the Canopic and Sebennytic channels of the Nile. Here he blockaded them for eighteen months. At last he drained the canal *454 B.C.* and turned aside the water, so that the Greek ships were left high and dry, and almost the whole island was reconnected with the banks. Thus the Persians were able to march across to the island. The Greeks, having burned their ships, retreated to Byblos, where they capitulated to Megabyzus and were allowed to depart. An exhausting march through the western desert brought them to friendly Cyrene, where they found means of returning to their homes. Inaros who kindled the revolt was crucified, though his life had been spared by the terms of the capitulation. Soon afterwards a relief squadron of 50 triremes arrived from Athens and her naval allies. It was attacked by the powerful Phoenician fleet in the Mendesian mouth of the Nile, and only a few ships escaped. The Persian authority was restored throughout the land; the day for Greek control of Egypt had not yet come.[10]

But though the Athenians lost ships and treasure in this daring, ill-fated enterprise, their empire was now at the height of its power. They were even able to make the disaster in Egypt a pretext for converting the Delian confederacy into an undisguised Athenian empire. The triumphant Persian fleet might sail into the Aegean sea; Delos was not a safe treasury; the funds of the league must be removed to the Athenian Acropolis.

The empire of Athens now included a continental as well as a maritime dominion. *Extent of Athenian empire, 456-449 B.C.* The two countries which marched on her frontiers, Boeotia and Megara, had accepted her control. Beyond Boeotia, her dominion extended over Phocis and Locris to the pass of Thermopylae. In Argos her influence was predominant, Aegina had been added to her Aegean empire, the ships of Aegina to her navy. Through the alliance with Megara, the conquest of Aegina, and the capture of Troezen, the Saronic gulf had almost been converted into an Attic lake.

The great commercial city of the Isthmus *Expeditions to the Corinthian Gulf, 455 and 453 B.C.* was the chief and most dangerous enemy of Athens, and the next object of the policy of Pericles was to convert the Corinthian Gulf into an Attic lake also, and so hem in Corinth on both her seas. The possession of the Megarid and Boeotia, and especially the station at Naupactus, gave Athens control of the northern shores of the gulf, from within the gate up to the Isthmus. But the southern seaboard was still entirely Peloponnesian; and outside the gate, on the Acarnanian coast, there were posts which ought to be secured. The general Tolmides made a beginning by capturing the Corinthian colony Chalcis, opposite Patrae. Then Pericles himself conducted an expedition to continue the work of Tolmides. Having failed to reduce Sicyon he laid siege to Oeniadae, an important and strong-walled centre on the Acarnanian coast, but was unable to take it. Though no military success was gained, the expedition created a sensation, and it seems to have led to the adhesion of the Achaean cities to the Athenian alliance. It is *Acquisition of Achaea between 453 and 446* certain at least that shortly afterwards Achaea was an Athenian dependency; and for a few years Athenian vessels could sail with a sense of dominion in the Corinthian as well as in the Saronic Gulf.

Conclusion of Peace with Persia

The warfare of recent years had been an enormous strain on the resources of Athens, but the Egyptian disaster indirectly enabled her to secure more direct control of the tribute of the allies. She wanted a relief from the strain, but after the expedition of Pericles three or four years elapsed before peace was concluded. During that interval there seems to *Five Years' Truce* have been a cessation from military operations.

*Thirty
Years'
Peace of
Argos and
Sparta,
452-1 B.C.*

Then Cimon, who may have been specially recalled to Athens, negotiated a truce, which was fixed for five years, between the Athenians and Peloponnesians. At roughly the same time Lacedaemon and Argos concluded a treaty of peace for thirty years.

*Pericles
and Cimon*

As soon as the peace was arranged, Athens and her allies were able to resume their warfare against Persia, and to no man could that warfare be more safely or fitly entrusted than to the hero of the Eurymedon river. Pericles may have been well pleased to use Cimon's military experience; and an amicable arrangement seems to have been made, Cimon undertaking not to interfere with the policy of Pericles. Gossip said that Cimon's step-sister had much to do with bringing to pass the reconciliation. Elpinice was indeed a colourful person, one of the very few Athenian women of the fifth century who are more than shadows to us. She was suspected of being too familiar with Polygnotus the famous Thasian painter whom Cimon brought to Athens, and her portrait was said to have been painted for the head of Ladike in his picture of the *Sack of Troy* in the Painted Portico. Her relations with her step-brother Cimon were also the subject of much gossip and it is not surprising that she was divorced by her distinguished husband Callias, who had won chariot victories at Olympia and was to negotiate peace with Persia. Feminine charms, however, were not needed to persuade Cimon and Pericles to work together in 451. Both knew that Athens' first objective must be to undo the damage done by the disaster in Egypt.

*Campaign
in Cyprus*

The Phoenician fleet, which had put down the Egyptian rebellion, was afterwards sent to re-establish the authority of Artaxerxes in the island of Cyprus; and accordingly Cimon sailed thither with a squadron of 200 vessels. He detached 60 to help a princelet who had succeeded in defying the Persians in the fens of the Delta of the Nile; for the Athenians, even after their calamity, had not entirely abandoned the thought of Egyptian conquest. Then he laid siege to Cition. It was the last enterprise of the man who had conducted the war against Persia ever since the battle of Mycale. He died during the blockade; and his death marks the beginning of a new period in which hostilities between Greek and Persian slumber. But one final success was gained. Raising the siege of Cition, because there was no food, the fleet arrived off Salamis, and the Greeks gained a double victory by sea and land over the Phoenician and Cilician ships.

*Death of
Cimon,
450-49
B.C.*

*Necessity
of peace*

But this victory did not encourage the Athenians to continue the war. We have no glimpse of the counsels of their statesmen at this moment, but the facts of the situation enable us to understand their resolution to make peace with the Great King. The events of recent years had proved to them that it was beyond the strength of Athens to carry on war at the same time, in any effectual way, with the common enemy of all the Greeks and with her rivals among the Greeks themselves. It was therefore necessary to choose between peace with Persia and peace in Greece. But an enduring peace in Greece could only be purchased by the surrender of those successes which Athens had lately gained. Corinth would never acquiesce, until she had won back her old predominant position in her western gulf; so long as she was hemmed in, as Athens had hemmed her in, she would inevitably seize any favourable hour to strike for her release. Some Athenian politicians would have been ready to retreat from the positions which had been recently seized and whose occupation was most galling to Corinth. But Pericles, who had won those positions, was a strong imperialist. The aim of his statesmanship was to increase the Athenian empire and to spread the political influence of Athens within the borders of Greece. He was unwilling to let any part of her empire go, for the sake of earning new successes against the barbarian. The death of Cimon, who had been the soul of the Persian war, may have helped Pericles to carry through his determination to bring that war to an end. And the Great King on his side was disposed to negotiate; for the Greek victory of Cyprian Salamis had been followed by the revolt of Megabyzus, the general who had quelled the insurrection of Egypt.

*Policy of
Pericles*

Accordingly peace was made with Persia. There is a dark mist about the negotiations, so dark that it has been questioned whether a formal treaty was ever concluded. But there can be no reasonable doubt that Athens came to an understanding with Artaxerxes and that peace ensued; and it is equally certain that there was a definite contract, by which Persia undertook not to send ships of war into the Aegean, and Athens gave a similar pledge securing the coasts of the Persian empire against attack. An embassy from Athens must have waited on the Great King at Susa, and the terms of the arrangement must have been put in writing. But, whatever were the diplomatic forms of the agreement, both parties meant peace, and peace was maintained. It has been called the Peace of Callias; for it was generally believed that the chief am-

*Peace with
Persia
negotiated,
c. 449 B.C.*

Struggle of Greek and Phoenician in Cyprus

bassador was Callias, the richest man at Athens and the husband of Cimon's sister.[11]

The first act in the strife of Greece and Persia thus closes. All the cities of Hellas which had come under barbarian sway had been reunited to the world of free Hellenic states, except in one outlying corner. The island of Cyprus had been one of the prizes for which the Athenians had fought Persia. The victory of the Eurymedon had laid the foundation for a vigorous offensive in the east, and for more than ten years the winning of Cyprus had been one of the main objectives of Athenian policy. By the terms of the Peace Athens resigned her claims. The Greek cities of Cyprus were left to struggle with the Phoenicians as best they might, and the Phoenicians soon got the upper hand and held it for many years. They tried to extirpate Greek civilisation from the island, but Greek civilisation was a hardy growth, and we shall hereafter see Greek dynasties again in power.

Prevalence of Phoenicians after the Peace

Athenian Reverses. The Thirty Years' Peace

Athens loses Boeotia

The peace with Persia was not, however, followed by further Athenian expansion within the defined limits; on the contrary, some of the most recent acquisitions of the Athenian empire began to fall away. Orchomenus and Chaeronea and some other towns in western Boeotia were seized by exiled oligarchs, and it was necessary for Athens to intervene promptly. The general Tolmides went forth with a wholly inadequate number of troops. He took and garrisoned Chaeronea but did not attempt Orchomenus. On his way home he was set upon by the exiles from Orchomenus and some others in the neighbourhood of Coronea, and defeated. He was himself slain; many of the hoplites were taken prisoners; and the Athenians resigned Boeotia in order to obtain their release. Thus the battle of Coronea undid the work of Oenophyta.

Battle of Coronea, 447 B.C.

Athens had little reason to regret this loss, for dominion in Boeotia was not really conducive to the consolidation of her empire. To maintain control over the numerous city-states of the Boeotian country would have been a constant strain on her military resources, which would hardly have been remunerative. The loss of Boeotia was followed by the loss of Phocis and Locris. It was strange enough that Phocis should fall away. A few years before the Phocians had taken possession of Delphi. The Spartans had sent an army to rescue the shrine from their hands and give it back to the Delphians; but as soon as the Spartans had returned home, an Athenian army came and restored the sanctuary to the Phocians. It was a Sacred War, but so conducted that it did not make a breach of the Five Years' Truce. Yet, although their position at Delphi seemed to depend on the support of Athens, the Phocians now deserted her alliance. The change was due to an oligarchical reaction in the Phocian cities, consequent on the oligarchical rising in Boeotia.

Sacred War, 448 B.C.

The defeat of Coronea dimmed the prestige of Athenian arms, and still more serious results ensued. Euboea and Megara revolted at the same moment; here too oligarchical parties were at work. Pericles, who was a General, immediately went to Euboea with the regiments of seven of the tribes, while those of the remaining three marched into the Megarid. But he had no sooner reached the island than he was overtaken by the news that the garrison in the city of Megara had been massacred and that a Peloponnesian army was threatening Attica. He promptly returned, and his first object was to unite his forces with the troops in the Megarid, which were under the command of Andocides. But king Pleistoanax and the Lacedaemonians were, between them, commanding the east coast-road. Andocides was compelled to return to Attica by creeping round the corner of the Corinthian Gulf at Aegosthena and passing through Boeotia. The troops were guided by a man of Megara named Pythion, and the gratitude of the three tribes 'whom he saved by leading them from Pagae, through Boeotia, to Athens' was recorded on his funeral monument. The stone has survived, and the verses written upon it are a touching reminiscence of a moment of great peril.[12] But when the whole army united in Attica, the peril was passed. The return of Pericles had disconcerted king Pleistoanax, who commanded the Lacedaemonians, and having advanced only as far as the Thriasian plain he withdrew, deeming it useless to strike at Athens. Pericles was thus set free to carry out the reduction of Euboea. Histiaea, the city in the north of the island, was most hardly dealt with, probably because her resistance was most obstinate; the people were driven out, their territory annexed to Athens; and the new settlement of Oreus took the place of Histiaea. In other cases the position of each state was settled by an agreement; and the terms 'negotiated' with Chalcis, much stiffer than those given earlier to Erythrae, are still preserved on stone.[13] The alarm of the Athenians is reflected in widespread reductions of tribute which they

Loss of Megara

March of Andocides

Reduction of Euboea

allowed to their subject states; they feared that the example of Euboea might spread. The truce of five years was now approaching its end, and peace was felt to be so indispensable that they resigned themselves to purchasing a more durable treaty by considerable concessions. They had lost Megara but they still held the two ports, Nisaea and Pagae. These, as well as Achaea and Troezen, they agreed to surrender, and on this basis a peace was concluded for thirty years between the Athenians and the Peloponnesians. All the allies of both sides were enumerated in the treaty, and it was stipulated that neither Athens nor Lacedaemon was to admit into her alliance an ally of the other, while neutral states might join whichever alliance they chose. Aegina was to remain tributary to Athens but her autonomy was guaranteed.

The Thirty Years' Peace, 446-5 B.C.

It was a humiliating peace for Athens and perhaps would not have been concluded but for the alarm which had been caused by the inroad of the Peloponnesians into Attic territory. While the loss of Boeotia was probably a gain, and the evacuation of Achaea might be lightly endured, the loss of the Megarid was a serious blow. For, while Athens held the long walls and the passes of Geranea, she had complete immunity from Peloponnesian invasions of her soil. Henceforth Attica was always exposed to such aggressions. The attempt which she had made to win a land-empire had succeeded only for a brief space; the lesson was that she must devote her whole energy to maintaining her maritime dominion. It was a gloomy moment for the Athenians; and it must have required all the tact and eloquence of Pericles to restore the shaken confidence and revive the drooping spirits, but Euboea at all events was safe. While he made the most of the reduction of Euboea, Pericles may have also dwelt on the prospects of the Attic sea-empire. He may have elated them by words such as he is reported to have used at a later moment of despondency. 'Of the two divisions of the world accessible to man, the land and the sea, there is one of which you are absolute masters, and have, or may have, the dominion to any extent you please. Neither the Great King nor any nation on earth can hinder a navy like yours from penetrating whithersoever you choose to sail.'

The Imperialism of Pericles, and the Opposition to his Policy

The cities of the Athenian alliance might have claimed, when the Persian war was ended, that the 'Confederacy' should be broken up and that they should resume their original and rightful freedom. It was indeed a critical moment for Athens and it is probably at this time that, on the motion of Pericles, Athens addressed to the Greek world invitations to a Panhellenic Congress. She invited the Greek states to send representatives to Athens for the purpose of discussing certain matters of common interest: the restoration of the temples which had been burnt by the Persians, the payment of the votive offerings which were due to the gods for the great deliverance, and the taking of common measures for clearing the seas of piracy—this was the programme which Athens proposed to the consideration of Greece. The invitation did not go to the west, for the Italiots and Siceliots were not directly concerned in the Persian war, but it went to all the cities of old Greece and to the cities and islands which belonged to the Athenian empire. If the congress had been successful it would have inaugurated an amphictiony of all Hellas under Athenian leadership. But this type of panhellenism was not to the taste of Sparta and it is doubtful whether such a realist as Pericles can have been surprised when it miscarried. The Athenian envoys were re-buffed in the Peloponnese, the conference did not meet.[14]

Proposed Pan-hellenic Congress, ? 449 B.C.

Pericles, however, now had a new sanction to maintain the empire. The Greek world had been invited to discuss other means of maintaining peace in the Aegean and had not responded. Athens would retain the resources of her empire to maintain her fleet. Her temples had to be rebuilt. They had been burnt in the common cause; they would be rebuilt from the common funds, the accumulated reserve of the League treasury.

This policy met with fierce opposition both inside and outside Athens. Inside Athens the opposition had found a new leader. Cimon had been primarily a general, with little flair for the subtleties of politics. His kinsman, Thucydides, son of Melesias, who now rallied the opponents of Pericles, was first and foremost a politician. He was the first to concentrate his supporters in Assembly meetings and to organise a continuous and concerted opposition.[15] Most of the party attacked the imperialist policy of Pericles because they realised that it was the foundation of extreme democracy, but there were among them some genuine panhellenists who had real sympathy with the allies and who distrusted any step that was likely to keep Athens and Sparta apart. The party had a strong case. They

Opposition to Pericles

maintained that the tribute should be reserved for the purpose for which it had been levied, and that Athens had no right to use it for her own ends. 'Greece is surely suffering sore insult and manifest tyranny, when she sees that with the monies contributed perforce for the war we are gilding and adorning our city like a wanton woman, decking her with costly statues and offerings and thousand-talent temples.' But Pericles could claim that while Athens afforded protection to the allies she had the right to use their money; and the ambitious building programme, with its promise of splendour for the city and profitable employment for the workers, was too popular with the masses to be defeated on a vote.

Discontent in the empire

In the empire opposition was no less serious. The tribute quota lists show that even before the uprisings of 446 Athens had to weather a severe crisis. For the year 449-8 no list of quotas was inscribed on the great pillar and the natural inference has been drawn that for this year, perhaps pending the outcome of the Congress, tribute was suspended. But whatever the explanation of the missing list, the normal system was resumed for the year 448-7. The list of this year gives clear evidence of widespread discontent. A considerable number of cities brought no tribute, others paid only part of what was due; others paid late. The Athenian reaction, however, was vigorous. A decree was passed providing for the tightening up of collection: recognised seals were to be used by the allies to secure the money and a separate statement sent so that no plea could be made of loss in transit. The effect of the increased pressure can be seen in the list of the next year, which includes not only a normal number of contributions but also back payments by the defaulters of the previous year.[16]

It is in this general context that two further acts of advanced imperialism should probably be placed. Among the measures which Pericles initiated to strengthen the empire of his city, none was more important in its results than the system of settling Athenian citizens abroad. Precedents had already been made when Athenians were settled on land confiscated from the Chalcidians of Euboea in 506, and when, after the Persian War, Athenians were settled on the island of Scyros and in Eion at the mouth of the Strymon. The policy was now more widely extended. In some cases the Athenians formed a garrison to watch allies who had revolted or who seemed restless. Such were the cleruchies sent, probably in 450, to Naxos, Andros, and perhaps Carystus at the south end of Euboea, which seem to have been disaffected in the years following the transference of the treasury from Delos to Athens. The cleruchy established by Pericles on the Chersonese in 447 had different objectives. This peninsula was vital to Athens since it controlled the corn route from the Euxine, and it also had good farming land. Athens had occupied the peninsula in the time of Pisistratus with the good excuse that the natives needed protection from Thracians pressing down from the north. The Thracian danger was again serious and the main duty of the thousand settlers established by Pericles in 447 was to ensure the security of the peninsula; at the same time the wall which Miltiades, who had led out the original settlers, built across the isthmus was restored. The sending of cleruchs to Lemnos and Imbros at about the same time was an additional safeguard.[17]

The cleruchs thus settled overseas were drawn from the two lowest property classes; the grant of land raised the *thetes* to the hoplite class and relieved Athens of what was in peacetime a superfluous population. But they remained Athenian citizens and could be called on for military service and probably for taxation. Colonies were formally different from cleruchies.[18] They were independent cities with their own government bound by religious and moral ties to the mother city but deciding their own policies. Two Athenian colonies are known in this period; one was Thurii, a special Panhellenic colony in the west which will be discussed later. The Athenian element at Thurii was small and the colony ultimately became too independent. The second colony, Brea, is known from an inscription which preserves some of the regulations governing the foundation. It is specifically laid down in an amendment that the colonists are to be drawn from the *zeugitae* and *thetes*, and troops returning from an expedition (probably in Euboea in 446) are to be eligible for enrolment. Provision is made for the distribution of land and the allocation of reservations for the gods. Unfortunately this colony has no history and even its site is not beyond dispute. It was presumably intended to strengthen the Athenian position in the economically important Thraceward area, for one of the clauses of the decree prescribes that 'if anyone invades the colony's territory the cities are to bring help as sharply as possible according to the regulations laid down concerning the Thraceward cities when —— was secretary'.[19] This policy of overseas settlement strengthened Athens' hold on her empire; but it was

Enforcement of Athenian coinage

strongly resented by the allies and is included in all the fourth-century attacks on Athenian imperialism. When Athens set out to attract a new maritime league in the fourth century she found it politic to renounce formally any attempt to take land publicly or privately in the territories of her allies. No less significant of Athens' imperial mood at this time is a decree enforcing the use of Athenian coins, weights, and measures throughout the empire, and forbidding the minting of silver coins in allied cities, while allowing electrum coinages to be continued.[20] There had been an increasing tendency since the establishment of the Delian Confederacy for the smaller cities to adopt Athenian coinage with its wide commercial reputation, but many states still preferred to retain a coinage with their own state symbol. They were now forced to conform. Non-Attic coins were to be called in and brought to Athens to be reminted: henceforth Athenian coinage only must be used. This sweeping act may have facilitated the development of trade in the Aegean, but it increased still further the economic dominance of the Piraeus. Silver for coinage could be secured at several points: Athenian coinage had mainly to be bought with goods at Athens.

Most Athenian citizens were naturally attracted by a policy of expansion which made their city great and powerful without exacting heavy sacrifices from themselves. The day had not yet come when they were unwilling to undertake military service, and they were content as long as the cost of maintaining the empire did not tax their purses. The empire furthered the extension of their trade and increased their prosperity. The average Athenian citizen was not hindered by his own full measure of freedom from being willing to press, with as little scruple as any tyrant, the yoke of his city upon the necks of other communities. So long as the profits of empire were many and its burdens light, the Athenian democracy would feel few searchings of heart in adopting the imperialism of Pericles.

Policy of Pericles

That imperialism was indeed of a lofty kind. The aim of the statesman who guided the destinies of Athens in these days of her greatness was to make her the queen of Hellas; to spread her sway on the mainland as well as beyond the seas; and to make her political influence felt in those states which it would have been unwise and perhaps impossible to draw within the borders of her empire. The full achievement of this ideal would have meant the union of all the Greeks, a union held together by the power

of Athens but having a natural support in a common religion, common traditions, common customs, and a common language.

The firmness of Athens to the allies in the years immediately following peace with Persia helped her to survive the crisis of 446 without the disintegration of the empire, and the formal recognition of that empire in the peace by Sparta may well have discouraged the internal opposition to Pericles. In 443 their leader Thucydides was ostracised and a new phase of Athenian politics developed.

The Restoration of the Temples

The motive of the buildings at Athens under Pericles

With the collapse of the Panhellenic Congress it remained for Athens to carry out that part of the programme which concerned herself, and restore in greater splendour the temples of her city and her land. We shall miss the meaning of the architectural monuments which now began to rise under the direction and influence of Pericles, if we do not clearly grasp their historical motive and recognise their immediate connection with the Persian war. It devolved upon the city, as a religious duty, to make good the injuries which the barbarian had inflicted upon the habitations of her gods and fully to pay her debt of gratitude to heaven for the defeat of the Mede. And seeing that Athens had won her great empire through that defeat, the gods might well expect that she would perform this duty on no small scale and in no niggardly spirit. In this, above all, was the greatness of Pericles displayed, that he discerned the importance of performing it on a grand scale. He recognised that the city by ennobling the houses of her gods would ennoble herself; and that she could express her own might and her ideals in no worthier way than by the erection of beautiful temples. His architectural plans went farther than this, and we can see that he was influenced by the example of the Pisistratids; but the chief buildings of the Periclean age, it should always be remembered, were, like the Athenian empire itself, the direct consequence of the Persian invasion.[21]

450-30 B.C.

One of the finest memorials of the Persian war had probably been completed before peace was made with Persia. This was the gigantic statue of Athena Promachos, wrought in bronze by Phidias.[22] The goddess stood near the west brow of her own hill, looking south-westward, and her helmet and the tip of her spear flashing in the sun could be seen far off at sea. But the great transformation of the

Athena Promachos, before 450

9.2 The Athenian Acropolis, with the Areopagus in foreground and Mount Hymettus in background

9.3 The Parthenon from the south-west

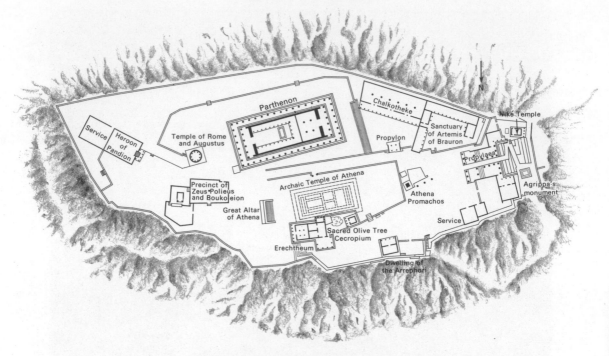

Service

Heroon
of
Pandion

Temple of Rome
and Augustus

Parthenon

Chalkotheke

Propylon

Sanctuary
of Artemis
of Brauron

Niké Temple

Propylaea

Agrippa's
monument

Precinct of
Zeus Polieus
and Boukoleion

Archaic Temple of Athena

Athena
Promachos

Great Altar
of Athena

Sacred Olive Tree

Cecropium

Service

Erechtheum

Dwelling of
the Arrephori

N

19.   THE ATHENIAN ACROPOLIS

9.4 Model of the Athenian Acropolis (see note, p. 554)

9.5   Poseidon, Apollo, Artemis, from the Parthenon frieze

Temple of Athena Polias (the 'Parthenon'), 447-32 B.C.

Acropolis began only after the peace. Nothing was so pressing as to carry to completion the new house of the goddess, which had been begun after Marathon but was destroyed by the Persians while building was in process. The work was now resumed on the same site and the same foundations, but it was resumed on an entirely different plan, drawn up by the gifted architect Ictinus. The new temple was slightly broader but considerably shorter than it would have been if the old design had been carried out, and instead of foreign Parian marble native Attic from the quarries of Pentelicus was employed. Callicrates, another expert architect, superintended the execution of the plan which Ictinus had conceived. It is not within our province to enter here into the architectural beauties of this perfect Dorian temple, which came afterwards to be generally known as the Parthenon. The building contained two rooms, between which there was no communication. The eastern room into which one entered from the pronaos was the temple proper, and contained the statue of the goddess. It was about a hundred feet long and was hence officially called the *Hecatompedon*.

The door of the small western room was on the west side of the temple. This chamber was perhaps designed for the habitation of invisible maidens who attended the maiden goddess; it is at least certain that it was called the *Parthenôn*. It is easy to imagine how a word which designated as the room of the Maidens part of the house of the Maiden could soon come to be associated popularly with the whole building, and the name Parthenon came to mean for the ordinary ear, in defiance of official usage, the temple of Athena Parthenos, and not the chamber of her virgins.[23]

The statue of Athena by Phidias

The goddess stood in her dwelling, majestic and smiling, her colossal figure arrayed in a golden robe, a helmet on her head, her right hand holding a golden Victory, and her left resting on her shield, while the snake Erichthonius was coiled at her feet. It was a wooden statue covered with ivory and gold—ivory for the exposed flesh, gold for the raiment—and hence called *chryselephantine*. It was wrought by the Athenian sculptor of genius who has given his name to the plastic art of the Periclean age, Phidias, the son of Charmides.[24] He had already made his fame by the Athena

229

9.6 Two knights, from the Parthenon frieze

Promachos and another beautiful statue of the goddess of the city, which the outsettlers who went forth to colonise Lemnos dedicated on the Acropolis. The Lemnian Athena was wrought in bronze and it revealed Athena to her people in the guise of their friend, while the image of the Parthenon showed her rather as their queen.

To Phidias too was entrusted the task of designing and carrying out those plastic decorations which were necessary to the completion of a great temple. With the metopes of the lofty entablature, from which Centaurs and Giants stood out in high relief, the great master had probably little to do, but he will at least have designed the two pediments and the frieze which ran round the wall of the temple, within the colonnade. *The pediments* The triangle above the eastern portal was adorned with the scene of the birth of Athena, who has sprung from the head of Zeus, at the rising of the sun and the setting of the moon; and Iris the heavenly messenger was shown, going forth to carry the good news to the ends of the world. The pediment of the western end was occupied with the passage in the life of the goddess that specially appertained to Attica—her triumph on the Acropolis in her contest with her rival Poseidon for the lordship of the land. The olive which came forth from the earth by her enchantment was probably shown; and we should like to believe that at the northern and southern ends reclined the two river gods, Eridanus and Ilisus, each at the side which was nearest his own waters. The subject of the wonderful *The frieze* frieze which encircled the temple from end to *of cella* end was the most solemn of all the ceremonies which the Athenians performed in honour of their queen. At the greater Panathenaic festival, every fourth year, they went up in long procession to her temple to present her with a new robe. The advance of this procession, *The Pan-* starting from the western side, and moving *athenaic* simultaneously along the northern and south- *procession* ern sides, to meet at the eastern entrance, was vividly shown on the frieze of the Parthenon. Walking along the peristyle and looking upwards, the spectator saw the Athenian knights—beautiful young men—on

9.7   The temple of Athena Nike

horseback, charioteers, citizens on foot, musicians, cattle and sheep led for sacrifice, stately maidens with sacred vessels, the nine archons of the city, all advancing to the house of Athena where she entertains the celestials on her feast-day. The high gods are seated on thrones, Zeus on one side of Athena, Hephaestus on the other; and near the goddess is a robe—perhaps the old robe —in the hands of a priest.

The old temple

Athena Polias had now two houses side by side on her hill. For the old restored temple was not destroyed, nor was her old image removed from it. But in her character of Victory, yet another small habitation, by the architect Callicrates, was decreed for her about the same time, on the bastion which the hill throws out on its south-western side. It was an appropriate spot for the house of Victory. The Athenian standing on that platform saw Salamis and Aegina near him; his eye ranged along the Argolic coast, to the distant citadel of Corinth and the mountains of the Megarid; under the shadow of Victory he could lose himself in reveries of memory and dreams of hope. The motive of the temple, as a memorial of the Persian war, was written clear in the

Temple of Athena Nike

frieze. Whereas the sculptures of other temples of this period alluded only indirectly to that great struggle, by the representation of mythical wars—such as the war of Greek and Amazons, or of Lapiths and Centaurs, or of gods and giants, on the frieze of Athena Nike a battle between the Greeks and Persians is portrayed. The decree for the temple was carried soon after the Peace of Callias, but the actual building was delayed for some twenty years.[25]

But there were other shrines of other gods in Athens and Attica which had been wrecked by the Persians, and which were now to be restored. From the west side of the Acropolis, as one looks down on the western quarter of the city, no building is so prominent, or can ever have been so prominent, as the Dorian temple of Pentelic marble which crowns the hill of Colonus. It is the temple which 'the sons of Hephaestus' built for their sire, the god of handicraftsmen, who was always worshipped with special devotion at Athens and is here associated with Athena. It is significant that on the frieze of the Parthenon he sits next the lady of the land. This house of Hephaestus is the only Greek temple that

The temple of Hephaestus (popularly called the Theseum)

231

9.8 The temple of Hephaestus (see note, page 554)

9.9 The temple of Poseidon, Sunion

The temple of Sunion is not a ruin. A little later, a marble temple of Poseidon, designed by the same architect, rose on the extreme point of southern Attica, the promontory of Sunion. The Persian invasion had probably been fatal to the old temple of poros-stone. Here the sea-god, 'to whom men pray at Sunion', seems to have had his own house, looking down upon his own domain. The same characteristic features have been seen in the temple of Nemesis at Rhamnus, the last to be begun of the three.[26] *(Σουνι-άρατος)*

At the other extremity of the Attic land, the shrine of the goddesses of Eleusis had likewise been destroyed by the barbarians. Rebuilding was begun under Pericles; Ictinus made the design and Coroebus carried it out. The new Hall of Mysteries was built of the dark stone of Eleusis; one side of it was formed by the rock of the hill under which it was built; and the stone steps around the walls would have seated about 3000. As the place was close to the Megarian frontier, a strong wall with towers was erected round the precincts of the shrine, so that the place had the aspect of a fortress. *The Eleusinian telesterion*

These splendid buildings required a large outlay of money, which was drawn mainly from the tribute reserve.[27] The opposition, as has been seen, challenged this use of the allies' money for Athenian temples, but was overridden. Expenditure, however, was not limited to temples and statues for the gods. A programme of social building was also developed. In the days of Cimon's ascendency the people still looked naturally to the aristocratic houses for patronage, and Cimon in particular had a reputation for liberality: in the fully developed democracy the state provided for all its citizens the essential amenities of a citizen's life such as gymnasia and baths.[28] This side of the building programme has been overshadowed by the great works on the Acropolis, but it represents an important aspect of Periclean social policy. The extravagance of the social building programme was, we may think, a natural target for the opposition and one of the main issues which led to the ostracism of Thucydides. The most spectacular of the buildings, which were not primarily of a religious character, dates certainly from this time. A great Hall of Music or *Odeon*, intended for the musical contests which had recently been added to the Panathenaic celebrations, was erected on the east side of the Theatre of Dionysus. Its roof, made of the masts and yard-arms of captured Persian ships, was pointed like a tent, and wits compared it to the helmet of Pericles the strategos. 'The *Cratinus on Pericles (in the Thrattai)* trial by sherd is over,' says someone in a play which the comic poet Cratinus put on the stage at this time; 'so here comes Pericles, our peak-headed Zeus, with the Odeon set on his crown.'

The new Propylaea Though Cimon, when he constructed the southern wall of the Acropolis, left the earlier entrance-gate facing south-westward, it was too small and unimposing to relieve the frowning aspect of the walled hill. A more worthy approach, worthy of the new Parthenon, was devised by the architect Mnesicles. The buildings designed by Mnesicles occupied the whole west side of the hill. In the centre, on the brow of the height and facing westward, was to be the entrance with five gates, and on either side of this two vast columned halls—reaching to the north and south brinks of the hill—in which the Athenians could walk sheltered from sun and rain. Thrown out on the projecting cliffs in front of these halls were to be two spacious wings, flanking the ascent to the central gate. But the plan of Mnesicles took no account of the sanctuaries on the south-western part of the Acropolis, on which his new buildings would encroach. The southern colonnade would have cut short the precinct of Artemis Brauronia and the adjacent southern wing would have infringed on the enclosure of Athena Nike. On the north side there were no such impediments. The priests of these goddesses raised objections to the execution of the architect's plan at the expense of their sacred precincts, and in consequence

the grand idea of Mnesicles was only partly carried out. But even after the building had been begun, Pericles and his architect never abandoned the hope that the scruples of the priests might ultimately be overcome; and, while they omitted altogether the southern colonnade and reduced the proportions of the southern wing, they built in such a way that at some future time the structure might be easily enlarged to the measures of the original design. On the northern side, too, the idea of Mnesicles was not completed, but for a different reason. The covered colonnade was never built; it was left to the last, and, when the time came, Athens was threatened by a great war and deemed it unwise to undertake any further outlay on building. But the north-western wing was built and was adorned with *Pinacotheca* paintings. The greatest paintings that Athens possessed were however not on the hill but in buildings below; and they belonged to a somewhat earlier age. It was Cimon who brought Polygnotus of Thasos to Athens, and it was *Polygnotus at Athens, c. 470-465* when Cimon was in power that he, in collaboration with Micon, another eminent painter, decorated with life-size frescoes the new Theseum and the Anaceum, on the north side of the Acropolis, and the walls of the Painted Portico in the Agora. We have *Poecile Stoa (p. 161)* already cast a glance at the picture of the Battle of Marathon. The most famous of the pictures of the Thasian master were executed, after he had left Athens, for the hall of the Cnidians at Delphi. Their subjects were the *Visit of Odysseus to the Underworld* and the *Sack of Troy*.

If it was vain for Athens to hope that Greece would yield her any formal acknowledgment of headship, she might at all events have the triumph of exerting intellectual influence even in the lands which were least ready to admit her claims. And in the field of art she partly fulfilled the ambition of Pericles, who, when he could not make her the queen, desired that she should be the instructress, of Hellas. When Phidias had completed the great *Phidias goes to Olympia, c. 438 B.C.* statue of Athena in gold and ivory and had seen it set up in the new temple, he left Athens, invited by the men of Elis, to make the image for the temple of Zeus at Olympia. For five years in his workshop in the Altis the Athenian sculptor wrought at the 'great chryselephantine god', and the colossal image which came from his hands was probably the highest creation ever achieved by the plastic art of Greece. The Panhellenic god, seated on a lofty throne, and clad in a golden robe, held a Victory in his right hand, a sceptre in his

9.10 Apollo, from the west pediment of the temple of Zeus at Olympia (see note, page 554)

left. He was bearded, and his hair was wreathed with a branch of olive. Many have borne witness to the impression which the serene aspect of this manifest divinity always produced upon the heart of the beholder. 'Let a man sick and weary in his soul, who has passed through many distresses and sorrows, whose pillow is unvisited by kindly sleep, stand in front of this image; he will, I deem, forget all the terrors and troubles of human life.' An

9.11   Metope from the temple of Zeus at Olympia: Athena, Hercules, Atlas (see note, page 554)

9.12   'I belong to Phidias' (see note, page 554)

Athenian had wrought, for one of the two great centres of Hellenic religion, the most sublime expression of the Greek ideal of godhead. Nor was Phidias the only Athenian artist who *(Temple of* worked abroad; we also find the architect *Apollo at* Ictinus engaged in designing a temple of *Phigalia)* Apollo in Arcadia at Bassae.

The Piraeus. Growth of Athenian Trade

The Piraeus had grown enormously since it *The* had been fortified by Themistocles; it was now *Piraeus* one of the great ports and markets 'in the midst of Hellas', and Pericles took in hand to make it a greater and fairer place. There was one weak point in the common defences of Piraeus and Athens. Between Munychia and the extreme end of the southern wall which ran down to the strand of Phaleron, there was an unfortified piece of marshy shore,

9.13   Temple of Apollo, Bassae

The middle Long Wall where an enemy might land at night. This defect might have been remedied by building a cross-wall, but a wholly different plan was adopted. A new long wall was built, running parallel and close to the northern wall, and, like it, joining the fortification of Piraeus with the 'upper city,' as Athens was locally called. The southern or Phaleron wall consequently ceased to be part of the system of defence and was allowed to fall into disrepair. Round the three harbours ship-sheds were constructed, in which the vessels could lie high and dry; and on the wharfs and quays new storehouses and buildings of various kinds arose for the convenience of shipping and trade. On the east side of the great Harbour the chief traffic was carried on in the Place of *Emporion* Commerce. This mart was marked off by boundary stones, some of which are still preserved, and was subject to the control of a special board of officers. The most famous of the buildings in the Place of Commerce was the colonnade known as the

Deigma or Show-place, where merchants showed their wares. But Pericles was not content with the erection of new buildings; the whole town, which crept up the slopes of Munychia from the quays of the great Harbour, was laid out on a completely new system, which created considerable interest in Greece. It was the rectangular system, on which the main streets run parallel and are cut by cross streets at right angles. The Piraeus was the first town in Europe where this plan was adopted, which we now see carried out on a large scale in many modern cities. The idea was due to Hippodamus, an architect of Miletus, a man of a speculative as well as practical turn, who tried with less success to apply his principles of symmetry to politics, and sketched the scheme of a model state whose institutions were as precisely correlated as the streets of his model town.

The increase of Athenian trade was largely due to the decline of the merchant cities of Ionia, as well. as to the blow which was

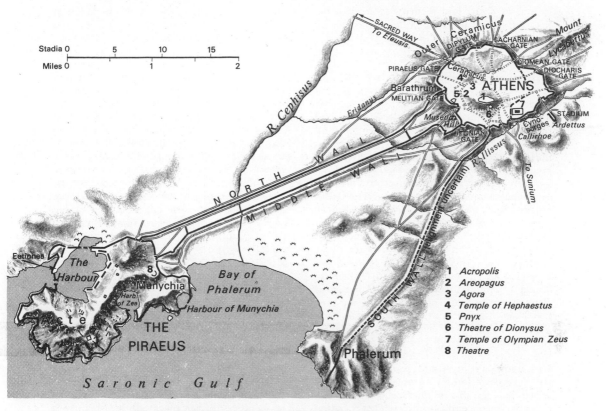

1 Acropolis
2 Areopagus
3 Agora
4 Temple of Hephaestus
5 Pnyx
6 Theatre of Dionysus
7 Temple of Olympian Zeus
8 Theatre

20. ATHENS AND THE PIRAEUS (see note, page 555)

struck to Phoenician commerce by the victory of Greece over Persia. The decay of Ionian commerce is strikingly reflected in the tribute-records of the Athenian Confederacy, where the small sums paid by the Ionians are contrasted with the larger tributes of the cities on the shores of the Propontis. Lampsacus contributes twice as much as Ephesus. Both trade and industry migrated from the eastern to the western and northern shores of the Aegean; and as this change coincided with the rise of her empire, it was Athens that it chiefly profited. The population of Athens and her harbour multiplied; and about this time the whole number of the inhabitants of Attica seems to have been about 315,000—perhaps more than twice as large as the population of the Corinthian state.[29] But nearly half of these inhabitants were slaves; for one consequence of the growth of manufactures was the inflowing of slave 'hands' into the manufacturing towns. In towns where the people subsisted on the fruits of agriculture the

(Tribute of Lampsacus, 12 tals.; of Ephesus, 6)

demand for slaves remained small. It should be observed that, although Greece, and especially Athens, consumed large quantities of corn brought from beyond the seas, this did not ruin the agriculture of Greece; the costs of transport were so great that home-grown corn could still be profitable.

Except in remote or unusually conservative regions, money had now entirely displaced more primitive standards of exchange and valuation. Most Greek states of any size issued their own coins, and their money at this time was in almost all cases silver. Silver had become plentiful, and prices had necessarily gone up. Thus the price of barley and wheat had become two or three times dearer than a hundred years before. Far more remarkable was the increase in the price of stock. In the days of Solon a sheep could be bought for a drachma; in the days of Pericles, its cost might approach fifty drachmae. As money was cheap, interest should have been low; but mercantile enterprise was so active, the demand for

Money plentiful

Rise of prices

237

Rate of interest

capital so great, and security so inadequate, that the usual price of a loan was twelve per cent.

Athenian Enterprise in Italy

Athenian trade in the west

In the far west Athens was spreading her influence and pushing her trade. She supplied the Etruscans with her red-figured pottery, and there was a market for these products of her industry even in the remote valley of the Po. Her ships brought back metalwork from Tuscany, carpets and cushions from Carthage, corn, cheese and pork from Sicily. The Greek cities of Sicily had gradually adopted the Attic standard for their currency; and in the little Italian republic on the Tiber, which was afterwards destined to make laws for the whole world, the fame of the legislation of Solon was so high that envoys were sent to Athens to obtain a copy of the code. Thus Athens had stepped into the place of Chalcis; she was now the chief Ionian trader with Italian and Sicilian lands. Her rival in this western commerce was Corinth, but she was beginning to outdistance the great Dorian merchant-city. In this competition Athens had one advantage. By the possession of Naupactus she could control the entrance to the Corinthian gulf—a perpetual menace to Corinth; while the hatred which existed between Corinth and her colony Corcyra prevented this island from being as useful as it should have been to the Corinthian traffic with the west. On the other hand, Corinth had the advantage of having important colonies in the west, with which she maintained intimate relations, especially Syracuse; and these maritime cities were centres of her trade and influence. Next to Athens herself, Syracuse was probably the largest and most populous city in the Greek world. Athens had no colonies and no such centres. The disadvantage seems to have been felt by Themistocles, for there are several indications that he was interested in the west. He named two of his daughters Sybaris and Italia and, before the battle of Salamis, threatened that the Athenians would emigrate to Siris, which had been destroyed by neighbours, if the Peloponnesians abandoned the narrow waters. Corcyra also, on the western route, was under obligation to him. But after the Persian invasion other men and other policies held the stage. At length the opportunity came, when Pericles was at the head of affairs; here, as in other cases, it fell upon him to execute ideas of Themistocles.

The chance preservation of the fragment of a decree tells us that while Athens was reaching the height of her power in the First Peloponnesian War she made alliance with Segesta in the west of Sicily. It is a reflection of her influence in the west and the foundation of her ultimate disaster in Sicily, but no military commitments were yet undertaken.[30] Some time after the peace with Persia we find Athens making alliances with Leontini in Sicily and Rhegion on the straits of Messena, but again the influence of Athenian prestige against any growing threat from Syracuse rather than military help was secured by the alliance. At roughly the same time an even better opportunity offered. The men of old Sybaris, who since the destruction of their own city by Croton had dwelt in neighbouring cities, thought that they might at length return to build a new Sybaris on the old site; but within five years their old foes, the men of Croton, drove them out. They then invited Athens and Sparta to join them in regaining their city. For Sparta the offer had no attraction; but Athens seized her chance and a small band of Athenians and allies was sent out.

Alliance with Segesta, 458-7 B.C.

Leontini and Rhegium

Resettlement of Sybaris

Foundation of New Sybaris

But the men of old Sybaris were not content to stand on an equal footing with the colonists who had come to help them from the mother-country. They thought that their old connection with the place entitled them to a privileged position; they claimed an exclusive right to the most important offices in the state. Such claims could not be tolerated; a battle was fought; and the Sybarites were driven out. But there was then a pressing need for men; and for the second time an appeal was made to Athens, but this time from her own children.

To the second appeal Athens, under the guidance of Pericles, responded by an enterprise on a still greater scale. All Greece was now invited to take part in founding a Panhellenic colony. In carrying out this project the right-hand man of Pericles was the Seer and Interpreter (*Exegetes*) Lampon, who was closely connected with the Eleusinian worship and was the highest authority in Athens on all matters pertaining to religion. He obtained from the Delphic god an oracle touching the new colony; it was to be planted where men could drink water by measure and eat bread without measure. At Athens the enemies of Pericles opposed the project, and especially the Panhellenic character which he sought to impress upon it. Cratinus brought out a play deriding Lampon, and asking whether Pericles was a second Theseus who wanted to synoecise

Drapetides of Cratinus

Colony of Thurii, 443 B.C.

the whole of Greece. But Greece responded to the Athenian proposal, and the colony went out under the guidance of Lampon. Not far from the site of Sybaris they found a stream gushing from a bronze pipe, which was locally known as the Bushel. Here clearly was the measured water to which the oracle pointed; while the land was so fruitful that it might well be said to furnish bread without measure. The place was named Thurii, and the new city was designed by Hippodamus, the architect who had re-planned the Piraeus. The constitution of Thurii was naturally a democracy; but though the influence of the Athenian model might be recognised, the colony adopted not the laws of Solon, but those of Zaleucus, the lawgiver of Locri. Some years after the foundation, the question was asked, Who was the founder? and the Delphic god himself claimed the honour. The coins of Thurii were stamped with Athena's head and an olive branch; and the place became, as it was intended, a centre of Athenian influence in Italy, although the Attic element in the population failed to maintain its predominance.

Athenian Policy in Thrace and the Euxine

But Athens had greater and more immediate interests in the eastern sea where she succeeded Miletus than in the western where she challenged Corinth. The importance of the imports from the Pontus, especially corn, fish, and wood, was more vital than that of the wares which came to her from the west; and hence there was nothing of higher consequence in the eyes of a clear-sighted statesman than the assurance of the line of communication between Athens and the Euxine sea, and the occupation of strong and favourable points on the coasts of the Euxine itself. The outer gate of the Euxine was secured by the possession of the Chersonese which Pericles had strengthened, and the inner gate by the control of Byzantium and Chalcedon, members of the Athenian Confederacy. In the Euxine, Athens relied on the Greek towns which, fringing the shores at distant intervals, looked to her for support against the neighbouring barbarians. The corn-market in the Athenian agora was sensitive to every political movement in Thrace and Scythia; and it was necessary to be ever ready to support the ships of trade by the presence of ships of war. The growth of a large Thracian kingdom under Teres and his son Sitalces demanded the attention of Athenian

Rise of Thracian kingdom, c. 450 B.C.

statesmen to these regions more pressingly than ever. The power of Teres reached to the Danube and his influence to the Dnieper; for he married his daughter to the king of the neighbouring Scythians.

It was in order to impress the barbarians of the Euxine regions with a just sense of the greatness of the Athenian sea-power that Pericles sailed himself to the Pontus, in command of an imposing squadron. Of that voyage we know little.[31] It is recorded that he visited Sinope and that in consequence of his visit the Athenians gained a permanent footing at that important point. It is probable that he also sailed to the Cimmerian Bosphorus and visited the Archaeanactid lords of Panticapaeum, who were distinguished for many a long year by their abiding friendship to Athens in her good and evil days alike. As Panticapaeum was the centre of the Euxine corn trade, this intimacy was of the highest importance.

Pericles visits the Euxine, c. 436 B.C.

The union of the Thracian tribes under a powerful king constrained Athens also to keep a watchful eye upon the north coast of the Aegean and the eastern frontier of Macedonia. The most important point on that coast from both a commercial and a strategic point of view was the mouth of the Strymon, where the Athenians possessed the fortress of Eion. Not far from the mouth was the bridge over which much of the trade between Thrace and Macedonia passed to and fro; and up the Strymon valley ran the chief roads into the interior. The mountains of the neighbourhood were famous for their timber and for the veins of gold and silver stored in their recesses; the Macedonian king Alexander had tapped a mine near Lake Prasias which yielded daily a silver talent. In the days of Cimon, Athens had attempted to strengthen Eion by establishing a colony at the Nine Ways, by the Strymon bridge. We saw how that attempt roused the opposition of Thasos, whose interests it menaced; and though Thasos was subdued, the colony of the Nine Ways was destroyed by the neighbouring barbarians. Thirty years later Pericles resumed the project with greater success. Hagnon, son of Nicias, led forth a colony of Athenians and allies and founded a new city, surrounded on three sides by the Strymon, and called its name Amphipolis. It flourished and became, as was inevitable, the most important place in the district. But a considerable proportion of the population was drawn from Greek cities of the neighbourhood, a local feeling grew up unfavourable to the mother-country, and the city

Attemt to colonise the Nine Ways, 465 B.C. Foundation of Amphipolis, 437-6 B.C.

was lost to Athens within fifteen years of its foundation.

The Revolt of Samos

Political position of Pericles

After the ostracism of Thucydides, Pericles reigned, the undisputed leader of Athenian policy, for nearly fifteen years. He ruled as absolutely as a tyrant, and folk might have said that his rule was a continuation of the tyranny of the Pisistratids. But his position was entirely constitutional, and it had the stablest foundation, his moral influence over the sovereign people. He had the power of persuading them to do whatever he thought good, and every year for fifteen years after his rival's banishment he was elected one of the generals. Although all the ten generals nominally possessed equal powers, yet the man who possessed the supreme political influence and enjoyed the confidence of the people was practically chief of the ten and had the conduct of foreign affairs in his hands. Pericles was not irresponsible; for at the end of any official year the people could decline to re-elect him and could call him to account for his acts. When he had once gained the undisputed mastery, the only forces which he used to maintain it were wisdom and eloquence. Whatever devices he may have employed in his earlier career for party purposes, he rejected now all vulgar means of courting popularity or catching votes. He believed in himself; and he sought to raise the people to his own wisdom, he would not stoop to their folly. The desire of autocratic authority was doubtless part of his nature; but his spirit was fine enough to feel that it was a greater thing to be leader of free men whom he must convince by speech than despot of subjects who must obey his nod. Yet this leader of democracy was disdainful of the vulgar herd; and perhaps no one knew more exactly than he the weak points in a democratic constitution. There is no better equipment for the highest statesmanship than the temper which holds aloof from the public and shows a front of good natured indifference towards unfriendly crticism; and we may be sure that this quality in the temperament of Pericles helped to establish his success and maintain his supremacy.

Pericles was a man of finer fibre than Themistocles, but he was not like Themistocles a statesman of originative genius. He originated little; he elaborated the ideas of others. He brought to fulfilment the sovereignty of the people which had been fully established in principle long ago; he raised to its height the empire which had been already founded. As an orator he may have had true genius; of that we cannot judge. It was his privilege to guide the policy of his country at a time when she had poets and artists who stand alone and eminent not only in her own annals and those of Greece, but in the history of mankind. The Periclean age, the age of Sophocles and Euripides, Ictinus and Phidias, was not made by Pericles. But Pericles, though not creative, was one of its most interesting figures. Perhaps his best service to Greece was one which is often overlooked: the preservation of peace for twelve years between Athens and her jealous continental neighbours—an achievement which demanded statesmanship of no ordinary tact.

In his military operations he seems to have been competent, though we have not material to criticise them minutely; he was at least generally successful. Five years after the Thirty Years' Peace, he was called upon to display his generalship. Athens was involved in a war with one of the strongest members of her Confederacy, the island of Samos. The occasion of this war was a dispute which Samos had with another member, Miletus, about the possession of Priene. It appears that Athens, some years before, had settled the constitution of Miletus and placed a garrison in the city; and yet we now find Miletus engaged in a struggle with a non-tributary ally, and, when she is worsted, appealing to Athens. The case shows how little we know of the various orderings of the relations between Athens and her allies and subjects. One would have thought the decision of such a case would have rested with Athens from the first. On the appeal, she decided in favour of Miletus, and Pericles sailed with 44 triremes to Samos where he overthrew the aristocracy, carried away a number of hostages, and established a democratic constitution, leaving a garrison to protect it. The nobles who fled to the mainland returned one night, captured the garrison and handed them over to the Persian satrap of Sardis, with whom they were intriguing. They also recovered the hostages who had been lodged in the island of Lemnos. Athens received another blow at the same time by the revolt of Byzantium.

Revolt of Samos, 440 B.C.

Revolt of Byzantium

Pericles sailed speedily back to Samos and invested it with a large fleet. Hearing that a Phoenician squadron was coming to assist the Samians, he raised the siege and with a part of his armament went to meet it. During his absence the Samians gained some successes against the Athenian ships which were anchored close to the harbour. At the end of two weeks Pericles returned; either the Phoenicians had not appeared after all, or they had been induced to sail home. Well-nigh 200 warships now blockaded Samos, and at the end of nine months the city surrendered. The Samians undertook to pull down their walls, to surrender their ships, and pay a war indemnity which amounted to 1500 talents or thereabouts. They became subject to Athens and were obliged to furnish soldiers to her armies, but they were not made tributary.

Siege and reduction of Samos, 439 B.C.

The Athenian citizens who fell in the war received a public burial at Athens. Pericles pronounced the funeral oration, and it may have been on this occasion that he used a famous phrase of the young men who had fallen. The spring, he said, was taken out of the year.

Byzantium also came back to the confederacy. It had been a trying moment for Athens; for she had some reason to fear Peloponnesian intervention. Sparta and her allies had met to consider the situation; and the Corinthians afterwards claimed, whether truly or not, that they deprecated any interference, on the general principle that every state should be left to deal with her own rebellious allies. However the Corinthians may have acted on this occasion, it was chiefly the commercial jealousy existing between Athens and Corinth that brought on the ultimate outbreak of hostilities between the Athenians and Peloponnesians, which led to the destruction of the Athenian empire.

Temporary restrictions on Comedy

It seems that during the excitement of the Samian war, Pericles deemed it expedient to place some restraints upon the licence of the comic drama. What he feared was the effect which the free criticisms of the comic poets on his policy might have, not upon the Athenians themselves, but upon the strangers who were present in the theatre and especially upon citizens of the subject states. The precaution shows that the situation was critical; though the restraints were withdrawn soon afterwards, for they were contrary to the spirit of the time. Henceforward the only check on the comic poet was that he *might* be prosecuted before the Council of Five Hundred for 'doing wrong to the people', if his jests against the officers of the people went too far.

Comedy had grown up in Athens out of the mummeries of masked revellers who kept the feasts of Dionysus by singing phallic songs and flinging coarse jests at the folk. It was not till after the Persian war that the state

recognised it. Then a place was given at the great festival of Dionysus to competitions in comedy. To the three days which were devoted to the competitions of tragedies a fourth was added for the new contest. The comic drama then assumed form and shape. Magnes and Chionides were its first masters; but they were eclipsed by Cratinus, the most brilliant comic poet of the age of Pericles.

472-1 B.C.

There is no more significant symptom of the political and social health of the Athenian state in the period of its empire, than the perfect freedom which was accorded to the comic stage, to laugh at everything in earth and heaven, and splash with ridicule every institution of the city and every movement of the day, to libel the statesmen and even jest at the gods. Such licence is never permitted in an age of decadence even under the shelter of religious usage. It can only prevail in a free country where men's belief in their own strength and virtue, in the excellence of their institutions and their ideals, is still true, deep, and fervent; then they can afford to laugh at themselves. The Old Comedy is a most telling witness to the greatness of Athens.

Higher Education.   The Sophists

Since the days of Nestor and Odysseus, the art of persuasive speech was held in honour by the Greeks. With the rise of the democratic commonwealths it became more important, and the greater attention which was paid to the cultivation of oratory may perhaps be reflected in the introduction of a new class of proper names, which refer to excellence in addressing public assemblies. The institutions of a Greek democratic city presupposed in the average citizen the faculty of speaking in public, and for anyone who was ambitious for a political career it was indispensable. If a man was hauled into a law-court by his enemies and did not know how to speak, he was like an unarmed civilian attacked by armed soldiers. The power of clearly expressing ideas in such a way as to persuade an audience was an art to be learned and taught. But it was not enough to gain command of a vocabulary; it was necessary to learn how to argue, and to exercise one's self in the discussion of political and ethical questions. There was a demand for higher education.

New class of names (e.g. Pythagoras, Anaxagoras)

This tendency of democracy corresponded to the growth of that spirit of inquiry which had first revealed itself in Ionia in the field of natural philosophy. The study of nature

Science

had passed into a higher stage in the hands of two men of genius, whose speculations have had an abiding effect on science. Empedocles distinguished the 'four elements', and explained the development of the universe by the forces of attraction and repulsion which have held their place till today in scientific theory. He also foreshadowed the doctrine of the survival of the fittest. Democritus, of Abdera, a man of vast learning, originated the atomic theory, which was in later days popularised by Epicurus, and still later by the Roman Lucretius. The scientific imagination of Democritus generated the world from atoms, like in quality but different in size and weight, existing in void space. Such advances in the explanation of nature implied and promoted a new conception of what may be called 'methodised' knowledge, and this conception was applied to every subject. The second half of the fifth century was an age of technical treatises; oratory and cookery were alike reduced to systems; political institutions and received morality became the subject of scientific inquiry. Desire of knowledge had led the Greeks to seek more information about foreign lands and peoples; they had begun both to know more of the world and to regard it with a more critical mind; enlightenment was spreading, prejudices were being dispelled. Herodotus, who was far from being a sceptic, fully appreciates the instructiveness of the story which he tells, how Darius asked some Greeks for what price they would be willing to eat the dead bodies of their fathers. When they cry that nothing would induce them to do so, the king calls a tribe of Indians who eat their parents and asks them what price *they* would accept to burn the bodies of their fathers. The Indians exclaim against the bare thought of such a horror. Custom, Pindar had said and Herodotus echoes, is king of the world; and men began to distinguish between custom and nature. They felt that their own conventions and institutions required justification; the authority of usage and antiquity was not enough; and they compared human society with nature. The appeal to nature led indeed to very opposite theories. In the sight of nature, it was said, all are equal; birth and wealth are irrelevant; therefore the state should be built on the basis of perfect equality. On the other hand, it was argued that in the state of nature the strong man subdues the weaker and rules over them; therefore monarchy is the natural constitution. But it matters little what particular inferences were drawn; for no attempt was made to put them into

practice. The main point is that the questioning spirit was active; there were clever men everywhere, who refused to take anything on authority; who always asked, how do you know? and claimed to discuss all things in heaven and earth.

It was in this atmosphere of critical inquiry and scepticism that Greece had to provide for the higher education of her youth, which the practical conditions of the democracy demanded. The demand was met by teachers who travelled about and gave general instruction in the art of speaking and in the art of reasoning, and, out of their encyclopaedic knowledge, lectured on all possible subjects. They received fees for their courses, and were called Sophists, of which name perhaps our best equivalent is 'professors'. Properly a sophist meant one who was eminently proficient in some particular art—in poetry, for instance, or cookery. As applied to the teachers who educated the youths who were able to pay, the name acquired a slightly unfavourable colour—partly owing to the distrust felt by the masses towards men who know too much, partly to the prejudice which in Greece always existed more or less against those who gave their services for pay, partly too to the jealousy of those who were too poor to pay the fees and were consequently at a great disadvantage in public life compared with men whom a sophist had trained. But this haze of contempt which hung about the sophistic profession did not imply the idea that the professors were impostors, who deliberately sought to hoodwink the public by arguments in which they did not believe themselves. That suggestion—which has determined the modern meaning of 'sophist' and 'sophistry'—was first made by the philosopher Plato, and it is entirely unhistorical.

The sophists

The sophists did not confine themselves to teaching. They wrote much; they discussed occasional topics, criticised political affairs, diffused ideas; and it has been said that this part of their activity supplied in some measure the place of modern journalism. But the greatest of the professors were much more than either teachers or journalists. They not only diffused but set afloat ideas; they enriched the world with contributions to knowledge. They were all alike rationalists, spreaders of enlightenment; but they were very various in their views and doctrines. Gorgias of Leontini, Protagoras of Abdera, Prodicus of Ceos, Hippias of Elis, Socrates of Athens, each had his own strongly marked individuality. To Socrates, who has a place apart from the others,

Their writings

Prodicus

Supplices 196

Protagoras

His flight from Athens (415 B.C.)

we shall revert in a later chapter. Prodicus of Ceos was a pessimist; and it was doubtless he whom the poet Euripides meant by the man who considered the ills of men to be more in number than their good things. It was Prodicus who invented the famous fable of Heracles at the crossway choosing between virtue and pleasure. Of all the sophists Protagoras was perhaps the greatest. He first distinguished the parts of speech and founded the science of grammar for Europe. His activity as a teacher was chiefly at Athens, where he seems to have been intimate with Pericles. The story that Pericles and Protagoras spent a whole day arguing on the theory of punishment—a question which is still unsettled—illustrates the services which the sophists rendered to speculation. The retributive theory of justice, which logically enough led to the trial and punishment of animals and inanimate things, was called in question; and a counter-theory started that the object of punishment was to deter. Protagoras was a victim of the religious prejudices of the Athenians. He wrote a theological book, which he published by reading it aloud before a chosen audience in the house of his friend Euripides. The thesis of the work is probably contained in the first sentence: 'In regard to the gods I cannot know that they exist, nor yet that they do not exist; for many things hinder such knowledge—the obscurity of the matter, and the shortness of human life.' Protagoras may have himself *believed* in the gods; what he asserted was that their existence could not be a matter of *knowledge*. Unluckily the book itself has perished. For a certain Pythodorus came forward as the standard-bearer of the state religion and accused Protagoras of impiety. The philosopher deemed it wise to flee from Athens; he sailed for Sicily and was lost at sea. When Euripides makes the choir of Thracian women in his play of *Palamedes* cry bitterly, 'Ye have slain, O Greeks, ye have slain the all-wise nightingale of the Muses, that did no wrong', the poet was thinking of the dead friend who had come from the Thracian city. The sale of the book of Protagoras was forbidden in Athens, and all copies that could be found were publicly burned.

The case of Protagoras was not the only case of the kind. Years before, the philosopher Anaxagoras had been condemned for impiety; years after, Socrates would be condemned. These cases show that the Athenians were not more enlightened than other peoples, or less prejudiced. The attitude of Protagoras to theology was perfectly compatible with a fervent devotion to the religion of the state; but an Athenian jury was not sufficiently well-educated to discern this. When we admire the spread of knowledge and reasoning in the fifth century, we must remember that the mass of citizens was not reached by the new light; they were still conservative in religion, suspicious and jealous of the training which could be got only by sons of the comparatively well-to-do or those who were exceptionally intellectual.

Gorgias of Leontini

Gorgias was a philosophical thinker and a politician, but he won his renown as an orator and a stylist. He taught Greece how to write a new kind of prose—not the cold style which appeals only to the understanding, but a brilliant style, rhythmic, flowery in diction, full of figures, speaking to the sense and imagination. In the inscription of a statue which his grand-nephew erected to him at Olympia, it is said: 'No mortal ever invented a fairer art, to temper the soul for manlihood and virtue.' Wherever he went he was received with enthusiasm; we shall presently meet him as an ambassador at Athens.

Euripides

His critical spirit

The sophists were the chief, the professional expounders of the intellectual movement. But the exaltation of reason had a no less powerful supporter in the poet Euripides. He used the tragic stage to disseminate rationalism; he undermined the popular religion from the very steps of the altar. By the necessity of the case he accomplished his work indirectly, but with consummate dexterity. Aeschylus and Sophocles had reverently modified religious legend, adapting it to their own ideals, interpreting it so as to satisfy their own moral standard. Euripides takes the myths just as he finds them and contrives his dramas so as to bring the absurdities into relief. He does not acquiesce, like the older tragic poets, in the ways of the gods with men; he is not content to be a resigned pessimist. He will receive nothing on authority; he declines to bow to the orthodox opinions of his respectable fellow-countrymen, on such matters as the institution of slavery or the position of women in society. He refuses to endorse the inveterate prejudice which prevailed even at Athens in favour of noble birth. But perhaps nothing is so significant as his attitude to the contempt which the Greeks universally felt for other races than their own. Nowhere is Euripides more sarcastic than when, in his *Medea*, he makes Jason pose as a benefactor of the woman whom he has basely betrayed, on the ground that he has brought her out of an obscure barbarian home

243

and enabled her to enjoy the privilege of—living in Greece.

Yet we need not go to the most daring thinkers, to Euripides and the sophists, to discern the spirit of criticism at work. The Periclean age has left us few more significant, and certainly no more beautiful, monuments than a tragic drama which won the first prize at the great Dionysia a few years after the Thirty Years' Peace. The soul of Sophocles was in untroubled harmony with the received religion; but, living in an atmosphere of criticism and speculation, even he could not keep his mind aloof from the questions which were debated by the thoughtful men of his time. He took as the motive of his *Antigone* a deep and difficult question of political and of ethical science—the relation of the individual citizen to the state. What shall a man do if his duty of obedience to the government of his country conflicts with other duties? Are there any obligations higher than that of loyalty to the laws of his city? The poet answers that there are such—for instance, certain obligations of religion. He justifies Antigone in her disobedience to the king's decree. The motive lends itself to dramatic treatment, and never has it been handled with such consummate art as by him who first saw its possibilities. But it is worth observing that the *Antigone*, besides its importance in the history of dramatic poetry, has a high significance in the development of European thought, as the first presentation of a problem which both touches the very roots of ethical theory and is, in daily practice, constantly clamouring for solution.

The Antigone 442 or 441 B.C. March-April

CHAPTER 10

The War of Athens with the
Peloponnesians (431–421 B.C.)

The empire and commercial supremacy of Athens had, as we have seen, swiftly drawn a war upon herself and Greece. That war had been indecisive; it had taught her some lessons, but it had not cooled her ambition or crippled her trade, and it was therefore inevitable that she should have to fight again. We have now to follow the second phase of the struggle, up to the culmination of that antagonism between Dorian and Ionian, of which the Greeks of this period never lost sight.

The Prelude of the War

The incidents which led up to the 'Peloponnesian War' are connected with two Corinthian colonies, Corcyra and Potidaea: Corcyra which had always been an unfilial daughter; Potidaea which, though maintaining friendly relations with Corinth, had become a member of the Athenian Confederacy.

(1) One of those party struggles in an insignificant city, which in Greece were often the occasion of wars between great states, had taken place in Epidamnus, a colony of Corcyra. The people, harassed by the banished nobles and their barbarian allies, asked help from their mother-city. Corcyra refused, and Epidamnus turned to Corinth. The Corinthians sent troops and a number of new colonists. The Corcyraeans, highly resenting this interference, demanded their dismissal and, when the demand was refused, blockaded the isthmus of Epidamnus. Corinth then made preparations for an expedition against Corcyra; and Corcyra in alarm sent envoys to Corinth, proposing to refer the matter for arbitration to such Peloponnesian states as both should agree upon. But the Corinthians refused the arbitration and sent a squadron of 75 ships with 2000 hoplites against the Corcyraeans. The powerful navy of Corcyra consisted of 120 ships, of which 40 were besieging Epidamnus. With the remaining 80 they won a complete victory over the Corinthians outside the Ambracian gulf and on the same day Epidamnus surrendered. During the rest of the year Corcyra had command of the Ionian sea and her triremes sailed about damaging the allies of Corinth.

But Corinth began to prepare for a greater effort against her powerful and detested colony. The work of preparation went on for two years. The report of the ships she was building and the crews she was hiring frightened Corcyra. For, while Corinth had the Peloponnesian league at her back, Corcyra had no allies, and belonged neither to the Athenian nor to the Spartan league. It was her obvious policy to seek a connection with Athens, and she determined to do so. The Corinthians, hearing of this intention, tried to thwart it, for they had good reason to fear a combination of the Athenian with the Corcyraean navy. The envoys of Corcyra and Corinth appeared together before the Assembly of Athens. The arguments which Thucydides has put into their mouths express clearly the bearings of the situation and the importance of the decision for Athens. The main argument for accepting the proffered alliance of Corcyra depends on the assumption that war is imminent. 'The Lacedaemonians, fearing the growth of your empire, are eager to take up arms, and the Corinthians, who are your enemies, are all-powerful with them. They begin with us, but they will go on to you, that we may not stand united against them in the bond of a common enmity. And it is our business to strike first, and to forestall their designs instead of waiting to counteract them.' On this assumption, the alliance of Corcyra offers great advantages. It lies conveniently on the route to Sicily, and it possesses one of the only three considerable navies in Greece. 'If the Corinthians get hold of our fleet, and you allow the two to become one, you will have to fight against the united navies of Corcyra and the Peloponnese. But if you make us your allies, you will have our navy in addition to your own ranged at your side in the impending conflict.' The reply of the Corinthian ambassadors was weak. Their appeal to certain past services that Corinth had rendered to Athens could hardly have much effect, for there was nothing but jealousy between the two cities. They might deprecate, but they could not disprove, the notion that Athens would soon have a war with the Peloponnese on her hands. And as for justice, Corcyra could make as plausible a case as Corinth. The most cogent argument for Corinth was that if Athens allied herself with Corcyra she would take a step which if not in itself violating the Thirty Years' Peace would necessarily involve a violation of it.

Defensive alliance of Athens with Corcyra

After two debates the Assembly agreed to an alliance with Corcyra, but of a defensive kind. Athens was only to give armed help in case Corcyra itself were threatened. By this decision she avoided a direct violation of the treaty. Ten ships were sent to Corcyra with orders not to fight unless Corcyra or some of the places belonging to it were attacked.[1] A great and tumultuous naval engagement ensued near the islet of Sybota, between Leucimme, the south-eastern promontory of Corcyra, and the Thesprotian mainland. A Corcyraean fleet of 110 ships was ranged against a Corinthian of 150—the outcome of two years of preparation. The right wing of the Corcyraeans was worsted, and the ten Athenian ships, which had held aloof at first, interfered to prevent its total discomfiture. In the evening the sudden sight of 20 new Athenian ships on the horizon caused the Corinthians to retreat, and the next day they declined battle. This seemed an admission of defeat and justified the Corcyraeans in raising a trophy; but the Corinthians also

Battle of Sybota, 433 B.C. (late summer)

raised a trophy, for they had come off best in the battle. They returned home then and on their way captured Anactorion, which Corcyra and Corinth held in common. Corinth treated the Corcyraeans who had been taken captive in the battle with great consideration. Most of them were men of importance and it was hoped that through them Corcyra might ultimately be won over to friendship with Corinth. It will be seen afterwards that the hope was not ill-founded.

(2) The breach with Corinth forced Athens to look to the security of her interests in the Chalcidic peninsula, where Corinth had a great deal of influence. The city of Potidaea, which occupies and guards the isthmus of Pallene, was a tributary ally of Athens but received its annual magistrates from its mother-city, Corinth. Immediately after the battle of Sybota, Athens required the Potidaeans to raze the city-walls on the south side where they were not needed for protection against Macedonia, and to abandon the system of Corinthian magistrates. The Potidaeans refused; they were supported by the promise of Sparta to invade Attica, in case Potidaea were attacked by Athens. But the situation was complicated by the policy of the Macedonian king, Perdiccas, who had been formerly the friend of Athens but was now her adversary, because she had befriended his brothers who were leagued against him. He conceived and organised a general revolt of Chalcidice against Athens and even persuaded some of the Chalcidians to pull down their cities on the coast and concentrate themselves in the strong inland town of Olynthus. The Bottiaeans also, centred on Spartolus, joined the rebels. Thus the revolt of Potidaea, while it has its special causes in connection with the enmity of Athens and Corinth, under another aspect forms part of a general movement in that quarter against the Athenian dominion.

Revolt of Potidaea from Athens

(433 B.C.)

432 B.C.

The Athenians began operations in Macedonia, but soon advanced against Potidaea and gained an advantage over the Corinthian general, Aristeus, who had arrived with some Peloponnesian forces. The Athenians then invested the city. So far the Corinthians had acted alone. Now, seeing the danger of Potidaea, they took active steps to incite the Lacedaemonians to declare war against Athens.

Battle of Potidaea, c. Sept. 432 B.C.

Pericles knew that war was coming, and he promptly struck—not with sword or spear, but with a more cruel and deadly weapon. Megara had assisted Corinth at the battle of Sybota; the Athenians passed a measure excluding the Megarians from the Athenian

Megarian Decree, 432 B.C., autumn

Agora and the ports of their empire. The decree spelt economic ruin to Megara, and Megara was an important member of the Peloponnesian league; the Athenian statesman knew how to strike.[2] The comic poet sang how

> The Olympian Pericles in wrath
> Fulmined o'er Greece and set her in a broil
> With statutes worded like a drinking catch:
>   No Megarian on land
>   Nor in market shall stand
> Nor sail on the sea nor set foot on the strand.

First Assembly at Sparta

The allies appeared at Sparta and brought formal charges against Athens of having broken the Thirty Years' Peace and committed various acts of injustice. The most violent speech came from the Corinthians who attacked the basic nature of Athenian imperialism and demanded action rather than words. They were supported by the Megarians who complained bitterly about the decree against them. Behind the scenes the Aeginetans, who dared not come out into the open, did what they could to bring matters to a head, claiming that the independence guaranteed to them by the Thirty Years' Peace was being violated by Athens.[3] Some Athenian envoys who were at Sparta—ostensibly for other business—were given an opportunity of replying. But arguments and recriminations were superfluous; it did not matter in the least whether Athens could defend this transaction or Corinth could make good that charge. For in the case of an inevitable war the causes openly alleged seldom correspond with the motives which really govern. It was not the Corcyraean incidents, or the siege of Potidaea, or the Megarian decree that caused the Peloponnesian War, though jointly they hastened its outbreak; it was the fear and jealousy of the Athenian power. The only question was whether it was the right hour to engage in that unavoidable struggle. The Spartan king, Archidamus, advised delay. 'Do not take up arms yet. War is not an affair of arms, but of money which gives to arms their use and which is needed above all things when a continental is fighting against a maritime power. Let us find money first, and then we may safely allow our minds to be excited by the speeches of our allies.' But the ephors were in favour of war. Sthenelaidas, in a short and pointed speech, put the question, not, Shall we declare war? but Has the treaty been broken and are the Athenians in the wrong? It was decided that the Athenians were in the wrong, and this decision necessarily led to a

declaration of war. Sparta's allies, however, were not committed to war by the decision of the Spartan Assembly; to ensure their support a majority vote at a formal meeting of the members of the Peloponnesian league was needed. Sparta at this point consulted Delphi and having been assured that Apollo supported their cause they summoned their allies to Sparta. At this meeting the Corinthians spoke with considerably more restraint, for to win the vote they had to convince the small states of the interior, who were not directly concerned, that war was in their interest. Two arguments were therefore emphasised: that the states of the interior depended on Corinth and other coastal towns to secure the imports they needed from outside the Peloponnese and to market their exports; and that the resources of the Peloponnesians guaranteed victory. A majority voted for war.

Second Assembly

Thucydides chose the setting well for his brilliant contrast between the characters and spirits and aims of the two great protagonists who now prepare to stand face to face on the stage of Hellenic history. He makes the Corinthian envoys, at the first assembly in Sparta, the spokesmen of his comparison. 'You have never considered, O Lacedaemonians, what manner of men are these Athenians with whom you will have to fight, and how utterly unlike yourselves. They are revolutionary, equally quick in the conception and in the execution of every new plan; while you are conservative—careful only to keep what you have, originating nothing, and not acting even when action is most necessary. They are bold beyond their strength; they run risks which prudence would condemn; and in the midst of misfortune they are full of hope. Whereas it is your nature, though strong, to act feebly; when your plans are most prudent, to distrust them; and when calamities come upon you, to think that you will never be delivered from them. They are impetuous and you are dilatory; they are always abroad, and you are always at home. For they hope to gain something by leaving their homes; but you are afraid that any new enterprise may imperil what you have already. When conquerors, they pursue their victory to the utmost; when defeated, they fall back the least. Their bodies they devote to the country, as though they belonged to other men; their true self is their mind, which is most truly their own when employed in her service. When they do not carry out an intention which they have formed, they seem to have sustained a personal bereavement; when an enterprise succeeds

The contrast, drawn by Thucydides, between the Athenians and Lacedaemonians

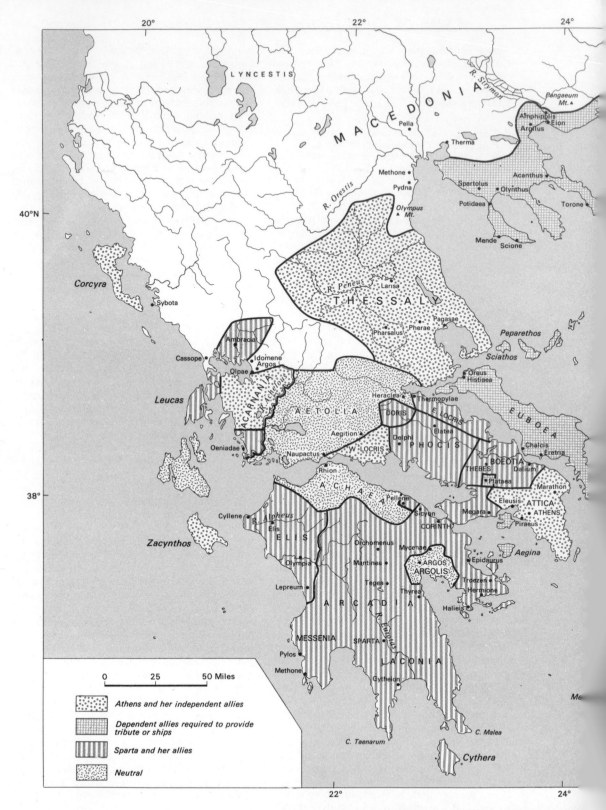

21. THE ALLIANCES AT THE BEGINNING OF

The map legend reads:

- Athens and her independent allies
- Dependent allies required to provide tribute or ships
- Sparta and her allies
- Neutral

0   25   50 Miles

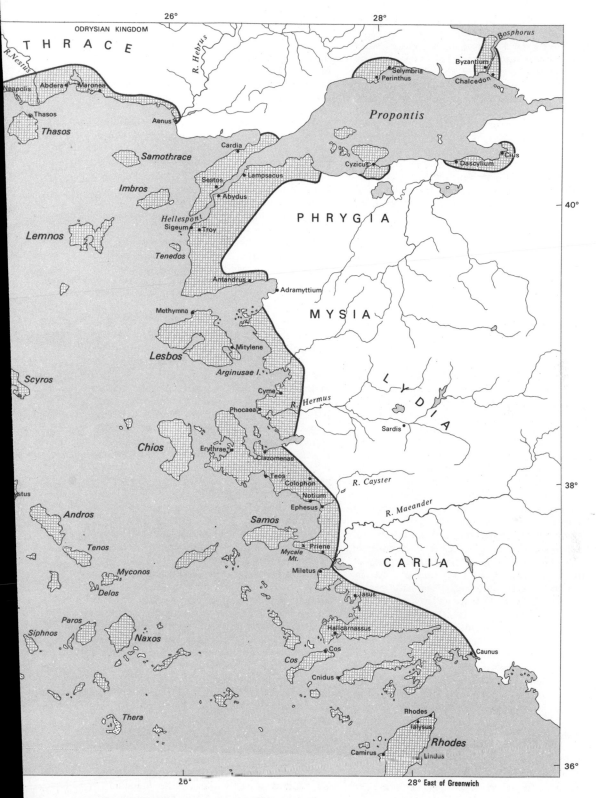

ODRYSIAN KINGDOM

T H R A C E

R. Nestus

Bosphorus

Neapolis Abdera Maronea

Byzantium

•Selymbria

Perinthus

Chalcedon

Propontis

Thasos

Thasos

Aenus

•Cius

Cardia

Samothrace

Cyzicus

•Dascylium

Imbros

Sestos•

•Lampsacus

•Abydus

    P H R Y G I A

40°

Hellespont

Sigeum• •Troy

Lemnos

Tenedos

•Antandrus

•Adramyttium

Methymna•   M Y S I A

Scyros

Lesbos •Mitylene

L Y D I A

Arginusae I.

Cyme•

Phocaea• *R. Hermus*

Chios Erythrae•

•Sardis

Clazomenae•

ystus •Teos *R. Cayster* 38°

Colophon•

•Notium

Ephesus• *R. Maeander*

Andros *Samos*

Tenos •Priene

Mycale C A R I A

Myconos Mt.

Delos Miletus•

•Jasus

Paros

Siphnos *Naxos* Halicarnassus•

•Cos

Cos

Cnidus•

•Caunus

Thera Rhodes•

•Ialysus

Rhodes

Camirus• •Lindus

36°

LOPONNESIAN WAR (see note, page 555)

they have gained a mere instalment of what is to come; but if they fail, they at once conceive new hopes and so fill up the void. With them alone to hope is to have, for they lose not a moment in the execution of an idea. This is the lifelong task, full of danger and toil, which they are always imposing upon themselves. None enjoy their good things less, because they are always seeking for more. To do their duty is their only holiday, and they deem the quiet of inaction to be as disagreeable as the most tiresome business. If a man should say of them, in a word, that they were born neither to have peace themselves nor to allow peace to other men, he would simply speak the truth.'

Diplomatic futilities

On the present occasion, however, the Athenians did not give an example of that promptness in action which is contrasted in this passage with the dilatory habits of the Spartans; we shall presently see why. It was the object of Sparta to gain time; accordingly she sent embassies to Athens with trivial demands. She required the Athenians to drive out the 'curse of the goddess', which rested on the family of the Alcmaeonidae. This was a raking up of history, two centuries old—the episode of Cylon's conspiracy; the point of it lay in the fact that Pericles, on his mother's side, belonged to the accursed family. Athens replied by equally trivial demands—the

(Above, p. 200)

purification of the curse of Athena of the Brazen House, and of the curse of Taenarus, where some Helots had been murdered in the temple of Poseidon. These diplomatic gestures, which served the purpose of Sparta by gaining time, were followed by an ultimatum, in the sense that Athens might still have peace if she restored the independence of the Hellenes. There was a peace party at Athens, but Pericles carried the day. 'Let us send the ambassadors away,' he said, 'giving them this answer: That we will not exclude the Megarians from our market and harbours, if the Lacedaemonians will not exclude foreigners, whether ourselves or our allies, from Sparta; for the treaty no more forbids the one than the other. That we will concede independence to the cities, if they were independent when we made the treaty, and as soon as the Lacedaemonians allow their subject states to be governed as they choose, not for the interest of Lacedaemon but for their own. Also that we are willing to offer arbitration according to the treaty. And that we do not want to begin the war, but intend to defend ourselves if attacked. This answer will be just and befits the dignity of the city.

We must be aware, however, that the war will come; and the more willing we are to accept the situation, the less ready will our enemies be to lay hands upon us.' Pericles was in no haste to draw the sword; he had delivered a blow already by the Megarian decree.

The peoples of Greece were parted as follows on the sides of the two chief antagonists. Sparta commanded the whole Peloponnese, except her old enemy Argos and Achaea, where Pellene alone was on the Peloponnesian side; she commanded the Isthmus, for she had both Corinth and Megara; in northern Greece she had Boeotia, Phocis, and Locris; in western Greece, Ambracia, Anactorion, and the island of Leucas. In western Greece, Athens was supported by the Acarnanians, Corcyra, and Zacynthus, as well as the Messenians of Naupactus; in central Greece she had Plataea; and these were her only allies beyond her confederacy.

Resources of Athens and the Peloponnesians

Athens' strength lay in her fleet, large and well trained. In addition to the ships of Lesbos and Chios and the possible help from Corcyra she had 300 triremes of her own. Her fleet had a long tradition of active fighting and had maintained annual patrols in the Aegean even in peace. The nucleus of her crews was Athenian but the numbers needed were too large to be supplied from the citizen body alone, and a considerable proportion of her rowers were recruited in the islands, where men who had few chances to earn a livelihood at home were glad to earn good pay in a service with great traditions. On the Peloponnesian side the Corinthians alone were a naval power and their failure at Sybota had emphasised their weakness. They had had little experience of fighting and their ships and crews were outclassed. On land, however, the Peloponnesians had an immense advantage. With their Boeotian allies they could put into the field at least 30,000 men without using reserves, and the Lacedaemonians were still the best hoplites in Greece. Against them the Athenians had a field force of 13,000 hoplites with 1200 cavalry, including mounted archers, and a reserve force, including metics, of 16,000.

Scarcely less important to Athens than her armed forces were her financial reserves.[4] More than 1200 talents had been spent on crushing the revolt of Samos, and it was clear that war with the Peloponnesians would involve heavier and more expensive commitments. Pericles well knew that the efficiency of a navy depended in large part on regular and high pay and that war could not be financed on emergency measures; he had therefore deliberately aimed at maintaining a reserve for the inevitable clash. As war drew near special measures were taken to restrict expenditure. The building programme on the Acropolis was halted; further expenditure beyond a low annual limit from the reserve was made subject to a special vote of sanction in the Assembly. The treasures in money and kind of the other gods in the city below the Acropolis and throughout Attica had been concentrated on the Acropolis, where they would be safe from invading Peloponnesians and readily available if the state needed to use them. After the Peace of Callias the principle had been established that the tribute could be used for Athenian purposes, and it was the accumulation of tribute that formed the bulk of the reserve. It had been given to the safe keeping of Athena and is described in documents as 'the sacred moneys of Athena'. Spending from this reserve for war purposes involved loans from the goddess; a strict record had to be kept and the interest on the debts was carefully calculated. In this reserve when war broke out there were some 6000 talents, and Athens could expect an annual income from home sources and the empire of some 1000 talents. From the experience of the Samian revolt, Athens in 431 seemed likely to be able to finance war without resorting to extreme measures.

The Peloponnesians were in a much weaker position. They had no financial reserves and no common war chest. Their organisation was well adapted to land operations but they lacked the essential financial basis for naval warfare. The Corinthians could talk lightly of attracting the allies from the Athenian crews by higher pay, but in their hearts they knew that these were empty words. Not until Persian subsidies were secured could the Peloponnesians keep large fleets for long periods at sea.

General View of the War. Thucydides

Perspective of the war of Athens with the Peloponnesians

The war on which we are now entering is a resumption, on a somewhat greater scale, of the war which was concluded by the Thirty Years' Peace. Here too the Corinthians are the most active instigators of the opposition to Athens. The Spartans are but half-hearted leaders, and have to be spurred by their allies. The war lasts ten years, and is concluded by the Peace of Nicias. But hostilities begin again and pass for a time to a new scene of warfare, the island of Sicily. This war ends with the

battle of Aegospotami, which decided the fate of the Athenian empire. Thus during fifty-five years Athens was contending for her empire with the Peloponnesians, and this conflict falls into three distinct wars: the first ending with the Thirty Years' Peace, the second with the Peace of Nicias, the third with the battle of Aegospotami. But while there is a break of thirteen years between the first war and the second, there is hardly any break between the second war and the third. Hence the second and the third, which have been united in the History of Thucydides, are generally grouped closely together and called by the common name of the 'Peloponnesian War'. This name is never used by Thucydides; but it shows how Athenian the sympathies of historians have always been. From the Peloponnesian point of view the conflict would be called the 'Attic War'.

Three periods: (1) 460–445 B.C.; (2) 431–421; (3) 420–404

It will not be amiss to repeat here what the true cause of the struggle was. Athens was resolved to maintain, in spite of Greece, her naval empire, and thus far she was responsible. But there is no reason to suppose that she had any design of seriously increasing her empire; and the idea of some modern historians that Pericles undertook the war in the hope of winning supremacy over all Hellas is contrary to the plain facts of the case.

This war has attained a celebrity in the world's history which, considering its scale and its consequences, may seem unmerited. A domestic war between small Greek states may be thought a slight matter indeed, compared with the struggle in which Greece was arrayed against the might of Persia. But the Peloponnesian war has had an advantage which has been granted to no other episode in the history of Hellas. It has been recorded by the first and the greatest of Greek critical historians. To read the book which Thucydides, the son of Olorus, has bequeathed to posterity is in itself a liberal education; a lesson in politics and history which is, as he aimed to make it, 'a possession for ever'. Only a few years can have separated the day on which Herodotus completed his work and the day on which Thucydides began his. But from the one to the other there is a sheer leap. When political events have passed through the brain of Herodotus, they come out as delightful stories. With the insatiable curiosity of an inquirer, he has little political insight; he has the instinct of a literary artist, his historical methods are rudimentary. The splendid work of Herodotus has more in common with the epic poets who went before him than the

The History of Thucydides

Contrast of Thucydides with Herodotus

historians who came after him. When he began to collect material for his history, the events of the Persian invasion were already encircled with a halo of legend, so that he had a subject thoroughly to his taste. It is a strange sensation to turn from the naïve, uncritical, entrancing storyteller of Halicarnassus to the grave historian of Athens. The first History, in the true sense of the word, sprang full-grown into life, like Athena from the brain of Zeus; and it is still without a rival. Severe in its detachment, written from a purely intellectual point of view, unencumbered with platitudes and moral judgements, cold and critical, but exhibiting the rarest powers of dramatic and narrative art, the work of Thucydides is at every point a contrast to the work of Herodotus. Mankind might well despair if the science of criticism had not advanced further since the days of Thucydides; and we are not surprised to find that when he deals, on the threshold of his work, with the earlier history of Greece, he fails to carry his sceptical treatment far enough and accepts some traditions which on his own principles he should have questioned. But the interval which divides Thucydides from his elder contemporary Herodotus is a whole heaven; the interval which divides Thucydides from a critic of our own day is small indeed. Reserved as he is, Thucydides cannot disguise that he was a democrat of the Periclean school; he makes no secret of his admiration for the political wisdom of Pericles.

It must be granted that the incidents of the war would lose something of their interest, that the whole episode would be shorn of much of its dignity and eminence, if Thucydides had not deigned to be its historian. But it was not a slight or unworthy theme. It is the story of the decline and fall of the Athenian empire, and at this period Athens is the centre of ecumenical history. The importance of the war is not impaired by the smallness of the states which were involved in it. For in these small states lived those political ideas and institutions which concerned the future development of mankind far more than any movements in barbarous kingdoms, however great their territory.

The war of ten years, which now began, may seem at first sight to have consisted of a number of disconnected and haphazard incidents. But both the Athenians and the Peloponnesians had definite objects in view. Their plans were determined by the nature of their own resources and by the geography of the enemy's territories.

Key to the operations of the war

The key to the war is the fundamental fact that it was waged between a power which was mainly continental and a power which was mainly maritime. From the nature of the case, the land-power is obliged to direct its attacks chiefly on the continental possessions of the sea-power, while the sea-power has to confine itself to attacking the maritime possessions of the land-power. It follows that the small land army of the sea-power, and the small fleet of the land-power, are each mainly occupied with the work of defence, and are seldom free to act on the offensive. Hence the maritime possessions of the maritime power and the inland possessions of the continental power are not generally the scene of warfare. These considerations simplify the war. The points at which the Peloponnesians can attack Athens with their land forces are Attica itself and Thrace. Accordingly Attica is invaded almost every year, and there is constant warfare in Thrace; but the war is hardly ever carried into the Aegean or to the Asiatic coast, except in consequence of some special circumstance, such as the revolt of an Athenian ally. On the other hand the offensive operations of Athens are mainly in the west of Greece, about the islands of the Ionian sea and near the mouth of the Corinthian gulf. That was the region where they had the best prospect, by their naval superiority, of detaching members from the Peloponnesian alliance. Thrace, Attica, and the seas of western Greece are therefore the chief and constant scenes of the war. There are episodes elsewhere, but they are to some extent accidental.

Pericles had completely abandoned the policy of continental enterprise which had led up to the Thirty Years' Peace. That enterprise had been a departure from the policy, initiated by Themistocles, of concentrating all the energy of Athens on the development of her naval power. Pericles returned to this policy without reserve, and he appears, at the outbreak of the war, under the inspiration of the Salaminian spirit. Athens is now to show the same extreme independence of her land, the same utter confidence in her ships, which she had shown when the Mede approached her borders. 'Let us give up lands and houses,' said Pericles, 'but keep a watch over the city and the sea. We should not under any irritation at the loss of our property give battle to the Peloponnesians, who far outnumber us. Mourn not for houses or lands, but for men; men may give these, but these will not give men. If I thought that you would listen to me, I would say to you: Go yourselves and destroy them, and thereby prove to the Peloponnesians that none of these things will move you.' For 'such is the power which the empire of the sea gives'. This was the spirit in which Pericles undertook the war.

The policy of sacrificing Attica was neither rash nor perverse; it was only part of a well-considered system of strategy, for which Pericles has been severely blamed. His object was to wear out the enemy, not to attempt to subjugate or decisively defeat him. He was determined not to court a great battle, for which the land forces of Athens were manifestly insufficient: on land Boeotia alone was a match for her. He adopted the strategy of 'exhaustion', as it has been called—the strategy which consists largely in manoeuvring and considers the economy of one's own forces as solicitously as the damaging of the enemy; which will accept battle only under certain conditions; which is always on the watch for favourable opportunities, but avoids great risks. The more we reflect on the conditions of the struggle and the nature of the Athenian resources, the more fully will the plan of Pericles show itself as the strategy uniquely suitable to the circumstances. Nor will the criticism that he neglected the land defences of Attica, and the suggestion that he should have fortified the frontier against invasions, bear close examination. The whole Athenian land army would have been required to garrison both the Megarian and Boeotian frontiers, and there would have been no troops left for operations elsewhere. Nor would it have been easy for a citizen army to remain on duty, as would in this case have been necessary, for a large part of the year. It was quite in accord with the spirit of the patient strategy of Pericles that he refrained from the temptation of striking a blow at the enemy, when they had resolved on war but were not yet prepared. One effective blow he had indeed struck, the decree against Megara; to damage the enemy commercially was an essential part of his method. Within a few years this method would doubtless have been crowned with success and brought about a peace favourable to Athens, but for untoward events which he could not foresee.

The Theban Attack on Plataea

Theban night attack on Plataea (March 431 B.C.)

The declaration of war between the two great states of Greece was a signal to smaller states to profit by the situation for the gratification of their private enmities. On a dark moonless night, in the early spring, a band of 300 Thebans entered Plataea, invited and admitted by a small party in the city. Instead of at once attacking the chiefs of the party which supported the Athenian alliance, they took up their post in the Agora and made a proclamation, calling upon the Plataeans to join the Boeotian league. The Plataeans, as a people, with the exception of a few malcontents, were cordially attached to Athens; but they were surprised, and in the darkness of the night exaggerated the numbers of the Thebans. They acceded to the Theban demand, but in the course of the negotiation discovered how few the enemies were. Breaking down the party-walls between their houses, so as not to attract notice by moving in the streets, they concerted a plan of action. When all was arranged, they barricaded the streets leading to the Agora with waggons and then attacked the enemy before dawn. The Thebans were soon dispersed. They lost their way in the strange town and wandered about, pelted by women from the housetops, through narrow streets deep in mud, for heavy rain had fallen during the night. A few clambered up the city wall and cast themselves down on the other side. But the greater number rushed through the door of a large building, mistaking it for one of the town-gates, and were thus captured alive by the Plataeans. A few escaped who reached an unguarded gate and cut the wooden bolt with an axe which a woman gave them.

The 300 were only the vanguard of a large Theban force which was advancing slowly in the rain along the 8 miles of road which lay between Thebes and Plataea. They were delayed by the crossing of the swollen Asopus river, and they arrived too late. The Plataeans sent out a herald to them requiring them to do no injury to Plataean property outside the walls, if they valued the lives of the Theban prisoners. According to the Theban account, the Plataeans definitely promised to restore the prisoners, when the troops evacuated their territory. But the Plataeans afterwards denied this, and said that they merely promised (without the sanction of an oath) to restore the prisoners in case they came to an agreement after negotiation. It matters little. The Plataeans as soon as they had conveyed all their property into the city, put their prisoners to death, 180 in number. Even on their own showing they were clearly guilty of an act of bad faith, which is explained by the deep hatred existing between the two states. A message had been immediately sent to Athens. The Athenians seized all the Boeotians in Attica and sent a herald to Plataea bidding them not to injure their prisoners; but the herald found the Thebans dead. The Athenians

Theban prisoners executed

Athens supports Plataea

immediately set Plataea ready for a siege. They provisioned it with corn; removed the women, children, and old men; and sent a garrison of 80 Athenians.

The Theban attack on Plataea was a glaring violation of the Thirty Years' Peace, and it hastened the outbreak of the war. Greece was now in a state of intense excitement at the approaching struggle of the two leading cities; oracles abounded; and a recent earthquake in Delos was supposed to be significant. Public opinion was generally favourable to the Lacedaemonians, who seemed to be the champions of liberty against a tyrannical city.

Both sides meditated enlisting the aid of Persia. The Lacedaemonians negotiated with the states of Italy and Sicily, for the purpose of obtaining a large navy to crush the Athenians. But this scheme also fell through; the cities of the west were too busy with their own political interests to send ships and money to old Greece. Athens indeed had also cast her eyes westward, and when she embraced the alliance of Corcyra, she seems to have been forming connections with Sicily. At all events, in the same year ambassadors of Rhegion and Leontini appeared together at Athens, and at the same meeting of the Assembly alliances were renewed with both cities on the proposal of Callias.[5] The object of Chalcidian Leontini was doubtless to gain support against Corinthian Syracuse, while the motive of Rhegion may have been connected with the affairs of Thurii, the rebellious daughter of Athens herself. But these alliances led to no action of Athens in the west for six years to come.

Treaties of Athens with Leontini and with Rhegion, 433 B.C.

The Plague

First invasion of Attica, 431 B.C.

When the corn was ripe, in the last days of May, king Archidamus with two-thirds of the Peloponnesian army invaded Attica. From the Isthmus he had sent on Melesippus to Athens, if even at the last hour the Athenians might yield. But Pericles had persuaded them to receive no embassies, once the enemy were in the field; the envoy had to leave the borders of Attica before the sun set. And Thucydides, after the manner of Herodotus, marks the formal commencement of the war by repeating the impressive words which Melesippus uttered as he stood on the frontier: 'This day will be the beginning of great sorrows to the Greeks.' Archidamus then laid siege to Oenoe, a fortress on Mount Cithaeron, but failed to take it, and his delay gave the Athenians time to complete their preparations. They brought into the city

their families and their goods, while their flocks and herds were removed to the island of Euboea. The influx of the population into the city caused terrible crowding. A few had the homes of their friends, but the majority improvised shelters in the vacant spaces and housed themselves, as the peace-party bitterly said, in barrels and vultures' nests. They seized temples and shrines, and even the ancient enclosure of the Pelargicon on the north-west of the Acropolis was occupied, though its occupation was deprecated by a dark oracle. Subsequently the crowding was relieved when the Piraeus and the space between the Long Walls were utilised.

Archidamus first ravaged the plain of Eleusis and Thria. He then crossed into the Cephisian plain by the pass between Mounts Aegaleos and Parnes, and halted under Parnes in the deme of Acharnae, whence he could see, in the distance, the Acropolis of Athens. The proximity of the invaders caused great excitement in Athens and roused furious opposition to Pericles, who would not allow the troops to go forth against them—except a few flying columns of horse in the immediate neighbourhood of the city. Pericles had been afraid that Archidamus, who was his personal friend, might spare his property, either from friendship or policy; so he took the precaution of declaring to his fellow-citizens that he would give his lands to the people, if they were left unravaged. The invader presently advanced northward, between Parnes and Pentelicus, to Decelea, and proceeded through the territory of Oropus to Boeotia.

The Athenians meanwhile had been operating by sea. They had sent 100 ships round the Peloponnese.[6] An attack on Methone, on the Messenian coast, failed; the place was saved by a daring Spartan officer, Brasidas, who by this exploit began a distinguished career. But the fleet was more successful further north. The important island of Cephallenia was won over, and some towns on the Acarnanian coast were taken. Measures were also adopted for the protection of Euboea against the Locrians of the opposite mainland. The Epicnemidian town of Thronion was captured, and the uninhabited island of Atalanta, over against Opus, was made a guard station. More important was the drastic measure which Athens adopted against her subjects and former rivals, the Dorians of Aegina. She felt that they were not to be trusted, and the security of her positions in the Saronic gulf was of the first importance. So she drove out the Aeginetans and settled the island with a cleruchy of her

Athens wins Cephallenia and Sollion Locrian expedition

End of the Aeginetans

Aegina becomes part of Attica

own citizens. Aegina thus became, like Salamis, annexed to Attica. Just as the Messenian exiles had been befriended by Athens and given a new home, so the Aeginetan exiles were now befriended by Sparta and were settled in the region of Thyreatis, in the north of Laconia. Thyreatis was the Lacedaemonian answer to Naupactus.

When Archidamus left Attica, Pericles provided for emergencies of the future by setting aside a reserve fund of money, and a reserve armament of ships. There had been as much as 9700 talents in the treasury, but the expenses of the buildings on the Acropolis and of the war at Potidaea had reduced this to 6000.[7] It was now decreed that 1000 talents of this amount should be reserved, not to be touched unless the enemy were to attack Athens by sea, and that every year 100 triremes should be set apart, with the same object.

Funeral of those slain in the war

In winter the Athenians, following an old custom, celebrated the public burial of those who had fallen in the war. The bones were laid in ten cypress coffins and were buried outside the walls in the Ceramicus. An empty bed, covered with a pall, was carried, for those whose bodies were missing. Pericles pronounced the funeral Panegyric. It has not been preserved, but the spirit and general argument of it have been reproduced in the oration which Thucydides, who must have been one of the audience, has put in his mouth.

The ideal Athens adumbrated by Pericles

'There is no exclusiveness,' he said, 'in our public life, and in our private intercourse. We are not suspicious of one another, nor angry with our neighbour if he does what he likes; we do not put on sour looks at him which, though harmless, are not pleasant. And we have not forgotten to provide for our weary spirits many relaxations from toil; we have regular games and sacrifices throughout the year; at home the style of our life is refined; and the delight which we daily feel in all these things helps to banish melancholy. Because of the greatness of our city the fruits of the whole earth flow in upon us; so that we enjoy the goods of other countries as freely as of our own.

'Then again our military training is in many respects superior to that of our adversaries. Our city is thrown open to the world, and we never expel a foreigner or prevent him from seeing or learning anything, of which the secret if revealed to an enemy might profit him. We rely not upon management or trickery, but upon our own hearts and hands. And in the matter of education, whereas they from early youth are always undergoing laborious exercises which are to make them brave, we live at ease, and yet are equally ready to face the perils which they face.

'If we prefer to meet danger with a light heart but without laborious training, and with a courage which is gained by habit and not enforced by law, are we not greatly the gainers? For we do not anticipate the pain, although, when the hour comes, we can be as brave as those who never allow themselves to rest; and thus too our city is equally admirable in peace and in war. For we are lovers of the beautiful, yet simple in our tastes, and we cultivate the mind without loss of manliness. Wealth we employ, not for talk and ostentation, but when there is a real use for it. To avow poverty with us is no disgrace; the true disgrace is in doing nothing to avoid it. An Athenian citizen does not neglect the state because he takes care of his own household; and even those of us who are engaged in business have a very fair idea of politics. We alone regard a man who takes no interest in public affairs, not as a harmless, but as a useless character; and if few of us are originators, we are all sound judges of a policy. The great impediment to action is, in our opinion, not discussion, but the want of that knowledge which is gained by discussion preparatory to action. For we have a peculiar power of thinking before we act and of acting too, whereas other men are courageous from ignorance but hesitate upon reflection.'

Then the speaker goes on to describe Athens as the centre of Hellenic culture and to claim that 'the individual Athenian in his own person seems to have the power of adapting himself to the most varied forms of action with the utmost versatility and grace'. And, he continues, 'we shall assuredly not be without witnesses; there are mighty monuments of our power which will make us the wonder of this and of succeeding ages; we shall not need the praises of Homer or any other panegyrist whose poetry may please for the moment, although his representation of the facts will not bear the light of day. For we have compelled every land and every sea to open a path for our valour, and have everywhere planted eternal memorials of our friendship and of our enmity. Such is the city for whose sake these men nobly fought and died; they could not bear the thought that she might be taken from them; and every one of us who survives should gladly toil on her behalf. I would have you day by day fix your eyes upon the greatness of Athens, until you become filled with the love of her; and when you are impressed by the spectacle of her glory, reflect that this empire has been acquired by men who knew their duty and had the courage to do it, who in the hour of conflict had the fear of dishonour always present to them, and who, if ever they failed in an enterprise, would not allow their virtues to be lost to their country, but freely gave their lives to her as the fairest offering which they could present at her feast. The sacrifice which they collectively made was individually repaid to them; for they received again and again each one for himself a praise which grows not old and the noblest of all sepulchres—I speak not of that in which their remains are laid, but of that in which their glory survives and is proclaimed always and on every fitting occasion both in word and deed. For the whole earth is the sepulchre of famous men; not only are they commemorated by columns and inscriptions in

their own country, but in foreign lands there dwells also an unwritten memorial of them, graven not on stone but in the hearts of men. Make them your examples.'

We are reminded of an earlier monument from the middle of the century. A beautiful relief, found on the Acropolis, shows the helmeted Athena, leaning on her spear, with downcast head, and gazing gravely at a slab of stone. It is an attractive interpretation that she is sadly engaged in reading the names of citizens who had recently fallen in defence of her city, perhaps in the First Peloponnesian War.

The 'Mourning Athena'

Next year the Peloponnesians again invaded Attica, and extended their devastations to the south of the peninsula as far as Laurion. But the Athenians concerned themselves less with this invasion; they had to contend with a more awful enemy within the walls of their city. The Plague had broken out. Thucydides, who was stricken down himself, gives a terrible account of its ravages and the demoralisation which it produced in Athens. The art of medicine was in its first infancy, and the inexperienced physicians were unable to treat the unknown virulent disease, which defied every remedy and was aggravated by the overcrowding, in the heat of summer. The dead lay unburied, the temples were full of corpses; and the funeral customs were forgotten or violated. Dying wretches were gathered about every fountain, seeking to relieve their unquenchable thirst. Men remembered an old oracle which said that 'a Dorian war will come and a plague therewith'. But the Greek for plague (*loimós*) was hardly distinguishable from the Greek for famine (*limós*)—at the present day they are identical in sound; and people were not quite sure which was the true word. Naturally the verse was now quoted with *loimos*; but, says Thucydides, in case there comes another Dorian war and it is accompanied by a famine, the oracle will be quoted with *limos*.

430 B.C., Invasion of Attica

The Great Plague

Oracle: λοιμός or λιμός?

The same historian—who has given of this pestilence a vivid description, unequalled by later narrators of similar scourges, Procopius, Boccaccio, Defoe—declares that the plague originated in Ethiopia, spread through Egypt over the Persian empire, and then reached the Aegean. But it is remarkable that a plague raged at the same time in the still obscure city of central Italy which was afterwards to become the mistress of Greece. It has been guessed with some plausibility that the infection which reached both Athens and Rome had travelled along the trade-routes from Carthage.

Origin of the plague

10.1 The mourning Athena

Effect of
the plague
on the
Athenian
population

The Peloponnese almost entirely escaped. In Athens the havoc of the pestilence permanently reduced the population. The total number of Athenian citizens (of both sexes and all ages) was about 140,000 in the first quarter of the fifth century. Prosperity had raised it to 172,000 by the beginning of the war; but the plague brought it down below the old level which it never reached again.[8]

Sea opera-
tions of
Athenians

As in the year before, an Athenian fleet attacked the Peloponnese, but this time it was the coasts of Argolis—Epidaurus, Troezen, Hermione, Halieis. The armament was large, 4000 spearmen and 300 horse; it was under the command of Pericles; and it aimed at the capture of Epidaurus, while the Epidaurian troops were absent with their allies in Attica. The attempt miscarried, we know not why; and it is hard to forgive our historian for omitting all the details of this ambitious enterprise, which would have been, if it had succeeded, one of the most important exploits of the war. For Epidaurus occupied an invaluable strategic position. It would have been a useful base for raiding the territory of Corinth and Megara; it would have threatened Peloponnesian armies advancing into Attica; and it might have served as a tempting bait to Argos. For Epidaurus was part of the heritage of Temenus, and its independence was an index of Argive weakness. Should neutral Argos rejoin her old ally the balance of power would be decisively shifted in Athens' favour.

At the end of the summer hostilities broke out in the west of Greece. Before the war the inhabitants of Amphilochian Argos, driven out by the Ambraciots, had, with their allies the Acarnanians, appealed for help to Athens. Athens had sent Phormio with 30 ships to restore the position.[9] The Ambraciots were sold into slavery and the city restored to Amphilochians and Acarnanians, who became grateful allies. Now, taking advantage of the general unsettlement, the Ambraciots tried to recover the lost ground, but though they overran the countryside they could not take the city. A show of force by Athens was needed and Phormio was sent with 20 ships to hold guard at Naupactus. From this station he could watch the north-west and guard the entrance to the Crisaean Gulf.

Surrender
of
Potidaea

·In Thrace meanwhile the siege of Potidaea had been prosecuted throughout the year. The inhabitants had been reduced to such straits that they even tasted human flesh, and in the winter they capitulated. The terms were that the Potidaeans and the foreign soldiers were to leave the city, the men with one garment, the women with two, and a sum of money was to be allowed them. Athens soon afterwards colonised the place. The siege had cost 2000 talents.

Meanwhile the Athenians had been cast into such despair by the plague that they made overtures for peace to Sparta. Their overtures were rejected, and they turned the fury of their disappointment upon Pericles, who had returned unsuccessful from Epidaurus. He was suspended from the post of *strategos* to which he had been elected in the spring and was fined. But soon the mood of the people changed again and he was reinstated; he was in truth indispensable. All the courage, all the patience, all the eloquence of the great statesman were demanded at this crisis. He had to convince Athens that the privileges of her imperial position involved hardships and toils, and that it was dangerous for her to draw back. The position of the imperialist is always vulnerable to assaults on grounds of morality, and the peace party at Athens could make a plausible case against the policy of Pericles. But the imperial instinct of the people responded, in spite of temporary reactions, to his call. Athens was not destined to be guided by him much longer. He had lost his two legitimate sons in the plague, and he died about a year later. In his last years he had been afflicted by the indirect attacks of his enemies. These attacks began with a charge against Phidias, who had worked closely with Pericles on the Parthenon, of mishandling the money allocated for his grand chryselephantine statue of Athena. On this charge he was acquitted, but he was apparently found guilty of sacrilege for inserting portrait heads of himself and Pericles in the *Battle against the Amazons* on Athena's shield. He is said by Plutarch to have died in prison at Athens, but if, as is generally held, his trial was in 438/7, the year in which his cult statue was dedicated, Plutarch must be ignored, for it is now certain that Phidias worked at Olympia on his cult statue of Zeus after he had completed work on his Athena. The next to suffer was Anaxagoras, who had played a considerable part in the intellectual development of Pericles. He was prosecuted under a decree brought forward by Diopeithes, a champion of religious orthodoxy, that anyone who refused to believe in the supernatural and offered instruction about the heavenly bodies should be liable to impeachment. Anaxagoras, against whom the· decree was clearly directed, had to leave Athens and withdrew to Lampsacus where he left a flourishing school of philosophy. Even more

Pericles
deposed
from office
of general,

Death of
Pericles
(autumn
429 B.C.).
Attacks
upon him.
(1) Trial
of Phidias.
(2) Trial of
Anax-
agoras.
(3) Trial of
Aspasia,
the mis-
tress of
Pericles.
The
younger
Pericles
legitimised

personal was the attack against Aspasia with whom Pericles had lived for some fifteen years. She was charged with impiety but the pleading of Pericles procured her acquittal, and in the last year of his life the people passed a decree to legitimise her son. The latest words of Pericles express what to the student of the history of civilisation is an important feature of his character—his humanity. 'No Athenian ever put on black for an act of mine.'[10]

The Siege and Capture of Plataea

Third year of the war, 429 B.C.

In the next summer Archidamus was induced by the Thebans, instead of invading Attica, to march across Cithaeron and lay siege to Plataea. Like Elis itself, the Plataean land was sacred—in memory of the great deliverance of Hellas which had been wrought there; and the Spartan king, when he set foot upon it, called the gods to witness that the Plataeans had first done wrong. He proposed to the Plataeans that they should evacuate their territory until the end of the war; they might count their trees and their possessions, and all should then be restored to them intact. Having consulted Athens, which promised to protect them, the Plataeans refused, and Archidamus began the siege. The Athenians, however, were true to the policy of avoiding continental warfare, and notwithstanding their promises sent no help. Plataea was a very important position for the Peloponnesians to secure. It commanded the road from Megara to Thebes, by which communications between the Peloponnese and Boeotia could be maintained most easily without entering Attica.

Site of Plataea

The visitor to Plataea must not suppose that the city which Archidamus besieged extended over the entire ground plan which now meets his eye. For he sees the circuit of the city as it existed a century later, occupying the whole surface of the low triangular plateau on which the town stood. The Plataea of Archidamus corresponds probably to the southern and higher part of the space occupied by the later town. The wall of the older Plataea cannot have been much more than a mile long, for the small garrison—400 Plataeans and 80 Athenians—could never have maintained a longer line of defence in a place where nature had done almost nothing to assist them.

The mound

Having surrounded the city with a palisade to prevent any one from getting out, Archidamus employed his army in building a mound against the southern wall. They worked for seventy days and seventy nights. The Plataeans endeavoured to counteract this by raising the height of their own wall, opposite the mound, by a structure of mud-bricks in a wooden frame. They protected the workmen by screens of hide against burning arrows. But as the mound rose higher and higher a new device was tried. They made a hole in the wall and drew out the earth from the mound. The Peloponnesians met this device by putting into the gap clay packed in baskets of reed; this could not be drawn away quickly like the loose earth. Another plan was then devised by the besieged. They dug a subterranean mine under the wall to some distance beneath the mound, and drew the earth away as they had done before. This effectually retarded the progress of the mound, for, though the besiegers were numerous, they had to carry the earth from a considerable distance. The Plataeans resorted to yet another device. From the two extremities of that portion of the wall which they had raised in height, they built an inner wall, in crescent shape, projecting inwards; so that if the outer wall were taken, the Peloponnesians would have all their labour over again. They also showed ingenuity in frustrating the battering-rams which the besiegers brought against the walls. They placed two poles on the top of the wall, projecting over it; to the ends of these poles they attached a huge beam by means of iron chains. When the engine approached, they let go the beam, which snapped off the head of the battering-ram. The besiegers then made an attempt to set the town on fire. They heaped up faggots along the wall close to the mound, and kindled them with brimstone and pitch. If the prevalent south wind had been blowing down the slopes of the mountain, nothing would have saved the Plataeans from the tremendous conflagration which ensued and rendered the wall unapproachable by the besiegers.

Stratagems of the besieged. (1) Raising of the wall. (2) Removing the earth through wall; (3) by a mine

(4) The inner wall

The battering-rams

The fire

When this device failed the Peloponnesians saw they would have to blockade Plataea. They built a wall of circumvallation, about 100 yards from the city, and dug two fosses, one inside and one outside this wall. Then Archidamus left part of his army to maintain the blockade during the winter. The blockaders, of whom about half were Boeotians, established a communication by means of fire signals with Thebes. At the end of another year, the Plataeans saw that they had no longer any hope of help from Athens, and their food was running short. They determined to make an attempt to escape.

The wall of the Peloponnesians looked like a single wall of immense thickness, but it

Blockade, autumn 429 to summer 427

Plan of escape. Winter (? Dec.) 428 B.C.

actually consisted of two walls, 16 feet apart. The middle space, which served as quarters for the garrison, was roofed over, and guard was kept on the roof. Along the top there were battlements on each side, and at every tenth battlement there was a tower which covered the whole width from wall to wall. There were passages through the middle of the towers but not at the sides. On wet and stormy nights the guard used to leave the battlements and retire under the shelter of the towers. The escape was attended with much risk and less than half the garrison attempted it. The plan was carefully calculated. They determined the height of the wall by counting and recounting the number of layers of bricks in a spot which had not been plastered; and then constructed ladders of exactly the right length. On a dark night, amid rain and storm, they stole out, crossed the inner ditch, and reached the wall unnoticed. They were lightly equipped, and while their right feet were bare the left were shod, to prevent slipping in the mud. Twelve men, led by Ammeas, ascended first, near two adjacent towers. They killed the guard in each tower and secured the passages, which they held until all their companions had mounted and descended on the other side. One of the Plataeans, in climbing up on the roof, knocked a brick from one of the battlements; its fall was heard, and the alarm was given. All the besiegers came out on the wall, but in the blackness they could not discover what it was, and no one dared to move from his own place. Moreover the Plataeans in the city distracted their attention, by sallying out on the side opposite to that on which their friends were escaping. The Peloponnesians lit their danger signals to Thebes, but this had also been foreseen by the Plataeans, who by lighting other beacons on their own wall confused the signals of their enemies. But what the Plataeans had most to fear was an attack from a band of 300 men, whose duty it was to patrol outside the wall. While the last of the Plataeans were descending, they arrived with lights. They were thus illuminated themselves and a good mark for the arrows and darts of the Plataeans who were standing along the edge of the outer ditch. This ditch was crossed with difficulty; it was swollen with rain and had a coat of ice too thin to bear. But all got over safely except one archer who was captured on the brink.

The escape was perhaps effected on the north side of the city. The fugitives at first took the road to Thebes, to put their pursuers off the scent, but when they had left Plataea about a mile behind them, they struck to the right

and reached the road from Thebes to Athens near Erythrae. Two hundred and twelve men reached Athens; a few more had started but had turned back before they crossed the wall. This episode is an eminently interesting example of the survival of the fittest; for a melancholy fate awaited those who had not the courage to take their lives in their hands. In the following summer want of food finally forced them to capitulate to the Lacedaemonians. Five men were sent from Sparta to decide their fate. But their fate had been already decided through the influence of Thebes. Each prisoner was merely asked, 'Have you in the present war done any service to the Lacedaemonians or their allies?' The form of the question implied the sentence, and it was in vain that the Plataeans appealed to the loyalty of their ancestors to the cause of Hellas in the Persian war, or implored the Lacedaemonians to look upon the sepulchres of their own fathers buried in Plataean land and honoured every year by Plataea with the customary offerings. They were put to death, 200 in number, and 25 Athenians; and the city was razed to the ground. The Peloponnesians now commanded the road from Megara to Thebes. *Surrender of Plataea, 427 B.C.*

It is hard to avoid reproaching the Athenians for their failure to come to the relief of their old and faithful ally, and maintaining a position so important for communication between the Peloponnese and Boeotia. Their failure to bring help at the beginning of the siege may be explained by their sufferings from the plague which still prevailed. And in the following year a more pressing danger diverted their attention, the revolt of a member of their maritime confederacy.

Revolt of Mytilene

Archidamus had invaded Attica for the third time and had just quitted it, when the news arrived that Mytilene and the rest of Lesbos, with the exception of Methymna, had revolted. This was a great and, as it might seem to Athens, an unprovoked blow. It was not due to any special grievance. The oligarchical government of Mytilene confessed that the city was always well-treated and honoured by Athens. The revolt is all the more interesting and significant on this account. It was a protest of the Hellenic instinct for absolute autonomy against an empire such as the Athenian. The sovereignty of the Lesbian cities was limited in regard to foreign affairs; their relations with *Fourth year of the war, 428 B.C.*

other members of the confederacy were subject to control on the part of Athens; and their ships were required for Athenian purposes. Such restraints were irksome, and as they had seen the free allies of Athens, most recently Samos, gradually transformed into subjects, they might fear that this would presently be their own case too. The revolt had been meditated for some years;[11] it was hastened in the end, before all the preparations were made—such as the closing of the harbour of Mytilene by a mole and chain—because the design had been betrayed to Athens by enemies in Methymna and Tenedos. The Athenians, on the first news, sent ships under Cleïppides to surprise Mytilene at a festival of Apollo, which all the inhabitants used to celebrate outside the walls; but the Mytilenaeans received secret intelligence and postponed the feast. The Lesbians had a large fleet; and the Athenians were feeling so severely the effects of the plague and of the war that the rebellion had a good prospect of success if it had been energetically supported by the Peloponnesians.

Lesbian envoys at Olympia Envoys who were sent to gain their help pleaded the cause of Lesbos at the Olympian games which were celebrated that year. At the most august of the Panhellenic festivals, by the banks of the Alpheus, it was a fitting occasion to come forward among the assembled Greeks as champions of the principle of self-government which it is the glory of Greece to have taught mankind. And as Mytilene had no grievance beyond the general injustice of Athens in imposing external limitations on the autonomy of others, her assertion of that principle carried the greater weight. Lesbos was accepted into alliance, but it was a long time before any help was given. The Spartans ordered their allies to assemble at the Isthmus and themselves made preparations for hauling triremes across the Isthmus from the Corinthian gulf, intending to attack Athens by land and sea; but there was no response from the allies. They were engaged in bringing in the harvest and in no mood for fighting.

Synoecism of Mytilene The revolt from Athens was accompanied by a constitutional change within the borders of Lesbos itself. Except Methymna in the north, the other cities in the island—Antissa, Eresus, and Pyrrha on her land-locked bay—agreed to merge their own political individualities in the city of Mytilene. By the constitutional process known as synoecism, Mytilene was now to be to Lesbos what Athens was to Attica. The citizens of Pyrrha, Eresus, and Antissa would henceforward be citizens of Mytilene. Lesbos, with Methymna indepen-

dent and hostile, would now be what Attica was before the annexation of Eleusis.

Autumn, 428 B.C. Meanwhile the Athenians had blockaded the two harbours of Mytilene, and Paches soon arrived with 1000 hoplites to complete the investment. He built a wall on the land side of the city. At this time the Athenians were in sore want of money, for their funds had been seriously strained, especially by the expenses of the siege of Potidaea. As a measure of economy the hoplites sent from Athens to reinforce the besiegers were required to take the oars themselves. A small squadron was sent at the same time to the Carian district to levy tribute from states which had defaulted, a dangerous mission which met with no success. The tribute of the empire was increased by a new, extraordinary, assessment and at home they resorted to the expedient of raising money by a property tax.

The Elisphora (property tax), 428 B.C. This tax, now introduced for the first time in the war, differed in object and nature from the property tax of the sixth century. In the first place, it was not imposed permanently but only to meet a temporary crisis; secondly, it was to be used for purely military purposes; thirdly, it was imposed on all property and not merely on land. Only the very poor were exempt. *Probably a tax on capital* The tax yielded, in the first year, 200 talents and was frequently reimposed. The urgent need justified it, but it increased the bitterness of the oligarchs and helped to strain the allegiance of the moderates. It was probably first introduced by Cleon, who may have been this year a member of the Council;[12] it became associated with the policy of the demagogues.

427 B.C., first months Towards the end of the winter, the Spartans sent a man, named Salaethus, to assure the people of Mytilene that an armament would be dispatched to their relief. He managed to elude the Athenians and get into the city. The spirits of the besieged rose, and when summer came *May* 42 ships were sent under the command of Alcidas, and at the same time the Peloponnesians invaded Attica for the fourth time, hoping to distract the attention of the Athenians from Mytilene. The besieged waited and waited, but the ships never came, and the food ran short. Salaethus, in despair, determined to make a sally, and for this purpose armed the mass of the people with shields and spears. But the people, when they got the arms, refused to obey and demanded that the oligarchs should bring forth the corn and that all should share it fairly; otherwise, they would surrender the city. This drove the government *Surrender of Mytilene* to anticipate the chance of a separate negotiation on the part of the people; and they preferred to capitulate. Their fate was to be decided at Athens, and meanwhile Paches was to put no man to death.

The expedition of Alcidas

The fleet of Alcidas had wasted time about the Peloponnese, and on reaching the island of Myconos received the news that Mytilene was taken.[13] He sailed to Erythrae and there it was proposed to Alcidas that he should attack Mytilene, on the principle that men who have just gained possession of a city are usually off their guard. Another suggestion was that a town on the Asiatic coast should be seized and a revolt stirred up against Athens in the Ionian district. But these plans were far too good and daring for a Lacedaemonian admiral to adopt. He sailed southward, was pursued by Paches as far as Patmos, and retired into the Peloponnesian waters where he was more at home.

People of Mytilene sentenced to death

The ringleaders of the revolt of Mytilene were sent to Athens, and along with them the Spartan Salaethus, who was immediately put to death. The Assembly met to determine the fate of the prisoners, and decided to put to death not only the most guilty who had been sent to Athens, but the whole adult male population, and to enslave the women and children. A trireme was immediately dispatched to Paches with this terrible command.

The fact that the Athenian Assembly was persuaded to press the cruel rights of war so far as to decree the extinction of a whole population shows how deep was the feeling of anger against Mytilene. Many things contributed to render that feeling particularly bitter. The revolt had come at a moment when Athens was hard pressed by the plague and the war. All except the poorest Athenian had suffered in their pockets through the tax which it had been necessary to impose. And the imperial pride of the people had been wounded by the unheard-of event of a Peloponnesian fleet sailing in the eastern waters, of which Athens regarded herself as the sole mistress. But above all it was the revolt not of a subject, but of a free ally. Athens could more easily forgive the rebellion of a subject state which tried to throw off her yoke, than repudiation of her leadership by a nominally independent confederate. For the action of Mytilene was in truth an indictment of the whole fabric of the Athenian empire as unjust and undesirable. And the Athenians felt its significance. The mere unreasoning instinct of self-preservation suggested the policy of making a terrible example. It was another question whether this policy was wise.

New class of statesmen

The calm sense of Pericles was no longer there to guide and enlighten the Assembly.

We now find democratic statesmen of a completely different stamp coming forward to take his place. The Assembly is swayed by men of the people—men engaged in trade, like Cleon, the leather-merchant; Eucrates, the rope-seller; Hyperbolus, the lamp-maker. These men had not, like Aristides, Cimon, and Pericles, family connections to start and support them; they had no aristocratic traditions as the background of their democratic policy. They were self-made; they won their influence in the state by the sheer force of cleverness, eloquence, industry, and audacity. A man like Cleon, the son of Cleaenetus, whom we now meet holding the unofficial position of leader of the Assembly, must, to attain that eminence, have regularly attended in the Pnyx; he must have mastered the details of political affairs; he must have had the courage to confront the Olympian authority of Pericles, and the dexterity to make some palpable hits; he must have studied the art of speaking and been able to hold his audience. Cleon and the other statesmen of this new type are especially interesting as the politicians whom the advanced democracy produced and educated. It would be a grievous error and injustice to suppose that their policy was determined by mere selfish ambition or party malice. Nearly all we know of them is derived from the writings of men who not only condemned their policy but personally disliked them as low-born upstarts. Yet though they may have been vulgar and offensive in their manners, there is abundant evidence that they were able, and there is no proof that they were not generally honest, politicians. To those who recalled the dignity of Pericles, the speeches of Cleon or Hyperbolus may have seemed violent and coarse; but Cleon himself could hardly have outdone the coarseness and the violence of the personalities which Demosthenes heaped on Aeschines in a subsequent generation.

These new politicians were for the most part strong imperialists, and Cleon seems to have taken fully to heart the maxim of Pericles, to keep the subject allies 'well in hand'. It was under his influence that the Assembly vented its indignation against Mytilene by such a ruthless sentence. But when the meeting had dispersed, a partial reaction set in. Men began, in a cooler moment, to realise the inhumanity of their action and to question its policy. The envoys of Mytilene, who had been permitted to come to Athens to plead her cause, seeing this change of feeling, induced the authorities to summon an extraordinary

Second meeting of the Assembly

Arguments of Cleon

Speech of Diodotus

meeting of the Assembly for the following morning, to reconsider the decree. Cleon again came forward to support it on the grounds of both legal justice and good policy. Thucydides represents him as openly asserting the principle that a tyrannical city must use tyrannical methods, and rule by fear, punishing her allies without mercy. The chief speaker on the other side was a certain Diodotus, whose name has won immortality by his action at this famous crisis. Diodotus handled the question entirely as a matter of policy. Cleon had deprecated any appeal to the irrelevant considerations of humanity or pity; Diodotus, carefully avoiding such an appeal, deprecates on his own side with great force Cleon's appeal to considerations of justice. The Mytilenaeans have deserved the sentence of death: certainly; but the argument is entirely irrelevant. The question for Athens to consider is not what Mytilene deserves, but what it is expedient for Athens to inflict. 'We are not at law with the Mytilenaeans and do not want to be told what is just; we are considering a matter of policy, and desire to know how we can turn them to account.' He then goes on to argue that as a matter of fact the penalty of death is not a deterrent, and that the result of such a severe punishment will be injurious to Athens. A city which has revolted, knowing that whether she comes to terms soon or late the penalty will be the same, will never surrender; money will be wasted in a long blockade; and 'when the place is taken, it will be a mere wreck'. Moreover, if the people of Mytilene, who were compelled to join with their oligarchical government in rebelling, are destroyed, the popular party will everywhere be alienated from Athens.

Sentence revoked

The reasoning of Diodotus, which was based on sound views of policy, must have confirmed many of the audience who had already been influenced by the emotion of pity. But even still the Assembly was nearly equally divided, and the supporters of Diodotus won their motion by a very small majority. The ship which bore the sentence of doom had a start of about a day and a night; could it be overtaken by the trireme which was now dispatched with the reprieve? The Mytilenaean envoys supplied the crew with wine and barley, and offered large rewards if they were in time. The oarsmen continued rowing while they ate the barley, kneaded with wine and oil, and slept and rowed by turns. The first trireme, bound on an unpleasant errand, had sailed slowly. It arrived a little before the other. Paches had the decree in his hand and was about to execute it,

when the second ship sailed into the harbour, and the city was saved.

Execution of Mytilenaean ringleaders

The wrath of Athens against her rebellious ally was sufficiently gratified by the trial and execution of those Mytilenaeans who had been sent to Athens as especially guilty.

Cleruchy at Mytilene

Having taken away the Lesbian fleet and razed the walls of Mytilene, the Athenians divided the island, excluding Methymna, into 3000 lots of which 300 were consecrated to the gods. The rest they allocated to Athenian cleruchs, but by a special concession the Mytilenaeans were allowed to work the land themselves at an annual rent of two minae for each lot. The cleruchs presumably lived on the rents in Mytilene.[14]

Warfare in Western Greece. Tragic Events in Corcyra

Course of events in western Greece. 429 B.C.

While the attention of Greece was directed upon the fortunes of Plataea and Mytilene, warfare had been carried on in the regions of the west, and the reputation of the Athenian navy had risen higher. The Ambraciots had persuaded Sparta to send an expedition against Acarnania; if the Peloponnesians firmly established themselves there, they might win the whole Athenian alliance in the west. Cnemus was sent with 1000 hoplites in advance; he made an attempt on the important town of Stratus but was forced to retreat. Meanwhile a Peloponnesian fleet was to sail from Corinth to support him. It consisted of 47 ships, and had to pass Phormio, who was guarding the entrance of the Corinthian gulf with only 20. Phormio let them sail into the open sea, preferring to attack them there. The Spartan ships were serving primarily as transports and were not well equipped for battle, but to reach Acarnania they had first to engage the Athenians. Their superiority in numbers, however, gave them confidence and to offset the superior seamanship of the Athenians they adopted a defensive formation in a circle, which would protect them from the favourite Athenian tactic of cutting through the enemy line and ramming his ships in the flank. Phormio in response continued to row round the Spartan circle, threatening always to strike and so forcing their ships into an increasingly narrow space; then when the morning breeze, for which he was waiting, came down from the gulf and unsettled the Spartan ships he dashed in and gained a complete victory, capturing 12 ships. The government at Sparta could not understand how skill could gain such an

First naval victory of Phormio

Second naval victory of Phormio

advantage over far superior numbers; they sent commissioners to make an inquiry; and Cnemus was told that he must try again and be successful. A reorganised Peloponnesian fleet took up a position at Panormus in Achaea, and Phormio was stationed at Rhion on the opposite coast. The object of Cnemus was to lure or drive the enemy into the gulf where their skill in handling their ships would be less decisive than in the open sea. With this purpose he sailed towards Naupactus, and Phormio in alarm sailed along the coast to protect the place. As the Athenian ships moved near the land in single file, the enemy suddenly swung round and rowed down upon them at their utmost speed. The 11 ships which were nearest Naupactus had time to run round the right Peloponnesian wing and escape; the rest were driven aground. Twenty Peloponnesian vessels on the right were in the meantime pursuing the 11 Athenian, which were making for Naupactus. A Leucadian ship was far in advance of the others, closely pursuing an Athenian which was lagging behind. Near Naupactus a merchant vessel lay in their way, anchored in the deep water. The Athenian trireme rowed round it, struck her pursuer amidships, and sank her. This brilliant exploit startled the Peloponnesians who were coming up singing a paean of victory; the front ships dropped oars and waited for the rest. The Athenians, who had already reached Naupactus, saw the situation and immediately bore down and gained another complete victory.

A defeat

turned into a victory at Naupactus

If this able admiral, Phormio, had lived, he might have extended Athenian influence considerably in western Greece. But, after a winter expedition which he made in Acarnania, he silently drops out of history, and, as we find his son Asopius sent out in the following summer at the request of the Acarnanians, we must conclude that his career had been cut short by death. Asopius made an unsuccessful attempt on Oeniadae and was slain in a descent on Leucas. The peninsula of Leucas, and the Acarnanian Oeniadae, surrounded by marsh at the mouth of the river Achelous, were two main objects of Athenian enterprise in the west. Leucas was never won, but four years later Oeniadae was forced to join the Athenian alliance.

Asopius in the west, 428 B.C.

Oeniadae, 424 B.C.

Affairs at Corcyra, 427 B.C.

Corcyra herself was to be the next scene of the war in the Ionian Sea. The prisoners whom Corinth had taken in the Epidamnian war had been released on the understanding that they were to win over Corcyra from the Athenian alliance, and their intrigues were effectual in dividing the state and producing a sanguinary revolution. The question between the Peloponnesian and the Athenian alliance was closely bound up with the cleavage between the oligarchical and the democratic party. The intriguers in the Corinthian interest and their faction formed a conspiracy to overthrow the democratic constitution. Their first step was to prosecute Peithias, the leader of the people, on the charge of scheming to make Corcyra a subject of Athens. He was acquitted, and retorted by summoning their five richest men to take their trial for cutting vine-poles in the sanctuaries of Zeus and Alcinous. They were fined a stater for each pole: such a heavy fine that the culprits sat as suppliants in the sanctuary, imploring that they might pay by instalments. The prayer was refused, and in desperation they rushed into the senate-house and slew Peithias and 60 others who were with him.

Murder of the popular government, 427 B.C. Civil war in Corcyra

The oligarchy now had the upper hand, and they attacked the people, who fled to the acropolis and the Hyllaic harbour. The other harbour, which looks towards the mainland, along with the agora and the lower parts of the city were held by the oligarchs. Next day reinforcements came to both sides: to the people, from other parts of the island; and to the oligarchs, from the mainland. Fighting was soon resumed and the people had the advantage. In order to bar their way to the arsenal, the oligarchs set fire to the houses and buildings in the neighbourhood of the agora.

Next day 12 Athenian ships under Nicostratus arrived from Naupactus. He induced the two parties to come to an agreement, but the democrats persuaded him to leave five Athenian ships to ensure the preservation of order, for they did not trust their opponents. Nicostratus was to take five Corcyraean ships instead, and the crews of them were chosen from the oligarchs; they were in fact to be hostages for the behaviour of their fellows. But they feared they might be sent to Athens and fled to the refuge of a temple. Nicostratus could not induce them to stir. The people regarded this distrust as a proof of criminal designs, and armed anew. The rest of the oligarchs then fled to the temple of Hera, but the democrats induced them to cross over to an islet off the coast.

Arrival of the Athenians

Four or five days later a Peloponnesian fleet of 53 ships arrived under Alcidas, who had just returned from his expedition to Ionia. In a naval engagement outside the harbour the Corcyraeans fought badly, and the Athenians were forced to retreat; but the Peloponnesians did not follow up their success and soon afterwards, hearing that an Athenian armament of 60 ships was on its way, returned home.

The democratic party was now in a position to take vengeance on its enemies, who had gratuitously disturbed the peace of the city and sought to submit it to the yoke of its ancient enemy. The most vindictive and inhuman passions had been roused in the people by the attempt of the oligarchs on their liberty, and they now gave vent to these passions without regard to honour or policy. The 400 suppliants had returned from the island and were again under the protection of Hera. Fifty of them were persuaded to come forth to take their trial, and were executed. The rest, seeing their fate, aided each other in committing suicide; some hung themselves on the trees in the sacred enclosure. Eurymedon arrived with the Athenian fleet and remained seven days. During this time, the Corcyraeans slew all whom they suspected of being opposed to the democracy, and many victims were sacrificed to private enmity. 'Every form of death was to be seen, and everything, and more than everything that commonly happens in revolutions, happened then. The father slew the son, and the suppliants were torn from the temples and slain near them; some of them were even walled up in the temple of Dionysus and there perished. To such extremes of cruelty did revolution go; and this seemed to be the worst of revolutions because it was the first.' Eurymedon looked on and did not intervene.

While the democracy cannot be excused for these horrible excesses, the fact remains that the guilt of causing the revolution rests entirely with the oligarchs. The chief victims of the democratic fury deserve small compassion; they had set the example of violence. The occurrences at Corcyra made a profound impression in Greece, reflected in the pages of Thucydides. That historian has used the episode as the text for deep comments on the revolutionary spirit which soon began to disturb the states of the Greek world. Party divisions were encouraged and aggravated by the hope or fear of foreign intervention, the oligarchs looking to the Lacedaemonians, and the democrats to the Athenians. In time of peace these party struggles would have been far less bitter. This acute observation is illustrated by a famous modern instance, the French Revolution, where the worst outrages of the revolutionaries were provoked by foreign intervention. In that great Revolution too we can verify the Greek historian's analysis of the

The revolutionary spirit

effect of the revolutionary spirit, when it runs wild, on the moral nature of men. The revolutionaries 'determined to outdo the report of all who had preceded them by the ingenuity of their enterprises and the activity of their revenges. The meaning of words had no longer the same relation to things, but was changed by them as they thought proper. Reckless daring was held to be loyal courage; prudent delay was the excuse of a coward; moderation was the disguise of unmanly weakness; to know everything was to do nothing. Frantic energy was the true quality of a man. The lover of violence was always trusted and his opponent suspected.' It was dangerous to be quiet and neutral. 'The citizens who were of neither party fell a prey to both; either they were disliked because they held aloof, or men were jealous of their surviving.' The laws of heaven as well as of civilised societies were set aside without scruple amid the impatience of party spirit, the zeal of contention, the eagerness of ambition, and the cravings of revenge. These are some of the features in the delineation which Thucydides has drawn of the diseased condition of political life in the city-states of Greece.

But the sequel of the Corcyraean revolution has still to be recorded. About 600 of the oligarchs who escaped the vengeance of their opponents established themselves on Mount Istone in the north-east of the island, and easily becoming masters of the open country they harassed the inhabitants of the city for two years. Then an Athenian fleet, of which the ultimate destination was Sicily, under the command of Eurymedon and Sophocles, arrived at Corcyra; and the Athenians helped the democrats to storm the fort on Mount Istone. The oligarchs capitulated on condition that the Athenian people should determine how they were to be dealt with. The generals placed them in the island of Ptychia, on the understanding that, if any of their number attempted to escape, all should be deprived of the benefit of the previous agreement. But the democrats were afraid that the prisoners would not be put to death at Athens, and they were determined that their enemies should die. A foul trick was planned and carried out. Friends of the prisoners were sent over to the island, who said that the generals had resolved to leave them to the mercy of the democrats, and advised them to escape, offering to provide a ship. A few of the captives fell into the trap and were caught starting. All the prisoners were immediately handed over to the Corcyraeans, who shut them up in a large building.

Corcyraean oligarchs on Istone

427-5 B.C.

Fall of Istone, 425 B.C.

Massacre of the oligarchs

They were taken out in batches of 20, and made to march, tied together, down an avenue of hoplites, who struck and wounded any whom they recognised as a personal enemy. Three batches had thus marched to execution, when their comrades in the building, who thought they were merely being removed to another prison, discovered the truth. They called on the Athenians, but they called in vain. Then they refused to stir out of the building or let any one enter. The Corcyraeans did not attempt to force their way in. They tore off the roof, and hurled bricks and shot arrows from above. The captives, absolutely helpless, began to anticipate the purpose of their tormentors by taking their own lives, piercing their throats with the arrows which were shot down, or strangling themselves with the ropes of some beds which were in the place or with strips of their own dress. The work of destruction went on during the greater part of the night; all was over when the day dawned; and the corpses were carried outside the city. Thus ended the Corcyraean revolution, and the last scene was more ghastly even than the first. Eurymedon had less excuse, on this occasion, for refusing to intervene than he had two years before, since the prisoners had surrendered to the Athenians. It was said that he and Sophocles were ready to take advantage of the base trick of the democrats, because, unable to take the captives to Athens themselves, being bound for Sicily, they could not bear that the credit should fall to another. The oligarchical faction at Corcyra was now utterly annihilated, and the democrats lived in peace.

Campaigns of Demosthenes in the west

Aetolian expedition, 426 B.C.

During the Corcyraean troubles, the war had not rested in western Greece. An Athenian fleet under the general Demosthenes had sailed round the Peloponnese and attacked the 'island' of Leucas. Demosthenes was an enterprising commander, distinguished from most of his fellows by a certain originality of conception. On this occasion, the idea of making a great stroke induced him to abandon the operations at Leucas—though the Acarnanians thought he might have taken the town by blockade—and engage in a new enterprise on the north of the Corinthian gulf. Most of the lands between Boeotia and the western sea—Phocis, Locris, Acarnania—were friendly to Athens. But the hostility of the uncivilised Aetolians rendered land operations in those regions dangerous. Demosthenes conceived the plan of reducing the Aetolians so that he could then operate from the west on Doris and Boeotia without the danger of his communications being threatened in the rear. His idea, in fact, was to bring the Corinthian gulf into touch with the Euboean sea. The Spartans, it is to be observed, were at this very time concerning themselves with the regions of Mount Oeta. The appeals of Doris on the south, and Trachis on the north, of the Oetaean range, for protection against the hostilities of the mountain tribes, induced the Lacedaemonians to send out a colony, which was established in Trachis not very far from the Pass of Thermopylae under the name of Heraclea. A colony was an unusual enterprise for Sparta, but Heraclea had a more important significance and intention than the mere defence of members of the amphictiony. It was a place from which Euboea could be attacked; and it might prove of the greatest service, as an intermediate station, for carrying on operations in the Chalcidic peninsula. The fears which the foundation of Heraclea excited at Athens were indeed disappointed. Heraclea never flourished; it was incessantly assailed by the powerful hostility of the Thessalians and its ruin was completed by the flagrantly unjust administration of the Lacedaemonian governors. But its first foundation was a serious event; and it seems highly probable that Demosthenes, when he formed his plan, had before his mind the idea of threatening Heraclea and Boeotia from the south by the occupation of Doris. But his plan, attractive as it might sound, was eminently impracticable. The preliminary condition was the subjugation of a mountainous country, involving a warfare in which Demosthenes was inexperienced and hoplites were at a great disadvantage. The Messenians of Naupactus represented to him that Aetolia, a land of unwalled villages, could easily be reduced. But the Messenians had their own game to play. They suffered from the hostilities of their Aetolian neighbours and wanted to use the ambition of the Athenian general for their own purpose.

Colony of Heraclea

The Acarnanians, who were deeply interested in the defeat of Leucas, were indignant with Demosthenes for not prosecuting the blockade and refused to join him against Aetolia. Starting from Oeneon in Locris, the Athenians and some allies—not a large force—advanced into the country, hoping to reduce several tribes before they had time to combine. But the Aetolians had already learned his plans and were collecting a great force. The main chance of Demosthenes lay in the co-operation of the Ozolian Locrians, who knew the Aetolian country and mode of warfare and were armed in the Aetolian fashion. Demosthenes committed the error of not waiting for them and was consequently unable to deal with the Aetolian javelin-men. At Aegition, rushing down from the hills they wrought havoc among the invaders who had captured the town. A hundred and twenty Athenian hoplites fell—'the very finest men whom the city of Athens lost during the war'. Demosthenes did not dare to return to Athens.[15] He remained at Naupactus and soon had an opportunity of retrieving his fame.

[Aegition = Velu-chovos ?]

The Lacedaemonians answered this invasion of Aetolia by sending 3000 hoplites under Eurylochus against Naupactus. Five hundred of these troops came from Heraclea, the newly-founded colony. Naupactus, ill-defended, was barely saved by the energy of Demosthenes, who persuaded the Acarnanians to send reinforcements. Eurylochus abandoned the siege and withdrew to the neighbourhood of Calydon and Pleuron in southern Aetolia for the purpose of joining the Ambraciots in an attack upon Argos. Winter had begun when the Ambraciots descended from the north into the Argive territory and seized the fort of Olpae, which stands, a little north of Argos, on a hill by the sea, and was once used as a hall of justice by the Acarnanian league. Demosthenes was asked by the Acarnanians to be their leader in resisting this attack, and a message for help was sent to 20 Athenian vessels which were coasting off the Peloponnese. The troops of Eurylochus marched from the south across Acarnania and joined their allies at Olpae. The Athenian ships arrived in the Ambracian gulf, and with the reinforcements which they brought Demosthenes gave battle to the enemy between Olpae and Argos, annulling by a skilfully contrived ambuscade the advantage which they had in superior numbers. Eurylochus was slain, and the Peloponnesians delivered themselves from their perilous position—between Argos and the Athenian ships—by making a secret treaty with Demosthenes, in which the Ambraciots were not included. It was arranged that they should retreat stealthily without explaining their intention to the Ambraciots. It was good policy on the part of Demosthenes, for by this treacherous act the Lacedaemonians would lose their character in that part of Greece. The Peloponnesians crept out of Olpae one by one, pretending to gather herbs and sticks. As they got farther away, they stepped

Demosthenes saves Naupactus

and Amphilochian Argos

Battle of Olpae

Truce; the Peloponnesians desert the Ambraciots, who are slaughtered

out more quickly, and then the Ambraciots saw what was happening and ran out to overtake them. The Acarnanians slew about 200 Ambraciots, and the Peloponnesians escaped into the land of Agraea. But a heavier blow was in store for Ambracia. Reinforcements of that city, ignorant of the battle, were coming to Olpae. Demosthenes sent forward some of his troops to lie in ambush on their line of march. At Idomene, some miles north of Olpae, there are two peaks of unequal height. The higher was seized in advance by the men of Demosthenes; the Ambraciots when they arrived encamped on the lower. Demosthenes then advanced with the rest of his troops and attacked the enemy at dawn, when they were still half asleep. Most were slain, and those who escaped at first found the mountain paths occupied. Thucydides says that during the first ten years of the war 'no such calamity happened within so few days to any Hellenic state', and he does not give the numbers of those who perished, because they would appear incredible in proportion to the size of the state. Demosthenes might have captured the city if he had pushed on, but the Acarnanians did not desire a permanent Athenian occupation at their doors; they were content that their neighbour was rendered harmless. A treaty of alliance for 100 years was concluded between the Acarnanians, with the Amphilochians of Argos, and the Ambraciots. Neither side was to be required by the other to join against its own allies in the great war, but they were to help each other to defend their territories. Some time afterwards Anactorion, and then Oeniadae, were won over to the Athenian alliance.

Anactorion, 425 B.C. Oeniadae, 424 B.C.

Nicias and Cleon. Politics at Athens

The success against Ambracia compensated for the failure in Aetolia, and Demosthenes could now return to Athens. His dashing style of warfare and his bold plans must have caused grave mistrust among the older, more experienced, and more commonplace commanders. Nicias, the son of Niceratus, who seems to have already won, without deserving, the chief place as a military authority at Athens, must have shaken his head over the doings of Demosthenes in the west. Nicias, a wealthy conservative slave-owner, who hired out his slaves profitably for work in the silver-mines of Laurion, was one of the mainstays of that party which was out of sympathy with the intellectual and political progress of Athens,

Nicias

and bitterly opposed to the new politicians like Cleon who wielded the chief influence in the Assembly.

The ability of Nicias was irretrievably mediocre; he would have been an excellent subordinate officer but he had not the qualities of a leader or a statesman. Yet he possessed a solid and abiding influence at Athens, through his impregnable respectability, his superiority to bribes, and his scrupulous superstition, as well as his acquaintance with the details of military affairs. This homage paid to mediocre respectability throws light on the character of the Athenian democracy and the strength of the conservative party. Nicias belonged to the advocates of peace and was well-disposed to Sparta, so that for several reasons he might be regarded as a successor to Cimon. But his political opponents, though they constantly defeated him on particular measures, never permanently undermined his influence. He understood the political value of gratifying in small ways those prejudices of his fellow-citizens which he shared himself, and he spared no expense in the religious service of the state. As Thucydides says, he thought too much of divination and omens. He had an opportunity of displaying his religious devotion and his liberality on the occasion of the purification of Delos, which was probably undertaken to induce Apollo to avert a recurrence of the plague. The dead were removed from all the tombs, and it was ordained that henceforth no one should die or give birth to a child on the sacred island. Those who were near to either should cross over to Rheneia. The Athenians revived in a new form the old festival, celebrated in the Homeric hymn to Apollo, the festival to which 'the long-robed Ionians gathered, and made thee glad, O Phoebus, with boxing, dancing, and song'. The games were restored, and horse-races introduced for the first time. Four years later the purification was perfected by the removal of all the inhabitants, and the Persians accorded them a refuge at Adramyttion.

Conducting such ceremonies, Nicias was in his right place. Unfortunately such excellence had an undue weight, and it should be noted that this is one of the drawbacks of a city-state. In a large modern state, the private life and personal opinions of a statesman have small importance and are not weighed by his fellow-countrymen in the scale against his political ability, save in rare exceptional cases. But in a small city the statesman's private life is always before men's eyes, and his political position is distinctly affected, according as he shocks or gratifies their prejudices and predilections. A mediocre man is able, by judicious conforming, to attain an authority to which his brains give him no claim. Pericles was indeed so strong that his influence could survive attacks on his morality and his unorthodoxy. Nicias maintained his position because he never shocked the public sense of decorum and religion by associating with an Aspasia or an Anaxagoras. The Athenian people combined in a remarkable degree the capacity of appreciating both respectability and intellectual power; their progressive instinct was often defeated by conservative prejudices.

Though Nicias was one of those Athenians who were not in full sympathy with the policy of Pericles, and approved still less of the policy of his successors, he was thoroughly loyal to the democracy. But an oligarchical party still existed, secretly active, and always hoping for an opportunity to upset the democratic constitution. This party, or a section of it, seems to have been known at this time as the 'Young Party'. It included, among others who will appear on the stage of history some years later, the orator Antiphon, who was now coming into public notice in connection with some sensational lawsuits. Against the dark designs of this party, as well as against the misconduct of generals, Cleon was constantly on the watch; he could describe himself in the Assembly as the 'people's watch-dog'. But at present these oligarchs were harmless; so long as no disaster from without befell Athens, they had no chance; all they could do was to make common cause with the other enemies of Cleon, and air their discontent in anonymous political pamphlets. Chance has preserved us a work of this kind, written in one of these years by an Athenian of oligarchical views. Its subject is the Athenian democracy, and the writer professes to answer on behalf of the Athenians the criticisms which the rest of the Greeks pass on Athenian institutions.[16] 'I do not like democracy myself,' he says, 'but I will show that from their point of view the Athenians manage their state wisely and in the manner most conducive to the interests of democracy.' The defence is for the most part a veiled indictment; it displays remarkable acuteness, with occasional triviality. The writer has grasped and taken to heart one deep truth, the close connection of the sea-power of Athens with its advanced democracy. It is just, he remarks, that the poor and the common folk should have more influence than the noble and rich; for it is the common folk that row the ships and make the city powerful, not the

Purification of Delos, 426 B.C.

Quadrennial festival established at Delos

The oligarchical party

οἱ νεώτεροι

Antiphon

The pseudo-Xenophontic Ἀθηναίων πολιτεία, c. 424 B.C.

hoplites and the well-born and the worthy. Highly interesting is his observation that slaves and metics enjoyed what he considered unreasonable freedom and immunity at Athens: 'Why, you may not strike one of them, nor will a slave make way for you in the street.' And his malicious explanation is interesting too: the common folk dress so badly that you might easily mistake one of them for a slave or a metic, and then there would be a to-do if you struck a citizen. There is perhaps also a touch of malice in the statement that the commercial empire of Athens, which brought to her wharves the delicacies of the world, was affecting her language, as well as her habits of life, and filling it with foreign words.

An important feature in the political history of Athens in these years was the divorce of the military command from the leadership in the Assembly, and the want of harmony between *Cleon's* the chief Strategoi and the Leaders of the *position* People. The new men who swayed the Assembly had no military training or capacity, and they were always at a disadvantage when opposed by men who spoke with the authority of a strategos on questions of military policy. Until recent years the post of General had been practically confined to men of property and good family. But a change ensued, perhaps soon after the death of Pericles, *Eupolis on* and men of the people were elected. The *the new* comic poet Eupolis, in a play called the *Demes* *generals* —in which the great leaders, Miltiades and Themistocles, Aristides and Pericles, are summoned back to life that they may see and deplore degenerate Athens—meditates thus on the contrast between latter-day generals and their predecessors:

> Men of lineage fair
>   And of wealthy estate
>   Once our generals were,
>   The noble and great,
> Whom as gods we adored, and as gods they guided and guarded the state.

> Things are not as then.
>   Ah, how different far
>   A manner of men
>   Our new generals are,
> The rascals and refuse our city now chooses to lead us to war!

Cleon was a man of brains and resolution. Hitherto his main activity had been in the law-courts, where he called officers to account and maintained the safeguards of popular government. If he was to be more than an opposition leader, he must be ready to undertake the post of strategos; and, supported by the experience of an able colleague, he need not disgrace himself. An understanding, therefore, between Cleon and the enterprising Demosthenes was one which seemed to offer advantages to both; acting together they might damage both the political and the military position of Nicias.

The Athenian Capture of Pylos

It was probably through the influence of Cleon that Demosthenes, though he received *425 B.C.* no official command, was sent to accompany the fleet of 40 ships which was now ready to start for the west, under Eurymedon and Sophocles. We have already seen this fleet at Corcyra assisting the people against the oligarchical exiles who had established themselves on Mount Istone. Demosthenes accompanied the expedition without any official command. He had a plan in his head for establishing a military post in the western Peloponnese; and he was allowed to take advantage of the sailing of the fleet and use it according to his discretion. Arriving off the coast of Messenia, Demosthenes asked the commanders to put in at Pylos, but they had heard that the Peloponnesian fleet had already reached Corcyra, and demurred to any delay. But chance favoured the design of Demosthenes. Stress of weather drove them into the harbour of Pylos, and then Demosthenes pressed them to fortify the place. The task was easy, for the place was naturally strong and there was an abundance of material, stone and timber, at hand. The commanders ridiculed the idea. 'There are many other desert promontories in the Peloponnese,' they said, 'if you want to waste the money of the city.' But the stormy weather detained the ships; the soldiers were idle; and at length, for the sake of something to do, they adopted the project of Demosthenes and fell to the work of fortifying Pylos.

The features of the scene, which was now *Topo-* to become illustrious by a striking military *graphy of* episode, must be clearly grasped. The high *Pylos and* promontory of Pylos or Coryphasion was on *Sphacteria* three sides encompassed by water. Once it had been an island, but at this time it was connected with the mainland on the north side by a low sand-bar. If we go further back into prehistoric days, Pylos had been part of a continuous line of coast-cliff. In this line three rents were made, which admitted the sea behind the cliff and isolated the islands of Pylos and Sphacteria. Accumulation of sand gradually covered the most northern breach and reunited Pylos with the mainland, but the other openings were never filled up and Sphacteria still remains an island. Originally Pylos and Sphacteria, when they had been severed, formed the sea-wall of one great land-locked bay. Before the present reclamation work Pylos was also connected with the mainland at its southern end by a sand-bar, north of which was a lagoon. Most modern writers have assumed that this sand-bar was a comparatively late formation and that in the classical period the bay was uninterrupted, but a more detailed examination has revealed buildings of the Roman and Hellenistic period on the 'sand-bar' and traces of occupation within the 'lagoon'.[17] It follows from what has been said that there were two entrances into the bay: the narrow water which divides Pylos from Sphacteria, and the wide passage which severs the southern point of Sphacteria from the opposite mainland. We must distinguish yet another smaller bay on the north side of the Pylos hill. The sand-bar which there connects Pylos with the mainland is of crescent shape and forms the little circular basin of Buphras, dominated by the height of Pylos on the south and a far lower, nameless hill on the north.

The length of Pylos is less than a mile. On the sea-side it was hard to land, and the harbour side was strongly protected by steep cliffs. Only in three places was it found necessary to build walls: (1) at the south-east corner, where the cliffs slope down to the channel for about 100 yards; (2) along the shore on the south-west side close to the entrance to the bay, for 400 or 500 yards; (3) the northern defence of the position consisted of a line of land cliffs, which required no artificial fortification except at the western

Athenian fortifications of Pylos

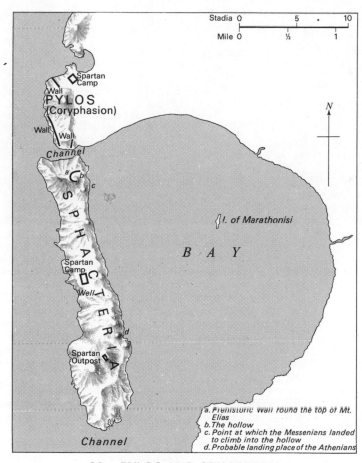

Stadia 0   5   .   10
Mile 0   ½   1

Spartan Camp
PYLOS (Coryphasion)
Wall
Wall Wall
Channel

SPHACTERIA
a
b
c

I. of Marathonisi

B A Y

Spartan Camp
Well
d
Spartan Outpost

Channel

a. Prehistoric wall round the top of Mt. Elias
b. The hollow
c. Point at which the Messeniens landed to climb into the hollow
d. Probable landing place of the Athenians

22. PYLOS AND SPHACTERIA

10.2 Pylos and Sphacteria, from the air

extremity, where they decline before they reach the sea; here another wall was built. One of the soldiers present vividly described to Thucydides the manner in which the fortifications were wrought. 'Being unprovided with iron tools they brought stones which they picked out, and put them together as they happened to fit; if they required to use mortar, having no hods, they carried it on their backs, which they bent so as to form a resting-place for it, clasping their hands behind them that it might not fall off.' In six days the work was finished, and the fleet went on its way, leaving Demosthenes with five ships to hold Pylos.

The Lacedaemonian army under Agis had invaded Attica earlier than usual, before the corn was ripe. Want of food, wet weather, and then perhaps the news from Pylos, decided them to return to Sparta after a sojourn of only two weeks within the Attic borders. They did not proceed immediately to Pylos, but another body of Spartans was sent on; requisitions for help were dispatched to the Peloponnesian allies; and the 60 ships at Corcyra were hastily summoned. These ships succeeded in eluding the notice of the Athenian fleet which had now reached Zacynthus. In the meantime Demosthenes, beset by the Spartan troops, sent two of his ships to overtake the fleet and beg Eurymedon to return to help him.

The object of the Lacedaemonians was to

Arrival of Lacedae-monians by land and sea

Siege of Pylos

blockade the hill of Pylos by land and sea, and to prevent new Athenian forces from landing. They probably established their camp on the north side of Pylos, so that no ships entering the bay of Buphras could bring help to the fort. They were moreover afraid that the Athenians might use the island of Sphacteria as a basis for military operations, and accordingly Epitadas occupied Sphacteria with 420 Lacedaemonians and their Helots. It would have been easy to block the narrow entrance to the bay between Pylos and the island; but there was little use in doing so, as the Athenian ships would be able to enter by the entrance at the south of the island, a passage about three-quarters of a mile wide—far too wide to block with so small a fleet.

Attack on Pylos

The Lacedaemonians then prepared to attack the place, before help could come to the Athenians. Demosthenes posted the greater part of his force to guard the northern line of defence and the south-eastern corner, while he himself with 60 hoplites and some archers took his stand on the edge of the south-western shore, which though rocky and perilous was the spot where the enemy had the best prospect of effecting a landing. Thrasymelidas was the name of the Spartan admiral. He had 43 ships, which he brought up in relays, the crews fighting and resting by turns. The great danger was that of running the vessels on reefs. Brasidas, who commanded one of the ships, was the leading spirit. 'Be not sparing of timber,' he cried to those who seemed to draw back from the rocks; 'the enemy has built a fortress in your country. Sacrifice the ships, and force a landing.' But in trying to disembark he was wounded and lost his shield. It was washed ashore and set up in the trophy which the Athenians afterwards erected. The Spartan attack, which was re-

repelled

newed on two subsequent days, was repelled. It was a singular turn of fortune, says Thucydides, which drove the Athenians to repel the Lacedaemonians, who were attacking them by sea from the Lacedaemonian coast, and the Lacedaemonians to fight for a landing on their own soil, now hostile to them, in the face of the Athenians. For in those days it was the great glory of the Lacedaemonians to be an inland people distinguished for their military prowess, and of the Athenians to be a nation of sailors and the first naval power in Hellas.

Arrival of Athenian fleet

The fleet from Zacynthus, now augmented to 50 ships by some reinforcements, at length arrived. But finding the shores of the bay of Buphras and the island of Sphacteria occupied, they withdrew for the night to the isle of Prote which was some miles distant. The next morning they returned, determined to sail into the harbour, if the enemy did not come out to meet them. The Lacedaemonians were preparing their ships for action, evidently intending to fight in the bay. The Athenians therefore rowed in by both entrances; some of the enemy's vessels which were able to come out to meet them were captured; and a tremendous struggle ensued close to the shore. The Athenians were tying the empty beached ships to their own and endeavouring to drag them away, the Lacedaemonians dashed into the sea and were pulling them back. The Lacedaemonians knew that, if they lost their ships, the party on the island of Sphacteria would be cut off. Most of the empty ships were saved, but the fleet was so far damaged and outnumbered that the Athenians were able to blockade Sphacteria.

Battle in the harbour

The interest of the story now passes from Pylos to Sphacteria. The blockade of Demosthenes and his Athenians in Pylos by the Spartans has changed into a blockade of Epitadas and his Spartans in Sphacteria by the Athenians. The tidings of this change in the situation caused grave alarm at Sparta and some of the ephors came themselves to see what measures could be taken. They decided that nothing could be done for the relief of the island, and obtained from the Athenian generals a truce for the purpose of sending ambassadors to Athens to ask for peace. The terms of this truce were as follows:—

Second stage of the episode: blockade of Sphac-teria

Truce

The Lacedaemonians shall deliver into the hands of the Athenians at Pylos the ships in which they fought, and shall also bring thither and deliver over any other ships of war which are in Laconia; and they shall make no assault upon the fort either by sea or land. The Athenians shall permit the Lacedaemonians on the mainland to send to those on the island a fixed quantity of kneaded flour, viz. two Attic quarts of barleymeal for each man, and a pint of wine, and also a piece of meat; for an attendant half these quantities; they shall send them into the island under the inspection of the Athenians, and no vessel shall sail in by stealth. The Athenians shall guard the island as before, but not land, and shall not attack the Peloponnesian forces by land or sea. If either party violate this agreement in any particular, however slight, the truce is to be at an end. The agreement is to last until the Lacedaemonian ambassadors return from Athens, and the Athenians are to convey them thither and bring them back in a trireme. When they return, the truce is to be at an end, and the Athenians are to restore the ships in the same condition in which they received them.

Athens rejects Spartan proposals of peace

In accordance with these terms, 60 ships were handed over and the ambassadors went to Athens. They professed the readiness of Sparta to make peace and pleaded for generous treatment on the part of Athens. At heart most of the Athenians were probably anxious for peace. But the Assembly was under the influence of Cleon, and he, as the opponent of Nicias and the peace-party, urged the Athenians to propose terms which could hardly be accepted. It might seem indeed an exceptionally favourable moment to attempt to undo the humiliation of the Thirty Years' Peace and win back some of the possessions which had been lost twenty years ago. Not only Nisaea and Pagae, the harbours of the Megarid, but Achaea and Troezen, were demanded as the purchase of the lives of the Spartans on Sphacteria. The embassy returned to Pylos disappointed, and the truce came to an end. But the Athenians refused to give back the 60 ships, on the pretext of some slight infraction of the truce on the part of the Lacedaemonians.

Protracted blockade

The blockade proved a larger and more difficult matter than the Athenians had hoped. Reinforced by 20 more triremes from Athens, they lay round the island, both in the bay, and, except when the wind was too high, on the seaside; and two ships kept continually cruising round in opposite directions. But their vigilance was eluded, and Sphacteria was secretly supplied with provisions. Large sums were offered to any who succeeded in conveying meal, wine, or cheese to the island; and Helots who did such service were rewarded with freedom. When a strong wind from the west or north drove the Athenian ships into the bay, the daring crews of provision-boats beat recklessly into the difficult landing-places on the seaside. Moreover some skilful divers managed to reach the shores of the island—drawing skins with poppy-seed mixed with honey, and pounded linseed. But this device was soon discovered and prevented.

And besides the difficulty of rendering the blockade complete in a high wind, the maintenance of it was extremely unpleasant. As there was no proper anchorage, the crews were obliged to take their meals on land by turns—generally in the south part of Sphacteria, which was not occupied by the Spartans. And they depended for their supply of water on one well, which was in the fort of Pylos. The supply of food was deficient, for it had to be conveyed round the Peloponnese. At home the Athenians were disappointed at the

Impatience at Athens

protraction of the siege, and grew impatient. They were sorry that they had declined the overtures of the Lacedaemonians, and there was a reaction of feeling against Cleon. That statesman took the bold course of denying the reports from Pylos, and said—with a pointed allusion to the strategos Nicias—that if the Generals were men they would sail to the island and capture the garrison. 'If I were commander,' he added, 'I would do it myself.' The scene which follows is described in one of the rare passages where the most reserved of all historians condescends to display a little political animosity. 'Seeing that the people were murmuring at Cleon, Nicias stood up and offered, on the part of his colleagues, to give Cleon any force he asked for and let him try.' Cleon—says Thucydides—'at first imagined that the offer of Nicias was only a pretence and was willing to go; but finding that he was in earnest, he tried to back out and said that not he but Nicias was general. He was now alarmed, for he never imagined that Nicias would go so far as to give up his place to him. Again Nicias bade him take the command of the expedition against Pylos, which he formally gave up to him in the presence of the Assembly. And the more Cleon declined the proffered command and tried to retract what he had said, so much the more the multitude, as their manner is, urged Nicias to resign and shouted to Cleon that he should sail. At length, not knowing how to escape from his own words, he undertook the expedition and, coming forward, said that he was not afraid of the Lacedaemonians and that he would sail without withdrawing a single man from the city, if he were allowed to have the Lemnian and Imbrian forces now at Athens, the auxiliaries from Aenus who were targeteers, and 400 archers from other places. With these and with the troops already at Pylos he gave his word that he would either bring the Lacedaemonians alive within twenty days or kill them on the spot. His vain words moved the Athenians to laughter; nevertheless the wiser sort of men were pleased when they reflected that of two good things they could not fail to obtain one—either there would be an end of Cleon, which they would have greatly preferred, or, if they were disappointed, he would put the Lacedaemonians into their hands.'

Cleon sent as commander to Pylos

The story is almost too good to be true. But whether Cleon desired the command or had it thrust upon him against his will, his words which moved the Athenians to laughter were fully justified by the event. He chose

Demosthenes as his colleague; and, invested with the command by a formal vote of the Assembly, he immediately set sail with special light-armed troops.

Nature of Sphacteria

In the meantime Demosthenes, wishing like Cleon to bring matters to an issue, was meditating an attack upon Sphacteria. This island is about 2¾ miles long. At the northern extremity rises a height, higher than the acropolis of Pylos over against it, the east side descending, a sheer cliff, into the water of the bay. Some of the Spartans had naturally occupied the summit, but the chief encampment of their small force was in the centre of the island, close to the only well; and an outpost was set on a hill farther to the south. An assault was difficult not only because the landing-places on both sides were bad, but because the island was covered with close bush, which gave the Spartans, who knew the ground, a great advantage. Demosthenes had experienced in Aetolia the difficulties of fighting in a wood. But one day, when some Athenians were taking their noonday meal on the south shore

Burning of the wood

of the island, the wood was accidentally kindled, and, a wind arising, the greater part of the bush was burnt. It was then possible to see more clearly the position and the numbers of the Lacedaemonians, and when Cleon arrived, the plan of attack was matured.

Athenian forces land on Sphacteria

Embarking at night all their hoplites in a few ships, Cleon and Demosthenes landed before dawn on the south of the island, partly on the sea side and partly on the harbour side, near the spot where the Lacedaemonians had their outpost. The whole number of troops that landed must have been nearly 14,000, against which the Spartans had only 420 hoplites and perhaps as many Helots. And yet a high military authority described the Athenian enterprise as mad. The truth seems to be that it could hardly have succeeded if the Spartan commander had disposed his forces to the best advantage, posting watches at all possible landing-places and organising a proper system of signals.

The attack

The outpost was at once overpowered, and light-armed troops advanced towards the main Spartan encampment, along a high ridge on the harbour side of the island. Others moved along the low shore on the sea side, so that when the main body of the Spartans saw their outpost cut to pieces and began to move southward against the Athenian hoplites, they were harassed on either side by the archers and targeteers, whom, encumbered by their arms and in difficult ground, they were unable to pursue. And the attacks of these light-armed troops, as they grew more fully conscious of their own superiority in numbers and saw that their enemy was growing weary, became more formidable. Clouds of dust arose from the newly burnt wood—so Thucydides reports the scene from the vivid description of an eye-witness—and there was no possibility of a man's seeing what was before him, owing to the showers of arrows and stones hurled by their assailants which were flying amid the dust. And now the Lacedaemonians began to be acutely distressed, for their felt cuirasses did not protect them against the arrows, and the points of the javelins broke off where they struck them. They were at their wits' end, not being able to see out of their eyes or to hear the word of command, which was drowned by the cries of the enemy. Destruction was staring them in the face, and they had no means or hope of deliverance.

Distress of the Spartans

At length it was determined that the only chance lay in retreating to the high hill at the north of the island. About a mile had to be traversed to the foot of the hill, but the ground was very difficult. The endurance and discipline of the Spartan soldiers was conspicuously displayed in this slow retreat which was accomplished, with but a small loss, under a burning sun, by men who were suffering from thirst and weary with the distress of an unequal battle. When they had reached and climbed the hill the battle assumed another aspect. On the high ground, no longer exposed on their flanks, and finding a defence in an old Cyclopean wall, which can still be traced round the summit, the Lacedaemonians were able to repel their assailants; and they were determined not to surrender. At length a Messenian captain came to the Athenian generals and said that he knew a path by which he thought he could take some light-armed troops round to the rear of the Spartans. The hill on its eastern side falls precipitously into the bay; but the fall is not direct. The summit slopes down into a hollow, about 50 yards wide, and then the hill rises again into the cliff which falls sheer into the water. But at the south end of the cliff there is a narrow gorge by which it is possible to climb up into the hollow. Embarking in a boat on the eastern side of the island, the Messenians reached the foot of the gorge and climbed up with difficulty, unseen by the Spartans, who neglected what seemed an impracticable part of the hill, and then ascending the summit suddenly appeared above the Lacedaemonians, who were ranged in a semicircle below on the western and northern slopes. The Athenians now invited

Spartan retreat to the hill (now Mount Elias)

The Messenian plan

273

the defenders to capitulate, and with the consent of their friends on the mainland they laid down their arms. Two hundred and ninety-two, of the 420, survived and were brought to Athens, and of these some 120 were Spartan citizens. The high opinion which the Greek world held of the Spartan spirit was expressed in the universal amazement which was caused by this surrender. Men had thought that nothing could induce the Lacedaemonians to give up their arms.

Cleon had performed his promise; he brought back the captives within twenty days. The success was of political rather than military importance. The Athenians could indeed ravage Lacedaemonian territory from Pylos, but it was a greater thing that they had in the prisoners a security against future invasions of Attica and a means of making an advantageous peace when they chose. It was the most important success gained in the war, and it was a brilliant example of the valuable successes that can be gained, as it were accidentally, in following that system of strategy which Pericles had laid down at the beginning of the war. This stroke of luck increased the influence of Cleon, and enabled him to support a drastic step to strengthen the financial position of Athens, which was becoming alarming.

More than 4000 talents had already been borrowed from the reserve and, though steps had been taken to increase revenue when Lesbos revolted, the drain was continuing and the end was not in sight.[18] Cleon seems to have been particularly concerned with the financing of the war and it was no doubt under his influence that it was decided to strengthen the position at the expense of the allies. The decree providing for a new assessment of tribute was passed in the Assembly after the dramatic success at Sphacteria, but the main lines had probably been worked out by Cleon earlier. We possess numerous fragments of the stone recording the decree and, below it, the list of cities with their new assessment. The main character is clear: 'Since the tribute has become too small, they (the jurors) shall join with the Council in making the current assessments . . . They shall not assess a lower tribute on any city than it was paying before, unless because of impoverishment of the country there is a manifest inability to pay more.' These instructions were faithfully followed. Many cities had their tribute doubled or trebled; few escaped increase. Cities that had long discontinued payment were included, and more than a

hundred names were added of cities which are not known to have paid before, including a large group of cities in the Euxine and the stubborn island of Melos. The total of the assessment by these measures was increased to nearly 1500 talents. But this total is in part illusory, for many of the cities waited on events, and in the following years Athens was not able to display the necessary force overseas. Borrowings, though on a reduced scale, had to continue. A sharp increase in tribute was necessary to maintain the offensive, but it was an act of ruthless imperialism. It increased discontent among the allies, who found sympathy from some of Cleon's opponents in Athens.[19]

10.3 The Victory of Paeonius

While the allies were to be more heavily burdened, Cleon raised the jurors' fee from two to three obols. It would be a mistake to consider this measure a mere bid for popularity. We shall hardly be wrong in regarding it as an attempt to relieve the distress which the yearly invasions of Attica and losses of the harvests inflicted upon the poorer citizens. Meanwhile Nicias managed to retrieve his military reputation. In the autumn of 425 he led an army into Corinthian territory, gained a partial victory at Solygea, and then went on to the peninsula of Methana, between Troezen and Epidaurus. He built a wall across the isthmus and left a garrison in Methone. In the following year, he made the more important acquisition of the island of Cythera, from which he was able to make descents upon Laconia. The loss of Cythera was in itself more serious for Sparta than the loss of Pylos, but owing to the attendant circumstances the earlier event made far greater stir. The Athenians had now three bases of operation in the Peloponnese—Pylos, Cythera, and Methone.

425 B.C. Activity of Nicias

424 B.C. Capture of Cythera

To none was the discomfiture of the Spartans in Messenia sweeter than to the Messenian exiles who had borne their part in the work of that memorable day. At Olympia there is a figure of Victory, hovering aloft in the air, amid wind-blown drapery, while an eagle flies below her. It is the work of the sculptor Paeonius, and it was dedicated by the Messenians in the Altis of Zeus, with part of the spoil they stripped from the hated usurpers of their land.

Victory of Paeonius

The Athenian Capture of Nisaea

In each of the first seven years of the war Attica was invaded, except twice; on one occasion the attack on Plataea had taken the place of the incursion into Attica, and, on another, the Peloponnesian army was hindered by earthquakes from advancing beyond the isthmus. Every year by way of reply the Athenians invaded the Megarid twice, in spring and in autumn. The capture of Pylos affected both these annual events. The invasion of Attica was discontinued, because Athens held the Spartan hostages; and the elation of the Athenians at their success induced them to undertake a bolder enterprise against Megara.

429 B.C.

426 B.C.

Minoa, now a hill on the mainland but then an island, lay at the entrance to the harbour of Nisaea. It was separated from Nisaea by a narrow channel, protected by two projecting

Capture of Minoa, 427 B.C.

towers. Nicias had destroyed these towers three years before and had fortified Minoa so as to blockade completely the port of Nisaea. The Megarians then depended entirely on the port of Pagae and their communications with the Crisaean Gulf. They were hard pressed; their distress was vividly portrayed in the comedy of the *Acharnians* which was put on the stage two years later. The situation became almost intolerable when a domestic sedition led to the expulsion of a small party who seized Pagae and cut off Megara from importing food on that side too. It became a question of either allowing the exiles to return or submitting to Athens. Those who knew that the return of their rivals from Pagae would mean their own doom opened secret negotiations with Athens and offered to betray Megara and Nisaea. The Long Walls and Nisaea were held by a Peloponnesian garrison. The generals Hippocrates and Demosthenes organised the enterprise. While a force of 4000 hoplites and 600 horse marched overland by Eleusis, the generals sailed to Minoa. When night fell, they crossed to the mainland. There was a gate in the eastern wall close to the spot where it joined the fortification of Nisaea, and near the gate there was a hollow out of which earth to make bricks had been dug. Here Hippocrates and 600 hoplites concealed themselves, while Demosthenes, with some light-armed Plataeans and a band of the youthful Peripoloi or Patrollers of Attica, took up a position still nearer the gate, in a sacred enclosure of the war-god, Enyalios. The conspirators had long matured their plan for admitting the Athenians. As no boat could openly leave the harbour, owing to the occupation of Minoa, they had easily obtained permission of the commander of the Peloponnesian garrison to carry out through this gate a small boat on a cart at night, for the alleged purpose of privateering. They used to convey the boat to the sea along the ditch which surrounded Nisaea, and, after a midnight row, return before dawn and re-enter the Long Walls by the same gate. This became a regular practice, so that on the night fixed for executing the conspiracy they carried out the boat without exciting any suspicion. When the boat returned, the gate was opened, and Demosthenes, who had been watching for the moment, leapt forward and forced his way in, assisted by the Megarians. They kept the gate open till Hippocrates arrived with his hoplites, and when these were inside the Long Walls were easily secured, the garrison retreating into Nisaea. In the morning the main body of the Athenians arrived. A scheme for

424 B.C.

the betrayal of Megara had been concerted. The conspirators urged their fellow-citizens to sally forth and do battle with the Athenians; they had secretly arranged that the Athenians should rush in, and had anointed themselves with oil, as a mark by which they should be known and spared in the assault. But their political opponents, informed of the scheme, immediately rushed to the gates and declared decisively that they should not be opened; the battle would have to be first fought inside. The delay apprised the Athenians that their friends had been baffled, and they set about blockading Nisaea. Their energy was such that in two days the circumvallation was practically completed, and the garrison, in want of food (for their supplies were derived from Megara), capitulated. Thus the Long Walls, which they had built themselves, and the port of Nisaea had passed again into the hands of the Athenians. They were not, however, destined to take the city on the hill. The Spartan general Brasidas, who was recruiting in the north-east regions of the Peloponnese for an expedition to Thrace, hastened to the relief of Megara and was joined

by forces from Corinth and Boeotia, to whom the defence of Megara was vital. An indecisive skirmish took place; the Athenians did not care to risk a battle and they resolved to be content with the acquisition of Nisaea. Soon afterwards there was a revolution in Megara. The exiles from Pagae were received back; they soon got the power into their hands and murdered their enemies. A narrow oligarchical constitution was established. The new order of things, says Thucydides, lasted a very long time, considering the small number of its authors.

Athens fails in Boeotia

The recovery of Nisaea, which had been lost by the Thirty Years' Peace, was a solid success and it seemed to the ambitious hopes of the two generals who had achieved it the first step in the recovery of all the former conquests of their city. Hippocrates and Demosthenes induced Athens to strive to win back what she had lost at Coronea. But Boeotia was not like Megara; and an attempt on Boeotia was an

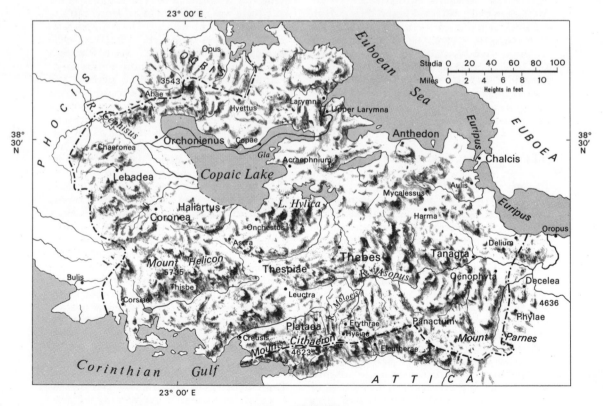

23. BOEOTIA

unwise reversion to the early continental policy which Pericles had definitely abandoned. The dream of a second Oenophyta was far less likely to come true than the threat of a second Coronea. And the enterprise was a departure from the Periclean strategy, of which Nicias was the chief exponent, and it is significant that Nicias took no part in it. Moreover at this moment Athens, as we shall see, ought to have concentrated her forces on the defence of her Thracian possessions which were in grave jeopardy. The Boeotian, like the Megarian, plan was formed in concert with native malcontents who wished to overthrow the oligarchies in the cities, to establish democratic governments, and probably dissolve the Boeotian Confederacy. At this time the Confederacy was governed by 11 Boeotarchs, four of whom were chosen by Thebes, and a federal council representing the various districts of Boeotia and divided into four panels.[20]

Plan for invading Boeotia

The new Boeotian plan, in which Demosthenes was now concerned, did not involve such extensive operations and combinations as that which he had conceived when he invaded Aetolia. But the two plans resembled each other in so far as each involved operations from the Crisaean Gulf. Demosthenes, having sailed to Naupactus and gathered a force of Acarnanians, was to go on to secure Siphae, the port of Thespiae, on the shore of a promontory beneath Mount Helicon. On the same day, the Athenian army under Hippocrates was to enter Boeotia on the north-east and seize the temple of Apollo at Delium, which stood on the seacoast over against the Lelantine plain in Euboea. At the same time Chaeronea, the extreme west town of the land, was to be seized by domestic conspirators. Thus on three sides the Boeotian government was to be threatened; and the same day was fixed for the three attacks. But the scheme was betrayed by a Phocian, and frustrated by the Boeotarchs, who occupied Siphae and Chaeronea with strong forces and made a general levy of the Boeotians to oppose the army of Hippocrates. It mattered little that Demosthenes made a mistake about the day fixed for the attack; he found himself opposed by a Boeotian force and could only retire. None of the internal movements in the Boeotian cities, on which the Athenians had counted, took place.

Battle of Delium 424 B.C.

Hippocrates, however, had time to reach and fortify Delium. He had a force of 7000 hoplites and over 20,000 light-armed troops. A trench, with a strong rampart and palisade, was drawn round the temple, and at noon on the fifth day from their departure from Athens the work was completed. The army then left Delium, to return home. When they crossed the frontier and entered the Athenian territory of Oropus, at about a mile from Delium, the hoplites halted, to wait for Hippocrates, who had remained behind to give final directions to the garrison of the temple; the light-armed troops proceeded on their way to Athens. The hoplites were interrupted in their rest by a message from Hippocrates, ordering them to form instantly in array of battle, as the enemy were upon them. The Boeotian forces had been concentrated at Tanagra, about 5 miles from Delium, and they had been persuaded by Pagondas, one of the Theban Boeotarchs, to follow and attack the Athenians in their retreat although they had left Boeotia. After a rapid march, Pagondas halted where a hill concealed him from the view of the Athenians and drew up his army. It consisted of 7000 hoplites—the same number as that of the enemy—1000 cavalry, and over 10,000 light-armed men. The Thebans occupied the right wing, in the unique formation of a mass 25 shields deep; the other contingents varied in depth. The Athenian line was formed with the uniform and regular depth of eight shields. Hippocrates had arrived and was moving along the lines encouraging his men, when the enemy, who had for some time been visible on the crest of the hill, raised the Paean and charged down. The extreme parts of the wings never met, for watercourses lay between them. But the rest pushed shield against shield and fought fiercely. On the right the Athenians were victorious, but on the left they could not sustain the enormous pressure of the massed Theban force, especially as the Thebans were probably man for man stronger than the Athenians through a laborious athletic training. But even the victory on the right was neutralised through the sudden appearance of a squadron of cavalry, which Pagondas, seeing the situation, had sent unobserved round the hill. The Athenians thought it was the vanguard of another army and fled. Hippocrates was slain and the army completely dispersed.

The battle of Delium confirmed the verdict of Coronea.

Subsequent negotiations

The Boeotians were left masters of the field, but Delium itself was still held by the invader. This led to a curious negotiation. The Athenians demanded their dead, and the Boeotians refused permission to take them unless they evacuated the temple of Apollo. Now if there was an international custom which was universally recognised among the Greeks, even among the barbarous Aetolians, it was the obligation of the victor to allow his defeated opponents to remove and bury their dead, unconditionally. This custom had the sanction of religious feeling and was seldom violated. But in this case the Boeotians had a pretext for departing from the usual practice. They alleged that the Athenians had on their side violated the laws of Hellenic warfare by seizing and fortifying the sanctuary of Delium and living in it, as if it were unconsecrated—using even the sacred water. There seems little doubt that the conduct of the Boeotians was a greater departure from recognised custom than the conduct of the Athenians. The herald of the Athenians made what seems a foolish reply, to the effect that Delium having been occupied by the Athenians was now part of Attic soil, and that they showed the customary respect for the temple, so far as was possible in the circumstances. 'You cannot tell us to quit Boeotia,' he said, 'for the garrison of Delium is not in Boeotia.' The Boeotians made an appropriate answer to the quibble: 'If you are in Boeotia, take what is yours; if you are in your own land, do as you like.' The dead were not surrendered, and the Boeotians settled down to the blockade of Delium.

Capture of Delium, seventeen days after the battle

They took the place by a curious device. They sawed in two and hollowed out a great beam, which they joined together again very exactly, like a flute, and suspended a vessel by chains at the end of the beam; the iron mouth of a bellows directed downwards into the vessel was attached to the beam, of which a great part was itself overlaid with iron. This machine they brought up from a distance on carts to various points of the rampart where vine stems and wood had been most extensively used, and when it was quite near the wall they applied a large bellows to their own end of the beam and blew through it. The blast, prevented from escaping, passed into the vessel, which contained burning coals and sulphur and pitch; these made a huge flame and set fire to the rampart, so that no one could remain upon it. The garrison took flight and the fort was taken. The Boeotians no longer refused to surrender the dead, who included rather fewer than 1000 hoplites.

The War in Thrace.
Athens loses Amphipolis

The defeat of Delium eclipsed the prestige of Athens, but did not seriously impair her strength, and was balanced by the success of a diplomatic mission to Persia. When the war had broken out the Athenians had no reason to fear Persia, with whom they had made a formal peace, but it was clearly in Sparta's interest, especially in view of her financial weakness, to enlist Persian help. Spartan envoys were intercepted in 430 but others got through, as the Athenians discovered in the late summer of 425 when they arrested a Persian envoy bound for Sparta. In his despatch the Persian king complained that it was impossible to know what precisely the Spartans had in mind. The Athenian reaction was to send envoys to Susa. At Ephesus these envoys heard that Artaxerxes had died and so they returned to Athens. When his successor Darius was firmly established a second mission was sent out, and early in 423 the peace was renewed.[21]

Peace with Persia renewed

The year, however, ended badly with a sequence of serious reverses in the north. The war in Thrace was always complicated by the neighbourhood of the kingdoms of Thrace and Macedonia. Before the fall of Potidaea the Athenians had formed an alliance with Sitalces, king of Thrace, and made his son Sadocus an Athenian citizen. The realm of Sitalces extended from the Strymon to the Euxine; its coast-line began at Abdera and ended at the mouth of the Ister. The revenue of tribute both from Greek towns and barbarians amounted, in the reign of his successor, to more than 400 talents—counting only what was paid in the shape of coin. The alliance with Athens seems to have lasted till the king's death. An Athenian ambassador from Thrace, in the *Acharnians* of Aristophanes, reports to the Assembly:

The Thracian kingdom

425 B.C.

> We passed our time
> In drinking with Sitalces. He's your friend,
> Your friend and lover, if ever there was one,
> And writes the name of Athens on his walls.

Perdiccas, the shifty king of Macedonia, played a double game between Athens and Sparta. At one time he helped the Chalcidians against Athens, at another he sided with Athens against her revolted allies. In 429 combined operations had been planned between Athens and Sitalces. Sitalces was to lead the Thracian tribesmen against Perdiccas and to help in the reduction of the Chalcidic rebels. A huge Thracian army was mustered and invaded Macedonia. The territory was laid waste, but for some reason which Thucydides does not adequately explain the Athenian force did not arrive, and the Thracians withdrew. Throughout all changes of fortune, the city of Methone, situated to the south of the mouth of the Haliacmon, held to Athens with unshaken

Double dealings of Macedonia

Methone

fidelity, though the varying relations between Athens and Perdiccas must have seriously affected the welfare of the Methonaeans. Some decrees relating to Methone have been preserved on a marble, adorned with a relief of the Athenian Demos seated, stretching out his hand to the Demos of Methone, who stands accompanied by a dog. In the first decree, probably of 430, Methone is given the special privilege of remission of tribute with the exception of the *aparche* paid to Athena; and Perdiccas, who is nominally at peace with Athens, is required to refrain from interfering with Methone's trade by sea or land. Envoys are to proceed to Perdiccas to reconcile the parties. In a second decree the Methonaeans are allowed to import corn up to a stated amount from Byzantium.[22] But the drastic increase in the tribute assessment of 425 probably made Athens more unpopular among the allies.

Chalcidians and Macedonia appeal to Sparta

Perdiccas and the Chalcidians (of Olynthus) feared that the success of Pylos might be followed by increased activity of the Athenians in Thrace, and they sent an embassy to Sparta, requesting help, and expressing a wish that Brasidas might be the commander of whatever auxiliary force should be sent. It was wise policy for Sparta to threaten her rival in Thrace at this juncture, though the prospect of any abiding success was faint. No Spartans went, but 700 Helots were armed as hoplites; the government was glad to take the opportunity of removing another portion of this dangerous element in the population. Having obtained some Peloponnesian recruits and having incidentally, as we have already seen, saved Megara, Brasidas marched northward to the new colony of Heraclea.

Character of Brasidas

Brasidas was a Spartan by mistake. He had nothing in common with his fellows, except personal bravery, which was the least of his virtues. He had a restless energy and spirit of enterprise, which received small encouragement from the slow and hesitating authorities of his country. He had an oratorical ability which distinguished him above the Lacedaemonians, who were notoriously unready of speech. He was free from political prejudices, and always showed himself tolerant, just, and moderate in dealing with political questions. Besides this, he was simple and straightforward; men knew that they could trust his word implicitly. But the quality which most effectually contributed to his brilliant career, and perhaps most strikingly belied his Spartan origin, was his power of winning popularity abroad and making himself personally liked by

strangers. In Greece, the Spartan abroad was a proverb for insolence and misbehaviour. Brasidas shone out, on a dark background, by his frank and winning manners.

Brasidas at Acanthus

His own tact and rapid movements, as well as the influence of Perdiccas, enabled Brasidas to march through Thessaly, which was by no means well disposed to the Lacedaemonians. When he reached Macedonia, Perdiccas required his assistance against Arrhabaeus, the king of the Lyncestians, in Upper Macedonia. Brasidas was impatient to reach Chalcidice, and he contrived to make a separate arrangement with Arrhabaeus and abstained from invading Lyncestis, to the disappointment of Perdiccas. He then marched against Acanthus, situated on the base of the peninsula of Acte. The mass of the Acanthians were perfectly content with the position of their city as a member of the Athenian Confederacy; they had no grievance against Athens; and they were unwilling to receive the overtures of Brasidas. They were, however, induced by a small party to admit Brasidas alone into the city and give him a hearing in the Assembly. From his lips the Acanthians learned the Lacedaemonian programme, and Thucydides has given the substance of what he said. 'We declared at the beginning of the war that we were taking up arms to protect the liberties of Hellas against Athens, and for this purpose we are here now. You have a high repute for power and wisdom, and therefore a refusal from you will retard the good cause. Every city which joins me will retain her autonomy; the Lacedaemonians have pledged themselves to me on this point by solemn oaths. And I have not come to be the tool of a faction, or to enslave the many to the few; in that case we should be committing an act worse than the oppression of the Athenians. If you refuse, and say that I have no right to thrust an alliance on a people against its will, I will ravage your land and force you to consent. And for two reasons I am justified in doing so. The tribute you pay to Athens is a direct and material injury to Sparta, for it contributes to strengthen her foe; and secondly, your example may prevent others from embracing freedom.' When Brasidas retired, there was a long debate; much was said on both sides. The manner of Brasidas had produced a favourable impression; and the fear of losing the vintage was a powerful motive with many for acceding to his demand. The vote was taken secretly and the majority determined to detach themselves from Athens, though they had no practical grievance and were not enthusiastic for the change. Sparta's natural friends here as in other cities were the oligarchs.

Acanthus was an Andrian colony, and its action led to the adhesion of two other Andrian colonies, Stagira and Argilus; and the relations which Brasidas established with Argilus led to the capture of the most important of all Athenian posts in Thrace, and among the most important in the whole Athenian empire, the city of Amphipolis. This place, of which the foundation has been already recorded, had diminished the importance of Argilus and roused the jealousy of the Argilians, although some of the colonists were of Argilian origin. The coming of Brasidas offered Argilus an opportunity, for which she had been waiting, against the Athenians of Amphipolis. After a cold wintry night march, Brasidas found the Bridge of the Strymon defended only by a small guard, which he easily overpowered. Amphipolis was completely unprepared, but Brasidas did not venture to attack the city at once; he expected the gates to be opened by conspirators within, and meanwhile he made himself master of the territory.

(See above, p. 239)

That a place of such first-rate importance as Amphipolis should be found unprepared at a time when an energetic enemy like Brasidas was actively engaged against other Athenian cities in the neighbourhood seemed a criminal negligence on the part of the two Strategoi to whom defence of the Thracian interests of Athens was entrusted. These were Thucydides, the son of Olorus, and Eucles. It was inexcusable in Eucles, who was in Amphipolis, to leave the Bridge without an adequate garrison; and it was considered culpable of Thucydides, who had mining interests in the district, not to have moved up the Athenian squadron from the island of Thasos. A message was sent at once to Thucydides; that officer hastened back with seven triremes and reached the mouth of the Strymon in the evening of the same day. But in the meantime Brasidas had offered the inhabitants of Amphipolis such easy terms that they were accepted. He promised every citizen who chose to remain equal political rights, without any loss of property; while all who preferred to go were allowed five days to remove their possessions. Had the Amphipolitans known how near Thucydides was, they would probably have declined to surrender. Thucydides arrived just too late. But he preserved Eion, at the mouth of the river, and repelled an attack of Brasidas.

The true blame for the loss of Amphipolis probably rests not on the General, who was in a very difficult position, but on the Athenians,

Revolt of Amphipolis (424 B.C.)

Negligence of Thucydides the historian;

who, instead of making adequate provision for the defence of Thrace, were misled by the new strategy of Demosthenes into the unsuccessful expedition to Boeotia. It must be remembered that Thucydides was responsible for the safety of the whole coast of Chalcidice and Thrace; that at any moment he might be summoned to defend any part of it from Potidaea to the Chersonese; that therefore either Eion or Thasos was a suitable centre for his headquarters; and that Eion had the disadvantage of having no harbour.

It may be that we are indebted to the fall of Amphipolis for the great history of the war. The Athenians attributed the loss of one of their most valuable possessions to the neglect of their generals. Thucydides was sentenced to banishment, and it is probable that Cleon, to whom he bore no goodwill, was instrumental in drawing down upon him a punishment which possibly was not deserved. But in his exile the discredited general became the greatest of Greek historians. If he had remained at Athens and continued his official career he might not have concentrated his whole mind on his history. By travelling in foreign lands, among the enemies of Athens and in neutral states, Thucydides gained a large knowledge of the Hellenic world and wrote from a wider point of view than he could have done if he had only had an Athenian experience. 'Associating,' he says himself, 'with both sides, with the Peloponnesians quite as much as with the Athenians, because of my exile, I was thus enabled to watch quietly the course of events.' Judged in this way, the fall of Amphipolis, a great loss to Athens, may have been a great gain to the world.

his banishment

Having secured the Strymon, Brasidas retraced his steps and subdued the small towns on the high eastern tongue of Chalcidice. The Andrian Sane and another place held out, and their obscurity saved them. Brasidas hastened on to gain possession of Torone, the strongest city of Sithonia. A small party of the citizens invited and expected him; but the rest of the inhabitants and the Athenian garrison knew nothing of his coming until the place was in his hands. Torone was a hill city by the sea. Besides its walls, it had the protection of a fort on a height which rose out of the water and was connected with the city by a narrow neck of land. This fortress, known as Lecythus, was occupied by an Athenian garrison. Brasidas halted within about half a mile of the city before daybreak. Seven bold soldiers, lightarmed and carrying daggers, were secretly

Reduction of Acte

Capture of Torone, 424-3 B.C.

introduced by the conspirators. They killed the sentries on the top of the hill, and then broke down a postern gate and undid the bars of the great gate near the market-place, in order that the men without might rush in from two sides. A hundred targeteers who had drawn near to the walls dashed in first, and when a signal was given Brasidas followed with the rest. The surprise was complete. Fifty Athenian hoplites were sleeping in the agora; a few were cut down, but most escaped to the fort of Lecythus, which was held for some days and then captured.

Brasidas called an assembly of the Toronaeans, and spoke to them in words which sounded strange indeed, falling from the mouth of an Hellenic victor. He told them that he had not come to injure the city or the citizens; that those who had not aided in the conspiracy to admit him would be treated on a perfect equality with the others; that the Lacedaemonians had never suffered any wrong from Torone; and that he did not think the worse of those who opposed him.

Negotiations for Peace

Athenian inactivity

In the meantime the Athenians had taken no measures to check the victorious winter-campaign of Brasidas. Their inactivity was due to two causes. The disaster of Delium had disheartened them and rendered the citizens unwilling to undertake fresh toil in Thrace. In Greek history we must steadfastly keep in view that we are reading about citizen soldiers, not about professional soldiers; and that the temper of the time, whether of confidence or dismay, modifies all the calculations of military and political prudence. Secondly, the peace party, especially represented by the generals Nicias and Laches, took advantage of this depression to work in the direction of peace. The possession of the Spartan captives gave the means of coming to terms with Sparta at any moment, but it was clear that they could not now conclude a peace on such favourable terms as would have been possible a year before. If an able statesman, like Pericles, had at this time possessed the confidence and guided the counsels of the Athenians, he would have persuaded them to postpone all thoughts of peace until the success of Brasidas had been decisively checked and the prestige of Athens in some degree retrieved. This was obviously the right policy, which would have enabled Athens to win the full advantage of the captives of Sphacteria. It was a policy which

Cleon, a far abler politician than any of his opponents, must have preached loudly in the Assembly. But the Athenians were not in a mood to weigh considerations of policy; they were swayed by the feelings of the hour, which were flattered by the arguments of the military experts; and they decisively inclined to peace.

Sparta desires peace

The Lacedaemonians were more deliberately set on peace than the Athenians. Their anxiety to recover the Sphacterian captives increased, and on the other hand they desired to set a term to the career of Brasidas in Chalcidice. They wished to take advantage of the considerable successes he had already won, to extort favourable conditions from Athens before any defeat should undo or reverse his triumphs. Nor was the news of his exploits received at Sparta with unmixed feelings of pleasure. They were rather regarded with jealousy and distrust. The victories had not been won by an army of Spartan citizens, but by the brilliant un-Spartan qualities of Brasidas and a force of which the effectiveness entirely depended on its leader. Brasidas had broken through the fetters of Lacedaemonian method, and his fellow-citizens felt that he was a man of different fibre from themselves, and suspected and disliked him accordingly. Moreover the personal influence of king Pleistoanax was thrown weightily into the scale of peace. This king had been banished just before the Thirty Years' Peace, on the ground that he had taken bribes to spare Attica when he invaded it after the deliverance of Megara. He had lived for nearly twenty years in western Arcadia on the mountain of Lycaeon, beside the dread sanctuary of Zeus, of which it was told that whosoever entered it lost his shadow and died before the year was out. Even here Pleistoanax was afraid for his life. His house was half within the precincts, so that in case of danger he could retire into the sacred place without passing his door. But he had influence at Delphi, and whenever the Spartans consulted that oracle they were always bidden to take back into their own land the seed of the demigod, the son of Zeus, or else they would have to plough with a silver share. The Lacedaemonians at length recalled him, and re-enthroned him as king with ancient and most solemn ceremonies. But his enemies now vexed him with the charge of having bribed the Pythian priestess to procure his recall. Pleistoanax conceived that such charges would fall to the ground if he satisfied the people by negotiating a permanent peace and restoring as speedily as possible the prisoners from their captivity in Athens to their impatient friends at home. And, as a matter of fact, Sparta had everything to gain from making peace at once, unless she was prepared to adopt the imperial policy of Athens, against which it had been hitherto her rôle to protest. Such a policy might for a time have met with some success if she had put her whole confidence in Brasidas, but must soon have been checked by the naval superiority of her rival.

Pleistoanax and Nicias understood each other; and Nicias, a man of commonplace ability and possessed by one idea, played into the hands of Sparta. It was not, however, an easy matter to arrange the exact terms of a durable pacification, while it was important for Athens that the negotiation should be made before she experienced any further losses in Thrace. Accordingly the two states agreed on a truce for a year, which would give them time to arrange quietly and at leisure the conditions of a permanent peace. The truce and some of its conditions were suggested by Athens; the terms were drawn up at Sparta and accepted by the Spartan Assembly, and were then conveyed to Athens, where they were proposed for the acceptance of the Athenian Assembly by Laches. The clauses were the following: (1) Free access to the Delphic oracle was ensured to all, for Athens had been debarred from consulting it during the war. (2) Both parties guaranteed the protection of the treasures of Delphi. (3) During the truce both parties should keep what they had, the Athenians retaining Pylos, Cythera, Argolic Methana, Nisaea, and Minoa. (4) The Lacedaemonians were not to sail, even along their own coasts, in warships or in merchant vessels exceeding a certain size (12 tons). (5) The free passage of envoys, for the purpose of arranging a peace, was provided for. (6) Neither party was to receive deserters. (7) Disputes, in case they arose, were to be decided by arbitration.

The truce was sworn to. But in the meantime an event happened in Chalcidice which was to disappoint the pacific calculations of the statesmen at Athens and Sparta. The city of Scione, on the western prong of the Chalcidian fork, revolted from Athens and invited Brasidas in, much to that general's surprise. For it was far more hazardous for the towns on the peninsula of Pallene to defy the authority of Athens than for any others; since by the strong city of Potidaea, which stretched entirely across the narrow isthmus, they were isolated and as much exposed to the full force of Athenian power as if they had been islanders. The arrival of Brasidas and the words he spoke to them wound up the men of Scione to the highest pitch of enthusiasm; they set a golden crown on his head, as the liberator of Hellas, and their admiration for him personally was shown by casting garlands on him, as if he were a victorious athlete—so great was his popularity.

At this point an Athenian and a Lacedaemonian commissioner arrived to announce the truce, which had in fact been concluded two days before Scione revolted. The Athenians refused to admit Scione to the benefit of the armistice until the authorities at home had been consulted. There was deep indignation at Athens when the news of the defection of Scione arrived; it was practically the rebellion of 'islanders' relying on the land-power of Sparta. Cleon was able to take advantage of this exasperation and carry a decree that Scione should be destroyed and all the male inhabitants slain. This incident brings out in an interesting way the geographical difference between the three sea-girt promontories of Chalcidice as to their degrees of participation in the insular character. Acte, with its steep inhospitable shores, is far more continental than insular; Sithonia partakes of both natures more equally, is more strictly a half-island; Pallene is more an island than part of the mainland. And we see the political importance of such geographical differences: the loss of Scione produced an irritation at Athens which the loss of Torone could not inspire.

The revolt of Scione was followed by that of the neighbouring town of Mende and, although this happened distinctly after the truce had been made, Brasidas did not hesitate to accept the alliance of Mende, his plea being that in certain points the Athenians themselves had broken the truce. The case of Mende differed from that of Scione, for the revolt was the doing not of the people but of an oligarchical faction. Brasidas was then obliged to join Perdiccas in another expedition against Arrhabaeus, king of the Lyncestians. The fact that the Macedonian monarch was contributing to the pay of the Peloponnesian army rendered it necessary for Brasidas to co-operate in an enterprise which was of no interest to the Greeks. Arrhabaeus was defeated in a battle, but a reinforcement of Illyrians came to his help, and the warlike reputation of Illyria was so great that their approach produced a panic among the Macedonians and the whole army of Perdiccas fled, leaving the small force of Brasidas to retreat as best it could. He was in great jeopardy, but effected his retreat successfully. The incident led to a breach between

Brasidas and the Macedonians; Perdiccas changed sides once more, and proved his new friendship to Athens by preventing Lacedaemonian troops, which had been sent to join Brasidas, from crossing Thessaly.

The truce observed except in Thrace

Brasidas returned to Torone and found that an Athenian armament of 50 ships, under Nicias and Niceratus, had recovered Mende and was besieging Scione. Everywhere else the truce was observed, and by tacit consent the hostilities in Thrace were not allowed to affect the rest of Greece. But it was inevitable that they should frustrate the purpose for which the truce had been concluded. It was impossible that negotiations with a view to the definitive peace should proceed in exactly the same way as had been originally contemplated; by the end of the year there was a marked change in public feeling at Athens and the influence of Cleon was again in the ascendant. After his spectacular triumph at Sphacteria he had been elected general in 424, but he seems to have been less at ease with the small board of generals than in the Boule or the Assembly, and the attempts on Megara and Boeotia were designed and carried out by Hippocrates and Demosthenes. Cleon had little chance of distinguishing himself, and when the elections were held in 423 the Athenians were moving towards peace; he was not re-elected.[23] But the deterioration of the situation in Thrace gave him his second chance and he was elected once more in 422.

Cleon re-appointed general

If Nicias had played into the hands of Sparta, Brasidas had played into the hands of Cleon, and effectually embarrassed the home government. His conduct first in regard to Scione and then in regard to Mende was indefensible and entirely governed by personal considerations. The gold crown of Scione seems to have acted like a potent spell in arousing his ambition, and he began to play a war-game of his own. His policy was the more unhappy, as he was perfectly aware that it was impossible to protect the cities of Pallene against the fleets of their indignant mistress. He effectually hindered the conclusion of peace, which his city sincerely desired. Brasidas and Cleon, Thucydides says, were the chief opponents of the peace; but while the motives of Brasidas were purely personal, the policy of Cleon, whatever his motives may have been, was statesmanlike. He adopted the principle of Pericles that Athens must maintain her empire unimpaired, and he saw that this could not be done without energetic opposition to the progress of Brasidas in Thrace. The charge of Thucydides that Cleon desired war, because he could not so easily conceal his own dishonesty in peace, does not carry the least conviction. When the truce expired, Cleon was able to carry a resolution that an expedition should be made to reconquer Amphipolis. It does not appear whether he was himself anxious for the command, in consequence of his previous success at Pylos, or whether the opposition and lukewarmness of the strategoi practically forced him into it. But it is certain that all possible difficulties were thrown in his way by Nicias and the peace party, who in their hearts doubtless hoped for the complete failure of his enterprise.

Summer 422 B.C.

Battle of Amphipolis and Peace of Nicias

Cleon set sail with 30 ships, bearing 1200 Athenian hoplites, 300 Athenian cavalry, as well as allies. Taking some troops from the force which was still blockading Scione, he gained a considerable success at the outset by taking Torone and capturing the Lacedaemonian governor; Brasidas arrived too late to relieve it. Cleon went on to the mouth of the Strymon and made Eion his headquarters, intending to wait there until he had augmented his army by reinforcements from Thrace and Macedonia.

Site of Amphipolis

Not far from its mouth the stream of the Strymon expands into the lake Kerkinitis (now drained); on narrowing again into its proper channel it is forced to bend to the westward in order to skirt a hill, and forms a great loop, before it disgorges its waters into the sea close to the walls of Eion. In this loop the high city of Amphipolis stood, the river serving as its natural defence, so that it required fortifications only on the eastern side. On the right bank of the river, to the west of the town, rose the hill of Cerdylion; on the east were the heights of Pangaeus. A ridge joined Pangaeus with the hill of Amphipolis, and the wall of the city crossed the ridge. The Strymon Bridge was outside the south-western extremity of the wall; but, since the place had passed into the hands of Brasidas, a palisade had been built connecting the wall with the bridge. Brasidas with some of his forces took up a commanding position on the hill of Cerdylion, from which he had a wide view of the surrounding country, while other troops remained in Amphipolis under the command of Clearidas, whom he had appointed governor. Their hoplites numbered about 2000.

The discontent and murmurs of his troops forced Cleon to move prematurely. The soldiers had grumbled at leaving Athens under an utterly inexperienced commander to face a general like Brasidas, and they were now displeased at his inaction. In order to do something, Cleon led his army to a hill north of the city wall, where he could obtain a view of the country beyond, and, as he saw Brasidas on Cerdylion, he had no fear of being attacked.[24] But Brasidas was resolved to attack, before reinforcements should arrive; and, seeing the Athenians move, he descended from Cerdylion and entered Amphipolis. The Athenians could

observe the whole army gathered within the city and Brasidas himself offering sacrifice at the temple of Athena; and Cleon was presently informed that the feet of men and horses, ready to sally forth, could be seen under one of the gates. Having verified this fact for himself, Cleon gave the signal to wheel to the left and retreat to Eion; it was the only possible line of retreat and necessarily exposed the unshielded side to an enemy issuing from the city. But he made the fatal mistake of not preparing his men for action, in case they should be forced to fight; he rashly calculated that he would have time to get away. Hence when Brasidas, *Battle*

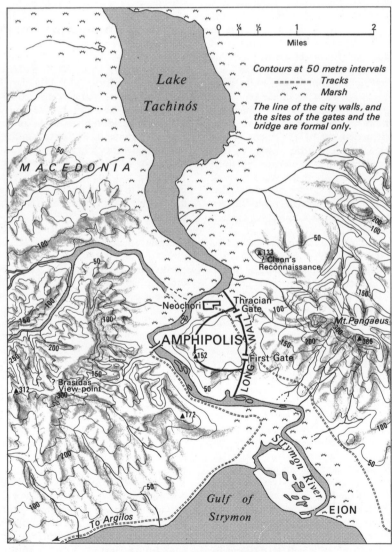

24. ENVIRONS OF AMPHIPOLIS

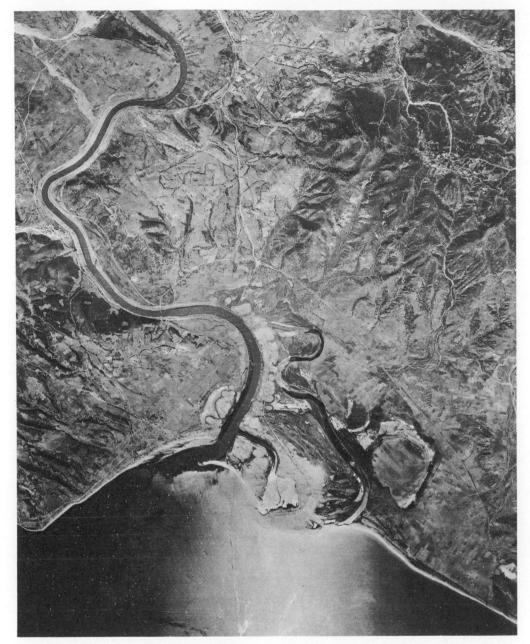

10.4 Amphipolis and district, from the air

with 150 hoplites, came forth from one of the gates, ran up the road, and charged the Athenian centre, the left wing, which was in advance, was struck with terror and took to flight. At the same time the rest of the garrison of Amphipolis, led by Clearidas, had issued from a more northerly gate and attacked the Athenian right. Here a stand was made, though Cleon, unused to the dangers of warfare, proved himself no better than many of his hoplites, who were said to be the flower of the army. He fled and was shot down by a targeteer. But Brasidas was also doomed to die. As he was turning to assist Clearidas, he

Death of Cleon

Death of Brasidas

received a mortal wound and was carried into the city. He lived long enough to be assured of the utter rout of the foe; but his death had practically converted the victory into a defeat. The people of Amphipolis gave him the honours of a hero; they made him their founder, and removed all the memorials of the true founder of their colony, the Athenian Hagnon. Sacrifices were offered to Brasidas, and yearly games celebrated in his honour.

Result of the battle—peace

The death of Brasidas removed the chief obstacle to peace; for no man was competent, or disposed, to resume his large designs in Thrace. The defeat and death of Cleon gave a free hand to Nicias and the peace party. The peace party were in truth far more responsible for the disaster than Cleon, whom they had placed in a false position. Thus the battle of Amphipolis led immediately to the conclusion of peace; and the comic poet could rejoice

(Aristophanes)

in the destruction of the pestle and mortar—Cleon and Brasidas—with which the spirits of War and Tumult had pounded the cities of Greece. But the desire for peace seems to have been even stronger at Sparta than at Athens, where there was a certain feeling, in spite of the longing for a rest from warfare, that the lustre of the city was tarnished and something strenuous should be done. Menaces of invading Attica were required to apply the necessary pressure; though they could hardly have been seriously contemplated, as long as the captives were in an Athenian prison.

422-1 B.C.

Negotiations were protracted during autumn and winter, and the peace was definitely concluded about the end of March.

Peace of Nicias, 421 B.C. (March)

The Peace, of which Nicias and Pleistoanax were the chief authors, was fixed for a term of fifty years. Athens undertook to restore most of the posts which she had occupied during the war against the Peloponnesians: Pylos, Cythera, Methana, Atalanta, and Pteleon in Thessaly. But she insisted upon retaining Sollion and Anactorion, and the port of Nisaea. The Lacedaemonians engaged to restore Amphipolis, and to relinquish Argilus, Stagira, Acanthus, Scolus, Olynthus, Spartolus. These cities were to be guaranteed independence provided that they paid tribute to Athens—not, however, at the exorbitant rate recently fixed, but according to the original assessment of Aristides. Moreover, the border fortress of Panacton, on Mount Cithaeron, which the Boeotians had recently occupied, was to be restored to Athens. Certain towns in the possession of Athens, such as Torone, were to be dealt with at the discretion of Athens. All captives on both sides were to be liberated.

Corinth, Megara, Boeotia refuse to accept the Peace

It appeared immediately that the situation was not favourable to a durable peace, for, when the terms were considered at Sparta by a meeting of the members of the Peloponnesian League, Corinth, Boeotia, Megara, and Elis, Sparta's strongest allies all voted against acceptance; but the smaller states, who had nothing to gain by a continuation of the war, ensured a majority for the peace. Corinth was indignant that Sollion and Anactorion were left in Athenian hands; Megara was furious that she was not to recover Nisaea; Boeotia refused to hand over Panacton, and Elis resented Spartan interference in her dispute with the border town of Lepreon. Yet Athens could hardly have demanded less. The consequence was that the Peace was only partial; those allies which were politically of most consequence refused to accept it, and they were joined by Elis; the diplomacy of Nicias was a complete failure, so far as it aimed at ensuring an abiding peace. But since the deepest cause of the war lay in the commercial competition between Athens and Corinth, and since the interests of Sparta were not at stake, the treaty might seem at least to have the merit of simplifying the situation.

Cleon's policy justified, if the Periclean imperialism was justified

But if we admit the justification of the imperial policy of Pericles, then the policy of vigorous action advocated by Cleon was abundantly justified. It may safely be said that if the conduct of the state had rested entirely with Cleon, and if the military talents of the city had been loyally placed at his disposal, the interests of Athens (as Pericles understood them) would have been far better served than if Nicias and his party had been allowed to manage all things as they willed without the restraint of Cleon's opposition. Few statesmen of the merit of Cleon have come before posterity for judgment at such a great disadvantage, condemned by Thucydides, held up to eternal ridicule by Aristophanes. If we allow for the personal prejudice of Thucydides, these testimonies only show that Cleon was a coarse, noisy, ill-bred, audacious man, offensive to noblemen and formidable to officials—the watch-dog of the people. Nothing is proved against his political insight or his political honesty. The portrait of Aristophanes in the *Knights* carries no more historical value than, nowadays, a caricature in a comic paper. He too had suffered from the assaults of Cleon, who

had dragged him to the Senate House,
And trodden him down and bellowed over him,
And mauled him till he scarce escaped alive.

The Peace, 421 B.C.

The Peace of Nicias was celebrated by a

play of Aristophanes, which admirably expresses the exuberant joy then felt at Athens, but carefully avoids the suggestion of any noble sentiment that may have quickened the poet's delight in the accomplishment of the policy he had advocated. So Cleon's friends might have said; but we judge Aristophanes unfairly, if we misapprehended the comic poet's function. Comedy did not guide public opinion, but rather echoed it; comedy set up no exalted ideal or high standard of action. The best hits were those which tickled the man in the market-place and more or less responded to his thoughts. Aristophanes had his own political prejudices and predilections; but as a son of Athens he was assuredly proud of the great place which her democracy had won for her in the world. It was the nature and the business of his muse to distort in the mirror of comedy the form and feature of the age.

CHAPTER 11

The Decline and Downfall of the Athenian Empire

New Political Combinations with Argos

Sparta and Athens form a defensive alliance

Sparta had good reasons for desiring peace: the prospect in the Peloponnese gave her no little concern. Mantinea had been gradually enlarging her boundaries southwards, and that could not be permitted. Elis was sulky and hostile because, in a quarrel with Lepreon, Sparta had supported her rival. Far more serious than these minor vexations was the circumstance that the treaty of peace with Argos was about to expire. It had been a consideration of supreme importance for Sparta, when she entered upon the war with Athens, that for the next ten years she was secure on the side of her old Peloponnesian rival. But there was now the chance that Athens and Argos might combine, and there was urgent need, as Argos had not agreed to renew the treaty, to come to terms with Athens. These reasons which recommended the peace to Sparta ought to have prevented Athens from consenting to it. The settlement was a complete failure. Not only did the Corinthians and the other chief allies refuse to accede to it, but the signatories found themselves unable to carry out the terms they had agreed upon. The Chalcidians refused to surrender Amphipolis, and the Spartans could not compel them. Athens therefore justly declined to carry out her part of the bargain. As a way out of this deadlock, the Spartans, impatient at all costs to recover the Sphacterian prisoners, conceived the device of entering into a defensive alliance with their old enemy. This proposal, warmly supported by Nicias, was accepted, and the captives were at length restored—Athens still retaining Pylos and Cythera.

This alliance between Sparta and Athens led directly to the dissolution of the Peloponnesian league. Corinth, Mantinea, and Elis, considering themselves deserted by their leader, broke with her and formed an alliance with Argos, which now enters upon the scene. The Chalcidians of Thrace joined. There was, however, little reason to fear or hope that the intimacy between Sparta and Athens could be long or strong, seeing that Athens insisted on keeping Cythera and Pylos until Amphipolis should be restored to her and the other states should accede to the Peace. In the following year these unstable political combinations were upset by a change in the balance of parties at Athens, and by the triumph of the anti-Athenian war-party at Sparta. The opposition to Nicias was led by Hyperbolus, a man of the same class and same kind of ability as Cleon; a comic poet—and no statesman was such a favourite butt of comedy as Hyperbolus—described him as a Cleon in hyperbole. But the movement against peace was now strengthened by the accession of a young man of high birth, brilliant intellect, and no morality—Alcibiades, son of Cleinias. Educated by his kinsman Pericles in democratic traditions, he was endowed by nature with extraordinary beauty and talents, and by fortune with the inheritance of wealth which enabled him to indulge an inordinate taste

Disruption of Peloponnesian league

420 B.C.

Hyperbolus

Alcibiades

for ostentation. He had shocked his kinsfolk and outraged the city, not by his dissoluteness, but by the incredible insolence which accompanied it. The numerous anecdotes of his petulance, which no one dared to punish, need not all be true; but they illustrate the fact that undue respect for persons of birth and wealth had not disappeared in the Athenian democracy. Alcibiades was feared and courted, and pursued by lovers of both sexes. He fought with bravery at Delium, where his life was saved by his friend Socrates the philosopher. It was a celebrated friendship. Intellectual power and physical courage were the only points of likeness between them; socially and morally, as well as in favour and fortune, they were as contrasted as two men well could be. Though Socrates took no interest in politics, he was an unequalled dialectician, and an aspiring statesman found his society a good training for the business of political debate. Alcibiades indeed had not in him the stuff of which true statesmen are made; he had not the purpose, the perseverance, or the self-control. An extremely able and dexterous politician he certainly was; but he lacked that balance which a politician, whether scrupulous or unscrupulous, must have in order to be a great statesman. Nor had Alcibiades any sincere belief in the democratic institutions of his country, still less any genuine sympathy with the advanced democratic party whose cause he espoused. When he said—as Thucydides makes him say—at Sparta, at a later stage of his career, that democracy is 'acknowledged folly', he assuredly expressed what he felt in his heart. Yet at this time his ultimate aim may have been to win such a place as that which Pericles had held, and rule his country without being formally her ruler. At all events he saw his way to power through war and conquest.

Alcibiades chosen strategos, 420 B.C. Alliance with Argos Epidaurian War, 419 B.C.

The accession of Alcibiades should have been particularly welcome to the radical party, not so much on account of his family connections or his diplomatic and rhetorical talents, but because he had a military training and could perform the functions of strategos. Unfitness for the post of strategos was, as we have seen, the weak point in the position of men like Hyperbolus and Cleon. But the rise of Alcibiades threatened the eclipse of Hyperbolus, whose influence over the common people was undermined by the popular appeal of the brilliant young aristocrat who kept the best stables in Athens, and the relations between these two politicians sowed the seeds of a bitter feud which was to be carried on against Alcibiades by Androcles and Cleophon,

the successors of Hyperbolus. But this was not yet apparent. When Alcibiades was elected a strategos and Nicias was not re-elected, the prospects of the radical party looked brighter. The change was immediately felt. Athens entered into an alliance with Argos, and her allies Elis and Mantinea, for a hundred years;[1] and the treaty was sealed by a joint expedition against Epidaurus. Sparta assisted Epidaurus, and then the Athenians declared that the Lacedaemonians had broken the Peace.

The new policy of Athens received a check by the return of Nicias to power and the refusal of the people to re-elect the adventurous Alcibiades; but the alliance with Argos was not broken off. Sparta, alarmed by the activity of Argos against Epidaurus, resolved to strike a blow, and sent forth in summer an army under King Agis to invade the Argive land. The allies gathered at Phlius, and Corinth, which had no longer any reason to hold aloof, sent a contingent. The Argive troops under Thrasyllus, with their Mantinean and Elean allies, were in every way inferior to the enemy; yet concentrating close to Nemea, they could easily defend the chief pass from the north into the plain of Argos. But Agis out-manoeuvred them. Sending the Boeotians along the main road by Nemea, he led his own troops by a difficult mountain path, from the west, and descended into the plain by the valley of the Inachus; the Corinthians and Phliasians he sent over by another pass. Thus the Argives were hemmed in between two armies and cut off from their city. They left their position near Nemea and came down into the plain; the Boeotians appear not to have followed. The soldiers of both Thrasyllus and Agis were confident of victory, but the generals were of another mind. Agis, as well as his antagonist, considered his position precarious, and consequently they came to terms, concluding a truce for four months. On both sides there was a loud outcry against the generals, and Thrasyllus was nearly stoned to death by his disappointed soldiers.

Athenian forces now arrived at Argos, 1000 hoplites and 300 cavalry under Laches and Nicostratus, accompanied by Alcibiades as an ambassador.[2] Alcibiades induced the allies to disregard the truce, on the technical ground that, not having been accepted by the Athenians, it was not valid. The allied troops accordingly crossed the mountains into Arcadia and won Orchomenus. The Mantineans now wished to advance against Tegea, but the men of Elis were more anxious to attack Lepreon, whose independence they resented.

418 B.C.

Spartan invasion of Argolis

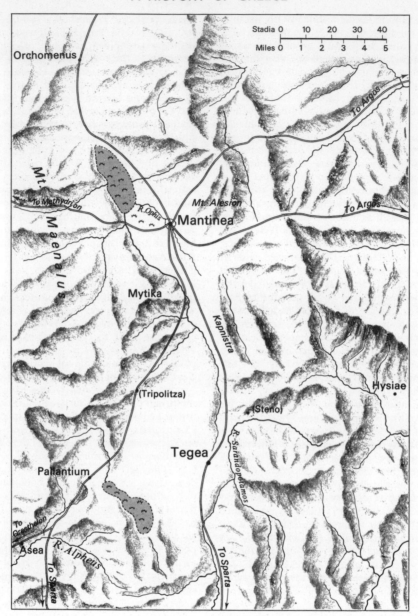

25. PLAIN OF MANTINEA

Outvoted, they withdrew their forces, and the remaining allies proceeded to Mantinea. Meanwhile the Spartans, shaken by the news of the capture of Orchomenus and warned from friends inside the city that the loyalty of Tegea could no longer be depended on, led out their forces and ordered their Arcadian allies to meet them on the route to Tegea.

They also sent for reinforcements to their stronger allies, but the Corinthians and Boeotians would have had to pass through hostile territory and the time was too short.

When the Spartans advanced to the border of Mantinea, the Mantineans and their allies took up a defensive position on the slope of Mount Alesion to the east of the city. Agis at

Battle of Mantinea, 418 B.C.

first intended to attack uphill but he changed his plans and withdrew to Tegeate territory, where he diverted a river course to threaten Mantinea with flooding. This brought the Mantineans and their allies down to the plain and Agis, returning with his army, was surprised to find his enemies drawn up in battle line. The Spartans proved their excellent discipline by a rapid formation of their own line, with the Sciritae on the left wing, next to them the troops who had served under Brasidas in Chalcidice, then the Spartan divisions, and on the right the Tegeates. There were cavalry on both wings. Opposite them the Mantineans were on the right, next to them their Arcadian allies, in the centre the specially trained Argive corps of 1000, and next to them the rest of the Argives; the left wing was held by the Athenians.

The Spartans won the battle, but their success was endangered, and its completeness diminished, by a hitch which occurred at the outset. There was a tendency in all Greek armies, when engaging, to push towards the right, each man fearing for his own exposed right side and trying to edge under the screen of his neighbour's shield. Consequently, an army was always inclined to outflank the left wing of the enemy by its own right. On this occasion, Agis observed that the Mantineans, who were on the right wing of the enemy, stretched far beyond his own left wing, and fearing it would be disastrously outflanked and surrounded, gave a signal to the troops of his extreme left to make a lateral movement further towards the left; and at the same time he commanded two captains on his right to move their divisions round to fill up the gap thus created. The first order was executed, but the two captains refused to move. The result was that the extreme left was isolated and utterly routed, while a band of 1000 chosen Argives dashed through the gap. On the right, however, the Lacedaemonians were completely victorious over the Athenians and other allies. The Athenians would have been surrounded and utterly at the mercy of their foes, if Agis had not recalled his troops to assist his discomfited left wing. Both Laches and Nicostratus fell.

Results of the battle The Lacedaemonians returned home and celebrated the feast of the Carnean Apollo in joy. The victory did much to restore the prestige of Sparta, which had dwindled since the disaster of Sphacteria. The public opinion of Greece had pronounced Sparta to be stupid and inert; it now began to reconsider its judgement. But the victory had

direct political results: it transformed the situation in the Peloponnese. One of those double changes which usually went together, a change in the constitution and a change in foreign policy, was brought about at Argos. *Argos joins Sparta* The democracy was replaced by an oligarchy, and the alliance with Athens was abandoned for an alliance with Sparta. Mantinea, Elis, and the Achaean towns also went over to the victor. Athens was again isolated.

It was probably at this juncture that the advanced democrats in Athens made an attempt *Ostracism of Hyperbolus, 418-7 B.C.* to remove from their way the influential man who was their chief opponent, Nicias. It had been due to his counsels that Argos had not been more effectively supported; there was probably a good deal of dissatisfaction at Athens; and when Hyperbolus proposed that a vote of ostracism should be held he had good grounds to hope that there would be a decision against Nicias, and no apparent reason to fear for himself. He might calculate that most of the supporters of Nicias would vote against the more dangerous Alcibiades. The calculation was so well grounded that it missed its mark, for Alcibiades, seeing the risk which threatened him, deserted Hyperbolus and the democratic party, and allied himself with Nicias. So it came about that Hyperbolus was ruined by his own machination; all the followers of Nicias and Alcibiades wrote *his* name on their sherds, and he was banished for ten years.[3] His political career had ended. This was the last case of ostracism at Athens; the institution was not abolished, but it became a dead letter.

The new alliance of the pious and punctilious Nicias, champion of peace, with the profane and unstable Alcibiades, bent on enterprises of war, was more unnatural than that between the high-born noble and the lamp-maker. But Nicias seems to have been to some small extent aroused from his policy of inactivity. *417 B.C.* We find him undertaking an expedition against Chalcidice, where nothing had been done since the Peace, except the capture of Scione *421 B.C.* and the execution of all the male inhabitants.

Nicias failed in an attempt on Amphipolis; *Conquest of Melos, 416 B.C.* but in the following year an enterprise in the southern Aegean was attended with success. The island of Melos had resolutely stood outside the Athenian empire, unlike her neighbour Thera who was compelled to pay tribute when war broke out. Athens probably demanded tribute from Melos at the same time; but, far from complying, she actually contributed money to the Spartan fleet which sailed to the relief of Lesbos.[4] In 426 Nicias took a small force to the island but, failing to secure a quick success, he withdrew. In 425 we find Melos listed in the Island panel with the high assessment of 15 talents, but still she stood firm. Now, under the influence of Alcibiades, the Athenians resolved to end the matter. The town of Melos was invested in the summer by land and sea, and surrendered unconditionally in the following winter. All the men of military age were put to death, the other inhabitants were enslaved, and the island was colonised by Athenians.

Athenian cleruchs

The conquest of Melos is remarkable, not for the rigorous treatment of the Melians, which is merely another example of the inhumanity which we have already met in the cases of Plataea, Mytilene, Scione, but for the unprovoked aggression of Athens, without any tolerable pretext. By the curious device of constructing a colloquy between Athenian envoys and the Melian government, Thucydides has brought the episode into dramatic relief. In this scene the Athenians assert in frank and shameless words that it was a law of nature that the strong rule over the weaker. This was a doctrine which it was Hellenic to follow, but unusual to enunciate in all its nakedness; and in the negotiations which preceded the blockade no Athenian spokesmen would have uttered the undiplomatic audacities which Thucydides ascribes to them. The historian has artfully used the dialogue to indicate the overbearing spirit of the Athenians, flown with insolence, on the eve of an enterprise which was destined to bring signal retribution and humble their city in the dust. Different as Thucydides and Herodotus were in their minds and methods, they had both the same, characteristically Hellenic, feeling for a situation like this. The check of Athens rounded the theme of the younger, as the check of Persia had rounded the theme of the elder, historian; and, although Nemesis, who moves openly in the pages of Herodotus, is not acknowledged by Thucydides, she seems to have cast a shadow here.

Emphasis laid by Thucydides on the conquest of Melos

During the years immediately succeeding the Peace there are some signs that the Athenians turned their attention to matters of religion, which had perhaps been too much neglected during the war. It may have been in these years that they set about the building of a new temple for Athena and Erechtheus, concerning which we shall hear again at a later stage. It may have been at this time that Asclepius, the god of healing, came over with his snake from Epidaurus, and established himself in a sanctuary under the south slope

Temple of Athena Polias (see below, p. 312). The Asclepieum

of the Acropolis. And it was probably soon after the Peace that a resolution was carried imposing a new tax upon the fruits of the earth for the maintenance of the worship of Eleusis. The farmers of Attica were required to pay $\frac{1}{600}$ th of every medimnus of barley and $\frac{1}{1200}$ th of every medimnus of wheat. The same burden was imposed upon the allies; and the Council was directed to invite 'all Hellenic cities whom it seemed possible to approach on the matter' to send first-fruits likewise.[5]

The Eleusinian decree (medimnus = 1½ bushels), 418 B.C.

The Western Policy of Athens

During the fifth century the eyes of Athenian statesmen often wandered to western Greece beyond the seas. There are signs of growing influence as early as the days of Themistocles and we have seen how under Pericles a western policy definitely began in alliances with Segesta, Leontini and Rhegion. One general object of Athens was to support the Ionian cities against the Dorian, which were predominant in number and power, and especially against Syracuse, the daughter and friend of Corinth. The same purpose of counteracting the Dorian predominance may be detected in the foundation of Thurii. But Thurii did not effect this purpose. The colonists were a mixed body; other than Athenian elements gained the upper hand; and, in the end, Thurii became rather a Dorian centre and was no support to Athens. It is to be observed that at the time of the foundation of Thurii, and for nearly thirty years more, Athens is seeking merely influence in the west, she has no thought of dominion. The growth of her connection with Italian and Sicilian affairs was forced upon her by the conditions of commerce and the rivalry of Corinth.

The treaties with Leontini and Rhegion had led to no immediate interference in Sicily on the part of the Athenians. The first action came six years later, on an appeal for help from both cities. Leontini was struggling to preserve her independence against Syracuse, her southern neighbour. All the Dorian cities, with the exception of Acragas and Camarina, were on the side of Syracuse, while Leontini had the support of Rhegion, Catane, Naxos, and Camarina. The continued independence of the Ionian element in western Greece might seem to be seriously at stake. The embassy of the Leontines was accompanied by the greatest of their citizens, Gorgias, the professor of eloquence, whose fame and influence were Panhellenic. We may well believe

Condition of Sicily, 427 B.C.

that when the embassy arrived the Athenians were far more interested in the great man than in his mission; that they thronged in excitement to the Assembly, caring little what he said, but much how he said it. His eloquence indeed was hardly needed to win a favourable answer. Athens was convinced of the expediency of bringing Sicily within the range of her politics. It was important to hinder corn and other help being conveyed from thence to her Peloponnesian enemies; it was important to prevent Syracuse, the friend of Corinth, from raising her head too high; and already adventurous imaginations may have pressed beyond the thought of Athenian influence, and dreamed-of Athenian dominion, in the west. Hyperbolus seems to have especially interested himself in the development of a policy in the western Mediterranean. Aristophanes ridicules him for contemplating an enterprise against Carthage herself.[6]

Sicilian expedition under Laches, 427 B.C.

A force of 20 ships was sent out, under the command of Laches. It achieved little, but if it had been followed up it might have led to much. Messana was induced to join Athens, who thus obtained free navigation of the Straits. The old alliance with Segesta was renewed, but a severe check was experienced in an attempt to take Inessa. The poor success of this expedition must partly, at least, be set down to the dishonesty of the general Laches and his treasurer. Cleon seems to have called Laches to account for his defalcations on his return; and a comic poet jested how Laches ate up the Sicilian cheese—Sicily was famous for her cheeses—with the help of his treasurer, the cheese-grater.[7] Meanwhile the Athenians in response to an appeal from their Sicilian allies for stronger support had appointed a new commander, Pythodorus, and had decided to send out 40 triremes in 425 to reinforce their small fleet. But their intention was not yet the reduction of Sicily.

Expedition of Eurymedon and Sophocles, 425 B.C.

The episode of Pylos and the operations at Corcyra may be regarded as causes which ruined Athenian prospects in Sicily. For these affairs detained the fleet of 40 ships which was bound for the west under the command of Eurymedon and Sophocles, and the delay led to the loss of the one thing which the expedition of Laches had gained, the adhesion of Messana. This city, cleft by adverse political parties, revolted; and the fleet, when at last it came, accomplished nothing worthy of record. Its coming seems rather to have been the occasion for the definite shaping of a movement among almost all the Sicilian states towards peace—a movement unfavourable to

the Athenian designs. When the Athenian generals invited the cities to join in the war against Syracuse, they were answered by the gathering of a congress at Gela, where delegates from all the Siceliot cities met to discuss the situation and consider the possibility of peace. The man who took the most prominent part at this remarkable congress was Hermocrates of Syracuse. He developed what has been justly described as a Siceliot policy. Sicily is a world by itself, with its own interests and politics, and the Greeks outside Sicily should be considered as strangers and not permitted to meddle in the affairs of the island. Let the Sicilian cities settle their own differences among themselves, but combine to withstand intervention from Athens or any other external power. Thus the policy of Hermocrates was neither local nor Panhellenic, but Siceliot. It has been compared to the 'Monroe doctrine' of the United States. The policy was, indeed, never realised, and we shall see that Hermocrates himself was driven by circumstances to become eminently untrue to the doctrine which he preached. But the Congress of Gela was not a failure; the Athenians had to accept the position and return to Athens, where the Assembly, flushed with the triumph of Sphacteria, fined Eurymedon and banished his two colleagues. Soon afterwards trouble arose in Leontini. The oligarchs, threatened by radical measures, called in Syracuse, drove out the democrats and then themselves transferred to Syracuse. Athens saw an opportunity to intervene and sent Phaeax, a prominent orator, with two colleagues, to build up a general alliance against Syracuse. The envoys, after a promising beginning, failed at Gela, and Athens, now moving to a peace mood, did no more until the year of the conquest of Melos.

Congress of Gela, 424 B.C.

The Sailing of the Sicilian Expedition. First Operations in Sicily

In that year there arrived at Athens an appeal for help from Segesta, at war with her stronger southern neighbour, Selinus. The appeal was supported by the Leontine democrats, who had no longer a city of their own. Athens sent envoys to Sicily for the purpose of reporting on the situation and spying out the resources of Segesta, which had undertaken, if the Athenians would send an armament, to provide the expenses of the war. The ambassadors returned with 60 talents of uncoined

Embassy of Segesta, 416 B.C.

11.1 Temple of Apollo, Segesta

silver and glowing stories of the untold wealth of the people of Segesta. They described the sacred vessels of gold and the rich plate of the private citizens. Alcibiades and all the younger generation were in favour of responding to the appeal, and of vigorously supporting the causes of Segesta against Selinus, of the Leontines against Syracuse. Nicias wisely opposed the notion, and set forth the enormous cost of an expedition which should be really effective. The people, however, elated by their recent triumph over Melos, were fascinated by the idea of making new conquests in a distant, unfamiliar world; the ordinary Athenian had very vague ideas of what Sicily meant; and, carried away by dreams of a western empire, he paid no more attention to the discreet counsels of Nicias than to vote a 100 triremes instead of the 60 which were originally asked for.

Athenians vote expedition to Sicily

But having committed the imprudence of not listening to Nicias when his caution was, from the highest point of view, wisdom, the people went on to commit the graver blunder of electing him as a commander of the expedition of which he disapproved. He was appointed as General along with Alcibiades and Lamachus.[8] This shows how great was the consideration of his military capacity, and he was doubtless regarded as a safe makeweight against the adventurous spirit of his colleagues. But though Nicias had shown himself capable of carrying out that Periclean strategy which Athens had hitherto adopted, his ability and temperament were wholly unsuited to the conduct of an enterprise of conquest demanding bolder and greater operations.

(See above, p. 253)

When the expedition was ready to sail, in the early summer, a mysterious event delayed it. One morning in May it was found that the square stone figures which stood at the entrance of temples and private houses in Athens, and were known as Hermae, had been mutilated.[9] The pious Athenians were painfully excited. Such an unheard-of sacrilege seemed an evil omen for the Sicilian enterprise, and it was illogically argued that the act betokened a conspiracy against the state. The enemies of Alcibiades seized the occasion and tried to implicate him in the outrage. It was said that a profane mockery of the Eleusinian Mysteries had been enacted in his house—a charge which may well have been true; and it was argued that he was the author of the present

The mutilation of the Hermae, 415 B.C.

sacrilege and prime mover in a conspiracy against the democracy. It did not appear why a conspirator should thus advertise his plot. But though the theory hardly hung together, it might be good enough for an excited populace. Alcibiades demanded the right of clearing himself from the charge, before the fleet started. In this case, his acquittal was certain, as he was deemed necessary to the enterprise; and his enemies, aware of this, procured the postponement of his trial till his return. The fleet then set sail, and in the excitement of its starting, the sacrilege was almost forgotten. Thucydides says that no armament so magnificent had ever before been sent out by a single Greek state. There were 134 triremes, and an immense number of smaller attendant vessels; there were 5100 hoplites; and the total number of combatants was well over 30,000. For cavalry they relied on their Sicilian allies; only 30 horse went with the fleet.

Sailing of the fleet

A halt was made at Rhegion, where disappointments awaited them. Rhegion adopted a reserved attitude which the Athenians did not expect. The government said that their conduct must be regulated by that of the other Italiot states. This looks as if the Italiots were aiming at a policy of joint interests, such as that which the Siceliots had discussed at the Congress of Gela. In the next place, the Athenians had relied on the wealth of Segesta for supporting their expedition, and they now learned that their spies had been deceived by simple tricks. Gilt vessels of silver had been displayed to them as solid gold; and the Segestaeans, collecting all the plate they could get from their own and other cities, had passed the same service from house to house and led the envoys to believe that each of the hosts who sumptuously entertained them possessed a magnificent service of his own.

This discovery came as an unwelcome surprise to soldiers and commanders alike. It was a serious blow to the enterprise, but no one, not even Nicias, seems to have thought of giving the enterprise up. What then was to be done? A council of war was held at Rhegion. Nicias advocated a course which involved risking and doing as little as possible—to sail about, make some demonstrations, secure anything that could be secured without trouble, give any help to the Leontines that could be given without danger. Alcibiades proposed that active attempts should be made to win over the Sicilian cities by diplomacy, and that then, having so strengthened their position, they should take steps to force Selinus and

The council of war at Rhegion

Syracuse to do right by Segesta and Leontini. Both Nicias and Alcibiades kept in the forefront the ostensible object of the expedition, to right the wrongs of Leontini and Segesta. But Lamachus, who was no statesman or diplomatist but a plain soldier, regarded the situation from a soldier's point of view. Grasping the fact that Syracuse was the real enemy, the ultimate mark at which the whole enterprise was aimed, he advised that Syracuse should be attacked at once, while her citizens were still unprepared. Fortunately for Syracuse, the bold strategy of Lamachus did not prevail; he had no influence or authority except on the field; and, failing to convince his colleagues, who perhaps despised him as a mere soldier, he gave his vote to the plan of Alcibiades.

Naxos and Catane were won over; the Athenian fleet made a demonstration in the Great Harbour of Syracuse and captured a ship. But nothing more had been done, when a mandate arrived from Athens recalling Alcibiades, to stand his trial for impiety. The people of Athens had reverted to their state of religious agony over the mutilation of the Hermae, and the mystery which encompassed it increased their terrors. A commission of inquiry was appointed; false statements were lodged; numbers of arrests were made. Andocides, a young man of good family, was one of the prisoners, and he at length resolved to confess the crime and give the names of his accomplices. His information was readily believed; the public agitation was allayed; and all the prisoners whom he accused were tried and put to death. He was himself pardoned and soon afterwards left Athens. But it is not certain, after all, whether the information of Andocides was true; Thucydides declares that the truth of the mystery was never explained.

Recall of Alcibiades

It was, indeed, never known for certain who the actual perpetrators were; so far the affair remained a mystery. But the purpose of the deed and the source of its inspiration can hardly be doubtful. It occurred on the eve of the Sicilian expedition, and can have had no other intention than to hinder the expedition from sailing, by working on the superstitions of the people. If we ask then, who above all others were vitally concerned in preventing the sailing of the fleet, the answer is obvious, Corinth and Syracuse. We are justified in inferring that the authors of the outrage—to us their names would be of only subordinate interest—were men suborned by Corinth, in receipt of Corinthian silver. In the

Meaning of the Hermae mystery

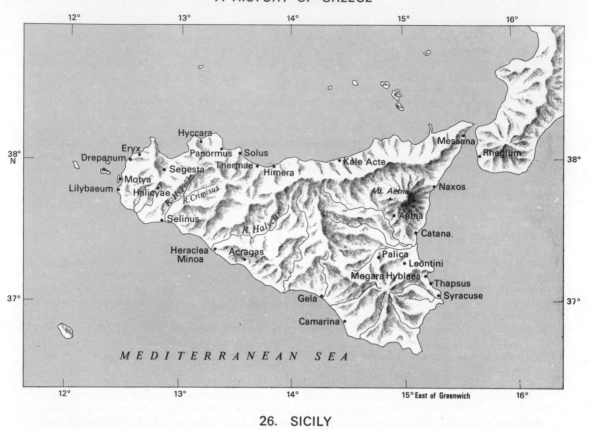

26. SICILY

main point, the mutilation of the Hermae is assuredly no mystery.

The investigations in connection with the Hermae led to the exposure of other profanations, especially of travesties of the Eleusinian mysteries, in which Alcibiades was involved. His enemies of both parties deemed that it was the time to strike. Thessalus, the son of Cimon, preferred the impeachment, which began thus: 'Thessalus, son of Cimon, of the deme Laciadae, impeached Alcibiades, son of Cleinias, of the deme Scambonidae, of wrongdoing in respect to the two goddesses, Demeter and Core, by parodying the mysteries and displaying them to his comrades in his own house, wearing a dress like that which a hierophant with the mysteries wears, and calling himself hierophant.' The trireme *Salaminia* was sent to summon Alcibiades to return, but with instructions to use no violence. Alcibiades might have refused, but he did not do so. He went with the *Salaminia* as far as Thurii, where he made his escape and went into voluntary exile. The Athenians con-

demned him to death, along with some of his kinsfolk, and confiscated his property.

In Sicily, when Alcibiades had gone, the rest of the year was frittered away in a number of small enterprises, which led to nothing. At length, when winter came, Nicias aroused himself to a far more serious undertaking. By a cunning stratagem he lured the Syracusan army to Catane for the purpose of making an attack on the Athenian camp, which they were led to believe they would take unawares, while in the meantime the Athenians had gone on board the fleet and sailed off to the Great Harbour of Syracuse. Nicias landed and fortified his camp on the south-west side of the harbour, near the point of Dascon, just south of the temple of the Olympian Zeus, which he was scrupulous to treat with profound respect. When the Syracusans returned, a battle was fought, the first battle of the war. The Athenians had the disadvantage of having no cavalry whatever, but the woeful want of discipline which prevailed in the ranks of the enemy outbalanced the advantage they had

Athenian victory

from 1200 horse. A storm of rain and lightning helped the Athenians to break their untrained antagonists, but the cavalry stood the Syracusans in good stead by protecting their retreat.

A success had now been gained, but Nicias was incapable of following it up. On the following day he ordered the whole army to embark and sail back to Catane. He had numbers of excellent reasons—the winter season, the want of cavalry, of money, of allies; and in the meantime Syracuse was left to make her preparations. 'The Athenian fleet and army was to go on falling away from its freshness and vigour. All Sicily was to get more and more accustomed to the sight of the great armada sailing to and fro, its energies frittered away on small and mostly unsuccessful enterprises, and, when it did strike something like a vigorous blow, not daring to follow it up.'

The winter was employed by both parties in seeking allies. The Sicels of the island for the most part joined Athens. Camarina, wooed by both Athens and Syracuse, remained neutral. It is in the Assembly of Camarina that Thucydides makes Hermocrates reassert the doctrine of a purely Siceliot policy, which he had formulated ten years before at Gela, while an Athenian envoy develops in its most naked form the theory of pure self-interest, reminding us of the tone which the Thucydidean Athenians adopted in the Melian dialogue. A train had been laid for the capture of Messana before Alcibiades had been recalled, but when the time came for making the attempt, it failed. Alcibiades began his terrible vengeance on his country by informing the Syracusan party in Messana of the plot.

It seemed, indeed, as if a fatality dogged Athens in her conduct of the expedition which she had so lightly undertaken. If she had committed the command to Alcibiades and Lamachus, without Nicias, it would probably have been a success, resulting in the capture of Syracuse. But, not content with the unhappy appointment of Nicias, she must go on to pluck the whole soul out of the enterprise by depriving it of Alcibiades. That active diplomatist now threw as much energy into the work of ruining the expedition as he had given to the work of organising it. He went to Sparta, and was present at the Assembly which received a Syracusan embassy, begging for Spartan help. He made a vigorous and effective speech. He exposed the boundless plans of Athenian ambition, aiming at conquests in the west (including Carthage), which should enable them to return and conquer the Peloponnese. These had perhaps been the dreams of Alci-

Alcibiades at Sparta; his speech

biades himself, but they had certainly never taken a definite shape in the mind of any sober Athenian statesman. Alcibiades urged the Spartans especially to take two measures: to send at once a Spartan general to Sicily to organise the defence—a general was far more important than an army—and to fortify Decelea in Attica, a calamity which the Athenians were always dreading. 'I know,' said the renegade, 'the secrets of the Athenians.' Thucydides shows what defence Alcibiades might have made for his own vindictive—it can hardly be called treacherous—conduct. The description of the Athenian democracy as 'acknowledged folly' may well have been a phrase actually used by Alcibiades. Intense hostility animated the exile, but one asks, did he act merely to gratify this feeling, or had he not further projects for his own career? If we may trust the speech which Thucydides ascribes to him, his ultimate aim was to win back his country. With Spartan help, presumably, he was to rise on the calamity of Athens, and, we may read between the lines, the 'acknowledged folly' was to be abolished. One can hardly see a place for Alcibiades except as a second Pisistratus.

The speech of this powerful advocate turned the balance at a most critical point in the history of Hellas. The Lacedaemonians, who were wavering between the policies of neutrality and intervention, were decided by his advice, and appointed an officer named Gylippus to take command of the Syracusan forces. Corinth too sent ships to the aid of her daughter city.

Since the sailing of the expedition, Athens was in a mood of adventurous speculation and sanguine expectancy, dreaming of some great and wonderful change for the better in her fortunes. Aristophanes made this mood of his countrymen the motive of a fanciful comedy, entitled the *Birds,* which he brought out at the Great Dionysia. Some have sought to detect definite political allusions in the story of the foundation of Cloudcuckootown by the birds of the air, under the direction of two Athenian adventurers, Persuasive and his follower Hopeful; but this is to misapprehend the intention of the drama and to do wrong to the poet's art. The significance of the *Birds* for the historian is that it exhibits with good-humoured banter the temporary mood of the Athenian folk.

The Birds of Aristophanes, 414 B.C. March to April

Siege of Syracuse, 414 B.C.

The Island of Syracuse, the original settlement of Archias, always remained the heart and

414 B.C.

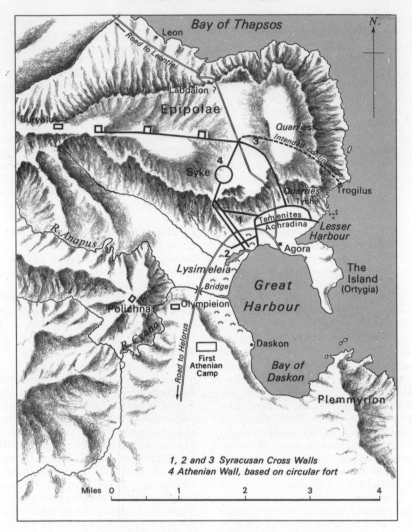

27. THE ATHENIAN SIEGE OF SYRACUSE

centre of the city. However the city might extend on the mainland opposite, the island was always what the Acropolis was to Athens, what Larisa was to Argos; it was even called the acropolis. The island had been connected with the mainland in the sixth century by a mole, and the city had gradually extended round the shore of the Little harbour and up the slope towards the cliffs of Epipolae, forming the two districts of Achradina and Tyche, which were enclosed by a circuit of walls. But the great plateau of Epipolae above the city, forming a large triangle with the high point of Euryalus as its vertex, remained unoccupied. Earlier maps assign the district of

Achradina to the east end of this plateau and assume that, when Dionysius later built his wall round Epipolae, the whole area had been occupied. But a thorough re-examination of the site and the literary sources has shown that what was thought to be the wall enclosing Achradina is in fact an old quarry, and that no evidence of occupation exists. Its dominating position made Epipolae a key point in the strategy of the siege.

The Syracusans did something, though not perhaps as much as they might, to prepare for a siege. They reformed their system of military command and replaced their 15 generals by Hermocrates and two colleagues who were given supreme power. They fortified the precinct of Apollo Temenites, which was just outside the wall of Achradina, and also strengthened Polichna, the fort south of the hill, near the shrine of Olympian Zeus.

The first brief operation of the Athenians against Syracuse had been made on the table-land west of the Great Harbour. With the second act, which began in the ensuing spring, the scene changes to the north, and the hostilities are enacted on the heights of Epipolae. Hermocrates had realised the necessity of guarding these heights. It was accordingly fixed that a great review should be held of all the fighting population, and a force of 600 was to be chosen for the guard of Epipolae. But the hour had almost passed. At the very moment when the muster was being held below in the meadows on the banks of the Anapus, the Athenians were close at hand. The fleet had left Catane the night before, steered for the bay on the north side of Epipolae, and set down the army at a landing-place within less than a mile from the height of Euryalus. The soldiers hastened up the ascent and were masters of Epipolae before the Syracusan host knew what was happening. The six hundred made an attempt to dislodge them, and were repulsed with great loss. The Athenians then fortified a place called Labdalon, near the north cliffs; they have been criticised for not rather fortifying Euryalus.

The Athenians seize Epipolae

The plan of the siege was to run a wall across Epipolae and down the cliff to the harbour in the south.[10] This would cut off communications by land, while the fleet which was stationed at Thapsus, ready to enter the Great Harbour, would cut off communications by sea. For this purpose, a point was chosen in the centre of the intended line of wall, and a round fort, 'the Circle' (*kyklos*), was built there, from which the wall was to be constructed eastward and southward. The Syracusans, having made a vain attempt to stop the building of the wall, set themselves to build a counter-wall, beginning at the Temenites and running westward, to intercept the southern wall of the Athenians and prevent its reaching the harbour. The Athenians did not try to hinder them, and devoted themselves entirely to the building of their own wall north of the Round Fort; this seemed at first of greater consequence than the southern section, since they had to consider the maintenance of communications with their fleet at Thapsus. But though they were apparently not concerning themselves with the Syracusan builders, they were really watching for a good opportunity.

The Athenian wall

First Syracusan counter wall

The carelessness of the Syracusans soon gave the looked-for chance. An attack was made on the counter-wall and it was utterly destroyed. The generals then began to look to the southern section of their own wall, and, without waiting to build it on the side of the Round Fort, they began to fortify the southern cliff, near the temple of Heracles, above the marshy ground on the north-west side of the great harbour.

The Syracusans then began a second counter-work, not on the hill but over this low swampy ground, to hinder the Athenians from bringing their wall down from the cliff to the harbour. This work was not a wall, which would not have been suited to the swampy ground, but a trench with a palisade. At the break of day, the Athenians led by Lamachus descended into the swamp and destroyed the Syracusan works. But what was gained was more than undone by what followed. Troops sallied out of Syracuse; a battle was fought; and Lamachus—the hero Lamachus, as comic poets called him in derision while he lived, in admiration when he died—exposed himself rashly and was slain. This was the third great blow to the prospect of Athenian success. Nicias had been appointed; Alcibiades had been recalled; now Lamachus was gone. To make things worse, Nicias himself was ill.

Death of Lamachus

The southern Athenian wall advanced southward in a double line, and the fleet had now taken up its station in the Great Harbour. The Syracusans, not realising how much they had gained in the death of Lamachus, were prematurely in despair; they changed their generals and were prepared to make terms. Nicias, strangely swerving from his wonted sobriety, was prematurely elated; he thought that Syracuse was in his hands and made the fatal mistake of neglecting the completion of the wall on the north side. His neglect was the more culpable as he had received information of the help that was coming for Syracuse from the mother-country. But alike in his normal mood of caution and in his abnormal moment of confidence, Nicias was doomed to do the wrong thing.

All thought of capitulation was abandoned when a Corinthian captain named Gongylus reached Syracuse with the news that Corinthian ships and a Spartan general were on their way. That general had indeed given up the hope of being able to relieve Syracuse, which, from the reports of Athenian success that had reached him, was thought to be past helping; but he had sailed on to the coast of Italy with the aim of saving the Italiot cities. At Locri,

Gylippus learned that Syracuse might still be saved, since the northern wall was not yet completed. He immediately sailed to Himera and collected a land force, supplied by Gela, Selinus, and Himera itself, and marched over- **Arrival of** land to Syracuse. He ascended the hill of **Gylippus** Epipolae by the same path on the north side which had been climbed by the Athenian army when they seized the heights; and without meeting any opposition advanced along the north bend of the hill to Syke and entered the city. Such was the result of the gross neglect of Nicias. If the wall had been finished, the attempt of Gylippus would never have been made; if Euryalus had been fortified, the attempt would probably have failed.

Gylippus immediately undertook the command of the Syracusan army, and inspired the inhabitants with new confidence. He was as unlike the typical Spartan as Nicias was unlike the typical Athenian. He had all the energy and resourcefulness of Brasidas, though without that unique soldier's attractive personality. He set himself instantly to the work of the defence, and his first exploit was the capture of the fort Labdalon. But the great object was to prevent the Athenians from hemming in the city by completing the northern section of their wall, and this could be done only by building **Third** a new counter-wall. The Athenians themselves **Syracusan** began to build vigorously, and there was a race **counter-** in wall-building between the two armies. As **wall** the work went on, attacks were made on both sides with varying success. In the end, the Syracusan builders prevailed; the Athenian wall was turned, and never reached the eastern coast. This was not enough for Gylippus. His wall was continued to reach Euryalus, and four forts were erected on the western part of the hill, so that Syracuse could now hinder help from reaching the Athenians by the path by which Gylippus had himself ascended. In the meantime Nicias had occupied Plemmyrion, the headland which, facing the Island, forms the lower lip of the mouth of the Great Harbour. Here he built three forts and established a station for his ships, some of which were now dispatched to lie in wait for the expected fleet from Corinth. The Syracusans made a sort of answer to the occupation of Plemmyrion by sending a force of cavalry to the fort of Polichna to guard the southern coast of the harbour. But, though the Athenians commanded the south part of Epipolae and the entrance to the harbour, the Syracusan wall from Syke to Euryalus had completely changed the aspect of the situation for Syracuse from despair to reasonable hope.

The winter had now come and was occupied with embassies and preparations. Gylippus spent it in raising fresh forces in Sicily. Camarina, so long neutral, at length joined Syracuse, who had in fact all Greek Sicily on her side, except her rival Acragas, who persistently held aloof, and the towns of Naxos and Catane. Appeals for help were again sent to the Peloponnese. Corinth was still unremitting in her zeal; and Sparta had sent a force of 600 hoplites—Neodamodes and Helots. Thebes and Thespiae also sent contingents.

We must go back for a moment to Old Greece. The general war is being rekindled there, and the war in Sicily begins to lose the character of a collateral episode and becomes merged in the larger conflict, in which greater interests than those of Syracuse and Sicily are at stake. The Spartans had come to the conclusion that they had been themselves the wrongdoers in the earlier war, and the Athenian successes, especially the capture of Pylos, had been a retribution which they deserved. But now the Athenians had clearly committed a wrong in their aggression on Sicily, and Sparta might with a good conscience go to war against her. The advice of Alcibiades to fortify Decelea **413 B.C.** was adopted: a fort was built and provided with **Occupa-** a garrison under the command of king Agis. **tion of** From Mount Lycabettus at Athens one can see **Decelea** the height of Decelea through the gap between **by the** Pentelicus on the right and Parnes, of which **Spartans** Decelea is an outlying hill, on the left. It was a good position for reaching all parts of Attica, which could no longer be cultivated, and at the same time maintaining easy communications with Boeotia.

But while the Peloponnesians were carrying **Appeal of** the war once more to the very gates of Athens, **Nicias for** that city was called upon to send forth a new **help** expedition to the west on a scale similar to the first. Nicias wrote home a plain and unvarnished account of the situation. We are expressly told that he adopted the unusual method of sending a *written* despatch instead of a verbal message; it was all-important that the Athenian Assembly should learn the exact state of the case. He explained that, since the coming of Gylippus and the increase of the numbers of the garrison and the building of the counter-wall, the besiegers had become themselves besieged. They even feared an attack on their own element, the sea, and their ships had become leaky and the crews fallen out of practice. Further successes of the enemy might cut off their supplies, now derived from the cities of Italy. One of two things must be done: the enterprise must be abandoned or a new armament, as strong as the first, must be sent out at once. Nicias also begged for his own recall, on the ground of the disease from which he suffered. The Athenian people repeated its previous recklessness by voting a second expedition, and by refusing to supersede Nicias, in whom they had a blind and touching trust. They appointed Eurymedon and Demosthenes as commanders of the new armament.

The Second Expedition

413 B.C. Freeman's judgment

'The original interference of Athens in the local affairs of Sicily, her appearance to defend Segesta against Selinus and the Leontines against Syracuse, has grown into a gigantic struggle in which the greater part of the Hellenic nation is engaged. The earlier stage of the Peloponnesian War has begun again with the addition of a Sicilian war on such a scale as had never been seen before. In that earlier stage Sicilian warfare had been a mere appendage to warfare in Old Greece. Now Sicily has become the centre of the struggle, the headquarters of both sides.'

For Sicily itself, the struggle was now becoming a question of life and death, such as the Persian invasion had been for Greece. Syracuse, under the guidance of Hermocrates and Gylippus, put forth all her energy in the organisation of a fleet, and in the spring she had a navy numbering 80 triremes. The crews were inexperienced, but they could remember that it was under the pressure of the Persian danger that Athens herself had learned

Sea battle

her sea skill. Gylippus determined to attack the Athenian station at Plemmyrion by land and sea. By sea the Syracusans were defeated, but while the naval battle was being fought in the harbour, a land force under Gylippus had marched round to Plemmyrion and captured the forts on the headland. The Athenian ships were thus forced back to their station close to their double wall on the north of the harbour, of which the entrance was now commanded by the Syracusans. The Athenians were thus besieged both by land and sea, and could not venture to send ships out of the harbour except in a number sufficient to resist an attack. Presently the new Syracusan sea-power achieved the important success of capturing off the Italian coast some ships bringing supplies from Athens.

At length the news came that the great fleet under Eurymedon and Demosthenes was on its way. It consisted of 73 triremes; there were 5000 hoplites and large numbers of slingers and javelin men. The chance of Syracuse lay in attacking the dispirited forces of Nicias before the help arrived, and it was obviously the policy of Nicias—a congenial policy—to remain inactive. The Syracusans made a simultaneous assault on the walls by land and on the naval station below the walls by sea. The land attack was beaten off, but two days' fighting by sea resulted in a distinct victory for Syracuse. The Great Harbour was too small for the Athenians to win the advantage of their superiority in seamanship, and their ships were not adapted for the kind of sea-warfare which was possible in a narrow space. The effective use of the long light beaks depended on the possibility of manoeuvring. The Syracusans had shaped the beaks of their vessels with a view to the narrow space, by making them short and heavy. On the day after the victory, the fleet of Eurymedon and Demosthenes sailed into the Great Harbour.

Syracusan sea-victory

Demosthenes saw at once that all was over, unless the Syracusan cross-wall were captured. An attempt to carry it from the south was defeated, and the only alternative was to march round the west end of the hill and ascend by the old path near Euryalus. It was a difficult enterprise, guarded as the west part of Epipolae was by the forts, as well as the wall, and by a picked body of 600 men who were constantly keeping watch. A moonlight night was chosen for the attempt. The Athenians were at first successful. One fort was taken and the 600 under Hermocrates himself were repelled. But when one part of their force received a decisive check from the Thespians, the disorder spread to the rest, and they fell back everywhere, driven down the hill on the top of their comrades who had not yet reached the summit. Some, throwing away their shields, leapt from the cliffs. About 2000 were slain.

Fruitless attacks on the Syracusan cross-wall

(August)

These failures damped the spirits of the army, and Demosthenes saw that no profit could be won by remaining any longer where they were. The only wise course was to leave the unhealthy marsh, while they had still command of the sea, and before the winter came. At Syracuse they were merely wasting strength and money. But though Demosthenes had the sense of the army and the sense of the other commanders with him, he could not persuade Nicias to adopt this course. The same quality of nature which had made Nicias oppose the counsel of Lamachus to attack Syracuse now made him oppose the counsel of Demosthenes to leave Syracuse. Fear of responsibility was the dominant note in the character of Nicias. He was afraid of 'Polydamas and the Trojan women', he was afraid of the censure, perhaps the condemnation, of the Athenian Assembly. Nor would he even accept the compromise of retiring to Catane and carrying on the war on a new plan. Demosthenes and Eurymedon, being two to one, should have insisted on instant departure, but they foolishly yielded to the obstinacy of their senior colleague. In a few days, however, events overbore the resolution of Nicias himself. Gylippus arrived at Syracuse with new contingents he had collected in the island; and Peloponnesian and Boeotian reinforcements, after a long roundabout journey by way of Cyrene, at length reached the Great Harbour. Nicias gave way and everything was ready for departure. But on the night on which they were to start, the enemy suspecting nothing, the full moon suffered an eclipse. The superstitious army regarded the phenomenon as a heavenly warning, and cried out for delay. Nicias was not less superstitious than the sailors. Unluckily his best prophet, Stilbides, was dead, and the other diviners ruled that he must wait thrice nine days (for the next full moon). There was perhaps a difference of opinion among the seers, and Nicias decided to be on the safe side by waiting the longer period. Never was a celestial phenomenon more truly disastrous than that lunar eclipse. With the aid of Nicias, it sealed the doom of the Athenian army.

Eclipse of the moon, August 27

Departure postponed

Religious rites occupied the next few days. But meanwhile the Syracusans had learned of the Athenian intention to abandon the siege; their confidence was raised by the implied confession of defeat; and they resolved not to be content with having saved their city, but to destroy the host of the enemy before it could escape. So they drew up their fleet, 76 ships, in the Great Harbour for battle; and 86 Athenian ships moved out to meet them. The Athenians were at a disadvantage as before, having no room for manoeuvring; and, centre, right, and left, they were defeated. The general Eurymedon was slain. The left wing was driven back on the marshy north-west shore of the harbour, between their own wall and Dascon. A force under Gylippus endeavoured to advance along the swamp of Lysimelea and prevent the crews of their ships from landing, but he was driven off by the Etruscan allies of Athens who had been sent to guard the shore here. Then there was a battle for the ships, and the Syracusans succeeded in dragging away 18.

Sea-fight in the Harbour, Sept. 3

The defeat broke the morale of the Athenian army; the victory crowned the confidence of their enemies. The one thought of the Athenians was to escape—the eclipse was totally forgotten; but Syracuse was determined that escape should be made impossible. The mouth of the Great Harbour was barricaded by a line of ships and boats of all kinds and sizes bound together by chains and connected by bridges. The fate of the Athenians depended on their success in breaking through that barrier. They abandoned their posts on the hill and went on board their ships. At this critical moment Nicias revealed the best side of his character. He left nothing undone that could hearten his troops. We are told that, after the usual speech, still thinking, 'as men do in the hour of great struggles, that he had not done, that he had not said half enough', he went round the fleet in a boat, making a personal appeal to the trierarch of each ship. 'He spoke to them, as men will at such times, of their wives and children and the gods of their country; for men do not care whether their words sound commonplace, but only think that they may have some effect in the terrible moment.' The paean sounded, and the Athenian lines sailed forth together across the bay to attack the barrier. When they reached it, Syracusan vessels came out against them on all sides. The Athenians were driven back into the middle of the harbour, and the battle resolved itself into an endless number of separate conflicts. The battle was long, and wavered. The walls of the Island, the slopes of Achradina above, were crowded with women and old men, the shores below with warriors, watching the course of the struggle. Thucydides gives a famous description of the scene; one would think that he had been an eye-witness. 'The fortune of the battle varied, and it was not possible that the spectators on the shore should all receive the same impression of it. Being quite close and having different points of view, they would some of them see their own ships victorious; their courage would then revive, and they would earnestly call upon the gods not to take from them their hope of deliverance. But others, who saw their ships worsted, cried and shrieked aloud, and were by the sight alone more utterly unnerved than the defeated combatants themselves. Others again who had fixed their gaze on some part of the struggle which was undecided were in a state of excitement still more terrible; they kept swaying their bodies to and fro in an agony of hope and fear, as the stubborn conflict went on and on; for at every instant they were all but saved or all but lost. And while the strife hung in the balance, you might hear in the Athenian

Blocking of the Harbour, Sept. 6-8

Last battle in Harbour, Sept. 9

army at once lamentation, shouting, cries of victory or defeat, and all the various sounds which are wrung from a great host in extremity of danger.' The conflicting emotions of suspense, agony, triumph, despair, which swayed to and fro, in the breasts of thousands, round and over the waters of the Great Harbour on that September day, have been lifted out of the tide of time and preserved for ever by the genius of Thucydides.

In the end the Athenians gave way. They were driven back to the shelter of their own wall, chased by the foe. The crews of the remnant of the navy—which amounted to 60 ships—rushed on shore as best they could. The land forces were in a panic; no such panic had ever been experienced in an Athenian army. Thucydides compares the situation to that of the Spartans at Sphacteria. The generals did not even think of asking for the customary truce to bury the corpses which were strewn over the waters of the bay. Demosthenes proposed that they should make another attempt to pass the barrier at daybreak; their ships were even now rather more numerous than those of the enemy; but the men positively refused to embark. Nothing remained but to escape by land. If they had started at once, they would probably have succeeded in reaching shelter at Catane or inland among the friendly Sicels. But Hermocrates contrived a stratagem to delay their departure, so as to give him time to block the roads. Taking advantage of the known fact that there were persons in Syracuse who intrigued with the besiegers, he sent some horsemen who rode up within earshot of the Athenian camp, and pretending to be friends stated that the roads were guarded and that it would be well to wait and set out better prepared. The message was believed. The Athenians remained the next day, and the Syracusans blocked the roads.

Retreat of Athenians, Sept. 11

In his picture of the sad start of the Athenians on their forlorn retreat, Thucydides outdoes his wonderful powers of description. They had to tear themselves away from the prayers of their sick and wounded comrades, who were left to the mercy of the enemy. They could hardly make up their minds to go. The bit of hostile soil under the shelter of their wall had come to seem to them like their home. Nicias, notwithstanding his illness, rose to this supreme occasion as he had never risen to another. He tried to cheer and animate the miserable host—whose wretched plight was indeed of his own making—by words of hope. They set forth, Nicias leading the van,

Demosthenes the rear, along the western road which crosses the Anapus and passes the modern village of Floridia. The aim was to reach Sicel territory first, and then get to Catane as they could; for it would have been madness to attempt the straight road to Catane round the west of Epipolae under the Syracusan forts. The chief difficulty in their way was a high point called the Acraean cliff, approached by a rugged pass, which begins near Floridia. It was not till the fourth day that, having toiled along the pass under constant annoyance from javelin men and horsemen, they came in sight of the cliff, and found that the way was barred by a wall, with a garrison of Syracusan hoplites behind it. To attempt to pass was impossible; they retreated on Floridia in a heavy thunderstorm. They now moved southwards, and abandoning the idea of reaching the Sicel hill-land from this point, marched to the Helorine road. which would take them in the direction of Gela. During the sixth day's march a sort of panic seems to have Sept. 16 fallen on the rear of the army under Demosthenes; the men lagged far behind and the army was parted in two. Nicias advanced with his division as speedily as he could. There were several streams to cross, and it was all-important to press on before the Syracusans had time to block the passages by walls and palisades. The Helorine road approaches the shore near the point where the river Kakyparis (R. Cassibie) flows into the sea. When they reached the ford, the Athenians found a Syracusan band on the other side raising a fortification. They drove the enemy away without much difficulty (R. Elanici, or Caval-lata?) and marched as far as the river Erineos, where they encamped for the night. On the next morning a Syracusan herald arrived with news. The rear of the army had been surrounded the day before, in the olive garden of Polyzalus, through which the Helorine road passed, and had been forced to surrender. The lives of the 6000 men were to be spared. Demosthenes did not condescend to make terms for himself, and when the capitulation had been arranged he sought death by his own hand, but the enemy, who desired to secure a captive general, intercepted the stroke. Having sent a messenger, under a truce, to assure himself of the truth of the tale, Nicias offered terms to the Syracusans—that the rest of the army should be allowed to go free on condition that Athens should repay the costs of the war, the security being a hostage for every talent. The terms were at once rejected. The Syracusans were bent on achieving the glory of leading the whole army captive. For that day the miserable Sept. 17

army remained where it was, worn out with want of food. Next morning they resumed the march and, harassed by the darts of the enemy, made their way to the stream of the Assinaros. Here they found a hostile force on the opposite steep bank. But they cared little for the foe, for they were consumed with intolerable thirst. They rushed down into the bed of the river, struggling with one another to reach the water. The Syracusans who were pursuing came down the banks and slaughtered them unresisting as they drank. The water was soon foul, but muddy and dyed with blood as it was, they drank notwithstanding and fought for it.

Sept. 18

(R. Falconara)

Athenians surrender

At last Nicias surrendered. He surrendered to Gylippus, for he had more trust in him than in the Syracusans. The slaughter, which was as great as any in the war, was then stayed and the survivors were made prisoners. It seems that a great many of the captives were appropriated for their own use by the individual victors, and their lot may have been comparatively light. But the fate of the state prisoners was cruel. Seven thousand were thrown into the stone-quarries of Achradina— deep, unroofed dungeons, open to the chills of night and the burning heat of the day—on a miserable allowance of food and water. The allies of the Athenians were kept in this misery for seventy days; the Athenians themselves were doomed to endure the torture for six months longer, throughout the whole winter. Such was the vengeance of Syracuse upon her invaders. The prisoners who survived the ordeal were put to work in the public prison or sold. Some were rescued by young men who were attracted by their manners. Others owed mitigation of their lot, even freedom, to the power which an Athenian poet exercised over the hearts of men, in Sicily as well as in his own city. Slaves who knew speeches and choruses of the plays of Euripides by heart, and could recite them well, found favour in the sight of their masters; and we hear of those who, after many days, returned to their Athenian homes and thanked the poet for their deliverance.

Treatment of the prisoners

Fate of Nicias and Demosthenes

Some mystery has hung round the fate of the two generals, Demosthenes and Nicias, but there is no doubt that they were put to death without mercy, and some reason to suppose that they were not spared the pain of torture. Hermocrates and Gylippus would have wished to save them, but were powerless in face of the intense feeling of fury against Athens which animated Syracuse in the hour of her triumph. If a man's punishment should be proportionate not to his intentions but to the positive sum of mischief which his conduct has caused, no measure of punishment would have been too great for the deserts of Nicias. His incompetence, his incredible bungling, ruined the expedition and led to the downfall of Athens. But the blunders of Nicias were merely the revelation of his own nature, and for his own nature he could hardly be held accountable. The whole blame rests with the Athenian people, who insisted on his playing a part for which he was utterly unsuited. It has already been observed that one dominant note of the character of Nicias was fear of responsibility. Throughout the whole war there was no post which so absolutely demanded the power of undertaking full responsibility as that of commander in this great and distant expedition. And yet Nicias was chosen. The selection shows that he was popular as well as respected. He was popular with his army, and he seems to have been hardly a sufficiently strict disciplinarian. It has been well said that in the camp he never forgot that the soldiers whom he commanded had votes in the Ecclesia which they might use against himself when they returned to Athens. Timid as a general, timid as a statesman, hampered by superstition, the decorous Nicias was a brave soldier and an amiable man, whose honourable qualities were the means of leading him into a false position. If he had been less scrupulous and devout and had been endowed with better brains, he would not have ruined his country. 'Given the men a people chooses,' it has been said, 'the people itself, in its exact worth and worthlessness, is given.' In estimating the character of the Athenian people, we must not forget their choice of this hero of conscientious indecision.

So deep is the pity which the tragic fate of the Athenians excites in us that we almost forget to sympathise with the Syracusans in the joy of their deliverance. Yet they deserve our sympathy; they had passed through a sore trial, and they had destroyed the powerful invader who had come to rob them of their freedom. To celebrate the anniversaries of their terrible victory they instituted games which they called Assinarian, after the river which had witnessed the last scene.

Institution of the Assinarian games

In connection with these games, some beautiful coins were struck. Perhaps there is nothing which enlists our affections for Syracuse so much as her coins. And it was at this very period that she brought the art of engraving coin-dies to perfection. Never in any country, in any age of the world, was the

The coin-engravers of Syracuse

art of engraving on metal practised with such high inspiration and such consummate skill as in Sicily. No holy place in Hellas possessed diviner faces in bronze or marble than the faces which the Sicilian cities circulated on their silver money. The greatest of the Sicilian artists were Syracusan, and among the greatest of the Syracusan were Evaenetus and Cimon. The die-engraver's achievements may seem small, compared with the life-size or colossal works of a sculptor, yet, as creators of the beautiful, Evaenetus and his fellows may claim to stand in the same rank as Phidias. Their heads of Persephone and of the water-nymph Arethusa encircled by dolphins, their wonderful four-horsed chariots, seem to invest Syracuse with a glory to which she hardly attained. In the years after the defeat of Athens there were several issues of large ten-drachm medallions, modelled on those 'Damareteion' coins which had commemorated Gelon's victory at Himera. The engraving of these was committed to Cimon and Evaenetus and a nameless artist—perhaps a greater than either —of whom a single medallion, an exquisite Persephone crowned with barley, was found on the slopes of Aetna.

New issues of 'Damareteion, 412-406 B.C.

Consequences of the Sicilian Catastrophe

Was the Sicilian expedition a foolish undertaking?

The Sicilian expedition was part of the general aggressive policy of Athens which made her unpopular in Greece. Unjust that policy was; but this enterprise was not more flagrantly unrighteous than some of her other undertakings, and it had the plausible enough pretext of protecting the weaker cities in the west against the stronger. More fruitful is the question whether the expedition was justified from a purely political point of view. It is often said that it was a wild venture, an instance of a whole people going mad, like the English people in the matter of the Crimean War. It is hard to see how this view can be maintained. If there were ever an enterprise of which the wisdom cannot be judged by the result, it is the enterprise against Syracuse. All the chances were in its favour. If the advice of Lamachus had been taken and Syracuse attacked at once, there cannot be much doubt that Syracuse would have fallen at the outset. If Nicias had not let precious time pass and delayed the completion of the wall to the northern cliff of Epipolae, the doom of the city would have been sealed and Gylippus could never have entered. The failure was due to nothing in the

character of the enterprise itself, but entirely to the initial mistake in the appointment of Nicias. And it was quite in the nature of things that the Athenian sea-power, predominant in the east, should seek further expansion in the west. An energetic establishment of Athenian influence in that region was recommended by the political situation. It must be remembered that the most serious and abiding hostility with which Athens had to reckon was the commercial rivalry of Corinth; and the close alliance of Corinth with her Dorian daughters and friends in the west was a strong and adequate motive for Athenian intervention. The necessity of a counterweight to Corinthian influence in Sicily and Italy had long ago been recognised; some attempts had been made to meet it; and when peace with Sparta set Athenian forces free for service outside Greece and the Aegean, it was natural that the opportunity should be taken to act effectively in the west.

The infatuation of the Athenian people was shown not in willing the expedition, but in committing it to Nicias—instead of Demosthenes, who was clearly marked out for the task—and then in recalling Alcibiades. These blunders seemed to point to something wrong in the constitution or in its working. They did in fact show that an expedition of that kind was liable to be mismanaged when any of the arrangements connected with its execution depended on a popular assembly, or might be interfered with for party purposes. To Thucydides it was clear that the primary mistakes were political, not military.

Cause of the failure

After the disaster of the Assinaros there was a feeling that some change must be made in the administration. Athens was hard pressed by the Lacedaemonian post at Decelea, which stopped cultivation in Attica and forced the Athenians to send their supplies from Euboea round the dangerous rocky promontory of Sunion rather than by the much shorter overland route. Decelea also became a refuge for deserting slaves. Of these slaves, who numbered about 20,000, we can hardly doubt that many belonged to the gangs which worked in the mines of Laurion. In any case, one most disastrous effect of the seizure of Decelea was the closing of the mines, since even southern Attica was at the mercy of the Lacedaemonians. Thus one of the chief sources of Athenian revenue was cut off; she was robbed of her supply of 'Laureot owls'; and in a few years we find her melting gold dedicatory offerings to make gold coins, and even coining in copper, thinly plated with silver.[11]

Closing of the mines of Laurion, 413 B.C. Gold coinage at Athens (407); copper coinage (406)

11.2   The rocky promontory of Sunion

Extra-ordinary adminis-tration of the Pro-buloi at Athens

Thus the treasury was at a low ebb, and there were no men to replace those who were lost in Sicily. It was felt that the committees of the Council of Five Hundred were hardly competent to conduct the city through such a crisis; a smaller and more permanent body was required; and the chief direction of affairs was entrusted to a board of Ten, named *Probuloi*, which practically superseded the Council for the time being.

Shortly before this a change had been made in the system of tribute payment. The fixed assessment was replaced by a tax of 5 per cent on all imports and exports carried by sea to or from the harbours of the empire. It was thought that this duty would produce a larger

Tribute of the Con-federacy tem-porarily abolished

income than the tribute, and that it might seem a more equitable principle for payment, for it would be paid by those who had profited most from the growth of Aegean trade under the Athenian thalassocracy. Its effectiveness, however, depended on the requisite display of strength by Athens. No doubt there was considerable scope for disputing the amount due; at all events the old system of tribute was restored as soon as the first substantial Athenian victory gave grounds again for confidence.[12]

The financial pressure was shown by the dismissal of a body of Thracian mercenaries who had arrived too late to sail to Sicily. They returned home under the conduct of Diitrephes, who was instructed to employ them, on the road, in any way he could against the enemy. Sailing northward between Euboea and the mainland, they disembarked on the coast of Boeotia, and reaching the small town of Mycalessus at daybreak, captured it. The Thracians showed their barbarity in massacring all the inhabitants, men, women, and children, beasts of burden and every living thing they saw. They broke into a large school. The boys had only just gone in; they were all slaughtered. 'Nothing was ever so unexpected and terrible.'

Reforms did not avert the dangers which threatened Athens. The tidings of the great calamity which had befallen the flower of her youth in Sicily moved Hellas from end to end. The one thought of enemies, neutrals and subjects alike, was to seize the opportunity of shattering the power of Athens irretrievably. Messages came from some of the chief allies, from Euboea, from Lesbos, from Chios, to Agis at Decelea, to the ephors at Sparta, declaring that they were ready to revolt, if a Peloponnesian fleet appeared off their coasts. A fleet was clearly necessary to do the work that was to be done; a naval policy was forced upon Sparta by the case. It was decided that 100 ships should be equipped, of which half, in equal shares, were to be supplied by Sparta and Boeotia. Athens also spent the winter in building triremes, and fortified Cape Sunion to protect the arrival of her corn-ships.

King Agis, while he was at Decelea, possessed the right of sending troops wherever he chose. He received the overtures from Euboea and Lesbos and promised assistance. But Spartan interference in these islands was deferred owing to the more pressing demands of Chios, which were addressed directly to Sparta and were backed by the support of a great power, whose voice for many years had not been heard in the sphere of the politics of Hellas. Persia now enters once more upon the stage of Greek history, aiming at the recovery of the coast cities of Asia Minor, and for this purpose playing off one Greek power against another. The Sicilian disaster suggested to Tissaphernes, the satrap of Sardis, and to Pharnabazus, the satrap of Hellespontine Phrygia, that it was the moment to wrest from Athens her Asiatic dominions. This must be done by stirring up revolt and by a close alliance with Sparta. Each satrap was anxious to secure for himself the credit of having brought about such a profitable alliance, and each independently sent envoys to Lacedaemon, Pharnabazus urging action in the Hellespont, Tissaphernes supporting the appeal of Chios. The Chian demand, which had the powerful advocacy of Alcibiades, carried the day.

Persia comes on the stage again

In the following summer the rebellion against Athens actively began. The appearance of a few Spartan ships was the signal for the formal revolt of Chios, and then in conjunction with the Chian fleet they excited Miletus, Teos, Lebedus to follow in the same path. Methymna and Mytilene lost little time in joining the movement and were followed by Cyme and Phocaea. The Athenian historian has words of commendation for the city which played the chief part in this rebellion. 'No people,' says Thucydides, 'as far as I know, except the Chians and Lacedaemonians (but the Chians not equally with the Lacedaemonians), have preserved moderation in prosperity, and in proportion as their city has gained in power have gained also in the stability of their government. In this revolt they may seem to have shown a want of prudence, yet they did not venture upon it until many brave allies were ready to share the peril with them, and until the Athenians themselves seemed to confess that after their calamity in Sicily the state of their affairs was hopelessly bad. And, if they were deceived through the uncertainty of human things, the error of judgement was common to many who, like them, believed that the Athenian power would speedily be overthrown.'

412 B.C.

Revolt of Athenian allies

This successful beginning led to the Treaty of Miletus between Sparta and Persia. In the hope of humbling to the dust her detested rival, the city of Leonidas now sold to the barbarian the freedom of her fellow-Greeks of Asia. The Persian claim was that Athens had usurped the rights of the Great King for nearly seventy years over the Asiatic cities, and that arrears of tribute were owing to him. Sparta recognised the right of the Great King

Treaty of Miletus

to all the dominion which belonged to him and his forefathers, and they agreed to carry on the war jointly against Athens and to prevent the Athenians drawing any money or other benefits from cities that had belonged to Persia. It may be said for Sparta that she merely wanted to get the money at the time, and had no intention of honourably carrying out her dishonourable undertaking, but hoped to rescue the Greek cities in the end. But the treaty of Miletus opened up a new path in Greek politics, which was to lead the Persian king to the position of arbiter of Hellas.

Warfare in 412-11 B.C.

Meanwhile Athens had not been idle. Short of money, she had been forced to pass a measure to touch the reserve fund of 1000 talents. She blockaded a Corinthian fleet, destined for Chios, on the Argolic coast; she laid Chios itself waste, and blockaded the town; she won back Mytilene, and gained some successes at Miletus. But Cnidus rebelled; the Peloponnesians gained an advantage in a naval engagement at the small island of Syme, and this was followed by the revolt of Rhodes.

Battle of Syme (Jan.? 411)

This island was still divided between the territories of the three cities of Lindus, Ialysus, and Camirus, but a few years after the revolt the foundation of the island's future power was laid by the synoecism of the three communities in the common city of Rhodes. By the spring of 411 the situation was that Athens had her northern and Hellespontine confederacy intact, but that on the western coast of Asia little of importance remained to her but Lesbos, Samos, Cos, and Halicarnassus. She was confronted by a formidable Peloponnesian fleet, supported by Persia and by a considerable reinforcement from Sicily— 22 vessels under Hermocrates, the return of Syracuse for her deliverance.

It could not be said indeed that all things had gone smoothly between Persia and Lacedaemon. Differences had arisen as to the amount of the subsidies, and a new treaty was concluded in which the King's right to recover territory was limited to Asia and a specific clause was introduced about the payment of ship crews. In the meantime

Alcibiades leaves Sparta, 412 B.C. (autumn)

Alcibiades had been cultivating the friendship of Tissaphernes at Miletus, and had on that account become an object of suspicion at Sparta. He had a bitter enemy in King Agis, whose wife he had seduced. Seeing that his life was in danger, he had left Miletus and gone to the court of the satrap, where he began a new series of machinations with a view to his own return to Athens. Indeed his work at Sparta had now been done, and political changes which were in the air at Athens invited the formation of new schemes. The man who had done much to bring about the alliance of Tissaphernes with Sparta now set himself to dissolve that union and bring about an understanding between the satrap and Athens.

The Oligarchic Revolution

At Athens in these months there was distress, fear, and discontent. How deeply the people felt the pressure of the long war is revealed in the comedy of *Lysistrata* or 'Dame Disbander' which the poet Aristophanes brought out at this crisis. The heroine unites all the women of the belligerent cities of Greece in a sex strike to force the men to make peace. Under the ribald humour there is here and there a note of pathos not to be found in the poet's earlier peace plays, the *Acharnians* and the *Peace*. War is not a time for marrying and giving in marriage. 'Never mind us married women,' says Lysistrata; 'it is the thought of the maidens growing old at home that goes to my heart.' 'Do not men grow old too?' asks a Probulos who argues with her. 'Ah, but it is not the same thing. A man, though his hair be grey, can soon pick up a young girl; but a woman's season is short, and if she miss her chance then, no one will marry her.'

The Lysistrata of Aristophanes, 411 B.C., Jan.-Feb.

But the fear of Persia was the shadow which brooded darkest over Athens at this time, and there was also a lurking suspicion of treachery, a dread that the oligarchical party were planning a revolution or even intriguing with the enemy at Decelea. Two months after the *Lysistrata*, at the great feast of Dionysus, Aristophanes brought out a play whose plot had nothing to do with politics— the 'Celebrants of the Thesmophoria'. But the fears that were in the hearts of many were echoed by the poet, when his chorus called upon Athena, 'the sole keeper of our city', to come as *the hater of tyrants*.

Thesmophoria-zusae (March to April, 411 B.C.)

Lovers of the democracy might well pray to the guardian lady of the city. The opportunity for which the oligarchs had waited so long had come at last. For outside their own ranks there was a large section of influential men who were dissatisfied with the existing forms of government and, though opposed to oligarchy, desired a modification of the constitution. There was a fair show of reason for arguing that the foreign policy had been mismanaged

The moderate revolutionists

by the democracy and that men of education and knowledge had not a sufficient influence on the conduct of affairs. While Athens was winning battles, or even holding her own, there was little prospect of the common people accepting change; but radical democracy depended ultimately on money, and the disastrous Syracusan expedition had almost exhausted the treasury. Moreover there had probably been a change in the balance of voting power by 412. At Syracuse the losses among the *thetes* in the ships had probably been heavier than among the hoplites, and in the Athenian forces based on Samos there were more sailors than soldiers. The weakness of the moderates was that they had not sufficiently studied the tactics of revolution and had not agreed any specific constitutional objectives. Later, Theramenes became their leader and worked out a mixed form of constitution which combined oligarchic and democratic elements, but in the early stages he was outwitted by the extremists.[13]

Thera-
menes.

The extreme oligarchs, though the ideal of Theramenes was not theirs, were ready in the first instance to act in concert with the moderate party for the purpose of upsetting the democracy. The soul of the plot was Antiphon of Rhamnus, an eloquent orator and advocate, who had made his mark in the days of Cleon. He was unpopular, on account of his undisguised oligarchical views; the historian Thucydides describes him as 'a man who in virtue fell short of none of his contemporaries'; and by *virtue* is meant disinterested and able devotion to his party. Other active conspirators were Pisander, who had been in old days a partisan of Cleon, and Phrynichus, who was one of the commanders of the fleet stationed at Samos. The prospects of the movement were good; it was favoured by the Probuli and by most of the officers of the fleet. Moreover, the Athenians—as they had shown already by the appointment of the Probuli— were in a temper, with the fear of Persia before their eyes, to sacrifice their constitution if such a sacrifice would save the city. Alcibiades had entered into negotiations with the officers at Samos, promising to secure an alliance with Tissaphernes, but representing the abolition of democracy as a necessary condition. Most of the oligarchical conspirators were pleased with the scheme, and even the army was seduced by the idea of receiving pay from the Great King. Some indeed of the more sagacious thought they saw through the designs of Alcibiades; and Phrynichus, who himself

Antiphon

aspired to be the leader of the revolution, detected a rival and tried by various intrigues to thwart him. Alcibiades was certainly no friend of oligarchy; but it was his policy in any case to upset the existing democracy, which would never recall him. If an oligarchy were established, he might intervene to restore the democracy, and in return for such a service all would be forgiven. But he would have to be guided by events.

Pisander was sent to Athens to prepare the way for the return of Alcibiades and a modification of the democracy. The people were at first indignant at the proposals to change the constitution and recall the renegade; the Eumolpidae denounced the notion of having any dealings with the profaner of the Mysteries. But the cogent argument that the safety of Athens depended on separating Persia from the Peloponnesians, that this could be managed only by Alcibiades, and that the Great King would not trust Athens so long as she was governed by a popular constitution, had its effect; and there was moreover powerful but secret influence at work through the Hetaeriae or political clubs. It was voted that Pisander and other envoys should be sent to negotiate a treaty with Tissaphernes and arrange matters with Alcibiades.

Pisander
at Athens

(Feb. ?)

It appeared at once that Alcibiades had promised more than he could perform. There had indeed been a serious rupture between Tissaphernes and Sparta. Lichas, a Spartan commissioner who conferred with the satrap, denounced the terms of the treaties. He pointed out the monstrous consequences of the clause which assigned to the king power over all the countries which his ancestors had held; for this would involve Persian dominion over Thessaly and other lands of northern Greece. On such terms, he said, we will not have our fleet paid, and he asked for a new treaty. Tissaphernes departed in anger. But when it came to a question of union with Athens, Tissaphernes showed that he did not wish to break with the Peloponnesians. He proposed impossible conditions to the Athenian envoys, and then made a new treaty with the Spartans, modifying the clause to which Lichas objected. The territory which the Spartans recognised as Persian was now expressly confined to Asia.

Sparta and
Tissa-
phernes

But though the reasons for a revolution, so far as they concerned Tissaphernes and Alcibiades, seemed thus to be removed, the preparations had advanced so far that the result of the mission of Pisander produced no effect on the course of events. The conspirators did

The
revolution
at Athens

not scruple to use menaces and even violence; Androcles, a strong democrat, who had been prominent in procuring the condemnation of Alcibiades, was murdered. Some others of less note were made away with in like manner; and there was a general feeling of fear and mistrust in the city. But there was a widespread conviction that the existence of Athens was at stake and that some change in the constitution was inevitable. The news that Abydus and Lampsacus had revolted may have hastened the final act. Pisander hurried back to Athens, where he found the people frightened and tense. He persuaded the Assembly to appoint ten commissioners to draw up proposals for reform and report to the Assembly. On the appointed day the Assembly was summoned to meet at Colonus, outside the walls, where unarmed citizens would feel insecure because of the Spartan force at Decelea. The commissioners made no proposals for a new constitution but recommended that anyone who wished should be allowed to bring proposals forward and that the *graphe paranomon,* which provided for the prosecution of proposers of measures contrary to existing laws, should be suspended. At this point 'a motion was carried to abolish all the existing magistracies and the payment of magistrates, and to choose a presiding body of five; these five were to choose a hundred and each of the hundred was to co-opt three others. The four hundred thus selected were to meet in the council chamber, they were to have absolute authority and might govern as they deemed best. The five thousand were to be summoned whenever the four hundred chose.'[14] The setting, the tactics, the text had been thought out with care; Pisander was the actor but the producer behind the scenes was Antiphon, and the intention was to ensure that the extreme oligarchs could control events. All power was vested in the council of four hundred. Lip service was paid to the moderates by the inclusion in the constitution of the five thousand as an Assembly, but this Assembly was only to meet when it suited the four hundred to convene them; the five thousand in fact were never summoned, nor was a roll of their members ever published. The people had been too intimidated at Colonus to demonstrate, but there might be resistance when they recovered; the four hundred therefore decided to act at once. A legal date had been laid down for the transference of power, but on the same day as the meeting at Colonus they entered the council house with daggers and a bodyguard of a hundred young supporters and dismissed the democratic council of five hundred.

Fall of the Four Hundred. The Polity. The Democracy Restored

Rule of the Four Hundred, June-Sept.

For more than three months the Four Hundred governed the city with a high hand, and then they were overthrown. Their success had been largely due to the absence of so many of the most democratic citizens in the fleet at Samos, and it was through the attitude of the fleet that their fall was brought about. The sailors rose against the oligarchic officers and the oligarchs of Samos, who were conspiring against the popular party and had murdered the exile Hyperbolus. The chief leaders of this reaction were Thrasybulus and Thrasyllus, who persuaded the soldiers and sailors to proclaim formally their adhesion to the democracy and their hostility to the Four Hundred. The Assembly, which had been abolished at Athens, was called into being at Samos, and the army, representing the Athenian people, deposed the Generals and elected others. The Athenians at Samos felt that they were in as good a position as the Athenians at Athens, and they hoped still to obtain the alliance of Persia, through the good offices of Alcibiades, whose recall and pardon were formally voted. Thrasybulus fetched Alcibiades to Samos, and he was elected a General. The hoped-for alliance with Persia was not effected, but it was at least something that Tissaphernes did not use the large Phoenician fleet which he had at Aspendus against the Athenians, and that his relations with the Peloponnesians were becoming daily worse. He went to Aspendus, but he never brought the ships, and it was a matter of speculation what the object of his journey was. Thucydides records his own belief that Tissaphernes 'wanted to wear out and to neutralise the Hellenic forces; his object was to damage them both, while he was gaining time in going to Aspendus, and to paralyse their action and not strengthen either of them by his alliance. For if he had chosen to finish the war, finished it might have been once for all, as any one may see.' The Athenians at Samos now proposed to sail straight to Athens and destroy the Four Hundred. The proposal shows how much the fleet despised the Peloponnesian navy, which, under its incompetent admiral Astyochus, had been spending the summer in doing nothing. But to leave Samos would have been madness, and Alcibiades saved them from the blunder of sacrificing Ionia and the Hellespont. Negotiations were begun with the oligarchs at Athens, and Alcibiades expressed himself satisfied with the Assembly of Five Thousand, but insisted that the Four Hundred should be abolished.

As a matter of fact the overtures from Samos were welcome to the majority of the Four Hundred, who were dissatisfied with their colleagues and their own position. The nature of an oligarchy which supplants a democracy was beginning to show itself. 'The instant an oligarchy is established,' says Thucydides, 'the promoters of it disdain mere equality, and everybody thinks that he ought to be far above everybody else. Whereas in a democracy, when an election is made, a man is less disappointed at a failure because he has not been competing with his equals.' Moreover, the Four Hundred were at first professedly established as merely a temporary government, preliminary to the establishment of a polity which would be less an oligarchy than a qualified democracy. Such a polity was the ideal of Theramenes, and he was impatient to constitute it. Thus there was a cleavage in the Four Hundred, the extreme oligarchs on one side, led by Antiphon and Phrynichus, the moderate reformers on the other, led by Theramenes. While the moderates had the support of the army at Samos behind them, the extreme party looked to the enemy for support and sent envoys to Sparta for the purpose of concluding a peace. In the meantime they fortified Eetionea, the mole which formed the northern side of the entrance to the Great Harbour of Piraeus. The object was to command the entrance so as to be able either to admit the Lacedaemonians or to exclude the fleet of Samos.

Movement against the Four Hundred

When the envoys returned from Sparta without having made terms, and when a Peloponnesian squadron was seen in the Saronic gulf, the movement against the oligarchs took shape. Phrynichus was slain by an unknown assassin in the Agora.[15] The soldiers who were employed in building the fort at Eetionea were instigated by Theramenes to declare against the oligarchy, and after a great tumult at the Piraeus the walls of the fort were pulled down, to the cry of 'Whoever wishes the Five Thousand, and not the Four Hundred, to rule, let him come and help'. Nobody in the crowd really knew whether the Five Thousand existed as an actually constituted body or not. When the fort was demolished, an Assembly was held in the theatre on the slope of Munychia; the agitation subsided, and peaceable negotiations with the Four Hundred ensued. A day was fixed for an Assembly in the theatre of Dionysus, to discuss a settlement on the basis of the constitution of the Five Thousand. But on the very day, just as the Assembly was about to meet, the appearance of a Lacedaemonian squadron, which had been hovering about, off the coast of Salamis, produced a temporary panic and a general rush to the Piraeus. It was only a fright, so far as the Piraeus was concerned, but there were other serious dangers ahead, as every one saw. The safety of Euboea was threatened, and the Athenians depended entirely on Euboea, now that they had lost Attica. The Lacedaemonian fleet—42 ships under Agesandridas—doubled Sunion and sailed to Oropus. The Athenians sent 36 ships under Thymochares to Eretria, where they were forced to fight at once and were utterly defeated. All Euboea then revolted, except Oreus in the north, which was a settlement of Athenian cleruchs.

Revolt of Euboea (early in September)

At no moment perhaps—since the Persian War—was the situation at Athens so alarming. She had no reserve of ships, the army at Samos was hostile, Euboea, from which she derived her supplies, was lost, and there was feud and sedition in the city. It was a moment which might have inspired the Lacedaemonians to operate with a little vigour both by land and sea. Athens could not have resisted a combined attack of Agis from Decelea and Agesandridas at the Piraeus. But the Lacedaemonians were, as Thucydides observes, very convenient enemies, and they let the opportunity slip. The battle of Eretria struck, however, the hour of doom for the oligarchs. An Assembly in the Pnyx deposed the Four Hundred and voted that the government should be placed in the hands of a body consisting of all those who could furnish themselves with arms, which body should be called the Five Thousand. Legislators (*nomothetae*) were appointed to draw up the details of the constitution, and all pay for offices was abolished. Most of the oligarchs escaped to Decelea, and one of them betrayed the fort of Oenoe on the frontier of Boeotia to the enemy. Two—Antiphon and Archeptolemus—were executed.

(Sept.) 'Polity' or moderate democracy established at Athens

The chief promoter of the new constitution was Theramenes. Thucydides praises it as a constitution in which the rule of the many and the rule of the few were fairly tempered.[16] It was the realisation of the ultimate intentions of most of those who had promoted the original resolution. It is certain that Theramenes, from the very beginning, desired to organise a polity, with democracy and oligarchy duly mixed; his acquiescence in a temporary oligarchy was a mere matter of necessity; and the nickname of *Cothurnus*—the loose buskin that fits either foot—given to him by the oligarchs was not deserved.

In the meantime the supine Spartan admiral Astyochus had been superseded by Mindarus, and the Peloponnesian fleet, invited by Pharnabazus, sailed for the Hellespont. The Athenian fleet under Thrasybulus and Thrasyllus followed, and forced them to fight in the straits. The Athenians, with 76 ships, were extended along the shore of the Chersonese, and the object of the Peloponnesians, who had ten more ships, was to outflank and so prevent the enemy from sailing out of the straits, and at the same time to press their centre in upon the land. The Athenians, to thwart this intention, extended their own right wing, and in doing so weakened the whole line. The Peloponnesians were victorious on the centre, but Thrasybulus, who was on the right wing, took advantage of their disorder in the moment of victory and threw them into panic. The engagement on the Athenian left was round the Cape of Cynossema, out of sight of the rest of the battle, and resulted after hard fighting in the repulse of the Peloponnesians. This victory heartened the Athenians; it was followed immediately by the recovery of Cyzicus, which had revolted. Mindarus had to send for the squadron which lay in the waters of Euboea, but only a remnant reached him: the rest of the ships were lost in a storm off Mount Athos. Another Athenian success at Abydus closed the military operations of the year, but owing to lack of funds the fleet had to disperse for the winter. Tissaphernes was dissatisfied with the success of Athens, and when Alcibiades paid him a visit at Sardis during the winter, he arrested him. But Alcibiades made his escape.

The Peloponnesians were now vigorously supported by Pharnabazus, who was a far more valuable and trustworthy ally than Tissaphernes. In the spring Mindarus laid siege to Cyzicus, and the satrap supported him with an army. The Athenian fleet of 86 ships succeeded in passing the Hellespont unseen, and in three divisions, under Alcibiades, Theramenes, and Thrasybulus, took Mindarus by surprise. After a hard-fought battle by both land and sea, the Athenians were entirely victorious, Mindarus was slain, and about 60 triremes were taken or sunk. This annihilated the Peloponnesian navy. A laconic despatch, announcing the defeat to the Spartan ephors, was intercepted by the Athenians: 'Our ships are lost; Mindarus is gone; the men are starving; we don't know what to do'.[17] Sparta immediately made proposals of peace to Athens on the basis of

the *status quo*. It would have been wise of Athens to accept the offer, and obtain relief from the pressure of the garrison at Decelea. But there is no doubt that the feeling in the navy was entirely against a peace which did not include the restoration of the power of Athens in the Aegean and Asia Minor; and the victory of Cyzicus seemed to assure the promise of its speedy recovery, notwithstanding the purse of Pharnabazus. The Spartan overtures were rejected.

The victory of Cyzicus led to a restoration of the unity of the Athenian state, which for a year had been divided into two parts, centred in Athens and Samos. The democratic party at Athens, encouraged by the success of the thoroughly democratic navy, were able to upset the polity of Theramenes and restore the democracy with the unlimited franchise and the Cleisthenic Council of Five Hundred.[18] The most prominent of the leaders of this movement was Cleophon the lyremaker, a man of the same class as Hyperbolus and Cleon, and endowed with the same order of talent. Like Cleon he was a strong imperialist, and he was now the mouthpiece of the prevailing sentiment for war. His financial ability seems to have been no less remarkable than that of Cleon. The remuneration of offices, which was an essential part of the Athenian democracy, was revived as a matter of course; but Cleophon instituted a new payment, for which his name was best remembered by posterity. This was the 'Two-obol payment'.[19] Though we know that it was introduced by Cleophon, it is not recorded for what purpose it was paid or who received it. Some have supposed that it was simply the wage of the judges—that the old fee of three obols was revived in the reduced form of two obols. But this can hardly be the case. The two-obol payment is mentioned in a manner which implies that it was something completely novel. The probability is that it was a disbursement intended to relieve the terrible pressure of the protracted war upon the poor citizens whose means of livelihood was reduced or cut off by the presence of the enemy in Attica; and we may guess that the pension of two obols a day was paid to all who were not in the receipt of other public money for their services in the field, on shipboard, or in the law courts. To give employment to the indigent by public works was another part of the policy of Cleophon, who herein followed the example of Pericles. In the first years of this statesman's influence the building of a new temple of Athena on the Acropolis, probably begun after the Peace of

Battle of Cynossema, 411 B.C.

Battle of Cyzicus, 410 B.C.

Restoration of Athenian democracy

Diobelia

The new temple of Athena Polias (so-called Erechtheum)

312

11.3 The Erechtheum

Nicias, but abandoned during the Sicilian expedition, was continued. It was close to the north cliff, on the site of the royal palace of Mycenaean days, and seems to have been designed to replace the oldest temple of Athena, which held the ancient wooden statue of the goddess. This new temple Athena shared with Erechtheus and, though less magnificent than the Parthenon, it was the true centre of the city's worship of her patron goddess. Detailed accounts of the money paid to the craftsmen and labourers, citizens, metics, and slaves, who worked on the building and its sculptures, have survived and it is interesting to find that the sculptors of the panels of the frieze were paid at standard piece rates.[20] That this graceful Ionic temple with the Porch of the Maidens should be completed in years of sore need is a striking tribute to Athenian resilience. And in this new confidence the old system of tribute was restored.

The years following the rejection of the Spartan overtures were marked by operations in the Propontis and its neighbourhood. The Athenians, under the able and strenuous leadership of Alcibiades, slowly gained ground. At Chrysopolis a toll station was established at which ships coming from the Euxine had

Recovery of Thasos; occupation of Chrysopolis, 410 B.C.; recovery of Colophon by Thrasyllus, 409 B.C.;

to pay one-tenth of the value of their freight. Then Selymbria was won back,[21] Chalcedon was besieged and made tributary, and finally Byzantium was starved into capitulation, so that Athens once more completely commanded the Bosphorus. Meanwhile Pharnabazus had made an arrangement to conduct Athenian envoys to Susa for the purpose of coming to terms with the Great King. Much of the ground that had been lost in the Thraceward area was also recovered. Thasos had come out in revolt in 411 and the democracy had been replaced by a strong oligarchy; but Neapolis, the most important of the Thasian colonies on the mainland, remained loyal to Athens and helped her to fight back. Thrasybulus, with a small Athenian fleet, succeeded in blockading the island, opposition developed against the oligarchy, and in 407 the Athenians were able to dictate terms. The decree can still be read in which the Athenian Assembly showed its gratitude to Neapolis.[22] Nearer home, however, Athens lost Nisaea to the Megarians; and Pylos was at length recovered by Sparta.

As the distinctive feature of the last eight years of the Peloponnesian War was the combination between Persia and Sparta, we may divide this period into three parts, according

Athenians lose Pylos and Nisaea, 409 B.C.; capture of Chalcedon and Byzantium, 408

Three
periods of
co-
operation
between
Persia and
Peloponn-
esians:
(1)
412-11,
(2) 410-7,
(3) 407-5

to the nature of the Persian co-operation. During the first two years it is the satrap Tissaphernes who supports the Peloponnesian operations, and Athens loses nearly all Ionia. Then the satrap Pharnabazus takes the place of Tissaphernes as the active ally of the Peloponnesians; the military operations are chiefly in the Hellespont; and Athens gradually recovers many of her losses. But the affairs of the west had begun to engage the attention of the Great King, Darius, who, aware that the jealousy of the two satraps hinders an effective policy, sends down his younger son Cyrus to take the place of Tissaphernes at Sardis, with jurisdiction over Cappadocia, Phrygia, and Lydia. The government of Tissaphernes is confined to Caria. The arrival of Cyrus on the scene marks a new turning-point in the progress of the war.

Gorgias at
Olympia,
408 B.C.
(July to
August)

It was a strange sight to see the common enemy of Hellas ranged along with the victors of Plataea against the victors of Salamis. It was a shock to men of Panhellenic feeling, and it was fitting that at the great Panhellenic gathering at Olympia a voice of protest should be raised. Men of western Hellas beyond the sea could look with a calmer view on the politics of the east, and it was a man of western Hellas, the Leontine Gorgias himself, who lifted up an eloquent voice against the wooing of Persian favour by Greek states. 'Rather,' he said, 'go to war against Persia.'

Downfall of the Athenian Empire

Lysander

Prince Cyrus was zealous, but his zeal to intervene actively and furnish pay to the Peloponnesian seamen might have been of little use were it not for the simultaneous appointment of a new Spartan admiral, who possessed distinguished ability and inordinate ambition. This was Lysander, who was destined to bring the long war to its close. He gained the confidence of his seamen by his care for their interests, and he won much influence over Cyrus by being absolutely proof against the temptation of bribes—a quality at which an oriental greatly marvelled. But in prosecuting the aims of his ambition Lysander was perfectly unscrupulous, and he was a skilful diplomatist as well as an able general.

Alcibiades
at Athens,
summer,
407 B.C.

While Cyrus and Lysander were negotiating, Alcibiades, after an exile of eight years, had returned to his native city. He had been elected strategos, and had received an enthusiastic welcome. Time had, in some measure, dulled the sense of the terrible injuries which he had inflicted on his country, and his share in the recent recovery of the Hellespontine cities had partly at least atoned. But it was rather hope for future benefits than forgiveness for past wrongs that moved the Athenians to let bygones be bygones. They trusted in his capacity as a general, and they thought that by his diplomatic skill they might still be able to come to terms with Persia. So a decree was passed, giving him full powers for the conduct of the war, and he was solemnly freed from the curse which rested upon him as profaner of the Eleusinian rites. He had an opportunity of making his peace with the divinities of Eleusis. Ever since the occupation of Decelea, which he had done so much to bring about, the annual procession from Athens along the Sacred Way to the Eleusinian shrine had been suspended, and the mystic Iacchus had been conveyed by sea. Under the auspices of Alcibiades, who protected the procession by an escort of troops, the solemnity was once more celebrated in the usual way. It is possible that, if he had been bold enough to seize the opportunity of this tide of popularity, he might have established a tyranny at Athens; but he probably thought that such a venture would hardly be safe until he achieved further military or diplomatic successes. The opportunity was lost, and did not recur. A slight incident completely changed the current of feeling in Athens. An Athenian fleet was at Notion, keeping guard on Ephesus, and Lysander succeeded in defeating it and capturing 15 ships. Though Alcibiades was not present at the battle, he was responsible, and lost his prestige at Athens, where news of a decisive victory was confidently expected. New generals were appointed immediately, and Alcibiades withdrew to a castle on the Hellespont which he had provided for himself as a refuge in case of need. Conon succeeded him in the chief command of the navy.

(Sep-
tember)

Battle of
Notion,
spring,
406 B.C.

During the following winter the Peloponnesians organised a fleet of greater strength than they had had for many years—140 ships; but Lysander had to make place for a new admiral, Callicratidas. The Peloponnesians at first carried all before them. The fort of Delphinion in Chios, and the town of Methymna in Lesbos were taken; Conon, who had only 70 ships, was forced into a battle outside Mytilene and lost 30 triremes in the action. The remainder were blockaded in the harbour of Mytilene. The situation was critical, and Athens did not underrate the danger. The gold and silver dedications in the temples of the Acropolis were melted to defray the

Battle of
Arginusae,
406 B.C.

costs of a new armament; freedom was promised to slaves, and citizenship to resident aliens, for their services in the emergency; and at the end of a month Athens and her allies sent a fleet of 150 triremes to relieve Mytilene. Callicratidas, who had now 170 ships, left 50 to maintain the blockade and sailed with the rest to meet the foe. A great battle was fought near the islets of the Arginusae, south of Lesbos, and the Athenians were victorious. Seventy Spartan ships were sunk or taken, and Callicratidas was slain. An untimely north wind hindered the victors from rescuing the crews of their wrecked ships, as well as from sailing to Mytilene to destroy the rest of the hostile fleet.

Trial of
the
generals

The success had not been won without a certain sacrifice; 25 ships had been lost with their crews. It was believed that many of the men, floating about on the wreckage, might have been saved if the officers had taken proper measures. The commanders were blamed; the matter was taken up by politicians at Athens; the generals were suspended from their office and summoned to render an account of their conduct. They shifted the blame on the trierarchs; and the trierarchs, one of whom was Theramenes, in order to shield themselves, accused the generals of not having issued the orders for rescue until the high wind made the execution impossible. We are not in a position to judge the question; for the decision must entirely depend on the details of the situation, and as to the details we have no certainty. It is not clear, for instance, whether the storm was sufficiently violent to prevent any attempt at a rescue. The presumption is, however, that the Athenian people were right in the conviction that there had been criminal negligence somewhere, and the natural emotion of indignation which they felt betrayed them into committing a crime themselves. The question was judged by the Assembly and not by the ordinary courts. Two sittings were held, and the eight generals who had been present at Arginusae were condemned to death and confiscation of property. Six, including Thrasyllus and Pericles, son of the great statesman, were executed; the other two had prudently kept out of the way. Whatever were the rights of the case, the penalty was unduly severe; but the worst feature of the proceedings was that the Assembly violated a recognised usage of the city by pronouncing sentence on all the accused together, instead of judging the case of each separately. Formally illegal indeed it was not; for the supporters of the generals had not the courage to apply the *Graphe Paranomon*.

Protests had no effect on the excited multitude, thirsty for vengeance.[23] It was an interesting incident that the philosopher Socrates, who happened on the fatal day to be one of the prytaneis, objected to putting the motion. All constitutions, democracy like oligarchy and monarchy, have their own dangers and injustices; this episode illustrates the gravest kind of injustice which a primary Assembly, swayed by a sudden current of violent feeling and unchecked by any responsibility, sometimes commits—and repents.

The victory of Arginusae restored to the Athenians the command of the eastern Aegean, and induced the Lacedaemonians to repeat the same propositions of peace which they had made four years ago after the battle of Cyzicus: namely, that Decelea should be evacuated and that otherwise each party should remain just as it was. Through the influence of the demagogue Cleophon, who is said to have come into the Assembly drunk, the offer was rejected. Nothing was left for the Spartans but to reorganise their fleet. Eteonicus had gathered *Conspiracy of the reed-bearers at Chios* together the remnants of the ships and gone to Chios, but he was unable to pay the seamen, who were forced to work as labourers on the fields of Chian farmers. In the winter this means of support failed; threatened by starvation, they formed a conspiracy to pillage the town of Chios. The conspirators agreed to carry a reed-stick in order to recognise one another. Eteonicus discovered the plot, but there were so many reed-bearers that he shrank from an open conflict, and devised a stratagem. Walking through the streets of Chios, attended by 15 armed men, he met a man who suffered from ophthalmia, coming out of a surgeon's house, and seeing that he had a reed-stick, ordered him to be put to death. A crowd gathered and demanded why the man was put to death; the reply was, 'Because he had a reed-stick'. When the news spread, every reed-bearer was so frightened that he threw his reed away. The Chians then consented to supply a month's pay for the men, who were immediately embarked.

This incident shows that money had ceased to flow in from Persia. It was generally felt *Lysander in command again, 405 B.C.* that if further Persian co-operation was to be secured and the Peloponnesian cause restored, the command of the fleet must again be entrusted to Lysander. But there was a law at Sparta that no man could be navarch a second time. On this occasion the law was evaded by sending Lysander out as secretary, but on the understanding that the actual command lay with him and not with the nominal admiral.

Lysander visited Cyrus at Sardis, asserted his old influence over him, and obtained the money he required. With the help of organised parties in the various cities, he soon fitted out a fleet. An unlooked-for event gave him still greater power and prestige. King Darius was very ill, his death was expected, and Cyrus was called to his bedside. During his absence, Cyrus entrusted to his friend Lysander the administration of his satrapy, and the tribute. He knew that money was no temptation to this exceptional Spartan, and he feared to trust such power to a Persian noble.

With these resources behind him, Lysander speedily proved his ability. Attacked at Ephesus by the Athenian fleet under Conon, he declined battle; then, when the enemy had dispersed, he sailed forth, first to Rhodes, and then across the Aegean to the coast of Attica, where he had a consultation with Agis. Recrossing the Aegean, he made for the Hellespont and laid siege to Lampsacus. The Athenian fleet of 180 ships reunited and followed him thither. Lampsacus had been taken before they reached Sestos, but they determined now to force him to accept the battle which he had refused at Ephesus, and with this view proceeded along the coast till they reached Aegospotami, 'Goat's rivers', an open beach without harbourage, over against Lampsacus. It was a bad position, as all the provisions had to be fetched from Sestos at a distance of about two miles, while the Peloponnesian fleet was in an excellent harbour with a well-supplied town behind. Sailing across the strait, the Athenians found the enemy drawn up for battle but under orders not to move until they were attacked, and in such a strong position that an attack would have been unwise. They were obliged to return to Aegospotami. For four days the pattern recurred. Each day the Athenian fleet sailed across the strait and endeavoured to lure Lysander into an engagement; each day its efforts were fruitless. From his castle in the neighbourhood Alcibiades descried the dangerous position of the Athenians, and riding over to Aegospotami earnestly counselled the generals to move to Sestos. His sound advice was received with coldness, perhaps with insult. When the fleet returned from its daily cruise to Lampsacus, the seamen used to disembark and scatter on the shore. On the fifth day Lysander sent scout ships which, as soon as the Athenian crews had gone ashore for their meal, were to flash a bright shield as a signal. When the signal was given, the whole Peloponnesian squadron, consisting of about 200 galleys,

rowed rapidly across the strait and found the Athenian fleet defenceless. There was no battle, no resistance. Twenty ships, which were in a condition to fight, escaped; the remaining 160 were captured at once. It was generally believed that there was treachery among the generals, and it is possible that Adeimantus, who was taken prisoner and spared, had been bribed by Lysander. All the Athenians who were taken, to the number of three or four thousand, were put to death. The chief commander Conon, who was not among the unready, succeeded in getting away. Greek ships usually unshipped their sails when they prepared for a naval battle, and the sails of the Peloponnesian triremes had been deposited at Cape Abarnis, near Lampsacus. Informed of this, Conon boldly shot across to Abarnis, seized the sails, and so deprived Lysander of the power of an effective pursuit. It would have been madness for the responsible commander to return to Athens with the tidings of such a terrible disaster; and Conon, sending home 12 of the 20 triremes which had escaped, sailed himself with the rest to the protection of Evagoras, the king of Salamis in Cyprus. Never was a decisive victory gained with such small sacrifice as that which Lysander gained at Aegospotami.

The tidings of ruin reached the Piraeus at night, and 'on that night not a man slept'. The city remembered the cruel measure which it had once and again meted out to others, as to Melos and Scione, and shuddered at the thought that even such measure might now be meted out to itself. It was hard for the Athenians to realise that at one blow their sea-power was annihilated, and they had now to make preparations for sustaining a siege. But the blockade was deferred by the policy of Lysander. He did not intend to attack Athens but to starve it into surrender, and with this view he drove to Athens all the Athenian cleruchs whom he found in the islands in order to swell the starving population. Having completed the subjugation of the Athenian empire in the Hellespont and Thrace, and ordered affairs in those regions, Lysander sailed at length into the Saronic gulf with 150 ships, occupied Aegina, and blockaded the Piraeus. At the same time the Spartan king Pausanias entered Attica, joined forces with Agis, and encamped in the Academe, west of the city. But the walls were too strong to attack, and at the beginning of winter the army withdrew, while the fleet remained near the Piraeus. As provisions began to fail, the Athenians made a proposal of peace, offering to resign their empire and become allies of Lacedaemon. The envoys were turned back at Sellasia; they would not be received by the ephors unless they brought more acceptable terms; and it was intimated that the demolition of the Long Walls for a length of ten stades was an indispensable condition of peace. It was folly to resist, yet the Athenians resisted. The demagogue Cleophon, who had twice hindered the conclusion of peace when it might have been made with honour, first after Cyzicus, then after Arginusae, now hindered it again when it could be made only with humiliation. An absurd decree was passed that no one should ever propose to accept such terms. But the danger was that such obstinacy would drive the enemy into insisting on an unconditional surrender; for the situation was hopeless. Theramenes undertook to visit Lysander and endeavour to obtain more favourable conditions, or at all events to discover how matters lay. His real object was to gain time and let the people come to their senses. He remained three months with Lysander, and when he returned to Athens he found the citizens prepared to submit on any terms whatever. People were dying of famine, and the reaction of feeling had been marked by the execution of Cleophon, who was condemned on the charge of evading military service. Theramenes was sent to Sparta with full powers. It is interesting to find that during these anxious months a decree was passed recalling to Athens an illustrious citizen who had been found wanting as a general, but whose genius was to make immortal the war now drawing to its close—the historian Thucydides.

An assembly of the Peloponnesian allies was called together at Sparta to determine how they should deal with the fallen foe. The general sentiment was that no mercy should be shown; that Athens should be utterly destroyed and the whole people sold into slavery. But Sparta never felt the same bitterness towards Athens as that which animated Corinth and Thebes; she was neither a neighbour nor a commercial rival. The destruction of Athens might have been politically profitable, but Sparta, with all her faults, could on occasion rise to nobler views. She resolutely rejected the barbarous proposal of the Confederacy; she would not blot out a Greek city which had done such noble services to Greece against the Persian invader. That was more than two generations ago, but it was not to be forgotten; Athens was saved by her past. The terms of the Peace were: the Long Walls and fortifications of the Piraeus were to be destroyed; the Athenians lost all their foreign possessions, but remained independent, confined to Attica and Salamis; their whole fleet, with the exception of 12 triremes, was forfeited; all exiles were allowed to return; Athens became the ally of Sparta, pledged to follow her leadership. When the terms were ratified, Lysander sailed into the Piraeus. The demolition of the Long Walls immediately began. The Athenians and their conquerors together pulled them down to the music of flute-players; and the jubilant allies thought that freedom had at length dawned for the Greeks. Lysander permitted Athens to retain 12 triremes, and, having inaugurated the destruction of the fortifications, sailed off to reduce Samos.

When the Aegean world realised that Athenian sea power was irreparably broken, it seemed unlikely that Sparta would meet with any resistance from Athenian allies; but Samos had stood firm. Her democracy, established after the revolt of 440-439, had been generously treated by Athens and from 411 she had been the main base of the Athenian fleet. Athens showed her appreciation of this almost reckless loyalty by offering Athenian citizenship to all Samians and undertaking to include Samos in any peace negotiations. In a sense this was a hollow gesture, for Athens herself was doomed, but when the Athenian democracy was restored the original decree was reaffirmed.[24] But by then Samos had been forced to capitulate. An oligarchy had been established with Spartan support and the democratic supporters of Athens had been driven into exile. In view of their violent suppression of the oligarchs in 411 it is a tribute to Sparta that they were not put to death.

It is not to be supposed that all Athenians were dejected and wretched at the terrible humiliation which had befallen their native city. There were numerous exiles who owed their return to her calamity; and the extreme oligarchic party rejoiced in the foreign occupation, regarding it as an opportunity for the subversion of the democracy and the reestablishment of a constitution like that which had been tried after the Sicilian expedition. Theramenes looked forward to making a new attempt to introduce his favourite polity. Of the exiles, the most prominent and determined was Critias, son of Callaeschrus, and a member of the same family as the lawgiver Solon. He was a man of many parts, a pupil of Gorgias and a companion of Socrates, an orator, a poet,

Athens submits

Conditions of Peace imposed on Athens

404 B.C. April

and a philosopher. A combination was formed between the exiles and the home oligarchs, a common plan of action was organised, and the chief democratic leaders were presently seized and imprisoned. The intervention of Lysander was then invoked for the establishing of a new constitution and, awed by his presence, the Assembly passed a measure proposed by Dracontides, that a body of Thirty should be nominated for the purpose of drawing up laws and managing public affairs until the code should be completed.[25] The oligarchs did not take the trouble to repeal the law which would expose the proposer of the measure to prosecution by the Graphe Paranomon; they felt sure of their power. Critias, Theramenes, and Dracontides were among the Thirty who were appointed.

The ruin of the power of Athens had fallen out to the advantage of the oligarchical party, and it has even been suspected that the oligarchs had for many years past deliberately planned to place the city at the mercy of the enemy, for the ulterior purpose of destroying the democracy. The part played by Theramenes in the condemnation of the generals who had the indiscretion to win Arginusae, the parts he subsequently played in negotiating the Peace and in establishing the oligarchy, the serious suspicions of treachery in connection with the disaster of Aegospotami, have especially suggested this conjecture. The attempt of the Four Hundred on a previous occasion to come to terms with Sparta may be taken into account, and the comparatively lenient terms imposed on Athens might seem to point in the same direction. One thing seems certain. The oligarchical party had been distinctly aiming at peace, and the repeated opposition of Cleophon (impolitic, as we have seen) indicates that he suspected oligarchical designs. It must also be admitted that the conduct of the Athenians in fixing their station at Aegospotami, and delivering themselves to the enemy like sheep led to the altar, argues a measure of folly which seems almost incredible, if there were not treachery behind; and the suspicion is confirmed by the clemency shown to Adeimantus. It must, however, be acknowledged that it is hard to understand how the treason could have been effectually carried out without the connivance of Conon, the commander-in-chief; yet no suspicion seems to have been attached to him. The whole problem of the oligarchical intrigues of the last eight years of the war remains wrapped in far greater mystery than the mutilation of the Hermae.

Rule of the Thirty and Restoration of the Democracy

The purpose for which the Thirty had been appointed was to frame a new constitution; their powers, as a governing body, were only to last until they had completed their legislative work. The majority of them, however, with Critias, who was the master spirit, had no serious thoughts of constructing a constitution; they regarded this as merely a pretext for getting into power, and their only object was to retain the power in their own hands, establishing a simple oligarchy. In this, however, they were not absolutely unanimous. One of them at least, Theramenes, had no taste for pure oligarchy, but was still genuinely intent on framing a polity, tempered of both oligarchic and democratic elements. This dissension in the views of the two ablest men, Critias and Theramenes, soon led to fatal disunion.

The first measures of the Thirty were, however, carried out with cordial unanimity. A Council of Five Hundred was appointed, consisting of strong supporters of oligarchy, and was invested with the judicial functions which had before belonged to the people. A body of Eleven, under the command of Satyrus, a violent, unscrupulous man, was appointed for police duties, and the guard of the Piraeus was committed to a body of Ten. The chief democrats, who on the fall of Athens had opposed the establishment of an oligarchy, were then seized, tried by the Council, and condemned to death for conspiracy. So far there was unanimity, but at this point Theramenes would have stopped. At such times, moderate counsels have small chance of winning, ranged beside the extreme policies of resolute men like Critias, who had come back in a bitter and revengeful spirit against democracy, relentlessly resolved to exercise an absolute despotism and expunge all elements of popular opposition. A polity on the broad basis which Theramenes desired was as obnoxious to Critias as the old democracy—into which, he was convinced, it would soon deviate. He and his colleagues were therefore afraid of all prominent citizens of moderate views, whether democratic or oligarchic, who were awaiting with impatience the constitution which the Thirty had been appointed to prepare—the men on whom the polity of Theramenes, if it came into existence, would mainly rest.

The Thirty had announced as part of their programme that they would purge the city of

Tyranny

wrongdoers. They put to death a number of men of bad character, including some notorious informers; but they presently proceeded to execute, with or without trial, not only prominent democrats, but also men of oligarchic views who, though unfriendly to democracy, were also unfriendly to injustice and illegality. Among the latter victims was Niceratus, the son of Nicias. To the motives of fear and revenge was soon added the appetite for plunder, and some men were executed because they were rich, while many fled, happy to escape with their lives. Even metics, who had little to do with politics, were despoiled; thus the speech-writer Lysias and his brother Polemarchus, who kept a lucrative manufactory of shields, were arrested, and while Lysias succeeded in making his escape, Polemarchus was put to death. And while many Athenians were removed by hemlock or driven into banishment, others were required to assist in the revolting service of arresting fellow-citizens, in order that they might thereby become accomplices in the guilt of the government. Thus the philosopher Socrates and four others were commanded with severe threats to arrest an honest citizen, Leon of Salamis. Socrates refused without hesitation to do the bidding of the tyrants; the others were not so brave. Yet Socrates was not punished for his defiance; and this immunity was perhaps due to some feeling of piety in the heart of Critias, who had been one of his pupil-companions; a feeling which might be safely indulged, as the philosopher was neither wealthy nor popular.

Attitude of Thera-menes

To these judicial murders and this organised system of plundering, Theramenes was unreservedly opposed. The majority of the Council shared his objections and he would have been able to establish a moderate constitution but for the ability and strength of Critias. His representations, indeed, induced the Thirty to broaden the basis on which their power rested by creating a body of 3000 citizens, who had the privilege of bearing arms and the right of being tried by the Council. All outside that body were liable to be condemned to death by sentence of the Thirty, without a trial. The body of 3000 had practically no political rights, and were chosen so far as possible from known partisans of the government, the staunchest of whom were the thousand knights. This measure naturally did not satisfy Theramenes; his suggestions had, in fact, been used with a purpose very different from his—to secure, not to alter, the government.

The exiles

In the meantime the exiles whom the oligarchy had driven from Athens were not idle. They had found refuge in those neighbouring states—Corinth, Megara, and Thebes—which had been bitter foes of Athens, but were now undergoing a considerable change of feeling. Dissatisfaction with the high-handed proceedings of Sparta, who would not give them a share in the spoils of the war, had disposed them to look with more favour on their fallen enemy, and to feel disgust at the proceedings of the Thirty, who were under the aegis of Lysander. They were therefore not only ready to grant hospitality to Athenian exiles, but to lend some help towards delivering their city from the oppression of the tyrants. The first step was made from Thebes. Thrasybulus and Anytus, with a band of 70 exiles, seized the Attic fortress of Phyle, in the Parnes range, close to the Boeotian frontier, and put into a state of defence the strong stone walls, whose ruins are still there. The Thirty led out their forces—their faithful knights and Three Thousand hoplites—and sat down to blockade the stronghold. But a timely snowstorm broke up the blockade; the army retired to Athens, and for the next three months or more nothing further was done against Thrasybulus and the men of Phyle.

Thrasy-bulus seizes Phyle, c. Dec. 404 First expedition of the Thirty against Thrasy-bulus, Dec. 404 or Jan. 403

The oligarchs were now in a dangerous position, menaced without by an enemy against whom their attack had failed, menaced within by a strong opposition. They saw that the influence of Theramenes, who was thoroughly dissatisfied with their policy, would be thrown into the scale against them, and they resolved to get rid of him. Having posted a number of devoted creatures, armed with hidden daggers, near the railing of the council-house, Critias arose in the assembled Council and denounced Theramenes as a traitor and conspirator against the state—a man who could not be trusted an inch in view of those repeated tergiversations which had won him the nickname of the 'Buskin'. The reply of Theramenes, denouncing the policy of Critias and his colleagues, is said to have been received with applause by most of the Council, who really sympathised with him. Critias, seeing that he would be acquitted by the Council, resorted to an extreme measure. He struck the name of Theramenes out of the list of the Three Thousand, and then along with his colleagues condemned him to death—since those who were not included in the list could not claim the right of trial. An appearance of legality seems to have been given to this act. A law was passed—presumably on the spot—that

Death of Thera-menes, c. Jan. 403

319

persons who had opposed the Four Hundred in 411 B.C., or taken part in destroying the fort at Eetionea, should be excluded from the constitution.[26] Theramenes leapt on the sacred Hearth and appealed for protection to the Council; but the Council was stupefied with terror, and at the command of Critias the Eleven entered and dragged the suppliant from the altar. He was borne away to prison; the hemlock was immediately administered; and when he had drunk, he tossed out a drop that remained at the bottom of the cup, as banqueters used to do in the game of kottabos, exclaiming, 'This drop for Critias the fair!' There had perhaps been a dose of truth in the reproaches which the gentle Critias had hurled at him across the floor of the council-chamber. Theramenes may have been shifty and unscrupulous where means and methods were concerned. But in his main object he was perfectly sincere. He was sincere in desiring to establish a moderate polity which should unite the merits of both oligarchy and democracy, and avoid their defects. There can be no question that he was honestly interested in trying this political experiment. And the very nature of this policy involved an appearance of insincerity and gave rise to suspicion. It led him to oscillate between the democratic and oligarchical parties, seeking to gain influence and support in both, with a view to the ultimate realisation of his middle plan. And thus the democrats suspected him as an oligarch, the oligarchs distrusted him as a democrat. In judging Theramenes, it seems fair to remember that a politician who in unsettled times desires to direct the state into a middle course between two opposite extremes can hardly avoid oscillation more or less, can rarely escape the imputation of the Buskin.[27]

After the death of Theramenes, the Thirty succeeded in disarming, by means of a stratagem, all the citizens who were not enrolled in the list of the Three Thousand, and expelled them from the city. But with a foe on Attic ground, growing in numbers every day, Critias and his fellows felt themselves so insecure that they took the step of sending an embassy to Sparta, to ask for a Lacedaemonian garrison. The request was granted, and 700 men, under Callibius, were introduced into the Acropolis. The Thirty would never have resorted to this measure except under the dire pressure of necessity; for not only was it unpopular, but they had to pay the garrison out of their own chest.[28]

Spartan garrison occupies the Acropolis

It was perhaps in the first days of the month of May that it was resolved to make a second attempt to dislodge the democrats from Phyle. A band of the knights and the Spartan garrison sallied forth, but near Acharnae they were surprised at night and routed with great loss by Thrasybulus. This incident produced considerable alarm at Athens, and the Thirty had reason to fear that many of their partisans were wavering. Deciding to secure an eventual place of refuge in case Athens should become untenable, they seized Eleusis and put about 300 Eleusinians to death. This measure had hardly been carried out when Thrasybulus descended from Phyle and seized the Piraeus. He had now about 1000 men, but the Piraeus, without fortifications, was not an easy place to defend. He drew up his forces on the hill of Munychia, occupying the temples of Artemis and the Thracian goddess Bendis, which stood at the summit of a steep street; highest of all stood the javelin-men and slingers, ready to shoot over the heads of the hoplites. Thus posted, with his prophet by his side, Thrasybulus awaited the attack of the Thirty, who had led down all their forces to the Piraeus. A shower of darts descended on their heads as they mounted the hill, and, while they wavered for a moment under the missiles, the hoplites rushed down on them, led by the prophet, who had foretold his own death in the battle and was the first to perish. Seventy of the enemy were slain; among them Critias himself. During the truce which was then granted for taking up the dead, the citizens on either side held some converse with one another, and Cleocritus, the herald of the Eleusinian Mystae, impressive both by his loud voice and by his sacred calling, addressed the adherents of the Thirty: 'Fellow-citizens, why do you seek to slay us? why do you force us into exile? us who never did you wrong. We have shared in the same religious rites and festivals; we have been your school-fellows and choir-fellows; we have fought with you by land and sea for freedom. We adjure you, by our common gods, abandon the cause of the Thirty, monsters of impiety, who for their own gains have slain in eight months more Athenians than the Peloponnesians slew in a war of ten years. Believe that we have shed as many tears as you for those who have now fallen.' This general appeal, and individual appeals in the same tone, at such an affecting moment, must have produced an effect upon the half-hearted soldiers of the Thirty, who had now lost their

Second expedition against Phyle, beginning of May, 403 B.C.

Battle of Munychia

Death of Critias

able and violent leader. There was dissension and discord not only among the Three Thousand and the Council, but among the Thirty themselves. It was felt that the government of the Thirty could no longer be maintained, and that if the oligarchy was to be rescued a new government must be installed. A general meeting of the Three Thousand deposed the Thirty and instituted in their stead a body of Ten, one from each tribe. One member of the Thirty was re-elected as a member of the new government, but the rest withdrew to the refuge which they had provided for themselves at Eleusis. The new body of Ten represented the views of those who were genuinely devoted to oligarchy, but disapproved of the extreme policy of Critias and his fellows. They failed to come to terms with Thrasybulus, who was every day receiving reinforcements both in men and arms; the civil war continued; and it soon appeared that it would be impossible for Athens to hold out against the democrats in the Piraeus without foreign aid.

The first board of Ten

An embassy was accordingly dispatched by the Ten to Sparta, and about the same time the remnant of the Thirty at Eleusis sent a message on their own account for the same purpose. Both embassies represented the democrats at Piraeus as rebels against the power of Sparta. The Lacedaemonian government, through the influence of Lysander, was induced to intervene in support of the Ten. Lysander assembled an army at Eleusis, and 40 ships were sent under Libys, his brother, to cut off the supplies which the democrats received by sea. The outlook was now gloomy for Thrasybulus and his company; but they were rescued by a disunion within the Lacedaemonian state. The influence of Lysander, which had been for the last years supreme, was perceptibly declining; the king Pausanias was his declared opponent, and many others of the governing class were jealous of his power, vexed at his arrogance, perhaps suspicious of his designs. The oligarchies which he had created at Athens and in the other cities of the Athenian empire had disgraced themselves by misgovernment and bloodshed, and the disgrace was reflected upon the fame of their creator. Lysander had hardly begun his work when Pausanias persuaded the ephors to entrust to himself the commission of restoring stability at Athens, and Lysander had the humiliation of handing over to his rival the army which he had mustered. A defeat convinced Thrasybulus

Oligarchs appeal to Sparta (late spring, 403) Sparta intervenes

Pausanias in command

that it would be wise to negotiate; and on the other hand Pausanias deposed the irreconcilable Ten, and caused them to be replaced by another Ten of more moderate views. Both parties then, the city and the Piraeus alike, submitted themselves to Spartan intervention, and Sparta, under the auspices of king Pausanias, acquitted herself uncommonly well. A commission of 15 was sent from Lacedaemon to assist the king, and a reconciliation was brought about. The terms were a general and mutual pardon for all past acts; from which were excepted only the Thirty, the Ten who had held the Piraeus under the Thirty, the Eleven who had carried out the judicial murders perpetrated by the Thirty, and the Ten who had succeeded the Thirty. All these excepted persons were required to give an account of their acts if they wished to remain at Athens. Eleusis was to form an independent state, and any Athenian who chose might migrate to Eleusis within a specified time.

Second board of Ten

End of the civil war in Attica

The evil dream of Athens was at last over: a year and half of oligarchical tyranny, and foreign soldiery on the Acropolis. She owed her deliverance to the energy of Thrasybulus and the discretion of Pausanias. Pausanias displayed his discretion further by not meddling with the reconciled parties in their settlement of the constitution. It was decreed, on the motion of Tisamenus, that 'lawgivers' should be appointed to revise the constitution, and that in the meantime the state should be administered according to 'the laws of Solon and the institutions of Draco'. There also was an idea afloat of making the possession of landed property a qualification for political rights.[29] But it was a totally unpractical idea. Such a test would have excluded rich men; it would have included many of the fourth class. In the end, no new experiment was tried. The lawgivers restored the old democracy with its unlimited franchise, and Athens entered upon a new stage of her career. The amnesty was faithfully kept: the democrats did not revenge themselves on the supporters of the oligarchical tyranny. But it was easier to forgive than forget; and for many years after the reconciliation a distinction was drawn, though not officially, yet in the ordinary intercourse of life, between the 'men of the city' and the 'men of the Piraeus'—the men who had fought for freedom and those who had fought against it. That was almost inevitable; and so long as the oligarchs held Eleusis, there might even be some ground for suspecting the loyalty of their old sup-

Sept., B.C. 403

Nomothetes appointed. Provisional arrangement

porters. After about two years of independent existence, Eleusis was attacked by Athens; the Eleusinian generals were captured and put to death, and the town resumed its old place as part of Attica. Henceforward, for almost three generations, the Athenian democracy was perfectly secure from the danger or fear of an oligarchical revolution. That hideous nightmare of the Thirty had established it on a firmer base than ever.

CHAPTER 12

The Spartan Supremacy and the Persian War

The Spartan Supremacy

Sparta drawn into founding an empire

Sparta had achieved the task which she had been pressed to undertake, and had undertaken somewhat reluctantly, the destruction of the Athenian empire. It was a task which, though not imposed by the unanimous voice of Greece, appealed to a most deeply-seated sentiment of the Greeks, their love of political independence. The Athenian empire had been an outrage on that sentiment, and, apart from all calculations of particular interest, the humiliation of the great offender must have been regarded, even by those who were not her enèmies, with an involuntary satisfaction. The avowed aim of Sparta throughout had been to restore their liberty to those states which had been 'enslaved' by Athens, and to protect the liberty of those whom her ambition threatened. Now that this object was accomplished as fully as could be desired it would have been correct for Sparta to retire into her old position, leaving the cities which had belonged to the Athenian empire to arrange their own affairs—if her deeds were to be in accordance with her professions. The alternative course for a state in the position of Sparta was to enter frankly upon the Athenian inheritance, and pursue the aims and policy of Athens as an imperial power. Other states might have adopted this course with advantage both to themselves and Greece; for Sparta it was impossible. And so when Sparta, unable from the nature of her institutions and the character of her genius to tread in the footsteps of her

fallen rival, nevertheless resolved to take under her own control the cities which she had gone forth to liberate, she not only cynically set aside her high moral professions, but entered on a path of ambition which led to calamity for herself and distress for Greece. The main feature of Greek history for the thirty years after Aegospotami is Sparta's pursuit of a policy of aggrandisement beyond the Peloponnese; the opposition which this policy calls forth leads both to the revival of Athens as a great power and to the rise of Thebes. In the end Sparta is forced to retire into the purely Peloponnesian position for which her institutions fitted her. In the making of those institutions, an activity beyond the Peloponnese had not been contemplated, and they were too rigid to be adapted to the enlarged sphere of an Aegean dominion. Nothing short of a complete revolution in the Spartan state could have rendered her essay in empire a success, but the narrow Spartan system was too firmly based in the narrow Spartan character to suffer such a revolution.

We may wonder how far the general who had placed his country in the position of arbitress of Greece appreciated the difficulty of reconciling the political character of Lacedaemon with the rôle of an imperial city. Un-Spartan as he was in many respects, Lysander had possibly more enlightened views on the administration of an empire than his countrymen. A story is told that when Callibius, the Spartan harmost of Athens, was knocked down by a young athlete whom he had insulted, and

Unfitness of Sparta for empire

appealed to Lysander, he was told that he did not know how to govern free men. To deal with free men abroad was what the average Spartan could not do, yet it was such men as Callibius that Lysander had to use for the establishment of the empire which he had resolved to found. In each of the cities which had passed from Athenian into Spartan control, a government of ten members was set up, and its authority was maintained by a Lacedaemonian *harmost* with a Lacedaemonian garrison. The cities were thus given over to a twofold oppression. The foreign governors were rapacious and were practically free from home control; the native oligarchies were generally tyrannical and got rid of their political opponents by judicial murders; and both the decarchs and the harmost played into each other's hands. Lysander exercised with a high hand and without farsightedness the dictatorship which was his for the time and might at any hour be taken from him. He was solely concerned to impose a firm military despotism on the states which had been rescued from the Athenian Confederacy.

It is obvious that the Athenian and Spartan empires had little in common. They were, first of all, sharply contrasted through the fact that the Spartan policy was justified by no public object like that to which the Confederacy owed its origin. And this contrast was all the more flagrant, considering that after the battle of Aegospotami there was the same demand for a Panhellenic confederacy, with the object of protecting the Asiatic Greeks from Persia, as there had been after the battle of Mycale. But so far from connecting her supremacy with such an object, Sparta had abandoned the Asiatic Greeks to the Great King as the price of Persian help. Athens had won her power as the champion of the eastern Greeks; Sparta had secured her supremacy by betraying them. In the second place, the methods of the two states in exercising their power were totally different. The grievances against Athens, though real, were mainly of a sentimental nature. Athens had deprived the Confederate cities of autonomy: there were few complaints of rapine or oppression. But under the Lacedaemonian supremacy men suffered from positive acts of injustice and violence, and might seek in vain at Sparta for redress. The spirit of the system which Lysander instituted may be judged from the statement that the will of any Spartan citizen was regarded as law in the subject states. The statement comes from a friend of Lacedaemon.

The position of power which Lysander had

*De-
carchies*

*Harmosts
(= 'regu-
lators')*

*Contrast
between
Athenian
and
Spartan
empires*

*Lysander's
recall*

attained in the eyes of the world, and enjoyed without moderation, could not fail to excite jealousy and apprehension at Sparta itself. He held a sort of royal court at Samos, and the Samians accorded him divine honours by calling after his name a feast which had hitherto been a feast of Hera. He was recalled to Sparta, and he obeyed the summons, bearing a letter from the satrap Pharnabazus to justify him. But when it was opened, instead of being an encomium, it was found to be a deed of accusation; and Lysander was covered with ridicule as the victim of a Persian trick. He was permitted to escape from the situation on the plea of visiting the temple of Zeus Ammon in the Libyan oasis, in accordance with a vow. But his work remained. Lacedaemon upheld her uncongenial military despotism, modifying Lysander's system only so far as not to insist on the maintenance of the decarchies, but to permit the cities to substitute other forms of government, under the aegis of the harmost. Diodorus, probably exaggerating considerably, tells us that more than 1000 talents were levied each year from the empire in tribute. The receipt of such an income was a political innovation, and its administration involved money transactions of a nature and on a scale which would have been severely condemned by 'Lycurgus'. The admission into the treasury of a large sum of gold and silver which had been brought to Sparta by Lysander was a distinct breach of the Lycurgean discipline. Thus, inflexible as the Spartan system was, the necessities of empire compelled it to yield at one point, and a point where attack is especially insidious.

403 B.C.

The supremacy of Sparta lasted for a generation, though with intervals in which it was not effective, and its history for more than half of the period is mainly determined by her relations with Persia. As it had been through Persia that she won her supremacy, so it was through Persia that she lost it, and through Persia that she once more regained it.

*404-371
B.C.*

*394 B.C.
387-6
B.C.*

The Rebellion of Cyrus and the March of the Ten Thousand

We now come to an episode which takes us into the domestic history of Persia, out of the limits of Greek geography into the heart of the Persian empire. On the death of Darius, his eldest son Artaxerxes had succeeded to the throne, notwithstanding the plots of his

*Cyrus and
Tissa-
phernes*

mother Parysatis, who attempted to secure it for her younger and favourite son Cyrus. In these transactions Tissaphernes had supported Artaxerxes and, when Cyrus returned to his satrapy in Asia Minor, Tissaphernes was set to watch him. False suspicions and calumnies frequently lead to the actual perpetration of the crimes which they attribute; and perhaps if he had not been suspected, Cyrus would not have formed the plan of subverting his brother and seizing the kingship. But it is far more likely that from the first Cyrus had hoped and resolved to succeed to his father's throne. For his success he relied largely on an army of Greek mercenaries which he began to enlist. The revolutions which had passed over Greek cities in recent years, both in Asia and Europe, threw into the military market large numbers of strong men eager for employment and pay. They were recruited for the prince's service by Clearchus, a Spartan, who had held the post of harmost, but had been repudiated and expelled by the ephors when he attempted to make himself tyrant of Byzantium, like a new

Pausanias. Moreover, the Lacedaemonian government, which owed much to Cyrus, was induced to support him secretly, and sent him —avowedly for another purpose—seven hundred hoplites. The army which Cyrus mustered when he set forth on his march to Susa comprised a large body of oriental troops, and about 13,000 Greeks, of which 10,600 were hoplites.[1]

Cyrus takes the field, spring, 401 B.C.

The purpose of the march was at first carefully concealed from the troops, nor was the secret communicated to any of the officers except Clearchus. The hill tribes of Pisidia were often troublesome to Persian satraps, and their reduction furnished a convenient pretext. Among those who were induced, by the prospect of high pay under the generous Persian prince, to join this Pisidian campaign was Xenophon, an Athenian knight, who was one of the pupils and companions of the philosopher Socrates. His famous history of the *Anabasis* or Up-going of the Greeks with Cyrus, and their subsequent retreat, has rendered the expedition a household word. The charm of the

Xenophon

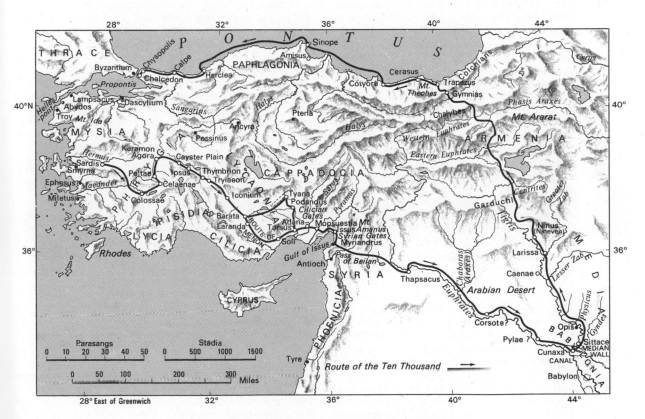

28. THE MARCH OF THE TEN THOUSAND

Anabasis depends on the simple directness and fulness with which the story is told, and the great interest of the story consists in its breaking new ground. For the first time we are privileged to follow step by step a journey through the inner parts of Asia Minor, into the heart of the Persian empire beyond the Euphrates and the Tigris. There is a charm of actuality in the early chapters, with their recurring phrases, like brief entries in a diary—the days' marches from one city to another, the number of parasangs, and the lengths of the halts, all duly set out. 'Hence Cyrus marches two stages, ten parasangs, to Peltae, an inhabited city; and here he remained three days.'

March through Asia Minor

Setting forth from Sardis, Cyrus took the south-easterly road, which led across the upper Maeander to the Phrygian Colossae, where he was joined by the troops of one of his Greek captains, the Thessalian Menon; and thence onward to Celaenae, where he awaited the arrival of Clearchus. So far, the march had been straight to the ostensible destination, the country of Pisidia; but now Cyrus turned in the opposite direction, and, descending the Maeander, marched northward to Peltae and Keramon Agora or Potters' Mart. Then eastward, to the city called Cayster-Plain, close to the fort of Ipsus. Here the Greeks demanded their arrears of pay, and Cyrus had no money to satisfy them. But he was relieved from the difficulty, which might well have proved fatal to his enterprise, by the Cilician queen Epyaxa, wife of Syennesis IV, who arrived well laden with money. Her coming must have been connected with private negotiations between Cyrus and the Cilician governor. As the route of Cyrus lay through Cilicia, a country barred on all sides by difficult passes, it was of the greatest moment for Cyrus to come to an understanding with the ruler; and on the other hand it was the policy of Syennesis so to order his ways that whether Cyrus succeeded or failed he might in either event be safe. As the plan of Cyrus was still a secret, it was a prudent policy to entrust the delicate negotiations to no one less safe than the queen. Having pacified the demands of his Greek mercenaries, Cyrus proceeded (by Thymbrion and Tyriaeon) to Iconium; and thence by the road, which describes a great southern curve through Lycaonia, to Tyana. The Greeks were allowed to plunder Lycaonia, a rough country with rough people, as they passed through it. The arrangement with Syennesis seems to have been that he should make a display of resisting Cyrus, and Cyrus make a display of

Keramon Agora (now Iskam Keui)

circumventing him. To carry out this arrangement, Menon's division, accompanied by the queen Epyaxa, diverged from the route followed by the rest of the army and crossed the Taurus into Cilicia by a shorter route. Perhaps they struck off at Barata and passed by Laranda, on a road that led to Soli. Thus Syennesis, who, as a loyal servant of the Great King, hastened to occupy the Cilician gates, the pass for which the main army of Cyrus was making, found himself taken in the rear by Menon. It was therefore useless to remain in the pass, and he retreated to a mountain stronghold: what more could a loyal servant of the Great King be expected to do? The army of Cyrus then coming up from Tyana, by Podandus, found the impregnable pass open, and descended safely to Tarsus, where it met Menon. The city and palace of the prince of Cilicia were pillaged; this perhaps was part of the pretence. It was at all events safe now for Syennesis to enter into a contract with Cyrus (a compulsory contract, the Great King would understand) to supply some money and men.

It must have been dawning on the Greek troops for some time past, and at Tarsus they no longer felt any doubt, that they had been deceived as to their ultimate destination. They had long ago passed Pisidia, the ostensible object of their march, and the true object was now clear to them. They flatly refused to advance further. It was a small thing to be asked to take the field against the forces of the Great King; but it was no such light matter to be asked to undertake a march of three months into the centre of Asia. To be at a distance of three months from the sea-coast was a terrible idea for a Greek. Clearchus, a strict disciplinarian—a man of grim feature and harsh voice, unpopular with his men—thought to repress the mutiny by severity; but the mutiny was too general to be quelled by coercion. Then he resorted to a stratagem, which he carried out with admirable adroitness. Calling his soldiers together, he stood for some time weeping before he spoke. He then set forth the cruel dilemma in which their conduct had placed him; he must either break his plighted faith with Cyrus or desert them; but he did not hesitate to choose: whatever happened, he would stand by them, who were 'his country, his friends, and his allies'. This speech created a favourable impression, which was confirmed when Cyrus sent to demand an interview with Clearchus and Clearchus publicly refused to go. But the delight of the troops was changed into perplexity when Clearchus asked them what they proposed to do: they were no longer the soldiers of Cyrus, and could not look to him for pay, provisions, or help. He (Clearchus) would stand by them, but declined to command them or advise them. The soldiers—some of them in the secret confidence of their captain—discussed the difficulty, and it was decided to send a deputation to Cyrus, to ask him to declare definitely his real intentions. Cyrus told the deputation that his purpose was to march against his enemy Abrocomas—Persian general in Syria—who was now on the Euphrates, and offered higher pay to the Greeks, a daric and a half instead of a daric a month. The soldiers, finding themselves in an awkward pass, agreed to continue the march—reluctant, but hardly seeing any other way out of the difficulty; though many of them must have shrewdly suspected that they would deal with Abrocomas on the Euphrates even as they had dealt with the hillmen of Pisidia.

Issus; new reinforce-ments The march was now eastward by Adana and Mopsuestia, across the rivers Sarus and Pyramus, and then along the coast to Issus, where Cyrus found his fleet. It brought him 700 hoplites sent by the Lacedaemonians. Here too he was reinforced by 400 Greek mercenaries who had deserted from the service of the Persian general Abrocomas, the enemy of Cyrus, who had fled to the Euphrates instead of holding the difficult and fortified passes from Cilicia into Syria, as a loyal general of the Great King should have done. So Cyrus now, with his Greek troops increased to the total number of 14,000, passed with as much ease through the Syrian gates, owing to the cowardly flight of Abrocomas, as he had before passed through the Cilician gates, owing to the prudent collusion of Syennesis. The Syrian gates are a narrow pass between the end of Mount Amanus and the sea, part of the coast road from Issus to Myriandrus. At Myriandrus the Greeks bade good-bye to the sea, little knowing how many days would pass, how many terrible things befall them, before they hailed it again. They crossed Mount Amanus by the pass of Beilan, which Abrocomas ought to have guarded, and in a twelve days' march, passing by the park and palace of Belesys, satrap of Syria, they reached Thap- Arrival at Thapsacus sacus and beheld the famous Euphrates. Here a new explanation was necessary as to the object of the march, and Cyrus had at last to own that Babylon was the goal—that the foe against whom he led the army was the Great King himself. The Greek troops murmured loudly and refused to cross the river; but their murmurings here were not like their murmurs at Tarsus, for they had guessed the truth long since, and their complaints were only designed to extort promises from Cyrus. The prince agreed to give each man a present of five minae at the end of the expedition—more than a year's pay at the high rate of a daric and a half. But while the rest of the Greeks were making their bargain, Menon stole a march on them, inducing his own troops to cross the river About August 1 first—a good example, for which Cyrus would owe him and his troops particular thanks. Abrocomas had burned the ships, but the Euphrates was—a very unusual circumstance at that season—shallow enough to be forded; a fact of which Abrocomas was conceivably aware. The army accordingly crossed on foot and continued the march along the left bank— an agreeable march until they reached the river Chaboras, beyond which the desert of 'Arabia' began: a plain, Xenophon describes it, smooth as a sea, treeless; only wormwood and scented shrubs for vegetation, but alive with all kinds of beasts strange to Greek eyes, wild asses and ostriches, antelopes and bustards. The tramp through the desert lasted thirteen days, and then they reached Pylae, at the edge of the land of Babylonia, fertile then with its artificial irrigation, now mostly a barren wilderness. Soon after they passed Pylae, they became aware that a large host had been moving in front, ravaging the country before them.

Artaxerxes on his part had made somewhat Prepara-tions of Arta-xerxes tardy preparations to receive the invaders. It seems indeed to have been hardly conceived at the Persian court that the army of Cyrus would ever succeed in reaching Babylonia. The city of Babylon was protected by a double defence against an enemy approaching from the north—by a line of wall and a line of water, both connecting the Euphrates with the Tigris. The enemy would first have to pass the Wall of Media, 100 feet high and 20 feet broad, built of bricks with bitumen cement, and would then have to cross the Royal Canal, before they could reach the gates of Babylon. To these two lines of defence a third was now added, in the form of a trench about forty miles long, joining at one end the Wall of Media and at the other the Euphrates, where a space of not more than seven yards was left between the trench and the river. To defend a country so abundantly guarded by artificial fortifications, the king was able to muster immediately an army of about 40,000; but this did not seem enough when the danger became imminent, and orders were sent to Media that the troops of that province should come to the aid of Babylonia. There was some delay in the arrival of these forces, and Artaxerxes probably did not wish to risk an action until their arrival had made his immense superiority in numbers overwhelming. This may explain the extraordinary circumstance that when the army of Cyrus came to the fosse which had been dug expressly to keep them out, they found it undefended, and walked at their ease over the narrow passage between the trench and the river.

Battle of Cunaxa (summer, 401)

But now it was hardly possible for Artaxerxes to let his foes advance further, though there was still no sign of the troops from the east. Two days after passing the trench, the army of Cyrus reached the village of Cunaxa, and suddenly learned that the king's host was approaching. The oriental troops under Ariaeus formed the left wing of Cyrus, who himself occupied the centre with a squadron of cavalry; the Greeks were on the right, resting on the river Euphrates. The Persian left wing, commanded by Tissaphernes, consisted of cavalry, bowmen, and Egyptian footmen, with a row of scythe-armed chariots in front. The king was in the centre with a strong bodyguard of horse. Cyrus knew the oriental character, and he knew that if the king fell or fled, the battle would be decided and his own cause won. He accordingly formed a plan of battle which would almost certainly have been successful, if it had been adopted. He proposed that the Greeks should shift their position further to the left—to a considerable distance from the river—so that they might immediately attack the enemy's centre where the king was stationed. But Clearchus, to whom Cyrus signified his wishes, made decided objections to this bold and wise plan. Unable to rise, like Cyrus, to the full bearings of the situation, he ruined the cause of his master by pedantically or timorously adhering to the precepts of Greek drill-sergeants, that it is fatal for the right wing to allow itself to be outflanked. And besides the consideration which Cyrus had in view, the advantage of bringing about with all speed the flight of Artaxerxes, there was another consideration which would not have occurred to Cyrus, but which ought to have occurred to Clearchus. The safety of Cyrus himself was a matter of the first importance to the Greeks—how important we shall see in the sequel. It was useless for the Greeks to cut down every single man in the Persian left, if while they were sweeping all before them the prince for whom they fought were slain. Cyrus did not press the matter, and left it to Clearchus to make his own dis-

Greeks victorious;

positions. The onset of the Greeks struck their enemies with panic before a blow was struck. On the other side, the Persian right, which far outflanked the left wing of Cyrus, was wheeled round, so as to take the troops of Ariaeus in the rear. Then Cyrus, who was already receiving congratulations as if he were king on account of the success of the Greeks, dashed forward with his 600 horse against the 6000 who surrounded Artaxerxes. The impetuous charge broke up the guard, and, if the prince had kept command over his passions, he would have been the Great King within an hour. But unluckily he caught sight of his brother, whom he hated with his whole soul, amid the flying bodyguard. The bitter passion of hatred overmastered him, and he galloped forward, with a few followers, to slay Artaxerxes with his own hand. He had the satisfaction of wounding him slightly with a javelin; but, in the confused fighting which ensued, he was himself wounded in the eye by a Carian soldier and, falling from his horse, was quickly killed. The news of his death was the signal for the flight of his Asiatic troops.

Cyrus slain

The vivid narrative of Xenophon, who took part in the battle, preserves the memory of these remarkable events. At the time he saw little of the battle, and he could have known little of the arrangements and movements of the Persians. But before he wrote his own book, he had the advantage of reading a book written by another Greek, who had also witnessed those remarkable events, but from the other side. This was Ctesias, the court physician, who was present at the battle and cured Artaxerxes of the breast-wound which Cyrus had dealt him. The book of Ctesias is lost, but some bits of his story have drifted down to us in the works of later writers who had read it, and afford us a glimpse or two into the Great King's camp and court about this eventful time.[2]

The work of Ctesias

For the Greek band, which now found itself in the heart of Persia, surrounded by enemies on every side, the death of Cyrus was an immediate and crushing calamity. But for Greece it was probably a stroke of good fortune—though Sparta herself had blessed the enterprise. Cyrus was a prince whose ability was well-nigh equal to his ambition. He had proved his capacity by his early successes as satrap; by the organisation of his expedition, which demanded an exceptional union of policy and vigour, in meeting difficulties and surmounting dangers; by his recognition of the value of the Greek soldier. Under such a sovereign, the Persian realm

Ability of Cyrus; possible consequences of his success

would have flourished and become once more a menace to the freedom of the European Greeks. Who can tell what dreams that ambitious brain might have cherished, dreams of universal conquest to be achieved at the head of an invincible army of Greek hoplites? And in days when mercenary service was coming into fashion, the service of Cyrus would have been popular. Whatever oriental craft and cruelty lurked beneath, he had not only a frank and attractive manner but a generous nature, which completely won such an honest Greek as Xenophon, the soldier and historian. Cyrus knew how to appreciate the Greeks, he recognised their superiority to the Asiatics in the military qualities of steadfastness and discipline, and this undisguised appreciation was a flattery which they were unable to resist. If Cyrus had come to the throne, his energy and policy would certainly have been felt in the Aegean world; the Greeks would not have been left for the next two generations to shape their own destinies, as they did, little affected by the languid interventions of Artaxerxes. Perhaps the stubborn stupidity of Clearchus on the field of Cunaxa, with his hard-and-fast precepts of Greek drill-sergeants, saved Hellas from becoming a Persian satrapy.

Greeks refuse to surrender

But such speculations would have brought little comfort, could they have occurred, to the 10,000 Greeks who, flushed with the excitement of pursuit, returned to hear that the rest of their army had been defeated, to find their camp pillaged, and then to learn on the following morning that Cyrus was dead. The habit of self-imposed discipline which Cyrus knew so well how to value stood the Greeks in good stead at this grave crisis; and their easy victory had given them confidence. They refused to surrender at the summons of Artaxerxes. For him their presence was extremely awkward, like a hostile city in the midst of his land, and his first object was at all hazards to get them out of Babylonia. He therefore parleyed with them, and supplied them with provisions. The only desire of the Greeks was to make all the haste they could homeward. By the road they had come it was nearly 1500 miles to Sardis; but that road was impracticable, for they could not traverse the desert again unprovisioned. Without guides, without any geographical knowledge—not knowing so much as the course of the Tigris—they had no alternative but to embrace the proposal of Tissaphernes, who undertook to guide them home by another road, on which they would be able to obtain provisions.

Following him—but well in the rear of his troops—the Greeks passed the Wall of Media, and crossed two navigable canals, before they reached the Tigris, which they passed by its only bridge, close to Sittace. Their course then lay northward, up the left bank of the Tigris. They passed from Babylonia into Media and, crossing the lesser Zab, reached the banks of the greater Zab without any incident of consequence. But here the distrust and suspicion which smouldered between the Greek and the Persian camps almost broke into a flame of hostility, and Clearchus was driven into seeking an explanation with Tissaphernes. The frankness of the satrap disarmed the suspicions of Clearchus; Tissaphernes admitted that some persons had attempted to poison his mind against the Greeks, but promised to reveal the names of the calumniators, if the Greek generals and captains came to his tent the next day. Clearchus readily consented, and induced his four fellow-generals—Agias, Menon, Proxenus, and Socrates—to go to Tissaphernes, though such blind confidence was ill justified by the character of the crafty satrap. It was a fatal blunder—the second great blunder Clearchus had made—to place all the Greek commanders helplessly in the power of the Persian. Clearchus had been throughout an enemy of the Thessalian Menon; and it may be that he suspected Menon of treason and that his desire to convict his rival in the tent of Tissaphernes blinded his better judgment. The five generals went, with 20 captains and some soldiers; the captains and soldiers were cut down, and the generals were fettered and sent to the Persian court, where they were all put to death.

Treacherous seizure of Clearchus and the generals

Tissaphernes had no intention of attacking the Greek army. He had led them to a place from which it would be extremely difficult, if not impossible, to return to Greece, and he imagined that when they found themselves without any responsible commanders they would immediately surrender. But if in the first moments of dismay the prospect seemed hopeless, the Greeks speedily rallied their courage, chose new generals, and resumed their northward march. It was the Athenian Xenophon, a man of ready speech and great presence of mind, who did most to infuse new spirit into the army and guide it amidst the perils and difficulties which now beset it. Though he had no rank, being merely a volunteer, he was elected a general, and his power of persuasion, united with practical sense, won for him a remarkable ascendency over the men. He tells us how, on the first dreary night after the betrayal of the generals, he dreamed that he saw a thunderbolt striking his father's house and flames wrapping the walls about. This dream gave him his inspiration. He interpreted it as showing the plight in which he and his fellows were; the house was in extreme danger, but the light was a sign of hope. And then the thought was borne in on him that it was foolish to wait for others to take the lead, that it would be well to make a start himself.

It was bold indeed to undertake a march of uncertain length—terribly long—without guides and with inexperienced officers, over unknown rivers and uncouth mountains, through the lands of barbarous peoples. The alternative would have been to found a Greek city in the centre of Media; but this had no attraction: the hearts of all were set upon returning to the Greek world. It would take too long to tell the full story of the adventures of their retreat; it is a chronicle of courage, discipline, and reasonableness in the face of perils which nothing but the exercise of those qualities in an unusual measure would have been able to surmount. Their march to the Carduchian mountains, which form the northern boundary of Media, was harassed by the army of Tissaphernes, who however never ventured on a pitched battle. When they *Kurdistan* entered Carduchia, the Greeks passed out of the Persian empire; for the men of these mountains were independent, wedged in between the satrapies of Media and Armenia. The passage through this wild country was the most dangerous and destructive part of the whole retreat. The savage hillsmen were implacably hostile, and it was easy for them to defend the narrow precipitous passes against an army laden with baggage, and fearing, at every turn of the winding roads, to be crushed by rocky masses which the enemy rolled down from the heights above. After much suffering and loss of life, they reached the stream of the *Buhtan-* Centrites, a tributary of the Tigris, which *Tchai* divides Carduchia from Armenia. The news of their coming had gone before; and they found the opposite bank lined with the forces of Tiribazus, the Armenian satrap. The Carduchian hillsmen were hanging on their rear, and it needed a clever stratagem to cross the river safely. It was now the month of December, and the march lay through the snows of wintry Armenia. They had terrible struggles with cold and hunger; but they went unmolested, for they had made a compact with Tiribazus, undertaking to abstain from pillage. The direction of the march lay northwestward; they crossed the two branches of

the Euphrates, and their route perhaps partly corresponded to that which a traveller follows *They cross* at the present day from Tavriz to Erzerum. *the Kara* When they had made their way through the *Su and* territories of the martial Chalybes and other *Murad Su* hostile peoples, they reached a city—a sign that at last they were once more on the fringe of civilisation. It was the city of Gymnias, a *Gumish* thriving place which perhaps owed its existence to neighbouring silver mines. Here they had a friendly welcome, and learned with delight that they were not many days' journey south of Trapezus. A guide undertook that they should have sight of the sea after a five days' march. 'And on the fifth day they came to Mount Theches, and when the van reached the summit a great cry arose. When Xenophon and the rear heard it, they *Reach the* thought that an enemy was attacking in front; *Euxine* but when the cry increased as fresh men *Sea* continually came up to the summit, Xenophon thought it must be something more serious, and galloped forward to the front with his cavalry. When he drew near, he heard what the cry was—*The Sea, the Sea!*' The sight of the sea, to which they had said farewell at Myriandrus, and which they had so often despaired of ever again seeing, was an assurance of safety at last attained. The night watches in the plains of Babylonia or by the rivers of Media, the wild faces in the Carduchian mountains, the bleak highlands of Armenia, might now fade into the semblances of an evil dream.

A few more days brought the army to *At* Trapezus—to Greek soil and to the very shore *Trapezus* of the sea. Here they rested for a month, *(first* supporting themselves by plundering the *months of* Colchian natives, who dwelled in the hills *400 B.C.)* round about, while the Greeks of Trapezus supplied a market. Here they celebrated games and offered their sacrifices of thanksgiving to Zeus Soter—in fulfilment of a vow they had made on that terrible night on the Zab after the loss of their generals.

Ten thousand Greek soldiers dropped down from the mountains, like a sudden thunderbolt from heaven, were a surprise which must have caused strange perplexity to the Greeks of the coast—to Trapezus and her sister Cerasus, and to their common mother Sinope. It was a somewhat alarming problem: more than a myriad soldiers, mostly hoplites, steeled by an ordeal of experience such as few men had ever passed through, but not quite certain as to what their next step should be, suddenly knocking at one's gates. And they were not an ordinary army, but rather a democracy of 10,000 citizens equipped as soldiers, serving no king, responsible to no state, a law unto themselves, electing their officers and deciding all matters of importance in a sovereign popular assembly—as it were, a great moving city, moving along the shores of the Euxine; what might it, what might it not, do? For one thing, it might easily plant itself on some likely site within the range of Sinope's influence, and conceivably out-top Sinope herself.

Xenophon thinks of founding a new city

But the Ten Thousand themselves thought only of home—the Aegean and the Greek world. Could they have procured ships at once, they would not have tarried to perplex Sinope and her daughter cities. To Xenophon, who foresaw more or less dimly the difficulties which would beset the army on its return to Greece, the idea of seizing some native town like Phasis and founding a colony, in which he might amass riches and enjoy power, was not unwelcome; but when it was known that he contemplated such a plan, though he never proposed it, he well-nigh forfeited his influence with the army. In truth, a colony at Phasis, in the land of the Golden Fleece, founded by the practical Xenophon, might have been the best solution of the fate of the Ten Thousand. The difficulties which they had now to face were of a different kind from those which they had so successfully surmounted, demanding not so much endurance and bravery as tact and discretion. Now that they were no longer in daily danger of sheer destruction, the motive for cohesion had lost much of its strength. If we remember that the army was composed of men from different Greek states, brought together by chance, and that it was now united by no bond of common allegiance but was purely a voluntary association, the wonder is that it was not completely disorganised and scattered long before it reached Byzantium. It is true that the discipline sensibly and inevitably declined; and it is true that the host dissolved itself at Heraclea into three separate bands, though only to be presently reunited. But it is a remarkable spectacle, this large society of soldiers managing their own affairs, deciding what they would do, determining where they would go, seldom failing to listen to the voice of reason in their Assemblies, whether it was the voice of Xenophon or of another.

Cohesion of the army

The last stages of the retreat, from Trapezus to Chalcedon, were accomplished partly by sea, partly by land, and were marked by delays, disappointments, and disorders. It might be expected that on reaching Chalcedon the army

It reaches Chalcedon

would have dispersed, each man hastening to return to his own city. But they were satisfied to be well within the Greek world once more, and they wanted to replenish their empty purses before they went home. So they still held together, ready to place their arms at the disposal of any power who would pay them. To Pharnabazus, the satrap of the Hellespontine province of Persia, the arrival of men who had defied the power of the Great King was a source of alarm. He bribed the Lacedaemonian admiral Anaxibius, who was stationed at the Bosphorus, to induce the Ten Thousand to cross over into Europe. Anaxibius achieved this by promises of high pay; but the troops, who were admitted into Byzantium, would have pillaged the city when they discovered that they had been deluded, if Xenophon's presence of mind and persuasive speech had not once more saved them from their first impulse. After this they took service under the Thracian prince Seuthes, who employed them to reduce some rebellious tribes. Seuthes was more perfidious than Anaxibius, for he cheated them of the pay which they had actually earned. But better times were coming. War broke out—as we shall presently see—between Lacedaemon and Persia, and the Lacedaemonians wanted fighting men. The impoverished army of Cyrus, now reduced to the number of 6000, crossed back into Asia, and received an advance of pay. Here our interest in them ends, if it did not already end when they reached Trapezus—our interest in all of them, at least, except Xenophon. Once again Xenophon had intended to leave the army since its return to civilisation, and he had steadfastly refused all proposals to elect him commander; but his strong ascendancy among the soldiers and his consequent power to help them had rendered it impossible for him on each occasion to abandon them in their difficulties. Now he was at last released, and returned to Athens with a considerable sum of money. It is probable that his native city, where his master Socrates had recently suffered death, proved uncongenial to him; for he soon went back to Asia to fight with his old comrades against the Persians. When Athens presently became an ally of Persia against Sparta, Xenophon was banished, and more than twenty years of his life were spent at Scillus, a Triphylian village, where the Spartans gave him a home. Afterwards the sentence of exile was revoked, and his last years were passed at Athens.

At By- zantium

Employed by Sparta, 399 B.C.

Career of Xenophon

Xenophon lives at Scillus in Triphylia till 070 B.C.

On a country estate near that Triphylian village, not far from Olympia, Xenophon settled down into a quiet life, with abundant leisure for literature; and composed, among other things of less account, the narrative of that memorable adventure in which Xenophon the Athenian had played such a leading part. Of the environment of his country life in quiet Triphylia he has given a glimpse, showing us how he imprinted his own personality on the place. He had deposited in the great temple of Artemis at Ephesus a portion of a ransom of some captives taken during the retreat, to be reserved for the service of the goddess. This deposit was restored to him at Scillus, and with the money Xenophon bought a suitable place for a sanctuary of Ephesian Artemis. 'A river Selinus flows through the place, just as at Ephesus a river Selinus flows past the temple; and in both streams there are fishes and shellfishes, but in the place at Scillus there is also all manner of game. And Xenophon made an altar and a temple, with the sacred money, and henceforward he used every year to offer to the goddess a tithe of the fruits of his estate, and all the citizens and neighbours, men and women, took part in the feast. They camped in tents, and the goddess furnished them with meal, bread, wine, and sweetmeats, and with a share of the hallowed dole of the sacrifice, and with a share of the game. For Xenophon's lads and the lads of the neighbours used to hunt quarry for the feast, and men who liked would join in the chase. There was game both in the consecrated estate and in Mount Pholoe—wild swine, and gazelles, and stags. That estate has meadow-land and wooded hills—good pasture for swine and goats, for cattle and horses; and the beasts of those who travel from Sparta to the Olympian festival—for the road wends through the place—have their fill of feasting. The temple, which is surrounded by a plantation of fruit trees, is a small model of the great temple of Ephesus; and the cypress-wood image is made in the fashion of the Ephesian image of gold.' Here Xenophon could lead a happy, uneventful life, devoted to sport and literature and the service of the gods.

Significance of the expedition of Cyrus

At a casual glance the expedition of Cyrus may appear to belong not to Greek but to Persian history; and the retreat of the Ten Thousand may be deemed matter for a book of adventures. But the fascinating story of the up-going and the home-coming of Xenophon and his fellows is in truth no digression. It has been already pointed out how vitally the interests of Hellas, according to human calculation, were involved in the issue of Cunaxa; and how, if the arbitrament of fortune on that battlefield had been other, the future of Greece might have been other too. But the whole episode—the up-going, the battle, and the home-coming—has an importance, by no means problematical, which secures it a certain and conspicuous place in the procession of Greek history. It is an epilogue to the invasion of Xerxes and a prologue to the conquest of Alexander. The Great King had carried his arms into Greece, and Greece had driven him back; that was a leading epoch in the combat between Asia and Europe. The next epoch will be the retribution. The Greeks will carry their arms into Persia, and Persia will fail to repel them. The success of Alexander will be the answer to the defeat of Xerxes. For this answer the world has to wait for five generations; but in the meanwhile the expedition of the soldiers of Cyrus is a prediction, vouchsafed as it were by history, what the answer is to be. Xenophon's *Anabasis* is the continuation of Herodotus; Xenophon and his band are the forerunners of Alexander. And this significance of the adventure, as a victory of Greece over Persia, was immediately understood. A small company of soldiers had marched unopposed to the centre of the Persian empire, where no Greek army had ever won its way before; they had defeated almost without a blow the overwhelming forces of the King within a few miles of his Babylon; and they had returned safely, having escaped from the hostile multitudes, which did not once dare to withstand their spears in open warfare. Such a display of Persian impotence surprised the world; and Greece might well despise the power whose resources a band of strangers had so successfully defied. No Hellenic city indeed had won a triumph over the barbarian; but all Hellenic cities alike had reason to be stirred by pride at a brilliant demonstration of the superior excellence of the Greek to the Asiatic in courage, discipline, and capacity. The lesson had, as we shall see, its immediate consequences. Only a year or two passed, and it inspired a Spartan king—a man, indeed, of poor ability and slight performance—to attempt to achieve the task which fate reserved for Alexander. But the moral effect of the Anabasis was lasting, and of greater import than the futile warfare of Agesilaus. Considering these bearings, we shall have not said too much if we say that the episode of the Ten Thousand, though a private enterprise so far as Hellas was concerned, and though enacted beyond the limits of the Hellenic world, yet occupies a more eminent place on the highway of Greek history than the contemporary transactions of Athens and Sparta and the other states of Greece.

War of Sparta with Persia

The enterprise of Cyrus had immediately affected the position and prospects of the Greek cities of Ionia. In accordance with their contract the Spartans had handed over the Asiatic cities to Persia, retaining only Abydus, on account of its strategic importance. Cyrus, however, bidding for Greek support, had instigated the Ionian cities to revolt from their satrap, Tissaphernes, and to place themselves under his protection. Tissaphernes was in time to save Miletus, but all the other cities received Greek garrisons, and thus, when Cyrus disappeared into the interior of Asia, they had practically passed out of Persian control. After the defeat of Cyrus at Cunaxa, Tissaphernes returned to the Aegean coast as governor of all the districts which had been under Cyrus, and with the general title of commander of Further Asia, implying supremacy over the adjacent satrapies. His first concern was to recover the Greek cities of the coast, and he attacked Cyme. The Asiatic Greeks were greatly alarmed, and they sent to Sparta an appeal for her protection.

The relations of Sparta to Persia were no longer the same, since the help given to Cyrus was an act of war against the king. The successful march of the Ten Thousand inspired Greece with a feeling of contempt for the strength of the Persian empire. The opportunity of plundering the wealthy satrapies of Pharnabazus and Tissaphernes was a bait for Spartan cupidity; the prospect of gaining signal successes against Persia appealed to Spartan ambition. These considerations induced Sparta to send an army to Asia, and this army was increased by the remains of the famous Ten Thousand, who (as already stated) crossed over from Thrace and entered the service of Sparta. Much might have been accomplished with a competent commander, but the general Thibron was unable to maintain discipline among his men, and the few successes achieved fell far short of Sparta's reasonable hopes. Thibron was superseded by Dercyllidas, a man who had the repute of being unusually wily. Taking advantage of a misunderstanding between the two satraps, Dercyllidas made a truce with Tissaphernes and marched with all his forces into the province of Pharnabazus, against whom he had a

Tissaphernes, as commander of Asia, plans to recover the Greek cities

which appeal to Sparta

Sparta sends an army, 400 B.C.

under Thibron (400-399 B.C.), who is succeeded by Dercyllidas (399 B.C.)

personal grudge. A recent occurence rendered it possible for him to get into his hands the Troad—or Aeolis, as it was called—with speed and ease. The government of this region had been granted by Pharnabazus to Zenis, a native of Dardanus. When he died, leaving a widow, a son, and daughter, Pharnabazus was about to choose another subsatrap, but the widow, whose name was Mania, presented a petition that she should be permitted to fill the post which her husband had held. 'My husband,' she argued, 'paid his tribute punctually, and you thanked him for it. If I do as well, why should you appoint another? If I am found unsatisfactory, you can remove me at any moment.' She fortified her arguments by large presents of money to the satrap, his officers, and concubines, and won her request. She gave Pharnabazus full satisfaction by her regular payments of tribute, and under her vigorous administration the Aeolid became a rich and well-defended land. A body of Greek mercenaries was maintained in her service, and immense treasures were stored in the strong mountain fortresses of Scepsis, Gergis, and Cebren. She even reduced some coast towns in the south of the Troad, and took part herself, like the Carian Artemisia, in military expeditions. But she had for son-in-law an ungrateful traitor, Meidias of Scepsis, whom she treated with trust and affection. In order to possess himself of her power, he strangled her, then killed her son, and laid hold of the three fortresses which controlled the district, along with all the treasure. But Pharnabazus refused to recognise the murderer of Mania, and sent back the gifts of Meidias with the message: 'Keep them till I come to seize both them and you. Life would not be worth living if I avenged not the death of Mania.'

As Meidias was expecting with alarm the vengeance of Pharnabazus, the Spartan army appeared on the scene. Dercyllidas became master of the Aeolid without any opposition, since the garrisons of the cities did not acknowledge Meidias—excepting only the forts of Scepsis, Gergis, and Cebren. The garrison of Cebren soon surrendered; at Scepsis, Meidias came out to a conference, and Dercyllidas, without waiting to confer, marched up to the gates of the town, so that Meidias, in the power of the enemy, could do nothing but order them to be opened; and his unwilling orders likewise threw open the gates of Gergis. His own private property was restored to Meidias, but all the treasures of Mania were appropriated by the Spartan general; for the property of Mania belonged to her master Pharnabazus,

The Troad

Mania,

murdered by her son-in-law

Dercyllidas gains the Troad;

and was therefore the legitimate booty of the satrap's enemy. This booty supplied Dercyllidas with pay for his 8000 soldiers for nearly a year, and it was noticed that the conduct of the heroes of the Anabasis showed a signal improvement from this time forward. The Aeolid now served the Spartans against the satrapy of Pharnabazus somewhat as Decelea had served them in Attica; it was a fortified district in the enemy's country. Sparta, hoping that these successes would induce Persia to make terms and acquiesce in the freedom of the Greek cities, concluded truces with Tissaphernes and Pharnabazus, and sent up ambassadors to Susa to treat with the Great King. Dercyllidas meanwhile crossed into Europe and occupied himself with restoring the crosswall which defended Sestos and the other cities of the Chersonese against the incursions of the Thracians, the inhabitants gladly furnishing pay and food to the army. On returning to Asia, the Spartan commander captured, after a long siege, the strong town of Atarneus. Then by special orders from home he proceeded to Caria.

(398 B.C.)

(398 B.C.)

besieges and captures Atarneus (398-7 B.C.); goes to Caria (397 B.C.)

The Spartan overtures were heard unfavourably at Susa, for the King had been persuaded by his able satrap Pharnabazus to prosecute the war by sea. The Spartans could not cope in mere numbers with the fleet which Phoenicia and Cyprus could furnish him, but everything would depend on the commander. Here fortune played into his hands. There was an enemy of Sparta, an experienced naval officer, who was ready to compass heaven and earth to work the downfall of her supremacy. The Athenian admiral Conon, whom we last saw escaping from the surprise of Aegospotami, was burning to avenge the disgrace of that fatal day. He had found hospitality and protection at the court of Evagoras, king of the Cyprian Salamis, and through him had entered into communication with Ctesias, the Greek physician, whom we met at Cunaxa. Ctesias had the ear of the queen-mother Parysatis, and through her influence and the advice of Pharnabazus Conon was appointed to command a fleet of 300 ships which was prepared in Phoenicia and Cilicia. Under his command, such a numerous navy was extremely formidable, but the Lacedaemonian government does not seem to have realised the danger, owing perhaps to their experience of the ineffectiveness of previous Persian armaments; and they committed the mistake of throwing all their vigour into the land warfare and neglecting their sea-power, which was absolutely vital for the maintenance of their

Conon

appointed commander of a Persian fleet

supremacy. But when Conon, not waiting for the complete equipment of the fleet, sailed to Caunus in Caria with 40 ships, the Spartans were obliged to move. They sent a fleet of 120 ships under Pharax from Rhodes to blockade Caunus and Conon's ships in the harbour, and ordered Dercyllidas to Caria. The joint forces of Tissaphernes and Pharnabazus first raised the siege of Caunus and then confronted Dercyllidas in the valley of the Maeander. A panic which seized some of the troops of the Spartan general might have been fatal, but the reputation of the Ten Thousand, whose valour Tissaphernes had experienced, rendered that satrap unwilling to risk a battle, and a conference issued in an armistice. Conon meanwhile was able to win over Rhodes, which had given useful service to Sparta since 411. At his instigation the leading oligarchs were cut down and an anti-Spartan democracy instituted.[3] But Sparta had now decided to conduct the war with greater vigour, and Dercyllidas had to make way for no less a successor than one of the kings.

Armistice

Agesilaus, who now comes upon the scene, had been recently raised to the regal dignity in unusual circumstances. When Lysander retired from public affairs to visit the temple of Zeus Ammon, he had neither discarded ambition nor lost his influence. He conceived the plan of making a change in the Spartan constitution which can hardly be described as less than revolutionary. The idea was that the kingship should be no longer confined to the Eurysthenid and Proclid families in which it was hereditary by law, but that the kings should be elected from all Heraclids. The scheme to make the office elective, instead of hereditary, was momentous. It meant immediately that Lysander should hold the military functions which belonged to the kings, the command of the army abroad, *for life;* he could no longer be deposed or recalled at the end of a term of office. And in the hands of a man like Lysander this permanent office might become something very different from what it was in the hands of the ordinary Proclid or Eurysthenid; the proportion between the power of king and ephor might be considerably shifted. Lysander's project might well have proved the first step to a sort of *principate,* which might have partially adapted Spartan institutions to the requirements of an imperial state. Lysander did not conceive the possibility of carrying this bold innovation by a *coup d'état;* his plan was to bring religious influence to bear on the authorities, and he secretly employed his absence from Sparta in

Agesilaus Revolutionary scheme of Lysander

attempting to enlist the most important oracles in favour of his design. But the oracles received his proposal coldly; it sounded far too audacious. He succeeded, however, in winning over some of the Delphic priests, who aided him to invent oracles for his purpose: a rumour was spread that certain sacred and ancient records were preserved at Delphi, never to be revealed until a son of Apollo appeared to claim them; and at the same time people began to hear of the existence of a youth named Silenus, whose mother vouched that Apollo was his sire. But the ingenious plot broke down; at the last moment one of the confederates did not play his part, and the oracles bearing on the Spartan *The plot* kingship were never revealed. Lysander then *abandoned* abandoned his revolutionary idea, and took advantage of the death of king Agis to secure the sceptre for a man whom he calculated he could direct and control. The kingship descended, in the natural course, on Leotychidas, the son of Agis; but it was commonly believed that this youth was illegitimate, being really the son of Alcibiades. There were doubts on *Accession* the matter but the suspicion was strong enough *of* to enable the half-brother of Agis, Agesilaus, *Agesilaus,* supported by the influence of Lysander, to *398 B.C.* oust his nephew and assume the sceptre.

His Lysander was deceived in his man; the new *character* king was not to be the kingmaker's tool. Agesilaus had hitherto shown only one side of his character. He had observed all the ordinances of Lycurgus from his youth up; had performed all duties with cheerful obedience; had shown himself singularly docile and gentle; had never asserted or put himself forward among his fellow-citizens. But the mask of Spartan discipline covered a latent spirit of pride and ambition which no one suspected. Agesilaus, though strong and courageous, was of insignificant stature and lame. When he claimed the throne, an objection was raised on the ground of his deformity, for an oracle had once solemnly warned Lacedaemon to beware of a halt reign. But like all sacred weapons this oracle could be blunted or actually turned against the adversaries. The god did not mean, said Lysander, physical lameness; but the reign of one who was not truly descended from Heracles. Yet those Spartans who believed in literal interpretation of divine words were ill content with the preference of Agesilaus.

The new king displayed remarkable discretion and policy by his general demeanour of deferential respect to the other authorities. This had the greater effect, as the kings were generally wont to make up by their haughty manners for their want of real power. Agesilaus made himself popular with everybody, and he maintained as king the simplicity which had marked his life as a private citizen. He was unswervingly true to his friends; but this virtue declined to vice, when he upheld his partisans in acts of injustice.

Not long after his accession, a serious *Domestic* incident occurred which gives us a glimpse of *condition* the social condition of the Lacedaemonian state *of Sparta* at this period and shows that while the government was struggling to maintain its empire abroad, it was menaced at home by dangers which the existence of that empire rendered graver every year. Commerce with the outside world and acquisition of money had promoted considerable inequalities in wealth; and in consequence the number of Peers or fully enfranchised Spartan citizens was constantly diminishing, while the class of those who had become too poor to pay their contribution to the *syssitia* was proportionally growing. These disqualified citizens were not degraded to the *The* rank of Perioeci; they formed a separate class *Inferiors* and were named Inferiors; a stroke of luck might at any moment enable one of them to pay his subscription and restore him to full citizenship. But the Inferiors naturally formed a class of malcontents; and the narrow, ever narrowing, oligarchy of Peers had to fear that they might make common cause with the Perioeci and Helots and conspire against the state. Such a conspiracy was hatched, but was detected in its first stage through the efficient system of secret police which was established at Sparta. The prime mover seems to have been a young man of the Inferior class named *Conspiracy* Cinadon, of great strength and bravery. The *of* ephors learned from an informer that Cinadon *Cinadon,* had called his attention in the market-place *397 B.C.* to the small number of *Spartans* compared with the multitude of their *enemies*—one perhaps in a hundred. All alike, Inferiors, Neodamodes, Perioeci, Helots, were, according to Cinadon, his accomplices; 'for hear any of them talk about the Spartans, he talks as if he could eat them raw.' And when Cinadon was asked where the conspirators would find arms, he pointed to the shops of the ironsmiths in the market-place, and added that every workman and husbandman possessed tools. On the ground of information which was perhaps more precise than this, the ephors sent for Cinadon, whom they had often employed on police service, and sent him on a mission of this kind, but with an escort which arrested him on the road, put him to the torture, and wrung from him the names of his accomplices.

It would have been dangerous to arrest him in Sparta and so spread the alarm before the names of the others were known. Asked why he conspired, Cinadon said: 'I wished to be inferior to none in Sparta.' He was scourged round the city and put to death with his fellows.

Recollecting the histories of other states we cannot forbear wondering that an ambitious general like Lysander did not attempt to use for his own purposes this mass of discontent, into which Cinadon's abortive conspiracy opens a glimpse. There was something in the Spartan air which made a Peer rarely capable of disloyalty to the privileges of his own class.

Asiatic Campaigns of Agesilaus. Battle of Cnidus

396 B.C. It was arranged that Agesilaus should take the place of Dercyllidas and that he should take with him a force of 2000 Neodamodes, and a military council of 30 Spartans, including Lysander.

In the Spartan projects at this juncture we can observe very clearly the effect of the episode of the expedition of Cyrus and the Ten Thousand in revolutionising the attitude of Greece towards Persia and spreading the idea that Persia was really weak. The Spartan leaders seemed to have regarded the lands of the Great King as a field of easy conquest for *Highflying* a bold Greek. King Agesilaus, especially, who *plans of* now began to disclose the consuming quality *Agesilaus;* of ambition, dreamed of dethroning the Great King himself, and felt no doubt that he would at least speedily deliver the Asiatic coast from Persian control. But he lived sixty years too soon and in any case this respectable Spartan was not the man to settle the 'eternal question'. He regarded himself as a new Agamemnon going forth to capture a new Troy; and, to make the illusion of resemblance complete, he sailed with part of his army to Aulis, to offer sacrifice there in the temple of Artemis as the 'king of men' had done before the sailing of the Greeks to Ilium. If Agesilaus had subverted the Persian empire, the sacrifice at Aulis would have seemed an interesting instance of a great man's confidence in his own *his display* star. But the performance of Agesilaus can *at Aulis* only provoke the mirth of history, especially as the solemnity was not successfully carried out. The Spartan king had not asked the permission of the Thebans to sacrifice in the temple, and a body of armed men interrupted the pro-

ceedings and compelled him to desist. It was an insult which Agesilaus never forgave.

Lysander expected that the real command in the war would devolve upon himself, and on arriving in Asia he acted on that assumption. He was soon undeceived. Agesilaus had no intention of being merely a nominal chief, and he checked his councillor's self-sufficiency by invariably refusing the petitions which were presented to him through Lysander. This policy was effectual; Lysander, smarting under the humiliation, was sent at his own request on a separate mission to the Hellespont, where he did useful work for Sparta. The *396 B.C.* satraps in the meantime had renewed with Agesilaus the truce they had made with Dercyllidas, but it was soon broken by Tissaphernes. Agesilaus made a feint of *Campaign* marching into Caria, and then suddenly, when *of Agesi-* Tissaphernes had completed his dispositions *laus in* for defence, turned northwards to Phrygia and *Phrygia* invaded the satrapy of Pharnabazus. Here he *(autumn)* accomplished nothing of abiding importance but secured a vast quantity of booty, with which he enriched his friends and favourites— it was no temptation to himself. The historian Xenophon, who has left us a special work on the life and character of Agesilaus, tells many anecdotes of this campaign, to illustrate the merits of his hero. Those incidents which bring *Anecdotes* out his humanity have more than a personal *of* interest for us, they must be taken in connec- *Agesilaus* tion with the general fact that the Greeks of the fourth century were more humane than the Greeks of the fifth. We are told that Agesilaus protected his captives against ill-usage; they were to be treated as men, not as criminals. Sometimes slave-merchants, fleeing out of the way of his army, abandoned on the roadside little children whom they had bought. Instead of leaving these to perish by wolves or hunger, Agesilaus had them removed and given in charge to natives who were too old to be carried into captivity. But Agesilaus did not scruple to use the captives, without regard to their feelings, as 'object-lessons' for his own soldiers. At Ephesus, where the winter was passed in drill, he conceived the idea of showing his troops the difference between good and bad training. He caused the prisoners to be put up for auction naked, so that the Greek soldiers might see the inferior muscles, the white skin, and the soft limbs of the Asiatics whose bodies were never exposed to the weather nor hardened by regular gymnastic discipline. The spectacle impressed the Greeks with their own superiority; but it was an outrage, though not intended as such, on the

Campaign
in Lydia,
395 B.C.
(spring)

Death of
Tissa-
phernes

Second
invasion of
the satrapy
of Pharna-
bazus by
Agesilaus
(autumn)

captives, for, while all Greeks habitually stripped for exercise, Asiatics thought it a shame to be seen naked.

Having organised a force of cavalry during the winter, Agesilaus took the field in spring, and gained a victory over Tissaphernes on the Pactolus, near Sardis. The general ill-success of Tissaphernes was made a matter of complaint at Susa. The queen-mother Parysatis, who had never forgiven him for the part he played in the disaster of her beloved Cyrus, made all efforts to procure his downfall, and Tithraustes was sent to the coast to succeed him and put him to death. An offer was now made by Tithraustes to Agesilaus, which it would have been wise to accept. He was required to leave Asia, on condition that the Greek cities should enjoy complete autonomy, paying only their original tribute to Persia. Agesilaus could not agree without consulting his government at home, and an armistice of six months was concluded—an armistice with Tithraustes, not with Persia; for Agesilaus was left free to turn his arms against Pharnabazus.

In his second campaign in Phrygia, the Spartan king was supported by a Paphlagonian prince named Otys, as well as by Spithridates, a Persian noble whom Lysander had induced to revolt. The province was ravaged up to the walls of Dascylion, where Pharnabazus resided, and the Spartan troops wintered in the rich parks of the neighbourhood, well supplied with birds and fish. The train of Pharnabazus, who moved about the country with all his furniture, was captured; but a dispute over the spoil alienated the oriental allies of Agesilaus, who was the more deeply chagrined at their departure, as he was warmly attached to a beautiful youth, the son of Spithridates. The Greek occupation of Phrygia was brought to an end by an interesting scene—an interview between the Persian satrap and the Lacedaemonian general. Agesilaus arrived first at the appointed place and sat down on the grass to wait. Then the servants of Pharnabazus appeared and began to spread luxurious carpets for their master. But Pharnabazus seeing the simple seat of Agesilaus went and sat down beside him. They shook hands, and Pharnabazus made a speech of dignified remonstrance. 'I was the faithful ally of Sparta when she was at war with Athens; I helped her to victory; I never played her false, like Tissaphernes; and now, for all this, you have brought me to such a plight that I cannot get a dinner in my own province save by picking up what you leave. All my parks and hunting grounds and houses you have

ravaged or burnt. Is this justice or gratitude?' After a long silence, Agesilaus explained that being at war with the Great King he had to treat all Persian territory as hostile; but invited the satrap to throw off his allegiance and become an ally of Sparta. 'If the king sends another governor and puts me under him,' said Pharnabazus, 'then I shall be glad to become your friend and ally; but now, while I hold this post of command for him, I shall make war upon you with all my strength.' Agesilaus was delighted with this becoming reply. 'I will quit your territory at once,' he said, 'and will respect it in future, so long as I have others to make war upon.' Farewells were said and Pharnabazus rode away; but his handsome son, dropping behind, said to Agesilaus, 'I make you my guest,' and gave him a javelin. Agesilaus accepted the proffered friendship and gave in exchange the ornaments of his secretary's horse. The incident had a sequel. In later years this young Persian, ill-treated by his brothers, fled for refuge to Greece, and did not seek in vain the protection of his guest-friend Agesilaus.

His success in Phrygia rendered Agesilaus more than ever disposed to attempt conquests in the interior of Asia Minor. But in the meantime he had mismanaged matters of greater moment. Before he marched against Pharnabazus, he had received a message from Sparta, committing to him the supreme command by sea. The preparation of an adequate fleet was urgent. Conon, with 80 sail—the rest of the armament was not yet completed—had induced Rhodes to revolt and had captured a corn fleet which an Egyptian prince had dispatched to the Lacedaemonians.[3] Agesilaus took measures for the equipment of a fleet of 120 triremes at the expense of the cities of the islands and coast-land; but he committed the blunder of entrusting the command to Pisander, his brother-in-law, a man of no experience. After his Phrygian expedition, Agesilaus had been himself recalled to Europe for reasons which will presently be related; while Pharnabazus went to discharge the functions of joint-admiral with Conon, who had visited Susa in person, to stimulate Persian zeal and obtain the necessary funds. In the middle of the summer the fleet of Conon and Pharnabazus, having left Cilician waters, appeared off the coast of the Cnidian peninsula. The numbers are uncertain, but the Persian fleet was overwhelmingly larger than that of Pisander, who sailed out from Cnidus to oppose it with desperate courage. The result could not be doubtful. Pisander's Asiatic contingents de-

(395 B.C.)

Battle of
Cnidus
(August
394 B.C.)

serted him without fighting, and of the rest the greater part were taken or sunk. Pisander fell in the action. The Greek cities of Asia expelled the Spartan garrisons and acknowledged the overlordship of Persia. Thus Conon, in the guise of a Persian admiral, avenged Athens and undid the victory of the Aegospotami in a battle which was almost as easily won. The maritime power of Sparta was destroyed, and the unstable foundations of her empire undermined.

Sparta at the Gates of the Peloponnese (the 'Corinthian War')

At the same time, she was suffering serious checks nearer home. While Agesilaus was meditating his wonderful schemes against Persia, war had broken out in Greece between Sparta and her allies, and the turn it took rendered it imperative to recall him from Asia. It is necessary to go back a little to explain.

After the battle of the Goat's River, Sparta had kept for herself all the fruits of victory. She had taken over the maritime empire of her prostrate foe and enjoyed its tribute. Her allies had got nothing, and yet they had made far greater sacrifices than Sparta herself throughout the Peloponnesian war. Any demands made by Corinth and other allies who had borne the burden and heat of those years were haughtily rejected. Lacedaemon felt herself strong enough to treat her former friends with contempt. She further exhibited her despotic temper by her proceedings within the Peloponnese against those who had displeased her. Elis had given her repeated and recent grounds of offence, and Elis was now *Fate of Elis, 399 B.C.* chastised. King Agis invaded and ravaged the country, and imposed severe conditions on the Eleans. They were deprived of their Triphylian territory, of Cyllene their port, and of other places; and were compelled to pull down the incomplete fortifications of their city. The only grace accorded to them was that they should still have the privilege of conducting the Olympian festival. The Spartans indulged *The Messenians* another grudge by expelling from Naupactus and Cephallenia the residue of the Messenians, who had settled in those places.

Spartan activity north of Thermopylae The exercise of authority within the Peloponnese was regarded by Sparta as an ordering of her own domain; but she also began vigorously to assert her power in the north of Greece. She resuscitated into new life her colony of Heraclea, near Thermopylae, and pushing into Thessaly she placed a Lacedaemonian garrison and harmost in Pharsalus.

Mission of Timocrates, 396 B.C. When war broke out between Persia and Sparta, it was the policy of Persia to excite a war in Greece against her enemy and fan the smouldering discontent of the secondary Greek powers into a flame. The satrap Pharnabazus sent a Rhodian agent, named Timocrates, with 50 talents to bribe the leading statesmen of the chief cities to join Persia in a league of hostility against Sparta.[4] Timocrates visited Argos, Corinth, Thebes, and Athens, and gained over some of the most influential people. But it really required only an assurance of Persian co-operation, and then a favourable occasion, to raise a general resistance to the ascendency of Lacedaemon. Already the anti-Spartan elements were strong at Argos, Corinth, and Thebes; and at Athens feeling was rising. While the oligarchs opposed any action against Sparta, extreme democrats, led by Epicrates and Cephalus, urged a bold policy: the more moderate Thrasybulus, conscious of the Spartan harmost at Aegina, preserved an uneasy balance. But when news came of Conon's activities, a ship with arms and equipment was sent off to him secretly: the action was publicly disowned, but further support was sent to Conon. The issue was forced by the anti-Spartan group in Thebes. A border dispute arose between Phocis and Western Locris; the Phocians appealed to Sparta, the Locrians to Thebes. The Thebans invaded Phocis, and when required by Sparta *Outbreak of war in Boeotia* to submit the case to arbitration, refused to negotiate. Sparta accepted the challenge. A double invasion of Boeotia was arranged, king Pausanias advancing from the south, and Lysander coming down from Heraclea, from the north.

Athens combines with Thebes Thus threatened, Thebes turned for aid to her old enemy. The prospect of Persian support, and the increasing activity of Conon, had strengthened the war party at Athens; and the protection that Thebes had afforded to Thrasybulus and his men was still remembered. The Assembly seized the opportunity for attempting to break free from Spartan rule. The decision was felt to be bold, since the Piraeus was unfortified; but there was also a feeling that the tide was at the flood—Conon was sailing the south-eastern seas, Rhodes had revolted, the moment must not be lost. So there was concluded an 'eternal alliance between the Boeotians and Athenians'; the phrase, pregnant with the irony of history, has been preserved on a fragment of the original treaty-stone, and it shows the hopes of the hour.[5]

When Lysander approached Boeotia, he was joined by Orchomenus, which was always bitterly hostile to Theban supremacy in Boeotia. He and Pausanias had arranged to meet near Haliartus, which is about half-way between Thebes and Orchomenus. It is uncertain whether Lysander was too soon or Pausanias too late; but Lysander arrived in the district of Haliartus first and attacked the town. From their battlements the men of Haliartus could descry a band of Thebans coming along the road from Thebes, some time before the danger was visible to their assailants; and they suddenly sallied forth from the gates. Taken by surprise and attacked on both sides, Lysander's men were driven back, and Lysander was slain. His death was a loss to Sparta, which she could not make good. He had made her empire such as it was; and she had no other man of first-rate ability. But the death of the Spartan Lysander was no loss to Greece.

Pausanias soon came up, and his first object was to recover the body of his dead colleague. He was strong enough to extort this from the Thebans and Haliartians, but an Athenian army came up at the same moment to their assistance, under the leadership of Thrasybulus. Pausanias was in a difficult predicament. To fight meant to incur defeat, but to acknowledge weakness by asking for a burial truce was galling to Spartan pride. A council of war, however, decided to beg for a truce; and when the Thebans, contrary to usage, would grant it only on condition that the Peloponnesian army should leave Boeotia, the terms were accepted. The Spartans vented their sorrow for the loss of Lysander in anger against their king. He was condemned to death for having failed to keep tryst with Lysander and for having declined battle. It is not clear whether the first charge was well founded; as for the second, no prudent general could have acted otherwise. Pausanias, who had discreetly refrained from returning to Sparta, spent the rest of his life as an exile at Tegea.

The result of this double blow to the Spartans—their prestige tarnished and their ablest general fallen—was the conclusion of a league against her. Thebes and Athens were now joined by Corinth and Argos. This alliance was soon increased by the adhesion of the Euboeans, the Acarnanians, the Chalcidians of Thrace, and other minor states. Perhaps the most active spirit in this insurgent movement was the Theban Ismenias. This leader succeeded in expelling the Spartans from their northern post Heraclea and in spreading the Theban alliance among the peoples of those regions. Sparta lost her foothold in Thessaly, and the Phocians, who were under the protection of a Spartan harmost, were defeated. Sympathy with Thebes against Sparta was also shown in the Aegean. The revolt of Rhodes and the victory of Cnidus were followed by the formation of a Maritime League. At this period a number of cities issued alliance coins with a common obverse type derived from Thebes, the infant Heracles strangling the snakes; the reverse was reserved for each city's civic device. Rhodes, Iasus, Cnidus, Ephesus, Samos, Byzantium, Cyzicus, Lampsacus are known to us and there may have been others. The same pro-Theban type is also found at this time in the west on coins of Zacynthus and Croton.[6]

Thus the situation of Greece and the prospects of Sparta were completely changed. The allies, when spring came, gathered together their forces at the Isthmus, and it was proposed by one bold Corinthian to march straight on Sparta and 'burn out the wasps in their nest'. But there were too many strategists present, and valuable time was wasted. The Lacedaemonians were able to advance through Arcadia to Sicyon, from which place they crossed over, by Nemea, to the southern shores of the Saronic gulf—a movement somewhat hampered by the allies, who had reached Nemea. The allies then took up a post near Corinth, and a battle was fought. The number of combatants on each side was unusually large for a Greek battle. The Lacedaemonian hoplite contingent totalled 6000, and was supported by some 10,000 allies from Elis, Sicyon, Epidaurus and its neighbours, Tegea, and Pellene; the Confederates had mustered some 24,000 hoplites, with a correspondingly larger force of cavalry and light-armed.[7] The Confederates' right defeated the Spartan allies, but the Spartans outflanked and broke the Athenians on the left. The Spartan divisions kept good order, checked their pursuit, wheeled round and caught the Argives, Boeotians, and Corinthians, returning from victory. The one-sided action that followed decisively confirmed the Spartan victory. The losses of the Confederates were more than twice as great as those of their foes. Some unrecorded feat of arms was achieved in this battle by five Athenian horsemen who lost their lives; and in the burying-ground outside the Dipylon Gate of Athens we may still see the funeral monument of one of these 'five knights',

Siege of
Haliartus

Death of
Lysander

Confederation
against
Sparta

The Confederates
at the
Isthmus,
spring,
394 B.C.

Battle of
Corinth
(July)[8]

12.1   Grave monument of Dexileos

Dexileos, a youth of twenty, who is portrayed, according to Greek habit, not in the moment of his death but in the moment of victory, spearing a hoplite who has fallen under his horse's hoofs.[8] Strategically, the Confederates lost nothing, the victors gained nothing, by the battle of Corinth. The Isthmus was left under the control of the Confederates, who were now free to oppose Agesilaus in Boeotia.

Return of Agesilaus to Europe   For Agesilaus was bearing down on Boeotia. The battle of Haliartus and the events which followed had decided the ephors to recall him from Asia, his presence being more pressingly needed in Europe; and with a heavy heart he was constrained to abandon his dazzling visions of Persian conquest. Agamemnon had to return to Mycenae without having taken Troy. He marched overland by a route which no army had traversed since the expedition of Xerxes, through Thrace and Macedonia. At

Amphipolis he received the news of the victory of Corinth, not excessively inspiriting. But even as he marched the fate of his country's empire was being decided. The victory of Conon at Cnidus was fatal to the ambitions of Agesilaus. When his army reached Chaeronea the sun suffered an eclipse; and the meaning of the phenomenon was explained by the news, which presently arrived, of the battle of Cnidus. To conceal from his army the full import of this news was the first duty of the general; and the second was to hasten on a battle, while it could still be concealed. Agesilaus had been reinforced by some contingents from Lacedaemon, as well as by troops from Phocis and Orchomenus; but his main force consisted of the soldiers whom he had brought from Asia, among whom were some of the famous Ten Thousand, including Xenophon himself. The Confederate army which had fought at Corinth was now in Boeotia, though hardly in the same strength, as a garrison must have been left to defend their important position near the Isthmus. The Confederates established their camp in the district of Coronea, a favourable spot for blocking against a foe the road which leads to Thebes from Phocis and the valley of the Cephisus. On the field where the Boeotians had thrown off Athenian rule half a century before, Athenians and Boeotians now joined to throw off the domination of Lacedaemon. Agesilaus advanced from the Cephisus. He commanded his own right wing, and the Argives who were on the Confederate left fled before him without striking a blow. On the other side, the Thebans on the Confederate right routed the Orchomenians on the Lacedaemonian left. Then the two victorious right wings wheeling round met each other, and the real business of the day began. The object of Agesilaus was to prevent the Thebans from joining and rallying their friends. The encounter of the hoplites is described as incomparably terrible by Xenophon, who was himself engaged in it. Agesilaus, whose bodily size was hardly equal to such a fray, was thrown to the ground, and rescued by the bravery of his bodyguard. The pressure of the deep column of the Thebans pushed a way through the Lacedaemonian array. Agesilaus was left master of the field; he erected a trophy, and the Confederates asked for the burial truce. But though the battle of Coronea, like the battle of Corinth, was a technical victory for the Spartans, history must here again offer her congratulations to the side which was, superficially, defeated. In the chief action of

Eclipse of sun, August 14, 394 B.C.

Battle of Coronea, 394 B.C.

the day, the Thebans had displayed superiority and thwarted the attempt of their enemy to cut them off. It was a great moral encouragement to Thebes for future warfare with Lacedaemon. And immediately, it was a distinct success for the Confederates. When an aggressor cannot follow up his victory, the victory is strategically equivalent to a repulse. Agesilaus immediately evacuated Boeotia— that was the result of Coronea. He crossed over to the Peloponnese from Delphi, as the Confederates commanded the road by Corinth.

Spartans blockaded in the Peloponnese

It was round Corinth that the struggle of the next years mainly centred, in fitting accordance with the object of the war. Sparta was fighting for domination beyond the Peloponnese; her enemies were fighting to keep her within the Peloponnese. The most effective way of accomplishing this design was to hold the gates of the peninsula, between the Corinthian and Saronic gulfs, and not let her pass out. With this view long walls were built binding Corinth, on the one hand with its western port Lechaeon, and on the other with its eastern port at Cenchreae. Thus none could pass from the Peloponnese into Northern Greece without dealing with the defenders of these fortifications. Never had Lacedaemon been more helpless—almost a prisoner in her peninsula, and her maritime empire dissolved. This momentary paralysis of Lacedaemon proved the salvation of Athens.

393 B.C. Pharna- bazus on the Greek coast

The restoration of Athens to her place among the independent powers of Greece at this juncture came about by curious means. The satrap Pharnabazus, who had done so much to aid Lysander in destroying her, now helped to bring about her resurrection. He had not forgiven Sparta for the injury which Agesilaus had inflicted on his province, and this rankling resentment was kept alive by the circumstance that, while the other Asiatic cities had unanimously declared against Sparta after the battle of Cnidus, Abydus alone held out against himself under the Spartan Dercyllidas. He exhibited his wrath by accompanying Conon and the fleet, in the following spring, to the shores of Greece, to ravage the Spartan territory and to encourage and support the Confederates. A Persian satrap within sight of Corinth and Salamis was a strange sight for Greece. His revengefulness stood Athens in good stead. When he returned home, he allowed Conon to retain the fleet and make use of it to rebuild the Long Walls of Athens and fortify the Piraeus. He even supplied money to inflict this crushing blow on Sparta, a blow which completely undid the chief result of the

Rebuilding of the Long Walls of Athens

Peloponnesian war. The two long parallel walls connecting Athens with the Piraeus were rebuilt;[9] the port was again made defensible; and the Athenians could feel once more that they were a free and independent people in the Greek world. Conon, who had been responsible for their deliverance, erected a temple to the Cnidian Aphrodite in the Piraeus, as a monument of his great victory.[10] Never since the day of Salamis was there such cause for rejoicing at Athens as when the fortifications were completed at the end of the autumn. As rebuilder of the walls, Conon might claim to be a second Themistocles. But the comparison only reminds us of the change which had come over Greece in a hundred years. It was through Persian support that Athens, now under the auspices of Conon, regained in part the position which she had won by her championship of Hellas against Persia under the auspices of Themistocles. She did not regain her former ascendancy or her former empire, but she was restored to an equality with the other powerful states of Greece; she could feel herself the peer of Thebes, Corinth, and Argos, and of Sparta, now that Sparta had fallen from her high estate. The Athenians could now calmly maintain that defiance which they had boldly offered to Sparta by their alliance with Thebes. About the same time the northern islands of Lemnos, Imbros, and Scyros seem to have been reunited to Athens, and she recovered her control of Delos which the Spartans had taken from her.[11] Chios too became her ally.

It was of vital importance to the Lacedaemonians to gain command of the gates of the Peloponnese by capturing some part of the line of defence; and thus Corinth becomes the centre of interest. The Lacedaemonians established their headquarters at Sicyon, and from this base made a series of efforts to break through the lines of Corinth—efforts which were ultimately successful. Unluckily the chronology is obscure, and it cannot be decided whether these operations were partly concurrent with, or altogether subsequent to, the rebuilding of the Long Walls of Athens. In Corinth itself there was a considerable party favourable to Sparta. This party seems to have arranged a plot for violently overthrowing the oligarchy which was in power; but the design was suspected and prevented by the government, who caused the friends of Sparta to be massacred in cold blood, in the market-place and theatre, on the last day of the feast of Euclea. The Corinthian government at the same time drew closer the bonds which attached it to the enemies of Sparta. By a

Union of Corinth and Argos (392 B.C.)

341

remarkable measure Corinth and Argos united themselves into a federal state; the boundary stones were pulled up; the citizens enjoyed common rights. It would be interesting to know how this federal constitution was framed, but such a union had no elements of endurance —it was merely a political expedient.

Praxitas at Corinth

A considerable number of the philo-Laconian party had escaped; some still remained in the city, and these now managed to open a gate in the western wall and admit Praxitas, the commander at Sicyon, with a Lacedaemonian *mora* of 600 hoplites. Praxitas secured his position between the two walls by constructing a ditch and palisade across the intermural space, on the side of Corinth. The

Battle of the Long Walls

Corinthians and their allies came down from the city, the palisade was torn up; a battle was fought; and the Lacedaemonians, completely victorious, captured the town of Lechaeon, though not the port. Praxitas then pulled down part of the walls, and made incursions into the Corinthian territory on the side of the Saronic bay. But when winter set in, he disbanded his army, without making any provision for keeping the command of the Isthmus; and the Athenians came, with carpenters and masons, and repaired the breach in the walls.

Mercenary troops: their growing importance

A warfare of raids was at the same time constantly carried on by the hostile parties, from their posts at Corinth and Sicyon. In this warfare a force of mercenaries, trained and commanded by the Athenian Iphicrates, was especially conspicuous. They were armed as peltasts, with light shield and javelin, and this armour was far better suited for the conditions of camp life and the duties of the professional soldier, than the armour of a hoplite. The employment of mercenaries had been growing —destined ultimately to supplant the institution of citizen armies. It was the wilder

Reforms of Iphicrates

parts of Greece, like Crete, Aetolia, Acarnania, that chiefly supplied the mercenary troops. Iphicrates of Rhamnus, an officer of great energy and talent, recognised the importance of the professional peltast as a new element in Hellenic warfare, and immortalised his name in military history by reforming the peltast's equipment. His improvements consisted in lengthening the sword and the javelin, and introducing a kind of light leggings, known as 'Iphicratid' boots. It is difficult to appreciate the full import of these changes, but they were clearly meant to unite effectiveness of attack with rapidity of motion.

Agesilaus captures Lechaeon, 391 B.C.

This enterprising officer and his peltasts won the chief honours of the 'Corinthian War'.

Agesilaus had been sent out to gain some more permanent successes than those which had been achieved by Praxitas. His brother Teleutias co-operated with him by sea; the Long Walls were stormed, and the port of Lechaeon was captured. In the following year he went forth again. It was the time of the Isthmian festival, and the games were about to be held in the precincts of Poseidon at the Isthmus. Agesilaus marched thither, interrupted the Corinthians and Argives who were beginning the celebration, and presided at the contest himself. When he retired, the Corinthians came and celebrated the festival over again; some athletes won the same race twice.

(390 B.C., spring)

Agesilaus then captured the port of Piraeon, on the promontory which forms the northern side of the inmost recess of the Corinthian gulf. The importance of this capture lay in the fact that Piraeon connected Corinth with her allies in Boeotia; its occupation was a threat to Boeotia, and the Boeotians immediately sent envoys to Agesilaus. The position was now reversed; the Spartans commanded the Isthmus passage, and by possessing Sicyon, Piraeon, Lechaeon, as well as Sidon and Crommyon on the Saronic gulf, they entirely closed in Corinth, except on the side of Argolis. But if Agesilaus felt himself the arbiter of Greece, his triumph was short.

Spartans capture Piraeon

In the garrison at Lechaeon there were some men of Amyclae, whose custom and privilege it was to return to their native place to keep the local feast of Hyacinthus. The time of this feast was now at hand, and they set out to return home by Sicyon and Arcadia, the only way open to them. But as it was not safe for a handful of men to march under the walls of Corinth, they were escorted most of the way to Sicyon by a *mora* of 600 Lacedaemonian hoplites. As this escort was returning to Lechaeon, Iphicrates and his peltasts issued from the gates of Corinth and attacked them. The heavy spearmen were worn out by the repeated assaults of the light troops with which they were unable to cope, and a large number were destroyed. This event, though less striking and important, bore a resemblance to the famous calamity of Sphacteria. In both cases, Spartan warriors had been discomfited in the same way by the continuous attacks of inaccessible light troops; and in both cases a blow was dealt to the military prestige of Lacedaemon. The success of Iphicrates was a suggestive sign of the future which might be in store for the professional peltast. To Agesilaus the news came at a moment when he was regarding

The light troops of Iphicrates vanquish Spartan hoplites

with triumphant arrogance his captives and the Theban envoys. His pride was changed into chagrin; the army was plunged into sorrow; and only the relatives of those soldiers who had fallen in the battle moved about with the jubilant air of victors. Leaving another division as a garrison in Lechaeon, Agesilaus returned home, skulking through Sicyon and the Arcadian cities at night, in order to avoid unkind remarks. Piraeon, Sidon, and Crommyon were soon recovered by Iphicrates; and the garrison of Lechaeon seems to have done no more than keep the gates of the Peloponnese open. This was the result of the 'Corinthian' war. Sparta had succeeded in breaking down the barrier which was to shut her out from North Greece, but she had sustained a serious loss and damage to her reputation.

The King's Peace

Efforts towards a peace, 392 B.C.

We must now turn from the Isthmus of Corinth to the eastern coasts of the Aegean. The Lacedaemonians ascribed the success of their opponents to the support of Persia, and drew the conclusion that their chance lay in detaching Persia to their own side. With this view they had dispatched Antalcidas to open negotiations with Tiribazus. The proposals of Sparta were (1) that the Hellenic cities of Asia should be subjects of the king; this was the price of Persian help; (2) that all other Hellenic cities should be independent; this was aimed at the Confederates—at the supremacy of Thebes in Boeotia, and at the union of Corinth with Argos. The Athenians and their allies sent Conon and other envoys to counteract the mission of Antalcidas, and perhaps it was at this time also that they sent the orator Andocides to Sparta to consider terms of peace. Both the mission of Andocides and the mission of Antalcidas were alike unsuccessful. Tiribazus, who was favourable to Sparta and threw Conon into prison, was recalled; and his successor Struthas had no Spartan leanings. The object of Antalcidas was indeed ultimately reached, but its attainment was postponed for four or five years, and the war went on as before.

Warfare in Asia;

The military events of these years are not of great interest, and our knowledge of them is meagre. In Asia, the Spartan cause revives. Thibron is sent out once more, and though he sustains a severe defeat at the hands of Struthas, it is not until he has won over Ephesus, Magnesia, and Priene. Soon Cnidus

and Samos follow the example of these cities. Agesilaus invades Acarnania, and forces the Acarnanians to join the Lacedaemonian league; his colleague Agesipolis carries out one of those invasions of Argolis which lead to nothing. Then the Spartans use Aegina as a base for harassing Attica, and a warfare of surprises is carried on between the harmosts of Aegina and Athenian admirals. The harmost Gorgopas captured four ships of an Athenia squadron; the Athenian Chabrias then landed on Aegina, laid an ambush, and killed Gorgopas. Teleutias, the brother of Agesilaus, was sent to Aegina soon afterwards. He made an attack on the Piraeus at daybreak, and towed away some of the ships lying in the harbour. In old Greece the war was on the whole advantageous to Sparta, though no decisive success was gained.

in Europe

But the most important event was the recovery of Athenian dominion on the Propontis. At this moment Athens was in great financial straits, for she had ceased to receive Persian subsidies. When an indirect impost of $\frac{1}{40}$th had been tried and found insufficient, a direct war-tax was levied. For the Athenians had determined to operate both in the south and in the north—in the south to assist their friend Evagoras, King of Salamis in Cyprus, who was revolting from the Great King; in the north to recover control of the route to the Euxine Sea. Thrasybulus, the restorer of the democracy, sailed with a fleet of 40 ships to the Hellespont, and won over to the Athenian alliance the islands of Thasos and Samothrace, the Chersonese, and the two cities which commanded the Bosphorus—Byzantium and Chalcedon. Proceeding to Lesbos, he defeated and slew the Spartan harmost, and established Athenian supremacy over most of the island. He also won Clazomenae. The original object for which he had been sent out was to assist Rhodes in maintaining her independence against the efforts of Sparta to regain the mastery of the island. But to act with effect it was necessary to raise money, and the Athenian fleet coasted round Asia Minor, levying contributions. These exactions appear to have been a renewal of the tax of 5 per cent which Athens imposed on the commerce of her allies towards the end of the Sicilian expedition.[12] It seemed like the beginning of a new empire. Aspendus in Pamphylia was one of the places visited, and the visit was fatal to Thrasybulus. The violent methods of his soldiers enraged the inhabitants; they surprised him at night in his tent and slew him. Athens had now lost the two men of action to whom, since the death of Pericles, she owed

Taxation at Athens: (1) Euripides' tax of $\frac{1}{40}$th;

(2) war tax, 390, 389 B.C.

389 B.C.

Death of Thrasybulus (388 B.C.)

most, Conon and Thrasybulus. Conon, who soon after his imprisonment by Tiribazus died in Cyprus, had broken down the maritime dominion of the Lacedaemonian oppressor and had given Athens the means of recovering her independence and her sea-power. Thrasybulus had given to the Athenian democracy a new life and breathed into it a new spirit of conciliation and moderation. He strikes us—we know too little of him—as an eminently reasonable citizen, one of those men who command general confidence, and are not biassed by prejudice or ambition. The virtues of Thrasybulus were moral rather than intellectual. After his death insinuations were made against his integrity; and one of his friends named Ergocles was found guilty of embezzlement of money collected on the expedition of Thrasybulus and was put to death. But the statements of an advocate—and we have no other evidence—carry no weight.

The success of Thrasybulus in re-establishing a toll for the advantage of Athens on merchandise passing through the Bosphorus was almost immediately endangered by Anaxibius, whom Sparta promptly sent out to act against Athens and Pharnabazus. He deprived *388 B.C.* Athens of her tolls by seizing the merchant vessels. Iphicrates was dispatched to oppose him with 1200 peltasts, and the Hellespont became the scene of the same kind of warfare of raids and surprises which we saw carried on at Aegina. At last Iphicrates saw a favourable opportunity for a decisive blow. Anaxibius had gone to place a garrison in Antandrus, which he had just won over. Iphicrates crossed by night from the Chersonese and laid an ambush on the return route, near the gold mines of Cremaste. The troops of Anaxibius marched in careless order, traversing the narrow mountain passes in extended single file, without the slightest suspicion that an enemy lay in the way. Suddenly, as they were coming down from the mountains into the plain of Cremaste, the peltasts of Iphicrates leaped out. Anaxibius saw at a glance that the case was desperate. The scattered hoplites had no chance against the peltasts. 'I must die here,' he said to his men, 'my honour demands it; but do you save yourselves.' A devoted youth who constantly accompanied him fell fighting by his side. This exploit of Iphicrates ensured the command of the Hellespont and Bosphorus to Athens.

Unfortunately for Athens the political situation changed, and other great powers intervened. At the beginning of the fourth century there were three great powers which aimed at supremacy over portions of the Greek world—Persia, Sparta, and the tyrant of Syracuse, Dionysius. At first, however, it was not a case of these three great powers uniting in a sacred alliance for the suppression of liberty. Dionysius did not intervene in the east; and Persia and Sparta contested the supremacy over the Asiatic Greeks. Thus Persia, in the cause of her own supremacy in Asia, made common cause with liberty elsewhere. The general military failure of Sparta forced her to seek a reconciliation with Persia on the basis of abandoning Asia. One of the obstacles to the accomplishment of this object was the influence of the satrap Pharnabazus who cherished bitter hostility to the country of Dercyllidas and Agesilaus. On the other hand, Athens had taken an ambiguous step which could not fail to create distrust and resentment at the Persian court. If Athens was indebted to Persia for the restoration of *Athens* her walls, she had also been befriended and *votes to* supported by Evagoras, the friend of Conon, *assist* and she had bestowed upon him her citizen- *Evagoras,* ship in recognition of his services.[13] Thus, *390 B.C.* when he revolted from Persia, Athens was in an embarrassing position. The support of Persia against Sparta was all-important to her. Artaxerxes was her ally; but Evagoras was her citizen too, and a Greek. Against her own *Spartan* apparent interests, Athens sent ten ships to *diplomacy* assist her Cypriot friend; and, though they *at Susa* were captured by a Lacedaemonian admiral and never actually served against the Persians, the incident was calculated to dispose the Great King to entertain the overtures of Sparta. The diplomatist Antalcidas went up to Susa and renewed his proposals. Backed by the influence of Tiribazus he overcame the reluctance of Artaxerxes, who was personally prepossessed against Sparta, and induced him to agree to enforce a general pacification, on the same conditions which had been proposed before. Opposition on the part of Pharnabazus was removed by summoning him to court to marry a daughter of Artaxerxes.

The diplomacy of Sparta was successful not *Sparta* only at Susa, but also at Syracuse, and *supported* obtained an auxiliary force of 20 triremes from *by* the tyrant Dionysius. *Syracuse*

With the support of the west and the east, Sparta was able to force the peace upon Hellas. When Antalcidas and Tiribazus returned to the coast, they found Iphicrates blockading the Spartan fleet at Abydus. Antalcidas dexterously rescued the fleet from *387 B.C.* this predicament, and was able, when the Syracusan vessels joined him, as well as

Persian reinforcements, to blockade the Athenians in the Hellespont and prevent corn vessels from reaching Athens. The coasting trade of Attica was at the same time suffering grievously through the raids from Aegina, which have already been mentioned. Hence peace was expedient for Athens, and the allies could not think of continuing the war without her. The representatives of the belligerents were summoned to Sardis, and Tiribazus read aloud the edict of his master, showing them the royal seal. It was to this effect:

The peace which the King sent down, 387-6 B.C.

'King Artaxerxes thinks it just that the cities in Asia, and the islands of Clazomenae and Cyprus, shall belong to him.[14] Further, that all the other Greek cities, small and great, shall be autonomous; except Lemnos, Imbros, and Scyros, which shall belong to Athens, as aforetime. If any refuse to accept this peace I shall make war on them, along with those who are of the same purpose, both by land and sea, with both ships and money.'

(386 B.C.)

The representatives were to report to the cities the terms of the peace, and then meet at Sparta to declare their acceptance. All accepted; but the Thebans raised a difficulty by claiming to take the oath on behalf of all the Boeotian cities as well as of themselves. Such a proposal would clearly place the Boeotian cities in a different class from the other cities of Greece, which took the oath each for itself. It was an attempt to assert the dependence of the Boeotian communities on Thebes, whereas one of the chief objects of the peace was to assert their autonomy. Agesilaus was secretly pleased with the opposition of Thebes: he hoped that the Thebans would persist in it and give him the opportunity of attacking and subduing their detested city. But they submitted in time and disappointed his vengeance.

The King's Peace was inscribed on stone tablets, which were set up in the chief sanctuaries of the Greek states. There was a feeling among many that Greece had suffered a humiliation in having to submit to the arbitration of Persia. Both Spartans and Athenians had alike used Persian help when they could get it, but never before had the domestic conflicts of Hellas been settled by barbarian dictation and under a barbarian sanction. It was Sparta's doing. She constituted herself the minister of the Great King's will in order to save her own position; and the Greeks of Asia were left to endure oriental methods of government. Athens, though she had lost what Thrasybulus had won for her, was allowed to retain her old insular dependencies in the North Aegean, a concession which shows that it was thought necessary to bribe her into accepting the peace, and that Sparta was more eagerly bent on weakening the other confederates. In truth, the main objects were to break up the Boeotian league and to separate the Argives from Corinth.

CHAPTER 13

The Revival of Athens and her Second League

High-handed Policy of Sparta

The gates of the Peloponnese were again open to Sparta without dispute; she was supported by Persia, and she had no complications in Asia to divide her energy. Accordingly she was able to renew the despotic policy which had been inaugurated for her by Lysander. Arcadian Mantinea was the first to suffer. The Mantineans were accused of various acts of disobedience and disloyalty to Sparta, and commanded to pull down their walls. When they refused, king Agesipolis—son of the exiled Pausanias—marched out against them. The city of Mantinea stood in a high plain, without any natural defences, depending entirely on its walls of unburnt brick. The river Ophis flowed through the town; and, a blockade proving tedious, Agesipolis dammed the stream at the point of issue. The water rose and undermined the walls; and when one of the towers threatened to fall, the people surrendered. Their punishment was severe. Mantinea ceased to be a city and was broken up into its five constituent villages. Those who originally belonged to the *village* of Mantinea remained on the site of the city; the rest had to pull down their houses and move each to the village where his property was. The loss of civic life meant to a Greek the loss of all his higher interests.

Agesilaus, who had once set out to destroy the Persian power, zealously supported the King's Peace. When someone suggested that it was at least curious to find the Spartans medizing, he rejoined, 'Rather say that the Persians are laconizing'. Each way of putting it expressed a measure of the truth. But some of the Lacedaemonians, including king Agesipolis, were opposed to the recent policy of their government, and thought it wrong to abandon the Greeks of Asia. Some years after the Peace, there seems to have been floating in the air a vague idea, which might or might not take shape, of organising another Asiatic expedition. It was to animate this idea that the Athenian orator Isocrates published a festal speech when the Greek nation was assembled at the Olympian festival. He advocated a grand Panhellenic union against Persia, under the common headship of Sparta and Athens—Sparta taking the command by land, Athens by sea. It was the third occasion on which a renowned master of style had broached the same idea at the same gathering-place. Nearly 30 years before, it had been recommended by the florid eloquence of Gorgias; more recently it had been advocated with gracious simplicity by Lysias; and now the rich periods of Isocrates urged it once more upon Greece. The project—in the ideal form in which Isocrates imagined it—was at this moment chimerical. A hundred years earlier, it had been hard enough to achieve a practical co-operation between Greek powers of equal strength and pretensions, in a war of defence; it was hopeless to think of such co-operation now for a war of aggression. Sparta and Athens were quarrelling, as the orator complains, over the tribute of the

The dissolution of the city of Mantinea (386-5 B.C.)

The Panegyric of Isocrates (composed 381), 380

(See above, p. 314; and below, p. 349)

Evagoras of Cyprus

Cycladic islands; neither was likely to yield to the other without a clear award of war. And other troubles were brewing in another quarter.

The contest of east and west had been going on meanwhile in Cyprus, an island whose geographical situation has marked it out, like Sicily, to be a meeting-place of races. We have already met a man who played an eminent part in that struggle, Evagoras the king of Salamis. He belonged to the Teucrid family which had reigned there in the days of Darius and Xerxes, but had been supplanted by a Phoenician dynasty about the middle of the fifth century. Evagoras, crossing over from the Cilician Soli, won back the sceptre of his race by a daring surprise. He governed with conspicuous moderation, discretion, and success—setting himself to the work of reviving the cause of Hellenism, which had lost much ground during the past half-century, and pursuing this task by entirely peaceful means. After Aegospotami, the city of Evagoras became the refuge for large numbers of Athenians who had settled down in various parts of the Athenian empire and could no longer remain securely in their homes. For the first sixteen years of his reign Evagoras was a faithful tributary of the Great King, and we have seen how his influence at Susa assisted Conon. But soon after the battle of Cnidus he became involved in war, both with Persia and with some of the Phoenician cities in the island. The Peace expressly recognised the sovereignty of Artaxerxes over Cyprus and, as soon as it was concluded, Persia began to concentrate her forces against Evagoras and a recalcitrant king of Egypt, with whom Evagoras was leagued. A severe defeat at sea shut Evagoras up in Salamis; but he held out so stubbornly, and the war had already cost Persia so much, that Tiribazus agreed to leave him his principality, on condition that he should pay tribute 'as a slave to his lord'. Evagoras refused; he would only pay it as one king to another. The negotiations were ruptured for a moment on this point of honour, but a dispute between the satrap and his subordinate general resulted in the removal of Tiribazus, and his successor permitted Evagoras to have his way.

411-10 B.C.

386 B.C.

(Acoris) 386-4 B.C.

381 B.C.

His death

The Salaminian ruler had thus gained a moral triumph. He did not survive it many years, and the story of his death is curious. A certain man named Nicocreon formed a plot against his life and being detected was forced to fly. He left a daughter behind him in Salamis under the care of a faithful eunuch. This servant privily acquainted both Evagoras and his son Pnytagoras with the existence of this young lady and her uncommon beauty, and undertook to conduct them to her bedchamber, each without the knowledge of the other. Both kept the assignation and were slain by the eunuch, who thus avenged his master's exile. Another son of Evagoras, named Nicocles, succeeded him, and pursued the same Hellenizing policy. One of the great objects of these enlightened princes was to keep their country in touch with the intellectual and artistic movements of Greece. Nicocles was a student of Greek philosophy, and a generous friend of Isocrates, to whose pen we are indebted for much of what we know of the career of Evagoras.

374 B.C.

Towards the close of the almost single-handed struggle of Salamis against Persia, the attention of Greece was directed to the north of the Aegean, and for a while the oriental question almost passes out of the pages of Greek history. Yet it was destined that from that very region on the north-west corner of the Aegean should issue the force which would not only reclaim for European influence Cyprus and all the Greek cities of Asia, but bear Greek light into lands of which Agesilaus had never dreamed. That force was being forged in the Macedonian uplands; and some who were children when Isocrates published his Panegyric against the Barbarian lived to see the Barbarian succumb to a Greek power.

Macedonia, 383 B.C.

It was indeed only indirectly that the southern Greeks had now to concern themselves with their backward brethren of Macedonia. One of the chief obstacles to the development of this country was its constant exposure to the attacks of its Illyrian neighbours. For protection king Amyntas—the great-grandson of Alexander—had, soon after his succession, concluded a close defensive and commercial alliance for fifty years with the Chalcidian league, which had been formed by Olynthus against Athens in the Peloponnesian War and now included most of the Greek towns of Chalcidice.[1] Almost immediately, however, he was forced to withdraw before an Illyrian invasion; but at the moment of his retreat Amyntas handed over to the Chalcidians the lower districts of Macedonia and the cities lying round the Thermaic gulf. The Macedonian cities readily embraced a union which could protect them against the Illyrians, and the league spread from the maritime towns up the country, including even Pella. Perfect equality and brotherhood between the members was the basis of this Chalcidian con-

? 392 B.C.

The Chalcidian Confederacy

347

federacy. All the cities had common laws, common rights of citizenship, intermarriage, and commerce; Olynthus did not assume a privileged position for herself. The neighbouring Greek cities were also asked to join, and some of them, Potidaea for instance, accepted the offer. But it was always a sacrifice for a Greek city to give up its hereditary laws and surrender any part of its sovereignty, whatever compensating advantages might be purchased; and there was consequently more reluctance among the Chalcidians than among the less developed Macedonians to join the league. The Olynthians, as their work grew, conceived the idea of a confederate power which should embrace the whole Chalcidic peninsula and its neighbourhood. Once this ambition took form, it became necessary to impose their proposition by force upon those who declined to accept it freely. The strong cities of Acanthus and Apollonia resisted, and sent envoys to Sparta to obtain her help. Moreover Amyntas had recovered his throne, and when the Olynthians refused to abandon the cities which he had handed over to them, he too looked for aid to Sparta.[2] These appeals directed the eyes of Greece upon the Chalcidian confederacy. It was the Lacedaemonian policy to oppose all combinations and keep Greece disunited—a policy which was popular, in so far as it appealed to that innate love of autonomy which made it so difficult to bring about abiding federal unions in Greece. The ambassadors had little difficulty in persuading the Lacedaemonians and their allies that the movement in Chalcidice was dangerous to the interests of Sparta, and should be crushed at the outset; and they argued that the very liberality of the principles on which it was founded made the league more attractive and therefore more dangerous. Whether the league was a party to the King's Peace is not known, nor is the legal position important; Sparta and her allies considered that their interests were involved. A vote of assistance to Acanthus and Apollonia was passed, and a small advance force was immediately sent under Eudamidas. Though unable to meet the confederate army in the field, this force was sufficient to protect the cities which had refused to join the league, and it even induced Potidaea to revolt.

The citadel of Thebes seized by the Spartans, 382 B.C.

The expedition against the Chalcidian Confederacy led unexpectedly to an important incident elsewhere. Phoebidas, the brother of Eudamidas, was to follow with larger forces, and, as the line of march lay through Boeotia, a party in Thebes favourable to Sparta thought to profit by the proximity of Spartan troops for the purpose of a revolution. Leontiadas, the most prominent member of this party, was then one of the polemarchs. He concerted with Phoebidas a plot to seize the Cadmea—the citadel of Thebes—on the day of the Thesmophoria; for on that day the citadel was given up to the use of the women who celebrated the feast. The plot succeeded perfectly; the acropolis was occupied without striking a blow; the oligarchical Council was intimidated by Leontiadas; and his colleague, the other polemarch Ismenias, was arrested. The leading anti-Spartans fled from Thebes, and a government friendly to Sparta was established. This was a great triumph for Sparta, a great satisfaction to Agesilaus, although, as a violation of peace, it caused a moment's embarrassment. Was the government to recognise the action of Phoebidas and profit by it? Spartan hypocrisy compromised; Phoebidas was heavily fined for his indiscretion, and the Cadmea was retained. Then Ismenias was tried by a body of judges representing Sparta and her allies, and was condemned on charges of Medism and executed. That Sparta, after the King's Peace, should condemn a Theban for Medism, was a travesty of justice.

With the fortress of Thebes in her hands, Sparta had a basis for extending her power in central Greece and might regard her supremacy as secured. She restored the city of Plataea, which she had herself destroyed nearly fifty years before, and gathered all the Plataeans who could be found to their old home. But her immediate attention was fixed on the necessity of repressing the dangerous league in the north of Greece, and continuing the measures which had been interrupted by the enterprise of Phoebidas in Boeotia. Teleutias, the popular brother of Agesilaus, was sent to conduct the war, but although he was aided by Amyntas and by Derdas, a prince of Upper Macedonia, who supplied good cavalry, it proved no easy matter to make headway against the league. In front of the walls of Olynthus, Teleutias sustained a signal defeat and was himself slain. Agesipolis, who was next sent out at the head of a very large force, caught a fever in the intolerable summer heat. He was carried to the shady grove of the temple of Dionysus at Aphytis, but he died there; and his body, stowed in honey, was brought home for burial. His successor, Polybiadas, was more successful. He forced the Olynthians to sue for peace and dissolve their league. They and all the Greek cities of the peninsula were constrained to join the Lacedaemonian alliance,

Restoration of Plataea, 382-1 B.C.

(381 B.C.)

(380 B.C.)

Suppression of the Chalcidian League, 379 B.C.

and the maritime cities of Macedonia were restored to Amyntas. Thus Sparta put down an attempt to overcome the system of isolation, which placed Greek cities at a great disadvantage when they had barbarian neighbours. If Sparta had not happened to be so strong at this moment, the Chalcidian league might have grown into a power which would have considerably modified the development of Macedonia. All that Sparta did, although for a moment it made her power paramount in northern Greece, fell out ultimately to the advancement and profit of Macedon.

Sparta tyrannises over Phlius; blockade, 381-79 B.C.

About the same time, the Lacedaemonians were making their heavy hand felt in the Peloponnese. Soon after the King's Peace they had forced the Phliasians to recall a number of banished aristocrats. Disputes arose about the restoration of confiscated property, and the exiles appealed to Sparta, where they had a zealous supporter in Agesilaus. War was declared; Agesilaus reduced the city of Phlius by blockade, and compelled it to receive a Lacedaemonian garrison for six months, until a commission of one hundred, which he nominated, should have drawn up a new constitution.

Thus the Lacedaemonians, in alliance with the tyrant Dionysius and the barbarian Artaxerxes, tyrannised over the Greeks for a space. Some demonstrations were made, some voices of protest were raised, in the name of the Panhellenic cause.

(388 B.C.) Olympiac oration of Lysias

At the Olympian festival which was held just before the King's Peace, the Athenian orator Lysias warned the assembled Greeks of the dangers which loomed in the east and in the west, from Persia and from Sicily, and uttered his amazement at the policy of Lacedaemon. A magnificent deputation had been sent by Dionysius to this festival, and the inflammatory words, perhaps the direct instigation, of the speaker incited some enthusiastic spectators to attack the gorgeous pavilion of the Syracusan envoys. The outrage was prevented, but the occurrence shows the beginning of that tide of feeling to which Isocrates appealed, eight years later, when in his festal oration he denounced the Lacedaemonians, as sacrificing the freedom of Greece to their own interests and treacherously aiding foreigners and tyrants.

Even Xenophon, the friend of Sparta's king, the admirer of Sparta's institutions, is roused to regretful indignation at Sparta's conduct, and recognises her fall as a just retribution. 'The Lacedaemonians, who swore to leave the cities independent, seized the acropolis of Thebes, and they were punished by the very men, single-handed, whom they had wronged, though never before had they been vanquished by any single people. It is a proof that the gods observe men who do irreligious and unhallowed deeds.' In this way the pious historian introduces the event which prepared the fall of Sparta and the rise of Thebes.

Alliance of Athens and Thebes

The deliverance of Thebes

The government of Leontiadas and his party at Thebes, maintained by 1500 Lacedaemonians in the citadel, was despotic and cruel, like that of the Thirty at Athens. Fear made the rulers suspicious and oppressive, for they were afraid of the large number of exiles who had found a refuge at Athens and were awaiting an opportunity to recover their city. Athens was now showing the same goodwill to the fugitives from Thebes which Thebes, when Athens was in a like plight, had shown to Thrasybulus and his fellows. One of the exiles, named Pelopidas, of more than common daring and devotion, resolved to take his life in his hands, and found six others to associate in his plans. No open attack was to be thought of; Thebes must be recovered by guile, even as by guile it had been won. There were many in Thebes who were bitter foes of the ruling party, such as Epaminondas, the beloved friend of Pelopidas, but most of them considered the time unripe for any sudden stroke for freedom. Yet a few were found ready to run the risk; above all Phyllidas, who was the secretary of the polemarchs and therefore the most useful of confederates, and Charon, a citizen of good estate, who offered his house as a place of hiding for the conspirators. The day on which the two polemarchs, Archias and Philippus, were to go out of office was fixed for the enterprise.

379-8 B.C. (winter)

On the day before, Pelopidas and his six comrades crossed Cithaeron in the guise of huntsmen and, nearing Thebes at nightfall, mixed with the peasants who were returning from the fields, got safely within the gates, and found safe hiding in the house of Charon. The secretary Phyllidas had made ready a great banquet for the following night, to which he had bidden the outgoing polemarchs, tempting them by the promise of bringing in some highborn and beautiful women. During the carouse a messenger came with a letter for Archias, and said that it concerned serious affairs. 'Business to-morrow,' said Archias, placing it under his pillow. On the morrow it was found that this letter disclosed the conspiracy. The polemarchs then called for the women, who were waiting in an adjoining room. Phyllidas said that they declined to appear till all the attendants were dismissed. When no one remained in the dining hall but the polemarchs and a few friends, all flushed with wine, the women entered and sat down beside the lords. They were covered with long veils; and even as they were bidden lift them and reveal their charms, they buried daggers in the bodies of the polemarchs. For they were none other than Pelopidas and his fellows in the guise of women. Then they went and slew in their houses Leontiadas and Hypatas, the two other chief leaders of the party, and set free the political prisoners. When all this was done, Epaminondas and the other patriots, who were unwilling to initiate such deeds themselves, accepted the revolution with joy. When day dawned, an assembly of the people was held in the Agora, and the conspirators were crowned with wreaths. Three of them, including Pelopidas, were appointed polemarchs, and a democratic constitution was established.

The rest of the exiles and a body of Athenian volunteers presently arrived, on the news of the success. The Spartan commander of the Cadmea had sent hastily, on the first alarm, for reinforcements to Thespiae and Plataea, but those that came were repelled, outside the gate. Then in the first flush of success the patriots resolved to storm the Cadmea, strong as the place was. But the labour and the danger were spared them. Amazing as it may seem, the Lacedaemonian harmosts decided to capitulate at once. Two of these commanders were put to death on their return to Sparta, and the third was banished. King Cleombrotus was immediately sent with an army to Boeotia, but accomplished nothing.

Cadmea surrendered

Athens was formally at peace with Sparta, and was not disposed to break with her, however great the secret joy felt at the events in Boeotia. But the march of the Athenian volunteers to Thebes was an awkward incident, the more so as there were two generals among them. Lacedaemonian envoys arrived to demand explanation and satisfaction, and their statements were reinforced by the nearness of the army of king Cleombrotus. There was indeed nothing to be said for the conduct of the two strategi. They had abused their position and brought their city into danger and embarrassment. We can only approve the sentence of the Athenians, which executed one and banished the other.

Athens disowns the action of the Athenian volunteers, and punishes the generals

But if these Athenian generals were indiscreet, it was as nothing beside the indiscretion of a Lacedaemonian commander, which now precipitated the breach between the two states. A not ignoble sympathy might have been pleaded by the two Athenians; but no excuse could be urged for the rash enterprise of the Spartan harmost of Thespiae, who aspired to be a second Phoebidas. His name was Sphodrias, and he conceived the plan of making a night march to Athens and surprising Piraeus on the land side. To seize Piraeus, the centre of Athenian trade, would be a compensation for the loss of Thebes. But the plan was, if not misconceived, at least poorly executed. Day dawned when he had hardly passed Eleusis, and there was nothing to do but to turn back. He retreated, laying waste the districts through which he passed.

The raid of Sphodrias

This unprovoked aggression roused tempers at Athens. The envoys had not yet gone; they were immediately thrown into prison, but escaped by declaring that the Spartan government was not responsible for the raid, and would speedily prove its innocence by the condemnation of Sphodrias. The assurance was belied; Sphodrias was not condemned. His son and the son of Agesilaus were lovers, and the king's influence saved him. Agesilaus is reported to have said: 'Sphodrias is guilty, of course; but it is a hard thing to put to death a man who, as child, stripling, and man, lived a life of perfect honour; for Sparta needs such soldiers.' This miscarriage of justice was a grave mistake of policy, and the high-handed insolence of the Spartan oligarchs was set in a more glaring light by contrast with the fair-mindedness which the Athenian people had displayed in promptly punishing their own generals. It was debated at the time, and has been debated since, whether Sphodrias acted wholly of his own accord; some thought that the suggestion came from king Cleombrotus, and the theory was started that the Thebans were the prime instigators—an unlikely theory, which was evidently based on the fact that Thebes was the only gainer by the raid.[3] It seems most probable that the private ambition of Sphodrias, who thought he had a chance of emulating Phoebidas, was alone responsible.

The raid and acquittal of Sphodrias drove Athens, against her will, into war with Sparta and alliance with Thebes; it stirred her for a while to leave her rôle of neutral spectator and assume that of an active belligerent. For the next six years Athens and Sparta were at war, though such a war was contrary to the interests of both states, but especially to the interests of Sparta.

Alliance of Athens with Thebes, 378 B.C.

The Second Athenian League and the Theban Reforms

Second Athenian Confederacy

The raid of Sphodrias was the direct occasion of the Second Athenian Confederacy. For many years back, ever since the battle of Cnidus, Athens had been gradually forming bonds of alliance with various states in Thrace, in the Aegean, and on the coasts of Asia Minor. The breach with Sparta induced her now to gather together these separate connections into a common league, with the express object of protecting the independence of the Greek states against the oppression of Sparta. When men thought of the old Confederacy of Delos, they might fear that the second Athenian league would be soon converted into a second Athenian empire. But Athens anticipated such alarms by establishing the confederacy on a different system, which provided safeguards against the dangers of Athenian preponderance *378-7 B.C.* and encroachment. In the archonship of Nausinicus, Aristoteles of the deme of Marathon proposed in the Assembly a decree which embodied the principles of the league.[4] The rule of Persia over the Greeks of Asia was explicitly recognised, so that the field of operations was to be European Greece and the Islands. The league, which was purely defensive, was constituted in two parts, Athens on one side, her allies on the other. The allies had their own synedrion or congress, which met in Athens, but in which Athens had no part. Both the synedrion of the Confederates and the Athenian Assembly had the right of initiating measures, but no measure passed by either body was valid until it had been approved by the other body also. While this system gave Athens a weight and dignity equal to that of all her allies together, it secured for the allies an independence which they had not possessed under the old league, and they had the right of absolute veto on any Athenian proposal which they disliked. It was necessary for the members of the league to form a federal fund; their payments were called *syntaxeis* ('contributions'), and the word *phoros* ('tribute'), which had odious memories connected with the confederacy of Delos, was avoided. It was especially enacted that the practice of settling Athenians in the lands of the allies, which had formerly helped and supported the Athenian empire, was not to be permitted. No Athenian was to acquire home or farm, 'by purchase or mortgage, or any other means whatever', in the territory of any of the confederates. But the administration of the federal fund and the leadership of the federal forces were in the hands of Athens.

Good fortune has preserved to us the original stone, shattered into about 20 pieces, with the decree which founded the confederacy, and we find the purpose of the league definitely declared: 'To force the Lacedaemonians to allow the Greeks to enjoy peace in freedom and independence, with their lands unviolated.' It was no doubt Callistratus, the ablest statesman and orator of the day, who did most to make the new scheme a success; but, though *Callistratus* he may be called the Aristides of the Second Confederacy, Callistratus certainly did not mean the combination against Sparta as seriously as Aristides meant the combination against Persia. The policy which Callistratus generally pursued was based on harmony with Sparta and antagonism to Thebes. It is sometimes said that at this period there were two parties contending for the guidance of the foreign policy of Athens, one friendly and the other obstinately hostile to Boeotia. But though Thebes had some friends at Athens we have no good grounds for speaking of a Theban or Boeotian party. It might be truer to say that there was an anti-Spartan faction, which might often seek a Theban alliance as a means to an end. At this juncture Callistratus was astute enough to see not only that it would be useless to oppose the feeling against Sparta, but also that an opportunity which might never recur was offered for increasing the power of Athens. He therefore abandoned for the time his pro-Spartan policy, and threw himself heartily into a scheme of which the most remarkable feature was union with Thebes.

The chief cities which first joined the new league were Chios, Byzantium, Mytilene, Methymna, and Rhodes, with whom Athens already had alliances; then most of the towns of Euboea joined, and—what was most important and wonderful—Thebes enrolled her name in the list of confederates.[5] The Thracian cities, the Chalcidic League, and several other states, including Corcyra, Jason the despot of Pherae in Thessaly, and Alcetas a prince of Epirus, presently brought up the whole tally of members to about 70.[6] But though the league, drawn on such liberal lines, evoked some enthusiasm at first, and the adhesion of Thebes gave its inauguration a certain *éclat*, it had no vital elements of growth or permanence, and never attained high political importance. The fact is that the true interest of Athens, as Callistratus knew, was peace with Sparta, and was consequently repugnant to the avowed object of the confederacy. Hence the confederacy was doomed either to disintegrate, or to become the tool of other designs of Athens as soon as Sparta had been taught a lesson and the more abiding interest of Athens could safely assert itself again over the temporary expedient of an unnatural alliance with Thebes.

It was a moment at which the chief Greek states were setting their houses in order. Thebes was making herself ready for a new career; Sparta was remodelling her league and Athens her finances. The property tax, which *Eisphora or property tax at Athens* had been introduced in the fourth year of the Peloponnesian War, was revived, and a new assessment of property was made. The tax was voted, as special need arose, in the form of a percentage of each man's assessment, usually one per cent. But Athenian capital had declined sharply since the fifth century. In 428 alone the tax had realised 200 talents: between 378 and 355 little more than 300 talents was collected. For the purpose of levying the tax the whole body of citizens was divided into 20 symmories, and the richest citizens in each symmory were responsible to the treasury for the total sum due on the properties of all the citizens who belonged to it.[7] By this means the State relieved itself from the friction which is generally caused by the collection of direct imposts, and the revenue accruing from the tax was realised more promptly and easily than if the government had to deal immediately with the individual citizens. Thus Athens tried the novel experiment of a system of joint responsibility, such as in later days was to be *(Roman Empire)* established in an empire of which Athens was only an insignificant town.

At Thebes the attention of the government was chiefly bestowed on military affairs. A *Sacred Band* ditch was dug and a rampart raised round part of the Theban territory as a defence against the inevitable Lacedaemonian invasions. But this precaution was of small moment in comparison with the creation of a new troop of 300 hoplites, all chosen young men of the noblest families, who had proved their eminent strength and endurance in a long training in the wrestling school. Each man had his best friend beside him; so that the Sacred Band, as it was called, consisted of 150 pairs of comrades, prepared to fight and fall together. In battle, it was to be the spearhead of the attack. At the same time, we may be sure, much was done to improve the army in other points. Opportunely for Thebes *Epa-minondas* there had arisen, to guide her to success when her chance came, a man of rare ability, in whom nature seemed to have united the

best features of Greek character and discarded the defects. This was Epaminondas, the friend of Pelopidas. He was a modest, unambitious man, who in other circumstances would probably have remained in obscurity, unobtrusively fulfilling the duties of a citizen and soldier. But the revolution stimulated his patriotism and lured him into the field of public affairs, where his eminent capacity, gradually revealing itself, made him, before eight years had passed, the most influential man in his city. He had devoted as much time to musical as to gymnastic training; unlike most of his countrymen, he could play the lyre as well as the Theban flute; and he had a genuine interest in philosophical speculation. A Tarentine friend, who had been much in his company, maintained that he never met a man who knew more and talked less than Epaminondas. But the Theban statesman could speak when he chose, or when the need demanded; and his eloquence was extremely impressive. Exceptional in his indifference to the prizes of ambition, he was also exceptional in his indifference to money, and he died poor. Not less remarkable was his lack of that party spirit which led to so many crimes in Greece. He could not share in strong political hatred or lust for revenge, and we have already seen that his repugnance to domestic blood-shed kept him from taking a part in the fortunate conspiracy of Pelopidas.

The Battle of Naxos and the Peace of Callias

The following eight years are marked by a *378-1 B.C.* successful defensive war of Thebes against Spartan invasions; by a decrease of Spartan prestige; by the extension of the Theban supremacy over the rest of Boeotia. At the same time, Athens prosecutes a naval war against the Lacedaemonian Confederacy and gains considerable successes; but the strain on her resources which this war entails, and a growing jealousy of Thebes, combine to induce *Boeotia invaded by Agesilaus,* her to come to terms with Sparta.

Two invasions of Boeotia conducted by *378, 377 B.C.* Agesilaus himself in successive summers achieved nothing; and the Thebans had the *Defeat and death of Phoebidas,* satisfaction of slaying Phoebidas, who had *377 B.C.* won his fame by the capture of their acropolis. The other king, Cleombrotus, did even less *Cleombro-tus* than Agesilaus, for he found the passes of *marches to* Cithaeron held by the enemy, and could not *Cithaeron,* enter Boeotia. After this, the Thebans had *373 B.C.*

time to attack the Boeotian cities and drive out the Spartan garrisons; so that by the end of four years the Boeotian confederacy once more extended over most of Boeotia, the local governments being overthrown and the foreign harmosts expelled. Only in the extreme west, in Orchomenus and Chaeronea, were the Lacedaemonians able to hold their ground. In the course of this revival of the Boeotian league a notable exploit by Pelopidas and the Sacred Band is recorded. At Tegyra, on the road from Orchomenus to Locris, in a narrow pass, the Thebans routed twice as many Lacedaemonian troops, and slew both the Spartan generals. As in the case of all Spartan defeats, the moral effect was of far greater import than the actual loss in the field. Perhaps it was about this time that Athens won back Oropus, which had been lost to her in the year of the Four Hundred.

Battle of Naxos, 376 (September)

In the meantime there had also been war on the seas. When the invasion of Boeotia fell out so badly, Sparta had equipped a naval armament to cut off the corn ships which carried grain to Attica from the Euxine. The ships reached Geraestus, the south point of Euboea; but a fleet of 60 triremes under the Spartan Pollis hindered them from rounding the Cape of Sunion, and Athens was threatened with famine. Eighty triremes were speedily fitted out and sent forth from the Piraeus, under the command of Chabrias, to recover the mastery of the sea. Chabrias sailed to Naxos, important at this time to Sparta as her chief ally among the Cyclades, and beleaguered the city. Pollis hurried to the rescue, and a battle was fought in the sound between Paros and Naxos. The Athenians gained a complete victory, and only 11 of the Lacedaemonian vessels escaped. Even these would have been disabled, had not Chabrias desisted from the action, for the purpose of saving some of his own men who were overboard or in disabled ships. The lesson which the Athenian people taught its generals after the battle of Arginusae had not been forgotten. Though the battle of Naxos had not the important consequences of the battle of Cnidus, it was more gratifying to Athens. The Cnidian victory had been won indeed under the command of an Athenian, but by Persian men and ships; the victory gained by Chabrias was entirely Athenian. It led immediately to an enlargement of the Confederacy. The triumphant fleet sailed round the Aegean, enrolled 17 new cities, and collected a large sum of money. Athens had also to reassert her authority at Delos. For the inhabitants of the island who chafed at

Insurrectionary movement at Delos, 376 B.C.

the administration of their temple by the Athenian *amphictiones,* as the sacred overseers were entitled, had attempted, doubtless with Lacedaemonian help, to recover control of the sanctuary. An interesting entry in the Delian accounts of these years tells how seven ringleaders of the movement were punished by fines and perpetual banishment 'for having led the amphictiones forth from the temple and beaten them'.[8]

Next year, the fleet was sent to sail round the Peloponnese under the command of Timotheus, son of Conon. This circumnavigation of the Peloponnese was an assertion by Athens that her naval power was once more dominant; it was intended to frighten Sparta, to extend Athenian influence in western Greece, and to act in the Corinthian Gulf, in case the Spartans tried to throw an army into Boeotia by the port of Creusis. The islands of Corcyra and Cephallenia, the king of the Molossi, some of the Acarnanians, were won over to the Athenian alliance by the discreet policy of Timotheus, who also gained a trifling victory over some hostile ships. But there was a darker side to this triumphant expedition. The cost of the war was proving to be greater than Athens could well bear, and Timotheus failed to obtain from home the money required to pay his seamen. In this strait, he was obliged to ask each trierarch to advance seven minae for the payment of his crew; and Athens herself sent a request to Thebes for some contribution towards the expense of the naval operations, on the ground that the enterprise of Timotheus had been undertaken partly at Theban instigation. The refusal of this demand, along with a growing jealousy of Theban success, and the somewhat grave financial difficulties of the moment, combined to dispose Athens towards peace with Sparta; and this was in fact her wisest policy. Negotiations were opened and carried to a successful issue; but the peace was no sooner made than it was broken. For Timotheus, who was ordered to return home from Corcyra and reluctantly obeyed, halted at Zacynthus on his way, landed some Zacynthian exiles who were with him, and fortified a post for them on the island. The settlement of democratic exiles was enrolled in the Athenian Confederacy, and 'the people of the Zacynthians at Nêllon' appears as the last of the additions to the list of members on the Confederacy stone. The Zacynthians straightway complained to Sparta; Sparta demanded satisfaction from Athens, and when this was refused the incident was treated as a breach of contract and the war was resumed.

376 B.C. Expedition of Timotheus

Peace, 374

The first object of Sparta was to regain her power in the west, and undo the work of Timotheus. The best of the winnings of that general had been Corcyra, and Corcyra once more became the scene of a 'Peloponnesian' war. With the help of their confederates, including Corinth, the Lacedaemonians launched an armament of 60 ships, conveying 1500 mercenary hoplites, to gain possession of the island; and at the same time a message was dispatched to Dionysius of Syracuse requesting his aid, on the ground that Sicily had her interests in Corcyraean politics. The armament was commanded by the Spartan Mnasippus. He drove the Corcyraean fleet into the harbour, which he blocked with his own ships, and he invested the city by land, so that the supplies of the inhabitants were cut off. The island was a rich prize for the soldiers, to whose depredations it was now given over, and so plentiful was the wine that the troopers would drink none that was not of the finest sort. Urgent messages were sent to Athens by the Corcyraeans, who soon began to feel the pinch of famine. So great was the misery that slaves were cast out of the gates; even some citizens deserted, but were whipped back to the walls by the Lacedaemonian commander. But he, thinking that he had the city in his hands, grew careless in his confidence, and from the watch-towers on their walls the besieged could observe that the watch was sometimes relaxed. An opportune moment was seized for a sally, which resulted in a more complete success than they looked for. The professional soldiers, who had not been paid and who detested their general, showed no zeal in withstanding the hot onslaught of the desperate men who poured forth from the gates. Mnasippus was slain, the besiegers fell back to their camp and the Corcyraeans were safe until the coming of the expected help from Athens. But they did not have to wait until that tardy help came, for the Lacedaemonians evacuated the island almost immediately after the defeat. Then at last the Athenian fleet sailed into the roads of Corcyra.

It was from no want of goodwill on the part of the Athenian people that the help had not come in time to save Corcyra much of the misery which she had suffered. A tale hangs by the delay of the fleet. On the first appeal, it was resolved to send 60 ships at once, and 600 peltasts were sent in advance and successfully introduced into the city. It was fitting that Timotheus should return to the scene of his former achievements, and the command of the fleet was entrusted to him.

He found himself in an awkward position, owing to one of the gravest defects in the machinery of Athenian administration. The people had voted a certain measure, appointing him to carry it out, but had omitted to vote or consider the necessary ways and means. It consequently devolved upon Timotheus to find the men and the money. For this purpose he cruised with some of his ships in the Northern Aegean, visiting Thessaly, Macedonia, and Thrace, while the main part of the fleet awaited his return at the island of Calauria. But meanwhile the need of Corcyra was acute, and more pressing messengers were arriving in Athens. The long tarrying of the general excited public indignation; his appointment was annulled; and Iphicrates, in conjunction with Chabrias and Callistratus, was charged to sail at once to Corcyra.

Callistratus was the most eloquent orator of the day. Chabrias, a tried soldier who had served under Cypriot and Egyptian kings, we have already met as the victor of Naxos. Iphicrates, who had come to the front by his boldness and success in the Corinthian war, had for the last fifteen years served as a captain of peltasts under the princes of Thrace, and had married a daughter of king Cotys. A comic poet gives a picturesque description of his barbaric wedding.[9] In the market-place a plentiful feast is set out for a throng of wild-haired Thracians. There are immense brazen cauldrons of broth, and the king, girding himself up, serves it with his own hands in a golden basin. Then the wine and water are mixed in the bowls, and the king goes around tasting each bowl, until he is the first to get drunk. But an adventurous life among the 'butter-eating' barbarians does not seem to have wholly satisfied Iphicrates. He served the King of Persia in Egypt and then returned to Athens, and this expedition to Corcyra seems to have been his first service after his return. It was well and capably performed. The people in their excitement gave him a freer hand than they had given to Timotheus. He was able to put hard pressure on the trierarchs; he was allowed to impress seamen and to make use of the ships which guarded the Attic coast, and even the two sacred vessels, the *Salaminia* and *Paralus*. By these unusual efforts a fleet of 70 triremes was put together, but before it was quite ready to sail Timotheus returned. His cruise had been successful in raising money and men, and adding new members to the Confederacy, but it was thought that neither necessity nor success could excuse the singular inopportuneness of the delay. Ill-luck seemed to wait upon Timotheus. The funds which he brought back proved insufficient to meet the obligations which they ought to have defrayed, and a fraud was suspected. Iphicrates and Callistratus, his political rivals, lodged an indictment against him but, as they had to sail immediately to the west, the trial was postponed till the autumn.

372 B.C.
Capture
of the
reinforce-
ments from
Syracuse

On his way out Iphicrates learned the news of the deliverance of Corcyra, so that he was able to send back those ships whose true duty was the defence of Attica. But there was still work to be done. The appeal which the Lacedaemonians sent to the tyrant Dionysius had not been in vain, and ten Syracusan triremes were even then approaching Corcyra. They stopped at a point in the north of the island to rest the crews after the long voyage; and there Iphicrates, whose scouts had watched for their approach, captured them, all but one vessel. This prize raised the welcome sum of 60 talents, but it was not long before Iphicrates, even as Timotheus, found himself embarrassed for want of money. Callistratus went back to Athens, promising to persuade the people either to keep the fleet regularly paid or to make peace. Meanwhile the crews of Iphicrates obtained subsistence by labour on the Corcyraean farms.

Trial of
Timotheus,
373 (Nov.)

If Corcyra had fallen, there can be little question that Timotheus would have been sacrificed to the displeasure of the Athenian people. But the good tidings from the west restored the public good-humour, and this was fortunate for the discredited general. His trial came on towards the end of the year. His military treasurer was tried at the same time, found guilty of malversation, and condemned to death. But Timotheus himself was acquitted. He had indeed unusually powerful support. Two foreign monarchs had condescended to come to Athens to bear testimony in his favour, the Epirot king Alcetas, and Jason the despot of Thessalian Pherae. It was through Timotheus that these potentates had joined the Athenian league; and it was through them that he had been able to transport across Thessaly and Epirus the 600 peltasts who had been sent in advance to Corcyra. The interest of Jason—of whom more will have to be said presently—was particularly effective. Timotheus entertained these distinguished guests in his house in Piraeus, but he was obliged to borrow bedding, two silver bowls, and other things from his rich neighbour, the banker Pasion, in order to lodge them suitably.[10] Though acquitted, Timotheus was discredited in public opinion, and he soon left Athens to take service in Egypt under the Great King.

Sparta had lost heart at the decisive check which she had received in Corcyra, and the discouragement was increased by a series of terrible earthquakes, in which Poseidon seemed to declare his wrath. She was therefore disposed towards peace, and she thought to bring peace about, as before, through the mediation of Persia. Antalcidas was once more sent up to the Persian court. But this intervention from without was not really needed. Athens, uneasy under the burdens of the war and feeling jealousy of Thebes rather than bitterness against Sparta, was also well inclined to peace, and the influential orator Callistratus made it the object of his policy. The recent aggressions of Thebes against the Phocians, who were old allies of Athens, tended to estrange the two cities; and to this was added the treatment of that unfortunate little frontier town, Plataea, by her Theban enemies. Restored Plataea had been forced to join the Boeotian confederacy, but she was secretly scheming for annexation to Attica. Suspecting these plots, Thebes determined to forestall them, and a small Theban force, surprising the town one day when the men were in the fields, took possession of it and drove all the Plataeans from Plataean soil. Many of the dispossessed found a refuge at Athens, where Isocrates took up their cause and wrote his *Plataeic Discourse*, a denunciation of Thebes. This incident definitely, though not formally, loosened the bonds between the two northern powers.

Plataea
seized by
Thebes

The peace overtures came from Athens and her Confederacy. When the Lacedaemonian allies met at Sparta in spring, three Athenian envoys appeared at the congress. Of these the chief spokesman was Callistratus, and one of his associates was Callias, Torchbearer of the Eleusinian Mysteries, who had also worked to bring about the abortive peace three years before. Thebes likewise sent ambassadors, one of whom was Epaminondas. The basis of the peace which was now concluded was the principle which had been affirmed by the King's Peace, the principle of the autonomy of every Hellenic city. The Athenian and Lacedaemonian Confederacies were thus both rendered invalid. No compulsion could be exercised on any city to fulfil engagements as member of a league. Cities might co-operate with each other freely so far as they chose, but no obligation could be contracted or enforced. Yet while Athens and Sparta resigned empire, they mutually agreed to recognise each other's predominance, that of Athens by sea,

371 B.C.
Peace of
Callias

The
Boeotian
question

that of Sparta on land—a predominance which must never be asserted by aggression and must always be consistent with the universal autonomy.

The question immediately arose whether the Boeotian League was condemned by this doctrine of universal autonomy. Sparta and Athens, of course, intended to condemn it. But it might be pleaded that the Confederacy of Boeotian cities under the presidency of Thebes was not on the same footing as the Confederacies which had been formed, for temporary political purposes, without any historical or geographical basis of union, under the presidencies of Athens and Sparta. It might be contended that Boeotia was a geographical unity, like Attica and Laconia, and had a title to political unity too, especially as the League was an ancient institution. The question came to the issue when it was the turn of Thebes to take the oath. Her representative Epaminondas claimed to take it on behalf of the Boeotian cities; and Thebes, represented by him, was not so easily cowed as when she made the same claim at the conclusion of the King's Peace. He seems to have developed the view that Boeotia was to be compared to Laconia, not to the Lace-daemonian Confederacy; and when Agesilaus asked him, curtly and angrily: 'Will you leave each of the Boeotian towns independent?' he retorted: 'Will you leave each of the Laconian towns independent?' The name of Thebes was thereupon struck out of the treaty.

Thebes
excluded

There was an argument as well as a sting in this retort of Epaminondas. The argument was: Sparta has no more right to interfere in the internal affairs of Boeotia than we have to interfere in the domestic administration of Laconia; Laconia, Boeotia, Attica, each represents a distinct kind of constitution, and each constitution is justified; the union of Boeotia in a federation is as natural as the union of Attica in a single city, as legitimate as the union of Laconia in its subjection to the Spartan oligarchy. The union of Boeotia, like the union of Laconia, could not have been realised and could not be maintained without the perpetration of outrages upon the freewill of some communities. Yet it is hardly legitimate for one state to say to another: 'We have committed certain acts of violence, but you must not interfere; for at a remote period of history which none of us remember, your ancestors used even more high-handed methods for similar purposes, and you now maintain what they established.' But the tyrannical method by which Laconia was governed

was certainly a weak point in the Spartan armour; and the reply of Epaminondas may have well set Greece thinking over a question of political science. Setting aside the arguments of diplomacy, the point of the situation was this: Thebes could never become a strong power, the rival of Sparta or of Athens, except at the head of an united Boeotia, and it was the interest of Athens and Sparta to hinder her from becoming such a power.

So far as the two chief contracting parties were concerned, this bargain—which is often called the 'Peace of Callias'—put an end to a war which was contrary to the best interests of both. They were both partly to blame, but Sparta was far more to blame than her old rival. Her witless policy in overlooking the raid of Sphodrias had caused the war, for it left to Athens no alternative but hostility. At the end of four years, they seemed to have come to their senses; they made peace, but they were stupid enough to allow the incident of Zacynthus to annul the bargain. Three more years of fighting were required to restore their wits. But although Athens was financially exhausted by her military efforts, the war had brought its compensations to her. The victory of Naxos, the circumnavigation of the Peloponnese and the revival of her influence in Western Greece were achievements which indisputably proved that Athens was once more a first-rate Hellenic power, the peer of Sparta; and this fact was fully acknowledged in the Peace of Callias. But the true policy of Athens—from which the raid of Sphodrias had forced her—was that of a watchful spectator; and this policy she now resumes, though only for a brief space, leaving Sparta and Thebes in the arena. As for Sparta, she had lost as much as Athens had gained; the defeat of Naxos, the defeat of Tegyra, the failure at Corcyra, had dimmed her prestige. After the King's Peace she had begun her second attempt to dominate Greece; her failure is confessed by the Peace of Callias. If a third attempt was to be successful, it was obvious that it must begin by the subjugation of Thebes.

Positions
of Athens
and Sparta

Athens under the Restored Democracy

When Pericles declared that Athens was the school of Greece, this was rather his ideal of what she should be than a statement of a reality. It would have surprised him to learn that, when imperial Athens fell from her throne, his ideal would be fulfilled. This was what actually happened. It was not until Athens lost her empire that she began to exert a decisive influence on Greek thought and civilisation. This influence was partly exerted by the establishment of schools in the strict sense—the literary school of Isocrates and the philosophical school of Plato—which attracted to Athens men from all quarters of the Hellenic world. But the increase in the intellectual influence of Athens was largely due to the fact that she was becoming herself more receptive of influence from without. She was becoming Hellenic as well as Athenian; she was beginning to become even something more than Hellenic. This tendency towards cosmopolitanism had been promoted by philosophical speculation, which rises above national distinctions; and it is manifested variously in the Panhellenism of Isocrates, in the attitude of such different men as Plato and Xenophon towards Athens, in the increasing number of foreign religious worships established at Athens or Piraeus, in a general decline of local patriotism, and in many other ways. There was perhaps no institution which had a wider influence in educating Greek thought in the fourth century than the theatre; its importance in city life was recognised by practical statesmen. It was therefore a matter of the utmost moment that the old Athenian comedy, turning mainly on local politics, ceased to be written, and a new school of poets arose who dealt with subjects of general human interest. Here Athens had a most effectual instrument for spreading ideas. And the tragedies of the fourth century, though as literature they were of less note and consequence than the comedies, were not less significant of the spirit of the time. They were all dominated by the influence of Euripides, the great teacher of rationalism, the daring critic of all established institutions and beliefs. And the comic poets were also under his spell.

Influence of Athens on Greece

Growth of individualism

It can easily be seen that the cultivation of these wider sympathies was connected with the growth of what is commonly called 'individualism'. The citizen is no longer content to express his religious feelings simply as one member of the state, and, since his own life has thus become for him something independent of the city, his attitude to the city is transformed. His duty to his country may conflict with his duty to himself as a man, and thus patriotism ceases to be unconditionally the highest virtue. Again, men begin to put to themselves, more or less explicitly, the question whether the state is not made for the

individual and not the individual for the state. It followed that greater demands were made upon the state by the citizen for his own private welfare, and that the citizen, feeling himself tied by no indissoluble bond to his country, was readier than formerly to seek his fortune elsewhere. Thus we find Athenian officers acting independently of their country, in the pay of foreign powers.

A vivid exaggerated description of this spirit has been drawn by Plato in one of his famous contributions to political science, the *Republic*.

13.1 Socrates

'The horses and asses,' he says, 'have a way of marching along with all the rights and dignities of free men; and they will run at anybody whom they meet in the street if he does not leave the road clear for them: and all things are just ready to burst with liberty.' When he describes the excessive freedom of democracy, he is dealing with the growth of individualism, as a result of freedom in its constitutional sense; but his argument that individualism is the fatal fruit of a democratic constitution rests largely on the double sense of the word 'freedom'. The notable thing is that no man did more to promote the tendencies which are here deplored by Plato than Plato himself and his fellow philosophers. If any single man could be held responsible for the inevitable growth of individualism, it would be perhaps Euripides; but assuredly, next to Euripides, it would be Plato's revered master, Socrates, the son of Sophroniscus.

Socrates, the sculptor, son of Sophroniscus (born c. 469 B.C.)

When the history of Greece was being directed by Pericles and Cleon, Nicias and Lysander, men little dreamed either at Athens or elsewhere that the interests of the world were far more deeply concerned in the doings of one eccentric Athenian who held aloof from public affairs. The ideas which we owe to Socrates are now so organically a part of the mind of civilised men that it is hard to appreciate the intellectual power which was required to originate them. Socrates was the first champion of the supremacy of the intellect as a court from which there is no appeal; he was the first to insist that a man must order his life by the guidance of his own intellect. Socrates was thus a rebel against authority as such, and he shrank from no consequences. He did not hesitate to show his companions that an old man has no title to respect because he is old, unless he is also wise; or that an ignorant parent has no claim to obedience on the mere account of the parental relation. Knowledge and truth, the absolute sovereignty of the understanding, regardless of consequences, regardless of all prejudices connected with family or city—this was the ideal of Socrates, consistently and uncompromisingly followed.

His spirit

His method

But men using their intellects often come to different conclusions. The command issued by an authority which Socrates may reject has been, directly or ultimately, the result of some mental process. It is manifest that we require a standard of truth and an explanation of the causes of error. The solution of Socrates is, briefly, this: when we make a judgement, we compare two ideas; and in order to do so correctly it is obvious that these ideas must be clear and distinct; error arises from comparing ideas that are undefined and vague. Definition was thus the essential point—and it was an essential novelty—in the Socratic method for arriving at truth. Its necessity is a commonplace now, and we have rather to guard against its dangers.

Definitions

Founder of utilitarianism

The application of this method to ethics was the chief occupation of Socrates, for the interests of human life and its perplexities entirely absorbed him. In the history of ethics his position is supreme; he was the founder of utilitarianism. He arrived at the doctrine by analysing the notion of 'good'; the result of his analysis was that 'the good is the useful'. Closely connected was the principle that virtue is happiness, and this was the basis of the famous Socratic paradox that no man willingly does wrong, but only through ignorance, for there is no man who would not will his own happiness. It is easy to point out the errors of this startling statement; it is perhaps easier to forget how much wrong-doing is due to the confused thinking of clouded brains and the ignorance of untrained minds.

Attitude to theology

The man who had no respect for authority was not likely to except the gods from the range of his criticism, and the popular religion could not sustain examination. Socrates was as little orthodox as Anaxagoras and other 'impious' philosophers; but he made no new departure in the field of theology. He doubtless believed in the existence of a God; but as to the nature of the divine principle he was probably what we call an 'agnostic', as he certainly was in regard to the immortality of the soul.

His scepticism and irony

Socrates then was the originator of a new logical method, the founder of utilitarianism, and, above all, the unsparing critic of all things in heaven and earth—or rather on earth only, for he disdained things in heaven as uninteresting and irrelevant—a fearless critic, undeterred by any feeling of piety or prejudice. He never wrote anything, he only conversed. But he conversed with the ablest young men of the day who were destined afterwards to leave a name for themselves as thinkers; he communicated to them—to Plato, to Aristippus, to Euclides—his own spirit of scepticism and criticism; he imbued them with intellectual courage and intellectual freedom. He never preached, he only discussed; that was the Socratic method—dialectic or the conversational method. He did not teach, for he professed to have no knowledge; he would only confess that he was exceptional in knowing that he knew nothing: this was the Socratic irony. He went about showing that most popular notions, as soon as they are tested, prove to be inconsistent and untenable; he wished to convince every man he met that his convictions would not stand examination. We can easily conceive how stimulating this was to the young men, and how extremely irritating to the old. Haunting the marketplaces and the gymnasia, Socrates was always ready to entrap men of all ages and ranks into argument, and many a grudge was owed him by reverend and conceited seniors, whose foggy minds he exposed to ridicule by means of his prudent interrogations. Though no man ever taught more effectually than Socrates, he was not a teacher, he had no course of lectures to give, and therefore he took no fee. Herein lay his distinction from the sophists, to whom by his speculation, his scepticism, his mastery of argument, his influence over young men, he naturally belongs, and with whom he was generally classed. He soon became a notorious figure in the streets of Athens; nature had marked him out among other men by his grotesque satyr-like face.

Criticism of democracy

Though he was the child of democracy, born to a heritage of freedom in a city where the right of free discussion was unrestrained, the sacred name of democracy was not more sheltered than anything else from the criticism of Socrates. He railed, for instance, at the system of choosing magistrates by lot, one of the protections of democracy at Athens. He was unpopular with the mass, for he was an enemy of shams and ignorance and superstition. Honest democrats of the type of Thrasybulus and Anytus, who did their duty but had no desire to probe its foundations, regarded him as a dangerous freethinker who spent his life in diffusing ideas subversive of the social order.

His teaching suspected and unpopular

They might point to the ablest of the young men who had kept company with him, and say: 'Behold the fruits of his conversation! Look at Alcibiades, his favourite companion, who has done more than any other man to ruin his country. Look at Critias, who, next to Alcibiades, has wrought the deepest harm to Athens; who, brought up in the Socratic circle, first wrote a book against democracy, then visited Thessaly and stirred up the serfs against their masters, and finally, returning here, inaugurated the reign of terror. Look, on the other hand, at Plato, an able young man, whom the taste for idle speculation, infused by Socrates, has seduced from the service of his country. Or look at Xenophon, who, instead of serving Athens, has gone to serve her enemies. Truly Socrates and his propaganda have done little good to the Athenian state.' However unjust any particular instance might seem, it is easy to understand how considerations of this kind would lead many practical unspeculative men to look upon Socrates and his ways with little favour. And from their point of view they were perfectly right. His spirit, and the ideas that he made current, were an insidious menace to the cohesion of the social fabric, in which there was not a stone or a joint that he did not question. In other words, he was the active apostle of individualism, which led in its further development to the subversion of that local patriotism which had inspired the cities of Greece in her days of greatness.

He receives the approval of Delphi

And this thinker, whose talk was shaking the Greek world in its foundations, though none guessed it, was singled out by the Delphic priesthood for a distinguished mark of approbation. In the truest oracle that was ever uttered from the Pythian tripod it was declared that no one in the world was wiser than Socrates. We do not know at what period of the philosopher's career this answer was given, but, if it was seriously meant, it showed a strange insight which we should hardly have looked for at the shrine of Delphi. The motive of the oracle concerning the wisdom of Socrates is an unsolved problem. If it were an attempt to enlist his support, in days when religion was threatened by such men as Anaxagoras, it shows an unexpected perception of his importance, united with a by no means surprising blindness to the significance of his work.

Trial of Socrates, 399 B.C.

Socrates died five years after the fall of the Athenian empire, and the manner of his death set a seal upon his life. It was thought that the philosopher, who had been the friend of Critias, was a danger to the democracy, and should be removed; but the political motive was kept in the background. Anytus, the honest democratic politician who had been prominent in the restoration of the democracy, came forward, with some others, as a champion of the state religion, and accused Socrates of impiety. The accusation ran: 'Socrates is guilty of crime, because he does not believe in the gods recognised by the city, but introduces strange supernatural beings; he is also guilty, because he corrupts the youth.' The penalty proposed was death; but the accusers had no desire to inflict it; they expected that, when the charge was lodged in the archon's office, Socrates would leave Attica, and no one would have hindered him from doing so. But Socrates was full of days—he had reached the age of seventy—and life spent otherwise than in conversing in the streets of Athens would have been worthless to him. He surprised the city by remaining to answer the charge. The trial was heard in a court of 501 judges, the king-archon presiding, and the old philosopher was found guilty by a majority of 60. It was a small majority, considering that the general truth of the accusation was undeniable. According to the practice of Athenian law, it was open to a defendant when he was condemned to propose a lighter punishment than that fixed by the accuser, and the judges were

His death

required to choose one of the two sentences. Socrates might have saved his life if he had proposed an adequate penalty, but he offered only a small fine, and was consequently condemned, by a much larger majority, to death. He drank the cup of doom a month later, discoursing with his disciples as eagerly as ever till his last hour. 'I am persuaded that it was better for me to die now, and to be released from trouble.'

13.2   Plato

Plato's Apology

The actual reply of Socrates at his trial has not been preserved, but we know its tone and spirit and much of its tenor. For it supplied his companion Plato, who was present, with the material of a work which stands absolutely alone in literature. In the *Apology of Socrates*, Plato has succeeded in catching the personality of the master and conveying its stimulus to his readers. There can be no question that this work reproduces the general outline of the actual defence, which is here wrought into an artistic form. And we see how utterly impossible it was for Socrates to answer the accusation. He enters into an explanation of his life and motives, and has no difficulty in showing that many things popularly alleged against him are false. But with the actual charge of holding and diffusing heterodox views he deals briefly and unsatisfactorily. He was not condemned unjustly—according to the law. And that is the

Socrates justly condemned

intensity of the tragedy. There have been no better men than Socrates, and yet his accusers were perfectly right. It is not clear why their manifesto for orthodoxy was made at that particular time, but it is probable that twenty years later such an action would have been a failure. Perhaps the facts of the trial justify us in the rough conclusion that two out of every five Athenian citizens then were religiously indifferent. In any case the event had a wider than a merely religious significance. The execution of Socrates was the protest of the spirit of the old order against the growth of individualism.

Seldom in the course of history have violent blows of this kind failed to recoil upon the striker and serve the cause they were meant to harm. Socrates was remembered at Athens with pride and regret. His spirit began to exercise an influence which the tragedy of his death enhanced. His companions never forgave the democracy for putting their master to death; he lived and grew in the study of their imaginations; and they spent their lives in carrying on his work.

They carried forward his work, but they did not realise what they were doing. They had no suspicion that in pursuing those speculations to which they were stimulated by the Socratic method they were sapping the roots of Greek city life as it was known to the men who fought at Marathon. Plato was a true child of Socrates, and yet he was vehement in condemning that individualism which it had been the lifework of Socrates to foster. Few sights are stranger than Plato and Xenophon turning their eyes away from their own free country to regard with admiration the constitution of Sparta, where their beloved master would not have been suffered so much as to open his mouth. It was a distinct triumph for the Lacedaemonians when their constitution, which the Athenians of the age of Pericles regarded as old-fashioned machinery, was selected by the greatest thinker of Athens as the nearest existing approach to the ideal. Indeed the Spartan organisation, at the very time when Sparta was making herself detested throughout Greece, seems to have attracted general admiration from political thinkers. It attracted them because the old order survived there—the citizen absolutely submissive to the authority of the state, and not looking beyond it. Elsewhere they were troubled by the problem of reconciling the authority of the state with the liberty of the individual citizen; at Sparta there was no such trouble, for the state was absolute. Accordingly they saw in

Sparta the image of what a state should be; just because it was relatively free from that individualism which they were themselves actively promoting by their speculations in political philosophy. How freely such speculations ranged at this time is illustrated by the fact that the fundamental institution of ancient society, slavery, was called in question. It had indeed been called in question by Euripides, and the heterodox 'modern' views of Euripides were coming into fashion. One thinker expounded the doctrine that slavery was unnatural. Speculation even went so far as to stir the question of the political subjection of women. The *Parliament of Women,* a comedy of Aristophanes, ridicules women's rights; and in Plato's ideal *Republic* women are on a political equality with men. Socialistic theories were also rife, and were a mark for the mockery of Aristophanes in the same play. Plato seized upon the notion of communism and made it one of the principles of his ideal state. But his object was not that of the ordinary 'collectivist', to promote the material well-being of all; but rather to make his citizens better, by defending them against poverty and ambition. Before he died, Plato had come to the conviction that communism was impracticable, and in the state which he adumbrated in his old age he recognised private property—though he vested the ownership not in the individual but in the family.

Lyco-phron's view of slavery. Aristo-phanes' Ecclesi-azusae, (392– 389 B.C.) Communism in Plato's Republic. Private property in the Laws

In this period—during the fifty years after the battle of Aegospotami—the art of writing prose was brought to perfection at Athens; and this is closely connected with the characteristic tendency which has engaged our attention. While Socrates and others had been bringing about a revolution in thought, the Sicilian Gorgias and other professors of rhetoric or style had been preparing an efficient vehicle for diffusing ideas. Prose is the natural instrument of criticism and argument; it is a necessary weapon for intellectual persuasion; and therefore the fourth century is an age of prose. The circumstance that the great Athenian poets of the fifth century had no successors in the fourth does not prove any decline in brains or in imagination. If Plato had been born half a century earlier he would have been a rival of Aeschylus and Sophocles. If Aeschylus and Sophocles had been born two or three generations later they would have expressed their genius in prose. Euripides, who came under the influence of the critical spirit, seems sometimes like a man belated; he uses the old vehicle to convey thoughts for which it was hardly suited. It must always be remembered

Develop-ment of prose

that the great dramatic poems of the fifth century bore an inalienable religious character; and, as soon as the day came when the men of the highest literary gifts were no longer in touch with the received religion, drama of the old kind ceased to be written. That is why the fourth century is an age of prose; tragic poetry owes its death to Euripides and the Socratic spirit. The eager individualism of the age found its natural expression in prose, whose rhythmical periods demanded almost as much care and art as poetry; and the plastic nature of the Greek language rendered it a most facile instrument for the purposes of free thought and criticism.

Thus Athens became really a school for Greece, as soon as that individualism prevailed which Pericles had unwittingly foreshadowed in the very same breath: 'I say that Athens is the school of Hellas, and that the individual Athenian in his own person seems to have the power of adapting himself to the most varied forms of action with the utmost versatility and grace.'

It must never be forgotten that it is to the democratic Athenian law-courts that the perfecting of Attic prose was mainly due. This institution had, as we saw, called into being a class of professional speech-writers. But there were many who were not content with learning off, and reciting in court, speeches which a speech-writer like Lysias wrote for them, but wished to learn themselves the art of speaking. For those who aspired to make their mark in debates in the Assembly, this was a necessity. The most illustrious instructor in oratory at this period was Isocrates. But the school of Isocrates had a far wider scope and higher aim than to teach the construction of sentences or the arrangement of topics in a speech. It was a general school of culture, a discipline intended to fit men for public life. Questions of political science were studied, and Isocrates likes to describe his course of studies as 'philosophy'. But it was to Plato's school in the Academy that the youths of the day went to study 'philosophy' in the stricter sense. The discipline of these two rival schools—for there was rivalry between them, though their aims were different—was what corresponded at Athens to our university education. And the pupils of Isocrates, as well as those of Plato, had to work hard. For thoroughness of method was one of the distinctive characteristics of Isocrates. His school attained a Panhellenic reputation; pupils came to him from all quarters of the world. 'Our city,' he says, 'is regarded as the established teacher of all who

Higher education at Athens: Plato and Isocrates

speak or teach others to speak. And naturally so, since men see that our city offers the greatest prizes to those who possess this faculty—provides the most numerous and various schools for those who, having resolved to enter the real contests, desire a preparatory discipline—and further affords to all men that experience which is the main secret of success in speaking.' The tone of the teaching of Isocrates harmonised with the national position which he held. He took a large view of all things; there was nothing narrow or local in his opinions. And not less important than the width of his horizon was the high moral tone in which his thoughts were consistently pitched. Isocrates discharged not only the duties which are in modern times discharged by university teachers, but also the functions of a journalist of the best kind. Naturally nervous and endowed with a poor voice, he did not speak in the Assembly, but when any great question moved him he would issue a pamphlet, in the form of a speech, for the purpose of influencing public opinion. We may suspect that the Athenians appreciated these publications more for their inimitable excellence of style than for their political wisdom.

Isocrates as a pamphleteer

A highly remarkable passage of Isocrates expresses and applauds the wide-minded cosmopolitanism which was beginning to prevail in Greece. He says that 'Athens has so distanced the rest of the world in power of thought and speech that her disciples have become the teachers of all other men. She has brought it to pass that the name of Greek should be thought no longer a matter of race but a matter of intelligence; and should be given to the participators in our culture rather than to the sharers of our common origin.' Thirty or forty years earlier, no one perhaps, except Euripides, would have been bold enough to speak like that. But Isocrates did not see that this enlightenment which he admires was closely connected with the decay of public spirit which he elsewhere deplores. It is curious to find the man who approves of citizenship of the world looking back with regret to the days of Solon and proposing to revive the old powers of censorship which the court of the Areopagus possessed over the lives of Athenian citizens.

Cosmopolitanism in the Panegyric Speech of Isocrates. 381 B.C.

Idealisation of 6th century, Athens

(Areopagitikos, 355-4 B.C.)

The form and features of an age are wont to be mirrored in its art, and one effective means of winning a concrete notion of the spirit of the fourth century is to study the works of Praxiteles and compare them with the sculptures which issued from the workshop of Phidias. Just as the citizen was beginning to

Individualistic character of the art of 4th century

assert his own individuality as more than a mere item in the state, so the plastic artist was emancipating his art from its intimate connection with the temples of the gods, and its subordination to architecture. For in the fifth century, apart from a few colossal statues like those which Phidias wrought for Athens and Olympia, the finest works of the sculptor's chisel were to decorate frieze or pediment. In the fourth century the architect indeed still required the sculptor's service; Scopas, for instance, was called upon in his youth to decorate the temple of Athena Alea at Tegea, in his later years to make a frieze for the tomb of a Carian prince; but, in general, the sculptor developed his art more independently of architecture, and all the great works of Praxiteles were complete in themselves and independent. And, as sculpture was emancipating itself from the old subordination to architecture, so it also emancipated itself from the religious ideal. In the age of Phidias, the artist who fashioned a god sought to express in human shape the majesty and immutability of a divine being; and this ideal had been perfectly achieved. In the fourth century the deities lose their majesty and changelessness; they are conceived as physically perfect men and women, with human feelings though without human sorrows; they are invested with human personalities. The contrast may be seen by looking at the group of gods in the frieze of the Parthenon, and then at some of the works of Praxiteles: the Hermes, which was set up in the temple of Hera at Olympia, and is preserved there; the Aphrodite of Cnidus—a woman shrinking from revealing her beauty as she enters the bath; or the Satyr, with the shape of a man and the mind of a beast. Thus sculpture is marked by 'individualism' in a double sense. Each artist is freer to work out an individual path of his own; and the tendency of all artists is to portray the individual man or woman rather than the type, and even the individual phase of emotion rather than the character.

The general spirit of the Athenians in their political life corresponds to this change. Men came more and more to regard the state as a means for administering to the needs of the individual. We might almost say that they conceived it as a co-operative society for making profits to be divided among the members; this at least was the tendency of public opinion. They were consequently more disinclined to enter upon foreign undertakings which were not either necessary for the protection and promotion of their commerce or likely to fill their purses. The fourth century was therefore for Athens an age of less ambition and glory, but of greater happiness and freedom, than the fifth.

Athenian commerce

The decisive circumstance for Athens was that, while she lost her empire, she did not lose her commerce. This was a cruel blow to Corinth, since it was to destroy Athenian trade that Corinth had agitated for war. The fact shows on how firm foundations Athenian commerce rested. The only rival Athens had to fear was Rhodes, which was becoming a centre of traffic in the south-eastern Mediterranean, but was not destined to interfere seriously with Athenian trade for a long time yet. The population of Attica had declined; plague and war reduced the number of adult male citizens from at least 40,000 to some 22,000. But that was not unfortunate, for there were no longer outsettlements to receive the surplus of the population; and even with the diminished numbers there was a surplus which sought employment in foreign mercenary service. The mercantile development of Athens is shown by the increase of the Piraeus at the expense of the city, in which many plots of ground now became deserted,

Banks

and by the growth of private banks. It had long been a practice to deposit money in temples, and the priesthoods used to lend money on interest.[11] This suggested to money-changers the idea of doing likewise; and Pasion founded a famous house at Athens, which operated with a capital of fifty talents, and had credit at all Greek centres of commerce. Thus business could be transacted by exchanging letters of credit instead of paying in coin; and the introduction of this system, even on such a small scale, shows the growth of mercantile activity. Money was now much more plentiful, and prices far higher, than before. This was due to the large amount of the precious metals, chiefly gold, which had been brought into circulation in the Greek world in the last quarter of the fifth century. The continuous war led to the coining of the treasures which had been accumulating for many years in temples; and the banking system circulated the money which would otherwise have been hoarded in private houses. But, although the precious metals became plentiful, the rate of

Rate of interest

interest did not fall; men could still get 12 per cent for a loan of their money. This fact is highly significant; it shows clearly that industries were more thriving and trade more active, and consequently capital in greater demand. The high rate of interest must always be remembered when we read of a

Greek described as wealthy with a capital which would nowadays seem small.

Socialism

Communistic ideas were a consequence, perhaps inevitable, of the growth of individualism and the growth of capital. The poorer citizens became more and more acutely alive to the inconsistency between the political equality of all citizens and the social and economic advantages enjoyed by the rich. Political equality seemed to point to social equality as its logical sequel; in fact, full and equal political equality could not be secured without social equality also, since the advantages of wealth necessarily involve superiorities in political influence. Thus, just as in modern Europe, so in ancient Greece, capital and democracy produced socialists, who pleaded for a levelling of classes by means of a distribution of property by the state. Aristophanes mocked these speculations in his *Parliament of Women* and his *Wealth*.

Ecclesiazusae, 389 B.C.; Plutus. 388 B.C.

The idea of communism which Plato develops on lines of his own in the *Republic* was not an original notion of the philosopher's brain, but was suggested by the current communistic theories of the day. It is well worthy of consideration that the Athenians did not take the step from political to social democracy; and this discretion may have been partly due to the policy of those statesmen who, doubtless conscious of the danger, regarded the theoric fund as an indispensable institution.

Assembly pay (introduced before 389 B.C.)

The changed attitude of the individual to the state is shown by the introduction of payment for attending the meetings of the Assembly. The original obol a meeting was soon raised to two obols and then, before 391, to three obols. Finally the pay was raised to a drachma for ordinary meetings and a drachma and a half for the sovereign meeting of each prytany, which was reserved for special business, and apt to be less exciting.[12] The remuneration for serving in the law-courts was not increased; it was found that half a drachma was sufficient to draw applicants for the judge's ticket. Payment for the discharge of political duties was part of the necessary machinery of the democracy, but the distribution of 'spectacle-money' to the poor citizens was a luxury which involved an entirely different principle. It is uncertain when the practice of giving the price of his theatre ticket to the poor Athenian was first introduced. It has been attributed to Pericles, but it is possible that it was not introduced till Athens began to recover after the fall of her empire. In any case, the principle became established in the fourth century of distributing 'theoric' moneys, which were supposed to be spent on religious festivals; the citizens came to look forward to frequent and large distributions; the surplus revenue of the state, instead of being saved for emergencies, was placed in the theoric fund; and this theoric fund became so important that *ὁ ἐπὶ τὸ* it ultimately required a special minister of *θεωρικόν* finance to manage it. Those statesmen under whose guidance the theoric doles were most liberal had naturally the greatest influence with the mass of the citizens; and consequently finance acquired a new importance, and financial ability was developed in a very high degree. The state thus assumed the character of a commercial society; dividends were a political necessity, and in order to meet it heavier taxation was demanded. We have seen how, when war broke out with Sparta, in the year in which the Second Athenian Confederacy was formed, a property-tax was imposed, and the properties of the citizens were assessed anew for this purpose.

Thus the state provided for the comfort of its poorer citizens at the expense of their wealthier fellows. It is, as it were, publicly recognised as a principle of political science that the end of the state is the comfort and pleasure of its individual members; and everything has to be made subordinate to this principle, which is outwardly embodied in the theoric fund. This principle affected the foreign policy of Athens, as we have already observed. When she took the step of sending outsettlers to Samos and elsewhere, in defiance of the public opinion of Greece, her chief motive was doubtless material profit.

The constitution in the 4th century

Constitutionally, the restored Athenian democracy was a remarkable success. The difficulties which the democratic statesmen encountered after the overthrow of the Thirty had been treated with a wisdom and moderation which are in striking contrast with the violence and vengefulness shown in other Greek states at similar crises. Most democratic men of means had been robbed of property under the tyranny of the oligarchs, and the property had been sold. Were the purchasers to be compelled to restore it without compensation? Were all the acts of the Thirty to be declared illegal? Such a measure would have created a bitter and discontented party in the state. Some of the chief democratic leaders voluntarily resigned all claim to compensation for the property they had lost, and this example promoted a general inclination on both sides towards concession and compromise.[13] The wisdom and tact displayed in this matter was not the least of the services

which Thrasybulus and his fellows rendered to their country. No oligarchical conspiracy endangered the domestic peace of Athens again; no citizen, if not a philosophical speculator, called the democracy in question. Even Isocrates, who had little sympathy with the political tendencies of his day, can hold no public brief for oligarchy. In extolling an earlier Athens he has laboriously to emphasise the true democratic nature of the constitution before the reforms of Ephialtes.

At this epoch the laws were revised, and the register of citizens was revised. A new alphabet also was introduced as the official script of the state. The old Attic alphabet, with its hard-worked vowels doing duty for more than one sound, was discontinued; and henceforward the stones which record the public acts of the Athenian people are inscribed in the Ionic alphabet, with separate signs for the long and short *e* and *o*, and distinct symbols for the double consonants.[14] The constitution was left practically unaltered, but some 20 years later a change was made in the presidency of the Assembly, which had hitherto belonged to the *prytaneis* or board of Ten, selected every seven days from the presiding tribe in the Council. The close organic relation between the Council and Assembly required that members of the Council should preside in the Assembly; but the presidency of the Assembly was now divorced from the presidency of the Council and invested in a body of nine *proedroi*, selected one from each of the nine tribes which were not presiding.[15] This change was obviously designed to form a check on the administration. The presiding tribe in the Council could no longer deal directly with the Assembly, but was obliged to present its measures to the people through an intermediate body, which belonged indeed to the Council but not to its own part of the Council.

It is plain that Athens needed at this period not men of genius or enthusiasm, but simply men of ability, for the conduct of her affairs. She had no great aims to achieve, no grave dangers to escape, which demanded a Pericles or a Themistocles; a man of genius would have found no scope in the politics of Athens for two generations after the fall of her empire. Men of great ability she had, men who were thoroughly adequate to the comparatively unambitious rôle which she had wisely imposed upon herself—Agyrrhius, Callistratus, and afterwards Eubulus. To us they are all shadowy figures. Agyrrhius inaugurated the *Agyrrhius*

Introduction of the Ionic alphabet in the archonship of Euclides, 403-2 B.C.

Change in the presidency of the Assembly

The nine proedroi

profit-system which afterwards resulted in the institution of the theoric fund; and it was he who opposed and discredited the extreme anti-Spartan policy of the heroes of Phyle. His nephew Callistratus enjoyed a longer career and played a greater part in the affairs of Greece, conspicuous as the founder of the Second Confederacy, as the negotiator of the Peace of Callias, and then as the opponent of Epaminondas. His policy throughout was consistent and reasonable. He aimed at rendering Athens powerful enough to be independent of Sparta; he desired that Sparta and Athens should stand side by side as the two leading states in Greece; and he recognised that the nearness of Attica to Boeotia necessarily laid upon Athens the policy of opposing the aggrandisement of Thebes.

Calli-stratus

Agyrrhius and Callistratus might once and again fill the office of strategos; but, like Cleon and Hyperbolus, they exercised their influence as recognised—practically, official—advisers of the Assembly. The art of war became every year more and more an art, and little could be accomplished except by generals who devoted their life to the military profession. Such were Timotheus, the hero of Leucas; Chabrias, the victor of Naxos; and above all Iphicrates, whom we have met in so many places and in so many guises. Timotheus was a rich man; his father Conon had left him a fortune, and he could afford to serve his country and his country only. But Chabrias and Iphicrates enriched themselves by taking temporary service under foreign masters; Iphicrates even went so far as to support the Thracian king, whose daughter he had married, against Athens. All these military men preferred to dwell elsewhere than at Athens.

Military men

Abroad they could live in luxury and ostentation; while at Athens men lived simply and moderately, and public opinion was unfavourable to sumptuous establishments. The attitude of the generals to the city became much more independent when the citizens themselves ceased to serve abroad regularly, and hired mercenaries instead. The hiring of the troops and their organisation devolved upon the general, and he was often expected to provide the means for paying them too. Here we touch on a vice in the constitutional machine, which was the cause of frequent failures in the foreign enterprises of Athens during this period. No systematic provision was made that, when the people voted that a certain thing should be done, the adequate moneys at the same time should be voted. Any one might propose a decree, without responsibility for its execution; and at the next meeting of the Assembly the people might refuse to allow the necessary supplies, or no one might be ready to move the grant. In the same way, supplies might be cut off in the middle of a campaign. This defect had not made itself seriously felt in the fifth century, when the leading generals were always statesmen too, with influence in the Assembly; but it became serious when the generals were professional soldiers whom the statesmen employed. During the ten years after the Peace of Callias, Athens was actively engaged in a multitude of enterprises of foreign aggrandisement; but she achieved little, and the reason is that her armaments were hardly ever adequate. The difficulties of her financiers, who had always to keep a theoric reserve, must be taken into consideration.

CHAPTER 14

The Hegemony of Thebes

Jason of Pherae. The Battle of Leuctra

For a hundred years Athens and Sparta had been rivals for the leading rôle in Greece, and now the Peace of Callias had formally adjusted an equilibrium between them. But this dual system was threatened from the very outset by formidable dangers. It was clear that new forces had arisen within the last few years which would dispute the leadership of Greece with the two older states. There had been a development of military power in the north, and two cities had come into dangerous prominence, Thebes and Pherae.

Of the rise of Pherae we know less than of the rise of Thebes. At the time of the Peace of Callias we make the sudden discovery that the Thessalian cities which were usually in a state of feud have been united and that Thessaly has consequently become one of the great powers of Greece. This was the doing of one man. There had arisen at Pherae a despot, who was not merely vigorous and warlike, but whose ambition ranged beyond the domestic politics of Thessaly and sought to play a great part on the wider stage of Greece. Jason had established his dominion by means of a well-trained body of 6000 mercenaries, and also doubtless by able diplomacy. The most influential citizen of Pharsalus exposed at Sparta the ambitious and menacing views of Jason, and urged the importance of checking his career before he became too powerful; but Sparta, pressed by other more importunate claims, declined to interfere. Then Pharsalus yielded to the solicitations of Jason, and helped to install him as *Tagus* of a united

Thessaly. The power of the despot extended on one side into Epirus, where Alcetas, prince of the Molossi, became his vassal; and on the other side to Macedonia.

A monarch, endowed with uncommon political and military ability, at the head of all Thessaly, with the best cavalry in Greece at his command, seemed likely to change the whole course of Hellenic affairs. That he aimed at becoming the first power in Greece there can be no question; nor, considering the weakness and jealousies of the southern Greek states, would this object, with his resources, be difficult of achievement. But, if his ambition was not bounded by Thessaly, neither was it confined to Greece. His dream was to lead Greece against Persia and overthrow the power of the Great King. How serious he was in his great projects is shown by the fact that he set about building a navy. Thessaly was again to become a sea-power, as in the days of legendary story, when the Argo ventured forth from the land-locked bay of Iolcus.

The power of Sparta had evidently declined, but she was still regarded as the leading state in Greece; and it was the first object of Jason to weaken her still further and dethrone her from that place. His second immediate object was to gain control of the key of southern Greece—the pass of Thermopylae; and as this was commanded by the Spartan fortress of Heraclea, these two objects were intimately connected. His obvious policy was to ally himself with Sparta's enemy, Thebes; and Thebes, in her isolated position, leapt at his alliance. The treaty between the Boeotian and Thessalian federations was probably concluded not long before the Peace of Callias.

Jason of Pherae

371 B.C.

366

*Sparta
(contrary
to treaty)
orders
Cleom-
brotus to
march
against
Thebes,
371 B.C.
Protest of
Prothous*

According to the terms of that Peace, all parties were to recall their armaments from foreign countries and their garrisons from foreign towns. Athens promptly recalled Iphicrates from Corcyra, but Sparta on her side failed to fulfil the contract. King Cleombrotus had, shortly before, led an army to Phocis, and now, instead of disbanding it, he was ordered to march against Thebes and compel that state to set free the Boeotian cities. One voice, perhaps, in the Spartan assembly was raised against this violation of the recent oaths, a violation which was also unfair to the allies who served in the Lacedaemonian army. But in this hour Sparta was led on, as one of her admirers said, by a fatal impulse inspired by the gods; the feeling of hatred against Thebes, diligently fostered by Agesilaus, swept away all thoughts of policy or justice; and the voice which was raised for justice and policy was scornfully cried down. The duel between Thebes and Sparta was inevitable; and all Greece, confident in Spartan superiority, looked to see Thebes broken up into villages or wiped out from among the cities of Greece. Even Thebes herself hardly hoped for success. But Sparta would have done well to disband the army of Cleombrotus and organise a new force with the help of those allies who were willing to support her.

The object of Cleombrotus, who was posted near Chaeronea, in the gate between Phocis and Boeotia, was to reach Thebes; and, as we have seen in the case of former military operations in this country, his direct road lay along the western and southern banks of Lake Copais, by Coronea and Haliartus. The aim of the Thebans was to prevent him from reaching his objective; and they posted their forces near to Coronea, where, nearly a quarter of a century before, a confederate army had way-laid Agesilaus. But Cleombrotus disappointed his enemy; he marched southward by a difficult road round Mount Helicon to Thisbe, and thence pounced on the port of Creusis, which he captured along with 12 Theban ships in the harbour; and having by this swift stroke secured his rear, he advanced northward along the road to Thebes.

*Position of
the armies
at Leuctra*

When he reached the height of Leuctra, he found that the way was barred by the Theban army. Leuctra lies on the hills which form the south limit of a small plain, somewhat more than half a mile broad, traversed by the brook of the upper Asopus. The road from the coast to Thebes crosses it and ascends the hills on the northern side, where the Boeotarchs and their army were now drawn up. The round top of one of these low hills, just east of the road, was levelled and enlarged to form a smooth platform. Here the Theban hoplites of the left wing were posted, and the artificial mound marks their place to this day. The numbers of the two hosts are uncertain; the Lacedaemonians, in any case considerably superior, may have been about 11,000, the Thebans about 6000 strong. But the military genius of one of the Boeotarchs, now for the first time fully revealed, made up for the deficiency in strength. Instead of drawing out the usual long and shallow line, Epaminondas made his left wing deep. This wedge, 50 shields deep, of irresistible weight, with the Sacred Band under the captaincy of Pelopidas in front, was opposed to the Spartans who, with Cleombrotus himself, were drawn up on the right of the hostile army. It was on his left wing that Epaminondas relied for victory: the shock between the Spartans and Thebans would decide the battle; it mattered little about the Boeotians on the centre and right, whom he could not entirely trust.[1] The Thespians, who were present by constraint, were at the last moment permitted to depart; but their retreat was cut off and they were driven back to the camp by the Phocians and other of the Lacedaemonian allies, who, by detaching themselves for this purpose, weakened their own army without effecting a useful result.

*Tactics of
Epami-
nondas*

The battle began with an engagement of the cavalry. In this arm the Lacedaemonians were notoriously weak; and now their horsemen, easily driven back, carried disorder into the line of foot. Cleombrotus, who was confident of victory, then led his right wing down the slopes—the centre and left being probably impeded in their advance by the cavalry; and on his side Epaminondas with the Theban left moved down from their hill, deliberately keeping back the rest of the line. The novel tactics of Epaminondas decided the battle. The Spartans, 12 deep, though they fought ever so bravely, could not resist the impact of the Theban wedge led by Pelopidas. King Cleombrotus fell, and after great slaughter on both sides the Thebans drove their enemies up the slopes back to the camp. In other parts of the field there seem to have been little fighting or slaughter; the Lacedaemonian allies, when they saw their right wing worsted, retired without more ado.

*Battle of
Leuctra,
July 371
B.C.*

A thousand Lacedaemonians had fallen, including 400 Spartans; and the survivors acknowledged their defeat by demanding the customary truce to take up the dead. It might be thought that they would have immediately retreated to Creusis, the place of safety which the dead king had prudently provided in their rear. It is not likely that the enemy, whom they still considerably outnumbered, would have attempted to stop their way, or even to harass them seriously from behind. The Thebans could hardly realise the victory which they had never expected; it was more than enough to have defeated the Lacedaemonians in the open field, to have slain their king, and to have compelled them to evacuate Boeotia. But the Lacedaemonian army remained in its entrenchments on the hill of Leuctra, in the expectation of being reinforced by a new army from Sparta and retrieving the misfortune. A messenger was sent home with the inglorious tidings, and the shock was borne there with that studied self-repression which only the discipline of Sparta could inculcate in her citizens. The remaining forces of the city were hastily got together and placed under the command of Archidamus, son of Agesilaus. Some of the allied states sent aid, and the troops were transported by ship from Corinth to Creusis.

Position at Leuctra after the battle

Army of relief under Archidamus. Reception of the news at Athens

But all this took time, and meanwhile Thebes had not been idle. Two messengers were sent with the good news to Athens and to Thessaly. At Athens the wreathed messenger was received with an ominous silence. The Theban victory was distinctly unwelcome there; it opened up an indefinite prospect of warfare and seemed likely to undo the recent pacification; while the Athenians were far less jealous of Sparta than of Thebes. At Pherae the tidings had a very different reception. Jason marched forthwith to the scene of action, at the head of his cavalry and mercenaries, flying so rapidly through Phocis that the Phocians, his irreconcilable enemies, did not realise his presence until he had passed. He cannot have reached Leuctra until the sixth or seventh day after the battle. The Thebans thought that with the help of his forces they might storm the Lacedaemonian entrenchment, dangerous though the task would be. But by the policy of Jason the humiliation already inflicted on Sparta was enough; the annihilation of the enemy or any further enhancement of the Theban success would have been too much. He dissuaded the Thebans from the enterprise, and induced them to grant a truce to the Lacedaemonians, with leave to retire unharmed. This the Lacedaemonians were now forced to accept, notwithstanding the approach of reinforcements. For their position was totally altered through the

Jason of Pherae marches to Leuctra

Truce The Lacedaemonians evacuate Boeotia

presence of the seasoned troops of Jason, and it was clear that the enemy would not wait to attack them till the expected reinforcements arrived. The retreat was carried out at night, for the leaders suspected the good faith of their opponents. On the coast the defeated troops met the army of Archidamus, which had come in vain, and all the forces were disbanded.

Such were the circumstances of the Lacedaemonian evacuation of Boeotia after the battle of Leuctra, according to the historian whose authority we are naturally inclined to prefer. But the memory of Xenophon might have misled him in regard to some of the details, and there was another account from which it might be inferred that events moved more rapidly. There is something to be said for the view that the army of Archidamus was not dispatched as a relief force after the battle of Leuctra, but was already on its way before the battle was fought; that Cleombrotus had the alternative of waiting for Archidamus before he ventured on an engagement, and that his visit to Creusis was, in fact, connected with the expected arrival of reinforcements; that Jason too was hastening to support the Thebans, and that the messenger who bore the news of victory met him on his southward march. On this view the truce might have been concluded on the morrow of the battle, and we avoid the difficulty of supposing that the defeated army decided to remain for a week on the hill of Leuctra, when the road to Creusis was open behind them.[2]

Another view of the evacuation of Boeotia

The question is of little moment except in so far as it concerns the movements of the Tagus of Thessaly. The significance of the sequel of the battle lies in the prominent part which he played as a mediator; and we should very much like to know whether his original purpose was to fight side by side with his Theban allies. We also hear darkly of his avowed intention to bring help by sea, and we are tempted to speculate at what point the new Thessalian navy would have acted at this crisis.

Jason's fleet

Jason returned to his northern home, but on his way he dealt another blow at Sparta on his own account, by dismantling Heraclea, the fort which controlled the pass of Thermopylae. He thus encompassed an object of great importance for his further designs—which he soon began to unfold. He fixed on the next celebration of the Pythian festival as a time to display his greatness and his power to the eyes of assembled Hellas. He sent mandates around to the Thessalian cities to prepare oxen, sheep, and goats for the sacrifice at Delphi, offering a gold

Jason at Thermopylae

His schemes

crown as a prize for the fairest ox. And he issued commands that the armed host of the Thessalians should be ready to march with him to keep the feast. He proposed to usurp the rights of the Amphictionic board and himself preside over the games. A rumour was set afloat that he intended to seize the treasures of the temple, but it is hard to believe that an aspirant to the hegemony of Greece would have perpetrated an act so manifestly impolitic. Apollo told the Delphians, who were fluttered by the report, that he would himself guard his treasure.

But the priests were soon to breathe freely; the Phocians were to be spared the mortification of seeing the hated Thessalian in their land. One day Jason held a review of his cavalry, and afterwards sat to hear petitions. Seven young men, to all appearance wrangling hotly, drew near to lay their dispute before him, and slew him where he sat. The death of Jason meant the end of all his plans. The unity of Thessaly, the high position which it had attained among the Greek powers, depended entirely on him. The brothers who succeeded to his place were slight, insignificant men, without the ability, even if they had possessed the will, to carry out his far-reaching designs. It is the bare truth to say that the blades of the seven young men changed the course of history. Jason was well on his way to attaining in eastern Greece the supreme position which his great fellow-despot Dionysius held in the west. Nor is it extravagant to suppose that under him Thessaly might have accomplished part of the work which was reserved for Macedonia. Politically, indeed, his work is to be condemned. He had not laid the foundations of a national unity in Thessaly; the unity which he had achieved was held only by military force and by his own genius. We cannot congratulate a statesman on a result the stability of which hangs on the chances of his own life. In this respect Jason stands in the same rank with Epaminondas.

The death of the Thessalian potentate decided that, of the two northern states which had recently risen into prominence, Boeotia, not Thessaly, should take the place of Sparta.

The significance of the battle of Leuctra is perhaps most clearly revealed in the fact that, during the wars between Sparta and Thebes which followed it, the parts hitherto played by the two states are reversed. Thebes now becomes the invader of the Peloponnese, as Sparta before had been the invader of Boeotia. Thebes is now the aggressor; it is as much as Sparta can do to defend her own land. The significance of Leuctra is also displayed in the effect which it produced upon the policy of Athens, and in its stimulating influence on the lesser Peloponnesian states, especially Arcadia, which was wakened up into new life.

The supremacy of Thebes was the result of no overmastering imperial instinct and was inspired by no large idea, but it brought about some beneficial results. Sparta had grievously abused the dominion which had fallen into her hands, and the period of Theban greatness represents the reaction against the period of Lacedaemonian oppression. The two objects of Theban policy are to hinder Sparta from regaining her old position in the Peloponnese, and to prevent the revival of Jason's power in Thessaly.

Although no express record has been handed down as to constitutional changes, there is some evidence which has suggested the belief that the Thebans drew tighter the bond which united the Boeotian communities by transforming the federation into a national state.[3] Thebes seemingly became in Boeotia what Athens was in Attica; the other cities, Coronea, Thespiae, Haliartus, and the rest, were uncitied and became as Marathon and Eleusis; their citizens exercised their political rights in an Assembly at Thebes. If this be so, we may suspect that Epaminondas played the part of legendary Theseus; but the new constitution had no elements of stability, and it endured but for a few years.

Policy of Thebes in Southern Greece, Arcadia and Messenia

The defeat of a Lacedaemonian army in the open field by an enemy inferior in numbers was a thrilling shock to the Greeks, who regarded it as part of the order of nature that the Spartan hoplites should be invincible except in front of an overwhelmingly larger force. The event was made more impressive by the death of king Cleombrotus; a Spartan king had never fallen in battle since Leonidas laid down his life at the gates of Greece. The news agitated every state in the Peloponnese. The harmosts, whom Sparta had undertaken to withdraw three weeks before, when she signed the Peace, were now expelled from the cities; there was a universal reaction against the local oligarchies which had been supported by Sparta and had excited universal discontent; and these democratic revolutions flooded the land with troops of dangerous exiles. The contagion spread even to Argos, though Sparta had no influence there, and broke out with such violence that many citizens were cudgelled to death by the infuriated people.[4]

Pan-Arcadian League

But it was in Arcadia that the most weighty political results followed. A general feeling, which had perhaps been growing for some years back, now took definite shape, that the cities of Arcadia must combine together to oppose a united front to Lacedaemonian pretensions. The only way in which each city could hope to preserve her independence against the power of Sparta was by voluntarily surrendering a portion of that independence to a federal union of her sister cities. The most zealous advocate of the Pan-Arcadian idea was the Mantinean Lycomedes, a native of the district which had been more cruelly used than all others by the high-handed policy of Sparta. The fall of Sparta was the signal for the Mantineans to rebuild their walls, desert their villages, and resume the dignity and pleasures of city life. The old king Agesilaus had the insolence to remonstrate; he requested them at least to ask the gracious permission of Sparta, but he had no power to enforce his request.

Rebuilding of Mantinea, 370 B.C., spring

The Mantineans resolved that their city should not again be captured, as king Agesipolis had captured it, by means of its own river. They dug a new bed, so that the Ophis when it approached the south-eastern wall parted into two channels and, having described a great loop, reunited its waters on the north-western side. In this loop the city of Mantinea rose again, and by this means the river, which had proved itself a danger, was forced to become a fortification, entirely encompassing the walls. The stone foundations of the wall enable us to trace the circuit of the city, but they were only the base for a superstructure which, like the buildings of the town, was of mud-brick. The ten gates were curiously constructed, no two alike, yet all elaborations of a principle which was adopted by the builders of the fortress of Tiryns—the principle of exposing the undefended right side of an approaching enemy to the defenders who manned the walls and flanking towers. The general design may be best grasped by conceiving the wall not as a continuous circle but as composed of ten separate pieces, which did not join but overlapped, while the gates connected the overlapping ends.

Mantinea, arisen from her ruins, and the other towns of Arcadia—with the important exceptions of Tegea, Orchomenus, and Heraea—now agreed to form a Pan-Arcadian union and constitute a federal state. Several reasons made it expedient to establish a new seat as the federal capital of the country. The Arcadian cities were too small for the purpose. The selection of one of them would have excited the jealousies of the others, and it was intended that there should be no Thebes in the Arcadian state. The site chosen for the new city was in the western of the two large plains which define the geographical character of central Arcadia. It lay, in a long narrow irregular shape, on both sides of the river Helisson. Not far off rose Lycaeon, the mountain to which the Arcadian folk attached their most sacred associations; and in the centre of the market-place was built a shrine of Zeus of that holy hill. The town was entitled to its name of Megalopolis, or Great City, by the large circuit of its double wall, a circuit of five miles and a half—a somewhat rough piece of work, built of stone in the lower courses and brick above, and furnished with towers at intervals.

Foundation of Megalopolis (date uncertain, 371-369 B.C.)

It must be kept in view that Megalopolis had a double character. It was to be the federal capital, but it was also to be one of the federal cities. Apart from its relation to all Arcadia, it had a special relation to its own plain. The change which had come to pass in the eastern plain, so long ago that no man could tell when, by the founding of Tegea and Mantinea, now followed in the western plain. The village communities of the surrounding districts were induced to exchange their separate existence for joint life in a city. Lying close to the north-western frontier of Laconia, Megalopolis would be a bulwark against Sparta on this side, corresponding to Tegea on the north. It is natural to compare it with Mantinea, which arose in its new shape at the same time. Both cities seem to have had a similar system of fortification, double walls of stone and brick, strengthened by towers; but Megalopolis, which was the larger, was also the stronger by nature. For Mantinea lay on a dead level: all its strength was due to art; Megalopolis lay on sloping irregular ground, offering hills of which the architect could take advantage. The difference is illustrated by the fact that the little theatre in Mantinea rested on a stone substructure, while the huge theatre in Megalopolis is cut out of a hill.

The Federal Constitution was modelled on the ordinary type of democratic constitutions.[5] There was an Assembly, which met at stated periods to consider all important questions. Every citizen of the federal communities was a member of this Assembly, of which the official title was the *Ten Thousand*. The name indicates an approximate, not an exact, number, like the Five Thousand in the constitution of Thera-

Assembly of the Myrioi

menes at Athens. We have no information as to the working of this body, but from the analogy of other ancient federations it is probable that the votes were taken by cities, the vote of each city being determined by the majority of the votes of those of its citizens who were present. The Ten Thousand made war and peace, concluded alliances, and sat in judgment on offenders against the League. *Council* There was also a *Council,* and this body had doubtless the usual executive and deliberative functions which belonged to the Greek conception of a Council.

On the south side of the river stood the Thersilion, the federal building in which meetings of the Arcadian league were held. The foundations of this spacious covered hall have been laid bare, and display an ingenious arrangement of the internal pillars, converging in lines whereby as few as possible of a crowded audience might be hindered from seeing and hearing. It is an attempt to apply the principle of the theatre to a covered building. The Thersilion stood close in front of the hill from which the theatre was hewn, and the place of political deliberation seemed part of the same structure as the place of dramatic spectacles. For the Doric portico, which adorned the southern side of the federal house, faced the audience; the orchestra in which the chorus danced and the actors sometimes played stretched from the circle of seats up to the steps of the portico. Such was the original arrangement, changed in later years; and it illustrates the fact that the stone theatres which began to spring up throughout Greece in the fourth century were intended as much for political assemblies as for theatrical representations.

The river Helisson divides Megalopolis into two nearly equal parts; and it would seem that this division corresponded to the double character of the place.[6] The city of Megalopolis, in the strict sense, was on the northern side; there was the market-place, on the bank of the river; there was the hall in which the *Buleu-* Council of the Megalopolitan state met to-*terion* gether. But the southern half of Megalopolis was federal ground; here was the federal Hall of Assembly, here was the theatre, which was in fact an open-air hall for federal meetings. *Eparitoi* Here, we may suppose, were the dwellings of *(federal* the permanent armed force, 5000 strong, which *army)* was maintained by the Federation; here were lodgings for the 'Ten Thousand' when they assembled to vote on the affairs of the Arcadian state.

Tegea had hitherto been a sort of Laconian outpost, and a revolution was necessary to *Tegea joins* bring about its adhesion to the new federation. *the* With the help of a Mantinean band, the philo-*League,* Laconian party was overthrown, and 800 exiles *370 B.C.* sought refuge at Sparta. This blow stung Sparta to action. She might brook the resuscitation of Mantinea, she might look on patiently at the measures taken by the presumptuous Arcadians for managing their own affairs; but it was too much to see Tegea, her steadfast ally, the strong warder of her northern frontier, pass over to the camp of the rebels. Agesilaus led an army into Arcadia, and displayed the resentment of Sparta by ravaging the fields of Mantinea; but neither he nor the federal forces risked a conflict.

In view of this Spartan invasion, which came to so little, the Arcadians had sought the help of foreign powers. Their first appeal was made to Athens. The news of Leuctra had excited in that city mixed feelings of pleasure and jealousy. The humiliation of Sparta opened up a prospect of regaining empire, notwithstanding the undertakings of the recent peace; but the triumph of Thebes was unwelcome and dangerous. These hopes and fears spurred Athens to new activity. Shortly *Close of* after the battle of Leuctra she showed her *371 B.C.* appreciation of the changed condition of Greece by inviting delegates from the Peloponnesian cities to pledge themselves anew to the King's Peace (which, it must always be remembered, was the basis of the Peace of Callias) and to pledge themselves to one another for mutual help in case of hostile attack. Elis, refusing to recognise the autonomy of some of her subjects, was forced to hold aloof, but most of the other states swore to the alliance. It was a contract between Athens and her allies on one side, and the former allies of Sparta on the other. By virtue of this act of alliance, Athens was bound to help Mantinea and the Arcadian cities whenever they were threatened by an invasion. But it appeared that, though ready to usurp the place of Sparta, she was not ready to renew the war with her old rival. Perhaps in the course of the nine or ten months which had run since the congress at Athens there had been a change of feeling; the violence of the democratic movements in the Peloponnese may have caused disgust; certain it is that Athens refused the Arcadian appeal; she seems to have contemplated a policy of neutrality.

The rebuff at Athens drove Arcadia into the arms of Thebes. The battle which had been fought to secure the unity of Boeotia had been the means of promoting the unity of Arcadia,

371

and there was a certain fitness in the northern state coming to the aid of its younger fellow. But it was not mere sympathy with federal institutions that induced Thebes to send a Boeotian army into the Peloponnese. To keep Sparta down and prevent her from recovering her influence was the concern of Thebes, and a united Arcadia was the best instrument that could be devised for the purpose. At this juncture, the situation in northern Greece permitted Thebes to comply with the Arcadian request. The Phocians and Ozolian Locrians, the Locrians of Opus, the Malians, had sought her alliance after Leuctra, and even the Euboeans had deserted to her; so that all central Greece, as far as Cithaeron, was under Boeotian influence. But if the request had come some months sooner, it would have been impossible to grant it, for Jason of Pherae was then alive, preparing to march to Delphi, and the Boeotian forces could not have left Boeotia.

Boeotians invade Laconia

It was already winter when the Theban army, led by Epaminondas, accompanied by his fellow Boeotarchs, arrived in Arcadia to find that Agesilaus had withdrawn from the field. But, though the purpose of the expedition was thus accomplished, the Arcadians persuaded Epaminondas not to return home without striking a blow at the enemy. To invade Laconia and attack Sparta herself was the daring proposal—daring in idea at least, for within the memory of history no foeman had ever violated Laconian soil, the unwalled city had never repelled an assault. There was little danger, with an army of such size as that which was now assembled, and a march to the gates of Sparta would drive home the lesson of Leuctra. The invaders advanced in four divisions by four roads, converging on Sellasia, and met no serious attempt to block their way; some neodamodes and Tegeate exiles were annihilated by the Arcadians. Sellasia was burnt, and the united army descended into the plain on the left bank of the Eurotas. The river which separated them from Sparta was swollen with winter rains, and this probably saved the city, for the bridge was too strongly guarded to be safely attacked. Epaminondas marched southward a few miles further, as far as Amyclae, where he crossed the stream by a ford. But Sparta was now saved. On the first alarm of the coming invasion, messages had flown to the Peloponnesian cities which were still friendly; and these—Corinth, Sicyon, Phlius, Pellene, and the towns of the Argolic coast—had promptly sent auxiliary forces. The northern roads being barred by the enemy, these forces were obliged to land on the eastern shore of Laconia and make their way across Mount Parnon. They reached the Eurotas bridge, after the invaders had moved to Amyclae, and their coming added such strength to the defence of Sparta that Epaminondas did not attack it, but contented himself with marching up defiantly to its outskirts. It was indeed a sufficient revenge even for Theban hatred to have wounded Sparta as none had wounded her before, to have violated the precinct of the Laconian land. The consternation of the Spartans at a calamity which, owing to the immunity of ages, they had never even conceived as possible, can hardly be imagined. The women, disciplined though they were in repressing their feelings when sons or husbands perished in battle, now fell into fits of distress and despair; for, unlike the women of so many other Greek cities, they had never looked upon the face of an enemy before. Old Agesilaus, who loathed the Theban above all other names, was charged with the defence; and his task was the harder, since he had to watch not only the foe, but the disaffected. Freedom had been promised to 6000 helots who came forward to serve, but this aid was a new danger.

It is needless to say that the loss of a few hundred soldiers on the field of Leuctra had nothing to do with the impotence displayed by Sparta at this crisis. And if Leuctra had been won by superior generalship, it was not inferior generalship that exposed Laconia. The disease lay far deeper. The vigour of Sparta was decaying from the mere want of men; it has been calculated that at this time there were not more than 1500 with full citizenship. Not merely constant warfare, but, far more, economic conditions, brought about this decline in numbers. Since money had begun to flow into Laconia, and since a new law permitted citizens to alienate their holdings, the inevitable result ensued: the small lots which meagrely supported each Spartan were gathered into large estates, and with the lots the citizens disappeared. This disease which was sapping the energies of his enemy cannot have escaped the view of Epaminondas, and his next step is significant.

Depopulation of Sparta

Having ravaged southern Laconia, from the banks of the Eurotas to the foot of Taygetus, as far as Gytheion—where they failed to take the arsenal—the allies returned to Arcadia. But, though it was midwinter, their work was not over yet; a far greater blow was still to be inflicted on Sparta. Epaminondas led them now into another part of the Spartan territory, the ancient Messenia. The serfs, who belonged

Foundation of Messene, winter, 370-69 B.C.

to the old Messenian race, arose at their coming, and on the slopes of Mount Ithome the foundations of a new Messene were laid by Epaminondas. The ancient heroes and heroines of the race were invited to return to the restored nation; the ample circuit of the town was marked out, and the first stones placed, to the sound of flutes. Ithome was the citadel, and formed one side of the town, whose walls of well-wrought masonry descended the slopes and met in the plain below. The Messenian exiles who had been wandering over the Greek world had now a home once more.

Messene, like Megalopolis, was founded by 'synoecising' the districts round about. But its political position was entirely different from that of Megalopolis. Messene was not a federal capital; it was the Messenian state—a city with the whole country for its territory. Corone and Methone were not cities like Mantinea and Clitor; they were places like Brauron and Marathon; their inhabitants possessed the citizenship of Messene, but it was only under Mount Ithome that they could exercise their citizen-rights. The relation of Messene to Messenia was that of Athens to Attica, not that of Megalopolis to Arcadia.

Thus not only a new stronghold but a new enemy was erected against Sparta in Sparta's own domain. All the land west of Taygetus (except the coastal towns of Asine and Cyparissia) was subtracted from the Spartan dominion; more than half her serfs became the freemen of a hostile state. Under the auspices of Thebes an old act of injustice was undone, and the principle of autonomy was strikingly affirmed. But, besides the glory which Thebes won by so popular an act, besides the direct injury inflicted on Sparta and the establishment of a hostile fort, the policy of Epaminondas was calculated to produce a result of greater importance: the loss of Messenia would accelerate that process of decline in the Spartan state, which had already advanced so far. The fewer the lots, the fewer the citizens, according to the indissoluble connection between land and citizen-rights on the Lycurgean system.[7] It was high time for Sparta to reform her constitution.

The stone which bears witness to the invasion of Laconia

The Arcadians celebrated this memorable invasion of Laconia by dedicating with part of the spoil a group of statues to the Delphian god.[8] The verses of dedication signify that the indigenous people from sacred Arcadia, having laid Lacedaemon waste, set up the monument as a witness to future generations. The statues are gone, but the verses on their stone have been recovered.

In the meantime Sparta had begged aid from Athens, and Athens had decided to depart from her position of neutrality. A vote was passed, strongly supported by the orator Callistratus, to send the entire force of the city under Iphicrates to assist Sparta. This was evidently the most politic course for Athens to adopt. Sparta was a necessary makeweight against Thebes. Nor is it doubtful that, notwithstanding all their rivalries, no such antipathy parted Athens from Sparta as that which existed between the two states and Thebes. Iphicrates marched to the Isthmus and occupied Corinth and Cenchreae, thus commanding the line of Mount Oneion. His object, it must be clearly understood, was not to prevent the enemy from leaving the Peloponnese, but to protect the rear of his own army marching into a hostile country. He advanced into Arcadia, but found that the Thebans and their allies had left Laconia, and Sparta was no longer in danger. He therefore drew back to Corinth, and harassed the Boeotian army on its return march, without attempting to bar its passage. For the object of the Athenian expedition was simply to rescue Sparta—not, except so far as Sparta's danger might demand, to fight with the Thebans.

Athens sends an army to rescue Sparta

Theban army returns home, spring, 369 B.C.

But the hasty vote to march to the rescue was soon followed by a deliberate treaty of alliance, and Athens definitely ranged herself with Sparta against Boeotia and Arcadia. She was already meditating schemes of extending her empire; she was nourishing the hope of recovering the most precious of all her former imperial possessions, the Thracian Amphipolis. With such designs it was impossible to remain neutral; and, as we shall see, there was some danger of a collision with Thebes in Macedonia.

Alliance of Athens and Sparta, spring, 369 B.C.

Fighting went on in the Peloponnese between the Arcadians and the allies of Sparta, and a few months later Epaminondas (who had been re-elected Boeotarch in his absence at the beginning of the year) appeared again at the head of the Boeotian army. The Spartans and Athenians had occupied the line of Mount Oneion; this time the object was to keep out the Thebans. But Epaminondas broke through their lines, joined his allies, won over Sicyon and Pellene, but failed to win Phlius. New help for Sparta arrived at this moment from overseas. Twenty ships bearing 2000 Celtic and Iberian mercenaries came from her old ally, the tyrant of Syracuse, to whom she had once sent aid in an hour of peril, and who had more than once sent aid to her. Their coming seems to have decided Epaminondas to return home, though he had accomplished but little, and his

Second expedition of Epaminondas into the Peloponnese

political opponent Meneclidas took advantage of the general disappointment to indict him for treason. The result was that Epaminondas was not re-elected Boeotarch for the following year.[9]

To establish her supremacy, Thebes was adopting the same policy as Sparta. She placed a harmost in Sicyon; as the Boeotian cities had formerly been garrisoned by Sparta, the Peloponnesian cities were now to be garrisoned by Thebes. Messenia and Arcadia were to be autonomous, but the Thebans desired to be regarded as both the authors and preservers of that autonomy. As a mistress, distant Thebes might be more tolerable than neighbouring Lacedaemon; but the free federation of Arcadia determined to be free in more than name. Sparta was now sunk so low that the Arcadians —with friendly Messene on one side, and friendly Argos on the other—could hope to maintain their liberty with their own swords, without foreign aid. Their leading spirit Lycomedes animated them to this resolve of independence and self-reliance. 'You are the only indigenous natives of the Peloponnese, and you are the most numerous and hardiest nation in Greece. Your valour is proved by the fact that you have been always in the greatest request as allies. Give up following the lead of others. You made Sparta by following her lead; and now if you follow the lead of Thebes, without yourselves leading in turn, she will prove perhaps a second Sparta.' In this mood the Arcadians displayed a surprising activity and achieved a series of successes. The two important cities, Heraea in the west, and Orchomenus in the north, which had hitherto stood aloof, were forced to join the league, which now became in the fullest sense Pan-Arcadian. Some of the northern villages of Laconia were annexed, and the Triphylian towns sought in the league a support against the hated domination of Elis. The federal forces were active in the opposite quarters of Argolis and Messenia. Against all this activity Sparta felt herself helpless. But a second detachment arrived from her friend, the tyrant of Syracuse, and thus reinforced she ventured to take the field, and marched into the plain of Megalopolis. But the expedition was suddenly interrupted; time had been wasted, and the Syracusan force, in accordance with its orders, was obliged to return to Sicily. Its way lay through Laconia, in order to take ship at Gytheion, and the enemy tried to cut it off in the mountain defiles. The Spartan commander Archidamus, who was in the rear, hastened to the rescue and dispersed the Arcadians with

Spring, 368 B.C.

Sparta receives help from Dionysius

The tear-less battle, 368 (late summer?)

great loss. Not a single Lacedaemonian was killed, and the victory was called the 'tearless battle'. The joy displayed in Sparta over this slight success showed how low Sparta had fallen.

It may be thought that Dionysius might have kept his troops at home, if they were charged to return before they had well time to begin to fight. But the truth is that these troops were for some months inactive in Greece, while an attempt was being made to bring about a general peace. The initiative came from Ariobarzanes, the Persian satrap of Phrygia, who sent to Greece an agent well furnished with money; and this move on the part of Persia was probably suggested by Athens. The Syracusan sovereign also intervened in the interests of peace, and the stone remains on which the Athenians thanked Dionysius and his sons for being 'good men in regard to the people of Athens and their allies, and helping the King's Peace'.[10] Thus the King's Peace was the basis of the negotiations of the congress which met at Delphi. Both Athens, which was doubtless the prime mover, and Sparta were most anxious for peace; but each had an ultimate condition from which she would not retreat. Sparta's very life seemed to demand the recovery of Messenia, and Athens had set her heart on Amphipolis. But neither condition would be admitted by Thebes, and consequently the negotiations fell through. They led, however, to independent negotiations of various states with Persia, each seeking to win from the king a recognition of its own claims. Pelopidas went up to Susa on behalf of Thebes to obtain a royal confirmation of the independence of Messenia. The Athenians sent envoys to convince the king of their rights to Amphipolis. Arcadia, Elis, and Argos were also represented. Pelopidas was entirely successful. The king issued an order to Greece, embodying the wishes of Thebes: Messenia and Amphipolis to be independent, the Athenians to recall their warships. The question of Triphylia—whether it was to be dependent on Elis or a part of Arcadia—was decided in favour of Elis; this decision in a matter of absolute indifference to Persia was clearly due to Pelopidas, and indicates strained relations between Thebes and Arcadia. Pelopidas returned with the royal letter, but it found no acceptance in Greece, either at the congress of allies which was convoked at Thebes, or when the document was afterwards sent round to the cities. Arcadia would not abandon Triphylia, and Lycomedes formally protested against the policy of Thebes.

Congress of Delphi, 368 B.C. (summer)

Greek envoys at Susa, 367 B.C.

Persian rescript

*Third
expedition
of Epa-
minondas
into the
Pelopon-
nese,
366 B.C.*

The answer of Thebes to this defiance of her will was an invasion of the Peloponnese. The line of Mount Oneion was still defended, but negligently, and Epaminondas passed it with Argive help. His object was not to depress Sparta further, for Sparta was now too feeble to be formidable, but to check the pretensions of Arcadia. And this could only be done through strengthening Theban influence in the Peloponnese by winning new allies. Accordingly, Epaminondas advanced to Achaea, and easily gained the adhesion of the Achaean cities.

*Achaea
won and
lost,
366 B.C.*

But the gain of Achaea was soon followed by its loss. Counter to the moderate policy of Epaminondas, the Thebans had insisted on overthrowing the oligarchical constitutions and banishing the oligarchical leaders; these exiles from the various cities banded together, and recovered each city successively, overthrowing the democracies and expelling the harmosts. Henceforward Achaea was an ardent partisan of Sparta.

*Sicyon:
Euphron
becomes
tyrant,
368 B.C.*

The unsettled state of the Peloponnese was conspicuously shown by the events which took place at Sicyon. When the Theban harmost was installed in the acropolis, the oligarchy had been spared; but soon afterwards one of the chief citizens, named Euphron, brought about the establishment of a democracy, and then, procuring his own election as general, organising a mercenary force, and surrounding himself with a bodyguard—the usual and notorious steps of a despot's progress—made himself master of the city and harbour. The Arcadians had helped Euphron in his first designs, but the intrigues of his opponents were so skilful that Arcadia again intervened and restored to Sicyon the exiles whom the tyrant had driven out. Euphron fled

Expelled,

from the city to the harbour, which he surrendered to the Lacedaemonians; but the Lacedaemonians failed to hold it. Sicyon, however, was not yet delivered from her tyrant.

*restored
366-5 B.C.*

He was restored by the help of Athenian mercenaries. Afterwards, seeing that he could not maintain himself without the support of Boeotia, he visited Thebes, and was slain on the Cadmea in front of the Hall of Council by two Sicyonian exiles who had dogged him. His assassins were tried and acquitted at Thebes, but at Sicyon his memory was cherished and he was worshipped as a second founder of the city. The fact shows that under the rule of Euphron the masses of the people were happier than under the political opponents whom he had so mercilessly treated. His son succeeded to his power.

*Thebans
seize
Oropus,
366 B.C.*

The expedition of Epaminondas was attended with results which were in the end injurious to Thebes. The relations with Arcadia became more and more strained. But in the same year Oropus was wrested from Athens and occupied by a Theban force. The Athenians were unable to cope alone with Thebes; they called on their allies, but none moved to their aid. The moment was seized by Arcadia.

*Alliance of
Arcadia
with
Athens,
366 B.C.*

Lycomedes visited Athens and induced the Athenians, smarting with resentment against their allies, to conclude an alliance with the league. Thus Athens was now in the position of being an ally of both Arcadia and Sparta, which were at war with each other; and Arcadia was the ally of Athens and Thebes, which were also at war with each other. The visit of Lycomedes incidentally led to a disaster for Arcadia which outweighed the benefit of the alliance. The ambassador, on his way back,

*Murder of
Lyco-
medes*

was slain by some exiles into whose hands he fell, and the league lost its ablest statesman.

This change in the mutual relations among the Greek states, brought about by the seizure of Oropus, was followed by another change, brought about by an Athenian plot to seize Corinth. The object was to secure permanent control over the passage into the Peloponnese. But the plot was discovered and foiled by the Corinthians, who then politely dismissed the Athenian soldiers stationed at various posts in the Corinthian territory. But by herself Corinth would have been unable to resist the

*Partial
peace of
366-5 B.C.*

combined pressure of Thebes on one side and Argos on the other; and, as Sparta could not help her, she was driven to make peace with Thebes. She was joined by her neighbour Phlius and by the cities of the Argolic coast; all these states formally recognised the independence of Messenia, but did not enter into any alliance with Thebes or give any pledge to obey her headship. They became, in fact, neutral.

It was a blow to Sparta, who still refused to accept a peace on any terms save the restoration of Messenia. The Messenian question gave political speculators at Athens a subject for meditation. Was the demand of Sparta just? Isocrates argued the case for Sparta in a speech which he put in the mouth of king Archidamus. Another orator, Alcidamas, vindicated in reply the liberty of the Messenians and declared a principle which was far in advance of his time, 'God has left all men free; nature has made no man a slave'.

*Summary
of the
situation*

If we survey the political relations of southern Greece at this epoch, we see Thebes, supported by Argos, still at war with Sparta, who is supported by Athens; Achaea actively siding with Sparta; Elis hostile to Arcadia; the Arcadian league at war with Sparta, in alliance with Athens, in alliance with, but cool towards, Thebes, and already—having lost its leader Lycomedes—beginning to fall into disunion with itself.

The peace with Corinth and others of the belligerent states marks the time at which Peloponnesian affairs cease to occupy the chief place in the counsels of Thebes, and her most anxious attention turns to a different quarter. For Sparta is disabled, and the mistress of Boeotia recognises that the struggle for headship will be with Athens. While events were progressing in the Peloponnese, as we have seen, Athens was busily engaged in other parts of the world with a view to restoring her maritime empire; and we have now to see how she succeeded, and how Thebes likewise was pushing her own supremacy in the north.

Policy and Action of Thebes in Northern Greece

Death of Amyntas

The same year which saw the death of Jason of Pherae saw the death of his neighbour and ally Amyntas of Macedonia. We have seen how Amyntas had to fight for his kingdom with the Chalcidian league; how he was driven out of his land and restored; and how the league was crushed by the power of Sparta. Both Jason and Amyntas were succeeded by an Alexander. At Pherae, the power first passed to Jason's brothers, of whom one murdered the other and was in turn murdered by his victim's son— Alexander, whose reign was worthy of its sanguinary inauguration. The Thessalian cities refused to bow down to the supremacy of Pherae, now that Pherae had no man who was worthy to be obeyed; and to resist Alexander of Pherae they invoked the aid of Alexander of

369 B.C.

Macedonia. The aid was given, and Larissa, Crannon, and other cities passed under Macedonian control. But this was not the purpose of the Thessalians, to exchange a native for a foreign ruler; and accordingly they invoked the help of Thebes against both Alexanders alike. It was sound policy on the part of Thebes to

First expedition of Pelopidas to Thessaly, 369 B.C.

accede to the request. It was impossible to discern yet what manner of man the successor of Jason might prove to be; and it was important, from the Boeotian point of view, to hinder the reunion of Thessaly under a monarch. The conduct of an expedition was entrusted to Pelopidas, who brought Larissa

and other towns in the northern part of Thessaly under a Theban protectorate.

At the same time the Thessalians sought to strengthen their position by a federal union— a political experiment which had been tried in Thessaly before. The little we know of the league which was established about this time suggests rather the revival of an old system than a new creation. The country was divided into four political divisions corresponding to the old geographical districts; at the head of each was a polemarch, who had officers of horse and foot under him; and at the head of the league was an archon, elected if not for life at least for longer than a year. Thus the organisation was military; but there are indications that it grew out of an old amphictionic association. There is no reason to think that Pelopidas had more to do with the establishment of the Thessalian federation than Epaminondas with that of the Pan-Arcadian league; the part of Thebes in either case was simply to support and confirm.

Thessalian league

Tetrads

Archon

Macedonia offered no obstacles to the operations of Pelopidas in Thessaly, for it was involved in a domestic struggle. One of the nobles, Ptolemy of Alorus, rebelled against the king, and was supported by the king's unnatural mother Eurydice. The two parties called upon Pelopidas to adjudicate between them, and he patched up a temporary arrangement and concluded a Theban alliance with Macedonia. Hardly had he turned his back when Ptolemy murdered Alexander and married Eurydice. But it seemed as if the paramours would not be permitted to reap the profits of their crime. Another pretender to the throne had gathered an army of mercenaries and occupied all the land along the Chalcidian frontier. Help, however, was at hand. An Athenian fleet was cruising in the Thermaic gulf, under the command of Iphicrates. The queen visited the admiral on the coast, accompanied by her two sons, Perdiccas and Philip—the brothers of Iphicrates, since he had been adopted as a son by Amyntas— and persuaded him to help her in her need. By his exertions the pretender was expelled, and the succession of Perdiccas was secured under the regency of Ptolemy.

Murder of Alexander of Macedon, 369-8 B.C.

Revolt of Pausanias

Intervention of Iphicrates

The interests of Athens on the Chalcidian and the adjacent coasts had forced her to keep an ever-watchful eye on political events in Macedonia and to seek influence at the court of Aegae. The intervention of Iphicrates was not the first case in which Athenian power had settled a dynastic question. His settlement lasted longer than that of Pelopidas; we may conjecture that the opportune appearance of the Athenian fleet was due to the circumstance that Thebes had interfered. But Thebes was resolved to continue her interference, and oust the Athenian influence. Pelopidas, again dispatched to the north, compelled the regent Ptolemy to enter into alliance with Thebes and assure his fidelity by furnishing a number of hostages. Among the young Macedonian nobles who were sent as pledges to Thebes was the boy Philip, who was destined to be the maker of Macedonia, and was now to be trained for the work in the military school of Boeotia, under the eye of Epaminondas himself.

Second expedition of Pelopidas to Macedonia and Thessaly, 368 B.C.

Having thus brought Macedonia within the circle of the Theban supremacy, Pelopidas on his way home visited the camp of the tyrant of Pherae. But he did not know that Alexander had become the ally of Athens—an inevitable combination, since it was the interest of both to oppose Theban expansion in the north. Supported by Athens, the despot could defy Thebes, and he detained his visitor Pelopidas as a hostage. A Boeotian army marched to rescue the captive; but a contingent of 1000 men arrived by sea from Athens, and the invaders, who were commanded by incompetent generals, were out-manoeuvred and forced to retreat. Epaminondas was serving as a common hoplite in the ranks, and but for his presence the army would have been lost. The soldiers unanimously invited him to take the command, and he skilfully extricated them from a dangerous position and managed their safe retreat. This exploit secured the re-election of Epaminondas as Boeotarch, and he immediately returned to Thessaly at the head of another army to deliver his friend. It was necessary to apply a compulsion severe enough to frighten the tyrant, but not so violent as to transport him with fury, which might be fatal to his prisoner. This was achieved by dexterous military operations, and Pelopidas was released in return for a month's truce. It seems probable that at the same time Epaminondas freed Pharsalus from the rule of Pherae. But it was not the interest of Thebes to overthrow the tyrant or even limit his authority to his own city. It was well that he should be there, as a threat to the rest of Thessaly; it was well that Thessaly should be unable to dispense with Theban protection. The power of Alexander extended over Phthiotis and Magnesia, and along the shores of the Pagasaean Bay, and to neighbouring towns like Scotussa. His tyranny and brutality seem to have been extreme, though the anecdotes of his cruelty cannot be

Pelopidas detained by the despot of Pherae

Theban invasion of Thessaly to rescue Pelopidas, 368 B.C. (autumn), unsuccessful

Second invasion of Thessaly to rescue Pelopidas, 367 B.C. (first months), successful

implicitly trusted. We read that he buried men alive, or sewed them up in the hides of wild beasts for his hounds to tear. We read that he massacred the inhabitants of two friendly cities. We read that he worshipped as a divine being the dagger with which he had slain his uncle, and gave it the name of 'Sir Luck'—an anecdote indicating a strain of madness which often attends the taste for cruelty. Excellently invented, if not true, is the story that, having seen with dry eyes a performance of the *Troades* of Euripides, a drama unutterably sad, the tyrant sent an apology to the actor, explaining that his apparent want of emotion was due to no defect in the acting, but to a feeling of shame that tears for the sorrows of Hecuba should fall from the eyes of one who had shown no pity for so many victims.

Tychon

'What's Hecuba to him?'

It has been said that the chief desire of Athens at this time was to regain the finest jewel of her first empire, Amphipolis. The fleet, under Iphicrates, was cruising and watching, with this purpose in view; but the hopes of success—which depended much on the goodwill of Macedonia—were lessened by the ties which Ptolemy had contracted with Thebes. And, besides losing Macedonian support, Athens was impeded by the cities of the Chalcidian league, who now broke away from the Athenian alliance and made a treaty with Amphipolis.

Meanwhile Athens began to act in the eastern Aegean. The opportunity was furnished by the revolt of her friend Ariobarzanes, the satrap of Phrygia. It was the policy of Athens to help the satrap without breaking with the Great King, from whom she still hoped to obtain a recognition of her claim to Amphipolis. A fleet of 30 galleys and 8000 troops was sent under her other experienced general Timotheus, and he accomplished more in the east than Iphicrates had accomplished in the north. He laid siege to Samos, on which Persia had laid hands, contrary to the King's Peace, and took it at the end of ten months. At the same time he lent assistance to Ariobarzanes, who had to maintain himself against the satraps of Lydia and Caria; and as a reward for these services Athens obtained the cession of two cities in the Thracian Chersonese—Sestos and Crithote.

366 B.C. (367 B.C.)

Timotheus sent to Asia Minor, 366 B.C. He captures Samos, 365 B.C.

Of these acquisitions Sestos was of special value, from its position on the Hellespont, securing to Athens control at this point over the ships which supplied her with corn from the Euxine coasts. But more than this, she now regained a foothold in the peninsula which Miltiades had won for her, and she hoped to

Athens gets Sestos

make it entirely her own up to a line drawn across the isthmus north of Cardia, marked at one point by an altar of 'Zeus of Boundaries'. Timotheus himself began the work of expansion by annexing Elaeus near the southern extremity. Thus Athens began to revive her old empire, but in Samos she revealed her designs even more clearly. This island was not treated as a subject ally, but was appropriated as Athenian territory. Settlers were sent from Athens to occupy Samos, and thus the system of cleruchies, which had been the most unpopular feature of the first Confederacy and had been expressly guarded against at the formation of the second Confederacy, was renewed.[11] It did not indeed violate the letter of the constitution of the league, which only bound Athens not to force settlers upon members of the league; but it was distinctly a violation in spirit. The treatment of Samos showed Greece that Athens was bent on rising again to her old Imperial position, while the second Confederacy was based on the principle that she had renounced such pretensions for ever.

Delighted with the achievements of Timotheus, the Athenians appointed him to command the fleet which had been operating for years on the Macedonian coast under Iphicrates, whose failure was strikingly contrasted with the success of Timotheus. It must be remembered that while Iphicrates was hindered by the hostility of the regent of Macedon, Timotheus was helped by the friendship of the satrap of Phrygia; but Timotheus possessed a diplomatic dexterity which Iphicrates never displayed. And now fortune favoured the diplomatist. Shortly before his new appointment, the regent Ptolemy was assassinated by the young king Perdiccas, who thus avenged his brother Alexander. The change in the holders of power led to a change in policy. Macedonia freed itself from the influence of Thebes, and the young king sought the support of Athens. And so Timotheus, not only untrammelled by Macedonian opposition, but even aided by Macedonian auxiliaries, set about the reduction of towns around the Thermaic gulf.[12] He compelled Methone and Pydna to join the Athenian confederacy, and in the Chalcidic peninsula he made himself master of Potidaea and Torone. The acquisition of these Chalcidic towns was valuable in itself, and Potidaea was occupied by Athenian settlers; but the main purpose of the general was to weaken the resources of Olynthus, which, at the head of the Chalcidian states, gave powerful support to its ally Amphipolis,

Murder of the regent Ptolemy; Perdiccas in power, 365 B.C.

Successes of Timotheus in the Chalcidic region (364-2 B.C.)

the supreme objective coveted by Athens, whose rights to it had been recently recognised by the Persian king. A famous mercenary captain named Charidemus, who had previously served under Iphicrates, was now secured again by Timotheus; but two efforts to capture Amphipolis were repelled. The work of Brasidas was not destined to be undone.

It was high time for Thebes to interfere. If the successes of Timotheus were allowed to continue, Athens would soon recover Euboea, and the adhesion of that island was, from its geographical position, of the highest importance to Boeotia. But in order to check the advance of her neighbour it would be necessary for Thebes to grapple with her on her own element. By the advice of Epaminondas, in spite of the opposition of Meneclidas, it was resolved to create a navy and enter upon the career of a sea-power. This was a momentous decision, which demanded a careful consideration of ways and means. Given the problem, to break the power of Athens, there can be no question that Epaminondas advised the only possible method of solving it. But it might be well to consider whether its solution was a necessity for Thebes. The history of Boeotia had marked it out as a continental power, and it would have been wiser to consolidate its power on the mainland. The maintenance of a navy involved financial efforts which could not be sustained by any but a great commercial state, and the cities of Boeotia had little trade. It was the natural antipathy of the two neighbours, far more than any mature consideration of her own interests, that drove Boeotia to take this indiscreet step. Yet the step had immediate success. A hundred triremes were built and manned and sent to the Propontis under the Boeotarch Epaminondas.

Boeotian navy

364 B.C.

The sailing of this fleet was a blow to Athens, not from any victory that it gained—there was no battle—but from the support and encouragement which it gave to those members of the Confederacy which were eager to break their bonds. The establishment of the cleruchs on Samos had created great discontent and apprehension among the Athenian allies, and they wanted only the support of a power like Thebes to throw off the federal yoke. Byzantium openly rebelled; Rhodes and Chios negotiated with Epaminondas; and even Ceos, close to Attica itself, defied Athens.[13] When the Theban fleet returned home, Chabrias recalled Ceos to its allegiance, and a new treaty was drawn up; but a second rebellion had to be put down at Iulis before the island acquiesced in Athenian control. The expedition of Epami-

Revolts of Athenian allies. 364 B.C. Revolts of Ceos, 364 and 362 B.C.

nondas also served to support the enemies of Athens, who opposed her advance in the Chersonese—namely the free city of Cardia, and the Thracian King Cotys, who was aided by his son-in-law Iphicrates. This general, superseded by Timotheus, had not ventured to return to Athens, and now sided with her enemies.

Third expedition of Pelopidas to Thessaly, 364 B.C.

While the young Theban navy went forth to oppose Athens in the Propontis, a Theban army had marched against the ally of Athens, Alexander of Pherae, who, backed by a strong mercenary force, had pressed heavily on the Thessalians. Once more, but for the last time, Pelopidas entered Thessaly at the head of an army to assist the Federation. Before he left Thebes, the sun suffered an eclipse, and this celestial event, interpreted by the prophets as a sign of coming evil, cast a gloom over his departure.

Eclipse of the sun, July 13

Battle of Cynos-cephalae

At Pharsalus he was joined by forces of the Thessalian league, and immediately advanced against Pherae itself. Alexander came forth to meet him with a large force, and it was a matter of great importance, for the purpose of barring the Theban advance, to occupy the heights known as the Dog's Heads, on the road from Pharsalus to Pherae. The armies reached the critical spot nearly at the same time, and there was a rush for the crests. The Theban cavalry beat off the cavalry of the enemy, but lost time in pursuing it, and in the meantime the infantry of Alexander seized the hills. In the battle which followed the object of the Thebans was to drive the enemy from this position. Having been repeatedly repelled, Pelopidas, anticipating the tactics of Alexander, at length won the summit by a combined assault of horse and foot, and forced the enemy to give way. But in the moment of victory he sighted the hated despot who had kept him in prison and, yielding to an irresistible fit of passion, he forgot the duties of a general and rushed against his enemy. Alexander withdrew into the midst of his guards, and Pelopidas, plunging desperately after him, was overwhelmed by numbers. It was even so that Cyrus threw away his victory at Cunaxa. The death of Pelopidas was not fatal to his followers, who routed the enemy with heavy loss; but it was a sore blow to his own Thebes, of which he had been the deliverer and strong pillar, and to Thessaly, of which he had been the protector. In the following year an army was sent against Pherae and avenged his death. Alexander was obliged to relinquish all his possessions except his own city, and to submit to the hegemony of Thebes.

Death of Pelopidas

Pherae becomes a Boeotian dependency, 363 B.C.

It was about this time that Thebes shocked the Hellenic world by the destruction of her venerable rival, the Minyan Orchomenus. Some Theban exiles induced the horsemen of Orchomenus to join them in a plot to subvert the constitution. But the hearts of the principal conspirators failed them before the day of action came, they informed the Boeotarchs; the horsemen were promptly seized and condemned to death; and the Assembly passed a resolution to raze Orchomenus and enslave its people. The Thebans rejoiced at a fair pretext to satisfy the hatred of ages upon their unhappy neighbour. The men were slain because they resisted; the rest of the folk were enslaved. If the moderate and humane Boeotarch, who was then in the Hellespontine regions, had been present to control the counsels of his country, the crime would possibly never have been committed.

The destruction of Orchomenus, 364 B.C.

The Battle of Mantinea

While Thebes was intent on opposing Athens, now her only serious rival, she had kept aloof from the Peloponnese. But the course of affairs there was soon to demand a new intervention. The interest now centres on the relations of Elis with Arcadia; and the decisive element in the situation is the rift in the Arcadian league, perceptibly widening every month.

Her rights over Triphylia were the chief question of political importance for Elis. They had been recognised in the Persian rescript, but Arcadia refused to admit them and Thebes did not interfere. Thus Elis found herself in the same plight as Sparta in regard to the Arcadian league. It had always been a principle of Lacedaemonian policy to preserve against Elis the independence of her two southern neighbours, the Pisatans and the Triphylians. But now, for the sake of winning an ally, Sparta was only too ready to renounce this policy and recognise the Elean claim. It was in the nature of things that the two states should combine to recover Messenia and Triphylia. And so Sparta's prospect changed for the better: enemies had risen up against Arcadia on the north and on the west, and Thebes held aloof. The Spartans had recently gained a welcome success in the recovery of Sellasia, with the help of a force which had been sent to their aid by the second Dionysius of Syracuse.

The Triphylian question

Besides Triphylia there were certain places on the mountainous frontier between Elis and Arcadia to which Elis professed to have claims. One of these was Lasion, in the high plateau of

Outbreak of war between Elis and Arcadia, 365 B.C.

379

First Arcadian invasion of Elis, 365 B.C.

Pholoe, north-east of Olympia. The Eleans occupied the district, but were speedily driven out by the Pan-Arcadian *eparitoi*, who were always ready for such emergencies. The plains of Elis were far more assailable than the highlands of Arcadia, and the Arcadians were able to carry the war to the very heart of their foe. The Olympian festival would fall next year, and they were resolved that it should not be celebrated under the time-honoured presidency of Elis. They marched to Olympia, and occupied and fortified the Hill of Cronus, which looks down upon the Altis. Then they made an attack on the unwalled city of Elis, in concert with the democratic faction. But the attempt at a revolution failed and the Arcadians were repulsed. In the following year a second invasion reduced the Eleans to such distress that they implored Sparta to make a diversion and draw off the Arcadian forces. In answer to this prayer Archidamus occupied Cromnon, a fort which commands the road from Megalopolis to Messenia, with a garrison of 200 men. The importance of this step is shown by the fact that not only did the Arcadians promptly leave Elis, but they were also joined by allies, Argives as well as Messenians, to besiege Cromnon. A Spartan post there cut off the communication between the Arcadian and the Messenian capitals and was a threat to both. Archidamus at first tried to create a second diversion by ravaging northern Laconia, which was now politically part of Arcadia. When this failed, he made an attempt to relieve Cromnon but was driven back with some loss. A second attempt at rescue would have ben successful if it had been better concerted, but it led to the capture of almost the whole garrison—an event which ten years before would have sent a shock through the Hellenic world, but now seemed an ordinary occurrence.

Second Arcadian invasion, 364 B.C.

The Arcadians were again free to continue their designs in Elis. The time of the Olympian games was approaching, and the people of Pisa, the ancient possessors of the sanctuary, who had by no means forgotten the rights which Elis had usurped in days long gone by, were installed as presidents of the festival. It was fully expected that the feast would not pass without battle and bloodshed. The hill of Cronus had been occupied for a year by the Arcadian garrison, but now the whole army of the federation, as well as 2000 spearmen from Argos and 400 cavalry from Athens, arrived to protect the solemn celebration. The day came round and the games began. The horse race was run and won. The next contest

The Olympian games, 364 B.C., July, celebrated by the Pisatans (Ol. 104)

was the pentathlon, which demanded excellence in five different kinds of athletic prowess—in running, wrestling, hurling the javelin, throwing the disc, and leaping. The first event, the race, was over when the company became aware that the men of Elis were marching up to the bank of the Cladeus, which bounded the western side of the Altis. The soldiers took up their position on the opposite bank, but the games went on. Those competitors who had not failed in the race proceeded to the wrestling; but as the spectators, when the alarm was given, moved from the race-course into the Altis, to be nearer the scene of action, the wrestling match was held in the open space between the race-course and the Great Altar, under the terrace of the Treasure-houses. The Eleans, who were supported by an Achaean force, performed a sacrifice, and then, charging across the stream with unexpected boldness, drove back the Arcadian and Argive line into the Altis. A battle ensued in the southern part of the holy precinct, between the Hall of Council and the great Temple of Zeus. But the colonnades of these and other adjacent buildings gave shelter and points of vantage to the defenders; and the Eleans, when their captain fell, retired across the stream to their camp. The Arcadians improvised a fortification on the western side of the Altis, using for this purpose the tents of the spectators; and the men of Elis, seeing that it would be useless to repeat their attack, returned home, obliged to content themselves with declaring the festival to be null and void, and marking the year in their register as an 'An-Olympiad'. The religious sentiment of Greece was outraged by these violent scenes at a sanctuary which belonged to all Greece rather than to any single state; and there can be no question that the general sympathy—independently of all political considerations—was on the side of Elis, whose presidency was regarded in Hellas as part of the order of nature, and was strongly adverse to the Arcadian intruders supporting with arms the antiquated rights of Pisa. But it was far worse when the Arcadians began to make free use of the sacred treasures of Olympia, for the purpose of paying the federal army. This was an act of sacrilegious spoliation which could not be defended, and it was disastrous to the Arcadian Federation.

Battle in the Altis

Spoliation of the Olympian treasures

It was inevitable that, when the first impulse of enthusiasm which drove the Arcadian cities to unite together had spent itself, the old jealousies would emerge again and imperil the Pan-Arcadian idea. So it was that the two

Divisions in the Arcadian League

neighbours, Mantinea and Tegea, whose common action had been the chief cause of the federal union, began to resume something of their traditional enmity. The scandal of Olympia gave Mantinea, who was jealous of Megalopolis also, a fair opportunity to secede from the League, which had put itself so signally in the wrong. This step necessarily involved the consequence that Mantinea would definitely range herself with the other camp in the Peloponnese—with Sparta, Elis, and Achaea. And thus the traditional policies of Mantinea and Tegea were reversed. Tegea, the support of Sparta, had become the life and soul of the anti-Spartan movement; Mantinea, the state which Sparta had uncitied, was now Sparta's support. Though the Arcadian Assembly resented and tried to punish the protest of Mantinea, the pressure of public opinion induced it to forbid any further plundering of the Olympian sanctuaries.

When this resolution was taken, the weakness of the Arcadian League was exhibited. There was no money in the federal treasury to pay the standing army, and without this army it would be impossible for Arcadia to maintain herself against enemies on three sides—not to speak of disaffected Mantinea—without the protection of Thebes. But there was a strong feeling throughout the country against a Theban protectorate, and a large number of wealthy Arcadians who shared this feeling proposed to solve the difficulty by enrolling themselves in the corps of *Eparitoi* and serving without pay. Occupying this position, they would be able to dictate the policy of the League. There was little doubt that the predominance of this party would soon bring Arcadia into alliance with Sparta, which was no longer dangerous to Arcadian liberty. But such a political revolution would be fatal to Theban influence, which rested on the antagonism between Arcadia and Sparta; it might even imperil the independence of Messenia.

Fourth Theban invasion of the Peloponnese 362 B.C.

To meet this danger of an alliance between Sparta and Arcadia, Thebes was constrained to send a fourth expedition into the Peloponnese. It was imperative to support the Theban party in Arcadia. Both parties alike were probably satisfied with the resolution of the Assembly to make peace with Elis and acknowledge her rights at Olympia. Each city swore to the peace. At Tegea the solemnity of the oath led to an incident. Arcadians from other places had gathered together for the occasion, which they celebrated by feast and merriment. The commander of the Boeotian garrison ordered the gates to be shut, and

arrested the leaders of the anti-Theban party. Most of the Mantineans present had left the town at an early hour, but there were a few among the prisoners; and the energetic protests of Mantinea frightened the faint-hearted harmost into releasing all his prisoners and excusing his act by a false explanation. The *coup* had doubtless been planned long beforehand, and consent obtained from the highest quarter. Epaminondas, when complaint was made at Thebes, approved the act of arrest and condemned the act of release. At the same time he declared to the Arcadian League that it had no right to make peace with Elis without consulting Thebes. 'We will march into Arcadia,' he said, 'and assist our friends.'

The threat was seriously meant, and the friends and enemies of Thebes prepared for war. Athens, the ally of both Sparta and Arcadia, could now fulfil without difficulty the double obligation, by supporting those Arcadians who were on Sparta's side. The common dread of Thebes was reflected in the quintuple alliance which Athens (with her allies), Mantinea, Elis, Achaea, and Phlius formed for the sake of mutual protection. Part of the text of this treaty is preserved to us on fragments of one of the original marble copies.[14] It is worthy of remark that the Mantineans, who seem to have been the only Arcadian community that entirely dissociated itself from the government at Megalopolis, appear in the treaty as 'the Arcadians'—thus claiming to be the true representatives of their country.

The quintuple alliance, summer, 362 B.C.

The Boeotian force in its full strength, accompanied by all the allies of central Greece who were pledged to follow Thebes into the field, went forth under Epaminondas to bring back the unruly Peloponnesians under Boeotian control. The Phocians alone refused to go; the terms of the alliance which bound them to Boeotia obliged them to bear aid only if Boeotia were itself attacked.[15] When he reached Nemea, Epaminondas halted his army, in the hope of intercepting the forces which Athens prepared to send to her allies. But the Athenian forces did not come and he advanced to Tegea, the chief centre of Theban influence in the peninsula, which he had appointed as the meeting-place for all his allies—Arcadian, Argive, and Messenian. His enemies were also gathering to the rival city of Mantinea, and a Spartan army under old Agesilaus was expected there. Epaminondas marched to attack them before the Spartans and Athenians arrived, but found their position too strong and retired to his camp in Tegea. Learning that

March of Epaminondas to Sparta

Agesilaus had already set out, he determined to strike a second blow at Sparta. He would have found the place as unprotected as 'a nest of young birds' if his plan had not been thwarted by a Cretan runner who carried the news to Agesilaus. The king immediately returned on his steps; and when Epaminondas after a night's march reached Sparta, he found it prepared and defended. Baffled in this project by an incalculable chance, Epaminondas promptly resolved to attempt another surprise. He foresaw that the army at Mantinea would immediately march to the rescue of Sparta, and that Mantinea would consequently be inadequately guarded. His camp at Tegea commanded the direct road from Mantinea to Sparta, so the enemy would be obliged to march by the longer western road. Moving

He returns to Tegea

rapidly he reached Tegea, where he rested his hoplites, but he sent on his cavalry to surprise Mantinea. The army had departed, as he calculated, and the people were out in the fields, busy with the harvest. But in the same hour in which the Theban horse approached from the south, a body of Athenian cavalry had reached the city. They had not yet eaten or drunk, but they rode forth and drove the

Cavalry battle at Mantinea

assailants back. The conflict between the two weary troops of horsemen was sharp and was marked by the death of Gryllus, the son of Xenophon the historian.

The allied army, learning that Sparta was no longer in danger, soon returned from its fruitless excursion to its former post, now reinforced by both the Spartan and Athenian contingents. Foiled in his two projects of surprise, Epaminondas was obliged to attack the united enemy at Mantinea; the difficulty of supplying his army with provisions, and the anxiety of his allies to return home as soon as possible, rendered it imperative to bring the campaign to a swift decision. The enemy occupied the narrow part of the plain, south of Mantinea, where ridges of the opposite mountains approach each other. The object of Epaminondas was to sweep them out of his way and take the city but, instead of marching straight for the gap, he adopted a strategical movement which puzzled his antagonists. He led his army north-westwards to a point in the hills near the modern Tripolis, and then moved a short distance along the skirts of the mountain so as to approach the right wing of the foe. He then halted and formed in battle array. The enemy were deceived by the indirect advance. Seeing him march obliquely towards the hills, they concluded that he would not attack that day and, even when he changed his

direction and advanced towards them, they persisted in their false opinion.

Epaminondas adopted the same tactics by which he had won at Leuctra. On the left he placed the Boeotian hoplites, under his own immediate command, in a deep column, destined to break through the right wing of the enemy before the rest of the armies could come to blows. The oblique advance, besides its chief purpose of deceiving the enemy, had the further advantage of assisting the peculiar tactics of the general; for when he formed his line there was obviously a far greater distance between his right and the hostile left than that which divided his left from the hostile right. The Mantineans (since it was their territory) had the place of honour on the extremity of the enemy's right wing, and the Lacedaemonians were next to them; the Athenians were on the farthest left; and both wings were protected by squadrons of horse. Epaminondas placed his own cavalry in deep column in front of the deep column of infantry. But there was one danger against which he had to guard. When the Boeotian column charged, the Athenian left might wheel round and attack it on the unshielded side—a movement which could be executed owing to the distance dividing them from his own right. To meet this danger, he sent a body of horse and foot to occupy rising ground, out in the plain, considerably in advance of his line; this body could attack the Athenians in the rear if they tried such a movement.

Dispositions of Epaminondas

With an extraordinary lack of perception, the Lacedaemonians and their allies witnessed these manoeuvres without understanding their drift, and it was not until Epaminondas began to advance in full march against them that they realised his meaning and rushed tumultuously to arms. All fell out as he designed. His cavalry routed their cavalry, and the force of his wedge of hoplites, led by himself, broke through the opposing array and put the Lacedaemonians to flight. It is remarkable indeed how the tactical lesson of Leuctra seems to have been lost on the Spartans. The men of Achaea and Elis and the rest, when they saw the flight of the right wing, wavered before they came into collision with their own opponents. It is not quite clear what happened, but here again Mantinea seems to repeat Leuctra: the charge of the Theban left decided the battle; with the exception of cavalry engagements, there was but little and desultory fighting along the rest of the line.

It was a great Theban victory, and yet a chance determined that this victory should be

Death of Epaminondas

the deathblow to the supremacy of Thebes. As he pursued the retreating foe, at the head of his Thebans, Epaminondas received a mortal thrust from a spear. When the news spread through the field, the pursuit was stayed and the effect of the victory was undone; the troops fell back like beaten men. 'So striking a proof has hardly ever been rendered, on the part of soldiers towards their general, of devoted and absorbing sentiment. All the hopes of this army, composed of such diverse elements, were centred in Epaminondas; all their confidence of success, all their security against defeat, were derived from the idea of acting under his orders; all their power, even of striking down a defeated enemy, appeared to vanish when those orders were withdrawn.' And there was no one to take his place. In his dying moments, before the point of the fatal spear was extracted, Epaminondas asked for Iolaidas and Daiphantus, whom he destined as his successors. He was told that they were slain. 'Then,' he said, 'make peace with the enemy.' Peace was made on condition that things should remain as they were; Megalopolis and Messenia were recognised—the abiding results of Theban policy. In this peace Sparta would not acquiesce; she still persisted in refusing to recognise the independence of Messenia, but her allies would not listen to her protests. As Xenophon remarked: 'Greece was more unsettled and disturbed after the battle than before.'

The work of Epaminondas

The military genius of Epaminondas, the qualities of mind and character which distinguished him among his countrymen, and the actual work which he accomplished in the deliverance of Messenia and the support of Arcadia, must not be allowed to obscure the fact that his political faculty was mediocre. What could be done by the energy and ability of a general, or by the discretion of a magistrate, that he did; but he failed to solve the fundamental problems which demanded solution at the hands of a statesman who aimed at making his country great. It was necessary to create an efficient machinery, acting on definite principles, for conducting the foreign affairs of Boeotia—like the machinery which existed at Sparta. This was the only possible substitute for brains, which were not plentiful in Boeotia; Epaminondas could not hope to communicate any part of his own virtue to his successors. It was necessary to decide whether it was possible or desirable for Boeotia to enter into competition with Athens as a maritime power. If the decision were affirmative, it was of capital importance to organise the navy on a

sound financial foundation. There is no sign that Epaminondas grappled with the problems of government and finance; his voyage to the Propontis was an experiment which had no results. Nor does he seem to have taken steps to secure Boeotia on the side of her dangerous Phocian neighbours, though he had the insight to organise anew the Amphictionic League and make it an instrument of Theban policy. Above all, he did not succeed in accomplishing the first thing needful, the welding together of Boeotia into a real national unity. He aspired to expand Boeotia into an empire; the worst of it was that no one had come before him to make it into a nation. That which mythical Lycurgus and Theseus had done for Sparta and Athens had never been done for Thebes by any of her numerous heroes. Epaminondas seems to have attempted to unify Boeotia; if he had known how to build such an unity on solid foundations, he might have bestowed on Thebes a future of glory which he would not have lived to see. But his ambition—for his country, not for himself—was too impatient and imaginative. The ardour of his patriotism drove him to enter upon paths of policy which his countrymen felt no compelling impulse to pursue; the successes of Thebes were achieved by his brains, not by her force. He bore his country aloft on the wings of his genius, but did not impart to her frame the principle of that soaring motion; so that when the shaft pierced the heart of her sustainer, she sank to the earth, never to rise again. Epaminondas was a great general; he was not a great statesman.

The Last Expedition of Agesilaus

To no one in Greece can the supremacy of Thebes have come as a sorer trial than to the Spartan king Agesilaus. He who had once dreamed of conquering Persia had lived to see his own inviolable land twice trodden by an invader, his own city quake twice before an enemy at her doors. But he had at least the consolation of outliving the triumph of the Theban and seeing the brief supremacy pass away. The death of Epaminondas of which he could not mistake the significance did not restore Messenia or give Sparta any immediate power; but with Epaminondas dead and Arcadia spent, Sparta had now a prospect of regaining something of her old influence. With her own diminished population she could do little; it would be necessary to follow the general example and take mercenary forces

Sparta in want of money

into her pay; but to do this a well-filled treasury was needed. Accordingly we find Sparta, as well as Athens, busy beyond the sea, taking part in the troubles which in these years agitated the western portion of the Persian kingdom, and lending help to the satraps and dynasts who were rebelling against the Great King. The object of Athens was territory, the object of Sparta was money.

365 B.C.

While Timotheus had been engaged in winning Samos, Agesilaus had visited Asia Minor and done his utmost in support of Ariobarzanes —for the sake of gold. And after the battle of Mantinea, he again went forth in a guise which differed little from that of a mercenary in foreign service.

The revolt in the Persian empire

The borders of Western Asia, from the Hellespont to the Nile, were in revolt against the Great King. The expedition of Cyrus was only the first of a series of rebellions which troubled the reign of Artaxerxes. We have seen how Cyprus rebelled and was subjugated, but Egypt still defied the Persian power, and its success set a bad example to the satraps of the adjoining countries. The Athenian general Chabrias had helped the Egyptians to strengthen their country by a scientific system of defences, but he was recalled to Athens after the King's Peace; and the Athenian

373 B.C.

whom we next find in Egypt is fighting on the other side—the freelance Iphicrates, giving sound military advice to the Persian commander, which the Persian commander does not follow. Soon after this the satraps of Asia began to rebel—first in Cappadocia, then in Phrygia, then successively in Ionia, Caria, and Lydia—and the insurrection extended to Phoenicia and Syria. A scheme of co-operation was formed between the satraps and the Egyptian king Tachos, who had recently come to the throne, and Sparta decided to support this coalition. Athens held aloof, but Chabrias went once more to Egypt as a volunteer.[16]

Agesilaus in Egypt, 361 B.C.

At the head of 1000 men, and accompanied by 30 Spartans as advisers, Agesilaus set sail for the Nile. It is said that the small figure, the lame leg, and the plain dress of the experienced old soldier made a bad impression in Egypt; in any case he was not given the supreme command of the army as he expected. When a sufficient force was gathered, Tachos,

accompanied by Agesilaus and Chabrias, made an expedition to Phoenicia, to act there against the Persian troops; but they were obliged to return almost immediately in consequence of a revolt against Tachos, headed by his cousin Nektanebos. The Spartan king, who considered that he had been slighted by Tachos, supported the rival; and Tachos fled to Susa and made his peace with the Persian monarch. Another competitor then arose but was defeated by the effective support which Agesilaus gave to Nektanebos. In consequence of these struggles for the Egyptian throne nothing was done against Persia, and the great coalition signally failed. Ariobarzanes of Phrygia, the friend of Timotheus, was betrayed and crucified; another satrap was murdered; the rest made their submission to their king. By 358 Western Asia was entirely subject to Artaxerxes.

But Sparta had won from the futile project what she really wanted. She might shelter her dignity under the pretext that she had gone forth to punish the Persian king for recognising the independence of Messenia, but every one knew that her motive was to replenish her treasury. Nektanebos presented her with 230 talents, in return for the support of Agesilaus. It was the last service the old king was destined to perform for his country. Death carried him off—he was eighty-four years old—at the Harbour of Menelaus on the way to Cyrene, and his embalmed body was sent home to Sparta.

Death of Agesilaus, winter, 361-0 B.C. (?)

Though not in any case a great man, though not in the same rank as Lysander, Agesilaus had been for forty years a prominent figure in Greece. There is something melancholy about his career. He could remember the outbreak of the Peloponnesian War; he had seen the triumph of Sparta, and had conducted her policy during a great part of thirty years of supremacy; and then, as an old man, he shared in her humiliation. He had begun by dreaming of the conquest of Persia; he had been forced to abandon such dreams; and he had translated his ardour into a bitter hatred against a Greek city. It is tragic to see him, at the age of eighty-three, going forth against Persia once more, not now for conquest or glory, but to earn by any and every means the money needed by his indigent country.

CHAPTER 15

The Syracusan Empire and the Struggle with Carthage

We have seen how the war in Greece, in its last stage, after the collapse of the Sicilian expedition, ceased to be a mere domestic struggle among Greek states and became part of the greater struggle between Greek and barbarian. We have now to see how the strife of Greek and barbarian was renewed at the same moment in the west. It is indeed remarkable how these two episodes in the great conflict between Asia and Europe run parallel though separate courses in the fifth century. The victory of Himera, which beat back the Carthaginian invader from Sicily, was won in the same year which saw the repulse of the Persian invader from Greece. After these triumphs of Hellas, both Persia and Carthage had long lain quiescent, and left the Greek cities of east and west to live undisturbed at war or in peace among themselves. It was not till the greatest city of eastern and the greatest city of western Hellas came to blows and wore one another out in the conflict, that the barbarians, discerning the propitious hour, once more made their voices heard in the Greek world. Sicily with an exhausted Syracuse, the Aegean with an exhausted Athens, invited Carthage and Persia alike to make an attempt to enlarge their borders at the expense of the Greek.

Carthaginian Destruction of Selinus and Himera

After Syracuse had achieved the repulse and utter confusion of Athens, it might have seemed likely that she would succeed in founding a Sicilian empire. Her first task would be to reduce Catane and Naxos; and, when this was done, the other cities, including luxurious Acragas, would hardly be able to resist. This prospect was disappointed by the intervention of a foreign enemy. But though the victory of Syracuse over Athens did not lead to a Syracusan empire, as the victory of Athens over Persia had led to an Athenian empire, it was followed, as in the case of Athens, by a further advance in the development of democracy. Had Hermocrates remained at Syracuse, in possession of his old influence, a change in this direction would hardly have been made. But he was appointed to command the auxiliary fleet which Syracuse sent to Sparta's help in the Aegean, and when he had gone the democratic mood of the citizens, excited by their recent efforts, vented itself in a decree pronouncing the deposition and banishment of Hermocrates. This was the work of his political opponent Diocles, who was a thoroughgoing democrat. Diocles bore the same name as a far earlier lawgiver—belonging to the same class and age as Charondas and Zaleucus—who had drawn up the laws on which the Syracusan constitution rested. The accidental identity of name led in subsequent ages to a confusion, and we find later writers ascribing to the democratic reformer who rose into prominence now the legislation of his ancient namesake. In his popular innovations Diocles borrowed ideas from the enemy whom his country had just overthrown. The Athenian use of lot in the appointment of magistrates was adopted. Hitherto the generals were also the presidents of the sovereign assembly, and had the unrestricted power of dismissing it at discretion. Diocles seems to have taken away this political function from the generals and assigned the presidency of the assembly to the new magistrates, but with much smaller powers. The presidents, as we shall presently see, were able only to fine a speaker who was out of order; they could not silence him or break up the assembly.

Such was the position of the greatest Sicilian city—a full-blown democracy, but without her chief citizen to whom above all others she owed the deliverance from her danger—when the island was exposed for the second time to a Carthaginian invasion. The occasion of the war was the same which had brought about the Athenian invasion—the feud between Selinus and Segesta concerning some fields on their common frontier. In both cases, the dispute of these towns was a pretext, not the deeper cause. As Athens thought that the time had come for extending her empire in the west, so Carthage decided that the day had dawned for asserting anew her power in Sicily; and there were those who had not let fade the memory of the humiliation endured at Himera seventy years before and longed to take a late revenge.

Segesta, with no Athens to protect her now, ceded the disputed lands; but Selinus went on to make further demands, and the Elymian city appealed to Carthage. One of the two shophets or judges in that republic was Hannibal, the grandson of Hamilcar, who had been slain at Himera. The desire for vengeance, long deferred, dominated Hannibal, now almost an old man; and his influence persuaded the Senate to accept Segesta's offer to become a Carthaginian dependency in return for Carthaginian help. A grand expedition was fitted out, and Hannibal was named commander. Sixty warships were got ready, with a large convoy of transports and strong forces of foot and horse.[1] The fleet was not intended

to take a part in the offensive warfare; it was stationed at Motya to be a protection for Phoenician Sicily and a security in case of a reverse. The army landed at Lilybaeum and marched straight to Selinus. This city had never been besieged before within the memory of its folk; immunity had made it secure and the fortifications had been neglected. For more than two generations the Selinuntines had been building a temple of vast proportions to

Apollo, or perhaps Olympian Zeus, when they were brought face to face with the sudden danger from Carthage. The house of the god was never completed; of the 'pillars of the giants' which were to support the massive roof, some stand in their places on the eastern hill, but the great drums and the capitals of others must be looked for some miles away, in the quarries from which they were hewn, left there when the Carthaginian destroyer came.[2] There was no time to repair adequately the walls of the acropolis, on the central hill. Hannibal surrounded it and a breach was soon made; but the place was not in the enemy's hands for nine days, owing to the stubborn resistance which the inhabitants were able to offer in the narrow streets. The Siceliot sister cities were not prompt in aid; Syracuse promised to come to the rescue, and sent a force under Diocles, which arrived too late. Selinus was the first Siceliot city which was stormed and sacked by the barbarian; she was not to be the last. The people were slaughtered without mercy; only some women and children who took refuge in the temples were spared (not from any respect of the holy places) and carried into bondage. Those who escaped from the sack fled to Acragas. Thus Selinus fell, after a brief life of two centuries and a half.

Hannibal had now done the work which Carthage had given him to do; but he had still to do the work which he had imposed upon himself. His real motive, in undertaking the public duty of the Selinuntine war, was to carry out the private duty of avenging his ancestor. Against Selinus he had no personal grudge, and there he did not carry the work of destruction further than military considerations required. The buildings on the western hill, where he had pitched his camp, suffered much, but the injuries sustained by the temples on the acropolis and on the eastern hill are due, not to Hannibal's army, but to the earthquakes of later ages. It was to be different in the case of the city which he now turned to attack. At Selinus, Hannibal was merely the general of Carthage; at Himera, he was the grandson of Hamilcar.

Hannibal planned to capture Himera by his land forces alone; and in this absence of a Carthaginian fleet Hannibal's siege of Himera differs from Hamilcar's. The Greeks of Sicily were now bestirring themselves; the terrible fate of one of their chief cities had aroused them to a sense of their peril. The naval power which was supporting Sparta in the Aegean had been long ago recalled; and a force of 5000, including 3000 Syracusans, under

Diocles, came to the relief of Himera. This city had time to prepare for the danger which she must have foreseen. But the besiegers, by means of mines, opened a breach in the wall and, although they were repelled and the defenders made a successful sally, the prospects of Himera looked black, when the fleet of 25 ships, which had returned from the Aegean, appeared in front of the city. Hannibal saved the situation by a stratagem. He spread abroad a report that he intended to march on Syracuse and take it unprepared. Diocles, thoroughly deceived, decided to return home and carry off the citizens of Himera, leaving the empty town to its fate. He induced half the population to embark in the ships, which, as soon as they had set the passengers in safety at Messana, were to return for the rest. Diocles and his army departed in haste, not even waiting to ask Hannibal for the dead bodies of those who had fallen in fight outside the walls; and for this neglect he was greatly blamed. When Hannibal saw that half his prey had escaped him, he pressed the siege more vehemently, determined to force an entry before the ships returned. On the third day, *Third day of the siege* the returning vessels were sighted by the Himeraeans. It seemed that Hannibal was to be baulked of his revenge. But before the ships could reach the harbour, the Spanish troops of Hannibal burst through the breach, and the town was in the hands of the avenger. On the spot where Hamilcar, according to the story, had offered up his life to the gods of his country, a solemn rite was held; 3000 men, who had survived the first indiscriminate slaughter, were sacrificed with torture to appease his shade. Himera, the offending city, was swept utterly out of the world and its place knew it no more.

Having thus accomplished his duty to his country and his gods, Hannibal returned triumphant to Africa. The position which Carthage won in Sicily by this year's work, and her new policy of activity there, are reflected in the coinage of Segesta and Panormus. The transformation of Segesta into a Carthaginian dependency was displayed by the fact that she ceased to coin her own money. But Carthage also showed that she intended to keep a firmer hand on her Phoenician dependencies. These cities had hitherto paid homage to Hellenic influences by adopting a coinage of *New coinage at Panormus with mysterious legend— Ziz* Hellenic character, with Hellenic inscriptions. This coinage now comes to an end at Panormus, and is replaced by a coinage, of Greek type indeed, but with a Phoenician legend—the word *Ziz*. The change seems to have been

made just before the invasion, and it was significant of an anti-Greek movement. But the curious thing is that Himera—the city which was to be one of the first victims of the new policy heralded in this numismatic reform—abandoned her old coinage with the cock, and struck a new coinage with a seahorse, on the Punic model of Panormus. Are *Change in Himera's coinage* we to suppose that Himera, aware of the peril which menaced her, thought to avert it by a timely approach of friendship to her Phoenician neighbour, and that this coinage was part of a policy of Punicism, intended to be only temporary?

Syracuse, although she had sought to do something for Selinus and had done something for Himera, felt no call to come forward as a champion against the new aggressive policy of Carthage. It was reserved for one of her citizens to attempt on his private responsibility the warfare which she declined to undertake against the Phoenician foe. The exile Hermocrates returned to Sicily, enriched by the gifts of the satrap Pharnabazus. His own city *Return of Hermocrates, 408 B.C.* refused to withdraw the sentence of banishment, for a man of his views and abilities seemed dangerous to the democratic constitution. Hermocrates then resolved to earn his recall by performing conspicuous services to the Hellenic cause in Sicily—by winning back the Greek territory which the Phoenician had taken, by carrying Greek arms into Phoenician territory itself. He had built five triremes, he *His warfare against the Phoenician cities. Selinus reoccupied* had hired 1000 mercenaries, and he was joined by 1000 Himeraean fugitives. With these he marched to the spot where Selinus had once been, and made the place a centre for a 'crusade' against the Phoenician. He repaired the fortifications of the acropolis on the central hill; and the remains of the well-built wall betray, by the capitals of columns used in the building, the circumstances of its erection. The adventure prospered; the band of Hermocrates soon increased to 6000, and he was able to devastate the lands of Motya and Panormus and to drive back the forces which came out to meet him. In the same way he ravaged the territory of Solus and the now Carthaginian Segesta. These successes of Hermocrates were of greater significance than the actual injury dealt to the enemy. He had done what had not been done before since the days of Dorieus: he had broken into the precincts of Phoenician Sicily, and set an example to many subsequent leaders.

Hermocrates was bent above all things on *Hermocrates at Himera. 407 B.C.:* regaining his own country. Diocles and his political opponents were still powerful in the city and able to hinder the revulsion of feeling which his successes caused from having any practical effect. Accordingly he made another attempt to soften the hearts of his fellow-citizens. It was a well-calculated move. He marched to the ruins of Himera, collected the unburied bones of the soldiers of Diocles which Diocles had neglected, and sent them on waggons to Syracuse, himself remaining as an exile outside the Syracusan borders. He hoped to awaken the religious sentiment of the citizens in his own favour and at the same time to turn it against his rival. The bones were received and Diocles was banished; but Hermocrates was not recalled. Having failed to secure his restoration by persuasion, the exile resolved to achieve it by force, and he was encouraged by his numerous partisans in Syracuse. He was admitted with a small band at the gate of Achradina, and posted himself in the adjacent agora waiting for the rest of his forces to arrive. But they tarried too long; the people, learning that Hermocrates was in the city, rushed to the market-place; the small band was soon overcome and Hermocrates was slain. The Syracusans in these days were inspired with an instinctive rather than well-founded dread of tyranny, and this dread was stronger than admiration for Hermocrates. Their instinct was right: tyranny was approaching, but *he* was not the man. They little guessed that their future master was an obscure follower of Hermocrates, who was wounded that day in the agora and left for dead.

Carthaginian Conquest of Acragas

The private warfare of Hermocrates in western Sicily had naturally provoked the anger of the Carthaginians. Embassies passed between Carthage and Syracuse, Carthage regarding Syracuse as answerable for the acts of a Syracusan. But diplomacy was merely a matter of form; the African republic had resolved to make all Greek Sicily subject to her rule. She made ready another great expedition—as great as if not greater than that which had been sent against Selinus; and at the same time she took the novel step of founding a colony on Sicilian soil. If Hermocrates had lived, Himera might have been partially restored like Selinus; but the destroyers of Himera now founded a city in the neighbourhood which was to take Himera's place. On the hill above the 'hot baths of the Nymphs', whereof Pindar sings, the Carthaginian colonists built their town. But it was not destined to retain its Phoenician character. The Greeks who were admitted to dwell in it transformed it before long into a Greek city; the *Thermae* of Himera preserved the memories of Himera, and the people were known as Thermites or Himeraeans indifferently.

Acragas, the city which faces Carthage, was the first object of attack to the invaders who now came to conquer and enslave all Greek Sicily. Since her defeat by Syracuse in 445, Acragas had held aloof from all struggles in the island and was now at the height of her prosperity. But she was enervated by peace and luxury, and when the day of trial came she was found wanting. How far her citizens were prepared to endure the hardships of military life may be inferred from the law—passed with a view to the present peril—that none of the men in the watch-towers should have more than a mattress, two pillows, and a quilt. Such were the austerities of the men of Acragas. But at least they paid homage to the different discipline of Sparta. They invited Dexippus, a Spartan who was then at Gela, to undertake the conduct of the defence. A body of Campanian mercenaries was hired; and they could rely on the assistance of their old rivals the Syracusans, as well as of the other Greek cities, who were fully conscious that the peril of Acragas was their own. And Acragas herself behaved well. Notwithstanding her habits of ease, and her old practice of holding aloof, she refused the tempting offer of the invader that she should now purchase immunity by remaining neutral. She was true to her own race; she might remain indifferent when it was a struggle between Dorian and Ionian, but it was another case when the whole of Sicilian Hellas was threatened by the Phoenician.

The army of Carthage was again under the command of Hannibal, who felt that he was too old for the work, and was assisted by his cousin Himilco. Fragments of an Athenian decree show that the Carthaginians sent envoys to Athens at this time, a most unexpected development; but the Athenians were much too pre-occupied with their own troubles to intervene again in Sicily.[3] Hannibal pitched his main camp on the right bank of the river Hypsas, south-west of the city, and stationed some forces in another small camp on the eastern hill, beyond the river Acragas, to act against Greek aid coming from the east. The point of attack was the part of the western wall close to the chief western gate. But the ground, though lower here, was still difficult

he sends the bones of the dead to Syracuse;

he breaks into Syracuse and is slain

(Dionysius)

Foundation of Carthaginian colony at Thermae, 407 B.C.

(Termini)

Preparations of Acragas

406 B.C.

Siege of Acragas

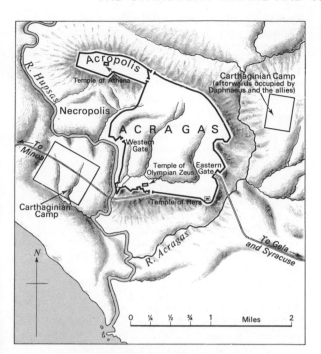

29.   THE SIEGE OF ACRAGAS

The causeway

for a besieger, and Hannibal determined to raise an immense causeway from which the wall could be more effectively attacked. The tombs of the neighbouring necropolis supplied stones for the work; but, as the tomb of Theron was being broken down, it was shaken by a thunderbolt, and the seers advised that it must be spared. Then a pestilence broke out in the Carthaginian camp and carried off Hannibal himself. It seemed that the gods were wroth and demanded a victim; Himilco lit the fires of Moloch and sacrificed a boy. The causeway was then completed, but no further injury was done to the sepulchres.

Plague Death of Hannibal

Relief army arrives

An army was already on its way to the relief of Acragas—30,000 foot and 5000 horse from Syracuse, Gela, and Camarina. When they approached the city they were met by the forces which had been placed for this purpose on the eastern hill; a battle was fought, a victory gained, and the Greek army took possession of the lesser Carthaginian camp. Meanwhile the routed barbarians fled for refuge to the main camp, and their flight lay along the road beneath the southern wall of the city. There was a general cry to sally forth and cut them off, but the generals refused. The moment was lost; but presently the people, yielding to an impulse which the

generals could not resist, went forth from the eastern gates to meet their victorious allies. A strange scene followed. A tumultuous assembly was held outside the walls; the Acragantine commanders were accused of failing in their duty, and when they tried to defend themselves the fury of the people burst out and four generals were stoned to death. The direction of the defence seems now to have been shared by Dexippus within the city and Daphnaeus, the commander of the Syracusan troops, without. Though the hostile camp was too strong to be attacked, the prospect looked favourable for Acragas. The Punic army, diminished though it had been by the plague, suffered acutely from lack of supplies, and it seemed certain that hunger and mutinous soldiers would soon force Himilco to raise the siege. But he learned that provision-ships were coming from Syracuse to Acragas; he sent in haste for the Carthaginian vessels at Panormus and Motya, put out to sea with 40 triremes, and intercepted the supplies. This not only saved his own position, but even reversed the situation. The besieged city now began to suffer from scarcity of food, and as soon as supplies began to run short, the weak point in the position of the Acragantines was displayed. They had found it necessary to rely on mercenaries, and hired men were not likely to serve long when rations ran short: the Campanians were easily induced to transfer their services from Acragas to Carthage. But this was not all. It was commonly believed that Dexippus—incapable, like most Spartans abroad, of resisting a bribe—received 15 talents from Himilco and induced the Italiot and Siceliot allies to desert Acragas as a sinking ship. But whatever the conduct of Dexippus may have been, the discredit of this desertion cannot rest entirely with him.

Acragantines murder their generals

Mercenaries and allies desert Acragas

The defence, which had been maintained for eight months with foreign aid, was now left to the men of Acragas alone. They showed at once that they were shaped of different stuff from the men of Selinus. Overcome with despair, they resolved to save their lives and abandon their city and their gods. Such a resolution, taken by the people of a great city, is unique in Greek history. It did not befit the men who had rejected the overtures of Hannibal, but it was what we might expect from the men who murdered their generals. They marched forth at night, men, women, and children, without let or hindrance from the enemy. The old and sick could not set out on the long journey to Gela, the place of refuge, and were left behind; some too re-

Flight of the Acragantines

mained who chose to perish at Acragas rather than live in another place. The army of Himilco entered the city in the morning and sacked it, slaying all whom they found, and despoiling and burning the temples. The great house of Olympian Zeus—the largest Greek temple in Europe—was still unfinished, and the sack of Himilco decided that it should never be completed. But Acragas was not to be destroyed like Selinus; it was intended to be a Carthaginian city in a Carthaginian Sicily. Himilco made the place his winter quarters; Gela would be the next object of his attack, when the spring came round.

406-5 B.C.

Rise of Dionysius

For the catastrophe of Acragas the chief blame was laid upon the Syracusan generals, who deserted her in the critical hour. The Acragantines were not slow to make them responsible for their own unheroic flight. At Syracuse itself there was a feeling that these generals were hardly the men to meet the great crisis in which Sicily now stood, and there was one man who saw in the crisis the opportunity of his own ambition. It was Dionysius, a man of obscure birth, who had been a clerk in a public office. He had been a partisan of Hermocrates, by whose side he had stood in the last fatal fray and had been wounded and left for dead. Recently he had marked himself out by his energy and bravery before the walls of Acragas. He saw the incompetence of the democratic government of his city; he saw that in the present peril it might be overthrown, and he determined to overthrow it. An assembly was held to consider the situation. Dionysius arose and in a violent harangue accused the generals of treachery. His language was intended to stir up the hearers to fury; he called upon the people to rise up themselves and destroy the traitors without trial. His violence transgressed the constitutional rules of the assembly, but the presidents had no power to bridle him; they imposed a fine—the only resource they had—but a wealthy friend, Philistus the historian, came forward and paid the fine, bidding the speaker go on, for as often as a fine was imposed he would pay it. Dionysius carried his point. The generals were deposed, and a new board was appointed, of which Dionysius was one. This was only the first step on the road which was to lead to the *tyrannis*. His next success was to procure the recall of the partisans of Hermocrates who had been condemned to exile; these old comrades

Dionysius:

comes forward for the first time; his violent speech

Philistus the historian. The despot's progress: (1) Dionysius general;

might be useful to him in his designs. At the same time he sought to discredit his colleagues; he kept entirely apart from them and spread reports that they were disloyal to Syracuse. Presently he openly accused them, and the people elected him sole general with sovereign powers to meet the instant danger. This office, held before, as we have reason to think, by Gelon and Hieron, did not set him above the laws; nor was the office illegal, though extraordinary it may be compared to the Roman dictatorship. But it was the second step to the tyranny. The next step, as history taught him —the story of Pisistratus, for instance—was to procure a bodyguard. The Assembly at Syracuse, which had perhaps begun to repent already of having placed so much power in the hands of one man, would certainly not have granted such an instrument of tyranny. But Dionysius was ingenious; he saw that the thing might be done elsewhere. He ordered the Syracusan army to march to Leontini, which, it will be remembered, was now a Syracusan dependency. He encamped near the town, and during the night a rumour was spread abroad that the general's life had been attempted and he had been compelled to seek refuge in the acropolis. An assembly was held next day, nominally an assembly of Syracusan citizens, which, when Dionysius laid bare the designs of his enemies, voted him a bodyguard of 600; this he soon increased to 1000; and he had won over the mercenaries to his cause.

(2) Dionysius στρατηγὸς αὐτοκράτωρ;

(3) gets a bodyguard

These were the three steps in the 'despot's progress' which rendered Dionysius lord and master of Syracuse: his intrigues had won him first a generalship, then sole generalship with unlimited military powers, and finally a bodyguard. Syracuse, unwilling and embarrassed, submitted with evident chagrin, but was dominated by the double dread of the mercenaries and the Carthaginians. The democracy of course was not formally overthrown; Dionysius held no office that upset the constitution. Things went on as at Athens under Pisistratus: the Assembly met and passed decrees and elected magistrates.

Democratic constitution formally continues

The justification of the power of Dionysius lay in the need of an able champion to oppose Carthage, and his partisans represented him as a second Gelon. But though Dionysius was in later years to prove himself among the chief champions of Hellenic Sicily against the Punic power, his conduct at this crisis did not fulfil the hopes of those who thought to compare him with the hero of Himera. The Carthaginians were already encamped at Gela. Their first act was to remove a colossal bronze

Siege of Gela, 405 B.C.

390

statue of Apollo which stood, looking over the sea, on the hill to the west of the city. The Geloans defended their walls with courage and zeal, and when Dionysius arrived with a large army of Italiots and Siceliots and a fleet of 50 ships to co-operate, it seemed as if Gela would escape the doom of Acragas. An excellent plan was arranged for a combined attack on the Carthaginian camp, which lay on the west side of the town. The plan failed, because the concert was not accurately carried out. The Siceliots who were to assault the eastern side of the camp arrived late on the spot and found the enemy, who had already repelled the attack of the Italiots and the fleet on the southern and western sides, free to meet them in force. This hitch in the execution of the plan was hardly a mere blunder. Dionysius with his mercenaries had undertaken to issue from the western gate of Gela and drive away the besiegers, while the rest of his army were attacking the camp. It seems, however, that Dionysius took no part in the fighting, and alleged that he was retarded by difficulties in crossing the town from the eastern to the western gate. We shall probably do no injustice to Dionysius if we conclude that it was through his dispositions that the Siceliots failed to act in concert with the Italiots. The action which he took after the defeat shows that he was half-hearted in the work. He decided in a private council, as Diocles had decided at Himera, that the defence must be abandoned and the whole people of Gela removed. At the first watch of the night he sent the multitude forth from the city, and followed himself at midnight. His way to Syracuse led by Camarina, and here too Dionysius ruled that the whole people must forsake their home. The road to Syracuse was full of the crowds of helpless fugitives from the two cities.

It was generally thought that these strange proceedings of Dionysius were carried out in collusion with the barbarians; that he had deliberately betrayed to them Gela, which might have been defended, Camarina, which had not yet been attacked. The Italiot allies showed not their disgust only, but their apprehension that the war was practically over, by marching immediately home. The horsemen of Syracuse seized the occasion for a desperate attempt to subvert the new tyrant. They rode rapidly to the city, plundered the house of Dionysius, and maltreated his wife although she was the daughter of Hermocrates. When Dionysius heard the news, he hastened to Syracuse with a small force. He reached the gate of Achradina by night and, being refused

Plan of concerted attack; its failure

Strange conduct of Dionysius

Gela and Camarina evacuated

Suspicions of good faith of Dionysius

Revolt of the horsemen,

admittance, burned it down with a fire of reeds supplied by the neighbouring marsh. In the market-place he easily overmastered a handful of opponents; the remnant fled to Etna, which now became, 'in a better cause, what Eleusis was to Athens after the overthrow of the Thirty'.

put down by Dionysius Etna

In what concerns the charge that the Syracusan tyrant had a secret understanding with Carthage, there is a strong case against him; the events are scarcely intelligible on any other view. But it was no more than a temporary disloyalty to the cause of Hellas and Europe, for which he was hereafter to do great feats. His first motive was the selfish motive of a tyrant. He wanted time to lay stable foundations for his still precarious power at Syracuse; and he judged that it would be a strong support to obtain a recognition of his power from the Carthaginian republic. The Punicism of the lord of Syracuse was not more unscrupulous than the Medism of the ephors of Sparta, to which it is the western parallel.

Policy of Dionysius

The treaty, which was now agreed upon between Himilco and Dionysius, was drawn up on the basis of *uti possidetis*. Each party retained what it actually held at the time. Syracuse acknowledged Carthage as mistress of all the Greek states on the northern and southern coasts, and also of the Sican communities. Acragas, what was left of Selinus, Gela, and Camarina, were all to be henceforward under Carthaginian control; and, on the north coast, Carthage had advanced her frontier to include the territory of Himera in which she had planted her first colony. But not all these cities were to hold the same relation to their mistress. Acragas and Selinus, like Thermae, were subjects in the full sense of the word, but Gela and Camarina were to be only tributary and unwalled cities. The Elymian towns are not mentioned, but we have seen how Segesta became a subject of Carthage by her own act, and we can hardly doubt that Eryx was forced into the same condition.

The treaty between Carthage and Dionysius, 405 B.C.

Carthaginian Sicily:

subjects and tributaries

The terms of the treaty provided for the independence of the Sicel communities and of the city of Messana. But it provided also for the independence of Leontini, and this was a point in which it departed from the basis *uti possidetis,* Leontini being a dependency of Syracuse. It was clearly a provision extorted from Dionysius, and intended by Himilco to be a source of embarrassment to Syracuse. On the other hand, as a counter-concession, nothing was said about the dependence of Naxos or Catane, so that Syracuse might have

Independent states: position of Leontini

a free hand to deal with her old enemies, without fear of violating the treaty. Such was the new arrangement of the map of Sicily at the end of the second Carthaginian invasion. An accidental consequence of that invasion had been to establish Dionysius as tyrant of Syracuse. This consequence enabled Himilco to bring his work to a conclusion more easily and quickly than he had hoped; he could not foresee that the undoing of his work would be the ultimate result. The Carthaginians guaranteed to maintain the rule of Dionysius, who was soon to prove one of their most powerful foes. For Dionysius this guarantee, 'the Syracusans shall be subject to Dionysius', was the most important clause in the treaty—some suppose that it was a secret clause. It was for the sake of this recognition and the implied promise of support that he stooped to betray Sicilian Hellas. We shall see how he redeemed this unscrupulous act of expediency by creating the most powerful Hellenic state in the Europe of his day.

Clause of guarantee

First Years of Dionysius

For half a century after the fall of Athens it seemed likely that the destinies of Europe would be decided by a Greek city in the western Mediterranean. Under her new lord Dionysius, Syracuse had become a great power, a greater power than any that had yet arisen in Europe. In strength and dominion, in influence and promise, she outstripped all the cities of the mother-country; and, in a general survey of the Mediterranean coasts, she stands out clearly as the leading European power. The Greek states to which the Persian King sent down his Peace were now flanked on either side by two great powers, and a political prophet might have been tempted to foretell that the communities of old Greece were doomed to perish between the monarchies of Susa and Syracuse, which threatened their freedom on the east and on the west. Those who were tempted to spy into the future might have conjectured that the ultimate conflict with Persia was reserved for a Sicilian conqueror, who should one day extend his dominion over eastern Greece and the Aegean and, as autocrat of Europe, oppose the autocrat of Asia. Though this was not to be, though the expansion of Sicily was arrested, and the power which was to subdue Asia arose on the borders of Old Greece, yet we shall see that in many ways the monarchy of Dionysius foreshadowed

Great position of Syracuse

the monarchy of Philip and Alexander. It is in Sicily, not in Old Greece, that we see the first signs of a new epoch, in which large states are to take the place of small, and monarchy is to supersede free institutions.

The tyranny of Dionysius lasted for thirty-eight years, till the end of his life. All that time it was maintained by force; all that time it was recognised as a violation of the constitution and an outrage on the freedom of the people. The forms of the constitution were still maintained; the folk still met and voted in the Assembly; and Dionysius was either annually re-elected, or permanently appointed, general with absolute powers. But all this was pure form; his position was a fact, which had no constitutional name, and which made the constitution meaningless. And it was by compulsion and not of their freewill that the mass of the citizens continued to obey him; his bodyguard of foreign mercenaries was the support of his power. More than one attempt was made to throw off the yoke, but his craft and energy defeated the most determined efforts of his adversaries. Yet the unusual ability of Dionysius would not have availed, more than the spearmen who were ever within call, to extend his unlawful reign to a length which a tyrant's reign seldom reached, if he had not discovered and laid to heart what may be called a secret of tyranny. While he did cruel and oppressive deeds for political purposes, he never committed outrages to gratify personal desires of his own. He scrupulously avoided all those acts of private insolence which have brought the reigns of Greek tyrants into such ill repute. Many a despot had fallen by the hand of fathers or lovers, whom the dishonour of their nearest and dearest had spurred to the pursuit of vengeance at the risk of their own lives. Dionysius avoided this mistake; his crimes and his enemies were political. When his son seduced a married woman, the discreet tyrant rebuked him. 'It is well for you to chide me,' said the young man, 'but you had not a tyrant for your father.' 'And if you go on doing this sort of thing,' retorted Dionysius, 'you will not have a tyrant for your son.' This notable moderation of Dionysius in private life was perhaps the chief cause of the duration of his tyranny; beyond the common motive of patriotism, men had no burning personal wrongs to spur them to plot his death. But, besides this discretion which made his government tolerable, his successes abroad counted for something, and it was more than once borne in on Syracuse that his rule was necessary to protect her against her enemies. And we shall

The statecraft of Dionysius, and the secret of his long reign

see that Dionysius was fully conscious that it conduced to his own safety that there should be enemies against whom she needed a protector.

*Fortifica-
tion of the
Island*

The first concern of the new tyrant was to establish himself in a stronghold. As we have seen, the acropolis of Syracuse was not, as in other cities, the hill, but the Island; and it was the Island which Dionysius made his fortress. He built a turreted wall on the north side of the isthmus so as to bar the Island off from the mainland, and he built two castles, one close to, if not on, the isthmus, the other at the southern point of the island. Whoever entered the Island from Achradina had to pass under five successive gates; and no one was allowed to dwell within the island fortress except those whom Dionysius regarded as his own friends and supporters. The scheme of fortifications took in the Lesser Harbour, which, with its new docks, became under Dionysius the chief arsenal of the Syracusan naval power. The mouth of this port was entirely closed by a mole, the galleys passing in and out through a gate, which was only wide enough to allow one to pass at a time.

Besides these defences of stone, Dionysius strengthened his position by dealing rich rewards to confirm in their allegiance his friends and hirelings, and by forming a class of New Citizens out of enfranchised slaves. The forfeited estates of his enemies supplied him with the means of carrying out both these acts of policy.

*Revolt
against
Dionysius*

It was not long before he had an unwelcome occasion of putting to the test both the walls of his fortress and the hearts of his followers. The most favourable opportunity for any attempt to overthrow the tyrant was when the Syracusan army was in the field. When the citizens had arms in their hands and were formed in military ranks, the word of a patriot could more easily kindle them to action than when they were engaged in their peaceable occupations at home. Dionysius led out the army against Herbessus, one of the cities of the Sicels. Mutinous talk passed from mouth to mouth, and the disaffected citizens slew one of the tyrant's officers who rebuked them. Then the mutiny broke out loud and free. Dionysius hastened to Syracuse and shut himself up in his fastness; the rebel citizens followed and laid siege to their own city.

*Siege of
Syracuse,
403 B.C.*

They sent messages to Messana and Rhegion, asking these cities to help them to win back their freedom; and 80 triremes came in answer to their help. By sea and land they pressed Dionysius so hard in his island fortress that his case seemed desperate, and some of his mercenary troops went over to the enemy. Dionysius called a council of his most trusted friends. Some bade him flee on a swift horse; others counselled him to stay till he was driven out. Heloris used a phrase which became famous: 'Sovereign power is a fair winding-sheet.' Dionysius followed the counsel of those who bade him stay, but he resorted to a piece of craft which was more successful than he could well have hoped. He entered into negotiation with his besiegers and asked for permission to quit Syracuse with his own goods. They willingly agreed to the proposal and allowed him five triremes, and they were so convinced of his good faith that they dismissed a company of cavalry which had come to their aid from Etna. But, meanwhile, Dionysius had sent a secret message to the Campanian mercenaries of Carthage, who had been left by Himilco in some part of Sicily. Twelve hundred in number, they were permitted to come to the help of the tyrant, whose lordship had been recognised and guaranteed by Carthage in the recent treaty. The besiegers, thinking that the struggle was over, had half abandoned the siege and were in complete disorder; the Campanians occupied the hills of Epipolae without resistance; Dionysius sallied forth, and decisively, though without much shedding of blood, defeated the rebels in the neighbourhood of the theatre—a quarter of the city which we now find for the first time called *Neapolis*. Dionysius used his victory mildly. Many of the rebels fled to Etna and refused to return to Syracuse, but those who returned were received kindly and not punished. As for the Campanians, to whom Dionysius owed his rescue, they did not return to the service of Carthage, but made a new home in the west of Sicily, in the Sican town of Entella. They induced the inhabitants to admit them as new citizens, and one night they arose and slew all the men and married the women. Thus was formed the first Italian settlement on Sicilian soil.

*Revolt
suppressed
by Cam-
panian
help*

*Entella;
first
Italian
settlement
in Sicily.
Designs of
Dionysius
on the
Sicels*

When the revolt broke out, we saw Dionysius aiming an attack at a Sicel city. The first step in the expansion of Syracusan power, which was the object of the tyrant's ambition, was the reduction of the Greek cities of the eastern coast and the neighbouring Sicel towns. The Sicel towns were putting on more and more of an Hellenic character, and the reign of Dionysius marks a stage of progress in their Hellenization. We get a glimpse of political parties striving in Sicel just as in

Greek cities; and we find Henna ruled by a tyrant of Greek name. To attack the Sicels was indeed a breach of the treaty with Carthage; but for the present Dionysius gained no success which obliged Carthage to intervene. He entered Henna indeed, but only to overthrow the local tyrant and leave the inhabitants to enjoy their freedom; he attacked Herbita, but his attack was fruitless. With the Greek cities which stood in his way he was *Etna* more successful. First of all he captured Etna, *taken* the refuge of Syracusan exiles and malcontents, and these dangerous enemies dispersed. Then he turned against the two Ionian cities, Catane and Naxos. In fear of such an attack Catane *Alliance of* had taken the precaution of allying herself with *Catane and* Syracuse's former vassal, Leontini. The sole *Leontini,* record we have of this alliance is a beautiful *404 B.C.* little silver coin, with a laurelled head of Apollo and the names of the two cities—one of an issue which was struck in token of the *Catane and* treaty. But the support of Leontini did not *Naxos* avail. Both Catane and Naxos were won by *taken by* gold, not by the sword; traitors opened the *treachery* gates to the Dorian tyrant.

In his treatment of these cities Dionysius showed himself in his worst light. All the *Fate of* inhabitants of Naxos and Catane alike were *Catane and* sold as slaves in the Syracusan slave-market. *Naxos* Catane was given over to Campanian mercenaries as a dwelling-place, and thus became the second Italian town in Sicily. But the city of Naxos, the most ancient of all the Siceliot cities, was not even given to a stranger to dwell in; the walls and the houses were destroyed; the territory was bestowed upon the Sicels, the descendants of the original possessors; and a small settlement near the old site *(The* barely maintained the memory of the name. *Naxian* Dionysius was one of the ablest champions of *Neapolis)* Greek Sicily against the Phoenician, yet here he appears in the character of a destroyer, dealing to Greek civilisation blows such as we should expect only from the Phoenician enemy. It is certain indeed that the severity of the doom which he meted out to these cities was meant to serve a purpose, for wanton severity was never practised by Dionysius. We may *Recovery* suspect what that purpose was. The conquest *of Leontini* of Naxos and Catane was of far less consequence to the lord of Syracuse than the recovery of Leontini. To win back this lost Syracusan possession was the first object of all in the eyes of a Syracusan ruler. Dionysius had already called upon the Leontines to surrender, but in vain, and perhaps he thought that the siege of the place would be long and tedious. When he pronounced the doom of Naxos and

Catane, he was in truth besieging Leontini with most effectual engines; and when he approached with his army and summoned the Leontines to migrate to Syracuse and become his subjects under the name of Syracusan citizens, they did not hesitate to prefer that unwelcome change to the risk of faring still worse than the folks of Catane and Naxos.

If we glance over Sicily at this moment, it comes upon us as a shock to discover that of all the cities of Greek Sicily which enjoyed sovereign powers at the time of the Athenian invasion, there remained now not a single independent community, outside Syracuse herself, with the exception of Messana, who still kept watch upon her strait. The Carthaginians and Dionysius between them had swept all away.

The recovery of the Leontine territory was a success which probably gratified the Syracusans as well as their master. It was indeed a direct defiance of Carthage, for the treaty had guaranteed the independence of Leontini. But Dionysius knew that a struggle with Carthage *Fortifica-* must come, and was not unwilling that it *tion of* should come soon. He determined to equip *Epipolae* Syracuse against all enemies who should come against her, and we next find him engaged in fortifying the city on an enormous scale. The fortification of the Island had been intended mainly for his own safety against domestic enemies; but the works which he now undertook were for the city and not for the tyrant. The Athenian siege of Syracuse taught him lessons which he had taken to heart. It taught him that the commanding heights of Epipolae must not be left for an enemy to seize, and therefore that it must become part of the Syracusan city, enclosed within the circuit of the Syracusan wall.[4] It taught too the decisive importance of the western corner at Euryalos, and the necessity of constructing a strong fortress at that point, which has been called 'the key of Epipolae and of all Syracuse'. The walls were built in an incredibly short space of time by 60,000 freemen, under the supervision of Dionysius himself. He seems to have inspired the citizens with the ambition of making their city the most strongly fortified place in the whole Greek world. The northern wall, from Tycha to Euryalos, a distance of more than three miles, was completed in twenty days. The striking ruins of the massive castle of Euryalos, with its curious underground chambers, are a memorial indeed of a tyrant's rule; but they are more than that: they are a monument of Greek Syracuse at the period of her greatest might—when she became for a moment the greatest power in Europe.

It was no small thing to have carried out this enormous system of fortifications which made Syracuse the vastest of all Greek cities, but Dionysius showed his surpassing energy and resource in preparing for offensive as well *Improve-* as for defensive warfare. In military innova- *ments of* tions he is the forerunner of the great *Dionysius* Macedonians and the originator of the methods *in warfare* which they employed. He first thought out and taught how the heterogeneous parts of a military armament—the army and the navy, the cavalry and the infantry, the heavy and the light troops—might be closely and systematically co-ordinated so as to act as if they were a single organic body. He first introduced, his engineers first invented, the catapult, which, if it did not revolutionise warfare in general like the discovery of gunpowder, certainly revolutionised siege warfare, and introduced a new element into military operations. An engine which hurled a stone of two or three hundredweight for a distance of two or three hundred yards was extremely formidable at close quarters. In naval warfare he has been credited with the invention of quadriremes and quinqueremes, but this must remain doubtful.[5] He largely increased the fleet, which seems to have numbered about 300 warships.

First Punic War of Dionysius

First When his preparations were complete, Dion- *Punic* ysius went forth to do what no Greek leader *War,* in Sicily had ever done before. He went forth *398-7 B.C.* not merely to deliver Greek cities from Phoenician rule, but to conquer Phoenician Sicily itself. Marching along the south coast he was hailed as a deliverer by the Greek dependencies of Carthage, both by the tributary towns Gela and Camarina, and by the subject town of Acragas. Thermae on the northern coast likewise joined him, and of the two Elymian towns, Eryx received his overtures, while Segesta remained faithful to her Punic mistress. At the head of a host, which for a Greek army seems immense— 80,000 foot, it is said, and more than 3000 horse—Dionysius advanced to test his new *Siege of* siege engines on the walls of Motya. This *Motya* city, which now for the first and for the last time becomes the centre of a memorable episode in history, was like the original Syracuse, an island town; but, though it was joined to the mainland by a causeway, the

town did not like Syracuse spread to the mainland. It was surrounded entirely by a wall, of which traces still remain; and the bay in which it lay was protected on the sea side by a long spit of land. The men of Motya were determined to withstand the invader to the uttermost, and the first measure they took was to insulate themselves completely by breaking down the causeway which bound them to the mainland. Thus they hoped that Dionysius would have to trust entirely to his ships to conduct the siege, and that he would be unable to make use of his artillery. But they did not know the enterprise of Dionysius *The mole* nor the excellence of his engineers. The tyrant was determined to assault the city from solid ground, and to bring his terrible engines close to the walls. He set the crews of his ships to the work of building a mole far greater than the causeway which the Motyans had destroyed; the ships themselves, which he did not destine to play any part in the business of the siege, he drew up on the northern coast of the bay. The mole of Dionysius at *(Compare* Motya foreshadows a more famous mole which *the mole of* we shall hereafter see erected by a greater *Alexander* than Dionysius at another Phoenician island *the Great* town, older and more illustrious than Motya. *at Tyre,* *p. 460)*

While the mole was being built, Dionysius made expeditions in the neighbourhood. He won over the Sicans from their Carthaginian allegiance, and he laid siege to Elymian Segesta and Campanian Entella. Both these cities repelled his attacks, and leaving them under blockade he returned to Motya when the solid bridge was completed. In the meantime, Carthage was preparing an effort to rescue the menaced city. She tried to cause a diversion by sending a few ships to Syracuse, and some damage was caused to ships that were lying in the Great Harbour. But Dionysius was not to be diverted from his enterprise; he had doubtless foreseen such an attempt to lure him away, and knew that there was no real danger. Himilco, the Carthaginian admiral, seeing that Dionysius was immovable, sailed with a large force to Motya and entered the bay, with the purpose of destroying the Syracusan fleet, which was drawn up on the shore. Dionysius seems to have been taken by surprise. For whatever reason, he made no attempt to launch his ships; he merely placed archers and slingers on those which would be first attacked. But he brought his army round to the peninsula which forms the western side of the bay, and on the shores of this strip of land he placed his new engines. The catapults hurled deadly volleys of stones upon Himilco's ships, and the novelty of these crushing missiles, which they were quite unprepared to meet, utterly disconcerted the Punic sailors, and the Carthaginians retreated. Then Dionysius, who was no less ready to treat earth as water than to turn sea into land, laid wooden rollers across the neck of land which formed the northern side of the bay, and hauled his whole fleet into the open sea. But Himilco did not wait to give him battle there; he went back to Carthage, and the men of Motya were left unaided to their fate.

As the site of the island city required a special road of approach, so its architecture demanded a special device of assault. Since the space in the city was limited, its wealthy inhabitants had to seek dwelling-room by raising high towers into the air; and to attack *(The helepoleis)* these towers Dionysius constructed siege towers of corresponding height, with six storeys, which he moved up near the walls on wheels. These wooden *belfries*, as they were called in the Middle Ages, were not a new invention, but they had never perhaps been built to such a height before, and it is not till the Macedonian age, which Dionysius in so many ways foreshadows, that they came into common use. It was a strange sight to see the battle waged in mid-air. The defenders of the stone towers had one advantage; they were able to damage some of the wooden towers of the enemy by lighted brands and pitch. But the arrangements of Dionysius were so well ordered that this device had little effect; and the Phoenicians could not stand on the wall which was swept by his catapults, while the rams battered it below. Presently a breach was made, and the struggle began in earnest. The Motyans had no thought of surrender; they defended their streets and houses inch by inch. Missiles rained on the heads of the Greeks who thronged through, and each of the lofty houses had to be besieged like a miniature town. The wooden towers were wheeled within the walls; from their topmost storeys bridges were flung across to the upper storeys of the houses, and in the face of the desperate inhabitants the Greek soldiers rushed across these dizzy ways, often to be flung down into the street below. At night the combat ceased; both besiegers and besieged rested. The issue was indeed certain, for however bravely the Motyans might fight, they were far outnumbered. But day after day the fighting went on in the same way, and Motya was not taken. The losses on the Greek side were great, and Dionysius became impatient. Accordingly he planned a night assault, which the Motyans did not look for,

and this was successful. By means of ladders a small band entered the part of the town which was still defended, and then admitted the rest of the army through a gate. There was a short and sharp struggle, which soon became a massacre. The Greeks had no thought of *Capture of* plunder, they thought only of vengeance. *Motya, and* Now for the first time a Phoenician town had *massacre,* fallen into their hands, and they resolved to *398 B.C.* do to it as the Phoenicians had done to Greek cities. They remembered how Hannibal had dealt with Himera. At length Dionysius stayed the slaughter, which was not to his mind, since every corpse was a captive less to be sold. Then the victors turned to spoil the city, and its wealth was abandoned to them without any reserve. All the prisoners were sold into slavery, except some Greek mercenaries, whose treachery to the Greek cause was expiated by crucifixion. A Sicel garrison was left in the captured city.

After this achievement, which had no pre- *Second* cedent in Sicilian history, Dionysius retired for *campaign* the winter to Syracuse. Next spring he *of Diony-* marched forth again to press the siege of *sius, 397* Segesta, which was still under blockade. In *B.C.* the meantime the fall of Motya had awakened Carthage into action; she saw that she must bestir herself, if she was not to let her whole Sicilian dominion slip out of her hands. Himilco was appointed Shophet and entrusted *Cartha-* with the work of saving Punic Sicily. He *ginian* collected a force, which seems to have been at *expedition* least as large as that which Dionysius had *to Sicily,* brought into the field, and set sail with *397 B.C.* sealed orders for Panormus. A small portion of the armament was sunk by Leptines, brother of Dionysius, who was in command of the Syracusan fleet; but the main part disembarked in safety. And then events happened in rapid succession, which are hard to explain. Himilco first gains possession of Eryx by *Himilco* treason; then he marches to Motya and *takes Eryx* captures it; and when Motya is lost, Dionysius *and Motya* raises the siege of Segesta and returns to Syracuse. The loss of Eryx could not be provided against; but it is hard to discern why Dionysius should have made no attempt to relieve Motya, whose capture had cost him so much the year before, or why he should have allowed the Carthaginian army to march from Panormus to Eryx and Motya without attempting to intercept it. He could not have more effectually pressed the siege of Segesta than by dealing a decided check to Himilco. Not knowing the exact circumstances, not knowing even the number of the two armies, we can hardly judge his action; but it may be suspected that Dionysius was by nature a man who did not care to risk a pitched battle, unless the advantage were distinctly on his own side. It is to be remembered that he won nearly all his successes by sieges and surprises, by diplomacy and craft, and that the name of this great military innovator is not associated with a single famous battle in the open field. When he had once allowed Motya to be taken, his retreat is not surprising, for he had no base in the western part of the island, and we are told that his supplies were failing. He had now lost all that he had won in the first campaign.

End of Motya. Foundation of Lilybaeum (Marsala)

Motya, however, was wiped out as a Phoenician city, though it was not to be a Greek or Sicel stronghold. Himilco, instead of restoring the old colony, founded a new city hard by to take its place. On the promontory of the mainland which forms the south side of the Motyan bay arose the city of Lilybaeum, which was henceforward to be the great stronghold of Carthaginian power in the west of the island. The sea washed two sides of the town, and the walls of the other two sides were protected by enormous ditches cut in the rock. The history of Lilybaeum is the continuation of the history of Motya; but it was not destined to be taken either by a Greek or a Roman besieger.

Himilco takes and destroys Messana

Having driven the invader from Phoenician Sicily, and having laid the foundations of a new city, Himilco resolved to carry his arms into the lands of the enemy and to attack Syracuse itself. But he did not go directly against Syracuse. Before he attempted that mighty fortress, he would try the easier task of capturing Messana which would be no mean vengeance for the fall of Motya. The walls of Messana had been allowed to fall into decay, and the place was an easy prey for the Carthaginians, but the greater part of the inhabitants escaped into fortresses in the neighbouring hills. The Carthaginian general had to wreak his vengeance on the stones. He razed the walls and the buildings, and the work was done so well that no man, we are told, would have recognised the site.

If the triumphant demolition of the Sicilian city which watched the strait was a sore blow to the Hellenic cause, Himilco sought at the same moment to deal another blow to that cause by the foundation of a new Sicilian city in another place. It was his policy to cultivate the friendship of the Sicels and to foment the dislike which they felt towards the lord of Syracuse. Dionysius too had sought to win influence over the native race, and we saw how he gave them the territory of Naxos. The Carthaginian general grasped at the idea of erecting a new town for these very Sicels of Naxos, on the heights of Taurus which rise above the old site. Such was the strange origin of the strong city of Tauromenion, with its two rock citadels, one of the fairest sites in Sicily. It was the second foundation of Himilco in the same year; and both his foundations were destined signally to prosper. Lilybaeum became more famous than Motya, and Tauromenion has had a greater place in history than Naxos. As a founder of cities Himilco has a high title to fame; he was, like Dionysius, a creator as well as a destroyer. The creation of new cities and the destruction of old, by Greeks and Phoenicians alike, was a characteristic feature of this epoch.

Foundation of Tauromenion

Dionysius was preparing in the meantime to protect Syracuse. He committed the command of the fleet, which appears to have been now about 200 strong, to his brother Leptines; and fleet and army together moved northward to Catane. In the waters near the shore of Catane a naval battle was fought, and the Greek armament was defeated with great loss. It was indeed far outnumbered by the fleet of the Phoenicians, who also used their transport vessels as warships; but the cause of the disaster was the bad generalship of Leptines, who did not keep his ships together. The rout was witnessed by Dionysius from the shore, and it might have been retrieved by a victory on the land. Himilco and his army had not yet arrived on the scene, for an eruption of Etna had made the direct road impassable and forced them to make a long détour. Dionysius again shrank from risking a battle, though his men were eager to fight; he retreated to the walls of Syracuse. This city was the last bulwark of Greek Sicily, and with it the cause of Greek civilisation was in jeopardy. It was a moment at which the Syracusans might well sue for help from their fellow-Greeks beyond the sea. Dionysius dispatched messages to Italy, to Corinth, and to Sparta, imploring urgently for help.

Sea-fight at Catane

Retreat of Dionysius

It was not long before the victorious Carthaginian fleet sailed into the Great Harbour, and the Carthaginian army encamped hard by, along the banks of the Anapus. The mass of the host encamped as well as it could in the swamp, but the general pitched his tent on the high ground of Polichna, within the precinct of the Olympian Zeus. This insult to the religion of Hellas was followed up by a more awful sacrilege, when Himilco pillaged the temple of Demeter and Kore on the southern slope of Epipolae.

Punic siege of Syracuse

When the barbarians began to perish in the plague-stricken marsh, the pestilence was imputed to the divine vengeance for these acts of outrage. The besiegers must have sat for no brief space before the walls of Syracuse. The messengers of Dionysius had time to reach the Peloponnese and return with help—30 ships under a Lacedaemonian admiral. Himilco had time to build three forts to protect his army and his fleet—one near his own quarters at Polichna, one at Dascon, on the western shore of the harbour, and one at Plemmyrion. After the arrival of the auxiliaries, the capture of a Punic cornship was the occasion of a small naval combat in the harbour; only a few of the Carthaginian ships were engaged, and the Syracusans were victorious.

Feeling in Syracuse against the tyrant

Within the town there was deep dissatisfaction with Dionysius and his conduct of the war, and the citizens thought that they might reckon on the sympathy of their Peloponnesian allies with an attempt to cast off the tyrant's yoke. At an assembly which the tyrant convened the feeling of dissatisfaction broke forth openly. But the movement of revolution was checked by the Peloponnesians, who said that their business was to help Dionysius against the Carthaginians, not to help the Syracusans against Dionysius. So the danger passed over, but the tyrant had a warning, and he put on winning manners and courted popularity.

Plague in Carthaginian camp

The deadly airs of the swamp, in the burning heat of summer, were doing their work. The army of Himilco was ravaged by pestilence; soon the soldiers fell so fast that they could not be buried. The hour had now come for the men of the city to complete the destruction which their fens had begun. It was just such a case as called forth the energy and craft of the ruler of Syracuse and showed him at his best. He devised his attack with great skill. Eighty ships, under Leptines and the Spartan captain, were to attack the Carthaginian fleet, which was anchored off the shore of Dascon. He himself led the land forces, marching by a roundabout road on a moonless night, and suddenly appeared at dawn on the west side of the Punic camp. He ordered his horsemen and a thousand mercenaries to attack the camp here; but the horsemen had secret commands to abandon the hired soldiers once they were in the thick of the fight and ride rapidly round to the east of the camp, where the true attack was to be made. The attack on the west was only a feint, to distract the attention of the enemy from the

Dionysius attacks the Carthaginians

other side; and for this purpose Dionysius sacrificed the lives of the mercenaries whom he did not trust. The real attack on the east was made on the forts of Dascon and Polichna. Dascon was assailed by the horsemen along with a special force of triremes which had been sent across the bay; Dionysius himself went round to lead the attack on Polichna. The plan was carried out with perfect success. The thousand mercenaries were cut to pieces, the forts were captured, and the victory on land was crowned by the destruction of the Carthaginian fleet. The Syracusan ships bore down upon the enemy before they had time fully to man their vessels, much less to row well out to sea, and the beaks of the triremes crashed into defenceless timber. There was slaughter, but hardly a fight; and then the land troops, fresh from *their* victory, rushed down to the beach and set fire to the transports and all vessels which had not left the shore. A wild scene followed. A high wind spread the flames; the cables were burnt; and the bay of Dascon was filled with drifting fireships, while amid the waters despairing swimmers were making for the shore.

Defeat of Carthaginians

Fate had indeed delivered the barbarians into the hands of the Greeks; and the Greeks were determined to exact the uttermost vengeance and extirpate the destroyers of Messana. Dionysius had proved himself the successor of Gelon: the double victory of Dascon was worthy to be set beside the victory of Himera. But Dionysius was not capable of absolute sincerity in the part he played as the champion of Hellas; he could not act to the end as a Syracusan patriot with singleness of heart. This was the fatality of his position as a tyrant, conscious that his autocracy rested on unstable foundations. He fought against Carthage, but it was always with the resolve that the power of the Carthaginians should not be annihilated in Sicily. The Punic peril was a security for his tyranny, by making him necessary to Syracuse. The Syracusans must look to him as their protector against the ever-present barbarian enemy. This was another secret of tyranny discovered by Dionysius. The Punic subtlety of Himilco, enlightened by passages in the tyrant's past career, gave him no doubt a shrewd idea of this side of his policy; the Carthaginian saw that his hope of safety lay in bargaining with Dionysius. Secret messages passed, and Dionysius agreed to allow Himilco along with all those who were Carthaginian citizens to sail away at night. In payment for this collusion he received three hundred

Double-dealing of Dionysius

His policy in regard to Carthage

Escape of Himilco by collusion of Dionysius

talents. Dionysius recalled his reluctant army from their assaults on the camp, and left it in peace for three days. On the fourth night Himilco set sail with 40 triremes, leaving his allies and his mercenaries to their fate. It was an act of desertion which was likely to repel mercenary soldiers from the Carthaginian service in the future; and this was doubtless foreseen by the crafty tyrant. But the squadron of fugitive triremes did not escape untouched. The noise of the oars as they sailed out of the Harbour was detected by the Corinthian allies, and they gave the alarm to Dionysius. But Dionysius was purposely slow in his preparations to pursue, and the impatient Corinthians sailed out without his orders and sank some of the hindmost of the Punic vessels. Having connived at the escape of Himilco, the tyrant was energetic in dealing with the remnant of Himilco's host.[6] The Sicel allies had escaped to their own homes, and only the mercenaries were left. These were slain or made slaves, with the exception of a band of strong and valiant Iberians who were taken into the service of the tyrant.

Thus ended the first struggle of Dionysius with Carthage, and it ended in a complete triumph for the Greek cause. The dominion of the African city was now circumscribed within its old western corner; and the greater part of the rest of Sicily was subject, directly or indirectly, to the rule of the lord of Syracuse. Both from Greek and from barbarian Sicily, a famous city had been blotted out; but Motya had been revived in Lilybaeum, and Messana was soon to rise again upon her ruins.

Second Punic War, and Sicel Conquests of Dionysius

The equivocal policy of Dionysius towards Carthage was manifested clearly enough in the course which he pursued after his great victory. It was the most favourable moment that had yet come in the struggle of centuries for driving the barbarians out and making Sicily a Greek island from the eastern to the western shore. Carthage could not readily gather together such another armament as that which had been destroyed. No patriot leader who was devoted to the Greek cause heart and soul, with singleness of aim, would have failed to follow up the great success by an invasion of western Sicily. But the preservation of his own precarious despotism was the guiding principle of Dionysius; and he saw in the barbarian corner of the island a palladium of his power.

The next Punic War broke out five years later, and part of the meantime had been occupied by Dionysius in extending his power over the Sicels. He annexed to his dominion Morgantina, Cephaloedion, and Henna itself; he made treaties with the tyrants of Agyrion and Centuripa, and with other places. But among all the Sicel towns, that which it was most important for him to win was the new foundation of the Carthaginian on the heights of Taurus. He laid siege to Tauromenion in the depth of winter. Operations of war in the winter season are one of the features of the reign of Dionysius, which separate it from the habits of older Greece and link it to the age of the Macedonian monarchy. The tyrant himself led his men on a wild and moonless night up the steep ascent to the town. One of the citadels was taken, and the assailants entered the place. But the Syracusan band was outnumbered and surrounded, 600 were killed, and the rest were driven down the cliffs. Of these Dionysius was one; he reached the bottom barely alive, after that precipitous descent.

Sicel conquests of Dionysius between 396 and 393 B.C.

Unsuccessful assault on Tauromenion

In the course of the extension of his power on the northern coast, Dionysius had advanced to the limits of the Phoenician corner, and had won possession, through domestic treachery, of Solus, the most easterly of the three Phoenician cities. Of the circumstances we know nothing, but the conquest would seem to have been rather a piece of luck than part of any deliberate plan of aggression on the part of the Greek tyrant. No treaty appears to have been concluded between Carthage and Syracuse after the defeat of Himilco, so that the capture of Solus was not a violation of peace, but only an occasion for the reawakening of hostilities which had been permitted to sleep by tacit consent. At all events, it must have had something to do with the renewal of the war—a renewal for which our records assign no causes.

Conquest of Solus

At the opening of the second war we find a Carthaginian general commanding the Phoenician forces of the island, but without any troops, so far as we know, from Africa. The general was Mago, who in the previous war had been commander of the fleet. His army was doubtless considerably inferior to the forces which Dionysius could muster; certain it is that on this occasion Dionysius did not hesitate to give him battle and did not fail to defeat him. Carthage saw that she must make a more vigorous effort, and she gave Mago a large army—80,000 men, it is said—to retrieve his ill success. To meet the invader, Dionysius

Second Punic War, 392 B.C.

Victory of Dionysius

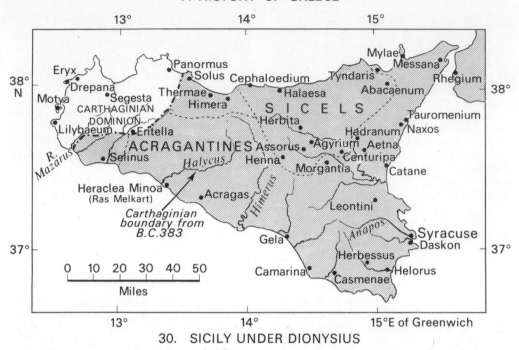

30. SICILY UNDER DIONYSIUS

League of Dionysius with Agyris

entered into a close league with the strongest Sicel power in the land, his fellow-tyrant Agyris of Agyrium. This is the special feature of the second Punic War: the cause of Europe is upheld by a federation of the two European powers of the island, Sicel and Greek. The Carthaginian army advanced into Sicel territory, seeking to win the Sicel towns. But Agyris and his men waged a most effectual manner of warfare, cutting off all the foraging parties of the enemy and thus starving them by degrees. This they were able to do from their knowledge of their native hills. But it seems that the Syracusans were dissatisfied with this slow method, which was thoroughly to the taste of Dionysius. What happened is not clear, but we learn that the Syracusans marched away from the camp, and that Dionysius replaced them by arming the slaves. Then the Greeks and the Sicels must have won some unrecorded success, or the Carthaginian host must have been already terribly deplenished by the want of food, for we next find Mago suing for peace.

Terms of the Peace

This peace, although it is said to have been based on the treaty which Dionysius had made twelve years before, was in truth altogether different, for the parts of the two powers were reversed. All the Greek communities of Sicily were now placed under the direct or indirect power of Syracuse. The Carthaginian power was confined to the western corner.

Nothing is said of Solus; it must have been now handed over to Carthage, if Mago had not already recovered it by arms. But the most striking provision of the treaty is that which placed 'the Sicels' under the rule of Dionysius. Nothing is said of Agyrium, and we are almost driven to wonder whether there was here any treachery to Agyris, of whom we hear nothing further. But there was a special clause touching Tauromenion; and acting on this clause Dionysius immediately took possession of the town, expelled the Sicels, and established in the fortress one of those mercenary settlements which were characteristic of his age. Such was the end of the two Punic wars, which were in truth rather but a single war broken by an interval of quiescence.

Dionysius wins Tauromenion

The Empire of Dionysius

Having made himself master of all Greek Sicily, the lord of Syracuse began to extend the compass of his ambition beyond the bounds of the island.[7] He began to plan the conquest of Greek Italy. Hitherto the Sicilian cities, though they had constant dealings with the colonies of the Italian mainland, had never sought there, or anywhere out of their own island, a field for conquest or aggression. The restriction of Siceliot ambition to Sicilian territory was the other side of the doctrine preached by Hermocrates that the Siceliots should not allow Greeks from beyond the sea to interfere in the affairs of Sicily. Here, as in other things, Dionysius was an innovator; he set the example of enterprises of conquest beyond the sea. Into the enterprise of Italian conquest he was naturally led on by his dealings with the fellow-cities of the strait, Messana and Rhegion.

Messana restored 396 B.C. (Messenians driven from Naupactus, 400-1 B.C.) Foundation of Tyndaris by Dionysius, 395 B.C.

For Messana was a city once more; it had been rebuilt by Dionysius himself. He settled in it colonists from Locri and Medma in Italy, and 600 Messenians from old Greece, who had been wandering about homeless since Sparta had driven them from Naupactus. But this favour to the Messenians displeased the Spartans, and as Dionysius was anxious to maintain the friendship of Sparta he yielded to their protests. He removed the exiles from Messana, but he made for them a secure though less illustrious home. He founded the city of Tyndaris on a high hill to the west of Mylae, and fortified it strongly; the walls and towers, which still remain, are a good specimen of the fortifications of Dionysius.

The restoration of Messana and the foundation of Tyndaris were no pleasant sight to the Ionian city across the strait; these new cities seemed to Rhegion a Syracusan menace. The men of Rhegion sought to make a counter-move by founding a city themselves between Tyndaris and Messana. They gathered together the exiles from Catane and Naxos and settled them on the peninsula of Mylae; but the settlement lasted only for a moment: almost immediately the town of Mylae was captured by its neighbours of Messana, and the exiles were driven out to resume their wanderings.

Foundation of Mylae, 394 B.C.

Apart from his political hostility to Rhegion, Dionysius is said to have borne it a private grudge. He had asked the men of Rhegion to give him one of their maidens to wife, and they had answered that they would give him none but the hangman's daughter. Locri, Rhegion's neighbour, then granted him the request which Rhegion refused; Locri was his faithful ally; and now, when the conclusion of peace with Carthage left him free to pursue his Italian designs, it was Locri that he made his base of operations. The first object was to capture Rhegion; its position on the strait dictated this, apart from all motives of revenge or hatred. Accordingly starting from Locri with army and fleet, he laid siege to Rhegion by land and sea. But the confederate cities of the Italian coast came to the assistance of a member of their league; the Italiot armament worsted the fleet of Dionysius in or near the

Rhegion besieged, 391 B.C.

Naval defeat of Dionysius

strait, and Dionysius escaped with difficulty to the opposite coast.

Rhegion was thus relieved, and Dionysius now directed his hostilities against the Italiot federation. He made an alliance with the Lucanians, to the intent that they and he should carry on war in common against the Italiot cities, they by land and he by sea. In accordance with this treaty, the Lucanians invaded the land of Thurii. The men of Thurii retorted by invading Lucania in considerable force; but they sustained a crushing defeat at the hands of the barbarians. Most of the Thurians were slain, but some escaped to the shore and swam out to ships which they happened to see coasting along. By a curious chance, the ships were the fleet of Syracuse, and Leptines, the tyrant's brother, was once more the commander. He received the fugitives, and did more; he landed and ransomed them from the Lucanians. He did even more than this: he arranged an armistice between the Lucanians and the Italiots. In acting thus, he clearly went beyond his powers; he had been sent to co-operate with the Lucanians against the Italiots, and he had no right to conclude an armistice in such circumstances, without consulting his brother. It is not surprising that Dionysius deposed him from the command.

Alliance of Dionysius with the Lucanians: joint operations, 390 B.C.

Thurians defeated by Lucanians

Leptines concludes an armistice and is deposed

In the following year Dionysius took the field himself. He opened the campaign by laying siege to Caulonia, the northern neighbour of Locri. The Italiots, under the active lead of Croton, collected an army of 15,000 foot and 2000 horse, and entrusted the command to Heloris, a brave exile of Syracuse, who bitterly hated the tyrant who had banished him. The federal army marched forth from Croton to relieve Caulonia and, when Dionysius learned of its approach, he decided to go forth to meet it, for his own forces, 20,000 foot and 3000 horse, were considerably superior. Luck favoured him. Near the river Elleporus which flows into the sea between Caulonia and Croton, the tyrant heard that the enemy were encamped within a distance of 5 miles, and he drew up his men in battle array. Heloris, less well-informed, rode forward in front of his main army, with a company of 500 men, and suddenly found himself in the presence of the Syracusan host. Sending back a message to hasten the rest of his army, he and his little band stood firm against the onset of the invaders. Heloris fell himself, and the main army, coming up company by company, in haste and disorder, was easily routed by Dionysius. Ten thousand fugitives escaped to a high hill, but it was a poor hill of refuge, for

Dionysius besieges Caulonia, 389 B.C.

Battle of the Elleporus, 389 B.C.

*Dionysius'
politic act
of mercy*

there was no spring of water and they could not hold out. The next morning they begged Dionysius, who kept watch around the hill throughout the night, to set them free for a ransom. Dionysius refused; he would accept only unreserved surrender. But he was cruel only to grant them a greater mercy than they could themselves have dared to ask. When they came down the hill, Dionysius himself counted their number with a wand as they filed past him, and each man thought that his fate would be bondage if not death. But Dionysius let them all depart, without even exacting a ransom. This act of mercy, which was notable as compared not only with other acts of the tyrant, but with the ordinary practice of the age, produced a great sensation. There is no reason for imputing it to a magnanimous impulse; it was a deliberate act of policy. Dionysius did not wish to be generous, but he wished to be regarded as generous and win over the Italiot cities. For this purpose he made up his mind to sacrifice

*His treaties
with the
Italiot
cities*

10,000 ransoms. His wisdom was soon proved. The communities to which the captives belonged gratefully voted him golden crowns, and made separate treaties with him. In this way he accomplished his purpose; with Rhegion, Caulonia, and Hipponion he still remained at war, but these states were now isolated and the league was broken up. Rhegion bought off his hostilities for the time by surrendering its fleet. Caulonia was captured and abolished, and its territory given to Locri; Hipponion was likewise taken and destroyed; but the peoples of both these cities were transplanted to Syracuse and became Syracusan citizens.

But Dionysius had not yet finished with Rhegion. He created a pretext for renewing hostilities and he laid siege to the city. The men of Rhegion had now no friends to help them, but, under their general Phyton, whom the tyrant vainly endeavoured to bribe, they held out for ten months, and were reduced to surrender in the end by starvation. Dionysius

*Sub-
mission of
Rhegion,
capture of
Caulonia,
389 B.C.
Capture of
Hipponion,
388 B.C.*

*Capture of
Rhegion,
387 B.C.*

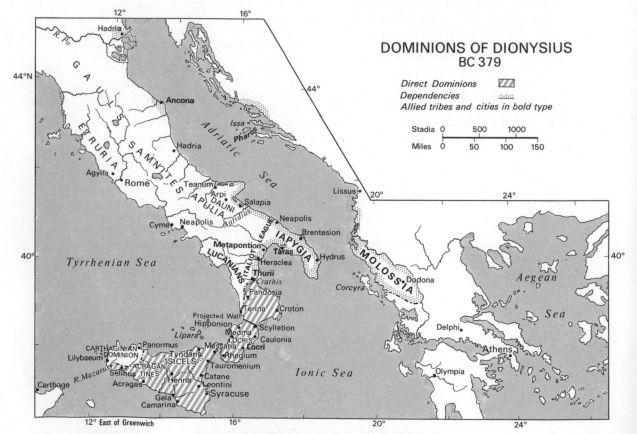

31. DOMINIONS OF DIONYSIUS 379 B.C.

accepted ransoms for those who could find the money; the rest of the inhabitants were sold. Phyton was selected for special vengeance. He was scourged through the army and then drowned with all his kin. Thus Dionysius gained what hitherto had been one of his most pressing desires—possession of the city which had so long hated and defied him. He was now master of both sides of the strait and held the fortress which was the bulwark of Greek Italy. Eight years later he captured Croton, and his power in Italy reached its greatest height.

The Adriatic schemes of Dionysius

But in the meanwhile the restless ruler of Syracuse had turned his eyes to a region of enterprise further afield. The needs of his treasury, if nothing else, bent his attention to commerce. Dionysius saw an opening for Sicilian commerce along the eastern and western coasts of the Adriatic sea, in whose waters the ships of Corcyra, Athens, and Taras had been the main traders, and he set about making the Adriatic a Syracusan lake, by means of settlements and alliances. He founded settlements in Apulia, which he probably hoped ultimately to incorporate in his dominion. He settled a colony and fixed a naval station in the island of Issa, whose importance as a strategic post has been more than once illustrated in subsequent history.

Issa

Pharos
Ancona

He took part with the Parians in colonising Pharos, on an island not far from Issa. A Syracusan colony was planted at Ancona, and, even if the colonists were, as they are said to have been, exiles and enemies of Dionysius, we may be sure that the merchant ships of Syracuse were welcome at the wharfs of Ancona. The northern goal of these merchant ships was near the mouth of the Po, at a spot where there was already a mart for diffusing Greek merchandise in Cisalpine Gaul, and beyond the Alps into northern Europe. This

Hadria

was the Venetian Hadria, city of marshes and canals, which was now colonised by Dionysius, to be in some sort—as has been aptly observed —a forerunner of Venice itself. It was in one of these outlying posts of the Hellenic world that the historian to whom we owe our best knowledge of the Sicilian history of this time probably wrote his works. Philistus had held posts of high trust under Dionysius and had even been the commandant of the Syracusan citadel; but in later years he incurred his master's displeasure or suspicion, and chose as his place of banishment some city on the Adriatic, possibly Hadria. In connection with these Adriatic designs, about which we have only the most fragmentary records, Dionysius

formed an alliance with Alcetas of Molossia, whose unstable position in his own kingdom made him willing to be a dependent on the strong ruler of Syracuse. Thus Dionysius made his influence predominant at the gates of the Adriatic.

Molossia

The Syracusan empire—we may survey it, when it reached its widest extent—consisted, like most other empires, partly of immediate dominion and partly of dependent communities. The immediate dominion was both insular and continental; it included the greater portion of Sicily and the southern peninsula of Italy, perhaps as far north as the river Crathis. But this dominion was not homogeneous, in the relations of its various parts to the government at Syracuse. There was first of all the old territory of the Syracusan republic. There were secondly, a number of military settlements; an institution of Dionysius which has been compared to the military colonies of Rome. Such, for example, was Croton on the mainland; such in Sicily were Henna and Messana; such was Issa in the Adriatic. Outside these direct subjects was the third class of the allied cities, which, though absolutely subject to the power of Dionysius, had still the management of their less important affairs in their own hands. To this class belonged the old Greek cities of Sicily—like Gela and Camarina; new colonies, like Tyndaris; some Sicel states like Agyrium and Herbita.

*Greatest extent of Syracusan Empire Its character
I. Immediate dominion
(a) Territory of Syracuse
(b) Military Colonies
(c) Allied cities*

Beyond the sphere of direct dominion stretched the sphere of dependencies—the allies, whose bond of dependence was rather implied than formally expressed. Here belonged the cities of the Italiot league, Thurii and the rest, north of the Crathis river; here belonged some of the Iapygian communities in the heel of Italy; and here the kingdom of Molossia beyond the Ionian sea, and some Illyrian places on the Adriatic coast. The Crathis may be regarded as the line between the two, the outer and the inner, divisions of the empire of Dionysius. But it is remarkable that at one time he planned a wall and ditch which should run across the isthmus from Scylletion to the nearest point on the other sea—a distance of about 20 miles—and thus sever, as it were, the toe of Italy from the mainland and make it a sort of second Sicily.

II. Dependencies

Scheme of fencing off the extremity of Italy

The acquisition and maintenance of this empire, the building of ships and ship-sheds, the payment of mercenary soldiers, the vast fortifications of Syracuse, both of the island and of the hill—all this, along with the ordinary

The finances of Dionysius

expenses of government and the state of a tyrant's court, demanded an enormous outlay. To meet this outlay Dionysius was forced to resort to extraordinary expedients. He oppressed the Syracusans by burdensome taxation. He imposed special taxes for war, special taxes for building ships; and he introduced an onerous tax on cattle. It is said that the citizens paid yearly into the treasury at the rate of 20 per cent of their capital. Later sources embellished the financial theme. He issued, they said, debased tetradrachms of tin instead of silver and, in one case of financial need, paid a debt by placing on each coin an official mark which made it worth the double of its true value. But the most that the numismatists can confirm is the issue of electrum pieces which in the west amounted to the employment of adulterated gold. There is, however, little doubt that Dionysius was an unscrupulous rifler of temples. Thus, when he took Croton, he carried off the treasures of a temple of Hera. In an earlier year he sailed like a pirate to Etruria, swooped down on a rich temple at the port of Agylla, and bore off booty which amounted to the value of 1500 talents. The plunder of a sanctuary on distant barbarian shores might seem a small thing, but no awe of divine displeasure restrained Dionysius from planning a raid upon the holiest place of Hellenic worship. He formed the design of robbing the treasury of Delphi itself, with Illyrian and Molossian help, but the plan miscarried. It is little wonder that the tyrant had an evil repute in the mother-country.

Death of Dionysius. Estimate of his Work

Outbreak of Third Punic War, 383 B.C.

It was only for a moment that the dominion of the Syracusan despot reached its extreme limits. He had hardly won the city and lands of Croton, when his borders fell back in the west of his own island. A new war with Carthage had broken out, and this time, if Dionysius was not the first to draw the sword, he at least provoked hostilities. He entered into alliances with some of the cities dependent on Carthage—possibly Segesta or Eryx. Of the campaigns we know almost nothing, except their result. First we find Carthage helping the Italiots with whom the tyrant was at war. Next we find a Carthaginian force in Sicily commanded by Mago. In a battle fought at Cabala—a place unknown—the Syracusans won a great victory and Mago was killed. While negotiations for peace were proceeding,

Battle of Cabala. Battle of Cronion, 379 B.C. Peace, 378 B.C.

another battle was fought at Cronion near Panormus, and fate reversed her award. Dionysius was defeated with terrible loss and compelled to make a disadvantageous peace. The boundary of Greek against Punic Sicily was withdrawn from the river Mazarus to the river Halycus. This meant that the deliverer of Selinus and Thermae gave back those cities to the mercies of the barbarian. At the mouth of the Halycus, the old Greek foundation of Heraclea Minoa now became, under the corresponding Punic name Ras Melkart, one of the chief strongholds of Punic power.

Ras Melkart

Just ten years later, ten years in which the history of Sicily is a blank, Dionysius essayed to retrieve the losses which the disastrous battle of Cronion had brought upon him. He made war once more upon Carthage, and for the second time he invaded Punic Sicily. He delivered Greek Selinus; he won Campanian Entella; and captured Elymian Eryx along with its haven Drepanon. He then attempted, we may almost say, to repeat the great exploit of his first war. There was no more a Motya to capture, but he laid siege to Lilybaeum, which had taken Motya's place. But he was compelled to abandon the attempt—the fortress was too strong; and his ill-success was soon crowned by the loss of a large part of his fleet, which was carried out of the harbour of Drepanon by an enterprising Carthaginian admiral.

Fourth Punic War, 368 B.C.

It was the last undertaking of the great 'ruler of Sicily'. He did not live to conclude the peace which probably confirmed the Halycus as the boundary between Greek and barbarian. His death was connected with a side of his character which has not yet come before us. The tyrant of Syracuse has a place, though it is a small place, in literary history. He was a dramatic poet, and he frequently competed with his tragedies in the Athenian theatre. He won third, he won even second prizes; but his dearest ambition was to be awarded a first place. That desire was at length fulfilled; his failure at Lilybaeum and the loss of his ships at Drepanon were compensated by the news that the first prize had been assigned to his *Ransom of Hector* at the Lenaean festival. He celebrated his joy by an unwonted carouse; his intemperance was followed by a fever, and a soporific draught was administered to him which induced the sleep of death.

Death of Dionysius, 367 B.C.

Dionysius as a tragic poet

Dionysius did not stand wholly aloof from the politics of elder Greece. His alliance with Sparta, and the help which he received from her at the siege of Syracuse, involved him in obligations to her which he fulfilled on more

Relations of Sicily to Eastern Greece

than one occasion; and in the regions of Corcyra his empire came into direct contact with the spheres of some of the states of the mother-country. But these political relations are an unimportant part of his reign. His reign, as a whole, lies apart from the contemporary politics of elder Greece. Yet, from some points of view, it possesses more significance in Greek, and in European, history than the contemporary history of Sparta and Athens.

Signification cance of Dionysius in history Champion of Europe against the Semite

In the first place, Dionysius stands out as one of the most prominent champions of Europe in the long struggle between the Asiatic and the European for the possession of Sicily. He did what no champion had done before: he carried the war into the enemy's precinct. He well-nigh achieved what it was reserved for an Italian commonwealth actually to achieve, the reclaiming of the whole island for Europe, the complete expulsion of the Semitic intruder.

Extra-Sicilian Empire

In the second place, he stands out as the man who raised his own city not only to dominion over all Greek Sicily but to a transmarine dominion, which made her the most powerful city in the Greek world, the most potent state in Europe. The purely Sicilian policy is flung aside, and Syracuse becomes a continental power, laying one hand on that peninsula to which her own island geographically belongs, and stretching out the other to the lands beyond the Adriatic. And, thirdly, this empire,

Anticipation of the Macedonian monarchies Military improvements Deification

though it is thinly disguised like the later empire of Rome under constitutional forms, is really a monarchical realm, which is a foreshadowing of the Macedonian monarchies and an anticipation of a new period in European history. Again in the art of war Dionysius inaugurated methods which did not come into general use till more than half a century later; some of his military operations seem to transport us to the age of Alexander the Great and his successors. In another way too Dionysius anticipated the age of those monarchs; statues were set up representing him in the guise of Dionysus, the god by whose name he was called. Here indeed he did not stand alone among his contemporaries; the Spartan Lysander also had been invested with attributes of divinity.

Dionysius not a Hellenizer First signs of the expansion of the Italian race

But in one respect Dionysius was far from being a forerunner of the Macedonian monarchs: he was not an active or deliberate diffuser of Hellenic civilisation. On the contrary he appears rather as an undoer of Hellenic civilisation. He destroys Hellenic towns, and he replaces Hellenic by Italian communities; he cultivates the friendship of Gauls and

Lucanians, to use them against Greeks, not to make them Greeks. This side of the policy of Dionysius, the establishment of Italian settlements in Sicily, points in a different direction; it points—unintentionally, indeed, so far as he was concerned—to the expansion of Italy and to the Italian conquest of Sicily which was to be accomplished more than a century after his death.

Dionysius then has the significance of a pioneer. But there is something else to be said. Original and successful as he was, great things as he did, we cannot help feeling that he ought to have done greater things still. A master of political wisdom, an originator of daring ideas, a man of endless energy, remarkably temperate in the habits of his life, he was hampered throughout by his unconstitutional position. The nature of tyranny imposed limitations on his work. He had always to consider first the security of his own uncharted rule; he could never forget the fact that he was a hated master. He could therefore never devote himself to the accomplishment of any object or the solution of any problem with the undivided zeal which may animate a constitutional prince who need never turn aside to examine the sure foundations of his power. We saw how the tyrant's warfare against Carthage was affected by these personal calculations. The Syracusan tyranny accomplished indeed far more than could have been accomplished by the Syracusan democracy; Dionysius as a tyrant accomplished what he could never have accomplished as a mere statesman governing by legitimate influence the counsels of a free assembly. But he illustrates—and all the more strikingly, as the pioneer of the great monarchies of the future—the truth to which attention has been called before, that the tyrannies and democracies of Greek cities were in their nature not adapted to create and maintain large empires.

Why Dionysius did not do more

Dionysius the Younger

The empire of Dionysius, which he had made fast, to use his own expression, 'by chains of adamant'—a strong army, a strong navy, and strong walls—descended to his son, Dionysius, a youth of feeble character, but not without amiable qualities, but of the nature that is easily swayed to good or evil and is always dependent on advisers. At first he was under the influence of Dion, who had been the most trusted minister of the elder Dionysius in the latter part of his reign, holding the office of

Dionysius II., 367 B.C.

Dion, brother-in-law and son-in-law of Dionysius the elder

admiral, and allied by a double marriage with the tyrant's family. The tyrant had married Dion's sister Aristomache; and Dion married one of the daughters of this marriage, Arete, his own niece. The other daughter was given to Dionysius, her half-brother. Another man, possessing the pride, wealth, and ability of Dion, might have sought to fling aside Dionysius, and if he did not seize the tyranny himself, even if only to secure it for the sons of his sister, the brothers of his wife, Hipparinus and Nysaeus. But Dion was not like

His political aspirations

other men; his aspirations were loftier and less selfish. His object was not to secure tyranny for any man, but to get rid of tyranny altogether. But this was not to be done by a revolution; the democracy which would have risen on the ruins of the despotism would have been in Dion's eyes as evil a thing for

Plato's influence on Dion

Syracuse as the despotism itself. For Dion had imbibed, and thoroughly believed in, the political teaching of his friend Plato, the philosopher. His darling project was to establish at Syracuse a constitution which would so far as possible conform to the theoretical views of Plato, and which would probably have taken the shape of a limited kingship, with some resemblance to the constitution of Sparta. And this could never have been brought about by a pure vote of the Syracusan people; the ideal constitution must be imposed upon them for their own good. The sole chance lay in persuading a tyrant to impose limitations on his own absolute power and introduce the required constitution. 'Give me,' says Plato himself, 'a city governed by a tyranny, and let the tyrant be young, with good brains, brave, and generous, and let fortune bring in his way a good lawgiver'—then a state has a chance of being well governed. Dion saw in young Dionysius a nature which might be moulded as he wished—a nature, perhaps, which he missed in his own nephews, Hipparinus and Nysaeus. He devoted himself loyally to Dionysius, who looked up to his virtue and experience, and he set himself to interest the young ruler in philosophy and make him take a serious view of his duties. But his chief hope lay in bringing the tyrant under the attraction of the same powerful personality which had exercised a decisive and abiding influence over himself. Plato must come to Syracuse and make the tyrant a philosopher. The treatment which Plato had

c. 388 B.C.

experienced on the occasion of a previous visit to Sicily, at the hands of the elder Dionysius, was not indeed such as to encourage him to return. But he yielded, reluctantly, to the pressing invitation of the young ruler and the urgent solicitations of Dion, who represented that now at last the moment had come to call an ideal state into actual existence.

Plato's second visit to Sicily

It was the vision of a 'dreamer dreaming greatly'; and that a statesman of Dion's practical experience and knowledge of human nature should have allowed himself to be guided by such a dream may seem strange to us, to whom the history of hundreds of societies throughout a period of more than two thousand years has brought disillusion. It has indeed seemed so curious that some have concluded that Dion was throughout plotting to dethrone Dionysius—that the philosophical scheme was part of the plot, and Plato an unconscious tool of the conspiracy. But the good faith of Dion seems assured. We must remember that a state founded on philosophical principles was a new idea, which was not at all likely to seem foredoomed to failure to anyone who was enamoured of philosophy; for such a state had never been tried, and consequently there was no example of a previous failure. On the contrary, there was the example of Sparta as a success. The political speculators of those days always turned with special predilection to Sparta as a well-balanced state, and it was believed that her constitution and discipline had been called into being and established for all time by the will and fiat of a single extraordinarily wise lawgiver. Why then should not Dionysius and Dion, under the direction of Plato, do for Syracuse what Lycurgus had done for Lacedaemon? And Dion doubtless thought that his own experience would enable him to adjust the demands of speculation to the rude realities of existence.

Serious intention to form an ideal state

No welcome could have been more honourable and flattering than that which Plato received. He engaged the respect and admiration of Dionysius, and the young tyrant was easily brought to regard tyranny as a vile thing and to cherish the plan of building up a new constitution. The experiment would probably have been tried, if Plato, in dealing with his pupil, had acted otherwise than he did. The nature of Dionysius was one of those which are susceptible of impressions and capable of enthusiasm, but incapable of persevering application. If Plato had contented himself with inculcating the general principles which he has expounded with such charm in his *Republic*, Dionysius would in all likelihood have attempted to create at Syracuse a dim adumbration of the ideal state. It is hardly likely that it would have been long maintained: still, it would at least have been tried. But Plato insisted on

Plato's course of instruction

imparting to his pupil a systematic course of philosophical training, and began with the science of geometry. The tyrant took up the study with eagerness; his court was absorbed in geometry; but he presently wearied of it. And then influences which were opposed to the scheme of Dion and Plato began to tell.

Philistus recalled: opposed to Dion's scheme

One of the first acts of the new reign had been to recall from exile the historian Philistus. He was entirely averse to the proposed reforms, and wanted the tyranny to continue on its old lines. He and his friends insinuated that the true object of Dion was to secure the tyranny for one of his own nephews, as soon as Dionysius had laid it down. They did everything to turn Dionysius against Dion, and at last an indiscreet letter of Dion gave them the means of success. Syracuse and Carthage were negotiating peace, and Dion wrote to the Carthaginian Judges not to act without first consulting him. The letter was intercepted, and though its motive was doubtless perfectly honest it was interpreted as treason. Dion was banished from Sicily, but was allowed to retain his property, and the party of Philistus won the upper hand. Plato remained for a while in the island; Dionysius was jealous of the esteem which he felt for Dion and desired above all things to win the same esteem for himself. But the philosopher's visit had been a failure; he yearned to get back to Athens, and at length Dionysius let him go.

Banishment of Dion

Plato returns to Athens

So ended the notable scheme of founding an ideal state, the realisation of which would have involved the disbandment of the mercenary troops and thereby the collapse of the Syracusan empire. It is easy to ridicule Plato for want of tact in his treatment of the young tyrant; it is easy to flout him as a pedant for not distinguishing between an Academy and a Court. But Plato was perfectly right. The only motive which had brought him to Sicily was to prepare the way for founding a state fashioned more or less according to his own ideal. Now the first condition of the life of such a state was that a king should be a philosopher. Therefore, as Dionysius—not Plato—was to be king in the new state, it was indispensable that Dionysius should become a philosopher. Plato had not the smallest interest in imparting to the tyrant a superficial smattering of philosophy, enough to beguile him into framing a Platonic state. For that state would have been still-born, since it lacked the first condition of life, a true philosopher at its head. If Dionysius had not the stuff of a true, but only of a sham, philosopher, it was useless to make the experiment. Plato adopted the only reasonable course; he was true to his own ideal.

Dion

Strange as it may appear after such experiences, Plato seems to have returned once more to Sicily, at the urgent invitation of Dionysius. He can have had no more expectations of making a philosopher out of the tyrant, and his chief motive must have been to bring about the recall of Dion and reconcile him to Dionysius, who appears to have lured the philosopher by the hope that this might be accomplished. Plato was received and entertained with as great honour as before, but his visit was fruitless. Probably the tyrant ascertained that Dion was in the meantime using his wealth to make silent preparations for winning his way back to Syracuse and overthrowing the tyranny. Dionysius therefore took the precaution of confiscating Dion's property, and then Plato returned to Athens as soon as he could. Dion also betook himself to Old Greece and made Athens his headquarters. Presently the tyrant committed a needless act of tyranny: he compelled Dion's wife Arete to marry another man. At length Dion decided that the time for action had come. With a very small force, packed into not more than five merchant ships, he set sail from Zacynthus, to encounter the mighty armaments of Dionysius. His coming was expected, and the admiral Philistus had a fleet in Italian waters to waylay him. But Dion sailed straight across the open sea to Pachynus. His plan was to land in Western Sicily, collect what reinforcements he could, and march on Syracuse. It was a bold enterprise, but Dion knew that the character of the tyrant was feeble, and that the Syracusans longed to be delivered from his tyranny. Driven by a storm to the Libyan coast, the ships of the deliverer finally reached Heraclea Minoa, now a Carthaginian port in southwestern Sicily. Here they learned that Dionysius had departed for Italy with 80 ships, and they lost no time in marching to Syracuse, picking up reinforcements, both Greek and Sicel, on their way. The Campanian mercenaries who were guarding Epipolae were lured away by a trick and, making a night march from Acrae, Dion and his party entered Syracuse amid general rejoicings. The Assembly placed the government in the hands of 20 generals, Dion among them. The fortress of Epipolae was secured; no part of Syracuse remained in possession of Dionysius except

Third visit of Plato to Syracuse

Dion at Athens

357 B.C. Dion sails for Sicily, August

Enters Syracuse

Dionysius holds the Island

the Island, and against this Dion built a wall of defence from the Greater to the Lesser Harbour. Seven days later Dionysius returned.

While Syracuse was rocking with the first enthusiasm at her deliverance, the deliverer was the popular hero. But Dion was not a man who could hold the affections of the people, for he repelled men by his exceeding haughtiness. And it was seen too that he was determined masterfully to direct the Syracusans how they were to use their freedom. Dionysius, shut up in the Island, resorted to artifices to raise suspicion against him in the minds of the citizens, and a rival appeared on the scene who possessed more popular *Heraclides* manners than Dion. This was a certain Heraclides, whom the tyrant had banished, and who now returned with an armament of ships and soldiers. The Assembly elected him admiral. Dion undid this act on the ground that his own consent was necessary, and then came forward himself to propose Heraclides. This behaviour alienated the sympathies of the citizens; they did not want another autocrat. Soon afterwards Heraclides won an important sea-fight, defeating Philistus, who had returned from Italy with his squadron. *Death of* The old historian himself was captured and *Philistus* took his own life. Dionysius thus lost his best support, and presently he escaped from the Island, taking his triremes with him, but leaving a garrison of mercenaries and his young son Apollocrates in command, an unenviable position.

Soon after this the influence of Dion sank so low that the Syracusans deposed him from the post of general, and appointed 25 new generals, among them Heraclides. They also refused to grant any pay to the Peloponnesian deliverers who had come with Dion. The *Dion* Peloponnesians would have gladly turned *withdraws* against the Syracusans if Dion had given the *to Leontini,* signal; but Dion, though self-willed, was too *356 B.C.* genuine a patriot to attack his own city, and he retired to Leontini with 300 devoted men.

The Syracusans then went on with the siege of the island fortress, and so hard pressed was the garrison that it determined to surrender. Heralds had been already sent to announce the decision to the Syracusans, when in the early *Arrival of* morning reinforcements arrived—soldiers and *Nypsius* provisions, brought by a Campanian of Naples, by name Nypsius, who, eluding the enemy's ships, sailed into the Great Harbour. The situation was changed, and negotiations were immediately broken off. At first fortune favoured the Syracusans. Heraclides put out to sea and won a second sea-fight, sinking or capturing whatever warships had been left behind by Dionysius or were brought by Nypsius. At this success the city went wild with joy and spent the night in carousing. Before the dawn of day, when soldiers and generals were alike sunk in a drunken sleep, Nypsius and his troops issued from the gates of the island and, surmounting the cross-wall of Dion by scaling-ladders, slew the guards and took possession of Lower Achradina and the Agora. All this part of the city was sacked. Full license was given to the mercenaries, and they carried off women and children and all the property they could lay hands on. Next day all the citizens who had taken refuge in Epipolae and the Upper Achradina, looking helplessly at what had been done, and seeing that the barbarians were beginning their horrible work again, voted to call Dion to the rescue. Messengers riding as swiftly as they could reached Leontini towards *Dion* evening. Dion led them to the theatre, and *recalled,* there before the gathered folk the envoys told their tale and implored Dion and the Peloponnesians to forget the ingratitude of Syracuse and come to her help. Dion made a moving speech; he would in any case go, and if he could not save his city he would bury himself in her ruins; but the Peloponnesians might well refuse to stir for a people which had treated them so badly. A shout went up that Syracuse must be rescued, and for the second time Dion led the Peloponnesians to her deliverance. They set out at once, and a night march brought them to Megara, 5 or 6 miles from Syracuse, at the dawn of day. There dreadful news reached them. Nypsius, knowing that the rescue was on its way and deciding that no time was to be lost, had let loose his barbarians again into the city at midnight. They no longer thought of plunder, but only of slaying and burning. At this news the rescuing army hurried on to save what might still be saved. Entering by the Hexapylon on the north, Dion cleared his way before him through Achradina, *rescues* and reached the cross-wall which he had *Syracuse* himself built as a defence against the Island. It was now broken down, but behind its ruins Nypsius had posted a body of his mercenaries, and this was the scene of the decisive struggle. Dion's men carried the wall, and the enemy was driven back into the fortress of Ortygia.

The opponents of Dion, who had not fled, were humbled. Heraclides pleaded for pardon, and Dion was blamed for not putting him to death. It was at all events foolish magnanimity which consented to the arrangement that Dion should be general with full power on land, and

Heraclides by sea. The old dissensions soon broke out, and presently we find a Spartan named Gaesylus reconciling the rivals and constraining Heraclides to swear solemnly to do nothing against Dion.

Surrender of the Island

Nypsius seems to have disappeared from the scene, and it was not long before the son of Dionysius, weary of the long siege, made up his mind to surrender the Island to Dion. During all these dreadful events Dion's sister Aristomache and his wife Arete had been kept in the Island. Dion now took back his wife.

The time at last came for Dion to show what his political aims really were. He professed to have come to give Syracuse freedom; but the freedom which he would have given her was not such as she herself desired. The Syracusan citizens wanted the restoration of their democracy, but to Dion democracy seemed as bad a form of government as tyranny. If, taught by experience, he no longer dreamed of a Platonic state, he desired to establish an aristocracy, with some democratic limitations, and with a king, or kings, as in Sparta. With this purpose in view he sent to Corinth for helpers and advisers; and he expressed his leanings to the Corinthian oligarchy by an issue of coins, with a flying horse, modelled on the Pegasi of Corinth. But though Dion hoped to establish a state in which the few should govern the many, he made a grave mistake in not immediately placing himself above the suspicion of being a selfish power-seeker—a possible tyrant. The Syracusans longed to see the fortress of the tyrant demolished, and if Dion had complied with their wish he might have secured for himself enduring influence. But though he did not live in the fortress he allowed it to remain, and its existence seemed a standing invitation to tyranny. Dion had no intention of allowing the Syracusans to manage their own affairs, and the enjoyment of power corrupted him. His authority was only limited by the joint command of Heraclides, and at last he was brought to consent that his rival should be secretly assassinated. After this he was to all purposes tyrant, though he might repudiate tyranny with his lips.

Dion's political aim:

a modified aristocracy

Dion becomes a tyrant

Plot of Callippus;

Among those who had come with him from older Greece to liberate Syracuse was a pupil of Plato named Callippus; and this man plotted to overthrow Dion, who trusted him implicitly. Aristomache and Arete suspected him and taxed him with treachery; nor were they assured until he had taken the most solemn oath that a mortal could take. He went to the precinct of the great goddesses

his oath

Demeter and Persephone; the priest wrapped him in the purple robe of the queen of the underworld and gave him a lighted torch; in this guise he swore that he plotted no evil design against Dion. But so little regard had Callippus for religion that he chose the festival of the Maiden by whom he had sworn for the execution of his plot. He employed some men of Zacynthus to murder Dion, and then seized the power himself.

Murder of Dion, 354 B.C., June

The tyranny of Callippus lasted for about a year. Then, while he was engaged in an attack on Catane, the two sons of the elder Dionysius by his second wife, Hipparinus and Nysaeus, came to Syracuse and won possession of Ortygia. These brothers were a worthless pair, drunken and dissolute. Hipparinus held the island for about two years; then he was murdered in a fit of drunkenness, and was succeeded by Nysaeus, who ruled Ortygia five years longer. It is not certain how far these tyrants were able to assert their authority over Syracuse outside the precincts of the Island.

Tyranny of Callippus, 354-3 B.C.; of Hipparinus, 353-1 B.C.; of Nysaeus, 351-46 B.C.

During all these changes Dionysius was living at Locri, the native city of his mother, and ruling it with a tyrant's rod. His cruelty, and the outrages which he committed on the freeborn maidens of the city, provoked universal hatred. At length he saw the chance of recovering Syracuse. Leaving his wife and daughters at Locri with a small garrison, he sailed to Ortygia and drove out Nysaeus. As soon as he had gone the Locrians arose and easily overcame his mercenaries. The enormities of which the tyrant had been guilty may best be measured by the brutal thirst of vengeance which now consumed the citizens of Locri. The wife and daughters of Dionysius were submitted to the most horrible tortures and insults before they were strangled; the sea was sown with their ashes.

Second tyranny of Dionysius, 346 B.C.

Fate of his wife and daughters

Timoleon

At this moment tyrannies flourished in Sicily. Besides Syracuse, the cities of Messana, Leontini, and Catane, and many Sicel towns were under the yoke of tyrants. Syracuse was at least half free; Dionysius held only the Island. But the Syracusans, for lack of another leader, looked for help and guidance, in their struggle against their own tyrant, to the man who had made himself lord of Leontini. This was a certain Hiketas who was a follower of Dion, but after Dion's death caused his wife and sister to be drowned while they were sailing to the Peloponnese. This Hiketas

Hiketas

Sicilian
appeal to
Corinth

was aiming at becoming himself lord of Syracuse, and he hoped to accomplish his purpose with the help of Carthage. But he veiled his designs, and he supported an appeal which the Sicilian Greeks now addressed to Corinth. It was an appeal for help both against the plague of tyranny which was rampant in Sicily and against the Carthaginians, who were preparing a great armament to descend upon the troubled island. The Syracusans selected Hiketas as their general.

Corinth's
response

Timoleon

Corinth, ever a solicitous mother to her colonies, was ready to respond to the appeal, and the only difficulty was to find a suitable commander. Someone in the assembly, by a sudden inspiration, arose and named Timoleon, the son of Timodemus. Belonging to a noble family, and notable by his personal qualities, Timoleon was living under a strange cloud, through a deed which some highly praised and others severely blamed. He had saved his brother's life in battle at the risk of his own; but, when that brother afterwards plotted to make himself tyrant, Timoleon and some friends put him to death. His mother and many others abhorred him as guilty of a brother's blood, while others admired him as the slayer of a tyrant. In the light of his later deeds, we know that Timoleon was actuated by the highest motives of duty when he consented to his brother's death. Ever since that terrible day he had lived in retirement, but when his name was mentioned in the Assembly all approved, and Teleclides, a man of influence, expressed the general thought by saying, 'We shall decide that he slew a tyrant, if he is successful; that he slew his brother, if he fails.' The enterprise was to be Timoleon's ordeal.

The
sailing of
Timoleon,
344 B.C.

With ten ships of war, a few fellow-citizens, and about 1000 mercenaries, Timoleon crossed the Ionian sea, guided, it was said, by the track of a flaming torch, the emblem of the Sicilian goddesses Demeter and Persephone. At Rhegion, now free from the rule of tyrants, he met with a warm welcome. But he found a Carthaginian fleet awaiting him there, and likewise ambassadors from Hiketas, who demanded that the ships and soldiers should be sent back to Corinth, since the Carthaginians would not permit them to cruise in Sicilian waters. As for Timoleon himself, Hiketas would be pleased to have his help and counsel. Timoleon had no thought of heeding such a message. It was not to set up the rule of Hiketas at Syracuse that he had come, or to submit to the dictation of the enemies of Hellas. But the difficulty was to leave the

roadstead of Rhegion in face of the Punic fleet. Here Timoleon showed caution and craft. He pretended to agree to the proposals, but he asked that the whole matter and the intentions of Hiketas should be clearly stated in the presence of the people of Rhegion. With their connivance time was wasted, and the Carthaginians and the ambassadors of Hiketas were detained in the Assembly, until the Corinthian ships had put out to sea, Timoleon himself slipping away just in time to embark in the last of them. He made straight for Tauromenion.

Timoleon
comes to
Tauro-
menion

It will be remembered that Tauromenion, planted by Himilco to be a Sicel city, had been taken by Dionysius to be a home for his mercenaries. Amid the troubles after the tyrant's death it had gained its independence, and a citizen named Andromachus had become the foremost man in its public affairs. Andromachus induced his fellow-citizens to offer a home to the homeless Naxians whose parents Dionysius had so cruelly dispossessed. The Naxians came back to the hill which looked down on the place of their old city; Naxos revived in Tauromenion. And the Naxians were the first Sicilians to welcome the deliverer of Sicily to her shores. Timoleon's first success was at Hadranum, the Sicel town where the great Sicilian fire-god Hadranus had his chief abode. The men of Hadranum were at discord among themselves; some would summon Hiketas, others invited Timoleon, and both Hiketas and Timoleon came. It was a race between them to get to Hadranum first. Timoleon, the later to arrive, surprised the enemy as they were resting outside the town, and defeated them, although in numbers they were five to one. The gates of the city were then thrown open and Hadranum became the headquarters of Timoleon's army. Soon afterwards Hiketas suborned two men to assassinate the Corinthian leader, but the plot was frustrated at the last moment, and henceforth the belief gained ground that Timoleon was hedged about by some divine protection. The fire-god of Hadranum too had shown by miraculous signs that he approved of the stranger's enterprise. Other cities now allied themselves with Timoleon, and presently Dionysius sent a message to him, proposing to surrender the Island, and asking only to be allowed to retire in safety to Corinth, with his private property. The offer was at once accepted; the fortress, and the mercenaries who guarded it, and all the war gear were transferred to Timoleon. Dionysius lived the rest of his life at Corinth in harmless obscurity.

Settlement
of Naxians
there by
Andro-
machus

Battle of
Hadra-
num

The end of
Dionysius

Many anecdotes were told of the trivial doings of the fallen lord of Sicily and his smart sayings. When some one contrasted his fortune with that of his father, he remarked, 'My father came into power when democracy was hated, but I when tyranny was envied.'

Having won Ortygia sooner and more easily than could have been hoped, it remained for Timoleon to liberate the rest of Syracuse, which was in the hands of Hiketas. But Hiketas had powerful allies. A hundred and fifty Carthaginian ships, under the command of Mago, sailed into the Great Harbour, and a Carthaginian force was admitted into Syracuse. The Corinthian commander in the Island—Timoleon himself still lived at Hadranum—was hard pressed; but presently Mago and Hiketas went off to besiege Catane, and Neon making a successful sally occupied Achradina. At the same time reinforcements from Corinth, which had been for some time delayed in Italy by the Carthaginian fleet, arrived in Sicily. It was now time for Timoleon himself to appear at Syracuse. He pitched his camp on the south side, on the banks of the Anapus. Then he had another piece of luck. The Greek mercenaries, both his own and those of Hiketas, used to amuse their idle hours by fishing for eels at the mouth of the river; and as they had no cause to quarrel, though they were ready to kill each other for pay, they used to converse amicably on such occasions. One of Timoleon's soldiers observed that the Greeks ought to combine against the barbarians, and the words coming to the ears of Mago caused him to conceive suspicions of Hiketas; he suddenly sailed off with all his fleet, but when he reached Carthage he slew himself and his countrymen crucified his corpse. This story, however, can hardly be the whole explanation of Mago's strange behaviour.

Thus freed from his most formidable enemy, Timoleon soon drove Hiketas from Epipolae, and Syracuse was at length completely free. The Syracusans had found a deliverer who did not, like Dion, seek to be their master, and the fortress of Dionysius was pulled down. This act of demolition seemed the seal and assurance of their deliverance. But the city was depopulated and desolate, grass grew in the market-place; and the first task of the deliverer was to repopulate it with new citizens. The Corinthians made proclamations at the festivals of older Greece, inviting emigrants to resettle Syracuse; men whom the tyrants had banished flocked back, and 60,000 men in all gathered both from west and east, with women and children, and restored the strength of the city. The laws of Diocles were issued anew, and the democratic constitution was revived and in some respects remodelled. The most important innovation was the investing of the *amphipolos* or priest of Olympian Zeus with the chief magistracy. The priest was annually elected and gave his name to the year; but, as he was chosen by lot out of three clans, his promotion to be the first magistrate of the republic was a limitation of the democracy. Such was the renovation of Syracuse; and her debt to Corinth in the winning of freedom was reflected in the issue of coins with the Corinthian Pegasus on the obverse.

Timoleon then went on to do for other towns in Sicily what he had done for Syracuse. Many tyrants submitted; even Hiketas, who had withdrawn to Leontini. There was also work to be done against the Carthaginians, who were intent upon recovering lost ground and were preparing for another great effort to drive the Greeks out of Sicily. Five years after Timoleon had landed in the island, a large armament sailed from Carthage and put in at Lilybaeum. It consisted of 200 galleys and 1000 transports; there were 10,000 horses—some for war-chariots; and the total number of the infantry was said to be 70,000. The flower of the host was the 'Sacred Band' of 2500 Carthaginian citizens, men of birth and wealth. Hamilcar and Hasdrubal, the commanders, decided to march right across Sicily against Syracuse. But Timoleon did not await them there; he would try to encounter them west of the Halycus, in Punic not in Greek territory. Collecting such an army as he could —it amounted to no more than 10,000—he set out. On the march he was deserted by 1000 mercenaries who clamoured for arrears of pay and murmured at being led against such overwhelming odds; and only with difficulty could he persuade the rest to go on. The Carthaginians were encamped on the west bank of the Crimisus, a branch of the river Hypsas, not that which washes Acragas, but that which flows through the territory of Selinus. The city of Entella, now held by Campanians, was situated on the Crimisus, and it may be that the Punic army had halted with the hope of taking it.

The field of the battle which was now fought between the Greeks and Phoenicians on the banks of the Crimisus is unknown. In the morning the Greeks ascended a hill which divided them from the river, and on their way they met mules laden with wild celery, a herb which was used to wreathe sepulchral slabs.

Carthaginians at Syracuse supporting Hiketas

Syracuse repeopled

Democracy

Coinage

Tyrants suppressed in Sicily

Carthaginian expedition against Sicily, 339 B.C.

Battle of the Crimisus (June)

(σέλινον)

411

The soldiers were depressed by an incident which seemed ominous; but of the same herb were made the crowns of victors in the Isthmian games, and Timoleon hastened to interpret the chance as an augury of victory. He wreathed his head with the celery, and the whole host followed his example. Then two eagles appeared in the sky, one bearing a serpent—another fortunate omen. The Greeks halted on the hilltop, striving to pierce the mist which enveloped the ground below them, and when it melted away they saw the enemy crossing the stream. The war-chariots crossed first, and behind came the Sacred Band. Timoleon saw that his chance lay in attacking before the whole army had crossed. He sent down his cavalry to lead the attack and himself followed with the foot. The war-chariots prevented the horses from approaching the Sacred Band; so Timoleon ordered the cavalry to move aside and assail the flank of the foe, leaving the way clear for the infantry. It is not recorded how the infantry swept away the war-chariots, but they succeeded in reaching the Sacred Band. The Carthaginians, firm and immovable, withstood the onset of the spears; and the Greeks, finding that all their thrusting could not drive back or pierce the shield wall, flung down their spears and drew their swords. In the sword fight it was no longer a matter of weight and courage; skill and swift movements told, and the Greeks, superior in these qualities, utterly outfought the Sacred Band. Meanwhile the rest of the Punic army had crossed the river, and although the flower of it was destroyed, there were still enormous numbers to deal with. But fortune followed Timoleon. Clouds had gathered and were hanging over the hills, and suddenly there burst forth a tempest of lightning and wind-driven rain and hail. The Greeks had their backs to the wind; the rain and hail drove into the faces of the enemy, who in the noise could not hear the commands of their officers. When the ground became muddy, the lighter armour of the Greeks gave them a great advantage over their foes, who floundered about, weighed down by their heavy mail. At length the Carthaginians could no longer stand their ground, and when they turned to fly they found death in the Crimisus. Rapidly swollen by the rain, the river was now rushing along in a furious torrent, which swept men and horses to destruction. It is said that 15,000 prisoners were taken and that 10,000 men had been killed in the fight, not counting those who perished in the river; rich spoils of gold and silver were taken in the camp. The choicest of the arms were sent to the Isthmus to be dedicated in the temple of Poseidon.

Timoleon had gained a victory which may be set beside Gelon's victory at Himera. But he did not follow it up; he made no attempt to cut short the Phoenician dominion in Sicily. Perhaps his inaction was due less to unwillingness than to embarrassments which threatened Syracuse. The tyrant of Catane, *Tyranny reviving is suppressed* who had gone over to Timoleon, declared against him; Hiketas seems to have seized again the tyranny at Leontini; and Timoleon found himself engaged in a war with these two tyrants, Mamercus and Hiketas, who were aided by Carthaginian mercenaries. At last both the tyrants were captured. The Syracusans put them both to death, and slew the wife and daughter of Hiketas, in retaliation for the murder of the wife and sister of Dion. The Messanians also put to death their oppressor Hippon with torture, and the schoolboys were taken to the theatre to witness a tyrant's death. Other cities under the yoke of tyranny were likewise liberated, and some depopulated towns, like Acragas and Gela, *Peace with Carthage* were colonised. After twenty years of troubles Sicily was to have a respite now. Carthage made peace, the Halycus being again fixed as the frontier, and she undertook to do nothing to uphold tyrants in Greek cities.

Timoleon had now delivered Sicily both from domestic despots and from foreign foes, and having achieved his task he laid down the powers which had been granted to him for its performance. Among the great men in Greek history he holds a unique place, for the work which he accomplished was inspired neither by selfish ambition nor by patriotism. He sought no power for himself; he laboured in a strange land for cities which might adopt him but were not his own. Patriotism, indeed, in the widest sense, might stimulate his ardour, when he fought for Hellas against the Phoenician. But of Greek leaders who achieved as much as he, there is none whose conduct was, like Timoleon's, wholly guided by simple devotion to duty. The Syracusans gave him a property near Syracuse, and there he dwelt till his death, two years after his crowning victory. Occasionally he visited the city when the folk wished to ask for his counsel, but he had become blind and these visits were rare. He was lamented by all Greek Sicily, and at *The Timo-leonteion* Syracuse his memory was preserved by a group of public buildings called after him.

The land had rest for twenty years after Timoleon's death; the direct results of his work did not amount to more than that. A tyrant arose then of a worse type than the elder Dionysius, and his hand was heavy upon Sicily. But the career of Agathocles lies outside the limits of this history.

Events in South Italy

In these days, troubles and dangers beset the Greeks of Italy no less than their brethren of Sicily. On the mainland, as in the island, the Hellenic name seemed likely to be blotted out —there by the Phoenicians and the Italian mercenaries, here by the native races. The power of the elder Dionysius had kept at bay the Lucanians, the Messapians, the Iapygians, and other neighbours who pressed on Great Greece; but when his son was attacked by Dion, the Syracusan empire dissolved of itself, and the barbarians of Italy, having no great power to fear, began anew to descend from the mountains on the Greek settlements of the coast. A number of tribes in the toe of the peninsula banded themselves together in a league with their federal capital at Consentia; and this Brettian league, as it was called, aimed at subduing all the Greek cities of the promontory. Terina, Hipponion, New Sybaris on the Traeis, and other places were captured. Men were not blind to the danger which menaced Western Hellas, of being sunk under a tide of barbarism; one of the objects of Plato and Dion had been to drive all the barbarian mercenaries out of Greek Sicily. But in Italy the peril was greatest, and there was urgent need of help from without. The appeal of Syracuse to her mother Corinth, and the coming of Timoleon, put it into the mind of Taras, hard beset by the neighbouring peoples, to ask for help from her mother Sparta. The appeal came at a favourable moment. Sparta was not in a position to undertake any political scheme at home, and king Archidamus eagerly embraced the chance of leading the fight for Hellas against the barbarians of the West, even as his father Agesilaus, sixty years ago, had fought against the barbarians of the East.[8] He got together a band of mercenaries, chiefly from the Phocian survivors of the Sacred War, and sailed to Italy.

The Brettian league

c. 356 B.C.

King Archidamus sails to Italy, 343 B.C.

For four or five years seemingly he strove against the barbarians, but without winning any decisive success, and was finally killed at Mandonion in a battle with the Lucanians. The ineffectual expedition of Archidamus was a striking contrast to the brilliant achievements of Timoleon. But Taras was not ungrateful for his efforts. She had commemorated her appeal to Sparta by minting beautiful gold pieces, on which the infant Taras was shown supplicating Poseidon of Cape Taenarus.[9] The tragic issue of that appeal suggested a motive for another series of coins, and called forth one of those pathetic allusions which Greek art could achieve with matchless grace. Taras is represented riding on his dolphin and sadly contemplating a helmet; it is the helmet of the Spartan king who had fallen in his service.

Battle of Mandonion, 338 B.C.

Taras was soon forced to seek a new champion. She invited Alexander of Molossia, the uncle of Alexander the Great, and this king saw and seized the chance of founding an empire in the West—of doing there on a small scale what his nephew was accomplishing on a mighty scale in Asia. He was an able man and success attended his arms. On the east coast of Italy he subdued the Messapians, and pushed as far north as Sipontion, which he captured. In the west he smote the Brettian league, seizing Consentia and liberating Terina. His power was so great in the south that Rome made a treaty with him, and it is possible that his designs reached to Sicily.

Expedition of Alexander of Epirus, 334 B.C.

But a coin issue from Taras shows that Alexander was taking firm hold of his allies. On the obverse is the oak-crowned head of Zeus of Dodona, on the reverse a thunderbolt and spear-head with the legend 'Alexander, son of Neoptolemos'.[10] Taras, her freedom menaced, renounced her alliance. War ensued, Thurii upholding Alexander. The barbarians profited by these struggles to rise against their conqueror, and a battle was fought at Pandosia. During the engagement, a Lucanian exile in the Tarentine army stabbed the king in the back, and the design of an Epirote empire bestriding the Adriatic perished with him. This was not long after the overthrow of the Persian monarchy on the field of Gaugamela. But Alexander's work had not been futile; henceforward Taras was able to keep the upper hand over her Italian neighbours.

Battle of Pandosia, 331-30 B.C. Alexander's death

CHAPTER 16

The Rise of Macedonia

After the battle of Mantinea, when Thebes retired from her aggresive policy, Athens stood forth as the most important state in Old Greece. She would have been free to devote all her energies to re-establishing her power on the coasts of the northern Aegean and by the gates of the Pontic waters, and would doubtless have successfully achieved this main object of her policy, if two outlying powers had not suddenly stepped upon the scene to thwart her and cut short her empire. These powers, Caria and Macedon, lay in opposite quarters of the Greek world. Both were monarchies, both were semi-Hellenic. Macedon was a land-power; Caria was both a land-power and a sea-power, but it was as a sea-power that she was formidable to Athens. Of the two, it was Caria which seemed to Greece the country with a future and to Athens the dangerous rival. Of Macedonia little account was taken by the civilised world, and Athens expected that she could always manage her. No prophet in his happiest hour of clairvoyance could have predicted that within thirty years Caria would have sunk back into insignificance, leaving nothing to posterity save the sepulchre of her prince, while Macedon would bear the arts and wisdom of Hellas to the ends of the earth.

Athens regains the Chersonese and Euboea

The death of Epaminondas delivered Athens from her most dangerous and active enemy, but the intrigues which he had spun against her in the north bore results after his death. Alexander of Pherae, who had become the ally of the Thebans, seized the island of Peparethus with his pirate ships, and defeated an Athenian armament under Leosthenes. He then repeated the daring enterprise of the Spartan Teleutias, sailing rapidly into the Piraeus, plundering the shops, and disappearing as rapidly with ample spoil. The Athenians replied by making a close defensive and offensive alliance with the federal state of the Thessalians. The stone of the treaty is preserved. The allies of both parties are included. The Thessalians bind themselves not to conclude the war against Alexander without the Athenians, and the Athenians on their side 'without the president (archon) and league of the Thessalians'; and the treasurers of Athens are directed to pull down the stêlê on which the former alliance with Alexander had been inscribed.[1]

Thessalian alliance of Athens

But the Athenians vented their indignation within their own walls. Since the capture of Oropus there had been signs of smouldering discontent at the conduct of affairs. Callistratus had been indicted and acquitted in the matter of Oropus, but his credit had been roughly shaken and Alexander's insult to the city at her very doors excited the popular wrath to such a pitch that the statesman as well as the defeated admiral was condemned to death and escaped only by a timely flight. Thus the ablest Athenian statesman of the fourth century passed from the stage, and no sympathy followed him. Some years later he ventured to return from his Macedonian exile, hoping that the anger of his countrymen would have passed away. Their anger had passed, but it had not been replaced by regret. On reaching Athens he sought the refuge of suppliants at the altar of the Twelve Gods; but no voice was raised

Condemnation and exile of Callistratus, 361 B.C.

to save him, and the executioner carried out the sentence of the people. The Athenians were always austere masters of their statesmen, and it sometimes appears to us—though in truth we seldom have sufficient knowledge of the circumstances to justify a confident judgment—that they unreasonably expected a harvest where no seed had been sown.

The Thracian Chersonese

The public indignation which had been aroused by the daring stroke of the tyrant of Pherae was inflamed by the bad tidings which came from Thrace. King Cotys, the reviver of the Odrysian power, had succeeded in laying hold of Sestos and almost the whole peninsula which guards the entrance to the Propontis, in spite of the Athenian fleet. Soon afterwards the old king was murdered and his son Cersobleptes was challenged by two rivals. This was advantageous to Athens, as she could play off one Thracian prince against another.[2] The territory on the Propontis fell to Cersobleptes, who was supported by the Euboean Charidemus, a mercenary captain who had frequently been employed in the service of Athens, and had married, like Iphicrates, a daughter of the Thracian king. Cersobleptes engaged to hand over to Athens the entire Chersonese, except Cardia, 'the enemy of Athens', which was to remain independent. But there was no fleet on the spot to enforce the immediate fulfilment of the promise, and when an admiral was presently sent out he was defeated by Charidemus. At length a capable man was sent, Chares, a daring, dissolute, and experienced soldier, who speedily captured Sestos and punished the inhabitants for their unfaithfulness by an unmerciful slaughter.[3] Cersobleptes was forced to change his attitude, and the peninsula was recovered. The Athenians, adopting the same policy which they had followed in Samos, sent outsettlers to the Chersonese. In the same year Euboea was won back to the Athenian league, and there even seemed a fair prospect of accomplishing what of all things would have rejoiced them most, the recovery of long-lost Amphipolis.[4] But their new scheme against Amphipolis may be said to open, in a certain way, a new chapter in the history of Greece.

Death of king Cotys, 360-59 B.C.

Cersobleptes and his brothers succeed Cotys

357 B.C. Recovery of the Chersonese and settlement of cleruchs

Recovery of Euboea, 357 B.C.

Philip II of Macedonia

The man for whom Macedonia had waited long came at last. We have met earlier kings of that ambiguous country—Hellenic, and yet not Hellenic: Alexander playing a double part at Plataea; Perdiccas playing, with consummate skill, a double part in the war of Sparta and Athens. But now the hour of Macedonia has come, and we must look more closely at the cradle of the power which was destined to change the face not only of the Greek but of the oriental world.

In their fortress of Aegae the Macedonian kings had ruled for ages with absolute sway over the lands on the northern and north-western coasts of the Thermaic Gulf, which formed Macedonia in the strictest sense. The Macedonian people and their kings were of Greek stock, as their traditions and the scanty remains of their language combine to testify. They were a military people, and they extended their power westward and northward over the peoples of the hills, so that Macedonia in a wider sense reached to the borders of the Illyrians in the west and of the Paeonians in the north. These hill tribes, the Orestians, Lyncestians, and others, belonged to the Illyrian race, and they were always seeking to cast off the bond of subjection which attached them to the kings of Aegae. In Illyria and Paeonia they had allies who were generally ready to support them in rebellion; and the dangers which Macedonia had constantly to encounter and always to dread from half-subjugated vassals and warlike enemies had effectually hindered her hitherto from playing any conspicuous part in the Greek world.

Macedonia

Thus the Macedonian kingdom consisted of two heterogeneous parts, and the Macedonian kings had two different characters. Over the Greek Macedonians of the coast the king ruled immediately; they were his own people, his own 'Companions'. Over the Illyrian folks of the hills he was only overlord; each was subject to its own chieftain, and the chieftains were his unruly vassals. It is clear that Macedonia could never become a great power until these vassal peoples had been completely tamed and brought under the direct rule of the kings, and until the Illyrian and Paeonian neighbours had been taught a severe lesson. These were the tasks awaiting the man who should transform Macedonia. The kings had made some efforts to introduce Greek civilisation into their land. Archelaus, who succeeded Perdiccas, had been a builder and a roadmaker, and, following the example of Greek tyrants, he had succeeded in making his court at Pella a centre for famous artists and poets. Euripides, the tragic poet; Timotheus, the most eminent leader of a new school of music; Zeuxis the painter; and many another, may have found pleasure and relief in a change from the highly civilised cities of the south to a new and fresher atmosphere, where

King Archelaus

there were no politicians. It is sometimes said that Macedonia was still in the Homeric stage of development. The position of the monarch, however, was different from that of the Homeric king. Though he was the religious head of the state and led the army in war, his power was not absolute. He had to observe traditional law. Moreover it was the assembled Macedonians who decided the succession, and it was only on their authority that a capital charge could be heard. This was the charter of Macedonian liberty. Fighting and hunting were the chief occupations of this vigorous people. A Macedonian who had not killed his man wore a cord round his waist; and until he had slain a wild boar he could not sit at table with the men. Like the Thracians, they drank deep; Bacchic mysteries had been introduced; it was in Macedonian air, on the banks of Lake Ludias, that Euripides drew inspiration for his *Bacchae*.

Perdiccas sole king, 365 B.C.;

slain 359 B.C.

We have seen how Perdiccas slew his guardian and stepfather Ptolemy, and reigned alone. Six years later the Illyrians swooped down upon Macedonia, and the king was slain in battle. It was a critical moment for the kingdom; the land was surrounded by enemies, for the Paeonians at the same time menaced it in the north, and from the east a Thracian army was advancing to set a pretender on the throne. The rightful heir, Amyntas, the son of the slain king, was a child. But there was one man in the land who was equal to the situation—this child's uncle, Philip; and he took the government and the guardianship of the boy into his own hands. We have already met Philip as one of the hostages who were carried off to Thebes. He had lived there for a few years, and drunk in the military and political wisdom of Epaminondas and Pelopidas. We do not know why he was allowed to return to his home soon after the death of Ptolemy; perhaps it was thought that his affections had been firmly won by Thebes and that he would be more useful to her in Macedonia.

Philip, guardian of Amyntas, 359 B.C.

Philip returns to Macedonia, 364 B.C.

Philip was twenty-four years old when he was called upon to rescue his country and the dynasty of his own house. The danger consisted in the number of his enemies—foreign invaders, and domestic pretenders, and pretenders supported by foreign powers. Philip's first step was to buy off the Paeonians by a large sum of money, his next to get rid of the pretenders. One of these, Argaeus, was assisted by Athens with a strong fleet. Philip defeated him, and did all in his power to come to terms with Athens. He released without ransom the Athenians whom he had made prisoners in the

Philip disposes of the pretenders, 359 B.C.;

battle, and he renounced all claim to the possession of Amphipolis, which his brother king Perdiccas had occupied with a garrison. Gold easily induced the Thracians to desert the pretender whom they had come forth to support.

But the Paeonians were quieted only for the moment, and the Illyrians were still in the land, threatening Macedonian towns. It was necessary to deal with these enemies once and for all, and to assert decisively the military power of Macedon. Philip had new ideas on the art of war, and he spent the winter in remodelling and training his army. When spring came round he had 10,000 foot-soldiers and 600 horsemen, thoroughly disciplined and of great physical strength. With this force he marched against the Paeonians and quelled them in a single battle. He then turned against the Illyrians, who refused to evacuate the towns they held in the Lyncestian territory. A great battle was fought, in which Philip tested his new military ideas; the Illyrians left 7000 on the field, and the vassals of the highlands, who had supported the invaders, were reduced to abject submission.

defeats the Paeonians, 358 B.C. (spring); the Illyrians, 358 B.C.

When he had thus established his power over his dependencies and cleared the land of enemies, Philip lost little time in pushing eastward, on the side of Thrace. The motive for this rapid advance was the imperative necessity of obtaining gold. Without gold Philip could not develop his country or carry out his military schemes. The Macedonians were not a commercial people, and therefore his prospects depended on possessing land which produced the precious ore. In Mount Pangaeus on his eastern frontier there were rich sources of gold; and, incited by him, a number of people from the opposite island of Thasos, where the art of mining was well understood, had crossed over to Crenides near the mountain and formed a settlement. But in order to control the new mines it was indispensable to become master of the great fortress on the Strymon, the much-coveted Amphipolis. The interests of Philip thus came into direct collision with the interests of Athens. When Philip advanced with his army against their city the Amphipolitans appealed earnestly to Athens for help.[5] But the Athenians were preoccupied with troubles in Euboea and in the Chersonese, no help was sent, and Amphipolis soon fell. But Philip, anxious not to offend Athens unnecessarily, released Athenian prisoners captured in the town. There are some grounds for believing that a secret agreement was made with Philip, probably before the fall

Thasian settlement at Crenides, 359 B.C.

of Amphipolis, that he would hand over Amphipolis to Athens in return for Pydna on the Thermaic Gulf which had joined the Athenian Alliance.[6] It is certain that no formal agreement, open or secret, was reached for such an exchange but Philip may have given Athenian envoys the impression that this was his intention.

When Philip had taken Amphipolis, he converted the Thasian settlement of Crenides into a great fortress, which he called after his own name, Philippi. He had thus two strong stations to secure Mount Pangaeus; and the yield of the gold mines, which were soon actively worked, amounted to at least 1000 talents a year. No Greek state was so rich. The old capital, Aegae or Edessa, was now definitely abandoned, and the seat of government was established at Pella, the favourite residence of Archelaus. This coming down from Aegae to Pella is significant of the opening of a new epoch in Macedonian history.

Philip takes Pydna and Potidaea, c.B.C. 356; his alliance with Olynthus

Not long afterwards Philip captured Pydna. If the seizure of Amphipolis was an injury to Athens, the capture of Pydna was an insult. He then took Potidaea but, instead of keeping it for himself, handed it over to the Olynthians, to whom he also ceded Anthemus. The Olynthians, alarmed by his operations on the Strymon, had made proposals to Athens for common action against Macedon. The Athenians, trusting Philip, had rejected the overtures. But when they found that they had been duped, they would have been ready and glad to co-operate with Olynthus; and it was to prevent such a combination that Philip dexterously propitiated the Olynthians—intending to devour them on some future day. With the exception of Methone, the Athenians had no foothold now on the coasts of the Thermaic Gulf.

They formed alliances with the Thracians of the west, who were indignant at the Macedonian occupation of Crenides, and with the Paeonian and Illyrian kings, who were smarting under their recent discomfitures.[7] But Philip prevented the common action of the allies. He forced the Paeonians to become his vassals; Parmenio, his ablest general—his only general, he used to say himself—inflicted another overwhelming defeat on the Illyrians; and the Thracians, again bought off, renounced their rights to Mount Pangaeus.

Defeat of Illyrians, 356 B.C., autumn

But the successes cost Philip little. Having established his mining town, he assumed the royal title, setting his nephew aside, and devoted himself during the next few years to the consolidation of his kingdom, and the creation of a national army. It was in these years that he made Macedonia. His task, as has been already indicated, was to unite the hill tribes, along with his own Macedonians of the coast, into one nation. The means by which he accomplished this was military organisation. He made the highlanders into professional soldiers and kept them always under arms. Caught by the infection of the military spirit, seduced by the motives of emulation and ambition, they were to forget that they were Orestians or Lyncestians, and blend into a single homogeneous Macedonian people. To complete this consummation would be a work of years, but Philip conceived the project clearly and set about it at once. 'A professional army with a national spirit—that was the new idea.'[8] Both infantry and cavalry were indeed organised in territorial regiments; perhaps Philip could not have ventured at first on any other system. But common pride and common desire of promotion, common hope of victory, tended to obliterate these distinctions, and they were done away with under Philip's son. The heavy cavalry were called 'Companions' of the king and 'Royal' soldiers, and they were more honourable than the infantry. Among the infantry there was a special corps of *hypaspistae*, including a royal guard.[9]

The making of Macedonia

Hetairoi

Hypaspists

The famous Macedonian phalanx, which Philip drilled, was merely a modified form of the usual battle-line of Greek spearmen. The men in the phalanx stood freer, in a more open array, and used a longer spear; so that the whole line, though still cumbrous enough, was more easily wielded, and the effect was produced not merely by the sheer pressure of a heavy mass of men but by the skilful manipulation of weapons. Nor was the phalanx intended to decide a battle, like the deep columns of Epaminondas; its function was to keep the front of the foe in play, while the cavalry, in wedge-like squadrons, rode into the flanks. It was by these tactics that Philip had won his victory over the Illyrians.

But Greece paid little heed to the things which Philip was doing. The Athenians might indeed encourage his Illyrian and Paeonian enemies, and urge the Thracians to drive him from Mount Pangaeus but, though he had outwitted them, they could not yet see that he was an enemy of a different stamp from a Cotys or a Cersobleptes; having managed Macedonia for a hundred years, they had little doubt that as soon as they had the time to spare they would easily manage it again. When Philip married Olympias, the daughter of an Epirot prince, the event could cause no sensation; the birth of a

Birth of Alexander, summer, 356 B.C.

son a year later stirred no man's heart in Greece; for who, in his wildest dreams, could have foreseen in the Macedonian infant the greatest conqueror who had yet been born into the world? If it had been revealed to men in that autumn that a power had started up which was to guide history into new paths, they would have turned their eyes not to Pella but to Halicarnassus.

Mausolus of Caria

Caria, like Macedonia, was peopled by a double race, the native Carians and the Greek settlers on the coast. But the native Carians were further removed than the Illyrians from the Greeks: the Illyrians spoke a tongue of the same Indo-Germanic stock as the Greeks; the Carians belonged to an older race which held the region of the Aegean before Greeks and Illyrians came. Yet the Carians were in closer touch with Greece than the Greeks of Macedonia. The Greeks of Caria were always abreast of Greek civilisation, and they had assimilated and tutored the natives of the land.[10] Tralles and Mylasa were to all appearance Greek towns; Greek was the dominant language of the country. A province of the Persian empire, Caria had yet a certain independent bond of union among her cities in an Amphictionic League which met in the temple of Zeus at Lagina. It was a religious union, though it might be used for purposes of common political action. But political unity was given to Caria not by federation but by monarchy.

Hecatomnus, c. 395-90 to 377 B.C.

A citizen of Mylasa named Hecatomnus succeeded in establishing his rule over the whole land soon after the death of Tissaphernes, and the Great King esteemed it prudent policy to acknowledge the 'dynast of Caria' as his official satrap. Both Hecatomnus and his son Mausolus, who succeeded to his power, never failed to pay their tribute to the treasury of Susa or to display the becoming submission to the Persian king; only once—as we have seen—when all the western satraps rebelled, did Mausolus fall short in his loyalty. The Carian Dynasts—they never assumed the royal title—

Extra-constitutional position of the Carian tyrants

thus secured for themselves a free hand. With the constitutions of the Carian cities their sovereignty did not interfere. Thus even in their own city, Mylasa, the popular Assembly still passed decrees, and these decrees were ratified not by Mausolus but by the 'Three Tribes'—perhaps a sort of aristocratic council.[11] In fact Hecatomnus and Mausolus held in relation to the Carian states an analogous

position to that which Pisistratus and his sons held in the Athenian state; they were the actual rulers but officially they did not exist. The differences were that the Carian dynast held the official position of Persian satrap and was 'tyrant' of a number of states which were independent of each other.

These native satraps brought the Greek towns of the coast, Halicarnassus, Iasus, Cnidus, perhaps Miletus itself, gradually under their power; and Mausolus annexed the neighbouring land of Lycia. Thus at the time of Philip's accession to the throne of Macedonia, a rich and ambitious monarchy had arisen on the south-eastern shores of the Aegean. To develop his power, it was desirable for Mausolus to win the lordship of the islands adjacent to his coasts, and it was clearly necessary to form a strong navy. The change of the satrap's residence from inland Mylasa to Halicarnassus on the sea is thus politically significant; Caria was to become a sea-power. Mausolus built himself a strong castle on the little island of Zephyrion in front of the city, and constructed two harbours, one for ships of war, the other for trading ships.

The great islands of Rhodes, Cos, and Chios, which Mausolus especially coveted, belonged to the Athenian alliance. But recently there was much discontent at the Athenian supremacy, and there were good grounds for this feeling. The reversion to the policy of cleruchies in neighbouring Samos, as well as in distant Potidaea, excited apprehensions for the future; and the exactions of the rapacious and irresponsible mercenaries whom Athens regularly employed, but did not regularly pay, caused many complaints. There were moreover strong oligarchical parties in these states which would be glad to sever connection with Athens. The

Revolt of Chios, Cos, and Rhodes, 357 B.C.

scheme of the Carian prince was first to induce these islands to detach themselves from Athens and then to bring them under his own control. He fanned the flame of discontent, and the three islands jointly revolted from the Athenian alliance and were supported by Byzantium.[12]

Athenian attack on Chios; death of Chabrias 357 B.C.

Athens immediately sent naval forces to Chios under Chabrias and Chares, two of the generals of the year, and the town was attacked by land and sea. But in trying to enter the harbour, Chabrias, who led the way, was assailed on all sides and fell fighting. Thus the Athenians lost the most gallant of their soldiers—a commander of whom it was said that he never spared himself and always spared his men. The attack on Chios was abandoned, and the Chians, much elated, and commanding a fleet of 100 ships, proceeded to aggressive

356 B.C.

Battle of Embata

Trial of Timotheus and Iphicrates, 355 B.C. (?)

Con-demnation of Timotheus; his death

Chares in Asia Minor, 355 B.C.

warfare against the Athenian cleruchs and blockaded Samos. With only 60 ships Chares could do nothing, and another 60 were hastily sent under the command of Timotheus and Iphicrates. Under three such generals much might be expected from such a fleet, but more would probably have been accomplished under any one of them alone. They relieved Samos and made an unsuccessful diversion to the Propontis, hoping to take Byzantium. Then they sailed to Chios, and concerted a plan of attack in the strait between the island and the mainland. But the day proved stormy, and the two veteran admirals, Iphicrates and Timotheus, decided that it would be rash to fight. Chares, however, against their judgment, attacked the enemy and, being unsupported, was repulsed with loss.

The ineffectual operations of two such tried and famous generals were a cruel disappointment to the Athenians, who had given them an adequate fleet. Chares, furious at the behaviour of his colleagues, formally accused them of deliberate treachery, and was supported by the orator Aristophon. The charge was that they had received bribes from the Chians and the Rhodians. Counter-charges were brought against Chares by Timotheus and Iphicrates, but the sympathies of Athens were altogether given to the commander who erred on the side of boldness. Iphicrates, however, had less political influence and therefore fewer enemies than Timotheus, and he knew how to conciliate the people; he was accordingly acquitted. Timotheus, always haughty and unpopular, probably assumed a posture as haughty and unbending as ever, Aristophon probably pressed him hard, and he was fined 100 talents. Rich as he was he was unable to pay this enormous sum, and he withdrew to Chalcis where he died soon afterwards. Thus within twelve months the Athenians lost the two men, Chabrias and Timotheus, who had built up their second empire. They afterwards recognised that the measure which they had dealt out to Timotheus was hard, and they permitted his son—who had himself been tried and acquitted on the same charge—to settle the fine by a payment of ten talents.

Chares now sailed out as sole commander to sustain the war against the rebel allies; but he went unfurnished with money to pay his troops. He found the means of supplying this deficiency in the disturbed state of Asia Minor.[13] The satrap of Hellespontine Phrygia, Artabazus, had rebelled, but was not strong enough to hold his own against the king's troops. Chares came to his rescue, gained a

brilliant victory over the satraps who were arrayed against him, and received from the grateful Artabazus money which enabled him to pay and maintain the army. The victory and the money pleased the Athenians, but Artaxerxes was deeply incensed. The news presently reached Athens that the Great King was equipping a vast armament in Syria and Cilicia to avenge the audacity of Chares. How much truth there was in this report it is impossible to say, but it evoked an outburst of patriotism and supplied the Athenian orators with material for invectives and declamations. Men began to talk in earnest of realising the dream of Isocrates, of convoking a Panhellenic congress and arming Hellas against the barbarian. Demosthenes, who was now beginning to rise into public notice, delivered at this juncture a speech which was more to the point than many of his later more famous orations. He showed that the alarm was premature and that the notion of sending round appeals to the cities of Greece was foolish: 'your envoys will do nothing more than rhapsodise in their round of visits.' The truth was that Athens could in no case think of embarking at this juncture on a big war; she had not the means.[14] Isocrates himself raised his voice for peace in a remarkable pamphlet, distinguished by the nobility of tone and the width of view which always mark his writings. It was a scathing condemnation of Imperialism. Passing from the momentary state of affairs, he looked out into the future and boldly declared that the only salvation for Athens lay in giving up her naval empire. 'It is that,' he said, 'which brought us to this pass; it is that which caused the fall of our democracy.' He showed the calamities which the empires of Athens and Sparta had drawn upon themselves and Greece. But it is to be observed that, when a moment had come at which his favourite plan of a common attack on Persia seemed at length feasible, he was wise enough not to advise it. He looks to Thrace, not to Persia, to find lands for endowing those needy Greeks who were roving about for subsistence.

In the end prudent counsels prevailed; Chares was recalled, negotiations were opened with the revolted allies, and a peace was made. Athens recognised the independence of the three islands, Chios, Cos, and Rhodes, and of the city of Byzantium. It was not long before Lesbos also severed itself from the Athenian alliance, which thus lost all its important members in the eastern Aegean; and in the west Corcyra fell away about the same time.

All happened as Mausolus foresaw. He

Demo-sthenes' speech On the Symmories

Isocrates on the Peace, 355 B.C.

(404 B.C.)

Peace, 354 B.C.

helped the oligarchies to overthrow the popular governments, and then gave them the protection of Carian garrisons. But the prince did not live to develop his empire. Soon after the success of his policy against Athens he died, leaving his power to his widow Artemisia. The opportunity was seized by the democrats of Rhodes to regain their freedom, and they appealed to Athens. After what had passed they had little right to expect a hearing; and under the influence of the wise and pacific statesmen who now controlled the Assembly, their appeal was refused—in spite of the hot and somewhat sentimental pleadings of Demosthenes, who upheld the extraordinary doctrine that Athens was bound, whenever she was called upon, to intervene to support democracy against oligarchy.[15] Artemisia soon recovered her grip on Rhodes.

Death of Mausolus, 353 B.C.

Rhodes appeals to Athens 353 or 351 B.C.

Caria remained for another twenty years under dynasts of the house of Hecatomnus, until it submitted to Alexander the Great. The expansion of the Carian power, which seemed probable under the active administration of Mausolus, was never fulfilled. Though we know nothing of his personal character, the appearance of Mausolus is familiar to us from his splendid portrait. The colossal statue, made,

The statues of Mausolus and Artemisia (in the British Museum)

at latest, soon after his death, represents a man of a noble cast of face, of a type presumably Carian, certainly not Greek, and with the hair curiously brushed back from the brow. This statue stood, along with that of Artemisia, within the sepulchral tomb which he probably began and which she certainly completed. Such a royal tomb seems to take us back to the days of prehistoric Greece; it strikes one almost like a glorified resurrection of one of the old chamber sepulchres of the Leleges which are strewn about the Halicarnassian peninsula. It rose above the harbour at Halicarnassus, conspicuous from the sea, crowned with a chariot on its apex. The building was adorned with friezes, wrought by four of the most illustrious sculptors of the day, of whom Scopas himself was one. The precious fragments of these works of art are the legacy which the Carian realm has bequeathed to mankind— these and a new word which the tomb of Mausolus added to the vocabularies of Europe.

The tomb of Mausolus

Sculptures (in British Museum) Origin of 'Mausoleum'

Phocis and the Sacred War

In the meantime, another of the states of northern Greece seemed likely to win the position of supremacy which Thessaly had seemed on the eve of winning, and which Boeotia had actually held for a few years. Phocis now came forward in her turn and enjoyed a brief moment of expansion and conquest—a flashlight which vanished almost as soon as it appeared. In succession to the national leaders, Jason of Pherae and Epaminondas of Thebes, we now meet Onomarchus of Elatea.

Into this career of aggrandisement Phocis was thrust by the aggresion of her neighbours rather than lured by the lust of conquest. The Phocians had never been zealous adherents of the Boeotian alliance, which they were forced to join after the battle of Leuctra, and they cut themselves loose from it after the death of Epaminondas. But though Thebes could no longer maintain her wider supremacy in Greece, an independent Phocis was a source of constant danger to her in her narrower supremacy in Boeotia, as the western cities of the land could always find in Phocis a support for their own independence. It was therefore deemed necessary by the politicians of Thebes to strike a blow at their western neighbours. One of the instruments of which Epaminondas had made use to promote his city's influence in the north was the old Amphictionic League, which for a hundred years had never appeared

Position of Phocis

16.1 Mausolus and Artemisia

420

on the scene of history. At an assembly of this body, soon after Leuctra, the Thebans accused the Spartans of having seized the Cadmea in time of peace. The Spartans were sentenced to pay a fine of 500 talents; the fine could not indeed be exacted, but they were doubtless excluded from the temple of Delphi. The Thebans resolved to wield against Phocis the same engine which they had wielded against Sparta. The nature of the pretext is uncertain, but it was not difficult to find a misdemeanour which would seem grave enough to the Thessalians and Locrians, inveterate enemies of Phocis, to justify a sentence of condemnation.[16] A number of rich and prominent Phocians were condemned to pay large fines for sacrilege, and when these sums were not paid within the prescribed time the Amphictions decreed that the lands of the defaulters should be taken from them and consecrated to the Delphian god, and a tablet with the inscribed decree was set up at Delphi.

Sparta fined

Phocians fined

The men who were implicated in the alleged sacrilege determined to resist, and they appealed to their fellow-countrymen, in whatever form of federal assembly the Phocian cities used to discuss their common interests, to protect themselves and their property against the threatened danger. The man who took the lead in organising the resistance was Philomelus, a wealthy citizen of Ledon. He discerned clearly that mercenaries would be required to defend Phocis against her enemies —Boeotians, Locrians, and Thessalians—and made the bold and practical proposal that Delphi should be seized, since the treasures of Delphi would supply at need the sinews of war. It is hardly likely that he openly avowed the true reason of the importance of seizing Delphi; it was enough to assert the old rights of the Phocians over rocky Pytho—rights for which he could appeal to the highest authority, the sacred text of Homer—and to point out that the Delphians were implicated in the unjust decrees of the Amphictions. The proposals of Philomelus were adopted, and he was appointed general of the Phocian forces, with full powers. His first step was to visit Sparta, not only as the enemy of Thebes, but as being in the same case as Phocis, lying under an Amphictionic sentence which had recently been renewed and confirmed. King Archidamus welcomed the proposals of the Phocian plenipotentiary, but Sparta stood in a rather awkward position. Hitherto she had always supported the Delphians in maintaining their independence against Phocian claims—as, for instance, when in the days of Pericles she

Philomelus

450 B.C. sqq.

restored them to their shrine after the Phocians with Athenian aid had dispossessed them. It would consequently have been a flagrant inconsistency in Spartan policy to turn against the Delphians now, so Archidamus did not openly avow his sympathy with the Phocian cause, but privately he supported it by placing 15 talents in the hands of Philomelus. With this sum and 15 talents from his own purse Philomelus was able to hire some mercenaries, and with their help to seize Delphi. The Locrians of neighbouring Amphissa, whom the Delphians had summoned to their aid, arrived too late and were repulsed. Philomelus did no hurt to the people of Delphi, excepting only the clan of the Thracidae, bitter anti-Phocians, whom he put to death.

Phocians seize Delphi, 356 B.C.

The first object of Philomelus was to enlist Hellenic opinion in his favour. He had the secret sympathy of Sparta, and he might count on the friendship of Athens, who had always been an ally of Phocis and was now an enemy of Thebes. He sent envoys to Sparta, to Athens, to Thebes itself, to explain the Phocian position. These envoys were instructed to say that in seizing Delphi the Phocians were simply resuming their rights over the temple, which belonged to them and had been usurped by others, and to declare that they would act merely as administrators of the Panhellenic Sanctuary, and were ready to allow all the treasures to be weighed and numbered and to be responsible to Greece for their safety. In consequence of these embassies Sparta came forward from her reserve and openly allied herself with Phocis, while Athens and some smaller states promised their support. The Thebans and their Amphictionic friends resolved to make war.

In the meantime, Philomelus had fortified the Delphic sanctuary by a wall, and had collected an army of 5000 men, with which he could easily hold the position. It was his wish that the oracular responses from the mystic tripod should continue to be given as usual to those who came to consult Apollo, and he was anxious above all to receive some voice of approval or encouragement from the god. But the Delphian priestess was stubborn to the Phocian intruder, and refused to prophesy. He tried to seat her by force upon the tripod, and in her alarm she bade him do as he would. He eagerly seized these words as an oracular sanction of his acts. It soon became necessary to raise more money for paying the mercenaries, and for this purpose Philomelus, refraining as long as he could from touching the treasures of the shrine, levied a contribution

Philomelus fortifies Delphi;

and defeats the Locrians

from the rich Delphians. At first he had to deal only with the Locrians, whom he finally defeated in a hot battle near the Phaedriad cliffs which rise sheer above Delphi. The loss of the Locrians was heavy; some of them, driven to the edge, hurled themselves down the cliffs.

Thebes prepares to act

This victory forced the Thebans to prepare actively to intervene. The Amphictionic assembly met at Thermopylae, and it was decided that an Amphictionic army should enforce the decree of the league against the Phocians and rescue Delphi from their power. Philomelus, with the forces which he had, might have held his own against the Locrians, but not against the host which would now be arrayed against him. There were only two means of saving Phocis. One was the active support of Athens or Sparta, or both; the other was the organisation of a large army of mercenaries. As neither Athens nor Sparta showed willingness to give any immediate assistance, nothing remained but the other alternative. And that, as Philomelus must have foreseen from the beginning, would not be possible without the control of far larger sums of money than could either be contributed by the Phocian cities or extorted from the Delphian proprietors. No resource remained but to make use of the treasures of the temple. At first Philomelus was scrupulous: he only *borrowed* from the god enough to meet the demand of the moment. But, as habit blunted the first feelings of scrupulousness, and as needs grew more pressing, the Phocians dealt as freely with the sacred vessels and the precious dedications as if they were their own. By offering large pay Philomelus assembled an army of 10,000 men, who cared little whence the money came. An indecisive war with the Thebans and Locrians was waged for some time, till at length the Phocians suffered a severe defeat near Neon on the north side of Mount Parnassus. The general fought desperately, and was driven, covered with wounds, to the verge of a precipice where he had to choose between capture and self-destruction. He hurled himself from the cliff and perished.

Battle of Neon, 354 B.C.; death of Philomelus

Onomarchus succeeds Philomelus

The Thebans imagined that the death of Philomelus meant the doom of the Phocian cause, and they retired after the battle. But it was not so. In Onomarchus of Elatea, who had been associated with him in the command of the army, he had a successor as able as himself. The retreat of the enemy gave Onomarchus time to reorganise the troops and collect reinforcements, and he not only coined the gold and silver ornaments of the temple but

beat the bronze and iron donatives into arms for the soldiers. He then entered upon a short career of signal successes. Westward, he forced Locrian Amphissa to submit; to northward he reduced Doris; and crossing the passes of Mount Oeta he made himself master of Thermopylae, and captured the Locrian Thronion near the eastern gate of the pass. Eastward, he took possession of Orchomenus and restored those of the inhabitants who had escaped the sword of the Thebans ten years before.

The Thebans meanwhile were hampered by want of money, and, having neither mines like Philip nor a rich temple like Phocis, they decided to replenish their treasury by sending out a body of troops on foreign service. We have already seen Sparta and Athens raising money by the same means, and the Theban soldiers who now went forth under Pammenes hired themselves out to the same Persian satrap Artabazus, for whom the Athenian Chares had won a victory over the army of the king. Pammenes was equally successful, but it does not seem that his expedition profited the Boeotian treasury, for he presently became suspected by Artabazus, who threw him into prison.

Among the most important uses to which Onomarchus applied the gold of Delphi was the purchase of the alliance of the tyrants of Pherae. By this policy Thessaly was divided; and the Thessalian league, beset by the hostility of Pherae, was unable to co-operate with the Thebans against Phocis. But the Thessalians, being hard pressed, turned for help to their northern neighbour, Philip of Macedon, and his intervention south of Mount Olympus marks a new stage in the course of the Sacred War.

Philip's capture of Methone, 353 B.C. He enters Thessaly; 352 B.C.

Philip had lately deprived Athens of her last ally on the Thermaic Gulf by the capture of Methone, the Athenian expedition of relief coming too late to save it. He readily acceded to the request of the Thessalians to act as their general: it was a convenient occasion to begin the push southward and lay the foundation of Macedonian supremacy in Greece, plans which were now coming within the range of practical effort. Against the forces which Philip led to the support of the Thessalian league it was hopeless for Lycophron of Pherae to stand alone; the tyrant was lost unless he were helped by those who had already furnished him with gold. Nor did the Phocians leave him unsupported: the strength of Onomarchus was now so great that he could spare a force of 7000 men for a campaign in the north. But his

defeats a Phocian army;

*suffers two
defeats and
is expelled
from
Thessaly
by Ono-
marchus*

brother Phayllus, to whom he entrusted the command, was beaten out of Thessaly by Philip. Then Onomarchus himself took command of the whole Phocian host (about 20,000), to rescue his ally. Far superior in numbers, he defeated the Macedonian army in two battles with serious loss. Philip was compelled to withdraw into Macedonia, and Onomarchus delivered Thessaly into the hands of Lycophron.

*Height of
the
Phocian
sup-
remacy,
353-2 B.C.*

Coronea

At this moment the power of the Phocians was at its height. Their supremacy reached from the shores of the Corinthian Gulf to the slopes of Olympus. They were masters of the pass of Thermopylae and they had two important posts in western Boeotia, for in addition to Orchomenus they won Coronea immediately after the Thessalian expedition. If all these things had occurred at some other epoch, the Phocian power might have endured for a time, and the name of their able leader might have been more familiar to posterity. But Onomarchus had fallen on evil days. He and his petty people were swept away in the onward course of a greater nation and a greater leader.

*Philip
drives the
Phocians
from
Thessaly*

Philip of Macedon speedily retrieved the humiliation which he had suffered at the hands of his Phocian foes. In the following year he descended again into Thessaly and Onomarchus took the field again to support his ally or dependent. In the preceding campaign Philip had captured the port of Pagasae and placed in it a Macedonian garrison. It was important not only for Pherae, but for Athens, that this post should not remain in his hands, and Chares was sent with an Athenian fleet to assist the Phocians in recovering it. The decisive battle was fought at a place unknown, near the Pagasaean Gulf. The numbers of the infantry were nearly equal, but Philip's cavalry and his tactics were far superior. More than a third of the Phocian army was slain or made prisoner, and Onomarchus was killed. Pherae was then captured and Lycophron driven from the land; and Philip, having thus become master of Thessaly, prepared to march southward for the purpose of delivering the shrine of Apollo from the possession of the Phocians, whom he professed to regard as sacrilegious usurpers.

Phocis was now in great need, and her allies—Sparta, Achaea, and Athens—at length determined to give her active help. The Macedonian must not be permitted to pass Thermopylae. The statesman Eubulus, whose influence was now predominant at Athens, and was chiefly directed to the maintenance of peace, acted promptly on this occasion, and

*Eubulus
rescues
Phocis*

sent a large force under Nausicles to defend the pass. Philip at once recognised that it would be extremely hazardous to attempt to force the position, and he retired. He was a prince who knew when to wait and when to strike. Thus Phocis was rescued for the time; she was indebted both to Sparta and Achaea who had sent her aid, but most of all to Athens.

In supporting Phocis, the Spartans had objects of their own in view. They had not abandoned their hopes of winning back Messenia and destroying Megalopolis. It was therefore their policy to sustain Phocis, in order that Phocis might keep Thebes so fully occupied that they would have a free hand in the Peloponnese without fear of Theban interference. The successes of Onomarchus in his first Thessalian campaign encouraged Sparta to prepare for action, and Megalopolis, made aware of the danger, applied to Athens for help. It was a request which no practical statesman could have entertained, and it had no chance of being granted under the régime of as wise a head as Eubulus. Orators like Demosthenes, who constituted themselves the opponents of Eubulus, might invoke the old principle that it was the policy of Athens to keep Sparta weak. But this was an obsolete maxim, for there was now no serious prospect of Sparta becoming formidably strong. It was no concern of Athens to meddle in the Peloponnese now. Her true policy was to keep on friendly terms with Sparta, and in conjunction with her to support the Phocian state against Thebes, Thessaly, and Macedon. This was the policy which Eubulus followed.

*Megalo-
polis
applies to
Athens,
end of
353 B.C.*

*Demo-
sthenes'
speech for
the Mega-
lopolitans*

The war broke out in the Peloponnese soon after the check of Philip at Thermopylae. While Athens held aloof, Achaea and Elis, Phlius and Mantinea, supported Sparta, and the Phocians sent 3000 men to her help. But all these forces were outnumbered by the Messenians, Arcadians, and Argives, to whom the Thebans had sent considerable aid. A series of engagements were fought. They were almost all indecisive, but they rescued Messenia and the Arcadian capital, and frustrated the plans of Sparta.

*War in
the Pelo-
ponnese,
352 B.C.*

The death of Onomarchus devolved the leadership of the Phocian league upon his brother Phayllus. At first the Phocians barely maintained their posts in western Boeotia, but presently—after the return of the auxiliaries whom they had sent to the Peloponnese— they invaded Epicnemidian Locris and laid siege to Naryx, which they ultimately captured. Thus Phayllus maintained the power of Phocis for about two years; then he was carried

Phayllus

352-1 B.C.

Phalaecus

off by disease, and was succeeded by his nephew, Phalaecus, son of Onomarchus. Under Phalaecus the war dragged on for a few more years, without any notable achievement, the Thebans winning battles of no importance and ravaging Phocis, the Phocians retaining their grip on western Boeotia.

The position and policy of Phocis

The rise of Phocis to its momentary position as one of the leading powers in Greece depended on two conditions—the possession of Delphi and the possibility of hiring mercenaries. It is therefore clear that Phocis could not easily have come to the front before the fourth century, when mercenary service had come widely into vogue. But these two essential features of the Phocian power, the occupation of Delphi and the employment of mercenary troops, gave it a bad name. Historians echo the invectives of the enemies of Phocis, and give the impression that during the Sacred War the sanctuary of Apollo was in the hands of sacrilegious and unscrupulous barbarians. Tales were told how the dedicatory offerings were bestowed upon the loose favourites of the generals—how Philomelus gave a golden wreath to a dancing girl, or Phayllus a silver beaker to a flute-player. It matters little whether such scandals are true or false; if true, they would only show that the generals were not above petty peculations. But the Phocians were not alien desecrators of the shrine of Apollo. They could establish as good a claim to Delphi as many claims founded on remote events in the past, and they certainly desired to maintain the Panhellenic dignity and sanctity of the shrine and the oracle as high as ever under their own administration. But they regarded Delphi not only as a Panhellenic sanctuary, but as a national sanctuary of Phocis—somewhat in the same way as Athens employed the treasures of her temples for national purposes of defence in the Peloponnesian war. So Phocis felt justified in employing the treasures of Apollo for the national interest of Phocis. Throughout all, the Phocian statesmen could have maintained that they were only borrowing from the god loans which would be gradually paid back after the restoration of peace.

Among the original documents inscribed on stone at Delphi, a striking disproof has been found of the old view which conceived the Phocians of Onomarchus and Phayllus as a band of robbers holding their orgies in a holy place. The temple of the god which had been built by the Alcmaeonids was destroyed by an earthquake nearly twenty years before the Phocian usurpation. The work of rebuilding had been begun, perhaps soon after, but had advanced slowly, and when Philomelus seized Delphi the completion of the temple was still far off. The work was carried out under a commission of 'Temple-builders', in which all the Amphictionic states were represented, and this body administered a fund set apart for the building. During the Phocian usurpation the council of Temple-builders still held their meetings; the work still went on; the skilful artisans in Corinth and elsewhere wrought the stone material and transferred it to Delphi, as if nothing had happened; the payments were made, as usual, from the fund; and the accounts were kept—we have some of them still.[17] Those Amphictionic states which were at war with Phocis, like Thebes and Thessaly, were naturally not represented at the meetings of the board of the Temple-builders, but Delphian members were always present; and after Locris had been conquered by Phayllus we find Locrians also attending the meetings. Thus the completion of the temple of Apollo was not suspended while the Phocians held the sanctuary; and the Dorian and Ionian states continued to take their part in the Panhellenic work of supervising the structure, as if nothing had happened to alter the centre of the Greek world.

The building of the temple of Apollo not interrupted during the Phocian occupation

373 B.C. Council of Naopoioi

The Advance of Macedonia

The Macedonian monarch was now master not only of the Thermaic Gulf and the mouth of the Strymon but of the basin of Pagasae, and he was beginning to create a fleet. His marauding vessels, let loose in the northern Aegean, captured the cornships of Athens, descended on her possessions and dependencies—Lemnos, Imbros, and Euboea—and once even insulted the coast of Attica itself. The most important interests of Athens centred on the Hellespont and Propontis, and it was obviously her policy to form a close combination with the Thracian king Cersobleptes, with a view to offering common resistance to the advance of the new northern power on the Thracian side. It was an effort in this direction when Aristocrates proposed a resolution in honour of Charidemus, the adventurer who had become the brother-in-law and the chief minister of the Thracian king. The resolution was impeached as illegal, and the accuser was supplied with a speech by the young politician Demosthenes. The legal objections were probably cogent, but the opponents of the

Demosthenes' speech against Aristocrates, 352 B.C.

proposal might wisely have confined themselves to this aspect of the question. They went on to impugn the expediency of the measure, and the speech of Demosthenes against Aristocrates was calculated, so far as a single speech could have a political effect, to alienate a power which it was distinctly the interest of Athens to conciliate.

Philip in Thrace, 352 B.C., autumn

But it mattered little. No sooner had Philip returned from Thessaly than he moved against Thrace. Supported by a rival Thracian prince and by the cities of Byzantium and Perinthus, he advanced to the Propontis, besieged Heraeon-Teichos the capital of Cersobleptes, and forced that potentate to submit to the overlordship of Macedon. The movements of Philip had been so rapid that Athens had no time to come to the rescue of Thrace. When the news arrived there was a panic, and a force was voted to save the Chersonese. But a new message came that Philip had fallen ill; then he was reported dead, and the sending of the fleet was postponed. Philip's illness was a fact: it compelled him to desist from further operations, and the Chersonese was saved.

Submission of Cersobleptes to Philip

Position of Philip at the end of 352 B.C.

Eight years had not elapsed since Philip had mounted the throne of Macedon, and he had shifted the balance of power in Greece and altered the whole prospect of the Greek world, for those who had eyes to see. He had created an army and a thoroughly adequate revenue, and he had made himself lord of almost the whole sea-board of the northern Aegean from the defile of Thermopylae to the shores of the Propontis. The only lands which were still excepted from his direct or indirect control were the Chersonese and the territory of the Chalcidian league. He was ambitious to secure a recognised hegemony in Greece; to hold such a position as had been held by Athens, by Sparta, and by Thebes in the days of their greatness; to form, in fact, a confederation of allies, which should hold some such dependent relation towards him as the confederates of Delos had held towards Athens. Rumours were already floating about that his ultimate design was to lead a Panhellenic expedition against the Persian king—the same design which was ascribed to Jason of Pherae.

His Hellenism

Though the Greek states regarded Philip in a certain sense as an outsider, both because Macedonia had hitherto stood aloof from their politics and because absolute monarchy was repugnant to their political ideas, it must never be forgotten that Philip desired to identify Macedonia with Greece, and to bring his own country up to the level of the kindred peoples which had so far outstripped it in civilisation. Throughout his whole career he regarded Athens with respect; he would have given much for her friendship, and he showed that he regarded it as one of his misfortunes that she compelled him to be her enemy. He was himself imbued with Greek culture and, if the robust Macedonian enjoyed the society of the rough boon companions of his own land with whom he could drink deep, he knew how to make himself agreeable to Attic philosophers or men of letters whom he always delighted to honour. He chose an accomplished man of letters, Aristotle of Stagira, who had been educated at Athens, to be the instructor of his son Alexander. This fact alone sets Philip in a true light, as a conscious and deliberate promoter of Greek civilisation.

Greece saw with alarm the increase of the Macedonian power, though men were yet far from apprehending what it really meant. No state had been directly hit except Athens— though the day of Chalcidice was at hand, and it was now too late for Athens to retrieve her lost position, either alone or with any combination she could form, against a state which possessed an ample revenue and a well-drilled national army, under the sovereign command of the greatest general and diplomatist of the day. The only event which could now have availed to stay the course of Macedon would have been the death of Philip. But the Athenians did not grasp this; they still dreamed of recovering Amphipolis. Their best policy would have been peace and alliance with Macedonia. There can be little question that Philip would have gladly secured them the Chersonese and their cornships, for the possessions of the Chersonese had not the same vital importance for him as Amphipolis, or as the towns around the Thermaic Gulf.

Position of Athens

In these years, Athens was under the guidance of a cautious statesman, Eubulus, who was an extremely able minister of finance. He was appointed chancellor of the Theoric Fund for four years, and this office, while it was specially concerned with the administration of the surplus of revenue which was devoted to theoric purposes, involved a general control over the finances of the state. He pursued a policy of peace, yet it was he who struck the one effective blow that Athens ever struck at Philip, when she hindered him from passing Thermopylae. But Eubulus wisely refused to allow Athens to be misled into embarking in unnecessary wars in the Peloponnese or Asia Minor, and frankly accepted the peace which had concluded the war of Athens with her allies. The mass of the Athenians were well content

Eubulus, in charge of the Theoric Fund, 354-50 B.C., and probably, 350-346 B.C.

to follow the counsel of a dexterous financier, who, while meeting fully all the expenses of administration, distributed large dividends of festival-money. The news of Philip's campaign in Thrace may have temporarily weakened his influence: it was felt that there had been slackness in watching Athenian interests in the Hellespontine regions, and his opponents had a fair opportunity to inveigh against an inactive policy.

Demo-sthenes, born c. 384 B.C.

 The most prominent among these opponents was Demosthenes, who had recently made a reputation as a speaker in the Assembly. The father of Demosthenes was an Athenian manufacturer, who died when his son was still a child; his mother had Scythian blood in her veins. His guardians dealt fraudulently with the considerable fortune which his father had left him, and when he came of age he resolved to recover it. For this purpose he sat at the feet of the orator Isaeus and was trained in law and rhetoric. Though he received but a small portion of his patrimony, the oratory of

Demosthenes owed to this training with a practical purpose many qualities which he would never have acquired under the academic instruction of Isocrates. He himself used to tell how he struggled to overcome his natural defects of speech and manner, how he practised gesticulation before a mirror and declaimed verses with pebbles in his mouth. In the end he became as brilliant an orator as the Pynx had ever cheered; perhaps his only fault was a too theatrical manner. His earlier political speeches are not monuments of wisdom. He came forward as an opponent of the policy of Eubulus, and so we have already met him supporting the appeals of Rhodes and Megalopolis. The advance of Philip to the Propontis gave him a more promising occasion to urge the Athenians to act, since their own interests were directly involved. And the *His first Philippic* effort of Demosthenes was more than adequate: the harangue, which is known as the *First Philippic*, one of his most brilliant and effective speeches, calls upon the Athenians to brace themselves vigorously to oppose Philip 'our enemy'. He draws a lively picture of the indifference of his countrymen and contrasts it with the energy of Philip 'who is not the man to rest content with what he has subdued, but is always adding to his conquests, and casts his snare around us while we sit at home postponing'. Again: 'Is Philip dead? Nay, but he is ill. What does it matter to you? For if this Philip die, you will soon raise up a second Philip by your apathy.' Demosthenes proposed a scheme for increasing the military forces of the city, and the most essential part of the scheme was that a force should be sent to Thrace of which a quarter should consist of citizens, and the officers should be citizens. At present the numerous officers whom they elected were kept for services at home: 'You choose your captains, not to fight but to be displayed like dolls in the market-place.'

 Demosthenes was applauded, but nothing was done. His ideal was the Athens of Pericles, but he lived in the Athens of Eubulus. In the fourth century the Athenians were quite capable of holding their own among their old friends and enemies, the Spartans and Thebans and the islanders of the Aegean; with paid soldiers and generals like Iphicrates and Chares they could maintain their position as a first-rate power. But against a large, vigorous land-power with a formidable army their chances were hopeless, for since the fall of their empire the whole spirit of the people had tended to peace and not to war. They were no longer animated by the idea of empire, and the

16.2 Demosthenes

memories of the past, which Demosthenes might invoke, were powerless to stir them to action. The orations of Demosthenes, however carefully studied, however imbued with passion, could not change the character of his countrymen; their spirit did not respond to his, and, not being under the imperious dominion of an idea, they saw no reason for great undertakings. Nor was the condition of Athens as bad as the opponent of Eubulus painted it. Under the administration of Eubulus the fleet was increased, the building of a new arsenal was begun, new ship-sheds were made, and the military establishment of Athens was in various ways improved. She was still the great sea-power of the Aegean, and strong enough to protect her commercial interests.

Peace of the Chalcidian league with Athens, ?352-1 B.C.

The next stage in the development of Macedonia was the incorporation of Chalcidice, and as soon as Philip recovered from his illness he turned his attention to this quarter. If the Olynthians had treated Philip honourably they would probably have been left as a self-governing community, with their territory intact, dependent on Macedonia. But they treated both Athens and Philip badly. They first made a close alliance with Philip to rob Athens, and then, when they had received from Philip Anthemus and Potidaea, they turned round and made peace with Athens, a power with which Philip was at war, and recognised the right of Athens to Amphipolis.[18] At the time Philip was otherwise engaged, but three years later he sent a demand to Olynthus, that they should surrender his half-brother, a pretender to the Macedonian throne, to whom they had given shelter. The demand was refused and Philip marched against Chalcidice. One after another the cities of the Olynthian confederacy opened their gates to him; if they refused, like Stagira, they were captured.

Philip reduces Chalcidice, 349 B.C.

Alliance of Athens with the Olynthians

In this crisis Olynthus sought an alliance with Athens, and on this occasion both the leaders of the Athenian Assembly and the advocates of a war policy found themselves in harmony. It was during the debates on the question of alliance that Demosthenes pronounced his Olynthiac orations, which were animated by the same spirit as his Philippic, and were in fact Philippics. At this juncture the Athenians seem to have been sufficiently awakened to the necessity of action to embolden Demosthenes to venture the unpopular suggestion that the Theoric Fund should be devoted to military purposes, and he repeats his old plea for citizen-soldiers. An alliance was concluded and mercenaries were dispatched to the Chalcidian peninsula under Chares and Charidemus (who had left the service of Cersobleptes). More troops would certainly have followed, and Philip might have been placed in some embarrassment, especially as Cersobleptes had rebelled. But he diverted the concern of Athens in another direction, and so divided her forces. He had long been engaged in intrigues in Euboea, and now Eretria revolted and drove out Plutarch, the tyrant who held the city for Athens. Neighbouring Chalcis, and Oreus in the north, followed the example; Euboea was in a state of revolt. It is just possible that, if Athens had left Euboea alone, and concentrated all her military power in Chalcidice, she might have saved Olynthus for a time. The division of her forces was certainly fatal, and Demosthenes deserves great credit for opposing any interference in Euboea. But the Athenians would have been strong-minded indeed if they had done nothing to regain the neighbouring island, while they dispatched all their troops to support an ally. The expedition to Euboea, which was now entrusted to the general Phocion, might better never have been sent, but beforehand there seemed no reason why it should not succeed. Phocion's only exploit was to extricate himself from a dangerous position at Tamynae by winning a battle, but he returned to Athens without having recovered any of the rebellious cities. The enemy had taken a number of prisoners, for whose ransom Athens had to pay 50 talents, and it was decided that there was nothing for it but to acknowledge the independence of Euboea, with the exception of Carystus, which remained loyal.

Revolt of Euboea

Expedition to Euboea, spring, 348 B.C.

Euboea declared independent

Meanwhile Philip was pressing Olynthus hard, and urgent appeals were sent to Athens. This time Demosthenes had his way, and 2000 citizen-soldiers sailed for the north. But it was too late. Olynthus was captured before they reached it, and Philip showed no mercy to the city which had played him false. The place was destroyed and the inhabitants scattered in various parts of Macedonia, some set to work as slaves in the royal domains. The other cities of the confederacy were practically incorporated in Macedonia, but they still continued to exist as cities and manage their local affairs. There was no question of their extermination.

Fall of Olynthus, 348 B.C.

Demosthenes had opposed the expedition to Euboea, and thereby hangs a story. He had a bitter enemy in a rich man, named Meidias, who was a supporter of Eubulus. Their personal hostility was reawakened in the debates over

427

the Euboean question, and Meidias seized the occasion of the great Dionysiac feast to put a public affront on his enemy. Demosthenes had undertaken the duty of supplying a chorus for his tribe, and on the day of the performance, when he appeared in the sacred robe of a choregus, Meidias struck him in the face. The outrage involved contempt of a religious festival, and Demosthenes instituted proceedings against his insulter. The speech which he composed for the occasion contains fine scathing invective. The description of Meidias vulgarly displaying his wealth may be quoted to illustrate contemporary manners. 'Where,' Demosthenes asks, 'are his splendid outlays? For myself, I cannot see unless it be in this—that he has built a mansion at Eleusis large enough to darken all the neighbourhood—that he keeps a pair of white horses from Sicyon, with which he conducts his wife to the mysteries or anywhere else he fancies—that he sweeps through the market-place with three or four lackeys all to himself, and talks about his cups and drinking-horns and bowls, loud enough to be heard by the passers-by.' But Demosthenes consented to compromise for a small sum before it was brought to an issue, and there can be little question that his consent was given from political motives. On the capture of Olynthus the different parties drew together and agreed to co-operate; and this new political combination rendered it necessary for Demosthenes, however reluctant, to patch up the feud with Meidias.

The Peace of Philocrates

Her recent military efforts had exhausted the revenue of Athens; there was not enough money in the treasury to pay the judges their daily wage; peace was clearly a necessity, and this must have been fully recognised by Eubulus. But there was great indignation at the fall of Olynthus, and the feeling that a disaster had been sustained was augmented by the fact that there were a considerable number of Athenians among the captives. Accordingly the pressure of popular opinion, which was for the moment strongly aroused against Philip, induced Eubulus to countenance the dispatch of envoys to the cities of the Peloponnese for the purpose of organising a national resistance in Hellas against the man who had destroyed Olynthus. It is probable that this measure was advocated by Demosthenes, for in later years a national resistance to Philip was his favourite idea. It was

an effort foredoomed to failure, as Eubulus knew perfectly well; yet it served his purpose, for it protected him against suspicions of being secretly friendly to Philip. On this occasion the orator Aeschines, famous as the antagonist of Demosthenes, first came prominently forward. He had begun life as an usher in a school kept by his father, had become a tragic actor, and finally a public clerk. He was now sent to rouse the Greeks of the Peloponnese against Macedonia, and he used such strong language in disparagement of Philip, especially at Megalopolis, that no one could accuse him of 'philippizing'. The mere fact that envoys were sent to Megalopolis—whose application for help had so recently been rejected by Athens—is enough to cast suspicion on the whole round of embassies as a farce, got up to satisfy public opinion at home. Demosthenes, like other politicians, saw the necessity of peace and worked towards it.

Philip desired two things, to conclude peace with Athens and to become a member of the Amphictionic Council. Towards this second end a path was prepared by the Thebans, who along with the Thessalians addressed an appeal to Philip that he would undertake the championship of the Amphictionic League and crush the Phocians. In Phocis itself there had recently been domestic strife: Phalaecus had been deposed from the generalship, but he had a party of his own and he held Thermopylae with the strong places in its neighbourhood. When it was noised abroad that Philip was about to march southward in answer to the Theban prayer, the Phocians invited Athens and Sparta to help them once again to hold the gates of Greece. Both Athens and Sparta again responded to the call, but the call had come from the political opponents of Phalaecus, and he refused to admit either Spartan or Athenian into the pass. Phalaecus seems to have previously assisted the enemies of Athens in Euboea, and statesmen at Athens might now feel some uneasiness as to whether he would not turn traitor and surrender the pass to Philip. It was another reason for acquiescing in the necessity of making peace.

The first overtures came from Athens. Ten Athenian envoys, and one representative of the Synedrion of Athenian allies, were sent to Pella to negotiate terms of peace with the Macedonian king. Among the envoys were Philocrates, who had proposed the embassy, Aeschines, and Demosthenes. The terms to which Philip agreed were that Athens and Macedon should each retain the territories of which they were actually in possession at the time the peace was concluded; the peace would be concluded when both sides had sworn to it. Both the allies of Macedonia and those of Athens were to be included, with two exceptions: Philip refused to treat with Halus in Thessaly—a place which he had recently attacked—or with the Phocians, whom he was determined to crush.

By these terms, which were perfectly explicit, Athens would surrender her old claim to Amphipolis, and on the other hand Philip would recognise Athens as mistress of the Chersonese. The two exceptions which Philip made were inevitable. Halus indeed was a trifle which no one heeded, but it was an essential part of the Macedonian policy to proceed against Phocis. To the envoys, whom the king charmed by his courteous hospitality at Pella, he privately intimated that he was far from being ill-disposed to the Phocians; and perhaps a few of them hoped that there was something in the assurance. But in truth the Athenian statesmen troubled themselves little about Phocis; some of them, like the Theban proxenos Demosthenes, were more disposed to lean towards Thebes. It would be necessary to keep up the appearance of protecting an ally—though relations with that ally had recently grown somewhat strained—but neither Eubulus nor Demosthenes would for a moment have dreamed of forgoing the peace for the sake of supporting Phocis against her enemies.

Peace accepted and sworn to at Athens, 346 B.C. March

There were a few Thracian forts, belonging to Cersobleptes, which Philip was anxious to capture before the peace was made; and, when the envoys left Pella, he set out for Thrace, having given them an undertaking to respect the Chersonese. The envoys returned home bearing with them a friendly letter from Philip to the Athenian people, and they were followed in a few days by three Macedonian delegates, appointed to receive the oaths from the Athenians and their allies. How important this negotiation was for Philip is proved by the fact that two of these deputies were the two greatest of his subjects, Parmenio and Antipater. On the motion of Philocrates the Peace was accepted by Athens on the terms which Philip offered, though there were dissentient voices against the exclusion of Phocis and Halus; but the murmurs of the opposition were silenced by the plain speaking of Eubulus, who showed that if the terms were rejected the war must be continued.[19] And some of the ambassadors disseminated the unofficial utterances of Philip, that he would not ruin the Phocians and that he would help Athens

to win back Euboea and Oropus. The upshot was that Phocis was not mentioned in the treaty; she was tacitly, not expressly, excluded.

The Peace was now concluded on one side, and it remained for the envoys of Athens to administer the oath to Philip and his allies. It was to the interest of Athens that this act should be accomplished as speedily as possible, for Philip was entitled to make new conquests until he swore to the Peace, and he was actually engaged in making new conquests in Thrace. The same ambassadors who had visited Macedonia to arrange the terms of a treaty now set forth a second time to administer the oaths.

Second embassy from Athens to Philip sets out in April, 346 B.C.

Meanwhile Philip had taken the Thracian fortresses which he had gone to take, and had reduced Cersobleptes to be a vassal of Macedonia. When he returned to Pella, he found not only the embassy from Athens, but envoys from many other Greek states also, awaiting his arrival with various hopes and fears. He was beginning to be recognised as the arbiter of northern Greece.

So far as the formal conclusion of the Peace went, there was no difficulty. But the Athenian ambassadors had received general powers to negotiate further with Philip, with a view to some common decision on the settlement of the Phocian question and northern Greece. The treaty was a treaty of 'peace and alliance', and if Philip could have had his way the alliance would have become a bond of close friendship and co-operation. And it was in this direction that Eubulus and his party were inclined, cautiously, to move. Athens might have now taken her position as joint arbitrator with Philip in the settlement of the Amphictionic states. Both Philip and Athens had a common interest in reducing the power of Thebes; and, if it was the interest of Athens that Phocis should not be utterly destroyed, Philip had no special enmity against Phocis, whose strength was now exhausted—the Phocian 'sacrilege' was a convenient pretext to interfere and step into the place of Phocis in the Delphian Amphictiony. A common programme was discussed and might easily have been concerted between Philip and the ambassadors. To treat the Phocians with clemency and to force Thebes to acknowledge the independence of the Boeotian cities would have been the basis of common action; the restoration of Plataea was mentioned; and while Philip promised to secure the restitution to Athens of Euboea and Oropus, Athens would have supported the admission of Macedonia into the Amphictionic Council. Aeschines was the chief mouthpiece of the counsels of Eubulus. But the project of an active alliance was opposed strenuously by Demosthenes and, as Demosthenes had great and daily increasing influence with the Athenian Assembly, it would have been unsafe for Philip to conclude any definite agreement with the majority of the embassy. The policy of Demosthenes was to abandon the Phocians to their fate and to draw closer to Thebes, so that, when his city had recovered from her financial exhaustion, Thebes and Athens together might form a joint resistance to the aggrandisement of Macedonia. In consequence of this irreconcilable division, which broke out in most unseemly quarrels among the ambassadors, nothing more was done than the administration of the oath. The envoys accompanied the king into Thessaly, and at Pherae the oath was administered to the Thessalians, his allies. The envoys returned to Athens, leaving Philip to proceed on his own way.

Embassy returns to Athens, June, 346 B.C.

It now remained to be seen whether Eubulus would carry the Assembly with him in favour of a rational policy of co-operation with Macedon, or would be defeated by the brilliant oratory of his younger rival. Philip's course of action would depend on the decision of the Assembly.

It was a calamity for Athens that at this critical moment there was no strong man at the helm of the state. The Assembly was swayed between the opposite counsels of Demosthenes, whose oratory was irresistible, and of Eubulus, whose influence had been paramount for the past eight years. When the ambassadors returned, Demosthenes lost no time in denouncing his colleagues, as having treacherously intrigued with Philip against the interests of the city. His denunciation was successful for a moment, and the usual vote of thanks to the embassy was witheld. But the success was only for a moment; Aeschines and his colleagues defended their policy triumphantly before the Assembly, and it was clear that the programme which they had discussed with Philip would have been satisfactory to the people. The Assembly decreed that the treaty of peace and alliance should be extended to the posterity of Philip. It further decreed that Athens should formally call upon the Phocians to surrender Delphi to the Amphictions, and should threaten them with armed intervention if they declined. Demosthenes appears to have made no opposition to this measure against the Phocians, and it seemed that the policy of co-operation with Philip was about to be realised.

Philip in the meantime advanced southward. The pass of Thermopylae · was held by Phalaecus, who had been reinforced by some Lacedaemonian troops; but Phalaecus had opened secret negotiations with Pella some months before, and the hostile vote of the Athenians decided him to capitulate on condition of departing unhindered where he would.

Thermopylae opened to Philip, July

Before he reached Thermopylae, Philip had addressed two friendly letters to Athens, inviting her to send an army to arrange the affairs of Phocis and Boeotia. Indisposed as the Athenian citizens were to leave Athens on military service, they lent ready ears to the absurd terrors which Demosthenes conjured up, suggesting that Philip would detain their army as hostages. Accordingly they contented themselves with sending an embassy (on which Demosthenes declined to serve) to convey to Philip an announcement of the decree which they had passed against the Phocians. Thus swayed between Eubulus and Demosthenes, the Athenians had done too much or too little. They had abandoned the Phocians, and at the same time they resigned the voice which they should, and could, have had in the political settlement of northern Greece.

As it was clear that Philip could not trust Athens, owing to the attitude of Demosthenes, he was constrained to act in conjunction with her enemy, Thebes. The cities of western Boeotia, which had been held by the Phocians, were restored to the Boeotian confederacy. The doom of the Phocians was decided by the Amphictionic Council which was now convoked. If some of the members had had their way, all the men of military age would have been cast down a precipice; but Philip would not have permitted this, and the sentence was as mild as could have been expected. The Phocians were deprived of their place in the Amphictionic body, and all their cities (with the exception of Abae) were broken up into villages, so that they might not again be a danger to Delphi. They were obliged to undertake to pay back, by instalments of 60 talents a year, the value of the treasures which they had taken from the sanctuary.[20] The Lacedaemonians were also punished for the support which they had given to Phocis, by being disqualified to return either of the members who represented the Dorian vote. The place which Phocis vacated in the Council was transferred to Macedonia, in recognition of Philip's services in expelling the desecrators of the temple.

Fate of the Phocians

The Athenian declaration against Phocis

exempted Athens from the penalty which was inflicted on Sparta at this Amphictionic meeting. But this was small comfort, and when the Athenians realised that they had gained nothing and that Thebes had gained all she wanted, they felt with indignation that the statesmanship of their city had been unskilful. The futility of their policy had been mainly due to Demosthenes, who had done all in his power to thwart Eubulus; and he now seized the occasion to discredit that statesman and his party. He encouraged his fellow-countrymen in the unreasonable fear that Philip would invade Attica, and the panic was so great that they brought their families and movable property from the country into the city. The fear was soon dispelled by a letter from Philip himself, but Demosthenes had succeeded in creating a profound distrust of Philip, and there was soon an opportunity of expressing this feeling.

An occasion offered itself to Philip almost immediately to display publicly to the assembled Greek world the position of leadership which he had thus won. It so happened that the celebration of the Pythian games fell in the year of the Peace. It will be remembered how Jason of Pherae, when he had made himself ruler of Thessaly, was about to come down to Delphi and assume the presidency of the Pythian feast, when he was cut down by assassins. The ambitions and plans of Pherae had passed to Pella, and Greece, which had dreaded the claims of the Thessalian tyrant, had now to bend the knee before the Macedonian king. Athens sulked; she sent no deputy to the Amphictionic meeting which elected Philip president for the festival, no delegates to the festival itself. This marked omission was a protest against the admission of Macedonia to the Amphictionic League, and Philip understood it as such. But he did not wish to quarrel with Athens; he hoped ultimately to gain her goodwill, and instead of marching into Attica, whither his Thessalian and Theban friends would have only too gladly followed him, he contented himself with sending an embassy to notify to the Athenian people the vote which made him a member of the Amphictiony and to invite them to concur. The invitation was in fact an ultimatum. Eubulus and his party had lost their influence in the outburst of anti-Macedonian feeling which Demosthenes had succeeded in stirring up. But the current had gone too far, and Demosthenes had some difficulty in allaying the spirits which he had conjured up. The Assembly was ready, on the slightest encouragement, to refuse its concurrence to the

Pythian games, 346 B.C.: Philip president

Inconsistency of Athens

Demosthenes' speech on the Peace

Amphictionic decree, and Demosthenes was forced to save the city from the results of his own agitation by showing that it would be foolish and absurd 'to go to war now for the shadow at Delphi'. Rarely had Athens been placed in such an undignified posture—a plight for which she had to thank the brilliant orator whom a malignant fate had sent to guide her on a futile path. From this time forward Demosthenes was the most influential of her counsellors.

Neither Demosthenes, the eloquent speaker, nor Eubulus, the able financier, saw far into the future. The only man of the day perhaps who grasped the situation in its ecumenical aspect, who descried, as it were from without, the place of Macedonia in Greece and the place of Greece in the world, was the nonagenarian Isocrates. He had never ventured to raise his voice in the din of party politics; and, when he condescended to give political advice to Greece, it was easy for the second-rate statesman as well as the party hack to laugh at a mere man of study stepping into a field where he had no practical experience. But Isocrates discerned the drift of events, where the orators who madly declaimed in the Pnyx were at fault; and the view which he took of the situation after the conclusion of the Peace of Philocrates simply anticipated the decrees of history. He explained his view in an open letter to king Philip. He had, long since, seen the endless futility of perpetuating that international system of Greece which existed within the memory of men: a number of small sovereign states, which ought by virtue of all they had in common to form a single nation, divided and constantly at feud. The time had come, he thought, to unite Greece, now that there had arisen a man who had the brains, the power, and the gold to become the central pivot of the union. Sovereign and independent the city states would of course remain, but they might be drawn together into one fold by a common hope and allegiance to a common leader. And under such a leader as Philip there was a great programme for Greece—not a mere programme of ambition, undertaken for the sake of something to do, but an enterprise which was urgently needed to meet a pressing social danger. We have already seen how Greece was flooded for many years past with a superfluous population who went about as armed rovers, attached to no city, hiring themselves out to any state that needed fighting men, a constant menace to society. A new country to colonise was the only remedy for this overflow of Greece, as

The political insight and foresight of Isocrates

431

Isocrates recognised. And the new country must be won from the barbarian. The time had come for Hellas to take the offensive against Persia, and the task appointed for Philip was to lead forth the hosts of Hellas on this splendid enterprise. If he did not destroy the whole empire of the Great King, he might at least annex Asia Minor 'from Cilicia to Sinope' to the Hellenic world and appropriate it to the needs of the Hellenic people.[21]

Ten years later the fulfilment of this task which Isocrates laid upon Philip was begun, not indeed by Philip himself, but by his successor. We shall see in due time how the fulfilment surpassed the utmost hopes of the Athenian speculator. But it is fair to note how justly Isocrates had discerned the signs of the times and the tendency of history. He saw that the inveterate quarrel between Europe and Asia, which had existed since the 'Trojan war', was the great abiding fact; he foresaw that it must soon come to an issue; and throughout the later part of his long life he was always watching for the inevitable day. The expedition of Cyrus and the campaign of Agesilaus were foreshadowings of that day, and it had seemed for a moment that Jason of Pherae was chosen to be the successor of Agamemnon and Cimon. Now the day had come at last; the choice of destiny had fallen upon the man of Macedonia. And Isocrates knew that this expansion of Greece would meet Greece's chief practical need. It is instructive to contrast his sane and practical view of the situation of Greece with the chimerical conservatism of some of his contemporaries. This conservatism, to which the orator Demosthenes gave a most noble expression, was founded on the delusion that the Athens of his day could be converted by his own eloquence and influence into the form and feature of the Periclean city. That was a delusion which took no account of the change which events had wrought in the Athenian character; it was a noble delusion which could have misled no great statesman or hard-headed thinker. It did not mislead Isocrates; he appreciated the trend of history, and saw the expansion of Greece, to which the world was moving.

Interval of Peace and Preparations for War (346–1 B.C.)

Having gained for Macedonia the coveted place in the religious league of Greece, Philip spent the next year or two in improving his small navy, in settling the administration of Thessaly, and in acquiring influence in the Peloponnese. It may fairly be said that Thessaly was now joined to Macedonia by a personal union. The Thessalian cities elected the Macedonian king as their *archon*—the old name of tagus with its Pheraean associations was avoided—and he set four governors over the four great divisions of the country. South of the Corinthian Isthmus, Philip adopted the old policy of Thebes, offering friendship to those states which needed a friend to stand by them against Sparta. His negotiations gained him the adhesion of Messenia and Megalopolis, Elis and Argos. In Megalopolis they set up a bronze statue of Philip, while Argos had a special tie with Macedon, since she claimed to be the original home of the Macedonian kings. *Philip elected archon of Thessaly; four tetrarchies of Thessaly*

Nor did Philip yet despair of achieving his chief aim, the conciliation of Athens. No one knew how to bribe better than he, and we may be sure that he gave gold without stint to his Athenian supporters. The Athenians naturally preferred peace to war, and the political party which was favourable to friendly relations with Philip was still strong and might at any moment regain its power. The influence of the veteran Eubulus, who seems to have withdrawn somewhat from public affairs, was on that side; there were Aeschines and Philocrates, who had been active in the negotiation of the Peace; and there was the incorruptible soldier Phocion, who was a remarkable figure at Athens, although he had no pretensions to eminence either as a soldier or as a statesman. He was marked among his contemporaries as an honest man, superior to all temptations of money; and, as the Athenians always prized this superhuman integrity which few of them attempted to practise, they elected him forty-five times as strategos, though in military capacity he was no more than a respectable sergeant. But his strong common sense, which was impervious to oratory, and his exceptional probity made him a useful member of his party. *The Peace-party at Athens*

There was one man in Athens who was firmly resolved that the peace should be no abiding peace, but a mere interval preparatory to war: Demosthenes, supported by Hypereides, Lycurgus, and others, spent the time in inflaming the wrath of his countrymen against Philip and in seeking to ruin his political antagonists. These years are therefore marked by a great struggle between the parties of war and peace, the influence of Demosthenes being most often in the ascendancy and ultimately emerging victorious. *The War-party*

*Demo-
sthenes
impeaches
Aeschines,
346-5 B.C.*

After Philip's installation in the Amphic-tionic Council, Demosthenes lost no time in striking a blow at his opponents. He brought an impeachment against Aeschines for receiving bribes from the Macedonian king and betraying the interests of Athens in the negotiations which preceded the Peace. Men's minds were irritated by the triumph of Thebes, and Demosthenes might have succeeded in inducing them to make Aeschines a scapegoat, if he had not committed a fatal mistake. He associated with himself in the prosecution a certain Timarchus, whose early life had been devoted to vices which disquali-fied him from the rights of a citizen; and thus Aeschines easily parried the stroke by bringing an action against Timarchus and submitting his private life to an annihilating exposure. The case of Demosthenes was thereby dis-credited, and he was obliged to let it drop for the time.

*Aeschines
against
Timar-
chus*

*Demo-
sthenes in
the Pelo-
ponnese,
344 B.C.*

A year or so later we find Demosthenes taking part in a mission to the cities of the Peloponnese to counteract by his oratory the influence of Philip. But his oratory roused no echoes, and Philip had good reason to complain of invectives which could hardly be justified from the lips of the representative of a power which was at peace and in alliance with Macedonia. An embassy came from Pella to remonstrate with the Athenians on their obstinate misconstruction of Macedonian motives, and Demosthenes seized the occasion to deliver one of his uncompromising anti-Macedonian harangues. The basis of his reasoning in this Philippic, and in the political speeches which followed it during the next few years, is the proposition that Philip desired and intended to destroy Athens. It was a proposition of which he had no valid proof; and it was actually untrue, as the sequel showed.

*The
Second
Philippic*

We are not told what answer Athens sent to Pella, but it would seem that she complained of the terms of the recent Peace as unfair, and insisted on her right to Halonnesus. This island off the coast of Thessaly, a place of no value whatever, had belonged to the Athenian Confederacy, but it had been seized by pirates, and the pirates had been expelled by Philip's soldiers. Philip sent an embassy with a courteous message, requesting Athens to propose emendations in the terms of the Peace, and offering to give her Halonnesus. But the place was of so little consequence to Athens, or anyone, that it served as an excellent pretext for diplomatic wrangling, and Demo-sthenes could persuade the people to refuse

*Halon-
nesus*

Halonnesus as it was offered, and demand that it should not be 'given' but 'given back'. Besides the 'restoration' of this worthless island, Athens made the proposal that the basis of the Peace should be altered, and that each party should retain, not the territories which were actually in its possession when the treaty was concluded, but the territories which lawfully belonged to it. This proposal was preposterous: no peace can be made on a basis that leaves open all the debated questions which it is the object of the treaty to settle. Athens also complained of the Thracian fortresses which Philip captured and retained after the negotiation had begun. On this question Philip was legally in the right, but he offered to submit the matter to arbitration. Athens refused the offer on the plea that suitable arbiters could not be found. She thus showed that she was not in earnest; her objection was as frivolous as her proposal. Demosthenes was responsible for the attitude of the city, and his intention was to keep up the friction with Macedonia and prevent any conciliation.

The ascendancy which Demosthenes and his fellows had now won emboldened them to make a grand attack upon their political opponents, and thereby deal Philip an effective blow. Hypereides brought an accusation of treachery against Philocrates, whose name was especially associated with the Peace, and so formidable did the prospect of the trial seem, in the current state of popular opinion, that Philocrates fled, and was condemned to death for contempt of court. Encouraged by this success, Demosthenes again took up his indictment against Aeschines; but Aeschines stood his ground, and one of the most famous political trials of antiquity was witnessed by the Athenian public. We can still hear the two rivals scurrilously reviling each other and vying to deceive the judges, for they published their speeches after the trial, to instruct and perplex posterity. It is in these documents, burning with the passions of political hatred, that the modern historian picking his doubtful way through lies and distortions of fact, has to discover the course of the negotiations which led to the Peace of Philocrates.

*Impeach-
ment and
flight of
Philo-
crates,
343 B.C.*

*Impeach-
ment of
Aeschines,
343 B.C.*

The speech of Demosthenes, in particular, is a triumph in the art of sophistry. No politician ever knew better than he how short is the memory of ordinary men for the political events which they have themselves watched and even helped to shape by their votes and opinions; and none ever traded more audaciously on this weakness of human

*Demo-
sthenes
on the
malversa-
tion of the
embassy*

nature. Hardly four brief years after the Peace was made, Demosthenes, confident that his audience will remember nothing accurately, ventures lightly to falsify facts which had so lately been notorious in the streets of Athens. Disclaiming all responsibility for a peace which he had himself worked hard to bring about but now seeks to discredit, he discovers that the Phocians were basely abandoned and imputes their fate to Aeschines. Against Aeschines there was in fact no case; the charge of receiving bribes from Philip was not supported by any actual evidence. The reply of Aeschines, which as an oratorical achievement is not inferior to that *Aeschines* of his accuser, rings less falsely. Eubulus and *acquitted* Phocion, men of the highest character, supported Aeschines, but the public feeling was so hostile to Philip at this juncture that the defendant barely escaped.

That Aeschines and many others of his party received money from Philip we may well believe—though the reiterations of Demosthenes are no evidence. But to receive money from Philip was one thing and to betray the interests of Athens was another. It had to be proved that a politician had sacrificed the manifest good of his country, or deserted his own political convictions, for a sackful of silver or gold before he could be considered unconditionally a traitor. Public opinion in Greece thought no worse of a man for accepting a few talents from foreigners who were pleased with his policy; although those few public men—Demosthenes was not among them—who made it a rule never to accept an obol in connection with any political transaction were respected as beings of superhuman virtue. Philip, who unlocked many a city by golden keys, was doubtless generous to the party whose programme was identical with his own interests, and it may be that Aeschines and others, who were not in affluent circumstances, would have been unable to devote themselves to public affairs if the king had not lined their wallets with gold.

Alliances Meanwhile Philip was seeking influence and *of Athens* intriguing in the countries which lay on either *with* side of Attica—in Megara on the west, and *Megara* Euboea on the north-east. An attempt at a *and* revolution in Megara was defeated, and the *Chalcis,* city allied itself with its neighbour and old *343-2 B.C.* enemy Athens, but in Euboea the movements *Philo-* supported by Macedonia were more successful. *Mace-* Both in Eretria and in Oreus oligarchies were *donian* established, really dependent on Philip. But *oligarchies* in Chalcis, which from its strategic position *in Euboea*

was of greater importance, the democracy held its ground and sought an equal alliance with Athens, to which Athens gladly consented.

Events in another quarter of Greece now caused a number of lesser Greek states to rally round Athens, and so bring within the field of near possibilities a league such as it was the dream of Demosthenes to form against Macedonia. By his marriage with an Epirot *Philip in* princess, it naturally devolved upon Philip to *Epirus* intervene in the struggles for the Epirot throne which followed her father's death. He espoused the cause of her brother Alexander against her uncle Arybbas, marched into the country, and established Alexander in the sovereignty. Epirus would now become dependent on Macedonia, and Philip saw in it a road to the Corinthian Gulf and a means of reaching Greece on the western side. His first step was to annex the region of Cassopia (between the rivers Acheron and Oropus) to the Epirote league of which his brother-in-law was head; and his eyes were then cast upon Ambracia, which stood as a barrier to the southward expansion of Epirus. But the place which he desired above all was doubtless Naupactus, the key to the Corinthian Gulf, now in the hands of the Achaeans. For pursuing his schemes in this quarter his natural allies were the Aetolians. They too coveted Naupactus and would have held it for him—and they were the enemies of the Ambraciots and Acarnanians, whom he hoped to render dependent on Epirus. The evident designs of Philip alarmed all these peoples, and not only Ambracia, Acarnania, and Achaea, but Corcyra also, sought the alliance of Athens.

Philip, however, judged that the time had not come for further advances on this side, and some recent movements of Cersobleptes decided him to turn now to one of the greatest tasks which were imposed upon the expander of Macedonia—the subjugation of Thrace. Since the Persians had been beaten out of Europe, Thrace had been subject to native princes, some of whom—Teres, Sitalces, Cotys —we have seen ruling the whole land from the Strymon's to the Danube's mouth. It was now to pass again under the rule of a foreigner, *Thracian* but its new lords were Europeans who would *expedition* lead Thracian soldiers to avenge upon Asia *of Philip,* the oriental yoke which had been laid upon *summer,* their ancestors. Of the Thracian expedition of *342 B.C.;* Philip we know as little as of the Thracian *spring,* expedition of Darius. Unlike Darius, he did *341 B.C.* not cross the rivers of the north or penetrate into any part of Scythia, but his campaign lasted ten months and he spent a winter in the field in that wintry land, suffering from sickness as well as from the cold. In war Philip never spared himself either hardship or danger. Demosthenes in later years described his reckless energy, ruthless to himself, in a famous passage: 'To gain empire and power he had an eye knocked out, his collar-bone broken, his arm and his leg maimed; he abandoned to fortune any part of his body she cared to take, so that honour and glory might be the portion of the rest.'

Philippopolis founded (Plovdiv)

The Thracian king was dethroned, and his kingdom became a tributary province of Macedon. There is still in the land a city which bears Philip's name, and is the most conspicuous memorial of that great and obscure campaign. Phillippopolis on the Hebrus was the chief of the cities which the conqueror built to maintain Macedonian influence in Thrace.

This conquest was not an infringement of the Peace, for Cersobleptes had not been admitted to the treaty as an ally of Athens. But it affected nearly and seriously the position of Athens at the gates of the Black Sea. The Macedonian frontier was now advanced to the immediate neighbourhood of the Chersonese, and Athens had no longer Thracian princes to wield against Philip. The prospect did not escape Demosthenes, and he resolved to force on a war—though both his own country and Philip were averse to hostilities. Accordingly he induced Athens to send a few ships and mercenaries, under a swashbuckler named Diopeithes, to protect her interests in the Chersonese. There had been some disputes with Cardia concerning the lands of the Athenian outsettlers, and Diopeithes lost no time in attacking Cardia. Now Cardia had been expressly recognised as an ally of Philip in the Peace, and thus the action of Diopeithes was a violation of the Peace. The admiral followed up this aggression by invading some of Philip's Thracian possessions, and Philip then remonstrated at Athens. Their admiral was so manifestly in the wrong that the Athenians were prepared to disown his conduct, but Demosthenes saved his tool and persuaded the people to sustain Diopeithes. He followed up his speech on the Chersonese question, which scored this success, by a loud call to war—the harangue known as the Third Philippic. The orator's thesis is that Philip, inveterately hostile to Athens and aiming at her destruction, is talking peace but acting war; and, when all the king's acts have been construed in this

Demosthenes' speech on the Chersonese, 341 B.C. Third Philippic

light, the perfectly sound conclusion is drawn that Athens should act at once. The proposals of Demosthenes are to make military preparations, to send forces to the Chersonese, and to organise an Hellenic league against 'the Macedonian wretch'.

Envoys were sent here and there to raise the alarm. Demosthenes himself proceeded to the Propontis and succeeded in detaching Byzantium and Perinthus from the Macedonian alliance. At the same time Athenian troops were sent into Euboea; the governments in Oreus and Eretria were overthrown, and these cities joined an independent Euboeic league, of which the Synod met at Chalcis. The island was thus liberated from Macedon without becoming dependent on Athens.

Demosthenes at Byzantium, 341 B.C. The Euboeic Federation, 341 B.C.

All these acts of hostility were committed without an overt breach of the Peace between Athens and Philip. But the secession of Perinthus and Byzantium was a blow which Philip was not prepared to take with equanimity. When he had settled his Thracian province, he began the siege of Perinthus by land and sea. There was an Athenian squadron in the Hellespont which barred the passage of the Macedonian fleet, but Philip caused a diversion by sending land troops into the Chersonese, and by this stratagem got his ships successfully through. The siege of Perinthus marks, for eastern Greece, the beginning of those new developments of the art of besieging which in Sicily had long since been practised with success. But all the engines and rams, the towers and the mines of Philip failed to take Perinthus on its steep peninsular cliff. His blockade on the sea side was inefficient, and the besieged were furnished with stores and men from Byzantium. The Athenians were still holding aloof. They had addressed a remonstrance to Philip for violating the Chersonese and capturing some of their ships. Philip replied by a letter in which he rehearsed numerous acts of Athenian hostility to himself. But the decisive moment came when the king suddenly raised the siege of Perinthus and marched against Byzantium, hoping to capture it by the unexpectedness of his attack. Athens could no longer hold aloof when the key of the Bosphorus was in peril. The marble tablet on which the Peace was inscribed was pulled down; it was open war at last. A squadron under Chares was sent to help Byzantium, and Phocion presently followed with a second fleet. Other help had come from Rhodes and Chios, and Philip was compelled

Philip lays siege to Perinthus, 340 B.C.

then to Byzantium

to withdraw into Thrace, baffled in both his undertakings. It was the first triumph of Demosthenes over the arch-foe, and he received a public vote of thanks from the Athenian people.

But one wonders that the naval power of Athens had not made itself more immediately and effectively felt. The Macedonian fleet was insignificant: it could inflict damage on merchant-vessels or raid a coast, but it had no hold on the sea. The Athenian navy was 300 strong and controlled the northern Aegean, and yet it seems that in these critical years there was no permanent squadron of any strength stationed in the Hellespont. Naval affairs had been by no means neglected. Eubulus had seen to the building of new ship-sheds and had begun the construction of a magnificent arsenal, close to the harbour of Zea, for the storage of the sails and rigging and tackle of the ships of war. But these luxuries were vain, if the ships themselves were not efficient, and the group-system on *The naval* which the ships were furnished worked badly. *reform of* Demosthenes had long ago desired to reform *Demo-* this system, which had been in force for *sthenes* seventeen years. The 1200 richest citizens were liable to the trierarchy—each trireme being charged on a small group, of which each member contributed the same proportion of the expense. If a large number of ships were required, the group might consist of five persons; if a small number, of fifteen. This system bore hardly on the poorer members of the partnership, who had to pay the same amount as the richer, and some were ruined by the burden. But the great mischief was that these poorer members were often unable to pay their quota in time and consequently the completion of the triremes was delayed. The influence of Demosthenes was now so enormous that he was able, in the face of bitter opposition from the wealthy class, to introduce a new law by which the cost of furnishing the ships should fall on each citizen in proportion to his property. Thus a citizen whose property was rated as exceeding 30 talents would henceforward, instead of having to pay one-fifth or perhaps one-fifteenth of the cost of a single trireme, be obliged to furnish three triremes and a boat.

So popular was Demosthenes, by the successes of Euboea and Byzantium, that he was able to accomplish a still greater feat. Years before he had cautiously hinted at the expediency of devoting the Festival Fund to military purposes; he now persuaded the

Athenians to adopt this highly disagreeable measure. The building of the arsenal and ship-sheds was interrupted also, in order to save the expenses.

Philip in the meantime had again withdrawn *Philip in* into the wilds of Thrace. The Scythians near *Thrace,* the mouth of the Danube had rebelled, *340-339* and he crossed the Balkan range to crush *B.C.* them. In returning to Macedon through the land of the Triballi, in the centre of the peninsula, he had some hard fighting in the mountains and was severely wounded in the leg. But Thrace was now safe, and he was free to deal with Greece.

Battle of Chaeronea

Philip had no longer the slighest prospect of realising the hope, which he had cherished both before and after the Peace of Philocrates, of establishing friendly relations with Athens. The influence of the irreconcilable orator was now triumphant; through the persistent agitation of Demosthenes, coldness and quarrelling had issued in war, and Macedonia had received a distinct check. There was nothing for it now but to accept the war and bring the Macedonian cavalry into play. There were two points where Athens could be attacked effectively, at the gates of her own city and at the gates of her granary in the Euxine. But a land-power like Macedonia could not operate effectively in the Propontis, unless aided by allies which possessed an effective navy; and Philip had experienced the truth of this when he laid siege to Perinthus and Byzantium. And in that quarter he had now to reckon not only with the Athenian sea-power but with the small navies of the Asiatic islands, Rhodes, Cos, and Chios, which had recently come to the rescue of the menaced cities. For these island states calculated that if Philip won control of the passage between the two continents he would not only tax their trade, but would soon cross over to the conquest of Asia Minor, and their fleets would then be appropriated to form the nucleus of a Macedonian navy. Now that Athens had been awakened from her slumbers, it was abundantly evident that the only place where Macedonia could inflict upon her a decisive blow was Attica.

On her side Athens had lightly engaged in *Dangerous* a war for which she had not either fully *position of* counted the cost or meditated an adequate *Athens* programme. In truth the Athenians had no craving for the war; and they were not driven to it by an imperious necessity, or urged by an irresistible instinct, or persuaded by a rational conviction of its expediency. The persistent and crafty agitation of Demosthenes and his party had drawn them on step by step; their natural feeling of irritation at the rise of a new great power in the north had been sedulously fed and fostered by that eloquent orator and his friends till it had grown into an unreasoning hatred of the Macedonian king. whose character, aims, and resources were totally misrepresented. But now that war was declared, what was to be the plan of action? Athens had not even an able general who could make an effective combination. She controlled the sea, and it was something that Euboea had shaken off the Macedonian influence. In Chalcis, Athens had a point of vantage against Boeotia, and from Oreus she could raid the Thessalian coast and operate in the bay of Pagasae. But when Philip advanced southward, and passed Thermopylae, which was in his hands, the Athenian superiority at sea was of no use, for his communications were independent of the sea. There was no means of offering serious opposition if he marched on Attica, and the citizens were hardly likely at the bidding of Demosthenes to take to their ships as they had done at the bidding of Themistocles. If events fell out according to the only probable forecast which could be made—on the assumption of Demosthenes that the invasion of Attica and ruin of Athens were the supreme objects of Philip—the Athenians had to look forward to the devastation of their country and the siege of their city. How was this peril to be met? They were practically isolated, for they had no strong continental power to support them; what could Megarians or Corinthians, Ambraciots or Achaeans, do for them against the host of Philip and his allies? 'Ah, if we were only islanders!' many an Athenian must have murmured in these critical years. It was the calamity of Athens, as it has been the calamity of Holland, that she was solidly attached to the continent. Now that the crisis approaches nearer, it is borne in upon us more and more how improvident the policy of Athens had been. If she had accepted Macedonian friendship and kept a strong naval force permanently in the Propontis, assuring herself of undisputed control of her own element, she would have been perfectly safe. The constant presence of a powerful fleet belonging to a predominant naval state may be in itself a strategic success equivalent to a series of victories. But, though we have almost no notices of the movements

of the Athenian triremes at this time, we cannot help suspecting that the naval power of Athens was inefficiently handled.

Demosthenes had never had a free hand until the siege of Byzantium; till then, he could do little more than agitate. When at length he became in the full sense of the word the director of Athenian policy, his energy and skill were amazing. But we cannot help asking with what hopes he was prepared to undertake the responsibility of bringing an invader into his country and a besieger to the walls of his city. The answer is that he rested his hope on a single chance. From the beginning of his public career Demosthenes had a strong leaning to Thebes; it has been already mentioned that he was Theban proxenos at Athens. This was a predilection which he needed to be very careful of airing, for the general feeling in his city was unfriendly to Thebes. The rhetorical tears which Demosthenes shed over the fate of the Phocians were not inconsistent with his attachment to the enemies of Phocis, for he never raised his voice for the victims of Theban hatred until their fate was sealed. The aim of his policy was to unite Athens in alliance with Thebes. It was a difficult and doubtful game. Could Thebes be induced to turn against her Macedonian ally, who had recently secured for her the full supremacy of Boeotia, and who, she might reasonably reckon, would continue to support her as a useful neighbour to Attica? On this chance, and a poor chance it seemed, rested the desperate policy of Demosthenes. If Thebes joined Philip, or even gave him a free passage through Boeotia, Attica was doomed. But if she could be brought to desert him, her well-trained troops, joined with those of Athens, might successfully oppose his invasion.

The invasion was not long delayed, and it came about in a curious way. During the recent Sacred War, the Athenians had burnished anew and set up again in the sanctuary of Delphi the donative which they had dedicated after the victory of Plataea, being gold shields with the inscription, 'From the spoils of Persians and Thebans, who fought together against the Greeks'. Such a re-dedication, while Delphi was in the hands of the Phocians, who had been condemned as sacrilegious robbers, might be regarded as an offence against religion; at all events, the Thebans and their friends had an excellent pretext to revenge themselves on Athens for that most offensive inscription, which had perpetuated the shame of Thebes for a century and a half. The

Theban leanings of Demosthenes

Meeting of the Amphictionic Council, autumn, 340 B.C.

Speech of
Aeschines,
who retorts
sacrilege
on the
Locrians

Thebans themselves did not come forward, but their friends of the Locrian Amphissa arranged to accuse the Athenians at the autumn session of the Amphictionic Council and propose a fine of 50 talents. At this session Aeschines was one of the Athenian deputies and he discovered the movement which was afoot against his city. He was an able man and he forestalled the blow by dealing another. The men who had been incited to charge Athens with sacrilege had been themselves guilty of a sacrilege far more enormous: they had cultivated part of the accursed field which had once been the land of Crisa. Aeschines arose in the assembly and, in an impressive and convincing speech which carried his audience with him, called upon the Amphictions to punish the men who were responsible for this impious act. On the morrow at break of day the Amphictions and the Delphians, armed with pickaxes, marched down the hill to lay waste the places which had been unlawfully cultivated, and, as they did so, were assaulted by the Amphissians, whose city is visible from the plain. The Council then resolved to hold a special meeting at Thermopylae, in order to consult on measures for the punishment of the Locrians, who, to their former crime, had added the offence of violating the persons of the Amphictionic deputies.

By his promptness and eloquence the Athenian orator had secured a great triumph. He had completely turned the tables on the enemies, Amphissa and Thebes, who must have been prepared to declare an Amphictionic war against Athens, in case she declined, as she certainly would have done, to pay the fine. They calculated of course on the support of Philip of Macedon. But it was now for Athens to take the lead in a sacred war against Amphissa; and it was a favourable opportunity for her to make peace with Philip—so that the combination should be Philip and Athens against Thebes, instead of Philip and Thebes against Athens. It was not to be expected that this advantage which Aeschines had gained would be welcome to Demosthenes, for it was the object of Demosthenes to avoid an embroilment with Thebes. Accordingly he persuaded the people to send no deputies to the special Amphictionic meeting and take no part in the proceedings against Amphissa. He upbraided Aeschines with trying to 'bring an Amphictionic war into Attica'—a strange taunt to the man who had prevented the declaration of an Amphictionic war against Athens.

Athens
does not
follow up
the lead
of
Aeschines

Thus, although the attack upon Athens must have been prepared at Theban instigation, the incident was converted through the policy of Demosthenes into a means of bringing Athens and Thebes closer together. Athens and Thebes alike abstained from attending the special meeting. The Amphictions, in accordance with the decisions of that meeting, marched against the Amphissians, but were not strong enough to impose the penalties which had been decreed. Accordingly, at the next autumn session, they determined to invite Philip to come down once more to be leader in a sacred war.

The Am-
phictions
proceed
against
Amphissa,
339 B.C.
The Am-
phictions
call in
Philip,
338 B.C.,
spring

Philip did not delay a moment. An Amphictionic war, from which both Athens and Thebes held aloof, was a matter which needed prompt attention. When he reached Thermopylae, he probably sent on, by the mountain road which passes through Doris to Amphissa, a small force to occupy Cytinion, the chief town on that road. Advancing himself through the defile of Thermopylae into northern Phocis, he seized and refortified the dismantled city of Elatea. The purpose of this action was to protect himself in the rear against Boeotia, and preserve his communications with Thermopylae, while he was operating against Amphissa. But while he halted at Elatea he sent ambassadors to explore the intentions of Thebes. He declared that he intended to invade Attica, and called upon the Thebans to join him in the invasion, or, if they would not do this, to give his army a free passage through Boeotia. This was a diplomatic method of forcing Thebes to declare herself; it does not prove that Philip had any serious intention of marching against Attica, and his later conduct seems to show that he did not contemplate such a step.

But in Athens, when the news came that the Macedonian army was at Elatea, the people fell into extreme panic and alarm. It would seem that Philip's rapid movements had brought him into central Greece far sooner than was expected; and the news of his arrival, which must have been transmitted by way of Thebes, was accompanied by the rumour that he was about to march on Athens. And thus the Athenians in their fright connected the seizure of Elatea with the supposed design against themselves, although Elatea had no closer connection than the pass of Thermopylae with an attack on Athens. For a night and a day the city was filled with consternation, and these anxious hours have become famous in history through the genius of the orator Demosthenes, who in later years recalled to

Alarm at
Athens

the people the scene and their own emotions by a picturesque description which no orator has surpassed.

On the advice of Demosthenes, the Athenians dispatched ten envoys to Thebes; everything depended on detaching Thebes from the Macedonian alliance. And it seemed at least possible that this might be effected. For though there were probably few in Thebes who were inclined to be friendly to Athens, there was a party of some weight which was distinctly hostile to Macedonia. Moreover, there was a feeling of soreness against Philip for having seized Nicaea, close to Thermopylae, and replaced its Theban garrison by Thessalians. The envoys, of whom Demosthenes was one, were instructed to make concessions and exact none.

The ambassadors of Athens and Macedon met in the Boeotian capital, and their mesages were heard in turn by the Theban assembly. It would be too much to say that the fate of Greece depended on the deliberations of this assembly, but it is the mere truth that the Theban vote not only decided the doom of Thebes itself, but determined the shape of the great event to which Greece had been irresistibly moving.

In considering the situation which the rise of Macedon had created we have hitherto stood in Pella or in Athens; we must now for a moment take our point of view at Thebes. The inveterate rivalry and ever-smouldering hate which existed between Thebes and Athens was a strong motive inducing Thebes to embrace an opportunity for rendering Athens harmless. But it would require no great fore-sight to see that, by weakening her old rival, Thebes would gravely endanger her own position. So long as Philip had a strong Athens to reckon with, it was in his interest to treat Thebes with respect, but if Athens were reduced to nothingness Thebes would be absolutely in his power, and probably his first step would be to free the cities of Boeotia from her domination. To put it shortly, the independent attitude which Thebes had hitherto been able to maintain towards her friend Macedonia depended on the integrity of Athens. Thus the positions of Thebes and Athens were remarkably different. While Athens could with impunity stand alone as Philip's enemy, when Thebes was Philip's friend, Thebes could not safely be Philip's friend unless Athens were his enemy. The reason for this difference was that Athens was a sea-power, less dominant than in the fifth century, but still formidable.

To a Theban statesman then, possessing any foresight, the subjugation of Athens would have been feared as the prelude to the supression of Thebes, and it would have seemed wiser to join in a common resistance to Philip. This sound reasoning was quickened by the eloquence of Demosthenes and the offers of Athens. The Athenians were ready to pay two-thirds of the expenses of the war; they abandoned their claim to Oropus, and they recognised the Boeotian dominion of Thebes—a dominion which they had always condemned before as an outrage on the rights of free communities. But professing now, through the mouth of Demosthenes, to be the champion of Hellenic liberty, Athens scrupled little to sacrifice the liberties of a few Boeotian cities. By these concessions she secured the alliance of Thebes, and Demosthenes won the greatest diplomatic success that he had yet achieved—the consummation to which his policy had been directed for many years.

The allies occupied the passes leading from Phocis into Boeotia and detached a strong force under Chares to bar the road from the Gulf of Corinth through Amphissa and Doris. In the summer Philip, reinforced, made a lightning campaign through Phocis, defeated Chares, captured Amphissa, and seized Naupactus to gain direct access to the Gulf. The Greeks, now threatened in their rear, fell back to the plain of Chaeronea. Philip, advancing through the pass of Parapotamii from which the allies had withdrawn, found them guarding the way to Thebes and prepared to give him battle. He had 30,000 foot soldiers and 2000 horse, perhaps slightly outnumbering his foes.

Their line extended over about three and a half miles, the left wing resting on Chaeronea and the right on the river Cephisus. The Theban hoplites, with the Sacred Band in front, under the command of Theagenes, did not occupy the left wing, as when Epaminondas led them to victory at Leuctra and at Mantinea, but were assigned the right, which was esteemed the post of honour. In the centre were ranged the troops of the lesser allies, Achaeans, Corinthians, Phocians, and others, whom Demosthenes boasted of having rallied to the cause of Hellenic liberty. On the left stood the Athenians under three generals, Chares, Lysicles, and Stratocles, of whom Chares was a respectable soldier with con-siderable experience and no talent, while the other two were incompetent. Demosthenes himself was serving as a hoplite in the ranks.

Of the battle we know less perhaps than of

any other equally important engagement in the history of Greece. But we can form a general notion of the tactics of Philip. The most formidable part of the line against him was the Theban infantry, and accordingly he posted on his own left wing the phalanx, with its more open order and long pikes, to try its strength against the most efficient of the old-fashioned hoplites of Greece. On the flank of this wing he placed his heavy cavalry, to ride down upon the Thebans when the phalanx had worn them out. The cavalry was commanded by Alexander, now a lad of eighteen, and, many hundred years after, 'the oak of Alexander' was shown on the bank of the river. The right wing was comparatively weak, and Philip planned that it should gradually give way before the attack of the Athenians and draw them on, so as to divide them from their allies. This plan of holding back the right wing reminds us of the tactics of Epaminondas, but the use of cavalry to decide the combat is the characteristic feature of Philip's battles.

The Athenians pressed forward, fondly fancying that they were pressing to victory, and Stratocles in the flush of success cried, 'On to Macedonia!' But in the meantime the Thebans had been broken by Alexander's horsemen: their leader had fallen, and the comrades of the Sacred Band were making a last hopeless stand. Philip could now spare some of his Macedonian footmen, and he moved them so as to take the Athenians in flank and rear. Against the assault of these trained troops the Athenians were helpless. One thousand were slain, 2000 captured, and the rest ran, Demosthenes running with the fleetest. But the Sacred Band did not flee. They fought till they fell, and it is their heroism which has won for the battle of Chaeronea its glory as a struggle for liberty. When the traveller, journeying on the highway from Phocis to Thebes, has passed the town of Chaeronea, he sees at the roadside the tomb where those heroes were laid, and the lion, now reconstructed which was set up to keep a long ward over their bones.

Signifi-cance of battle of Chaeronea (1) mili-tary;

An epitaph which was composed in honour of the Athenian dead suggested the consolation that God alone is sure of success—men must be prepared to fail. It is true, but in this case the failure cannot be imputed to the chances of war. When the allies opened the campaign the outlook was not hopeless; if they had been led by a competent general they might have reduced the Macedonian army to serious straits amid the valleys of Phocis and the hills of Locris. But to oppose to a Philip, the best

they had was a Chares. The war was really decided in Locris by the strategical inferiority of the Athenian and Theban generals; and the inevitable sequel of the blunders there was the catastrophe in Boeotia. The advantage in numerical strength with which the allies started had been lost, and when they faced such an outstanding general in open battle at

16.3   The Lion of Chaeronea, restored

(2) political

Chaeronea defeat was inevitable. Men must be prepared to fail when they have no competent leader.

If the chances of another issue to the battle of Chaeronea have been exaggerated, the significance of that event has been often misrepresented. The battle of Chaeronea belongs to the same historical series as the battles of Aegospotami and Leuctra. As the hegemony or first place among Greek states had passed successively from Athens to Sparta, and to Thebes, so now it passed to Macedon. The statement that Greek liberty perished on the plain of Chaeronea is as true or as false as that it perished on the field of Leuctra or the strand of the Goat's River. Whenever a Greek state became supreme, that supremacy entailed the decline of some states and the dependency or subjection of others. Athens was reduced to a secondary place by Macedon, and Thebes fared still worse; but we must not forget what Sparta, in the day of her triumph, did to Athens, or the more evil things which Thebes proposed. There were, however, in the case of Macedonia, special circumstances which seemed to give her victory a more fateful character than those previous victories which had initiated new supremacies.

Greek feelings towards Macedon

For Macedon was regarded in Hellas as an outsider. This was a feeling which the southern Greeks entertained even in regard to Thessaly when Jason threatened them with a Thessalian hegemony; and Macedonia, politically and historically as well as geographically, was some steps further away than Thessaly. If Thessaly was hardly inside the inner circle of Hellenic politics, Macedonia was distinctly outside it. To Athens and Sparta, to Corinth and Argos and Thebes, the old powers, who, as we might say, had known each other all their lives as foes or friends, and had a common international history, the supremacy of Macedonia seemed the intrusion of an upstart. And, in the second place, this supremacy was the triumph of an absolute monarchy over free commonwealths, so that the submission of the Greek states to Macedon's king might be rhetorically branded as an enslavement to a tyrant in a sense in which subjection to a sovereign Athens or a sovereign Sparta could not be so described. For these reasons Chaeronea sent a new kind of thrill through Greece. And the impression that there was something unique in Philip's victory might be said to have been confirmed by subsequent history, which showed that the old Greek commonwealths had had their day and might never again rise to be first-rate powers.

The Synedrion of the Greeks. Philip's Death

Isocrates just lived to hear the news of Chaeronea and died consoled for the fate of his fallen fellow-citizens by the thought that the unity of Hellas was now assured. But in fact a Greek unity, such as he dreamed of, was by no means assured. The hegemony of Macedonia did as little to unite the Greek states or abolish the separatist tendency as the hegemony of Athens or of Sparta. But we must see how Philip used his victory.

Philip harsh to Thebes;

He treated Thebes just as Sparta had treated it when Phoebidas surprised the citadel. He punished by death or confiscation his leading opponents; he established a Macedonian garrison in the Cadmea, and broke up the Boeotian league, giving all the cities their independence and restoring the dismantled towns of Orchomenus and Plataea. But if his dealing with Thebes did not go beyond the usual dealing of one Greek state with its vanquished rival, his dealing with Athens was unusually lenient. The truth was that Athens did not lie defenceless at his feet. He might invade and ravage Attica but, when he came to invest Athens and Piraeus, he might find himself confronted by a task more arduous than that which had thwarted him at Perinthus and Byzantium. The sea-power of Athens saved her and not less, perhaps, the respect which Philip always felt for her intellectual eminence. Now, at last, by unexpected leniency, he might win what he had always striven for, the moral and material support of Athens. And in Athens men were now ready to listen to the voices which were raised for peace. The policy of Demosthenes had failed, and all desired to recover the 2000 captives and avert an invasion of Attic soil. There was little disposition to listen to Hypereides, who proposed to arm all disenfranchised citizens, metics, and slaves. Among the captives was an orator of consummate talent, named Demades, who belonged to the peace party and saw that the supremacy of Macedon was inevitable. An anecdote was noised abroad that Philip, who spent the night after the battle in wild revelry, came reeling drunk to the place where his prisoners were and jeered at their misfortune, making merry, too, over the flight of the great Demosthenes. But Demades stood forth and ventured to rebuke him: 'O king, fortune has given you the rôle of Agamemnon, and you play the part of Thersites!' The words stung and sobered the drunken victor; he flung away his garlands and all the gear of his revel, and set

lenient to Athens

Demades

441

the bold speaker free. But whether this story be true or not, Demades was politically sympathetic with Philip and was sent by him to negotiate peace at Athens.

Terms of Peace between Athens and Macedonia

Philip offered to restore all the prisoners without ransom and not to march into Attica. The Athenians on their side were to dissolve what remained of their confederacy and join the new Hellenic union which Philip proposed to organise. In regard to territory, Oropus was to be given to Athens, but the Chersonese was to be surrendered to Macedonia. On these terms peace was concluded, and the Athenian people thought that they had come off well. Philip sent his son and two of his chief officers to Athens with the bodies of the Athenians who had been slain. They were received with great honour, and a statue of the Macedonian king was set up in the Agora, a token of gratitude which was probably genuine. Demosthenes himself afterwards confessed with a snarl that Philip had been kind.

Philip in the Peloponnese

It was now necessary for Macedonia to win the recognition of her supremacy from the Peloponnesian states. Philip himself marched into the Peloponnese and met with no resistance. Sparta alone refused to submit, and the conqueror bore down upon her, with the purpose of forcing on her a reform of the constitution and the abolition of her peculiar kingship, which seemed to him like a relic of the dark ages. But something mysterious happened which induced him to desist from his purpose, and a poet of Epidaurus, who was at that time a boy, told in later years how the god Asklêpios had intervened to save the Spartan state—

Isyllus of Epidaurus

> What time king Philip unto Sparta came,
> Bent on abolishing the royal name.[22]

But Sparta, though her kings were saved, had to suffer at the hands of Philip what she had before suffered at the hands of Epaminondas —the devastation of Laconia and the diminution of her territory. The frontier districts on three sides were given to her neighbours, Argos, Tegea, Megalopolis, and Messenia. Having thus displayed his arms and power in the south, the Macedonian king invited all the Greek states south of Thermopylae to send delegates to a congress at Corinth; and, with the sole exception of Sparta, all the states obeyed.

Synedrion at Corinth, 338 B.C.

It was a Federal congress—the first assembly of an Hellenic Confederacy, of which the place of meeting was to be Corinth and Macedonia the head.[23] The aim of the Confederacy was understood from the first; but it would seem that it was not till the second

meeting, a year later, that Philip announced his resolve to make war upon Persia, on behalf of Greece and her gods, to liberate the Greek cities of Asia, and to punish the barbarians for the acts of sacrilege which their forefathers had committed in the days of Xerxes. It was the formal announcement that a new act in the eternal struggle between Europe and Asia was about to begin, and Europe, having found a leader, might now have her revenge. The federal gathering voted for the war and elected Philip general with supreme powers. It was arranged what contingents in men or ships each city should contribute to the Panhellenic army, the Athenians undertaking to send a considerable fleet.

Comparison of the Synedrion of the Isthmus of 480 B.C. with that of 338 B.C.

The league which was thus organised under the hegemony of Macedon had the advantage of placing before its members a definite object to be accomplished, and, it might be thought, a common interest. But if Themistocles found it hard to unite the Greek states by a common fear, it was harder still for Philip to unite them by a common hope; and the idea which Macedon promulgated produced no Panhellenic effort, and awakened but small enthusiasm. Yet the Congress of Corinth has its significance: it is the counterpart of that earlier congress which met at the Isthmus, when Greece was trembling at the thought of the barbarian host which was rolling towards her from the east. She had so long since ceased to tremble that she had almost forgotten to remember before the day of vengeance came; but with the revolution of fortune's wheel, that day came duly round, and Greece met once more on the Isthmus to concert how her ancient tremors might be amply avenged.

Unity of Greece not achieved

The new league did not unite the Greeks in the sense in which Isocrates hoped for their union. There was a common dependency on Macedon, but there was no zeal for the aims of the northern power, no faith in her as the guide and leader of Greece. Each state went its own private way; and the interests of the Greek communities remained as isolated and particular as ever. A league of such members could not be held together, and the peace which the league stipulated could not be maintained, without some military stations in the midst of the country; and Philip established three Macedonian garrisons at important points: at Ambracia to watch the west, at Corinth to hold the Peloponnese in check, and at Chalcis to control north-eastern Greece.

Philip's garrisons in Greece

The designs of Philip probably did not extend beyond the conquest of western Asia Minor, but it was not fated that he should achieve

Parmenio, Amyntas, and Attalus invade Asia Minor, 336 B.C.

this himself. In the spring after the congress, his preparations for war were nearly complete, and he sent forward an advance force under Parmenio and other generals to secure the passage of the Hellespont and win a footing in the Troad and Bithynia. The rest of the army was soon to follow under his own command.

But Philip, as a frank Corinthian friend told him, had filled his own house with division and bitterness. A Macedonian king was not expected to be faithful to his wife; but the proud and stormy princess whom he had wedded was impatient of his open infidelities. Nor was her own virtue above suspicion, and it was even whispered that Alexander was not Philip's son. The crisis came when Philip fell in love with a Macedonian maiden of too high a station to become his concubine—

Philip divorces Olympias and marries Cleopatra

Cleopatra, the niece of his general Attalus. Yielding to his passion, he put Olympias away and celebrated his second marriage. At the wedding feast, Attalus, bold with wine, invited the nobles to pray the gods for a *legitimate* heir to the throne. Alexander flung his drinking-cup in the face of the man who had insulted his mother, and Philip started up, drawing his sword to transfix his son. But he reeled and fell, and Alexander jeered, 'Behold the man who would pass from Europe to Asia, and trips in passing from couch to couch!' Pella was no longer the place for Alexander. He took the divorced queen to Epirus, and withdrew himself to the hills of Lyncestis until Philip invited him to return. But the restless intrigues of the injured mother soon created new debates, and when a son was born to Cleopatra it was easy to arouse the fears of Alexander that his own succession to the throne was imperilled. Philip's most urgent desire was to avoid a breach with the powerful king of Epirus, the brother of the injured woman. To this end he offered him his daughter in wedlock, and the marriage was to be celebrated with great pomp in Pella on the eve of Philip's departure for Asia. But it was decreed that he should not depart: Olympias was not one to hesitate at crime, and a tool was easily found to avenge the wrongs of the wife and assure the succession of the son. A certain Pausanias, an obscure man of no merit, had been grossly wronged by Attalus and was madly incensed against the king, who refused to do him justice. On the wedding day, as Philip, in solemn procession, entered the theatre a little in advance of his guards, Pausanias rushed forward with a Celtic dagger and struck him down at the gate. The assassin

Murder of Philip, 336 B.C. (summer)

was caught and killed, but the real authors of the plot were not discovered. Her enemies later accused Olympias of the crime, but the charge comes from tainted sources. Alexander reaped the fruits, but was not responsible. There were dark whispers against him, but the loyalty of Philip's two leading generals, Antipater and Parmenio, is sufficient evidence of his innocence.

To none of the world's great rulers has history done less justice than to Philip. This failure in appreciation has been due to two or perhaps to three causes. The overwhelming greatness of a son greater than himself has overshadowed him and drawn men's eyes to achievements which would never have been possible without the firm foundations built up by Philip. In the second place, we depend for our knowledge of Philip's work almost entirely on the Athenian orators, and especially on Demosthenes, whose main object was to misrepresent the king. And we may add, thirdly, that we possess no account of one of the greatest and most difficult of his exploits, the conquest of Thrace. Thus through chance, through the malignant eloquence of his opponent, who has held the ears of posterity, and through the very results of his own deeds, the maker and expander of Macedonia, the conqueror of Thrace and Greece, has hardly held his due place in the history of the world. The importance of his work cannot be fully understood until the consequences which it devolved upon his son to carry out have been studied. The work of Alexander is the most authentic testimony to the work of Philip.

Injustice done to Philip by posterity

But there was one notable man of the day whose imagination grasped the ecumenical importance of the king of Macedon. A pupil of Isocrates, Theopompus of Chios—who played some part in the politics of his own island—was inspired by the deeds of Philip to write a history of his own time, with Philip as its central figure. In that elaborate work, the loss of which is irreparable, Theopompus exposed candidly and impartially the king's weaknesses and misdeeds; but he declared his judgement that Europe had never produced so great a man as the son of Amyntas.

The Philippic Histories of Theopompus

It is part of the injustice to Philip that the history of Greece during his reign has so often been treated as little more than a biography of Demosthenes. Only his political opponents would deny that Demosthenes was the most eloquent of orators and the most patriotic of citizens, but that oratory in which he excelled was one of the curses of Greek politics. The art of persuasive speech is indispensable in

Demosthenes as an orator

a free commonwealth, and when it is wielded by a statesman or a general—a Pericles, a Cleon, or a Xenophon—is a noble as well as useful instrument. But once it ceases to be a merely auxiliary art, it becomes dangerous and hurtful. This is what had happened at Athens. Rhetoric had been carried to such perfection that the best years of a man's youth were absorbed in learning it, and when he entered upon public life he was a finished speaker, but a poor politician. Briefly, orators took the place of statesmen, and Demosthenes was the most eminent of the class. They could all formulate striking phrases of profound political wisdom; but their school-taught lore did not carry them far against the craft of the Macedonian statesman. The men of mighty words were as children in the hands of the man of mighty deeds. The Athenians took pleasure in hearing and criticising the elaborate speeches of their orators; and the eloquence of Demosthenes, though it was thoroughly appreciated, imposed far less on such connoisseurs than it has imposed upon posterity. The common sense of a plain man could easily expose his sophistries; he said himself that the blunt Phocion was the 'chopper' of his periods.

Demosthenes used his brilliant gift of speech in the service of his country, but he used it unscrupulously and according to his light—the light of a purblind patriotism. He could take a lofty tone—he professed to regard Philip as a barbarian threatening Hellas and her gods—but there is no need to show that, judged from the point of view of the history of the world, his policy was retrograde and retarding. We cannot, perhaps, fairly criticise him for not having seen, even as fully as Isocrates, that the day for the expansion of Greece had come, and that no existing Greek commonwealth was competent to conduct that expansion; or if he did vaguely see it, for having looked the other way. Yet all he saw, or at least all he cared, was that the increase of Macedonia meant the curtailment of Athens; and his political life was one long agitation against Macedonia's resistless advance. But it was nothing more than a busy and often brilliant agitation, carried on from day to day and from month to month, without any comprehensive plan. A fervent patriot does not make a great statesman. Demosthenes could devise reforms in special departments of the administration; he could admonish his fellow-citizens to be up and doing; but he did not grapple seriously with any of the new problems of the day; he did not originate one fertile political idea. A statesman of genius might conceivably have infused fresh life into Athens by effecting some radical change in her constitution and finding for her a new part to play. The fact that no such statesman arose is perhaps merely another aspect of the fact that her part as a chief actor was over. It has often been said that the Demosthenic Athenians were irreclaimable. They certainly could not have been reclaimed by Demosthenes, for Demosthenes, when all is said, was a typical Demosthenic Athenian.

The policy of Demosthenes

CHAPTER 17

The Conquest of Persia

Alexander's First Descent on Greece

On his accession to the throne of Macedon, Alexander found himself menaced by enemies on all sides. The members of the Confederacy of Corinth, the tributary peoples of the province of Thrace, the inveterately hostile Illyrians, all saw in the death of Philip an opportunity, not to be missed, for undoing his work; and in Asia, Attalus, the father of Cleopatra, espoused the claim of Cleopatra's infant son. Thus Alexander stood within a belt of dangers like that by which his father, at the same crisis in *his* life, had been encompassed; and the difference of the means which father and son adopted to deal with the danger showed the difference in temperament between the two men. If Alexander had followed the slow and sure methods of his father, he would have bought off the barbarians of the north, effected a reconciliation with Attalus, and deferred the Greek question till he had thoroughly established his power in Macedonia; then, by degrees, he could have recovered in a few years the dominion which Philip had won and undertaken the expedition against Persia which Philip had planned. But such cautious calculation did not suit the bolder genius of Philip's son. He refused to yield to any of his enemies; he encountered the perils one after another, and overcame them all.

First of all, he turned to Greece, where the situation looked serious enough. Athens had hailed the news of Philip's death with undisguised joy, and at the instance of Demosthenes had passed a decree in honour of his murderer's memory. Trumpets were sounding for war; messengers were flying to Attalus and to

17.1 Alexander the Great

445

Persia; and Greece was incited to throw off the Macedonian yoke. Ambracia expelled her garrison, and Thebes attempted to expel hers.

Importance of Thessaly

But the insurrection of Thessaly was of far greater importance than the hostile agitations in the southern states. The Thessalian cavalry was an invaluable adjunct to the Macedonian army, and it was of more material consequence to a Macedonian king to be the archon of the Thessalian Federation than to be acknowledged as general of the Confederacy of Corinth. Yet it was hardly altogether the need of quickly securing Thessaly that urged Alexander to deal with Greece before he dealt with any other portion of his empire. He wished above all things to save Greece from herself. His timely appearance, before the agitation could develop into a fully declared rebellion, might prevent the cities from committing any irreparable action, which would necessitate a ruthless punishment, or even harsh measures. He would march south, not to chastise or judge the Greeks, but to conciliate them and obtain recognition as successor to his father's place in the amphictiony of Delphi and in the league of Corinth.

336 B.C., late summer

He advanced to the defile of Tempe, but found it strongly held by the Thessalians. Instead of attempting to carry a position which was perhaps impregnable, he led his army farther south along the coast, and cutting steps up the steep side of Ossa he made a new path for himself over the mountain and descended into the plain of the Peneus behind his enemy. Not a drop of blood was shed. A Thessalian assembly elected Alexander to the archonship, and he guaranteed to the communities of the land the same rights and privileges which they had enjoyed under his father. The conciliation of Thessaly led, without a blow, to the adhesion of its southern neighbours, Malis and Dolopia. At Thermopylae the young king was recognised by the Amphictiony, and as he marched southward not a hand was raised against him; he had swooped down so quickly that nobody was ready to resist. The Athenians sent a repentant embassy, which the king received kindly without any reference to the public jubilations over his father's murder, and the Congress of the Confederacy met at Corinth to elect Alexander general in his father's place.

Alexander elected General of the Greeks

Alexander was chosen supreme general of the Greeks for the invasion of Asia, and it was as head of Hellas, descendant and successor of Achilles, rather than as Macedonian king, that he desired to go forth against Persia. But his election by the Greek Confederacy at Corinth had more of historical fitness than political significance. The contingents which the Greek states furnished as members of the league were small, and the idea of the expedition failed to arouse any national feeling. Yet the welcome, though half-hearted and hypocritical, which was given to Alexander at Corinth, and the vote, however perfunctory, which elected him leader of the Greeks, were the fitting prelude to the expansion of Hellas and the diffusion of Hellenic civilisation, which destiny had chosen him to accomplish.[1] He was thus formally recognised as what he in truth was, the representative of Greece. Of all those who thronged at Corinth round the royal youth, to observe him with curious gaze or flatter him with pleasant words, some may have foreseen that he would be a conqueror of many lands, but none can have suspected how his conquests would transform the world; for few realised that the world was waiting to be transformed. Outside the gates of Corinth, according to a famous story, the king found the eccentric philosopher Diogenes, sitting in the barrel which served him as a home, and asked him to name a boon. 'Stand out of the sun,' was the brief reply of the philosopher. 'Were I not Alexander,' said the king to his retinue, 'I should like to be Diogenes.' The incident may never have happened, but the anecdote happily brings face to face the enthusiast who carried individual liberty to the utmost verge of independence and the enthusiast who dreamed of making his empire conterminous with the globe. For the individualism which Diogenes caricatured was sister to the spirit of cosmopolitanism which Alexander's empire was to promote.

Meanwhile some domestic dangers had been cleared violently out of his path. His stepmother, her father, and her child had all been done away with. Attalus had been murdered in Asia, in accordance with the king's commands. But Alexander was not responsible for the death of Cleopatra and her infant. This was the work of Olympias, who, thirsty for revenge, caused the child to be slaughtered in its mother's lap, and forced Cleopatra to hang herself by her own belt.

Alexander's Campaigns in Thrace and Illyria

There were symptoms of trouble in Thrace; there were signs of a storm brewing in the Illyrian quarter; and it would have been impossible for the young king to invade Asia with Thrace ready to revolt in his rear and Mace-

Alexander marches against the Triballi, 335 B.C.

donia exposed to attack from the west. It was indispensable to teach the Thracians a lesson, and especially the Triballi, who had never been humbled for the check which they had inflicted on Philip. The Triballi lived beyond the Haemus, and when Alexander, having crossed Mount Rhodope, reached the foot of one of the western passes of Mount Haemus, he found the steep defile defended by mountaineers. They had hauled up a multitude of their war-chariots to the top of the pass, in order to roll them upon the Macedonians and then, rushing down themselves, to fall upon the disordered array. There was no other way of crossing the mountain, and the mountain must be crossed. Alexander showed here again the same temper and the same resource which he had shown at Tempe; when he had made up his mind that an object must be attained, he never hesitated to employ the boldest or most novel means. He ordered the infantry to advance up the path, opening the ranks when possible to let the chariots roll through, but when that was impossible, he directed them to fall on their knees and, holding their shields locked together, to form a roof on which the chariots could fall and roll harmlessly away. The device was successful. The chariot wheels thundered over the locked shields, and notwithstanding the shock not a man was killed. When the barbarians had exhausted these ponderous missiles, the pass was easily taken, and the Macedonians descended into the country of the Triballi. At the news of Alexander's approach the Triballi had sent their wives and children to an island named Peuce, in the Danube; and then, waiting until he advanced into their land, stole behind him to seize the mountain passes in his rear. Learning of this movement, Alexander marched rapidly back, forced the enemy to fight and dispersed them with great loss. He then proceeded on his way to the bank of the Danube. He had foreseen that it might be necessary to operate on that river, perhaps to make a demonstration in the country of the Getae on the northern bank; and he had prepared for this emergency by adopting the same plan as Darius in his famous Thracian expedition. He instructed his ally Byzantium to dispatch ships to sail up the river. The garrison in the island of Peuce were supported by a host of Scythian friends on the left bank of the stream, and Alexander saw that with his few Byzantine ships it would be hopeless to attack the island until he had secured the Scythian shore. The problem was to throw his troops across the river without the enemy's knowledge, and this must be done in the

darkness of one night. The ships were too few in number; but all the fishing-boats in the neighbourhood were collected, and tent-skins filled with hay were tied firmly together and strung across the stream. Landing on the other bank, led by the king himself, a large band of horse and foot advanced under the cover of the long corn at dawn of day, and the barbarian host arose to see the Macedonian phalanx bearing down on them. Startled as much by the frightening speed of their foe as by the formidable array which faced them, they withdrew into their poorly fortified town and, when Alexander followed them at the head of his cavalry, they fled with all their horses could carry into the wilds of the north. Empire beyond the Danube was not sought by Alexander, and he did not pursue. He marked the term of his northern conquest by sacrificing solemnly on the banks to Zeus Soter, Heracles, and the river-god himself.

This exploit led to the surrender of the Triballi in the island, and all the neighbouring tribes south of the river hastened to assure the king of their submission. There came also from unknown homes far up the river, or perhaps in the Dalmatian mountains, an embassy of Celts, huge-limbed, self-confident men, who had heard of Alexander's deeds and were eager to be his friends. They swore alliance with him in a form still used by the Irish Gaels a thousand years later. 'We will keep faith unless the sky fall and crush us or the earth open and swallow us or the sea rise and overwhelm us'.[2] 'Braggarts!' said Alexander afterwards. But before two generations had passed away these men of mighty limbs and mighty words were destined to roll down in a torrent upon Greece and Asia, and to wrest for their own habitation a part of Alexander's conquests.

Alexander's work was done in Thrace, but as he marched homewards he learned that the Illyrians were already in the gate of Macedonia, and that not a moment must be lost if the country was to be saved from an invasion. Philip had secured the Macedonian frontier on the Illyrian side by a number of fortresses, near the sources of the Haliacmon and Apsus; and Pelion, which was the strongest of these strongholds, the key-fortress of the mountain gate, had now fallen into the hands of Clitus, the Illyrian chief. To reach Pelion as quickly as possible, before the arrival of the Taulantines, a tribe in alliance with Clitus, was the object of Alexander. His march was threatened by the Autariats, another hostile folk, whom Clitus had engaged to waylay him; but this danger was prevented by the friendly king of the

Shipka Pass

On the Danube, May

The embassy of the Celts

(Subsequent settlement of Celts in Galatia)

The Illyrian danger

Alexander marches to Pelion

447

Agrianes, who invaded the Autariat territory and fully occupied the fighting-men. Marching rapidly up the valley of the Erigonus, Alexander encamped near Pelion. The heights around were covered with Illyrians, and Clitus, as was the custom of his people before a battle, sacrificed three boys, three maidens, and three black rams. But before they came to the actual attack, the hearts of the Illyrians failed them, and deserting all their points of vantage and leaving their sacrifice incomplete, they retired into the fastness. Alexander intended to blockade the place next day by a circumvallation, but the Taulantines arrived in a large force, and he saw that his men were too few to deal at once with the enemies both within and without the walls, nor were his provisions *The Mace-* sufficient for a protracted siege. It was *donian* absolutely necessary to withdraw from his *troops* present position; but it was a task of extreme *extricate* peril to retreat in these defiles, with hostile *themselves* Pelion in the rear and Taulantine troops *from a* occupying the slopes and heights. This task, *dangerous* however, was carried out successfully, through *position* the amazingly swift and skilful manoeuvring of the highly drilled Macedonian soldiers; the enemy were driven from their flanking positions, and the river was crossed with much trouble yet without the loss of a man. At the other side of the river, Alexander's communications were safe; he could obtain provisions and reinforcements as he chose, and might wait, at his ease, for an opportunity to strike. The moment soon came. The enemy, seeing in Alexander's retreat a confession of fear, neglected all precautions and formed a camp without rampart or outpost before the gates of the fortress. Taking a portion of his army and bidding the rest follow, Alexander set out at night and surprised the slumbering *Mace-* camp of the barbarians. A carnage followed and *donian* a wild flight, and the Macedonians pursued to *victory* the Taulantine mountains. At the first alarm, Clitus rushed into the gates of Pelion and set the town on fire, before he joined the flight.

This discomfiture of the Illyrians was a no less striking proof of Alexander's capacity than his exploits in Thrace. These months of incessant toil had earned him a rest, but there was to be no rest yet for the young monarch. Even as the news of the Illyrian danger had reached him before he left Thrace, so now, while he was still at Pelion, the news came that Thebes had rebelled. He must now speed to Greece as swiftly as seven days before he had sped to the Illyrian hills. No need was more pressing than to crush this revolt before it spread.

Alexander's Second Descent on Greece

The agitation against Macedon had not ceased *Greek* during the past year in the cities of Greece, *cities* and it was now fomented by the gold and the *negotiat-* encouragement of Persia. Five years earlier, at *ing with* the outbreak of the war, Athens had sent *Persia* ambassadors to Susa begging for subsidies *against* from Artaxerxes, but the Great King would *Macedonia* not break with Philip then and sent them away with 'a very haughty and barbarous letter' of refusal. The Phrygian satrap, however, perhaps on his own responsibility, sent useful help to Perinthus in its peril, and Persia gradually awoke to the fact that Macedonia was a dangerous neighbour. The new king, Darius, saw the necessity of embarrassing Alexander in Europe, so as to keep him as long as possible from crossing into Asia, where the Macedonian forces under Parmenio were holding their own. For this purpose he stirred up thoughts of war in Greece and sent subsidies to the Greek states. To many cities these overtures were welcome, but especially to Thebes, under the shadow of the Macedonian garrison. Three hundred talents were offered to Athens and publicly declined; but Demosthenes privately accepted them, to be expended in the interests of the Great King. It is not probable that any city entered into a formal contract with Persia, but the basis of the negotiations was the King's Peace, of fifty years ago, the Greeks admitting the rights of the Persian empire over their brethren in Asia, who on their part were awaiting with various feelings the approach of the Macedonian deliverer.

As the patriots had often prayed for the *Report of* death of Philip, so now they longed for the *Alex-* death of his youthful son, an event which might *ander's* have hurled back Macedon into nothingness *death* for ever. Rumours soon spread that the wish was fulfilled. Alexander was reported to have been slain in Thrace; Demosthenes produced a man who had seen him fall; and the Theban fugitives in Athens hastened to return to their native city and incite it to shake off the Macedonian yoke. Two captains of the garrison were caught outside the Cadmea and murdered, and the Thebans then proceeded to *Thebans* blockade the citadel by a double rampart on *blockade* the south side, where there was no city wall *the* outside the wall of the citadel. Greece res- *Cadmea* ponded to the Theban lead, which Demosthenes, Lycurgus, and the other Athenian patriots had prompted and encouraged. There were movements against Macedon in Elis and Aetolia; the Arcadians marched forth to the

Isthmus; and the Athenians sent arms to Thebes, though they sent no men. The hopes of the patriots ran high; the fall of the Cadmea seemed inevitable.

Alexander at Onchestus

Suddenly a report was whispered in Thebes that a Macedonian army was encamped a few miles away at Onchestus. As Alexander was dead, it could only be Antipater—so the Theban leaders assured the alarmed people. But messengers soon came, affirming that it was certainly Alexander. Then, said the leaders, since King Alexander is dead, it can only be Alexander of Lyncestis.

But it was indeed the king Alexander. In less than two weeks he had marched from Pelion to Onchestus, and on the next day he stood before the walls of Thebes. He halted first on the north-eastern side of the city, near the sanctuary of the Theban hero, Iolaus; he would give the citizens time to make their submission. But they were in no mind to submit, and some of their light-armed troops, rushing out of the gates, attacked the outskirts of the Macedonian camp. On the morrow Alexander moved his whole army to the south side of the city, and encamped close to the Cadmea, without making any attack on the walls, still hoping that the city would surrender. But the fate of Thebes was precipitated by one of his captains, by name Perdiccas, who was in charge of the troops which guarded the camp on the side of the Cadmea. Stationed within a few yards of the Theban earthworks, Perdiccas, without waiting for orders, dashed through the outer rampart aand fell upon the Theban guards. He was supported by a fellow-officer; and Alexander, when he observed what had happened, sent archers and light troops to their aid. The Thebans who manned the rampart were driven along the gully, which, running along the east side of the Cadmea, passes the temple of Heracles outside the walls. When they reached this temple they rallied and turned on their assailants and routed them back along the 'hollow road'. But as they pursued, their own ranks were broken, and Alexander, watching for the moment, brought his phalanx into action and drove them within the Electran gate. They had no time to shut the gate before some Macedonians pushed in along with the fugitives; and there were no men on the walls to shoot the enemy down, for the men who should have defended the walls had been sent to the blockade of the citadel. Some of the Macedonians, who thus entered, made their way to the Cadmea, and joining with the garrison they sallied out close to the Ampheion, where the main part of the Theban forces was

Capture of Thebes, beginning of Sept. 335 B.C.

drawn up. Others, having mounted the bastions, helped their friends outside to climb the walls, and the troops thus admitted rushed to the market-place. But the gate was now in the possession of the Macedonians; the city was full of them; and the king himself was everywhere. The Theban cavalry was broken up, and fled through the streets and the open gates into the plain; the foot soldiers saved themselves as they could; and then a merciless butchery began. It was not the Macedonians who were zealous in the work of slaughter, but the old enemies of Thebes, the Phocians, the Plataeans and other Boeotian peoples, who now took their vengeance upon the proud city of the seven gates for the wrongs and insults of many generations. Six thousand lives were taken before Alexander stayed the slaughter. On the next day he summoned the Confederates of Corinth to decide the fate of the rebellious city. The judges meted out to Thebes the same measure which Thebes would have once meted out to Athens. The sentence was that the city should be levelled with the dust and her land divided among the Confederates; that the remnant of the inhabitants, with the women and children, should be sold into slavery, except the priests and priestesses of the gods, and those citizens who had bonds of guest-right with the Macedonians; and that the Cadmean citadel should be occupied by a garrison. The severe sentence, showing how deeply the masterful city was abhorred, was carried out; and among the ruined habitations on which the Macedonian warders looked down from the fortress walls, only one solitary house stood, making the desolation seem more desolate, the house of Pindar, which Alexander expressly spared.

The destruction of Thebes

The Boeotian cities were at length delivered from the yoke of their imperious mistress; Plataea and Orchomenus rose again from their ruins. The fall of Thebes promptly checked all other movements in Greece: the Arcadian forces withdrew from the Isthmus, Elis and Aetolia hastened to abandon their hostile attitude. The news reached Athens during the festival of the Mysteries. The solemnity was interrupted, and in a hurried meeting of the Assembly it was resolved, on the proposal of Demades, to send an embassy to welcome Alexander on his safe return from his northern campaign, and to congratulate him on the just punishment which he had inflicted upon Thebes. The same people passed this decree who a few days before, on the proposal of Demosthenes, had resolved to send troops to the aid of that luckless city. Alexander de-

Athens congratulates Alexander on the fall of Thebes

manded—and it was a fair demand—that Demosthenes and Lycurgus and the other agitators who kept the hostility to Macedonia alive, and were largely responsible for the disaster of Thebes, should be delivered to him, for so long as they were at large there was no security that Athens would not entangle herself in further follies. When the demand was laid before the Assembly, Demosthenes epigrammatically expressed his own view of the situation by advising the people not to hand over their sheep-dogs to the wolf. Phocion said in downright words that Alexander must be conciliated at any cost: let the men whose surrender he demanded show their patriotism by sacrificing themselves. But it was finally decided that Demades, who had ingratiated himself with the Macedonian king, should accompany another embassy and beg that the offenders might be left to the justice of the Athenian people. Alexander, still anxious to show every consideration to Athens, withdrew his demand, insisting only on the banishment of the adventurer Charidemus, of Thracian notoriety.

With the fall of Thebes, Alexander's campaigns in Europe came to an end. The rest of his life was spent in Asia. The European campaigns, though they filled little more than a year, and though they seem of small account by the side of his triumphs in the east, were brilliant and important enough to have won historical fame for any general. In his two descents into Greece, first to conciliate and afterwards to punish; in his expedition to the Danube; and in his Illyrian campaign, he had given tokens of the rare strategic capacity, the originality of conception, the boldness of resolution, the rapidity of action, and those other qualities which served Alexander's genius and soon found a more spacious sphere for their manifestation when they bore him toward the unknown limits of the eastern world.

Preparations for Alexander's Persian Expedition. Condition of Persia

The scheme of Alexander's conquests

Having spent the winter in making his military preparations and setting in order the affairs of his kingdom for a long absence, Alexander set forth in spring for the conquest of Asia. Of his plans and arrangements we know almost nothing, but we may say with confidence that his scheme of conquest was well considered to take whatever came in his way. His original plan was afterwards merged in a second and larger scheme, of which he had no conception when he set out from Macedonia, for he had not the requisite geographical knowledge of central Asia. But in the first instance his purpose was to conquer the Persian kingdom, to dethrone the Great King and take his place, to do to Persia what Persia under Xerxes had tried to do to Macedonia and the rest of Hellas. To carry out this design the first thing needed was to secure Thrace in the rear, and that had been already done. In the conquest itself there were three stages. The first step was the conquest of Asia Minor; the second was the conquest of Syria and Egypt; and these two conquests, preliminary to the advance on Babylon and Susa, would mean not merely acquisitions of territory, but strategic bases for further conquest. The weak point in Alexander's enterprise was the lack of a fleet capable of coping with the Persian navy, which was 400 strong. Here the Confederacy of Corinth should have come to his help; Athens alone could have furnished over 200 galleys. And Alexander doubtless counted on ultimately obtaining the support of Athens and the other Greek cities. But he desired aid rendered with goodwill, and he made no effort to extort either ships or men. The loosely organised league of Corinth had undertaken to supply fixed contingents, but the fulfilment of these promises was not strictly exacted. *Want of a fleet*

To secure Macedonia against her neighbours and subjects during his absence, Alexander was obliged to leave a large portion, perhaps as much as one half, of the national army behind him. The government was entrusted to his father's minister, Antipater. It is said that the king made dispositions before his departure as one who expected never to return. He divided all his royal domains and forests and revenues among his friends, and when Perdiccas asked what was left for himself he replied, Hope. Then Perdiccas, rejecting his own portion, exclaimed, 'We who go forth to fight with you need share only in your hope.' The anecdote at least illustrates the enthusiasm with which Alexander infected his friends and officers on the threshold of a venture, of which the conception was almost as wonderful as its success. *Provisions for the government of Macedonia*

The Persian empire was weak and loosely knit, and it was governed now by a feeble monarch. Two generations had passed since Greece saw its weakness memorably demonstrated by the adventures of Xenophon's Ten *State of Persia*

Ochus (acceded, 358 B.C.) conquers Egypt

Thousand; and since then we have seen it, on the western side, paralysed by revolts. Artaxerxes Ochus displayed more strength than his predecessors. He re-established his power in Asia Minor, he quelled rebellions in Phoenicia and Cyprus, and even conquered Egypt, which had long defied the Persian efforts to regain it. The king, Nektanebos, was driven back from Pelusium to Memphis, and from Memphis he fled to Ethiopia. The Persian king had no thought of holding the land of the Nile by kindness; as soon as he had Memphis in his power he displayed the intolerance of the fire-worshipper. He drowned the holy bull, Apis, and inaugurated the ass as the sacred animal of Egypt. This stupid outrage made the Persian rule more detested than ever. Ochus was assassinated, the victim of a palace conspiracy; and after two or three years of confusion the throne passed to a distant member of the Achaemenid house, Darius Codomannus, destined to be the last successor of his great namesake. He was a mild and virtuous prince, beloved by his followers, but too weak, in both brains and will, for the task to which fate had doomed him.

Murder of Ochus, 338 B.C. Accession of Darius, 335 B.C.

Advantages on the side of Persia in the approaching struggle

It cannot be denied that if Darius had been able and experienced in war and capable of leading men, he would have had some enormous advantages. In the first place, there was the sheer weight of human bodies: though the size of his forces has been wildly exaggerated by ancient writers, at every stage of the war he heavily outnumbered Alexander's army. In the second place, while the coffers of Pella are said to have been emptied before Alexander set foot in Asia, the Great King commanded untold wealth—the treasury of Susa was full, and in the palace of Persepolis were hoarded inexhaustible stores of gold. In the third place, he had a navy which controlled the seaboard of Asia Minor, Syria, and Egypt, and ought, if it had been handled ably, to have placed insuperable obstacles in the way of an invader who had no adequate sea-power. And fourthly, although there was no cohesion in the vast empire or unity of centralisation, there was, for that very reason, little or no national discontent in the provinces. Egypt was an exceptional case. The other revolts which occurred from time to time were not national movements, but the disaffections of ambitious satraps. If the Persian monarch was not loved, at least he was not hated; and the warlike barbarians of the east, from far Hyrcania or the banks of the Oxus, were always ready to follow him and glad to fight in his cause. It was quite feasible, so far as the state of feeling in the provinces was concerned, to organise an effective defence of the empire. But all these advantages were wasted, for lack of a master mind and a controlling will. Multitudes were useless without a leader, and money could not create brains. Moreover Persia was behind the age in the art of warfare. She had not kept pace with the military developments in Greece during the last fifty years, and, though she could pay Greek mercenaries and though these formed in fact a valuable part of her army, they could have no effect on the general character of the tactics of an oriental host. The Persian commanders had no notion of studying the tactics of their enemy and seeking new methods of encountering them. They had no idea of shaping strategic plans of their own; they simply waited on the movements of the enemy. They trusted, as they had always trusted, with perfect simplicity, in numbers, individual bravery, and scythe-armed chariots. The only lesson which the day of Cunaxa had taught them was to hire mercenary Greeks. Tradition gives their number as 50,000, but it was probably substantially less.

Fatal shortcomings of Persia

The strength of the army which Alexander led forth against Persia is said to have been 30,000 foot and 5000 horse, thus preserving the large proportion of cavalry to infantry which was one of the chief novelties of Philip's military establishment. We have seen how Philip organised the national army of Macedonia, in the chief divisions of the phalanx, the special corps of hypaspists, and the heavy cavalry. Alexander led to Asia six regiments of the phalanx, and in the great engagements which decided the fate of Persia these formed the centre of his array. They were supported by Greek hoplites, both mercenary and confederate; the mercenaries were commanded by Menander, the confederates by Antigonus. The hypaspists, led by Nicanor, son of Parmenio, had their station on the right wing, and the first regiment of these was the royal guard, called the *agēma*. Philotas, another son of Parmenio, was commander of the heavy cavalry, in eight squadrons, one of which, the 'royal squadron' under Clitus, corresponded to the *agēma* of the hypaspists. This Macedonian cavalry was always placed on the right, while on the left rode the splendid Thessalian cavalry under Callas, with a corps of other Greek horse attached. Both the right and the left wings were strengthened by light troops, horse and foot, armed according to their national habit, from Thrace, Paeonia, and Illyria.

Alexander's army

Heavy infantry

Light Macedonian infantry

Cavalry

Light troops

Conquest of Asia Minor

Successes of Parmenio, 335 B.C.

The forces which had been operating in Asia under Parmenio while Alexander was detained in Europe had been endeavouring to establish a footing in Aeolis and Mysia and secure a base on the Propontis for further advance.[3] The Great King had empowered Memnon of Rhodes, an able mercenary captain, who in recent years had come to the front, to oppose the van of the Macedonian invasion. The most pressing need of the Persians was to recapture Cyzicus, which was in the hands of Parmenio. In this Memnon failed; but he occupied Lampsacus, he forced the Macedonians to raise the siege of Pitane and beat them back to the coast of the Hellespont. But he could not or did not press his advantage, and the shores where Alexander's army would land were safe in Macedonian possession.

The crossing of the Helles-pont, 334 B.C.

The fleet transported the army from Sestus to Abydus, while Alexander himself proceeded to Elaeus, where he offered a sacrifice on the tomb of Protesilaus, the first of the mythical Greeks who landed on the shore of Asia in the Trojan war, and the first who fell. Praying that he might be luckier than Protesilaus, Alexander sailed across to the 'Harbour of the Achaeans', and in the mid-strait made libations to Poseidon and the Nereids from a golden dish.

Alexander at Troy

The first to leap upon the Mysian strand, he crossed the plain of Troy and went up to the hill of Ilion, where he performed a sacrifice in the temple of Athena, in the poor town which stood on the ruins of seven prehistoric cities. It is said that he dedicated his own panoply in the shrine and took down from the wall some ancient armour, preserved there as relics of the war of Priam and Agamemnon. He sacrificed to Priam to avert his anger from one of the race of Neoptolemus; he crowned the tomb of Achilles his ancestor; and his bosom-friend Hephaestion cast a garland upon the grave of Patroclus, the beloved of Achilles. He commanded that Ilion should rise again from its ruins, as a favoured city enjoying the rights of self-government and immunity from taxation. These solemnities on the hill of Troy are significant as revealing the spirit which the young king carried into his enterprise. They show how he was imbued with Greek scriptures and Greek traditions; how his descent from Achilles was part of his life, part of his inspiration; how he regarded himself as chosen to be the hero of another episode in the drama of which the first act had been illustrated by the deeds of that glorious ancestor.

Meanwhile the satraps of the Great King had formed an army of about 40,000 men to defend Asia Minor. If he had entrusted the command to the Rhodian Memnon, it is possible that some effective defence might have been made, but he committed the characteristic blunder of a Persian monarch, and consigned the army to the joint command of a number of generals, including with Memnon several of the western satraps. The Persian commanders were jealous of the Greek, and against his advice they decided to risk a battle at once. Accordingly they advanced from Zelea, where they had mustered, to the plain of Adrastea, through which the river Granicus flows into the Propontis, and posted themselves on the steep right bank of the stream, so as to hinder the enemy from crossing. Alexander and his army advanced eastward from Abydus, and received the submission of Lampsacus, and then of Priapus, a town near the mouth of the Granicus. It was impossible for him to avoid the combat which the Persians desired; he could not march southward, leaving them in his rear. But he courted the combat even more than they, for the worst thing that could have befallen him (as Memnon knew well) was that the hostile army should persistently retire before him, eating up the provisions of the country as it retreated.

Advance of a Persian army to the Granicus

Advance of Alexander

With his heavy infantry in two columns and his horse on the wings, Alexander marched across the Adrastean plain. The Persians had made the curious disposition of placing their cavalry along the river bank and the Greek hoplites on the slopes behind. As cavalry in attack has a great advantage over cavalry in defence, Alexander saw that the victory could best be won by throwing his own squadrons against the hostile line. Parmenio advised him to wait till the following morning and cross the river at daybreak before the enemy were drawn up. 'I should be ashamed,' said the king, 'having crossed the Hellespont, to be detained by a miserable stream like the Granicus'; an answer such as Alexander loved to give, veiling under the appearance of negligent daring a self-confidence which was perfectly justified by his strategic insight.

Position of the armies

Drawing up his army in the usual way (which has been described above), with the six regiments of the phalanx in the centre, entrusting the left wing to Parmenio and commanding the right himself, Alexander first sent across the river his light cavalry to keep the extreme left of the enemy engaged, and then led his heavy Macedonian cavalry against the Persian centre. Alexander himself was in the thickest of the fight, dealing wounds and

Battle of the Granicus (334 B.C., May-June)

receiving blows. After a sharp mêlée on the steep banks, the Persian cavalry was broken and put to flight. The phalanx then advanced across the river against the Greek hoplites in the background, while the victorious cavalry cut them up on the flanks.

This victory, in winning which Alexander drank to the full the mad excitement of battle, cost few lives to the Macedonians and cleared out of their way the only army which was to oppose their progress in Asia Minor. But it was very far from laying Asia Minor at the conqueror's feet. There were strong places, which must be taken one by one—strong places on the coast, which could be supported by the powerful Persian fleet. Of all things, the Athenian navy would have best helped Alexander now, and he did not yet despair. After the skirmish of the Granicus, when he divided the spoil, he sent 300 Persian panoplies to Athens, as an offering to Athena on the Acropolis, with this dedication: 'Alexander, son of Philip, and the Greeks (except the Lacedaemonians), from the barbarians of Asia.' But Athens had no zeal for the cause of the Greeks and Alexander against the barbarians.

Sub-mission of Lydia

The victor entrusted the satrapy of Hellespontine Phrygia to Callas, making no change in the method of the Persian administration, and marched southward to occupy the satrapy of Lydia and the rock of Sardis, with its threefold wall. It was a little more than 200 years since Cyrus had overthrown the Lydian kingdom, and Sardis had become the chief centre of Persian power in the west. The citadel was strong and capable of a stout defence, but it now passed with its treasures unresistingly into the hands of the Greek conqueror. For this prompt submission the Lydians received their freedom and the ancestral constitution, which had been suspended during the long period of Persian domination. Alexander resolved to build a temple to the Olympian Zeus on the citadel. It was said that a thunder shower falling on the site of the royal palace showed him the fitting place for the sanctuary—the spot where a more famous thunder shower had quenched the pyre of the last Lydian king.

Parmenio's brother Asander was appointed satrap of Lydia, and Alexander turned to deal with the Ionian cities. It was his declared policy to free the cities from tribute, establish democracies and give them autonomy.[4] The democrats welcomed the Greek deliverer; but the oligarchs supported the Persian cause and, wherever they were in power, admitted Persian garrisons. In Ephesus the oligarchy had got the upper hand, but on the approach of Alexander's army the garrison left the city and the people began to massacre the oligarchs. Alexander pacified these troubles and established a democratic constitution. He stayed some time in the city, and during this sojourn the painter Apelles executed a famous picture of the king, wielding lightning in his hand, which was set up in the temple of Artemis.

Siege and capture of Miletus, 334 B.C.

The next stage in the advance of Alexander was Miletus, and here for the first time he encountered resistance. The Persian garrison was commanded by a Greek, who had at first meditated surrender but, learning that the Persian fleet was at hand in full force, decided to brave a siege. In an earlier episode of the struggle between Europe and Asia we witnessed memorable operations in the Latmian gulf and the Milesian harbours, which the retreat of the sea has blotted from the map. The isle of Lade, then associated with the triumph of Asia, was now to play a part in the triumph of Europe. The Macedonian fleet, of 160 ships, sailed into the bay and occupied the harbour of Lade before the great fleet of the enemy arrived. When the Persian vessels came and saw that they had been forestalled, they anchored off the promontory of Mycale. The city of Miletus consisted of two parts, an outer city which Alexander easily occupied as soon as he came up, and an inner city strongly fortified with wall and fosse. Alexander threw up a rampart round the inner city and placed troops in the island of Lade. Miletus was easily stormed by the Macedonian siege engines, and the fleet blocking the harbour hindered the Persian squadron from bringing help.

Parmenio had urged the king to risk a battle on the water, though the enemy's ships were nearly three to one, but Alexander rejected the advice. He had judged the whole situation, and had made up his mind that the Persian sea-power would have to be conquered on land. If Athens had sent him naval reinforcements it might have been otherwise, but he now despaired of active help from Greece and decided that it was a useless drain on his treasury to maintain 160 ships, too few to cope with the 400 of the enemy. Accordingly he disbanded the fleet after the fall of Miletus, and proceeded to blockade the sea by seizing all the strong places on the shores of the Eastern Mediterranean. The execution of this design occupied him for the next two years, but it brought with it the conquest of Asia Minor, Syria, and Egypt.

Alexander disbands his fleet

The manifest objection to the dissolution of

the naval force was that, in case a decisive defeat at the hands of the Great King should compel him to retreat, he would have no fleet to transport his army from Asia to Europe, and the fleet of the enemy, by occupying the straits at either end of the Propontis, could entirely cut him off. But Alexander trusted his own strategy; he knew that he would not be compelled to retreat.

As for Asia Minor, the next and the hardest task was the reduction of Caria and the capture of Halicarnassus. The remnant of the army which fled from the Granicus, and the Rhodian Memnon himself, had rallied here and rested their last hopes in the strong city of Mausolus, with its three mighty citadels. The Great King had now entrusted to Memnon the general command of the fleet and the coasts, and Memnon had dug a deep fosse round Halicarnassus, furnished the place with food for a long siege, and placed garrisons in the smaller neighbouring towns. Halicarnassus was to be the centre of a supreme resistance.

The last rulers of the dynasty of Mausolus

There had once been a chance that Alexander himself might have been, by a personal right, lord of Halicarnassus. The prince Pixodarus, one of the brothers of Mausolus, had wished to form an alliance of marriage with the house of Macedon, and Alexander had thought of offering himself as a bridegroom for his daughter. But Philip would not hear of such a match, and Pixodarus had given the maiden to a Persian noble, who had succeeded to the dynasty after his father-in-law's death. There was indeed another claimant to the dynasty,

Ada

Ada, wife and sister of Idrieus. She had succeeded her husband as ruler, and had been driven out by her brother Pixodarus. She now sought the protection of Alexander and, when he captured Halicarnassus, he assigned to her the satrapy of Caria. It was destined that women should represent Caria in the two great collisions of Greece with Persia, in the days of Alexander as in the days of Xerxes.

Siege of Halicarnassus, autumn, 334 B.C.

Having made a futile attack on Myndus, Alexander filled up the moat with which Memnon had encompassed Halicarnassus, and brought his towers and engines against the walls. A breach was made on the north-east side near to the gate of the road to Mylasa, but Alexander, who hoped to induce the town to surrender, forbore to order an attack. His hands were almost forced by two soldiers of the phalanx, who, one day drinking together in their tent and bragging of their prowess, flushed with wine and the zeal of rivalry, put on their armour and, marching up to the wall, challenged the enemy to come out. The men

on the wall seeing them alone rushed out in numbers, and the two were hard pressed till their comrades came to the rescue, and there was a sharp fight under the walls. But even now, Alexander would not order an attack on the breach, and the besieged built a new crescent wall connecting the two points between which the wall had been broken down, and maintained themselves behind it for a time. At length they made a great sally against the camp of the besiegers at two different places. On both sides they were driven back in confusion, and in their haste to shut the gates they left many of their fellows to perish. At this moment an assault would doubtless have carried the Macedonians within the walls, but Alexander gave the signal to retire, still intent on saving the city. Memnon saw that the prospect of holding out longer was hopeless, and he determined to withdraw the garrison to the citadel of Salmacis and the royal fortress on the island in the harbour. He fired the city at night before he withdrew, and the place was in flames when the Macedonians entered. Alexander destroyed what the fire spared, and left a body of mercenary soldiers under Ptolemy to blockade Salmacis and support the princess of Caria.

Division of the army

The cold season was approaching and Alexander divided his army into two bodies, one of which he sent under Parmenio to winter in Lydia, while he advanced himself with the other into Lycia. He gave leave to a few young officers who had been recently wedded to return to their Macedonian homes, charging them with the duty of bringing reinforcements to the army in spring, and appointing Gordion in Phrygia as the mustering-place.

Lycia submits

Advance through Pamphylia and Pisidia

Alexander met with no resistance from the cities of the Lycian League, and he left the constitution of the confederacy intact. From the rich frontier town of Phasēlis he advanced along the coast of Pamphylia, receiving the submission of Perge and Aspendus and other maritime cities; and then he turned inland from Perge, and fought his way through the Pisidian hills, taking with some trouble Sagalassus, the chief fastness of the Pisidian mountaineers. He descended to Celaenae, the strong and lofty citadel of the Phrygian satrapy and, leaving a garrison there, he marched on to Gordion on the Sangarius, the capital of the ancient kingdom of Phrygia.

Persian fleet in the Aegean

While he was winning the Lycian and Phrygian satrapies, he lost, for the moment, some points in the Aegean. Memnon, appointed commander of the Persian fleet, had taken Chios, reduced the greater part of

Lesbos, and laid siege to Mytilene. He died during the siege, but Mytilene soon surrendered, and then Tenedos was compelled to recognise the 'Peace which the king sent down'.[5] The great danger for Alexander was that these successes might encourage the Greeks to revolt, and ten Persian ships sailed as far west as Siphnos for the purpose of exciting a movement in Hellas. But eight of these vessels were captured by some Macedonian triremes which ran over from Chalcis, and the project of a Greek rising was not carried out.

At Gordion, 333 B.C. At Gordion, the appointed mustering place, Alexander's army re-united, and new troops arrived from Macedonia to replace those who had been left to garrison the subjugated countries and cities. On the citadel of Gordion stood the remains of the royal palaces of Gordius and Midas, and Alexander went up the hill to see the chariot of Gordius and the famous knot which fastened the yoke. Cord of the bark of a cornel-tree was tied in a knot which artfully concealed the ends, and there was an oracle that he who should loose it would rule over Asia. Alexander vainly attempted to untie it, and then drawing his sword cut the knot and so fulfilled the oracle.[6] From Gordion *Advance to Cilicia* Alexander marched by Ancyra into Cappadocia. Having received the submission of Paphlagonia and asserted rather than confirmed his authority over the Cappadocian satrapy, he marched southward to Tyana and the Cilician gates. It was well that Alexander should show himself for a moment in the centre of Asia Minor, but the reduction of these wild regions and of the southern coast of Pontus was a task which might safely be postponed. The Cilician gates might have easily been defended by the garrison which the satrap Arsames had posted in the pass. Alexander, with the hypaspists and some light troops, leaving the rest of his army in camp, marched up at night to surprise the station. As soon as the guards heard their approach they fled; and then Alexander at the head of his cavalry moved so rapidly on Tarsus that Arsames, amazed at his sudden appearance, fled without striking a blow.

At Tarsus Here a misadventure happened which wellnigh changed the course of history. After a long ride under a burning sun, the king bathed in the cool waters of the Cydnus, which flows through Tarsus. He caught a chill which resulted in violent fever and sleepless nights, and his physicians despaired of his life. But Philip of Acarnania, who was eminent for his medical skill, recommended a certain purgative. As he was preparing the draught in the king's tent, a letter was placed in Alexander's hands. It was from Parmenio and was a warning against Philip, alleging that Darius had bribed him to poison his master. Alexander taking the cup, gave Philip the letter to read, and, while Philip read, Alexander swallowed the medicine. His generous confidence was justified and under the care of Philip he soon recovered from his sickness.

Battle of Issus

The Great King had already crossed the Euphrates at the head of a vast host. He had let the invader subjugate Asia Minor, but he now came in person to bar his further progress. Alexander did not hurry to the encounter, and his delay, as we shall see, turned to his profit in an unexpected manner. Sending forward Parmenio with part of the army to secure the passes from Cilicia into Syria, Alexander himself turned to subdue western Cilicia. He first *Reduction of Cilicia* visited Anchialus, noted for the statue of the *At Anchialus* Assyrian king Sardanapalus, and the famous inscription: 'Sardanapalus founded Anchialus and Tarsus on the same day. But thou, O stranger eat, drink, and sport; all else is worthless.' Having seen this comment on his own ambitious dreams, Alexander went on to Soli, the city of 'solecisms', an ultimate Greek *At Soli* outpost, where men had almost forgotten Greek institutions and Greek speech. From here he made an excursion against the Cilician hill-folk, and reduced the whole district in seven days. He then returned eastward, and *At Issus, 333 B.C., Oct.* advanced to Issus under Mount Amanus.

Darius was on the other side of the mountains, in the plain of Sochoi, on ground which was highly favourable for deploying his host. There were two roads from Issus into Syria. One led directly over difficult mountainpasses, while the other wound along the coast to Myriandros and then crossed Mount Amanus. The second road, along which we formerly accompanied Cyrus and Xenophon, was now chosen by Alexander. Leaving his *At Myriander* sick at Issus, he marched forward to Myriandros, but was detained there by a violent storm of rain, for it was already the beginning of winter. The Great King, informed by Arsames of the rapid approach of Alexander, expected every day to see him descending from the mountains. And when he did not come, owing to the delays in Cilicia, it was thought that he held back through fear, and did not venture to desert the coast. Accordingly Darius and his

455

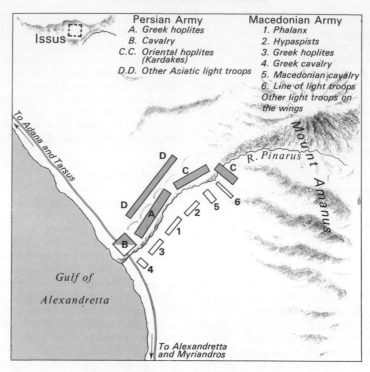

Persian Army
A. Greek hoplites
B. Cavalry
C.C. Oriental hoplites (Kardakes)
D.D. Other Asiatic light troops

Macedonian Army
1. Phalanx
2. Hypaspists
3. Greek hoplites
4. Greek cavalry
5. Macedonian cavalry
6. Line of light troops
Other light troops on the wings

32.   BATTLE OF ISSUS 333 B.C.

Advance of the Persians to Issus,

nobles decided to seek Alexander. The Persian army crossed the northern passes of Amanus and reached Issus, where they tortured and put to death the sick who had been left behind. Alexander cannot be blamed for this disaster, for he could not foresee that his enemies would commit such an incredible military error as to abandon the open position in which their numerical superiority would tell for a confined place where the movements of large masses would be cramped. To Alexander the news that Darius was at Issus was too good to be true, and he sent a boat to reconnoitre. When he was assured that the enemy had thus played into his hands, he marched back from Myriandros through the sea-gates into the little plain of Issus.

and return of Alexander

Position of the armies at Issus

The plain of Issus is cut in two by the stream of the Pinarus, which was to play the same part in the coming battle as the Granicus had played in the plain of Adrastea. Here, as in that first skirmish, it fell to Alexander to attack the Persians, whose plan was defensive; and here, as there, the Persians were defended by the natural entrenchment of a steep-banked river. The Macedonian columns defiled into the plain at dawn, and when Darius learned that they were approaching he threw across the

river his main cavalry force and light troops to cover the rest of the army while it arrayed itself for battle and to threaten the enemy's rear. The Persian front was composed of hoplites—some 15,000 Greek mercenaries, and regiments of orientals called *Kardakes*. Archers were stationed on the left in front of the *Kardakes* and light-armed on the extreme left wing, which touched the lower slopes of the mountains and curved round, following the line of the hill, so as to face the flank of the enemy's right wing. Darius himself was behind the centre. When the line was formed, the cavalry was recalled to the north of the river, and posted on the right wing, near the sea, where the ground was best adapted for cavalry movements.

Alexander advanced, his army drawn up on the usual plan, the phalanx in the centre, the hypaspists on the right. At first he placed the Thessalian as well as the Macedonian cavalry on the right wing, in order to strengthen his own cavalry attack, but when he saw that all the Persian cavalry was concentrated on the sea side, he was obliged to transfer the Thessalians to their usual position on his own left. In order to meet the danger which threatened the flank and rear of his right wing from the Persian

Arrangement of Alexander's troops

456

forces on the slope of the mountain, he placed a column of light troops on the extreme right, to form a second front. As in the engagement on the Granicus, the attack was to be made by the heavy cavalry on the left centre of the enemy's line.[7] But it was a far more serious and formidable venture. Those who had read the story of the battle of Cunaxa might despise an Asiatic multitude, but Darius had 15,000 Greek mercenaries who knew how to stand and fight. And if Alexander was defeated, his retreat was cut off.

Battle

The Persian left did not sustain Alexander's onset at the head of his cavalry. The phalanx followed more slowly, and in crossing the stream and climbing the steep bank the line became dislocated, especially at one spot, and the Greek hoplites pressed them hard on the river-brink. If the phalanx had been driven back, Alexander's victorious right wing would have been exposed on the flank and the battle lost; but the phalangites stood their ground obstinately, until the hypaspists were free to come to their help by taking their adversaries in the flank. Meanwhile Alexander's attack had been directed upon the spot where the Great King himself stood in his war-chariot, surrounded by a guard of Persian nobles. There was a furious mêlée, in which Alexander was wounded in his leg. Then Darius turned his chariot and fled, and this was the signal for a universal flight on the left. On the sea side the Persian cavalry crossed the river and carried all before them, but in the midst of their success the cry that the king was fleeing made them waver, and they were soon riding wildly back, pursued by the Thessalians. The whole Persian host was now rushing northward towards the passes of Amanus, and thousands fell beneath the swords of their pursuers.

Flight of Darius

Darius did not tarry—he forgot even his mother and his wife who were in the camp at Issus—and when he reached the mountain he left his chariot, his shield, and his royal cloak behind him, and mounting a swift mare rode for dear life.

Having pursued the Great King till nightfall and found his relics by the wayside, Alexander returned to the Persian camp. He supped in the tent of Darius, and there fell upon his ears a noise and the wailing of women from a tent hard by. He asked who the women were, and why they were lodged so near, and learned that it was the mother and wife and children of the fugitive king. They had been told that Alexander had returned with the shield and cloak of Darius, and, supposing that their lord was dead, had broken out into lamentation.

Alexander sent one of his companions to comfort them with the assurance that Darius lived, and that they would receive, while they were in Alexander's power, all the respect and consideration due to royal ladies; for Alexander had no personal enmity against Darius. No act of Alexander, perhaps, astonished his contemporaries more than this generous treatment of the family of his royal rival. His ideal hero Achilles would not have resisted the charm of the captive queen Statira, the most beautiful of women. But the charms of love had no temptation for Alexander, and his behaviour to the captives was prompted not only by his natively humane and generous feelings, but by the instinct and policy of a royal invader to display respect for royalty as such.

Thus was the Persian host, which had come to 'trample down' Alexander and his little army, annihilated on the plain of Issus. A city, which still retains the name of Alexander, was built in commemoration of the battle, at the northern end of the sea-gates. The road was now open into Syria; this was the immediate military result of the battle of Issus. Just as the small fight on the Granicus had cleared the way for the acquisition of Asia Minor, so the fight on the Pinarus cleared the way for the conquest of Syria and Egypt. The rest of the work would consist of tedious sieges. But the victory of Issus had, beyond its immediate results, immense importance through the prestige which it conferred on the victor. He had defeated an army considerably larger than his own, led by the Great King in person, whom he had driven back over the mountains in ignominious flight; and he had captured the mother of the Great King, and his wife and his children. Darius himself unbent his haughty Persian pride, when he had reached safety beyond the Euphrates, so far as to make the first overtures to the conqueror. He wrote a letter, in which he complained that Alexander was an unprovoked aggressor, begged that he would send back the royal captives, and professed willingness to conclude a treaty of friendship and alliance. It was much for a Persian king to bring himself to write this, but such a condescending appeal required a stern reply. We are fortunate enough to possess the text of Alexander's answer, which seems to have been published as a sort of manifesto to Europe as well as Asia. It was to this effect:

'Your ancestors invaded Macedonia and the rest of Greece and without provocation inflicted wrongs upon us. I was appointed leader of the Greeks, and crossed over into Asia for the purpose of avenging those wrongs;

Foundation of Alexandria at Issus (Alexandretta)

A state document of Alexander: letter to Darius, 333 B.C.

457

for you were the first aggressors. In the next place, you assisted the people of Perinthus, who were offenders against my father, and Ochus sent a force into Thrace, which was part of our empire. Further, the conspirators who slew my father were suborned by you, as you yourselves boasted in your letters. You with the help of Bagoas murdered Arses (son of Ochus) and seized the throne unjustly and contrary to the law of the Persians, and then you wrote unfavourable letters about me to the Greeks, to incite them to war against me, and sent to the Lacedaemonians and others of the Greeks, for the same purpose, sums of money (whereof none of the other cities partook, but only the Lacedaemonians); and your emissaries corrupted my friends and tried to dissolve the peace which I had brought about in Greece. Wherefore I marched forth against you who were the aggressor in the quarrel. I have overcome in battle, first your generals and satraps, and now yourself and your host, and possess your land, through the grace of the gods. Those who fought on your side and were not slain, but took refuge with me, are under my protection, and are glad to be with me, and will fight with me henceforward. I am lord of all Asia, and therefore you should come to me. If you are afraid of being badly treated, send some of your friends to receive sufficient guarantees. You have only to come to me to ask and receive your mother and wife and children, and whatever else you may desire. And for the future, whenever you send, send to me as to the Great King of Asia, and do not write as to an equal, but tell me whatever your need be, as to one who is lord of all that is yours. Otherwise I shall deal with you as an offender. But if you dispute the kingdom, then wait and fight for it again and do not flee; for I shall march against you wherever you may be.'

The treasures which Darius had brought with him into Syria had been sent for safety to Damascus when he crossed the passes of Mount Amanus. Accordingly Alexander sent Parmenio to take possession of them. Parmenio found at Damascus some Greek envoys who had arrived at the camp of Darius a short time before the battle—one Spartan, one Athenian, and two Thebans. Alexander detained the Spartan as a prisoner, kept the Athenian as a friend, and let the Thebans go free. His clemency to the Thebans was due to a certain compunction which he always felt for the hard measure dealt out to their city; a personal motive dictated his favour to the Athenian, Iphicrates, son of the great general of the same

Greek intrigues with the Persian king

name, whose memory was highly esteemed in Macedonia. The incident showed that Greece, which had openly chosen Alexander for her leader, was secretly intriguing with Persia. When it was known that Darius was crossing the Euphrates, men were hoping and praying at Athens that the Macedonians would be trodden down by the Persian host. A hundred fast-sailing Persian ships appeared at Siphnos, and Agis the Spartan king visited the commanders, asking for money and ships to carry out a project of rebellion against Macedonia. At Athens, Hypereides agitated for open war, but Demosthenes prudently counselled his fellow-citizens to wait until the expected catastrophe of Alexander had become an accomplished fact. Then the news came that the leader of the Greeks had won a brilliant victory, and Greece had to cloak her disappointment. The Persian squadron hurried back to save what could be saved on the Asiatic coast, and only 30 talents and 10 vessels could be spared for Agis, who used them to secure the island of Crete, which might prove a useful recruiting ground for the fleet.

Persian squadron at Siphnos Activity of Agis

Disappointment in Greece at the news of Issus

Conquest of Syria

It might seem that the course plainly marked out for the victor of Issus was to pursue and overwhelm Darius before he should have time to collect another army; and this is what Darius himself would have done if he had been Alexander. But it would have been a strategical error to plunge into the heart of the Persian empire, leaving Syria and Egypt unsubdued behind him and a Persian fleet controlling the coast. The victory of Issus did not seduce Alexander into swerving from his proper course; the strategic value of that victory was simply that it opened the gates to Syria and Egypt. As the subjugation of Asia Minor was the strategic condition of subjugating Syria and Egypt, so the conquest of Syria and Egypt was the strategic condition of conquering Mesopotamia and Iran. It was the more imperative to follow this logical order of conquest, since Phoenicia supplied the main part of the hostile navy, and nothing but the reduction of the Phoenician towns would effectually break the sea-power of Persia. No one could swoop more swiftly than Alexander when it was the hour to swoop; but never did he display his superior command of the art of war more signally than when he let the royal prey escape him and quietly carried out the plan of conquest which he had chosen.

Strategic plan of Alexander's conquest

The Persian kings had allowed the Phoenician traders to go on their own way, and meddled little with their prosperous cities so long as the Phoenician navy was at the disposal of Persia. If these strong and wealthy semi-insular cities of the coast, cut off as they were from the inner country by the high range of Lebanon, had formed a solid federal union, they might have easily succeeded in winning complete independence in the days of Persian decadence. But though Tyre, Sidon, and Aradus were bound together by a federal bond, their commercial interests clashed and their jealousies hindered a vigorous national effort. This had been illustrated by a recent experience. When Sidon revolted from Persia, in the reign of Artaxerxes Ochus, her two sister cities promised at a federal meeting to stand by her. But both Tyre and Aradus selfishly calculated that if Sidon were crushed and punished, her trade would come to themselves, and they left her to maintain the struggle alone. She succumbed to the power of Ochus, her town was burnt down, and she lost her rights as a city.

The divisions which prevented the Phoenicians from becoming a nation were profitable to Alexander. If their united fleet, which was now acting ineffectually in Aegean waters, had acted energetically in defence of their own coast against the Macedonian, their cities would have been impregnable even to Alexander. But those cities could not trust each other. Byblus, which had in some measure taken the place of Sidon, and Aradus sent their

submission to the conqueror of Issus; while dismantled Sidon, which still contributed some ships to the fleet, hoped to be reinstated in her old position by the favour of Persia's enemy. Her hope was not disappointed. Alexander restored to Sidon her constitution and her territory.

It cannot have been long after this that a kingling of Sidon was laid in a resting-place worthy of the great conqueror himself. His sculptured sarcophagus, dug up in a burying-ground of the Sidonian kings, is one of the most beautiful achievements of Greek art. But we may well associate this monument with Alexander, rather than with the obscure Phoenician for whose ashes it was made. For in two of the vivid scenes which are represented in coloured relief upon its sides, Alexander appears on horseback. One of these is a passage from the battle of Issus. There is a mêlée in the centre; the king charges on this side; a general, perhaps Parmenio, on that. The other scene is a lion-hunt, and here, if Alexander were not marked out by the royal fillet, we might almost recognise him by his eager straining face.

Alexander advanced southward towards Tyre. Ambassadors from this city met him on the road, professing the readiness of the Tyrians to do his will. Alexander expressed his intention of visiting the city, in order to sacrifice in the famous temple of Heracles. But a Macedonian visit was far from the wish of the men of Tyre. Persia was not yet subdued, and their policy was to await the event, and

17.2   Sidonian sarcophagus: Alexander at Issus (see note, page 554)

avoid compromising themselves by a premature adhesion to Macedonia. They felt secure on their island rock, which was protected by 80 ships, apart from the squadron which was absent in the Aegean. Accordingly they invited Alexander to sacrifice in Old Tyre on the mainland, but refused to 'receive either Persian or Macedonian into the city'.

captured; but it was not easy to say how, without a powerful navy, its capture could be achieved. This was perhaps the hardest military task that Alexander's genius ever encountered. The city, girt by walls of great height and magnificently strong masonry, stood on an island severed from the continent by a sound of more than half a mile in width. On the side which faced the mainland were the two harbours: the northern or Sidonian harbour with a narrow mouth, and the southern or Egyptian. It might seem utterly hopeless for an enemy, vastly inferior at sea, to attempt a siege of the island Rock. And in truth there was only one way for a land-power to set about the task. Those 1000 yards of water must be bridged over and the isle annexed to the mainland. Without hesitation Alexander began the building of the causeway. The first part of the work was easy, for the water was shallow; but when the mole approached the island, the strait deepened, the workmen came within range of the walls, and the difficulties of the task began. Triremes issued from the havens on either side to shoot missiles at the men who were at work. To protect them Alexander erected two towers on the causeway, and mounted engines on the towers to reply to the missiles from the ships. He attached to these wooden towers curtains of leather to screen both towers and workmen from the projectiles which were hurled from the city walls. But the men of Tyre were ingenious. They constructed a fire-ship filled with dry wood and inflammables, and choosing a day on which a favourable wind blew, they towed it close to the mole; the burning vessel soon wrapped the towers and all the engines in flames, and the triremes which had towed it up discharged showers of darts at the Macedonians who attempted to extinguish the fire. The Tyrians also rowed across from their island in boats and tore up the stakes at the unfinished part of the mole.

Siege of Tyre, Jan. to July, 332 B.C.

33. TYRE

To subdue Tyre was an absolute necessity, as Alexander explained to a council of his generals and captains which he called together. It was not safe to advance to Egypt, or to pursue Darius, while the Persians were lords of the sea; and the only way of wresting their sea-power from them was to capture Tyre, the most important naval station on the coast; once Tyre fell, the Phoenician fleet, which was the most numerous and strongest part of the Persian navy, would come over to Macedon, for the rowers would not row or the men fight when they had no habitations to row or fight for. The reduction of Cyprus and Egypt would then follow without trouble. Alexander grasped and never let go the fact that Tyre was the key to the whole situation.

It was easy to say that Tyre must be

Undismayed by this disaster, which seemed to show the hopelessness of the enterprise, Alexander only went to work more vigorously. It was necessary to take Tyre, and he was determined that Tyre should be taken. He widened the causeway throughout its whole length, so that it could accommodate more towers and engines, before he attempted to complete it. He saw that it would be necessary to support his operations from the causeway by operations from shipboard; and he went to Sidon to bring up a few ships which were stationed there. But at this moment the aspect of affairs was suddenly changed by the accession to Alexander of naval forces which enabled him to cope with Tyre at an advantage on her own element. The squadrons of Aradus and Byblus which were acting in the Aegean, learning that their cities had submitted to Alexander, left the fleet and sailed to Sidon, which the Macedonians had chosen as their naval station. These Phoenician ships were about 80; and at the same time there came nine ships from Rhodes and ten from Lycia and Cilicia. The adhesion of the kings of Cyprus presently followed, and reinforced the fleet at Sidon by 120 ships. With a fleet of about 250 triremes at his command, Alexander was now far stronger at sea than the merchants of Tyre, and, though the siege of the mighty stronghold was still a formidable task, it was no longer superhuman.

Embassy from Darius

While the fleet was being made ready in the roads of Sidon, and the engineers were fabricating new siege-engines to batter down the walls of Tyre, Alexander made an expedition at the head of his light troops to punish the native brigands who infested the hills of Antilebanon and made the traffic between the coast and the hinterland unsafe. Perhaps it was now that he received an embassy from the Great King, offering an immense ransom for the captives of the royal house, and the surrender of all the lands west of the Euphrates; proposing also that Alexander should marry the daughter of Darius and become his ally. The message was discussed in a council, and Parmenio said that if he were Alexander he would accept the terms. 'And I,' said the king, 'would accept them if I were Parmenio.' Alexander was resolved to carry out his plan of conquest to the end; he would agree to no compromise. He bade the ambassadors say that he would receive neither money nor provinces in lieu of the whole empire of Darius, for all the land and possessions of Darius were his; he would marry the daughter of Darius if he chose, whether Darius willed it or not; and if Darius wished for any favour he must come himself and ask it.

From Sidon Alexander bore down upon Tyre with his whole fleet, hoping to entice the Tyrians into an engagement. He commanded the right wing, while the left was committed to the charge of Craterus, and Pnytagoras the king of Cypriot Salamis. When the fleet hove in sight, the men of Tyre were astonished and dismayed. Before, they would gladly have given battle, but they saw that they had no chance against so many, and they drew up their triremes in close array to block the mouths of their harbours. Alexander set the Cyprian vessels on the north side of the mole to blockade the Sidonian harbour, and the Phoenicians on the south side to blockade the Egyptian harbour. It was opposite this harbour, on the mainland, that his own pavilion was placed.

The mole had now been carried up to the island, and engineers, the best that Phoenicia and Cyprus could furnish, had prepared the engines of war. All was ready for a grand attack on the eastern wall. Some of the engines were placed on the mole, others on transport ships or superannuated triremes. But little impression was made on the wall, which on this side was 150 feet high and enormously thick; and the besieged replied to the attack with volleys of fiery missiles from powerful engines, which were mounted on their lofty battlements. Moreover, the machine-bearing vessels could not come close enough to the walls for effective action; huge stones lying under the water hindered their approach. Alexander decided that these must at all cost be removed; and ships with windlasses were anchored at the spot in order to drag the boulders away. It was a slow task and was hampered by the Tyrians. Covered vessels shot out of the havens and cut the anchor-ropes of the galleys, so that they drifted away. Alexander tried to meet this by placing boats similarly decked close to the anchors; but even this failed, since Tyrian divers swam under water and cut the cables. The only resource was to attach the anchors with chains instead of ropes, and by this means the stones were hauled away and the ships could approach the wall.

The Tyrians now resorted to a last device. They spread the sails of all the ships which were riding at the entrance of the northern harbour, and behind this curtain of canvas, which screened them from the observation of the enemy, they manned seven triremes, three five-oared and three four-oared boats, with the coolest and bravest of their seamen, and waiting for the hour of noon, when the sailors of the besieging vessels used generally to disembark and Alexander himself used to retire to his tent, they rowed noiselessly towards the Cyprian squadron, which was taken completely by surprise, sank some of the vessels at once, and drove the rest onto the shore. It happened that on this day Alexander remained for a shorter time than usual in his pavilion; and when he returned to his station with the Phoenician ships on the south side of the mole, discovering what had happened, he stationed the main part of these ships close to the Egyptian harbour to prevent the enemy from making any movement on this side, and taking with him some five-oared boats and five swift-sailing triremes he sailed round the island. The men in the city saw Alexander and all that he did, and signalled to their own crews who were engaged in battering the stranded Cyprian vessels; but the signals were not seen or heard until Alexander was close upon them. When they saw him coming, they desisted from their work and made all speed for the haven, but the greater number of their boats were disabled by Alexander's vessels before they reached the harbour mouth. Henceforward the ships of Tyre lay useless in the harbours, unable to do anything for the defence of the island.

It was now a struggle between the engineers of Tyre and the engineers of Alexander. The wall opposite the mole defied all machines of battery and methods of assault, and the northern part of the same eastern wall, though the big stones had been cleared away from the water below it, proved equally invulnerable. Accordingly the efforts of the besiegers were united upon the south side near the Egyptian harbour. Here at length a bit of the wall was torn down, and there was fighting in the breach, but the Tyrians easily repelled the attack. It was an encouragement for Alexander, it showed him the weak spot, and two days later he prepared a grand and supreme assault.

Capture of Tyre, August, 332 B.C.

The vessels with the siege engines were set to work at the southern wall, while two triremes waited hard by, one filled with hypaspists under Admetus, the other with a phalanx regiment, ready as soon as the wall yielded to hurl their crews into the breach. Ships were stationed in front of the two havens, to force their way in at a favourable moment, and the rest of the fleet, manned with light troops and furnished with engines, were disposed at various points round the island, to embarrass and bewilder the besieged and hinder them from concentrating at the main point of attack. A wide breach was made, the two triremes were rowed up to the spot, the bridges were lowered, and the hypaspists, Admetus at their head, first mounted the wall. Admetus was pierced with a lance, but Alexander took his place, and drove back the Tyrians from the breach. Tower after tower was captured; soon all the southern wall was in the hands of the Macedonians, and Alexander was able to make his way along the battlements to the royal palace, which was the best base for attacking the city. But the city had been already entered from other points. The chains of both the Sidonian and the Egyptian harbours had been burst by the Cyprian and Phoenician squad-

rons; the Tyrian ships had been disabled; and the troops had pressed into the town. The inhabitants made their last stand in a place called the Agenorion. Eight thousand are said to have been slain, and the rest of the people, about 30,000, were sold into slavery, with the exception of the king, Azemilco, and a few men of high position, who were set at liberty.

The siege had been long and wearisome, but the time and the labour were not too dear a price. The fall of Tyre gave Alexander Syria and Egypt, and the naval supremacy in the eastern Mediterranean. He performed the sacrifice to Heracles in the temple to which the Tyrians had refused him access, and celebrated the solemnity with a torch procession and games. The communities of Syria and Palestine which had not submitted, like Damascus, after the victory of Issus, submitted now after the capture of Tyre, and he encountered no resistance in his southern march to Egypt until he came to the great frontier stronghold, Gaza, the city of the Philistines.[8]

Southward advance of Alexander

Defended by a stout wall, Gaza stood on high rising ground, and more than two miles of sand lay between the city and the seashore so that a fleet was no help to a besieger. The place had been committed by Darius to the care of Batis, a trusty eunuch, and had been well furnished with provisions for a long siege. Batis refused to surrender, trusting in the strength of the fortifications, and at the first sight the engineers of Alexander declared that the wall could never be stormed on account of the height of the hill on which it stood. But Alexander was now accustomed to overcome the insuperable, and the conqueror who sacked Tyre was not ready to turn away from the walls of Gaza. He could not leave such an important post on the line from Damascus to Egypt in the hands of the enemy. He ordered ramparts to be thrown up round the city, in order that the siege engines mounted on this elevation might be on a level with the wall. The best chance seemed to be on the south side, and here the work was pushed on rapidly. When the engines were placed in position, Alexander offered a sacrifice, and a bird of prey flying over the altar dropped a stone on the king's garlanded head. The soothsayer interpreted the meaning of the sign: 'O king, you will take the city, but you must take good heed for your own safety on this day.' Alexander was cautious for a while, but when the besieged sallied forth from the gates and attacked the Macedonians who were working the engines on the rampart, and pressed them hard, he rushed to their aid and was wounded in the shoulder by a dart

Siege of Gaza, Oct.-Nov. 332 B.C.

from a catapult. Thus part of the sign had come true; the other part was in time fulfilled. The engines which had been used in the siege of Tyre arrived by sea, the rampart was widened and raised to a greater height, and underground mines were dug beneath the walls. The walls yielded in many places to the mines and the engines, but it was not till the fourth attack that the Macedonians succeeded in scaling the breaches and entering the city. The slaughter was greater than in Tyre; the women and children were sold into slavery; and the place became a Macedonian fortress.

Conquest of Egypt

Alexander enters Egypt, c. Nov. 332 B.C.

Egypt was now absolutely cut off from Persia; the gate was open, and Alexander had only to march in. The Egyptians had not the vigour to offer any national resistance to the Greek invader; and Mazaces the Persian satrap, seeing Phoenicia and Syria in Alexander's power, the Macedonian navy in the roadstead of Pelusium, and no help at hand, thought only of making his submission and winning the conqueror's grace. Sending his fleet up the Pelusiac branch of the Nile to meet him at Memphis, Alexander journeyed thither by way of Heliopolis. In the capital of the Pharaohs, where he was probably proclaimed king, he sacrificed to Apis and the other native gods, and thereby won the goodwill of the people, who contrasted his piety with the bigotry of the Persian monarch Ochus, who had killed the sacred bull. But while the new king showed that he would treat the native religion and customs with respect, he also made it clear that Greek civilisation was now to pour into the exclusive regions of the Nile. He held athletic games and a poetical contest at Memphis, and the most famous artists from Greece came to take part in it.

At Memphis

Foundation of Alexandria, 331 B.C. Jan. (?)

From Memphis he sailed down the river to Canopus, and took a step which, if he had never performed another exploit in his life, would have made his name memorable for ever. He chose the ground, east of Rhacotis, between Lake Mareotis and the sea, as the site of a new city, over against the island of Pharos, famous in Homeric song, and soon to become more famous still as the place of the first lighthouse, one of the seven wonders of the world. The king is said to have himself traced out the ground plan of *Alexandria*—the market-place and the circuit of the walls, the sanctuary of Isis and the temples of the Hellenic gods. He joined the mainland with the island by a causeway seven stades (nearly a mile) in length, and thus formed two harbours. The subsequent history of Alexandria, which has held its position as a port for more than 2000 years, proves that its founder had a true eye in choosing the site of the most famous of his new cities. The greatness of the place as a market of the world far surpassed any purposes or hopes that Alexander could have formed, but his object in founding it can hardly be doubted. Alexandria was not intended to supersede Memphis as the capital of Egypt; it was intended to take the place of Tyre as the commercial centre of Western Asia and the Eastern Mediterranean. And there was a good reason for diverting the lines of traffic from the Phoenician to the Egyptian coast. It was naturally the policy of Alexander to transfer the trade of the world, so far as might be, into the hands of Greeks; but any new emporium rising on the ruins of Tyre or Sidon would have soon become predominantly Phoenician, owing to the Phoenician genius for trade, whereas on the Egyptian coast Greek traders would encounter no such rivalry. It was thus with a view to the commercial interests of his own race that Alexander founded the port of Egypt.

Amen Ra

In the official style of the Egyptian monarchy the Pharaohs were sons of Ammon, and as the successor of the Pharaohs Alexander assumed the same title. It was therefore necessary in order to regulate his position that an official assurance should be given by Ammon himself that Alexander was his son. To obtain such a declaration and satisfy fully the formalities required by the priests, Alexander undertook a journey to the oracular sanctuary of Ammon in the oasis of Siwah. And this motive is alone sufficient to explain the expedition. But it may well be that in Alexander's mind there was a vague notion that there was something divine about his own origin, something mystical in his mother's conception, and that, like Achilles, he was somewhat more than an ordinary man. Proceeding along the coast to Paraetonion, he was there met by envoys who conveyed the submission of Cyrene. By this acquisition the western frontier of the Macedonian empire extended to the border of the Carthaginian sphere of rule. Alexander then struck across the desert to visit the temple which was the most famous of all Egyptian temples, the temple as it was always called of Zeus Ammon. There were no tracks to guide the travellers, for the south wind had ploughed up the sand and obliterated the road-marks, and stories were told in the camp of miraculous guidance vouchsafed to the favourite of the god. Ptolemy,

Alexander's visit to temple of Zeus Ammon (first months of 331 B.C.)

son of Lagus, who was destined thereafter to rule over Egypt and Libya, recorded in his Memoirs that two snakes moved in front of the troops and showed the way, while Aristobulus, another companion of the king, spoke of the guidance of two crows. A certain mystery enveloped this expedition. It is said that Alexander told no man what he asked the god or what the god replied, save only that the answer pleased him. But it is certain that the priests had ensured that Ammon spoke and recognised him as his son. The very route by which Alexander returned to Memphis is uncertain, for the same two companions differ, Ptolemy stating that he went direct across the desert, and Aristobulus that he returned by Paraetonion.

Organisation of Egypt

At Memphis he organised the government of Egypt, entrusting it to two native nomarchs, and appointing separate Greek governors for the adjoining districts of Arabia and for Libya. But the control of the finances was placed in the hands of a special minister, Cleomenes of Naucratis. Several military commanders were also appointed, and it would seem that Alexander instituted this divided command as a safeguard against the danger of a rebellion. For, geographically situated as Egypt was, an ambitious commander might have a fair prospect of holding the country against his master; and its recent history as a Persian province had illustrated the difficulty of dealing with it. If this is so, Alexander inaugurated a policy which was followed, in later days and in another form, by his Roman successors.

Battle of Gaugamela, and Conquest of Babylonia

The new lord of Egypt and Syria returned with the spring to Tyre. The whole coastland was now in his possession, and he controlled the sea; the time had come to advance into the heart of the Persian empire. Having spent some months in the Phoenician city, busied with various matters of policy and administration, as well as with plans for his next campaign,

Alexander crosses the Euphrates and marches to the Tigris

he set forth at the head of 40,000 infantry and 7000 horse, and reached Thapsacus on the Euphrates at the beginning of August. The building of two bridges had been already begun, but the Persian Mazaeus, who was stationed with troops on the further shore, had hindered their completion. When Alexander arrived, he withdrew; the bridges were finished, and the army passed over. The objective of Alexander was Babylon. The more direct

route, considerably shorter, was to follow the Euphrates downstream; but the hardships suffered by Cyrus and the Ten Thousand had demonstrated the difficulty of maintaining supplies of food and wood from the thin strip of fertility between the deserts to east and west. Alexander chose the other road, across the north of Mesopotamia and down the Tigris on its eastern bank. Throughout the Asiatic campaigns of Alexander we are struck by the perfect organisation of his transports and supplies; but we are struck even more by the certainty of his movements through strange lands, as if he had a map of the country before him. His intelligence department must have been excellent and, though our records give us no intimations on the subject, it has been supposed with much plausibility that here the invader received help from the Jews, who ever since the Captivity were scattered about Media and Babylonia. It is certain that Alexander had shown special favour to the race of Israel at the foundation of Egyptian Alexandria; he had invited a Jewish colony to settle there, enjoying the rights of citizens, and yet living in a separate quarter and keeping their own national customs.

From some Persian scouts who were captured it was ascertained that Darius, with a yet larger multitude than that which had been crushed at Issus, was on the other side of the river, determined to contest the passage. Alexander crossed the Tigris, not at Nineveh, the usual place of crossing, but higher up at Bezabde. On the same night the moon went into eclipse, and men anxiously sought in the phenomenon a portent of the issue of the coming struggle for the lordship of Asia.

Eclipse of the moon, Sept. 20, 331 B.C.

Marching southward for some days, Alexander learned that Darius was encamped in a plain near Gaugamela on the river Bumōdus. The numbers of the army have again been grossly exaggerated but they were considerably larger than at Issus.[9] Having given his men four days' rest, Alexander moved on by night and halted on a hill looking down on the plain where the enemy lay. A council of war was held, and the question was discussed whether the attack should be made immediately; but Parmenio counselled a day's delay, for the purpose of reconnoitring fully the enemy's position and discovering whether covered pits had been dug or stakes laid in the ground. Parmenio's counsel was followed, and the troops pitched their camp in the order in which they were to fight. Alexander rode over the plain and found that the Persians had cleared it of all bushes and obstacles which might

Alexander reaches the plain of Gaugamela

Sept. 30

impede the movements of their cavalry or the effect of their scythed chariots.

The following night was spent by the Persians under arms, for their camp was unfortified and they feared a night attack. And a night attack was recommended by Parmenio, but Alexander preferred to trust the issue to his own generalship and the superior discipline of his troops, and not to brave the hazards of a struggle in the dark. He said to Parmenio 'I do not steal victory', and under the gallantry of this reply he concealed, in his usual manner, the prudence and policy of his resolve. A victory over the Persian host, won in the open field in the light of day, would have a far greater effect in establishing his prestige in Asia than an advantage stolen by night.

The Great King, according to custom, was in the *centre* of the Persian array, surrounded by his kinsfolk and his Persian bodyguard. On either side of them were Greek mercenaries, Indian auxiliaries with a few elephants, and Carians whose ancestors had been settled in Upper Asia. The centre was strengthened and deepened by a second line, composed of the Babylonian troops, and the men from the shores of the Persian Gulf, and the Uxians who dwelt east of Susa, and the Sitacenes. On the *left* wing, the Cadusians from the shores of the Caspian and the men of Susa were nearest the centre; next came a mixed host of Persian horse and foot; and at the extreme left were the troops from the far east, from Arachosia and Bactria. This wing was covered by 1000 Bactrian cavalry, 100 scythe-armed chariots, and the Scythian cavalry from the desert districts of Lake Aral. On the *right* were the contingents of the Caucasian peoples; the Hyrcanians and Tapurians from the southeastern shores of the Caspian; the Parthians, who were destined in the future to found a new oriental monarchy; the Sacae from the slopes of the Hindu-Kush; the Medes, and the dwellers in Mesopotamia and northern Syria.

Against this host, of which the cavalry alone is said to have been as numerous as all the infantry of the enemy, Alexander descended the hill in the morning. On his *left* wing—commanded as usual by Parmenio—were the cavalry of the Thessalian and confederate Greeks; in the *centre* the six regiments of the phalanx; and on the *right*, the hypaspists, and the eight squadrons of the Companions, the royal squadron of Clitus being at the extreme right. Covering the right wing were some light troops, spear-throwers and archers. The line was far outflanked on both sides by the enemy, and the danger which Alexander had most to fear, as at the battle of Issus, was that of being attacked in rear or flank—except that, whereas in the plain of Issus his right alone was threatened, here both wings were in peril. He sought to meet these contingencies by forming behind each wing a second line, which by facing round a quarter or half circle could meet an attack on flank or rear. Behind the *left* wing were placed Thracian foot and horse, some Greek confederate cavalry, and Greek mercenary cavalry; behind the *right*, the old Greek mercenaries under Cleander, the Macedonian archers, some of the Agrianian spear-throwers, the mounted pikemen, the light Paeonian cavalry—and, at the extreme right, to bear the brunt of a flank assault, the new Greek mercenaries under Menidas.

As he advanced, Alexander and his right wing were opposite to the centre of the enemy's line, and he was outflanked by the whole length of the enemy's left. He therefore bore obliquely to the right, and, even when the Scythian horsemen riding forward came into contact with his own light troops, he continued to move his squadrons of heavy cavalry in the same direction. Darius saw with anxiety that this movement would soon bring the Macedonian right outside the ground which he had carefully levelled and prepared for the action of his scythed chariots, and, as he had set no small part of his hopes in the deadly effect of these chariots, he commanded the Scythian and Bactrian cavalry to ride round and deliver a flank-charge, in order to hinder any further advance towards the right. The charge was met by the new mercenaries of Menidas; but they were too few, they were driven back, until the Paeonians and the old mercenaries were ordered to come to their support. Then the barbarians gave way, but in a short while, reinforced by more troops, they returned to the charge. The battle raged, and the Macedonians, far outnumbered, could do no more than hold their ground.

Meanwhile Darius had loosed his scythed chariots, to whirl destruction into the ranks of the Companions and hypaspists. But the archers and the Agrianian spear-throwers received them with showers of spears and arrows; some of these active hillsmen seized the reins of the horses and pulled the drivers from their seats, while the hypaspists, swiftly and undismayed, opened their ranks, and the terrible chariots rattled harmless through the gaps.

The whole Persian line was now advancing to attack, and Alexander was waiting for the moment to deliver his cavalry charge. He had

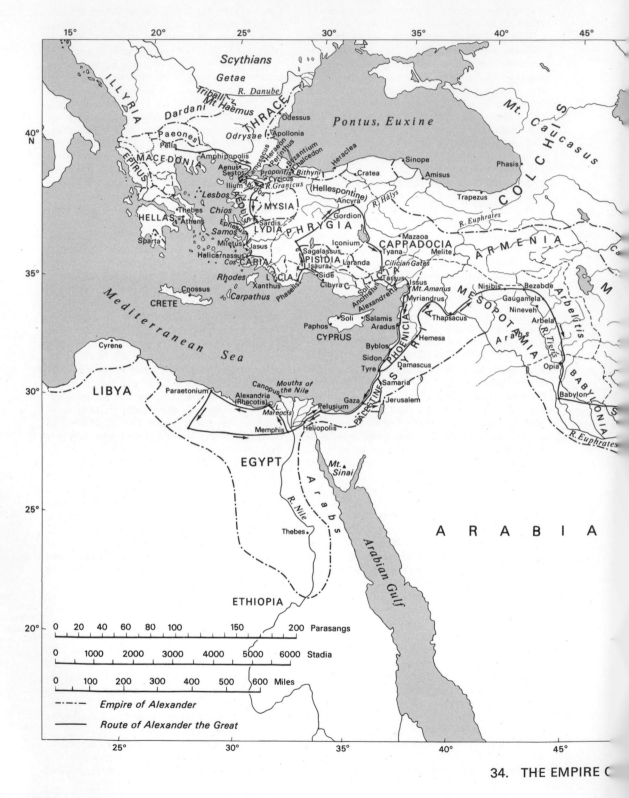

34. THE EMPIRE OF

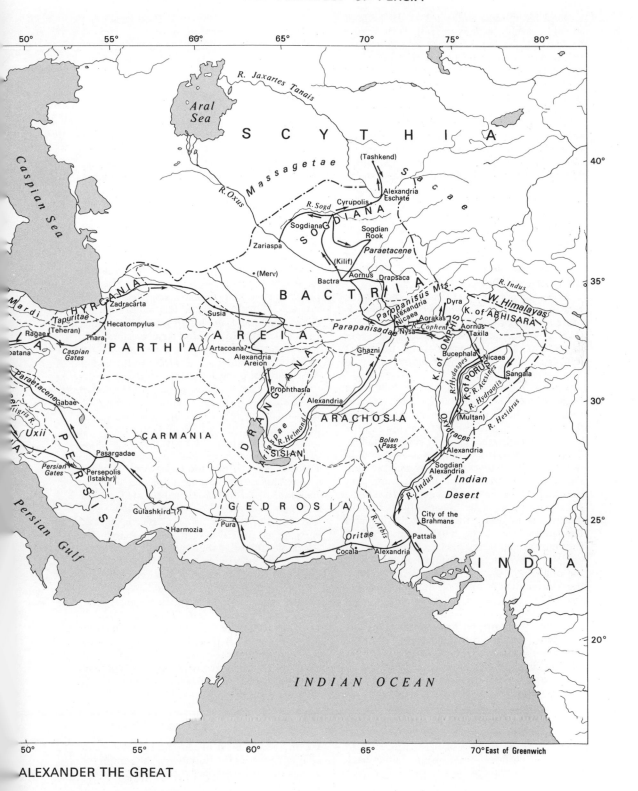

ALEXANDER THE GREAT

Charge of Alexander

to send his mounted pikemen to the help of the light cavalry, who were being hard pressed on the right by the Scythians and Bactrians; and as a counter-check to this reinforcement, squadrons of Persian cavalry were dispatched to the assistance of their fellows. By the withdrawal of these squadrons a gap was caused in the left wing, and into this gap Alexander plunged at the head of his cavalry column and split the line in two. Thus the left side of the enemy's centre was exposed and, turning obliquely Alexander charged into its ranks. Meanwhile the bristling phalanx was moving forward and was soon engaged in close combat with another part of the Persian centre. The storm of battle burst with wildest fury round the Persian king, and the story of Issus was repeated at Gaugamela. The Great King turned his chariot and fled. His Persians fled with him and swept along in their flight the troops who had been posted in the rear.

Flight of Darius

Thus the Persian centre and the neighbouring part of the left wing were cut down or routed by the phalanx, the hypaspists, and the Companions. And in the meantime, the severe struggle of the light cavalry on the uttermost left had also ended in victory for the Macedonians.

Gap in the phalanx

The regiments of the phalanx in their rapid advance had failed to keep abreast, and it would seem that when the regiment of Craterus, on the extreme left, was already far forward in the thick of the fight, the regiment commanded by Simmias, second from the left, was considerably in the rear. From his position Simmias saw that the Thessalian cavalry on the left wing were pressed hard by their adversaries, and he halted his regiment, in order apparently to make a movement to assist them. The Indian and Persian cavalry of the hostile centre rushed through the gap in the phalanx, but instead of exploiting their tactical advantage and attacking the phalanx in the rear they rode straight on the Macedonian camp to set the royal captives free. This gave the Greek mercenaries and Thracians of the rear line time to recover and regroup; they turned round, attacked the plunderers in the rear, and saved the camp. The enemy cavalry turned and in good order tried to cut their way back through the lines.

Attack on the Macedonian camp

Meanwhile Parmenio was hard pressed. The Mesopotamians and Syrians of the extreme Persian right had attacked his cavalry in the flank or rear. Parmenio sped a messenger to Alexander entreating aid, and Alexander desisted from the pursuit of his fleeing rival to restore the battle on his left wing. Riding back with his Companions he encountered a large body of cavalry, Persians, Parthians, and Indians, in full retreat, but in orderly array. A desperate conflict ensued, perhaps the most fearful in the whole battle, the Persians fighting not for victory but for life. Sixty of the Companions fell, but Alexander was again victorious and rode on to the help of Parmenio. But Parmenio no longer needed his help. Not the least achievement of this day of great deeds was the brilliant fighting of the Thessalian cavalry, who not only sustained the battle against the odds which had wrung from Parmenio the cry for aid, but in the end routed their enemy before Alexander could reach the spot. The battle was won, and the fate of the Persian empire was decided.

Victory on the Macedonian right

Alexander did not tarry on the field. He lost not a moment in resuming the chase which he had abandoned, and, riding eastward throughout the night on the tracks of the Persian king, he reached Arbela on the morrow. His experience after Issus was now repeated. He did not take the king, but found at Arbela his chariot, his shield, and his bow. Darius fled into the highlands of Media, and Ariobarzanes with part of the routed army hastened southward to Persia. Alexander did not follow either king or satrap, but pursued his way to Babylon.

Pursuit of Darius as far as Arbela

It might have been expected, and Alexander seems to have expected, that the men of Babylon, trusting in their mighty walls, would have offered to the victor of Gaugamela the same defiance which the men of Tyre offered to the victor of Issus. He was disappointed. When he approached the city, with his army arrayed for action, the gates opened and the Babylonians streamed out, led by their priests and their chief men. The satrap Mazaeus, who had fought bravely in the recent battle, surrendered the city and citadel. In Babylonia, Alexander followed the same policy which he had already followed in Egypt. He appeared as the protector of the national religions which had been depressed and slighted by the fireworshippers. He rebuilt the Babylonian temples which had been destroyed, and above all he commanded the restoration of the marvellous temple of Bel, with its eight stepped storeys, on which the rage of Xerxes had vented itself when he returned from the rout of Salamis. The Persian Mazaeus was retained in his post as satrap of Babylonia.

Babylon submits to Alexander

Conquest of Susiana and Persia

Having rested his army in the luxurious and wonderful city of the Euphrates, the conqueror advanced south-eastward to Susa, the summer

Alexander at Susa, Dec. 331 B.C.

residence of the Persian court. Susa had been already secured for him by Philoxenus, whom he had dispatched thither from Arbela with some light troops. In the citadel he found enormous treasures of gold and silver and purple. Among other precious things at Susa was the sculptured group of the tyrant-slayers, Harmodius and Aristogiton, which Xerxes had carried off from Athens; and Alexander had the pleasure of sending back to its home this historical monument, now more precious than ever through its own strange history.

Statue-group of Harmodius and Aristogiton

Though it was mid-winter, Alexander soon left Susa to accomplish one of the most arduous adventures that he ever undertook. He had won the treasures of Susa, but there were immense treasures still in the palaces of Cyrus and Darius in the heart of the Persian highlands, and these were guarded not only by the difficulties of the mountainous approaches, but by the army which Ariobarzanes had rescued from the overthrow of Gaugamela. Perhaps the reason for Alexander's haste in pressing on to Persia was the fear that Darius might descend with a new force from Media, if time were given him before Ariobarzanes was crushed. But whatever his reasons, it seemed to him of the greatest moment to secure Persia immediately. His road lay south-eastward, and when he had crossed the river Pasitigris, the first obstacle that he encountered was the independent tribe of the Uxian hillsmen, on whom the Persian kings themselves were accustomed to bestow gifts for their goodwill. The barbarians held the passes through which the road lay, but a night march by a difficult mountain path enabled Alexander to surprise them, and the Uxians henceforward were forced to pay yearly gifts to the lord of Asia— 100 horses, 500 draught oxen, and 30,000 sheep.

(Kārūn)

The Uxian pass

The Macedonian army was now in the midst of a region which was unknown to Greek charts. Alexander's advance is a march not only of conquest but of discovery, and opens a new epoch in the history of geographical science by revealing Central Asia to the knowledge of Europe.

Storming of the Persian Gates, Jan. 330 B.C.

Leaving half of his army with Parmenio to proceed more slowly along the main road, Alexander led the other half (including the Macedonians, both horse and foot) by a shorter path through the hills to the narrow defile which formed the entrance to Persia and was called the Persian Gates. Ariobarzanes was posted there with 40,000 foot and 700 horse, guarding the rocky pass which he had fortified by a wall. An attack, easily repelled,

showed Alexander that the pass was impregnable; yet it must be carried for this was the only road to the royal cities of Persia. For a moment Alexander was baffled; never perhaps—not even before Tyre—had he encountered a more desperate problem. But he learned from a prisoner of some extremely perilous paths leading round, through the forests which covered the mountains, to the back of the pass. At this season the snow made these paths more dangerous than ever, and they might well seem hopeless to men weighed down with heavy armour; but they were the only hope and Alexander did not hesitate. He left Craterus with part of the troops in front of the pass, with orders to attack as soon as he heard the Macedonian trumpets sounding from above on the other side. With the rest of his force, including most of the cavalry, three regiments of the phalanx, the hypaspists, and other light troops, he set forth at night, and marched quickly eleven miles along the precipitous snowy track, intersected frequently by deep gullies. When the point was reached at which he was to turn in order to descend on the Persian camp, he again divided his forces, and sent one division forward to bridge the river Araxes and cut off the Persian retreat. Taking the hypaspists, the royal squadron of the Companions, one regiment of the phalanx, and some light troops, he raced down upon the camp and destroyed or routed three successive sets of outposts before the day dawned. Instead of raising the alarm, the sentinels scattered on the mountain, and when the Macedonian trumpets sounded on the brink of his entrenchments, Ariobarzanes was taken completely by surprise. Attacked on both sides, in front by Craterus who stormed up the wall of rock, and in the rear by Alexander, the Persians were cut to pieces or fell over precipices in their flight. Ariobarzanes with a small band escaped into the mountains.

The royal palaces of Persia, to which Alexander now hurried with the utmost speed, stood in the valley of Mervdasht, fertile then but desolate at the present day, and close to the city of Istachr, which the Persians deemed the oldest city in the world. In Istachr itself there was a royal house too, but the great palaces stood some miles away, close beneath the mountain, upon a lofty platform against a background of black rock. The platform was mounted by magnificent staircases, and it bore, besides massive propylaea, four chief buildings—the small palace of Darius, the larger palace of Xerxes, and two great pillared halls. The impressive ruins tell a trained eye

The palaces of Persia (Persepolis)

how to reconstruct the general plan of the royal abode, and there can be no question that Achaemenian architecture had wrought here its greatest achievements, greater than the palace of Susa which Alexander had seen, greater than that of Ecbatana which he was soon to see. This cradle of the Persian kingdom, to which, city and palace together, the Greeks gave the name of *Persepolis*, was 'the richest of all the cities under the sun'. It is said that 120,000 talents were found in the treasury; an army of mules and camels was required to remove the spoils. This store of gold, so long withdrawn from use, was now suddenly to be restored to circulation and perturb the markets of the world.

Pasargadae

Not far off, two days' journey northward up the winding valley of the Murghab, was Pasargadae, the city of Cyrus. The maker of Persia built it close to the field where he had shattered the host of the Median king; and the place is still marked by his tomb, and the stones of other buildings, on some of which the traveller may read the words 'I am Cyrus the king, the Achaemenian'. In Pasargadae too Alexander found a store of treasure.

Jan.-April, 330 B.C.

For four months he made the Persian palaces his headquarters, during which time he received the submission of Caramania or Kirman, and made some excursions to punish the robbers who infested the neighbouring mountains. But

Burning of the palace of Xerxes

the most famous incident connected with the sojourn at Persepolis is the conflagration of the palace of Xerxes. This was a spectacular act of calculated policy. It symbolised the achievement of an objective. The Persian invasion of Greece had been avenged; the rule of the Achaemenids was ended. Later gossip embroidered the tale to detract from Alexander and heighten the moral. The story is that one night when Alexander and his companions had drunk deep at a royal festival, Thais, an Attic courtesan who was of the company, flung out among the tipsy carousers the idea of burning down the house of the hated enemy who had burned the temples of Greece. The mad words of the woman inspired a wild frenzy, and whirled the revellers forth, armed with torches, to accomplish the barbarous deed. Alexander hurled the first brand, and the cedar woodwork of the palace was soon in flames. But before the fire had done its work the king's head was cool, and he commanded the fire to be quenched. The great Xerxes had burnt the Acropolis: his own palace was to be burnt by a humble Athenian flute-girl.[10]

Death of Darius

In the meantime king Darius remained in Ecbatana, surrounded by the adherents who were faithful to him, chiefly the satraps of those lands which were still unconquered— Media itself and Hyrcania, Areia and Bactria, Arachosia and Drangiana. It is probable that after the Gaugamela battle Alexander hoped to receive some proposal from his defeated foe, more submissive and acceptable than that which had been sent after Issus. He would have been ready perhaps to leave to Darius the eastern part of his dominions, with the royal title, though as a dependent vassal, and to content himself for a while with the empire which he had won, including Susa and Persepolis. It may have been with the hope of receiving overtures that he tarried so long in Persia. But Darius gave no sign. Media was defensible; he had a large army from the northern satrapies; and he had Bactria as a retreat, if retreat he must.

The spring was advanced when Alexander left Persia for Ecbatana. The direct road did not lie by Susa, but much farther east through the land of Paraetacene. He made all speed, when the news reached him by the way, that Darius was at Ecbatana with a large army, prepared to fight. But when after a succession of forced marches he drew near to the city he found that Darius had fled eastward, following the women and heavy baggage which had been sent on to the Caspian Gates, and taking the treasures with him. When he reached the Median capital, Alexander was detained by the need of arranging certain matters before he pursued his rival into the northern wilds. The purpose of the League had now been achieved, and the League forces had the right to withdraw. He paid off the Thessalian troops and the other Greek confederates, giving them a handsome donative and a conduct to the Aegean; but any who chose to enrol themselves anew in his service and share in his further course of conquest might stay, and not a few stayed. Parmenio was entrusted with the care of seeing that the treasures of Persia were transported and safely deposited in the strong keep of Ecbatana, where they were to remain in charge of the treasurer Harpalus and a large body of Macedonian troops. Parmenio was then to proceed northward to Cadusia, and along the shores of the Caspian Sea, where he was to meet the king.

Alexander at Ecbatana

With the main part of the army Alexander hurried on, merciless to men and steeds, bent on the capture of Darius. His way lay by Ragae

(Rayy)

and, when he reached that place, a little to the south of the modern capital of Persia, he found that the fugitive was already well beyond the Caspian Gates, which lie a long day's journey to the east. Despairing of overtaking him, Alexander rested some days at Ragae before he advanced towards Parthia through the Caspian pass. But meanwhile fate was approaching Darius by another way. His followers were beginning to suspect that ill-luck dogged him and, when he proposed to stay and risk another battle instead of continuing his retreat to Bactria, none were willing except the remnant of Greek mercenaries, who were still faithful to the man who had hired them, and perhaps dreaded punishment as traitors to the Greek cause. Bessus, the satrap of Bactria, was a kinsman of the king, and it was felt by many that he might be able to raise up again the Achaemenian house, which Darius had been unable to sustain. A plot was formed; Darius was seized and bound in the middle of the night, set in a litter, and hurried on as a prisoner along the road to Bactria. This event disbanded his army. The Greek mercenaries went off northwards into the Caspian mountains, and many of the Persians turned back to find pardon and grace with Alexander. They found him encamped on the Parthian side of the Caspian Gates, and told him the new turn of events. When he learned that his old rival was a prisoner and that Bessus was now his antagonist, Alexander resolved on a swift and hot pursuit. Leaving the main body of the army to come slowly after, he set forth at once with his cavalry and some light foot, and sped the whole night through, not resting till next day at noon, and then another evening and night at the same breathless speed. Sunrise saw him at Thara. It was the place where the Great King had been put in chains, and it was ascertained from his interpreter, who had remained behind ill, that Bessus and his fellows intended to surrender Darius if the pursuit were pressed. There was the greater need for haste. The pursuers rode on throughout another night, men and horses dropping with fatigue. At noon they came to a village where the pursued had halted the day before, and Alexander learned that they intended to force a march in the night. He asked the people if there was no short way, and was told that there was a short way, but it was waterless. Alexander instantly dismounted 500 of his horsemen and gave their steeds to the officers and the strongest men of the infantry who were with him. With these he started in the evening, and having ridden

Darius seized by Bessus

The pursuit of Darius

about forty-five miles came up with the enemy at break of day. The barbarians were straggling, many of them unarmed; a few who made a stand were swept away, but most of them fled when they saw that it was Alexander. Bessus and his fellow-conspirators bade their prisoner—no longer, seemingly, in chains—mount a horse; and when Darius refused, they stabbed him and rode their ways, wounding the litter-mules too and killing the drivers. The beasts, sore and thirsty, strayed about half a mile from the road down a side valley, where they were found at a spring by a Macedonian who had come to slake his thirst. The Great King was near his last gasp. If he could have spoken Greek, or if the stranger had understood Persian, he might have found words to send a message of thanks to his conqueror for the generous treatment of his wife and mother who were then assuredly in his thoughts; afterwards men had no scruple in placing appropriate words in the mouth of the dying monarch. It is enough to believe that he had the solace of a cup of water in his supreme moments and thanked the Macedonian soldier by a sign. Alexander viewed the body, and is related to have thrown his own cloak over it in pity. It was part of his fair luck that he found Darius dead; for if he had taken him alive, he would not have put him to death, and such a captive would have been a perpetual embarrassment. He sent the corpse with all honour to the queen-mother, and the last of the Achaemenian kings was buried with his forefathers at Persepolis.

Spirit of Alexander's Policy as Lord of Asia

Before we follow Alexander on his marches of conquest and discovery into the regions which were then in European eyes the Far East, we may pause to observe his attitude as ruler and king; for the months which passed between the battle of Gaugamela and the pursuit of Darius were a critical period, which witnessed a remarkable change in his conception of his duty and in his political aims.

From the very beginning he had shown to the conquered provinces a tolerance which was not only prompted by generosity but based on political wisdom. He had not attempted to apply an artificial scheme to all countries, but had permitted each country to retain its national institutions. One general principle, indeed, he did adopt—the division of power—

Change in Alexander's aims

His tolerant policy

and this was a notable improvement on the Persian method. Under the Persian kingdom the satrap was usually sole governor, controlling not only the civil administration, but the treasury and the troops. Alexander in most cases committed only the internal administration to the governor, and appointed beside him, and independent of his authority, a financial officer and a military commander. This division of authority was a security against rebellion. We have already seen, in Egypt and Babylonia, how in matters of religion Alexander was, like all the Greeks, broadminded and tolerant.

His policy as successor of the Great King

But the Macedonian king, the commander-in-chief of the Greek confederates, had set forth as a champion of Greeks against mere barbarians, as a leader of Europeans against effeminate Asiatics, as the representative of a higher folk against beings lower in the human scale. All the Greeks and Macedonians who followed him regarded the east as a world to be plundered and rifled by their higher intelligence and courage, and considered the orientals as inferiors meant by nature to be their own slaves. 'Slaves by nature' they seemed to the political wisdom of Aristotle himself, Alexander's teacher; and the victories of Issus and Gaugamela were calculated to confirm the Europeans in their sense of unmeasured superiority. But, as Alexander advanced, his view expanded, and he rose to a loftier conception of his own position and his relation to Asia. He began to transcend the familiar distinction of Greek and barbarian, and to see that, for all the truth it contained, it was not the last word that could be said. He formed the notion of an empire, both European and Asiatic, in which the Asiatics should not be dominated by the European invaders, but Europeans and Asiatics alike should be ruled on an equality by a monarch, indifferent to the distinction of Greek and barbarian, and looked upon as their own king by Persians as well as by Macedonians. The idea begins to show itself after the battle of Gaugamela. The Persian lords and satraps who submit are received with favour and confidence; Alexander learns to know and appreciate the fine qualities of the Iranian noblemen. Some of the eastern provinces are entrusted to Persian satraps, for example Babylonia to Mazaeus, and the court of Alexander ceases to be purely European. With oriental courtiers, the forms of an oriental court are also gradually introduced; the Asiatics prostrate themselves before the lord of Asia; and presently Alexander adopts the dress of a Persian king at court ceremonies, in order to appear less a foreigner in the eyes of his eastern subjects. The idea which prompted this policy was new and bold, and it harmonised with the great work of Alexander—the breaking down of the barriers between west and east; but it was accompanied by a certain imperious self-exaltation, which we do not find in the earlier part of Alexander's career, and it involved him in troubles with his own folk. The Macedonians strongly disapproved of their king's new paths; they disliked the rival influence of the Asiatic nobles, and their prejudices were shocked at seeing Alexander occasionally assume oriental robes. The Macedonian royalty was indeed inadequate for Alexander's imperial position; but it is unfortunate that he had no other model than the royalty of Persia, hedged round by forms which were so distasteful to the free spirit of Greece. The life of Alexander was spent in solving difficult problems, political and military, and none was harder than this—to create a kingship which should conciliate the prejudices of the east without offending the prejudices of the west.

CHAPTER 18

The Conquest of the Far East

Hyrcania, Areia, Bactria, Sogdiana

Conquest
of
Hyrcania
(Tabar-
istan
and
Mazen-
deran),
330 B.C.

The murderers of Darius fled—Bessus to Bactria, Nabarzanes to Hyrcania—and the direction of their flight determined the course of Alexander's advance. He could not pursue Bessus while there was an enemy behind him in the Caspian region, and therefore his first movement was to cross the Elburz chain of mountains which separate the south Caspian shores from Parthia and subdue the lands of the Tapuri and Mardi. The Persian officers who had retreated into these regions submitted and were received with favour; the life of Nabarzanes was spared. The Greek mercenaries who had found refuge in the Tapurian mountains capitulated. All who had entered the Persian service, before the Synedrion of Corinth had pledged Greece to the cause of Macedon, were released; the rest were compelled to serve in the Macedonian army for the same pay which they had received from Darius. The importance of the well-wooded southern coast of the Caspian was understood by Alexander, and he sent orders to Parmenio at Ecbatana to take possession of the Cadusian territory on the south-western side of the sea.

(Astrabad,
near
Meshed)

He himself could not wait. Having rested a fortnight at Zadracarta and held athletic games, he marched eastward to Susia, a town in the north of Areia, and was met there by Satibarzanes, governor of Areia, who made his submission and was confirmed in his satrapy. Here the news arrived that Bessus had assumed the style of Great King with the name of Artaxerxes, and was wearing his turban 'erect'. Alexander started at once on the road to Bactria. His way would have lain by Merv; in

the wilds of Central Asia the beaten ways of traffic remain the same for thousands of years. But he had not gone far when he was overtaken by the news that Satibarzanes had revolted behind him. There was nothing to be done but to return and secure the province of Areia; for this province did not stand alone; it would certainly be upheld in its hostility by the neighbouring countries of Arachosia and Drangiana, which formed the satrapy of Barsaentes, one of the murderers of Darius. Hurrying back in forced marches with a part of his army, Alexander appeared before Artocoana, the capital of Areia, in two days; Satibarzanes galloped away to seek Bessus in Bactria, and his troops who fled to the mountains were pursued and overcome. There was no further resistance, and the conqueror marched southwards to Drangiana. His road can hardly be doubtful—the road which leads by Herat into Seistan. And it is probable that Herat is the site of the city which Alexander founded to be the capital and stronghold of the new province, Alexandria of the Areians. The submission of Drangiana was made without a blow; the satrap, who had fled to the Indians, was given up by them and put to death.

Alexandria
Areiôn
(Herat)
Occupa-
tion of
Drangiana

Execution
of
Barsaentes

At Prophthasia, the capital of the Drangiana, there followed a tragedy, of which we know too little to judge the rights and wrongs of the case. It came to Alexander's ears that Philotas, the son of Parmenio, was conspiring against his life. The king called an assembly of the Macedonians and stated the charges against the general. Philotas admitted that he had known of a plot to murder Alexander and said nothing about it, but this was only

(Near Nad
Ali in
Seistan)

The
conspiracy
of Philotas

one of the charges against him. The Macedonians, although many of them were ill-content with the developments of their king's policy in the east, found Philotas guilty, and he was pierced by their javelins. The son dead, it seemed dangerous to let the father live, whether he was involved or not in the treasonable designs of Philotas. A messenger was despatched with all speed to Media, bearing commands to some of the captains of Parmenio's army to put the old general to death. If the guilt of Philotas was assured—and we have no reason to doubt it—we can hardly, so far as Philotas is concerned, blame Alexander for his rigorous measures, which it must have been painful for him to adopt. A crime which might have been pardoned in Macedonia could not be dealt gently with in a camp in distant lands, where not only success but safety depended on loyalty and discipline. But the death of Parmenio was an arbitrary act of precaution against merely suspected disloyalty; there seem to have been no proofs against him, and there was certainly no trial.

Fate of Parmenio

In the meantime Alexander had changed his plans. Instead of retracing his steps and following the route to Bactria, which he had originally intended to take, he resolved to follow a circle, and marching through Afghanistan, subduing it as he went, he would cross the Hindu-Kush mountains and descend on the plain of the Oxus from the east. First he advanced southwards to secure Seistan and the north-western regions of Baluchistan, then known as Gedrosia. The Ariaspae, a peaceful and friendly people whom the Greeks called 'Benefactors', dwelt in the south of Seistan. Alexander passed part of the winter among them, gratified them by a small increase of territory, and made them free, subject to no satrap. The neighbouring Gedrosians volunteered their submission and a Gedrosian satrapy was constituted with its capital at Pura. When spring came, Alexander pushed north-eastward up the valley of the Halmand to Candahar. And in pronouncing the name of Candahar, we are perhaps pronouncing the name of the great conqueror; for the chief city which he founded in Arachosia was probably on the site of Candahar, which seems to be a corruption of its name, Alexandria. The way led on over the mountains, past Ghazni, into the valley of the upper waters of the Cabul river, and Alexander came to the foot of the high range of the Hindu-Kush. The whole massive complex of mountains which diverge from the roof of the

Alexander winters in Seistan, 330-29 B.C.

Alexandria in Arachosia

world, dividing southern from central, eastern from western Asia—the Pamirs, the Hindu-Kush, and the Himalayas—were grouped by the Greeks under the general name of Caucasus. But the Hindu-Kush was distinguished by the special name of Paropanisus, while the Himalayas were called the Imaus. At the foot of the Hindu-Kush he spent the winter, and founded another Alexandria to secure this region, somewhere to the north of Cabul; it was distinguished as Alexandria of the Caucasus. While he was in these parts he learned that Satibarzanes was still abroad in Areia, inflaming a rebellion. Some forces were sent to crush him; a battle was fought and Satibarzanes was killed.

Alexandria of the Caucasus (perhaps Houpian), 329-8 B.C.

The crossing of the Caucasus, undertaken in the early spring, was an achievement which, for the difficulties overcome and the hardships of cold and want endured, seems to have fallen little short of Hannibal's passage of the Alps. The soldiers had to content themselves with raw meat and the herb of silphion as a substitute for bread. At length they reached Drapsaca, high up on the northern slope—the frontier fortress of Bactria. Having rested his weary army, Alexander went down by the stronghold of Aornus into the plain, and marched through a poor country to Bactra, the chief city of the land, which has preserved its old site but has changed its name to Balkh.

(? Kunduz)

(Tashkurgan)

The pretender, Bessus Artaxerxes, had stripped and wasted eastern Bactria up to the foot of the mountains for the purpose of checking the progress of the invading army, but he fled across the Oxus when Alexander drew near, and his native cavalry deserted him. No man withstood the conqueror, and another province was added without a blow to the Macedonian empire. Alexander lost no time in pursuing the fugitive into Sogdiana. This is the country which lies between the streams of the Oxus and the Jaxartes. It was called Sogdiana from the river Sogd, which flows through the land and, passing near the cities of Samarcand and Bokhara, loses itself in the sands of the desert before it approaches the waters of the Oxus. Bessus had burned his boats and, when Alexander, after a weary march of two or three days through the hot desert, arrived at the banks of the Oxus, he was forced to transport his army by the primitive vehicle of skins, which the natives of Central Asia then used and still use today. Alexander's soldiers, however, instead of inflating the sheep-skins with air, stuffed them with rushes. They crossed the river at Kilif, where its banks contract to the width of

Occupation of Bactria

(R. Saravshan)

about two-thirds of a mile, and advanced on the road to Maracanda, the chief city of the country, easily recognised as Samarcand.

Bessus had no support north of the Oxus. He had some Sogdian allies, at the head of whom were Spitamenes and Dataphernes, but these men had no intention of sacrificing their country to the cause of the pretender. Thinking that Alexander's only object was to capture Bessus and that he would then withdraw from Sogdiana and fix the Oxus as the northern boundary of his dominion,

was scourged and sent to Bactra to await his sentence.

But Alexander did not arrest his march; he had made up his mind to annex Sogdiana. Not the Oxus but the Jaxartes was to be the northern limit of his empire. The inhabitants of the land called this river the Tanais. It is said that the Greeks were deceived into imagining that it was the same river as the familiar Tanais which discharges its waters into the Maeotic lake and hence regarded it as the boundary between Asia and Europe, and

River Jaxartes (Syr Darya)

(Don)

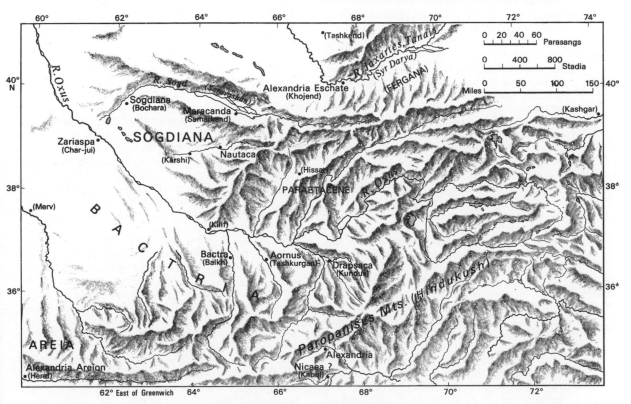

35. BACTRIA AND SOGDIANA

they sent a message to him offering to surrender the usurper. The king sent Ptolemy, son of Lagus, with 6000 men to secure Bessus, whom they found in a walled village, deserted by his Sogdian friends. By Alexander's orders he was placed, naked and fettered, on the right side of the road by which the army was marching. Alexander halted as he passed the captive and asked him why he had seized and murdered Darius, his king and benefactor. Bessus replied that he had acted in concert with other Persian nobles, in the hope of winning the conqueror's favour. He

thought that the herdsmen of the north, who dwelt beyond it, were the Scythians of Europe. But they can hardly have fallen into this error, for they imagined that the Caspian Sea was a gulf of the ocean, and the two errors are inconsistent.[1] Having seized and garrisoned Samarcand, the army pushed on north-eastward by the unalterable road which nature has marked out and occupied seven strongholds which the Sogdians had built as defences against invaders from the north. The road reaches the Jaxartes where that river issues from the chilly vale of Fergana and deflects its course to flow through the steppes. It was a point of the highest importance, for Fergana forms the vestibule of the great gate of communication between south-western Asia and China—the pass over the Tian-shan mountains, which descends on the other side into the land of Kashgar. Here Alexander, with strategic insight, resolved to fix the limit of his empire, and on the banks of the river he founded a new city which was known as Alexandria the Ultimate. There is no doubt about the situation; it is the later Khodjend.

Alexandria Eschate (Khodjend), 328 B.C.

The conqueror, judging from the ease with which he had conquered Arachosia and Bactria, seems not to have conceived that it might be otherwise beyond the Oxus. But the chiefs of Sogdiana were not as the Persian grandees; they were ready to fight for their freedom against the European invader. As he was designing his new city, Alexander received the news that the land was up in arms behind him. Spitamenes was the leader of the movement and was supported by Oxyartes and other leading Sogdians. The few Macedonian soldiers left in the seven strongholds had been overpowered, and the garrison of Samarcand was besieged in the citadel. A message had gone forth into the western wastes, and the Massagetae and other Scythian tribes were flocking to drive out the intruder. It was a dangerous moment for Alexander. He first turned to recover the fortresses and in two days he had taken and burned five of them. Cyrupolis, the largest and strongest, caused more trouble; but Alexander, with a few companions, contrived to creep under the wall by the bed of a dry stream and threw open a gate to the troops. The resistance of the inhabitants was furious, and the king was wounded in the mêlée. The fall of Cyrupolis was followed by the capitulation of the seventh fortress, and the remnant of the inhabitants of all these places were led in chains to take part in peopling the new Alexandria.

Sogdiana rises against Alexander

Summer, 328 B.C. (Uratübe)

The next task should have been the relief of Samarcand, but Alexander found himself confronted by a new danger and could send only a few thousand troops to help the besieged garrison. The herdsmen of the north were pouring down to the banks of the Jaxartes, ready to cross the stream and harass the Macedonians in the rear. It was impossible to move until they had been repelled and the passage of the river secured. The walls of Alexandria were hastily constructed of unburnt clay and the place made fit for habitation in the short space of twenty days.

Meanwhile the northern bank was lined by the noisy and jeering hordes of the barbarians, and Alexander determined to cross the river. The offerings were not favourable; they portended, said the seer, personal danger to the king; but Alexander would be mocked no longer. Bringing up his missile-engines to the shore, he dismayed the shepherds, who, when stones and bolts began to fall among them from such a distance and unhorsed one of their champions, retreated some distance from the bank. The army seized the moment to cross; the Scythians were routed, and Alexander, at the head of his cavalry, pursued them far into the steppes. Parched by the intense summer heat, the king was tempted to drink the foul water of the desert and he fell dangerously ill. Thus was the presage of the offerings fulfilled.

Luckily Alexander soon recovered, for bad news came from the south. When the relieving force approached Maracanda, Spitamenes had fled westward to the town of Sogdiana, which probably answers to Bokhara. The Macedonians marched after him, hoping to drive him utterly out of the land, but they were careless and the whole detachment was cut off. Learning of this disaster, Alexander hurried to Samarcand with cavalry and light troops, covering the distance, it is said, in three days—a forced march of between 50 and 60 miles a day, which seems almost impossible for foot soldiers, however lightly equipped, in the heat of a Sogdian summer. At his coming, Spitamenes, who had returned to the siege of Samarcand, again withdrew westward, and Alexander followed in pursuit. Visiting the spot where the unlucky corps had been cut down on the banks of the Sogd, the king buried the dead; then crossing the river, he pursued the fugitive chieftain and his Scythian allies to the limits of the waste. He swept on to Sogdiana, ravaging the land; then, marching south-westward to the Oxus, he crossed into western Bactria and spent the winter at Zariaspa. The Bactrian cities of Zariaspa and Bactra bore somewhat the same relation to one another as the Sogdian cities of Maracanda and Sogdiana.

Alexander in western Sogdiana; winters, 328-7 B.C., at Zariaspa (Charjui)

At Zariaspa, Bessus was formally tried for the murder of Darius and was condemned to have his nose and ears cut off and be taken to Ecbatana to die on the cross. The Greeks, like ourselves, regarded mutilation as a barbarous punishment, and it is not pleasant to find Alexander violating this sentiment. But the adoption of oriental punishments in dealing with orientals must be judged along with the

Fate of Bessus

adoption of other oriental customs. Every conqueror of an alien race finds himself in a grave embarrassment. Is he to offend his ideals and fall away from his convictions by acquiescing in outlandish usages antagonistic to his own? Or is he, stiff-necked and inflexibly true to the principles of his own civilisation, to remain out of touch with his new subjects? Is he to adopt the policy which will be most effective in administering the conquered land, or is he to impose a policy which works and is approved in his home-country, but may be *Oriental* useless or fatal elsewhere? Alexander did not *policy of* adopt the second method. It was the task of *Alexander;* his life to spread Greek civilisation in the East. But he saw that this could not be done by an outsider—a general of Hellas or king of Macedonia. He must meet the orientals on their own ground; he must become their king in their own way. The surest means of planting Hellenism in their midst was to begin by taking account sympathetically of their prejudices. Alexander therefore assumed the state of Great King, surrounded himself with Eastern forms and pomp, exacted self-abasement in his presence from oriental subjects, and adopted the maxim that the king's person was divine. He was the successor of Darius, and he regarded the murder of that monarch as a crime touching himself, inasmuch as it was a crime against royalty. It was therefore an act of deliberate policy that he punished the king-slayer in Eastern fashion, as an impressive example to his Eastern subjects.

unpopular The misfortune was that Alexander's *with the* assumption of oriental state, and the favour *Macedon-* which he showed to the Persians, were *ians* highly unpopular with the Macedonians. It was hard always to preserve a double face, one for his Companions, another for his Persian ministers. Nor was it Alexander's policy to maintain this difference for ever. He hoped ultimately to secure uniformity in the relations of Macedonians and Persians to their common king. Meanwhile, in the intervals of rest between military operations, discontent smouldered among the Macedonians. Though they were attached to their king, and proud of the conquests which they had helped him to achieve, they felt that he was no longer the same to them as when he had led them to victory at the Granicus. His exaltation over *327 B.C.* obeisant orientals had changed him, and the *(first* execution of his trusted general Parmenio was *months)* felt to be significant of the change. *Alexander at Samar-* These feelings of discontent accidentally *cand* found a mouthpiece about this time. Rebellious

movements in Sogdiana brought Alexander over the Oxus again before the winter was over, and he spent some time at Samarcand. One of the most unfortunate consequences of the long-protracted sojourn in the regions of the Oxus was the increase of drunkenness in the army. The excessively dry atmosphere in summer produces an intolerable and frequent thirst, and it was inevitable that the Macedonians should slake it by wine—the strong wine of the country—if they would not sicken themselves by the brackish springs of the desert or the noxious water of the towns. One night in the fortress of Samarcand the carouse lasted far into the night. Greek men of letters, who accompanied the army, sang the praises of Alexander, exalting him above the Dioscuri, whose feast he was celebrating on this day. Clitus, his foster-brother, flushed with wine, suddenly sprang up to denounce the blasphemy, and once he had begun the current of his feelings swept him on into a denunciation and disparagement of Alexander. It was to the Macedonians, he said—to men like Parmenio and Philotas—that Alexander owed his victories; he himself had saved Alexander's life at the Granicus. These were the two sharpest stings, and they stirred Alexander's blood to fury. He started to his feet and called in Macedonian for his hypaspists. None obeyed his drunken orders; Ptolemy and other banqueters forced Clitus out of the hall, while others tried to restrain the king. But presently Clitus made his way back and shouted from the doorway some insulting verses of Euripides, signifying that the army does the work and the general reaps the glory. The king leapt up, snatched a spear from the hand of a guardsman, and rushed upon his foster-brother. Drunk though he was, the aim was sure—Clitus sank dead to the *Murder of* ground. An agony of remorse followed. For *Clitus* three days the murderer lay in his tent, without sleep or food, cursing himself as the assassin of his friends. The army sympathised with his grief; they tried the dead man and resolved that he had been justly slain. The tragedy was attributed to the anger of Dionysus, because the day was his festival and the Dioscuri had been celebrated instead.

The tragic issue of this miserable drunken brawl is a lurid spot in Alexander's life, but it was a slight matter compared with an act which is said to have marked his invasion of Sogdiana. When we saw him first cross the Oxus in pursuit of Bessus we did not pause to witness his treatment of a remarkable town which lay on his way. The Branchidae, who had charge of the temple and oracle of Apollo 20 miles from Miletus, were charged with having betrayed the treasures of the sanctuary. Their lives were not safe from the anger of the Milesians, and Xerxes transported them into Central Asia, where no Greek vengeance could pursue them. They were established in Sogdiana, not far from the place where Alexander crossed—a solitary little settlement, which, though severed so long from Hellas, preserved its Greek religion and Greek customs, and had not forgotten the Greek speech. It is easy to imagine what excitement was stirred there by the coming of a Greek army. The folk came forth joyously to bid Alexander welcome and offer him their loyalty. But Alexander remembered only one thing— the ancestors of this people had committed a heinous crime against Apollo, and had sided with Persia against Greece. That crime had never been forgotten by the men of Miletus, and the king called upon the Milesians in his army to pronounce sentence upon the Branchidae. The Milesians could not agree, and Alexander himself decided the fate of the town. Having surrounded it with a cordon of soldiers, he caused all the inhabitants to be massacred and the place to be utterly demolished. Few of the children of the children's children of the original transgressors could have been still alive; most of the victims would have belonged to the fifth degree of descent. We cannot imagine a fouler enforcement of the savage principle that crimes of the fathers should be visited on distant generations. Such is the shocking story which has blackened Alexander's fame. Fortunately we can safely reject it as untrue; it was not related in the memoirs of the two oldest and best authorities, Ptolemy and Aristobulus. Alexander committed some cruel deeds but none so appalling as this massacre would have been.[2]

There were more hostilities in western **Bactria** and western Sogdiana, until at last, overawed by Alexander's success, the Scythians, in order to win his favour, slew Spitamenes. With this chieftain the resistance collapsed, and it only remained to reduce the rugged south-eastern regions of Sogdiana, which were called Paraetacene. The Sogdian Rock, which commands the pass into these regions, was occupied by Oxyartes, and a band of Macedonian soldiers captured it by an arduous night-climb. Among the captives was Roxane, the daughter of Oxyartes; and the love of Alexander, who had been always indifferent to women, was attracted by the beauty and

manners of the Sogdian maiden. It was characteristic of him that, nothwithstanding the reaction which such a marriage could be expected to provoke among the proud Macedonians, he resolved to make her his wife, and, on his return to Bactra after subjugating other fortresses in Paraetacene, he divided a loaf of bread with his bride according to the fashion of the country, and celebrated the nuptials. There was policy in this marriage as well as sentiment. It was symbolic of the union of Asia and Europe, of the breaking down of the barrier between barbarian and Hellene, and of Alexander's position as an oriental king.

About this time an attempt seems to have been made to adopt a common court ceremonial. The Persian nobles were not well pleased that, whereas they were compelled to abase themselves to the ground before the king, the Macedonians and Greeks were excused from the obeisance.[3] Most of the Greeks would have been pliant enough, but there was one prominent man of letters who stood out against the usage and drew upon himself displeasure by the utterance of bold truths. This was Callisthenes, a nephew of Aristotle. He was composing a history of the campaigns of Alexander, whose exploits he ungrudgingly lauded; he had joined the army, he used to say, to make *him* famous, not to win fame himself. It is related that Hephaestion and a number of others arranged a plan for surprising the king's guests at a banquet into making the obeisance. Alexander, raising his golden cup, drank to each guest in order—first to some of those who were privy to the plan; each arose and prostrated himself and was then kissed by the king. Callisthenes, when his turn came, drained the cup and went to receive the kiss, without doing obeisance; Alexander would not kiss him, and he turned away, saying, 'I go the poorer by a kiss!' Incidents of this kind created a coolness between the king and his historian. One of the duties of Callisthenes and the other philosophers and literary men who accompanied Alexander's progress was to educate the pages, the noble Macedonian youths who attended on the king's person; and over some of these Callisthenes had great influence. One day at a boar-hunt a page named Hermolaus committed the indiscretion of forestalling the king in killing a boar, and for this breach of etiquette he was flogged and deprived of his horse. Smarting under the dishonour, Hermolaus plotted with some of his comrades to slay Alexander in his sleep. But on the appointed night Alexander sat up carousing till dawn, and on the next day the plot was betrayed. The conspirators were arrested and put to death by the sentence of the whole army. Callisthenes was also arrested on the charge of being an accomplice and was afterwards hanged. Hermolaus was indeed one of his warmest admirers, but it is not clear what the evidence against the historian was. On the one hand, Ptolemy and Aristobulus asserted independently that the pages declared under torture that Callisthenes had incited them; on the other hand, Alexander is said to have stated in a letter that the torture had failed to elicit the name of any accomplice. The deeper cause may be that Alexander suspected Callisthenes as an agent of the anti-Macedonian party in Greece.

Callis-thenes charged with treason and executed

Before the end of summer, Alexander bade farewell to Bactria and set forth to the conquest of India. Three years had passed since the death of Darius, three unique years in the annals of the world. In that time the western conqueror had subdued Afghanistan, and cast his yoke over the herdsmen of the north as far as the river Jaxartes. He was the first and last western conqueror of Afghanistan; he was the first but not the last invader. He was the first European invader and conqueror of the regions beyond the Oxus, anticipating by more than two thousand years the conquests which have been achieved by a European power in modern times. His next enterprise anticipated a later conquest of north-western India. But Britain made her conquests from the south, Russia hers from the north; Alexander was the only European conqueror who marched straight from the west to the Indus and the Oxus.

Alex-ander's position among western conquerors of Asia

The Macedonian monarch's work in Bactria and Sogdiana was an unavoidable sequel of his succession to the Persian empire. He had to set up a barrier against the unsettled races of the waste, who were a perpetual menace to the civilisations of the south. He founded a number of settlements in these regions, not only to serve as military garrisons, but also probably with the hope of gradually training the herdsmen to more settled ways of life. If so, it was a vain hope. History has shown that there is only one means of forcing the shepherd races to become reluctant tillers of the soil. Not until they have been engulfed on all sides by civilisation, and driven within a narrow geographical area, will they adopt, under the stress of necessity, the regular and laborious life of agriculture. In the days of Alexander they had endless space behind them and an indefinite future before them.

The Conquest of India

In returning to Afghanistan, Alexander seems to have followed the main road from Balkh to Cabul, crossing the Hindu-Kush by a pass more westerly than that by which he had come. Reaching Alexandria in ten days, he went on to another town, Nicaea, which, if he had not refounded, he had at all events renamed, and which is possibly to be sought in Cabul itself. Here he stayed till the middle of November, finding much to do both in organising the province and in preparing for further advance. He had left a large detachment of his army in Bactria, but he had enrolled a still larger force, 30,000, of the Asiatics of those regions—Bactrians, Sogdians, Dahae, and Sacae. The host with which he was now to descend upon India must have been at least twice as numerous as the army with which he had crossed the Hellespont seven years before. It had increased as it rolled on, and the additions far more than counterbalanced the reductions caused by leaving detachments in each new province and the losses due to warfare or disease.

Halt at Nicaea (Cabul or Bagram?), 327 B.C.

During these years Alexander's camp was his court and capital, the political centre of his empire—a vast city rolling along over mountain and river through Central Asia. Men of all trades and callings were there, some indispensable for the needs of the king and his army, others drawn by the prospect of making profits out of the spoil-laden soldiers: craftsmen of every kind, engineers, physicians, and seers; cheapjacks and money-changers; literary men, poets, musicians, athletes, jesters; secretaries, clerks, court attendants; a host of women and slaves. In many of the halting-places athletic and musical contests were held, serving both to cheer the Greeks by reminding them of their home country and to impress the imagination of the barbarians. A Court Diary was regularly kept—in imitation of the court journal of Persia—by Eumenes of Cardia, who conducted all the political correspondence of Alexander.

Alex-ander's camp

Alexander had no idea of the shape or extent of the Indian peninsula, and his notion of the Indian conquest was probably confined to the basins of the Cophen and the Indus. He was not the first invader speaking an Aryan language who went down through the north-western hills into the plains of India. Centuries before, Aryan herdsmen had flowed down in successive waves and found an abiding home there. From Central Asia, from the regions of the Hindu-Kush, bringing

State of India

(R. Cabul)

with them their old hymns, some of which we still possess, they came down into the lands of the Indus, 'the glorious giver of wealth', and turned to a settled agricultural life. Strangely different was the civilisation which grew up in northern India among the men who called upon *Dyaus pitar* from that of their speech-brethren who worshipped *Zeus patêr* on the shores of the Aegean. The castes of the Brahmins and the warriors, the inhuman

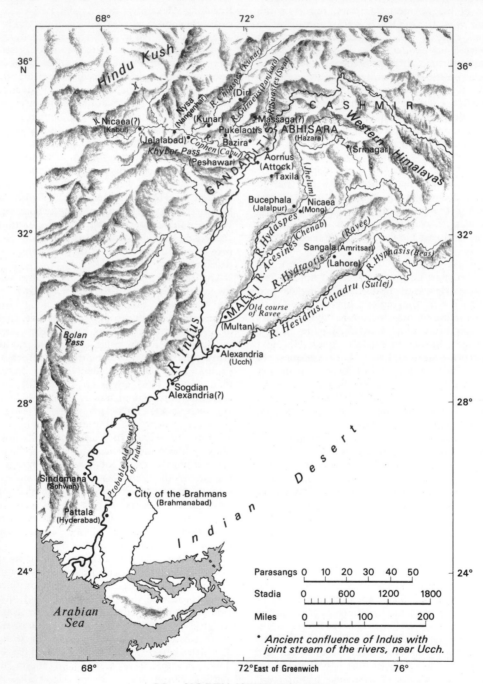

36. NORTH-WESTERN INDIA

asceticism of the Brahmin's life, the political influence of these religious men, must have seemed repulsive and outlandish to the free and cheerful temper of the Greeks. The great Darius had partially annexed the lands of the Indus, and they constantly supplied troops to his successors. Scylax of Caryanda had sailed down the Indus by his orders and probably published an account of the voyage.[4] The stories that were told about the wonders of India excited the curiosity of the Greek invaders. It was a land of righteous folks, of strange beasts and plants, of surpassing wealth in gold and gems. It was supposed to be the ultimate country on the eastern side of the world, bounded by Ocean's stream.

Omphis

At this time north-western India was occupied by a number of small heterogeneous principalities and village communities. The northern districts of the land between the Indus and the Hydaspes—the stream which we now call the Jhelum—were ruled by Omphis, a prince whose capital was at Taxila near the Indus. His brother Abisares was the ruler of Hazara and the adjacent parts of Kashmir. Beyond the Hydaspes was the powerful kingdom of Porus, who ruled as far as the Acesines or 'dark-hued', which we know as the Chenab, the next of the 'Five Rivers'. East of the Chenab, in the lands of the Ravee and the Bëas, were other small principalities, and also free 'kingless' peoples, who owned no master. These principalities and free communities differed much in manners and religion; they had no tendency to unity or combination; the free tribes feared and hated the princes; the princes strove with one another. And these states were not all of the same race. Most perhaps were Aryan; but some, like the Malli, belonged to the old 'Dravidian' stock, whom even in the Punjab the Aryans had not entirely dispossessed or subdued. An invader, therefore, had no common resistance to fear; he had to deal with the states one by one, and he could be assured that many would welcome him out of hatred for their neighbours. The prince of Taxila hoped great things from the Macedonian conqueror, especially the downfall of his rival Porus. He visited Alexander at Nicaea, laid himself and his kingdom at the great emperor's feet, and promised his aid in subduing India. Other chiefs on the hither side of the Indus also made submission.

(Takka cila)
(The Paurava)
(Asikni)

Aryans,

and Dravidians

Alexander's direct road from the high plain of Cabul into the Punjab lay along the right bank of the Cophen or Cabul river, through the great gate of the Khyber Pass.

But it was impossible to advance to the Indus without securing his communications, and for this purpose it was necessary to subjugate the river-valleys to the left of the Cabul, among the huge western spurs of the Himalaya mountains.

It was perhaps not far from Jelalabad that the army came to a city which was called Nysa. The name immediately awakened in the minds of all the Greeks the memory of their god Dionysus. For Mount Nysa was the mythical place where he had been nursed by nymphs when he was born from the thigh of Zeus. The mountain was commonly supposed to be in Thrace, but an old hymn placed it 'near the streams of Nile'; it had no place on the traveller's chart. But here was an actual Nysa; and close to the town was a hill whose name resembled *mêros*, the Greek word for 'thigh', and whose slopes were covered with the god's own ivy. Therefore Nysa, they said, was founded by Dionysus; the god had fared eastward to subdue India, and now Alexander was marching on his tracks. Everywhere on their further march the Greeks and Macedonians were alert to discover traces of the progress of the bacchic god.

Nysa (Nanghenhar)

For the purposes of this campaign Alexander divided his army. Hephaestion, taking three regiments of the phalanx, half the Macedonian cavalry, all the mercenary cavalry, advanced by the Khyber Pass, with orders to construct a bridge across the Indus. The king, with the rest of the army, including the light troops, plunged into the difficult country north of the river; and the winter was spent in warfare with the hardy hill-folks, especially the Aspasians and Assacenes, and in capturing their impregnable fortresses, in the district of the Kunar, in remote Chitral, and in the Panjkar and Swat valleys. Massaga, of the Assacenian people, in the Swat valley, was one of the most important strongholds that Alexander captured;[5] we cannot point it out on the map, but Dyrta, another fortress of the same people, may be fairly sought in Dir. The most wonderful exploit of all was the scaling and taking of the rock of Aornus, to which the Assacenes had fled for refuge after Alexander's successful operations in the Swat valley.[6] Perched high on the summit of Pir-sar, some 5000 feet above the Indus, this natural fortress had defied, so tradition ran, even Heracles. Using a local guide Alexander made the difficult ascent to an attacking base, filled in with a mound the ravine below the rock, brought his catapults into play and stormed the fortress. Even now a brief campaign in

Alexander's campaigns in Chitral, etc.

(Açrakas)

Aornus

481

Crossing of
the Indus
near
Attock,
326 B.C.

Buner was needed before the Assacenes could be safely left.

After this severe winter campaign the army rested on the nearer bank of the Indus until spring had begun, and then, with the solemnity of games and sacrifices, crossed the river and marched a three days' journey eastward to Taxila. The rich country of these Aryan husbandmen was a striking and pleasant contrast to the barren homes of the shepherds of Bactria and Sogdiana. The prince of Taxila met Alexander with obsequious pomp, and other lesser princes assembled at the city to do him homage. The administration of the recent conquests was now arranged. A new satrapy, embracing the lands west of the Indus, was established and entrusted to Philip, son of Machatas; Macedonian garrisons were placed in Taxila and some other places east of the Indus, and Philip was given the general command of these troops. This shows the drift of Alexander's policy. The Indus was to be the eastern boundary of his direct rule; beyond the Indus, he intended to create no new provinces, but only to form a system of protected states.

Alexander then marched by a southward road to the Hydaspes, where he was to meet the only power in the land which could hope to resist his progress. Porus had accepted the challenge and, having gathered an army from thirty to forty thousand strong, was encamped on the left bank of the river, to contest the crossing. Moreover, Abisares of Kashmir promised him aid, although he had sent marks of homage to Alexander. The boats which had been constructed on the Indus for transporting the troops were, by Alexander's orders, sawn in two or three pieces according to their size and conveyed on carts to the Hydaspes. After a march, which was made slow and laborious by the heavy tropical rain, the invaders encamped on the right bank of the river, near Jalalpur, and saw the lines of Porus on the opposite shore, protected by a multitude of elephants, his most formidable weapon of war. It was useless to think of crossing in the face of this host, for the horses, who could not endure the smell and noise of the elephants, would certainly have been drowned; and the men would have found it almost impossible to land, amid showers of javelins, on the slimy, treacherous edge of the stream. All the fords in the neighbourhood were watched. Alexander adopted various measures to deceive and puzzle the enemy. He collected large stores of corn, as if he had made up his mind to remain for many days

Alexander
and Porus
encamped
on the
Hydaspes

where he was; he spread the rumour that he intended to wait till the season of rains was over; and he kept his troops in constant motion, sending detachments hither and thither. Then one night his trumpets blew, his cavalry rode down to the edge of the water, and to the eyes of the enemy it seemed the whole army was about to cross. Porus moved his elephants up to the bank and drew up in line of battle. But it proved to be a false alarm. The same feint was repeated again and again. Each night the Macedonian camp was in motion as if for crossing; each night the Indians stood long hours in the wind and rain. But when he saw that the noise was never followed by action, Porus became weary of these useless nightly watches and disregarded the alarms of a faint-hearted foe. Alexander meanwhile was maturing a plan which he was able to carry out when he had put Porus off his guard.

About 16 miles upwards from the camp, the Hydaspes makes a bend, changing its course from south to westward, and opposite the jutting angle a thickly wooded island rose amid the stream, while a dense wood covered the right shore. Here Alexander determined to cross. He caused the boats to be conveyed thither and remade in the shelter of the wood close to a deep ravine; he had prepared skins stuffed with straw, such as he had used in passing the Oxus. When the time came, he took with him the hypaspists, two regiments of the phalanx, two battalions of the Companion cavalry with the royal squadron, the Indian and Scythian cavalry and the mounted archers, and the Agrianian javelin-men and the archers, and led them to the wooded promontory, marching at a considerable distance from the river in order to avoid the observation of the enemy. A sufficient force was left in the camp under the command of Craterus, with orders not to cross, unless Porus either moved his entire army from its present position or was defeated and routed. Three small detachments were posted at points between the camp and the island, to cross and help at the right moment. The king arrived at the appointed spot later in the evening, and throughout the wet stormy night he directed the preparations for passing the swollen stream.

Alexander's
artifice

The wind and rain, which had effectually concealed all the noise from the ears of hostile outposts on the bank, abated before dawn, and the passage began. Alexander led the way in a barque of 30 oars, and the island was safely passed; but land was hardly reached before they were sighted by Indian scouts, who galloped off at full speed to warn their chieftain. The king, who was the first to leap ashore, waited till the cavalry had been disembarked and marshalled, but on advancing he discovered that he had landed not on the bank but on an island which was parted from the bank by a small channel now swollen with rain. It was some time before a passage for wading could be found, and the water was breast-high. At last the whole force was safely landed on the bank, and Alexander arranged his men for the coming battle—the third of the three great battles of his life. He had with him only 6000 heavy infantry, about 4000 light foot, 5000 cavalry, including 1000 mounted archers. Taking all the cavalry with him, he rode rapidly forward towards the camp of Porus, leaving the infantry to follow. If the whole host of Porus should come out to meet him, he would wait for the infantry, but if the enemy showed symptoms of retreating, he would dash in among them with his superior cavalry. Presently he saw a troop coming; it was the son of Porus at the head of 1000 horsemen and 60 war-chariots, too late to impede the landing of the Macedonians. As soon as he perceived the small number of the foe, Alexander charged and easily drove them back, slaying the prince and four hundred of his men.

Battle of the Hydaspes

But Porus himself was advancing with his main army, having left a small force to guard the river-bank against Craterus. When he reached sandy ground, suitable for the movements of his cavalry and war-chariots, he drew up his line of battle. In front of all he placed 200 elephants at intervals of 100 feet, and at some distance behind them his infantry, perhaps up to 30,000, covering the intervals, but extending beyond the elephants on both flanks. On the wings he placed his cavalry, perhaps up to 4000, with his chariots in front of them, 150 on each wing. Alexander waited for his infantry to come up, then rested them so that they would be fresh for the battle, and made his dispositions. For the reconstruction of the decisive engagement we have to rely on Arrian, for the lesser sources provide no significant evidence of the tactics, but there are obscurities and omissions in his text.[7]

Alexander's general plan is clear enough. His greatest danger came from the elephants, whom his horses had not met in action and who would badly maul his infantry if they had to bear the main brunt of the battle. He therefore instructed Seleucus and the other infantry commanders to hold their line back while he struck first with the cavalry, which was considerably stronger than the Indians in numbers and experience. Porus' scouts had probably reported that Alexander's cavalry was massed on his right wing, for he seems to have brought his own cavalry round from his right wing to reinforce the left before battle was joined. Alexander first sent in his mounted archers to spread confusion among the Indian infantry's left wing which was not protected by elephants. He himself then led more than half his cavalry to launch the main attack. By riding to the right and so threatening to round the Indian cavalry and attack their infantry in the rear he drew the Indians away from their main forces. Meanwhile he had ordered Coenus with two cavalry battalions to ride as if he were intending to attack the Indian right wing, but when he saw the Indian cavalry being drawn to their left by Alexander he was to change direction, ride after them and attack their rear. This manoeuvre forced the Indians to reform their ranks into two fronts, and it was not long before they were driven back to shelter behind their elephants. Then those elephant riders who were on this side of the army drove the beasts against the Macedonian horses, and at the same time the Macedonian footmen rushed forward and attacked the animals which were now turned sidewards towards them. But the other elephants of the line were driven into the ranks of the hypaspists, and dealt destruction, trampling down and striking furiously. Heartened by the success of the elephants, the Indian cavalry rallied and charged but, beaten back by the Macedonian horse, who were now formed in a serried mass, they again sought shelter behind the wall of elephants. But many of the beasts were now furious with wounds and beyond control; some had lost their riders and in the mêlée they trampled on friends and foes alike. The Indians suffered most, for they were surrounded and confined to the space in which the animals raged, while the Macedonians could attack the animals on side or rear, and then retreat into the open when they turned to charge. At length, when the elephants grew weary and their charges were feebler, Alexander closed in. He gave the order for the hypaspists to advance in close array, shield to shield, while he, re-forming his squadrons, dashed in from the side. The enemy's cavalry, already weakened and dislocated, could not withstand the double shock and was cut to pieces. The hypaspists rolled on upon the enemy's infantry, who, though they had hitherto taken no serious part in the fight,

The Indian rally

soon broke and fled. Meanwhile the generals on the other side of the river, Craterus and the rest, discovering that fortune was declaring for Alexander, crossed the river without resistance and arrived in time to consummate the victory by pursuing the fugitives. Porus, who had shown himself a mediocre general but a most valiant soldier, when he saw most of his forces scattered, his elephants lying dead or straying riderless, did not flee—as Darius had twice fled—but remained fighting, seated on an elephant of commanding height, until he was wounded in the right shoulder, the only part of his body unprotected by mail. Then he turned round and rode away. Alexander, struck with admiration at his prowess, sent messengers who overtook him and induced him to return. The victor, riding out to meet the old prince, was impressed by his stature and beauty, and asked him how he would wish to be treated. 'Treat me like a king,' said Porus. 'For my own sake,' said Alexander, 'I will; ask for your own sake what you desire.' 'That,' replied Porus, 'containeth all.'

And Alexander treated his captive royally. He not only gave him back his kingdom, henceforward to be a protected state under Macedonian suzerainty, but largely increased its borders. This royal treatment, however, though it pleased the generous impulses of Alexander, was inspired by deep policy. He could rest the security of his rule beyond the Indus on no better base than the mutual jealousy of two moderately powerful princes. He had made the lord of Taxila as powerful as was safe; the reinstatement of his rival Porus would be the best guarantee for his loyalty. But on either side of the Hydaspes, close to the scene of the battle, two cities were founded, which would serve as garrisons in the subject land. On the right hand, the city of Bucephala, named after Alexander's horse, which died here—probably shortly before the battle—of old age and weariness; on the left, Nicaea, the city of victory.

Alexander's cities on the Hydaspes

Leaving Craterus to build the cities, Alexander marched northwards to subdue the Glausae, a hill-folk on the border of Kashmir, and at the same time to intimidate Abisares. Then skirting the hills, he crossed the Acesines, more than a mile and a half broad, with great peril and some loss, into the territory of a namesake and nephew of Porus. This Porus was at enmity with his uncle, who probably claimed overlordship over him; he had sent messages of submission to Alexander before the battle, but, disappointed and frightened at the favour which the conqueror

(Mong)
Alexander's advance through the Punjab

had shown his uncle, he fled eastward. Alexander himself hastened in pursuit, crossing the Hydraotis, which, unlike the Acesines, was easily passed, but he left Hephaestion to march southward and subdue the land of the younger Porus, as well as the free communities between the two rivers—all this northern portion of the 'doab' or interfluvial tract to be added to the realm of the elder Porus. The news that the Cathaeans, a free and warlike people, whom Porus and Abisares had, some time before, failed to conquer, were determined to give him battle, diverted Alexander from the pursuit. He advanced against their chief town Sangala, strongly walled and protected on one side by a hill and on the other by a lake. It was probably near Amritsar, to the north-west of Lahore. The Cathaeans, supported by some neighbouring tribes, had made a stockade with a triple line of waggons round the hill. After a severe struggle the entrenchment was carried and the defenders retreated into the city. They tried to escape across the lake under the cover of night, but Alexander discovered the plan and lined the shores with soldiers. Then the place was stormed; the neighbouring peoples submitted, and all this land was likewise placed under the lordship of Porus. Thus of the four river-bounded tracts which compose the Punjab, the largest, between Indus and Jehlum, belonged to Omphis of Taxila, while the three others, between Jehlum and Bëas, were assigned to Porus.

(Ravee)

Capture of Sangala

Alexander now advanced to the Hyphasis, or Bëas, and reached it higher up than the point where it joins the Sutlej to form the Çatadru or 'Hundred Streams'. It was destined to be the furthest landmark of his march. He wished to go farther and explore the lands of the Ganges, but an unlooked-for obstacle occurred. The Macedonians were worn out with years of hard campaigning and weary of this endless rolling on into the unknown. Their numbers had dwindled; the remnant of them were battered and grown old before their time. The terrible rains, which had beaten incessantly upon them since the crossing of the Indus and had made their labours doubly laborious, were the last weight in the scale. Their gear was worn out; the hoofs of their horses, as one of the campaigners described, were rubbed away by the long rough journeys; their arms were blunted and broken in hard combats; the bodies of the veterans were enveloped in Indian rags, for their Greek clothes were worn out. All yearned for their homeland in the west. They had won glory enough; why heap

The term of Alexander's march

The army refuses to advance

up toil on toil and peril on peril? On the banks of the Hyphasis the crisis came; the men resolved to go no farther, and their resolution was strengthened by the information that they would have to cross the Indian desert, a journey of eleven days, before they reached the fertile regions of the Ganges. At a meeting of the officers which Alexander summoned, Coenus was the spokesman of the general feeling. The king, not a little vexed, dismissed them, and summoning them on the morrow, declared that he intended to advance himself, but would constrain no man to follow him; let the Macedonians go back to Macedonia and tell how they abandoned their king in a hostile land. He retired to his tent and for two days refused to see any of his Companions, hoping that their hearts would be softened. But though his resentment made them unhappy, the Macedonians did not relent or go back from their purpose. On the third day Alexander offered sacrifices preliminary to crossing the river. But the victims—and this was assuredly no freak of chance—gave unfavourable signs. Then the king yielded and signified to the stubborn army that he had decided to return. When his will was made known, the way-worn veterans burst into wild joy; the greater part of them shed tears. They crowded round the royal tent, blessing the unconquered king, that he had permitted himself to be conquered for once, by his Macedonians. On the banks of the Hyphasis Alexander erected 12 towering altars to the 12 great gods of Olympus, as a thank-offering for having strewn his wonderful path with victories and led him safely within reach of the world's end.

Alexander's conception of the geography of Asia

Within reach of the world's end, and not to reach it—this was the disappointment which Alexander suffered at the Hyphasis. To understand fully the measure of this disappointment we must realise his geographical conceptions. Of the southern extension of Asia in the great Indian promontory, and Further India with its huge islands, he knew nothing; of the vastness of China, of the existence of Siberia he had not the least suspicion. He supposed that the Ganges discharged its waters into the ocean which bounded the earth on the east, as the Atlantic bounded it on the west; and he imagined that this eastern sea, washing the base of the further slopes of the Hindu-Kush and Pamir mountains, and rounding the northern shores of Scythia, was continuous with the Caspian. And just as he planned to navigate the southern ocean, from the mouth of the Indus to the Arabian Gulf,

or perhaps even round Libya to the Pillars of Heracles, plans to which we shall presently refer, so he probably dreamed of navigating the eastern ocean from the mouth of the Ganges and winning round to the shores of Scythia and Hyrcania. On annexation or effective conquest beyond the Hyphasis the mind of Alexander does not seem to have been bent. He had only a small army with him, for he had left large detachments on his way from the Jehlum to the Bëas; and he expected no hostilities from the tranquil dwellers of the Ganges. His expedition would have been in the first instance a journey of exploration; circumstances might have made it a march of conquest.

Alexander is often represented as a madman, dazzled by wild and whirling visions of dominion and glory, impelled by an insatiable lust of conquest for conquest's sake. But in judging his schemes, which in themselves seem wild to us who know the configuration of the earth, we must contract our imagination to the compass of his false notions and imperfect knowledge. If the form and feature of the earth were what he pictured it to be, twenty years would have sufficed to make his empire conterminous with its limits. He might have ruled from the eastern to the western ocean, from the ultimate bounds of Scythia to the shores of Libya; he might have brought to pass in the three continents a universal peace, and dotted the habitable globe with his Greek cities. Alexander was ambitious, but ambition did not blind him; he was perfectly capable of discerning shine from substance. The advance to the Indus was no mere wanton aggression, but was necessary to establish secure routes for Indian trade, which was at the mercy of the wild hill-tribes; and the subjugation of the Punjab was a necessity for securing the Indus frontier. The solid interests of commerce underlay the ambitions of the Macedonian conqueror. It is not without significance that Phoenician merchants accompanied his army.

Alexander retraced his steps to the Hydaspes, on his way picking up Hephaestion, who had founded a new city on the banks of the Acesines. On the Hydaspes, Craterus had not only built the two cities at the scene of the great battle, but had also prepared a large fleet of transports, which was to carry part of the army down the river to reach the Indus and the ocean. The fleet was placed under the command of Nearchus, and the king's own ship was piloted by Onesicritus, who afterwards wrote a book on Alexander's expedition.

The rest of the army, divided into two parts, marched along either bank, under Hephaestion and Craterus.

As they advanced they swept the southern portions of the doabs, reducing the tribes which did not submit. The only formidable resistance that they encountered was from the free and warlike tribe of the Malli, whose territory stretched on both sides of the Ravee. Having routed a large host of these Indians on the southern bank of the river, Alexander pursued them to their chief city, Sangala, whose site has not yet been identified. Since then the Ravee has changed its bed; in the days of Alexander it used to flow into the Chenab below Multan. Here he had a nearly fatal adventure. The city had been easily taken, and the Indians had retreated into the citadel. Two ladders were brought to scale the earthen wall, but it was found hard to put them in place beneath the shower of missiles *Siege of Sangala* from above. Impatient at the delay, Alexander seized a ladder and climbed up under the cover of his shield. Peucestas, who bore the sacred buckler from the temple of Ilion, and Leonnatus followed, and Abreas ascended the other ladder. When the king reached the battlement, he hurled down or slew the Indians who were posted at that spot. The hypaspists, when they saw their king standing upon the wall, a mark for the whole garrison of the fortress, made a rush for the ladders, and both ladders broke under the weight of the crowd. Only those three—Peucestas, Leonnatus, and Abreas— reached the wall before the ladders broke. His friends implored Alexander to leap down; he answered their cries by leaping down among the enemy. He alighted on his feet. With his back to the wall he stood alone against the throng of foes, who recognised the Great King. With his sword he cut down their leader and some others who ventured to rush at him; he felled two more with stones; and the rest, not daring to approach, pelted him with missiles. Meanwhile his three companions had cleared the wall of its defenders and leapt down to help their king. Abreas fell slain by a javelin. Then Alexander himself received a wound in *Alexander wounded* the breast. For a space he stood and fought, but at last sank on his shield fainting through loss of blood. Peucestas stood over him with the holy shield of Troy, Leonnatus guarded him on the other side, until rescue came. Having no ladders, the Macedonians had driven pegs into the wall, and a few had clambered up as best they could and flung themselves down into the fray. Some of these succeeded in opening one of the gates, and then the fort was taken. No man, woman, or child in the place was spared by the infuriated soldiers, who thought that their king was dead. But though the wound was serious, Alexander recovered. The rumour of his death reached the camp where the main army was waiting at the junction of the Ravee with the Chenab, and it produced deep consternation and despair. Reassuring letters were not believed; so Alexander caused himself to be carried to the banks of the Ravee and conveyed by water down to the camp. When he drew near, the canopy which sheltered his bed in the stern of the vessel was removed. The soldiers, still doubting, thought it was his corpse they saw, until the barque drew close to the bank and he waved his hand. Then the host shouted for joy. When he was carried ashore, he was lifted for a moment on horseback, that he might be the better seen by all, and then he walked a few steps for their greater reassurance.

This adventure is an extreme case of *Alexander's* Alexander's besetting weakness, which has *ander's* been illustrated in many other of his actions. *rashness in* In the excitement of battle, he was apt to *endanger-* forget his duties as a leader. Though one of *ing his* the most consummate generals that the world *person* has seen, he took a far keener delight in fighting in the thickest of the fray, or heading a charge of cavalry, than in manoeuvring an army or contriving strategical operations. His eyes and ears were ever filled

With the brilliance of battle, the bloom and the beauty, the splendour of spears.

He could not resist the temptations of danger, and he had hardly conducted a single campaign in which he had not been wounded. On the last and most flagrant occasion, when some of his intimate friends upbraided him for acting as a soldier instead of acting as a general, he was deeply hurt, for his conscience pricked him. To have endangered his own safety was a crime against the whole army.

The Malli made a complete submission, and *325 B.C.* their example was followed by the Oxydraces, their southern neighbours, who were also renowned for their warlike character. These lower parts of the Punjab were not added to the dominion of Porus, but were placed in direct dependence on the satrapy which had been committed to Philip. When Alexander had recovered from his wound, the fleet sailed downward past the junction of the Hyphasis, and the Indian tribes submitted, presenting to the conqueror the characteristic products of India, gems, fine draperies, tame lions and tigers. At the place where the united stream of the four lesser rivers joins the mighty flow of the Indus, the foundations were laid of a new Alexandria, to be the great trade centre between the Punjab and the territory of the lower Indus, and to be the bulwark of the southern frontier of the province of Philip. The next stage of the southward advance was the capital town of the Sogdi, which lay upon the river. Alexander refounded it as a Greek colony and built wharfs; it was known as the Sogdian Alexandria and was destined to be the residence of a southern satrapy which was to extend to the sea-coast. This province was committed to Peithon, the son of Agenor.

The principalities of the rich and populous land of Sind were distinguished from the states of the north by the great political power enjoyed by the Brahmins. Under the influence of this caste, which was vehemently opposed to the intrusion of the foreigners, the princes either defied Alexander or, if they submitted at first, speedily rebelled. The spring was spent in reducing these regions, and it was nearly midsummer when the king reached Patala at the vertex of the Indus delta. On the tidings of an insurrection in Arachosia, he had dispatched Craterus with a considerable portion of the army to march through the Bolan Pass into southern Afghanistan and put down the revolt. Alexander himself designed to march through Baluchistan, and Craterus was ordered to meet him in Kirman, near the entrance of the Persian Gulf. Another division of the army was to go by sea to the mouth of the Tigris. The king fixed upon Patala to be for the Indian empire what the most famous of his Alexandrias was for Egypt. He charged Hephaestion with the task of fortifying the citadel and building an ample harbour. Then he sailed southward himself to visit the southern ocean. It was the season at which the monsoons blow from the south-west, and the Macedonians, accustomed to the tideless midland sea, were at first much perplexed by the ebb and flow of the oceanic tide, at this time especially high and violent in the main arm of the river. Several ships were lost, but the sailors soon mastered the secret of the times and tides, and Alexander sailed out into the open sea. He sacrificed to Poseidon; he poured drink-offerings from a golden cup to the Nereids and Dioscuri, and to Thetis the mother of his ancestor Achilles, and then hurled the cup into the waves. This ceremony inaugurated his plan of opening a seaway for commerce between the West and the Far East. The enterprise of discovering this seaway was entrusted to Nearchus, an officer who was an intimate com-

panion of his own and possessed the confidence of the troops. Alexander started on his land-march in the early autumn, but Nearchus and the fleet were to wait till October, in order to be helped forward by the eastern monsoons.

Alexander's Return to Babylon

No enterprise of Alexander was so useless, and none so costly, as the journey through the desert of Gedrosia, the land which is now known as the Mekran. Of the inhospitable character of the country he must have had general information, but he had no idea of the hardships and terrors of the march which awaited him. His guiding motive in choosing this route was to make provisions for the safety of the fleet, to dig wells and store food at certain places along the coast. He also had in view the subjugation of the Oritae, a hardy warlike people who dwelled in the mountains on the eastern limit of the wilderness. But if it had been only a matter of subduing the Oritae, this could easily have been accomplished by an expedition from Patala. The march through the Mekran and the voyage of Nearchus were interdependent parts of the same adventure; and so timid were the mariners of those days that the voyage into unknown waters seemed far more formidable than the journey through the desert.

With perhaps 30,000 men, Alexander passed the mountain wall which protects the Indus delta, and crossing the river Arbis he reduced the Oritae to subjection. He chose their chief village Rambacia for the foundation of a colony, the Orite Alexandria; it was important to have stations on his projected ocean-route. Then he descended into the desert of Gedrosia. No resistance met him here, for there were no folk to resent his intrusion—only a few miserable villages in the hills, or more miserable fishing hamlets on the coast. The army moved painfully through the desert of rocks and sand, waterless and barren, and part of the scanty provisions that the foragers obtained had to be stored on the shore for the coming of the fleet. It was often almost impossible to step through the deep sinking sand; the pitiless heat rendered night marches necessary; and those marches were frequently of undue length, owing to the need of reaching a spring of water. Alexander himself is said to have trudged on foot and shared all the hardships of the way. It was doubtless the non-combatants and camp-followers who suffered most. At length the waste was crossed; and, leaving the coast regions, the remnant of the army marched north to Pura, the residence of the satrapy of Gedrosia. It is said that the survivors, exhausted and dishevelled, were the smaller part of the army which had set forth from India two months before; and the losses of that terrible Gedrosian journey exceeded the losses of all Alexander's campaigns. But this is probably a heightened statement of the calamities of the march.

Having rested at Pura, the king proceeded to Kirman, where he was joined by Craterus, who had suppressed the revolt in Arachosia. Presently news arrived that the fleet had reached the Kirman coast, and soon Nearchus arrived at the camp and relieved Alexander's anxiety. He too had a tale to tell of hardships and perils. The hostile attitude of the Indians, when Alexander's back was turned, had forced him to start a month before the season of the east winds, and contrary south winds kept him for twenty-four days in a haven at some distance to the west of the delta. Then a storm wrecked three of his ships near Cocala. During the rest of their voyage the seafarers suffered badly for want of sweet water and provisions. But the king was overjoyed that they had arrived at all. Nearchus was dismissed to complete the voyage by sailing up the Persian Gulf and the Pasitigris river to Susa; Hephaestion was sent to make his way thither along the coast; while Alexander himself marched through the hills by Persepolis and Pasargadae.

It was high time for Alexander to return. There was hardly a satrap, Persian or Macedonian, in any land, who had not oppressed his province by violence and rapacity; and some, in the expectation that the king would never come back from the Far East, had formed plots for establishing independent principalities. In Kirman, in Persis, and at Susa, the most pressing business of the king was to re-establish his authority by punishing without favour or mercy the governors and officers who were found guilty of treason and oppression. Many satraps were deposed or put to death; Atropates of Media was one of the few who had been faithful to his charge. But the military garrison of Media had not behaved so well; and none of Alexander's sentences at this juncture was more effective than the execution of two officers and 600 soldiers for having plundered the temples and sepulchres of that province. Of all evil deeds, that perhaps which most vexed the king was the opening and plundering of the sepulchre of Cyrus at Pasargadae; it was more than a common

sacrilege, it was an outrage against the majesty of kings. He tortured the Magians who were the guardians of the tomb, but did not discover the author of the outrage.

One guilty minister fled at Alexander's approach. This was Harpalus, who had once before been disloyal but had been forgiven and placed in charge of the financial administration of the empire. He squandered his master's money in riotous living at Babylon and, as the news of these scandals reached Alexander in India, he deemed it prudent to move westward. Taking a large sum of money, he went to Cilicia and, hiring a bodyguard of 6000 mercenaries, he lived in royal state at Tarsus with Glycera, an Athenian courtesan. On Alexander's return, Tarsus was not safe, and he fled to Greece, where we shall meet him presently.[8]

Having punished with a stern hand the misrule of his satraps, Macedonian and Persian alike, Alexander began to carry out schemes which he had formed for breaking down the barrier which divided East from West. He had unbarred and unveiled the Orient to the knowledge and commerce of the Mediterranean peoples, but his aim was to do much more than this; it was no less than to fuse Asia and Europe into a homogeneous unity. He devised various means for achieving this object. He proposed to transplant Greeks and Macedonians into Asia, and Asiatics into Europe, as permanent settlers. This plan had indeed been partly realised by the foundation of his numerous mixed cities in the Far East. The second means was the promotion of intermarriages between Persians and Macedonians, and this policy was inaugurated in magnificent fashion at Susa. The king himself married Statira, the daughter of Darius; his friend Hephaestion took her sister; and a large number of Macedonian officers wedded the daughters of Persian grandees. The nuptials were celebrated on the same day and according to the Persian fashion; Alexander is said to have feasted 9000 guests. Of the general mass of the Macedonians 10,000 are said to have followed the example of their officers and taken Asiatic wives; all those were liberally rewarded by Alexander. He looked forward to the offspring of these unions as a potent instrument for the further fusing of the races. It is to be noticed that Alexander, already wedded to the princess of Sogdiana, adopted the polygamous custom of Persia; and he even married another royal lady, Parysatis, daughter of Ochus. These marriages were purely dictated by policy; they were meant as an example, for Alexander never

The voyage of Nearchus, October–December, 325 B.C.

(? Karachi)

Misconduct of Alexander's governors, and his dealings with them

Flight of Harpalus

(p. 496) Alexander's policy: the fusion of Greeks and Asiatics;

means for accomplishing this: (1) transplantation and colonisation; (2) intermarriage;

came under the influence of women. The bridals of Susa were a lesson in political marriages on a vast scale.

(3) equal military service

But the most effective means for bringing the two races together was the institution of military service on a perfect equality. With this purpose in view, Alexander, not long after the death of Darius, had arranged that in all the eastern provinces the native youth should be drilled and disciplined in Macedonian fashion and taught to use the Macedonian weapons. In fact, Hellenic military schools were established in every province, and at the end of five years an army of 30,000 Hellenized barbarians was at the Great King's disposition. At his summons this army gathered at Susa, and its arrival created a natural, though unreasonable, feeling of discontent among the Macedonians, who divined that Alexander aimed at making himself independent of their services. His schemes of transforming the character of his army were also indicated by the enlistment of Persians, Bactrians, Areians, and other orientals in the Macedonian cavalry regiments, and the enrolling of nine distinguished Persians in the royal Agema itself. The general dissatisfaction was not allayed by the king's liberality in defraying all the debts of the soldiers.

Macedonian mutiny at Opis

Alexander left Susa for Ecbatana in spring. He sailed down the river Pasitigris to the Persian Gulf, surveyed part of the coast, and sailed up the Tigris, removing the weirs which the Persians had constructed to hinder navigation. The army joined him on the way, and he halted at Opis. Here he held an assembly of the Macedonians and formally discharged all those—about 10,000 in number —whom old age or wounds had rendered unfit for warfare, promising to make them comfortable for life. He fondly thought that his words would be welcomed with delight, but he was disappointed. The smouldering discontent found a voice now. The cry was raised, 'Discharge us all'; and some tauntingly added, 'Go and conquer with your father Ammon'. The king may well have been taken aback. The men who on the banks of the Hyphasis had declared themselves worn out with war and toil and sick with yearning for their homes were now indignant when he honourably discharged their veterans. Alexander leapt down from the platform into the shouting throng; he pointed out 13 of the most forward rioters and bade his hypaspists seize them and put them to death. The rest were cowed. Amid a deep silence the king remounted the platform and in a bitter speech

he discharged the whole army. Then he retired into his palace, and on the third day summoned the Persian and Median nobles and appointed them to posts of honour and trust which had hitherto been filled by Macedonians. The names of the Macedonian regiments were transferred to the new barbarian army. When they heard this, the Macedonians, who still lingered in their quarters, miserable and uncertain whether to go or stay, appeared before the gates of the palace. They laid down their arms submissively and implored admission to the king's presence. Alexander came out, and there was a tearful reconciliation. This dramatic incident possesses no historical importance like the action of the troops on the Hyphasis, and it is only significant in so far as it marks the last futile explosion of Macedonian sentiment against the liberal policy of the king, the final protest of men who knew that they would have to acquiesce in a new order of things. The reconciliation was sealed with another great feast at which Alexander sat with his Macedonians and Persians and men of standing from other races. All drew from the same mixing bowl and poured the same libations. Alexander prayed for harmony above all things and partnership in the empire between Macedonians and Persians.[9]

Veterans sent back to Macedonia

The veterans started for home under the leadership of Craterus and Polyperchon; they left behind the children whom Asiatic women had borne to them, the king promising to bring them up in Macedonian fashion. Craterus was to supersede Antipater as regent of Macedonia, and Antipater was to come out to Asia with a fresh supply of troops. This arrangement was desirable, on account of the estranged relations which existed between Antipater and the queen-mother, whose letters to Alexander were always teeming with mutual accusations.

Alexander at Ecbatana

The summer and early winter were spent at the Median capital. Here a sorrow, the greatest that could befall him, befell Alexander. Three thousand professional players or 'Dionysiac artists', as they were called, had arrived from Greece, and Ecbatana was festive with revels and dramatic exhibitions. In the midst of the gaiety, Hephaestion fell ill, languished for seven days, and died. Alexander was plunged into despair at losing his bosom friend; he fasted three days, and the whole empire went into mourning; it is said that he crucified the miserable physician whose skill had been found wanting. Inconsolable the lonely monarch might well be. He could have other companions, other faithful counsellors and devoted servants; but he knew that he would never

Death of Hephaestion; Alexander's grief

find another to whom he would be simply 'my friend Alexander' and not 'my lord the king'. The body was sent to Babylon to be burned; 10,000 talents were set apart for a funeral of unsurpassed magnificence.

Alexander set out for Babylon towards the end of the year, and on his way he enjoyed the excitement of hunting down the Cossaeans, a hill-folk of Luristan, who made brigandage their trade. The slaughter of these robbers, who were chased to their mountain nests, was described as an offering to the spirit of Hephaestion. As Alexander advanced to Babylon, ambassadors came to him from Libya, from the Lucanians and Bruttians of south Italy who feared vengeance for the death of Alexander of Epirus, his brother-in-law, and from the Etruscans. These embassies are attested by Arrian from a good source. He also adds the story (from inferior authorities) that Carthaginians also came and envoys from the Aethiopians, Scythians of Europe, Celts and Iberians. They brought their differences to Alexander: 'then especially did he appear to be lord of the whole earth and sea'. Certain Greek writers even included Rome in the list: 'when Alexander saw the bearing, the endurance and the free spirit of the Romans and learnt about their form of government, he prophesied something of their future greatness'. Rome, preoccupied with wars in Italy, can have sent no mission to Alexander. The invention is due to Greek flattery.

When Alexander approached within sight of Babylon, he was met by a deputation of priestly star-gazers who counselled him not to enter the city, for their god Bel had revealed to them that it would not be for his profit. He replied to the Chaldaeans with a verse of Euripides—'The best seer he who guesseth well', and entered at the head of his army. One of his first cares was to take measures for the rebuilding of the temple of Bel, unduly retarded by the wilful neglect of the Chaldaean priests, who were unwilling to appropriate their revenues to the purpose. It has been thought that their attempt to divert the king from entering Babylon may have been connected with their negligence.

Preparations for an Arabian Expedition. Alexander's Death

Ever since the successful voyage of Nearchus, the brain of Alexander had been filled with maritime enterprises. He was bent on the exploration of the northern and the southern oceans. He had already sent Heraclides and a company of shipwrights to the Hyrcanian mountains, to cut wood in the forests and build a fleet to navigate the Caspian Sea and discover its supposed communication with the eastern ocean. But his more immediate and serious enterprise was the circumnavigation and conquest of Arabia. His eastern empire was not complete so long as this peninsula lay outside it. He knew of the rich spice-lands of Arabia Felix, but he had no conception of the vast extent of the desert which renders a land invasion so difficult and so unremunerative. The possession of this country of sand, however, was not his main object; it was only an incident in the grand range of his plans. His visit to India and the voyage of Nearchus had given him new ideas; he had risen to the conception of making the southern ocean another great commercial sea like the Mediterranean. He proposed to make the seaboard of the Persian Gulf a second Phoenicia, and he sent to the Syrian coast for seamen to colonise the shores of the mainland and the islands. He hoped to establish a regular trade route from the Indus to the Tigris and Euphrates, and thence to the canals which connected the Nile with the Red Sea. If he had lived to accomplish this he might have renewed the project of king Necho and hewn a water-way through the neck of Suez. Mighty Babylon would then be in close connection with the new oceanic trade; argosies from Alexandria or Patala could sail into her wharves. Alexander destined Babylon to be the capital of his empire, and doubtless it was a wise choice. But its character was now to be transformed. It was to become a naval station and a centre of maritime commerce. Alexander set about the digging of a great harbour, with room for a thousand keels, and designed the building of shipsteads.

The fleet of Nearchus sailed up the Euphrates and met the king at Babylon. But this fleet was not sufficient for the approaching enterprise. Orders had been sent to Phoenicia for the building of new warships; 12 triremes, three quadriremes, four quinqueremes, and 30 of the smaller thirty-oared barques. These were constructed in pieces, conveyed overland to Thapsacus on the Euphrates, and there put together. Other ships, of cypress wood, were also built in Babylonia. The expedition was to set forth in the summer, and the king occupied part of the intervening time in a voyage down the Euphrates to visit the Pallacopas canal. The snows of winter melting in the late springtide on the north slopes of the Armenian mountains used to swell the waters of the Euphrates and force it to overflow its banks in the Babylonian plain. About 90 miles below Babylon a canal had been dug to drain the superfluous waters into the marshes which stretched for leagues and leagues south-westward. In the autumn the canal was closed by a sluice to prevent the water leaving its bed. But the sluice was out of working order, and Alexander devised a better place, connecting the canal with the river at a different point. He sailed up the canal, lost his way for a while among the swamps, and selected a site for a new city, whose building was immediately begun. We may guess that the city was meant to be the first of a string of fortresses stretching across the desert from Babylonia to the Red Sea.

On his return to Babylon, he found some new western troops which had arrived from Caria and Lydia, and also a body of 20,000 Persians who had been recruited by Peucestas. He proceeded to carry out a sweeping military reform, at which his mind must have been working for some time past. It was nothing less than a complete transformation of his father's phalanx—in fact, of the Hellenic hoplite system. Alexander had done much with the well-drilled phalanx; but his experience had taught him that it was far from being the ideal infantry. The advantages of its sheer weight and solid strength were more than counterbalanced by its want of mobility. Alexander invented a means of increasing the mobility with as little as possible diminution of the weight. He inserted the fresh body of 20,000 Persians into the Macedonian phalanx in the following way. The old depth of the file, 16 men, was retained, but of these only four were Macedonian pikemen—the men of the first three ranks and the hindmost man of all. The 12 intervening places—the fourth to the fifteenth ranks—were filled by Persians lightly armed with their native bows and javelins. This new phalanx required a new kind of tactics, which must have consisted in opening out the ranks, so as to allow the archers and javelin-men to deploy into the intervals and discharge their missiles, and then closing up again, in order to advance in a serried mass, each file bristling with three, no longer with five, spear-points. It was a thoroughly original idea, this combination of heavy and light troops into a tactical unity, but it would need all the skill of the great master to bring it to perfection. The strange thing is to find Alexander introducing this new system, which implied a complete change

Reform of the phalanx

in the drill, on the very eve of his setting forth on the Arabian expedition. We are tempted to think that he had already made experiments —perhaps with that army of 30,000 orientals, drilled in Macedonian fashion, who had come to him at Susa. The tactical reform had also its political bearings. It was another step in the direction of fusing the Macedonian and Persian together and marrying Europe with Asia.

There was one thing, very near to the king's heart, still to be accomplished before he set out—the funeral of Hephaestion. The oracle of Ammon had been consulted touching the honours which should be paid to the dead man, and had ordained that he might be honoured as a hero. In accordance therewith, Alexander ordered that chapels should be erected to Hephaestion in Egyptian Alexandria and other cities. Never were obsequies so magnificent as those which were held at Babylon; the funeral pyre, splendidly decked with offerings, towered to the height of 200 feet.

Funeral of Hephaestion, May 323 B.C.

All was in readiness at length for the expedition to the south. On a day in early June a royal banquet was given in honour of Nearchus and his seamen, shortly about to start on their oceanic voyage. As Alexander was retiring to his chamber at a late hour, a friend named Medius carried him off to spend the rest of the night in a bout of hard drinking. On the morrow he slept long; in the evening he dined with Medius, and another carousal followed. After a bath and a meal in the early hours of the morning, he fell into a feverish sleep. On awaking, he insisted upon preparing the daily sacrifices according to his wont; but the fever was still on him, he could not walk, and was carried to the altar on a couch. He spent the day in bed, actively engaged with Nearchus in discussing the expedition, which he fixed for four days hence. In the cool of the evening he was conveyed to the river and rowed across to a garden villa at the other side. For six days he lay here in high fever, but regularly performing the sacrifices and daily deferring the departure of the expedition. Then his condition grew worse, and he was carried back to the palace, where he won a little sleep, but the fever did not abate. When his officers came to him they found him speechless; the disease became more violent, and a rumour spread among the Macedonian soldiers that Alexander was dead. They rushed clamouring to the door of the palace, and the bodyguards were forced to admit them. One by one they filed past the bed of their young king, but he could not

Illness of Alexander, 16th day of Daesius (June 1.?);

17th;

18th;

19th-24th;

25th;

27th

491

speak to them; he could only greet each by slightly raising his head and signing with his eyes. Peucestas and some others of the Companions passed the night in the temple of Serapis and asked the god whether they should convey the sick man into the temple, if haply he might be cured there by divine help. A voice warned them not to bring him, but to let him remain where he lay. He died on a June evening, before the thirty-third year of his age was completed.[10] Such is the punctilious and authentic account of the last illness of Alexander, as it was recorded in the Court Diary; but it is not sufficient to enable us to discover the precise nature of the fatal disease.

Death of Alexander 28th of Daesius (= June 13)

The untimely deaths of sovereigns at particular junctures have often exercised an influence on the course of events; but no such accident has diverted the paths of history so manifestly and utterly as the death of Alexander. Twelve years had sufficed him to conquer western Asia, and to leave an impress upon it which centuries would not obliterate. And yet his work had only been begun. Many plans for the political transformation of his Asiatic empire had been initiated—plans which reveal his originality of conception, his breadth of grasp, his firm hold of facts, his faculty for organisation, his wonderful brain-power—but all these schemes and lines of policy needed still many years of development under the master's shaping and guiding hand. The unity of the realm, which was an essential part of Alexander's conception, disappeared upon his death. The empire was broken up among a number of hard-headed Macedonians, capable and practical rulers, but without the higher qualities of the founder's genius. They maintained the tolerant Hellenism which he had initiated—his lessons had not been lost upon them—and thus his work was not futile; the toils of even those twelve marvellous years smoothed the path for Roman sway in the East, and prepared the ground for the spread of a universal religion.

His work and what he might have done

It is impossible to write the history of Alexander so as to produce a true impression of his work, because, in the records which we have, the general and soldier fills the whole stage and the statesman is, as it were, hustled out. The details of administrative organisation are lost amidst the sounding of trumpets and the clashing of spears. But it is the details of administration and political organisation which the historical inquirer wants to know, and especially the constitution of the various new-founded cities in the Far East, those novel experiments which set Macedonian, Greek,

and oriental inhabitants side by side. By their silence on these matters the Companions of Alexander, who wrote memoirs about him, unwittingly did him a wrong, and hence there has largely prevailed an unjust notion that he only knew and only cared how to conquer.

It is hardly open to question that this brilliant leader of well-trained regiments would have advanced to the conquest of the West; nor can we doubt that, succeeding where one of his successors failed, he would have annexed *(Pyrrhus)* Sicily and Great Hellas, conquered Carthage, and overrun the Italian peninsula.[11] To apprehend what his death meant for Europe we need not travel farther in our speculations. To the Indies he would certainly have returned and carried out with fresh troops that project of visiting the valley of the Ganges which had been frustrated by his weary army. As it was, he had left no lasting impression upon Indian civilisation, and his successors soon abandoned their hold upon the Punjab. It is needless to add that if Alexander had lived another quarter of a century, he would have widened the limits of geographical knowledge. The true nature of the Caspian Sea would have been determined; the southern extension of the Indian peninsula would have been discovered; and an attempt would have been made to repeat the Phoenician circumnavigation of Africa. Nor could Alexander have failed, in his advanced position on the Jaxartes, to have learned some facts about the vast extension of the Asiatic continent to the east and north, and the curiosities of Chinese civilisation.

His sudden death was no freak of fate or fortune; it was a natural consequence of his character and his deeds. Into thirteen years he had compressed the energies of many lifetimes. If he had been content with the duties of a general and a statesman, laborious and wearing though those duties would have been both to body and to brain, his singularly strong constitution would probably have lasted him for many a long year. But the very qualities of his brilliant temper which most endeared him to his fellows, a warrior's valour and a love of good fellowship, were ruinous to his health. He was covered with scars, and he had probably never recovered from that terrible wound which had been the price of his escapade at Multan. Sparing of himself neither in battle nor at the symposion, he was doomed to die young.

Greece under Macedonia

The tide of the world's history swept us away from the shores of Greece; borne breathlessly along from conquest to conquest in the triumphant train of the Macedonian, we could not pause to see what was happening in the little states which were looking with mixed emotions at the spectacle of their own civilisation making its way over the earth. Alexander's victory at the gates of Issus and his ensuing supremacy by sea had taught many of the Greeks the lesson of caution; the Confederacy of the Isthmus had sent congratulations and a golden crown to the conqueror; and when, a twelvemonth later, the Spartan king Agis, a resolute man without any military ability, renewed the war against Macedonia, he got no help or encouragement outside the Peloponnese.[12] Some hot spirits at Athens proposed to support the movement, but the people were discreetly restrained not only by Phocion and Demades but by Demosthenes himself. Agis induced the Arcadians, except Megalopolis, the Achaeans, except Pellene, and the Eleians, to join him; and having mercenary troops besides, he got together a considerable army. It was easy to gain a few successes before the regent of Macedonia, then occupied with a rising in Thrace, had time to descend on the Peloponnese. The chief object of the allies was to capture Megalopolis, and the federal capital of Arcadia was in the strange position of being besieged by the Arcadian federates. Antipater, as soon as the situation in Thrace set him free, marched southward to the relief of Megalopolis, and easily crushed the allies in a battle fought hard by. Agis fell fighting, and there was no further resistance; Sparta sent up hostages to Alexander, who accorded the conquered Greeks easy terms.

Battle of Megalopolis, 331 B.C.

So long as Darius lived, many of the Greeks cherished secret hopes that fortune might yet turn against Alexander, and maintained clandestine intrigues with Persia. But on the news of his death such hopes expired, and tranquillity prevailed in Hellas. It was not till Alexander's return from India that anything happened to trouble the peace. And in the meantime Greece was experiencing a relief which she had needed for two generations. A field had been opened to her superfluous children, who were pouring by thousands, or rather tens of thousands, into Asia, to find careers, if not permanent homes.

Athens

For Athens the twelve years between the fall of Thebes and the death of Alexander were an interval of singular well-being. The conduct of public affairs was in the hands of the two most honourable statesmen of the day, Phocion and Lycurgus. Supported by the orator Demades, Phocion was able to dissuade the people from embarking on any foolhardy

enterprises; and Demosthenes was sufficiently clear-sighted not to embarrass, but, when required, to support, the policy of peace. Phocion probably did not grudge him the signal triumph which he won over his old rival, Aeschines, for this triumph had only a personal, and not a political, significance. Shortly before Philip's death, Ctesiphon had proposed to honour Demosthenes, both for his general services to the state and especially for his liberality in contributing from his private purse towards the repair of the city-walls, by crowning him publicly in the theatre with a crown of gold. The Council had passed a resolution to this effect; but Aeschines lodged an accusation against the proposer, whose motion technically exposed him to the Graphe Paranomon, and consequently the Council's resolution was not brought before the people. The matter remained in abeyance for about six years, neither party venturing to bring it to an issue, Aeschines by following up his indictment or Ctesiphon by forcing him to bring it into court. The collapse of the attempt of Agis to defy Macedonia probably encouraged Aeschines to face his rival at last. In a speech of the highest ability Aeschines reviewed the public career of Demosthenes, to prove that he was a traitor and responsible for all the disasters of Athens. The reply of Demosthenes, a masterpiece of splendid oratory, captivated the judges, and Aeschines, not winning one-fifth part of their votes, left Athens and disappeared from politics. It is not unfair to say that it was Demosthenes the orator, not Demosthenes the statesman, who convinced the Athenian judges. Apart from his Speech on the Crown, which has been described as the funeral oration on Greek freedom, Demosthenes fell almost silent during these years; he saw that public action on his part would be useless, but perhaps he worked underground.

Attitude of Demosthenes

Speeches on the Crown, 330 B.C.

In these two speeches in the matter of the crown, the most interesting passage is where Aeschines reflects on the changes which had recently come to pass over the face of the earth. We want to know what the Greeks thought of those startling changes, what they felt as they saw the fashion of the world passing and the things which had seemed of great weight and worth in Hellas becoming of small account. Aeschines thus utters their surprise:

Aeschines on the strange events of his time

'All manner of strange events, utterly unforeseen, have befallen in our lifetime. Our extraordinary experiences will seem to those who come after us like a curious tale of marvels. The king of the Persians, who dug the canal through Athos, who bridged the Hellespont,

493

who demanded earth and water from the Greeks, who dared in his letters to declare, "I am the lord of all the world from the rising to the setting of the sun", is at this moment struggling not for domination over other men, but to save his own life and limb. Thebes, even Thebes our neighbour, has been snatched, in the space of a single day, out of the midst of Hellas—justly, for her policy was false; but assuredly she was rather blinded by a heaven-sent infatuation than misled by human perversity. And the poor Spartans, who once were proud to be recognised as leaders of the Greeks, must now go up to Alexander as hostages and throw themselves upon the mercy of the potentate whom they wronged. Our own city, once the asylum of the Greek world, whither all men looked for help, has now ceased to strive for the leadership of the Greeks, for the very ground of her home is in danger.'[13]

Athenian activity in the west

The Macedonian empire had not yet lasted long enough to turn the traffic of the Mediterranean into new channels, and Athens still enjoyed great commercial prosperity. She sent a colony to some unknown place on the Adriatic seaboard, to be a base of protection against the Etruscan rovers, the big menacing eyes of whose pirate craft were a constant terror to traders in those seas.[14] And, although peace was her professed policy, she did not neglect to make provision for war, in case a favourable opportunity should come round for regaining her sovereignty on sea. Money was spent on the navy, which is said to have been increased to well-nigh 400 ships, and on new ship-sheds.

Skeuo-theke of Philo

The handsome 'marble storehouse for the hanging shipgear', designed by the architect Philo, was completed at the harbour of Zea. It was expressly provided that the cases which lined the walls and pillars of this cool triple-aisled arcade should be open, 'in order that those who pass through may be able to see all the gear that is in the gear-store'.

Financial ministry of Lycurgus

The man who was mainly responsible for this naval expenditure was Lycurgus. It is significant of the spirit of Athens at this time that while Phocion and Demades were the most influential men in the Assembly, the finances were in the charge of a statesman who had been so signally hostile to Macedonia that Alexander had demanded his surrender. In recent years considerable changes had been made in the constitution of the financial offices. Eubulus had administered as the president of the Theoric Fund. But now we find the control of the expenditure in the hands of a Minister of the Public Revenue, who was elected by the

people and held office for four years, from one Panathenaic festival to another. Lycurgus was entrusted with this post for twelve years—for the first period in his own name; for the two succeeding periods his activity was cloaked under the names of his son and another nominal minister. He acted, of course, in conjunction with the Council, but the influence of the more permanent and experienced minister upon that annual body was inevitably very great. The new system, it is evident, was a distinct improvement on the old. It was much better that the administration of the revenue should be managed by one competent statesman, unhampered by colleagues, and that his tenure of office should not be limited to a year. The post practically included the functions of a minister of public works, and the ministry of Lycurgus was distinguished by building enterprises. He constructed the Panathenaic stadion on the southern bank of the Ilissus. He rebuilt the Lycean gymnasium, where in these years the philosopher Aristotle used to take his morning and evening 'walks', teaching his 'peripatetic' disciples. It lay somewhere to the east of the city, under Mount Lycabettus. But the most memorable work of Lycurgus was the reconstruction of the theatre of Dionysus. It was he who built the rows of marble benches, climbing up the steep side of the Acropolis, as we see them today; and his original stage-buildings can be distinguished, amidst the ruins, from the mass of later additions and improvements. He canonised, as it were, the three great tragic poets, Aeschylus, Sophocles, and Euripides, by setting up their statues in the theatre, and by carrying a measure that copies of their works should be officially prepared and preserved by the state.

.338-326 B.C.

The stadion; the gymnasium at the temple of Apollo Lyceus;

theatre;

canonical copies of the tragic poets

In connection with the prosperity of Athens and her large public outlay, it is important to observe that the silver mines of Laurion, which had been closed when the Spartans occupied Decelea and had been neglected—for want of capital and enterprise—throughout the whole first half of the fourth century, had been re-opened and were working vigorously. The historian Xenophon had written a pamphlet on the subject of the mines as a neglected source of revenue, and it would be interesting to know whether the revival of the industry is to be ascribed directly or indirectly to the influence of his exhortations.

Working of the Laurion silver mines

Xenophon, De Vectī-gal., 355 B.C.

No sign of the times which followed the defeat of Chaeronea is more striking than the framing of a new system for drilling the young citizens of Athens in the duties of military life. The training began when a youth, having

The re-organisation of the ephebi, c. 336 B.C.

completed his eighteenth year, came of age and was enrolled in the register of his deme, and it lasted for two years.[15] During these two years the young citizen was known as an *ephēbos* and might not appear either as prosecutor or defendant in the law-courts except in a few cases expressly specified. The general supervision over all the Attic ephebi was committed to a marshal (*kosmētēs*), who was elected by the Athenian Assembly; and under him were ten

received from the city a shield and a spear. The second year was spent in patrolling the frontiers of the land and guarding the prisons. The garrison and patrol duties had always devolved upon the young men of Attica, but they were now organised into a new and thorough scheme of discipline—a mild Attic approach to the stern system of Sparta. It almost strikes one as a conscious effort to arrest the decline of the citizen army in the

18.1   The theatre of Dionysus, Athens

masters of discipline (*sōphrōnistai*), one for each tribe. The institution had a religious consecration. The first act in the service of the ephebi was solemnly to 'go round the temples' under the conduct of the masters. Then they served for a year on duty in the guard-houses at Munychia and along the coast, receiving regular military instruction from special drill-masters, who trained them in the exercises of the hoplites, and taught them how to shoot with bow and javelin and to handle artillery. The ephebi of each tribe ate together at barrack messes which were managed by the masters of discipline. At the end of the first year they appeared before an Assembly in the theatre, and, when they had made a public display of their proficiency in the art of warfare, each

face of the encroachments of the mercenary system. The ephebi in their characteristic dress, the dark mantle and the broad-brimmed hat, are a graceful feature in Athenian life and art from this time forward.

It is significant that the whole revival, stimulated by the disaster of Chaeronea, was marked by a religious character. Lycurgus, who belonged to the priestly family of the Eteobutads, was a sincerely pious man, and impressed upon his administration the stamp of his own devotion. Never for a hundred years had there been seen at Athens such a manifestation of zealous public concern for the worship of the gods. The two chief monuments of the Lycurgan epoch—the Panathenaic stadium and the theatre of Dionysus—were, it must always be remembered, religious, not secular, buildings.

Thus Athens discreetly attended to her material well-being and courted the favour of the gods, and the only distress which befell her was a dearth of corn.[16] But on the return of Alexander to Susa, two things happened which imperilled the tranquillity of Greece.

Restoration of exiles

324 B.C.

Alexander promised the Greek exiles—there were more than 20,000 of them—to procure their return to their native cities. He sent Nicanor to the great congregation of Hellas at the Olympian festival, to order the states to receive back their banished citizens. A general reconciliation of parties was a just and politic measure;[17] but it could be objected that, by the terms of the Confederation of Corinth, the Macedonian king had no power to dictate orders to the confederates in the management of their domestic affairs. Only two states objected, Athens and Aetolia; and they objected because, if the edict were enforced, they would be robbed of ill-gotten gains. The Aetolians had possessed themselves of Oeniadae and driven out its Acarnanian owners; by Alexander's edict the rightful inhabitants would now return to their own city and the intruders be dislodged. The position of Athens in Samos was similar; the Samians would now be restored to their own lands, and the Athenian settlers would have to go. Both Athens and Aetolia were prepared to resist.

Alexander's divinity

Another desire was expressed by Alexander at the same time, which was readily acquiesced in. He demanded that the Greeks should recognise his divinity.[18] Sparta is reported to have replied indifferently, 'We allow Alexander to call himself a god, if he likes.' There was not a sensible man at Athens who would have thought of objecting; even the bitterest patriots would have allowed him to be 'the son of Zeus or Poseidon, or whomever he chose'. If the Greeks of Corinth looked up to Alexander as their chieftain and protector— and this was actually their position in regard to him—there was no incongruity in the idea of officially acknowledging his divinity. Ever since the days in which an Homeric king 'was honoured as a god by the people', there was nothing offensive or outlandish to a Greek ear in predicating godhood of a revered sovereign or master. Divine honours had been paid to Lysander; and the Greeks, in complying with Alexander's desire, did not commit themselves more than the pupil of the Academy who erected an altar to his master Plato.

The Episode of Harpalus and the Greek Revolt

Harpalus in Greece, spring, 324 B.C.;

Meanwhile an incident had happened which might have induced some of the patriots to hope that Alexander's empire rested on slippery foundations. Harpalus had arrived off the coast of Attica with 5000 talents, a body of mercenaries, and 30 ships. He had come to excite a revolt against his master. A gift of corn had formerly secured him the citizenship of Athens, but the Athenians prudently refused to harbour him, coming in this guise. He sailed away to Cape Taenaron, always a refuge of adventurers, and leaving his men and ships there returned to Athens with a sum of about 700 talents. He was now received, since he did not come with an armed force, but after a while messages arrived both from Macedonia and from Philoxenus, Alexander's financial minister in western Asia, demanding his surrender. It would have been an act of war to protect the runaway treasurer and his stolen monies; but the Athenians, on the proposal of Demosthenes, adopted a clever device. They arrested Harpalus, seizing his treasure, and said that they would surrender him to officers expressly sent by Alexander, but declined to give him up to Philoxenus or Antipater. It was not long before Harpalus escaped; he returned to Taenaron and was shortly afterwards murdered by one of his fellow-adventurers.

his reception at Athens;

his death

The Harpalus scandal:

The stolen money was deposited in the Acropolis, under the charge of specially-appointed commissioners, of whom Demosthenes was one. It was known by report that the sum was about 700 talents, but Demosthenes and his fellows had strangely omitted to make any official entry or report of the amount. Suddenly it was discovered that only 350 talents were actually in the Acropolis. Charges immediately circulated against the influential politicians, that the other 350 talents had been received in bribes by them before the money was deposited in the citadel. Men of opposite sides were suspected; Demades, for example, as well as Demosthenes. But, apart from the suspicion of bribery, manifest blame rested upon Demosthenes for having grossly neglected his duty. He was responsible for the custody of the treasure, for which Athens was responsible to Alexander. He was bound to demand an investigation, and on his motion the people directed the Council of the Areopagus to hold an inquiry. Philoxenus furnished the account-book of Harpalus, which had come into his hands. By this evidence it was proved that 700 talents had been

bribery and peculation

delivered for safe-keeping in the Acropolis; the entries ceased at this point. It was also shown that certain Athenians had previously been bribed; but Demosthenes was not among them. Other evidence was necessary to show how the missing half of the 700 talents had disappeared. We do not know what this evidence was, but the Court of the Areopagus satisfied themselves that a number of leading statesmen had received considerable sums. Demosthenes appeared in their report as the recipient of 20 talents. The proofs against him were irrefutable, for he confessed the misdemeanour himself and sought to excuse it by the paltry and transparent subterfuge that he had taken it to repay himself for 20 talents which he had advanced to the Theoric Fund. But why should he repay himself, without any authorisation, out of Alexander's money, for a debt owed him by the Athenian state? There can be little doubt that Demosthenes took the money not for personal gratifications, but for the good of his party. It was all the more necessary for his party to clear themselves from implication in such corrupt transactions. We therefore find Hypereides coming forward as a public prosecutor of Demosthenes. We possess considerable portions of his speech; and we have in its complete form another speech, written for one of the other prosecutors by a miserable hack named Dinarchus. The charges against Demosthenes were twofold: he had taken money, and he had culpably omitted to report the amount of the deposit and the neglect of those who were set to guard it. For the second offence alone he deserved a severe sentence. The judges were not excessively severe, if we consider that his behaviour had placed the city in a most embarrassing position towards Alexander. He was condemned to pay a fine of 50 talents. Unable to pay it, he was imprisoned, but presently effected his escape. It was a venial offence in the eyes of Greece for a statesman to take a bribe, provided he did not take it to injure his country; and in view of public opinion the moral character of Demosthenes was little damaged by this tortuous transaction. He was not on a level with men like Nicias and Phocion, who were immune to such temptations; but then nobody ever supposed that he was incorruptible. Yet there were two circumstances which aggravated the case. The money which Demosthenes took was stolen money, which Athens was about to sequester for Alexander; and he was himself a commissioner responsible for its safety. It was far from being an ordinary case of corruption.[19]

Demosthenes a receiver of 20 talents

Condemnation of Demosthenes

If Alexander had lived, the Athenians might have persuaded him to let them remain in occupation of Samos; for he was always disposed to be lenient to Athens. When the news of his death came, men almost refused to credit it; the orator Demades forcibly said, 'If he were indeed dead, the whole world would have smelt of his corpse.' The patriots had been building on the slender hopes of some disaster, and the greatest disaster of all had befallen. It had been recognised as madness to defy the power of Alexander, but it did not seem rash to strike for freedom in the unsettled condition of things after his death. Athens revolted from Macedonia; she was joined by Aetolia and many states in northern Greece, and she secured the services of a band of 8000 discharged mercenaries who had just returned from Alexander's army. One of their captains, the Athenian Leosthenes, occupied Thermopylae, and near that pass the united Greeks gained a slight advantage over Antipater, who had marched southward as soon as he could gather his troops together. The Thessalian cavalry had deserted him, and no state in north Greece except Boeotia remained true to Macedonia. The regent shut himself in the strong hill-city of Lamia, which stands over against the pass of Thermopylae under a spur of Othrys; and here he was besieged during the winter by Leosthenes. These successes had gained some adherents to the cause in the Peloponnese, and if the Greeks had been stronger at sea that cause might have triumphed, at least for a while. But the strange thing was that, notwithstanding the improvements of recent years in her naval establishment, Athens seems to have been able to set afloat no more than 170 warships against 240 of Macedon. The brave general Leosthenes was hampered by a Council of War, in which the various allies were represented—reminding us of the days of the Persian invasion; yet, if a fatal stone had not put an end to his life during the siege, more would probably have been effected for the cause of the allies. In spring the arrival of Leonnatus, governor of Hellespontine Phrygia, at the head of an army, raised the siege of Lamia. The Greeks marched into Thessaly to meet the new army before it united with Antipater; a battle was fought, in which the Greeks had the upper hand, and Leonnatus was wounded to death. Antipater arrived the next day, and, joining forces with the defeated army, withdrew into Macedonia, to await Craterus, who was approaching from the east. When Craterus arrived, they entered Thessaly together, and in an engagement at

The Greek revolt against Macedonia, 323 B.C.

Antipater besieged in Lamia, 323-2 B.C.

Crannon, in which the losses on both sides were light, the Macedonians had a slight advantage. This battle apparently decided the war, but the true cause which hindered the Greeks from continuing the struggle was not the insignificant defeat at Crannon, but the want of unity among themselves, the want of a leader whom they entirely trusted. They were forced to make terms singly, each state on its own behalf.

Hypereides pronounced a funeral oration, distinguished by that lucidity of which he was a perfect master, over those who had fallen in this hopeless war; and gave his due—it is not for us to say that he gave more than his due—to Leosthenes, who 'succeeded in what he undertook, but not in excaping fate'. There is a fine passage which distorts indeed the historical perspective, but well displays the spirit of the patriots. 'In the dark underworld —suffer us to ask—who are they that will stretch forth a right hand to the captain of our dead? May we not deem that Leosthenes will be greeted with welcome and with wonder by those half-gods who bore arms against Troy? Ay, and there, I deem, will be Miltiades and Themistocles, and those others who made Hellas free to the glory of their names.'

Athens submitted when Antipater advanced into Boeotia and prepared to invade Attica. She paid dearly for her attempt to win back her power. Antipater was not like Alexander. He was an able man, warmly devoted to the royal house of Macedon, but he did not share in Alexander's sympathies with Greek culture, he had no soft place in his heart for the memories and traditions of Athens. He saw only that, unless strong and stern measures were taken, Macedonia would not be safe against a repetition of the rising which he had suppressed. He therefore imposed three conditions, which Phocion and Demades were obliged to accept: that the democratic constitution should be modified by a property qualification; that a Macedonian garrison should be lodged in Munychia; and that the agitators, Demosthenes, Hypereides, and their friends, should be surrendered.

Demosthenes had exerted eloquence in gaining support for the cause of the allies in the Peloponnese, and his efforts had been rewarded by his recall to Athens. As soon as the city had submitted, he and the other orators fled. Hypereides with two companions sought refuge in the temple of Aeacus at Aegina, whence they were taken to Antipater and put to death. Demosthenes fled to the temple of Poseidon in the island of Calauria.

When the messengers of Antipater appeared and summoned him forth, he swallowed poison, which he had concealed, according to one story, in a pen, and was thus delivered from falling into the hands of the executioner.

The constitutional change which was carried out at the dictation of the Macedonian general would have been judged by Aristotle an improvement. The institutions were not changed, but the democracy was converted into a 'polity' or limited democracy—such as Theramenes had striven for—by a restriction of the franchise. All citizens whose property amounted to less than 2000 drachmae were deprived of their civic rights. It is said that this measure erased 12,000 names from the citizen lists, and that 9000 citizens remained. A large number of the poorer people thus disfranchised left Attica and settled in Thrace, where Antipater gave them land; perhaps these settlers included some of the cleruchs from Samos, who were now turned adrift, being obliged to quit the island and make way for the rightful possessors.

Aristotle and Alexander

It was through an accident that Alexander was brought into contact with the one other man of his time whose genius was destined to move the world. Aristotle's father had been court physician of Amyntas II, and Aristotle was meant to follow his father's profession. At the age of seventeen he went to Athens, where he was under the guardianship of a certain Proxenus, to whose son Nicanor—the same Nicanor who made public Alexander's edict at Olympia—he afterwards betrothed his only daughter. At first Aristotle studied in the school of Isocrates, but when Plato returned from Sicily he came under the influence of that philosopher's idealism, and this decided him for the 'life of speculation', which he regarded—and it is the deliberate judgement of his mature years—as the only life that is perfectly happy. After Plato's death he spent some years on the north-eastern coasts of the Aegean, at Assos and Mytilene, and then received the call from Philip to undertake the education of the crown prince. As yet he had won no eminent reputation for wisdom or learning, and Philip probably chose him because his father had been connected with the Macedonian court. The instruction which Aristotle imparted to Alexander was perhaps chiefly literary and philological; he came as a tutor, not as a philosopher. We know nothing

18.2 Aristotle

of the mutual relations between the brilliant master and his brilliant pupil—they were men of different and hardly sympathetic tempers—but we may suspect that Aristotle was more disposed to curb than to spur on the ardent straining spirit of Alexander. Certainly the episode led to no such maintenance of intimacy afterwards as it might have led to if Plato had *c. 335 B.C.* been the teacher. On his return to Athens, Aristotle founded his school of philosophy, and the Lyceum soon took the place formerly occupied by the Academy, which ever since Plato's unhappy adventures in Sicily had withdrawn itself more and more from the public attention. He taught for twelve or thirteen years—and these years were doubtless the time of his most effective philosophical *Death,* activity—and died not long after the death of *322 B.C.* Alexander.

Never were there more wonderful years than these in which the brains of Alexander and *Debt of* Aristotle were ceaselessly working. It is not an *Europe to* overstatement to say that there is no one to *Aristotle* whom Europe owes a greater debt for the higher education of her peoples than to

Aristotle. The science of the laws of thought is still taught mainly as he first worked it out. There are no better introductions to ethical and political speculation than his fundamental treatises on ethical and political science. Nor was it a small thing that his system controlled the acutest minds of the Middle Ages, whose reasoning faculties, though cramped by the imminence of a narrowly interpreted theology, were of amazing power and subtlety.

But Aristotle, supreme as he was in abstract *Aristotle's* reasoning, zealous as he was in collecting and *prejudices,* appreciating concrete facts, was not without prejudices. As a boy, in the narrow self-satisfied community of little remote Stagira, he had imbibed the dislike which was openly or secretly felt towards Athens in all the *against* Chalcidian regions. And, though he settled at *Athens* Athens, he never overcame this distrust; he always remained a citizen of Stagira and lived in Athens as a stranger. This initial prejudice prevented him from ever judging with perfect impartiality the Athenian institutions, which he took as the type of democracy. He was also prejudiced against Macedonia. The Chalci- *and Mace-* dians looked upon their Macedonian neigh- *donia,* bours as far below themselves in civilisation; and Aristotle's experience of the court of Pella, where he must have been a spectator of the scandalous quarrels between Philip and Olympias, did not create a favourable impression. He was thus disposed to hold his sympathies entirely aloof from the enterprises of Alexander. But he not only failed to sympathise, he disapproved. For he was wedded to the idea of the small Greek republic; he condemned the large state. Moreover, he held firmly to the Hellenic conviction that Hellenes were superior *and* by nature to peoples of other race, and he was *barbarians* thus opposed to the most original and enlightened feature of Alexander's policy—the ruling of Greeks and barbarians on an equality. Owing to this attitude of coldness and distrust towards the Macedonians, he missed a great opportunity. Alexander's expedition threw open to science a new field of discovery in natural history, and we can imagine what endless pains the king would have given himself if Aristotle had urged him to collect extensive observations on the animal and vegetable kingdoms in the various countries and climates through which he passed.

It is a strange sensation to pass from the view *His ideal* of the state which Alexander was fashioning *state* to the sketch of an ideal state which was drawn by the most thoughtful of men at the same time. Aristotle envisages a little north-country city, situated in a compact, defensible

499

territory, close to the sea and yet not on the coast, having a harbour within easy reach but quite disconnected, so that the precincts of the city may not be contaminated and its people troubled by the presence of a motley crowd of foreigners, pedlars and mariners such as throng a seaport's quays. He will not have his city a centre of trade; it is to import and export only for the purposes of its own strict needs. It is to be a tiny city, the number of the citizens so limited that each one may be able to know all about each of the others. The citizens are to have equal rights; their early manhood is to be spent on military duties; when they come to middle life they are to be eligible for political offices; in their old age they are to act as priests. Subject to this citizen aristocracy, but entirely excluded from the franchise, are to be the artisans and merchants. Part of the land is to be public— the yield to be devoted to maintaining the worship of the gods and providing the public meals of the city; part is to be the private property of the citizens; and the fields are to be tilled by slaves or labourers of non-Hellenic race. Such was the little exclusive community which Aristotle designed, while his former pupil was setting in motion schemes for world-wide commerce, shattering the barriers which sundered nation from nation, building an empire which should include millions, founding cities composed of men of divers races, hewing his way through a maze of new political problems which were beyond Aristotle's horizon. The republic of Aristotle's wish is not quickened like Plato's by striking original ideas; it is a commonplace Greek aristocracy with its claws cut, carefully trimmed and pruned, refined by a punctilious education, without any expansive vitality, and like Sparta leaving no room for the free development of the individual citizens. If the cities of Hellas had been moulded and fashioned on the model of the city of the philosopher's wish, they would hardly have done what they did for European civilisation.

We may wonder whether Aristotle divined before his death that the Hellenic cities were not to have the last word in the history of men. More probably the untimely end of Alexander reassured him that the old fashion of things would soon go on again as before. The brilliant day of the Greek city states had indeed drawn to a close so suddenly that they could not be expected to grasp the fact; and no people that has ever borne the torch of civilisation has been willing, or even able, to recognise that the hour of relinquishing sovereignty has come. The Greeks may well be excused if they were reluctant to acquiesce in the vicissitude which forced them to sink into a subordinate place. But it is thus that the austere laws of history reward the meritorious. The republics of Greece had performed an imperishable work: they had shown mankind many things and, above all, the most precious thing in the world—fearless freedom of thought.

Chronological Table

B.C.

612	Fall of Nineveh. Nabopolassar of Babylonia and Cyaxares of Media conquer and divide Assyria.
c. 610	Foundation of Naucratis.
605	Nebucadnezar succeeds Nabopolassar.
c. 600	Athens wins Salamis from Megara, and settles Sigeum at mouth of Hellespont, successful in fighting against Mytilene.
	Sappho, Alcaeus, Pittacus, flourish at Mitylene.
	Periander tyrant of Corinth.
	Thrasybulus tyrant of Miletus.
594–3	Archonship of Solon. *Seisachtheia.*
594–89	Nubian expedition of Psammetichus II. Inscription of Greek mercenaries at Abu Simbel.
590–89	Sacred War against Crisa.
	Cleisthenes of Sicyon flourishes.
585	May 28: Eclipse of sun. Drawn battle of Cyaxares king of Media with Alyattes king of Lydia.
	Thales flourishes.
583–1	Archonship of Damasias at Athens.
582	First Pythiad.
572	Eleans win control of the Olympian games.
c. 570	Athenian War with Megara, capture of Nisaea.
569	Accession of Amasis to throne of Egypt.
562	Death of Nebucadnezar.
560	Croesus succeeds to throne of Lydia.
c. 560–50	War of Sparta with Tegea.
561–60	Archonship of Comeas. Pisistratus seizes tyranny at Athens.
c. 559–6	Miltiades becomes tyrant in Thracian Chersonese.
c. 550	Spartan conquest of Thyreatis.
548–7	Temple of Apollo at Delphi burnt down.
? 546	Cyrus king of Persia conquers Lydia and captures Sardis.
546–5	Persian conquest of Asiatic Greeks.
538	Cyrus takes Babylon.
528–7	Death of Pisistratus, succeeded by Hippias.
526	Polycrates, tyrant of Samos, abandons alliance with Amasis and joins Persia.
525	Death of Amasis king of Egypt.
	Persian conquest of Egypt: battle of Pelusion.
c. 525	Spartans attack Samos.
c. 523	Death of Polycrates.
522	Death of Cambyses king of Persia.
521	Accession of Darius.
520	First capture of Babylon by Darius.
519	Second capture of Babylon by Darius.
514	Conspiracy of Harmodius and Aristogiton.
c. 512	First European expedition of Darius: conquest of Thrace.
510	Fall of the Pisistratid tyranny. Spartans in Attica. Sybaris destroyed by Croton.
508–7	Archonship of Isagoras. Spartans under Cleomenes invade Attica; besieged in the Acropolis.
? 508–7	Principles of Cleistheines' reforms carried in Ekklesia.
506	Peloponnesian army invades Attica.
	Athens defeats (1) Boeotians, (2) Chalcidians: acquires Chalcidian plain and Oropus.
501	Institution of the *Ten* strategoi of the tribes at Athens.
499	Outbreak of Ionian revolt.
c. 498	Ionians and allies at Sardis: burning of Sardis.

B.C.

Crushing of revolt in Cyprus.	c. 497
Hipparchus archon at Athens.	496–5
Battle of Lade; Persians capture Miletus.	494
Battle of Sepeia (Spartans under Cleomenes defeat Argives).	c. 494
Archonship of Themistocles.	493–2
Mardonius subdues Thrace and Macedonia.	492
Trial of Miltiades.	c. 492
Gelon becomes tyrant of Gela.	c. 491
Spartans take hostages from Aegina. Battle of the Helorus.	c. 491
Expedition of the Persians under Datis against Greece. Destruction of Eretria. Battle of Marathon.	490
Expedition of Miltiades to Paros. Trial and death of Miltiades.	489
Death of Cleomenes.	c. 489
Victory of Gelon in chariot-race at Olympia.	488
Ostracism of Hipparchus the Pisistradid.	487
War of Athens with Aegina.	
Archons begin to be appointed by lot. Strategoi supersede the Polemarch.	487–6
Ostracism of Megacles. Pindar's *7th Pythian.*	486
Egypt revolts against Persia.	486–5
Death of Darius. Accession of Xerxes.	485
Ostracism of Xanthippus son of Ariphron.	484
Persia recovers control of Egypt.	484–3
Persians hew canal through Athos peninsula.	483
Rich silver strike in Laurion mining area.	483–2
Ostracism of Aristides.	482
Themistocles' decree to build a new Athenian fleet. Pythian victory of Hieron in horse-race.	482
Xerxes comes down to Sardis.	481
Spring: Athens recalls ostracised citizens.	480
August: Xerxes enters Greece. Battles of Artemisium and Thermopylae.	
September: Battle of Salamis.	
Olynthus given to the Chalcidians.	
Carthaginians invade Sicily. Battle of Himera.	
Mardonius in Attica. August: battle of Plataea and battle of Mycale. Ionians revolt from Persia. Athenians capture Sestos at end of winter 479/8.	479
Pausanias' expedition to Cyprus, Byzantium.	478
Death of Gelon: his brother Hieron succeeds to his power. Pythian victory of Hieron in horse-race. *3rd Pythian Ode* of Pindar.	
Foundation of Confederacy of Delos.	477
? Pausanias driven from Byzantium by Cimon.	
Fortification of Athens.	478–6
Lacedaemonian expedition to Thessaly. Victory of Hieron in horse-race at Olympia (*1st Olympian* of Pindar; *5th Ode* of Bacchylides).	476
Cimon captures Eion.	476–5
Battle of Cyme. Syracusan defeat of Etruscans.	474
Cimon conquers Scyros and recovers the bones of Theseus.	474
Olympian victories of Hieron in horse-race and Theron in chariot-race. *2nd and 3rd Olympians* of Pindar. The *Persae* of Aeschylus.	472
Athenians reduce Carystus. Ostracism of Themistocles. Death of Theron of Acragas. ? Synoecisms of Elis and Mantinea.	c. 472–1
Flight of Themistocles. ? Battle of Dipaea.	c. 471

B.C.

471–70 War of Hieron with Thrasydaeus of Acragas.

470 Pythian victory of Hieron in chariot-race. Pindar's *1st Pythian*. *4th Ode* of Bacchylides (?).

470–69 Revolt and reduction of Naxos (?).

468 Olympian victory of Hieron in chariot-race. *3rd Ode* of Bacchylides. Olympian victory of a boy of Tiryns in boxing.

Battle of the Eurymedon (?).

468–7 Argos reduces Tiryns (?).

467 Death of Hieron.

465 Revolt of Thasos.

465–4 Athenians attempt to colonise the Nine Ways (later Amphipolis); defeated by Thracians.

464 Earthquake at Sparta. Revolt of helots. Siege of Ithome. Accession of Artaxerxes to throne of Persia.

463 Surrender of Thasos.

463–2 Cimon in Messenia.

463–1 Ephialtes influential at Athens. The Areopagus deprived of its powers.

462–60 Argos reduces Mycenae (?). Pay introduced at Athens for the judges of the *heliaea*. Influence of Pericles begins.

461 Ostracism of Cimon.

461–60 Alliance of Athens and Argos. Megara joins the alliance. Long Walls built connecting Megara with Nisaea.

? 459 Athenian expedition to Cyprus diverted to support revolt of Egypt. Memphis captured (except central fort). Battles of Halieis, Cecryphalea, Aegina, Megara.

Capture of Ithome. Messenians settled at Naupactus.

458 *Oresteia* of Aeschylus. Zeugitae admitted to archonship.

457 Lacedaemonian expedition to Phocis and Boeotia. Battle of Tanagra. Athenian victory at Oenophyta, control of Boeotia (? except Thebes). Athenian Long Walls completed. Aegina surrenders, made to pay tribute.

Athenian conquest of Boeotia (battle of Oenophyta; autumn).

457–6 Athenian conquest of Aegina.

456 Megabyzus arrives in Egypt with army and fleet.

456–5 Expedition of Tolmides to Corinthian Gulf. Troezen and Achaea brought under Athenian control.

454 Expedition of Pericles to Corinthian Gulf. Unsuccessful Athenian intervention at Pharsalus. Final defeat in Egypt.

Treasury of confederacy of Delos transferred from Delos to Athens.

451 Five years' Truce between Athenians and Peloponnesians. Thirty years' Peace between Argos and Lacedaemon.

451–50 Pericles' decree requiring Athenian parentage on both sides for citizenship.

? 450 Cleruchs sent to Euboea, Naxos, and Andros.

450–49 Cimon in Cyprus. Death of Cimon at siege of Cition.

449–8 Peace with Persia. Sacred War. Athens invites the Greeks to restore the temples.

447 Parthenon begun.

Athens loses Boeotia (battle of Coronea).

B.C.

Cleruchs sent to the Chersonese (? and to Lemnos and Imbros).

Revolt and reduction of Euboea. Athens loses Megara. — 447–6

Thirty years' Peace between Athens and Peloponnesians. Foundation of New Sybaris. — 446–5

Foundation of Thurii. — 443

Ostracism of Thucydides, son of Melesias.

Revolt of Samos, and Byzantium. — 440–39

Chryselephantine Athena set up in the Parthenon. — 438

Foundation of Amphipolis. — 436

Pericles' expedition to Euxine. — *c.* 435

Sedition at Epidamnus. — 436–5

Sea-victory of Corcyra over Corinth (spring). — 435

Defensive alliance of Athens with Corcyra. Battle of Sybota. Treaties of Athens with Rhegion and Leontini renewed. — 433

Revolt of Potidaea. — 432

The 'Megarian decree' passed at Athens. Battle of Potidaea (*c.* Sept.).

The Spartan Assembly, and Peloponnesian League Conference declare for war.

First year of the Peloponnesian War.—Theban attack on Plataea (March). First Peloponnesian invasion of Attica (May). Athens wins Sollion and Cephallenia; takes Thronion and Atalanta: expels Aeginetans from Aegina. — 431

Second year of the War.—Outbreak of Plague at Athens. Second invasion of Attica. Expedition of Pericles to Argolis and failure at Epidaurus. Pericles deposed from strategia, tried, fined, and reappointed strategos. Phormio operates in the west. Surrender of Potidaea. — 430

Third year of the War.—Peloponnesians besiege Plataea. Sea-victories of Phormio in the Corinthian Gulf. Death of Pericles (autumn). — 429

Fourth year of the War.—Third invasion of Attica. Revolt of Mytilene. Introduction of war tax (*eisphora*). — 428

Fifth year of the War.—Fourth invasion of Attica. Surrender of Mytilene. Surrender of Plataea. Civil war breaks out in Corcyra. Athens captures Minoa. Expedition of Laches to Sicily. — 427

Sixth year of the War.—Aetolian expedition of Demosthenes. Battle of Olpae. Unsuccessful attempt by Athens to win Melos. Purification of Delos. — 426

Seventh year of the War.—Fifth invasion of Attica. Athenians send reinforcements to Sicily. Occupation of Pylos; and capture of Spartans on Sphacteria. Triumph of the democracy in Corcyra. Athens wins Anactorion, and occupies Methone. Athens more than doubles the tribute of her allies. Introduction of the triobolon for jurors. *Acharnians* of Aristophanes. Antiphon's *De Choreuta*. Congress of Gela. — 425

Eighth year of the War.—Athens wins Oeniadae; captures Nisaea, with the Long Walls of Megara, and Cythera. Athenian invasion of Boeotia; battle of Delion. Brasidas in Thrace. Revolt of Acanthus, Amphipolis, and other — 424

503

B.C.

cities. Banishment of Thucydides, the historian. *Knights* of Aristophanes.

423 *Ninth year of the War.*—Negotiations for peace. One year's truce (March). Revolt of Scione. *Clouds* of Aristophanes. Leontini annexed by Syracuse.

422 *Tenth year of the War.*—Battle of Amphipolis. Death of Brasidas and Cleon. Peace negotiations. *Wasps* of Aristophanes.

421 Peace of Nicias (March). *Peace* of Aristophanes. Capture of Scione.

421–20 Defensive alliance between Athens and Sparta.

420 Alliance of Athens with Argos, Elis, and Mantinea.

418 Battle of Mantinea. Argos forms alliance with Sparta.

417 Ostracism of Hyperbolus. Nicias in Chalcidice.

416 Conquest of Melos. Embassy of Segesta to Athens.

415 Mutilation of the Hermae at Athens. Athenian expedition to Sicily. Recall of Alcibiades.

414 Spring: *Birds* of Aristophanes. Siege of Syracuse. Gylippus arrives in Sicily.

413 Spartans occupy Decelea. Second Athenian expedition to Sicily. Great battle in the Syracusan Harbour (September 9). Disaster of the Athenians.

412 Revolt of Athenian allies. Treaty of Miletus (between Sparta and Persia). Alcibiades leaves Sparta.

411 Battle of Syme (January). Revolt of Rhodes. Pisander at Athens (*c.* February). Revolt of Abydus and Lampsacus (April). Assembly at Colonus and provision made for a new Constitution (May). Revolt of Thasos. Council of Four Hundred comes into office (early in June), and governs till September. Revolt of Euboea (September). Four Hundred overthrown and Polity established (September). Battle of Cynossema. *Lysistrata* and *Thesmophoriazusae* of Aristophanes. Evagoras becomes king of Salamis.

410 Battle of Cyzicus. Restoration of Democracy at Athens. [Pseudo-Lysias] *For Polystratus.*

409 Athens recovers Colophon: loses Pylos and Nisea. Carthaginian invasion of Sicily. Destruction of Selinus and Himera.

408 Athens recovers Chalcedon and Byzantium. Gorgias at Olympia. Warfare of Hermocrates in western Sicily.

407 Athens recovers Thasos. Alcibiades at Athens. Cyrus comes down to the coast. Death of Hermocrates. Foundation of Thermae. Lysander navarch.

406 Battle of Notion. Alcibiades deposed.
Battle of Arginusae. Trial of the Generals. Siege of Acragas.

406–5 Conspiracy of reed-bearers at Chios.

405 Lysander 'assistant' navarch. Cyrus called to Susa. Battle of Aegospotami (end of summer). Dionysius becomes tyrant of Syracuse; and makes peace with Carthage.

405–4 Blockade of Athens.

B.C.

Surrender of Athens. Long Walls pulled down (April). Psephism of Dracontides (summer) and rule of the Thirty. Thrasybulus seizes Phyle (December). Alliance of Catane and Leontini. — 404

First expedition of Thirty against Thrasybulus. Death of Theramenes. — 404–3

Lacedaemonian garrison at Athens. Second expedition against Thrasybulus (May). — 403

Thrasybulus seizes Piraeus. Battle of Munychia. King Pausanias at Athens. Fall of Thirty (September). Recall of Lysander. Lysias' *Against Eratosthenes.*

Revolt at Syracuse against Dionysius.

Archonship of Euclides. Ionian letters adopted. — 403–2

Sicel war of Dionysius. Reduction of Naxos and Catane. — 403–400

Expedition of Cyrus. Battle of Cunaxa (summer). — 401

Thimbron in Asia Minor (end of summer). — 400

Dercyllidas succeeds Thimbron, and gains the Troad. War of Sparta and Elis. Death of Socrates. — 399

Sparta makes truce with the satraps; sends embassy to Susa. Accession of Agesilaus. Dionysius captures Motya. — 398

Dercyllidas in the Chersonese; takes Atarneus (397, first months). — 398–7

Dercyllidas in Caria; makes truce with the satraps. Conon appointed commander of Persian fleet. Conspiracy of Cinadon at Sparta. — 397

Himilco's expedition to Sicily. Siege of Syracuse. Foundation of Lilybaeum.

First campaign of Agesilaus in Phrygia (autumn). Restoration of Messana. Acoris becomes king of Egypt. — 396

Sicel war of Dionysius. — 396–3

Campaign of Agesilaus in Lydia. Death of Tissaphernes. Second campaign of Agesilaus in Phrygia. Revolt of Rhodes. War breaks out in Boeotia. Battle of Haliartus and death of Lysander. Accession of Agesipolis at Sparta. Athens begins to rebuild her Long Walls. Foundation of Tyndaris. — 395

Confederation of Athens, Thebes, etc., against Sparta. — 395–4

Battle of Corinth (July). Battle of Cnidus (August). Eclipse of sun (August 14). Battle of Coronea (August). Foundation of Mylae. — 394

Completion of Long Walls of Athens. — 393

Union of Corinth and Argos. Battle of the Long Walls (of Megara). First embassy of Antalcidas to Susa. Second Punic War of Dionysius. — 392

Spartans capture Lechaeon. Dionysius besieges Rhegion. — 391

Agesilaus celebrates Isthmian games and captures Piraeon. Iphicrates gains a victory over Spartan hoplites. Teleutias captures an Athenian squadron. Evagoras revolts from Persia. Alliance of Athens with Evagoras and Acoris. Hecatomnus has become satrap of Caria (between 395 and 390). — 390

Successes of Thrasybulus in the Hellespont. Dionysius besieges Caulonia. Battle of the Elleporus. — 389

B.C.

388 Death of Thrasybulus (first months). Warfare of Anaxibius and Iphicrates in the Hellespont.

Speech of Lysias at Olympic games (July-August).

388–7 Second mission of Antalcidas to Susa.

387 Capture of Rhegion by Dionysius. Chabrias sent to help Evagoras.

387–6 The King's Peace.

386 Evagoras defeated at Cition. Chabrias in Egypt.

386–4 Persian siege of Cypriot Salamis.

386–5 Breaking up of Mantinea.

384 Orontes makes peace with Evagoras.

384–2 Formation of the Chalcidian Confederacy.

383–78 Third Punic War of Dionysius.

383 Death of Acoris.

382 Spartans seize citadel of Thebes (summer).

382–1 Restoration of Plataea.

381 Defeat of Spartans at Olynthus. Siege of Phlius begins. Persia concludes Peace with Evagoras. Accession of Nektanebos I in Egypt.

380 Accession of king Cleombrotus at Sparta. Olympic games for which Isocrates wrote his *Panegyric*.

379 Suppression of Chalcidian League. Battles of Cabala and Cronion in Sicily.

379–8 Spartans expelled from Theban citadel (winter). Raid of Sphodrias on Piraeus.

378 Alliance of Athens with Thebes. Boeotia invaded by Agesilaus. Iphicrates in Thrace. Peace of Syracuse with Carthage.

377 Foundation of Second Athenian Confederacy. Property tax at Athens.

377 Boeotia invaded by Agesilaus. Defeat of Phoebidas. Mausolus becomes satrap of Caria.

376 Battle of Naxos. Western expedition of Timotheus. Rebellion at Delos. Iphicrates in Persian service.

75–3 Iphicrates and Pharnabazus in Egypt. Jason of Pherae a member of Athenian League.

374 Peace between Athens and Sparta. Death of Evagoras; accession of Nicocles.

74–3 Peace broken. Lacedaemonians at Corcyra.

373 Iphicrates sent to Corcyra. Trial of Timotheus. Earthquakes in Greece; destruction of temple of Delphi (?).

371 Peace of Callias (June). Battle of Leuctra (July). Accession of Agesipolis II at Sparta.

1–69 Foundation of Arcadian League, and of Megalopolis.

370 Rebuilding of Mantinea. Death of Jason of Pherae. Accession of Cleombrotus II at Sparta.

0–69 First Boeotian invasion of Peloponnese, led by Epaminondas and Pelopidas.

369 Foundation of Messene (first months). Alliance of Athens and Sparta (spring). Second Boeotian invasion of Peloponnese, led by Epaminondas. First Thessalian expedition of Pelopidas.

69–8 Murder of Alexander of Macedon, and intervention of Iphicrates.

368 Heraea and Orchomenus join Arcadian League. Congress of Delphi (summer). Tearless Battle. Euphron tyrant of Sicyon. Second Thessalian expedition of Pelopidas, and his captivity.

First expedition to rescue him. Fourth Punic war of Dionysius.

Death of Dionysius I. Greek envoys at Susa. 367 Second expedition to rescue Pelopidas.

Ariobarzanes revolts from Persia.

Third Boeotian invasion of Peloponnese. 366 Thebans seize Oropus. Alliance of Athens with Arcadia. Death of Lycomedes. Timotheus in eastern Aegean. Isocrates' *Archidamus*.

Timotheus wins Samos. Murder of Macedonian 365 regent Ptolemy. Timotheus wins Potidaea and other towns of Chalcidian region. War breaks out between Arcadia and Elis.

Naval expedition of Epaminondas. Third Thes- 364 salian expedition and death of Pelopidas. Eclipse of sun, July 13. Battle of Cynoscephalae. Destruction of Orchomenus. Pisatans celebrate Olympian games; battle in the Altis. Athens obtains Sestos. Timotheus besieges Amphipolis.

Timotheus recovers Byzantium. Nektanebos I 363 succeeded by Tachos.

Timotheus again besieges Amphipolis. Revolts 363–2 of satraps against Persia.

Battle of Mantinea. Athenian fleet sent to Helles- 362 pont. Ariobarzanes crucified. Death of Epaminondas.

Agesilaus in Egypt. Accession of Nektanebos II. 361 Battle of Peparethus.

Death of Agesilaus (?). 361–60

Death of king Cotys, and division of Thrace. 360–59

Death of Perdiccas and accession of Amyntas. 359

Victories of Philip over Paeonians and Illyrians. 358 Death of Artaxerxes II; accession of Artaxerxes III, Ochus.

Athens recovers the Chersonese and Euboea. 357 Philip captures Amphipolis. Revolt of Chios, Cos, and Rhodes from Athens. Death of Chabrias. Dion returns to Sicily.

Illyrian victory of Philip. Battle of Embata. 356 Phocians seize Delphi. Revolt of Artabazus and Orontes. Arrival of Nypsius at Syracuse.

Philip captures Pydna and Potidaea. Birth of 356–5 Alexander. Composition of Xenophon's *De Vectigalibus*.

Chares in Asia Minor; defeats Tithraustes. 355 Isocrates' *De Pace*. Trial of Timotheus and Iphicrates (?).

Peace of Athens with Rhodes, Cos, etc. Isocrates' 355–4 *Areopagiticus*.

Battle of Neon. Death of Philomelus. Murder 354 of Dion.

Demosthenes' *On the Symmories*. Tyranny of 354–3 Callippus at Syracuse.

Eubulus in charge of the Theoric Fund. 354–50

Philip captures Methone. Power of Onomarchus 353 in Thessaly. Eubulus hinders Philip from attacking Phocis. Demosthenes' *For the Megalopolitans*. Death of Mausolus.

Hipparinus tyrant of Syracuse. 353–1

Cersobleptes of Thrace submits to Macedon. 352 Demosthenes' *Against Aristocrates*. Artabazus flees to Macedonia, and Artaxerxes makes peace with Orontes.

B.C.

505

B.C.

351 Revolt of Phoenicia against Persia; revolt in Cyprus. Demosthenes' *For the Freedom of the Rhodians* and *First Philippic*. Idrieus succeeds Artemisia in Caria. Nysaeus becomes tyrant at Syracuse.

350 Phocion in Cyprus helping to suppress revolt.

349 Phocion in Euboea. Philip reduces Chalcidice. Alliance of Athens with Olynthus. Demosthenes' *Olynthiacs*.

348 Euboea acknowledged independent. Philip captures Olynthus.

347 First Athenian embassy to Philip (end of year). Death of Plato.

346 The Peace of Philocrates. Second embassy to Philip (spring). Philip at Thermopylae. The Phocians crushed. Philip presides at Pythian games. Demosthenes' *De Pace*. Isocrates' *Letter to Philip*. Second tyranny of Dionysius II.

346–5 Demosthenes impeaches Aeschines. Aeschines' *Against Timarchus*.

345–3 Persia recovers Egypt.

344 Demosthenes in the Peloponnese. His *Second Philippic*.
Timoleon sails for Sicily. Battle of Hadranum.

343 Impeachments of Philocrates and Aeschines. King Archidamus II sails to Italy.

343–2 Alliance of Megara with Athens. Philip in Epirus. Aristotle goes to Macedonia as tutor of Alexander.

342–1 Philip's conquest of Thrace.

341 Athens sends Diopeithes to the Chersonese. Demosthenes' *On the Chersonese,* and *Third Philippic*. Demosthenes at Byzantium. The Euboic League.

340 Sieges of Perinthus and Byzantium. Naval reform at Athens. Violent proceedings at Amphictionic Council (autumn).

339 Thracian expedition of Philip. Amphictions determine to make war on Amphissa.
Battle of the Crimisus.

338 Philip descends into Greece. His campaign in Phocis and Locris. Battle of Chaeronea (August).
Philip in the Peloponnese. Synedrion of Corinth. Death of Isocrates. Battle of Mandonia.

338–7 Murder of Artaxerxes Ochus and accession of Arses.

338–4 Lycurgus minister of finance at Athens.

337 Second meeting of Synedrion of the Greeks at Corinth.

336 Macedonian forces sent into Asia Minor. Murder of Philip and accession of Alexander (summer).
Alexander's first descent into Greece; his election as general of the Greeks.

335 Alexander's campaign in Thrace and Illyria, and his second descent into Greece. Destruction of Thebes (October). Accession of Darius III, Codomannus. Memnon opposes the Macedonians in Asia Minor. Aristotle begins his teaching at Athens.

334 Alexander starts on his expedition against Persia (spring). Battle of the Granicus. Conquest of

Lydia. Siege of Miletus. Siege of Halicarnassus. Expedition of Alexander of Epirus to Italy.

Conquest of Lycia, Pamphylia, Pisidia. 334–3

Alexander at Gordion. Conquest of Cilicia. 333 Battle of Issus (November).

Siege of Tyre (January–July). Submission of 332 Syria and Judaea. Siege of Gaza (October). Conquest of Egypt.

Foundation of Alexandria. Submission of Cyrene. 331 Lunar eclipse, September 20; battle of Gaugamela (October 1). Alexander at Babylon (October); at Susa (December). Revolt of Agis crushed at battle of Megalopolis.

Battle of Pandosia. 331–30

Alexander in Persis (January–April); burning of 330 palace at Persepolis; at Ecbatana. Death of Darius (July). Conquest of Hyrcania, Areia, and Drangiana. Foundation of Alexandria Areion and Prophthasia. Execution of Philotas and Parmenio.
Aeschines' *Against Ctesiphon* and Demosthenes' *On the Crown*. Lycurgus' *Against Leocrates*.

Alexander winters in Drangiana. 330–29

Partial submission of Gedrosia. Conquest of 329 Arachosia. Foundation of the Arachosian Alexandria.

Alexander winters in the Cabul region. Founda- 329–8 tion of Alexandria under Caucasus.

Alexander comes to the Hindu-Kush; conquers 328 Bactria and Sogdiana. Foundation of Alexandria Eschate.

Alexander winters at Zariaspa. 328–7

Alexander at Samarcand (first months); murder 327 of Clitus. Conquest of eastern Sogdiana.
Alexander marries Roxane. Conspiracy of the pages, and execution of Callisthenes.
Alexander recrosses the Hindu-Kush, and prepares for Indian expedition.

Winter campaigns in the Kunar, Chitral, and 327–6 Swat regions.

Alexander crosses the Indus. Battle of the 326 Hydaspes. Conquest of the Punjab.

Conquest of the Malli. Foundation of towns on 325 the Lower Indus. Alexander sails in the Indian Ocean. His march through Gedrosia(August–October). Voyage of Nearchus (October–December).

Macedonian mutiny at Opis. Alexander at Ecba- 324 tana. Death of Hephaestion. Harpalus in Greece (spring). Restoration of exiles proclaimed at Olympic games (July–August). Harpalus' trial at Athens; speeches of Hypereides and Dinarchus.

Subjugation of the Cossaeans. 324–3

Alexander at Babylon. Funeral of Hephaestion 323 (May).
Death of Alexander (June 13). Greece revolts against Macedonia.

Siege of Lamia. 323–2

Battle of Crannon. Funeral oration of Hypereides. 322 Change of the Athenian Constitution. Death of Demosthenes (October). Death of Aristotle. Death of Lycurgus (?).

Abbreviations

AAA	*Athens Annals of Archaeology.*
AJA	*American Journal of Archaeology.*
AJP	*American Journal of Philology.*
Arch.	*Archaeology.*
Ath. Const.	*Aristotelian Constitution of Athens.*
ATL	*The Athenian Tribute Lists* by B. D. Meritt, H. T. Wade-Gery, A. F. McGregor. 4 vols. Cambridge, Mass., Princeton 1939–53.
BCH	*Bulletin de correspondance hellénique.*
BSA	*Annual of the British School at Athens.*
CAH	*The Cambridge Ancient History*, Cambridge, 1923– .
CQ	*Classical Quarterly.*
FGH	F. Jacoby, *Die Fragmente der griechischen Historiker*, Berlin and Leyden, 1923– .
GHI	*Greek Historical Inscriptions.*
Gomme, *HCT*	A. W. Gomme, *A Historical Commentary on Thucydides*, Oxford, 1945– .
Hesp.	*Hesperia.*
Hist.	*Historia, Zeitschrift für Alte Geschichte*, 1950– .
IG	*Inscriptiones Graecae.*
ILN	*Illustrated London News.*
JHS	*Journal of Hellenic Studies.*
Meiggs, *Empire*	R. Meiggs, *The Athenian Empire*, Oxford 1972.
ML	R. Meiggs and D. M. Lewis, *Greek Historical Inscriptions*, Oxford 1969.
NC	*Numismatic Chronicle.*
SEG	*Supplementum Epigraphicum Graecum.*
SIG	Dittenberger, *Sylloge Inscriptionum Graecarum* (3rd edition), Leipzig 1915–24.
Tarn	W. W. Tarn, *Alexander the Great*, Cambridge 1948.
Tod	M. N. Tod, *Greek Historical Inscriptions*, vol. II, Oxford 1948.

Select Bibliography

General History

George Grote, *A History of Greece* (1851–7), new ed., London 1888.

The Cambridge Ancient History III–VI, Cambridge 1923–

N. G. L. Hammond, *A History of Greece to 322 B.C.*², Oxford 1967.

M. L. W. Laistner, *A History of the Greek World from 479 to 323 B.C.*, London 1936.

A. R. Burn, *The Lyric Age of Greece,* London 1960.

V. Ehrenberg, *From Solon to Socrates,* London 1968.

C. G. Starr, *A History of the Ancient World,* Oxford 1965.

J. M. Cook, *The Greeks in Ionia and the East,* London 1962.

A. G. Woodhead, *The Greeks in the West,* London 1962.

M. I. Finley, *Ancient Sicily to the Arab Conquest,* London 1968.

Constitutional and Political History

G. Sinclair, *A History of Greek Political Thought,* London 1951.

V. Ehrenberg, *The Greek State,* Oxford 1960.

W. G. Forrest, *The Emergence of Greek Democracy,* London 1966.

E. A. Havelock, *The Liberal Temper in Greek Politics,* London 1957.

C. Hignett, *A History of the Athenian Constitution,* Oxford 1952.

A. H. M. Jones, *Athenian Democracy,* Oxford 1957.

J. K. Davies, *Athenian Propertied Families, 600–300 B.C.,* Oxford 1971.

P. J. Rhodes, *The Athenian Boule,* Oxford 1972.

J. A. O. Larsen, *Representative Government in Greek and Roman History,* Berkeley 1955.

J. A. O. Larsen, *Greek Federal States: Their Institutions and History,* Oxford 1968.

Social and Economic History

H. Michell, *The Economics of Ancient Greece*², Cambridge 1957.

J. Hasebroek, *Trade and Politics in Ancient Greece* (trans.), London 1933.

A. M. Andreades, *A History of Greek public finance,* Cambridge, Mass., 1933.

G. Glotz, *Ancient Greece at Work* (trans.), London 1926.

A. Zimmern, *The Greek Commonwealth*⁶, Oxford 1961.

A. French, *The Growth of the Athenian Economy,* London 1964.

W. K. Lacey, *The Family in Classical Greece,* London 1968.

A. R. W. Harrison, *The Law of Athens:* (1) *The Family and Property,* Oxford 1968; (2) *Procedure* (ed. D. MacDowell) Oxford 1971.

M. I. Finley (ed.) *Slavery in Classical Antiquity* (collected essays), Cambridge 1960.

T. B. L. Webster, *Athenian Culture and Society,* London 1973.

Military History

A. M. Snodgrass, *Arms and Armour of the Greeks,* London 1967.

A. M. Snodgrass, *Early Greek Arms and Weapons from the end of the Bronze Age to 600 B.C.,* Edinburgh 1964.

P. A. L. Greenhalgh, *Early Greek Warfare,* Cambridge 1973.

F. E. Adcock, *The Greek and Macedonian Art of War,* Berkeley 1957.

J. K. Anderson, *Military Theory and Practice in the Age of Xenophon,* Berkeley 1970.

W. K. Pritchett, *Ancient Military Practices,* Part I, Berkeley 1971.

J. S. Morrison and R. T. Williams, *Greek Oared Ships, 900–322 B.C.,* Cambridge 1968.

509

Art, Architecture, Coinage

Rhys Carpenter, *The Esthetic Basis of Greek Art of the Fifth and Fourth Centuries B.C.* (revised from 1921), Bloomington 1959.

Rhys Carpenter, *Greek Sculpture*, Chicago 1970.

G. M. A. Richter, *The Sculpture and Sculptors of the Greeks*[4], New Haven 1970.

W. B. Dinsmoor, *The Architecture of Ancient Greece*[3], New York 1950.

D. S. Robertson, *A Handbook of Greek and Roman Architecture*[2], Cambridge 1947.

I. T. Hill, *The Ancient City of Athens*, London 1953.

H. A. Thompson and R. E. Wycherley, *The Agora of Athens*, Princeton 1972.

C. T. Seltman, *Greek Coins*[2], London 1955.

C. M. Kraay, *Greek Coins*, with photographs by M. Hirmer, London 1966.

P. E. Arias, *A History of Greek Vase Painting* (trans. B. Shefton), London 1962.

R. M. Cook, *Greek Painted Pottery*[2], London 1972.

Religion

H. J. Rose, *Ancient Greek Religion*, London 1946.

W. K. C. Guthrie, *The Greeks and their Gods*, London 1950.

E. R. Dodds, *The Greeks and the Irrational*, Berkeley 1951.

H. W. Parke and D. E. W. Wormell, *The Delphic Oracle* (Vol. I, *The History of the Oracle*; II, *The Oracular Responses*), Oxford 1956.

H. W. Parke, *Greek Oracles*, London 1969.

Miscellaneous

A. Andrewes, *The Greeks*, London 1967.

The Greeks (ed. H. Lloyd-Jones), London 1962.

H. D. F. Kitto, *The Greeks*, Pelican 1951.

M. Cary, *The Geographical Background to Greek and Roman History*, Oxford 1949.

A. W. Gomme, *Essays in Greek History and Literature*, Oxford 1937.

H. T. Wade-Gery, *Essays in Greek History*, Oxford 1958.

A. J. Toynbee, *Some Problems in Greek History*, London 1971.

M. Cary and E. H. Warmington, *The Ancient Explorers*, London 1929.

A. J. Graham, *Colony and Mother City in Ancient Greece*, Manchester 1964.

H. I. Marrou, *History of Education in Antiquity*, trans. G. Lane, London 1956.

L. Casson, *Ships and Seamanship in the Ancient World*, Princeton 1971.

H. W. Parke, *Greek Mercenaries from the Earliest Times to the Battle of Ipsus*, Oxford 1933.

Athenian Studies (presented to W. S. Ferguson), Harv. Stud. Suppl. I, 1940.

Ancient Society and Institutions (presented to V. Ehrenberg), Oxford 1966.

Period Bibliographies

1. THE BRONZE AGE
CHAPTER 1

The mainland. The best introduction is E. Vermeule's *Greece in the Bronze Age,* Chicago 1964, combining acute scholarship with a lively style, comprehensive, well illustrated and with excellently full bibliographies. The excitement of the early discoveries can be recaptured from H. Schliemann's *Mycenae* (1868) and *Mycenae and Tiryns* (1880). The most rewarding individual sites are Mycenae and Pylos. G. Mylonas, the present director of operations, has published two useful books to keep pace with the progress of excavation: *Ancient Mycenae,* Princeton 1957 and *Mycenae and Mycenaean Civilization,* Princeton 1966. *Mycenae: an archaeological history and guide,* Princeton 1949, by A. J. B. Wace, who had conducted important excavations at Mycenae, is still valuable. Three volumes of the basic publication of Blegen's excavation at Pylos have now been issued; the first gives the history of the site and a catalogue of what was found in the various parts of the building (*The Palace of Nestor at Pylos in Western Messenia,* by C. W. Blegen and M. Rawson, Princeton 1966); in the second Mabel Lang describes, classifies, and allocates the many fragments of frescoes from the Megaron and other rooms. The third volume (1973) by Blegen and others covers the excavations outside the palace. *The Mycenaeans,* by Lord William Taylour, London 1964, is a good general review, well illustrated.

The main evidence for Mycenaean trade comes from the distribution of Mycenaean pottery, the chronology of which is the essential foundation for any historical interpretation. The basic work of classification was done by A. Furumark in two major studies indispensable for the specialist: *The Mycenaean Pottery: Analysis and Classification* (1941): *Chronology* (1942). *Greek Pottery in the Bronze Age* by A. D. Lacy, London 1967, liberally illustrated, is a useful introduction to the broad outlines. The following illustrate the use made of the pottery evidence:

> A. Wace and C. W. Blegen, 'Pottery as evidence for Trade and Colonization in the Aegean Bronze Age', *Klio* 32 (1939) 131–147.
> H. Kantor, 'The Aegean and the Near East in the Second Millennium B.C.', *AJA* 32 (1948) 17–103.
> A. Furumark, 'The Settlement of Ialysos and Aegean Prehistory', *Op. Arch.* 6 (1950) 150–271.
> F. Stubbings, *Mycenaean Pottery from the Levant,* Cambridge 1951.
> W. Taylour, *Mycenaean Pottery in Italy and Adjacent Areas,* Cambridge 1958.
> S. Immerwahr, 'Mycenaean Trade and Colonization', *Arch.* 13 (1960) 4–13.
> *The Mycenaeans in the Eastern Mediterranean,* Acts of the International Archaeological Congress in Cyprus, Nicosia 1972.

V. R. Desborough collects and analyses the archaeological evidence for the collapse of the Mycenaean world, and the phase that follows in *The Last of the Mycenaeans and Their Successors,* Oxford 1964; in *The Greek Dark Ages,* London 1972, he carries his survey and analysis down to *c.* 900 B.C.

The main concentration of archaeology on palaces and tombs tends to obscure the wider environment. A Minnesota expedition has set an excellent precedent in attempting to reconstruct the Bronze Age environment of Messenia with a team of experts in different fields, in *Messenia,* edd. W. A. MacDonald and George R. Rapp, Minneapolis 1972.

Crete. The four volumes of *The Palace of Minos* by Sir Arthur Evans, London 1921–36, lavishly illustrated and eminently readable, are still the foundation for the reconstruction of Minoan civilisation. *The Archaeology of Crete*, London 1939, by J. D. S. Pendlebury, is a useful summary and interpretation of the evidence then available, but much has since been added to modify the picture. M. S. Hood's *The Minoans*, London 1971, is a good short up-to-date account and provides useful bibliographies for the main sites; R. Hutchinson's *Prehistoric Crete*, Penguin 1962, is particularly good on the physical setting, but uneven as a general history. *Crete* (trs. from Greek), Cleveland 1966, by C. Platon, who was formerly Director of Antiquities in Crete, has excellent photographs and is particularly interesting on the practice and principles of excavation. J. W. Graham's *The Palaces of Crete*, Princeton 1962, analyses the construction and plans of the main palaces.

Mycenae and Crete. *Crete and Mycenae* by S. Marinatos (trs. by J. Boardman) with photographs by M. Hirmer, London 1960, is a good general survey, brilliantly illustrated; *Minoan and Mycenaean Art* by R. A. Higgins, London 1967, is a good general introduction. In spite of the fascination of the gems, figurines, paintings and cult places it is too early yet for any study of Minoan and Mycenaean religion to carry complete conviction; M. P. Nilsson's *The Minoan–Mycenaean Religion and its survival in Greek Religion*,[2] London 1950, is still the best account available.

Homer and History. H. L. Lorimer's *Homer and the Monuments*, London 1950, reviewed the archaeological evidence in depth up to 1939; a new edition would be welcome to accommodate the new evidence and new interpretations. *A Companion to Homer*, edited by Wace and Stubbings, London 1962, includes articles on literary, historical and archaeological aspects: see the substantial review by D. H. Gray in *Phoenix* 17 (1963) 293–300. M. I. Finley's *The World of Odysseus*, London 1956, is mainly concerned to point the contrast between the social background of the two epics and the Mycenaean world, a heresy that has almost become orthodox, though the current tendency is to prefer a later date than Finley's tenth century for the main setting. D. L. Page's *History and Homer's Iliad*, Berkeley 1959, is persuasive and stimulating, but less convincing on a second reading. R. H. Simpson and J. F. Lazenby in *The Catalogue of Ships in Homer's Iliad*, Oxford 1970, review the archaeological evidence for all the sites mentioned in the Catalogue and contend that, in general, it reflects Mycenaean conditions with certain anomalies affected by post-Mycenaean changes.

2. THE ARCHAIC PERIOD
CHAPTERS 2–6

Our evidence for the early centuries is exclusively archaeological and archaeology remains an important control in the second half of the period. Contemporary literary evidence begins with Homer and Hesiod in the eighth century and increases in importance with the poets of the seventh and sixth centuries. Homer is in a sense frustrating because his world is a composite of several periods and to isolate the eighth century ingredient is very difficult. The historian gets more help from Hesiod who gives us a realistic picture of the small-scale farmer's struggle to make ends meet: there is an edition of the *Works and Days* by T. A. Sinclair, London 1937. Hesiod also introduces us to the Greek passion for systematising myth and bringing order into orthodox religion (for which see the introduction to M. L. West's edition of Hesiod's *Theogony*, Oxford 1966). The lyric poets of the seventh and sixth centuries, especially Archilochus, Sappho and Alcaeus give us vivid glimpses of aristocrats, fighting, feuding and feasting against a background of growing political conflict. *Greek Lyric Poetry*[2] by C. M. Bowra, Oxford 1961, is a perceptive review and there is a good selection in R. Lattimore's *Greek Lyrics* (second ed.), Chicago 1960; his translations admirably interpret the poetry as well as the meaning of the original poems. For the sixth century Solon and Theognis describe more explicitly the political tensions in Athens and Megara.

For the historical narrative we depend largely on authors most of whom wrote considerably later than the events, and no continuous narrative survives. The pieces have to be threaded together from such writers as the geographer Strabo describing the Mediterranean world in the time of Augustus and referring incidentally to historical events; Aristotle in his *Politics*, quoting examples from history to illustrate his political analysis; and later historians like Diodorus (*c*. 50 B.C.) and Nicolaus of Damascus, contemporary of Augustus, who depended on Ephorus and other earlier historians who themselves had to rely mainly on oral tradition. Inscriptions of the period add a little colour but they do not become of major importance until public business is recorded on stone.

The Dark Age of Greece by A. M. Snodgrass, Edinburgh 1971, is a useful comprehensive review of the archaeology of the period and pottery, which is the excavator's main friend in establishing his chronology and in tracing the patterns of trade, is well served by three books which are important to anyone who wishes to study the period in depth: *Protogeometric Pottery* by V. Desborough, Oxford 1952; *Greek Geometric Pottery* by J. N. Coldstream, London 1968; *Necrocorinthia* (Corinthian Art in the archaic period) by H. G. G. Payne, Oxford 1931. *The Origins of Greek Civilization*, New York 1961, by C. G. Starr is a stimulating and controversial study of the creative forces at work in the Dark Age.

T. Dunbabin in *Western Greeks*, Oxford 1948, assembles the archaeological and literary evidence for the history of Sicily and South Italy from the beginning of Greek colonisation to 480 B.C. His much shorter study of *The Greeks and their Eastern Neighbours* (ed. J. Boardman), London 1957, traces the development of Greek penetration into the Eastern Mediterranean. On these foundations and' with the further accumulation of archaeological evidence and argument J. Boardman, in *The Greeks Overseas*, Penguin 1964, reviews the relations of the Greeks with other peoples in the East and West. D. Ridgeway, 'The First Western Greeks', in *Greeks, Celts and Romans*, London 1973, 5–36, sets the colony of Pithecusae in its archaeological context.

G. L. Huxley's *The Early Ionians*, London 1966, together with C. Roebuck's *Ionian Trade and Colonization*, New York 1959, provide a good introduction to the history of the East Greeks. Sparta still awaits a master-work, but W. G. Forrest's *A History of Sparta, 950–192 B.C.* is an interesting summary; Huxley's *Early Sparta*, London 1962, attaches more importance to Pausanias and other late sources than most historians would approve, but his arguments are ingenious and sometimes convincing. M. I. Finley's essay in *Problèmes de la Guerre en Grèce ancienne* (ed. A. Vernant, Paris 1968) is an excellent short analysis (in English) of the basic character of Spartan society. Crete, which remained outside the mainstream of Greek history in the classical period was more important in the archaic period as an intermediary between the Near East and the Peloponnese. Her political organisation is described by R. F. Willetts in *Aristocratic Society in Ancient Crete*, London 1955, and her social development in *Ancient Crete: a social history*, London 1965. Most important of all sources for Cretan social and political organisation during this period is the code of laws inscribed on a circular wall which was later used to support the auditorium of a theatre. Difficulties of language and law have given it to most students the remoteness of Egyptian hieroglyphics; Willetts, *The Law Code of Gortyn*, Berlin 1967, provides a much needed translation together with introduction and commentary. His translation is reproduced in *The Fifth Century B.C.* by N. Lewis.

Athens, for which our evidence is fullest, is generously treated in standard histories, and V. Ehrenberg's *From Solon to Socrates* draws attention to topics in which views are changing. Among them is Solon's legislation which has needed re-thinking now that it has become virtually certain that there was no Athenian coinage when Solon is assumed to have brought forward his reforms (594). *Solon the Liberator*, by W. J. Woodhouse, London 1938, remains the fullest discussion of the agricultural background, and K. Freeman's *The Work and Life of Solon*, Cardiff 1926, is still useful for her translation of all the fragments of Solon's poems.

3. THE FIFTH CENTURY CHAPTERS 7–11

The Persian War. *Herodotus* (with commentary by W. W. How and J. Wells, Oxford 1912) provides in his last three books (VII–IX) a continuous narrative of the defeat of Xerxes' invasion, and in 5.28 ff. a short account of the Ionian Revolt and the Marathon campaign. Later sources add very little that is reliable to Herodotus but Aeschylus' *Persae*, produced in 472, less than eight years after the battle of Salamis, offers an important control. G. B. Grundy's detailed study of the 480–79 war in *The Great Persian War and its Preliminaries*, London 1901, is still useful, particularly on topography. *Xerxes' Invasion of Greece*, by C. Hignett, Oxford 1962, is the best critical review of the literary evidence; A. R. Burn's *Persia and the Greeks*, London 1963, is a more lively account. Both would have profited from W. K. Pritchett's *Studies in Ancient Greek Topography*, Part I, Berkeley 1965.

The Pentekontaetia. The eventful period between the Persian War and the Peloponnesian War bristles with problems owing to the nature of our evidence. Thucydides gives only a short summary in 1.89–146, and it is the weakest section in his great history. Diodorus adds useful information, but he has no good source to follow, much of his chronology is arbitrary and he has poor critical judgment. Plutarch's *Lives* of *Themistocles, Aristides, Cimon,* and *Pericles* preserve valuable material from contemporary sources which have not survived together with distortions and fabrications of later writers concerned more with interesting their readers than worrying about the truth. Inscriptions now assume increased importance, for sufficient fragments of the tribute lists have been preserved to follow the general pattern of assessments. After the democratic reforms of Ephialtes we have also a series of important decrees illustrating Athenian imperial policy. Texts with commentary of the most significant documents are included in *Greek Historical Inscriptions*, by Meiggs and Lewis, Oxford 1969. The sources for the period other than Thucydides and the Aristotelian *Constitution of Athens* are collected in G. F. Hill, *Sources for Greek History* (revised ed. 1951) and there are good translations of many of them in *The Fifth Century B.C.*, by N. Lewis, Toronto 1971, which covers the whole century.

For the transition from Delian League to Athenian Empire modern writing owes most to *The Athenian Tribute Lists* by B. D. Meritt, H. T. Wade-Gery, M. F. McGregor (Cambridge, Mass. and Princeton 1939–53). In Vol. I the texts of the tribute lists and relevant inscriptions are described, illustrated and established; Vol. II reprints the texts and adds many more inscriptions together with a generous selection of literary passages concerned not only with the tribute lists but also with the general character of the empire. Vol. III is primarily a history of the tribute, but includes also discussions of other important problems of Athenian imperialism. G. E. M. de Ste Croix's well documented attack on Thucydides' view of the empire ('The Character of the Athenian Empire', in *Hist.* 3 (1954–5) 1–41) provides lively controversy, and an incentive to read *Thucydides and Athenian Imperialism* by T. de Romilly, Paris 1947, trans. by P. Thody, Oxford 1963. *The Athenian Empire* by R. Meiggs, Oxford 1972, combines a history of the conversion from league to empire with an analysis of the empire's institutions and nature. V. Ehrenberg's *Sophocles and Pericles*, Oxford 1954, is a short but interesting study of basic antagonisms in Periclean Athens. Two recent books discuss the causes of the Peloponnesian War: *The Origins of the Peloponnesian War* by G. E. M. de Ste Croix, London 1972, is a refreshingly controversial analysis of the issues; D. Kagan's *Outbreak of the Peloponnesian War*, Ithaca 1969, is a more orthodox narrative. On the cultural background, C. M. Bowra's *Periclean Athens* is an eloquent tribute to the many-sidedness of Athenian brilliance. *The Sophists* by W. K. C. Guthrie (from the second volume of his *History of Greek Philosophy*) 1971, describes the intellectual background of the second half of the century and the best short account of the building history of the century available in English is I. T. Hill's *The Ancient City of Athens*, London 1953.

The Peloponnesian War. Thucydides' critical narrative provides a firm foundation for the military and political history of the war, and A. W. Gomme's *Historical Commentary on Thucydides*, I–III (covering 1 to 5.28), Oxford 1945–56, continued by A. Andrewes and K. J. Dover (Vol. 4, 5.29–7, 1970) is very rewarding. Plutarch adds more colour, sometimes too much colour, in his *Lives of Pericles, Nicias, Alcibiades*, and *Lysander*. The best contemporary complement to Thucydides are the comedies of Aristophanes, who took equal pleasure in attacking demagogues and intellectuals. His *Acharnians* and *Knights* bring out the harsh realities of the early stages of the war and his *Peace* is a good companion to Thucydides' account of the unsettlement that followed the Peace of Nicias. A good series of Oxford commentaries has begun with *Peace* (M. Platnauer, 1964); *Clouds* (K. J. Dover, 1968); *Wasps* (D. M. MacDowell, 1971): V. Ehrenberg's *The People of Aristophanes* (second ed.), Oxford 1951, is a good general guide to the plays. K. J. Dover's *Aristophanic Comedy*, London 1972, discusses the setting, structure, and production of Old Comedy, and includes a useful summary of all the plays. Aristophanes

distrusts Cleon and the demagogues who followed him, and his attacks are meant to bite as well as amuse, but he poses as a good democrat who believes in the demos. A more cynical analysis of Athenian democracy is preserved in a tract on the Athenian constitution by an unknown oligarch who regards the democracy as the rule of the good by the bad, but has a grudging admiration for the way in which it preserves its dominance: (*The Athenian Constitution* (preserved with manuscripts of Xenophon); translation by N. Lewis in *The Fifth Century B.C.*, 49–51), a usefully wide-ranging selection of literary sources and inscriptions. M. Renault's novel, *The Last of the Wine*, has a convincing late fifth century background.

4. THE FOURTH CENTURY BEFORE ALEXANDER CHAPTERS 12–15

The main sources are Xenophon and Diodorus. Xenophon played a leading part in the retreat of the ten thousand after the death of Cyrus at the battle of Cunaxa. His account of the expedition (*The Anabasis*) throws considerable light on the general condition of the Persian empire, the way of life of the Greeks on the south coast of the Euxine, and the toughness of fourth-century Greek mercenaries. The *Hellenica* continues Greek history where Thucydides left off (411) down to the battle of Mantinea (362). His narrative lacks distinction but, though he has some strange omissions, he does not distort history in the interest of rhetoric. He admires Sparta and has no sympathy for Thebes, but these prejudices do not lead to a deliberate falsification of facts. Diodorus is considerably more valuable for the fourth than for the fifth century and provides a useful control. Fourth-century historical inscriptions are more numerous and better preserved than those of the fifth century: M. N. Tod's *Greek Historical Inscriptions*, Vol. II, Oxford 1948, provides useful commentaries on a good selection of the most important. For the rise of Macedon Diodorus is supplemented by the public speeches of Demosthenes and Aeschines, particularly the two pairs delivered in 343 and 330 (Dem. 19 and 18, Aesch. 2 and 3). Books in English on the fourth century before the period of Demosthenes are rare. *The Second Athenian Confederacy*, by F. H. Marshall, Cambridge 1905, is still good as far as it goes, but something more substantial is needed to match (or translate) S. Accame's *La lega Ateniese*, Rome 1941. T. T. B. Ryder's *Koine Eirene*, London 1963, analyses the evidence for one of the most pervading but least realised ideals of the fourth century, a general peace which all would accept.

There has been more continuous interest in the struggle against Macedon, and the modern reputation of Demosthenes has fluctuated considerably. Bury, like many other historians of the late nineteenth and early twentieth centuries, regarded him primarily as a politician who did not understand history and fought for the preservation of the city state when it had become an anachronism. The growing disenchantment with the nation state and the modern associations of appeasement have helped to make this interpretation less popular. W. J. Jaeger in *Demosthenes, the Origin and Growth of his Policy,* Berkeley 1938, is the most extreme champion of Demosthenes as the consistent fighter for freedom, but he is too ready to defend Demosthenes at all points. A. W. Pickard-Cambridge's *Demosthenes and the last days of Greek Freedom,* New York 1914, is a more balanced and realistic account. In defence of Demosthenes his failure is often attributed in large part to the decadence of the Athenians. G. L. Cawkwell, the leading English-writing contributor to Demosthenic studies, suggests that if we had to rely on speeches delivered in court for our assessment of fifth-century Athenians they might seem no better than Demosthenes' contemporaries (an interesting point, perhaps a little exaggerated). Three of his articles are reproduced in *Philip and Athens,* a useful collection of articles selected and introduced by S. Perlman, Cambridge and New York 1973. Cawkwell criticises Demosthenes not for the ends for which he worked, but for the means he advocated. He lacked judgment and did not realise the military strength of the Macedonian army. He tried to fight the wrong kind of war (see 'The Crowning of Demosthenes' in *CQ* 19 (1969) 168–80, and the earlier articles there cited).

5. ALEXANDER
CHAPTERS 17–18

Alexander, like Caesar and Napoleon, invites partisanship. In modern times he has become a philosopher king, a military adventurer; a dedicated Hellenist more Hellenic than the Hellenes; a half-civilised Macedonian; a generous idealist; a ruthless tyrant. Napoleon, Bismarck, and Hitler have not been without influence on interpretations. One reason for this great diversity in the portraits is the nature of the evidence. The earliest continuous history of Alexander that survives was written nearly three hundred years after his death: from earlier historians we have only scattered fragments. Those who had accompanied Alexander in responsible positions were likely to flatter him, but there are also ample traces of a hostile tradition later. Rhetoric in the late fourth and early third centuries was a dominant influence on the writing of history, and the exploits of Alexander gave ample opportunities for dramatisation, moralisation and invention. The histories that were most read were those that were the most entertaining to read and battle emotions were more appreciated than battle tactics. When divergent accounts of actual facts are found in the sources it is not always easy to decide which is right, unless we can see a clear motive for falsification and in many cases both versions will make sense as falsifications. There is a danger also of rejecting ugly stories because they are not in charcter, or suspecting the more generous versions for the same reason. This is particularly dangerous in Alexander who was a man of many moods, with a violent temper and sudden impulses, who could be both ruthless and generous. We should not expect complete consistency. In past generations the main tendency was to idealise Alexander, to over-estimate his Greekness and to see in him the great liberator who saw the narrowness of the the city state and thought in terms of a world where race distinctions were irrelevant. Modern scholars are now concentrating more on Alexander in his Macedonian context, and pay more attention to the hard drinking, physically tough Macedonians than to the Greek intellectuals who accompanied him. Camp life was probably more Macedonian than Greek. But Alexander was such a dominant figure that most of the secondary characters make little impression in the sources. A more systematic study of the marshals and administrators, and of the tensions between Alexander's contemporaries and the older and more experienced men whom he inherited from his father is building up a more realistic picture; but in the process there is perhaps a danger of underestimating the irrational and imaginative side of Alexander.

Source criticism must always play a large part in the debate because the value of our late sources depends largely on the identification of the earlier sources which they follow and our judgment of their value. The fragments of these lost historians have been collected by F. Jacoby in his *Fragmente der griechischen Historiker,* nos. 117–58. C. A. Robinson has provided translations of them in *The History of Alexander the Great,* vol. I, and L. Pearson in *The lost histories of Alexander the Great* (New York 1968) reviews the evidence for their date and value. The best of the continuous histories is Arrian's *Anabasis.* Arrian was a governor of the Roman province of Cappadocia in the second century A.D. He had had considerable experience of army affairs and administration and he tells us that his main sources were Ptolemy and Aristobulus, whom he chose because they both served under Alexander, and both wrote after his death. Ptolemy, who did not become prominent until the latter stages of the expedition, was made a member of Alexander's personal bodyguard in 330 and held military commands in India. At Alexander's death he was important enough to secure the rich satrapy of Egypt where he later became king and established the Ptolemaic dynasty. He was probably Arrian's main source for Alexander's battles, and there is little clear evidence of his falsifying facts in his own interest, but he may have been inclined to gloss over or omit the less creditable acts of Alexander. Of Aristobulus we know much less. He was commissioned by Alexander to restore the tomb of Cyrus and was presumably an architect or engineer, but he also showed a very knowledgeable interest in the trees, plants and animals of India. But he was described as a flatterer and was probably more than generous to Alexander. From these, and other sources intermittently used, Arrian has written a comparatively sober, but fast-moving and readable narrative. But the most popular of the Alexander historians in the late Hellenistic and Roman periods was Clitarchus of Alexandria who was certainly readable, but far from reliable. He was a pioneer of the dramatic school of historians, and cared more for his effects than for the truth, introducing novelistic episodes where possible and concealing the tactics of battle behind a colourful description of the more dramatic moments and the emotions of the troops. The marvels of India also gave him ample scope. Unfortunately the relative order of Ptolemy, Aristobulus, and Clitarchus is still a matter of continuing controversy, but it is at least possible that Clitarchus was the earliest of the three.

Arrian can be supplemented and in some cases corrected from less historical writers. Diodorus devoted a complete book of 118 chapters to the history of Alexander, but this was a very small part only of an encyclopaedic history of the known world from the earliest times to 54 B.C. There was little critical judgment in his work, but he preserves information that would otherwise be lost. His normal practice was to base his narrative on one main author at a time, and intermittently consult others, and in his book on Alexander he seems to have made extensive use of Clitarchus (there are useful notes and introduction in C. B. Welles' translation in the Loeb series). Unlike Diodorus, who was a Sicilian and wrote in Greek, Quintus Curtius Rufus was a Roman and his history was written in the first century A.D. under the emperor Claudius or Vespasian. He shares some of Diodorus' sources but preserves more of the hostile tradition. He cares more for dramatic effect than sober judgment and speeches, some of them very effective, play an important part in his narrative. Plutarch's *Alexander* (a good commentary by J. R. Hamilton, Oxford 1969) is very different in character from our other sources, for, as he himself emphasises, he is writing a biography and not history. He is primarily interested in Alexander's character and sees no reason to study the tactics of his battles or the details of his administration. He was a poor historian in that he lacked critical judgment but he read very widely and liked to use original sources. Unfortunately he was easily deceived and by no means all the letters of Alexander which he uses were written by Alexander.

The modern literature on Alexander has grown at a menacing rate, but there is an excellent analytical Bibliography by E. Badian in *Classical World* LXV (1971) 37–56 and 77–83. The most balanced general account is still U. Wilcken's *Alexander*, though it was first published in 1931 (an English translation by G. C. Richards in 1932); it has been reprinted in paperback with introduction, notes and bibliography, by E. N. Borza, New York 1967. The most influential major work in English has been W. W. Tarn's *Alexander the Great,* Cambridge 1948, in two volumes, the first a vivid narrative, and the second a long series of appendices on problems concerning the sources, the army, and the aims of Alexander. Tarn's wide learning and attractive style captivated his first readers, but many of his more important views have had to be abandoned. His portrait is now seen to be too idealised and very few would accept his passionate conviction that the idea of the Brotherhood of Man derives from Alexander. His second volume, however, still remains a mine of useful information and argument.

New life has been given to Alexander studies by Badian in a series of impressive articles (see his Bibliography referred to above, nos. 51, 93, 107, 112, 117, 118, 149, 150, 151, 173, 183). By directing closer attention to Alexander's Macedonian background and the secondary figures he has thrown new light on the central character, and successfully questioned some of the assumptions of established orthodoxy. The Alexander who emerges has more of the calculated ruthlessness of the stereotype tyrant, ancient and modern, than is generally attributed to him, and a less embittered generation may wish to revive interest in Alexander's idealism. But for any future reconstruction of Alexander's personality and achievement Badian's work will be invaluable. R. D. Milns' *Alexander the Great,* London 1968, and J. R. Hamilton's *Alexander the Great,* London 1973, make good use of Badian's work and, though designed for the general reader, are the best up-to-date introductions available to ancient historians. There is a good conspectus of varying modern views in two collections of articles: G. T. Griffith (ed.), *Alexander the Great : the Main Problems,* Cambridge 1966; *Greece and Rome,* 12 (1965) 113–239. J. R. Lane Fox's *Alexander the Great,* London 1973, covers more new ground and is particularly impressive in the use of oriental sources from which a more credible picture of the Persian empire is drawn.

Notes to Text

CHAPTER 1

1 R. J. Rodden, *Proceedings Prehist. Soc.* 28 (1962) 267.

2 *Hesp.* 38 (1969) 343–81, *Archaeology* 21 (1968) 4–9.

3 It used to be thought that in the second millennium, until the power of Crete collapsed, Mycenae had to rely mainly on the Lipari islands for obsidian but the large-scale analysis of samples has revealed no trace of Lipari obsidian in Mycenaean Greece. See C. Renfrew and others, *BSA* 60 (1965) 225–47.

4 For early developments in metallurgy in the islands, see C. Renfrew in *AJA* 71 (1967) 1–20.

5 The arguments for the revised dating are set out by D. B. Redford in *History and Chronology of the eighteenth Dynasty of Egypt,* reviewed by K. A. Kitchen in *Chronique d'Égypte* 43 (1969) 313–24.

6 J. Caskey, *Arch.* 8 (1955) 116–20.

7 J. Caskey, *Hesp.* 29 (1960) 285–303.

8 Excavation at Lefkandi was begun in 1964. The site was selected to throw light on this area in the period before the Lelantine War between Chalcis and Eretria. Some of the earliest pottery is thought to have Anatolian affinities. See the preliminary report, *Excavations at Lefkandi, Euboea, 1964–6,* by M. R. Popham and L. H. Sackett (published by the British School at Athens, Thames and Hudson, 1968); and a more general account by them in *Arch.* 25 (1972) 8–19.

9 The distribution of these non-Greek names is reviewed by C. W. Blegen and D. Haley in *AJA* 32 (1928) 146–54, who conclude that they fit the pattern of settlement in the early Helladic period.

10 Example from Cnossus (1.63 m.), Evans, *Palace of Minos II,* 632.

11 Hdt. 3. 122; Thuc. 1.4.

12 For a general survey of Minoan and Mycenaean trade with the east see bibliography p. 511.

13 For Trianda, A. Furumark, 'The Settlement at Ialysus and Aegean Prehistory', *Opusc. Arch.* 6 (1950) 150–271. For Samos, see V. Milojcil, *Samos,* vol. I: *Die Prähistorische Siedlung unter dem Heraion* (1961); for Miletus, C. Weickert, *Istanbuler Mitteilungen* 9–10 (1959–60) 1–96.

14 Hdt. 7. 169.

15 *Kythera,* edd. J. N. Coldstream and G. L. Huxley, London 1972.

16 Four settlements have been explored at Phylakopi, the earliest unwalled, the second and third 'pre-Mycenaean' fortresses, the fourth of the Mycenaean Age; *Excavations at Phylakopi in Melos,* British School at Athens 1904.

17 S. Marinatos, *Excavations at Thera* I (1968), II (1969), III (1970), IV (1971). See also his lecture 'Life and Art in Prehistoric Thera', *Proceedings of the British Academy* 57 (1971) 351–67.

18 A short account by the excavator J. Caskey in *Memorie del. 1° Congresso Internazionale di Micenologia* (1967) Rome, 1968, I. 68–72; *Arch.* 16 (1963) 284 f.

19 G. E. Mylonas in *HSCP* Suppl. 1. (1940) 11–36 ('Athens and Crete') has no difficulty in showing that Crete could not have exercised any control over the Greek mainland in the thirteenth century, but his arguments are not valid against an earlier date. It was only when Crete was at the height of her power that she could have exercised any control over Attica. We do not know enough about Athens in the sixteenth century to rule out hostilities between Crete and Athens then. Tradition also recorded (Paus. 1.19.4, 1.44.3 and Apoll. Rhod. 3. 15–18) that the Cretan fleet was stationed at the off-shore island of Minoa, when the Cretans were subduing the cities of the Megarid, though this story may have been invented to explain the name of the island.

20 For Minoan religion, *The Minoan-Mycenaean Religion and its survival in Greek Religion,*[2] London 1950, by M. P. Nilsson.

21 The first published statement concerning the decipherment of Linear B as a primitive form of Greek was by M. Ventris with the Cambridge philologist J. Chadwick in *JHS* 73 (1953) 84–103. The process of decipherment was described by Chadwick in *The Decipherment of Linear B*² (1967) and Ventris and Chadwick together produced a volume of texts with translations, including the most informative tablets from Cnossus, Pylos and Mycenae, with a general commentary, *Documents in Mycenaean Greek* (1956), a 2nd ed. (1973) with new material by J. Chadwick. For a short article by Ventris himself based on the tablet that was decisive in verifying his hypothesis see *Arch.* 7 (1954) 15–21. There has been a limited resistance to the claim that the language is Greek, but the great majority of scholars now accept it. Decipherment, however, is difficult, because almost all the texts are lists of names or inventories. The difficulties are explained by S. Levin, *The Linear B Decipherment, the controversy re-examined* (1964). For the historical value of the tablets see especially S. Dow and J. Chadwick, *CAH²*, ch. XIII (1971).

22 The Santorini eruption was first related to Cretan history by Sp. Marinatos when he was Director of Antiquities in Crete and his major statement from that period, in *Antiquity* 13 (1939) 425–39, is still important. Impressed by his own excavations along the north coast of the island and particularly by the extraordinary natural force displayed in the destruction of a large building at Amnisus, an important harbour town on the north coast, he suggested that the series of destructions along the coast were the result of the tremendous tidal wave (fashionably called *tsunami*, the Japanese name) that must have been an immediate result of the eruption. Judging by known parallels less violent this wave could have been up to 100 feet high and would have devastated the shipping and the settlements along the coast. Even the editors of *Antiquity* seemed to feel a little uncomfortable at such boldness but they hoped that the theory would be tested by selected excavations. The question came alive again when two scientists, after studying a large sample of deep-sea cores, published a paper on the nature, volume, and direction of the ash thrown up by the volcano, and its probable effects on Crete (D. Ninkovich and B. C. Heeze, *Santorini Tephra*, Colston Papers 17, 1965). Two years later Marinatos, now Director of the Greek Archaeological Service, began his very successful excavation of Akrotiri (see n. 17 above). Santorini at once became front page news and caught the public imagination, especially when it was linked with Plato's story of Atlantis, the fabulous island civilisation that was swallowed up by the sea. The pioneer in this hypothesis was K. T. Frost in *JHS* 33 (1913) 189–206. Two good books, splendidly illustrated, have developed this theme, and both describe the nature of the eruption in detail: A. G. Galanopoulos and E. Bacon, *Atlantis*, 1959 (stronger on volcanology); J. V. Luce, *The End of Atlantis*, 1939 (stronger on the Minoan background and on the identification with Plato's Atlantis).

Historians and archaeologists were more interested in the relation of the eruption to a massive series of destructions in Crete which had long been recognised as a major crisis in Minoan history. On the initiative of Marinatos an International Congress of experts in Minoan Studies and in Volcanology was convened to discuss the problems on the spot (a record of the conclusions of the conference by S. Hood in *Kadmos* 9 (1970) 98–106). There now seems to be general agreement that the evacuation of Akrotiri (c. 1500) must be separated from the main series of destructions in Crete by a substantial interval of not less than twenty years and Marinatos himself is convinced in his third report (1970) that the eruption followed very soon after the earthquake which caused the evacuation. J. Money, in *Antiquity* 46 (1972) 50–3, claims to have found a layer of humus immediately beneath the pumice, which would indicate such an interval. This needs more detailed confirmation from the excavators before it is accepted.

23 S. Marinatos, *Excavation at Thera* III (1970) 7 f.

24 Page's thesis was set out in *The Santorini Volcano and the Desolation of Minoan Crete*, London 1969. It would seem to be untenable unless *either* the pottery experts can convince themselves that the pottery of Akrotiri could be contemporary with the pottery of the destructions *or* the volcanologists will allow a substantial interval between the preliminary earthquake and the great eruption. Meanwhile the considerable amount of rebuilding that was needed in the palace of Cnossus c. 1500 should be the result of the earthquake that led to the abandonment of Akrotiri and closer examination may reveal other sites including Amnisus that were seriously damaged c. 1500. See S. Hood in *Kadmos* 9 (1970) 105 f. It should also be possible by further excavation to resolve the conflicting statements about the degree and length of depopulation in the eastern half of the island and to find out how the western half of the island, considerably less extensively explored than the east, fared in these crucial years. New light which might be decisive could also be thrown on the destruction by G. Cadogan's current excavations at Myrtos on the south eastern coast. The large country house on the site was violently destroyed c. 1450 and the destruction was accompanied by fire. The analysis of samples of carbonised wood and ashes has not yet provided decisive evidence of the nature of the destruction (*Antiquity* 46 (1972) 310). See also a review by E. Vermeule in *Arch.* 24 (1971) 130–5.

25 S. Hood, *The Minoans*, 55, interpreting the excavator's account in *BSA* 7 (1900–1) 123–9.

26 The controversy between Palmer and his critics has been continuous and lively since 1960. Archaeologists have tended to accept Evans' main conclusions. Many of those who can have no independent judgment on the archaeological evidence have been tempted by Palmer's historical reconstruction. For recent statements of his case see L. R. Palmer, *The Penultimate Palace of Knossos*, Rome 1969, and *A new guide to the Palace of Knossos*, London 1969.

27 M. V. Popham, *The Destruction of the Palace at Knossos, Studies in Mediterranean Archaeology*, vol. 12, Göteborg 1970.

28 A detailed and fully illustrated catalogue, G. Karo, *Die Schachtsgräber von Mykenai*, 1930–3.

29 *Myc. Congress* (see n. 18), I. 262–5.

30 A Cretan origin is advocated by S. Hood, *Antiquity* 34 (1960) 166–76, but see E. Vermeule (n. 34) 338 n. 7.

31 It would surely be unwise to build ambitious inferences from the translation in Ventris and Chadwick, *Documents* n. 257: 'Thus the *mayors* and their *wives* and the vice-*mayors* and key-bearers and supervisors of *figs* and *hoeing* will contribute bronze for *ships* and the points for arrows and spears'.

32 *Documents* (n. 21) pp. 194–205.

33 G. E. Mylonas, *Mycenae's Last Century of Greatness*, Sydney 1968.

34 E. Vermeule, *Greece in the Bronze Age*, 181 f. Mylonas (*Mycenae and the Mycenaean Age* (1966), 80–83) associates the building with the palace.

35 For the history and description of the site see C. W. Blegen and M. Rawson, *The Palace of Pylos*, Vol. I. By the same authors, *A Guide to the Palace of Nestor*, 1962.

36 E. Vermeule (n. 34) 127–30. For the site of Vapheio see *BSA* 55 (1960) 76.

37 Thuc. 1. 2.5, probably an exaggerated reaction from traditional panegyric.

38 *ILN* Nov. 28, Dec. 5, 1964, 859–61, 896–9. For the literary tradition see A. Schachtar, *Phoenix* 21 (1967) 1–10.

39 *AAA* 4 (1971) 161–3. The main chamber measures 10·52 m. × 6·24 m. and is 3·50 m. high.

40 E. Kenney, *Liverpool Annals of Art and Arch.* 22 (1935) 189–206. Gla is off the beaten track, but is one of the most fascinating and puzzling of Mycenaean sites. It deserves more attention than it has received, but there is a good short description in Vermeule (n. 34) 266.

41 The belief that tin was mined near Cirrha (O. Davies, *JHS* 49 (1929) 89–99) has not survived the demonstration by S. Benton, *Antiquity* 38 (1964) 138, that the 'tin' was bauxite. Tin was scarce in the Mediterranean area. The most accessible supply came from the east. There was a little tin with a mainly copper cargo in a ship wrecked off Cape Gelidonya in the late Bronze Age (see n. 44 below).

42 It used to be thought that the Mycenaean interest in Lipari derived from its obsidian but analysis has shown that none of the samples from Mycenaean sites that have been examined come from Lipari (see n. 3). Possibly the island was a market for metals from Etruria or even Spain.

43 W. Taylour, *Mycenaean Pottery in Italy and adjacent areas* (1958), 81–137.

44 A preliminary report in *AJA* 65 (1961) 267–76; final publication, *Trans. Am. Philosoph. Soc.* 57 (part 8), 1967.

45 An account of Ugarit and its relations with Minoans and Mycenaeans in C. F. A. Schaeffer, *The Cuneiform Texts of Ras Shamra*. For a portrait of Tyre at the beginning of the sixth century see *Ezekiel*, 27.

46 For Samos and Miletus see n. 13 above.

47 For the Hittite background see O. Gurney, *The Hittites*,[2] Penguin 1954, 246–58.

48 D. L. Page, *History and the Iliad*, Berkeley 1959; E. Vermeule (n. 34) 272.

49 The revised dating is based primarily on philological grounds. See Philo H. J. Houwink ten Lake, *The Records of the Early Hittite Empire*, Istanbul 1970.

50 For the analysis see H. W. Catling, *Archaeometry* 6 (1963) 1–9 (esp. 4–6) and *BSA* 58 (1963) 94–115. Criticisms answered, *Archaeometry* 9 (1966) 92–7; for the Berbati pottery, A. Akerström, *Myc. Congress* (n. 18) 48–53.

51 Vermeule (n. 34) 217 with pl. XLA–B.

52 W. Taylour, *AAA* 3 (1970) 72–80; *AJA* 75 (1971) 266–8. It was subsequently found that a neighbouring room was also used for some form of religious cult.

53 *Odyssey* 3. 43–4.

54 In the east the chariot was used for attack; in Homer's battle scenes it serves almost exclusively as transport. There is no firm contemporary evidence on pots or stelae for Mycenaean usage. P. A. L. Greenhalgh in *Early Greek Warfare*, ch. 1, argues that the Mycenaeans must have followed eastern practice, and that, in the eighth century, when chariot-fighting was obsolete, the function of the chariot in battle was inferred from the practice of the horsemen of the archaic period who dismounted to fight. But the terrain of Greece was considerably less well suited than the plains of Asia to mass chariots charging in line. In the text a compromise has been adopted.

55 Photographs of the two cuirasses in A. M. Snodgrass, *Arms and Armour of the Greeks* (1967) pl. 9 (p. 25), pl. 17 (p. 41).

56 C. W. Blegen, *Troy* IV (1958).

57 J. H. Breasted, *Ancient Records of Egypt* III. 580.

58 *Ugaritica* V. 78–89.

59 J. B. Pritchard, *Ancient Near Eastern Texts*[3] (1969) pp. 262 f.

60 A. J. B. Wace, *Mycenae* (1949) 98 f.

61 O. Broneer, *Hesp.* 38 (1939) 367–429.

62 Broneer, *Hesp.* 35 (1966) 346–62, 37 (1968) 25–35, but see p. 47, with n. 64.

63 E. French, *BSA* 58 (1963) 44–52.

64 C. P. Kardara (*AAA* 4 (1971) 85–9) has to exclude the stretch of wall in the area of the sanctuary of Poseidon (*Hesp.* 37 (1966) 25 ff.) and suggests that it may be an early wall associated with the *temenos*. But there is no other evidence of a Bronze Age sanctuary here.

65 Blegen in *Troy* IV (1958) and in his *Troy and the Trojans* (1964) dated the destruction near the middle of IIIB (*c.* 1240). In *Pylos* I, 422 he preferred a date 'about the middle of the thirteenth century or a trifle earlier'. D. Gray, reviewing *Troy* IV (*JHS* 82 (1962) 195–7) argued from the latest pottery for the end of IIIB; so also Mylonas in *Hesp.* 33 (1964) 363 f. Nylander (*Antiquity* 37

(1963) 7), after discussion with Furumark, preferred the beginning of IIIC.

66 C. Nylander, *Antiquity* 37 (1963) 6–11; M. I. Finley, *JHS* 84 (1964) 1–9, *Aspects of Antiquity*, 24–37.

67 V. Desborough, *The Last Mycenaeans and their Successors* (1964).

68 Rhys Carpenter, *Discontinuity in Greek Civilisation* (1966).

69 E. French *BSA* 58 (1963) 44–52.

70 *Iliad* 10. 261–5. A good example in A. W. Persson, *New Tombs at Dendra* (1942) 126.

71 *Iliad* 11. 632–7.

72 *Iliad* 2. 494–759. The catalogue is woven artificially into the context. A roll-call of the contingents could be expected at the beginning of the expedition, but is out of place in the tenth year. R. Hope Simson and J. F. Lazenby in *The Catalogue of the Ships in Homer's Iliad* (1970) review the archaeological evidence from all the places mentioned in the catalogue. Their conclusion is that the list mainly reflects Mycenaean conditions, but that some entries imply a twelfth century context.

73 There seems to have been no major destruction at the end of IIIB at Argos or Asine and in both there is apparent continuity through IIIC. See *Catalogue* (n. 72), 61–73. For Asine, *AAA* 4 (1971) 147–8.

74 Thuc. 1.12.3. Thucydides qualifies his statement by saying that some Boeotians had preceded the main body and it was they who took part in the Trojan expedition. This is probably an attempt to reconcile Homer with the general tradition. See *Catalogue*, 19–37.

75 *Iliad* 2. 645–652. Homer implies that the whole of Crete with its hundred cities was under a single command and that Cnossus which he mentions first was the capital. Gortyn is listed second, but it is very doubtful whether it became important before the Iron Age. The archaeological evidence for the period between the destruction of Cnossus (*c.* 1370) and the arrival in strength of the Dorians does not yet offer firm controls, but there is nothing to suggest that a Cretan contingent would be so large or important in the late thirteenth century. The impression of Crete given by the *Odyssey* (19. 172–7) is rather different. There are ninety (and not a hundred) cities and the mixture of languages is emphasised—Achaeans, Eteocretans, Cydonians, Dorians and Pelasgians. This is not good evidence that Dorians had reached Crete before the Trojan War or the main destructions on the mainland. See *Catalogue*, 111–16; J. T. Hooker, *JHS* 89 (1969) 60–71.

76 *Iliad* 6.168–9. Perhaps the symbols were pictorial.

77 *Odyssey* 8.1–25 (Phaeacians); *Iliad* 2. 207 f. (Thersites).

78 The account of the period following the destructions is based primarily on Desborough's review of the archaeological evidence (n. 67).

79 For Perati see Desborough, *The Last Mycenaeans*, 115 f. In Lefkandi there are two destructions

during IIIC. The first probably represents refugees from the mainland, *Excavations at Lefkandi*, 34 f.

80 V. Desborough, *Protogeometric Pottery* (1952).

81 The evidence is reviewed by J. M. Cook in *Greek Settlement in the Eastern Aegean and Asia Minor, CAH* II² ch. xxxviii (1961) and, more fully, by M. B. Sakellariou, *La migration grecque en Ionie*, Athens 1958. The Anglo-Turkish excavations at Old Smyrna have been particularly valuable in establishing the chronology of settlement, *BSA* 63–4 (1958–9) 1–181 (a historical summary in 9–34).

82 Hdt. 1.56.

83 Hdt. 1.143–8.

84 Thucydides (3.2.3) records the encouragement given by the Boeotians to the Aeolian Mytilenaeans in their revolt from Athens in 428.

85 Herodotus (1.144) attributes the exclusion of Halicarnassus from the Dorian festival to an individual's offence: the cause was certainly deeper. The names in a fifth-century Halicarnassus law about disputed property emphasise the great mixture in the population, Meiggs and Lewis, *Greek Historical Inscriptions*, 32.

86 Hdt. 1.171. The tradition that the Carians were pioneers in the development of Greek arms (the details vary) recur often in Greek writers, but the archaeological evidence does not seem to support it. See A. M. Snodgrass (*JHS* 84 (1964) 107–18) who suggests that it may derive from the prominence of Carian mercenaries in the seventh century. There is no trace of it in Homer.

87 See n. 50 above.

88 V. Karageorghis, *Salamis* 1.1.

89 Hdt. 1.1.

90 Hdt. 2.44.4.

91 Hdt. 6.47.2.

92 Hdt. 1.105.3.

93 Hdt. 5.59.

94 Thuc. 1.8.1.

95 Thuc. 6.2.6.

96 *Iliad* 6.289; 23.740–3.

97 *Odyssey* 15.115–8.

98 *Od.* 15.415.

99 *Od.* 14.288.

100 *Od.* 13.274 ff.

101 Ventris and Chadwick, *Documents* (n. 21) p. 136.

102 For a detailed review of the evidence see J. D. Muhly, 'Homer and the Phoenicians', *Berytus*, 19 (1970) 19–64.

103 J. N. Coldstream, *Greek Geometric Pottery*, 380. The earliest Greek pottery so far found at Motya is Protocorinthian of the last quarter of the eighth century.

104 I. Kings, 5.9.26–8.

105 E. Kunze, *Kretische Bronzereliefs* (1931). Some archaeologists prefer a seventh century date.

106 P. Cintas, *Manuel d'archéologie punique* I. 1970.

107 Bury, like the majority of his contemporaries, preferred an earlier date, in the late tenth or ninth century, and he assumed that the transmission was made in Ionia. It is only in the last two generations that we have come to realise from the growing volume of archaeological evidence that Euboea and the Greek mainland took the lead in reopening the sea lanes to the East. There are three main lines of enquiry for establishing the date of transmission. (1) At what date do the Phoenician letters correspond most closely with the earliest Greek letters? (2) What is the date of the earliest surviving Greek writing? (3) How soon were the Greeks in close enough contact with the Phoenicians in the East to adopt their alphabet? Arguments from letter forms are indecisive because, while some Greek letters correspond more closely to tenth-century or earlier Phoenician letters, some of the letter forms (such as *kappa* and *mu*) do not appear in Phoenician inscriptions until the ninth century. More dated Phoenician inscriptions are needed before the criterion can carry weight. On our present evidence the establishment of the settlement at Al Mina at the mouth of the Orontes seems to mark the beginning of the Greek penetration of the Eastern Mediterranean, and this should probably be dated near 800 (J. Boardman, *The Greeks Overseas*, 61 ff.).

The main reason why a date *c.* 750 has won increasing acceptance is the evidence of writing on pots. The earliest surviving inscription may still be on the Attic vase of the late Geometric period (*c.* 720) which proclaims that it shall be 'the prize of the dancer who dances more gaily than others'; but whereas, when Bury wrote, this vase stood out in splendid isolation there is now a considerable accumulation of graffiti on pots from the late eighth century and a more substantial inscription, which may even be a little earlier than the Attic vase, from the Euboean colony of Pithecusae on the island of Ischia (Meiggs and Lewis, *GHI*.I). It is possible that the earliest writing was on perishable materials such as papyrus, leather or wood and that the habit of writing on pots did not develop until comparatively late. Hammond, for example (*A History of Greece*,[2] 1967) prefers a date *c.* 850; but until evidence accumulates of closer contact with the Near East than the present archaeological evidence suggests the eighth century provides a more likely context. Al Mina, Rhodes and Crete have all been suggested as the birthplace of the Greek alphabet. R. Young (*Hesp.* 38 (1969) 252–96) has shown that the Greek alphabet was already being used by the Phrygians before the end of the eighth century, and that they are likely to have found it at Al Mina or some other position on the Syrian or Cilician coast. A late archaic inscription from Crete recently published concerns the appointment of a *poinikastes*, a man who does Phoenician things, and he is a scribe as distinct from a *mnemon*, a remembrancer. The verb *poinikazen* has also been preserved in two other Cretan inscriptions, and neither word has been found elsewhere (L. H. Jeffery and A. Morpurgo Davies, *Kadmos* 9 (1970) 118–54). This slightly strengthens the case for a Cretan origin, but the basic discussion of the origin and distribution of the Greek alphabet is still L. H. Jeffery's *The Local Scripts of Archaic Greece*, Oxford 1961.

CHAPTER 2

1 The Cyrenaean decree (Meiggs and Lewis, *GHI* 5) concerns the status of Theraeans resident in Cyrene in the early fourth century. The foundation document is quoted in order to establish their claim to citizenship, 'according to the provisions made by our ancestors': 'It was resolved by the Ecclesia: since Apollo unprompted bade Battus and the Theraeans colonise Cyrene, the Theraeans are resolved to send Battus as leader and king: and the Theraeans shall sail as his companions. They shall sail with equal rights from each household, one son from each, and the young men [shall be drawn from all the districts] and any other free Theraean who wishes may sail. And if the colonists establish their settlement any kinsman who sails afterwards to Libya shall be entitled to citizenship and office and to a share in land that has no owner. But if they do not establish their settlement and the Theraeans cannot help them and they are hard pressed by necessity for five years, then they may leave the land without fear for Thera, and they may take again their property and be citizens. And who so refuses to sail when the city despatches him shall be condemned to death and his property shall be state property .... On these terms they made oaths, both those that remained in Thera and those who sailed to establish the colony, and they made curses against those who transgressed the oath and did not abide by it .. .. They fashioned images of wax and burnt them, all standing in a circle, men, women, boys and girls, chanting imprecations, that he who did not abide by these oaths should be consumed and should dissolve like the images, himself, his descendants, and his property.' The main substance of the document seems to be original and is close to the version of Herodotus (4.153). Herodotus (4.156) also records that when, after their first disappointment, the colonists sailed home, the Theraeans refused to let them land. Colonisation was here the alternative to starvation.

2 Plutarch, *Greek Questions* 11 (*Moralia* 293B).

3 A. Blakeway in *BSA* 33 (1932–3) 180–91 made a strong case for the view that the natives of Sicily were trading with the Greeks before the Greek colonies were established. This conclusion was based on the belief that the earliest Greek pottery at Syracuse and other sites was earlier than the earliest pottery from the Greek colonies. French excavations at Sicilian Megara, however, have produced Greek pottery from the graves of colonists earlier than the pottery on which Blakeway relied, and there is no longer any firm evidence that trade preceded colonisation in Sicily, G. Vallet and J. F. Villard, *BCH* 76 (1957) 289–346.

4 The Euxine was also called the Axine or inhospitable ('Άξενος, Pind. Pyth. 4.203). The origin of the epithet is still disputed. A. C. Moorhouse, *CQ* 34 (1940) 123–8 and 41 (1948) 59–60, suggests that the name Πόντος Εὔξεινος, meaning friendly passage, was first used for the approaches to the inner sea and then transferred to the sea itself. W. S. Allen (*CQ* 42 (1948) 59–60) infers that it derives from an Avestan word *achsaena* meaning dark and that this name was given to the sea by early peoples of Iranian speech living on the north shore; this word sounded to the Greeks like ἄξενος and so, by a typical euphemism, became Εὔξεινος.

5 The context of the earliest Milesian colonies in the Euxine and the approaches to the Euxine is not quite certain. Eusebius dates Cyzicus, Sinope and her daughter-city Trapezus in the middle of the eighth century, nearly a hundred years before the occupation of Byzantium. His dating is usually dismissed, but the stories of the Argonauts show an early interest in the Euxine, and the Corinthian epic poet Eumelus mentioned the Borysthenes in his *Corinthiaca* (eighth or early seventh century). Small settlements at Sinope and Trapezus in search of metals would be intelligible in the eighth century, but no evidence earlier than the late seventh century has been found in excavations at Sinope. Even if there were settlements in the eighth century on the south shore of the Euxine the colonisation of the north shore and the development of the corn trade did not begin until the second half of the seventh century. The evidence is discussed by R. M. Cook in *JHS* 66 (1946) 67–98. See also J. A. Graham, *Bull. Inst. Class. Stud.* 5 (1958) 25–42.

6 The need for sheltered harbours developed comparatively late. Athens was content with the open sandy bay of Phaleron until the early fifth century. The Samian harbour was not protected by a mole until the tyranny of Polycrates (*c.* 530 B.C.).

7 The excavations at Motya, the earliest of the Phoenician colonies, have produced no evidence of settlement before the last quarter of the eighth century, after the first wave of Greek colonisation. The traditional date for the foundation of Carthage is 814 which is defended by P. Cintas, *Manuel d'archéologie punique I* (Paris, 1970). Most modern archaeologists prefer a date some two generations later.

8 The dates are based on Thucydides whose source is probably the fifth-century Syracusan historian Antiochus. These dates seem to be precise, but it is now widely believed that no precise dates were known and that the dates given by Thucydides were based on generations. This case was developed by R. van Compernolle, *Étude de chronologie et d'historiographie Siciliotes* (Brussels, 1960) and is fully discussed by K. J. Dover in A. W. Gomme's *Historical Commentary on Thucydides*, IV 198–210. The generation thesis can explain some Thucydidean dates satisfactorily, but not all. Thucydides' relative chronology has also been questioned at an important point by Vallet and Villard (see n. 3) who infer from the pottery evidence of their excavations at Megara that Megara was founded before Syracuse, *c.* 757. J. N. Coldstream in *Greek Geometric Pottery*, 322–7 and 168–9, maintains that the evidence of the pottery is not inconsistent with the Thucydidean dates.

9 Thucydides records the expulsion of Sicels from Syracuse in 6.3.2. For Eretria see n. 2.

10 The three surviving temples of Poseidonia (Paestum) are of striking scale and impressive workmanship. The earliest, the so-called Basilica, may date from the early sixth century, the temple of Ceres *c.* 510 B.C., and the temple of Poseidon *c.* 460 B.C. They suggest considerable wealth, probably derived from the overland trade route. Photographs and descriptions in F. Krauss, *Paestum*.

11 Thucydides (1.13.2) seems to imply that the trireme was invented by Corinth *c.* 700, but such an early date is difficult to reconcile with the long survival of penteconters. Herodotus implies that Polycrates, tyrant of Samos (from *c.* 535), began his rule with penteconters but later built triremes. The case for dating the invention of the trireme in the sixth century is argued by Davison, *CQ* 41 (1947) 18. For the reconstruction of a trireme, J. S. Morrison, *The Mariner's Mirror*, 27 (1941) 14. See also J. S. Morrison and R. T. Williams, *Greek Oared Ships, 800–323 B.C.*, 158–63.

12 Thucydides, who was particularly interested in the growth of sea power, dates this battle 'some 260 years before the end of this war' (1.13.4). It is more probable that he means the Peloponnesian War as a whole, than the Archidamian War (431–421).

13 The account given by Assurbanipal of the submission, the revolt, and the death of Gyges is as follows (translated from the Assyrian by G. Smith, *History of Assurbanipal*, p. 64; cp. p. 73):— Gyges, King of Lydia, a district which is across the sea, a remote place of which the kings my fathers had not heard speak of its name. The account of my grand kingdom in a dream was related to him by Assur, the God my creator. 'Of Assurbanipal, king of Assyria, the beloved of Assur, king of the Gods, lord of all, his princely yoke take'. The day he saw that dream his messenger he sent to pray for my friendship. That dream which he saw by the hand of the envoy he sent and repeated to me. From the midst of the day when he took the yoke of my kingdom, the Cimmerians, wasters of his people, who did not fear my fathers and me, and did not take the yoke of my kingdom, he captured, in the service of Assur and Ishtar, the Gods my lords. From the midst of the chiefs of the Cimmerians, whom he had taken, two chiefs in strong fetters of iron and bonds of iron, he bound, and with numerous presents he caused to bring to my presence. His messengers whom, to pray for my friendship, he was constantly sending, he wilfully discontinued; as the will of Assur, the God my creator, he had disregarded; to his own power he trusted and hardened his heart. His forces to the aid of Psammetichus (king) of Egypt, who had thrown off the yoke of my dominion, he sent; and I heard of it and prayed to Assur and Ishtar thus: 'Before his enemies his corpse may they cast, and may they carry captive his attendants.' When thus to Assur I had prayed he requited me. Before his enemies his corpse was thrown down, and they carried captive his attendants. The Cimmerians, whom by the glory of my name he had trodden under him, conquered and swept the whole of his country . . . (Ardys) his son sat on his throne, that evil work at the lifting up of my hands, the Gods my protectors in the time of the father his begetter had destroyed. By the hand of his envoy he sent word and took the yoke of my kingdom thus: 'The king whom God has blessed art thou; my father from thee departed and evil was done in his time; I am thy devoted servant, and my people all perform thy pleasure.'

14 The date of the earliest Greek coins is disputed. The primary evidence comes from a sealed deposit in the temple of Artemis at Ephesus, containing early crude coins with other objects. This deposit used to be dated *c.* 700, which was consistent with the attribution of the first mainland coinage to Pheidon of Argos, minting in Aegina *c.* 670. But the attribution of the Aeginetan turtles to Pheidon may be an arbitrary expansion by Ephorus of Herodotus who refers to Pheidon a system of weights and measures but does not mention coins. Archaeologists now incline to date the objects associated with the early coins in the temple of Artemis later (S. G. Robinson, *JHS* 71 (1951) 156–67) and this implies that the first coins were probably minted *c.* 650. Most numismatists would date the first Aeginetan turtles not earlier than 600: see W. L. Brown, *NC* 1950, 177–204.

15 For a good example of an overstruck Corinthian Pegasus, H. M. V. Sutherland, American Numismatic Society, *Museum Notes*, 3 (1948), Pl. iv. 2.

16 Herodotus (2.178) says that Amasis (570–25), having become a Philhellene, allowed the Greeks to settle in Naucratis and to those who did not wish to live there permanently but to trade there he gave land on which they could build altars and shrines for their gods. But the archaeological evidence shows that Naucratis was occupied by Greeks before Amasis became king, and Herodotus himself describes Amasis' rule as a reaction against the dependence of his predecessor on foreign troops. It is more likely therefore that Amasis *restricted* the Greeks to Naucratis. By the end of his rule, however, he was on good terms with the Greeks, married a Greek wife from Cyrene, made an alliance with Samos, and contributed handsomely to the building of a new temple for Apollo at Delphi. For the relation of archaeological evidence to the literary sources, R. M. Cook, *JHS* 57 (1937) 227–37.

17 *ML* 7. The Greeks were under the command of Psammetichus, son of Theocles: the father may have served under the first Psamatik and named his son after the Egyptian king. Three of the Greeks gave their origins as Ialysus, Teos, Colophon.

18 For the importance of African sheep, Homer, *Odyssey*, 4.85 ff: καὶ Λιβύην, ἵνα τ' ἄρνες ἄφαρ κεραοὶ τελέθουσι. τρὶς γὰρ τίκτει μῆλα τελεσφόρον εἰς ἐνιαυτόν. Silphium, was used as a purgative and also as a vegetable, Aristophanes, *Knights*, 895. Pindar's Fourth and Fifth Pythian Odes celebrate Arcesilas, last king of Cyrene, for his victory of 462 B.C. in the chariot race at Delphi.

19 For an interpretation of the scene on the cup see p. 552. Sparta had natural connections with Cyrene through her colony, Thera. Samos, also connected with Sparta (Hdt. 3.47), had trading associations with Cyrene.

20 Hdt. 1.63–7.

21 R. Joffroy, *Le Trésor de Vix* (Mon. et Mémoires, Fondation E. Piot, 48.1: Paris 1954). The letters on the rim are Laconian and this crater strongly resembles the Spartan gift to Croesus on the occasion of their alliance with Lydia *c.* 546, Hdt. 1.170.1: 'a crater of bronze with animals right round the neck and a capacity of three hundred amphorae'.

CHAPTER 3

1 For the archaeological evidence see V. Desborough, *The last Mycenaeans and their successors*, 88–90.

2 According to Herodotus (5.75) this regulation followed a disagreement of the two kings on an invasion of Attica (*c.* 506), which led to the humiliating abandonment of the expedition.

3 The Spartan statute is preserved by Plutarch, *Lycurgus* 6. Tyrtaeus (cited by Plutarch) paraphrased it as an oracle. It is a statute of the Spartan Assembly, perhaps based on or confirmed by an oracle. The main power rests with the Gerousia, the council of elders, and the kings (γερουσία σὺν ἀρχαγέταις). They bring proposals before the Assembly which is to meet at regular intervals. The people have the right to accept or reject, but the kings and elders can exercise a veto. The ephors are not mentioned in the document; it was probably not until the sixth century that they became a major force in the constitution. The definition of functions is likely to be the product of a period of stress, an alternative solution to the tyrannies at Sicyon and Corinth. It may have been a sequel to the shock of the Messenian revolt towards the middle of the seventh century. For a more detailed discussion of this Spartan statute see W. G. Forrest, *A History of Sparta* (1968) 40–60.

4 The Alexandrians had an ephor list which began in 757, but this was combined with the tradition that the office was instituted by King Theopompus in the First Messenian War, which cannot be dated so early (see n. 5). The office is also found in Thera, Cyrene, Euesperides, Italian Heraclea, and this suggests that it is an early institution. Like the Roman tribunes of the people their office gradually grew in importance until in the middle of the sixth century Chilon was said to have made the power of the ephors equal to that of the kings. His reputation outside Sparta is confirmed by his inclusion in the list of the seven men of the sixth century who were ranked highest in practical wisdom.

5 Tradition connected the founding of Rhegion (*c.* 730) with the beginning of the war, the founding of Taras (*c.* 707) with its end. The last Messenian victory at Olympia was dated to 736, the first Spartan victory to 716. Tyrtaeus says that Theopompus led the Spartans; a date towards the end of the eighth century suits his place in the Spartan king list. The only valuable ancient source for the conquest of Messenia is Tyrtaeus.

6 Tyrtaeus, a contemporary, says that the war of conquest was fought by 'our fathers' fathers'.

This might date the revolt to the middle of the seventh century, but the phrase cannot be pressed. The revolt reflects the general reaction against Dorians in the Peloponnese, clearly expressed also in the tyranny of Sicyon. The revival of Messenian independence in the fourth century stimulated 'traditions' about the great revolt. Pausanias and other late sources have been particularly infected by a romantic epic composed by Rhianus, a third-century Alexandrian scholar.

7 Aristotle (*Politics* 1306b) speaks of 'a state of society which is most often the result of war, as at Lacedaemon in the days of the Messenian War (ὑπὸ τὸν Μεσσηνιακὸν πόλεμον, meaning perhaps just after the war); this is proved from the poem of Tyrtaeus, entitled *Good Order*; for he speaks of certain citizens who were ruined by the war and wanted to have a redistribution of the land.'

8 No metal defensive arms—breastplate, helmet, or greaves have been found from the period between the collapse of the Mycenaean world and a well-made bronze corselet and helmet found in an Argive grave of the late eighth century. The first clear evidence of the phalanx comes from the so-called Chigi vase of Protocorinthian style *c.* 650. (*See* p. 95.) See A. M. Snodgrass, *Arms and Armour of the Greeks,* 86 ff. and 'The Hoplite Reform and History' in *JHS* 85 (1965) 110–22.

9 Archaeological evidence for early Sparta: *Artemis Orthia,* the account of British excavations on the site of a Spartan temple. Laconian pottery, Lane, *BSA* 34 (1933–4) 99–189.

10 The tribal organisation is attested in Tyrtaeus fr. 1, 12, but it is not clear to what period he refers. Thucydides (1.20.3) contradicts Herodotus' statement (9.53.2) that there was a Pitanate division, but Herodotus had been to Pitane and is probably right. When Thucydides wrote there had been a further change in the Spartan army system. In the Peloponnesian War Spartans and Perioeci were brigaded together.

11 Apollo himself debated whether Lycurgus was god or man in an oracle cited by Herodotus (1.65):

> Well-come, Lycurgus, come to my rich shrine,
> Whom Zeus loves well, and all celestials love;
> Shall I declare thee human or divine?
> Surely a god, if I know aught thereof.

12 This description of the population of Crete in Homer's *Odyssey* (19.175–9) is an embarrassment. Like other passages in both Homeric epics it reflects post-Mycenaean conditions. Dorians came to Crete from the Peloponnese, long after the Trojan War and the fall of Mycenae.

13 There is much confusion in the ancient sources concerning the date of Pheidon. Ephorus called him the tenth from Temenos, which to Ephorus would be *c.* 800–770; but while the king list might be genuine the date assumed for Temenos might be wrong. In another tradition, reflected in the Parian Marble, he is placed 100 years earlier (900–870); but this dating probably derives from the fiction that Pheidon was brother of Karanus, the founder of the Macedonian Kingdom, whose date

was pushed back into a more remote past for reasons of prestige. Herodotus speaks of Pheidon as father of a suitor for Agariste of Sicyon (*c.* 570). These various traditions are set out in How and Wells, *Herodotus*, 2.117. In view of the wide divergence the best approach is to attempt to fit the actions attributed to Pheidon into the historical setting that best fits them. The fullest account is given in Strabo, 358 (from Ephorus). Pheidon was the strongest man of his day. He reasserted the heritage of Temenus. He established a system of weights and measures and a coinage. Pausanias refers to an Argive defeat of Sparta at Hysiae in 669 (Paus. 2.24.6). It must be admitted, however, that this context for Pheidon rests on an emendation. Our text of Pausanias puts Pheidon's Olympiad in 748. Two further cautions may be added. When the seventh century date first won general acceptance it was thought that an important clue lay in the statement of Ephorus that Pheidon introduced coins as well as weights and measures. It was known that Aegina's turtles were the first mainland coinage and, as Aegina at various times seems to have been dependent on Argos, it was assumed that Pheidon could be dated by the earliest turtles, which were then thought to have been minted in the early seventh century. With the re-dating of Aegina's coins to *c.* 600 (ch. 2, n. 14) this argument can no longer be used; Ephorus' attribution of coins to Pheidon is a typical example of his irresponsible rationalising; it was his habit to improve on his sources, and it is very doubtful whether he had a source which differed from Herodotus. It is also strange, if Pheidon led the Argive army to victory at Hysiae, that his name is not associated with the battle. And the battle was fought in Argive territory; it looks more like the successful repulse of a Spartan invasion than the first stage in an Argive offensive. We also know rather more about the general condition of Argos than we did twenty years ago. The French excavations of geometric tombs at Argos suggest that in the second half of the eighth century Argos was more advanced materially than most of her contemporaries. These arguments are developed more fully by G. L. Huxley, who prefers an eighth century date, *BCH* 82 (1958) 588–601.

14 The story of the struggle of the Eleans and Pisatans for Olympia rests on Elean tradition. The certain facts seem to be that the Elean control of the games dates from 572 B.C., and that for some years earlier there was a struggle. The Eleans represented this struggle as begun by the Pisatans (Pausanias 6.22.4), they themselves having been in possession of Olympia since the Olympiad of Pheidon. But it may be questioned whether this is true. The mere fact that the Elean control of the festival is dated from 572 B.C. (Eusebius 1.198, ed. Schöne) makes it probable that till then the festival was administered by the Pisatans. The institution of the Ἑλλανοζίκαι as umpires, may be referred to 572 B.C. or shortly after. The site, history and monuments of Olympia are described in Pausanias 5.7–6.21.

15 For the dating and character of the two

temples of Hera, see W. B. Dinsmoor, *The Architecture of Ancient Greece*,[3] 43, 53–8.

16 Records of the Olympian victors seem to have been kept by the Eleans since the early part of the sixth century; but the Olympiad list, as a whole, with the dates of the eighth and seventh centuries, seems to have been first worked out by Hippias of Elis at the very end of the fifth century. The Olympiads were first used as a system of chronological reckoning in the third century by the Sicilian historian Timaeus.

17 For Corinthian pottery, and also other crafts, see H. G. G. Payne, *Necrocorinthia*.

18 M. N. Tod, *GHI* I, n. 2.

19 Herodotus (1.14.2) says that six gold craters presented by the Lydian king Gyges 'stand in the Corinthian treasury, and they weigh thirty talents. But to tell the truth this is not the treasury of the Corinthian state, but of Cypselus son of Eetion.'

20 The chest is described by Pausanias, 5.17.2–19.

21 Timaeus (quoted by Athenaeus 12.519b) recorded that the Sybarites wore Milesian woollen clothes, and that this was the origin of their friendship. Sybaris also commanded an important trade route across Italy to her colonies Siris and Pyxus on the western coast. This was a valuable alternative to the passage through the straits if either Rhegion or Messana was hostile.

22 Pliny (*Nat. Hist.* 4.10) in his description of the Peloponnese says: 'On one side was the Corinthian, on the other the Saronic Gulf. On one side of the narrow isthmus was Lechaeon, on the other side Cenchreae; it was a long and difficult voyage round for ships whose size made carriage by cart impossible.' Strabo also (380) refers to the Diolkos in passing, and Thucydides (3.15.1) shows that triremes could be carried across. Substantial stretches of the Diolkos were excavated in the middle fifties (*Athen. Mitt.* 71 (1956) 51–9; a short account with illustrations in *ILN* 19 Oct. 1957). From the sherds associated with the work and the form of the masons' letters the excavator attributed the work to Periander. This could give special point to a late source which says that Periander built triremes and used both seas (*FGH* 90. fr. 58).

23 Corcyra was hostile to Corinth before the tyranny but they seem to have come to terms before the death of Cypselus. Periander, however, had brought Corcyra under direct control (Hdt. 3.52) and, when they killed his son, he sent 300 sons of leading Corcyraeans to the court of Alyattes to be made eunuchs. They were, however, rescued on their way by the Samians and sent back to Corcyra (Hdt. 3.48).

24 Hdt. 5.67–8.

25 The site and monuments of Delphi are described by Pausanias, 10.9–32.

26 An interesting political interpretation of the Sacred War by W. G. Forrest, *BCH* 80 (1956) 33–52.

27 Hdt. 6.126–31.

28 For the flavour of Theognis, R. Lattimore, *Greek Lyrics*, pp. 26–31.

CHAPTER 4

1 Thuc. 2.15.1–3.

2 There is no firm evidence when Eleusis was incorporated in the Athenian state. It is generally held that this was not until the seventh century, but the two main arguments are weak. (1) In the *Hymn to Demeter*, which probably dates from the seventh century, there is no mention of the Athenians, but the context of the poem is Mycenaean and there is no reason why the Athenians should be mentioned. (2) Solon disappoints Croesus by telling him that he was not so blest by fortune as Tellus, because Tellus died while fighting against neighbours at Eleusis. The reference should be to a period not long before Solon, but fighting at Eleusis is not necessarily against an independent Eleusis. Megarians attacking Athens would come past Eleusis. Tradition knows about hostilities between the two communities in the Mycenaean period. Had Eleusis remained independent into the seventh century Thucydides should have mentioned it.

3 V. Desborough, *Protogeometric Pottery* (Oxford 1952).

4 J. N. Coldstream, *Greek Geometric Pottery* (London 1968).

5 W. G. Forrest, in 'The First Sacred War' *BCH* 80 (1956) 333–52, suggests that the Alcmaeonids were moderate progressives, opposed to extreme oligarchs and to tyranny. Cylon had been encouraged by Delphi in his bid for tyranny and it was the Cylonians, he suggests, who, with the help of Delphi, engineered the curse and drove the family from Athens. It is well attested that the Alcmaeonids supported Solon's legislation but they may not have become progressives until the curse undermined their position in the aristocracy.

6 Constitutional reforms are attributed to Draco by Aristotle (*Ath. Const.* 4). This Draconian constitution contains clear anachronisms and is invented by later oligarchic propaganda. Draco's political work, as the other sources imply, was confined to a codification of the laws.

7 The main sources for Solon are the Aristotelian *Ath. Const.*, and Plutarch, *Solon*. The most important of his poems are translated in R. Lattimore, *Greek Lyrics*[2], 18–23.

8 For the revised dating of the introduction of coinage to Greece see ch. 2, n. 14. For the chronology of the early stages of Athenian coinage, see C. M. Kraay, *NC* 1956, 43–68.

9 The assumption in the text that there could be private ownership of land in Attica in Solon's time is disputed. J. V. A. Fine (*Horoi*, *Hesp.* Suppl. 9, 1951) argued that the land was legally inalienable until the time of the Peloponnesian War, on the grounds that there was no literary evidence of mortgaging before the last quarter of the fifth century and no surviving mortgage stones before the fourth century. Hammond (*JHS* 81 (1961) 76–98) accepted Fine's conclusion with a modification, maintaining that the land in the central plain of Attica was the land originally allocated to the settlers and that these lots belonged to the *gene* and could not be allocated, whereas the rest of Attica could become private property. He drew attention to the statement of Aristotle (*Pol.* 1319a 11) that 'in the early days it was illegal in many cities to sell the first lots'. Hammond also sees confirmation of the main thesis in Thucydides' description of the evacuation of Attica at the beginning of the Peloponnesian War (Thuc. 2.16.2): 'They were depressed at the thought of forsaking their homes and their sanctuaries which had come down to them from their fathers and were the abiding memorials of their early constitution.' The strongest argument against this thesis is the complete absence of any reference to such a fundamental change in comedy or any other contemporary literary or epigraphic source. Aristotle may be referring primarily to colonies where there was practical point, as we have seen (above, p. 70), in preventing the colonists from returning home unless it was absolutely necessary. From Thucydides' statement we need infer no more than that most Athenian citizens still lived on the land and that most families had lived in the same village 'from time immemorial'.

10 The occupation was followed by fighting with Mytilene, which was terminated by Periander's arbitration, Strabo, 599–600. Mytilene later gained control, but Sigeum was recovered by Pisistratus, Hdt. 5, 94–5.

11 Solon's name probably occurred in the archon-list for 594/3 and this may have been the only evidence for dating his reforms in that year. If his appointment was a special one the date may not have been preserved. Arguments for a later date, perhaps in the seventies are given by C. Hignett, *A History of the Athenian Constitution*, 316.

12 Aristotle (*Ath. Const.* 8) says that 'Solon made the nine archons to be appointed by lot from (40) previously elected.' Later (ch. 22) he says that in 488/7 'they appointed the nine archons by lot from 500 previously elected by the demesmen, then for the first time after the tyranny.' These two passages can be reconciled by assuming that the lot, introduced by Solon, was abandoned under the tyranny and reintroduced in 488/7. But the main struggle for power in the period following Solon's reforms centred round the archonship, which was still the most important office in the state. It is probable that archons were elected until their power was substantially diminished in the period following Cleisthenes' reforms.

13 Unlimited appeal would make the system unworkable and would imply a much more advanced stage of democracy than Solon's other measures. Presumably appeal was limited to cases involving the major penalties of death, exile, and loss of citizen rights.

14 For the case against a Solonian Council of 400 see C. Hignett (n. 11) 92–6.

15 The fragmentary Chian inscription is discussed in *ML* 8.

CHAPTER 5

1 The accounts of Athens' wars with Megara are confused in the ancient sources. Plutarch (*Solon*, 9–10) associates Pisistratus with Solon in the conquest. Herodotus (1.59.4) refers the capture of Nisaea to Pisistratus, but makes no mention of Salamis. The Aristotelian *Ath. Const.* 17.2, drawing on a standard history of Athens, denies that Pisistratus had any part in Solon's war. Solon certainly wrote a poem rousing the Athenians to fight (quoted above, p. 122). Perhaps Salamis was won *c.* 600: further fighting broke out *c.* 570 with Megara in which Nisaea was captured and the Athenian hold on Salamis confirmed, largely as a result of Pisistratus' generalship.

2 The Spartan arbitration is connected by Plutarch with Solon's conquest of Salamis, but is probably much later. Plutarch includes among the five arbitrators a Cleomenes, who may be the Spartan king (*c.* 520–490). The short period after the expulsion of the tyrants from Athens (510), when both Megara and Athens accepted Spartan leadership, provides the most probable historical setting.

3 *ML* 14. There are crucial gaps in the decree as preserved. The subject of the main provisions has been restored to mean (a) the original Salaminians (οἰκοῦντας), (b) all Athenians who have acquired land on Salamis ('Aθεναιος), (c) new Athenian settlers (κλεροχος). Since hoplite service is demanded it is probable that the native population is not concerned, for they were not enrolled in the Attic demes and did not serve in the hoplite ranks. The regulations are similar to those adopted for later cleruchies: probably the decree is concerned with new Athenian settlers. The date can be inferred only from letter forms, probably late sixth or early fifth century. It is tempting to believe that, when the Cleisthenic democracy broke with Sparta, the Athenians felt anxious about Salamis, to which their main title was a recent Spartan arbitration. They may have sent settlers to strengthen their hold on the island.

4 Pisistratus may also have been affected by the curse that hung over the Alcmaeonids.

5 The beginning of Pisistratus' tyranny (561/0) and his death (528/7) are securely established. The dates of his two exiles are controversial, though the length of the second, ten years, is common to all sources. The figures in the Aristotelian *Ath. Const.* are inconsistent and require amendment. An alternative chronology, more consistent with the indications of Herodotus, dates the second exile 556–546. Herodotus implies (1.59–61) that the first two periods of tyranny were very short, and when, on the expulsion of Hippias, he says (5.65.3) that the Pisistratids 'ruled over the Athenians for 36 years', he probably refers to the period of continuous rule, 546–510.

6 The distribution of the land of his political opponents in exile to the landless would seem a natural step for Pisistratus to have taken, and many historians agree with Bury. There is, however, no ancient evidence for such a redistribution of land and the argument from silence, though not decisive, is strong.

7 *Ath. Const.* 16.4; Thuc. 6.54.5.

8 The earliest reference to the commission in the surviving sources is in Cicero (*De Oratore* 3.3.4.). Plato (*Hipparchus* 228B) says that Hipparchus first brought the Homeric epics to Athens and compelled the rhapsodes at the Panathenaea to recite them in proper sequence. It is not difficult to see how this statement was elaborated during the Hellenistic period into the establishment of an official text.

9 Pausanias (1.14.1) implies that Enneakrounos was in or near the Agora, but Thucydides (2.15.4–5) clearly places it south of the Acropolis. Pausanias has confused it with another fountain-house, also of the Pisistratid period, in the south-east corner of the Agora (H. Thompson, *Hesp.* 22 (1953) 29–35. A good discussion in Gomme, *HCT* 2.53–60).

10 Plutarch, *Greek Questions 5* (*Moralia* 292B), quotes the inscription set up on the banks of the Alpheus (at Olympia). The Tegeates are to expel Messenians and not to make them citizens. See F. Jacoby, *CQ* 38 (1944) 15.

11 A fragment of an Athenian archon list, inscribed in the late fifth century (*Hesp.* 8 (1939) 59–65, *ML* 6) shows that Hippias, Cleisthenes (the first letter is missing), Miltiades were archons in successive years from 526 to 524, and probably Pisistratus, son of Hippias, in 522 (. . . . . στρατος). It seems that Hippias began his rule with a general political reconciliation and the return of hostile nobles from exile. The reconciliation, however, did not last long. The Alcmaeonids were again in exile by 512.

12 Subscriptions were also obtained from foreign peoples in contact with the Greeks. Herodotus (2.180) says that Amasis, king of Egypt, contributed 1000 talents of alum (to protect the timbers against fire).

13 The original group, by Antenor, was carried to Persia in 480, and restored by Alexander or one of his successors (the sources differ). A new group, by Critias and Nesiotes, was set up at Athens immediately after the Persian War. For the base of this group see *Hesp.* 5 (1936) 355.

14 Bury, and others before and after him, assumed that when the Spartans drove out the Pisistratids from Athens they would have brought the Athenians into their league. For this there is no positive evidence, and relations between Athens and Sparta were soon very strained. Cleomenes had been responsible for the exile of Cleisthenes, and had attempted to overthrow the Athenian democracy. The Cleisthenic democracy had every reason to be anti-Spartan and feeling ran higher when the Spartans even attempted to restore Hippias.

15 Herodotus (6.66) is emphatic that Cleisthenes' appeal to the people was preceded by a personal struggle for leadership with Isagoras, and the *Ath. Const.* (13.5) specifically adds that the *hetairiae* (aristocratic social clubs) were the centre of the struggle. This is reflected in Herodotus' word for Cleisthenes' appeal to the people-*proshetairizetai* (makes the people his club). It does not necessarily follow that the form of the Cleisthenic constitution

was first conceived in 508. It is an extremely complicated structure and is more likely to have been thought out in the years of exile (and the calmer atmosphere of Delphi).

16 Normally the trittys was formed of contiguous demes, but there are some strange anomalies. The most conspicuous is the separation of the important deme Probalinthos, which in the fourth century supplied five Councillors, from its three cult partners in the Tetrapolis—Marathon, Oinoe, and Tricorynthos. These are grouped with Rhamnus which has its own distinctive cult. D. M. Lewis (*Hist.* 12 (1963) 22–40) suggests that Cleisthenes in grouping demes together attempted to weaken the political influence of local cults, and draws attention to the treatment of the Tetrakomoi. These four neighbours—Piraeus, Phaleron, Thymantidae, Xypete—like the members of the Tetraplis, had a common cult from early times; they were distributed between three separate trittyes.

17 The existence of the prytany system in the original organisation of the Cleisthenic Council is uncertain. From the fifties of the fifth century the normal prescript of published decrees includes, beside the name of the proposer, the name of the president, the prytany on duty, and the secretary; in a minority of cases the archon's name is included. In the fragmentary remains of the decrees that can be securely dated before 460 this form of prescript does not seem to be used and it is possible that the prytany system was first introduced as a strengthening of democratic procedures in the reforms of Ephialtes. One of the main features of his reforms was to strengthen the participation of the demos in politics which involved an increase in the business of the Assembly and therefore of the Council which prepared business for the Assembly (see P. J. Rhodes, *The Athenian Boule*, 16–19).

There is also uncertainty about the presidency of the Council and of the Assembly in the Cleisthenic democracy. In the developed democracy the president for the day was appointed by lot from the prytany on duty but this would have been a very drastic innovation sixty years earlier. It is perhaps more probable that the archon still, at first at any rate, presided. There is also speculation about the character of the archonship in this period. The statement of Herodotus (6.109.2) that the polemarch at the battle of Marathon owed his position to the lot is generally discounted, but J. L. Myres (*Herodotus*, 208) suggested that the lot in this case might refer not to the appointment of the archons but to the apportionment of the duties within the archonship. This suggestion has been carried further by E. Badian (*Anticthon* 5 (1971) 1–34) who suggests that the selection of the eponymous archon by lot from the elected archons was an integral part of the democratic reforms of Cleisthenes.

18 Herodotus (6.108.2) provides no date for the alliance between Athens and Plataea, but implies that Cleomenes and the Spartans were near at the time. The alliance has therefore been commonly dated in the period following the expulsion of Hippias when

Cleomenes was in Athens. Our text of Thucydides, 3.68.5, however, gives a precise date, 519–8, which could make good historical sense.

CHAPTER 6

1 A cuneiform text in the British Museum gives a detailed account of events preceding and following the fall of Nineveh, C. J. Gadd, *The Fall of Nineveh*. In the savage gloating of the Hebrew prophet Nahum one can feel the relief of the peoples that had suffered from Assyrian conquests: 'the horseman mounting, and the flashing sword, and the glittering spear; and a multitude of slain, and a great heap of carcases: and there is none end of the corpses. . . . There is no assuaging of thy hurt; thy wound is grievous: all that hear the bruit of thee clap the hands over thee; for upon whom hath not thy wickedness passed continually?' (from *Nahum*, ch. 3).

2 Alcaeus wrote a poem for his brother Antimenidas on his return from service with the Babylonian army (Diehl, fr. 50): 'You have come from the bounds of the earth, with the ivory hilt of your sword bound with gold, for you have fought as an ally with the Babylonian host and have wrought a mighty deed of valour, . . . slaying a warrior who lacked but a palm from five royal cubits.'

3 Tod, *GHI* I. 6.

4 The Phocaeans had played a leading part in developing trade with the west, where Massalia was their most important colony. Alalia in Corsica had been settled *c.* 560.

5 The Behistun inscription records the successful crushing of a long series of revolts by Darius in his first years. See R. G. Kent, *Old Persian Grammar, Texts* (with translations), *Lexicon*, 116 ff. 'Saith Darius the King: This is what was done by me after that I became King. A son of Cyrus, Cambyses by name, of our family—he was King here. Of that Cambyses there was a brother, Smerdis by name, having the same mother and the same father as Cambyses. Afterwards Cambyses slew that Smerdis. When Cambyses slew Smerdis, it did not become known to the people that Smerdis had been slain. Afterwards Cambyses went to Egypt. When Cambyses had gone to Egypt, after that the people became evil. After that the lie waxed great in the country, both in Persia and in Media and in the other provinces. A Magian, Gaumata by name, seized the kingdom. . . . After that Cambyses died by his own hand. . . . I with a few men slew that Gaumata the Magian, and those who were his foremost followers. I took the Kingdom. . . .' Throughout the narrative Darius emphasises that he is the servant of his god: 'I worshipped Ahuramazda. Ahuramazda bore me aid. What was by me commanded, that he made successful for me. What I did, all by the favour of Ahuramazda I did'.

For a description and illustration of the Behistun inscription and its setting see G. G. Cameron, *Arch.* 13 (1960) 162–71.

6 It is perhaps more likely that Darius had strategic rather than economic objectives. His empire was already wealthy and he did not lack gold.

Invasion from Scythia had earlier brought considerable unrest into Asia Minor; he may have had the double aim of advancing along the north Aegean and ensuring that no strong power developed north of the Euxine.

7 It is doubtful whether Miltiades, as Herodotus says, openly advocated the breaking down of the bridge. Had he done so he could hardly have been allowed to remain in control of the Chersonese. The story may have been invented when he was on trial at Athens after he had been driven out by the Persians following the collapse of the Ionian revolt.

8 Our only source is Herodotus who explains the expedition and its failure by personal motives. It is unlikely that the Persians warned the Naxians in advance; but friction between Greeks and Persians may have accounted for the failure.

9 A number of electrum coins of approximately the same weight with different obverses can be attributed to the revolt. It used to be thought that there was a federal coinage centrally minted (Seltman, *Greek Coins*,[2] 87 f.) but the large number of types makes it more probable that each city minted its own coins. However, the common standard pre-supposes a formal agreement in the interests of combined action. See Meiggs, *The Athenian Empire,* 7 and 441.

10 *ML* 12. Darius also praises the satrap for planting Syrian fruit trees in his satrapy, an interesting parallel to Roman activity in giving a wide distribution to the trees that they found in their provinces.

11 Herodotus (6.103–17) gives the earliest and fullest account of the battle; later ancient writers add little but exaggeration. The central problem is to explain why the battle took place. The most radical view is that the Persians had divided their force: while one division reduced Eretria, the other landed at Marathon to contain the Athenians. The Athenians attacked when Eretria fell so that they should not have to fight the united Persian force (F. Maurice, *JHS* 52 (1932) 13–24). This interpretation is dangerously different from Herodotus and is not supported by any ancient evidence. A less improbable variant is a division of forces after the Persians had landed at Marathon. The Athenians attacked when a large part of the Persian forces, including the cavalry, had embarked on their ships to sail round to Athens, while the remaining Persians held the Athenians at Marathon. Herodotus, however, is very explicit that the signal which induced the Persians to sail to Athens was flashed *after* the battle, and if a strong striking force including the cavalry had left Marathon the Persians would surely have remained on the defensive by the Great Marsh rather than accept battle at the south end of the plain.

The position of the armies before the battle is also controversial. The physical features of the area are admirably described and illustrated by W. K. Pritchett in *Marathon* (Univ. of Cal. *Publications in Class. Arch.* 4.137–96, 1960), with a further note in *Studies in Ancient Greek Topography* I (Berkeley, 1965) 23–33. The key should lie in the location of the Herakleion where the Greeks made their camp, but the site has not yet been identified. A stele, however, with inscriptions in archaic lettering, that must have originally stood in the sanctuary, was found roughly a mile from the burial mound at the south end of the plain. It had been moved from its original setting for re-use. It is rather more likely, as Vanderpool argues (*AJA* 70 (1966) 319–23) but by no means certain that the original site was not far away. The alternative is to place the Herakleion on the southern foothills of Mount Agrieliki. But Herodotus' account of the battle strongly suggests that the two battle lines were at right angles to the shore, and this too favours Vanderpool's reconstruction. There is now general agreement that the Soros, the great mound that covered the ashes of the dead, marks the position of the main action, where the two lines first met. Schliemann found earlier material in his excavation and thought that an old memorial was being re-used. Later excavations proved beyond doubt that the mound was built after the battle. A victory trophy (n. 12) marked the area near the Great Marsh where the Persian losses were heaviest. The river bed which now bisects the plain once featured prominently in debate but its course in 490 is very uncertain and, as it would have been dry when the battle was fought, it would not have proved a serious obstacle.

The absence of the Persian cavalry in Herodotus' account of the battle remains puzzling, for Herodotus emphasises the suitability of the plain for cavalry as a reason for landing at Marathon. There is a very late record explaining the words 'horsemen away' (χωρὶς ἱππεῖς) by the story that the Ionians in the Persian army signalled to the Greeks when Datis left that the cavalry had gone, whereupon Miltiades attacked. The fact that there is no other trace of such a good story in all the surviving references to the battle before the end of antiquity undermines its credibility. It is easier to believe that the Persian cavalry played no significant part in the action; Herodotus is not a military historian. For different accounts of the battle see Hignett and Burn (in the bibliography) and N. G. L. Hammond in *JHS* 88 (1968) 13–59 (reprinted with answers to critics in his *Studies in Greek History*, 170.

12 *Hesp.* 35 (1968) 93–106.

13 *ML* 18.

14 *ML* 19.

15 W. B. Dinsmoor, *The Architecture of Ancient Greece*,³ 196, 198. The temple is dated by the fragments of pottery from the foundation level. This temple and its successor, the Parthenon, were built on the site of the old Hecatompedon, the hundred-footer; the name remained attached to the site.

16 Paus. 1.15.1–3.

17 Bury, with others, assumed that when the Spartans drove out the Pisistratids from Athens they would have brought the Athenians into their league. Cleomenes, however, was driven out of Athens and the Cleisthenic democracy had every reason to be anti-Spartan. Cleomenes had been responsible for the exile of Cleisthenes and had attempted to overthrow the democracy. A little later the Spartans had even considered the restoration of Hippias. The Athenian appeal in 490 to Sparta should not be

regarded as evidence that Athens was in the Peloponnesian League (see ch. 5, n. 14). Sparta was the strongest military power in Greece and the Athenian action was a natural response to the crisis. It was perhaps made easier by the rise to power of the aristocratic Miltiades.

18 The fullest account of ostracism is J. Carcopino's *L'Ostracisme athénien*. For the value of the evidence from surviving ostraka see E. Vanderpool, *Ostracism at Athens* (Semple Lectures), 1970 and *ML* 21.

CHAPTER 7

1 Herodotus delights in catalogues and numbers, but his large figures are almost always irresponsible and it is misguided to attempt to rationalise them. For a realistic attempt to estimate numbers from the availability of water supplies and other practical aspects see F. Maurice, *JHS* 50 (1930) 210–35.

2 Herodotus relates elsewhere (7.6.2) that the Aleuadae, one of the most powerful princely families in Thessaly, had medised enthusiastically even before Xerxes crossed the Hellespont.

3 In 480 Troezen had welcomed and supported Athenian refugees. Some two hundred years after the event she set up this copy of the decree of Themistocles to recall her links with Athens in the great days, presumably to confirm or improve current relations. The discovery and publication of the inscription by Michael Jameson led to a flood of controversy which continues. No one can now believe that this is an accurate copy of a decree passed in 480. There are several certain anachronisms in the text such as the addition to the mover's name of patronymic and deme, unparalleled in the fifth century, and the use of the standard prescript of the developed democracy which is not found on Athenian inscriptions of the early fifth century; more important, the general epigraphic style, smooth and flowing, is in sharp contrast with the staccato economic phrasing of early Athenian decrees. But no decisive conclusion can be drawn from the language, for the Greeks did not demand literal accuracy in copies and modernisms could be expected. It is also difficult to believe that a true copy can have survived. It would not have been inscribed on stone and in the desperate crisis of 480 it is very unlikely that any Athenians would be thinking of preserving historic documents on papyrus.

Argument therefore centres primarily on the substance of the decree. Directions are given for (1) evacuation; (2) the manning of 200 ships with crews of 100; (3) the disposition of the ships when manned; (4) the departure of 'those who had been banished for ten years', i.e. those ostracised between 487 and 481 (see pp. 164–5) to Salamis. The first and third of these clauses, the evacuation before the fall of Thermopylae and the division of the fleet into two squadrons, one of which is to remain in home waters, are credible, though barely compatible with the account in Herodotus. The treatment of the ostracised is the more surprising. This clause does not refer, as many have assumed, to the recall of the ostracised; it implies that they are already back in

Athens. Other sources record a decree allowing the ostracised to return (*Ath. Const.* 22.8; Plut. *Them.* 11.1). Plutarch attributes the decree to Themistocles whose motive is to allow them 'to join with the rest of the citizens by word and deed in what is best for Greece'. In the Troezen decree they are sent away to Salamis 'until the people take a decision about them' and the motive is 'that all Athenians may be of one mind'. The implication is that, though a decree was carried to recall the ostracised, a significant number of Athenians did not trust them and did not therefore want them to be serving where they might make contact with the Persians. Such a reconstruction of the Athenian mood is by no means impossible, but less probable than the implications of Plutarch that the ostracised were accepted back without reservations. However, it is fair to add that this is a very odd clause to invent and it could have been preserved in the family traditions of families hostile to the ostracised. It is much more difficult to justify the detailed arrangements for the manning of the 200 ships. This presupposes that no steps had yet been taken to train crews, that no trierarchs had yet been appointed, that there were enough specialist officers recognised as such to divide amongst 200 ships (Jameson's suggestion in *Hist.* 13 (1963) 385–404) that the word *hyperesiae,* later used for specialists such as helmsmen, was used in this decree for ship crews is not convincing), and that the crews would be formed by dividing the total number of its citizens and foreigners 'into 200 companies by hundreds'. Such measures seem much closer to fourth century conditions than to the crisis of 480. The artificiality of these clauses makes it very difficult to put any great weight on any of the other clauses.

The most popular solution is to believe that the decree was invented when Athens was attempting to rouse the Greek states in the middle of the fourth century to unite against Philip of Macedon. In such a context a reminder of Greek resistance to Persia and particularly of the part played by Athens could be expected to stir emotions, and Demosthenes records that Aeschines in his tour of the Peloponnese to secure support against Philip quoted the decrees of Miltiades and Themistocles. From that period there was a definite text, and both Plutarch and Aristides quoted it in phrases that are close to the Troezen text, but they quote only from the first part of the decree. The elaborate details of manning the ships could not have been expected to raise the temperature of Arcadian audiences. They could be part of a revised edition of the decree. But even though the balance of argument is in favour of the decree being a forgery there remains the possibility that parts of it rest on genuine tradition. On this problem opinions will continue to differ. For a text and commentary see *ML* no. 23. Burn (pp. 364–77) has a translation and a detailed commentary. Hignett (pp. 458–68) is more decisively hostile.

4 A more radical reconstruction suggests that the Persian squadron which sailed round Euboea was despatched much earlier, before the Persians moved to Aphetae, and that it was wrecked by the same storm which wrecked a large part of the main fleet. The reconstruction in the text, based more closely on Herodotus, is to be preferred. There are two other possible explanations of the arrival after the storm of the 53 Athenian ships. They might have been part of a home fleet (as provided by the Troezen decree) joining the fleet at Artemisium when they realised that there was now no immediate danger to Attica; or they may be ships that were not satisfactorily completed when the Athenians sailed to Artemisium. It would have been extremely difficult for Athenian shipwrights to finish the construction of 200 new triremes between the passing of Themistocles' naval bill in 482 and the summer of 480.

5 Herodotus (7.219–20) says: 'After this (the news that the Immortals had forced the mountain pass) they divided. Part of the army left and dispersed to their various states. The remainder made ready to stand with Leonidas. There is another story that Leonidas sent them away, anxious that they should not be destroyed.' Herodotus prefers the more charitable version, but it is more probable that Leonidas intended to hold off the Immortals with the larger part of his force.

6 Delphi had given very little comfort to the Greeks and seems to have anticipated a Persian conquest. This story recounted by Herodotus is probably part of the attempt to restore the prestige of Delphi. Herodotus seems to forget it when, later in his history (9.42.3), he makes Mardonius before the battle of Plataea say: 'there is an oracle that the Persians are fated to come to Greece and plunder the temple of Apollo, and, after the plundering, all perish. With this knowledge we will not go to this temple nor attempt to plunder it, and so we shall not perish.' Xerxes had enough political sense not to antagonise Delphi unnecessarily; an authorised expedition against Delphi can be ruled out. An unauthorised raid is possible but unlikely.

7 This story is introduced in *Ath. Const.* 23.1 to explain the increase in the power and prestige of the Areopagus after the war. Cleidemus, who wrote a constitutional history of Athens early in the fourth century, makes Themistocles responsible for finding the money by searching the baggage of Athenians coming down to the Piraeus in their flight from Attica. Neither story is convincing.

8 Siris had been a Colophonian colony, but had been destroyed by its neighbours. Athens claimed to be the founder of the Ionian colonies, including Colophon, and therefore entitled to occupy land which belonged rightly to her daughter-state.

9 Herodotus seems to have no clear mental picture of the position of the fleets. He implies that the Persians lined the Attic coast, the Greeks facing them along the shore of Salamis. He makes the Corinthians, stationed in the middle of the line, withdraw in the middle of the battle, an operation which, if the fleets occupied the positions he gives them, would have been impossible. He does not mention the Persian turning squadron (Egyptians according to Diodorus). Aeschylus was an eye-witness and his account should be decisive. In his drama the Persians before the battle are outside the straits in three columns (στοῖχοι): they sailed in expecting easy victory and were confounded in the narrow waters. Other ships, he says, were sent round the island of Ajax. The Corinthians were probably detached to meet this turning squadron. Herodotus may, however, be right when he says that, even before Themistocles' message, Xerxes intended to sail in. He was full of confidence and a decisive action would have suited his mood better than a wiser but more delaying strategy.

10 For the Corinthian epitaph, *ML* 24.

11 There is no evidence for this festival in the fifth and fourth centuries, but it was still being celebrated in the Hellenistic and Roman periods.

12 Thuc. 1.132.2–3; *ML* 27.

13 *ML* 26.

14 Traditions were preserved of early Greek colonies in Sardinia at Calaris (Cagliari) and Olbia. After Malchus' invasion of Sicily Carthaginian armies operated in Sardinia (before 550). At the time of the Persian conquest and again during the Ionian revolt (Her. 1.170, 5.106, 124) Eastern Greeks still regarded the island, rich in corn and metals (the south-west district round Iglesias) as a possible land for conquest and settlement; but no attempt was made. During the fifth century the Carthaginians had firm control of the island.

15 After the collapse of the Ionian revolt some of the Samian oligarchs, who resented the treachery at the battle of Lade, sailed west with a few Milesians in answer to an invitation from Zancle to settle at Kale Akte (Fair Shore) on the neighbouring coast to the west. The Samians on their way past South Italy were persuaded by Anaxilas of Rhegion to seize Zancle in the absence of its army on an expedition. The Samians took possession, but to maintain their hold they had to strike a bargain with Hippocrates of Syracuse who had been called in by the Zanclaeans. This gave Anaxilas a good excuse to drive the Samians out after five years and take control of Zancle himself, changing its name to Messana after the Messenian origins of Rhegion. The change is nicely illustrated and dated by the coinage, S. E. G. Robinson, *JHS* 66 (1946) 13–20.

16 Herodotus regards the conjunction as accidental and Aristotle in his *Poetics* expressly quotes it as such. Ephorus, writing in the middle of the fourth century, is the first known source to postulate combined operations in east and west directed by Persia. It is doubtful whether Xerxes would have felt it necessary to tie down the western Greeks, but Carthage may have seized the opportunity to attack Sicily when it could expect no help from the motherland.

17 Pindar, *Pyth.* 1.71–75.

18 Hieron's victories in the games were: Horse-races at Delphi, 482, 478; horse-races at Olympia, 476, 472; chariot-race at Delphi, 470; chariot-race at Olympia, 468. See Pindar, *Ol.* 1; *Pyth.* 1, 3.

19 A tripod base dedicated by Gelon has been found at Delphi. Three other similar bases were found nearby, one bearing an inscription of Hieron. They may have been dedicated by the four brothers, but not necessarily at the same time, *ML* 28. The charioteer dedicated by Polyzalus probably commemorated a Pythian victory in 478. The first line now extant was cut on an erased surface and traces of the earlier lettering survive. It has been suggested that in 477 Polyzalus described himself as King of Gela. He combined with Theron against Hieron, but when Theron made his peace with Hieron, Polyzalus renounced the title, and it was erased from his dedication at Delphi. See Wade-Gery, *JHS* 53 (1933) 102.

CHAPTER 8

1 Thucydides (1.128–35) is our main source for Pausanias' career in and after 478, and there are serious difficulties in his account. If he had been as clearly guilty of Medism in 478 as Thucydides implies he surely would not have been tolerated so long, nor is the story that he proposed marriage to the king's daughter convincing. Herodotus' version that he aimed to marry the daughter of Megabates, cousin of King Darius, is more plausible. Herodotus (5.32) in saying 'if indeed the story about Pausanias is true', suggests there were those who did not believe the worst about Pausanias. It is more probable that there were no serious grounds for a charge of Medism before he was driven out of Byzantium and settled at Colonae in the Troad, and this may have been not earlier than 472. (See Meiggs, *The Athenian Empire*, pp. 465–8.) The most damning evidence quoted by Thucydides is the text of a letter sent by Pausanias to Xerxes in 478, and the king's reply. It is surprising that such a critical historian could have accepted these letters as genuine.

2 The recovery of Tiryns seems to be later than August 468, for in the list of Olympic victors (*Oxyrhynchus Papyri* 2.89) a Tirynthian is recorded as winner of the boys' boxing in that year.

3 The battles of Tegea and Dipaea cannot be securely dated. They are mentioned by Herodotus (9.35) in a list of five Spartan victories, between the battle of Plataea and the crushing of the Helot revolt. Themistocles may have helped to stir up this reaction against Sparta. When he was ostracised he went to Argos and 'paid visits to other parts of the Peloponnese' (Thuc. 1.135.3).

4 This view was first developed by the authors of *The Athenian Tribute Lists* (*ATL* 3.234–9).

5 A different view is taken by Hammond (*JHS* 87 (1967) 41–61) who argues that the league was bicameral. The allies, he thinks, voted separately in their own Council and their combined vote was equal to the vote of Athens. Reasons for preferring the traditional view are set out in Meiggs, *The Athenian Empire*, pp. 459–62.

6 For the composition of Athenian crews see Meiggs, *Empire*, 439 f.

7 This temple for which Plutarch (Them. 22.2) is our only source has now been almost certainly identified. See J. Strepsiades and E. Vanderpool, *Deltion Arch.* 19A (1964) 26–31.

8 *Hesp.* 7 (1938) 228–43.

9 The chronology of the ostracism, flight, and death of Themistocles is uncertain. The only firm element is his arrival in Persia after the death of Xerxes in 465. He was in Athens in 476 when he was choregos for Phrynichus' *Phoenician Women*, which revived memories of the Persian War. Aeschylus in his *Persae*, produced in 472, referred to his cunning message to Xerxes before the battle of Salamis, but this is not strong evidence that Themistocles was still in Athens. In his flight from Argos he passed the Athenian fleet besieging Naxos, and the revolt of Naxos is between the reduction of Carystus and the battle of the Eurymedon, which in turn is before the revolt of Thasos, securely dated in 465. Eurymedon is commonly dated in 469 to fit Plutarch's story that Cimon and his fellow generals were called on to act as judges when Sophocles won his first prize in 468 (Plut. *Cimon* 9.7–8); but Plutarch's story does not require this connection. If the Eurymedon is in 469 the revolt of Naxos cannot be later than 470, and this leaves a much longer interval for Themistocles in Ionia than the sources suggest. The difficulties are less if Naxos is dated in 467. The ostracism was probably between 472 and 470, and there is no difficulty in accepting a stay of up to five years in Argos.

10 Themistocles issued coins in his own name as governor of Magnesia. It is interesting, in view of his reputation, to note that two of the four specimens known are ancient forgeries, copper plated with silver: Seltman, *Greek Coinage*,[2] 108. At Lampsacus a festival was instituted in honour of Themistocles and still maintained in the Hellenistic period (text in G. F. Hill, *Sources for Greek History*, revised edition, p. 324, no. 122).

11 A scholiast, commenting on Aeschines, says that, after capturing Eion, the Athenians, presumably attempting to establish a colony on the site of the later Amphipolis, were destroyed by the Thracians. It is very doubtful whether any such attempt was made before the revolt of Thasos in 465. Eion remained Athenian.

12 This account of the Eurymedon is based on the brief record in Thucydides (1.100.1), supplemented by Plutarch (quoting the fourth century Callisthenes) *Cimon*, 12–13. Diodorus (11.60–62), following Ephorus, has wrongly associated an epigram referring to Cimon's last campaign in Cyprus with the Eurymedon, and makes Cimon first win a sea battle in Cyprus before crushing the Persians at the Eurymedon.

13 *ML* 40. Erythrae had probably medised and been recovered by Athens (the date, ? 453/2, depends on the restoration of the archon's name). An oath to be taken by members of the new Erythraean democratic Boule may be restored: 'I will serve as a councillor in the best and most just interests of the people of Erythrae and of Athens and her allies, and I will not desert the people of Athens nor follow anyone else deserting . . . and I will not receive back any of those who have taken refuge with the Medes without the authority of the Council and people of Athens; nor will I drive out

any of those who remain in Erythrae without the authority of the Council and people of Athens.'

14 In his review of Athenian resources at the beginning of the Peloponnesian War Thucydides (2.9.5) after listing the allies who contributed ships says that the rest provided troops and money, and in his record of the war he mentions the use of allied troops from various cities. It is doubtful whether any regular obligation to provide troops when required was introduced before the middle of the century.

15 See *ML* 52, translated in N. Lewis, *The Fifth Century B.C.*, 15. In taking the Greek word *ephesis* to mean compulsory reference Bury was in good company (cf. Gomme, *HCT*, 1.342), but the word normally means appeal, and always a second hearing. See *ML* p. 143.

16 Very few firm facts are recorded about Aristides after his work on the assessment of the allies. Plutarch records (*Aristides*, 3.5) that everyone in the theatre looked at Aristides when Aeschylus in his *Seven Against Thebes* seemed to refer to him. This was in 467, and he probably died soon after this. Traditions differed about his death (Plut. *Ar.* 26), but in one version he died in the Euxine while engaged on public business. He may have been trying to enrol the Greek cities of the Euxine in the Delian League.

17 According to Thucydides (1.101.2) the Spartans had actually promised to help Thasos by invading Attica. The promise was probably not given openly at a meeting of the Assembly, but perhaps by the ephors.

18 The date of the settlement of Messenians at Naupactus is disputed. According to our text of Thucydides (1.103.1) Ithome fell in the tenth year of the siege. Diodorus attributes the capture of Naupactus and the settlement of Messenians to Tolmides in 456–5. The advance of Athenian influence in central Greece after the victory of Oenophyta would provide a good context. But Thucydides seems careful to maintain chronological sequence, suggesting that the settlement preceded the alliance of Athens with Megara.

CHAPTER 9

1 Aeschylus, *Eumenides*, especially 681–710.

2 Many historians prefer a later date for the introduction of jurors' pay, cf. Gomme, *HCT* 1.327. The sources are indecisive, but the commissioners for the Athena Promachos were paid annually and this statue was begun not later than the early fifties. Payment for jury service was an essential condition for the effectiveness of fully democratic juries.

3 Aristophanes' *Wasps*, produced in 422, is a splendid caricature of jury service.

4 Aeschylus, *Eumenides*, 290–1.

5 *ML* 33. The list includes two generals, one seer, four citizen archers and 170 others. Normally all tribes were commemorated on a single monument. This exceptional record of a single tribe is due to the exceptional number of casualties. The year is the campaigning year, and probably the first year of the Egyptian expedition.

6 The tribute of Thasos was at first 3 talents only, but this low figure has probably a special explanation. From 443 (and possibly from the assessment of 446) the regular annual figure was 30 talents.

7 Sparta's strengthening of Thebes is not mentioned by Thucydides in his brief record of the campaign (1.107.2–108.2). The evidence comes from Diodorus 11.81.1–2.

8 *ML* 36. Fragments of the dedicatory inscription survive and can be completed from the text recorded by Pausanias, 5.10.4. It was a 'gift won from Argives and Athenians and Ionians'. The Athenian army had included contingents from some members of the Delian League.

9 *ML* 15.

10 Thucydides (1.110) clearly implies that the 200 ships, Athenian and allied, who went to Egypt stayed there till the end. Most historians now believe that the greater part of the fleet returned, after the initial successes, for the naval operations in the Saronic Gulf. The arguments are reviewed in Meiggs, *Empire*, 104–8, 373–6.

11 The Peace of Callias has been responsible for more articles in periodicals than any other topic in fifth century history (with the possible exception of the Melian Dialogue in Thucydides). The main argument for rejection is that there is no direct reference to it in Thucydides, nor in any other fifth century source. Positive evidence begins only in the fourth century when the intellectual climate was less critical. But all are agreed that, even if there were no formal agreement, hostilities were now ended and most would agree that the pattern of events in the forties implies that those who directed Athenian policy took it for granted that there would be no more fighting against Persia. Reasons for accepting the peace are given in Meiggs, *Empire*, 129 ff., 487 ff.

12 *ML* 51. Thucydides in his brief account does not mention the division of Athenian forces, but this is one of the rare cases in which Diodorus (12.5) fills a gap with reliable information. The Athenians, realising the vital importance of Megara, had imposed a garrison which was stationed in Megara. According to Thucydides all were killed except those who escaped to Nisaea, which presumably had also had an Athenian garrison. Andocides' force probably saved Pagae, Megara's port on the Corinthian Gulf, which was still in Athenian hands when peace was made with the Peloponnesians.

13 *ML* 52, translated in N. Lewis, *The Fifth Century B.C.*, 15 f.

14 The only evidence for the Congress Decree is a paraphrase in Plutarch's *Pericles* (17), which seems to derive from a definite document. Its authenticity, however, has been strongly questioned by R. Seager in *Hist.* 18 (1969) 129–40. As he points out some of the language and some of the terms seem much more appropriate to the fourth than to the fifth century: he suggests that it was a forgery of the period following the Peace of Philocrates (346) to strengthen opposition to Philip. If, however, it was invented at this time for the greater glory of Athens it is very odd that it was not quoted by the orators of the period. For a discussion of the arguments, leaning slightly towards authenticity, see Meiggs, *Empire*, 512–5.

15 Most of the little we know about this Thucydides comes from Plutarch, *Pericles* 12–14. See H. T. Wade-Gery's imaginative study of his character and policies in *Essays in Greek History*, 239–70.

16 The complex problems of the Tribute Lists of 449–6 are discussed in *ML*, pp. 133–8.

17 The Chersonese is included in Plutarch's list of cleruchies (*Pericles*, 11.5). The date is inferred from changes in tribute. In the assessments of 454 and 450 the peninsula was required to make a single payment of 18 talents. In 446 for the first time (there is no evidence for 449 and 448) the individual cities pay separately and the combined total is little more than 2 talents.

18 The difficulties of distinguishing between fifth-century cleruchies and colonies is fully discussed by P. A. Brunt, *Ancient Society and Institutions (Ehrenberg Studies)*, 71–92.

19 *ML* 49, where the view is accepted that Brea is to be identified with the 1,000 settlers sent out to live with the Bisaltae who are included in Plutarch's list of cleruchies (*Pericles*, 11.5). This would be near Argilus west of the Strymon mouth. There is, however, a fragment from the fourth century historian Theopompus which seems to imply that Brea was further west, in Chalcidice, D. Ashiri, *AJP* 9 (1969) 337–40.

20 *ML* 45. The decree specifies *silver* coins. The abundance of Cyzicene staters from the second half of the century, some of them with types clearly derived from Athens, shows that there was no ban on electrum coinages. Cyzicene staters were particularly popular in the Euxine and may have been privileged for that reason. Since no exceptions are made among the silver-minting states it seems that Chios, Samos and Lesbos, which were still contributing ships, were included in the ban. The importance attached by Athens to the decree is emphasised by the addition of a clause to the Bouleutic oath: 'If anyone mints silver coinage in the cities or does not use Athenian coins or weights or measures, but uses non-Athenian coins and weights and measures, I will punish and penalise him according to the terms of the former decree of Clearchus.' The date is controversial. The decree is reconstructed from a number of fragments found in different parts of the empire (for copies had to be publicly displayed in all the cities). It was formerly dated *c.* 420 on the strength of a parody in Aristophanes' *Birds*, 1040, and the fragments were considered to be consistent with this dating. A new fragment from Cos, however, was inscribed in Attic letters and the form of the sigma (with three bars instead of four, as later) would have been obsolete after 445. On this evidence a date in the early forties was widely preferred and the historical context would be appropriate. After making peace with Persia the Athenians had decided to use the tribute reserve for Athenian purposes and to embark on an ambitious building programme. Public payments to

Athenians would have to be in Athenian coins and the coin evidence shows that there was a dramatic increase in the minting of Athenian owls in the middle of the century (C. G. Starr, *Athenian Coinage, 480–49 B.C.*, especially ch. 4). S. E. G. Robinson, reviewing the evidence of all the allied coinages (*Hesp.* Suppl. 8 (1949) 324–46) accepted the early dating, but so much of the dating depends on style alone that the coins themselves cannot give a decisive answer. The main arguments of those who still prefer a much later date are (1) that the strong imperialism reflected in such a sweeping decree is out of place before the death of Pericles and (2) that the lettering and general style of the fragments (with the possible exception of the Cos fragment) favour the later dating. The first argument will not trouble those who believe that the forties was a critical period in the development of Athenian imperialism, when tough policies were deliberately pursued in order to prevent a dissolution of the alliance which peace with Persia might encourage. The epigraphic argument is stronger (particularly for the fragment from Aphytis, phot. *ATL* 2, pl. 6), but not decisive. Most difficulties would be resolved if a decree passed originally in the early forties was revived in the late twenties.

21 Writers of the fourth century and later refer to an oath taken by the Greeks before the battle of Plataea that they would leave the temples destroyed by the Persians in ruins as a memorial to the barbarians' sacrilege, and what was alleged to be a copy of the decree was actually inscribed and set up at Acharnae in the second half of the fourth century (Tod, *GHI* II, no. 204). The oath was ridiculed by Theopompus and has been widely discredited by modern historians, but the accumulating evidence from excavations in Athens has considerably strengthened support for its existence. Some special explanation is needed to explain why so many temples were left in ruins until the mid-century, before the great outburst of new building in the forties. The evidence in favour of the oath is set out in Meiggs, *Empire*, 504–7.

22 Fragments from the accounts of this statue published by the commissioners have been identified, *SEG* X. 243. They include payments for charcoal and logs for burning, tin, and wages, and show that the work lasted for nine years. The commission to Phidias is usually dated in the period shortly before Cimon's ostracism in 461, but if payment to jurors marked the beginning of payment for public service the Promachos will have been commissioned shortly after 461.

23 Rhys Carpenter, in a fascinating book (*The Architects of the Parthenon*: Penguin 1970) has advanced the revolutionary view that there was a pre-Periclean Parthenon designed by Callicrates which had advanced to the stage where the columns had been erected and some of the metopes had been prepared when Cimon died. Pericles then dismissed Callicrates and chose Ictinus to design a new temple re-using the Cimonian material. This involved dismantling the columns and re-erecting them at narrower intervals for a temple of different dimen-

sions, and cutting down the existing metopes to fit the new spacing. Callicrates, who had also been chosen by Cimonians to build a temple of Athena Nike to commemorate the victories, primarily of Cimon, against the Persians now had to wait until the death of Pericles before his temple could be begun. This thesis is supported by several converging arguments of unequal strength, but cumulatively impressive. Two points can be agreed: (1) The platform of the Periclean Parthenon was originally built for a temple which was begun after Marathon, and some of the column drums were already in place when the Persians destroyed all the buildings on the Acropolis. (2) Some of the material used in the Periclean temple is reused material. The heart of the problem is whether *all* the reused material can be attributed to the temple of the eighties, and no satisfactory answer can be expected until those few who are thoroughly familiar with the art and architecture of the period have had their say. It is a serious objection to the thesis that there is no trace of such a sensational change of plan in the surviving sources; but the argument from silence cannot be decisive, for so very little survives from the controversies that lay behind the Athenian buildings of the fifth century (Plutarch, *Pericles* 12 is the striking exception). When, however, Plutarch says in his catalogue of Periclean buildings that 'Callicrates and Ictinus worked on the Parthenon' (*Pericles*, 13.7) we can infer that the general assumption in his day was that the two architects worked on the same building. A Cimonian Parthenon would also be difficult to reconcile with a Plataean oath not to rebuild temples that were destroyed by the Persians and the arguments in favour of the oath are strong (see n. 21).

24 The accounts of the Parthenon (*IG* 1². 339–53 with *SEG* X. 246–56) show that work began in 447/6 and ended in 433/2. The main payments to the commissioners are made by the treasurers of Athena which indicates that the tribute reserve had been transferred to Athena and was now technically 'holy money'. For the account of 434/3, *ML* 59.

25 The dismantling, for the purpose of restoration, of the bastion on which the temple of Nike stands, showed beyond doubt that the temple was not built until work on the Propylaea was abandoned. The generally accepted date of the decree depends on the form of sigma which on our present evidence seems to be obsolete after 445, and the appropriateness of a frieze depicting Greeks fighting Persians to the ending of hostilities against Persia. A detailed discussion in Meiggs, *Empire*, 496–503; in brief, *ML* 44.

26 Dinsmoor, *Hesp.* IX (1940) 44–7.

27 Plutarch (*Pericles* 12) makes the use of the allies' money on the Parthenon and other buildings the central issue in the conflict between Pericles and Thucydides the son of Melesias. The surviving accounts of the Parthenon, the cult statue of Athena by Phidias, and the Propylaea show that the main payments to the comissioners were made by the treasurers of Athena. This would have been impossible unless the tribute reserve had been transferred to Athena. Athena's money, in principle dedicated money, becomes in practice the main Athenian reserve from which extraordinary expenditure in peace and war is drawn.

28 [Xen.] *Ath. Const.* 2.10.

29 The evidence for the total population can provide no more than a very rough estimate, with a considerable margin of error: the figures for the *thetes* and the slaves are particularly uncertain. The best discussion of the evidence is in A. W. Gomme's *The Population of Athens in the fifth and fourth centuries B.C.*, Oxford 1933: his estimate for the grand total is 315,000.

30 The date of the alliance is not certain, being based primarily on letter forms. Mattingly has advocated a context more than thirty years later, near the time of the great expedition to Sicily. References to Mattingly with discussion, *ML* 37.

31 The only account is in Plutarch, *Pericles* 20.

32 The claim of the Corinthians in their speech to the Athenian Assembly, as recorded by Thucydides, is very specific. 'When the votes of the Peloponnesians were divided on the question of support for the Samians, we openly opposed intervention maintaining that every state should control its own allies.' (Thuc. 1.40.5.)

CHAPTER 10

1 The published accounts of the two Athenian squadrons sent to Corcyra survive, *ML* 61. Payment to the first squadron (26 talents) was made on the thirteenth day of the first prytany of the archonship of Apseudes, mid-July 433. The second squadron received its grant (50 t.) three weeks later. The battle of Sybota was therefore fought at the end of August or early September.

2 For the full text see Tod, *GHI* I. 59.

3 We do not know the background to Aegina's complaints. Thucydides' statement implies that in the Thirty Years Peace there was a special clause guaranteeing Aegina's autonomy. The Megarian Decree banning Megarians from Aegina's ports was an infringement, but Athens may also have interfered in Aeginetan jurisdiction or possibly imposed a garrison. It is probably significant that Aegina's tribute payment in 432 (14 or 9 t.) is considerably less than her normal assessment (30 t.).

4 There are two main sources for Athenian finance in the Periclean period: (1) Two financial decrees (*ML* 58) moved by Callias (probably the general of 433/2 who was killed in Chalcidice) in 434/3 (*ML* 58). Their purpose was to put Athenian finances on a war footing. First they must do their duty to the gods. 'Now that the 3000 talents previously voted have been paid over to Athena on the Acropolis, they are to repay their debts to the other gods.' These are the gods of the temples of Attica and the lower city whose treasures are to be brought for safety to the Acropolis (with the exception of those such as Nemesis of Rhamnous which was a strong fortress), and a new board of treasurers of the other gods is to be appointed to take care of them. 200 talents are earmarked

for the repayment of the debts and the balance is to be spent on the two most vital foundations of Athenian strategy, the walls for defence and the docks for the fleet's offensive. Work on the Acropolis is to be brought to an end and a restriction is put on spending from the reserve. It seems clear from these decrees that the Athenian Assembly was already expecting war before mid-summer 433. (2) Thucydides (2.13) reports a review of Athenian resources by Pericles in 431, and it is significant that his statement of capital and income and potential reserves in the form of dedications precedes his analysis of Athenian manpower. At one important point the figures are controversial. According to the standard text: 'There were still 6000 talents on the Acropolis of coined money. The highest point of the reserve had been 9700 talents from which they had drawn for the Propylaea of the Acropolis and the other buildings and for Potidaea.' A different text is preserved in a scholiast on Aristophanes (*Plutus*, 1193): 'There was a regular standing amount of 6000 talents on the Acropolis. The greater part of this, actually 5700 talents, was in fact still there. There had been extra disbursements from it for the Propylaea and other buildings and for Potidaea.' This is the translation of the authors of *The Athenian Tribute Lists,* who prefer this text and give their reasons in *ATL* III 118–32. For criticisms see Gomme *HCT* II 26–33. Neither text is completely satisfactory but I prefer the standard text, mainly for two reasons: (a) ἀεί ποτε (always) is less convincing than ἔτι τότε (even then), because the reserve had not been maintained at a roughly constant level. More than 1400 talents had been withdrawn for the crushing of the Samian revolt (*ML* 55). (b) The Propylaea and *the* other buildings (τἀλλα οἰκοδομήματα) should refer to well-known buildings including the Parthenon. The Propylaea is specified because it was the most recent and, as a secular building, the most extravagant. Whether the Athenians ever had as much as 9700 talents on the Acropolis is another matter, but the peak point was probably reached before the major expenditures of the forties.

5 For these treaties see *ML* 63, 64. The prescripts of both decrees are inscribed on an erasure and the lettering of the main text of the Leontini alliance seems earlier than the prescript. The general assumption is that in 433/2 there was a renewal of treaties originally made in the forties, perhaps when Athens was intervening at Sybaris. For the difficulties in this view see *ML* p. 174.

6 For payments to the generals see *SEG* X. 223.

7 See n. 4 above.

8 The population figures are taken from Gomme, *The Population of Athens in the fifth and fourth centuries B.C.*, p. 26. The only reliable figures are those given by Thucydides for the hoplite forces and cavalry in 431 (Thuc. 2.13.6–8). The evidence for the number of *thetes*, which is of considerable importance for the understanding of Athenian politics, is almost negligible. From a citizen active hoplite force of 13,000 no less than 4400 died from the plague (Thuc. 3.87.3).

9 The date of the expedition, mentioned only by Thucydides (in retrospect, 2.68.7–8), is uncertain. Phormio's strong action in a district which Corinth regarded as her own preserve and against Ambraciots who were members of a Corinthian colony might suggest a later stage in the incidents leading up to the war, after the battle of Sybota, in 432. But Thucydides' account of this period is detailed and his silence is a strong argument against any date after 435. Some year between the revolt of Samos, when Corinth opposed intervention against Athens, and the outbreak of trouble at Epidamnus is more probable. Gomme, *HCT* II. 416, prefers an earlier date, in the fifties or early forties.

10 Thucydides says nothing of these attacks on Pericles' friends and many modern writers have dismissed them from this context. According to Philochorus (schol. Aristoph. *Peace,* 605, as emended by Jacoby) Phidias was tried in 438/7, and, when the story that this was the first of the incidents that led to war was introduced in the *Peace,* the chorus say that they have never heard it before. It is also widely believed that Anaxagoras was prosecuted by Thucydides son of Melesias in the middle of the century and left Athens some twenty years before the outbreak of war (see *CAH* V. 477–80). But the decree of Diopeithes seems to be aimed specifically at Anaxagoras and there is no doubt that Aspasia was brought to court. Thucydides ignored these attacks because, in his opinion, they did not affect the course of events. For the chronology of Anaxagoras' life see Meiggs, *Empire,* 435 f.

11 Thucydides (3.2.1.) says that the Mytilenaeans 'wanted to revolt even before the war, but the Spartans would not accept them'. This was presumably after the Samian revolt when they had sent ships to help Athens.

12 In Aristophanes' *Knights,* produced early in 424, the Paphlagonian (Cleon) boasts (774 ff.): 'When I was in your Council I produced an abundance of money for you in the treasury with my torturing, throttling and browbeating; and I cared nothing for anyone so long as I pleased you.' Cleon was a member of the Boule before 425/4, and finance was one of the main responsibilities of the Boule. The language is well suited to the pressure of a property tax and it may have been Cleon who persuaded the Boule to introduce the *eisphora.* It is probable that there was at the same time, in 428, a new assessment of the tributes to increase the allies' contribution to the war.

13 A Spartan inscription survives of donations by individuals and communities to a Spartan war fund. The contributors include friends of the Spartans in Chios and Ephesus (both members of the Athenian empire), and Melos which was neutral. These gifts may have been intended for the fleet of Alcidas. See *ML* 67.

14 Normally cleruchs occupied the land allotted to them. In Lesbos it may have been thought better to concentrate them as a garrison. A very fragmentary inscription (*ATL* II, p. 70) records regulations for Mytilene, including arrangements for the land. The tone is conciliatory. Private cases between Mytilenaeans and Athenians are to be governed by the same agreement as obtained before the revolt, and some measure at least of autonomy was granted. There is no trace of these cleruchs in the later stages of the war: they were probably withdrawn when Athens needed more troops for offensive campaigns.

15 For the Aetolian campaign see Woodhouse, *Aetolia,* 57 ff., 340 ff.

16 The author is unknown, the date probably between 431 and 424. For the character of the treatise see Gomme, *Harvard Studies,* Suppl. I (1940) 211–45; W. G. Forrest, *Klio* 52 (1970) 107–16; analysis and commentary by H. Frisch, *The constitution of the Athenians,* Copenhagen 1942; translated in N. Lewis, *The Fifth Century B.C.,* 51 ff.

17 For the topography of the area see W. K. Pritchett, *Studies in Ancient Greek Topography* I (Berkeley, 1965) 1–29.

18 The Athenian reserve was strictly Athena's money and all payments made from it were loans on which the interest was meticulously calculated. A long inscription (*ML* 72) preserves the report of the public auditors drawn up in 422, the end of a four-year financial period. It gives a summary of borrowings from 433 to 426, and a detailed account of the annual borrowings from 426 to 422. The entry for 426–5 begins: 'The treasurers (of Athena), Androcles of the deme Phlya and his colleagues, paid out to the hellenotamiae . . . for (the general) Hippocrates and his colleagues, in the prytany of Cecropis, when four days had passed, in the session of the Boule in which Megacleides was the first secretary, in the archonship of Euthynos, 20 talents. The interest accumulated on the payment (in the four-year period) was 5696 drachmae.' Annual borrowings from 433 to 426 had averaged over 700 talents and had been more than 1000 talents in the first two years of the war: the highest figure in the next four years was 261 talents in 426–5. For tables of loans and estimated annual withdrawals see *ML* pp. 214, 217.

19 For text and commentary see *ML* 69, and for a translation *ATL* III. 71. The total is well preserved with the exception of the first figure and was either 960–1000 talents or 1460–1500 talents. Sufficient details survive to confirm the higher total. The island figures are the best preserved and may be compared with the pre-war assessments given in brackets: Paros 30 t. (18); Naxos 15 (6¾); Andros 15 (6); Siphnos 9 (3); Eretria 15 (3); Ceos 10 (3). . . . The highest pre-war assessment was 30 t., paid by Aegina and Thasos. In the Thraceward district the two highest figures in 425 (probably for Abdera and Thasos) were 75 t. and 60 t.

20 A detailed description of the Boeotian constitution is provided by an unknown historian of the early fourth century, fragments of whose history (detailed and accurate, but dull) have been recovered in Egypt (*Hellenica Oxyrhincia,* XVI (XI) 2–4). Boeotia was divided into eleven districts, each of which provided a Boeotarch and 60 representatives to a Federal Council which was responsible for foreign policy. Thebes' position at this time was dominant as she provided four Boeotarchs, two on her own account and two to represent Plataea and the adjoining area. The individual states in Boeotia also had their own local governments for internal affairs, based on four rotating Councils for which there was a property qualification.

21 Thucydides does not mention this agreement with Persia, but the orator Andocides, 3 (*On the Peace*) 29 is explicit. His uncle Epilycus, he says, served on the mission which negotiated friendship for ever with the Great King. An inscription also survives honouring Heracleides of Clazomenae in connection with an embassy to the King and a treaty. See *ML* 70.

22 *ML* 65.

23 Cleon's election as general for 424/3, though doubted by Gomme (*HCT* III. 505 f., 526), is a certain inference from Aristophanes' *Clouds*, 581 ff.

24 For the identification of the hill, see Pritchett (n. 17), 41–3.

CHAPTER 11

1 Thucydides (5.47–8) gives a text of the alliance which differs only in minor variants from surviving fragments of the original stele, Tod, *GHI* 72.

2 Alcibiades was probably not elected general at the annual election in spring 418, but he seems to have become general after the battle (his name is probably to be restored in the accounts of 418–7, *ML* 77.17), perhaps in place of the dead Nicostratus. Athenian policy in this year is a good example of the kind of dangerous compromise that the Assembly was liable to adopt. The battle of Mantinea was the natural climax of Alcibiades' policy, but at the decisive point the Athenian force was too slow in starting, too small, and commanded by Laches and Nicostratus who were close associates of Nicias and can have had no sympathy with the policy. It was probably because this was realised by the Assembly that Alcibiades was specially appointed to accompany the expedition and take part in any negotiations.

3 Thucydides does not mention this ostracism in its context, though he refers to it in connection with the murder of Hyperbolus in 411. Later accounts differ and are confused. One tradition introduces Phaeax, a prominent speaker with aristocratic connections, as one of the principals (Plut. *Alcibiades*, 13.3). It seems to derive from a speech attributed in antiquity to Andocides (3), but more probably a fourth century forgery. Whatever part, if any, Phaeax played the main issue was thought to lie between Nicias and Alcibiades. Hyperbolus, however, was considerably more important politically than Thucydides' scathing obituary notice suggests: 'ostracised not because of his power or high standing, but because he was a contemptible man of whom the city was ashamed' (διὰ πονηρίαν καὶ αἰσχύνην τῆς πόλεως, 8.73.3).[1]

4 *ML* 67.

5 The decree regulating the offering of first-fruits at Eleusis, *ML* 73, is very well preserved, but the date, between 424 and 415, is uncertain.

There are strong arguments for a date shortly before the Peace of Nicias.

6 Aristophanes, *Knights*, 1300–4: 'They say that the triremes held a session and one of them, an elderly soul, said: "Haven't you heard, my dears, what is on in the city? They say that there's a demand for a hundred of us to sail to Carthage, from a worthless citizen, sourpuss Hyperbolus."' This is not evidence that an attack on Carthage was formally proposed in the Assembly, but it does suggest that western ambitions were in the air.

7 It is more probable that Aristophanes, in *Wasps*, 903 ff. is parodying an actual trial, but the scene could be simply comic invention.

8 It is interesting to find in a fragment from a contemporary decree that the Assembly first took a vote on whether the command should be given to a single general or shared (*ML* 78, fr. C). Distrust of Alcibiades led to the same disastrous compromise as in 418 (see n. 2 above).

9 Andocides, who was arrested but released after turning king's evidence, later wrote a full but tendentious account of the proceedings (Andoc. 1 *On the Mysteries*, with a good commentary by D. M. MacDowell). Those who were convicted were condemned to death and their property confiscated. Fragments of the records of the public sale of these properties have survived, *ML* 79. One of the most interesting entries is a list of slaves which had belonged to the metic Cephisodorus, with the prices they fetched (prices in drachmae, f = female:) Thracian (f.), 165; Thracian (f.), 135; Thracian, 170; Syrian, 240; Carian, 105; Illyrian, 161; Thracian (f.), 220; Thracian, 115; Scythian, 144; Illyrian, 121; Colchian, 153; Carian boy, 174; Carian child, 72; Syrian, 301; Maltese, 151; Lydian (f.), 185.

10 Modern plans of the siege of Syracuse are based on the topographical study by Knud Fabricius, *Das Antike Syrakus* (1932). He was the first to demonstrate that the inhabited area did not extend on to Epipolae and that the town wall was south of the cliffs. The intended line of the Athenian blockading wall is controversial. It is generally thought to run straight across Epipolae to the Bay of Thapsos which it reached by the cove of S. Panagia; for this is thought to be the site of Trogilus, where according to Thucydides the wall was to end (see K. J. Dover, *HCT* IV, p. 474), but the shortest line between the Great Harbour and the outer sea would run near the southern end of the cliffs, circling the town. Strong reasons for preferring this line are given by Peter Green, *Armada from Athens*, 191–6.

11 Silver objects from the Parthenon were converted into coin in 409/8. In 406 the Assembly decreed that the golden statues of Victory should be melted down (Aristophanes, *Frogs*, 720), the first gold coinage of Athens. By the end of the war most of Athena's dedications had been taken (Ferguson, *Treasurers of Athena*, 85), but the gold on the great chryselephantine cult statue in the Parthenon, which was included by Pericles in his survey of Athenian resources in 431, survived the war.

12 There is no explicit evidence for the restoration of the normal tribute system but it is implied in a statement by Xenophon (1.3.9) that Chalcedon, on surrender to the Athenians in 409, undertook 'to pay to the Athenians the tribute which she used to pay'. There has also been found a fragment of an assessment which is probably to be dated in 410, or possibly 406, Meiggs, *Empire,* 438.

13 We have two main accounts of the oligarchic revolution, in Thucydides and in the Aristotelian *Ath. Const.* They cannot be reconciled. The treatise represents the revolution as a constitutional reform: the 5000 are selected and appoint 100 commissioners who draft a provisional constitution for the emergency and a permanent constitution to follow. Thucydides, who was in exile but following events closely, describes the establishment of the 400 as a coup. They are appointed under intimidation at Colonus (deliberately chosen for the Assembly as being outside the walls and dangerous for all but hoplites owing to the threat from Spartan forces at Decelea): the 5000 are not enrolled; the extremists take control. Thucydides' account is vivid and convincing; it is certain that the 5000 played no significant part except in propaganda. Thucydides records what actually happened, the constitutional treatise records what a constitutionalist would like to think had happened. It is uncertain where the author found the two constitutions that he includes. They were neither of them adopted in practice but they are interesting as reflecting ideas that were current at the time. For an examination of the sources see Hignett, *A History of the Athenian Constitution,* 356 ff.

14 Thucydides' language (8.67.3) implies that arrangements had already been made or were made at Colonus, to enrol 5000. This is confirmed in a speech of 410 attributed to Lysias in defence of Polystratus who had been both a member of the 400 and an enroller of the 5000 (Lysias, 20.13).

15 A surviving inscription shows that the mystery of the murder of Phrynichus had not been completely cleared up by 409, *ML* 85.

16 Thucydides' praise is very emphatic: it was 'the best form of government that the Athenians had known, at least in my time' (since the reforms of Ephialtes). He merely outlines its nature. Though power was mainly in the hands of the hoplite class it is possible that the *thetes* retained a vote in the Assembly, though excluded from office, and perhaps in the law-courts, as suggested by G. E. M. de Ste Croix, *Hist.* 5 (1956) 1–23.

17 Xen. 1.1.23, reading ἔρρει τὰ κᾶλα (lit. timbers, cf. Aristophanes, *Lysistrata* 1253). Grote and Bury preferred ἔρρει τὰ καλά, 'our success is over', but this fits the other clauses less well.

18 Andocides 1.96 preserves the first action of the restored democracy, determined to prevent a repetition of oligarchic tyranny: 'If anyone overthrows the democracy at Athens or holds any office if the democracy is overthrown he shall be an enemy of the Athenians and he shall die.' To solemnise this resolution all Athenians were required, by tribes and demes, to take an oath over burning victims to abide by its provisions.

19 This *diobelia* is first recorded in the accounts of the Treasurers of Athena in 410/9, *ML* 84.

20 A report was presented to the people in 409 detailing the present state of the building (*IG* I² 372): 'The commissioners of the temple on the Acropolis in which is the ancient image . . . recorded as follows the state of the work on the temple, in obedience to the decree of the people proposed by Epigenes, according as they found it complete or incomplete, in the archonship of Diokles . . . The following parts of the temple we found unfinished. At the corner towards the Cecropium (the southwest corner): four wall blocks not placed, 4 feet long, 2 feet wide, 1 foot and a half thick . . . On the Porch adjoining the Cecropium the upper surfaces of three of the ceiling blocks over the maidens, 13 feet long, 5 feet wide, needed to be dressed.' It is clear from the very detailed report that the building had been abandoned when nearing completion. Large fragments of the expenditure on the completion of the temple are also preserved. They are considerably more detailed than the earlier accounts of the Parthenon (a sign of a more radical democracy). 9.10: 'To sawyers working by the day, to two men, each receiving a drachma a day, twelve days, to Rhadios living in Kollytos and his assistants, 24 drachmae. For sawing 14 8-foot timbers, 84 cuts, at two obols a cut, to Rhadios living in Kollytos, 28 drachmae.' 13. col. 2.32: 'For taking down and carrying away the scaffolding from the north wall, from which the figures of the frieze were fastened in place (three obols apiece to six men).' The normal day rate was one drachma as in the navy, and it is interesting to note that the sculptors of the frieze are paid on roughly the same level as skilled craftsmen and according to the piece at a standard rate. 17. col. 1.4: 'Praxias, living in Melite, the horse and the man appearing behind it and striking it in the flank, 120 drachmae; Antiphanes of Kerameis, the chariot and the youth, and the two horses being harnessed, 240 dr.; Phyromachus of Kephisia, the man leading the horse, 60 dr. . . . Iasos of Kollytos, the woman with the little girl leaning against her, 80 dr.' ('Living in Melite' = a metic resident in the deme Melite; 'of Melite' = an Athenian citizen enrolled in that deme, but not necessarily living in it.) There is a general medieval flavour about the following entry, 17. col. 2.28: 'Paid for offerings at the new moon, with the workmen—four dr. three ob.' Translations from Paton, *The Erechtheum* (a detailed account of the temple including translations of all the relevant documents).

21 The decree of the Assembly confirming in 407 the settlement made by the generals with Selymbria in 408 is partly preserved (*ML* 87). The terms were very conciliatory. The Selymbrians were allowed to choose their own constitution and Athenian moveable property lost during the war was not to be recoverable.

22 *ML* 89.

23 The savage action of the people can partly be explained by the great importance attached to the covering of the dead with earth. Feelings were inflamed because it was the season of the Apaturia, a family festival, and the relatives of the dead seamen wore black in mourning.

24 The original decree was passed in 405, *ML* 94. The Athenians resolved 'that the Samians shall be Athenians, while maintaining whatsoever constitution they choose . . . and when peace is made they shall take counsel together with the Athenians about all other matters.' When the Athenian democracy was restored the Assembly in 403/2 republished the original decree and with it two others reaffirming and extending it, but by then Samos was controlled by a pro-Spartan oligarchy, Tod, *GHI* II. 97.

25 A speech of Lysias (12.76) adds the important detail that of the thirty, ten were to be chosen by Theramenes, ten by 'the five ephors' (unofficially appointed by the oligarchs) and ten 'from those present'.

26 According to *Ath. Const.* 37 this law was passed at the same time as the law authorising the thirty to put to death anyone not included in the three thousand.

27 In the fourth century Theramenes seems to have become the patron saint of moderate oligarchy and the accounts of both oligarchic revolutions in *Ath. Const.* are distorted in his favour, but there were sharp differences of opinion about him during his lifetime. Thucydides admired his abilities (8.68.4): 'he was a good speaker and an intelligent man' (οὔτε εἰπεῖν οὔτε γνῶναι ἀδύνατος), but he seems to have regarded his active opposition to the four hundred as opportunism. For a more direct, but more biased, condemnation see Lysias 12.62–80. It is a mistake to expect complete consistency. Theramenes was at his best in his final scene, at his worst in the condemnation of the generals after the battle of Arginusae.

28 Bury, following Busolt, accepts the chronology of *Ath. Const.* 37.2: Xenophon places the appeal to Sparta and the sending of a Spartan garrison shortly after the election of the thirty and he is followed by Diodorus (14.4.3–4). This account by a contemporary is more likely to be right than the *Ath. Const.* which is biased in favour of Theramenes. The redating exonerates Theramenes from any responsibility for a very unpopular step.

29 Our evidence is a fragment of a speech opposing the measure, Lysias, 34.

CHAPTER 12

1 Xenophon puts the number of Asiatics with Cyrus at 100,000 and Artaxerxes' army at the battle of Cunaxa at 900,000. These figures are impossibly high: similar exaggerations appear in the descriptions of Xerxes' invasions and of the forces opposed to Alexander.

2 e.g. Diodorus, 14.22 ff.

3 The best account of the Athenian recovery of Rhodes is in *Ox. Hell.* XI (X), which puts the revolution in 395. Probably the Spartans attacked Caunus in 396.

4 According to Xenophon (*Hell.* 3.5.1), Timocrates was sent by Tithraustes, who succeeded Tissaphernes as satrap of Ionia and Lydia in 395, but this allows too short an interval before the outbreak of war. The account of *Ox. Hell.* VII.2 is to be preferred. This author makes Pharnabazus responsible and puts the commission in 396 (or possibly 397). He also gives the better account of the party tensions in the various states. According to him, as against Xenophon, the leaders of the war party in Athens, Cephalus and Epicrates, accepted money. But he emphasises that deep-lying resentment against Sparta was more important than Persian gold in shaping the alliance and bringing on war.

5 Tod, *GHI* II, 101. The concept of an alliance for all time instead of a specified number of years can be traced back to the sixth century in the west (*ML* 10), and there are western examples in the fifth century as in the Athenian alliances with Rhegion and Leontini in 433–2 (*ML* 63, 64), but the alliance between Athens and Boeotia is the first known mainland example. During the fourth century the formula becomes common and the same mood is reflected in an increasing desire for a common peace which would cover all Greek states. The main terms of the alliance are preserved: 'If anyone makes war against Athens by land or by sea the Boeotians shall send help with all their strength on the request of the Athenians and to the best of their ability; and if anyone makes war on Boeotia the Athenians shall send help with all their strength on the request of the Boeotians and to the best of their ability.'

6 For this coinage see Seltman, *Greek Coinage,*[2] 157.

7 Xenophon (*Hell.* 4.2.16–17) gives a total of only 7500 Spartan allies, but in his review of the forces he does not include the contingents from Tegea and Pellene in Achaea, whom he mentions in the fighting. Diodorus (14.83.1) has 23,000 for the infantry total on the Spartan side. Xenophon does not record the casualties. Diodorus puts them at 2800 of the confederates, 1100 of the Spartans and their allies.

8 Tod, 105. The name of Dexileos is also included in a casualty list of 11 cavalrymen who died at Corinth and one at Coronea, Tod, 104.

9 An inscription (Tod, 107) records payments for the hiring of teams to carry stones, and of iron tools in the archonship of Diophantus, 395/4. This shows that the rebuilding of the walls was begun before the battle of Cnidus in August 394.

10 Pausanias (1.1.3) refers to this temple commemorating the victory of Cnidus and explains: 'for the Cnidians honour Aphrodite more than all the other gods . . . and they call her Aphrodite of the Fair Voyage.'

11 A Spartan inscription, with the names of the two kings and the five ephors, commemorates the freeing of Delos from Athens after Aegospotami, (Tod, 99). Athens had recovered control by 390/89, *IG* II². 1634.

12 An Athenian decree of 387 (Tod, 114.7–8) dealing with the nature and extent of Athenian control over Clazomenae refers to the payment by Clazomenae of 'the 5% introduced by Thrasybulus.'

13 Evagoras became king of Salamis by a blood-less coup in 411 and helped Athens in the last phase of the Peloponnesian War. He was rewarded with Athenian citizenship in or soon after 410 (*IG* I². 113) and was honoured with a crown at the Dionysia in 393 in recognition of his goodwill towards Athens (Tod, 109).

14 In 387, shortly before the Peace of Antalcidas, the Athenians had been debating in their Assembly whether to establish an Athenian official and garrison in Clazomenae, or to allow Clazomenae to decide whether she wanted them (Tod, 114). The terms of the Peace put an abrupt end to Athenian inter-vention.

CHAPTER 13

1 A fragmentary copy of the alliance was found at Olynthus (Tod, 111). The Chalcidians are to be allowed to import from Macedonia pitch, con-structional timbers of all species and shipbuilding timbers, with the exception of silver fir. If the Chalcidian League (as opposed to private traders) needs fir they may export it after first notifying Amyntas and paying the necessary dues. Silver firs (ἔλαται) were throughout her history one of Macedonia's greatest economic assets, since the Aegean world was extremely poor in good softwoods that provided long lengths.

2 Amyntas recovered his throne, with the help of Athens (schol. Aeschines 2.26). An inscription survives from near the end of his reign which refers to an Athenian alliance, Tod, 129.

3 Xenophon (*Hell*. 5.4.20) says that the action of Sphodrias was prompted by the Thebans who wanted to involve Athens in their antagonism to Sparta. This is not a plausible explanation and Xenophon was notoriously prejudiced against Thebes.

4 It is one of his strangest omissions that Xenophon says nothing of the formation of this grand alliance, but from Diodorus (15.28.2–4) it is clear that the structure of the Confederation was first worked out with a small group of allies. The decree of Nausinicus came later when the main terms had been agreed and it was intended to attract new allies. Diodorus refers to it in 29.6, though he mentions only the clause renouncing public or private landholding by Athenians in the territory of allies.

5 In Diodorus Thebes entered the alliance after the main principles had been established but before the decree of Nausinicus, and that is why their name was entered on the stone in a different hand.

6 The procedure of admission to the Con-federation is well illustrated by the decree con-cerning Corcyra, Acarnania, and Cephallenia, ad-mitted in 375, Tod, 126: 'In order that the necessary action may be taken they shall bring the envoys before the demos and they shall put forward the resolution of the Boule, that the Secretary of the Boule shall record the names of the cities that have come to Athens on the common stele of the allies, and the Boule and the Generals and the Knights shall give oaths to the cities that have come; and

in the same way the allies shall swear the oath. And when these things are done the demos shall choose men, in such manner as shall be approved by the council of the allies, who shall receive oaths from the cities.' This general decree was followed by a more detailed agreement with Corcyra, Tod, 127, which includes: 'The Corcyraeans may not make peace or war without the agreement of the Athenians and a majority of the allies, and in other matters they shall act according to the decrees of the allies.' The name of Alcetas is clear on the stone, and the following name has been restored as Jason.

7 According to Polybius (2.62.2) the new assessment of Attica, covering all private property, landed and moveable, totalled 5730 talents. His figure is confirmed by Demosthenes (14.19) who rounds it off to 6000 talents. Many scholars have considered this figure much too low for all the private capital of Attica; Böckh suggested that it represented not the total capital but taxable capital and that Polybius had misunderstood his source. This view was based on passages in Demosthenes (27.7 and 29.59) which seemed to imply that for the richest citizens the taxable capital was one-fifth of their total assessment. On this basis Böckh estimated the capital value of private property in Attica at 30,000 to 40,000 talents, and inferred that this was graduated, the rich paying at a higher rate. Such evidence as we have, including a late parallel from Messene (*IG* V. 1. 1433) is against such a high figure, and Polybius should not be assumed to have made such a mistake unless there is firm evidence against him, cf. A. M. Andreades, *History of Greek Public Finance*, 334. No progressive taxation is known from the classical world, and the sources clearly imply that a common percentage was levied on all above a certain modest assessment. At some time before 361 (Dem. 50.8) the *proeisphora* was intro-duced, by which the richest citizens advanced the amount required and recovered their money from the members of the symmory. De Ste Croix (*Classica et Mediaevalia* 14 (1953) 42 ff.) has made a strong case for the introduction of this system at the same time as the symmories in 478/7. This makes good sense but is hard to reconcile with the statements of Demosthenes. All the evidence is quoted in R. Thomsen, *Eisphora*, but much of his argument is unconvincing.

8 Tod, 125.35–40. Each of the seven men found guilty was fined the considerable sum of 10,000 dr.

9 Anaxandridas in his *Protesilaus*, Kock, *Comi-corum Atticorum Fragmenta* II. 41.

10 Demosthenes 49.

11 The best surviving illustration of temple finance comes from accounts of the commissioners responsible for supervising the funds of the Delian gods. See Tod, 125, which includes a record of the interest received on loans, the interest owing from defaulters, and the new loans issued. 51.79 f.: 'From this balance (handed over from the previous year) we made loans to the following Delians on the same terms as those given to other borrowers from the consecrated funds of Delian Apollo.' See also the

well preserved accounts of the more modest temple of Nemesis at Rhamnous in Attica, *ML* 53.

12 There were difficulties already in the fifth century in getting a full meeting of the Assembly. On Assembly days the other entrances to the Agora were blocked and two policemen 'dragged' the Agora with a long ruddle-dyed rope between them to drive loiterers up to the Pnyx, Aristoph. *Acharnians*, 21 f. The *Ath. Const.* (41.3) is our evidence for the introduction of pay. 'After the prytanes had tried many devices to get the common people to come forward and give their votes, Agyrrhius first provided an obol a meeting, then Heracleides, "King" as he was called, made it two obols, and then again Agyrrhius three obols.' The first evidence of the three obol payment is in Aristophanes' *Parliament of Women*, produced in 392 or 391; in 11.299 ff. he registers his disgust: 'Away with the city people, who when they got only one obol for coming sat gossiping where the crowns are sold; now they crowd in.' 'When noble Myronides was in office no one would have had the effrontery to take pay for carrying on the state's affairs . . . but now they are anxious to get their three obols whenever they take part in public business.' The sovereign Assembly, κυρία ἐκκλησία was reserved for the people's approval of the magistrates in office, the review of the corn supply and of defence, the reading out of property confiscated by the state, impeachments, and applications for inheritances and wards of state, (*Ath. Const.* 43.4). It needed a higher incentive, because the business was mainly routine and less interesting.

13 Isocrates (*Callimachus,* 23) singles out Thrasybulus and Anytus.

14 The change from Attic to Ionic script became official in 403–2, but many earlier Attic documents had some Ionic letters in them, and a few public decrees towards the end of the century were exclusively Ionic.

15 The new procedure is first illustrated in the alliance with Chalcis in 377, Tod, 124: τῶν π]ροέδρων ἐπεψήφιζεν Πανταρετο[s.

CHAPTER 14

1 The tactics of the battle of Delium in 424 against Athens in some measure anticipated the tactics of Leuctra. The victory is commemorated by an epigram set up by one of the Boeotarchs who had held a command in the battle with two others, one of whom had accompanied Pelopidas in 379 when they returned from exile to Thebes and restored Theban independence. 'When the spear of Sparta was still strong Xenocrates (Boeotarch) won by the lot the duty of bearing the trophies to Zeus, not fearing the host from the Eurotas nor the Laconian shield. "The Thebans are mightier in war," proclaim the trophies of victory won by the spear at Leuctra, nor did we run second to Epaminondas in the race.' (Tod, 130.)

2 The alternative reconstruction is based on what might be a confused account in Diodorus 15.54, which says that Jason joined the Thebans before the battle and persuaded them to make a truce with Sparta. But when Cleombrotus had withdrawn and been joined by reinforcements led by Archidamus the joint forces returned and fought the battle.

3 The main evidence for the new federal Assembly comes from Diodorus who speaks of 'the Boeotians assembling in their Ecclesia' and voting (16.25.1). Elsewhere he calls this Assembly ἡ κοινὴ συνόδος τῶν Βοιώτων (15.80.2) and το κοινὸν τῶν Βοιώτων (16.85.3). The change is also illustrated in a decree of the late sixties (*SIG* 179) conferring the title of *proxenos* of the Boeotians on a Carthaginian (perhaps for helping them in building a new navy). This decree begins: 'It was resolved by the people . . .' The names of the Boeotarchs are also given, reduced from eleven to seven following the destruction of Orchomenus and Thespiae. The same procedure is reflected in another decree from this period, *IG* VII. 2408.

4 According to Diodorus (15.58) the demagogues stirred up the common people against the rich and eminent and this led to an oligarchic plot to overthrow the democracy. Names were revealed under torture and what began as mob justice on those thought guilty ended in the indiscriminate clubbing to death of anyone who was thought to be hostile to the democracy. Diodorus says that more than 1200 were killed.

5 The nearest parallel is the revised Boeotian constitution, which would have been the natural pattern to follow. 10,000 seems too small a figure for the whole of Arcadia if all citizens were eligible; attendance may both in Boeotia and Arcadia have been restricted to the hoplite classes. The main elements of the constitution are reflected in a decree making an Athenian '*proxenos* and benefactor'. 'It was resolved by the Council of the Arcadians and the ten thousand' . . . after the decree fifty names are listed: 'these were *demiourgoi*'. They represent the various communities, ten from Megalopolis, five from Tegea and Mantinea and the other communities except Maenalus (three) and Lepreum (two). Some think that these fifty formed the council, but the inscription suggests that they are distinct. *Demiourgos* is a normal title for magistrates in many Peloponnesian cities. It probably has that meaning here. The number is larger than we would expect for a federal magistracy, but considerably smaller than a council would be expected to have.

6 E. A. Gardner and others, *Excavations at Megalopolis* (Hellenic Society Suppl. Papers I: Macmillan, 1892).

7 The most revealing analysis of the decline in Spartan numbers is in Aristotle's *Politics* 1270a. 'Nearly two-fifths of the whole country are held by women: and this is because of the great number of heiresses and the large amount of dowries . . . As it now is a man may give his heiress to anyone he wishes and, if he dies without a will, his heir may give her to anyone he wishes. As a result, though the country could sustain 1500 cavalry and 30,000 hoplites, there were less than a 1000 citizens (when the Thebans invaded). Even a single shock was too much for the state; their lack of manpower was fatal.' It seems that families without sons to inherit must have been common in fourth century Sparta.

8 Arcadian statues to Apollo, Paus. 10.9.3. The inscription has been recovered; it ends:

τῶνδέ σοι ἐκγίνεται Λακεδαιμονίους δη[ιώσαντες]
'Αρκαδες ἐστησαν μνῆμ' ἐπιγινομένοις.

9 Bury's narrative is based on Diod. 15.72.2. There had probably been an earlier challenge to Epaminondas. Both Plutarch (*Pelopidas*, 25) and Pausanias (9.14.7) record a trial of both Epaminondas and Pelopidas after the first expedition into the Peloponnese in 470–69 on the ground that he had acted as Boeotarch after the expiry of his term of office. Such an attack after such spectacular success seems so unlikely that many historians have rejected it as a confused version of the second trial, but the details are circumstantial and the very strangeness of the charge is a slight argument against invention. Plutarch includes Pelopidas in the trial, and Pelopidas was in Thessaly during the second Peloponnesian campaign of Epaminondas. There may have been a formal ground for prosecution if, when the Theban army left Thebes, only a short campaign to strengthen the confidence of the Arcadians was intended, especially as it was winter. The invasion of Laconia and the establishment of Messene were not part of the original design and the campaign which should have been completed by the end of the year lasted some months into 369. Great men eclipse their contemporaries and Meneclidas, the main opponent of Epaminondas, according to Plutarch, is dismissed as a jealous demagogue. But the strength of the opposition is confirmed by the evidence of two inscriptions (*IG* VII. 2407, 2408) which show that during two years of the ascendancy of Epaminondas neither he nor Pelopidas were elected Boeotarchs. The opposition may have been in part at least directed against the new imperialism of Epaminondas. The prosecution of 469 can be accepted, but it is not surprising that it failed. There is a good review of the evidence by J. Wiseman in *Klio* 51 (1969) 177–99.

10 Tod, 133. The Athenian decree is in response to a despatch from Dionysius concerning 'the rebuilding of the temple (of Apollo at Delphi) and the peace'. The allies of Athens have been consulted and have authorised Athens to give whatever response she thinks fit.

11 There is no good evidence concerning the organisation of Athenian cleruchies in the fifth century. An inscription of 346, which gives an inventory of the dresses of the goddess Hera in her great temple at Samos, shows that the Samian cleruchy directly mirrored Athenian institutions with eponymous archon, council with *proedroi*, and treasurers, Hicks and Hill, *GHI*² 114.

12 An Athenian decree of 362, Tod 143, shows that Timotheus was helped by Menelaus, the Pelagonian, possibly king of the Lyncestians, who is praised 'since Timotheus reports that Menelaus the Pelagonian is fighting in person with him and

providing money for the war against the Chalcidians and against Amphipolis'. Operations must have continued into 362.

13 A well preserved inscription summarises Athenian relations with Ceos, Tod 142. The first revolt was signalised by the murder of an Athenian *proxenos* and the exile of pro-Athenians. When Chabrias withdrew, the new alliance stele was overthrown and supporters of Athens suppressed. The decree gives the terms of the new settlement in 362. Those who had been responsible for the second revolt are to be exiled from Ceos and Athens, and their property confiscated. But the general terms are generous: the Athenians and their allies (still important in the constitution of the Confederacy) take an oath to bury the past: Οὐ μνησικακήσω τῶν παρεληλυθότων πρὸς Κείους οὐδενός.

14 Tod, 144.

15 Hostility between Thebes and Phocis is also probably reflected in the expulsion from Delphi at this time of a group of men who were given refuge in Athens. Delphi was dominated by Thebes, and it is significant that six of the eleven listed in the Athenian decree held office at Delphi between 351 and 346. They were able to return when Thebes lost control of Delphi. See Hicks and Hill, *GHI*² 116.

16 There is a fragmentary record of an Egyptian embassy sent to Athens by Tachos, Hicks and Hill, *GHI*² 121; there is also an inscription on a votive monument to an Egyptian god near Memphis which includes five Athenian names and with them one each from the island of Nisyros, Boeotia, Cyrene, Caryanda in Caria, and Corinth. These may have been mercenaries serving under Chabrias, Hicks and Hill, *GHI*² 122. Strabo (760, 803) refers in passing to Χαβρίου χάραξ and Χαβρίου κώμη in the Delta, named presumably after the Athenian commander.

CHAPTER 15

1 According to Diodorus (13.54.1) there were 1500 transports. The size of Hannibal's force was 'according to Ephorus 200,000 infantry, 4000 horse; according to Timaeus not many more than 100,000'. As we have seen, all but very few of our sources for Greek history are irresponsible in dealing with large numbers.

2 Most archaeologists who have studied the building now think that work on the temple was discontinued *c.* 470.

3 All that can be reasonably inferred from the two fragments of the decree, *ML* 92, is that Carthaginian envoys had come to Athens and received a friendly welcome, and that the Athenians decided to send an Athenian embassy to Hannibal and Himilco. We do not know whether this was before or after the victory of Arginusae. Alcibiades was thought to have included an attack on the Carthaginians in his grand western designs, but after he had been recalled Nicias made friendly overtures to them in the hope of support (Thuc. 6.88.6).

4 The primary aim of Dionysius was not to enlarge the inhabited area but to deny the heights to an enemy and to provide protected camping ground for his large army.

5 The new principle in these ships, which dominated Hellenistic warfare, was to assign 4, 5 (or more) men to a single long oar. It is doubtful whether they were invented by Dionysius as they are not used in the Aegean until the last third of the fourth century, W. W. Tarn, *Hellenistic Military and Naval Developments*, 129; S. Casson, *Ships and Seamanship in the Ancient World*, 97 ff.

6 The account of this pact is based on Diodorus 14.75 6, who is circumstantial and explicit. Others have thought that it could not be in Dionysius' interest to let the Carthaginians escape, and that, since Himilco still held the fort of Plemmyrion which commanded the entrance of the harbour, he could have sailed out when he wanted. But Carthaginian morale was low and escape would have been very costly if the Greeks were prepared. The desertion meant the complete loss of faith in Himilco by his Sicilian allies, the abandonment of his mercenaries, and 300 talents could be usefully employed.

7 Dionysius is called ὁ Σικελίας ἄρχων, ruler of Sicily, in Athenian decrees honouring him, Tod, 108 (393 B.C.), 133 (368), 136 (367).

8 It is interesting to note that in 356 Isocrates had, somewhat inopportunely, urged Archidamus to lead an expedition against Persia, Isoc. *Letter 9*.

9 A. J. Evans, 'Horsemen of Tarentum', *NC* 9 (1889) pl. V.1, IV. 9. 10.

10 Ibid. Pl. VI. 7.

CHAPTER 16

1 Tod, 147.

2 Cersobleptes was challenged by Berisades and Amadocus, both probably members of the royal house. By Athenian mediation the kingdom was divided, Berisades taking the west and Amadocus the centre.

3 Two unfavourable agreements had been made by Athens with Cersobleptes (Dem. 23.167 and 171). Chares secured more satisfactory terms: Tod, 151 (Dem. 23.173). The cities of the Chersonese were recognised as Athenian allies: they had to pay contributions to the Confederacy, but also tribute to the Thracian kings, a double obligation which may go back to the fifth century.

4 The Euboean cities had joined the Athenian Confederacy early (377/6), but, after Leuctra, they followed Thebes. In 366 it was the tyrant of Eretria who seized Oropus and handed it to Thebes. With the decline in Theban prestige the pro-Athenian elements in Euboea became stronger. In 357 the Thebans sent a force to support their partisans, but the Athenians intervened and drove them out. Eretria, Chalcis, Carystus and Hestiaea came over to Athens: Tod, 153. Another decree (Tod, 154) records a new alliance with Eretria, guaranteeing her the protection of Athens and the allies if she is attacked. Cp.*IG*.ii.²149.

5 The embassy had been led by Stratocles and Hiero (Dem. 1.8). When Amphipolis had been captured Philip 'banished those who were hostile to him' (Diod. 16.8.2). A decree of the demos of Amphipolis survives, recording the permanent exile of Stratocles and Philon (otherwise unknown), Tod, 150.

6 The evidence of a secret agreement with Philip is unsatisfactory. Demosthenes, in his *Second Olynthiac* (2.5–6), reciting a catalogue of Philip's treacherous dealing, begins by describing how Philip persuaded the Athenians to reject the Olynthians when they wanted to negotiate an alliance with Athens: 'by saying that he would give Amphipolis to Athens and by inventing (κατασκευάσαι, precise meaning uncertain) the secret that was once on everybody's lips'. Later scholars explained the phrase by a passage in Theopompus (Jacoby *FGH* 113, frag. 30) according to which two Athenian envoys sent to negotiate friendship with Philip persuaded him secretly to exchange Amphipolis for Pydna. They reported to the Council but did not take the matter to the Assembly as it was important that Pydna should not know. De Ste Croix (*CQ* 13 (1963) 110–19) examines the difficulties of reconciling the two sources, emphasises rightly that no formal agreement could be made without the authority of the Assembly and concludes that there was no such secret agreement. There is, however, no difficulty in accepting a secret session of the Council, for which there is a good parallel in Andocides 2.19.

7 Tod, 157. The Athenian oath includes: 'And I will not end the war against Philip without the agreement of Cetriporis and his brothers and I will join with Cetriporis and his brothers in reducing the other places which Philip holds and I will join with Cetriporis and his brothers in destroying Crenides.' Crenides, the centre of Philip's gold mines, was of vital importance.

8 Hogarth, *Philip and Alexander of Macedon*, 51.

9 Alexander had three battalions of hypaspists, each 1000 strong. One of them was a royal guard, *agema*. In what respects they differed from the hoplites of the phalanx is not clear from the sources. It is misleading to call them light-armed, because they often share the work of the phalanx (Tarn, ii. 148). But they seem to have been more mobile and were probably not armed with the long *sarissa*.

10 The fact that the Carians saw much of the world in mercenary service, since the days of Psammetichus and Amasis, helped to keep the country abreast of civilisation.

11 Tod, 138 records three decrees passed by Mylasa in 367/6, 361/0, 355/4, dealing severely with conspiracies against Mausolus. The first decree's prescript runs: 'In the thirty-ninth year of Artaxerxes' reign, when Mausolus was satrap, it was resolved by the people of Mylasa at a regular assembly meeting, and confirmed by the three tribes.' A similar document from Iasus, *SIG* 169, is quoted by Tod.

12 The relations between Mausolus and the Greek cities is illustrated in a decree from Erythrae, Tod, 155. 'Since he has been good to our city, he shall be made proxenos, benefactor, and citizen.' His statue in bronze is to be set up in the Agora and a marble statue of his wife Artemisia in the temple of Athena.

13 Chares seems to have prevented the Byzantines from joining forces with the Aegean rebels: cp. *SIG* 199, a decree which honours a Sestian 'for reporting the expeditionary force prepared by Byzantium'.

14 Financial difficulties are reflected in an Athenian decree concerning the island of Andros, where in the general insecurity Athens had installed a garrison, contrary to the guarantees given when the Confederacy was formed in 377, Tod, 156: 'In order that Andros may be preserved for the demos of Athens and the demos of Andros and that the garrison in Andros may receive their pay from the contribution (of the allies) according to the decrees of the allies . . . the Athenians shall appoint one of the elected generals to be responsible for the security of Andros. And Archedemos shall exact from the island the moneys that they owe for the troops in Andros and he shall hand them over to the Athenian officer in charge in Andros in order that the troops may have their pay.'

15 Dionysius of Halicarnassus dated the speech 351/0. Bury, with others, preferred an earlier date, probably 353, primarily on the ground that Philip of Macedon was almost completely ignored in the speech and this might seem odd in the year of the fiery attack on Philip in the *First Philippic*. This argument from probability is not strong enough to discredit the explicit evidence of a good scholar. It would not have suited Demosthenes' case to stress the menace of Philip when he was pressing for armed intervention in Rhodes.

16 A list of contributions 'to the war which the Boeotians were waging on behalf of the temple at Delphi against those who profaned the temple of Pythian Apollo', was found at Thebes, Tod, 160. The payments cover three years and are not substantial. The largest contributions come from Byzantium which had made an alliance with Thebes on revolting from Athens. A Boeotian proxenos in Tenedos (a member of the Athenian alliance) contributed 1000 dr.

17 For the accounts of the Naopoioi (temple-builders) see *SIG* 236–53. Soon after the beginning of the war the building seems to have been interrupted for a few years. Tod, 169 gives the accounts of 346–4.

18 The prescript of an alliance between Athens and the Chalcidian League has been recovered (Tod, 119), but there is no firm evidence of its date.

19 The Peace of Philocrates marked a decisive point in Philip's rise to dominance and became the source of bitter political feuds in Athens, but we have to try to disentangle the true record from two speeches that were delivered in court three years after the events. By then the dramatic advantages that Philip had won from the peace were only too clear and both Demosthenes and Aeschines were anxious to disown responsibility. Neither gives a convincing report and almost certainly both deliberately lied. At the time both Aeschines and Demosthenes were convinced that peace must be made, and Philip must have made his views known to all the Athenian envoys. When they returned to Athens they knew that he would not include Phocis or Halus in the peace and that he wanted an alliance with Athens as well as peace. The envoys hoped that the Assembly would be realistic and accept Philip's conditions, but in case feeling should be stirred up against them Demosthenes carried a decree that the business should be settled quickly on Elaphebolion 18 and 19 (April 15 and 16), roughly a fortnight ahead. On the first day there would be a free debate, on the second the vote would be taken without further speeches. Meanwhile since the peace concerned the Athenian confederacy the allies, whose representatives were in Athens, had to discuss the issue and make their recommendations.

At the first day's meeting Philocrates proposed peace and alliance, excluding Phocis and Halus. There is no reason to believe that this did not represent the agreed views of all the envoys including Demosthenes and Aeschines, but they underestimated the hostility to Philip and the public concern for Phocis. The opposition found encouragement in the result of the allies' debate. The allies agreed to accept whatever peace terms the Athenians agreed to but recommended that no decision should be taken until the envoys who had been sent out to sound the attitude of other states returned to Athens, and that the peace should for three months be open to all states who wished to join. It seems that both Aeschines and Demosthenes, presumably realising the strength of popular feeling, spoke against Philocrates' motion.

But by the second day the situation had changed. Instead of an immediate vote there was a further debate. Philocrates' motion was bitterly attacked and emotional appeals were made to Athenian traditions and their proud record in the fifth century. The Assembly did not acquiesce until Eubulus convinced them that if they did not accept Philip's peace there could be no peace and they would have to provide men and money for further fighting. The decisive change was due to the intervention of Philip's envoys who made it clear that Philip would not consider the proposed modifications.

20 The accounts of the payments show that for five years (343–38) the Phocians paid 30 talents half-yearly, Tod, 172. In spring 337 they paid 10 talents only: perhaps the fine was reduced when Philip restored the Phocian central council, κοινόν, in 338. The last payment, making a total of 460 talents, was probably made in spring 322.

21 A crusade against Persia had been advocated before Isocrates by Gorgias and Lysias, but in less urgent terms. The idea of colonising Asia Minor west of the Sinope-Cilicia line was in the air when Isocrates wrote his open letter to Philip (5.120). After his defeat at Issus the Persian king offered to surrender this area to Alexander.

22 Wilamowitz-Möllendorff, *Isyllos von Epidaurus*, 30 ff.

23 For the oath see Tod, 177. It probably

accompanied the peace settlement and preceded the alliance and declaration of war against Persia. The members swear to maintain the new peace and resist war and revolution. After the oath the members are listed, with the number of votes assigned to them in the League Council. These are based on their relative strengths: e.g. Thessaly has 10 votes, Aetolia 5, Thasos with Samothrace 2.

CHAPTER 17

1   A speech has been preserved, *Concerning the Agreement with Alexander,* attributed wrongly to Demosthenes (17), but possibly by Hypereides. The speech is a protest against Alexander for restoring a tyrant's sons to Messene and infringing in other cases the independence of the members of the Synedrion. The agreement is said to provide 'that the members of the Synedrion and those appointed to maintain general security are to see that in the cities which share the peace there shall be no death sentences or exiles contrary to the existing laws of the cities, nor confiscation of property, redistribution of land, cancellation of debts, nor freeing of slaves to support revolution'. A fragment from the original publication of the agreement may have been recovered (Tod, 183), but the few surviving clauses from what was clearly a long document, concern only conditions of service of troops on campaign and when discharged.

2   For the Celtic oath see Tarn, *Alexander the Great,* I. 5–6.

3   There is very little evidence for Parmenio's progress in Asia Minor since his operations were overshadowed by the drama of Philip's assassination and of Alexander's first campaigns. In 336 he seems to have met with considerable success. Ephesus was won over and a statue of Philip set up in the great temple of Artemis; he also got control of Cyzicus and Lampsacus and in 335 was besieging Gryneion in Aeolis, but from this point he had to fall back on the defensive. The Persian King had sent an able Rhodian mercenary, Memnon, to restore the position and he met with considerable success. At Ephesus there was a reaction, anti-Macedonian elements in the city co-operated with the mercenaries, threw down the statue of Philip, exiled the friends of Alexander and set up an oligarchy. Gryneion was relieved and after a memorable dash over Mount Ida Memnon nearly succeeded in capturing Cyzicus. When Alexander crossed the Hellespont Parmenio held little more than a beach-head.

4   There is no firm evidence whether Alexander added the liberated Greeks to the Synedrion of Corinth. The large offshore islands which had remained independent of Persia even after the King's Peace in 387, were members, but doubt remains about the mainland cities. It is not clear how independent they were originally intended to be, nor how independent they actually became. In an inscription from Priene (Tod, 185) we find that Priene after liberation pays *syntaxis,* implying a free contribution, as in the Athenian Alliance of 377,

rather than *phoros,* tribute, which they had paid to Persia. But Alexander takes major decisions about the status of the inhabitants. In the harbour town of Naulochum citizens of Priene are to be free and keep their lands and houses, but those who are not citizens are to live in the surrounding villages which are to pay tribute. He can also say: 'It is my decision that [certain land] belongs to me'. Similarly when Chios after being temporarily controlled by an oligarchy imposed by the Persian fleet in 333, was recovered by the Macedonian fleet in 332 Alexander dictates the general lines of the settlement (Tod, 192). The Chians are to appoint commissioners 'to revise the laws in order to ensure that nothing remains which is inconsistent with democracy and the return of the exiles. . . . Of those who betrayed the city to the barbarians those who have already left Chios are to be exiled from all the cities that share the Greek peace (i.e. all members of the Synedrion) and shall be liable to summary arrest according to the decree of the Greeks; those who remain in Chios are to be taken to Greece and judged in the Synedrion of the Greeks.' So far he is acting as hegemon according to the spirit of the meeting at Corinth that asked him to lead the crusade against Persia. But he adds that if disputes arise between returning exiles and those in the city the issues must be referred to him. Meanwhile he installs a garrison which is to be maintained by Chios and specifies that they are to supply 20 ships to serve with his fleet. Alexander clearly was not restrained by constitutional scruples from dictating to the liberated Greeks. For a discussion of the evidence, see V. Ehrenberg, *Alexander and the Greeks* (1938) and E. Badian, *Ehrenberg Studies* (1966) 37–69.

5   This Persian naval campaign occupies very little space in surviving sources: in retrospect it seemed no more than a minor diversion, but if Issus and what followed is forgotten it can be seen that the expedition had serious objectives that were not unrealistic. There was considerable anti-Macedonian feeling in Greece and though the ruthless destruction of Thebes had made a deep impression on central Greece its deterrent force had been much less in the Peloponnese: Sparta had been openly and consistently hostile and even after Alexander's crushing victory at Gaugamela most of the Peloponnesians were prepared to fight under Spartan leadership. Before Issus the prospects must have seemed considerably brighter, for at the Granicus the main Persian army had not been committed and Greeks will have remembered how the progress of Agesilaus in Asia Minor was halted by the troubles in Greece which forced him to return. Memnon had shown his quality against Parmenio in 335 and the early successes in winning over Chios and most of Lesbos were very encouraging. But the death of the Greek Memnon and the transfer of the command to Persians who proved ineffective robbed the expedition of its main driving force and Alexander's victory at Issus was fatal to it. The best account is in Arrian 2.1–2 and 3.2.3 (for Chios see also Tod, 192).

6   The Gordian Knot. Tarn (ii.262) argues from the sources that the cutting of the knot with a sword

is the malicious invention of the hostile tradition, inconsistent with Alexander's respect for gods and oracles. Aristobulus (Arrian, 2.3) makes Alexander draw out the pole to find the end of the cord, implying that the knot was then untied.

7 Mahaffy (*Greek Life and Thought*, 32) made an interesting comparison between the tactics of Cromwell and Alexander: 'Each of them fought most of his battles by charging with his heavy cavalry on the right wing, overthrowing the enemy's horse, and then, avoiding the temptation to pursue, charging the enemy's infantry in flank and so deciding the issue.'

8 Josephus (*Antiquities*, 11.329–39) records a visit by Alexander to Jerusalem, but since there is no other mention of the visit in our surviving sources we can dismiss it as patriotic fiction. No fighting by the Jews is recorded; they probably submitted without a struggle.

9 Arrian (3.8.6), not usually given to wild exaggeration, gives the Persian numbers as 1,000,000 infantry, 40,000 cavalry, 200 chariots, and some 15 elephants. Diodorus (17.53.3) gives 800,000 infantry and 200,000 cavalry. Both Greek and Roman historians become irresponsible with numbers above 50,000. The Persian battle order at Gaugamela was captured, but it did not include numbers. This was probably the largest Persian army that had ever been brought to battle but we have no means of estimating even its approximate strength.

10 Arrian (5.7) attributes the burning of the palace to deliberate policy against the advice of Parmenio and as his narrative, based on Ptolemy and Aristobulus, both of whom served under Alexander, is in general much superior to the other surviving sources, Bury is in good company in accepting his account. The more discreditable version is given by Diodorus (17.70), Curtius Rufus (3.7), and Plutarch (*Alexander*, 38) and cannot be lightly dismissed. In the account of Curtius Rufus Alexander first gives over the city of Persepolis to the army to sack (so also Diodorus) and then leaves for a campaign in the Persian back country, from which he returns 30 days later. It is only then that the palace is burned. Plutarch, after giving in detail the story of Thais, adds: 'This is what some authors say happened, others say that the burning was deliberate policy. There is, however, general agreement that Alexander quickly changed his mind and ordered his men to extinguish the fire.' If Arrian is right, one can understand the hostile tradition inventing the discreditable version. But could it have been invented if Thais was not present at the burning, and, if Plutarch is right in saying that she was Ptolemy's mistress, would he have wished her to be associated with an event which was widely regretted? Ptolemy also had a vested interest in preserving and if possible improving the reputation of Alexander.

CHAPTER 18

1 The Caspian was certainly regarded as a gulf of Ocean by some Greeks for some time after Alexander. Aristotle, like Herodotus, knew it to be a lake; but whether his knowledge was widely spread among his contemporaries (including Alexander) is uncertain. See Tarn, ii. 16.

2 The massacre of the Branchidae is a very strange story to invent. The fullest account is in Curtius Rufus (7.5.28–35); Diodorus recorded it, but the passage is lost; there are minor variants in Plutarch and Strabo. There is no mention of the incident in Arrian from which it is inferred that it was not in his main sources, Ptolemy and Aristobulus. Tarn gives the most detailed reasons for its rejection (ii, 272–5), and the argument which he regards as decisive is the apparent contradiction in Herodotus. At the end of his account of the Ionian revolt in the reign of Darius ending with the capture of Miletus Herodotus says that the temple of Apollo at Didyma had been burnt to the ground and sacked by the Persians, and he does not mention the priests (Hdt. 6.19.3). He adds that the Milesian survivors were settled on the Persian Gulf near the mouth of the Tigris. 'It follows therefore that, if Herodotus be right, in Xerxes' time there were neither priests nor temple nor treasure at Didyma.' But could anyone have expected any credibility for the story if there was no Milesian settlement in Sogdiana, and, if there was, is not some special explanation needed for Milesians being in Sogdiana rather than on the Persian Gulf? It is perhaps possible to believe in a massacre without necessarily believing that Alexander was responsible, but the argument that the act would be completely out of character is dangerously circular.

3 To the Greeks prostration was confined to worship of the gods, but the Persians, while exalting the power and dignity of their kings, did not regard them as gods. The Achaemenids in their pronouncements emphasised that they were the servants of Ahuramazda.

4 The extant *Periplus*, ascribed to Scylax, is a later work under a false name.

5 According to Diodorus (17.84), Alexander was guilty of gross treachery on this occasion. This does not appear in the narrative of Arrian.

6 For the identification of Aornos see Sir Aurel Stein, *On Alexander's track to the Indus,* chs. XVI–XXI.

7 In describing the Indian battle line Arrian (5.15.7) says that Porus placed his 300 chariots (fitted with scythes) in front of his cavalry (150 on each wing). In his account of the battle the chariots are not even mentioned. It is reasonable to assume that they played no significant part in the fighting. Alexander may perhaps have drawn the Indian cavalry to their left to neutralise the chariots. The most controversial element in Alexander's tactics is the role of Coenus, who was dispatched ὡς ἐπὶ τὸ δέξιον. Bury, with Wilcken and others, took this to mean that Coenus with his two battalions was to ride to the right of Alexander, but this is virtually incompatible with Alexander's further instructions that when Coenus saw Alexander committed to battle he should attack the rear of the Indian cavalry. Others have taken the words to mean that Coenus was to attack the Indian right but this is even more

incompatible with the further instructions. The translation 'as if he were going to attack the right' (so Tarn, Fuller, Hammond) makes much better military sense.

8 Badian, in an important article (*JHS* 81 (1961) 16–43 = *Problems,* 106) sees a deeper significance in the purge that followed Alexander's return from India. The reason given by the sources for the executions is gross misconduct in the satrapies during Alexander's absence. The elimination of the army commanders in Media, Badian suggests, was more probably the ruthless striking at potential rivals. Cleander, the commander-in-chief, is the key figure. He had been second in command to Parmenio at Ecbatana when, following the execution of his son Philotas, Alexander ordered the killing of Parmenio. His instructions were sent to Cleander who carried them out. Cleander was the brother of Coenus, one of Alexander's leading marshals in the early years, who had played an important part in the defeat of Porus. Soon after that battle, when they had come to the river Hyphasis, the troops mutinied and Coenus pleaded for them. For once Alexander was unable to change their mood: this was the abrupt end of his Indian adventure and he was bitterly disappointed. Soon afterwards Coenus died, of a sickness according to Arrian (6.2.1). Badian suggests that Alexander was more probably responsible for a death that was so convenient to him. The murder of Cleander and his close associates will then have been a logical sequel.

Against this background the flight of Harpalus can be differently interpreted. Harpalus was a boyhood friend of Alexander and, not being fit for fighting, he was used in the administration, at first in charge of army finance (ἐπὶ χρημάτων), finally in charge at Ecbatana of the immense wealth that had come from the Persian treasuries. He had fled once earlier, before Issus (Badian suggests, *Hist.* 9 (1960) 245 f., that it may have been because he knew that Alexander was going to divide his work between two other men, who in fact replaced him). He retired to Megara, but Alexander begged him to return and finally persuaded him. He seems to have been a keen Hellenist, for he sent Greek texts to Alexander in India and attempted to establish Greek plants in Babylon, to which he had moved from Ecbatana. As Badian points out, he was almost certainly a member of the royal house of Elimiotis and Cleander had commanded the troops of that district. Though there is no evidence in the sources an association between Harpalus and Cleander is at least plausible. When the purge started Harpalus will have read the signs and fled before it was too late.

This exciting hypothesis may have some substance, but the case is perhaps overstated. After his stand for the troops at the Hyphasis Coenus must have been very popular, and to keep completely secret his murder, however cleverly contrived, would have been very difficult. We should expect at least a hint of foul play in the sources, for they include many traces of a strong hostile tradition. This tradition should also have had its own explanation of the general purge. It must also be admitted that Harpalus had good reason to fear the reckoning even if he was guiltless of any conspiracy or close association with Cleander. The accounts of his high living at Babylon are very circumstantial. There is no good reason for rejecting the story that he brought over two attractive mistresses, Pythonice and Glycera, in turn from Athens and that at the end he was living in royal style at Tarsus with Glycera. Is the story that he erected a bronze statue of her by the side of his own statue and that of Alexander at Rhossus (Clitarchus, *FGH* 137 frag. 30) completely without foundation?

9 Tarn (II. 434) attached considerable importance to the banquet of reconciliation at Opis. He believed that Alexander prayed there for the brotherhood of man. The crucial passage is in Arrian 7.11.9: εὔχετο δὲ τά τε ἄλλα [καὶ τὰ] ἀγαθὰ καὶ ὁμόνοιάν τε καὶ κοινωνίαν τῆς ἀρχῆς Μακέδοσι καὶ Πέρσαις. Tarn translates 'he prayed for the other good things, and for *Homonoia*, and for partnership in the realm between Macedonians and Persians.' But ὁμόνοιαν and κοινωνίαν are closely linked. *Homonoia* here is not a general conception of the brotherhood of man, but harmony between Macedonians and Persians.

10 Plutarch's detailed account of the last days of Alexander is taken from what he believes to be the Royal Diary and Arrian quotes the same source for his account which is very similar (7.25.1–26.3). It used to be held that Arrian drew his account from Ptolemy, who could have had access to an original Diary, but Pearson has given good reasons for regarding the Diary used by Arrian as a Hellenistic work, betrayed by the mention in both Arrian and Plutarch of a temple of Serapis whose cult, it was thought, was instituted by Ptolemy after Alexander's death (*Hist.* 3 (1954–5) 432 ff.). C. B. Welles (*Hist.* II (1962) 271–98) argued that the Serapis cult could be shown to be earlier than Ptolemy, but his arguments have been met by P. M. Fraser (*Opuscula Atheniensia* 7 (1967) 23–45). Pearson suggests that Plutarch's document comes from Strattis of Olynthus who is said to have written 'Five Books of Diaries of the Exploits of Alexander' (rather than 'Five Books on the Diaries of Alexander's Exploits'). Arrian's differences may be due to his having corrected this diary by reference to Ptolemy. The account, however, is very circumstantial and convincing and may ultimately go back to an original record. The date given by the Diary is the last day of the Babylonian month Daisias, June 10th, and this date is confirmed by a contemporary tablet of a Babylonian astronomical diary which includes the entry: 'Month II, Babylonian day 29 (= June 10–11) King dies'. A. E. Samuel (*Hist.* 14 (1965) 1–12) suggests that a detailed record was kept at Babylon following Babylonian custom.

11 Diodorus (18.4) used a source which gave a list of specific plans drawn up by Alexander. These included: (1) The construction of a fleet of 1000 warships larger than triremes in Phoenicia, Syria, Cilicia, Cyprus for a grand expedition against Carthage and the coastal peoples of Africa and Spain and westwards as far as Sicily, and the building of the harbours and docks needed for such a campaign. (2) The transfer of people from Asia to Europe and from Europe to Asia 'in order that the two greatest peoples should be linked in a harmony shared by all and friendship based on kinship'. (3) The building of a memorial of his father Philip in the form of a pyramid to rival the Great Pyramid in Egypt. Tarn, in a detailed analysis (ii. 38 ff.), finds several anachronisms in the list and concludes that it is a forgery from a much later period. He argues, for instance, that no one would have thought of building a pyramid outside Egypt before the second century B.C., and that the idea of a major coastal road is Roman in conception. The context of the invention, he thinks, is the emergence of Rome as an imperial Mediterranean power in the second century. Livy later speculates how Alexander would have fared against Rome (9.18). F. Schachermeyer (*Jahreshefte* 41 (1954) 118–40 = *Problems*, 322–44) has shown that Tarn's arguments are not decisive and that each individual plan can be defended. This, however, does not in itself prove that the document has respectable roots, and the context is extremely unconvincing. According to Diodorus, these plans were given in a written document by Alexander to Craterus when he was sent back to Macedonia with 10,000 discharged veterans in 324, and he was instructed to carry them out. The plans were not in fact carried out because Perdiccas, afraid of their extravagance, but not wishing to be held responsible for diminishing Alexander's glory, submitted them to a full meeting of Macedonians (that is, the army) and the meeting decided against them. Was Alexander at that time thinking that he might die soon? Was he the kind of man who would have made a long formal will of this kind? Is it not suspicious that Diodorus is our only evidence for such a document? But, while believing that the document is a forgery we can believe that Alexander was dreaming of western conquests. The Phoenicians had been the national enemies of the Greeks for a long time, not only in the eastern Mediterranean but also in Sicily: the defeat of the Carthaginians at the battle of Himera was a pendant to the defeat of Xerxes in Greece. No doubt Alexander should have settled down and attended to the major problems of consolidating his conquests and laying sound foundations for a stable administration, but Alexander was not that kind of man. His restless ambition would have driven him on to new adventure and exploration. So too Caesar in 44 should have concentrated on healing tensions at home and restoring confidence in the forms of government. Instead he concentrated most of his energy on planning a Parthian campaign.

12 Badian attached considerably more weight to Agis, regarding him not only as a great patriot, but as a brilliant general (*Hermes* 45 (1968) 170–92). About his persistence there is no doubt. Even though he had failed to get any substantial assistance from Persia and Alexander had won an overwhelming victory at Issus, he refused to resign himself to what the majority of Greeks must have regarded as the inevitable. He managed to secure a substantial number of the Greek mercenaries who had fought for Persia at Issus and probably increased their number by a successful campaign in Crete. But he had no reason to expect any assistance from outside the Peloponnese and the number and, more important, the quality of his troops could be no match for Antipater. It is true that Antipater had also to meet trouble in Thrace at this time (which may have been known to Agis), but past experience had shown that the Thracians could not be a serious threat. Agis' political judgment was poor, and a successful campaign in Crete, (Diod. 17.48.2: 'He reduced most of the cities and forced them to medise') of which we have no details, is inadequate evidence for the outstanding military ability which Badian attributes to him. Plutarch (*Agesilaus*, 15) says that in Alexander's camp the war in Arcadia was likened to a war of mice. I do not think that Badian's arguments would have convinced Bury.

13 Aeschines III, *Against Ctesiphon*, 132–4.

14 A report of the curators of the Attic dockyards (325–4 B.C.) refers to a decree establishing the colony (*IG*.ii² 1629; a long extract in Tod, 200). The report includes (217–32): 'In order that the people may also safeguard its own trade and corn transport and that, by the establishment of its own naval station, it may have protection against the Etruscans, and in order that Miltiades the oekist and the settlers may have a fleet of their own and that Greeks and barbarians who sail the sea may also sail into the Athenian naval station, with protection for their merchantmen. . . .' It is interesting to note that this Miltiades is of the same deme and *genos* as the earlier oekist of the Chersonese and the victor of Marathon.

15 The organisation of the ephebes is described in *Ath. Const.* 42. The ephebic oath to defend Attica and respect authority is quoted by Lycurgus (Leocr. 76) and an inscribed text was found at Acharnae in 1932 (Tod, 204). The oath is described as 'ancestral', but we do not know when it was instituted nor what preceded the late fourth century reform.

16 There is ample evidence for an acute shortage of corn in Greece from 330 to 326. An interesting stele was found in Cyrene in 1922 (Tod, 196) giving a list of states to which Cyrene sent grain, with the amounts sent, totalling 805,000 medimni. Athens received, and probably needed, the largest allocation, 100,000 medimni. Other epigraphic and literary evidence for the famine is cited by Tod.

17 Throughout the reigns of Philip and Alexander the Greek cities had suffered seriously from political feuds derived from attitudes to Macedon, and the exiling of the opposition when either party won control was common practice (foreshadowed on a lesser scale in the period of the Athenian Empire). When Sparta was able to dictate terms to Athens after her victory in the Peloponnesian War she demanded that all Athenian exiles, most of whom would be sympathetic to Sparta, should be restored. Many of the exiles whose return was decreed by Alexander would be former enemies of Macedon. Badian (*JHS* 81 (1961) 25–31 = *Problems*, 215–21) has argued that Alexander's primary concern in issuing the decree for the restoration of exiles was the potential danger from mercenaries without employment. As Badian has pointed out, Alexander had ordered the satraps to dismiss their private mercenary armies, with the result that many of them had become a menace to the countryside in Asia, and at Cape Taenaron in southern Laconia there was a large reservoir of mercenaries who were prepared to fight for anyone who could pay them. How important this factor was depends on the number of mercenaries who had been exiled from their cities. Those who had fought for the Persians at Issus would not have been able to return to their homes at once, but when Agis employed them to fight against Antipater they would have been welcomed back by most Peloponnesian states, and a considerable number of them must have been killed at the battle of Megalopolis. Throughout the fourth century poverty had been a more important incentive than politics for mercenary service. Alexander was probably thinking in more general terms. Political exiles were likely to try to force their way back and civil war could result; the cities remained unsettled and thereby weakened. The interests of both ruler and ruled required *homonoia*. Alexander, who rarely had the patience to consider carefully the practical difficulties of putting his ideas into effect, hoped to impose it.

18 Opinions remain sharply divided. J. D. Balsdon's thorough review of the evidence, which led him to reject deification (*Hist.* 1 (1950) 363–88 = *Problems*, 179–84) has exercised a strong continuing influence, but the climate of opinion seems to be changing. Tarn, who accepted a widely-held view that the decree about exiles was accompanied by a demand from Alexander that he should be recognised as a god, interpreted the demand as a political manoeuvre; the Greeks would be more ready to accept his instructions if they came from a god (Tarn, ii.370). There have been half-hearted attempts to support Tarn's interpretation, but it is now rightly rejected. The Greeks in their thinking and actions still drew a sharp distinction between human and divine. Nothing that Alexander said about his own status would seriously affect what they thought about his instructions. But the passages to which Bury refers (*Hyperides, c. Demonsthenem* 31.15 ff.; Plutarch, *Moralia*, 804 B; Aelian, *Varia Historia* 5.12) do suggest that at the least some states in Greece knew that Alexander wanted to be regarded as a god, nor should this surprise us. From the time of his visit to the oasis of Siwah he liked to be known as 'son of Zeus', but

neither the Greeks nor the Macedonians took this language literally or regarded it as a basis of worship. But there remained a mystery about what he had been told in the temple of Ammon and this may have led him to feel that he was not an ordinary mortal. In the period following his return from India there are increasing symptoms of megolamania. His morbid reaction to the death of Hephaestion, which removed the only friend whom he could securely regard as 'the friend of Alexander and not of the King', was followed by the ordering of a funerary monument that was to cost more than ten times as much as the Parthenon (even allowing for the rise in prices). He was planning in detail an expedition for the exploration and conquest of Arabia, and at the same time having a fleet built for a survey of the Caspian Sea. In a letter to Athens concerning Samos which Plutarch accepted as genuine, Alexander wrote 'I would not have given you that free and famous city, but you hold it as a gift from its former master, my *so-called* father', and Plutarch explains that he means Philip. Plutarch was easily deceived by forgeries and there were many forged documents in the Alexander historians. This statement about Samos, however, in which Athens had forcibly settled a cleruchy without reference to Philip, is strange language for a forger and, as Hamilton has shown (*CQ* 3 (1953) 151–7 = *Problems*, 235–41), it is reflected in a rescript from Polyperchon in 319: 'We give Samos to the Athenians since Philip also gave it to them.' But Philip only gave Samos to Athens in the sense that after his victory at Chaeronea he could have taken it away. Hamilton argues convincingly that the letter quoted by Plutarch was indeed written by Alexander, when Athens appealed to him against his decree restoring exiles which implied the return of Samians to Samos and the evacuation of the Athenian cleruchs.

19 The responsibility of Demosthenes is difficult to determine and has been hotly debated. His defence is lost; Hypereides' speech for the prosecution (a careful introduction in the Budé edition by G. Colin, 1946) is only in parts preserved. It is referred to by Hypereides, (Col. 13) but only as hearsay: 'At first, *apparently* (ὡς[ἔοι]κεν) he admitted that he had taken the money, but had used it for you, borrowing it for the Theoric fund. And Cnosion and his other friends went round saying that the prosecution would compel him to disclose what he did not wish to make public, that he had borrowed the money for the needs of government.' This is hearsay, but it sounds circumstantial. It is difficult to believe that Demosthenes, whatever his motives, was completely innocent.

Notes to Illustrations

1.4 These faience plaques form part of a mosaic which may have decorated a large chest. The majority of the fragments depict houses of two or three storeys, with framed windows and differing styles of construction, some at least apparently in well-coursed ashlar masonry. Other fragments from the same composition have trees, animals and warriors, possibly the prow of a ship, and what may be the sea. The scene is usually interpreted, not very convincingly, as an attack on a town. The fullest description is in *The Palace of Minos* I. 301–14.

1.11 This sarcophagus is carved out of a solid block of limestone and all four sides are painted on a plaster surface. In the long side illustrated a male figure stands stiffly in front of a building, on a lower plane than the others. He is probably the dead man in front of his tomb. Before him to the right is a sacred tree and a stepped altar. Three youths approach from the left, the first carrying a boat, the other two calves or bulls, all perhaps models. On the left a woman pours a liquid into a large bowl raised between two stepped bases on each of which stands a pole with a decorative double-axe on top of which perches a bird. A second woman, ornately crowned and in a handsome long dress, brings up two further containers of the liquid; this scene is accompanied by a man playing a seven-stringed lyre. On the second long side three women in long robes approach from the left while a man plays on the double pipes. In the centre is a calf on a table, bound up for sacrifice, and beneath the table goats waiting their turn. To the right a woman sets her hands on an altar reserved for offerings of fruit and libations, to judge from the dish of fruit and the jug above. Behind the altar is a tall pole surmounted by an elaborate double-axe, with a bird perched on it. At the extreme right is a shrine with horns of consecration and behind it a sacred tree. On each of the two short sides are two female figures, perhaps goddesses, in a chariot, one drawn by goats and the other by winged griffins.

No satisfactory parallel has been found for the scenes on this sarcophagus, and in some respects it seems more Egyptian than Minoan or Mycenaean. It probably represents religious honours paid to a dead prince. For a detailed discussion, see M. Nilsson, *Minoan and Mycenaean Religion,*[2] 426–43.

1.13 Too little remains of this crowded scene to reconstruct the action coherently but it clearly represents an attack on a walled city, almost certainly from the sea. The city stands on a rocky height and on the battlements women are emotionally involved in what goes on below, where slingers and archers are vigorously engaged, defending the city. Below them can be seen the caps or helmets of four men and the upper part of a man in a plumed helmet, possibly a steersman. They may be reinforcements coming to land. The illustration shows the largest fragment; the remaining small fragments are reproduced with it in a drawing in E. Vermeule's *Greece in the Bronze Age*, pl. 14. See also her detailed analysis, pp. 100–4.

1.14 Most of the gold disks found in the shaft graves have no holes for attachment and were made expressly to decorate the dead. Some, however, have holes and we can assume that they were worn by the living as well as by the dead. The designs are varied and have no religious significance.

1.21 A second gold cup from the same tholos tomb shows in one scene a bull trapped in a net and furiously struggling, and in the second scene an escaping bull trampling his captors.

1.22 This delicately carved ivory group (only 2½″ high) was found at the foot of the archaic temple, which probably occupied the site of a Mycenaean sanctuary. The two female figures are dressed as grand Mycenaean ladies, but we should expect such an elaborate composition to have religious significance. These may be the two Eleusinian goddesses, Demeter and Persephone, and the boy god may be Plutos, the god of abundance, who is sometimes represented as a young child.

1.25 This gravestone from Grave V in Circle A is enigmatic. A man in a two-wheeled chariot urges on his galloping horse. Attached to his side (it is not clear how) is a large sword. He seems to be naked, as is the second figure, who holds in his left hand what looks more like a club than a sword. Would there have been a second man in the chariot? Would there have been a second horse? What is the second man's role? The first two questions dissolve when one appreciates the difficulty of drawing two men and two horses in their proper positions. The third question remains difficult. The most generally accepted view is that the second figure is the enemy, with very poor chances of survival. Marinatos has suggested that this is a chariot race in funeral games, such as followed the death of Patroclus, and that the standing figure is in place of the normal turning mark. This would be an attractive solution if a better explanation of the standing figure could be found.

1.33 Lefkandi is a long plateau overlooking the sea between Chalcis and Eretria in Euboea, roughly equal in area to the citadel of Mycenae. The provisional historical conclusions are based on a survey of sherds on the surface, a series of trial trenches, and the detailed investigation of an area of 5 sq. m. dug down to bedrock. This evidence from the settlement site was supplemented by the examination of tombs in three cemeteries. The depth of the 5 sq. m. cut shown in the illustration is roughly 8 m. and the white tabs mark separate stratified levels. These cover a period from near the end of the Early Helladic period (*c.* 2100 B.C.) to the end of the Geometric period (*c.* 700) when the site was virtually abandoned. The darker colouring marks the extension of the Middle Helladic period, and in the Late Helladic period there are clear signs of a sharp expansion of population when pottery of the IIIc style was current. This is the period that follows the destruction of the mainland palaces and the evidence suggests that Lefkandi attracted refugees. From this period, however, there were signs of two large-scale destructions. The effect of the fire in one of these destructions can be seen in the short stretch of wall near the top of the photograph, which had been built to close a corridor. The large sun-dried bricks were baked hard and changed their colour from mud-grey to a brownish red.

2.1 and 2 The Geometric style of pottery was changing its character in the last quarter of the eighth century. The figured panel was claiming a more important place in the design and oriental influences arising from the opening of the eastern Mediterranean encouraged new subjects and new styles. The heraldic principle of composition with two animals flanking a pillar, a tree, or a deity, which is splendidly illustrated in the Lion Gate at Mycenae (pl. 1.16), has no place in Greek art of the Early and Middle Geometric periods. The Boeotian amphora (2.2), *c.* 700 B.C. is an early example of the return of the heraldic design from the East. The mistress of the animal kingdom, *potnia theron*, is shown with two large wings in place of arms. On each side of her is a ravening lion and a large fish

decorates her dress. Above on the left there is a bull protome and on the right an animal leg, both reflecting the standard sacrifice. Above the panel runs a thin band of water birds. The painter is not yet familiar with lions (for a very similar example from Attica see P. E. Arias, *A History of Greek Vase painting*, pl. 8), and his drawing is still geometric. The delicately worked golden necklace, made in Rhodes *c.* 670 B.C., shows the same eastern influence, but a marked advance from the crudities of the Boeotian amphora. A winged Artemis is flanked by considerably more lion-like lions.

2.3 This large pithos (height, 1·4 m.) was found on the island of Myconos in 1961 near the surface when a house was being reconstructed. It is one of a series of pithoi with reliefs that have been found in Boeotia and the islands. On the neck is the famous wooden horse, on wheels, with its load of Greek warriors, which the Trojans brought within their walls to their own ruin. The artist of the reliefs, anxious to display his ingenuity, shows the armed warriors inside the horse through a series of windows which would have roused the suspicions even of the Trojans. Some of the Greeks have already come out, and they are armed in pre-hoplite but post-bronze-age style. On the shoulder of the pithos are a series of gruesome metopes in three registers illustrating the harsh realities of the sack of Troy. Most of the scenes show a young boy being brutally butchered and in some of them a mother's frantic pleas are ruthlessly ignored. In other scenes women are either being put to the sword or led into captivity, and one metope shows Menelaus threatening Helen with his sword while holding her wrist to lead her away. For detailed description and illustration see M. Erwin *Archaeologikon Deltion*, 18.1 (1963) 37–75.

2.5 King Arcesilas II (569–8) is seated on an elaborate stool under which lies a tame cheetah. He watches the weighing, packing, and storage of wool but it is not clear whether the scene is on land with an awning for shade, the wool being taken to a storage cellar, or, more probable, on ship with sail, the wool being stored in the hold. Above the scales is a crane or stork in full flight. Two other birds are on the beam of the scale looking downwards and S. Benton (*Arch.* 12 (1959) 178–82) argues ingeniously that they are woodpeckers. Between them a monkey balances on the beam. To the left another bird swoops down. The figures are named and the guard of the store is appropriately Phylakos. This cup was made in the best period of Laconian pottery which at this time was one of the finest in Greece and widely distributed. Sparta had not yet become a closed society. It is appropriate that such a detailed familiarity with a Cyrenaean scene should be shown in Sparta, for Thera from which Cyrene had been founded was settled from Sparta. The shape and external decoration of the cup can be seen in P. E. Arias *A History of Greek Vase Painting*, pl. 74.

3.1 This protocorinthian oinochoe was found near Etruscan Veii. The photograph shows the uppermost of three registers. To the left a line of nine warriors march to battle preceded by an unarmed boy flute player. To the right two battle lines clash. The warriors have the hoplite's typical armour, large shield, single thrusting spear, bronze helmet, and corselet. In the middle register the Judgement of Paris is accompanied by scenes of a lion hunt, a parade of horses, and a chariot. In the lowest and smallest register there is a hunting scene showing hunters, dog, hares and fox. For detailed illustration *see* P. E. Arias, *op. cit.* pl. 16 and 17.

3.5 The two grooves for the wheels of the cart on which boats were carried across the isthmus give way in this illustration to two walls where there is a curving slope.

4.1 The scene on this vase is generally taken to represent Paris taking Helen on board ship for the journey home; others have interpreted it as a farewell scene, a warrior going to war. It is also uncertain whether the ship is an early bireme or the painter's only satisfactory method of showing the oarsmen on both sides of the vessel.

5.1 On this handsome black-figure Hydria, which was exported to Vulci in Etruria, seven maidens bring their water-carriers to a fountain house on the left. On the far left of the scene the fountain-house is named, καλερ[ο]ε κρενε, 'fair-flowing spring'. This was the open spring that Pisistratus had converted into the fountain house of Enneakrounos, with nine lion heads through which the water flowed. The maidens are named partly at least for decorative purposes, inscriptions on vases being particularly common at this period (*c.* 520). Above the water carriers the beauty of Hippocrates is commemorated: ηιποκρατες καλυς. The name is aristocratic but not uncommon. Fountain scenes on Attic vases became very fashionable in the third quarter of the sixth century, an interesting reflection of the popularity of Pisistratus' care for the water supply.

6.2 The Samian Heraeum was built on very marshy ground and is one of the few Mediterranean sites outside Egypt where dedications in wood have been preserved. This example is from the late seventh century and the facial types and general style are typical of east Greek work, with strong oriental influence. As E. Simon (*Die Götter der Griechen*, 53–4) points out, the attitude of Zeus to Hera is more reminiscent of Homer, *Iliad*, 346 ff., than of a marriage ceremony.

6.3 These figures in relief come from the eastern stairway of the great audience hall (Apadana) which Darius built, together with a royal palace, at Persepolis to mark the transfer of the capital of the Persian empire from Susa. The buildings were completed by Xerxes. The tributaries in the three registers cannot be securely identified, but they may be Bactrians at the top, Babylonians and Lydians.

6.4 This early Attic red-figure plate with a youthful rider in Scythian costume is to be dated in the last twenty years of the sixth century and can be compared with a slightly earlier plate by Epiktetus which has an unmounted archer in Scythian

costume (P. E. Arias, *op. cit.*, pl. 98). The subject may reflect a general interest in the Scythians who successfully frustrated Darius' invasion (see p. 152 ff.) and a subsequent raid by the Scythians on the Chersonese. Round the rim of the plate above the rider is a faint inscription which cannot be read in the photograph, celebrating the beauty of Miltiades. One would like this Miltiades to be the victor of Marathon in 490, who governed the Hellespont from *c.* 516 to *c.* 493, but the plate cannot be dated earlier than 520 and if, as is generally assumed, Miltiades of Marathon is to be identified with the archon of 524–3, he must have been considerably more than 20 years old in 520. Wade-Gery (*JHS* 71 (1951) 210–21) suggested that Miltiades might have been praised earlier on a plate commemorating his father Cimon's return from exile to Athens *c.* 530, and that this plate might be a copy of the original made some twenty years later, when Miltiades had to face a Scythian invasion of the Chersonese. It is easier to believe that there was a younger Miltiades who did not become famous later.

6.5 This Roman copy of a head of Themistocles was found at Ostia in 1951. Whether it derives from a contemporary sculpture is disputed. No other early fifth century portrait is recorded. For a detailed bibliography see R. Calza, *Scavi di Ostia V, 1 Ritratti*, no. 1.

7.2 Diodorus (11.26.3) explains the origin of the Damareteion. The Carthaginians honoured Damarete, the wife of Gelon, with a golden crown of 100 talents, because she had been influential in securing peace for them after their defeat at Himera. Having received the crown 'she minted a coinage that was called the Demareteion after her. It contained ten Attic drachmas, and was called the five-litre by the Sicilians from its weight.' Diodorus seems to imply that the coinage was in gold, but he does not expressly say so, and no gold coinage of this period has survived. The date and context, however, of the Damareteion have been questioned by C. M. Kraay in *Greek Coins and History*, ch. 2. In an examination of the evidence of hoards of Syracusan coin issues in the first half of the fifth century he argues that the Damareteion cannot be earlier than the sixties. His objections have not yet been convincingly met, but his explanation of Diodorus' 'mistake' is unsatisfactory. See *Num. Chron.* 1972, 1–24, for arguments against the thesis by R. T. Williams and Kraay's restatement. The significance of the running lion on the obverse is not clear. Bury, with others, interpreted it as symbolising the flight of the Carthaginians, but this explanation has been generally rejected because there is no evidence or parallel to support it. H. Ross Holloway, in the *American Num. Soc. Museum Notes and News* 11 (1964) 1–11, has suggested that the lion, also found on contemporary coins of Leontini, is in both cities a reference to the Emmenids of Acragas whose tyrant Theron was father of Damarete. The tyrant of Leontini has the same name as the father of Theron and may also be an Emmenid.

8.2 In this photograph of the Acropolis from the south, the lower buildings are considerably later than Cimon's wall. On the left is the theatre of Herodes Atticus, a very wealthy Greek who spent a considerable fortune on new public buildings in Greece in the second century A.D. It is now the regular setting for classical Greek plays and for concerts. The long stoa stretching to the right was the gift of Eumenes II, the second King of Pergamum (*c.* 195 B.C.).

9.4 The model of the Acropolis differs from the plan at one point. The plan preserves the original winding approach to the Acropolis by which the Panathenaic procession had always passed. The wide formal stairway is a Roman 'improvement'. It was more probably divided into two flights.

9.8 The Doric temple of Hephaestus stood on Colonus hill overlooking the Agora. The large circle in the foreground preserves the form of the *tholos,* where the tribal prytany on duty had their headquarters and dined together. The date of the building cannot be more firmly fixed than between 470 and 455; it may have accompanied the reforms of Ephialtes when the responsibilities of the Council of five hundred were increased (p. 215 f.). The Council House, *bouleuterion,* was behind and to the right (north-west) of the *tholos.* Other public buildings lined this western side of the Agora, including a temple of Apollo, the Stoa of Zeus, and, in the north-west corner of the Agora, the Stoa of the King Archon, the official head of the state religion.

9.10 and 11 The temple (at Olympia) of Zeus, who had previously shared Hera's temple, was completed together with its architectural sculptures before 457, for the Spartans dedicated a gilded shield with Medusa's head over one of the pediments of the temple to commemorate their victory at the battle of Tanagra (above, p. 220). A considerable proportion of the pediments and metopes survive. The east pediment depicted the preparations for the famous chariot race in which Pelops outwitted Oinomaos of Pisa to win control of Elis; Zeus is the central figure of the design. The contained tensions of the east pediment are balanced in the western pediment by the violent action of the battle between the uncivilised centaurs and the civilised Lapiths.

The place of Zeus is taken by his son Apollo, who calmly surveys the battle, prepared to see that the right side wins. Metopes are confined to the east and west faces, six on each, depicting the labours of Heracles, for he was by tradition the refounder of the Olympic Games.

All the sculptures share a common style and a master sculptor must have been responsible for the designs, but he remains nameless and even his origin is unknown. It is agreed that the work is not Attic and as there are no quarries of white marble in the Peloponnese the use of marble on this scale so early would not be expected in a Peloponnesian school. An island school, accustomed to work in Parian marble, perhaps produced these masterpieces. They come at the end of the early classical period, when archaic formulas had been left behind and the sculptor was becoming increasingly interested in the expression of emotions and a more adventurous approach to the portrayal of the human body in action. Polygnotus of Thasos, who is a contemporary of these sculptors and was the most admired painter of his day, had these same qualities. *See* Ashmole and Yalouris, *Olympia: the sculptures of the temple of Zeus,* London 1967.

9.12 This base with the name of Phidias, presumably incised by the sculptor himself, was found in the remains of Phidias's workshop at Olympia. The pottery associated with the abandonment of the workshop has been dated to the period of the Archidamian War. The unattractively shaped black ribbed, single-handled, mug to which the base belongs is illustrated in *Olympischen Forschungen* 5 (1964), pl. 64.

17.2 This sarcophagus was found in the largest and latest tomb of the royal cemetery of Sidon. It may have been made for King Abdalonymus who transferred his loyalty to Alexander after the Persian defeat at Issus. He is probably the central figure in the lion hunt and in the two other scenes on the small sides. In the side illustrated Alexander can be recognised on the left by the lion's head in place of helmet. The balancing figure on the right is probably Parmenio, who shared in the battle honours at Issus. For detailed photographs and discussion, *see* K. Schefold, *Der Alexander Sarkophag,* Berlin 1968.

Notes to Maps

20 There is not sufficient evidence to trace the precise course of the wall from Athens to Phaleron, which became obsolete when the middle wall was built in the Periclean period. Presumably when the long walls were originally built it was thought essential to protect Phaleron and the bay of Phaleron, but when the middle wall was built the situation had changed. A possible explanation is that triremes were still drawn up on the sandy shore of the bay of Phaleron and that the ship sheds of the Piraeus were not completed until the forties.

The continuation of the north wall by causeway and bridge over the main harbour belongs to the rebuilding of the walls by Conon in the fourth century.

21 Without increasing differentiations to the point of confusion the precise relations of all states at the beginning of the war cannot be recorded on the map. Thucydides (2.9.4) includes the island of Zacynthus at the mouth of the Corinthian Gulf in his list of Athenian allies. The neighbouring island of Cephallenia had not yet committed itself, but when the Athenian fleet approached the island in the summer of 431 'they won the Cephallenians over without a battle' (Thuc. 2.30–3). Thessaly also is absent from Thucydides' list, but when the Spartans first invaded Attica the Thessalians sent a cavalry force to support the Athenians 'in the light of their old alliance' (Thuc. 2.22). There is no evidence that they took any further part in the war.

Glossary

ACADEMY Originally a park and gymnasium on the outskirts of Athens, where, possibly as early as 385 B.C., a school was established by Plato; it survived as a corporate body until its dissolution by Justinian in A.D. 529.

AGEMA The royal guard of the Macedonian infantry.

AGORA Originally a place where the people assembled. Later, when a separate meeting-place was found for the Assembly, the Agora became the civic centre with the main administration buildings and temples. It was also a commercial centre with shops and stalls.

AMPHICTIONIES Leagues connected with temples and the maintenance of their cults.

AMPHORA A two-handled vessel with a neck considerably narrower than the body: most commonly pottery, but sometimes of bronze. Large, coarse, undecorated ware was used for storage and transport. Smaller decorated amphorae were used as decanters.

APARCHE The gift of a portion of something to a god, as the first-fruits of the harvest to the Eleusinian goddesses, or the sixtieth part of the tribute paid to Athens, which was given to Athena.

ARCHON A general title for an office-holder. At Athens it was given to the nine men with their secretary chosen annually to the chief magistracy. One of the ten was president of the state and gave his name to the year, the 'eponymous' archon.

AREOPAGUS The 'Hill of Ares' (the god of war) north-west from the Acropolis of Athens. The name was also given to the council composed of ex-magistrates who met there. This was the most powerful body in the state during the archaic period, but the radical reforms of 462/1 stripped it of political power and left it as a judicial court for trying cases of homicide and certain religious cases.

BOULE A council, which could be either oligarchic or democratic. In classical Athens there was a democratic Boule of 500 members chosen annually by lot, 50 from each tribe. Its main duty was to discuss and prepare measures to be laid before the Assembly (Ecclesia). *See also* prytaneis.

BOULEUTERION The Council Chamber.

CHOREGIA The office of the choregos, whose duty it was to defray the expenses of producing the chorus for a play; the office was borne by individual citizens of sufficient wealth.

CLERUCHS Literally 'holders of plots of land'. Most commonly used of settlements of Athenian citizens who were given land in the territory of 'allies' who had unsuccessfully revolted. The cleruchs retained Athenian citizenship.

DECARCHY A ruling body of ten. Applied especially to the oligarchic governments installed by Lysander in cities taken from the Athenian empire.

DEMES Local communities in Attica (about 175). They replaced the kinship unit as the basis of the Athenian democracy in the reforms of Cleisthenes. The deme had its own officials and assembly and had to maintain a register of citizens who had reached the age of 18. Change of residence did not involve a change of deme.

DEMIOURGOI In Homer's epics men in professions useful to the community, such as doctors, seers, minstrels, builders. Later a common title for magistrates, especially in Dorian states, not always having the same functions.

DIOBELIA A grant of two obols daily, probably introduced by Cleophon in 410 as a form of poor relief to those who suffered most from the Spartan control of Attica from Decelea.

DIPYLON A double gateway in a city wall, the best known being in the Cerameicus at Athens, through which passed the broad Panathenaic Way of the annual procession through the Agora to Athena on the Acropolis.

ECCLESIA An assembly of adult male citizens summoned as of right. In classical Athens, meetings were normally summoned by the Boule and held on the Pnyx. Each citizen had the right to speak and voting was by simple majority, generally by show of hands.

EISPHORA A property tax in ancient Greece, which varied in its method of assessment in different cities.

EPARITOI 'Selected men', the name given to the troops of the Arcadian Federation.

EPHEBES Athenian citizens between 18 and 20 who were required to undergo paramilitary training for two years.

EPHETAI An Athenian jury, 51 in number selected by lot from citizens over 50, concerned with homicide cases only.

EPHORS 'Overseers.' Magistrates in Sparta and other states associated with Sparta. At Sparta they were an annually elected board of five who acted as a check on the powers of the kings.

GENOS A clan consisting of families who claimed descent from a common ancestor, and forming part of a phratry.

GEROUSIA The council of elders at Sparta, consisting of 28 men of over 60 elected from aristocratic families, together with the two kings.

GRAPHE PARANOMON At Athens a prosecution for the offence of proposing in the assembly or council a decree contrary to an existing law.

HARMOST 'A man who arranges matters', the title given to men sent by Sparta to control affairs in cities which had revolted from Athens.

HEKTEMOROI 'Sixth-parters', a class of peasants in Athens before Solon, probably small freeholders who had fallen into default.

HELLENOTAMIAE 'Treasurers of the Greeks', a board of ten Athenians elected at Athens to manage the finances of the Delian League.

HELOTS Serfs in the Spartan state, descended from the earlier inhabitants. They worked the land and provided the labour which left Spartan citizens free to keep themselves fit for fighting. They considerably outnumbered citizens and the fear of revolts made Sparta very reluctant to undertake commitments outside the Peloponnese.

HERMAE In Athens squared pillars crowned with the head of Hermes, god of travellers, which were set up at street corners and in front of houses.

HETAIRIAE 'Associations of companions', most commonly used of aristocratic clubs which became political as well as social.

HETAIROI The 'companions', the Macedonian cavalry of Alexander, consisting of seven squadrons of 200 and a royal squadron of 300.

HIPPEIS 'Horsemen', the title given to the second of Solon's census classes. In classical times the Athenian hippeis were a select cavalry corps of 1000 men who could afford to maintain their own horses.

HOPLITES Heavy-armed infantry, designed to fight in close formation, and roughly corresponding to Solon's third census class of *zeugitae*. Their basic equipment was a metal helmet, breastplate and grieves, a thrusting spear, and a large, round shield. *See also* phalanx.

HYPASPISTS Alexander's own infantry, corresponding to the Companion cavalry, three battalions, each of 1000 men, and one of them, the *agema*, the royal foot-guard. They fought next to the phalanx in the battle line and were also used on special missions.

LEITOURGIAE Duties imposed on Athenian citizens of the wealthiest classes, e.g. providing a chorus for tragedy or comedy.

MEDIMNUS A standard measure of corn, about 1½ bushels.

MEGARON A large hall or room, most often used for the main public reception room in a Mycenaean palace.

METICS Resident aliens in a Greek city-state, who had acquired a status distinguishing them from other foreigners.

MORA A unit of the Spartan army, probably about 600.

NEODAMODES Helots who were freed by the Spartan state for good service, particularly in war.

NOMOTHETAE 'Law-setters.' In Athens a committee appointed to draft or revise laws.

OSTRACISM In Athens in the fifth century B.C. a method of banishing for ten years a prominent citizen who had become unpopular. If the assembly voted in favour of holding an ostracism, it was held in the Agora and the voter wrote on a potsherd the name of the man he wished to be banished.

PELTASTS Light armed troops, using small, round shields and light throwing spears. Their special usefulness was not exploited till the fourth century.

PENTECONTER A fifty-oared ship.

PENTAKOSIOMEDIMNOI 'Five hundred *medimni* men' at Athens, richest of the census-classes devised by Solon.

PERIOECI 'Neighbouring peoples.' Most commonly used with reference to Sparta, where the other towns of Laconia were controlled by Sparta, had to follow her policies, and fight with her in war. They managed their own local affairs and were not subject to the strict discipline of Spartan citizens.

PHALANX The heavy-armed infantry in order of battle, close-formed and up to eight ranks deep, relying on the concerted weight of their charge.

PHOROS A money levy paid by most members of the Delian Confederacy instead of providing ships for the allied navy.

PHRATRIAE Groups of clans. In the archaic period the genos, the phratry and the kinship tribe were the basic divisions of the state, replaced in the reforms of Cleisthenes by the deme, the trittyes and the local tribe.

PHYLE A tribe or family-division.

PNYX The hill west of the Acropolis at Athens on which from the sixth century the Assembly met.

POLEMARCH One of the nine Athenian archons appointed annually. Originally the commander of the army, he lost his military importance when in the early fifth century the command passed to the board of generals. His later duties were primarily judicial, especially concerned with metics and foreigners.

POLETAI 'Sellers', a board of ten at Athens annually appointed who were responsible for selling and leasing public property, including contracts for the collection of taxes and confiscated property.

POLIS The Greek city-state, which arose after the decline of the monarchical system, and remained the general rule in spite of the rise of tyrannies from time to time.

PROBOULOI 'Counsellors.' In 413 B.C., a time of crisis, the Athenians elected ten probouloi over 40 years of age, to recommend policies to the democratic council and assembly.

PROEDROI 'Chairmen.' From the fourth century the Athenians appointed a board of ten to help the president to control meetings of the Boule or the Assembly and to take the vote.

PROXENOS The equivalent of a diplomatic representative in a Greek state; the office was frequently hereditary and the holder had to be a member of the state in which he served and not of the state which he represented.

PRYTANEIS Following the reforms of Cleisthenes in Athens, the Boule each year consisted of 50 men chosen by lot from each of the ten Phylae; each group of 50 served as prytaneis, 'presidents', for one-tenth of the year—this period was called a Prytany. The period was reduced to one-twelfth of the year when the number of phylae was increased to 12 in 307 B.C. The Prytaneis were on duty every day and were responsible for arranging the meetings of the Boule and the Ecclesia. Each day one of the Prytaneis was chosen by lot to be chairman.

PSEPHISM A decree approved by vote (from *psephos*, a pebble).

RHYTON A drinking vessel in the form of a horn or animal's head.

SARCOPHAGUS 'Flesh-eater.' Coffin made either of wood or stone and often richly decorated.

SATRAP A Persian provincial governor with wide powers within his own province but owing allegiance to the Persian King.

SEISACHTHEIA 'A shaking off of burdens', the first act of Solon's reforms, a cancellation of debts and the prohibition of lending on the security of a person.

SHOPHET Title of the two chief magistrates at Carthage and other Phoenician cities.

SOPHISTS Teachers of rhetoric and the art of disputation. In the time of Plato the term took on a derogatory sense and came to mean a man who merely pretended to knowledge or attempted to make the worse appear the better cause.

STATER The standard term for the main unit of a city's coinage, but not used in Athens.

STOA A wide colonnade, often with two side wings. The name was given to the school of philosophy founded by Zeno (Stoics), because he and his successors taught in the Stoa Poicile.

STRATEGOS General. In Athens in the fifth century the ten generals were the most influential officials in the state. They were elected annually and not like the other magistrates appointed by lot; they sat with the council and played an important part in politics. In the fourth century they lost much of their political influence and became more like professional soldiers.

SYMMORY A group of citizens in fourth-century Athens formed for the purpose of simplifying the collection of taxes or for the provision of ships for the navy.

SYNOECISM The joining of several communities into one city-state as when the city of Rhodes was formed from the union of Lindos, Camirus, and Ialysus.

SYNTAXIS A voluntary contribution, as opposed to tribute (*phoros*).

SYSSITIA The system at Sparta whereby male citizens lived and messed together, providing their own contributions.

TAGOS Official title borne by the chief magistrate of Thessaly.

THEORIC FUND Originally a fund to enable poor people to attend the theatre, drawn from the surplus revenue of the year. It was later used more widely to benefit the poor. There was great resistance when it was proposed to use the fund for national defence and politicians were accused of using it as a bribe for support.

THEOROI The official title given to a city's representatives at another city's festivals.

THESMOTHETAE At Athens the six junior of the nine archons, their functions being mainly the control of the law courts.

THETES Hired labourer or serf. It was also the name given to Solon's lowest census class.

TRIERARCHY The system in fifth-century Athens whereby a wealthy citizen was chosen to undertake the command, equipment and maintenance of a trireme at his own expense. After 411 B.C. two citizens usually shared this duty.

TRIOBOLON 'A three obol piece.' The jurors were called three-obol men when Cleon raised their daily pay from two to three obols.

TRITTYES Thirty territorial divisions created by Cleisthenes, each of whose ten new phylae contained three, one from each of his three regions of Attica.

ZEUGITAE At Athens, before the time of Solon, the citizens of moderate means, roughly corresponding to the farmers. Solon used the name for his third census-class and they provided the bulk of the hoplites. From the time of Cleisthenes, members of this class could hold major offices and from 457 B.C. could be appointed archons.

GREEK COINAGE The main units were the obol, drachma, mina, talent. 6 obols = 1 drachma; 100 drachmae = 1 mina; 60 minae = 1 talent. A naval oarsman and a building worker both received 1 dr. daily in the late fifth century; the juror's pay was raised from 2 to 3 obols in 425. A trireme probably cost about 1 talent to build.

Index

Det Dr